# Time-Saver Standards for Interior Design and Space Planning

## Other McGraw-Hill Books of Interest

*Binder* • Corporate Facility Planning

*Breyer* • Design of Wood Structures

*Burden* • Entourage

*Callender* • Time-Saver Standards for Architectural Design Data

*Colley* • Practical Manual of Site Development

*De Chiara* • Handbook of Architectural Details for Commercial Buildings

*De Chiara* • Time-Saver Standards for Residential Development

*De Chiara and Callender* • Time-Saver Standards for Building Types

*De Chiara and Koppelman* • Time-Saver Standards for Site Planning

*Dines* • Landscape Perspective Drawing

*Ehrenkrantz* • Architectural Systems

*Halse and George* • Architectural Rendering

*Harris* • Dictionary of Architecture and Construction

*Harris and Dines* • Time-Saver Standards for Landscape Architecture

*Izenour* • Theater Technology

*Leach* • Photographic Perspective Drawing Techniques

*Merritt* • Building Design and Systems Handbook

*Merritt* • Standard Handbook for Civil Engineers

*Nolon and Dickinson* • Common Walls/Private Homes

*Simonds* • Landscape Architecture

*Spaulding and D'Elia* • Advanced Marketing Techniques for Architecture and Engineering Firms

*Wentling* • Housing By Lifestyle

# Time-Saver Standards for Interior Design and Space Planning

Joseph De Chiara
Julius Panero
Martin Zelnik

**McGraw-Hill, Inc.**
New York  St. Louis  San Francisco  Auckland  Bogotá
Caracas  Lisbon  London  Madrid  Mexico  Milan
Montreal  New Delhi  Paris  San Juan  Singapore
Sydney  Tokyo  Toronto

Library of Congress Cataloging-in-Publication Data

De Chiara, Joseph, date
    Time-saver standards for interior design and space planning/
Joseph De Chiara, Julius Panero, Martin Zelnik.
      p.     cm.
    Includes index.
    ISBN 0-07-016299-9
     1. Interior decoration—Standards—Handbook, manuals, etc.
    2. Interior architecture—Standards—Handbook, manuals, etc.
    I. Panero, Julius.  II. Zelnik, Martin, date.  III. Title.
    NK2110.D35 1991
    729—dc20                       91-15189

5678910 KPKP 99876543

ISBN 0-07-016299-9

*The sponsoring editor for this book was Joel Stein, the
editing supervisor was Stephen M. Smith, the designer
was Ron Lane, and the production supervisor was Suzanne
W. Babeuf. It was set in Univers Light.*

*Printed and bound by Arcata Graphics/Halliday.*

# Contents

Contributors     vii

Organizations     ix

Foreword     xi

Preface     xiii

1. **Planning and Design of Interior Spaces**     1

**Residential Spaces**     3

| | |
|---|---|
| Period furniture | 5 |
| Furniture dimensions | 44 |
| Living rooms | 61 |
| Dining rooms | 80 |
| Bedrooms | 87 |
| Bathrooms | 100 |
| Kitchens | 149 |
| Library/study | 190 |
| Family/recreation rooms | 196 |
| Laundry/sewing rooms | 200 |
| Closets/storage areas | 206 |

**Office Spaces**     221

| | |
|---|---|
| General offices and multiple workstations | 223 |
| Private offices | 231 |
| Electronic workstations | 241 |
| Conference rooms | 249 |
| Reception areas | 260 |
| Furniture, furnishings, and equipment | 278 |

**Hospitality Spaces**     305

| | |
|---|---|
| Restaurants | 307 |
| Bars | 346 |
| Hotels | 374 |

**Retail Spaces**     385

| | |
|---|---|
| Shops | 387 |
| Banks | 396 |
| Department stores | 401 |

**Public Restrooms, Toilets, and Coatrooms**     423

| | |
|---|---|
| Restrooms and toilets | 425 |
| Coatrooms | 460 |

**2. Construction Details and Finishes**    **467**

| | |
|---|---|
| Partitions and wall finishes | 469 |
| Floors and floor finishes | 516 |
| Doors | 566 |
| Ceilings | 641 |
| Stairs | 660 |
| Fireplaces | 724 |
| Lighting | 743 |

**3. Architectural Woodwork**    **779**

| | |
|---|---|
| Standard joinery and casework details | 781 |
| Woodwork details | 804 |
| Cornices and mouldings | 866 |
| Furniture hardware | 887 |

**4. Specialties**    **903**

| | |
|---|---|
| Plantscaping | 906 |
| Signage and graphics | 931 |
| Audio-visual systems | 949 |
| Auditorium seating | 961 |
| Security | 977 |
| Color theory | 998 |
| Window treatments | 1015 |
| Elevators | 1060 |
| Indoor recreation | 1069 |
| Accessories | 1075 |

**5. General Reference Data**    **1103**

| | |
|---|---|
| Space planning | 1106 |
| Human factors | 1110 |
| Floor and wall covering | 1122 |
| Fabric | 1130 |
| Electrical | 1132 |
| Columns, capitals, and entablatures | 1135 |
| Nails, screws, and bolts | 1136 |
| Mathematical data and formulas | 1139 |

| | |
|---|---|
| Credits | 1145 |
| Index | 1151 |

# Contributors

Marvin Affrime
Andrew Alpern, AIA
Amon & Graecen *Architects*
David Appel, DLF, IALD
Bertram L. Bassuk *Architect*
Anthony Beaumont *Architect*
Jeannie Bochette *Steelcase*
Louis Bowman *Architect*
Scott Bromley *Architect*
Bromley Jacobsen *Architecture and Design*
Jerry Caldari *Architect*
Toni Chi/Albert Chen Associates
Will Ching *Planning and Design*
Barbara Cianci, IALD
Cameron Clark *Architect*
Davis, Brody & Wisniewski *Architects*
Majorie Earthlife
Brad Elias, ASID
David Engel *Landscape Architect*
Engel/GGP *Landscape Architects*
Paul Eshelman, IDEC
Evans, Moore, Peterson & Woodbridge *Architects*
Charles D. Flayhan Associates, Inc.
Frank J. Forster *Architect*
Ulrich Franzen *Architect*
Gensler Associates
Franklin H. Gottschall
Adrienne Grad
Julius Gregory *Architect*
Albert Halse
Hochheiser Elias Design Group, Inc.
Caleb Hornbolstel *Architect*
Lees Horton
ISD Incorporated
Lawrence Israel, FAIA *Architect*
Francis Joannes *Architect*
Ely Jacques Kahn *Architect*
Mary Jean Kamin, ASID
William H. Kapple, AIA
Joseph Kleiman
Dorothy Lee
Sammy Lee *Architect*
Lori Lennon, ASID

Howard Litton, ASID
Steve Louie
Ronald Lubman *Architect*
Harry Lunstead Design, Inc.
Michael Lynn *Architect*
Michael Lynn & Associates
Nathan Jerry Maltz, AIA *Architect*
William M. Manley, FASID
Mays, Simpson & Hunsicker *Architects*
Merrill, Humble, and Taylor *Architects*
Montgomery Winecoff & Associates, Inc.
William Morgan, FAIA
Bernhardt E. Muller *Architect*
Richard J. Neutra *Architect*
Julius Panero *Architect*
Panero Zelnik Associates
Parish Hadley Associates, Inc.
Perkins & Will *Architects*
Dennis Piermont, ASLA
Nicholas Politis *Professor, Fashion Institute of Technology*
John Russel Pope *Architect*
William Pulgram *Architect*
Ramey, Himes & Buchner *Architects*
Antonin Raymond *Architect*
Frank Rispoli
Saarinin, Swanson & Saarinen *Architects*
Jacqueline Siles
The Space Design Group
Richard Stonis
William Tarr
Andrew J. Thomas *Architect*
Thompson, Robinson, Toraby, Inc.
Darius Toraby *Architect*
Michael Trencher *Professor, Pratt Institute*
Verna, Cook, Salomosky *Architects*
Walker & Gillette *Architects*
Walker Group/CNI
Leroy P. Ward *Architect*
Edgar I. Williams *Architect*
Charlie Wing
Martin Zelnik *Architect*
Simon B. Zelnik, FAIA *Architect*

# Organizations

A & J Washroom Accessories
Access America
Alvarado Manufacturing Co., Inc.
American Olean Tile Company
American Parquet Association
American Sanitary Partition Corporation
American Specialties, Inc.
American Standard, Inc.
Architectural Paneling, Inc.
Architectural Woodwork Institute
Armor Elevator Company
Ascente
Bauman
Brown Manufacturing Co.
Buckingham-Virginia Slate Co.
Camden Window and Millwork
Clairson International
Closet Maid Systems
Conde Nast Publications, Inc.
Culter Manufacturing Corp.
Curvoflite
Designers Sign Company
Dover Elevator Systems
Eggers Industries
Eljer Plumbingware Division of Wallace-Murray Corporation
Euroflair
Focal Point, Inc.
Formica Corporation
Franciscan Tile Company
General Electric Lighting
General Services Administration
Glencoe Publishing Co.
Habitat
Hafele
Hartco Flooring/Tibbals Flooring Co.
Haws
Herman Miller, Inc.
Hollow Metal Manufacturers Association
Horton Lees Lighting Designs, Inc.
Howe Furniture Company

Hussey Seating Company
Illinois Agricultural Experiment Station
Ilttala, Inc.
Indiana Limestone Institute of America
Insulated Steel Door Systems Institute
Intergraph Corporation
Interkal, Inc.
JG Furniture Systems, Inc.
Just Bulbs Ltd.
Kinney Shoe Corporation
Kirsch Division of Cooper Industries, Inc.
Kohler
Lapeyre Stair Co.
Lehigh Furniture Corporation
Library Bureau, Inc.
Maclevy Health and Fitness Products
Manville
Marble Institute of America, Inc.
Marvin Windows
McGraw-Hill, Inc.
McKinney/Parker
Merillat
Midwest Plan Service
Modernfold
National Association of Architectural Metal Manufacturers
National Association of Ornamental Metal Manufacturers
National Cathode Corp.
National Retail Merchants Association
National Terrazzo and Mosaic Association, Inc.
Nesson Lamps, Inc.
New York City Housing Authority
Nichols Publishing
Niland Company
Osram Corporation
PAM International
Parker/Nutone
Philips Lighting Co.
Phillips & Brooks, Inc.
Pittcon Softforms
Pittsburg Corning Corp.

Putnam Rolling Ladder Co., Inc.
Railex Corporation
Roberts Step-Lite Systems
Roppe Rubber Corporation
St. Charles Kitchens
Schlage Lock Company
Schulte
Selby Furniture Hardware Co., Inc.
Simon and Schuster
Sister Kenny Institute
Steel Door Institute
Steelcase
Sweet's Division of McGraw-Hill, Inc.

Tarkett
Tile Council of America, Inc.
Triangle Pacific Corp.
Western Wood Products Association
Whirlpool
White Consolidated Industries, Inc.
Winebarger Church Furniture
Woodwork Institute of California
United States Dept. of Agriculture
United States Dept. of Commerce
United States Dept. of Housing and Urban Development
United States Dept. of the Interior
United States Dept. of Transportation

# Foreword

A resource of incredible range and detail, this volume was compiled by three remarkably inspired designers and educators. Because of their great knowledge of interior design and their sensitivity to the subject matter, they have created the most comprehensive source book for the field ever.

The editors spent three years bringing this volume to fruition, culling the best project drawings by outstanding designers to illustrate much of the subject matter and tapping their own anthropometric expertise to address space planning and special function areas. They also address the importance of historic influence on present-day design with an impressive review of period furniture and interior details. All of these things have produced a reference work of such scope and inclusiveness that the reader will be relieved of many hours in the pursuit of details and information, time saved that can be used for more innovation and creativity in developing solutions for client needs.

The authority and abundance of this book are a testimony to the maturation of this profession of ours and to the editors' appreciation and understanding of its importance.

*Jack Lowery, FASID, IDEC*


My pleasure in being invited to write part of the Foreword swiftly changed to respect and, in turn, awe at the scope and depth of this book.

To say that it is an encyclopedic compilation and mass of information is obvious. But it is especially and uniquely user-friendly. It presents the written and illustrative data without a trace of pedantry; it meets a real need in our interior designer professional resources. The editors' effort, dedication, and patience, sustained during a period of over three years, are truly heroic. An astonishing number of hours of input have produced a reference of incalculable value.

I offer the same cautionary advice mentioned in the Preface: If the book is a wonderfully comprehensive reference and support for interior design standards, historical material, suggested plan and design criteria, and regulatory limitations, it is not—it will never be—a subsitute for the inspired, creative design act, for imaginative solutions are always driven by new cultural conditions, programs, and functional requirements.

So to all you designers: Continue to spin your dreams, but do not stray far from this great resource.

*Lawrence J. Israel, AIA, FISP*

# Preface

*Time-Saver Standards for Interior Design and Space Planning* is a professional handbook dealing with the planning, design, and detailing of interior spaces. Its primary goal is to provide, within a single reference, information that typically is found dispersed throughout a multitude of sources, including manufacturers' catalogs, technical literature, books dealing with historic styles, and documents and drawings from various projects.

This handbook can be used by the small and medium-size interior design or architectural firm to establish an instant reference library of design data and details by providing a broad selection of detail types and techniques. In addition, the large firm will be able to substantially augment and modify an existing library of details.

Perhaps the most unique feature of this handbook is the vast array of construction and woodwork details reproduced directly from actual working drawings contributed by some of the nation's leading interior design and architectural firms. It is this that makes the handbook particularly useful to the interior designer, architect, and student alike.

This book consists of five sections. The first, entitled Planning and Design of Interior Spaces, deals with residential, office, hospitality, and retail spaces in terms of the relevant planning, design, and detailing data specifically associated with each. The second section, entitled Construction Details and Finishes, deals with various basic interior construction components associated with most interior spaces. These components include partitions, wall openings, wall finishes, floors and floor finishes, doors, ceilings, stairs, fireplaces, and lighting. Details relevant to each component have been contributed by practicing interior designers and architects as well as manufacturers.

The third section, entitled Architectural Woodwork, deals with standard joinery and casework details, customized woodwork details, cornices and mouldings, and furniture hardware. The fourth section, entitled Specialties, deals with various specialized areas of equipment, systems, furnishings, and decoration, including signage and graphics, audio-visual systems, window treatments, and accessories. Information for these subject areas is drawn from manufacturers, suppliers, and designers.

The fifth section, entitled General Reference Data, provides the most comprehensive set of time-saving reference materials found in handbooks of this type, including tables, charts, formulas, and planning guidelines. Of particular interest to the architect, interior designer, and facility manager are tables that can be easily used to determine carpet and wall covering yardage. Charts and drawings relative to human factors and planning standards are also provided.

It should be noted that since the details and other information presented in this book have been compiled from so many different sources, it is difficult to ensure that all the data are entirely accurate or appropriate; for example, in some instances planning guidelines may reflect minimum acceptable standards and not necessarily ideal or preferred standards. In other instances the details indicated may have been perfectly adequate in the context of the total building design of which they were a part, but they may well require modification to reflect design conditions and the reader's intended use. It should also be noted that building codes, fire safety regulations, barrier-free standards, and many other laws governing the design and construction of buildings vary from state to state. Accordingly, the reader should consult all applicable local, state, and federal codes for conformance prior to applying any of the information contained in this book. Moreover, the reader is cautioned that the dimensional information provided in connection with furniture, equipment, appliances, accessories, etc., has been obtained from manufacturers and technical literature and thus varies from supplier to supplier and from source to source. Certain items may have been discontinued, others modified, and still others replaced. Although every effort has been made to ensure the reasonableness of the information, the reader is cautioned to consult the manufacturer of the item specified for current dimensional data.

The reader is also advised that most drawings and other illustrative material have been enlarged or reduced for reasons of page layout and page size. The reader is cautioned, therefore, to disregard any scale designations and not to scale the drawings in order to determine any additional dimensional information.

Finally, as mentioned before, the plans and details contained in this book were extracted from complete sets of actual working drawings prepared by many different contributors. They were selected both because they were representative of typical situations faced by the designer of interior spaces and because they were particularly informative. The authors would like to underscore the fact that these plans and details, as well as all the other material presented in this book, are intended to serve only as a helpful point of departure in connection with the design process, and not as a substitute for original thinking and creativity.

Although every effort has been made to present reasonably accurate information, the editors and publisher assume no liability or responsibility for damage to persons or property alleged to have occurred as a direct or indirect consequence of the use and application of any of the contents of this book. The reader is advised to view the subject matter primarily as guidelines for preliminary planning and detailing, and to properly review, modify, and process it to ensure conformance with local codes and practices and appropriateness of applicability.

*Joseph De Chiara*
*Julius Panero*
*Martin Zelnik*

# 1

# Planning and Design of Interior Spaces

# Residential Spaces

| | |
|---|---|
| Period furniture | 5 |
| Furniture dimensions | 44 |
| Living rooms | 61 |
| Dining rooms | 80 |
| Bedrooms | 87 |
| Bathrooms | 100 |
| Kitchens | 149 |
| Library/study | 190 |
| Family/recreation rooms | 196 |
| Laundry/sewing rooms | 200 |
| Closets/storage areas | 206 |

## THE EXTERIOR

THE 17th Century immigrants brought to America the building traditions of their native lands. The Parson Capen house (1683) at Topsfield, Mass., for example, closely resembles English houses of the same period. But the clapboards are typically American. In the panels at right are close-up details of the Early Colonial background.

### Moldings and trim

### Doorway surrounds

## THE LIVING ROOM

THIS living room is typical of those in the more elaborate Early Colonial homes. The crewel-embroidered curtains are blue-green with touches of red. This is taken up by the upholstery—blue-green damask for the sofas, red tapestry for the chairs. The Oriental rug and the portrait above the fireplace are both in tones of red, brown and yellow, with red dominant.

An alternative color scheme would have blue and yellow upholstery (needlework for the chairs, satin for the sofas). The walls would be pine-paneled, adorned with silver sconces, the curtains a bright cotton print in red, yellow, blue and white.

### Living-room fabrics

PETIT-POINT ON SATIN

NEEDLEWORK PANEL

NEEDLEPOINT TAPESTRY

### Wing chairs, sofas, armchairs, stools

Furniture made in America during the Early Colonial period (the seventeenth century and the first quarter of the eighteenth century) was necessarily, and possibly also by choice, of the simplest type. The early colonists, particularly those in New England, had not time or equipment to spare for any but the essentials of life.

Turning on the lathe was the simplest to achieve and thus the most common form of furniture decoration. It was also a process capable of infinite variations of design (some are shown in Fig. 1).

**Fig. 1 Motifs characteristic of Early Colonial furniture.**

## THE DINING ROOM

THE color scheme in this dining room is keyed to the low tones of the pine paneling and walnut furniture, the soft gleam of the smooth polished brass chandelier. The bannister back chairs have rush-bottom seats. Brilliant red and white printed cotton is used for the curtains. The hooked rug is in reds and greens.

Alternatively the curtains might be of red and yellow crewel embroidery, the upholstery of red brocade. In the panels at right are furniture and fabrics suited to an Early Colonial dining room.

### Dining-room fabrics

NEEDLEPOINT TAPESTRY

CUT VELVET

COTTON PRINT

### Dining tables, table chairs

OAK TABLE

TABLE CHAIRS —
THE BACK SWINGS
DOWN OVER THE ARMS

SIDE TABLE
WITH CABRIOLE LEGS

OVAL TABLE, QUEEN ANNE STYLE,
WITH CABRIOLE LEGS

MAPLE BUTTERFLY TABLE,
FROM NEW ENGLAND

PLANK-TOP REFECTORY TABLE

ENGLISH GATE-LEG TABLE C 1670

## THE BEDROOM

THIS little bedroom with its pine paneling and low ceiling is typical of the Early Colonial period. The bed, decorated with hangings of crewel work in an Oriental design, is the most important feature of the room. The chairs are upholstered in yellow damask. The green printed cotton used for the little draped window curtains is echoed by the greens in the hooked rug on the floor.

Alternatively the walls might be painted a dark gray-blue, the curtain material being a red printed cotton on a gray ground. The furniture is of walnut and oak.

### Bedroom fabrics

DAMASK

PRINTED CALICO

CREWEL EMBROIDERY BASED ON TREE OF LIFE DESIGN

### Beds, daybed, cradle

PRIMITIVE TRUNDLE BED

FOLDING PRESS BED

CANOPY BED

WALNUT FOUR-POSTER
C. 1710

PANELED CRADLE

DAYBED OF "CAIN" STYLE C.1690

Even the most costly furniture in this Early Colonial period was usually of solid wood unfinished except for stain or waxing. Veneering and shellacking, to gain carefully patterned graining and high finish, were still unexploited. The pine paneling on the walls might be left unfinished, waxed, or painted. Other woods near at hand in the forests and so commonly used were oak, birch, maple, and walnut. Generally, American work is patterned upon English work of 10 or 20 years earlier. In Pennsylvania and Delaware, which were settled by colonists of Swedish and German descent (in addition to the English), much of the simple furniture was painted with its motifs transferred from European peasant art.

In the later years of the Early Colonial period, when New Englanders were already beginning to trade with the Orient, much Chinese porcelain was imported. The Oriental influence was strong in textiles; the Tree of Life pattern was very popular at this period. Native textiles copied the patterns

## Armchair, side chairs

"CAIN" CHAIRS, FLEMISH SCROLLS AND FEET, CANE BACKS AND SEATS

BANNISTER BACK, SIMPLE TURNED LEGS

EARLY TYPE CABRIOLE LEGS

CANE SEAT, PLAIN SPLAT

LATE QUEEN ANNE TYPE, FLATTENED BALL AND CLAW FEET

BANNISTER BACK, SPANISH FEET

EARLY QUEEN ANNE TYPE WITH DUTCH SPLAT BACK

UPHOLSTERED CHAIR, WITH DUTCH FEET

SHELL CRESTING, SHALLOW SEAT

PIERCED BACK, BALL-AND-CLAW FEET

## Sideboards, dressers, chests

OAK SIDEBOARD CABRIOLE LEGS C 1650

LOW CHEST WITH DRAWERS

NEW ENGLAND OAK PRESS CUPBOARD

HEAVY OAK CHEST OF DRAWERS WITH APPLIED MOLDINGS

OAK SIDEBOARD, TWISTED LEGS

WILLIAM AND MARY TYPE GLASS-FRONTED CABINET

PENNSYLVANIA SPICE CUPBOARD C. 1700

WALNUT DRESSER, PANELED DOORS

## Dining-room accessories

WROUGHT-IRON ANDIRON

BRASS ANDIRON

SPICE BOX

PAINTED BELLOWS

SPOON RACK

CANDLESTICKS

17th CENTURY DUTCH WALL CLOCK

BRASS CANDELABRA

SILVER CANDLESTAND

SILVER SCONCE WITH RAISED EMBOSSED EDGE

WALNUT-FRAMED MIRRORS AMERICAN QUEEN ANNE STYLE, C. 1710

ETCHED MIRROR SCONCE, GLASS DRIP DISHES

## Chests, kas, highboy, chests of drawers

MAPLE CHEST OF DRAWERS

BOX TABLE OF OAK AND MAPLE C 1670

INLAID CHEST OF DRAWERS WITH DROP HANDLES

CHEST ON FRAME, DECORATED WITH SCRATCH CARVING

CONNECTICUT PAINTED CHEST

HIGHBOY WITH TRUMPET-TURNED LEGS

DUTCH KAS WITH BALL FEET

DUTCH KAS FROM NEW YORK PAINTED IN GRAY AND WHITE

## Desk, lowboys, night tables, stools

WALNUT CORNER CHAIR

OAK JOINT STOOL

LOWBOY IN BURL WALNUT

NIGHT TABLE

ARMCHAIR QUEEN ANNE STYLE

CANDLESTAND

STOOL WILLIAM AND MARY TYPE

NIGHT TABLE

CARVED OAK WRITING BOX C 1650

UPHOLSTERED JACOBEAN SIDE CHAIR

LOWBOY WITH SHELL FRONT

SLANT-TOP DESK ON A TURNED FRAME

## Bedroom accessories

WROUGHT-IRON CANDLESTAND

HOG-SCRAPER CANDLESTICK

CHINESE PORCELAIN

RUSH LIGHT STAND

MIRROR SCONCE WITH SHELL TOP

SMALL WALL MIRROR

MIRROR SCONCE

REFLECTOR CANDLESTICK

WALNUT DRESSING MIRRORS 1700 - 1710

DOUBLE CANDLESTAND WITH METAL SHADES

and colors of India, Persia, and China. The originals, or good copies of them, were usually imported from England.

The colors in common use were of a piece with the solid, sturdy furniture. They seldom escaped from the conventional round of blue, red, gold, and natural gray. The only exceptions were imported fabrics and the occa-

sional hard brilliance of the Chinese porcelain found in the great houses of the day. Whatever luxury there was at this time expressed itself in textiles and silver rather than in furniture. Settlers in the South, many of them English aristocrats, maintained a higher standard of comfort than those in the North; they imported most of their furniture and fabrics

from England and continued to do so for a long time.

Early Colonial furniture taken as a whole is sturdy, but not subtle. Furniture patterns in this country changed slowly. Paneling relieved the larger flat areas such as cupboard doors and drawer fronts. The latter were further decorated by quite elaborate fretted

# PERIOD FURNITURE

### 17th Century American: Colonial

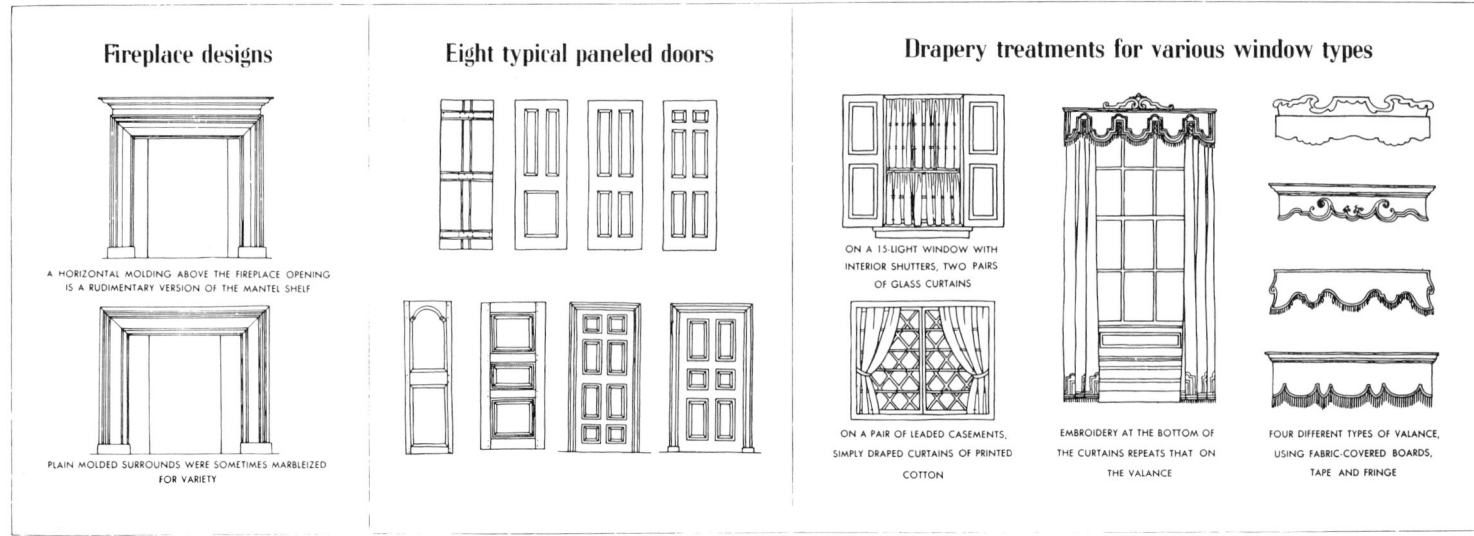

**Fireplace designs**

A HORIZONTAL MOLDING ABOVE THE FIREPLACE OPENING
IS A RUDIMENTARY VERSION OF THE MANTEL SHELF

PLAIN MOLDED SURROUNDS WERE SOMETIMES MARBLEIZED
FOR VARIETY

**Eight typical paneled doors**

**Drapery treatments for various window types**

ON A 15-LIGHT WINDOW WITH
INTERIOR SHUTTERS, TWO PAIRS
OF GLASS CURTAINS

ON A PAIR OF LEADED CASEMENTS,
SIMPLY DRAPED CURTAINS OF PRINTED
COTTON

EMBROIDERY AT THE BOTTOM OF
THE CURTAINS REPEATS THAT ON
THE VALANCE

FOUR DIFFERENT TYPES OF VALANCE,
USING FABRIC-COVERED BOARDS,
TAPE AND FRINGE

**Corner cupboards, cabinets, secretaries, chest**

BONNET-TOP
CABINET

WALNUT CHINA CABINET

CORNER CUPBOARD,
GOLD LACQUERED

QUEEN ANNE SECRETARY

RED LACQUERED SECRETARY
WITH PAINTED GLASS PANELS

MAHOGANY
CORNER CUPBOARD

RED LACQUER CHINA CABINET

HIGH CHEST,
WILLIAM AND MARY STYLE
C 1700

**Occasional tables, desk, lowboys, pedestals**

FOLDING TOP CARD TABLE

WALNUT BURL TABLE
WILLIAM AND MARY STYLE
C. 1690

QUEEN ANNE STYLE PEDESTALS

YARN WINDER

PINE HUTCH TABLE

NEW ENGLAND SPINNING WHEEL

LOWBOY WITH
TRUMPET-TURNED LEGS
AND CROSS STRETCHERS

CARVED OAK CHEST
ON LEGS

LOWBOY WITH
SHAPED APRON

LACQUERED LOWBOY
WITH CABRIOLE LEGS

TILE-TOP TABLE WITH
TRUMPET-TURNED LEGS
AND CROSS STRETCHERS

WALNUT DESK WITH BALL FEET

**Living-room accessories**

SILVER SCONCE

CANDLE BOX

BRASS ANDIRONS

CANDLE AND BETTY LAMP
TO BE SPIKED INTO WALL
OR CEILING BEAM

CANDLESTICK WITH
WROUGHT-IRON GUARD

ADJUSTABLE WOODEN STAND
FOR BETTY LAMPS

PIPE BOX

RUSH LIGHT HOLDER

WOODEN RATCHET
CANDLESTAND

EARLY DUTCH TYPE
WALL CLOCK

WALNUT-FRAMED MIRRORS
TOP PANEL OF ETCHED GLASS

BRASS AND DECORATED
MIRROR SCONCE

brass and wrought-iron hardware (see Fig. 1).

More carefully embellished than the earliest American furniture were the pieces imported by the colonists from their various homelands. These pieces, and the memories of others left behind, later served as models for American craftsmen. The dominant influence was Dutch, for the English had a Hollander, William of Orange, as king. He and his queen, Mary, gave their names to a style of which elaborate stretchers (particularly on highboys, lowboys, and occasional tables) and scrolled legs are among the most obvious characteristics.

Also from Dutch, Spanish, and Portuguese sources are derived most of the carved feet

**Chair backs**

CARVED YOKE

VOLUTE CRESTING

**Common types of leg**

TYPICAL
TURNED
LEGS

HOCK

PLAIN AND
DECORATED
CABRIOLE

FLEMISH
SCROLL

**Furniture hardware**

BRASS HANDLE AND KEY PLATE

DROP PULLS

BUTTERFLY
HINGE

H AND L
HINGE

**Common types of feet**

PORTUGUESE
SCROLL

DUTCH

DUTCH
CUSHION

BALL
WITH SHOE

SNAKE

BALL
AND CLAW

SPANISH

**Fig. 1** *(Continued)*

which distinguish this Early Colonial furniture and often give clues to its date and place of origin.

## THE EXTERIOR

The architectural details shown in the five panels at right are characteristic of the background for 18th Century Colonial decoration. As one of the finest houses of the period we have pictured (at right) "Westover" the great mansion erected by William Byrd in Charles City Co., Virginia. Typical of this period are the brick walls and chimneys, the stone or white painted brick trim. In the North wood was in more common use than brick for the exterior, and the interior wooden trim was finely detailed.

### Typical Colonial architecture

### Cornices and trim

TYPICAL McINTIRE DETAILS: CORNICE    DADO RAIL    ANOTHER CORNICE

### Interior doorways

SECTION AB

EARLY GEORGIAN
CLASSIC MOTIFS OF COLUMN AND SWAG

DOORWAY FROM KING'S CHAPEL, BOSTON

## THE LIVING ROOM

The furniture, fabrics and accessories shown in these panels are all suitable to the living room, and they are all typical of the 18th Century Colonial style.

The interior pictured at right is a fine Colonial living room carefully restored to its 18th Century state. The walls are Naples yellow, the columns and fireplace white. Red and green are dominant in the Oriental rug, dark greens and browns in the portrait above the fireplace. So the sofa is upholstered in striped satin, the armchair in yellow Venetian brocade, the wing chair in a printed linen. The urns are of Chinese porcelain.

Another color scheme might be: pearly gray walls, oyster white columns and fireplace. Red would be dominant in the Oriental carpet, dark greens and red in the portrait. There would be red damask on the sofa, green rep on the wing chair, and gold damask for the armchair.

### Decorating a Colonial living room

### Fabrics for curtains and upholstery

EMBROIDERY    SATIN    BLOCK PRINT

### Wing chairs, armchairs, sofas

CONNECTICUT WING CHAIR    PHILADELPHIA VERSION OF HEPPLEWHITE    MARTHA WASHINGTON CHAIR

CABRIOLE LEG SOFA    1760 - 1770    SETTEE CHIPPENDALE INFLUENCE

HEPPLEWHITE STYLE    PHILADELPHIA TYPE DESK CHAIR CABRIOLE LEG    PHILADELPHIA MAKE CHIPPENDALE STYLE

PHILADELPHIA TYPE WING CHAIR CHIPPENDALE INFLUENCE    MAHOGANY CHIPPENDALE SOFA

Whereas furniture of the Early Colonial period was often so primitive as to be referred to as "kitchen Colonial," in this succeeding era dignity and luxury prevail in the centers of taste. The furnishings reflect the fashionable contemporary styles of England and stately country homes, whether on New England farms or Virginian and Carolina plantations, followed these styles. This gave rise to a number of notable architects, craftsmen, and workers in metal and wood.

The eighteenth century Colonial period was the first of the really great eras in American cabinetmaking.

The manufacture of wallpaper in this country was begun by 1763. Before this it was from Europe. The "Pennsylvania fireplace" or "Franklin stove" was invented by Benjamin Franklin in 1742 and immediately became popular up and down the Atlantic seaboard. Philadelphia was a furniture style center, in fact the most active in the creation of taste, with Boston and Charleston following.

A number of artists and craftsmen of this period bear mentioning. Among the architects were Samuel McIntire, Charles Bulfinch, John James, Richard Mundy, Peter Harrison, John Kirk, and Isaac Royall. These men were greatly influenced by the English architects Isaac Ware, James Gibbs, Robert Morris, Abraham Swan, William Halfpenny, Batty Langley, and William Pain, who in turn were in debt to the Italian masters Palladio and Giacomo Leoni. Among the cabinetmakers were Moses Dodge, Stephen Dwight, Henry Hardcastle, Gilbert Ash, Robert Wallace, Charles Shipman, John Brinner, John Tremain, Charles Warham, John Brown, Bemsley Wells, Thomas and Benjamin Laskey, Jonathan Goodhue, and Job Trask. Among the upholsterers were Stephen Callow, Richard Wenman, Joseph Cox, and John Taylor; among the metalworkers were William Coffin, Wilkins, Joseph Liddell, William Bradford, John Bassett, and Peter Harby; and among the painters were John Singleton Copley, Joseph Blackburn, John

# DINING ROOM

The furniture and fabrics shown in the five panels at right would look well in any dining room; but for your guidance in the selection of materials and colors we illustrate at right a fine Colonial dining room as it might have appeared in the 18th Century.

The pine-panelled walls are colored a light ocher, the niches Chinese red. Curtains are French blue. Blue, rust and beige predominate in the Oriental rug, dark green, blue and black in the portrait over the fireplace. Table and chairs are of walnut, the sideboard of mahogany.

An alternative color scheme would be light blue-gray walls with cream niches. Curtains would be oyster white silk, the Oriental rug having a greenish tan background.

### Decorating a Colonial dining room

### Fabric for curtains and upholstery

BROCADE          PRINTED LINEN          STRIPED BROCADE

### Dining tables, consoles

MAHOGANY CONSOLE WITH MARBLE TOP AMER. CHIPPENDALE STYLE

CABRIOLE LEG, DROP LEAF DINING TABLE

PHILADELPHIA MAKE SHERATON INFLUENCE

AMERICAN HEPPLEWHITE DINING TABLE

AMERICAN HEPPLEWHITE

CONSOLE TABLE 1760 - 1770

EXTENSIBLE DINING TABLE 1770

# BEDROOM

In the bedroom at right, choice of color and textures was designed to achieve an impression of warmth and intimacy. The paneled walls are in two tones of gray-green, the ceiling ocher. Curtains are antique gray-green satin.

Furniture is walnut, except for the mahogany bed, which has a yellow taffeta spread. Fireside chairs are covered in crimson damask, side chairs in turkey work.

An alternative color scheme would be: warm gray walls with oyster white moldings. The ceiling would be cream, the carpet solid taupe, and the curtains of blue damask. The bed would have a white moire spread and blue valance. The side chairs would be upholstered in yellow damask, the wing chair in turkey work.

### Decorating a Colonial bedroom

### Fabrics for curtains, upholstery, canopy

PRINTED LINEN          TOILE DE JOUY          DAMASK

### Four-poster beds

MAPLE LOW POSTER BED

FIELD BED AND TESTER

FIELD BED AND TESTER

LATE 18TH CENTURY TYPE

Ramage, James Peale, and Charles Wilson Peale. Important manufacturers were, of wallpaper, Jackson of Battersea (England) and, of window and bottle glass, Baron Stiegel and Caspar Wistar.

Fabrics most commonly used during the Colonial period were damask, camblet, Indian gimp and binding, moreen (woolen drapery cloth), harrateen cloth, block-printed cotton and linen, cashmere, calico, dimity, durance, stout worsted cloth, turkey work (tufted "pilelike"), paduasoy (strong silk), soy, shalloon, watchet, linsey-woolsey, fustian, silk muslin, chintz, Indian calico, tabby, sarcanet, taffeta, horsehair, camak, bancours, and brocade.

Woods most commonly used were oak, ash, elm, red cedar, mahogany, walnut, maple, pine, and cherry.

The Chippendale style merges at one end with Queen Anne, at the other with Hepplewhite, Sheraton, and Duncan Phyfe. The Rococo mounts to its zenith and starts to decline within these years. Walnut has a new rival in mahogany. And American craftsmen produced pieces of a quality which compares favorably with English work.

## Armchairs, side chairs

## Sideboards, lowboys, chests

## Dining room accessories

## Chests, kas, secretary

## Wing chairs, armchairs, tables

## Bedroom accessories

Marble was imported until after the Revolution when domestic marbles began to be used. Marble chimney pieces, window sash, lead roofing, and hardware were all imported from London. The size of glass window panes gradually increased as the century progressed.

An order of small pilasters or columns supporting the mantel in a chimney piece was found only in imported work prior to the Revolution. Fireplace openings with neither cornice nor mantel shelf were long common. Ears on the architraves were almost universal, and a pediment (always broken) was very common. After 1760 the scroll pediment, or a similar treatment of the architrave, occurs.

# PERIOD FURNITURE
### 18th Century American: Colonial

## Fireplace designs

FINE COLONIAL CHIMNEY PIECE
SHELF 7'-11" WIDE, 5'-1" HIGH
WOOD OPENING 5'-4" WIDE,
3'-8" HIGH
WIDTH MIDWAY 6'-11"
3" PROJECTION

CHIMNEY PIECE IN THE
STYLE OF SAMUEL McINTIRE

SHELF 5'-1½" WIDE, 4'-0" HIGH
WOOD OPENING 3'-8" WIDE,
3'-0" HIGH
WIDTH MIDWAY 4'-11"
4" PROJECTION

## Window details

SMALLER DOUBLE HUNG WINDOW
PLACED ABOVE DADO  9 PANE SASH

MORE ELABORATE RECESSED TYPE WITH
WINDOW SEAT BELOW  12 PANE SASH

## Drapery treatments

CLASSIC TYPE OF DAMASK DRAPING USUALLY
ORNAMENTED WITH AN ELABORATE FRINGE

TYPE OF DRAPERY USUALLY DONE IN
TAFFETA AND LEFT PLAIN OR FRINGED

## Secretaries, highboy, clocks

HIGHBOY
CHIPPENDALE INFLUENCE

BRACKET CLOCK

CLOCK WITH
PAINTED GLASS PANEL

SECRETARY
WITH BOMBÉ BASE
ROCOCO

MAHOGANY
GRANDFATHER'S CLOCK

MAHOGANY BREAKFRONT
CHIPPENDALE STYLE

GRANDFATHER'S CLOCK
BY J. WILDER OF HINGHAM

## Desks, tables, firescreen

LATE
SOUTHERN COLONIAL
1760

WALL TABLE

POLE FIRE SCREEN
1775

MAHOGANY
SIDE TABLE

LATE
SOUTHERN COLONIAL
CARD TABLE

SLANT TOP DESK
1750

KNEEHOLE MAHOGANY DESK
RHODE ISLAND BLOCKFRONT

TIP TOP TEA TABLE
C. 1775

MAHOGANY CONSOLE TABLE

## Living room accessories

SANDWICH GLASS
OIL LAMP

GLASS DOLPHIN
CANDLESTICK

PEWTER
SCONCE

MINIATURE FRAMED
IN ROPE MOLDING

URN

PAUL REVERE SILVER TEAPOT
1789

COLONIAL
IN FULL ROCOCO SPIRIT
QUEEN ANNE INFLUENCE

PEWTER TEAPOT
1775

BRASS AND CRYSTAL SCONCE

CARVED AND GILT MIRROR

MAHOGANY
BOX

CANDELABRA
USED BY
GEORGE WASHINGTON

BRASS ANDIRONS 21" HIGH 25" LONG

CRYSTAL AND
WEDGWOOD
CANDELABRA

## THE EXTERIOR

As a typical mansion of the Federal period we show Mappa Hall in Trenton, N.Y. It was started in the closing years of the 18th Century and completed in 1809. The portico and the simple pediment exemplify the prevailing Classic trend. In the panels to the right are some typical details from the Federal period background

### Cornices and trim

CORNICE

UNDERSIDE OF CORNICE

CORNICE

CHAIR RAIL

WINDOW TRIM
AND DADO 1800

CORNICE

### Doorways for the interior

DOORWAY OF FEDERAL TYPE
GLASS FANLIGHT WITH LEAD CAMES

DOOR BY SAMUEL McINTIRE

## THE LIVING ROOM

This is a fine Federal interior in its original condition. The walls and woodwork are painted pistachio green. The curtains are of beige damask, the sofa upholstered in red and gold damask. Gold damask is used for the armchairs, yellow damask for the side chairs. The Oriental rug is wine red in tone, the furniture, mahogany. The clock is of ox-blood marble.

An alternate scheme would have light gray-blue walls and woodwork. The draperies would be yellow damask, the chairs upholstered in green damask. The furniture and fabrics shown in panels at right would also be suitable for the Federal living room

### Living room fabrics

SATIN DAMASK

VELOUR

SILK DAMASK

### Armchairs, side chair, sofas

SABER-LEG SOFA

ENGLISH REGENCY ARMCHAIR

SIDE CHAIR WITH HARP BACK
HAIR AND PAW FEET

SOFA BY PHYFE

SOFA CARVED BY SAMUEL McINTIRE
LOUIS XVI INFLUENCE

SHERATON TYPE CHAIR
MADE FOR GEORGE WASHINGTON
NOW IN CITY HALL, NEW YORK

ARMCHAIR
BY PHYFE

CANED BACK SETTEE BY PHYFE  c. 1805

The Federal style is at its most suave and elegant in the furniture of Duncan Phyfe, a Scotch cabinetmaker who arrived in New York about 1795. He did not originate a style; he translated prevailing fashions into fine craftsmanship. Thomas Sheraton, then the current English favorite, and the French Directoire cabinetmakers set the style. All these designers were profoundly influenced by a rediscovery of the classic splendors of Greece and Italy.

Reeding of table, chair, and sofa legs and other framing members gives elegance to Federal furniture. Contrasting color veneer is used to outline the edges of tables and desks and to lend interest to large plain surfaces.

CARVED
SUPPORTING POSTS

URN-SHAPED
TABLE POST

ROSETTE AT
CROSSING

LYRE FROM CHAIR BACK
STRINGS ARE BRASS
OR WHALEBONE

SIMPLE CHAIR SPLAT

OVOID CHAIR SPLAT

SABER
SOFA LEG

CORNUCOPIA
SOFA LEG

**Fig. 2  Motifs characteristic of Federal furniture.**

## THE DINING ROOM

IN THE dining room shown above the walls are mist gray, the chimneypiece ochre and white marble. The drapery and upholstery are both cherry silk damask. The Oriental rug is in tones of brown, blue and beige. The furniture is mahogany.

An alternate scheme would include: soft gray-green walls, beige silk damask curtains, red damask upholstery. The sconces, clock and picture frames would be gilt.

This original Federal period dining room will give you ideas for using the furniture and fabrics shown in the panels at right. Or reproductions of similar pieces are appropriate.

### Dining room fabrics

SATIN

PRINTED SILK

BROCATELLE

### Dining tables, side tables, console

PEDESTAL DINING TABLE

LYRE END TABLE BY PHYFE

CONSOLE WITH EGYPTIAN CARYATIDS

EXTENSION TYPE TABLE BY PHYFE

PEDESTAL DINING TABLE

SOFA TABLE BY PHYFE

FOUR SOFA TABLES JOINED TO FORM A DINING TABLE

FOLDING TOP OCCASIONAL TABLE

## THE BEDROOM

THIS bedroom shown above is typical of those found in fine houses during the Federal period. Walls, woodwork and chimneypiece are painted moss green. The upholstery is beige damask, except for yellow satin on the desk chair. The rug is in two tones of burgundy with a design of green, pink and white. On the walls are engravings in gilt frames.

An alternate color scheme would have walls and woodwork painted peach color. The rug would then be olive green with a design in yellow and pink. The upholstery would be blue, except for red satin on the seat of the desk chair. Other furniture and fabrics suitable for this room are shown at right

### Bedroom fabrics

SILK

SATIN

DAMASK

### Four-poster and other types of bed

FOUR-POSTER BED BY PHYFE

BED BY PHYFE, LOUIS XVI AFFINITY

MAHOGANY BED ONE OF A PAIR BY PHYFE

BED BY PHYFE FRENCH INFLUENCE

Another characteristic subtlety is the raised hairline of wood, known as a cock beading, which is used to finish off the edges of drawers. Phyfe used white wood linings for the drawers in his furniture, instead of the pine linings universally employed by other American cabinetmakers of this period.

Brass ornaments (probably for the most part imported) are used extensively on Federal pieces. They have brass feet and casters, ring handles, and other types of applied ornament. Toward the end of the period, about 1825, china and glass knobs began to supplant brass rings as drawer pulls.

The new United States was in its first throes of nationalism; consequently its emblem, the eagle, appears everywhere — on transparencies in windows, painted on fans, inlaid in mirrors, desks, knife boxes, and brass work. The "Spread Eagle" became a favorite tavern sign. All kinds of historic scenes and patriotic emblems appear as decoration on clocks.

And yet, the Classic influence was even stronger than the patriotic. Earthenware and porcelain such as Crown-Derby, Worcester,

## Armchairs, side chairs

TYPICAL CHAIRS OF AMERICAN FEDERAL DESIGN 1790-1830

## Sideboards, chests of drawers

BUTLER'S DESK BY PHYFE

CHEST OF DRAWERS, MAHOGANY AND SATINWOOD c. 1800

ENGLISH REGENCY SIDEBOARD EGYPTIAN INFLUENCE

DEEP-END SIDEBOARD BY PHYFE

SIDEBOARD BY PHYFE c. 1815

SIDEBOARD WITH REEDED LEGS IN THE PHYFE MANNER

MAHOGANY SIDEBOARD LION'S HEAD AND RING HANDLES

CHEST OF DRAWERS BY ALEXANDER SHAW

## Dining room accessories

WALL SCONCE FROM MOUNT VERNON

PORCELAIN BASKET BOWL

CRYSTAL TOP CANDLESTICK c. 1830

PINE AND METAL SCONCE c. 1800

CONVEX MIRROR WITH CRYSTAL CANDLE BRACKETS

SANDWICH MOLDED GLASS WHALE OIL LAMP

CHINESE LOWESTOFT JAR 1820

SILVER PLATED SCONCE

PORCELAIN URN

CLOCK, FRENCH EMPIRE STYLE

GILT SCONCE c. 1800

TORCHERE, PAINTED BLACK AND GOLD

SARCOPHAGUS GRATE

MIRROR IN GILT FRAME

## Dressing tables, wardrobe, chests

CHEST OF DRAWERS BY JOHN SEYMOUR MAHOGANY AND MAPLE VENEER

MAHOGANY DRESSING TABLE

CHEST OF DRAWERS BY SAMUEL McINTIRE

DRESSING TABLE BY PHYFE c. 1815

DRESSING TABLE MADE BY PHYFE FOR HIS DAUGHTER ELIZA

MAHOGANY BUREAU AND MIRROR BY WILLIAM HOOK

MAHOGANY WARDROBE

## Chairs, stools, tables, desks

ARMCHAIRS BY PHYFE

TAMBOUR WORKTABLE

UPHOLSTERED CHAIR BY PHYFE

NIGHT TABLE

WORK TABLE

SHERATON TYPE WRITING TABLE

FIGURED MAHOGANY CABINET DESK

BLACK AND GILT PAINTED CURULE CHAIR

MAHOGANY WINDOW SEAT CANED SEAT, CABRIOLE LEGS

STOOL SHERATON AFFINITY

## Bedroom accessories

MIRROR AND BRASS SCONCE

LAMP BASE

GLASS AND BRASS SCONCE

CHEVAL GLASS

BRASS SCONCE

BRASS DESK LAMP

SANDWICH GLASS LAMP

BASKET GRATE

PORCELAIN URN

WALL CLOCK

GILT MIRROR

CLOCK, GILT BRONZE ON A MARBLE BASE

ROSEWOOD FOOTSTOOL MOUNTED WITH ORMOLU

BRASS SCONCE ETCHED MIRROR BACK

and Wedgwood were molded in Classic forms and painted with delicate sepia figures in Classic robes. Silver and Sheffield plate (the latter replacing pewter) also followed Classic forms. Ireland sent Waterford glass.

Fabrics most used were damask, brocade, satin, taffeta, haircloth, toile de Jouy, printed cotton, and silk.

Woods most used were mahogany, cherry, and maple; and fruit woods in less splendid furniture. Curly maple often replaced the satinwood used in European models. After 1800 rosewood was used for the more costly furniture.

The Federal motifs derive almost exclusively from classical sources. The acanthus leaf, the lyre, the saber leg, the lion's mask and paw, the bowknot, rosettes, thunderbolts, trumpets, and drapery swags are all to be found on the list of standard Federal furniture motifs.

After the War of 1812, when the Federal era rose to its zenith of popularity, the laurel, cornucopia, and eagle motifs became especially popular. (See Fig. 2.)

Phyfe's treatment of the acanthus leaf is so typical that many of his pieces depend upon

# PERIOD FURNITURE
### 18th Century American: Federal

## Fireplace designs

CHIMNEY PIECE FROM BEACON HILL, BOSTON

CHIMNEY PIECE DESIGNED BY CHARLES BULFINCH

## Drapery treatments for five different types of window

FEDERAL DRAPERIES THROWN OVER TIEBACKS

SINGLE PANEL CURTAIN BALANCED WITH OTHER WINDOW

HEAVY MATERIAL FOR VALANCE, LIGHTER FOR DRAPERIES

RAISED CENTER VALANCE OF DIFFERENT COLOR

TYPICAL HEAVY FRINGES CONTRASTING COLOR LINING

## Secretaries, bookcases, cabinet, chest

MAHOGANY SECRETARY c. 1800

ROSEWOOD CABINET WITH GILT METAL GRILLES

TAMBOUR SECRETARY BY SAMUEL McINTIRE MAPLE, MAHOGANY, SATINWOOD

FAWN-COLORED BOOKCASE WITH GOLD DECORATION

CHEST ON CHEST BY SAMUEL McINTIRE

ROSEWOOD BOOKCASE MOUNTED WITH ORMOLU

SATINWOOD SECRETARY, REGENCY TYPE

## Desks, tables, piano, music desk

WALLTABLE BY PHYFE CROSSED LYRES SUPPORT

MAHOGANY DROP-LEAF TABLE BY PHYFE

LIBRARY TABLE BY PHYFE

FIVE-LEGGED CARD TABLE, FOLDING TOP

BLACK AND GILT PAINTED WRITING TABLE

OCCASIONAL TABLE c. 1800

DESK BY PHYFE

MAHOGANY MUSIC DESK c. 1800

WRITING DESK

PIANOFORTE PHYFE MAHOGANY CASE

MAHOGANY DESK c. 1800 SHERATON STYLE

## Living room accessories

CLASSIC PORCELAIN URN

GIRANDOLE 1821

SILVER AND GLASS LAMP

CONVEX MIRROR CARVED GILT FRAME c. 1810

BRONZE SCONCE

POLE SCREEN BY PHYFE

HOB-GRATE

SHELF CLOCK BY BENJAMIN MORREL 1816

WEDGWOOD CRYSTAL CANDLESTICK

MAHOGANY FOOTSTOOL

MIRROR IN TURNED AND GILT FRAME

CLOCK HEROIC CLASSIC INFLUENCE

this for their identification. It is simplified into a series of rounded grooves and ridges with a raised tapering ridge up the center.

The lyre was used to fill in the backs of chairs, to decorate the arms of sofas, and (split apart) to support mirrors on dressing tables. Two crossed lyres are used as support for a pedestal table.

TYPICAL FEDERAL TABLE LEGS

CARVED PANELS FROM CHAIR AND SOFA BACKS

WHEAT EARS TIED WITH BOWKNOT

CORNUCOPIAS TIED WITH BOWKNOT

SABER LEG

DOG'S FOOT CHAIR LEGS

LION'S FOOT IN BRASS

BRASS EAGLE FINIAL

LION'S MASK AND RING BRASS HANDLE

LAUREL

BED POST WITH ACANTHUS LEAF, AND WHORL ORNAMENT

**Fig. 2** *(Continued)*

## THE EXTERIOR

Typical of the better country houses in the second half of the 18th Century, is this design from Abraham Swan's *British Architect*, one of the many handbooks of builders' designs, which at this period carried news of architectural fashions from England to America. At right are close-up details of the Georgian background

### Moldings and trim

CORNICE OF FIREPLACE AT ONE CORNER OF THE MANTELSHELF

DADO RAIL

BASE MOLDING

CORNER OF A DOORHEAD WITH PULVINATED FRIEZE BELOW

MOLDINGS AROUND NICHES

CORNICE WITH ACANTHUS LEAF DECORATION AND MODILLIONS

### Interior doorway

CARVED PINE DECORATION COMBINES CLASSIC AND ORIENTAL MOTIFS

## THE LIVING ROOM

The pine-paneled walls in this characteristic Georgian living room are left unstained. The silk curtains are richly embroidered in many colors on a yellow ground which echoes the gilt frames used for pictures and mirrors. The crimson upholstery of the mahogany furniture is given added quality by the olive green carpet.

An alternative color scheme would be to have the walls painted dark gray-green with carving picked out in gold. The wall-to-wall carpet would be taupe, the upholstery of the wing chairs yellow Italian damask. In both color schemes needlepoint and natural leather would be used for upholstering other chairs in the room

### Living-room fabrics

CHINTZ

DAMASK

PRINTED SILK

### Armchairs, sofas, settees

TRIPLE CHAIR-BACK SETTEE, GOTHIC FRET SPLATS

DOUBLE CHAIR-BACK SETTEE, SWEPT WHORL TOP RAIL

CHIPPENDALE ARMCHAIR WITH CANTED ARMS

GEORGIAN TYPE DOUBLE CHAIR-BACK SETTEE

CHIPPENDALE WING CHAIR

UPHOLSTERED ARMCHAIR, CABRIOLE LEGS

CHIPPENDALE SOFA WITH CHINESE FRET

MAHOGANY CHIPPENDALE SETTEE

MAHOGANY CHIPPENDALE SOFA

Chippendale was a dominating factor in the history of Georgian furniture design and his name serves as a convenient tag for the period centering in the reign of the second of the three Georges who provide the period title. Yet this English cabinetmaker achieved eminence not so much by his own work as by that of his copyists.

They all used the designs in *The Gentleman and Cabinet-Makers' Director*, published by Chippendale in 1754. To fill this book Chippendale commandeered all the ideas he could lay his hands on and then embroidered them with his own fancy, adapted them to his own forms. He plundered the design manuals of China and the French rococo, of the ancient Gothic masters, and of his immediate predecessors in the English furniture trade.

### Georgian profiles

ROCOCO FRENCH

FRENCH BOMBE

CANTED CORNER

COMBINATION OF S AND C CURVES

### Common types of leg and foot

CARVED BRACKET FEET

CHINESE FRETTED

DECORATED CABRIOLE

FRETTED BRACKET FOOT

SCROLL FOOT

ROCOCO SPLAYED FOOT

CLUB FOOT

CLAW AND BALL FOOT

**Fig. 3   Motifs characteristic of Georgian furniture.**

From the craftsmen of the early eighteenth century Chippendale borrowed such tested forms as the cabriole leg, the claw-and-ball foot, and the typical acanthus leaf ornament. But to each of them he added a grace and charm of which the earlier furniture makers had never been capable.

Thomas Chippendale was a typical product of that brilliant English society which flourished during the mid–eighteenth century. He

## THE DINING ROOM

Hᴇʀᴇ the walls are pine-paneled, the wood being left its natural honey color. The consoles are also of pine. But brilliant against this pale background are the red damask curtains, and the mahogany furniture with its red and yellow striped silk upholstery.

Alternatively, the walls might be painted light blue as a background for yellow brocade curtains. The mahogany table and chairs stand on an Oriental rug which repeats colors found in the needlepoint upholstery. In the panels at right is furniture suitable for a room of this style

### Dining-room fabrics

CUT VELVET

CHINTZ

SILK BROCADE

### Armchairs, side chairs

ELABORATED SHELL BACK — CHINESE INFLUENCE IN DECORATION OF BACK SPLATS AND CABRIOLE LEGS — LADDER BACK — AMERICAN CHIPPENDALE SIMPLIFIED

OTHER CHARACTERISTIC EARLY GEORGIAN DESIGNS

CHIPPENDALE WITH CHINESE ORNAMENT

## THE BEDROOM

Cʜᴀʀᴀᴄᴛᴇʀɪsᴛɪᴄ of the Georgian period are the richly embroidered Chinese silk draperies and the delicately fretted four-poster bed in this room. The dominant tone is yellow, against which is posed green upholstery, with a gun-metal carpet for base, putty walls for background.

Alternatively the walls could be pale green, the carpet brown, the upholstery blue-green and yellow, the ceiling pale apricot. In the panels at right are other pieces suitable for a room of this type. Modern reproductions of such authentic pieces are available in good furniture stores

### Bedroom fabrics

CHINESE SILK BROCADE

PRINTED TAFFETA

PAINTED SATIN

### Four-poster and canopy beds

CHIPPENDALE FIELD BED WITH CANOPY

CHIPPENDALE BED WITH PAINTED SILK HANGINGS

CHIPPENDALE IN ROCOCO MANNER

COUCH BED DESIGNED FOR AN ALCOVE

was a contemporary of Josiah Wedgwood, the potter, and of Edmund Burke, the orator. Boswell and Johnson, Benjamin Franklin, Garrick, Gibbon, and Goldsmith, all added their wit and intelligence to the creation of a sturdy culture.

Thomas Chippendale served their changing taste and their fashionable whims. In his later years he was engaged in making furniture of classic, elegant simplicity for the brothers Adam. His earlier work to his own designs, his love of gilt and gaudy color, his fascination with the exotic — all typical of the age in which he lived — suggest that he might have made a brilliant stage designer.

Chippendale is the first personality in the history of furniture style. This was due less to his fine craftsmanship than to his ability as a publicist. He was the first cabinetmaker to publish a book of furniture designs. The influence of his *Director* was particularly strong in Philadelphia, but the American cabinetmakers usually simplified his exuberant ornament to suit their clients' taste and

## Dining tables, side tables, console

MAHOGANY SIDE TABLE WITH GILT GESSO EDGE

DINING TABLE WITH MODIFIED CHINESE DECORATION

SIDEBOARD TABLE WITH CHINESE PIERCED FRET DECORATION

PINE CARVED TABLE WITH MARBLE TOP

MAHOGANY TABLE WITH GILT GESSO EDGE

FRENCH ROCOCO-TYPE CONSOLE TABLE WITH GILT DECORATION AND MARBLE TOP

SIMPLE CABRIOLE-LEG DINING TABLE c. 1750

SERVING TABLE WITH CHINESE FRET DECORATION

CHINESE STYLE LACQUERED-TOP SIDE TABLE

FOLDING GATE-LEG TABLE

CLASSIC INFLUENCE IN LATER GEORGIAN SERVING TABLE

SIMPLE GATE-LEG TABLE OF EARLY PERIOD

## Pedestals, wine coolers

COMMODE WITH FOLDING TOP WHICH OPENS OUT TO FORM A TABLE

MAHOGANY METAL-LINED WINE COOLERS WITH BRASS ORNAMENT

"CHINESE" FRETTED PEDESTALS BY EDWARDS & DARLEY

## Dining-room accessories

MAHOGANY TEA CADDY WITH BRASS ORNAMENT

PORCELAIN

BRACKET CLOCK IN MAHOGANY WITH BRASS FITTINGS

PORCELAIN COFFEE POTS FANTASTIC CHINOISERIE

SILVER TEA URN

CANDLESTICKS IN SILVER IN BRASS

PIERCED SILVER FRUIT BASKET

MIRROR-BACK SCONCE 1775

CARVED AND GILT MIRROR

CRYSTAL CHANDELIER

CHANDELIER BY CHIPPENDALE IN THE "GOTHICK" TASTE

## Chests of drawers, secretary, desk

MAHOGANY CHEST OF DRAWERS FRENCH ROCOCO INFLUENCE

BOMBÉ WRITING TABLE

MAHOGANY WITH WATER-GILT, HAND-CHASED MOUNTS

MAHOGANY SECRETARY BY CHIPPENDALE

CHIPPENDALE CHEST-ON-CHEST

MAHOGANY CABINET WITH CHINESE DETAIL

CHIPPENDALE KNEE-HOLE CHESTS OF DRAWERS

MAHOGANY CHEST OF DRAWERS 1760

## Dressing tables, night stands, stools

CHIPPENDALE STOOLS

SHELL-TYPE CHAIR OF CARVED WOOD

MAHOGANY FIRESCREEN WITH TRIPOD POLE AND PETIT-POINT PANEL

CANDLESTAND BY CHIPPENDALE

RUSTIC WALL TABLE BY THOMAS JOHNSON

RIBBON BACK CHAIR

CHIPPENDALE MAHOGANY STAND

BASIN STAND

CANOPIED HANGING SHELVES

MAHOGANY NIGHT STANDS

FOLDING-TOP DRESSING TABLE BY INCE & MAYHEW

## Bedroom accessories

CHINESE PORCELAIN

CRYSTAL SCONCE

IRON GRATE WITH BRASS DECORATIONS

AESOP MIRROR BY CHIPPENDALE

CHINESE CHIPPENDALE MIRRORS, CARVED AND GILT

WALL BRACKET CHINESE CHIPPENDALE

GILT BRONZE CLOCKS CHINESE AND FRENCH ROCOCO IN STYLE

SILVER CANDLESTICK 1773

---

their workers' skill in carving. For it must be remembered that many of the published designs were too complex for reproduction in the solid, even by the most highly skilled English carvers. Such designs were intended for inspiration only.

The introduction of mahogany about 1725 was a fundamental influence on furniture design. Rosewood was another material in favor. Pine was used for paneling and also for intricate carving as, for example, on mirror frames. In the latter case it was usually gilt. Amboyna was occasionally used, mostly for inlays. But the considerable use of inlay is not found until the late Georgian period.

From China come the rectangular leg and an infinite variety of fretted ornament, as well as the more obviously Oriental pagoda forms. From the France of Louis XV come the elaborate combinations of foliated C and S scrolls so typical of the rococo style of ornament. These came to a lush flowering in furniture hardware and gilt mirror frames. Serpentine fronts and sides broke down

# PERIOD FURNITURE

### 18th Century English: Georgian

## Fireplaces and wall paneling

DESIGN BY THOMAS JOHNSON
IN THE "GOTHICK" TASTE

FIREPLACE WALL PANELED IN PINE, WITH A NICHE ABOVE
THE MANTEL AND A CUPBOARD ALONGSIDE.  c. 1750

## Drapery treatments for Georgian windows

THESE SIMPLE DRAPERIES SHOW UP THE FINE PROPORTIONS OF THE WINDOWS
AND PANELING AGAINST WHICH THEY ARE SET.
THEY WERE OFTEN OF VERY RICH, HEAVY MATERIALS.

## Secretaries, desks, bookcases

LIBRARY BOOKCASE BY CHIPPENDALE

FRENCH-STYLE
CHIPPENDALE DESK

MAHOGANY LIBRARY DESK
WITH OUT-SLOPING
CORNER PILASTERS

MAHOGANY BREAKFRONT
BY CHIPPENDALE  c. 1750

KNEEHOLE SECRETARY
WITH GLASS-FRONTED
BOOKSHELVES

SMALL SECRETARY
IN "GOTHICK" STYLE
c. 1750

DROP-FRONT SECRETARY

## Grandfather clocks, shelves, tables

POLE SCREEN
WITH PIERCED
TRIPOD BASE

PAGODA CHINA CABINET
1750

FOLDING-TOP
CARD TABLE
WITH CABRIOLE LEGS

CANOPIED WALL SHELVES
FOR KNICKKNACKS

TILT-TOP TABLE
WITH TRIPOD BASE

PIECRUST TRIPOD TABLE
BY CHIPPENDALE

MAHOGANY
BY CHIPPENDALE

INLAID WALNUT

LOUIS XV TYPE
WITH BRASS MOUNTS

CHIPPENDALE TEA TABLE
WITH GALLERY EDGE

## Living-room accessories

CHINESE PORCELAIN

BRASS FENDER

CHINESE TOLE
TEA JAR

CRYSTAL CANDELABRA

SILVER CANDLESTICK

CRYSTAL
CANDLESTICK

SILVER TEA URN

CARVED AND GILT
CHIPPENDALE MIRROR

CLASSIC MOTIFS
FOR A WALNUT MIRROR

GRATE IN "GOTHICK" STYLE

MAHOGANY MIRROR
BY CHIPPENDALE

even the solid rectangular forms of such traditionally four-square pieces as chests of drawers and tables. (For typical profiles and decorative motifs see Fig. 3.)

Romance was sought in the past as well as the East; the pointed Gothic arch and burgeoning crockets turn up in all kinds of furniture and decoration.

## Furniture hardware

PIERCED BRASS KEY PLATES AND
HANDLES OF BRASS AND GILT BRONZE

## Tripod-table posts

ACANTHUS
LEAF

FLUTING
AND WHORL

## Border moldings and frets

GOTHIC MOTIF

NULLING

BEADING

CHINESE MOTIFS

**Fig. 3**  *(Continued)*

## THE EXTERIOR

The exterior of a later Georgian house, such as the one shown above, would have been finished in cream-painted stucco with stone trim. The Classic detail was in carved stone or molded stucco. At right are details of the architectural background at this period.

## Wall paneling and painted decoration

FIREPLACE WALL IN THE LIBRARY OF SYON HOUSE, ISLEWORTH, ENGLAND
DESIGNED BY THE BROTHERS ADAM FOR THE DUKE OF NORTHUMBERLAND

## THE LIVING ROOM

GREEN brocade curtains, bound with gold, and green brocade upholstery on the sofa and adjacent chairs stand out brilliantly against the French white of these walls. A damask in tones of coffee and gold is used for the other chairs, a red moire for the other sofa. All these colors are repeated in the rug. The dark brown red of polished mahogany appears in the doors and furniture. Some of the smaller pieces are inlaid with satinwood.

Alternatively the walls might be pale pink with white moldings. Upholstery would be blue green except for the chairs by the fire in lemon yellow brocade and the sofa in gold satin.

### Living-room fabrics

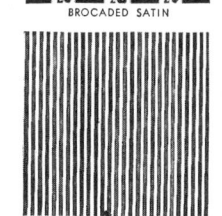

SILK AND LINEN DAMASK

BROCADED SATIN

SILK AND VELVET STRIPE

### Armchairs, love-seats, sofas

ADAM GILT SOFAS

CHARACTERISTIC ADAM ARMCHAIRS

SERPENTINE SOFA

SHERATON MAHOGANY SOFA

CHARACTERISTIC SHERATON ARMCHAIRS

HEPPLEWHITE MAHOGANY LOVE-SEATS

Chippendale went for inspiration to Chinese and Gothic decoration. The great designers of the later Georgian period — the brothers Adam, George Hepplewhite, and Thomas Sheraton — were entranced by the recently discovered Classic glories of Pompeii and Herculaneum, and by the slim prettiness in vogue at the French court.

The motifs most characteristic of the later Georgian period (see Fig. 4) are all of Classic origin: acanthus leaf and honeysuckle, ram's head, winged griffin and lion, laurel, and garland.

Characteristic of this period is the perfect coordination between architects, painters, and furniture designers. The four Adam brothers — John, Robert, James, and William, who trademarked themselves the Adelphi (Greek for brothers) — were Scots by birth, architects by profession. They did not consider their job at an end when they had designed the shell of a house. Every detail of furnishing, decoration, and lighting was especially designed by the Adams to give a rounded effect. Nothing was too small or unimportant to deserve their attention. The best craftsmen would then be employed to carry out their designs. Chippendale and Hepplewhite, perhaps Sheraton also, made furniture for the Adams.

All these designers followed Chippen-

| Furniture hardware | Chair and table legs | Pilaster capitals |
|---|---|---|

HEPPLEWHITE BRASS HANDLES — SHERATON BRASS HANDLES

CARVED AND TURNED DECORATION TYPICAL OF THE LATER GEORGIAN CABINET-MAKERS

SWAGS AND RAMS HEADS — THE WHEATSHEAF POPULAR IN AMERICA

**Fig. 4   Motifs characteristic of the later Georgian period.**

### THE DINING ROOM

THESE pale blue-green walls are relieved by grisaille paintings in delicate Classic taste. Gold appears in the leather chair seats, in the mirror above the consoles and in the binding of the white curtains. Green and beige enliven the carpet and painted ceiling design.

Alternatively the wall paintings might be brighter and more varied in color, including Naples yellow, mauve and green. Curtains and chair seats would be cherry, the ceiling painting cinnamon brown and white.

### Dining-room fabrics

SILK DAMASK

PRINTED COTTON

BROCATELLE

### Dining tables, consoles

MAHOGANY DINING TABLES BY SHERATON

HEPPLEWHITE CONSOLES COMBINED TO FORM A DINING TABLE

ADAM CONSOLE DECORATED WITH REEDING

ADAM CONSOLE DECORATED WITH PAINTED PANELS

ONE OF THE SIMPLEST OF ADAM DINING TABLES

TWO ADAM CONSOLES COMBINED TO FORM A DINING TABLE

EXTENSIBLE DINING TABLE BY ADAM

### THE BEDROOM

PALE colors are dominant here. The sofa, painted oyster white, is upholstered in apple green satin. The mahogany bed is covered in white taffeta trimmed with apple green, and the armchair upholstery is cinnamon and gold-striped damask. Curtains are white silk, gold-trimmed.

Alternatively the color scheme might be based on gold and white with blue green silk on the bed and yellow satin upholstery on the armchair for contrast. In the panels to the right are a number of authentic pieces which might be used in a Georgian bedroom such as this.

### Bedroom fabrics

SATIN BROCADE

SATIN DAMASK

CHINTZ

### Four-poster beds and canopies

CANOPY BY SHERATON

DRAPED FOUR-POSTER BY ADAM

CARVED MAHOGANY BED BY SHERATON

CANOPY BY ADAM

SOFA BED WITH CUPOLA BY SHERATON

dale's lead by publishing design handbooks for the use of other less experienced and less imaginative craftsmen in this country and in the English provinces outside London. Here is seen the changing fashion: lowboys are being supplanted by dressing tables, highboys by wardrobes. Color and inlay become more popular than carving, with Sheraton as the champion of inlay against painting.

Hepplewhite's work is usually characterized by his affection for curves, Sheraton's by a preference for straight lines. This was probably because Hepplewhite was more strongly influenced than Sheraton by contemporary French work, which was enlivened by a profusion of delicate curves. Of particular interest in Sheraton's work are his designs for ingenious folding and multi-

purpose furniture such as folding beds, combined bookcases and washstand, and couches that folded up to become tables. These were designed for use in those bedrooms which were now doubling as parlors during the day.

This later Georgian period has often been labeled the Age of Satinwood. All the designers eagerly exploited the possibilities of ve-

## Armchairs, side chairs

DESIGNED BY HEPPLEWHITE

DESIGNED BY SHERATON

DESIGNED BY THE BROTHERS ADAM

## Commodes, sideboards, cupboard

ADAM COMMODE OF CARVED MAHOGANY

REVOLVING MAHOGANY CUPBOARD

INLAID ADAM COMMODE WITH RECESSED FRONT

ADAM COMMODE WITH PAINTED DECORATION

ADAM SIDEBOARD GROUP WITH A PAIR OF PEDESTAL CUPBOARDS

SIDEBOARD BY THE BROTHERS ADAM

INLAID SATINWOOD COMMODE BY SHERATON

SIDEBOARD BY HEPPLEWHITE

SHERATON SIDEBOARD WITH INLAID SERPENTINE FRONT

ADAM SIDEBOARD OF MAHOGANY WITH BRASS RAILING

## Dining-room accessories

MIRROR FROM HEPPLEWHITE'S BOOK OF DESIGNS

ADAM WALL SCONCES IN BRASS

ADAM MIRROR WITH GILT DECORATION

INLAID MAHOGANY MANTEL CLOCK

GLASS AND METAL CANDLESTAND

HEPPLEWHITE GILT FRAME MIRROR

SMALL CRYSTAL CHANDELIER

BRONZE ADAM SCONCES INLAID WITH WEDGWOOD CHINA PLAQUES

WEDGWOOD URNS AND VASES

## Chests of drawers, wardrobes, commodes

HEPPLEWHITE INLAID MAHOGANY CHEST OF DRAWERS

ADAM COMMODE OF INLAID SATINWOOD WITH PANELING IN "ZUCCHI" STYLE

INLAID MAHOGANY SWELL-FRONT CHEST OF DRAWERS BY HEPPLEWHITE

WARDROBE OF CARVED PINE PAINTED

SERPENTINE CHEST OF DRAWERS BY HEPPLEWHITE

SHERATON CABINET OF SATINWOOD WITH TULIPWOOD BASE

INLAID SERPENTINE-FRONT COMMODE BY SHERATON

ADAM WARDROBE WITH DRAWERS BELOW

## Dressing tables, secretaries, candlestands

WASH-STAND BY SHERATON

SHERATON WRITING DESK, 1790

BEDSIDE TABLE BY HEPPLEWHITE

MAHOGANY DRESSING TABLE INLAID WITH MAPLE AND SATINWOOD

DESK OF PAINTED SATINWOOD WITH BRASS GRILLE

ADAM CANDLESTAND

CANDLESTANDS HEPPLEWHITE

POLE FIRE-SCREEN WITH PETIT-POINT PANEL

SATINWOOD CANDLESTAND BY SHERATON

TILT-TOP TABLE FOR SEWING AND WRITING BY SHERATON

TAMBOUR SECRETARY BY SHERATON

DRESSING TABLE BY SHERATON, 1770

## Bedroom accessories

WATERFORD GIRANDOLES

DRESSING TABLE MIRRORS BY HEPPLEWHITE

CRYSTAL AND PORCELAIN GIRANDOLE

TURQUOISE HONEY JAR

ADAM SCONCE IN BRASS

CARVED AND GILT MIRROR BY SHERATON

BRONZE AND CRYSTAL SCONCE

MARBLE AND BRONZE CLOCK

WEDGWOOD VASES

WATERFORD CANDLESTICK

MAHOGANY MANTEL CLOCK

ADAM MIRRORS WITH GESSO ORNAMENT

---

neering and inlay with woods such as satinwood and amboyna, ebony, sycamore, holly, kingwood, and lime. Ivory and brass inlay were often used to mark key plates.

Some of these motifs (the acanthus leaf, for example) had been in use by English designers for more than half a century. But now, reintroduced from Italy by means of measured drawings, they take on a fresh elegance. Italian painters were brought in — Pergolesi, Zucchi, and Cipriani — to provide the background of decoration. Angelica Kaufmann, a Swiss, filled their wreathed panels with neo-Classic figures.

Yet the solid tradition of English craftsmanship remained intact beneath all these changing fashions. The basic proportions remain almost inviolate. Hepplewhite attempted (in his own words) "to unite elegance with utility, and to blend the useful with the agreeable."

# PERIOD FURNITURE
## 18th Century English: Late Georgian

### Fireplace designs

ADAM MANTEL OF STATUARY MARBLE
AND ANTIQUE GREEN
BEVERLY HALL, ENGLAND, 1770

ADAM MANTEL OF WHITE, SIENNA
AND BROCATELLE MARBLE

### Interior doorways

DESIGNED BY PERGOLESI

DESIGNED BY THE BROTHERS ADAM

### Drapery treatments for Late Georgian windows

OUTSIDE THESE TALL WINDOWS
WERE SLENDER IRON BALCONIES

ELABORATE CORNICE OF METAL
OR OF CARVED, GILT WOOD

LAMBREQUINS, FABRIC-COVERED,
USED TO CUT DOWN DRAFTS

### Secretaries, bookcases, desks, cabinets

LIBRARY DESK BY SHERATON
OF INLAID SATINWOOD

ADAM WRITING TABLE
WITH ROLL TOP AT BACK

HEPPLEWHITE SECRETARY
INLAID MAHOGANY

HEPPLEWHITE SECRETARY

PAINTED CABINET
BY THE BROTHERS ADAM

MAHOGANY LIBRARY CABINET
BY SHERATON

SATINWOOD SECRETARY
MIRROR PANELS IN THE BOOKCASE DOORS

### Occasional tables, grandfather clocks

SHERATON LEATHER-TOPPED
CARD TABLE

HEPPLEWHITE SIDE TABLE
INLAID WITH TULIP
AND SATIN WOODS

SHERATON WALL TABLE

MAHOGANY GRANDFATHER CLOCKS
BY SHERATON

DROP-LEAF
OCCASIONAL TABLES

ADAM CONSOLE
PAINTED DECORATION, FOLDING TOP

ADAM PROJECTING-FRONT CONSOLE WITH
DELICATE CLASSIC DECORATION

SHERATON OCCASIONAL TABLES IN
MAHOGANY AND SATINWOOD

### Living-room accessories

WEDGWOOD
VASES

PAINTED
BRONZE AND CRYSTAL
SCONCES

PLASTER URN DESIGNED BY
THE BROTHERS ADAM

BILBOA MIRROR

ADAM MIRROR
WITH GILT DECORATION

BRASS AND CRYSTAL
SCONCE

ADAM MIRROR CANDLE
SCONCE

PEDESTAL
FOR ANTIQUE STATUES

CLASSIC DETAIL
IN BRONZE
AND MARBLE CLOCK

GILT WALL SCONCE
BY HEPPLEWHITE, 1785

### Decorative panels and roundels

PLASTER CEILING ENRICHMENTS

THE WINGED GRIFFIN
A POPULAR ADAM MOTIF

### Borders and friezes

ANTHEMION

URN AND SWAG

PATERAE

SWAG CORNICE

GUILLOCHE

CUP LION WITH FOLIATED TAIL AND OX SKULL

**Fig. 4**  *(Continued)*

## THE EXTERIOR

THE typical Directoire château shows French Renaissance tradition crossed with the newer Classic vogue. The center panel of this façade is of stone, the remainder in two shades of painted stucco, perhaps in such gay colors as salmon, tan and blue.

## Typical Directoire wall treatments

VERY SIMPLE PANELING ELABORATELY PAINTED WITH MULTICOLOR DECORATION OF CLASSIC AND EGYPTIAN DERIVATION

PLAIN COLOR DRAPERY PINNED UP WITH METAL ROSETTES PILASTERS AND CORNICE GILT

## THE LIVING ROOM

A CHARACTERISTICALLY pale range of colors keeps this room in period. The walls are a pinkish gray, the doors gray and gold. The curtains are oyster white bound in gray and the rug predominantly white except for green and gold in the center. Green recurs in the upholstery of the armchair, side chairs and sofa, and gold (satin) in the sofa and méridienne by the fireplace.

For added color the fireside pieces might be upholstered in red satin, the other furniture in gold and blue striped satin. In panels at right are other pieces suitable for such a room.

## Living-room fabrics

DAMASK

SATIN STRIPED DAMASK

TAPESTRY

## Settees, méridienne, sofas

MAHOGANY SOFA WITH BRASS MOUNTS LION FEET

MÉRIDIENNE DESIGNED FOR THE EMPRESS JOSEPHINE

SETTEE OF ITALIAN TYPE WITH SWAN AND LYRE BACK

DULL BLACK LOVE-SEAT WITH TAN STRIPING AND MAROON ROSETTES

SOFA FROM THE GRAND TRIANON AT VERSAILLES

ITALIAN-TYPE SETTEE PAINTED AND PARCEL GILT

SIMPLE DIRECTOIRE SETTEE UPHOLSTERED IN STRIPED SATIN

GOLD AND WHITE PAINTED SOFA WITH GOLD SATIN UPHOLSTERY

The Directoire was France's recovery period after the shock of a six-year revolution. The Directoire, established in 1795, lasted only a brief four years; but this was long enough for the designers to sketch in the outlines of a new style. Those outlines were to be filled in later as Directoire merged into Empire; these are but two stages in a single style.

With the rise of Napoleon to absolute power, the delicate style of the Directoire was taken over and developed "for the good of the State." It was to be made into a French national style thoroughly imbued with the political principles which were to guide the new state.

Imperial Rome was found to provide the dignity and impressiveness required in the

Friezes and borders

GREEK FRET

ROSETTES

SWANS AND BOWL

FLORIATED ROUNDEL

CLASSIC LEAVES AND FLOWER

Furniture hardware

BRASS HANDLES

BRASS KEY PLATES

Sofa ends

CARVED DOLPHIN

APPLIED BRASS DECORATION

**Fig. 5 Motifs characteristic of Directoire and Empire.**

prototype, so all the Imperial symbols were converted to use. The symmetrical shapes of heavy proportion were taken over unchanged, copied in wood instead of being reproduced in stone or bronze.

Most pieces displayed large surfaces of highly polished wood, usually mahogany. They were not, as a rule, decorated by molding or paneling, or even by carving. Ornamentation was almost always applied or inlaid. Most typically it took the form of gilded bas reliefs tacked to the smooth wood sur-

## PERIOD FURNITURE
### Late 18th–Early 19th Century French: Directoire and Empire

### THE DINING ROOM

THE rich brown of polished mahogany in this table is surrounded by chairs painted gold and white, upholstered in blue satin. The walls are painted oyster white picked out with yellow moldings. Above the doors are white Classic figure paintings with a blue background which is echoed in the blue taffeta curtains.

Alternatively the walls might be painted green with the cornice picked out in white and gold. The chairs would then be upholstered in red. Other pieces suitable for a room of this type are shown in the panels at right.

### Dining-room fabrics

PAINTED SILK

FIGURED VELVET, BRAID TRIM

BROCADE

### Side chairs, armchair

ARMCHAIR WITH LEATHER SEAT DESIGN INSPIRED BY ENGLISH PRECEDENT

FROM THE PALACE OF FONTAINEBLEAU

DESIGNED FOR NAPOLEON UPHOLSTERED WITH BEAUVAIS TAPESTRY

A GROUP OF MAHOGANY CHAIRS DESIGNED BY JACOB BROTHERS MANY WERE PAINTED WHITE. UPHOLSTERY WAS SATIN OR TAPESTRY

### THE BEDROOM

PINK WALLS decorated in white and gold provide a good background for this mahogany and rosewood furniture relieved with brass mounts. Fabrics are gayly colored here: blue taffeta for curtains and bed canopy, striped yellow and red satin for the chairs, and yellow satin for the two stools (which have white-painted frames).

An alternative color scheme would have dark beige walls, green taffeta for the curtains and bed canopy. Most of the furniture would be painted white and gold. At right are other pieces and fabrics suitable for this type of room.

### Bedroom fabrics

MOIRÉ

PRINTED SILK

SILK DAMASK

### Beds, chaises longues, méridiennes

MAHOGANY BED WITH SWAN AND LYRE DECORATION

MÉRIDIENNE OF MAHOGANY WITH BRONZE MOUNTS

CHAISE LONGUE WITH SWAN'S NECK DECORATION

MAHOGANY CHAISE LONGUE WITH BOLDLY PATTERNED RED UPHOLSTERY

PAINTED WOOD DIVAN

MAHOGANY COUCH UPHOLSTERED IN YELLOW SATIN

MÉRIDIENNE WITH GOLD AND WHITE FRAME, GREEN UPHOLSTERY

MAHOGANY BEDS WITH UPHOLSTERED ENDS

faces. Painted decoration was more commonly used on walls and ceilings than for furniture.

The general color scheme is rich, dark, and somewhat heavy. Rich deep mahogany, French polished and often stained red, was the favorite material. Rosewood and ebony were also in favor. Where other woods were used, their nature was concealed by staining to imitate the more popular species.

Round tables were popular. They usually stood on a pedestal or tripod vase. The top was commonly of porphyry or marble. Beds developed into Classic ceremonial couches with scrolled ends. The popular craze for all things Roman extended to include women's dresses and Lucullan banquets.

In the early (Directoire) part of the period fabrics were quite delicately colored, the decorative motifs still possessed some Gre-

cian delicacy of form, and much of the furniture was painted and gilt. Later, under Napoleon's fist, fabrics were usually in deep primary colors, the motifs of Imperial Roman heaviness, the furniture of dark red polished mahogany.

From each of his campaigns he brought home some new decorative motif which he would turn over to his craftsmen for use in the net batch of furniture made to his order.

## Pedestals

THESE STANDS, OF MAHOGANY AND BRONZE, WITH BRASS MOUNTS, WERE USED FOR DISPLAYING PLANTS AND STATUARY

## Wall tables, sideboards, consoles

CONSOLE TABLE WITH LEGS OF EGYPTIAN INSPIRATION

BRONZE MOUNTS ON A MAHOGANY CONSOLE

MARBLE TOP, GOLD AND WHITE PAINTED FRAME

PAINTED BLACK TOP AND GLOBES, EGYPTIAN INFLUENCE

MAHOGANY CONSOLES SUPPORTED BY BRONZE CARYATIDS WHICH ARE REFLECTED IN THE MIRROR PANEL AT BACK

SERVING TABLE OF SATINWOOD WITH MIRROR PANEL AT BACK

MAHOGANY SIDEBOARD WITH WHITE MARBLE TOP

CONSOLE WITH LOWER SHELF OF MARBLE, TOP SHELF INLAID WITH BRASS

MAHOGANY SIDE TABLES

## Dining tables

MAHOGANY-TOP TABLE, METAL LEGS

INLAID MARBLE TOP, LION FEET

SIMPLE TABLE WITH FLUTED LEGS ENGLISH PATTERN

MAHOGANY TABLE WITH LOTUS LEAF BASES FOR THE SUPPORTING COLUMNS

SATINWOOD TABLE SUPPORTED BY SPHINXES

## Dining-room accessories

BRONZE JARDINIERE IN BLACK AND GOLD

BRONZE LAMPS

CHASED BRASS CANDLESTICK AND WALL SCONCE

MARBLE URNS

BRASS READING LAMP WITH TOLE SHADE

PORCELAIN TABLE CENTRE ORNAMENT

BRASS ANDIRON

BRONZE CANDLESTICK

CRYSTAL AND BRONZE MIRROR-BACK SCONCE

PORCELAIN URNS

## Cabinets, chests of drawers, secretaries, desk

OAK COMMODE WITH LION BRACKETS

BOUDOIR WRITING DESK

DROP-FRONT SECRETARY WITH BRASS MOUNTS

MAHOGANY CHEST OF DRAWERS WITH LION-AND-RING HANDLES, SHIELD KEY-PLATES

BRASS-MOUNTED CONSOLE CABINET

LOW DROP-FRONT MAHOGANY SECRETARY

CABINET WITH MIRROR BACK PANEL AND CLASSIC PAINTED FIGURES ON DOORS

MAHOGANY CHEST OF DRAWERS WITH BRONZE MOUNTS AND GALLERY

FRUITWOOD CHEST OF DRAWERS WITH BRASS MOUNTS

## Dressing tables, stools, night tables, mirrors

DRESSING TABLE MIRROR WITH SPHINX HEAD SUPPORTS

WALNUT NIGHT TABLE

MAHOGANY NIGHT TABLE WITH PILLAR SUPPORTS

NIGHT TABLE WITH BRASS BUSTS, FEET AND KEY PLATE

DRESSING TABLE WITH BRONZE MOUNTS FOR THE LEGS

CANDLESTAND

BEDSIDE CHAIR

ADJUSTABLE PIER GLASS IN MAHOGANY STAND

BLACK PAINTED TABLE WITH GILT LINING

NIGHT TABLES WITH TAMBOUR DOORS

UPHOLSTERED PAINTED CHAIR

DRESSING STOOLS IN PAINTED MAHOGANY

## Bedroom accessories

BRASS READING LAMP WITH TOLE SHADE

MARBLE-BASE LAMP

BRONZE HEAD ON MARBLE STAND

BRASS WALL SCONCE

BRONZE CANDLESTICKS

TOLE VASES

GOLD AND MARBLE MANTEL CLOCK

PORCELAIN URNS

SMALL BRONZE WALL LAMP WITH TOLE SHADE

BRONZE SCONCE

FOOTSTOOLS WITH WHITE-PAINTED FRAMES UPHOLSTERED IN STRIPED SATIN AND TAPESTRY

The Egyptian campaign yielded an impressive collection of sphinxes, pyramids, obelisks, and lotus leaf capitals. From Italy came all the paraphernalia of Imperial Roman decoration, acanthus leaves, laurel wreaths, torches, winged victories, cornucopias, and the rest, including the famous wreath of bees Napoleon is usually accused of having appropriated from the arms of an old Italian family, the Barberini.

The early Empire pieces (Directoire) are simplified versions of the styles current under Louis XVI. These pieces have grace, simplicity, and charm. The hampering restrictions on foreign trade led to the use of native fruitwoods instead of mahogany.

# PERIOD FURNITURE
### Late 18th–Early 19th Century French: Directoire and Empire

### Fireplace designs

MARBLEIZED SURROUND
SLIDING METAL SCREEN IN FIREPLACE OPENING

GILT METAL APPLIED ORNAMENT
RELIEVES THIS SIMPLE DESIGN

### Interior Doorways

THE FRIEZE COMBINES CLASSIC
AND EGYPTIAN MOTIFS. PAINTED
DECORATION IN GREEN. GOLD AND BEIGE

PANELED DOOR WITH PAINTING OF
CLASSIC FIGURES ABOVE DECORATION IN
GOLD WHITE, BLUE AND YELLOW

### Drapery treatments for Directoire windows

SIMPLE LIGHT BLUE CURTAINS EDGED
WITH YELLOW BINDING TAPE
YELLOW TIEBACK

GREEN OVERDRAPERY
EDGED WITH GOLD AND
WHITE EMBROIDERY TAPE

WHITE SILK CURTAINS TRIMMED
WITH GOLD BRAID
SIMPLE WOODEN CORNICE BOARD

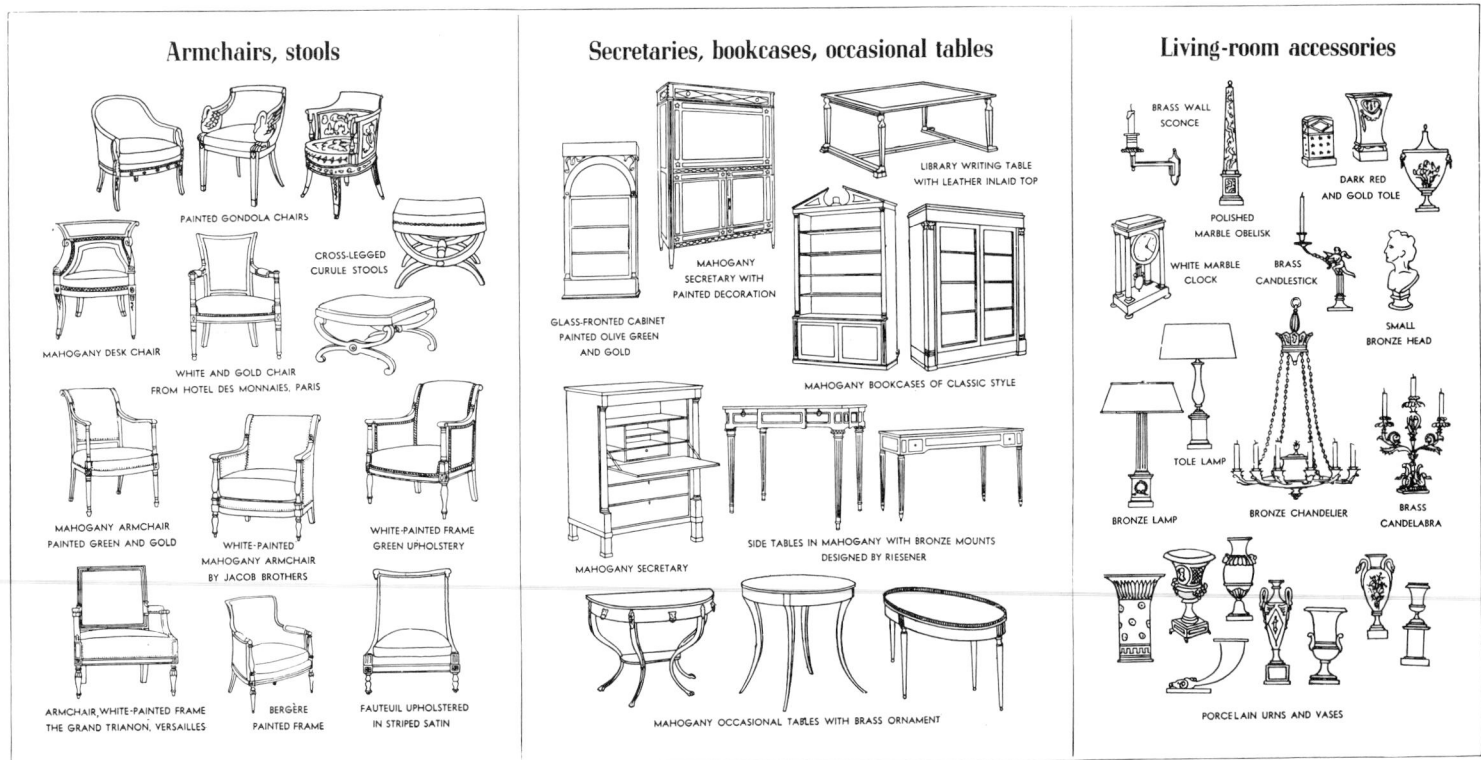

### Armchairs, stools

PAINTED GONDOLA CHAIRS

CROSS-LEGGED
CURULE STOOLS

MAHOGANY DESK CHAIR

WHITE AND GOLD CHAIR
FROM HOTEL DES MONNAIES, PARIS

MAHOGANY ARMCHAIR
PAINTED GREEN AND GOLD

WHITE-PAINTED
MAHOGANY ARMCHAIR
BY JACOB BROTHERS

WHITE-PAINTED FRAME
GREEN UPHOLSTERY

ARMCHAIR, WHITE-PAINTED FRAME
THE GRAND TRIANON, VERSAILLES

BERGÈRE
PAINTED FRAME

FAUTEUIL UPHOLSTERED
IN STRIPED SATIN

### Secretaries, bookcases, occasional tables

LIBRARY WRITING TABLE
WITH LEATHER INLAID TOP

GLASS-FRONTED CABINET
PAINTED OLIVE GREEN
AND GOLD

MAHOGANY
SECRETARY WITH
PAINTED DECORATION

MAHOGANY BOOKCASES OF CLASSIC STYLE

MAHOGANY SECRETARY

SIDE TABLES IN MAHOGANY WITH BRONZE MOUNTS
DESIGNED BY RIESENER

MAHOGANY OCCASIONAL TABLES WITH BRASS ORNAMENT

### Living-room accessories

BRASS WALL
SCONCE

DARK RED
AND GOLD TOLE

POLISHED
MARBLE OBELISK

WHITE MARBLE
CLOCK

BRASS
CANDLESTICK

SMALL
BRONZE HEAD

TOLE LAMP

BRONZE LAMP

BRONZE CHANDELIER

BRASS
CANDELABRA

PORCELAIN URNS AND VASES

### Typical legs, feet and arm

INVERTED
LYRE CHAIR LEG

TWO FORMS OF
LION'S PAW FOOT

BRONZE
TABLE SUPPORT

ROUND LEGS
AND FOOT

SPHINX SUPPORT
FOR UPHOLSTERED
FLAT CHAIR ARM

### Metal mounts and inlays

LAUREL
WREATH
INLAY

LAUREL AND
CORNUCOPIAS

FLYING VICTORY IN BAS RELIEF

URN WITH LION
SUPPORTS

TORCH
AND WREATHED
CLASSIC HEAD

WINGED SPHINXES

Fig. 5 *(Continued)*

FIG. 2
Rush Seated Bench.

PLAN

Corner Dresser

FIG. 3
Small Tea Table.

Low Post Bed  FIG. 1

FIG. 4
17th Century Arm Chair

FIG. 5

FIG. 6
Bow Back Windsor Arm Chair

FIG. 7

Pennsylvania Bread
Mixing Table.

FIG. 9
Tavern Table

FIG. 8
Bannister Back Side Chair

FIG. 11
Tilt Top Table.
With Snake Feet

FIG. 10
Pine Wing Chair

**Colonial style**

# PERIOD FURNITURE

**17th and 18th Century American: Colonial**

FIG. 13
TALL CLOCK.

FIG. 12
HIGHBOY

FIG. 14
TABLE CHAIR
EQUAL-RULE 6

FIG. 15
CHEST OF DRAWERS.

FIG. 16
GATE LEG TABLE

FIG. 17
LOVE SEAT

FIG. 18
SLANT TOP DESK

FIG. 19
TRESTLE TABLE

FIG. 20
BUTTERFLY TABLE

FIG. 21
TULIP AND ASTER CHEST.

FIG. 22
LADDER BACK SIDE CHAIR.

**Colonial style**

**FIG. 1**
DUNCAN PHYFE SIDE CHAIR. REEDED HORSESHOE SHAPED SEAT.

**FIG. 2**
SIDE CHAIR WITH LYRE BACK.

**FIG. 3**
DUNCAN PHYFE ARM CHAIR.

**FIG. 4**
TWO BACK SETTEE WITH LYRE ENDS. THESE MAY BE MADE WITH THREE BACKS & ARE SOMETIMES CANED. THEY SOMETIMES HAVE ANIMAL FEET.

**FIG. 5**
CONSOLE TABLE. VENEERED APRON.

**FIG. 6**
SEWING TABLE. THE SILK BAG IS FASTENED TO THE LOWER DRAWER WHICH HAS NO BOTTOM. THE SEMI-CIRCULAR ENDS ARE BOXES & THE LIDS HAVE INVISIBLE HINGES.

Though Duncan Phyfe Adapted Freely From The Work of Sheraton. Heppelwhite & Others He Developed A Distinct Style.

**FIG. 7**
LIBRARY TABLE WITH LYRE ENDS.

**FIG. 8**
SMALL VENEERED SIDEBOARD.

**FIG. 9**
LYRE BASE CARD TABLE
PLINTH

**FIG. 10**
DINING TABLE. THESE MAY BE MADE IN TWO, THREE OR FIVE SECTIONS. WIDE BOARDS MAY ALSO BE ADDED BETWEEN EACH SECTION TO LENGTHEN THE TABLES.

THE PRINCIPLE PIECES OF FURNITURE MADE BY PHYFE WERE CHAIRS, TABLES, SOFAS & SETTEES. HE ALSO MADE SIDEBOARDS, BEDSTEADS, MIRRORS, WASHSTANDS, WRITING DESKS, ETC. SOME OF HIS FAVORITE MOTIFS WERE THE LYRE, THE ACANTHUS LEAF, TURNED & REEDED LEGS, TURNED PEDESTALS SUPPORTED ON CURVED LEGS, & ANIMAL FEET OF BRASS. THE PRINCIPAL WOOD USED WAS MAHOGANY OFTEN VENEERED.

**Duncan Phyfe style**

# PERIOD FURNITURE
**16th Century English: Early Jacobean**

CHEST
FIG. 1

FIG. 2
CHEST ON FRAME

FIG. 3
CHEST of DRAWERS.

FIG. 4
COURT CUPBOARD

REFECTORY TABLE
FIG. 5

SETTLE     FIG. 6

FIG. 7
CROMWELLIAN CHAIR

SMALL TABLE
FIG. 8

FIG. 9  LONG FORM

FIG. 10
STOOL

**Early Jacobean period**

FIG. 12
JACOBEAN SIDE CHAIR

FIG. 11
CAROLEAN CHAIR

FIG. 13
BANNISTER BACK CHAIR

FIG. 14
WELSH DRESSER

FIG. 15
CROMWELLIAN SETTEE

FIG. 16
CHARLES II SETTEE

FIG. 17
MIRROR FRAME

Jacobean period

# PERIOD FURNITURE

### 17th Century English: William & Mary

**FIG. 1.**
WM. & MARY HIGHBOY. WITH TRUMPET TURNED LEGS.

**FIG. 2**
STOOL

**FIG. 3**
STRAIGHT TOP SECRETARY

**FIG. 4**
LOWBOY. THESE WERE THE DRESSING TABLES of THE PERIOD.

**FIG. 5**
WM. & MARY ARM CHAIR

**FIG. 6**
DOUBLE HOOD CHINA CABINET.

**FIG. 7**
LACQUERED CABINET.

**FIG. 8**
TALL CLOCK

**FIG. 9**
CARD TABLE.

William and Mary period

FIG. 1
HIGHBOY

FIG. 2
LOWBOY

FIG. 3
SMALL TABLE

FIG 4
SOFA

FIG. 5
HALL TABLE

FIG. 6
SMALL TEA TABLE

FIG. 7
LIGHT DROP-LEAF TABLE
Top 40" In Diameter When Open.

FIG. 8
GATE LEG TABLE

FIG. 9
ARM CHAIR
Seat 18" High
40 To 46" High
Seat 24" Wide 18" Deep

FIG. 10
SIDEBOARD
Top 22 By 72

FIG. 11
WRITING DESK

FIG. 12
FIG. 13
STOOL

SIDE CHAIR
Width of Seat 21"
Depth 17"
THE PROPER WOOD FOR QUEEN ANNE FURNITURE IS WALNUT. MAHOGANY WAS SOMETIMES USED.

**Queen Anne period**

# PERIOD FURNITURE

### 18th Century English: Georgian (Chippendale)

FIG. 1
CHEST OF DRAWERS

FIG. 2
HIGHBOY

FIG. 3
DESK

FIG. 4
TABLE OR SIDEBOARD

FIG. 5
CARD TABLE

FIG. 6
SWING LEG DINING TABLE.

FIG. 7
SECRETARY

FIG. 8
CAMEL BACK SOFA

FIG. 9
LAZY SUSAN

FIG. 10
FIRE SCREEN

FIG. 11
FOUR POST BED

FIG. 12
MIRROR

STANDARD SIZES FOR BEDS
INSIDE SIZES BETWEEN RAILS
35 WIDE & 78" & 50"x 78"
& 56"x 78.
RAILS ARE 2" THICK & BOX SPRINGS
& MATTRESS MAY BE PURCHASED
39"x82" & 54"x82" & 60"x82".
THE UPHOLSTERED BOX SPRINGS
ARE RABBETED TO SINK BELOW THE
RAIL & MAY BE BOUGHT WITH CUT-
OUT CORNERS TO FIT AROUND POSTS.

**Chippendale style**

FIG. 1
Oval Back With Straight Taper Legs.

Prince of Wales Feathers.

The Seats On The Best Chairs of This Type Are Slightly "Dished" That Is - Lower In The Center from Front To Back To Make Them More Comfortable.

FIG. 2
Shield Back Arm Chair

Egyptian Wing

FIG. 3
Shield Back With Moulded Taper Legs.

FIG. 4
Hepplewhite Sideboard With Border Veneered Drawers & Doors

Veneered Border

Plan of Top

FIG. 5
Dining Table In Three Sections. These Sections When Not In Use May Be Placed Against The Wall.

FIG. 6
Martha Washington Chair

Width At Seat 25

FIG. 7
Flat Top Knee Hole Desk

Flower Painted Panels

FIG. 8
Chest of Drawers.

Satinwood Veneer

French Foot

FIG. 9
Pembroke Table.

FIG. 10
Tambour Secretary.

FIG. 11
Card Table

FIG. 12
China Cupboard. Veneered & Inlaid.

Occasionally Lower

Inlay

Figured Veneer

13" Deep

18" Deep

Hepplewhite style

# PERIOD FURNITURE
18th Century English: Late Georgian (Sheraton)

**FIG. 1**
ARM CHAIR. FRONT LEGS & ARM SUPPORTS ARE REEDED.

**FIG. 2**
SIDE CHAIR WITH URN MOTIF IN BACK.

**FIG. 4**
BOW OR SWELL FRONT SHERATON CHEST OF DRAWERS.

**FIG. 3**
LATE SHERATON LIGHT SIDE CHAIR OF THE TYPE THAT BECAME VERY POPULAR IN AMERICA.

**FIG. 5**
LATE SHERATON CHEST OF DRAWERS WITH MIRROR

**FIG.7**
SECRETARY.

**FIG.6**
CHINA CABINET. FRENCH FEET

**FIG. 9**
CABINET

**FIG.8**
SIDEBOARD

**Sheraton style**

FIG. 1

THE LID OF THIS URN IS FASTENED TO A ROD BY MEANS OF WHICH IT MAY BE HELD SUSPENDED WHEN THE CONTENTS ARE TO BE REMOVED.

THE ORNAMENT ON THIS SIDEBOARD TABLE AS WELL AS THE PEDESTALS IS CARVED IN LOW RELIEF. THE HEIGHT OF THE TABLES MAY BE AS MUCH AS 36 IN WHICH CASE THE PROPORTIONS ARE VARIED ACCORDINGLY.

THESE PEDESTALS HAD SHELVES & DRAWERS TO HOLD VARIOUS KINDS OF DINING ROOM ACCESSORIES

BROTHERS ADAM SIDEBOARD WITH CHARACTERISTIC CLASSIC MOTIFS.

FIG. 2

BROTHERS ADAM SOFA

FIG. 3

LYRE BACK ARM CHAIR

FIG. 4
FIRE SCREEN

PAINTED SCREEN

PAINTED LEAVES

FRIEZE

BASE MOLD

BOOK CASE
FIG. 5

PLAN OF COMMODE

THE BROTHERS ADAM BEGAN THE CLASSICAL ERA IN FURNITURE OF THE EIGHTEENTH CENTURY. THE LINES AS VIEWED FROM THE FRONT WERE STRAIGHT. AS MAY BE SEEN ON THIS PLATE — THE PLAN VIEWS OF TABLES & COMMODES SHOW SHAPED FRONTS & OVAL FRONTS. THE VARIETY OF ORNAMENT USED WAS VERY GREAT. IT WAS RATHER ARCHITECTURAL IN CHARACTER HAVING BEEN INFLUENCED BY THE STUDIES OF ROMAN RUINS THAT ROBERT ADAM MADE.

WINDOW SEAT
FIG. 6

FIG. 7
COMMODE.

**Brothers Adam**

39

# PERIOD FURNITURE
## 18th Century English: Late Georgian (Brothers Adam)

ALL THE FURNITURE DESIGNED BY THE BROTHERS ADAM WAS BUILT BY OTHERS. HEPPLEWHITE, CHIPPENDALE & OTHERS EXECUTED THE COMMISSIONS. MOST OF THESE MAKERS WITH THE POSSIBLE EXCEPTION OF CHIPPENDALE WERE INFLUENCED BY THE WORK OF THESE ARTISTS.

WHILE THE FURNITURE IS VERY FORMAL IN CHARACTER IT IS ALSO VERY BEAUTIFUL & TASTEFUL. NO DETAIL WAS TOO SMALL TO RECEIVE THEIR ATTENTION. BESIDES THE ORDINARY PIECES THEY DESIGNED LIGHTING FIXTURES, UPHOLSTERY, & NUMEROUS ACCESSORIES.

GILDED COMPO ORNAMENT

GRIFFIN

FILIGREE

PAINTED FRIEZE

EGG & DART OR LEAF & DART CARVED MOULDING

34"

STRETCHERS

PLAN OF TABLE

MARBLE TOP

PAINTED APRON

**FIG. 9**
SIDE CHAIR

**FIG. 8**
CARVED GILT & PAINTED MIRROR & CONSOLE TABLE.

SATINWOOD VENEER

17" DEPTH OF SEAT INSIDE.

**ARM CHAIR**
**FIG. 10**

DEPTH OF SEAT OUTSIDE 17"

THE BROTHERS ADAM WERE ARCHITECTS & THE FURNITURE THEY DESIGNED WAS INTENDED FOR DEFINITE PLACES IN THE HOUSES THEY BUILT. FOR THIS REASON SOME OF THE PIECES WERE LARGE AS IS THE CASE OF PIECES SUCH AS THE TABLE & MIRROR SHOWN ABOVE. SOME BOOKCASES WERE MADE QUITE LONG. THE PROPORTIONS HOWEVER SEEM IN MOST CASES TO HAVE BEEN EXCELLENT. IT WAS ONLY BECAUSE OF A DESIRE TO HAVE EVERY DETAIL PERFECT IN THE HOUSES THEY BUILT THAT THEY DESIGNED THE FURNITURE FOR WHICH THEY ARE FAMOUS TODAY.

HAND PAINTED PANEL

THE DESIGN ON THIS APRON MAY BE PAINTED OR CARVED

**FIG. 11**
CABINET

TABLE **FIG. 12**

THE DOORS OF THESE CABINETS WERE OCCASIONALLY ON THE ENDS. THE HAND PAINTED PANEL WAS THE WORK OF A FAMOUS ARTIST.

**Brothers Adam**

*The Important Periods in the French Styles were Louis XIV, XV, & XVI.*

LOUIS XVI CHAIR BACKS SOMETIMES TAPERED TOWARD THE FLOOR — THAT IS THEY WERE WIDER AT THE TOP THAN AT THE FLOOR. IN THIS CASE THE BACK LEGS WERE SQUARE BELOW THE SEAT.

FIG. 1
LOUIS XIV ARM CHAIR

FIG. 2
LOUIS XVI ARM CHAIR

18" WIDE OR SQUARE
FIG. 3
LOUIS XV SEAT.

FIG. 4
LOUIS XIV SIDE CHAIR

16" SQ.
FIG. 5
LOUIS XVI SEAT.

LOUIS XIV FURNITURE IN PRINCIPLE OF DESIGN IS A CAREFUL COMBINATION OF STRAIGHT LINES & WELL STUDIED CURVES. LOUIS XV FURNITURE DEPARTS FROM THE STRAIGHT LINE ALTOGETHER. THE CURVELINEAR ELEMENT IS SUPREME IN THIS STYLE. THE LOUIS XVI STYLE SHOWS MORE EVENLY BALANCED DETAILS. STRAIGHT LINES & SIMPLE OUTLINES RETURNED.

THE FABRICS USED TO UPHOLSTER LOUIS XIV FURNITURE WERE TAPESTRIES. DAMASKS. CLOTH OF GOLD & SATINS. IN TAPESTRIES PICTORAL & RICH COLORED EFFECTS WERE USUAL. LOUIS XV PIECES WERE UPHOLSTERED WITH THE SAME MATERIALS AS GIVEN ABOVE. DECORATIVE MOTIFS DIFFERED SOMEWHAT. THE PICTORAL ELEMENT GAVE WAY TO THE HIGHLY DECORATIVE SHELL & LEAF MOTIFS. IN LOUIS XVI PIECES THE FABRICS WERE DECORATED WITH FORMAL FLOWER BOUQUETS. RIBBONS. GARLANDS OF DAINTY FLOWERS. CUPIDS. ETC. SOFT COLORS PREDOMINATE IN THIS STYLE.

FIG. 6
LOUIS XV CHAISE LONGUE FORMED BY COMBINING THREE PIECES OF FURNITURE

French styles

# PERIOD FURNITURE
### 16th and 17th Century Spanish

**FIG. 1**

VARGUENO

THESE CABINETS ORIGINATED IN SPAIN DURING THE 16TH CENTURY. THEY WERE OFTEN USED AS A DESK & ARE EASILY THE MOST IMPORTANT CONTRIBUTION OF SPAIN TO THE FURNITURE WORLD.

**FIG. 2**

THREE BACK SETTEE WITH TOOLED LEATHER BACK & SEAT FASTENED WITH LARGE HEADED BRASS NAILS  CIRCA.1700

TOOLED  LEATHER  BACK

TOOLED  LEATHER  SEAT

**FIG 3**

17TH CENTURY CHEST WITH CHIP CARVED PANELS LAID OUT IN GEOMETRIC DESIGNS INTERUPTED CHANNEL GROOVES ON LEGS. RAILS & STILES. SPANISH CHESTS VARY GREATLY IN CHARACTER. SOME ARE DESIGNED WITH ROUND LIDS. SOME ARE FASTENED TO TURNED LEGGED FRAMES. OTHERS ARE COVERED WITH TOOLED LEATHER OR CARVED IN GOTHIC MOTIFS. ETC.

**FIG. 4**

CUPBOARD OF THE 16TH CENTURY. RENAISSANCE PERIOD. THESE CUPBOARDS WERE USED TO HOLD FOOD SUCH AS BREAD & CHEESE & WINE.

**FIG. 5**

FRONT & END VIEWS OF TURNED LEGGED TABLE WITH WROUGHT IRON BRACES.

**FIG. 6**

18TH CENTURY SPANISH SIDE CHAIR.

**Spanish styles**

**TABLE 1  Period Style and Finishes**

| Period style | Associated styles | Walls and ceilings | Floors | Floor coverings |
|---|---|---|---|---|
| Early English<br>Tudor<br>Jacobean<br>Charles II | Italian Renaissance<br>Spanish Renaissance<br>William & Mary<br>Larger pieces of<br>Queen Anne | Oak panels<br>Rough plaster with oak trim<br>Parquetry ceilings | Hardwood stained, dark<br>strips and planks on<br>flooring<br>Stone<br>Tiles | Oriental and large-<br>patterned domestic rugs<br>Plain rugs |
| Anglo-Dutch<br>William & Mary<br>Queen Anne | Chippendale<br>Early Georgian<br>Louis XVI<br>Smaller pieces of<br>Jacobean, such as gate-leg<br>table or Windsor chair | Papered<br>Painted (in light tones)<br>Hung with fabrics<br>Paneled | Hardwood flooring<br>Parquetry | Oriental and large-<br>patterned domestic rugs<br>Plain rugs |
| Early Georgian<br>Chippendale | Chippendale<br>Early Georgian<br>Louis XVI<br>Smaller pieces of<br>Jacobean, such as gate-leg<br>table or Windsor chair | Painted dado<br>Painted<br>Paneled<br>Papered upper section | Hardwood flooring<br>Parquetry | Plain or small-patterned<br>rugs or carpets<br>Oriental rugs |
| Late Georgian<br>Adam<br>Hepplewhite<br>Sheraton<br>Empire<br>Federal | Chinese<br>Chippendale<br>Louis XVI<br>Duncan Phyfe<br>Directoire | Plain plaster<br>Painted<br>Papered<br>Large wood panels painted<br>Gesso ceilings | Hardwood flooring<br>Parquetry | Plain or small-patterned<br>rugs or carpets<br>Oriental rugs |
| Louis XIV, XV, and XVI | All late Georgian styles<br>1 or 2 pieces of Directoire | Large wood panels painted<br>and decorated<br>Wallpaper in Chinese<br>motifs | Hardwood flooring<br>Parquetry | Plain or small-patterned<br>rugs or carpets<br>Oriental rugs |
| Spanish Renaissance | Italian Renaissance<br>Early English<br>Louis XIV | Rough plaster painted<br>Ceilings same or beamed | Hardwood flooring<br>Tiles<br>Vinyls in tile pattern | Spanish or Oriental rugs |
| Early Colonial | All Early English styles<br>William & Mary<br>Queen Anne wing chair | Oak panels<br>Rough plaster with oak<br>Parquetry ceilings | Hardwood flooring or<br>planks<br>Vinyls in jaspe pattern | Braided or hooked rugs |
| Early American | Late Georgian<br>Chippendale<br>Queen Anne<br>Duncan Phyfe<br>French Provincial | Smooth plaster, light trim<br>Wallpaper, scenic and<br>Chinese designs<br>Paneling<br>Ceiling plaster | Dark hardwood flooring<br>Vinyls in plain or jaspe<br>patterns | Hooked, braided, Oriental,<br>or domestic rugs<br>Carpet, plain, two-toned<br>patterned |
| Modern | Swedish Modern<br>Chinese Chippendale | Painted solid colors,<br>striped, figured<br>Plain papers<br>Combinations of above | Hardwood flooring<br>Parquetry<br>Vinyls in modern pattern | Carpet<br>Rugs in solid colors,<br>geometric patterns |
| French Provincial | 18th-century<br>American<br>Colonial<br>Federal | Smooth plaster<br>Wallpaper in scenic or<br>geometric designs | Hardwood flooring<br>Parquetry | Aubussons<br>Homespun carpet, small-<br>patterned<br>Oriental rugs |
| Victorian | Colonial<br>William & Mary<br>Queen Anne | Large-patterned paper | Hardwood flooring | Carpet in large patterns<br>Oriental rugs |

# FURNITURE DIMENSIONS
Children's Furniture and Tables

## CHILDREN'S FURNITURE

| DIAPER CHANGER | POTTY CHAIR | FEEDING UNIT | HIGH CHAIR | SIDE CHAIR | ARM CHAIR | TABLE for 2 |
|---|---|---|---|---|---|---|
| H: 36" -42" | H: 12" - 13" | H: 24" - 26" | H: 36" - 40" | H: 24" - 26" | H: 23" - 25" | H: 20" - 22" |
| W: 32" - 42" | W: 16" - 17" | W: 24" - 28" | W: 18" - 22" | W: 14" - 16" | W: 14" - 16" | W: 24" - 30" |
| D: 21" - 24" | D: 14" - 16" | D: 24" - 25" | D: 18" - 20" | D: 15" - 17" | D: 16" - 17" | D: 24" - 25" |

TABLE for 4
H: 20" - 22"
W: 36" - 42"
D: 36" - 42"

## TABLES

| END/SIDE | END/SIDE | END/SIDE | LOW/COFFEE | LOW/COFFEE | LOW/COFFEE |
|---|---|---|---|---|---|
| H: 20" | H: 18" | H: 18" | H: 18: | H: 18" | H: 18" |
| W: 36" | W: 20" | Diam. 18" | W: 36" | W: 36" | Diam. 36" |
| D: 20" | D: 20" | | D: 24" | D: 36" | |

STOOLS
H: 18"
W: 18"
D: 18"

STOOLS
H: 38"
W: 18"
D: 20"

ENTRY/HALLWAY
H: 33"
W: 48"
D: 20"

## SOFAS

**Sectional sofa**

**Apartment-size sofa**

**Full-size sofa**

## LOVESEATS, LOUNGE CHAIRS, AND ARM CHAIRS

**Loveseat**

**Upholstered chair**

**Lounge chair**

**Arm chair**

**Side chair**

**Folding chair**

**Chaise lounge**

**Right corner**

**Left corner**

**Armless**

**Ottoman**

**Angled sectionals**

## FURNITURE DIMENSIONS
Bed/Mattress Types and Sizes

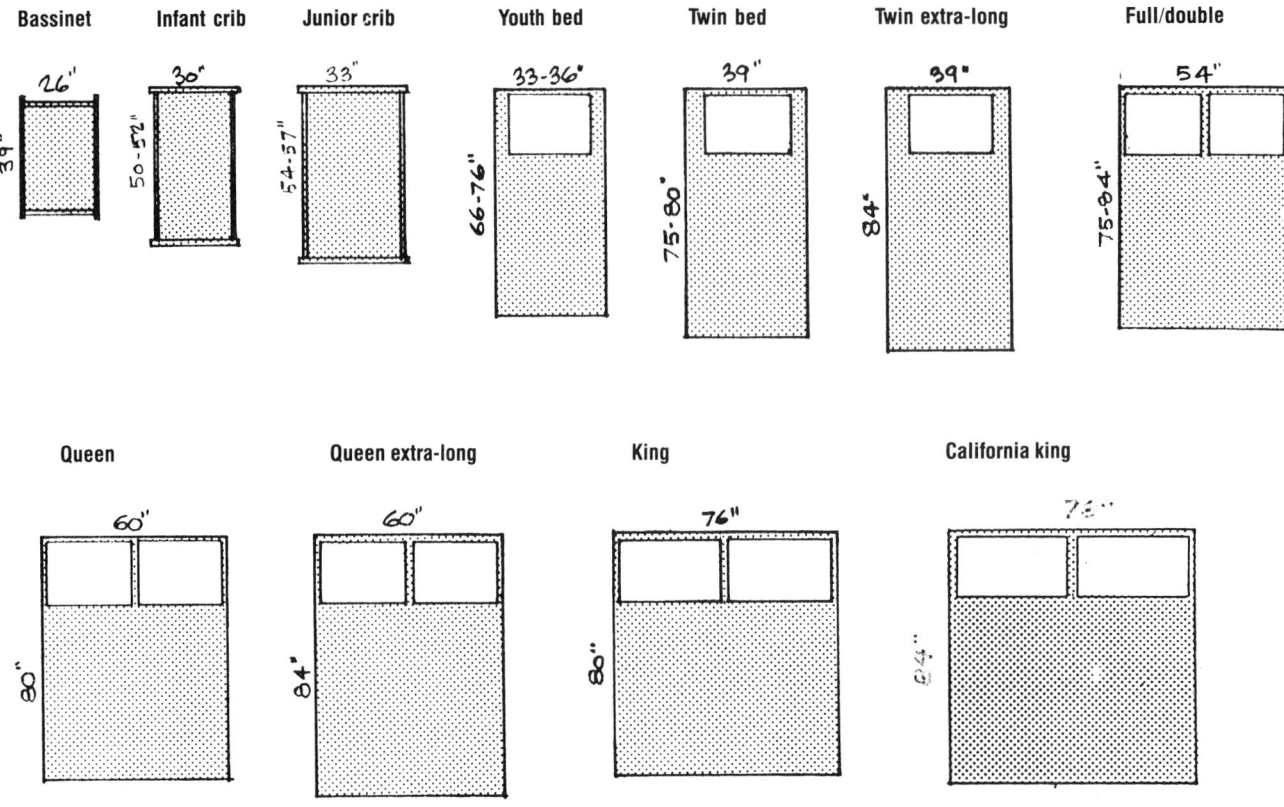

**Fig. 1**

Figure 1 provides the designer with an array of typical bed and mattress sizes with which rooms can be planned. Tables 1 and 2, however, suggest that within the bedding and mattress industries there exists a wide range of sizes from which to select. Many manufacturers use bed/mattress termi-nology that reflects different dimensional standards than that of other manufacturers. Ultimately, the designer, in consultation with the client, must verify exact measurements. Be sure to take your clients to see and test the bed or mattress selected. After all, they are the ones who will have to sleep on it.

**TABLE 1  Juvenile, Youth, and Adult Mattress Types and Sizes**

| | Width (in) | | Length (in) | |
| Mattress type | Min | Max | Min | Max |
|---|---|---|---|---|
| Bassinet | 17 | 23 | 36 | 40 |
| Portable crib | 22 | 26 | 45 | 52 |
| Junior crib | 24 | 32½ | 46 | 58 |
| Youth bed | 33 | 36 | 66 | 76 |
| Bunk bed | 30 | 33 | 75 | 76 |
| Dorm bed | 32 | 36 | 75 | 80 |
| Hospital bed | 36 | 36 | 75 | 80 |
| Narrow twin | 36 | 36 | 74 | 75 |
| Twin bed | 39 | 39 | 75 | 80, 84 |
| Full-size or double bed | 54 | 54 | 74 | 75 |
| Queen-size bed | 60 | 60 | 80 | 84 |
| King-size bed | 76 | 78 | 80 | 84 |
| Extra-long double | 54 | 54 | 80 | 80 |
| Super twin | 45 | 45 | 75 | 80 |

**TABLE 2  Pillow Types and Sizes**

| | Width (in) | | Length (in) | |
| Pillow type | Min | Max | Min | Max |
|---|---|---|---|---|
| Standard | 18 | 20 | 26 | 27 |
| Queen | 19 | 21 | 29 | 30 |
| King | 20 | 22 | 35 | 36 |

*Note:* Many manufacturers also make and sell undersized pillows for cribs and youth beds as well as oversized pillows for the larger beds.

## WATERBEDS

| Twin | Single | Double | Queen | King |

## SOFA BEDS/CONVERTIBLE SOFAS

96-in-diam round    Double/pull    Queen

## WALL AND SIDE BEDS

### Side

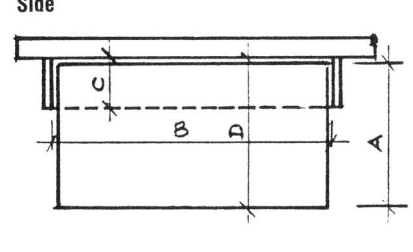

| A | B | C | D |
|---|---|---|---|
| Width of Bed | Width of Clear Door Opening | Depth From Back Of Closet To Back of Doors | Projection of Bed in Use From Back of Closet |
| 39" | 79" | 13" | 43½" |
| 48" | 79" | 13" | 52½" |
| 54" | 79" | 13" | 57" |

*HEIGHT: FLOOR TO TOP OF OPENING*
*44½" for 39" Bed. 53½" for 48" Bed. 59" for 54" Bed.*

### Wall

| A | B | C | D |
|---|---|---|---|
| Width of Bed | Width of Clear Door Opening | Depth From Back Of Closet To Back of Doors | Projection of Bed in Use From Back of Closet |
| 39" | 42" | 19" | 80" Standard 86" Extra Long |
| 54" | 57" | 19" | 80" Standard 86" Extra Long |
| 60" x 80" | 63" | 19" | 86" Queen |
| 76" x 80" | 79" | 19" | 86" King |

*HEIGHT: FLOOR TO TOP OF OPENING*
*80" - For 39" and 54" Beds of Standard 75" Length*
*86" - For Queen, King and Extra Long Beds 80" in Length*

# FURNITURE DIMENSIONS

## Audio-Visual Equipment

19-in television     Rear-projection television     Front-projection television     VCR     Laser disc player

Tape recorder     Turntable     Receiver     CD player     Storage rack

The shape of the viewing area is approximately as shown in Fig. 2. Its size is always based on the size of the image to be viewed. The human eye comprehends detail only within a limited cone angle (about 2½ minutes of arc), and the length of chord subtending this arc, i.e., the image of width, varies with its distance from the observer. Thus an object 20 feet away and 6 feet long appears the same as a similar object 10 feet away and 3 feet long. The size of the viewing area is determined by three dimensions:

- the minimum distance (1), which is the distance from the nearest part of the image to the eye of the closest viewer
- the maximum distance (2), which is the distance from the furthermost part of the image to the most distant viewer
- the maximum viewing angle (3), which is the angle between the projection axis and the line of sight of a person located as far from this axis as can be and still see all image detail in proper brilliance

Practical minimum and maximum distances are both expressed as multiples of the image width (W). They vary both with the medium being used and with the type and quality of material being projected, and may be affected also, in some degree, by personal preferences. They have not yet been precisely determined by scientific methods, and it's doubtful that such data would have much practical value anyway. The generally accepted values, resulting from numerous studies, are these:

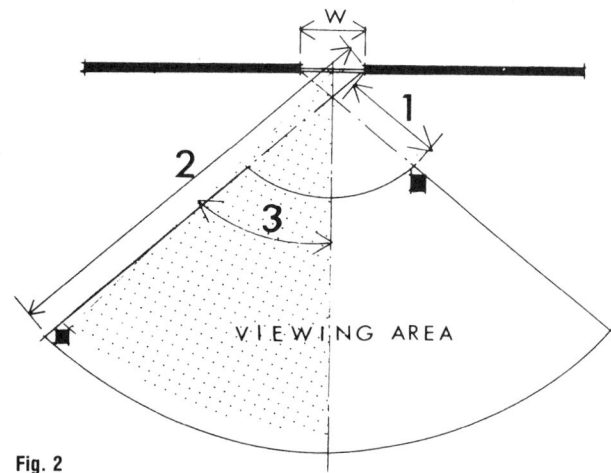

**Fig. 2**

| | Film, slides, and projected TV | TV receivers |
|---|---|---|
| Minimum distance | 2W | 4W |
| Maximum distance | 6W to 10W | 12W |

| Size of TV tube | Minimum viewing distance 4W | Maximum viewing distance 12W |
|---|---|---|
| 17 in | 4 ft 11 in | 14 ft 9 in |
| 19 in | 5 ft 1 in | 15 ft 2 in |
| 21 in | 6 ft 4 in | 19 ft 0 in |
| 23 in | 6 ft 6 in | 19 ft 4 in |
| 24 in | 7 ft 5 in | 21 ft 5 in |
| 27 in | 9 ft 8 in | 24 ft 5 in |

## FURNITURE DIMENSIONS

Fig. 3 Typical dining room furniture.

Fig. 4 Typical living room furniture.

### INGRAM HIGH CHAIR
DESIGNER:
Charles R. Macintosh
YEAR: 1900
MANUFACTURER:
Atelier International
DIMENSIONS:
18½"W x 17½"D x 59¼"H

### WASSILY CHAIR
DESIGNER:
Marcel Breuer
YEAR: 1925
MANUFACTURER:
Knoll International
DIMENSIONS:
30¾"W x 29"D x 28½"H

### KUBUS CHAIR
DESIGNER:
Joseph Hoffman
YEAR: 1910
DIMENSIONS:
36"W x 30½"D x 28½"H

### MR. CHAIR
DESIGNER:
Mies Van Der Rohe
YEAR: 1927
MANUFACTURER:
Stendig
DIMENSIONS:
21¾"W x 32¼"D x 32¼"H

### HAU KOLLER CHAIR
DESIGNER:
Joseph Hoffman
YEAR: 1911
DIMENSIONS:
35½"W x 32"D x 37"H

### LC1 SLING CHAIR
DESIGNER:
Le Corbusier
YEAR: 1928
MANUFACTURER:
Atelier International
DIMENSIONS:
23⅝"W x 25⅝"D x 25¼"H

### MIDWAY CHAIR
DESIGNER:
Frank Lloyd Wright
YEAR: 1914
MANUFACTURER:
Atelier International
DIMENSIONS:
16"W x 13"D x 35"H

### LC9 LOUNGE CHAIR
DESIGNER:
Le Corbusier
YEAR: 1928
MANUFACTURER:
Atelier International
DIMENSIONS:
22"W x 63"D

# FURNITURE DIMENSIONS
## 20th Century Classic Chairs

**CESCA ARMCHAIR**
DESIGNER:
Marcel Breuer
YEAR: 1928
MANUFACTURER:
Knoll International
DIMENSIONS:
22⅝"W x 21⅝"D x 31¾"H

**BARCELONA STOOL**
DESIGNER:
Mies Van Der Rohe
YEAR: 1929
MANUFACTURER:
Knoll International
DIMENSIONS:
23"W x 22"D x 14½"H

**BRNO ARMCHAIR**
DESIGNER:
Mies Van Der Rohe
YEAR: 1929
MANUFACTURER:
Stendig
DIMENSIONS:
18"W x 23"D x 31½"H

**CHAISE LOUNGE**
DESIGNER:
Mies Van Der Rohe
YEAR: 1931
MANUFACTURER:
Knoll International
DIMENSIONS:
23⅝"W x 47½"D x 37½"H

**LC2 ARMCHAIR**
DESIGNER:
Le Corbusier
YEAR: 1929
MANUFACTURER:
Atelier International
DIMENSIONS:
30"W x 27½"D x 26½"H

**ZIG-ZAG CHAIR**
DESIGNER:
Gerrit Rietveld
YEAR: 1934
MANUFACTURER:
Atelier International
DIMENSIONS:
14½"W x 17"D x 29"H

**BARCELONA CHAIR**
DESIGNER:
Mies Van Der Rohe
YEAR: 1929
MANUFACTURER:
Knoll International
DIMENSIONS:
30"W x 30"D x 30"H

**PAIMO CHAIR**
DESIGNER:
Alvar Aalto
YEAR: 1935
MANUFACTURER:
Palazetti
DIMENSIONS:
23½"W x 31½"D x 25"H

**BARREL CHAIR**
DESIGNER:
Frank Lloyd Wright
YEAR: 1937
MANUFACTURER:
Atelier International
DIMENSIONS:
21½"W x 22"D x 32"H

**MOLDED FIBERGLAS CHAIR**
DESIGNER:
Charles Eames
YEAR: 1949
MANUFACTURER:
Herman Miller
DIMENSIONS:
25"W x 25½"D x 31"H

**BUTTERFLY CHAIR**
DESIGNER:
Harday, Boner & Kurchan
YEAR: 1938
DIMENSIONS:
28"W x 27½"D x 35½"H

**DIAMOND CHAIR**
DESIGNER:
Harry Bertoia
YEAR: 1952
MANUFACTURER:
Knoll International
DIMENSIONS:
33¾"W x 28"D x 30½"H

**MOLDED PLYWOOD CHAIR**
DESIGNER:
Charles Eames
YEAR: 1946
MANUFACTURER:
Herman Miller
DIMENSIONS:
21½"W x 19¼"D x 29⅜"H

**LOUNGE CHAIR**
DESIGNER:
Charles Eames
YEAR: 1956
MANUFACTURER:
Herman Miller
DIMENSIONS:
32½"W x 32¾"D x 33½"H

**WOMB CHAIR**
DESIGNER:
Eero Saarinen
YEAR: 1948
MANUFACTURER:
Knoll International
DIMENSIONS:
40"W x 39"D x 35½"H

**OTTOMAN**
DESIGNER:
Charles Eames
YEAR: 1956
MANUFACTURER:
Herman Miller
DIMENSIONS:
26"W x 21"D x 15"H

# FURNITURE DIMENSIONS
## 20th Century Classic Chairs

**ALUMINUM GROUP CHAIR**
DESIGNER:
Charles Eames
YEAR: 1958
MANUFACTURER:
Herman Miller
DIMENSIONS:
28½"W x 24¾"D x 33¾"H

**LOUNGE CHAIR**
DESIGNER:
Richard Schultz
YEAR: 1966
MANUFACTURER:
Knoll International
DIMENSIONS:
26"W x 28¼"D x 26½"H

**SHERRIFF CHAIR**
DESIGNER:
Sergio Rodriguez
YEAR: 1958
MANUFACTURER:
OCA

**TUBO CHAIR**
DESIGNER:
John Mascheroni
YEAR: 1968
MANUFACTURER:
Vecta
DIMENSIONS:
32"W x 32"D x 32"H

**HAND CHAIR**
DESIGNER:
Pedro Freidberg
YEAR: 1963
MANUFACTURER:
Hand Crafted

**SAPPER COLLECTION**
DESIGNER:
Richard Sapper
YEAR: 1977
MANUFACTURER:
Knoll International
DIMENSIONS:
28⅜"W x 27½"D x 38½-41⅜"H

**PLATNER CHAIR**
DESIGNER:
Warren Platner
YEAR: 1966
MANUFACTURER:
Knoll International
DIMENSIONS:
36½"W x 25½"D x 30½"H

**BASIC OPERATIONAL**
DESIGNER:
Niels Diffrient
YEAR: 1979
MANUFACTURER:
Knoll International
DIMENSIONS:
25½"W x 21"D x 32½-36½"H

**NOTHING CONTINUES TO HAPPEN CHAIR**

DESIGNER:
Horward Meisper

YEAR: 1981

MANUFACTURER:
Art et Industrie

DIMENSIONS:
17"W x 16"D x 37"H

**OTTOMAN**

DESIGNER:
Niels Diffrient

YEAR: 1986

MANUFACTURER:
Sunar/Hauserman

DIMENSIONS:
25"W x 24"D x 17⅛"H

**LOUNGE CHAIR**

DESIGNER:
Michael Graves

YEAR: 1982

MANUFACTURER:
Sunar/Hauserman

DIMENSIONS:
32"W x 29"D x 29"H

**ED ARCHER CHAIR**

DESIGNER:
Philippe Starck

YEAR: 1987

MANUFACTURER:
Driade Italy

DIMENSIONS:
18½"W x 21½"D x 38½"H

**QUEENE ANNE CHAIR**

DESIGNER:
Robert Venturi

YEAR: 1984

MANUFACTURER:
Knoll International

DIMENSIONS:
26½"W x 23½"D x 38½"H

**STONE CHAIR**

DESIGNER:
James Kutasi

YEAR: 1988

MANUFACTURER:
James Kutasi Australia

DIMENSIONS:
19⅝"W x 19⅝"D x 35½"H

**JEFFERSON CHAIR**

DESIGNER:
Neils Diffrient

YEAR: 1986

MANUFACTURER:
Sunar/Hauserman

DIMENSIONS:
32⅜"W x 34"D x 43½"H

## FURNITURE DIMENSIONS
Traditional Bedroom and Dining Room Furniture

### BEDROOM FURNITURE

### DINING ROOM FURNITURE

*Elevations*

*Plans*

*Large Size* — 6'-0" to 7'-2"

*Medium Size* — 5'-0" to 6'-0"

*Small Size* — 4'-0" to 5'-0"

4'-0" to 5'-6"

**Sofas, couches, davenports, divans, lounges**

*Elevations*

*Plans*

*Large Size* — 3'-6" to 4'-6"

5'-0" to 6'-8"

*Medium Size* — 4'-6" to 5'-6"

*Small Size* — 3'-6" to 4'-6"

**Settees**

*Elevations*

*Plans*

All lengths to 7'-0"

up to 4'-6"

4'-0" to 5'-0"

5'-0" to 6'-10"

**Settle**

**Bench**

**Seats (Windsor)**

*Plan* — *Elevation* — 1'-6" to 2'-0"

*Plan* — *Elevation* — 1'-6" to 2'-0"

*Plan* — *Elevation*

*Bath Room* — *Plan* — *Elevation* — 10" to 13" dia.

**Dressing stools and benches**

# FURNITURE DIMENSIONS

## Traditional Desks, Bookcases, and Chests

**Desks**

**Secretary**

**Bookcases**

**Desks**

**Highboys**

**Lowboy**

**Cabinet or chest**

**Chests**

**Umbrella stand**

## UNUPHOLSTERED CHAIRS

**Kitchen chair**    **Side chair**    **Arm chairs**

**Windsor chairs**    **Dining room chairs**

## UPHOLSTERED CHAIRS

**Wing chair**    **Barrel chair**    **Arm chairs**

**Rocking chair**    **Club chair**    **Tavern chair**    **Side chair**

*Arm Posture Chair*    *Swivel Chair*    *Large - with arms*    *Jury Chair*    *Judge's Chair*    *Tablet Arm Chair*    *Coupon or Tel. Booth Chair*

**Office chairs**    **Special chairs**

# FURNITURE DIMENSIONS

**Traditional Tables**

Library table

Tea and coffee tables

Serving table

Night table

Dressing table

Occasional table

Card tables

Drop leaf and butterfly tables

Tilt table

Draw top tables

Candle stand

Gate leg tables

Hutch table

Console table

Stands

The size of living rooms and the furniture arrangements contained within such spaces vary dramatically, depending on the size of the dwelling, the economic status and lifestyle of the user, and the relationship of the room to other areas of the dwelling. With regard to the luxury end of the scale, there are few limitations and no attempt has been made to identify the endless planning options possible. There are, however, minimum requirements and basic planning considerations that are applicable whatever the size of the space.

## Minimum Requirements

A living room for a three- or four-bedroom dwelling unit requires more space for its occupants than one for a one- or two-bedroom dwelling unit. Luxury units will necessarily need more space to accommodate more furnishings. In any case, the minimum living room with no dining facilities should be approximately 180 ft² but preferably around 200 ft². Figures 1 and 2 show two living rooms with typical furniture groupings (no dining facilities).

Figure 3 shows a living room with one end used for dining. This area often is arranged in an "L" shape to achieve greater definition or privacy from the living activities. Dwelling units with three or more bedrooms should have separate dining rooms or clearly defined dining areas.

The minimum width of a living room should be 11–12 ft. This is extremely tight, however, and if at all possible the width should be at least 14 ft.

## Planning Considerations

Planning considerations should include adequate floor and wall space for furniture groupings, separation of trafficways from centers of activity, and ease of access to furniture and windows.

Circulation within the living room should be as direct as possible and yet not interfere with furniture placement. Ideally, there should be no through traffic. If such traffic is necessary, it should be at one end, with the remaining portion of the room a "dead-end" space.

During social activities, people tend to gather or congregate in relatively small groups. Desirable conversation distance is also relatively small, approximately 10 ft in diameter.

When the living room is combined with the dining area, the dining area should be offset into an alcove or be clearly identified as an entity in itself.

**Fig. 1   Typical furniture arrangement for a one- or two-bedroom apartment (12.5 ft x 16 ft, 200 ft²).**

**Fig. 2   Typical furniture arrangement for a three-bedroom apartment (12.5 ft x 20 ft, 250 ft²).**

**Fig. 3   Another typical furniture arrangement for a three-bedroom apartment (12.5 ft x 22 ft, 275 ft²).**

# LIVING ROOMS
### Circulation

(a)

(b)

(c)

(d)

**Fig. 4** When through traffic is unavoidable, pathways should skirt conversational or activity centers, as illustrated in *(a)*, *(b)*, and *(c)*. *(d)* illustrates a more ideal layout in which the entire room is bypassed.

**Fig. 5**

**Fig. 6**

**Fig. 7**

Figures 5 to 10 show various groupings and related clearances. Figure 5 shows that a space 12'6" x 15'6" should be provided in order to accommodate seating for five around a 56-in-diameter cocktail table. The piano, sofa, and cocktail table arrangement shown in Fig. 6 requires a space at least 11'0" x 16'0". Figure 7 suggests that a space at least 12'9" x 13'3" is required to accommodate a grouping to seat 6 or 7 persons, while Fig. 8 indicates that a corner arrangement for two requires a space at least 6'3" x 6'6".

When planning furniture arrangements, allowances for clearances should take into account the human dimension as well, as illustrated in Figs. 9 and 10.

It should be noted that these diagrams are not intended as models for complete living room layouts. They are intended only as guidelines to illustrate minimum clearances for preliminary planning purposes.

**Fig. 8**

**Fig. 9**

**Fig. 10**

CONVERSATION

UNRELATED ACTIVITIES

LISTENING TO MUSIC

WATCHING TELEVISION

SOFFIT

2 EQ. DOORS 3/4" BIRCH VENEER PLYWOOD @ STORAGE (SEE PG A5 FOR PAINT FINISH TOUCH LATCH)

CENTER ALL OPENINGS IN FRONT PANEL

REMOVABLE FRONT PANEL SEE DETAIL 4 THIS SHT.

BASE (SHIPPED SEPARATELY) BOLT TO CABINET IN FIELD

THREADED STUD GLUED TO BLOCKING
1 1/2" x 3 1/2" BLOCKING EXCEPT @ T.V.
PRE DRILL FRONT 3/4" PANEL TO RECEIVE STUDS & SECURE W/ WASHERS & WING NUTS

BACK PANEL OF STORAGE SHELF

COMPONENTS SHELF TYPICAL 3/4" PLYWOOD

REMOVABLE 3/4" PLYWOOD PANEL TYPICAL (2) HINGED DOORS W/ TOUCH LATCH & HIDDEN HINGES ABOVE

④ DETAIL REMOVABLE PANEL
3" = 1'-0"  PLAN

⑤ PLAN
1 1/2" = 1'-0"

① ELEVATION FRONT W/ PANEL
1 1/2" = 1'-0"

**Fig. 11** Working drawings of a media cabinet, including plans, elevations, and sections of the installation. The design of the cabinet should take into account the actual electronic and other equipment to be housed and the clearances involved for operation. Power outlets should be coordinated and located so as to conceal unsightly wires and cables.

2 — ELEVATION W/OUT PANEL
1½" = 1'-0"

3 — SECTION
1½" = 1'-0"

**Fig. 11** *(Continued)*

**Fig. 12** Working drawings of a library/living room, including a plan of the space, wall elevations, and some of the many details involved.

Fig. 12    (Continued)

D — D
Half·Full·Size

ELEVATION
Scale : ½" — 1' — 0"

DETAIL·OF·
PILASTER·&·CORNICE
1½"Scale :

A — A

DETAIL·of·MANTLE
Scale : 1½" — 1' — 0"

B — B

C — C

8 1/2" X 8 1/2" HEATER FLUE

3'-0"

2'-0"

FIXED DOOR

13" X 18" FLUE

3'- 3 5/8"

2'-6"

1'-8"

1'-2"

6"

FINISHED FL.

REINFORCED CONCRETE SLAB

CONCRETE BLOCK

**SECTION** 1/2" SCALE

THREE FIXED PANEL

ALL WALNUT VENEER DOORS

6'-8"

ADJUSTABLE SHELVES

12" RECORD SPACE

10" RECORD SPACE

HI-FI SPACE

FIREWOOD STORAGE

COLD AIR RETURN

**ELEVATION** 3/16" SCALE

DRAWERS

CLOSET

TWO FIXED DOORS

FIREW'D STORAGE

HOLLOW CORE DOORS

OUT-OF-SEASON CLOTHES CLOSETS

1'-4"

2'-11"

STORAGE

HANGROD

2'-0"

**PLAN** 3/16" SCALE

FIREBRICK HEARTH

FIXED PANEL OVER FIREPLACE

FIREBRICK LINING BACK, SIDES & HEARTH

3 1/2" X 3 1/2" X 1/4" STEEL ANGLE

7" X 10" ASH DUMP

3/4" PLYWOOD PANEL

3/4"

12 GAGE SHEET METAL FIRE GUARD BENT TACK WELD TO ANGLE

**SECTION** 1/2" SCALE

LINE OF CABINETS ABOVE

2'-11"

4 WF 13 COLUMN & LEADER ENCLOSED IN WOOD FRAME

HOLLOW CORE DOOR

3/8" PLYWOOD RECORD STORAGE DIVIDERS

24" DEEP SPACE FOR INSTALLATION OF HI-FI

3'-9"

6'-8"

1'-2 1/2"

CONTINUOUS FLUORESCENT LIGHTING, TOP & BOTTOM

3/4" PLYWOOD DOOR

HARDWOOD EDGE

2"

3/4"

**DETAIL** 1 1/2" SCALE

2'-6"

6"

3/8" PLYWOOD BASE

8 1/2" X 8 1/2" HEATER FLUE

3" DIA LEADER

8"

1'-4"

2'-4"

1'-8"

ASH DUMP

6"

4 WF 13 COLUMN COMPLETELY BURIED IN MASONARY FOR STIFFENING

8" 8" 4'-0" 8" 8"

2'-0"

**PLAN SECTION** 1/2" SCALE

Figure 13 shows a plan and elevations of modifications to an existing fireplace. Based on these drawings and inspection and measurement of existing conditions, the contractor prepares and submits shop drawings for the designer's approval. Since at least two trades are involved, coordination of the trades by the contractor and a thorough review of the shop drawings by both contractor and designer are essential. It is important, also, that modifications conform with all applicable codes. The extent of hearth extension, the materials used, and the distance of combustible materials from the fire box are among the numerous items governed by codes.

**Fig. 13**

**Fig. 14  Floor plan, elevations, and details of paneled living room/library.**

**EAST ELEVATION**

NOTE:
PROVIDE FLUSH ACCESS PANEL INSIDE CABINET
TO REMOTE LIGHTING CONTROLS

**SOUTH ELEVATION**

**Fig. 14** *(Continued)*

6'-0" MAX.
A.C. DUCT TO ROUGH WALL
A.C. SLOT IN CORNICE

6'-0" MAX.
A.C. DUCT TO ROUGH WALL
A.C. SLOT IN CORNICE

STEREO SPEAKER

STEREO SPEAKER

ADJUSTABLE SHELVES

ADJUSTABLE SHELVES

19'-8⅜"
EXIST. ROUGH

19'-3¾"
FINISH

CLOCK
OUTLET
@5'-6"A.FF

5'-11½"

2½" 1'-0" 2½"

4'-6¾"
7'-4¾"

2½" 1'-0" 2½"

5'-11½"

EQUAL TO BOOKCASE
ON EAST ELEVATION

EQUAL TO BOOKCASES
ON EAST ELEVATION

2½" EQ 2½"

2½" EQ 2½"

2½" EQ 2½"

2½" EQ 2½"

CAB.

CAB.

PHONE

A.C. DUCTS
8 x 10

10'-0½"

6'-7"

CLOCK
OUTLET
@5'-6"AFF

4½"
4/12
6
3'-8¾"
4¾" 1'-10½" 4¾"
7'-6"

REMOTE VIEWING
SENSOR
MUSIC
CONTROL
LITE
SWITCH

4"
4"
4"
4"

DIMMER SWITCHES (2)

2'-6"

1'-3¾"

2'-8"

2'-10"
1'-1½"

7½"

7½"

· NOTE:
· DOOR PANEL PROFILES TO
  MATCH WALL PANELS
· DOOR & JAMB TO BE FURNISHED & INSTALLED
  BY GENERAL CONTRACTOR

**Fig. 14** *(Continued)*

Fig. 14  *(Continued)*

Traditional: roll arms, loose-cushion back, kidney shape, solid base

Traditional: roll arms, fixed-cushion back, tailored skirt

Contemporary: curved arms, fixed-cushion back, solid base

Contemporary: dome arms, solid back, solid base

Traditional: roll arms, fixed-cushion back, tailored skirt

Traditional: roll arms, tufted

Traditional: roll arms, one-piece back, skirted base

Contemporary: slanted cushion arms, fixed-cushion back, solid base

Traditional: roll arms, one-piece back, solid base

Traditional: roll arms, loose-pillow back, shirred base

Contemporary: curved arms, fixed-cushion back, solid base

Contemporary: shaped sofa, shaped front view

Traditional: roll arms

Traditional: roll arms, loose-pillow back, tailored skirt

Traditional: roll arms

Traditional: roll arms, loose-cushion back, kidney shape, pleated skirt, solid base

Traditional: roll arms

Contemporary: shaped sofa, shaped base

Traditional: roll arms, fixed-cushion back, solid base

Contemporary: square arms, loose-cushion back, solid base

Contemporary: miscellaneous slanted arms

Traditional: roll arms, fixed-cushion back, shirred skirt

Traditional: roll arms, tufted

Traditional: roll arms, fixed-cushion back, tailored skirt

77

# LIVING ROOMS

**Planning Data: Sofas**

Contemporary: straight arms, one-piece back, open base

Traditional: roll arms, loose-pillow back, full skirt

Contemporary: shaped sofa, shaped plan

Contemporary: roll arms, fixed-cushion back, solid base

Traditional: roll arms, tufted

Contemporary: miscellaneous slanted arms

Contemporary: shaped sofa, partitioned back

Contemporary: curved arms, fixed-cushion back, solid base

Contemporary: square arms, loose-cushion back, solid base

Contemporary: straight arms, one-piece back, open base

Contemporary: miscellaneous slanted arms

Contemporary: dome arms, one-piece tufted back, solid base

Contemporary: roll arms, loose-cushion back, solid base

Contemporary: square arms, fixed-cushion back, open base

Contemporary: dome arms, loose-cushion back, solid base

Traditional: roll arms, fixed-cushion back

Contemporary: square arms, fixed-cushion back, open base

Contemporary: curved arms, fixed-cushion back, solid base

Contemporary: roll arms, fixed-cushion back, solid base

Contemporary: square arms, fixed-cushion back, open base

Contemporary: dome arms, solid back, solid base

Contemporary: wood frame arms and legs, one-piece curved back, open base

Contemporary: curved arms, fixed-cushion back, solid base

Traditional: roll arms, one-piece back, open base

Contemporary: slanted cushion arms, fixed-cushion back, open base

Contemporary: one-piece curved back and arms, wood legs, open base

Contemporary: slanted cushion arms, fixed-cushion back, open base

Contemporary: dome arms, solid back

Contemporary: square arms, fixed-cushion back, wood trim, open base

Traditional: roll arms, one-piece back, open base

Contemporary: dome arms, channel quilted back, seat, and arms, solid base

Contemporary: curved arms, fixed-cushion back, solid base

Traditional: roll arms, one-piece back, open base

Contemporary: curved arms, fixed-cushion back, solid base

Contemporary: modular

Contemporary: sofa/daybed

Contemporary: slanted cushion arms, fixed-cushion back, solid base

Contemporary: dome arms, one-piece tufted back and seat, solid base

Contemporary: roll arms, fixed-cushion back, soft skirt

Contemporary: shaped sofa, partitioned back

Contemporary: curved arms, fixed-cushion back, solid base

Contemporary: dome arms, solid back

# DINING ROOMS
**Furniture Clearances**

## SPATIAL CHARACTERISTICS AND ARRANGEMENT

### Requirement

Each living unit should contain space for the purpose of dining. This area may be combined with the living room or kitchen, or may be a separate room.

### Criterion

The amount of space allocated to dining should be based on the number of persons to be served and the proper circulation space. Appropriate space should be provided for the storage of china and large dining articles either in the dining area itself or in the adjacent kitchen.

Space for accommodating the following sizes of tables and chairs in the dining area should be provided, according to the intended occupancy, as shown:

*1 or 2 persons:* 2 ft 6 in by 2 ft 6 in
*4 persons:* 2 ft 6 in by 3 ft 2 in
*6 persons:* 3 ft 4 in by 4 ft 0 in or 4 ft 0 in round
*8 persons:* 3 ft 4 in by 6 ft 0 in or 4 ft 0 in by 4 ft 0 in
*10 persons:* 3 ft 4 in by 8 ft 0 in or 4 ft 0 in by 6 ft 0 in
*12 persons:* 4 ft 0 in by 8 ft 0 in
*Dining chairs:* 1 ft 6 in by 1 ft 6 in
*Buffet or storage unit:* 1 ft 6 in by 3 ft 6 in

Figures 1 to 6 show the minimum requirements of the U.S. Department of Housing and Urban Development.

### Commentary

Size of the individual eating space on the table should be based upon a frontage of 24 in and an area of approximately 2 ft$^2$. In addition, table space should be large enough to accommodate serving dishes.

Desirable room for seating is a clear 42 in all around the dining table. The following minimum clearances from the edge of the table should be provided: 32 in for chairs plus access thereto, 38 in for chairs plus access and passage, 42 in for serving from behind chair, 24 in for passage only, 48 in from table to base cabinet (in kitchen).

In sizing the separate dining room, provision should be made for circulation through the room in addition to space for dining.

The location of the dining area in the kitchen is desirable for small houses and small apartments. This preference appears to stem from two needs: (1) housekeeping advantages; (2) the dining table in the kitchen provides a meeting place for the entire family. Where only one dining location is feasible, locating the dining table in the living room is not recommended.

**Fig. 1   Dining room for 6-person, 3-bedroom living unit.**

**Fig. 2   Dining room for 8-person, 4-bedroom living unit.**

**Fig. 3   Table for 2, 2′6″ × 2′6″.**

**Fig. 4   Table for 4, 2′6″ × 3′2″.**

**Fig. 5   Table for 8, 4′0″ × 4′0″.**

**Fig. 6   Table for 8, 3′4″ × 6′0″.**

Fig. 7 *(a)* to *(e)* illustrate, in plan and elevation, seating requirements and clearances for various dining table arrangements. *(f)* and *(g)* illustrate clearance guidelines for a typical armless dining chair and a dining chair with arms, respectively. It should be noted that the clearances indicated relate to chairs with depth dimensions of 20″ and 22″; clearances should be adjusted depending on the chair size finally selected.

# DINING ROOMS
### Furniture Clearances

### A dining room for 12.
A hutch or buffet is typically about 18″ deep. A 42″ wide table is common. There is space behind the chairs to edge past one side and one end, and to walk past on the other side and end. Table space is 24″ per person, the minimum place setting zone. With arm chairs at the ends, allow an extra 2″ for each; add 4″ to the room length.

### Minimum width for table and chairs.
8′-8″ for 36″ wide table, 32″ on one side to rise from the table and 36″ on the other side to edge past. A 48″ long table seats 4 and requires 34.6 ft².

### Dining space with benches.
6′-6″ for benches on both sides of a 36″ table. A 48″ long table seats 4 and requires 26 ft².

**Fig. 8**

### Bench on one side.
7′-9″ for a bench on one side and chairs on the other. Seating for four requires 31 ft².

### Corner bench.
Benches on one side and one end, and two chairs on the other side, seat five at a 3′x4′ table in 44.5 ft².

## Bench and chair dining.

### Round tables.
A 36″ round table with four swivel chairs fit in a 5′-10″x5′-10″ or 34 ft² corner space.

Figures 8 and 9 show clearances and room sizes for various dining arrangements. Since these data come from two sources, there may be slight disparities in suggested dimensions for similar conditions. Since these illustrations are intended only as guidelines for preliminary planning purposes, either set of any differing dimensions can be used.

Fig. 9

# DINING ROOMS
**Furniture Clearances**

Fig. 10 Minimum clearances for dining areas. *(a)* One end of table against wall. *(b)* Serving from one end and one side of table.

To assure adequate space for convenient use of the dining area, not less than the following clearances from the edge of the dining table should be observed:

    32 in for chair plus access thereto
    38 in for chairs plus access and passage
    42 in for serving from behind chair
    24 in for passage only
    48 in from table to base cabinet (in dining-kitchen)

Fig. 11 Minimum clearances and circulation for combined living-dining areas.

# ROUND TABLES

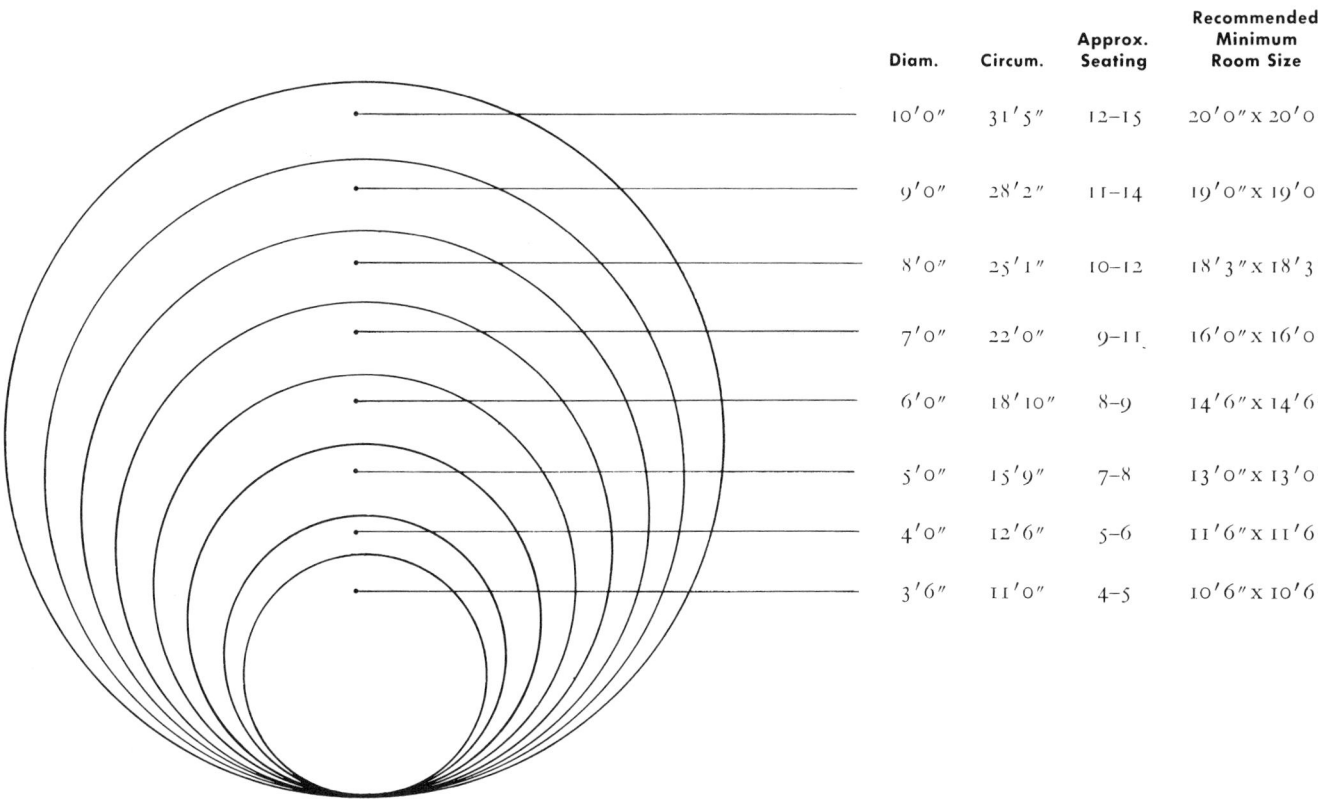

| Diam. | Circum. | Approx. Seating | Recommended Minimum Room Size |
|---|---|---|---|
| 10'0" | 31'5" | 12–15 | 20'0" x 20'0" |
| 9'0" | 28'2" | 11–14 | 19'0" x 19'0" |
| 8'0" | 25'1" | 10–12 | 18'3" x 18'3" |
| 7'0" | 22'0" | 9–11 | 16'0" x 16'0" |
| 6'0" | 18'10" | 8–9 | 14'6" x 14'6" |
| 5'0" | 15'9" | 7–8 | 13'0" x 13'0" |
| 4'0" | 12'6" | 5–6 | 11'6" x 11'6" |
| 3'6" | 11'0" | 4–5 | 10'6" x 10'6" |

# SQUARE TABLES

| W | L | Approx. Seating | Recommended Minimum Room Size |
|---|---|---|---|
| 5'0" | 5'0" | 8–12 | 13'0" x 13'0" |
| 4'6" | 4'6" | 4–8 | 12'0" x 12'0" |
| 4'0" | 4'0" | 4–8 | 11'6" x 11'6" |
| 3'6" | 3'6" | 4 | 10'6" x 10'6" |
| 3'0" | 3'0" | 4 | 9'0" x 9'0" |

**Fig. 12**  Seating capacities for round, square, rectangular, and boat-shaped tables of various sizes and the recommended minimum room sizes to accommodate each.

## DINING ROOMS
Dining Tables and Room Sizes

# RECTANGULAR TABLES

| W | L | Approx. Seating | Recommended Minimum Room Size |
|---|---|---|---|
| 6'0" | 28'0" | 28–30 | 18'0" x 40'0" |
| 6'0" | 26'0" | 26–28 | 18'0" x 38'0" |
| 6'0" | 24'0" | 24–26 | 18'0" x 36'0" |
| 5'0" | 22'0" | 22–24 | 15'0" x 32'0" |
| 5'0" | 20'0" | 20–22 | 15'0" x 30'0" |
| 4'6" | 18'0" | 18–20 | 13'6" x 27'0" |
| 4'6" | 16'0" | 16–18 | 13'6" x 25'0" |
| 4'6" | 14'0" | 14–16 | 13'6" x 23'0" |
| 4'0" | 13'0" | 12–14 | 12'0" x 21'0" |
| 4'0" | 12'0" | 12–14 | 12'0" x 20'0" |
| 4'0" | 11'0" | 10–12 | 12'0" x 19'0" |
| 4'0" | 10'0" | 10–12 | 12'0" x 17'0" |
| 4'0" | 9'6" | 8–10 | 12'0" x 16'6" |
| 3'6" | 9'0" | 8–10 | 10'6" x 16'0" |
| 3'6" | 8'6" | 8–10 | 10'6" x 15'6" |
| 3'6" | 8'0" | 8–10 | 10'6" x 15'0" |
| 3'6" | 7'6" | 6–8 | 10'6" x 14'6" |
| 3'6" | 7'0" | 6–8 | 10'6" x 14'0" |
| 3'0" | 6'6" | 6–8 | 10'0" x 13'6" |
| 3'0" | 6'0" | 6–8 | 10'0" x 13'0" |
| 2'6" | 5'6" | 4–6 | 9'0" x 12'6" |
| 2'6" | 5'0" | 4–6 | 9'0" x 12'0" |

# BOAT SHAPED TABLES

| W | L | Approx. Seating | Recommended Minimum Room Size |
|---|---|---|---|
| 3'5" | 8'0" | 8–10 | 10'0" x 15'0" |
| 3'8" | 9'0" | 8–10 | 11'0" x 16'0" |
| 3'11" | 10'0" | 10–12 | 12'0" x 17'0" |
| 4'3" | 11'0" | 10–12 | 13'0" x 19'0" |
| 4'7" | 12'0" | 12–14 | 14'0" x 21'0" |
| 4'11" | 14'0" | 14–16 | 15'0" x 23'0" |
| 5'3" | 16'0" | 16–18 | 16'0" x 26'0" |
| 5'7" | 18'0" | 20–22 | 17'0" x 29'0" |
| 6'0" | 20'0" | 20–24 | 18'0" x 32'0" |

**Fig. 12** *(Continued)*

Most of the clearances and bedroom sizes shown here are minimum and intended primarily for preliminary planning purposes. Some building codes permit rooms of even smaller sizes, while rooms in many private homes and luxury apartments are much larger. Moreover, in the final analysis lifestyle, the size and scale of furniture, the activities to be accommodated, and barrier-free design are all factors that should be taken into account during the design process.

Ideally, the recommended minimum bedroom size should be 10'0" x 12'0" exclusive of closets, while the recommended minimum size for a larger bedroom or master bedroom should be 12'0" x 16'0" exclusive of closets.

A larger proportion of the bedroom floor area is occupied by furniture than is the case with any other room; windows and doors account for a large percentage of the wall and partition space. These two factors complicate the planning of bedrooms, especially when the rooms are small.

Because of the room layout, some bedrooms with smaller areas better meet the needs than larger ones. The location of doors, windows, and closets must be properly planned to allow the best placement of the bed and other furniture.

Privacy, both visual and sound, are desirable for the bedroom. Children's bedrooms should be located away from the living room, because conversation in the living room prevents the children from sleeping. Closets should be used between all bedrooms wherever possible.

Each child needs a space that is his or her own to develop a sense of responsibility and a respect for the property rights of others. The ideal plan would provide a bedroom for each child, but since this is not always possible, there should be a bed for each.

The minimum room width shall be determined by the space required for the bed, activity space, and any furniture facing the bed. Widths less than 9'0" will usually require extra area to accommodate comparable furniture.

Aside from sleeping, the bedroom is the center of dressing and undressing activities. An interrelationship exists between dressing, storage of clothes, and the bedroom.

Inevitably, in a small apartment, it is not only economical but necessary to plan the use of the bedroom for more than one activity. It is essential to incorporate in the bedroom other functions such as relaxation, work, or entertainment.

A master bedroom should accommodate at least one double bed 4'6" x 6'6" or two single beds 3'3" x 6'6" each, one crib 2'4" x 1'5" if necessary, one dresser 3'6" x 1'10", one chest of drawers 2'6" x 1'10", one or two chairs 1'6" x 1'6" each, two night tables, and possibly a small desk or table 1'6" x 3'0". Figures 1 to 3 illustrate three configurations and the furniture clearances and room sizes required.

Ample storage is essential. Each bedroom requires at least one clothes closet. For master bedrooms, at least five linear feet of closet length is needed. For secondary bedrooms, at least three linear feet is needed. Clothes closets require a clear depth of two feet.

Each bedroom shall have at least one closet that meets or exceeds the following standards:

1. Depth: 2 feet clear
2. Length (for primary bedroom): 5 linear feet clear
3. Height:
    a. At least 5'4" clear hanging space
    b. Lowest shelf shall not be over 6'2" above the floor of room
4. One shelf and rod with at least 12 inches clear space above shelf
5. At least one-half the closet floor shall be level and not more than 12 inches above floor of adjacent room

DOUBLE BED · ONE CLOS.  10'-3"x12'-0"

**Fig. 1**

TWIN BED · SEPARATED  11'-0"x16'-0"

**Fig. 2**

TWIN BEDS ·· TWO CLOSETS  12'-4"x15'-6"

**Fig. 3**

# BEDROOMS

**Furniture Clearances and Arrangements**

**Fig. 4** *(a), (b)* Primary bedroom; *(c)* primary bedroom without crib.

## FURNITURE CLEARANCES

To assure adequate space for convenient use of furniture in the bedroom, not less than the following clearances should be observed (Figs. 4 and 5):

42 in at one side or foot of bed for dressing

6 in between side of bed and side of dresser or chest

## FURNITURE ARRANGEMENTS

The location of doors and windows should permit alternate furniture arrangements.

36 inches in front of dresser, closet, and chest of drawers

24 in for major circulation path (door to closet, etc.)

22 in on one side of bed for circulation

12 in on least used side of double bed. The least-used side of a single or twin bed can be placed against the wall except in bedrooms for the elderly.

**Fig. 5** *(a)* Single-occupancy bedroom; *(b)* double-occupancy bedroom.

Fig. 6 Although the recommended minimum size for a secondary bedroom is 10'0" x 12'0", these diagrams indicate how a double bed, night table, chair, and dresser can be accommodated in a room only 9'6" x 11'0".

Fig. 7 Double occupancy bedroom. Net area: 14.7 m² (160 ft²). The most likely occupants of this type of bedroom are adults, school-age children of the same sex, children of different sexes who are less than 9 years old, and preschoolers.

Fig. 8 Occupancy of a bedroom by more than two persons is not recommended. In cases where budgetary and/or space limitations offer no alternative, however, a dormitory arrangement may be necessary. The U.S. Department of Housing and Urban Development recommends the arrangement illustrated in this diagram.

# BEDROOMS
## Built-In Storage Details

SHELF ABOVE SEE DTL.

PLASTIC LAMINATE COUNTER W/ ¼" RADIUS NOSE EDGE

RECESSED FINGERPULL

PULL OUT SHELF STUDY ONLY W/ 2 DRAWERS BELOW

¾" PLYWOOD DRAWER FACE. PLASTIC LAMINATE FINISH

INTERIOR FINISH CLEAR LACQUER

RECESSED FINGERPULL

NOTE: 2 EQUAL DRAWERS ON GRANT EXTENSION SLIDES BEDR'S ONLY

2'-6"

1'-7" IN STUDY
2'-0" IN BEDROOM #4

(8) SECTION THRU FILE DRAWERS @ STUDY & BEDROOM #4
A12   1½" = 1'-0"

PLASTIC LAMINATE COUNTER TOP W/ ¼" RADIUS NOSE EDGE

RECESSED FINGERPULL

¾" PLYWOOD DOOR FACE W/ PLASTIC LAMINATE FINISH

DRILL HOLES 3" O.C. AND 6" FROM TOP & BOTTOM FOR SHELF PINS

2'-0"

2'-6"

(11) SECTION THRU CABINET @ BEDROOM #4
A12   1½" = 1'-0"

PLASTIC LAMINATE COUNTER W/ ¼" RADIUS NOSE EDGE

RECESSED FINGERPULL

¾" PLYWOOD DOOR W/ PLASTIC LAMINATE FINISH

DRILL HOLES ½" O.C. AND 6" FROM TOP & BOTTOM FOR SHELF PINS

¾" PLYWOOD SHELF

¾" PLYWOOD BASE

1'-7" IN STUDY
2'-0" IN BEDROOM #4

(9) SECTION THRU STORAGE CABINET @ STUDY & BEDROOM #4
A12   1½" = 1'-0"

PLASTIC LAMINATE COUNTER TOP W/ ¼" RADIUS NOSE EDGE

RECESSED FINGERPULL

¾" PLYWOOD DRAWER FACE. PLASTIC LAMINATE FINISH

BLOCKING AS REQ'D.

2'-0"

2'-0"

(12) SECTION THRU DESK DRAWER @ BEDROOM #4
A12   1½" = 1'-0"

LINE OF WALL

4" GRILLE SP-23

PLASTIC LAMINATE RADIATOR ENCLOSURE

¾" RADIUS NOSE EDGE

RECESSED FINGERPULL

'Z' CLIP

¾" PLYWOOD DOOR FACE

¾" PLYWOOD

MATTRESS N.I.C.

NEW A/C UNIT

2'-11"

REMOVEABLE BASE

PLAS. LAM.

GRILLE

¾" GYP. BD. INSULATION

1'-0"   6"

(10) SECTION THRU BANQUETTE @ BEDROOM #4
A12   1½" = 1'-0"

MIRROR

PLASTIC LAMINATE COUNTER TOP W/ ¼" RADIUS NOSE EDGE

RECESSED FINGERPULL

¾" PLYWOOD DRAWER FACE. PLASTIC LAMINATE FINISH

HAMPER DRAWER ON GRANT EXTENSION SLIDES

2'-0"

1'-0"

(13) SECTION THRU LAV. CAB. HAMPER @ BATHS #2,3 BDRM #4
A12   1½" = 1'-0"

# BEDROOMS

### Built-In Furniture

14 / A12  SECTION THRU CABINET @ BEDROOM #1  1½"=1'-0"

3 / A7  SECTION THRU RADIATOR COVER, TYP.  1½"=1'-0"

15 / A12  PLAN & ELEVATION OF PLATFORMS @ BED #1 & #4  1½"=1'-0"

1 / A7  PLAN: PLATFORMS FOR BEDS  ¼"=1'-0"

2 / A7  SECTION THRU PLATFORM

4 / A7  SECTION: ARMOIRE BEDROOM 1  1½"=1'-0"

- ¾" PLYWOOD
- ⅜" RADIUS HARDWOOD BULL NOSE
- ½" PLYWOOD BACK
- ¾" PLYWOOD
- ¾" PLYWOOD SIDES
- NOTE: LACQUER FIN. INSIDE & OUT. DRAWERS ON GRANT EXTENSION SLIDES W/ RECESSED FINGER PULLS
- PROVIDE FILE HANGER FOR LETTER SIZE FILES
- ¾" PLYWOOD BASE

2'-6"

2'-0"

5 / A6  SECTION THRU FILE CAB @ BEDROOM 1
1½"=1'-0"

- BULLNOSE 2 SIDES (BAR ONLY)
- ¾" PLYWOOD
- ⅜" RAD. HARDWOOD BULLNOSE
- NOTE: LACQUER FINISH @ BEDROOM 1, 5&6 & KITCHEN BAR & STUDY.

7 / A7  SECTION THRU DESK TOP-BDRM 1, BAR, STUDY
1½"=1'-0"

- VARIES: SEE CONSTRUCTION PLAN
- ¾" PLYWOOD
- ⅜" RADIUS HARDWOOD BULLNOSE
- NOTE: LACQUER FINISH @ DEN & LIVING ROOM PLASTIC LAMINATE @ STUDY

8 / A7  SECTION THRU BANQUETTE - TYPICAL
1½"=1'-0"

- ¾" PLYWOOD
- ½" PLYWOOD BACK
- NOTE: @ STUDY: 6 EQ. DOORS, 2 EQ. CAB. SECTIONS @ BDRM 2, 4 EQ. DOORS, 2 EQ. CABINET SECTIONS. CONCEAL HINGES, PLAS. LAM. FIN. INSIDE & OUT.
- NOTE: @ DEN: 4 EQ. DOORS 2 EQ. CABINET SECTIONS CONCEAL HINGES, LACQUER FINISH INSIDE & OUT.
- ¾" PLYWOOD SHELF
- DRILL HOLES 3" O.C. 6" FROM TOP & BOTTOM FOR SHELF PINS. PROVIDE 5 SHELVES @ DEN & 2 SHELVES @ STUDY & BEDROOM 2.
- LIGHT FIXTURE 'G'
- ¼" BLACK GLASS (@ DEN)
- ¾" PLYWOOD
- ⅜" RADIUS HARDWOOD BULLNOSE
- RECESSED FINGER PULL
- DRILL HOLES 3" O.C. 6" FROM TOP & BOTTOM FOR SHELF PINS
- ½" PLYWOOD BACK
- ¾" PLYWOOD
- ¾" PLYWOOD SHELF
- NOTE: 2 EQUAL DOORS. CONCEAL HINGES, BLANK PANEL BEHIND BANQUETTE. LACQUER FIN. INSIDE & OUT.
- BLOCKING AS REQ'D
- ¾" PLYWOOD
- ¾" PLYWOOD BASE
- PROVIDE BASE FILLER (LACQUER FIN) NEXT TO BANQUETTE.

3'-11½" @ STUDY & BEDROOM 2
4'-11½" @ DEN

1'-7½" @ DEN
1'-6" @ STUDY & BDRM 2

1'-9"

2'-0"

6 / A7  SECTION THRU CAB @ DEN WALL @ DEN, STUDY BDRM 2
1½"=1'-0"

ELEVATION · OF · CLOSET · DOORS & DRAWERS.

friction catches

adjustable shelves

friction catches

SECTION · THRO DRAWERS·

PLAN·

hanging · pole    drawers    · adjustable · shelves.

½" × ¾" hard wood slide

SECTION THRO · SLIDE

ceiling

½" × ¾" slide

PLAN · THRO DRAWERS·
scale : 3" = 1'—0"

3" scale PLAN SECTION · THRO · DOOR

3" scale SECTION · THRO · DRAWERS·

fin floor

# BEDROOMS
Plan and Elevation of Walk-In Closet

PLAN

Ⓐ

Ⓑ

NOTE: ALL HANG'G RODS
TO BE METAL

Ⓒ

Ⓓ

① ELEVATION
@ 1/4" = 1'-0"

TYPICAL HAT SHELVES
& COAT HANG RODS

SEE SCHEDULE

FIN. FL.

HARDWOOD CLEATS

1 1/16" ⌀ SATIN CHROME
HANGROD W/GARCY
#A3369 SOCKETS

FACE OF WALL

NOTE: PROVIDE WOOD GROUNDS
ON ALL PLASTER WALLS AND
WOOD OR METAL BLOCKING FOR
GYPSUM BOARD WALLS

① SECTION
@ 3" = 1'-0"

(a)

⑧ SECTION · NIGHT TABLE
A20  1 1/2" = 1'-0"

④ SECTION · DRESSER
A20  1 1/2" = 1'-0"

(b)

DOOR AS SCHEDULED

ALL SURFACES TO BE
PAINTED

COAT RAIL - POLISHED CHROME
HARDWOOD BLOCK'G.
ALL EXPOSED BLOCK'G TO BE
PAINTED

SEE CONSTR. PLAN
FOR WALL TYPES.

CLOSET

(c)

**Fig. 9** *(a)* illustrates a typical hat shelf and coat rod, while *(b)* shows relatively typical sections through a night table and a dresser. *(c)* illustrates a typical closet.

# BEDROOMS
## Closets

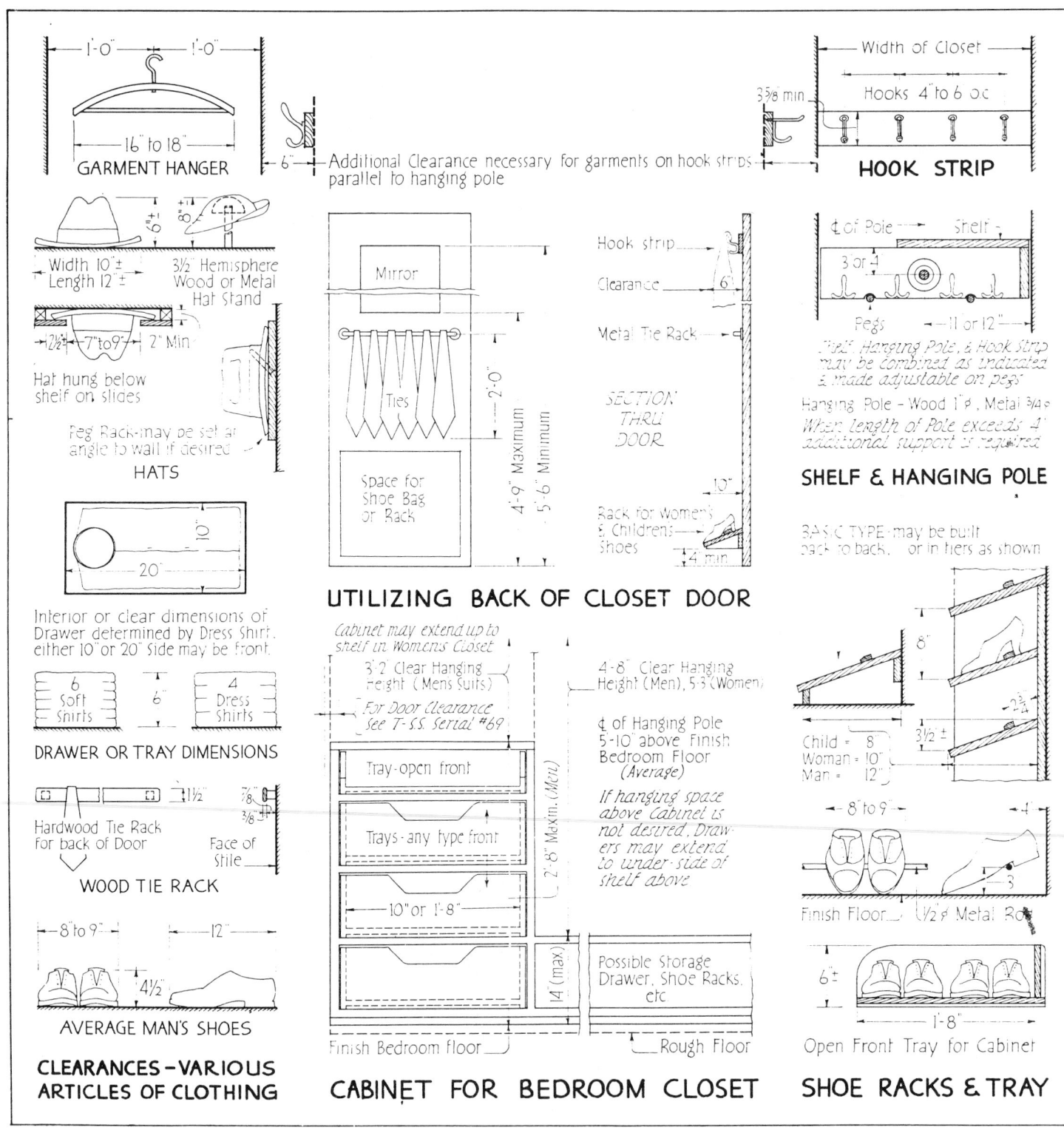

GARMENT HANGER

Additional Clearance necessary for garments on hook strips parallel to hanging pole

HOOK STRIP

HATS

Hat hung below shelf on slides

Peg Rack may be set at angle to wall if desired

SHELF & HANGING POLE

Interior or clear dimensions of Drawer determined by Dress Shirt, either 10" or 20" Side may be front.

DRAWER OR TRAY DIMENSIONS

Hardwood Tie Rack for back of Door

WOOD TIE RACK

AVERAGE MAN'S SHOES

CLEARANCES – VARIOUS ARTICLES OF CLOTHING

UTILIZING BACK OF CLOSET DOOR

SECTION THRU DOOR

Hook strip
Clearance
Metal Tie Rack
Rack for women's & Children's Shoes

CABINET FOR BEDROOM CLOSET

SHOE RACKS & TRAY

Open Front Tray for Cabinet

Ordinary treatment of space above door. Note poor access and waste space

2" to 3"

Space for Rack for Shoes

finished Ceiling Line

4'-8" (Men)
5'-3" (Women)
5'-10" (Average)

Floor Line

## SHALLOW CLOSETS

As much as possible of front walls should be doors to make entire length of shallow closets accessible.

Individual compartment with separate cabinet doors

Shelf & Hanging Pole

3'-2" (Men)

5'-6"

Space for Cabinet

May extend to shelf in Women's Closets

Short Garments & Suits

Long Garments & Dresses

Space for Cabinet, Shoe Drawers & Racks

Hook Strip space 6" extra

2'-0"

3'-4"    6"

2'-4" x 6'-8"

Approx 12 Garments on hangers

## MINIMUM CLOSET

Hook strips for Children's closets may be provided on rear of door or side walls & may be adjustable in height. (See Details)

12"   24"        Hook strip space 6" extra

16" desirable; Sliding Hangers available 10" to 24" and up.

2'-2" Hinged, folding or Sliding Doors

Sliding hanger-rods accommodate maximum number of garments without crushing.

## EXTREMELY SHALLOW

2' to 2'-6"

4'-8"

2'-2" x 6'-8"

Approx. 18 Garments on hangers

## FITTED CLOSET

Dead Storage

Pole    Cabinet

Provide 2" clearance for drawers at door jamb unless depth of closet permits complete removal

Shelves over   2'-0"   1'-2" or 2'-0"   Possible Extension

This dimension should equal twice depth of cabinet

Cabinet (10" or 20" front)

Hook Strip

## DEEP CLOSETS

Closet lights desirable; controlled preferably by door switch

Cupboard above is impractical because depth is extreme. One or two shelves may be provided

5'-10" or 5'-6"

Possible Cabinet

Closet floors should be flush with top of the door saddle.

# BATHROOMS
### Planning Data and Fixture Arrangements

A bathroom should have enough area to accommodate a lavatory, a water closet, and a bathtub or shower. Arrangement for fixtures should provide for comfortable use of each fixture and permit at least 90° door swing unless sliding doors are used.

The bathroom should be convenient to the bedroom zone, and accessible from the living and work areas. Linen storage should be accessible from the bathroom, but not necessarily located within the bathroom.

Each complete bathroom should be provided with the following:

1. Grab-bar and soap dish at bathtub
2. Toilet paper holder at water closet
3. Soap dish at lavatory (may be integral with lavatory)
4. Towel bar
5. Mirror and medicine cabinet or equivalent enclosed shelf space
6. In all cases where shower head is installed, provide a shower rod or shower door

Each half-bath should be provided with items 2 to 6 listed above.

## MINIMUM SHOWER CLEARANCES

|   | in | cm |
|---|---|---|
| A | 54 | 137.2 |
| B | 12 | 30.5 |
| C | 42 min. | 106.7 min. |
| D | 18 | 45.7 |
| E | 36 min. | 91.4 min. |
| F | 30 | 76.2 |
| G | 24 | 61.0 |
| H | 12 min. | 30.5 min. |
| I | 15 | 38.1 |
| J | 40–48 | 101.6–121.9 |
| K | 40–50 | 101.6–127.0 |
| L | 72 min. | 182.9 min. |

## DOUBLE LAVATORY CLEARANCES

|   | in | cm |
|---|---|---|
| A | 15–18 | 38.1–45.7 |
| B | 28–30 | 71.1–76.2 |
| C | 37–43 | 94.0–109.2 |
| D | 32–36 | 81.3–91.4 |
| E | 26–32 | 66.0–81.3 |
| F | 14–16 | 35.6–40.6 |
| G | 30 | 76.2 |
| H | 18 | 45.7 |
| I | 21–26 | 53.3–66.0 |

## WATER CLOSET

## BIDET

## BIDET AND WATER CLOSET

|   | in | cm |
|---|---|---|
| A | 12 min. | 30.5 min. |
| B | 28 min. | 71.1 min. |
| C | 24 min. | 61.0 min. |
| D | 52 min. | 132.1 min. |
| E | 12–18 | 30.5–45.7 |
| F | 12 | 30.5 |
| G | 40 | 101.6 |
| H | 18 | 45.7 |
| I | 30 | 76.2 |

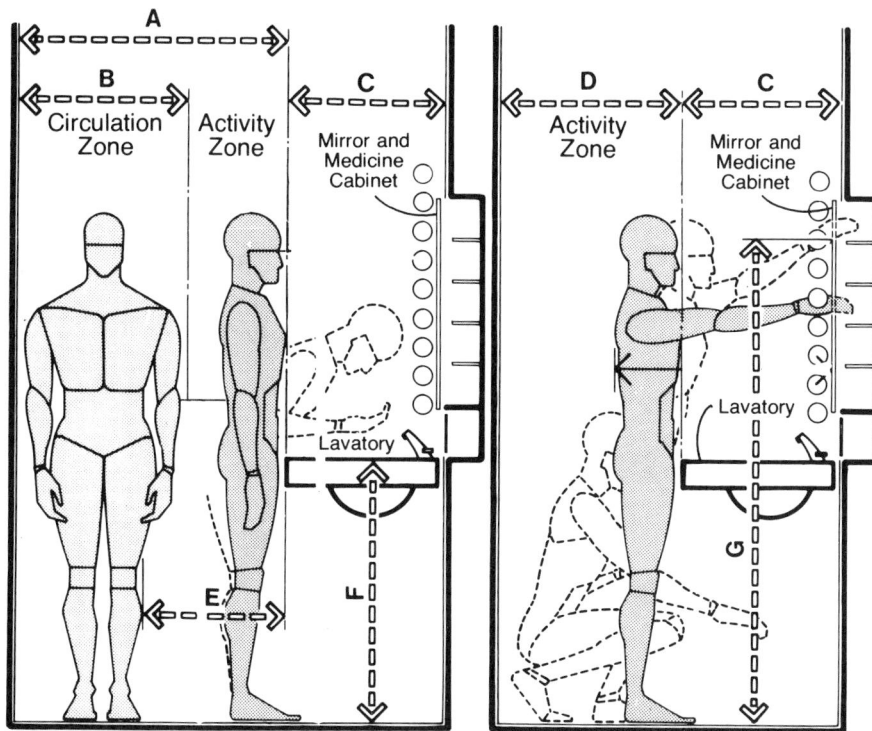

**Fig. 1 Lavatory: male anthropometric considerations.**

Figure 1 deals primarily with some of the more critical male anthropometric considerations. A lavatory height above the floor of 37 to 43 in, or 94 to 109.2 cm, is suggested to accommodate the majority of users. It should be noted, however, that common practice is to locate the lavatory in the neighborhood of 31 in above the floor. In order to establish the location of mirrors above the lavatory, eye height should be taken into consideration.

Figure 2 explores, in much the same manner, the anthropometric considerations related to women and children. Given the great variability in body sizes to be accommodated within a single family, a strong case can be presented for the development of a height adjustment capability for the lavatory. Until that is developed, there is no reason, on custom installations, why the architect or interior designer cannot take anthropometric measurements of the client to ensure proper interface between the user and the lavatory.

|   | in | cm |
|---|---|---|
| A | 48 | 121.9 |
| B | 30 | 76.2 |
| C | 19–24 | 48.3–61.0 |
| D | 27 min. | 68.6 min. |
| E | 18 | 45.7 |
| F | 37–43 | 94.0–109.2 |
| G | 72 max. | 182.9 max. |
| H | 32–36 | 81.3–91.4 |
| I | 69 max. | 175.3 max. |
| J | 16–18 | 40.6–45.7 |
| K | 26–32 | 66.0–81.3 |
| L | 32 | 81.3 |
| M | 20–24 | 50.8–61.0 |

**Fig. 2 Lavatory: female and child anthropometric considerations.**

# BATHROOMS
Typical Plans and Fixture Arrangements

Fig. 3   Two-fixture plans: water closet and washbasin.

Fig. 4   Three-fixture plans: water closet, washbasin and tub.

Fig. 5   Two- and three-fixture noncompartmented plans: water closet, washbasin, and shower.

Fig. 6   Four-fixture compartmented plans: water closet, tub, and two washbasins.

# BATHROOMS
## Typical Plans and Fixture Arrangements

### Minimum half-bath.
16 ft² is about minimum for standard fixtures; 4'-6"x4'-6" gives a more spacious feeling.

### Generous half-bath.
22.5 ft² is a generous half-bath. A wall-hung lavatory instead of a vanity squeezes into 2'-6" width and 16.3 ft².

### Corner toilet in a half-bath.
A corner toilet and a small lavatory fit 13.5 ft². Consider this idea for installing a half-bath in a closet or under a stairway.

### Corner shower.
A corner shower, toilet, and lavatory fit in 33 ft². Very little storage space available.

**Fig. 7 A wide array of two-, three-, four-, and five-fixture toilet plans.**

### Small, 3-fixture bathroom.
A small 3-fixture bathroom with limited storage in a built-in vanity meets basic bathroom requirements in a space 37.5 ft². The door is 32" wide for a person with a cane or crutches. This bathroom is too small for a wheelchair.

### Two-lavatory bathroom.
A 2-lavatory bathroom with adequate room at the toilet and each lavatory. Note storage space under the lavatories and in a floor-to-ceiling unit. Area: 63 ft².

### Separate tub and shower.
This plan also includes a bidet. Storage is in the 48" long vanity. Area: 75.3 ft².

### Large shower.
A generous 33"x48" shower is featured in this 32 ft² bathroom. Storage is under the 30" vanity and on shelves over the toilet.

### Corner square tub.
Although not usually a space saver, a square tub fits some situations better than a rectangular one. This 3-fixture bathroom has excellent storage but is only 59.5 ft².

### Large 3-fixture bathroom.
With fixtures in separate compartments, this layout can replace a second bath by accommodating more than one person at a time. It is as large as two bathrooms but costs less because of fewer fixtures and less plumbing. Area: 106 ft² plus hallway storage.

**Fig. 7** *(Continued)*

### Four-fixtures, two compartments.
Three people can use this bathroom at the same time. Consider a pocket door between the compartments. Even with generous storage space it takes only the same space as many non-compartmented bathrooms, about 80.5 ft².

### Five fixtures, three compartments.
This bathroom serves as two full bathrooms in 87 ft². Two doors to each compartment are undesirable. Limited storage space available.

# BATHROOMS

**Custom Designs**

Fig. 8 A variety of design possibilities for the more customized bathroom.

**Fig. 8** *(Continued)*

# BATHROOMS

**Custom Designs**

**Fig. 8** *(Continued)*

**Fig. 9   A selection of countertop lavatories.**

# BATHROOMS
## Lavatory Types and Dimensions

Fig. 10   A selection of wall-hung and pedestal-type lavatories.

Fig. 11    Another selection of lavatories.

# BATHROOMS
**Lavatory Types and Dimensions**

Fig. 11 *(Continued)*

Fig. 12    A selection of whirlpool baths.

# BATHROOMS

## Bathtub Types and Dimensions

Dimensions: 42″ x 37″ x 12″

Dimensions: 60″ x 31½″ x 16″

Dimensions: 60″ x 31½″ x 16″

Fig. 13    A selection of standard baths.

Fig. 14    A selection of waterclosets.

# BATHROOMS
### Bidet Types and Dimensions

**Fig. 15   A selection of bidets.**

# BATHROOMS

Plans, Elevations, and Details

PLAN

CORIAN TOP
LAV. & SPLASH

Ⓐ

Ⓓ

CERAMIC TILE
VERIFY SELECTION
W/OWNER

MARCHAND VALANCE
LIGHT
#27-109 & MED CAB.
& C-109 C

ALL CABINET &
DRAWER DOORS ARE
PLASTIC LAMINATE
NEVAMAR

Ⓑ

Ⓒ

**Three-fixture bathroom with tub**

FLORESTONE
SAFLOR MOLDED
STONE SHOWER
MODEL # 3232-1

CORIAN TOP
LAV & SPLASH

PLAN

Ⓐ

6 PEG COAT
HANGER

DOUBLE
HOOK

SHELF

MARCHAND MED. CABINET
& VALANCE LIGHT
14-109 AND MED CAB-
INET & C-109 B

ALL CABINET &
DRAWER DOORS ARE
PLASTIC LAMINATE.
NEVAMAR

Ⓒ

Ⓓ

Ⓑ

**Three-fixture bathroom with shower**

GUEST BATH

GUEST BATH
EAST

GUEST BATH
WEST

GUEST BATH
SOUTH

GUEST BATH
NORTH

**Four-fixture bathroom with tub and shower**

# BATHROOMS

Plans, Elevations, and Details

**Four-fixture bathroom with bidet and tub**

PLAN

Ⓐ  Ⓑ  Ⓒ

FURRED CEIL'G

Ⓓ  Ⓔ  Ⓕ

**Powder room**

PLAN

CORIAN TOP
LAV. & SPLASH

BATHROOM

CERAMIC SOAP DISH
TO MATCH TILE
(CONSULT OWNER)

Ⓐ

Ⓑ

Ⓕ

MARCHAND VALANCE
LIGHT
# 2T-109 & MED. CAB.
# C-109 C

ALL CABINET & DRAWER DOORS
ARE PLASTIC LAMINATE BY
NEVAMAR

Ⓒ

Ⓓ

Ⓔ

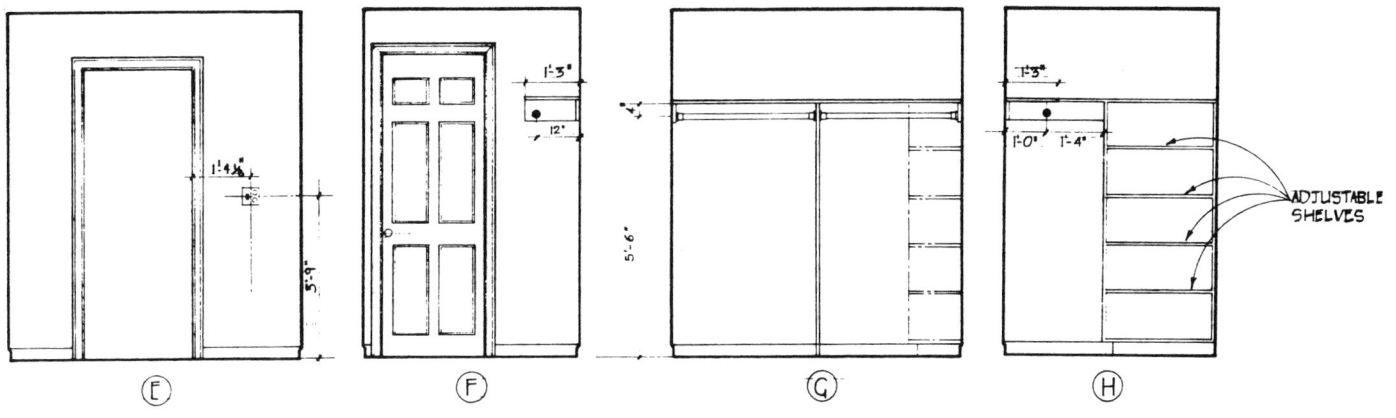

CORIAN TOP
LAV & SPLASH

// TILE SHELF

SHELVES

PLAN

Ⓐ

MARCHAND
VALANCE LIGHT
# 36-109

MIRROR

Ⓑ

Ⓒ

CERAMIC TILE
VERIFY W/OWNER

CERAMIC SOAP DISHES
TO MATCH TILE

Ⓓ

Ⓔ

Ⓕ

Ⓖ

ADJUSTABLE
SHELVES

Ⓗ

**Her bathroom**

# BATHROOMS

**Plans, Elevations, and Details**

LAMINATE TOP

FLORESTONE,
SAFLOR MOLDED STONE
SHOWER RECESS MODEL
# 4834-1

FOLD-DOWN
SEAT. DETAILS
TO FOLLOW

5½" DEEP
RECESSED TILED
SHAMPOO/SOAP
SHELF

TILE SHOWER
INTERIOR PER
OWNER/SELECTION

T.V. WIRE TO COME
THRU COUNTERTOP
TO T.V. UNIT

MARBLE LAV
TOP & SPLASH

PLAN

SHOE RACKS

ELECTRIC
TOWEL RACK

(A)                              (B)

MARCHAND
VALANCE LIGHT
# 36-109

LAMINATE TOP
(CONSULT OWNER
FOR COLOR)

MIRROR

ALL CABINET & DRAWER
DOORS ARE PLASTIC LAMINATE
NEVAMAR

(D)                              (E)

DRILL HOLES 3" OC. 6" FROM TOP
& BOTTOM FOR SHELF PINS

2) 3/4" PLYWOOD SHELVES, LACQUER FIN.

3/4" PLYWOOD, LACQUER FIN.

KINGSTON LIGHT FIXTURE
RECEPTICLE @ VANITY
LINE OF WALL TO ALIGN W/VAN. FACE

NOTE: 3 EQ. DOORS
2 UNEQUAL CAB. SECTIONS
CONCEAL HINGES, LACQUER
FINISH INSIDE & OUT.

3/4" MARBLE ON 3/4" PLYWOOD, 3/8" RADIUS
BULLNOSE (TYP.)

LACQUER FINISH DRAWER ON GRANT
EXTENSION SLIDES, NOTE: 3 EQ. DRAWERS

**18 / A6  MAKEUP VANITY & CAB ABOVE / MEDICINE CAB. BATH1**  1 1/2"=1'-0"

3/4" MARBLE ON 3/4" PLYWOOD
3/8" RADIUS BULLNOSE EDGE

3/4" PLYWOOD

NOTE: 4 EQUAL DOORS
3 UNEQUAL CAB. SECTIONS
CONCEAL HINGES, LACQUER
FINISH INSIDE & OUT.

NOTE: LAV-SEE SPECS.
ROUGH HIGH TO CONCEAL
PIPES IN CAB.

**19 / A6  LAV. VANITY, BATH 1**  1 1/2"=1'-0"

POP-UP DRAIN
HOT WATER
COLD WATER

LAV

**22 / A6  PLAN FITTINGS ARRANGEMENT @ LAV. BATH 2**  1 1/2"=1'-0"

STAINLESS STEEL #4 ON
3/4" PLYWOOD
3/8" RADIUS HARDWOOD
BULLNOSE

LAV. SEE SPECS. ROUGH
HIGH TO CONCEAL PIPES
IN CAB.

LARGE CLEAT NEEDED.
INSPECT WALL CONDITIONS
PRIOR TO COMMENCEMENT
OF WORK.

SS #4 ON 3/4" PLYWOOD

NOTE: 4 EQ. DRS., 2 EQ.
CAB. SECTIONS, CONCEAL
HINGES.

**23 / A6  LAV. VANITY, BATH 2**  1 1/2"=1'-0"

LINE OF CLG

STAINLESS STEEL #4
ON 3/4" PLYWOOD DOORS

3/4" PLY SIDE PANELS

1/2" PLY. BACK

NOTE: 2 EQUAL DOORS,
1 CAB. SECTION. CONCEAL
HINGES, TOUCH LATCH
PLAST. LAM. INSIDE

WASHER/DRYER UNIT

**2A / A6  SECTION THRU CAB OVER WASHER/DRYER UNIT**  1 1/2"=1'-0"

¢ OF SINK

SINGLE CONTROL LAV.
MIXER W/POP-UP KROIN
HV-3

SURFACE MOUNTED SINK
SEE SCHEDULE

PLASTIC LAMINATE
COUNTER TOP

**12 / A11  TYPICAL LAVATORY FITTINGS ARRANGEMENT**  1"=1'-0"

POP-UP DRAIN

ALIGN LAV. W/ ¢ OF
FITTINGS

DOUBLE CONTROL VALVE,
SWIVEL SPOUT, ROSETTES
AND HANDLES

UNDER THE COUNTER
MOUNTED SINK. SEE
SCHEDULE

STONE COUNTER TOP

NOTE: SINK ON LEFT
TO HAVE OPPOSITE
ARRANGEMENT

**17 / A11  LAVATORY FITTING ARRANGEMENT @ BATH #1**  1"=1'-0"
(SIMILAR BATH #5)

# BATHROOMS

### Vanities

KINGSTON LIGHT FIXTURE

PLASTIC LAM. ON 4" PLYWOOD SHELF

STAINLESS STEEL CLOTHES POLE

SOLID CORE DOOR

STAINLESS STEEL CLOTHES POLE @ DOORS 7 & 8 ONLY

DRILL HOLES 3" O.C.·6" FROM BOTTOM FOR SHELF PINS

PLASTIC LAM. ON 3/4" PLYWD. #SHELVES PER CLOSET ON DWG A8.

8' SINGLE ROD CLOSETS 3'-0"

17 / A6  TYPICAL CLOSET/SHELF CLOSET

POP UP DRAIN
HOT WATER
COLD WATER

LAV. 15" x 19"

ADDITIONAL LAV: GOOSENECK SPOUT W/ HOT & COLD HANDLES TO THE LEFT, NO POP UP DRAIN.

20 / A6  PLAN, FITTINGS ARRANGEMENT @ LAV. BATH 1

LINE OF LAV. VANITY BOTTOM
NOTE: HOLES TO BE CUT FOR PIPES.

3/4" PLYWOOD, MIRROR DOOR FACE, (ROUGH EDGES) TO BE FLUSH W/ ADJ. WALL

NOTE: TOUCH LATCH CONCEAL HINGES. CAB. TO BE INSULATED FOR SOUNDPROOFING AFTER INSTALLATION OF MOTOR.

LINE OF FLOOR

21 / A6  WHIRLPOOL MOTOR CAB.

MIRROR

(MARBLE) COUNTER TOP W/ 3/8" RADIUS NOSE EDGE

RECESSED FINGERPULL

3/4" PLYWOOD DRWR. FACE LACQUER FINISH. DRWR ON GRANT EXTENSION SLIDES

3/4" PLYWOOD DRWR. FACE 3/4" PLYWOOD SIDES

NOTE: DRAWER ON GRANT FULL EXTENSION SLIDES

ALIGN W/ TILE JOINT

NOTE: COLOR LACQUER EXTERIOR, CLEAR LACQUER INTERIOR

MARBLE

1 / A11  SECTION THRU LAV. CAB. @ BATH #1
1½" = 1'-0"

PLASTIC LAMINATE COUNTER, TOP W/ 3/4" RADIUS NOSE EDGE

KROIN SEAMLESS FORMED STEEL LAV.

CLEAR LACQUER INT. FINISH

2'-0"

CONCEAL ROUGHING IN CABINET

3/4" PLYWOOD DOOR FACE PLAS. LAM. FIN. CONCEAL HINGES

2"x2" WOOD @ 1'0.C ON BLOCKING TOP & BOTTOM PAINTED FINISH

NEW RADIATOR

MAGNETIC CATCH

2½" STL. STUD 5/8" GYP. BD

3 / A11  SECTION THRU LAV. CAB. @ BATH #4
1½" = 1'-0"

SEE DTL. A

PLASTIC LAMINATE COUNTER TOP W/ 3/4" RADIUS NOSE EDGE

RECESSED FINGERPULL

KROIN SEAMLESS FORMED STEEL LAV. EW-3 WHITE OVER THE COUNTER MOUNTED

3/4" PLYWOOD DOOR FACE PLASTIC LAMINATE FINISH CONCEAL HINGES

INTERIOR FINISH CLEAR LACQUER

2"x2" WOOD @ 1"0.C. ON BLOCKING TOP & BOTTOM PAINT FINISH

NEW RADIATOR

MAGNETIC CATCH

CONCEAL ROUGHING IN CABINET

2'-0" BATH #2, 6
1'-10" BATH #3

2 / A11  SECTION THRU LAV. CAB. @ BATH #2 & BATH #3, 6 (SIMILAR)
1½" = 1'-0"

MARBLE COUNTER TOP

RECESSED FINGERPULL

CAXTON VITREOUS CHINA RIMLESS LAVATORY WITH K-1010 CLAMP ASSEMBLY FOR MOUNTING UNDER COUNTER

3/4" PLYWOOD DOOR FACE. LACQUER FINISH CONCEAL HINGES CLEAR LACQUER INTERIOR

CONCEAL ROUGHING IN CABINET

2'-0"

5 / A11  SECTION THRU LAV. CAB. @ BATH #1
1½" = 1'-0"

5 DETAIL: VANITY HAMPER
A17 1½" : 1'-0"

6 DETAIL: MEDICINE CAB.
A17 1½" : 1'-0"

MIRROR
(TOP ALIGN W/ GROUT JOINT)
PLASTIC LAMINATE COUNTER TOP

¾" PLYWOOD DOOR FACE
PLASTIC LAMINATE FINISH
CONCEAL HINGES
INTERIOR FINISH CLEAR
LACQUER

6 SECTION THRU LAV. CAB. @ BATH #2 & BATH #3 (SIMILAR)
A11

7 SECTION: POWDER RM. VANITY
A17 1½" : 1'-0"

8 DETAIL: VANITY MASTER BATHROOM
A17 1½" : 1'-0"

STAINLESS STEEL COUNTER
TOP ON ¾" PLYWOOD W/ ¾"
RADIUS NOSE EDGE

ELKAY RLR-12 STAINLESS
STEEL SINK 12" Ø W/ INTEGRAL
S.S. COUNTER

RECESSED FINGERPULL
9.5.

¾" PLYWOOD DOOR FACE
PLASTIC LAMINATE FINISH
CONCEAL HINGES

2"x2" WOOD @ 1'-0 C. ON
BLOCKING TOP & BOTTOM
PAINT FINISH

NEW RADIATOR

MAGNETIC CATCH

7 SECTION THRU LAV. CAB. @ BATH #5
A11 1½" : 1'-0"

## BATHROOMS

**Accessory and Control Placement**

ELEVATION
OF TUB W/SHOWER

ELEVATION
OF TUB W/O SHOWER

SECTION AT SHOWER

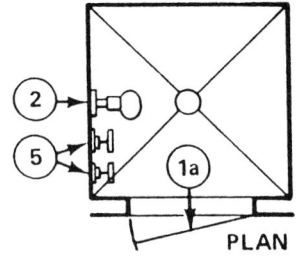

PLAN

1. SHOWER CURTAIN ROD: KEEP WITHIN INSIDE OF TUB OR SHOWER.

1a. ENCLOSURE DOORS: IF SWINGING DOORS ARE USED, PLACE HINGES ON THE SIDE OPPOSITE CONTROL VALVES.

2. SHOWER HEAD: SEE ELEVATION OF TUB AND SHOWER STALL FOR RECOMMENDED HEIGHTS.

3. GRAB BARS SHALL BE MANUFACTURED OF SHATTER-RESISTANT MATERIAL, FREE FROM BURRS, SHARP EDGES AND PINCH POINTS. KNURLING OR SLIP-RESISTANT SURFACE IS DESIRABLE.

4. RECESSED SOAP DISH SHALL BE FREE FROM BURRS AND SHARP EDGES. WHERE GRAB BAR IS AN INTEGRAL PART OF THE SOAP DISH, IT MAY HAVE A MINIMUM LENGTH OF 6 INCHES.

5. FAUCET SHALL BE MANUFACTURED OF SHATTER-RESISTANT MATERIAL, FREE FROM BURRS AND SHARP EDGES. ALL FAUCET SETS IN SHOWERS, TUBS AND LAVATORIES SHALL BE EQUIPPED WITH A WATER-MIXING VALVE DELIVERING A MAXIMUM WATER TEMPERATURE OF 110° ±5°F.

6. SHOWER STALL LIGHT: SHALL BE OF A VAPOR-PROOF FIXTURE WITH THE ELECTRICAL LIGHT SWITCH A MINIMUM OF 72 INCHES AWAY FROM SHOWER STALL.

2'-6"

5 SAW CUTS THRU FACE

PULLS

PLASTIC LAM.

SPLASH RETURN @ WALL

LAV.

3/4" RED OAK PLYWD. W/ RED OAK EDGES

3/8" F.R. PLYWD

3/4" F.R. PLYWD

DETAIL @ 3'-0"

4" BASE

1'-9"

TOILET ROOM CAB. ELEV.

TOILET ROOM CAB. SECT.

2'-0"

EQ.

EQ.

CL OF FIXTURE.

4" PLATE GLASS MIRROR W/ S.STL. FRAME. FULL HEIGHT FROM BACKSPLASH TO UNDERSIDE OF CLG.

PLASTIC LAM. FINISH.
BY: WILSONART
COLOR: KAHKI BROWN @ LADIES RM. D-60-15
BY: NEVAMAR
COLOR: BLACK PEARL S-6-14 T.

3/4" PLYWOOD.
(TYP.)

WD. BLOCKING.

NOTE:
ALL WOODWORK SHALL BE FIRE RETARDANT.

FIN. FLOOR.

2'-3" CLEAR.

DET. @ VANITY.
SCALE 1½" = 1'-0"

PROVIDE PIPE CHASE BELOW VANITY. G.C. TO COORDINATE W/ PLUMBER FOR EXACT PIPE LOCATIONS.

MIRROR

DOWEL & EPOXY
APRON TO FRAME

SECTION

NON STAINING CAULK

SHIM AS
REQ'D

BOWL

¾ PLYWOOD
EPOXY TO BOTT.
OF MARBLE TOP

1¼" x 1" BRASS OR SS PLATE
BOLT TO WOOD

WOOD OR
METAL FRAME

**SECTION "A"**
(NO SCALE)

Fig. 16   Typical details of a marble vanity-top installation.

NON STAINING CAULK

CER. BOWL

ROUT OUT ¾ PLYWOOD TOP
TO RECEIVE BOWL

LEAD EXPANSION SHIELD
USE WITH 1¼" THICK STOCK ONLY

1¼"

NON STAINING
CAULK

BOWL

METAL CLIP & SCREW
4 REQ'D

NON STAINING CAULK

WOOD BLOCKING
AS REQ'D

BOWL

WOOD SCREW

¾ PLYWOOD TOP

¾ PLYWOOD BRACE

**TYPICAL SECTIONS BOWL CARRIER**

TRIM RING

LAVATORY BOWL

MARBLE LAVATORY TOP

**PLAN**

TRIM RING

MARBLE LAVATORY TOP

LAVATORY BOWL

**ELEVATION**

SECT - "A"
NO SCALE

TRIM RING

MARBLE LAVATORY TOP

NOTE: Do not use oily putty or plumbing
sealants with marble.

**CONCEALED MARBLE EDGE**
SECTION

**Fig. 16**  *(Continued)*

## BATHTUB WALLS

### Wood or Metal Studs
#### Cement Mortar

3/4" TO 1 1/4"

- CERAMIC TILE
- BOND COAT
- MORTAR BED
- SCRATCH COAT
- METAL LATH
- MEMBRANE
- FLEXIBLE SEALANT
- TUB HANGER OR END GRAIN WOOD BLOCK
- BATH TUB
- FIREPROOFING WHEN REQUIRED (BY OTHER TRADE)
- WOOD OR METAL STUDS

**Recommended uses**

■ over dry, well-braced wood studs, furring, or metal studs
■ preferred method of installation over wood studs for bathtubs

### Glass Mesh Mortar Units

- CERAMIC TILE
- PRESANDED DRY-SET OR LATEX-PORTLAND CEMENT MORTAR
- GLASS MESH MORTAR UNIT
- WOOD OR METAL STUDS
- FLEXIBLE SEALANT
- TUB HANGER OR END GRAIN WOOD BLOCK
- BATH TUB
- FIREPROOFING WHEN REQUIRED (BY OTHER TRADE)

**Recommended use**

■ in tub enclosures and tub showers over dry, well-braced wood studs, furring, or metal studs

### Gypsum Board

- CERAMIC TILE
- LATEX-PORTLAND CEMENT MORTAR OR ADHESIVE
- WATER RESISTANT GYPSUM BOARD
- WOOD OR METAL STUDS
- FLEXIBLE SEALANT
- TUB HANGER OR END GRAIN WOOD BLOCK
- BATH TUB
- FIREPROOFING WHEN REQUIRED (BY OTHER TRADE)

1/4"

**Recommended use**

■ in tub enclosures and tub showers over water-resistant gypsum backing board on wood or metal studs

## TILE TUBS AND FOUNTAINS

### Membrane
#### Cement Mortar

- CERAMIC TILE
- NEAT CEMENT BOND COAT
- MORTAR BED
- SCRATCH COAT
- METAL LATH
- WATERPROOF MEMBRANE
- EXTERIOR GRADE PLYWOOD

3/4" TO 1 1/4"

**WOOD FORM**

3/4" TO 1 1/4"

- CERAMIC TILE
- NEAT CEMENT BOND COAT
- MORTAR BED
- SCRATCH COAT (IF NEEDED)
- METAL LATH
- WATERPROOF MEMBRANE
- CONCRETE TANK

**CONCRETE TANK
(Preferred)**

- REINFORCING

- WEEP HOLES
- CRUSHED TILE OR STONE

SLOPE TO DRAIN          SLOPE TO DRAIN

## SHOWER RECEPTOR RENOVATION

### Cement Mortar

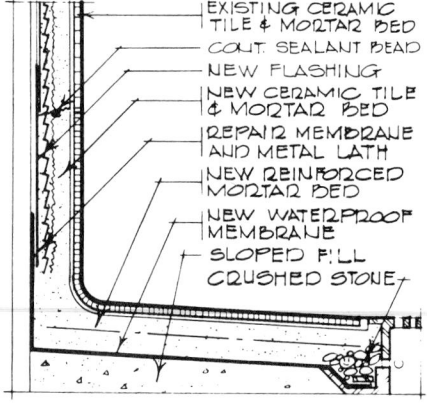

- EXISTING CERAMIC TILE & MORTAR BED
- CONT. SEALANT BEAD
- NEW FLASHING
- NEW CERAMIC TILE & MORTAR BED
- REPAIR MEMBRANE AND METAL LATH
- NEW REINFORCED MORTAR BED
- NEW WATERPROOF MEMBRANE
- SLOPED FILL
- CRUSHED STONE

**Recommended use**

■ over wood or concrete subfloors; where old shower pan has failed

**Requirements**

■ waterproof membrane required except in slab-on-grade installations where membrane may be omitted
■ slope tank so that membrane will slope to the drain
■ flange drain with weep holes required
■ wood framing, if used, should be pressure treated and designed to resist deflection and movement

## SHOWER RECEPTORS, WALLS

# Wood or Metal Studs

### Cement Mortar

- CERAMIC TILE
- BOND COAT
- REINFORCED MORTAR BED 1" to 1½"
- SHOWER PAN OR MEMBRANE
- SLOPED FILL WEEP HOLES
- CRUSHED TILE OR STONE

**Recommended use**
- over wood or concrete subfloors

### Glass Mesh Mortar Units

- CERAMIC TILE
- PRESANDED DRY-SET OR LATEX-PORTLAND CEMENT MORTAR
- GLASS MESH MORTAR UNIT
- WOOD OR METAL STUDS
- REINFORCED MORTAR BED 1" to 1½"
- SHOWER PAN OR MEMBRANE
- SLOPED FILL WEEP HOLES
- CRUSHED TILE OR STONE

**Recommended use**
- in showers over dry, well-braced wood studs, furring, or metal studs

### Gypsum Board
### Organic Adhesive

- CERAMIC TILE
- ADHESIVE
- WATER RESISTANT GYPSUM BOARD
- WOOD OR METAL STUDS
- FLEXIBLE SEALANT
- GALVANIZED METAL LATH
- TILE LINED SHOWER RECEPTOR

**Recommended use**
- in showers over water-resistant gypsum backing board on wood or metal studs

## COUNTERTOPS

# Wood Base

### Cement Mortar

- CUT WALL MORTAR AND METAL LATH HERE
- CERAMIC TILE
- BOND COAT
- MORTAR BED
- METAL LATH
- MEMBRANE
- WOOD BASE
- PUNCHED METAL STRIP

**Recommended uses**
- on countertops, drainboards, lavatory tops, etc.
- preferred method where sink or lavatory is to be recessed

### Thin-Bed

- CERAMIC TILE
- EPOXY OR ORGANIC ADHESIVE
- PLYWOOD

**Recommended use**
- on countertops where thin-set method is desired

### Glass Mesh  Mortar Unit

- CERAMIC TILE
- LATEX-PORTLAND CEMENT MORTAR
- GLASS MESH MORTAR UNIT
- PLYWOOD
- WATERPROOF MEMBRANE - TILE ADHESIVE

**Recommended uses**
- preferred thin-set mortar method on countertops, drainboards, lavatory tops, and similar uses
- preferred method where self-rimming sinks and lavatories are desired

**Fig. 18    Typical installation details for shower receptors, walls, and countertops.**

# BATHROOMS
Bathtub and Shower Details

5/8" GYP. BD. W.R. TYPE
2'-8⅝"
CERAMIC TILE, BULLNOSE @ EDGE
BLOCKING AS REQ.
NOTE: BUILD UP SILL TO BE FACED WITH FULL TILES IN ELEVATION

10 / A6  SILL DETAIL @ BATH 2  3"=1'-0"

2½" STEEL STUDS
3¾" x 3¾" CERAMIC TILE
5/8" GYP. BD. W.R. TYPE
CERAMIC TILE W/ 2 SIDES BULLNOSE
2⅜" x 9" WOOD GROUND
LINE OF CER. TILE FLOOR

11 / A6  WING WALL @ BATH 2 : TYP.  3"=1'-0"

FAST FILL W/ H & C HANDLES
ALL ROSETTES (NO PLATE)
(ON OPPOSITE WALL)
BULLNOSE EDGE, SEE
CERAMIC TILE
"STEEPING BATH" BY KOHLER, 36"x60" K-790-5
WOOD GROUND
2½" STEEL STUDS
5/8" GYP. BD. W.R. TYPE
NOTE: GROUT & CAULK AS REQ.
NOTE: PLATFORM HEIGHT
BLOCKING AS REQ.

12 / A6  SECTION : BATH @ BATH 2  1½"=1'-0"

SHOWER HEAD
SPEAKMAN CONTROL
STEAM MGT (BATH 1)
TILE FINISH : BATH 2
MARBLE TILE : BATH 1
NOTE: 4" SQUARE (FINISHED DIMENSION) CURB.
SPEAKERS
LEAD PAN

13 / A6  SECTION THRU SHOWER (TYP.)  ½"=1'-0"

V.I.F.
UP
5/8" MARBLE TILE
5/8" GYP. BD. W.R. TYPE
NOTE: CAULK AS REQ.
PLAN SECTION @ STEP
TYPICAL WING WALL

14 / A6  SECTION THRU MARBLE TILE WALL @ BATH 1  ½"=1'-0"

MARBLE TILE WALL BEYOND
2'-4½"
¾" MARBLE SILL, 3/8" RADIUS BULLNOSE
WOOD GROUND
2½" STEEL STUD
5/8" MARBLE TILES
5/8" GYP. BD. W.R. TYPE (2 LAYERS)
NOTE: CAULK AS REQ.
NEW RAISED FLOOR

15 / A6  SECTION THRU KNEE WALL & SILL @ BATH 1  1½"=1'-0"

NOTE: SEE PLAN, © RADIUS IS OUTSIDE OF TUB
LINE OF FLOOR IN RAISED PORTION OF BATHROOM
2'-4½"
BACK
LEG
APPROX. 3" FOR DRAINAGE
GLASS BLOCK
CAULKING
TOOLED EDGE
TYPICAL SILL DETAIL, GLASS BLOCK, SEE
¾" MARBLE
ISOLATION MEMBRANE (SEALANT)
¾" PLYWOOD
STRUCTURE
PLYWOOD CUT-OUT (TYP)
LEAD PAN
LINE OF EXISTING FLOOR
LEDGE
½" RAD. BULLNOSE

16 / A6  SECTION THRU BATHTUB @ BATH #1 (TYP.)  1½"=1'-0"

## SECTION: WHIRLPOOL BATH #1
12/A17   1"=1'-0"

12"Ø TOWEL BAR
BRUSHED CHROME

CERAMIC TILE

SETTING BED
BY W.P. CTR'BD

10 X 10 CERAMIC TILE

BUILD UP PLATFORM WITH
2x4 @ 16" O.C. DOUBLE
2x4'S OVER CORNERS.
WHIRLPOOL TUB

ALIGN W/TILE JT.

CERAMIC TILE
SETTING BED
3/4" PLYWOOD SUB FLOOR

DOUBLE 2x10 NOTCH
AS REQUIRED TO
ACHIEVE ELEVATION

EQUAL   EQUAL

SOLID BRIDGING
AS REQUIRED

## SECTION: WHIRLPOOL TUB, MASTER BATH
13/A17   1"=1'-0"

LINE OF WALL
EDGE OF FIREPLACE

ALIGN HEARTH
WITH INSIDE
OF FIREPLACE

SLAB

WHIRLPOOL JETS

DRAIN

SLAB MARBLE TOP

2x4 @ 12" O.C.
LEAD PAN CONT.

12x12 MARBLE TILE
SETTING BED

3/4" PLYWOOD

DOUBLE 2x10
FLOOR FRAMING

2'-0"

## SECTION: WHIRLPOOL TUB, MASTER BATH
14/A17   1"=1'-0"

7'-6" N.T.S.

SLAB MARBLE TOP

2x4 @ 12" O.C.

LEAD PAN

12x12 MARBLE TILE
SETTING BED
3/4" PLYWOOD SUBFLOOR

DOUBLE 2x10
FLOOR FRAMING

2'-0"

## SECTION: M. BATH SHOWER
10/A17   1"=1'-0"

MARBLE TILE
SETTING BED
3/4" PLYWOOD
4x4 POST

LINE OF WALL IN
FOREGROUND

LEAD SHOWER PAN

GLASS BLOCK
MARBLE TILE

MARBLE TILE
SETTING BED

FIN. FLR.

3/4" PLYWOOD

## BATHROOMS

Ceramic Tile Details

### TILE OVER TILE

## Interior Walls

CUT TRIM
TO FIT

NEW CERAMIC
TILE

BONDING
MATERIAL

EXISTING
TILE

**CASE I**

**CASE II**

NEW GYPSUM
BOARD OR
P.C. MORTAR

NEW CERAMIC
TILE

BONDING
MATERIAL

EXISTING
TILE

**CASE III**

NEW MORTAR

NEW CERAMIC
TILE

BONDING
MATERIAL

EXISTING TILE

**CASE IV**

## Interior Floors

NEW CERAMIC
TILE

GROUT

BONDING
MATERIAL

EXISTING FLOOR

### Recommended uses

■ for alteration of ceramic-tiled areas where modernization or a change of design is desired in residences, motels and hotels, restaurants, public rest rooms, etc.

■ also applicable to smooth floors of terrazzo, stone, slate, etc.

### Recommended uses

■ for alteration of ceramic-tiled areas where modernization or a change of design is desired in residences, motels and hotels, restaurants, public rest rooms, etc.

■ also applicable to smooth walls of marble, stone, slate, etc.

### Requirements

■ existing installation must be sound, well bonded, and without major structural cracks

### Materials, grouting, expansion joints, installation specifications

■ for organic adhesive installation see Method W223

■ for Dry-Set or latex-portland cement mortar installation see Method W202

■ for epoxy adhesive installation refer to manufacturer's literature

**Fig. 19   Typical installation details for tile over tile.**

## ACCESSIBILITY

It is essential that the design of interior spaces, as well as exterior spaces, be responsive to the needs of those having physical disabilities. There is a proliferation of state and local legislation in this regard, and, more recently, federal legislation (Americans with Disabilities Act of 1990), that provides design guidelines and requirements. The designer should become familiar with those codes and other requirements in her or his area prior to initiation of design and, where possible, go beyond the very minimum standards.

The design of the bathroom is perhaps one of those areas where the interface between the physically disabled and the interior space is the most critical. Accordingly, on this page and the following pages are design guidelines prepared by the Veterans Administration and the U.S. Department of Housing and Urban Development.

recommended self-supporting shelf and countertop

recommended additional connection for hand-held shower head

removable vanity cabinet in knee space

standard 5'-0" bathtub

reinforced areas for possible future grab bar installation

**Small Adaptable Bathroom in Conventional Configuration**

vanity cabinet removed and protection cover installed

hand-held shower and grab bars added as needed

ANSI/UFAS clear floor space at each fixture

exposed clear knee space under lavatory

clamp on tub seat added as needed

**Small Adaptable Bathroom in Adjusted Configuration**

## BATHROOMS
**Adaptable Bathrooms**

5'-0" min.

offset controls

clamp-on removable seat

7'-5" min.

This sample bathroom meets the minimum space requirements of both ANSI and UFAS; note, however, that the space is very small and many wheelchair users will have difficulty using such a bathroom. More space should be allocated when possible.

**A Small Bathroom with Adaptable Features Plan**

**A Small Bathroom with Adaptable Features Perspective**

recommended countertop lavatory on wall-mounted support brackets with pipe protection and appearance panel

reinforced areas for grab bar installation as needed

clamp-on tub seat

clear floor spaces as per ANSI/UFAS

vanity base cabinet (removed)

vanity cabinet
installed in knee
space

reinforced areas for
possible future grab
bar installation

offset controls

standard 5'-0" bathtub
with built-in seat

**Larger Adaptable Bathroom
in Conventional Configuration**

vanity cabinet
removed to
expose knee space

grab bars added
as needed

offset controls

built-in seat at
rear of tub

**Larger Adaptable Bathroom
in Adjusted Configuration**

## BATHROOMS

**Adaptable Bathrooms**

hand-held shower

clamp-on removable tub seat

wall rein-forcing areas

built-in seat

offset water valve

standard tub

**Standard Bathtub with Removable Seat**

**Standard Bathtub with Built-in Seat**

60"

30" min.

shower curtain

recommended additional water-proof floor area for water control

**ANSI Minimum Roll-in Shower**

greater stall depth for easier use

60"

42" min. recommended

**Preferred Deeper Roll-in Shower**

POWDER RM. PLAN WITH 27" REMOVABLE
VANITY CABINET

BATHROOM PLAN W/20" LAVATORY

BATHROOM TYPE WITH 24"
REMOVABLE VANITY CABINET

BATHROOM PLAN WITH 24"

REMOVABLE VANITY CABINET

X = THE OUTER EDGE OF THE WATER CLOSET WILL NOT EXTEND INTO THE CLEAR SPACE REQUIRED FROM THE DOOR OPENING.

2'-6" CLEAR AROUND SINK (ANSI 4.19.3.)

3'-0"x 4'-0" AROUND SHOWER (ANSI 4.21.2)

REMOVABLE SHOWER DOOR (ANSI 4.21.6)

SHOWER STALL WITH 4" MAX. CURB HEIGHT

SEAT (ANSI 4.21.3)

GRAB BAR (ANSI 4.21.4)

36"x 36" ADAPTABLE SHOWER STALL

MINIMUM BATHROOM REQUIRED

W/ADDITIONAL SHOWER

*Possible*
*wall locations* ------

**Clear Floor Space at Water Closets**

(a)
**Back Wall**

(b)
**Side Wall**

**Grab Bars at Water Closets**

**Clear Floor Space at Lavatories**

**Lavatory Clearances**

# BATHROOMS
## Wheelchair Accessible Clearances

Vanity

Combination bathtub/shower

Shower

Floor-mounted water closet

Typical bathroom arrangement

Shower seat

Lavatory

Bathtub

"Roll-in" shower

① PLAN: TYPICAL ADAPTABLE BATHROOM
A3  ½" = 1'-0"

② ELEVATION: TYPICAL ADAPTABLE BATHROOM
A3  ½" = 1'-0"

1A PLAN: TYPICAL ADAPTED BATHROOM
A3  ½" = 1'-0"

2A ELEVATION: TYPICAL ADAPTED BATHROOM
A3  ½" = 1'-0"

⑥ SECTION THRU THRESHOLD: TO COMPLY W/ ANSI 4.3.8
A3  FULL SIZE

**SYMBOL KEY:**
- ● Shower controls
- ◁ Shower head
- ⊕ Drain

**(a)**
**With Seat in Tub**

**(b)**
**With Seat at Head of Tub**

**Clear Floor Space at Bathtubs**

**(a)**
**With Seat in Tub**

**(b)**
**With Seat at Head of Tub**

**Grab Bars at Bathtubs**

(a)
36-in by 36-in
(915-mm by 915-mm) Stall

(b)
30-in by 60-in
(760-mm by 1525-mm) Stall

**Shower Size and Clearances**

**Shower Seat Design**

(a)
36-in by 36-in (915-mm by 915-mm) Stall

(b)
30-in by 60-in (760-mm by 1525-mm) Stall

**Grab Bars at Shower Stalls**

# BATHROOMS

### Wheelchair Accessible Design

**Fig. 1**

**RANGE CENTER**

**Fig. 2**

The height of a kitchen workcounter, the proper clearance between cabinets or appliances for circulation, the accessibility to overhead or undercounter storage, and proper visibility are among the primary considerations in the design of cooking spaces. All must be responsive to human dimension and body size if the quality of interface between the user and the components of the interior space are to be adequate. In establishing clearances between counters, the maximum body breadth and depth of the user of larger body size must be taken into account as well as the projections of the appliances. Refrigerator doors, cabinet drawers, dishwashing machine doors, and cabinet doors all project to some degree in their open position into the space within which the user must circulate and must be accommodated.

Standard kitchen counter heights manufactured are all about 36 in, or 91.4 cm. But such a height does not necessarily accommodate the body dimension of all users for all tasks. Certain cooking activities, for example, may be more efficiently performed from a standing position, but with a counter height less than 36 in. In overhead cabinets the upper shelves are usually inaccessible to the smaller person, while the lower shelves are usually inaccessible to most without bending or kneeling. The logical answer is the development of kitchen cabinet systems capable of total adjustability to accommodate the human dimension of the individual user. Such a system could accommodate not only those of smaller and larger body size, but also elderly and disabled people.

Figure 1 provides some general anthropometric data for establishing basic heights of cabinetry and appliances above the floor. Figures 2 and 3 show in more detail the interface of the human body and the kitchen environment.

| | in | cm |
|---|---|---|
| A | 48 min. | 121.9 min. |
| B | 40 | 101.6 |
| C | 15 | 38.1 min. |
| D | 21–30 | 53.3–76.2 |
| E | 1–3 | 2.5–7.6 |
| F | 15 min. | 38.1 min. |
| G | 19.5–46 | 49.5–116.8 |
| H | 12 min. | 30.5 min. |
| I | 17.5 max. | 44.5 max |
| J | 96–101.5 | 243.8–257.8 |
| K | 24–27.5 | 61.0–69.9 |
| L | 24–26 | 61.0–66.0 |
| M | 30 | 76.2 |
| N | 60 min. | 152.4 min. |
| O | 35–36.25 | 88.9–92.1 |
| P | 24 min. | 61.0 min. |
| Q | 35 max. | 88.9 max. |

Figures 2 and 3 illustrate the clearances related to range centers. Figure 2 indicates a minimum clearance between appliances of 48 in, or 121. 9 cm. The anthropometric basis for the clearances are amplified in Fig. 3.

The 40-in, or 101.6-cm, wall oven workzone clearance is adequate to accommodate the projected wall oven door, in addition to the maximum body depth dimension of the user. The standing figure shown in broken line, however, indicates both dimensionally and graphically that the 40-in clearance will not permit comfortable circulation when appliances on both sides are in operation at the same time. The range workzone clearance, also 40 in, is adequate to accommodate the open range door and the body size of the kneeling user.

An extremely important, but frequently overlooked, anthropometric consideration in kitchen design is eye height. In this regard, the distance from the top of the range to the underside of the hood should allow the rear burners to be visible to the user.

**RANGE CENTER**

Fig. 3

| | in | cm |
|---|---|---|
| A | 48 min. | 121.9 min. |
| B | 40 | 101.6 |
| C | 15 | 38.1 min. |
| D | 21–30 | 53.3–76.2 |
| E | 1–3 | 2.5–7.6 |
| F | 15 min. | 38.1 min. |
| G | 19.5–46 | 49.5–116.8 |
| H | 12 min. | 30.5 min. |
| I | 17.5 max. | 44.5 max |
| J | 96–101.5 | 243.8–257.8 |
| K | 24–27.5 | 61.0–69.9 |
| L | 24–26 | 61.0–66.0 |
| M | 30 | 76.2 |
| N | 60 min. | 152.4 min. |
| O | 35–36.25 | 88.9–92.1 |
| P | 24 min. | 61.0 min. |
| Q | 35 max. | 88.9 max. |

The U-shaped plan is the most efficient. When not broken, it provides the opportunity and floor space for several simultaneous activities. The corridor or gallery kitchen is typically accessible from both ends, often converting it from a work space to a corridor. It sometimes is closed off on one end, thereby creating a variation of the U-plan, which although small can produce a fairly comfortable kitchen.

The broken U-shaped plan often results from the necessity of locating a door along one or two of the three walls of a typical U-shaped scheme. The resulting through traffic reduces the compactness and efficiency of the plan.

The typical L-shaped kitchen allows for the location of a small breakfast area in the opposite corner.

**Fig. 4   U-shaped plans. If dishwasher is desired, it should be located at sink center.**

**Fig. 7   L-shaped plan. If dishwasher is desired, it should be located at sink center.**

**Fig. 5   Corridor plans. If dishwasher is desired, it should be located at sink center.**

**Fig. 6   Broken U-shaped plans. If dishwasher is desired, it should be located at sink center.**

# KITCHENS
### Typical Layouts

**U kitchen.**

Service Entry

10'–3" min

18' Perimeter

About 16'

STO   DW   S S   LS
RG
MW
R
P
D and C
T and C

**L kitchen.**

About 15'

10' to 11'

23' Perimeter

LS   DW   S S   R
RG
MW/
Util Cab
T and C
D and C
P

**Corridor kitchen.**

About 22'

4' min

20' Perimeter

MW   DW   S S   R
T and C
CT   OV   P   D
C

Service Entry

Traffic to Other Parts of House

**Broken U kitchen.**

About 13'

10' to 11'

18' Perimeter

4' min

D   MW/OV   DW   S S   LS
C
CT   R
Eating Bar
C C C C
P

Service Entry

**Fig. 8**   These diagrams illustrate further variations of the typical plans shown in Figs. 4 to 7. A triangle perimeter of 23'0" or less is usually indicative of a relatively efficient kitchen layout.

Cooking/baking

Oven

Range

Sink

Mixing Center

Refrigeration

OV and/or MW   RG   DW   S   S   R

18"–24"   36" min   48"–54"

**Minimum counter frontage.**
For combined work centers.

### Space Criterion

The size of the kitchen should be determined by the number of bedrooms provided in the living unit. Work centers for the following equipment, cabinets, and space for their use should be provided:

1. Range space with base and wall cabinet at one side for serving and storage of utensils and staples.

2. Sink and base cabinet with counter space on each side for cleanup. Wall cabinets for storage of dinnerware.

3. Refrigerator space with counter space at latch side of the refrigerator door.

4. Mixing counter and base cabinet for electrical appliances and utensil storage. Wall cabinet for staple storage.

### Recommended minimum edge distance

Equipment should be placed to allow for efficient operating room between it and any adjacent corner cabinet. At least 9 in from the edge of the sink and range and 16 in at the side of the refrigerator is recommended.

### Circulation space

A minimum of 40 in should be provided between base cabinets or appliances opposite each other. This same minimum clearance applies when a wall,

storage wall, or work table is opposite a base cabinet.

### Traffic

Traffic in the kitchen should be limited to kitchen work only. Serving circulation to the dining area should be without any cross traffic.

### Height of shelving and counter tops

1. Maximum height of wall shelving 74 in. Height of counter tops should be 36 in.

2. Minimum clearance height between sink and wall cabinet 24 in; between base and wall cabinets 15-in clearance.

ZERO BEDRM. KITCHENETTE

TWO BEDROOM LIVING UNIT KITCHENS

ONE BEDROOM KITCHENETTE

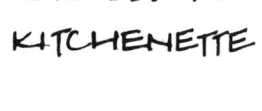

MIN. FRONTAGES FOR VARIOUS KITCHENS

THREE BEDRM. UNIT     FOUR BEDROOM UNIT

MIN. EDGE DISTANCES

# KITCHENS
## Storage and Cabinets

### KITCHEN STORAGE

Each kitchen or kitchenette should have (1) accessible storage space for food and utensils, (2) sufficient space for the average kitchen accessories, (3) sufficient storage space for those items of household equipment normally used and for which storage is not elsewhere provided.

width (w) in feet, times the depth (d) in feet, times the number of full-depth drawers equals area of drawer space

Area of Drawer Space

area to be included in base shelving where access is from one side = ½ depth of corner —where access is from both sides, allow full credit

Area of Corner Base Shelving

shelving that does not project past 60° may be included as required shelving

28" min.—sink
15" min.—other range—see detail of previous figure

shelving—note #1

| depth (inches) | min. spacing (inches) |
|---|---|
| 4 to 6 | 5 |
| 6 to 10 | 6 |
| 10 to 15 | 7 |
| 15 to 24 | 10 |

Height, Depth, and Spacing of Shelving and Countertop

| wall shelving | | | base shelving | | | countertop | | | drawers | | |
|---|---|---|---|---|---|---|---|---|---|---|---|
| 2 s. ft. | x 2 = | 4 s. ft. | 4 s. ft. | x 4 = | 16 s. ft. | 4 s. ft. | x 3 = | 12 s. ft. | 4 s. ft. | x 1 = | 4 s. ft. |
| 2.5 | x 2 = | 5 | 5 | x 3 = | 15 | 2.5 | x 1 = | 2.5 | 2.5 | x 4 = | 10 |
| 3 | x 3 = | 9 | 2 | x 2 = | 4 | total | | 14.5 s. ft. | total | | 14 s. ft. |
| 4 | x 3 = | 12 | total | | 35 s. ft. | | | | | | |
| total | | 30 s. ft. | | | | | | | | | |

**Fig. 9  Example: measurement of shelf and countertop areas.**

if more than ¾" increase clearance to cabinet by the additional amount

elevation
free-standing range

section

elevation

plan
built-in cooking unit

### CLEARANCES OVER COOKING RANGES

In Fig. 10, dimension A: 2 ft 6 in minimum clearance between the top of the range and the bottom of an unprotected wood or metal cabinet, or 2 ft 0 in minimum when the bottom of a wood or metal cabinet is protected.

Dimension B: 2 ft 0 in minimum when hood projection X is 18 in or more, or 1 ft 10 in min. when hood projection X is less than 18 in.

Dimension C: not less than width of range or cooking unit.

Dimension D: 10 in minimum when vertical side surface extends above countertops.

Dimension E: when range is not provided by builder, 40 in minimum.

Dimension F: Minimum clearance should be not less than 3 in.

Cabinet protection should be at least ¼ in asbestos millboard covered with not less than 28-gauge sheet metal (0.015 stainless steel, 0.024 aluminum, or 0.020 copper).

Clearance for D, E, or F should be not less than listed UL or AGA clearances.

**Fig. 10**

ABOVE SINK

ABOVE RANGE

ABOVE BASE CAB

Above a sink, plan for a minimum of 22 in. to the bottom of a wall cabinet. Since the wall behind a sink often holds a window, measurement for a cabinet is academic. But if wall space is minimal, a cabinet over the sink makes good sense.

The use of large pans, pancake flips and similar cooking maneuvers dictate a distance of 30 in. between rangetop and wall cabinet bottom. A fan mounted in the wall is the means here to exhaust cooking fumes to the outside.

A range of 15 in. to 18 in. is the proper span between standard base and wall cabinets. Opt for the 15 in. distance if you are 5 ft. 4 in. or less; a wider span if you're taller. The highest shelf: 6 ft. from the floor, is a reachable distance.

Kitchen activities become tiresome in poor light. A single fixture, centered on the ceiling is insufficient. Your need for light is greatest over the work centers. A good light there reduces the danger of cutting yourself; eases the task of monitoring color changes during a mix, and so on. The best place to install fixtures for this purpose is beneath the wall cabinets (with a shield to prevent glare when you're seated in the kitchen). A workable alternative is found in fixtures installed in an extended soffit. Plan for light above a rangetop and over the sink, as well. Choose incandescent, deluxe warm white or deluxe cool white lamps for the fixtures to avoid poor color rendition.

KITCHEN LIGHTING

**Utensil and General Storage**

Space for utensils includes storage for dishes, pots and pans, utensils, and appliances. With the increased use of such electrical appliances, their storage becomes a significant problem. General storage requires space for linens, towels, and kitchen supplies. Included in this category are brooms, mops, and other cleaning equipment and supplies.

**TABLE 1   Minimum Kitchen Storage Required**

| Item | 40 to 60 ft² Area — Kitchenette | |
| --- | --- | --- |
| | 0-bedroom living unit,* ft² | 1-bedroom living unit,* ft² |
| Total shelving in wall and base cabinets | 24 | 30 |
| Shelving in either wall or base cabinets | 10 | 12 |
| Drawer area | 4 | 5 |
| Countertop area | 5 | 6 |
| Item | 60 ft² Area and Over — Kitchen | |
| | 1- and 2-bedroom living units, ft² | 3- and 4-bedroom living units, ft² |
| Total shelving in wall and base cabinets | 48 | 54 |
| Shelving in either wall or base cabinets | 18 | 20 |
| Drawer area | 8 | 10 |
| Countertop area | 10 | 12 |

*Kitchen unit assemblies serving the kitchen function and occupying less than 40 ft² area in 0-BR living units shall not be less than 5 ft in length and shall provide at least 12 ft² of total shelving in wall and base cabinets. Drawer and countertop space shall also be provided. No room count is allowable for this type facility.

# KITCHENS

Cabinet Dimensions

HIGHEST SHELF ADVISABLE     ABOVE SINK     ABOVE RANGE     ABOVE CABINETS

COUNTER HEIGHT FOR STOOLS     COUNTER HEIGHT FOR CHAIRS

Depth of soffit, 12"-24"

Wall cabinet under soffit, 30" high

Depth of wall cabinet, 12" (not including door)

Average ceiling, 96" from floor

Outlet or light switch, 44" from floor

Countertop, 36" from floor (depending on countertop thickness)

Bottom of wall cabinet, 54" from floor (with 30" high wall cabinets)

Proper desk height, 31" from floor

Depth of base cabinet, 24" (not including door)

Depth of toe space, 2-3/8"

24" MAX. WITH WALL CABINET
30" MAX. WITHOUT WALL CABINET

72" MAX. HEIGHT TOP SHELF

24" MAX.

**Example of the proper dimensional limits and relative placement of kitchen base cabinets and wall cabinets**

## FRAMED CABINETRY

UTILITY CABINET
W/WALL CABINET

WALL CABINET

DOUBLE-FACED
WALL CABINET

BASE CABINET

DOUBLE-FACED
BASE CABINET

VANITY BASES

## FRAMELESS CABINETRY

UTILITY
CABINET

WALL
CABINET

DOUBLE-FACED
WALL CABINET

BASE
CABINET

DOUBLE-FACED
BASE CABINET

VANITY

# KITCHENS

**Cabinet Sizes**

FRAMED          FRAMELESS

## WALL CABINETS

Wall cabinets are available in heights of 42", 30", 24", 18", 15", and 12." Most cabinets are available in widths ranging from 9" to 48," in 3" increments. Framed wall cabinets are 12" deep, not including doors. Frameless wall cabinets are 12¾" deep, including doors.

## WALL BLIND CORNER CABINETS

Wall blind corner cabinets are available in heights of 42", 30" and 24." Most wall blind corner cabinets are available in widths of 24", 27", 30", 33", 36", 42", and 48."

## DOUBLE-FACE WALL CABINETS

Double-face wall cabinets are available in heights of 30", 24" and 18." Most are available in widths of 18", 24", 30", 36", 42" and 48." Framed cabinets are 13¹⁵⁄₁₆" deep with doors. Frameless are 13½" deep with doors.

## BASE CABINETS

All base cabinets are 34½" tall. Most are available in widths ranging from 9" to 48," in 3" increments. Framed base cabinets are 24" deep, not including doors. Frameless base cabinets are 24¾" deep, including doors.

Four-drawer base cabinets are available in widths ranging from 12" to 24," in 3" increments. Frameless base cabinets are also available in a three-drawer style in widths of 30" and 36."

## BASE BLIND CORNER CABINETS

All base blind corner cabinets are 34½" high. Most are available in widths of 24", 30", 36", 39", 42" and 48."

 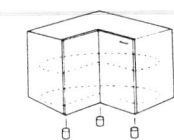

## SPECIALTY CABINETS

Lazy Susans:
36"-Wide

Range Hoods: (framed only)
36" & 30"-Wide

Wall What-Not Shelves: (framed only)
30"-High

Base Open Shelves: (framed only)
34½"-High

Pantries: (framed only)
36" x 66"

Utility Cabinets: (framed)
24" x 66"
18" x 66"
In 12" and 24" Depths

Utility Cabinets: (frameless)
24" x 65½"
18" x 65½"
In 12¾" and 24¾" Depths

Tilt-Out Range Hoods: (frameless only)
30" x 24"

Glass Door Wall Cabinets: (frameless only)
30" & 36"-Wide

Microwave Cabinets: (framed only)
30" x 21"

Microwave Shelves:
30" x 22⅝" (framed)
30" x 18" (frameless)

Oven Cabinets: (framed)
27" x 66"
30" x 66"
33" x 66"

Oven Cabinets: (frameless)
27" x 65½"
30" x 65½"
33" x 65½"

Up to six 6" drawers can be added to frameless oven cabinets.

WOOD
APRON PANEL

FINISHED
SIDES

LAMINATE
APRON PANEL

FINISHED
SIDES

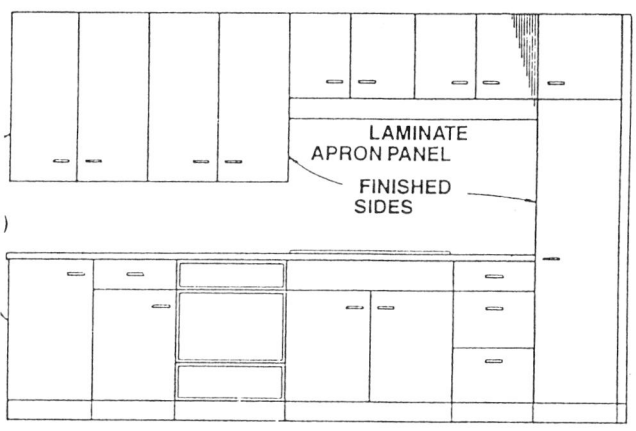

LAMINATE
APRON PANEL

FINISHED
SIDES

WOOD
APRON PANEL

FINISHED
SIDES

WOOD
APRON PANEL

FINISHED
SIDES

COUNTERTOP EDGED WITH
CONTOUR MOLDING

LAMINATE
APRON PANEL

FINISHED
SIDES

# KITCHENS
Cabinet Types and Dimensions

LAMINATE
APRON PANEL

FINISHED
SIDES

COUNTERTOP EDGED WITH
CONTOUR MOLDING

WOOD APRON
PANEL

FINISHED
SIDES

LAMINATE
APRON PANEL

FINISHED
SIDES

LAMINATE
APRON PANEL

FINISHED
SIDES

WOOD APRON PANEL

FINISHED
SIDES

WOOD
APRON PANEL

FINISHED
SIDES

# Sink Cabinets & Fronts

### SINK BASES

SB24 L or R
SF24 L or R
(Non-Trimmable)

SB27
SB30
SB33

SB36
SB42
SB48

### SINK FRONTS

– SF30 L or R

+ SF30     SF42
SF36       SF48

+ SF30 (Without L or R Available in Nordic™– Not Shown)
(Trimmable 3″ per side Except Nordic™ Non-Trimmable)

### CORNER SINK FRONT

36″      36″

* CSF36 L or R

# Oven Cabinets & Drop-In Range Fronts

### OVEN CABINETS

18″

96″
84″

4″

24″

37″
Max.
Cut
Out
Nordic™

60″
Max.
Cut
Out

A

DRWR
DRWR
DRWR

27″  24″

* OV24Dx96
* OV27Dx96
OV24D
OV27D

52″
Max.
Cut
Out

A

DRWR

27″  24″

+* OV24Sx96
+* OV27Sx96
+ OV24S
+ OV27S

### DROP-IN RANGE FRONT

30″

16″

* DORF30
(Trimmable
Height & Width)

### UNIVERSAL DROP-IN RANGE FRONTS

6″   24″   6″
     18″

22½″

34½″

* UDRF30
* UDRF36
(Trimmable Cut-Out)

# Utility Cabinets/Fronts & Pantry Cabinet

### UTILITY CABINETS/FRONTS

42″
30″

96″
84″

50″

4″

12″
24″

18″

24″

* UC1812x96    L or R
* UC1824x96    L or R
–* UCF1896     L or R
UC1812         L or R
UC1824         L or R
–* UCF18        L or R

* UC2412x96    L or R
* UC2424x96
–* UCF24x96
* UC2412
* UC2424
–* UCF24

### UTILITY CABINET SHELVES

16½″          10⅞″
22½″     22⅞″
(width)   UCS1812   (depth)
          UCS1824
          UCS2412
          UCS2424
(Shipped 1 Shelf with
4 Shelf Supports)

(Utility Fronts are
Non Trimmable)

### PANTRY CABINET

24″    24″

84″

* PC2424
(Includes – Lazy Susan
Shelves & Racks.) Available
in Oak Lines, Except Oakcrest,™
Euro,™ X-Line,™ & Spartan™

# Desk Cabinets

### DESK UNIT

DRWR
DRWR
DRWR

28¼″

* KDB15

### KNEEHOLE DRAWER

30″

7″    DRWR

6″            6″

* KD30
(Trimmable 3″ per side)

### DESK END PANEL

# KITCHENS

**Cabinet Types and Dimensions**

## BASE CABINETS

30½"
34½"
4"
24"

▲■ B9 L or R
(Concealed Drawer)

B12 L or R
B15 L or R
B18 L or R
B21 L or R
B24 L or R

B27    B36
B30    B42
B33    B48

## DRAWER BASE CABINETS

DRWR
DRWR
DRWR
DRWR

DB12
DB15
DB18
DB21
DB24

## SPECIAL DRAWER BASE CABINET

DRWR
DRWR
DRWR
DRWR

– DB18CB
(Includes — Cutting
Board, Cutlery Divider
& Metal Bread Box.)

## COMBINATION SINK BASE CABINETS

DRWR                    DRWR

⌐ A ⌐      B      ⌐ C ⌐

|      | A   | B   | C   |
|------|-----|-----|-----|
| –* SB60 | 15" | 30" | 15" |
| –* SB66 | 15" | 36" | 15" |
| –* SB72 | 18" | 36" | 18" |

▲ No Arched Door.
■ No Center Medallion. (Saxony)

## ROTATING CORNER BASE CABINET

36"
Wall Space
Required

36"
Wall Space
Required

34½"

■ CAR36

## BLIND CORNER BASE CABINETS

24"
3"
DRWR

(L-Shown, 3" Filler included, must use to allow doors to clear.)

BLB39 L or R (Pullable 6")
BLB42 L or R (Pullable 6")
* BLB48 L or R (Pullable 4")

## PENINSULA BASE CABINETS

24"
DRWR

24"
DRWR    DRWR

* PB24

* PB30
* PB36

(Drawers open on one side only in Peninsula Cabinet.)

## BLIND PENINSULA BASE CABINETS

DRWR
24"
3"
DRWR

(L-Shown, 3" Filler included, must use to allow doors to clear.)

* BLPB42 L or R (Pullable 6")
* BLPB48 L or R (Pullable 6")

## WALL CABINETS

       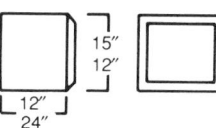

| | | | | | | | |
|---|---|---|---|---|---|---|---|
| * W1242 L or R | ▲■ * W930 L or R | * W2742 | W2730 | * W1224 L or R | W3024 | W2418 | W3015 * W3015x24 ■ W3012 |
| * W1542 L or R | W1230 L or R | * W3042 | W3030 | * W1524 L or R | * W3624 | W3018 | W3315 * W3315x24 ■ W3612 |
| * W1842 L or R | W1530 L or R | * W3342 | W3330 | * W1824 L or R | * W4224 | W3318 | W3615 * W3615x24 |
| * W2142 L or R | W1830 L or R | * W3642 | W3630 | * W2124 L or R | * W4824 | W3618 | |
| * W2442 L or R | W2130 L or R | * W4242 | W4230 | * W2424 L or R | | W4218 | |
| | W2430 L or R | * W4842 | W4830 | | | | |

## COMBINATION WALL CABINETS

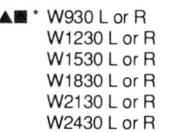

| | A | B | C |
|---|---|---|---|
| –* CWC60 | 15″ | 30″ | 15″ |
| –* CWC66 | 18″ | 30″ | 18″ |
| –* CWC72 | 21″ | 30″ | 21″ |

(Fixed Shelves)

## CORNER WALL CABINET

* CW2442 L or R
CW2430 L or R
(Fixed Shelves)

CWS2430 L or R
(2 Adjustable Rotary Shelves)

## BLIND CORNER WALL CABINETS

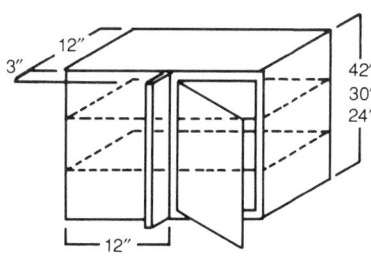

(L-Shown, 3″ Filler included, must use to allow doors to clear.)

* BLW2742 L or R     BLW2730 L or R     * BLW2724 L or R
* BLW3042 L or R     BLW3030 L or R     * BLW3624 L or R
* BLW3642 L or R     BLW3630 L or R
* BLW4242 (2 Doors) L or R     BLW4230 (2 Doors) L or R
* BLW4842 (2 Doors) L or R     * BLW4830 (2 Doors) L or R

## PENINSULA WALL CABINETS

* PW2430

| | | |
|---|---|---|
| * PW3030 | * PW3024 | * PW3018 |
| * PW3630 | * PW3624 | * PW3618 |
| | | * PW4218 |

## BLIND PENINSULA CORNER WALL CABINET

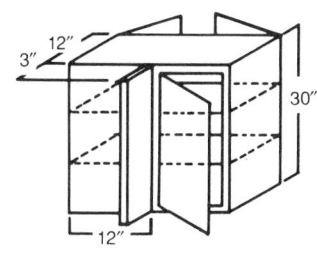

(L-Shown, 3″ Filler included, must use to allow doors to clear.)
* BLPW2730 L or R

## MICROWAVE CABINET

MW3035

A: 22″ Minimum    B: 13¾″ Minimum
28″ Maximum      19⅛″ Maximum

## MICROWAVE CABINET W/SHELF

MWS3035x12

# KITCHENS

## Cabinet Types and Dimensions

PARTIAL ELEVATION
SCALE: 3"=1'-0"

SECTION 'A'
SCALE: 3"=1'-0"

REFRIGERATOR ELEVATION
SCALE: 1"=1'-0"

SECTION OF WOOD PANEL FACING
SCALE: FULL SIZE

SECTION
SCALE: F.S.

SECTION
SCALE: F.S.

SECTION
SCALE: F.S.

WALL CABINET

BASE CABINET

① SECTION : TYPICAL KITCHEN CABINET @ DRAWERS
A4   1" = 1'-0"

② SECTION : KITCHEN CABINET @ GARBAGE DRAWER
A4   1" = 1'-0"

③ SECTION
A4   1" = 1'-0"

④ SECTION @ NEW WOOD DESK
A4   1" = 1'-0"

⑤/A4  KITCHEN CABINET · PLAN @ JAMB (TYPICAL)
FULL SIZE

STEEL PIVOT HINGE

¾" PLY DIVIDER (WHERE OCCURRING)
¾" X 3" CONT. WOOD FRAMING
¾" PLY RAIL
¼" X ¾" WOOD EDGE BAND GLUED & NAILED
1⅛" X 2¼" WOOD STILE MAXWELL M289
¼" X 1¼" WOOD CLEAT
¾" PLY PANEL

⑦/A4  KITCHEN CABINET · PLAN @ CORNER JAMB (TYPICAL)
FULL SIZE

¾" PLY SIDE
¾" X ¾" CONT. WOOD FRAMING
¾" PLY W/ EDGE BAND
1⅛" X 2¼" WOOD STILE MAXWELL M289
WOOD GLAZING BEAD MAXWELL M173
⅛" GLASS

⑥/A4  KITCHEN BASE CABINET @ DOOR · TYPICAL SECTION
FULL SIZE

1¾" MAPLE BUTCHER BLOCK
¾" X ¾" CONT. WOOD FRAMING
¾" PLY COUNTER FACE W/ EDGE BAND
STEEL PIVOT HINGE
1⅛" X 2¼" TOP RAIL MAXWELL M289
¼" X 1¼" WOOD CLEAT
¾" PLY PANEL
WOOD GLAZING BAR MAXWELL M291
¼" X 1¼" WOOD CLEAT
¾" X ¾" WOOD FRAMING
1⅛" X 3¼" BOTTOM RAIL : MAXWELL M290
STEEL PIVOT HINGE
¾" PLY BOTTOM OF CAB W/ EDGE BAND
¾" PLY BASE

⑧/A4  WALL CABINET · TYPICAL SECTION
FULL SIZE

1¼" X ¾" WOOD MOLDING DYKES #194
½" GYPSUM BD SOFFIT
¾" PLY CAB. TOP
¾" X ¾" WOOD FRAMING
¾" PLY FACE W/ EDGE BAND
STEEL PIVOT HINGE
1⅛" X 2¼" TOP RAIL MAXWELL M28
WOOD GLAZING BEAD MAXWELL M289
⅛" GLASS

# KITCHENS

Sink Types and Dimensions

### Ranges and Built-In Ovens

Freestanding ranges and built-in ovens come in a variety of sizes and configurations. Some of the larger ranges consist of modular cooktops providing anywhere from two to seven heating elements as well as modular grills, griddles, and even downdraft built-in ventilators. Normally, a minimum clearance of 30" is required above any range or cooktop, but the designer is cautioned to carefully verify local code requirements. Manufacturers' specifications should be carefully reviewed for rough opening requirements and any venting requirements, particularly for self-cleaning ovens.

### Dishwashers

Built-in, freestanding, and undersink dishwashers are fairly well standardized in terms of overall dimensions. Access to plumbing and waste lines is the major consideration, as is the method of securing the dishwasher in order to minimize vibration.

### Refrigerators

Refrigerator door swings and clearances are of critical importance. While a 90° door swing may provide sufficient room for a person to observe storage within a refrigerator or freezer, a 180° door swing may be required to clean a refrigerator and remove storage bins.

This is particularly true of the side-by-side door configuration. In addition, adequate clearance should be allowed between the sides and top of the refrigerator and any adjoining cabinetwork, especially if a built-in look is desired. The designer should check requirements with the manufacturer.

While these drawings can be used for preliminary planning, final dimensions and clearance must be verified with the manufacturer. Often overlooked are clearances for refrigerator handles or pulls as well as coils mounted at the rear of the refrigerator.

STANDARD FREESTANDING RANGE
W: 18" - 42"
D: 24" - 271/2"
H: 35" - 36"

BUILT-IN SINGLE OVEN
W: 20" - 24"
D: 21" - 24"
H: 22" - 28"

BUILT-IN OVEN/BROILER
W: 18" - 24"
D: 21" - 24"
H: 36" - 41"

BUILT-IN DOUBLE OVEN
W: 18" - 24"
D: 21" - 24"
H: 38" - 51"

STANDARD REFRIGERATOR
W: 18"          SINGLE DOOR
D: 24"
H: 68 1/2"

STANDARD REFRIGERATOR
W: 29 1/2" - 391/2" (SIDE BY SIDE)
D: 29" - 33"
H: 64" - 69 1/2"

STANDARD REFRIGERATOR
W: 24" - 331/2" (BOTTOM FREEZER)
D: 29" - 33"
H: 64" - 69 1/2"

STANDARD REFRIGERATOR
W: 24" - 33" (FREEZER AT TOP))
D: 273/4" - 32"
H: 631/2" - 681/2"

UNDER COUNTER DISHWASHER
W: 23" - 24"
D: 231/2" - 261/2"
H: 331/2" - 341/2"

FREE STANDING DISHWASHER
W: 23" - 24"
D: 231/2" - 261/2"
H: 331/2" - 341/2"

BUILT-IN /RECESSED REFRIGERATOR
W: 30" - 72"
D: 231/2" - 24"
H: 84"

# KITCHENS

**Appliances**

24" electric built-in double oven

24" electric built-in single oven

Gas built-in oven

Electric built-in single oven

27" electric built-in double oven

27" built-in microwave oven

30" electric built-in single oven

30" electric built-in double oven

30" built-in microwave oven

*Note:* Dimensions shown are for planning purposes only.

**Conventional electric cooktop**

**36″ electric cooktop**

**Glass cooktop**

**30″ solid elements/glass cooktop**

**36″ solid element/glass cooktop**

**30″ gas cooktop**

**30″ gas cooktop**

*Note:* Dimensions shown are for planning purposes only.

## DEFINITIONS & DETAILS FOR PLASTIC LAMINATE TOPS

**TOP MOUNT**

**SIDE OR BACK MOUNT**

**SQUARE BUTT JOINT.** Where the junction of the counter top or back and end splash is made by two separate pieces.

**COVE BACK SPLASH**
**SQUARE BUTT END SPLASH**

**COVE (Integral Cove).** A curved junction of the counter top and splash, formed by bending a continuous sheet of plastic.

**SELF EDGE CUSTOM GRADE**

**SELF EDGE PREMIUM GRADE (TOP LAP OVER EDGE)**

**SELF EDGE.** Application to the edge of plywood or particle-board core of a plastic laminate of the same pattern as the face surface.

**NO DRIP BULLNOSE**

**NO DRIP - TILT EDGE**

(Self-edged)

**NO-DRIP EDGE.** Where the edge is raised, formed by a continuous sheet of plastic - may be either "A", a bull-nosed edge, or "B", a tilt or wedge edge. This is not a continuous sheet of plastic.

**ROLLED EDGE.** Sometimes referred to as "Waterfall". Formed by a continuous sheet of plastic rolled over the edge, with no raised portion.

**WATERFALL.** Curved upper portion of the back splash and the curved edge of the top, formed with a continuous sheet of plastic.

**FULLY FORMED TOP**

**FULLY FORMED.** A counter top made with a continuous sheet of plastic, combining a no-drip bull-nose edge, integral cove, and waterfall back splash. Radius may be from 1/4" to 3/4".

### TYPES OF SINK INSTALLATIONS

Metal Sink Rim

Self Edge

### TYPES OF EDGING

**FLUSH METAL OR PLASTIC TEE TYPE EDGE**

**SNAP ON STAINLESS STEEL EDGE**

### TIGHT JOINT FASTENERS

Draw-Bolt

Fig. 11 Definitions and details for plastic laminate tops.

TOP SECTION WITH SHELF

¼″ WOOD MOULD
Acid Resistant Coated
if specified

SHELF

No. 10 – 2″ F.H. Screws 24″ o.c. Maximum
Parkerized or equal.

1x3 Cleat
cont. @ wall
by Cab. Inst.

SPLASH

SINK CUTOUT

Epoxy
Cement
Joint

½″ Standard
¼″ Minimum

Sink Wall

Wall Line

Attach to Cabinet with 1½″ P.H.
Screws No. 8 or 10–Cadmium Plated

1″

23″        6″

30″

TOP SECTION WITH SPLASH

SPLASH

6″

Epoxy Cement Joint

Wall Line

1″

1½″ P. H. Screws No. 8 or 10
Cadmium Plated

23″        6″

30″

FINISHED EDGE

Eased Edge

Relieved Corner

Drip Groove

BUTT JOINT

Color Matched Epoxy Cement

1/8″ Maximum

Fig. 12   Composition stone top and sink details.

WALLPAPER (CONSULT OWNER)

SILL - SEE DWG. N° 13

LAMINATE COUNTER TOP

SINK

SINK

SINK

DW

BUTCHER BLOCK - FLUSH W/LAMINATE

SUB-ZERO COMBINATION REFRIGERATOR-FREEZER, MODEL STAINLESS STEEL FINISH

GARLAND RANGE MODEL G 283 STAINLESS STEEL FINISH

A / A20   PLAN - KITCHEN
SCALE: ½" = 1'-0"

PULL OUT "DRAWER" TRASH BIN

C / A20   WEST KITCHEN ELEVATION
SCALE: ½" = 1'-0"

EAST          NORTH          WEST          SOUTH

F / A-20   KITCHEN ISLAND ELEVATIONS
SCALE: ½" = 1'-0"

ADJUSTABLE SHELVES

FURRED FINISHED WALL TO TOP OF CABINETS

PLASTIC LAM-
INATE CABINET
DOORS, COUNT-
ER TOPS AND
DRAWER DOORS

WALLPAPER

NOTE:
ALL SHELVES TO BE
ADJUSTABLE ON
CHROME PINS W/
HOLES DRILLED
1" O.C.

1/A20

EQ.     EQ.

1'-5"

PHONE
BOOK TYPE

EQ.    EQ.

EQ.     EQ.

2'-3"

EQ.
EQ.

5" CLEAR

4'-2" TYP.

FILING CABINET

WALL BASE (TYP.)

PLASTIC LAMINAT
CABINET DOORS,
COUNTER TOPS, AND
DRAWER DOORS, LAMINATED
COLOR & TEXTURE SELECTED
BY OWNER (TYP.)

B/A20  SOUTH KITCHEN ELEVATION
SCALE: 1/2" = 1'-0"

BRUSHED STAINLESS
STEEL TO MATCH RANGE,
RANGE HOOD.

2'-8"

5'-0" TYP. | 1'-8"

EQ.    EQ.

RANGE

D/A20  NORTH KITCHEN ELEVATION
SCALE: 1/2" = 1'-0"

FULL HEIGHT TILE
BACK SPLSH, TYP.
(CONSULT OWNER FOR SELECTION)

12" CLEAR

BIRCH VENEER - SEE NOTE № 2

WD. CLEAT

PLAST. LAM. UPPER CAB. DOOR
SEE NOTE № 1

SCRIBE

T5 LAMP

RIBBED ALKCORYLIC
SNAP-IN DIFFUSER

"ALKCO MNFCT'G. CO" - LITTLE INCH - UNDER CAB. FIXTURE

FINISHED KITCHEN WALL

PLAST. LAM. UNDERSIDE OF
OVER COUNTER CABINET - SEE NOTE № 1

1/A20  SECTION DETAIL @ UPPER CABINET  B
FULL SIZE

**(a)**
**Before Removal of Cabinets and Base**

**(b)**
**Cabinets and Base Removed and Height Alternatives**

**Counter Work Surface**

**(a)**
**Before Removal of Cabinets and Base**

**(b)**
**Cabinets and Base Removed
and Height Alternatives**

**Kitchen Sink**

**(a)**
**Side-Hinged Door**

**(b)**
**Bottom-Hinged Door**

SYMBOL KEY:
1. Countertop or wall-mounted oven.
2. Pull-out board preferred with side-opening door.
3. Clear open space.
4. Bottom-hinged door.

**Ovens without Self-Cleaning Feature**

ACCESSIBLE; BEFORE REMOVAL OF CABINETS AND BASE.    CABINETS AND BASE REMOVED, COUNTER HEIGHT LOWERED.

EXAMPLE OF ADAPTABLE KITCHEN –L– SHAPED PLAN

CABINETS AND BASE REMOVED, COUNTER HEIGHT LOWERED.

ACCESSIBLE ; BEFORE REMOVAL OF CABINETS AND BASE.

EXAMPLE OF ADAPTABLE KITCHEN –U– SHAPED PLAN

179

# KITCHENS

Wheelchair Accessible Design

Minimum-sized adaptable kitchen or kitchenette

Minimum-sized adaptable kitchen (galley type)

Kitchen clearance dimensions (not to scale)

adjustable height work
surface set at 36"
height with removable
base cabinet in knee
space

removable base cabinet
below sink in knee
space

adjustable height
counter with sink
mounted at 36" height

meets ANSI/UFAS
requirements for clear
floor space, storage,
controls, appliances,
doors

**Fig. 13  An adaptable kitchen in conventional configuration.**

## Requirements

The ANSI and UFAS standards require accessible and adaptable features which make the kitchen usable by most people. The fixed accessible features specified in ANSI 4.32.5 and UFAS 4.34.6 include requirements for doors, clearances, clear floor space, appliances, storage, controls, and knee space. The adaptable features are removable base cabinets at knee spaces and counters that can be adjusted in height or fixed at a lower than standard height.

The adaptable features for kitchens specified in the standards are shown in Figs. 13 and 14. In Fig. 13, the kitchen is shown in a standard configuration with the counter height at 36 inches and the knee spaces covered with base cabinets.

In Fig. 14, the kitchen has been adapted by exposing the knee spaces and lowering the work surface and sink counter segments. No other changes have been made to the kitchen.

Since removable base cabinets and adjustable height counters are not now products that are readily available for purchase, they are usually custom-made items.

lowered counter
segment with exposed
knee space

lowered sink and
counter segment with
exposed knee space

**Fig. 14  An adaptable kitchen in the adjusted configuration.**

## KITCHENS
**Wheelchair Accessible Design**

30" min.

adjustable height sink counter segment with removable base cabinet, and pipe protection and appearance screen

range with up-front controls

recommendation: position refrigerator so door can swing back 180°

adjustable height work surface counter segment with removable base cabinet

ANSI/UFAS complying refrigerator freezer with 50% storage within reach ranges
ANSI 2.34

30" min.

**Fig. 15   A small kitchen with adaptable features: plan.**

counter support bracket and appearance cover

removed base cabinet

ANSI/UFAS clear floor space

adjustable height work surface

removed base cabinet

**Fig. 16   A small kitchen with adaptable features: perspective.**

pantry — refrigerator —

removable base cabinets and adjustable height counter segment

shelves —

microwave oven —

base cabinets —

carts stored under counter —

overhead cabinets —

electronic media center —

rotating slide-out wire frame corner storage shelves

The kitchen shown in Figs. 17 and 18 is an example of a more elaborate kitchen having ANSI/UFAS accessible/adaptable features. This kitchen exceeds the ANSI/UFAS minimum requirements.

**Fig. 17  An elaborate kitchen with adaptable features: plan.**

refrigerator with large, low over head freezer

microwave within reach of a seated person

recommended longer wall cabinets for additional reachable storage over work surface

knee space and lowered work surface on adjustable supports

recommended special sink with shallow disposal bowl lets disposal fit despite required knee space

recommended wide lowered countertop at sink

low, up-front electrical receptacles

rotating, slide-out wire frame corner storage shelves

overhead cabinets

standard range with up-front controls

television and other electronic equipment mounted within reach of seated people

tambour doors for easy access to storage shelving

two rolling carts for food preparation and serving; also fit in knee space in work surface

telephone

extra electrical receptacles

**Fig. 18  An elaborate kitchen with adaptable features: perspective.**

# KITCHENS
**Wheelchair Accessible Design**

### Work Surfaces

People who use wheelchairs and other people who must or wish to sit down while preparing food need at least one work surface lower than the usual 36-in-high counter (Fig. 19).

The standards (ANSI 4.32.5.4 and UFAS 4.34.6.4) require that at least one 30-in-wide, adjustable-height work surface be provided in an adaptable kitchen, although a wider size is preferred. The wider work surface provides space for pots, dishes, and other utensils as well as small appliances, and makes it easier to work on several things at once or to cook using many ingredients.

lowered counter segment for work surface

**Fig. 19   Seated person at lowered work surface.**

recommended wide lowered work surface and knee space

60" min.

min. clear knee, work, and floor space required

30"

**Fig. 20   Use of a wider, lowered work surface.**

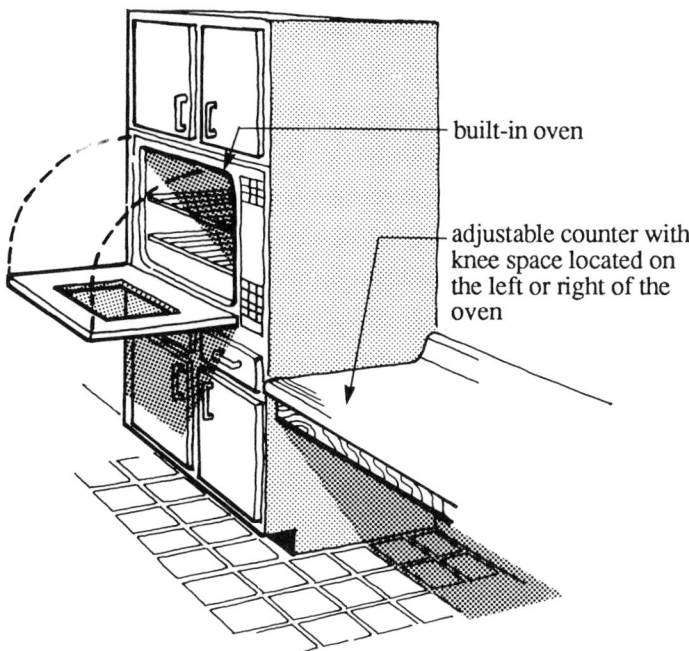

built-in oven

adjustable counter with knee space located on the left or right of the oven

**Fig. 21  Work surface at non-self-cleaning oven with drop-front door.**

**Work surfaces at ovens**  If a wall oven is installed, a lowered work surface with knee space should be installed next to the wall oven. The standards specify that when the wall oven is not self-cleaning, a knee space must be located next to the oven to permit a disabled person in a wheelchair to pull up close enough to clean the oven.

Even if a self-cleaning oven is installed, locating the knee space next to the oven makes it easier and safer for a disabled person to remove hot items from the oven.

When an oven with a side-opening door is used, a pull-out shelf located beneath the oven must be installed. The shelf is used as a transfer surface for dishes as they are placed into or taken out of the oven. When not needed, the shelf is pushed back into the oven cabinet (Fig. 23). When an oven with a drop-front door is used (Fig. 21), the pullout shelf is not needed because the door serves as a transfer shelf.

See ANSI 4.32.5.7 and UFAS 4.34.6.7 for dimensions and details of oven.

knee space allows someone to get close to oven

knee spaces not required if ovens are self-cleaning

**Fig. 22  Use of knee space next to oven.**

built-in oven

adjustable height counter segment on latch side of oven; this could also meet the adjustable work surface requirement

knee space and adjustable counter not required when oven is self-cleaning, but recommended

pull-out shelf 10" minimum in depth and full width of oven required with side opening door

**Fig. 23  Pull-out shelf at non-self-cleaning oven with side-opening door.**

# KITCHENS
**Wheelchair Accessible Design**

### Cooktops in Adjustable Height Counter Segments

ANSI 4.32.5.6 and UFAS 4.34.6.6 permit use of a standard range if the controls comply with ANSI 4.25 or UFAS 4.27. The controls must be placed along the front or the side of the range so that a seated person need not reach across a hot burner to adjust the controls (Fig. 24).

Some wheelchair users cannot use conventional ranges because the surface is too high and there is no knee space for maneuvering. Cooktops in lowered counter segments with knee space below allow some wheelchair users to get close enough to operate the controls and move heavy pots and pans (Fig. 25).

Cooktops with smooth surfaces are preferred by people with limited hand and arm strength because they can slide pots of hot food on and off the cooktop rather than lifting them over raised burners and knobs.

When a cooktop is installed in a lowered counter, the width of the counter segment and knee space should be at least 30 inches and should provide space to the side of the cooktop for utensils and maneuvering. An additional 30 inches to the side is recom-mended (Fig. 26).

When the knee space is under a cooktop, the standards require that the bottom of the cooktop be insulated to protect against accidental burns.

While this type of installation may be the only way that some people can cook, it does expose a person in a wheelchair to the hazard of spilling hot food in his/her lap. People who pull up beneath the cooktop must exercise extreme care and cool hot foods before moving them.

front-mounted controls

drop front conventional oven (self-cleaning preferred)

**Fig. 24   Standard range.**

optional lowered cooktop and counter segment

front- or side-mounted controls required

additional preferred space

surface and knee space wider than ANSI minimum

30" ANSI minimum

**Fig. 26   Lowered cooktop with knee space and wide counter.**

smooth ceramic surfaces allow easier sliding of pots and pans which can be safer than lifting

bottom of unit must be insulated and covered to prevent people from being burned

knee space provides essential maneuvering space for some people, but also creates a greater burn risk from hot food spilled in the lap

**Fig. 25   Use of cooktop with knee space.**

**Kitchen arrangements**

**Counter-mounted cook top**

**Sink**

**Knee-space clearance**

**Knee-recess work area**

**Disposal sink**

**Armrest clearance**

# KITCHENS
**Wheelchair Accessible Design**

REFRIG. TO COMPLY W/ ANSI 4.32.5.8
(TYPICAL LOCATION)

ADJUSTABLE HGT. SINK TO COMPLY
W/ ANSI 4.32.5.8 W/ REMOVABLE
CAB. BELOW

ADJUSTABLE HGT. WORK SURFACE
ADJACENT TO RANGE TO
COMPLY W/ ANSI 4.32.5.4
W/ REMOVABLE CAB BELOW

LINE OF WALL CABINETS OVER
TO COMPLY W/ 4.32.5.10

RANGE OVEN TO COMPLY W/
ANSI 4.32.5.6
(SELF CLEANING)

1/A4  PLAN : TYPICAL ADAPTABLE KITCHEN : LINEAR
½" = 1'-0"

REFRIG. (TYP. LOC.)

SINK W/ HGT. ADJUSTED & UNDER
-CABINET REMOVED

WALL CABINETS OVER

WORK SURFACE W/ HGT. ADJUSTED
& UNDER-CABINET REMOVED.

RANGE OVEN

1A/A4  PLAN : TYPICAL ADAPTED KITCHEN : LINEAR
½" = 1'-0"

WALL CABINETS TO COMPLY W/
ANSI 4.32.5.8

ADJUSTABLE HGT. COUNTERTOP
& SINK TO COMPLY W/
ANSI 4.32.5.4

REMOVABLE BASE CABINET

SUGGESTED FLEXIBLE SUPPLY
LINES.

SUGGESTED SLIP JOINT IN TAIL
PIECE / UNDERSINK WASTE &
HOT WATER PIPES TO BE INSULA-
TED OR OTHERWISE COVERED.

2/A4  SECTION : TYPICAL ADAPTABLE KITCHEN : LINEAR
½" = 1'-0"

WALL CAB.

SINK W/ UNDER-CABINET
REMOVED & HGT. ADJUSTED

SLIP JOINT & FLEXIBLE SUPPLY LINE
PERMIT HGT. VARIATION

UNDER-SINK WASTE & HOT WATER
PIPES TO BE INSULATED OR
OTHERWISE COVERED

2A/A4  SECTION : TYPICAL ADAPTED KITCHEN : LINEAR
½" = 1'-0"

RANGE/OVEN
WALL CABINETS
ADJUSTABLE HGT. SINK &
WORKTOP W/ REMOVABLE
CABINETS BELOW
REFRIG. (TYPICAL
LOCATION)

3/A4  ELEVATION : TYPICAL ADAPTABLE KITCHEN : LINEAR
½" = 1'-0"

RANGE OVEN
WALL CABINETS
SINK & WORK SURFACE ADJACENT
TO RANGE W/ UNDER-CABINETS
REMOVED & HGT. ADJUSTED
REFRIG. (TYPICAL LOCATION)

2'-6" MIN.   2'-6" MIN.

3A/A4  ELEVATION : TYPICAL ADAPTED KITCHEN : LINEAR
½" = 1'-0"

RANGE/OVEN TO COMPLY W/ ANSI 4.32.5.6 (TYPICAL LOCATION)

2'-0" MIN.

WALL CABINETS OVER:

ADJUSTABLE HGT. WORK SURFACE ADJACENT TO RANGE TO COMPLY W/ ANSI 4.32.5.4 REMOVABLE CABINET BELOW

2'-0" MIN.

ADJUSTABLE HGT. SINK TO COMPLY W/ ANSI 4.32.3.10 W/ REMOVABLE CAB. BELOW

TYPICAL LOCATION OF REFRIG. TO COMPLY W/ ANSI 4.32.3.10

④ **PLAN: TYPICAL ADAPTABLE KITCHEN : L-SHAPED**
A4  ½" = 1'-0"

RANGE/OVEN (TYP. LOC.)

2'-0" MIN.

LINE OF WALL CABINETS OVER

ADJ. WORK SURFACE W/ UNDER CABINET REMOVED & HGT. ADJUSTED

2'-0" MIN.

SINK W/ HGT. ADJUSTED & UNDER CABINET REMOVED.

REFRIG. (TYP. LOC.)

④A **PLAN: TYPICAL ADAPTED KITCHEN : L-SHAPED**
A4  ½" = 1'-0"

WALL CABINETS TO COMPLY W/ ANSI 4.32.3.10 (TYP. LOC.)

ADJ. HGT. SINK & WORKTOP W/ REMOVABLE CABINET BELOW

ADJ. HGT. WORKTOP ADJACENT TO RANGE W/ REMOVABLE CABINET BELOW

RANGE/OVEN (TYPICAL LOCATION)

4'-0" MAX.

SLIP JOINT IN TAIL PIECE & FLEXIBLE SUPPLY LINE

⑤ **ELEVATION: TYPICAL ADAPTABLE KITCHEN : L-SHAPED**
A4  ½" = 1'-0"

WALL CABS (TYP. LOC.)

SINK W/ HGT. ADJUSTED & UNDER CABINET REMOVED

RANGE/OVEN (TYP. LOC.)

WORKTOP W/ UNDER CABINET REMOVED & HGT. ADJUSTED

UNDERSINK WASTE & HOT WATER PIPES TO BE INSULATED OR OTHERWISE COVERED

3'-0" MAX.

2'-6"-3'-0"

4'-0" MAX.

2'-6" MIN.

⑤A **ELEVATION: TYPICAL ADAPTED KITCHEN : L-SHAPED**
A4  ½" = 1'-0"

REFRIG. (TYPICAL LOCATION)

WALL CABINETS (TYPICAL LOCATION)

ADJ. HGT. SINK & WORKTOP W/ REMOVABLE CABINET BELOW

ADJ. HGT. WORKTOP W/ REMOVABLE CABINET BELOW

2'-6" MIN.

⑥ **ELEVATION: TYPICAL ADAPTABLE KITCHEN : L-SHAPED**
A4  ½" = 1'-0"

REFRIG. (TYP. LOC.)

WALL CABINETS (TYP. LOC.)

SINK W/ UNDER CAB. REMOVED & HGT. ADJUSTED

WORKTOP W/ UNDER CAB. REMOVED & HGT. ADJUSTED.

2'-6" MIN.

⑥A **ELEVATION: TYPICAL ADAPTED KITCHEN : L-SHAPED**
A4  ½" = 1'-0"

It is difficult to develop precise formulas by which to design residential library shelving or to project the number of books that can be accommodated on a unit base because of the many variables involved. The size of books, the types of books and other reading materials, the reach limitations of the user, etc., all have an impact upon the design requirements.

It is possible, however, for preliminary planning purposes, to apply the broad guidelines indicated in Figs. 1 to 3. Seven volumes per foot of shelving can be used as a rule-of-thumb to project capacity. The height of the highest shelf above the floor should be limited to between 78 and 81 in; 24 in is the minimum height above the floor to gain access to a shelf without squatting. Limitations for shelving to serve children will differ and are indicated in Fig. 3.

**TABLE 1  Library Shelving: Volumes per Linear Foot of Shelf Based on Subject**
(Standard stack section 3 ft wide × 7½ ft high with 7 shelves)

| Subject | Volumes per foot of shelf | Volumes per single face section |
|---|---|---|
| Art (excluding oversize) | 7 | 147 |
| Nonfiction | 8 | 168 |
| Economics | 8 | 168 |
| Fiction | 8 | 168 |
| General literature | 7 | 147 |
| History | 7 | 147 |
| Law | 4 | 84 |
| Medical | 5 | 105 |
| Periodicals, bound | 5 | 105 |
| Public documents | 5 | 105 |
| Technical and scientific | 6 | 126 |
| Average for overall estimating | | 125 |

Fig. 1  Optimum shelving conditions for adults.

Fig. 2  Optimum shelving conditions for teenagers.

Fig. 3  Optimum shelving conditions for children.

① LIBRARY: PLAN
Ⓐ12   ½" = 1'-0"

② LIBRARY: NORTH ELEVATION
Ⓐ12   ½" = 1'-0"

③ LIBRARY: SOUTH ELEVATION
Ⓐ12   ½" = 1'-0"

- WOOD & GLASS CABINET W/ SHELVES OVER. SEE DWG. (A/12)
- ½" PLY. BACK ON ½" SHIMS
- WOOD PANEL DOOR: ¾" X 3¼" HDWD. FRAME ½" PLY PANEL
- ¾" PLY SHELF W/ ¾"X 1½" HDWD. LIP ON CONT BLCKNG
- 3 EQ. DRAWERS SEE NOTE ON DWG (A/12)
- ¾" PLY SHELF W/ ¾"X1½" HDWD. LIP ON CONT. BLOCKING
- 2 EQ. DRAWERS : SEE NOTE ON DWG (A/12)
- ¾"X6" HDWD. BASE ON CONT. BLOCKING
- PLY SPACE AS REQD.

(B/A12) LIBRARY : DETAIL @ NORTHEAST CABINET
1½" = 1'-0"

## DETAIL·OF·SHELVING·

7/8" Shelving 5'-0"

shelf

face of Cupboard below

·PLAN·

open

Section

6'-5"

2'-3"

3¾"

fin. floor

·PLAN·ON·
LINE "A-A"

3¾" jamb
2'-0⅛" Door
4¼" Center
2'-0⅛" Door
batten

1'-9⅛"
3"
1'-6⅛"
3¾"

Note: All·woodwork·in·Bookcase·and·Cupboards·is·White·Oak·

12"

plaster

wood

8'-3"
5'-0"
11¾"

4"
hinged    hinged
A        A
3¼" 2'-0⅛" 4¼" 2'-0⅛" 3¼"

· ELEVATION ·

plaster

8"  1'-1½"  7/8"
5/8"
3"
1'-6⅛"  ¾"

SECTION ·

PLAN SCALE 1/2" = 1'-0"

ELEVATION SCALE 1/2" = 1'-0"

SECTION A-A SCALE 3/4" = 1'-0"

3/8" EDGE BANDED

PAINTED PLYWOOD

SEC. B-B THROUGH BAR
SCALE 3/4" = 1'-0"

SECTION C-C THROUGH BAR SCALE 3/4" = 1'-0"

TRIM
1/2 FULL SIZE

SEC. D
SCALE 1/4" = 1'-0"

SEC. E
SCALE 1/4" = 1'-0"

3/8" PLYWOOD WITH EDGE BANDED

1/4" PLYWOOD

1/4" MIRROR APPLIED WITH ADHESIVE AND BRING FLUSH WITH TRIM EDGE

1/4" CLEAR FLOAT GLASS SHELVES 6" X 1'-10 1/4"

1/4" MIRROR APPLIED WITH ADHESIVE AND BRING FLUSH TO BUTT JOINT

1/4" MIRROR APPLIED WITH ADHESIVE AND BRING FLUSH TO BUTT JOINT AND TRIM

1/4" MIRROR APPLIED WITH ADHESIVE

1/4" MIRROR APPLIED WITH ADHESIVE AND BRING FLUSH WITH TRIM EDGE

3/8" PLYWOOD WITH EDGE BANDED

ADHESIVE

MIRROR

CARPET

## BUILT-IN BOOKSHELVES

Here is a simple method of building in bookshelves, bar units, etc., for residences and other types of buildings by using an egg-crate system. The front of the shelf is supported by the vertical members and the back of the shelf is nailed to the plywood back. These built-in bookshelves and bar unit were developed for a residence on the Eastern Shore of Maryland. In this design Hugh Newell Jacobsen, FAIA, divided the built-in bookcases into units of three shelf widths and introduced a recessed vertical divider 3" deep by 7 1/2" wide between bookcase units. The major trim piece is solid wood 1 1/8" X 1 1/8" with a 3/8" wide by 3/8" deep groove at the middle. This simple trim piece acts as framing for sides, top, and bottom of the bookshelves and also for the bar unit with glass shelves and mirrored back, sides, top, and bottom.

**TOP FIXTURES FOR
NO. 1 ROLLING LADDER**
No. 210—Roll Type Top Fixture
No. 230—Hook Slide Top Fixture

No. 230

CSNK

No. 210

BRASS HOOK

ADJUSTMENT 4

SECTION A-A
PRESSED STEEL FRAME

ALL WHEELS ARE
DIE CASTINGS

PUTNAM
ROLLING LADDERS

**BOTTOM FIXTURES FOR NO. 1 ROLLING LADDER**

PUTNAM
ROLLING LADDERS

WHEEL AND FRAME PRESSED STEEL
HUB DIE CASTING

No. 1 Bottom Fixture No. 270 Regular

WHEEL SECTION AT LINE A-A

PUTNAM
ROLLING LADDERS

No. 1 Bottom Fixture No. 270 Old Style

WHEEL SECTION AT A-A

**BRACKETS FOR TRACK**

| | No. 1 Track | |
| --- | --- | --- |
| | Roll Top No. 210 | Hook Slide No. 230 |
| Vertical Mount on Uprights | No. 14 | No. 14 H |
| Horizontal Mount | No. 27 | No. 27H |
| Top of Shelving Mount | No. 29 | No. 29H |

NO. 14

NO. 14H

CSNK FOR NO. 12 FH WOOD SCREW

NO. 27

CSNK FOR NO. 12 FH WOOD SCREW

NO. 27H

NO. 1 TRACK

CSNK FOR NO. 12
FH WOOD SCREW

NO. 29GR

SHOWING APPLICATION OF
END STOP TO ANY STYLE
BRACKET-RIGHT OR LEFT

CSNK FOR NO. 14 FH WOOD SCREW

NO. 29

CSNK HOLES

NO. 29H

PUTNAM
ROLLING LADDERS

# FAMILY/RECREATION ROOMS
### Arrangements and Clearances

### Recreational Activities

Indoor recreational activities invariably require definite spaces for equipment and clearances for using it. Not all games occupy floor areas indicated as necessary for those diagramed on this page. But if interiors are planned to accommodate large units of equipment such as that required for table tennis, and provide necessary playing clearances, spaces will be adequate for many other uses as well.

Dimensions of game equipment and floor areas required for its use are both subject to variation. Sizes noted here are comfortable averages, not absolute minima.

Clearances for playing bridge

Clearances for playing poker

Folded

Folded bridge table      Folded chair

Folded poker table

Fig. 1 Play room.

PING PONG

CARD PLAYING

POOL AND BILLIARDS

GYMNASTICS

**TABLE 1  Pool and Billiard Table Sizes (in feet)**

| Size | Where used |
|------|------------|
| 3 × 6 | Home |
| 3½ × 7 | Home |
| 4 × 8 | Home |
|  | Commercial standard in South America, Mexico, and Spain |
| 4½ × 9 | Popular U.S. commercial standard |
| 5 × 10 | U.S. professional standard |
| 6 × 12 | Commercial standard in Canada and England |

Standard ping pong table sizes are 3 ft x 6 ft; 3 ft 6 in x 7 ft 0 in; 4 ft 0 in x 8 ft 0 in; 4 ft 8 in x 8 ft 6 in; 5 ft 0 in x 9 ft 2 in; 5 ft 6 in x 10 ft 2 in; 6 ft 8 in x 12 ft 8 in.

# FAMILY/RECREATION ROOMS

**Residential Bar**

CONTINUOUS TUBE LIGHTING — PLASTER

PLAN AT PARTITION

REDWOOD: TRIM, DIVIDER PARTITIONS, & TOP, BOTTOM, SIDES

2 1/4" GLASS SHELVES

STOCK METAL STANDARD

1'-11"

2'-6"

2  1/4" x 1"  3/4"  1/2" x 1 1/2"

2'-0"

1/4" PLYWOOD

MATT WHITE PLASTIC LAMINATE  3/4"

3/4" PLYWOOD OR PARTICLE BOARD

1"

1/4" PLYWOOD

1-4"

1/2" PLYWOOD

1'-11 1/4"  1/2"

1-2 1/4"

## WALL SECTION

NOT TO SCALE

1/2" PLYWOOD  2"  VINYL BASE AND FLOOR TILE  4"

3/4" REDWOOD VENEER ON PLYWOOD

DARK BROWN LEATHERETTE

REDWOOD BURL VENEER 1/4" PLYWOOD

STAINLESS STEEL

3'-6"  9"  7'-7"  8'-6"  4'-6"

## ELEVATION  SCALE: 1/4" = 1'-0"

REFRID.

12'-6"

FROSTED GLASS LIGHT PANELS IN FURRED SOFFIT ABOVE

SINK

7'-4"

## PLAN  SCALE 3/16" = 1'-0"

1 3/4"  6"

2'-6 1/4"  3'-0"  2'-7"  2'-1 1/4"

3/4" REDWOOD VENEER ON PLYWOOD

2'-6"  HARDWOOD EDGE  4"

2 - 3/4" INTERMEDIATE BAR TOP SUPPORTS

MATT WHITE PLASTIC LAMINATE  3/4"

3/4" PLYWOOD PARTICLE BD.  1"

11"

1/2" PLYWOOD  1/2"

1'-7 1/4"

## BAR SECTION

NOT TO SCALE

2"  1/2" PLYWOOD

DARK BROWN LEATHERETTE  1/4" FOAM RUBBER

1'-6"

3/8"  3/4"

13/8"  6"

2 1/2"  2 3/4" 2 3/4"  5 1/2"

MATT WHITE PLASTIC LAMINATE

2" x 4" STUDS

1/4" PLYWOOD

1/4" PLYWOOD WITH REDWOOD BURL VENEER

STAINLESS STEEL

5"  5"

## RESIDENTIAL BAR

This small residential bar with double lighting was designed so that the back bar shelves would display all the types of bar glasses and the liquor bottles as a decorative element. Note how the recessed fluorescent tube fixtures indirectly light up all the glasses and the 2" open slot in the bottom shelf indirectly lights up the liquor bottles on the back bar shelf. The entire front bar has recessed light fixtures in the ceiling above; this allows for two different methods of lighting the bar area. Note also that the bar front is slightly padded with foam rubber and the entire bar top is finished with dark brown leatherette.

UPRIGHT PIANO SIZES

GRAND PIANO SIZES

SECTION THRU BAR CABINET

# LAUNDRY/SEWING ROOMS

**Laundry Room Layouts**

**Fig. 1   Angle arrangement.**

**Fig. 2   Conventional arrangement.**

**Fig. 3   Arrangement of ironing equipment based on flow of work.**

Scale 1:50

**Fig. 4.   Space around ironing board.**

## HOME LAUNDRY ACTIVITIES

Home laundry includes the processes from sorting through ironing of clothes and household linens, including pretreating, washing, drying, and sprinkling.

### General Planning Suggestions

1. It is desirable to plan space for specific laundry processes.
2. Moistureproof surfaces are needed for pretreating and sprinkling of clothes.
3. Drying areas should be accessible for use under all climatic conditions.
4. To control moisture in the room, dryers should be located to permit venting to the outside of the house.
5. Adequate storage for washing equipment and supplies should be located near the place of first use.
6. Facilities for hanging drip-dry garments after washing should be provided.
7. In locating the washing equipment consideration should be given to convenience of inter-related household activities, distances from the source of soiled clothes and the drying areas, and the isolation of clutter.

**TABLE 1   Space Requirements for Washer-Dryer Arrangements**

| Type and size of equipment | Auxiliary equipment | Work area, in | Total floor area, in Width | Total floor area, in Depth |
|---|---|---|---|---|
| Stacked arrangement: washer, 31 × 26 in; dryer, 31 × 26 in | Basket, 19-in diameter | 43 × 37 | 43 | 63 |
| Angle arrangement: washer 26 × 26 in; dryer, 31 × 26 in | Basket, 19-in diameter | 36 × 59 | 62 | 76 |
| Straight-line arrangement: washer, 26 × 26 in; dryer, 31 × 26 in | Basket, 19-in diameter | 36 × 66 | 62 | 66 |

Figures 1 and 2 illustrate arrangements of laundry equipment. Space needed by a single worker in front of equipment or between equipment placed opposite is indicated. Overall dimensions of areas will vary with type and size of equipment selected. No allowance has been made between the back of equipment and the wall for electrical, plumbing, and dryer vent connections. The space required will depend on the type of installation used.

Counter space is provided for sorting and folding three washer loads of clothes. The space under the counters has been used for bins, one for soiled clothing and the other for dry, clean articles that require further treatment before use or storage. Additional counter space can be provided by the tops of the dryer and washer, depending upon the type selected.

A tall storage cabinet for laundry supplies would complement each arrangement. In this cabinet, an ironing board, iron, mops, and buckets (needed for cleaning the laundry area) may also be stored.

Fig. 5   Automatic washer. A = 24–30 in, B = 26–30 in, C = 42 in, D = 36 in.

Fig. 6   Automatic dryer. A = 24–28 in, B = 24–26 in, C = 42 in, D = 36 in.

Fig. 7   Compact washer.

Fig. 8   Compact dryer.

Fig. 9   When space is limited, it may be possible to locate the laundry space next to a corridor.

Fig. 10   Clearance in front of automatic washer and dryer. If the space in front of the automatic washer and dryer is a corridor, this dimension should be increased to at least 1200 mm (4 ft). This will permit a second person to pass through when someone is doing the laundry. If a washer and dryer are located opposite each other, this dimension should also be 1200 mm (4 ft).

Fig. 11   Clearance in front of laundry tub.

Fig. 12   Clearance in front of sorting counter or table.

# LAUNDRY/SEWING ROOMS
### Laundry Room Layouts

### LAUNDRY LOCATION

The ideal location of the laundry space is a matter of preference. The laundry area may be separate or combined with the bathroom, the kitchen, the utility space, or the corridor. The most frequently mentioned advantages and disadvantages of these various options are listed below.

### Separate Laundry
### Advantages

A separate space can be used for other activities such as sewing and hobbies, if it is large enough.

Clothes may be hung for air drying without interfering with other household activities.

Noise from laundry appliances can be shut off from the rest of the dwelling.

Temporary holding or storage of clothing to be washed or ironed is made easier.

### Disadvantages

Providing this extra room increases the cost of the dwelling.

### Laundry in Combination with Bathroom
### Advantages

When the bathroom is located near the bedrooms, the washer and dryer are close to where most laundry originates. This facilitates gathering soiled articles and putting away clean linen and clothing.

Combining the laundry space with a half bathroom adjacent to the kitchen provides many of the advantages of a separate laundry room.

The tops of the laundry appliances provide useful horizontal space on which to lay clothes.

Floor and wall finishes in bathrooms are usually resistant to high humidities.

Usually, additional plumbing costs are minimal.

The bathroom sink may be used for hand washing.

Mechanical ventilation can be provided economically for both functions.

### Disadvantages

A bathroom will usually accommodate only washing and drying facilities. Other laundry related activities such as ironing, will have to be carried out elsewhere in the dwelling.

Occupants may wish to use the bathroom when laundry is being washed or dried.

## KEY

1. STORAGE CLOSET
2. CLOTHES CHUTE
3. SORTING SHELF
4. LAUNDRY TRAY
5. WASHING MACHINE
6. DRYER
7. IRONER
8. IRONING BOARD

### Laundry in Combination with Kitchen
#### Advantages

Suitable in housing for young families because the person doing the laundry can keep an eye on the washing machine while doing other jobs and supervising the children.

Direct access to the outside for clothes drying is likely to be easier than from laundries located in a basement or on a second storey.

Kitchen sinks are usually sizeable and can be used for laundering.

Additional plumbing costs are usually small.

#### Disadvantages

Danger of cross-contamination through the handling of dirty washing during food preparation.

Grease and cooking smells can be passed on to clean clothes.

Noise generated by running appliances cannot easily be shut off from the rest of the dwelling.

### Laundry in Combination with Utility Space in Basement
#### Advantages

Generally, as much space as needed can be provided.

Noise generated by running appliances can be easily shut off from the rest of the dwelling.

#### Disadvantages

Laundry must be carried up and down stairs, although automatic dryers have eased the problem of carrying heavy baskets of damp clothes to outdoor clotheslines.

### Laundry in Combination with Corridor
#### Advantages

The space is used more economically (Fig. 9).

The space above the appliances may be used as a linen closet.

The appliances can be hidden from sight when they are not in use; they can be recessed into the wall and enclosed with doors.

#### Disadvantages

Noise generated by running appliances cannot be easily shut off from the rest of the dwelling.

An alcove adjacent to a corridor will accommodate only a minimum-sized laundry area. Other laundry related activities, such as ironing, will have to be carried out elsewhere in the dwelling.

# LAUNDRY/SEWING ROOMS
### Laundry Room Layouts

### Planning for Efficiency

The sequence of laundering operations determines the planning of space and facilities and the placing of equipment. Convenience and time-and-step saving are easily achieved by placing the elements in their natural order of use: (1) clothes chute (with or without bins or hampers), (2) sorting table or counter, (3) washing machine, (4) laundry trays, (5) dryer, (6) ironer or mangle, (7) ironing board, (8) rack, "horse," or table for finished laundry. In addition, storage closet or cabinets will be necessary for soaps, powders, bluing, bleaches, starch, basket, clothespins, iron, etc.

### KEY

1. STORAGE CLOSET
2. CLOTHES CHUTE
3. SORTING SHELF
4. LAUNDRY TRAY
5. WASHING MACHINE
6. DRYER
7. IRONER
8. IRONING BOARD

KITCHEN AND LAUNDRY LAYOUT

LAUNDRY-SEWING-MENDING

### KEY

| | |
|---|---|
| CLOS. | STORAGE CLOSET |
| CH. | CLOTHES CHUTE |
| SORT. SH. | SORTING SHELF |
| TRAY | LAUNDRY TRAY |
| W.M. | WASHING MACHINE |
| DRY. | DRYER |
| IR'N | IRONER |
| IR. B'D | IRONING BOARD |

### General Planning Suggestions

1. An area especially planned for sewing, convenient to other activity areas, is desirable.

2. Most houses need storage space for sewing materials and equipment. The amount and kind of storage required varies according to the quality and frequency of sewing.

3. A minimum sewing area should include the machine, auxiliary work surfaces, a chair that permits freedom of motion, and storage arrangements. The work surface for layout and cutting may be outside the area for sewing machine operations and serve multiple purposes.

4. Consideration should be given to work surfaces at comfortable heights for the varying activities of sewing.

5. Light should be adequate for the activity.

**TABLE 2  Dimensions of Area for Layout and Cutting Garments**

| Measurement | Dimensions, in | |
| --- | --- | --- |
| | Minimum | Adequate |
| Working surface | | |
| Length | 56 | 72 |
| Width | | |
| Table, free-standing | 28 | 36 |
| Table obstructed on one side | 28 | 32 |
| Height | 34–40 (range) | 36 (median) |
| Clearance for worker | 18 | 24 |

**TABLE 3  Dimensions of Fitting Space**

| Use of Space | Minimum | Adequate |
| --- | --- | --- |
| Viewing in mirror: | | |
| Mirror dimensions, in | | |
| Width | 16 | 18 |
| Length | 42 | 60 |
| Top to floor | 70 | 72 |
| Clearance in front of mirror, ft | | |
| Width | 3 | 4 |
| Length | 6–8 | 10 |
| Clearance while fitting self, ft | 6 × 4 | |
| Clearance while being fitted, ft | 8½ × 4 | |
| Fitting garment on dress form, ft | 5 × 4 | 7 × 6 |

**Fig. 13  Mean heights and clearances for sewing machine use.**

**Fig. 14  Arrangement of sewing equipment based on flow of work.**

**Fig. 15  Sewing room.**

## CLOSETS/STORAGE AREAS

Figures 1 and 2 show the vertical clearances related to male and female closet and storage facilities. Wherever possible or practical, the closet shelf should be located within human reach. The height shown for the high shelf has been established based on fifth percentile male and female data in order to place it within reach of individuals of smaller body size. Any shelf located at a greater distance should be used primarily for storage that requires only infrequent access. The location of the shelf just above the rod is essentially a function of rod height. The clearance between the bottom of the shelf and the top of the rod should allow for easy removal of the hanger.

Figure 3 illustrates two various types of walk-in storage facilities. Undoubtably, it can be argued that the 36-in, or 91.4-cm, clearance shown between the hanging garment and the storage shelf or between opposite garments could be reduced about 50 percent. The authors contend, however, that in order to achieve any degree of comfort in the selection and removal of the desired garment, a minimum of 36 in should be maintained. The degree to which this dimension can be reduced is a question of the level of comfort the user is prepared to tolerate in exchange for the floor space saved. The two drawings of the plan view of the human figure illustrate clearances required for donning a coat or putting on a pair of stockings.

Fig. 1   Closet and storage facilities: male.

Fig. 2   Closet and storage facilities: female.

| | in | cm |
|---|---|---|
| A | 64–68 | 162.6–172.7 |
| B | 72–76 | 182.9–193.0 |
| C | 12–18 | 30.5–45.7 |
| D | 8–10 | 20.3–25.4 |
| E | 20–28 | 50.8–71.1 |
| F | 34–36 | 86.4–91.4 |
| G | 10–12 | 25.4–30.5 |
| H | 60–70 | 152.4–177.8 |
| I | 69–72 | 175.3–182.9 |
| J | 76 | 193.0 |
| K | 68 | 172.7 |
| L | 42 | 106.7 |
| M | 46 | 116.8 |
| N | 30 | 76.2 |
| O | 18 | 45.7 |

Fig. 3   Walk-in closet and storage facilities.

### CLOTHES CLOSETS

The capacity of a clothes closet depends upon the accessible length of rod. Three types of closets are common.

**Reach-in closet** The minimum front-to-back depth of space for hanging clothes is 24″. The accessible rod length is equal to the width of the door opening plus 6″ on each side.

**Edge-in closet** By providing an edge-in space of at least 18″, the accessible rod length can be much longer than the door width. This requires less wall space than a full front opening.

**Walk-in closet** This type provides rods on one or both sides of an access path at least 20″ wide. A wider access space within the closet may be used as a dressing area.

### Rod Lengths and Heights

The Minimum Property Standards of HUD (1973) require that each bedroom have a closet, with rod and shelf, with minimum dimensions of

For double-occupancy bedrooms:
24″ by 60″
For single-occupancy bedrooms:
24″ by 36″
For closet at entrance to house:
24″ by 24″

A more desirable front-to-back depth would be 28″ for bedroom closets and 30″ for entrance closets to accommodate bulky outer garments.

The average rod space per garment is about 2″ for women's clothing, 2¼″ for men's clothing, and 4″ for heavy coats.

Recommended heights of rods are 68″ for long robes, 63″ for adult clothing, and 32″ for children's clothing.

### Shelf Space and Lighting

The shelf is normally located 2″ above the rod, and another shelf may be located 12″ higher. Shelves higher than the rod may also be installed at the end of the closet.

A fluorescent fixture over the door is recommended for lighting a closet. Deluxe cool white tubes match daylight for selecting clothes.

## CLOSETS/STORAGE AREAS
### Clothes Closet Details

**Fig. 4  Bedroom closet designed for one person. This diagram shows dimensions for rods, shelves, and drawers to hold underwear, sweaters, shoes, hats, purses, and ties. Research shows that each person needs at least 48 inches of rod space for hanging clothing.**

**TABLE 1  Garment Dimensions**

| Men's garments | Allowance per garment, in | Women's garments | Allowance per garment, in |
|---|---|---|---|
| Heavy jackets and coats | 3 | Coats and jackets: | |
| Medium-weight jackets, coats, and raincoats | 2 | Heavy | 3 |
| Sweaters, light-weight jackets, and raincoats | 1 | Medium | 2 |
| Work pants: | | Light | 1 |
| Folded on hanger | 2¼ | Sweaters | 1¼ |
| Hung full length | 1¾ | Other garments: | |
| Other garments: | | Dress coats, winter | 3½ |
| Top coats | 2½ | Robes | 2 |
| Robes | 2 | Suits, wool (skirt under jacket) | 2½ |
| Suits (trousers full length under jacket) | 3 | Skirts | 1 |
| Trousers | 1½ | Jackets | 2 |
| Jackets | 2 | Blouses | 1 |
| Sweater jacket | 1 | House dresses | 1¾ |
| Shirts (all kinds) | 1½ | Other dresses: | |
| | | Average | 2 |
| | | Full-skirted | 2½ |
| | | Straight-line | 1¼ |

| Men's garments | Range of lengths, in | Women's garments | Range of lengths, in |
|---|---|---|---|
| Suit jackets, other jackets, shirts | 31–40 | Blouses, jackets | 25–35 |
| Trousers: | | Skirts, medium and short coats | 31–43 |
| Folded over hanger | 29–37 | Dresses, long coats, short robes | 48–55 |
| Full length | 47–53 | Long robes, long evening dresses | 61–68 |
| Overcoats, robes | 48–54 | | |

· ELEVATION · OF · DOORS ·

· SECTION · THRO · HANGING · SPACE ·

· SECTION · THRO · SHELVING · ·

· SECTION · THRO · SLIDING · TRAYS ·

PLAN

TYPICAL · DETAILS · OF · A · DRESSING · ROOM · WARDROBE

PLAN · THRO · TRAYS ·

SECTION · THRO · TRAYS ·

ELEVATION OF UNIT
@ 1/4" = 1'-0"

SHELVES & HANGROD
2A
O.A. LENGTH
(SEE SCHEDULE)
FIN. FLOOR

FACE OF WALL
STANDARDS SET FLUSH W/SIDES
END PANEL
INTERMEDIATE DIVIDERS
LINE OF SHELF EDGE
LINE OF TOP & BOTTOM EDGE
3'-6" MAX.

4D
@ 3" = 1'-0"

HARDWOOD CLEATS
NOTE: PROVIDE WOOD GROUNDS FOR ALL PLASTER WALLS
1-1/16" ø SATIN CHROME HANGROD W/ GARCY #A 3369 SOCKETS
FACE OF WALL

CLEAR LACQUER BIRCH PLYWOOD
1'-6"
1'-0"
1-1/2" ø S.S. HANGER ROD (CONTINUE)

1'-2⅛"

½"  1⅛"  12"  ¾"

¾" VENEERED PLYWD.

END BRACKET REQ'D;
INTERMEDIATE BRACKET 3'-6" o.c. MAX

S.S. HANGER ROD ¾" DIAM.

LINE OF CLOSET WALL

## CLOSET SHELF DETAIL

WHITE BIRCH SHELVES.
NATURAL LAQUER FINISH

HANG ROD

NORTH ELEVATION SPACE # 4A

**11** SCALE 3/8" = 1'-0"

GARCY B 3335 HANGROD
W/ B 3369 SOCKET

**12** SCALE 3" = 1'-0"

BIRCH
FILLER

WHITE BIRCH SHELVES
NATURAL LAQUER FINISH

GARCY B 3335 HANGROD
W/ B 3369 SOCKET.

COAT & HAT SHELVES
PART ELEVATION

**13** SCALE 3" = 1'-0"

HANGROD
SHELF

V.I.F.

ALIGN

IVES 326 MAGNETIC CATCH

1½"x2" PAINT GRADE BLOCKING

1¾" WD. DOOR W/PLAS. LAM. FINISH (PL-11)

101/AB-6

**PLAN SECTION AT COAT CLOSET**

ALIGN

STANLEY #327 HINGE TOP & BOT.

¾" PLYWD. W/ PLAS. LAM. FIN. (PL-11)

END BRACKET & (1) INTERMED. SUPPORT

S.S. HANGROD 1" DIAMETER

BOT. HINGE ¼" ABOVE CARPET

FLUSH PULL BY SUGATSUNE AMERICA, INC. #SP-48

1'-2¼"

3½"

½"

1½"

9'-0 3/8"

4'-7½"

**VERT. SECTION AT COAT CLOSET**

1'-6"

1½"

4"

1'-0"

7'-6" A.F.F.

CHROME HANG ROD

PROVIDE INTERMEDIATE SUPPORT FOR SPANS GREATER THAN 54"

## COAT CLOSET SHELF

ELEVATION · OF · CLOSET · DOORS & DRAWERS ·

· SECTION · THRO · DRAWERS ·

PLAN

SECTION THRO SLIDE

PLAN · THRO · DRAWERS ·
scale : 3" = 1' - 0"

PLAN SECTION THRO · DOOR

SECTION THRO · DRAWERS ·

ELEVATION · OF · CLOSETS · (DOORS · REMOVED)

· SECTION · THRO · TRAYS ·

· PLAN ·

SECTION · THRO SIDE · OF · TRAY

· SECTION · THRO · SHOE · SHELVING ·

PLAN SECTION THRO TRAYS

VERTICAL · SECTION THRO · TRAYS ·

ELEVATION OF STORAGE
CLOSETS 4'-0" OR LESS IN LENGTH
@ ¼" = 1'-0"

ELEVATION OF STORAGE
CLOSETS OVER 4'-0" IN LENGTH
@ ¼" = 1'-0"

4A @ 3" = 1'-0"

4B @ ½ FULL SIZE

4C @ 3" = 1'-0"

4 STORAGE CLOSET
SHELVING DETAILS

# CLOSETS/STORAGE AREAS
**Wire Basket and Shelving Systems**

# PANTRY

**Front View**
Multiple-stacked, wrap-around storage shelving. Optional baskets and door racks. (9″, 12″, 16″ and 20″ widths available)

**Top View**
All the shelving you'll ever need for full-size family food storage. Sliding baskets hold fruit, vegetables and other kitchen supplies. Optional door racks maximize storage area by utilizing all available space.

**Front View**
Multiple-stacked storage shelving. Optional full-height door storage rack. (9″, 12″, 16″ and 20″ widths available)

**Top View**
Standard pantry design provides ample shelving and storage for canned goods and other food items. Center pole gives extra support. Optional door racks provide easy access to your most needed items.

# HOUSEKEEPING/UTILITY ROOM

**Front View**
Double, full-width upper storage shelving with stacked storage shelving. (12″, 16″ widths available)

**Top View**
Makes housework easier to handle by storing household cleaning items just where you need them. Plenty of shelving space for cloths, detergents and brushes. Wide storage area holds vacuum cleaner, brooms, mops and small appliances.

**Front View**
Double, full-width storage shelving with side-mounted shelving and basket unit and optional door/wall storage rack. (12″, 16″ widths available)

**Top View**
Make a clean sweep of cleaning with full-length shelves that hold a variety of utensils. Storage baskets pack brushes, cloths and sundry items. Bottled detergents and cleaning products can be stored neatly and safely in optional door racks.

# BEDROOM APPLICATIONS

**Front View**
Single and double hang with upper storage, center pole support and shoe racks. (12″, 16″ widths available)

**Top View**
Combination convenience for single and double hanging clothes. The perfect his and hers closet. Extra wide shelf space for clothing, linen and blankets in your master bedroom. Plus lots of room for her long dresses and coats — his shirts, suits and slacks. Shoe racks on both sides.

**Front View**
Walk-In. Single and double hang with upper storage and central shelving unit with additional clearance and shoe racks. (12″, 16″ widths available)

**Top View**
Single hanging space for coats and other long garments. Double hanging convenience for shorter garments. Full shelves with central storage unit allow easy storage of sweaters, boots, sports equipment, tall and over-sized items. Tailor-made for couples with a 2nd bedroom.

# CHILDREN'S CLOSETS

**Front View**
Full-width, double hanging with lower shelving height. Sliding basket system and shoe racks. (12″, 16″ widths available)

**Top View**
Specially designed for the children's room. Extra low-hanging shelf makes it easy for kids to reach. Stores toys and sports equipment in easy-access sliding baskets. Shoe rack keeps sneakers and other footwear neatly organized.

**Front View**
Standard. Double hang with shoe rack and off-center pole support. (12″, 16″ widths available)

**Top View**
Makes kids stuff out of chaos in any teenager's room. Plenty of storage space for footballs, beach equipment, basketballs, skates and other cumbersome items. Doubles as storage area for dresses and coats. Conveniently placed hanging rod for all your teenager's clothing.

# LINEN

**Front View**
Multiple-stacked
linen shelving with
pole support and slid-
ing basket system.
(9," 12," 16" and 20"
widths available)

**Top View**
Four extra-wide
shelves for linen and
blankets. Storage
baskets slide out and
hold dish cloths, pil-
lowcases and smaller
items. The perfect
linen closet.

**Front View**
Multiple-stacked
linen shelving.
(9," 12," 16" and 20"
widths available)

**Top View**
Bathroom linen closet
stores towels, sheets
and cleaning supplies
in one easy-access area.

# FOYER/FRONT ENTRY CLOSET

**Front View**
Single hang with
upper storage and off-
center storage unit
and shoe racks. (12,"
16" widths available)

**Top View**
A welcome addition
to any home. Full-
width, upper storage
holds hats, gloves and
sweaters. Off-center
storage for umbrellas
and winter items.
Shelves, shoe racks
and generous hang-
ing space lets guests
know they're welcome.

**Front View**
Single hang with half-
length shoe racks and
upper storage. (12," 16"
widths available)

**Top View**
Holds coats, hats,
shoes and guest
clothing with care.
Upper storage area
for visitor's bags
and small cases.

# MASTER BEDROOMS

### Front View
**Walk-In. Single hang with upper storage and central shelving/basket unit and shoe racks. (12″, 16″ widths available)**

### Top View
**Keeps shoes, shirts and clothing neatly organized. Sliding baskets for easy access to linen, underwear, etc. Full-length clothes storage for dresses, shirts and suits. Ideal for master bedroom.**

### Front View
**Walk-In. Single and double hang with upper storage, central shelving and shoe racks. (12″, 16″ widths available)**

### Top View
**Hang dresses and coats on one side, suits and shorter garments on the other. Central shelving actually replaces a piece of furniture in the master bedroom!**

### Front View
**Single hang with upper storage and central shelving and basket unit, additional clearance and shoe racks. (12″, 16″ widths available)**

### Top View
**So well designed it actually replaces a piece of furniture! Four sliding baskets provide multiple storage capacity for shirts, underwear, socks and sweaters. Full-length clothes hanging space, full-width shoe racks and lots of shelf space make this system a must for your 2nd bedroom.**

### Front View
**Single hang with upper storage and full-width shoe racks. (12″, 16″ widths available)**

### Top View
**Doubles shelf/storage space. Single hanging for clothes, coats, shirts and jackets. Expands easily to accommodate future needs. Two full-length shoe racks.**

# Office Spaces

General offices and multiple workstations      223
Private offices      231
Electronic workstations      241
Conference rooms      249
Reception areas      260
Furniture, furnishings, and equipment      278

# INTRODUCTION

The amount of office space built during the past few decades can be measured in the hundreds of billions of square feet. Within these buildings, workers spend nearly half their waking hours and a third of their entire lives.

Over the life span of a typical office building, the same spaces may be occupied by a succession of different tenants, each with their own programmatic requirements. Consequently, interior spaces may be recycled and redesigned many times, simply to accommodate the changing needs of new corporate users. In many instances redesign may be necessitated solely by the effect of technological change on the methodology of transacting business. Moreover, the escalating costs of land acquisition and construction and the increasing scarcity of urban building sites make it essential that the redesign reflects an efficient, cost-effective utilization of space, as well as one that is responsive to the human factors involved. It is necessary, therefore, for the designer to be familiar not only with the general planning criteria associated with office design, but with the architectural detailing of some of the typical interior elements contained within these spaces.

Accordingly, this section includes general planning criteria and examples of actual working drawings of typical interior conditions, prepared by various design professionals. The details alluded to include such items as trading desks, elevated computer floors, library furniture, built-in storage cabinets, work counters, wall paneling, vanities, reception desks, and conference room elements. Also included are illustrations and dimensional data pertaining to typical office furniture, equipment, and electronic media storage.

The so-called general office takes on a variety of forms and configurations. In its simplest variation it may be nothing more complex than several standard desks with returns located within a room or space. In its more sophisticated and ergonomically designed form, the general office may be based on an open planning or office landscaping concept, involving a system of workstations. The workstations include desk surfaces, files, acoustic partitions, and a host of other optional components to suit the nature of the particular work tasks involved. The systems are extremely flexible, allowing the workstations to be configured in a variety of shapes. Provision for power and lighting is quite common.

The design of the general office, like the design of the private office, requires a knowledge of the basic dimensional requirements and clearances of the workstation and, where applicable, of the visitor seating to be accommodated.

In certain instances, where customized and/or built-in storage elements, work coun-

ters, credenzas, etc., are required, a knowledge of architectural woodworking, as may be related to the design of such elements, can be quite helpful.

Accordingly, this part includes basic planning criteria for general office design, in addition to examples of architectural woodwork details in connection with some of the more common customized components of general office spaces.

The basic workstation, as illustrated in plan in Fig. 1, is the fundamental building block in understanding the anthropometric considerations for the planning and design of the general office. The worktask zone must be large enough to accommodate the paperwork, equipment, and other accessories that support the user's function. The work/activity zone dimension, shown in Fig. 1, is established by the space requirements needed for use of the typical return. In no case should this distance be less than the 30 in, or 76.2 cm, needed to provide adequate space for the chair clearance zone. The visitor seating zone, ranging in depth from 30 to 42 in, or

76.2 to 106.7 cm, requires the designer to accommodate both the buttock-knee and buttock-toe length body dimensions of the larger user. If an overhang is provided or the desk's modesty panel is recessed, the visitor seating zone can be reduced due to the additional knee and toe clearances provided. The specific type and size of the seating (i.e., if it swivels or if it has casters) also influence these dimensions.

Figure 2 shows the typical workstation expanded into the basic U-shaped configuration. The work/activity zone dimension range is shown as 46 to 58 in, or 116.8 to 147.3 cm; additional space is needed to allow for drawer extension of the lateral file. Not only does it provide more storage, the lateral file unit is generally the same height as that of the worksurface and is often utilized as a supplementary worksurface. The distance between this unit and that of the primary worksurface must be sufficient to allow for movement and rotation of the chair.

Fig. 1  Basic workstation with visitor seating.

|   | in | cm |
|---|------|----------|
| A | 90–126 | 228.6–320.0 |
| B | 30–36 | 76.2–91.4 |
| C | 30–48 | 76.2–121.9 |
| D | 6–12 | 15.2–30.5 |
| E | 60–72 | 152.4–182.9 |
| F | 30–42 | 76.2–106.7 |
| G | 14–18 | 35.6–45.7 |
| H | 16–20 | 40.6–50.8 |
| I | 18–22 | 45.7–55.9 |
| J | 18–24 | 45.7–61.0 |
| K | 6–24 | 15.2–61.0 |
| L | 60–84 | 152.4–213.4 |
| M | 24–30 | 61.0–76.2 |
| N | 29–30 | 73.7–76.2 |
| O | 15–18 | 38.1–45.7 |

# GENERAL OFFICES AND MULTIPLE WORKSTATIONS

**Planning Data: Basic Workstations**

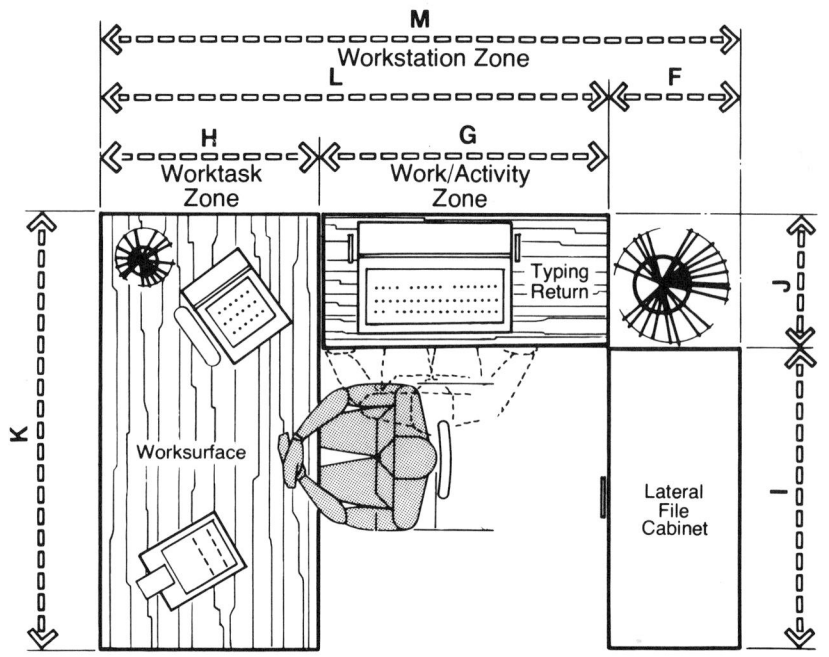

| | in | cm |
|---|---|---|
| **A** | 26–27 | 66.0–68.6 |
| **B** | 14–20 | 35.6–50.8 |
| **C** | 7.5 min. | 19.1 min |
| **D** | 29–30 | 73.7–76.2 |
| **E** | 7 min. | 17.8 min. |
| **F** | 18–24 | 45.7–61.0 |
| **G** | 46–58 | 116.8–147.3 |
| **H** | 30–36 | 76.2–91.4 |
| **I** | 42–50 | 106.7–127.0 |
| **J** | 18–22 | 45.7–55.9 |
| **K** | 60–72 | 152.4–182.9 |
| **L** | 76–94 | 193.0–238.8 |
| **M** | 94–118 | 238.8–299.7 |

**Fig. 2   Basic U-shaped workstation.**

**Minimum Square Footage Standards for the Open and Screened Workstation**

**The Nonautomated Task.** *Square footage workstation standards for the nonautomated task are developed primarily according to task profile, equipment, conferencing, and privacy requirements.*

**Open**
No requirement of equipment or task for privacy, concentration

**Screened**
Privacy required for reading, working, thinking, calculating, meetings, confidential phone calls, elimination of visual and acoustical distractions

---

**Task Profile:** Processing paper on work surface with quick turnaround.
- Continued flow of material is processed as it arrives at the workspace and is passed on to either another function or to group storage.
- Storage for permanent files and reference materials minimal.
- Reference material accessed infrequently. Telephone tasks may require concentration.

 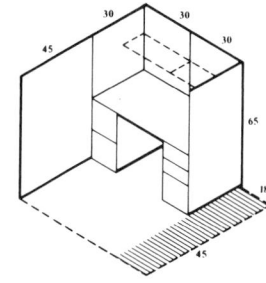

| | |
|---|---|
| No | Guest chair |
| 30 x 60 | Primary work surface |
| (76 x 152 cm) | |
| No | Secondary work surface |
| 3–4 | File drawers |
| 0–2 | Shelves |

**41 sq. ft.**

---

**Task Profile:** Typewriter the primary tool for processing paper.
- Continued flow of material is processed as it arrives at the workspace and is passed on to either another function or to group storage.
- Storage for permanent files and reference materials minimal.
- Reference material access may be frequent. Tasks may require concentration.

 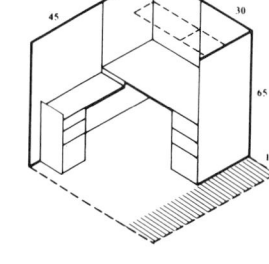

| | |
|---|---|
| No | Guest chair |
| 30 x 60 | Primary work surface |
| 18 x 42 | Secondary work surface |
| (46 x 107 cm) | |
| 3–4 | File drawers |
| 0–2 | Shelves |

**41 sq. ft.**

---

**Task Profile:** Typewriter the primary tool for processing paper.
- Continued flow of material is processed as it arrives at the workspace and is passed on to either another function or to group storage.
- Storage for permanent files and reference materials minimal.
- Reference material access may be frequent. Tasks may require concentration. Limited conferencing required at the workspace.
- Need to see and hear co-workers or subordinates of secondary priority.

 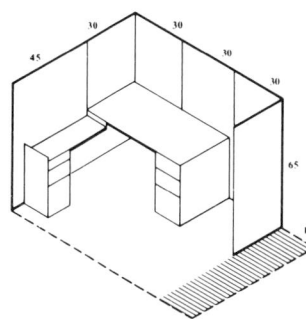

| | |
|---|---|
| 1 | Guest chair |
| 30 x 60 | Primary work surface |
| 18 x 42 | Secondary work surface |
| 3–4 | File drawers |
| 0–2 | Shelves |

**56 sq. ft.**

# GENERAL OFFICES AND MULTIPLE WORKSTATIONS

Planning Data: Basic Workstations

| The Nonautomated Task | **Open**<br>No requirement of equipment or task for privacy, concentration | **Screened**<br>Privacy required for reading, working, thinking, calculating, meetings, confidential phone calls, elimination of visual and acoustical distractions |
|---|---|---|

**Task Profile:** Same as 1 with addition of extended conferencing requirements at individual workstation.

| 2 | Guest chair |
|---|---|
| 30 x 60 | Primary work surface |
| No | Secondary work surface |
| 3–4 | File drawers |
| No | Shelves |

**65 sq. ft.**

**Task Profile:** Same as 3 with addition of extended conferencing requirements at individual workstation.

| 2 | Guest chair |
|---|---|
| 30 x 60 | Primary work surface |
| 18 x 42 | Secondary work surface |
| 3–4 | File drawers |
| No | Shelves |

**65 sq. ft.**

**Task Profile: Data Entry.**

□ Paper, material, or information processed and/or maintained.
□ Multiple reference sources may be used on a task.
□ Reference materials used frequently.
□ Limited volume of supplies and permanent records kept at the workspace.
□ Electronic equipment used for keeping records current, information inputting, and maintaining data and records.
□ Ability to see and hear co-workers may be desirable.
□ Tasks may also require screening for concentration.

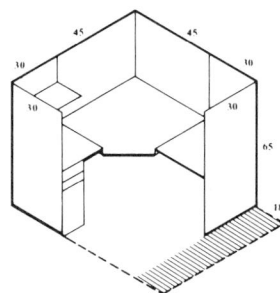

| No | Guest chair |
|---|---|
| 45 x 45<br>(114 x 114 cm) | Primary work surface |
| 30 x 30<br>(76 x 76 cm) | Secondary work surface |
| 1–2 | File drawers |
| 0–2 | Shelves |

**48 sq. ft.**

Fig. 3  Depending upon function, the sizes of individual and multiple workstations vary dramatically. Size of worksurface, length and depth of return, chair size, and circulation patterns all influence the gross square footage requirements.

# GENERAL OFFICES AND MULTIPLE WORKSTATIONS

**Planning Data: Multiple Workstations**

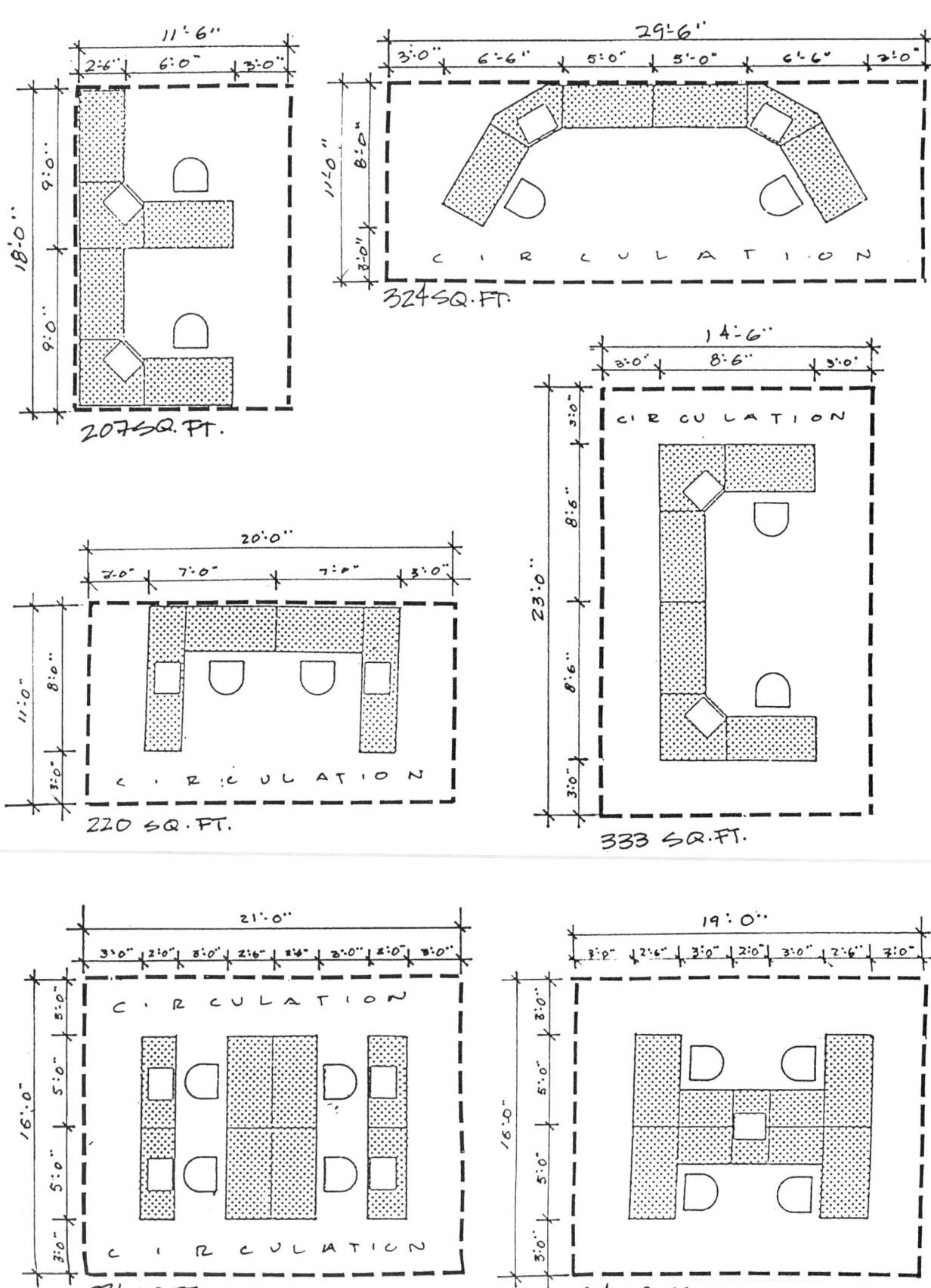

**Fig. 4** Floating or free-standing workstations tend to utilize more floor area than workstations placed against a wall or sharing the same wall panel. Clustering of workstations will ultimately result in the use of less floor area, but at the expense of major ergonomic considerations. Decisions relative to both acoustical privacy and personal space are often sacrificed in the name of economy.

# GENERAL OFFICES AND MULTIPLE WORKSTATIONS
## Planning Data: Multiple Workstations

**Fig. 5**

448 SQ. FT

Multiple workstations can result in efficient utilization of space and sharing of expensive computer terminals and equipment. If use of computer terminals is intensive, individual CRTs should be provided. Figures 5, 6, and 7 each show eight workstations, yet the setups range in area from 448 to 1012 ft². Furniture size, function, and ergonomic considerations all affect setup.

**Fig. 6**

760 SQ. FT

**Fig. 7**

1012 SQ. FT

# GENERAL OFFICES AND MULTIPLE WORKSTATIONS

Planning Data: Office Layout

Fig. 8   9 ft × 12 ft, 108 ft².

Fig. 9   9 ft × 14 ft, 126 ft².

Fig. 10   15 ft × 16 ft, 240 ft².

Fig. 11   12 ft × 25 ft, 300 ft².

Fig. 12   12 ft × 25 ft, 300 ft².

Fig. 13   18 ft × 25 ft, 414 ft².

Fig. 14   24 ft × 23 ft, 552 ft².

It is not unusual to have two or more persons share an enclosed office space. In planning this type of office space, both circulation and clearance become critically important. Door swings, the extension of file drawers, and points of entry must all be carefully considered.

The design of the private office requires a knowledge of the basic dimensional requirements and clearances of the executive workstation and, where applicable, of visitor seating accommodations. In certain instances where various aspects of the office interior are customized and/or built into the construction, a knowledge of architectural woodwork detailing is also desirable.

This page and the following pages include the necessary planning criteria required, as well as details of certain customized components.

Executive workstation and/or desk size and configuration can be customized depending on desired image, scale, and ambience. Desks are also available in generally accepted standard sizes. It is these standard desks that are most used in the design of the private office. Figure 1 illustrates the range of desk dimensions, chair dimensions, and clearances involved.

Many private executive offices are being designed with desks that do not conform

with the basic rectangular shape. Such a situation is illustrated in Fig. 2, which shows a circular executive desk. Such a desk is often selected if the executive in question plans to hold conferences within the office and prefers the psychology of having either visitors or employees gather around the worksurface in an egalitarian fashion. While a minimum desk size of 48 in, or 121.9 cm, is shown, this dimension is also influenced by the number of side chairs to be grouped around the desk.

A circular executive desk must be supported by supplementary credenza or file storage within easy reach of the executive chair. Side arm reach relative to the work/activity zone must always be studied carefully.

Figure 3 illustrates a typical circular lounge grouping found within an executive office. Providing for the appropriate leg clearance of 12 to 18 in, or 30.5 to 45.7 cm, is also determined by the sitting zone requirements. Buttock-knee length must also be considered.

| | in | cm |
|---|---|---|
| A | 30–39 | 76.2–99.1 |
| B | 66–84 | 167.6–213.4 |
| C | 21–28 | 53.3–71.1 |
| D | 24–28 | 61.0–71.1 |
| E | 23–29 | 58.4–73.7 |
| F | 42 min. | 106.7 min. |
| G | 105–130 | 266.7–330.2 |
| H | 30–45 | 76.2–114.3 |
| I | 33–43 | 83.8–109.2 |
| J | 10–14 | 25.4–35.6 |
| K | 6–16 | 15.2–40.6 |
| L | 20–26 | 50.8–66.0 |
| M | 12–15 | 30.5–38.1 |
| N | 117–148 | 297.2–375.9 |
| O | 45–61 | 114.3–154.9 |
| P | 30–45 | 76.2–114.3 |
| Q | 12–18 | 30.5–45.7 |
| R | 29–30 | 73.7–76.2 |
| S | 22–32 | 55.9–81.3 |

Fig. 1  Executive desk/visitor seating.

## PRIVATE OFFICES

**Executive Workstation**

| | in | cm |
|---|---|---|
| A | 77–88 | 195.6–223.5 |
| B | 30 | 76.2 |
| C | 46–58 | 116.8–147.3 |
| D | 22–28 | 55.9–71.1 |
| E | 24–30 | 61.0–91.4 |
| F | 24–28 | 61.0–71.1 |
| G | 2–3 | 5.1–7.6 |
| H | 20–22 | 50.8–55.9 |
| I | 48–60 | 121.9–152.4 |
| J | 92–116 | 233.7–294.6 |
| K | 36–42 | 91.4–106.7 |
| L | 6–9 | 15.2–22.9 |
| M | 24 | 61.0 |
| N | 42–60 | 106.7–152.4 |
| O | 36–48 | 91.4–121.9 |
| P | 57–78 | 144.8–198.1 |
| Q | 33–48 | 83.8–121.9 |
| R | 12–18 | 30.5–45.7 |
| S | 21–30 | 53.3–76.2 |
| T | 24–32 | 61.0–81.3 |

**Fig. 2   Circular executive desk.**

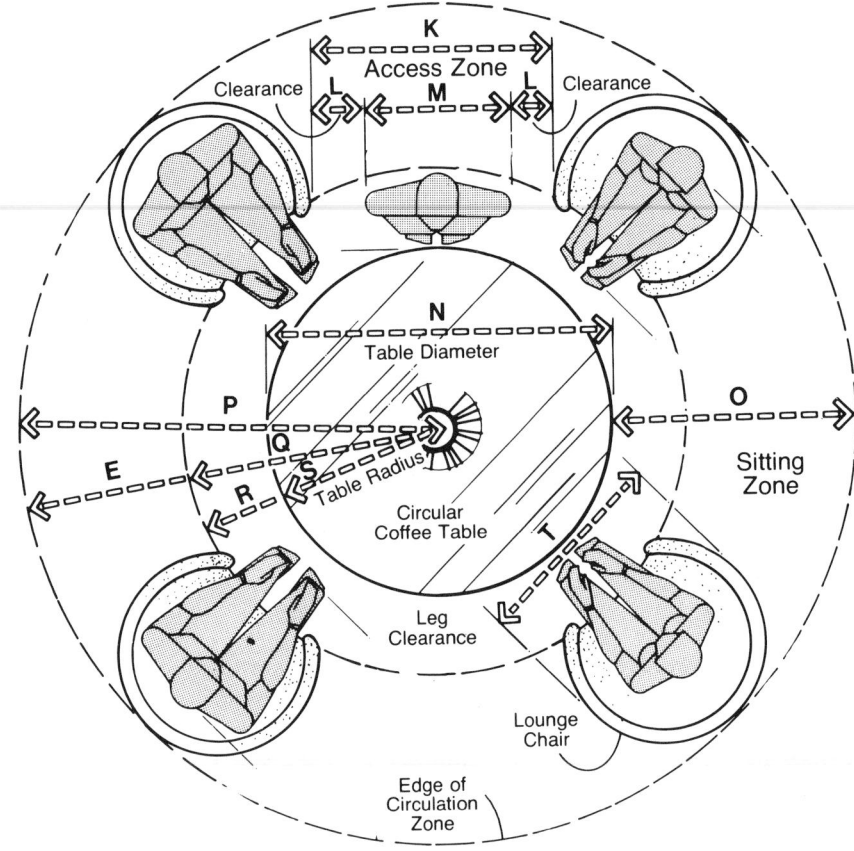

**Fig. 3   Circular lounge grouping.**

Fig. 4   12 ft × 15 ft, 180 ft².

Fig. 5   14 ft × 12 ft, 168 ft².

Fig. 6   13 ft × 12 ft, 156 ft².

Fig. 7   12 ft × 13 ft, 156 ft².

Fig. 8   9 ft × 15 ft, 135 ft².

Fig. 9   11 ft × 14 ft, 154 ft².

Fig. 10   10 ft × 11 ft, 110 ft².

Fig. 11   9 ft × 12 ft, 108 ft².

# PRIVATE OFFICES

**Planning Data: Typical Room Arrangements**

Fig. 12  16 ft × 21 ft, 336 ft².

Fig. 13  12 ft × 23 ft, 276 ft².

Fig. 14  15 ft × 18 ft, 270 ft².

Fig. 15  12 ft × 24 ft, 288 ft².

Fig. 16  12 ft × 16 ft, 192 ft².

Fig. 17  12 ft × 20 ft, 240 ft².

The private offices illustrated in Figs. 12 to 17 reflect middle to senior management functional, as well as status, requirements. Each office layout should be carefully reviewed with the client to ensure that all programmatic functions have been met. Offices of this size do not easily accommodate an independent conference function.

**Fig. 18** 14 ft × 22 ft, 308 ft².

**Fig. 19** 14 ft × 28 ft, 392 ft².

**Fig. 20** 19 ft × 33 ft, 627 ft².

**Fig. 21** Custom architectural woodwork, or "built-ins," is often required for executive offices. These architectural working drawings reflect the custom design of a storage wall for a partner in a law office. Careful analysis shows the incorporation of file, book, and coat storage within a floor-to-ceiling mahogany wood unit.

ADJUSTABLE PLYWD. SHELVES
W/MAHOGANY VENEER & HARDWD.
EDGES. DRILLED HOLES 1" O.C.
ON SIDE PANELS

PROVIDE 3/4" DRILL HOLE FOR
LIGHTING CONDUIT

FIXED SHELF W/2" HARDWD EDGE
(TO CONCEAL LIGHT)

ALCKO LITTLE INCH LIGHT FIXTURE
NO. 5F 50 · CONCEAL CORD BEHIND
TACK SURFACE
PROVIDE LOCK FOR CLOSET
1/2" HOMOSOTE TACK SURFACE
WRAPPED IN FABRIC
W/WIRE CHASE BEHIND
WOOD BLOCKING AS REQD
CONT. 3/4" JG MOLD
PAINTED TO MATCH
MILLWORK FIN.
FINGER ROUTE

MAHOGANY VENEER
WOOD END PANEL

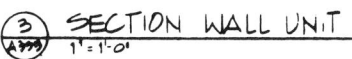

③ SECTION WALL UNIT
Ⓐ339  1" = 1'-0"

1/2" REVEAL AT CEILING (TYP.)

2'-0"

MAHOGANY VENEER
COUNTERTOP & ADJUSTABLE
SHELF W/HRDWD. EDGES

ALL EXPOSED INTERIOR
SURFACES TO BE MAHOGANY
VENEER.

BLOCKING AS REQ'D

④ SECTION OPEN SHELVING UNIT
Ⓐ339  1 1/2" = 1'-0"

1/2" REVEAL AT CEILING
SEE EDGE DETAIL A

(6) ADJUSTABLE PLYWD
SHELVES W/MAHOGANY
VENEER & HARDWD EDGES

SHIM TO WALL AS REQ'D

BLOCKING AS REQ'D

2'-1"

SHELF TO ALIGN
W/FIXED SHELF WITH
TACK LIGHT DRILL
HOLES AS REQ'D
SPACE 2" ON CENTER

SHELF TO ALIGN W/TOP
OF WORKTOP DRILL
HOLES AS REQ'D SPACE
2" ON CENTER

ALL EXPOSED
SURFACES TO BE
MAHOGANY VENEER

2 1/2"

MAHOGANY VENEER ON 2" BASE

⑦ SECTION - A UNIT SPECIAL
Ⓐ339  1" = 1'-0"

COUNTERTOP W/TYP.
HRDWD. EDGE DETAIL C

TOUCH LATCH
HARDWARE

3/4" PLYWD. W/HARDWD EDGES
FULL OVERLAP FLUSH DOORS
W/MAHOGANY VENEER HINGES:
OFFSET CONCEALED PIVOT TYPE
PROVIDE LOCKS ON FACE.
ADJUSTABLE MAHOGANY VENEER
SHELF ON METAL PINS. PROVIDE
HOLES 8" O.C. ON SIDEWALLS

BLOCKING AS REQ'D

MAHOGANY VENEER
ON 3/4" PLYWD. W/CLEAR
LACQUER FINISH ON
ALL EXPOSED SURFACES

⑤ SECTION THRU BASE CABINET
Ⓐ339  1 1/2" = 1'-0"

**Fig. 22** These details represent typical vertical sections taken through various storage components for the partner wall unit shown in Fig. 21. Careful attention must be given to integration of electronic equipment, electrical wiring, and task lighting.

LEGAL ASSISTANT WORKWALL

PARTNER'S WORKWALL @ KEYBOARD TRAY

PARTNER'S WORKWALL

**Fig. 23** In many instances, the utilization of standard wood moldings can enhance the overall appearance of an otherwise relatively simple workwall unit. Other cost-saving devices illustrated here are the application of a wood panel to a standard metal file and the use of a fabric-wrapped tack board. The incorporation of an undercabinet task light is almost always required.

**Fig. 24** These plan oblique drawings provide detailed design information to both client and architectural woodwork contractor. These drawings are particularly helpful when the office project for which these wall units are intended consists of many offices, and each office is to be customized within certain constraints.

# PRIVATE OFFICES

## Credenzas

**SECTION**

**SECTION**

**SECTION**

**Fig. 25**

Many private offices require the detailing of custom credenzas and storage units. The sophistication and complexity of such details can significantly influence the budget for the space as well as the time of installation. Figure 25 represents a "high-end" approach, while Fig. 26 is more appropriate for offices with a moderate budget.

New electronic technologies, together with the advent and proliferation of the microcomputer and the availability of inexpensive packaged software, have changed the complexion of the office workplace. The ergonomic considerations related to this new work environment have necessitated a re-evaluation of the traditional interface between the seated office worker and his or her workplace. It is essential that the design of this electronic workstation be responsive to human factors in order to avoid physical discomfort for the user. The location of the keyboard, angle of the visual display terminal, adjustability of the chair, field of vision, provisions for back support, and height of the seat above the floor are a few of the considerations in the design process.

This page and the following pages provide a variety of anthropometric and ergonomic planning data and details for use as reference in the design of the electronic workstation.

Figure 1 illustrates guidelines for use in establishing preliminary design assumptions for a workstation display console. Since the types of displays and the nature of the tasks associated with those displays can vary considerably, Fig. 1 cannot be taken too literally. The configuration shown, however, is fairly representational. Certain basic factors should be noted anthropometrically. The use of an adjustable chair will permit the eye height of the seated viewer to be raised or lowered to view the display, as may be required depending on body size. An adjustment range between 15 and 18 in, or 38.1 and 45.7 cm, should be adequate to accommodate the eye height sitting requirements of about 90 percent of all viewers. Adjustability, however, will be of little value if the vertical distance between the underside of the desk and the floor is insufficient to accommodate the knee height and thigh clearance when the seat is adjusted to the appropriate position. If such distance is not less than 26.5 in, or 67.3 cm, the majority of viewers will be accommodated.

The location of the top of the display should align with the standard sight line for optimum viewing conditions. Since the eye and the head can rotate within certain limitations and, in so doing, increase the area that can be scanned, displays can be located above the standard sight line when absolutely necessary. It should also be noted that the more perpendicular the normal sight line is to the display plane, the greater the viewing comfort. Accordingly, consideration should be given to sloping the display plane since the normal sight line is about 15° below the horizontal.

*Stature* is the vertical distance from the floor to the top of the head, measured while the subject stands erect, looking straight ahead.

*Elbow height* is the distance measured vertically from the floor to the depression formed at the elbow where the forearm meets the upper arm.

*Eye height* is the vertical distance from the floor to the inner corner of the eye, measured with the subject looking straight ahead and standing erect.

*Sitting height erect* is the vertical distance from the sitting surface to the top of the head with the subject sitting erect.

*Sitting height normal* is the vertical distance from the sitting surface to the top of the head, measured with the subject sitting relaxed.

*Eye height* is the vertical distance from the inner corner of the eye to the sitting surface.

*Shoulder height* is the distance taken vertically from the sitting surface to a point on the shoulder midway between the neck and acromion.

*Shoulder breadth* is the maximum horizontal distance across the deltoid muscles.

*Elbow to elbow* is the distance across the lateral surfaces of the elbows measured with elbows flexed and resting lightly against the body with the forearms extended horizontally.

*Hip breadth* is the breadth of the body as measured across the widest portion of the hips. Note that a hip breadth measurement can also be taken with the subject in a standing position, in which case the definition would be the maximum breadth of the lower torso.

*Elbow rest height* is the height from the top of the sitting surface to the bottom of the tip of the elbow.

*Thigh clearance* is the distance taken vertically from a sitting surface to the top of the thigh at the point where the thigh and the abdomen intersect.

*Knee height* is the vertical distance from the floor to the midpoint of the kneecap.

*Popliteal height* is the distance, taken vertically, from the floor to the underside of the portion of the thigh just behind the knee while the subject is seated with body erect. The knees and ankles are usually perpendicular, with the bottom of the thigh and the back of the knees barely touching the sitting surface.

*Buttock-popliteal length* is the horizontal distance from the rearmost surface of the buttock to the back of the lower leg.

*Buttock-knee length* is the horizontal distance from the rearmost surface of the buttocks to the front of the kneecaps.

*Buttock-toe length* is the horizontal distance from the rearmost surface of the buttocks to the tip of the toe.

*Buttock-heel length* is the horizontal distance from the base of the heel to a wall against which the subject sits erect with his leg maximally extended forward along the sitting surface. This is sometimes referred to as buttock-leg length.

*Vertical reach* is the height above the sitting surface of the tip of the middle finger when the arm, hand, and fingers are extended vertically.

*Vertical grip reach* is usually measured from the floor to the top of a bar grasped in the right hand while the subject stands erect and the hand within which the bar is grasped is raised as high as it can be conveniently without experiencing discomfort or strain.

*Side arm reach* is the distance from the center line of the body to the outside surface of a bar grasped in the right hand while the subject stands erect and the arm is conveniently outstretched horizontally without experiencing discomfort or strain.

*Thumb tip reach* is the distance from the wall to the tip of the thumb measured with the subject's shoulders against the wall, his arm extended forward, and his index finger touching the tip of his thumb.

*Maximum body depth* is the horizontal distance between the most anterior point on the body to the most posterior. Anterior points are usually located on the chest or abdomen while the posterior points are usually found in the buttock or shoulder region.

*Maximum body breadth* is the maximum distance, including arms, across the body.

| | in | cm |
|---|---|---|
| A | 16–18 | 40.6–45.7 |
| B | 16 min. | 40.6 min. |
| C | 18 min. | 45.7 min. |
| D | 15–18 adjust. | 38.1–45.7 |
| E | 26.5 min. | 67.3 min. |
| F | 30 | 76.2 |

**Fig. 1**

# ELECTRONIC WORKSTATIONS

**Planning Data: Anthropometrics**

■ Both the work surface and the display monitors must be lowered and raised as a unit with 31.8 cm of travel.

■ The work surface must be tilted anywhere between a horizontal position to 35° below horizontal. The work surface, at its lowest setting and with a 10° tilted angle, as is common in use, must be 63.5 cm in height at its front edge.

■ The work surface must raise to a horizontal height of 104 cm, accommodating a majority of people in a standing position.

■ The monitor screens must be tiltable to any position between 15° forward of vertical and 15° back. This lets the user adjust the screen to avoid reflective glare, and it accommodates various working positions of different lines of sight.

■ Adjustment controls designed for hand operation must be located within the operator's extended reach envelope.

■ All surfaces must have matte or dull finishes. This reduces the likelihood of reflective glare.

■ The workstation must be compact and relatively easy to move through a standard 81-cm doorway.

■ No structural components shall exist which inhibit the workstation's operation by users in wheelchairs, ensuring a barrier-free workstation.

■ Service personnel must have easy access to electrical components.

■ The digitizing surface must accommodate standard European and American D size drawings.

■ Screen depth of view must allow alphanumeric characters to be viewed at an angle between 20 and 28 arc minutes.

26 4 to 33 in. (67 to 83.8 cm) maximum reach

22 5 to 27 in. (57.2 to 68.6 cm) extended reach

15 to 19 in. (38.1 to 48.3 cm) normal reach

Frequently used items within easy reach

Extra worksurface and storage area

30° — Central field of view

60° — Extended field of view, maximum symbol recognition

120° — Binocular field of view, maximum color discrimination

Screen angle adjusts 15° from vertical, in either direction

—15° — 15°—

97.5 percentile male

2.5 percentile female

Table tilts down 0° to 35°

Table/monitor height adjusts through 12.5 in. (31.8 cm) range

28.5 in. (72.4 cm)     41 in. (104.1 cm)

*The Automated Task. Square footage workstation standards for the automated task are also developed primarily according to task profile, equipment, conferencing, and privacy requirements.*

**Open**
No requirement of equipment or task for privacy, concentration

**Screened**
Privacy required for reading, working, thinking, calculating, meetings, confidential phone calls, elimination of visual and acoustical distractions

### Task Profile: Data Retrieval.

□ Paper, material, or information processed, analyzed, and/or maintained.
□ Multiple reference sources may be used on a task.
□ Reference materials used frequently.
□ Limited volume of supplies and permanent records kept at the workspace.
□ Electronic equipment may be used for easy reference, retrieval, keeping records current, and maintaining data and records.
□ Additional equipment such as microfilm viewers may be required.
□ Ability to see and hear co-workers may be desirable.
□ Tasks may also require screening for concentration.

| | |
|---|---|
| No | Guest chair |
| 45 x 45 | Primary work surface |
| 30 x 45 | Secondary work surface |
| (76 x 114 cm) | |
| 3–4 | File drawers |
| 0–2 | Shelves |

**56 sq. ft.**

### Task Profile: Shared Tasks.

□ Paper, material, or information processed, analzyed, and/or maintained.
□ More than one task may be performed concurrently.
□ More than one operator uses same equipment.
□ Multiple reference sources may be used on a task.
□ Reference materials used may be used frequently.
□ Electronic equipment may be used for easy reference, inputting/maintaining data and records, retrieval, keeping records current.
□ Storage requirements vary according to task.

| | |
|---|---|
| No | Guest chair |
| 30 x 45 | Primary work surface |
| 30 x 60 | Secondary work surface |
| (76 x 152 cm) | |
| 1–2 | File drawers |
| 0–4 | Shelves |

**81 sq. ft.**

### Task Profile: Administrative Specialist/Secretarial.

□ Paper, material, or information processed, analyzed, and/or maintained.
□ More than one task may be performed concurrently.
□ Multiple reference sources may be used on a task.
□ Reference materials used frequently.
□ Electronic equipment may be used for easy reference, retrieval, keeping records current, inputting/maintaining data and records.
□ If supervising, ability to see subordinates may be desirable to direct activities.
□ If monitoring, visual access may be desirable.
□ Moderate amount of storage required at the workspace, that is, casework, client accounts, supplies.

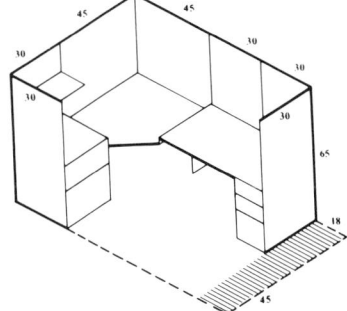

| | |
|---|---|
| No | Guest chair |
| 45 x 45 | Primary work surface |
| 30 x 60 | Secondary work surface |
| 3–4 | File drawers |
| 1–2 | Shelves |

**64 sq. ft.**

## ELECTRONIC WORKSTATIONS

| The Automated Task | Open | Screened |
|---|---|---|
| | No requirement of equipment or task for privacy, concentration | Privacy required for reading, working, thinking, calculating, meetings, confidential phone calls, elimination of visual and acoustical distractions |

### Task Profile: Administrative Specialist/Secretarial (+ Guest).

☐ Paper, material, or information processed, analyzed, and/or maintained.

☐ More than one task performed concurrently.

☐ Multiple reference sources used on a task.

☐ Reference materials used frequently.

☐ Limited volume of supplies and permanent records kept at the workspace.

☐ Electronic equipment may be used for easy reference, retrieval, keeping records current

☐ Tasks are complex enough to require concentration.

☐ Extensive use of telephone and additional equipment such as desk-top printer and micro-film viewer may be required.

☐ Need to see and hear co-workers is secondary priority.

☐ Limited conferencing required at workspace.

☐ If supervising, ability to see subordinates may be desirable to direct activities.

☐ If monitoring, visual access may be desirable.

| 1 | Guest chair |
|---|---|
| 45 x 45 | Primary work surface |
| 30 x 60 | Secondary work surface |
| 3–4 | File drawers |
| 1–2 | Shelves |

**80 sq. ft.**

### Task Profile: Word Processing.

☐ Time divided among administrative, processing paper, material, or information.

☐ More than one task may be performed concurrently.

☐ Multiple reference sources may be used on a task.

☐ Reference materials moderate but used frequently.

☐ Limited storage primarily for supplies.

☐ Ability to see and hear co-workers or subordinates is desirable.

☐ Typewriter and/or electronic equipment may be used to expedite processing and administrative tasks, for example, VDT, printer, transcriber, OCR, microfilm viewer, separate disk drives.

| No | Guest chair |
|---|---|
| 45 x 45 | Primary work surface |
| (114 x 114 cm) | |
| 30 x 45 | Secondary work surface |
| (76 x 114 cm) | |
| 3–4 | File drawers |
| 1–2 | Shelves |

**67 sq. ft.**

### Task Profile: Word Processing (+ Guest).

☐ Time divided among administrative, processing paper, material, or information, and limited conferencing at workspace.

☐ More than one task may be performed concurrently.

☐ Multiple reference sources may be used on a task.

☐ Reference materials moderate but used frequently.

☐ Limited storage primarily for supplies.

☐ Typewriter and/or electronic equipment (VDT, printer, and so on) may be used to expedite processing and administrative tasks.

☐ Tasks are complex enough to require concentration for analysis, or heavy equipment operations require acoustical screening.

☐ Work surface needed for organization of work.

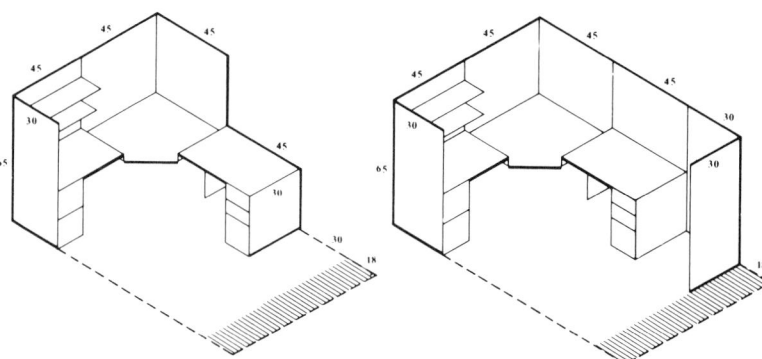

| 1 | Guest chair |
|---|---|
| 45 x 45 | Primary work surface |
| 30 x 45 | Secondary work surface |
| 3–4 | File drawers |
| 1–2 | Shelves |

**86 sq. ft.**

| The Automated Task | Open | Screened |
|---|---|---|
| | No requirement of equipment or task for privacy, concentration | Privacy required for reading, working, thinking, calculating, meetings, confidential phone calls, elimination of visual and acoustical distractions |

### Task Profile: Technical/Systems Analyst/ Programmer.
- Time divided among administrative, processing paper, material, or information, and limited conferencing at workspace.
- More than one task may be performed concurrently.
- Multiple reference sources may be used on a task.
- Reference materials may be extensive and used frequently.
- Ability to see and hear co-workers or subordinates desirable.
- Typewriter and electronic equipment (VDT, printer, and so on) may be used to expedite processing and administrative tasks.
- Moderate to extensive amount of storage required at the workspace for manuals, binders, computer printouts, coding sheets, supplies, permanent files, reference materials.

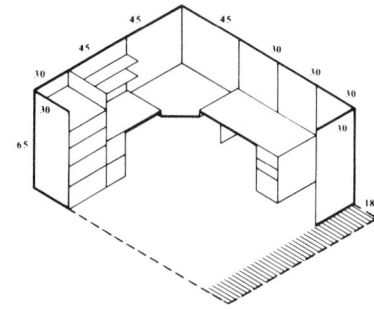

| 1 | Guest chair |
| 45 x 45 | Primary work surface |
| 30 x 60 | Secondary work surface |
| (76 x 152 cm) | |
| 6–8 | File drawers |
| 3–5 | Shelves |

**128 sq. ft.**

### Task Profile: Administrative/Managerial.
- Extensive conferencing at individual workspace.
- Analysis of reports, computerized materials, and so on.
- Varied tasks or projects performed simultaneously on an ongoing basis.
- Large amounts of storage extensively used.
- Storage for client/project files, reference manuals, documentation, correspondence.
- Telephone used extensively.
- Supervision of subordinates almost universal.
- Electronic equipment accommodation is secondary priority, used primarily for communication/electronic mail, scheduling.

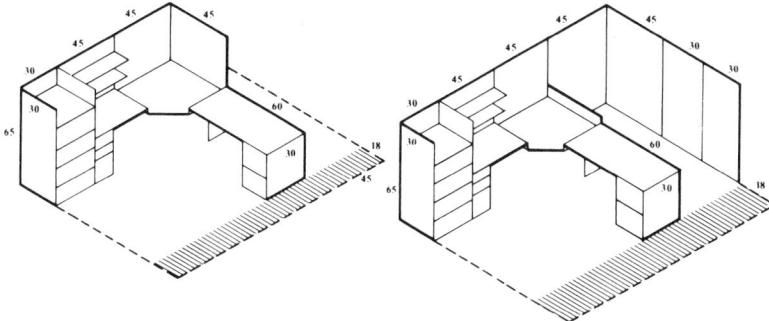

| 2 | Guest chair |
| 45 x 45 | Primary work surface |
| 30 x 60 | Secondary work surface |
| (76 x 152 cm) | |
| 5–8 | File drawers |
| 3–5 | Shelves |

**154 sq. ft.**

### Task Profile: Administrative/Total Enclosure.
- Extensive conferencing at individual workspace.
- Analysis of reports, computerized materials, and so on.
- Varied tasks on projects performed simultaneously on an ongoing basis.
- Large amounts of storage extensively used.
- Storage for client/project files, reference manuals, documentation, correspondence.
- Telephone used extensively.
- Supervision of subordinates almost universal.
- Electronic equipment accommodation is secondary priority, used primarily for communication/electronic mail, scheduling.
- Subject matter of job responsibilities requires confidentiality.

| 2 | Guest chair |
| 30 x 60 | Primary work surface |
| 20 sq ft | Secondary work surface |
| (15 sq m) | |
| 5–8 | File drawers |
| 3–5 | Shelves |

**150 sq. ft.**

A PLAN/SECTION TRADING DESK TYPE 'A'

B PLAN · 20TH FLOOR TRADING ROOM

C FRONT VIEW - TRADING DESK TYPE 'A'

246   Fig. 2   Technologically and electronically complex trading desks must be ergonomically correct in every respect. With little, if any, margin for error when designing and detailing multiple workstations of this type, a full-size mockup is always required.

**A** ERGONOMIC FACTORS - PLAN

- CONVEYOR BELT
- PHONE CONSOLE
- MODULAR OPEN STORAGE
- PERSONAL VDT
- SHARED VDT
- PERSONAL VDT
- WORK SURFACE
- KEYBOARDS
- FILE
- 6'-0"
- 6'-0"
- 6'-0"

**C** ELEVATION/SECTION

- CONVEYOR BELT
- 1'-2"
- 2'-2"
- VDT
- BEVELED EDGE
- ELECTRICAL RACEWAY
- ERGONOMIC CHAIR

**B** TYPICAL PLAN LAYOUT

- 12'-0"
- 12'-3 3/4" FINISHED ENDS
- CONVEYOR BELT

**DD** SECTION THRU TYPICAL DESK

- PLASTIC LAMINATE
- WIRE SCREEN ON UNDERSIDE OF GRILLES AT CONVEYOR DESKS
- INTERIOR PAINTED FLAT BLACK
- GROMMETS
- PLASTIC LAMINATE
- PACKER
- WIREMOLD BY ELECTRICIAN
- CORD SLOTS PAINTED EDGE
- V-GRADE PLASTIC LAMINATE
- 2x4 FRAMING
- AIR SLOTS PAINTED
- 4" DIAMETER 12 GAUGE STEEL PIPE W/ CHROME FINISH
- 3/8"x 1" STUD WELDED TO BOTTOM PLATE - HOLE TAPPED IN FLOOR
- BACK PANEL BEYOND
- 5 3/8"
- 3/8"
- 4 11/16"
- 4 11/16"
- 3 3/4"
- 3"
- 3" 3" 1 1/2"
- 13 7/16"
- 4 1/8"
- 19 7/8"
- 14 1/8"
- 1 1/2"
- 6 3/4"
- 18"
- 18°
- 1"
- 1 1/2" 1"
- 26 1/4"

① IPC TELEPHONE TURRET
CUT OUT · 2'-6½" × 8½"
③ REUTERS CRT · 15¾"
W × 9½" D × 12¾" H
④ ERICSON INTERCOM · CUT
OUT · 9" × 4½" HOLDER
11'9/16" × 5'3/16"

PLASTIC LAMINATE TYP.

LIGHT OILED OAK

REMOVABLE TOP IN CEN-
TER SECTION

BUTT JOINTS W/ QUIRK
REVEALS TYP.

PLASTIC LAMINATE TYP.

LIGHT OILED OAK

**Ⓐ** PLAN OF TREASURY TRADING TABLE

LIGHT OILED OAK
CHROME METAL
PLASTIC LAMIN.
LIGHT OILED OAK
CHROME METAL

**Ⓑ** PARTIAL ELEVATION

LAY-IN SPEAKER GRILL

NON-GLARE GLASS

SPEAKER

CRT

SPEAKER JACK BOX BY ELEC. CONTRACTOR

DICTATION SLIDE 1'-6"

DRAWERS 2'-3"

SURFACE ATD 'J' BOXES AS REQD BY ELEC CONTRACTOR

PENDAFLEX DRAWER 2'-3"

**ⒸⒸ** SECTION

IPC TELEPHONE TURRET

ERICSON INT-ERCOM · HAND-SET HOLDER & CABLE REEL

'J' BOXES AS REQD BY ELEC CONTRACTOR

STORAGE CABIN-ET W/ FIXED SHELF

**ⒹⒹ** SECTION

**Fig. 1  Square conference table.**

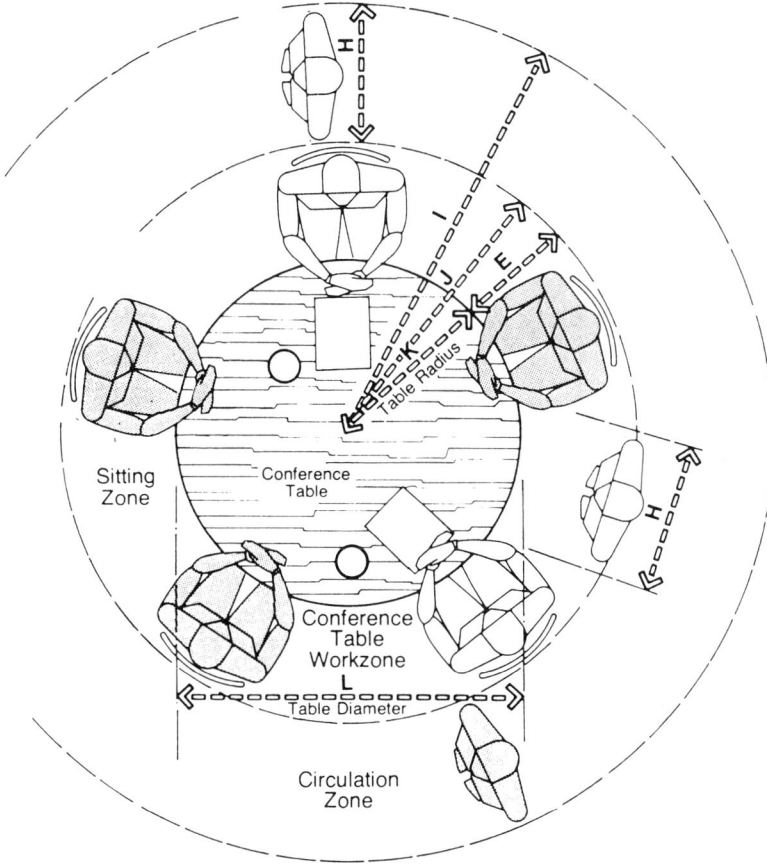

**Fig. 2  Circular conference table.**

Consideration must be given to clearances and circulation around the larger conference table, as indicated in Figs. 1 and 2. A minimum of 48 in, or 121.9 cm, is suggested from the edge of the table to the wall or nearest obstruction. This dimension under ordinary circumstance allows for a circulation zone beyond the sitting zone of 30 to 36 in, or 76.2 to 91.4 cm, based upon a maximum body breadth measurement of the larger person. The greater dimension is recommended to allow for the chair in a pulled-out position.

The actual dimensions of the conference table are a function of the number of people to be seated. The square table illustrated in Fig. 1 provides for eight people, with each side ranging from 54 to 60 in, or 137.2 to 152.4 cm. The larger dimension is more appropriate to accommodate people of larger body size and to allow for a more generous work zone for each person. This translates into 30 in, or 76.2 cm, per person, which constitutes a comfortable perimeter allocation. The circular table shown in Fig. 2 comfortably accommodates five people while allowing for a 30-in, or 76.2-cm, access zone between chairs. To accommodate both sitting zone and circulation zone, a space with a radius ranging from 72 to 81 in, or 182.9 to 205.7 cm, must be provided.

|   | in | cm |
|---|------|------------|
| A | 48–60 | 121.9–152.4 |
| B | 4–6 | 10.2–15.2 |
| C | 20–24 | 50.8–61.0 |
| D | 6–10 | 15.2–25.4 |
| E | 18–24 | 45.7–61.0 |
| F | 30–36 | 76.2–91.4 |
| G | 54–60 | 137.2–152.4 |
| H | 30 | 76.2 |
| I | 72–81 | 182.9–205.7 |
| J | 42–51 | 106.7–129.5 |
| K | 24–27 | 61.0–68.6 |
| L | 48–54 | 121.9–137.2 |

## CONFERENCE ROOMS

**Planning Data: Table Sizes and Seating Capacities**

Round conference tables offer the advantages of intimacy, "equality," and compactness. On the other hand, if status is an issue, or if one wall within the space is an audiovisual wall, this table shape can be less than satisfactory. The same problems can arise with a square conference table. In both instances, however, the total seating around each table shape must be viewed in the context of chair size, chair spacing, and tasks to be performed at the table.

## ROUND TABLES

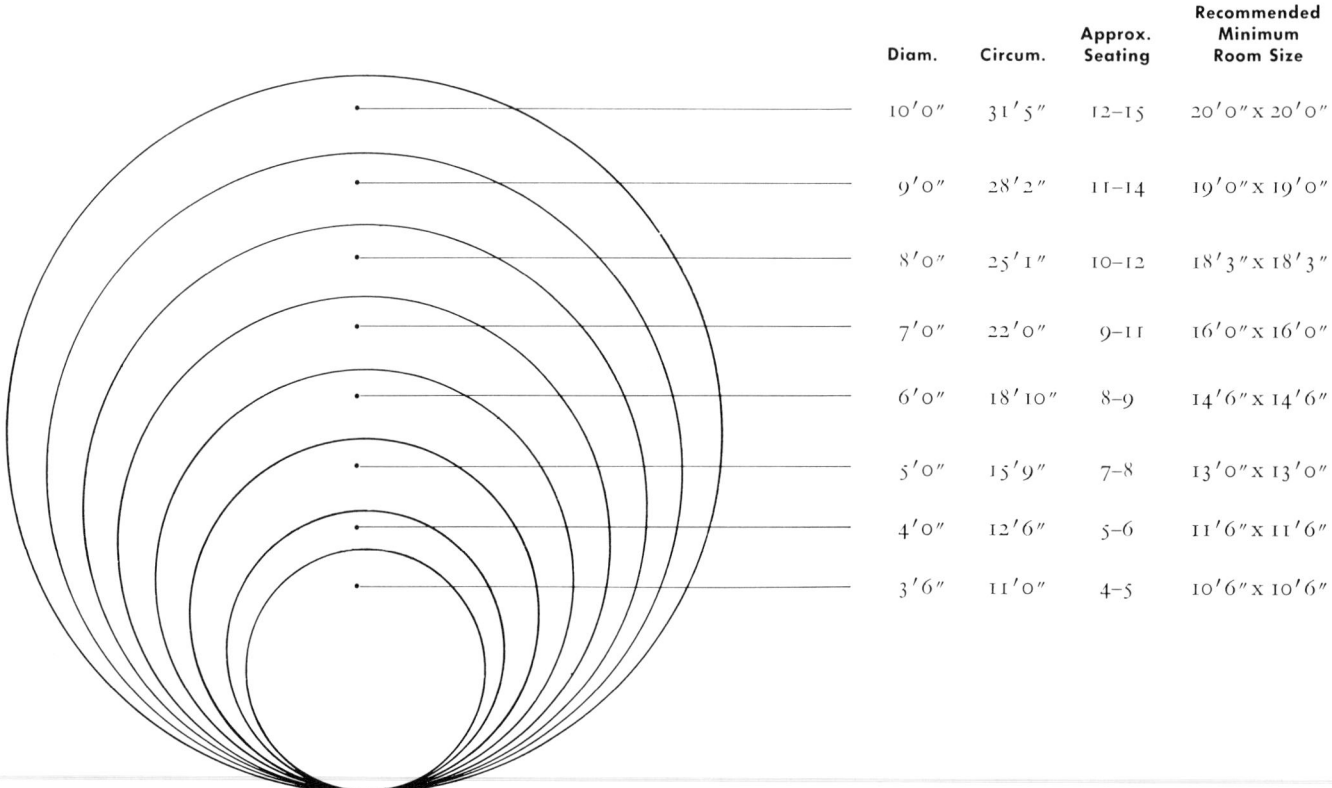

| Diam. | Circum. | Approx. Seating | Recommended Minimum Room Size |
|---|---|---|---|
| 10′0″ | 31′5″ | 12–15 | 20′0″ x 20′0″ |
| 9′0″ | 28′2″ | 11–14 | 19′0″ x 19′0″ |
| 8′0″ | 25′1″ | 10–12 | 18′3″ x 18′3″ |
| 7′0″ | 22′0″ | 9–11 | 16′0″ x 16′0″ |
| 6′0″ | 18′10″ | 8–9 | 14′6″ x 14′6″ |
| 5′0″ | 15′9″ | 7–8 | 13′0″ x 13′0″ |
| 4′0″ | 12′6″ | 5–6 | 11′6″ x 11′6″ |
| 3′6″ | 11′0″ | 4–5 | 10′6″ x 10′6″ |

## SQUARE TABLES

| W | L | Approx. Seating | Recommended Minimum Room Size |
|---|---|---|---|
| 5′0″ | 5′0″ | 8–12 | 13′0″ x 13′0″ |
| 4′6″ | 4′6″ | 4–8 | 12′0″ x 12′0″ |
| 4′0″ | 4′0″ | 4–8 | 11′6″ x 11′6″ |
| 3′6″ | 3′6″ | 4 | 10′6″ x 10′6″ |
| 3′0″ | 3′0″ | 4 | 9′0″ x 9′0″ |

Rectangular and boat-shaped conference tables lend themselves toward formal settings where status and hierarchy are important. Both table shapes are also more suitable in a room where an audiovisual wall is placed at one end of the space, or where speakers are making presentations. The boat-shaped table also offers greater visibility of others seated at the table, as well as ease of circulation around its perimeter.

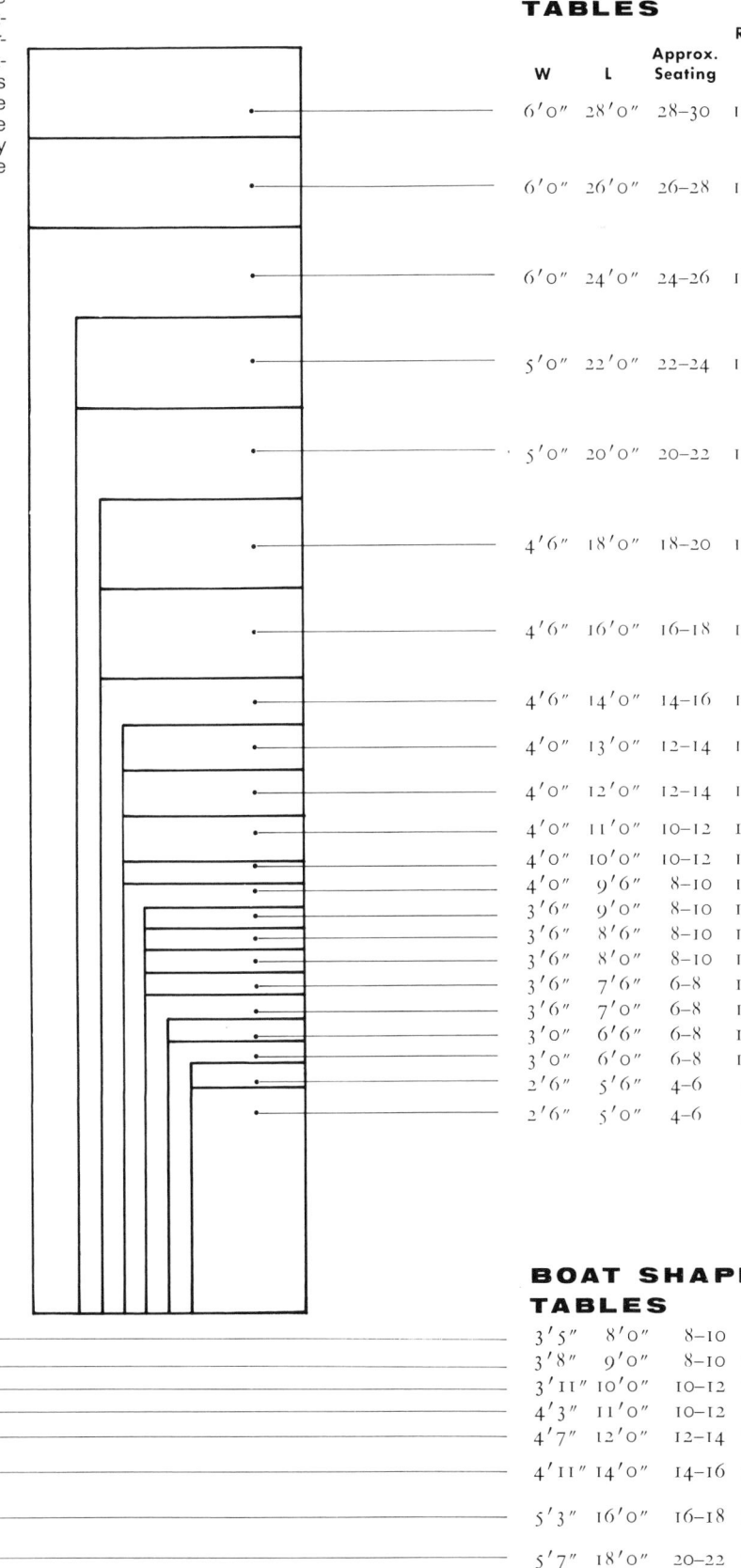

## RECTANGULAR TABLES

| W | L | Approx. Seating | Recommended Minimum Room Size |
|---|---|---|---|
| 6'0" | 28'0" | 28–30 | 18'0" x 40'0" |
| 6'0" | 26'0" | 26–28 | 18'0" x 38'0" |
| 6'0" | 24'0" | 24–26 | 18'0" x 36'0" |
| 5'0" | 22'0" | 22–24 | 15'0" x 32'0" |
| 5'0" | 20'0" | 20–22 | 15'0" x 30'0" |
| 4'6" | 18'0" | 18–20 | 13'6" x 27'0" |
| 4'6" | 16'0" | 16–18 | 13'6" x 25'0" |
| 4'6" | 14'0" | 14–16 | 13'6" x 23'0" |
| 4'0" | 13'0" | 12–14 | 12'0" x 21'0" |
| 4'0" | 12'0" | 12–14 | 12'0" x 20'0" |
| 4'0" | 11'0" | 10–12 | 12'0" x 19'0" |
| 4'0" | 10'0" | 10–12 | 12'0" x 17'0" |
| 4'0" | 9'6" | 8–10 | 12'0" x 16'6" |
| 3'6" | 9'0" | 8–10 | 10'6" x 16'0" |
| 3'6" | 8'6" | 8–10 | 10'6" x 15'6" |
| 3'6" | 8'0" | 8–10 | 10'6" x 15'0" |
| 3'6" | 7'6" | 6–8 | 10'6" x 14'6" |
| 3'6" | 7'0" | 6–8 | 10'6" x 14'0" |
| 3'0" | 6'6" | 6–8 | 10'0" x 13'6" |
| 3'0" | 6'0" | 6–8 | 10'0" x 13'0" |
| 2'6" | 5'6" | 4–6 | 9'0" x 12'6" |
| 2'6" | 5'0" | 4–6 | 9'0" x 12'0" |

## BOAT SHAPED TABLES

| W | L | Approx. Seating | Recommended Minimum Room Size |
|---|---|---|---|
| 3'5" | 8'0" | 8–10 | 10'0" x 15'0" |
| 3'8" | 9'0" | 8–10 | 11'0" x 16'0" |
| 3'11" | 10'0" | 10–12 | 12'0" x 17'0" |
| 4'3" | 11'0" | 10–12 | 13'0" x 19'0" |
| 4'7" | 12'0" | 12–14 | 14'0" x 21'0" |
| 4'11" | 14'0" | 14–16 | 15'0" x 23'0" |
| 5'3" | 16'0" | 16–18 | 16'0" x 26'0" |
| 5'7" | 18'0" | 20–22 | 17'0" x 29'0" |
| 6'0" | 20'0" | 20–24 | 18'0" x 32'0" |

# CONFERENCE ROOMS
**Planning Data: Table Sizes and Seating Capacities**

## CONFERENCE/MEETING ROOMS

### Solid Conference
For 20 people

4-30"x72" tables
2-30"x 60" tables

### Race Track
For 26 people

6-30"x72" tables
4-30" wide crescents

### Trapezoid/Round
For 12 people

6-30"x30"x30"x 60" tables

### V-Shape
For 20 people

### Boat Shape
For 28 people

## BANQUET ROOMS

### 60" diameter tables
Capacity: 180 people

| Table Size | Capacity | Centerline Spread |
|---|---|---|
| 48" dia. | 6 persons | 7'5" |
| 54" dia. | 6-8 persons | 7'10" |
| 60" dia. | 8-10 persons | 8'3" |
| 66" dia. | 10 persons | 8'8" |
| 72" dia. | 10-12 persons | 9'1" |

### 30" x 96" tables
Capacity: 180 people

| Table Size | Capacity |
|---|---|
| 30"x48" | 4-6 persons |
| 30"x60" | 6 persons |
| 30"x72" | 8 persons |
| 30"x96" | 10 persons |

### 18" x 72" classroom style tables
Capacity: 162 people

| Table Size | Capacity |
|---|---|
| 18"x60" | 2 persons |
| 18"x72" | 3 persons |
| 18"x96" | 4 persons |

Fig. 3   These conference tables are useful in making initial space planning allocations.

# CONFERENCE ROOMS

**Planning Data: Table Sizes and Seating Capacities**

Seats 8, 323 ft²

Seats 12, 324 ft²

Seats 12, 484 ft²

Seats 12, 532 ft²

Seats 50, 1058 ft²

**Fig. 4** These drawings provide the designer with a variety of conference room sizes, table shapes, floor areas, and seating capacities. They are useful in client discussions and in making preliminary area allocations. Chair size and circulation areas behind the chairs will, of course, cause overall dimensions to vary.

Seats 8, 272 ft²

Seats 10, 294 ft²

Seats 12, 338 ft²

Seats 18, 480 ft²

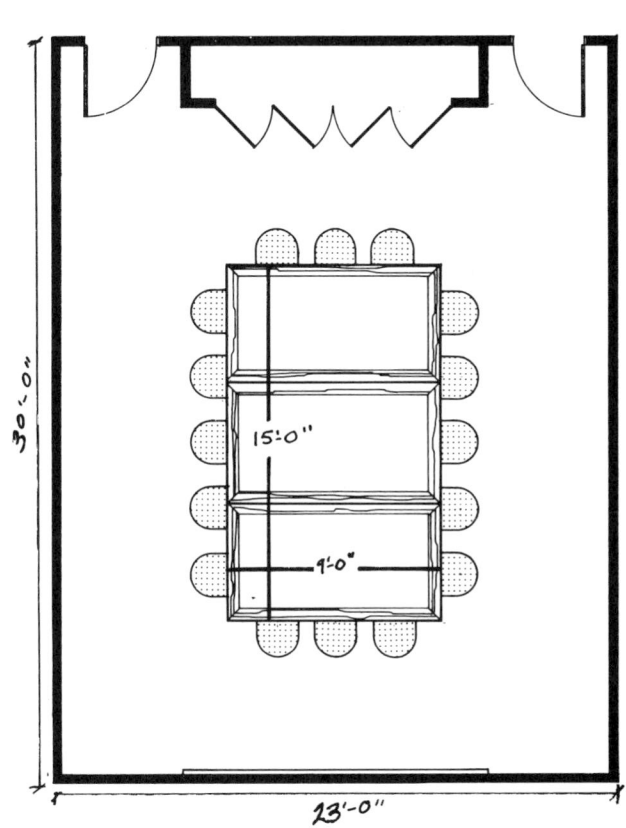

Seats 16, 690 ft²

# CONFERENCE ROOMS
## Table Base and Edge Treatments

It is important for the designer to understand and appreciate some of the important details that make up a conference table. The base treatments shown in Fig. 5 are but a few of the myriad possibilities. Perhaps even more important to consider are the finished edges of glass and wood conference tables, representative details of which are shown in Figs. 6 and 7. Other edge details could be made of marble, granite, or even leather. Fingers, hands, and arms make intimate contact with these edge details, something that should be carefully considered.

**Fig. 6    Glass edge treatment.**

**Fig. 5    Base treatment.**

**Fig. 7    Wood edge treatment.**

PLAN TABLE TOP

SECTION TABLE TOP

NOTE! FOR WELDED TAPERED CONN. PREPARE SUBSTRATE AS REQ'D
FOR WELDING. CLEAN & DRESS WELDS AS REQ'D.

PLAN-CONFERENCE TABLE

SECTION

TOP SECTION @ FIELD JOINT
CONFERENCE TABLE

TYPICAL SECTION CONFERENCE TABLE

SECTION THROUGH SUPPORT FRAME

FIELD JOINT SIDE SECTION CONFERENCE TABLE

SECTION AT CONFERENCE TABLE

SECTION AT CONFERENCE TABLE

Custom credenza units are often designed to complement the details of a conference table. They serve multiple functions, including storage, incorporation of electronic media equipment, display, and as a work surface. In addition, architectural woodwork is used to enclose existing convector covers and to frame window openings. It is important for the designer to consider providing ease of access to the heating and air-handling elements behind the woodwork, as well as allowing the appropriate flow of air.

**TYP. SECTION THRU CONF CENTER CREDENZA**

**SECTION THRU MILLWORK HEATING UNIT ENCLOSURE**

## RECEPTION AREAS

**Planning Data: Receptionist's Workstation**

Proper design of the reception area is critical in communicating an organization's desired corporate image. Reception spaces are both the first and last areas with which the visitor interacts and, accordingly, have considerable visual impact in communicating that image.

Not only must the reception space look attractive, but it must function properly as well. The two most important planning elements in this regard are the visitor's seating area and the receptionist's workstation or desk.

While most of the examples in this part are drawn from corporate interiors, the designer is urged to take into consideration the needs of special user groups who must interact with a receptionist. If small children are to communicate (or see or be seen), how high is the privacy wall? If a wheelchair-bound user is to approach the reception desk, is there room for the footrests to be accommodated? The designer must consider all user populations.

This part deals primarily with basic planning data relative to the design of a receptionist's workstation and furniture arrangements of the seating areas. Also included are related details directly from the working drawings of design firms.

For the purpose of privacy or security, the receptionist's workstation is often an area physically separated by built-in furniture and/or partitions. Figure 1 shows a counter height receptionist's workstation. While the relationship of worksurface to seat height is key, other anthropometric considerations are eye height and sitting height normal. The minimum height of the opening above the floor has been established at 78 in, or 198.1 cm. Sitting height and eye height are significant in providing unobstructed vision. Figure 2 de-

picts a desk height receptionist's workstation. The depth of the worksurface ranges from 26 to 30 in, or 66 to 76.2 cm, allowing for thumb tip reach required for the exchange of

papers and packages. Both Figs. 1 and 2 show in broken line an added counter top element often provided for security or as a visual screen of the work surface top.

**Fig. 1   Receptionist's workstation/counter height.**

| | in | cm |
|---|---|---|
| A | 40–48 | 101.6–121.9 |
| B | 24 min. | 61.0 min. |
| C | 18 | 45.7 |
| D | 22–30 | 55.9–76.2 |
| E | 78 min. | 198.1 min. |
| F | 24–27 | 61.0–68.6 |
| G | 36–39 | 91.4–99.1 |
| H | 8–9 | 20.3–22.9 |
| I | 2–4 | 5.1–10.2 |
| J | 4 | 10.2 |
| K | 44–48 | 111.8–121.9 |
| L | 34 min. | 86.4 min. |
| M | 44–48 | 111.8–121.9 |
| N | 54 | 137.2 |
| O | 26–30 | 66.0–76.2 |
| P | 24 | 61.0 |
| Q | 30 | 76.2 |
| R | 15–18 | 38.1–45.7 |
| S | 29–30 | 73.7–76.2 |
| T | 10–12 | 25.4–30.5 |
| U | 6–9 | 15.2–22.9 |
| V | 39–42 | 99.1–106.7 |

**Fig. 2   Receptionist's workstation/desk height.**

AS SHOWN @ M. 305, NO DIAMOND PATTERN @ M. 311. VERTICAL WD-2 ONLY.

11 PLAN - M. 305

12 ELEVATION

13 ELEVATION - LEFT

14 SECTION -

15 SECTION -

M. 311
M. 305

**Fig. 5**  More privacy can be achieved in the design of a reception desk when there is enclosure on three sides, as is shown here. When designing custom reception desks, it is important to fully understand the tasks that the person working there will be asked to perform, in order to provide for adequate storage, work surfaces at the appropriate height, the incorporation of electronic equipment, and task lighting.

## RECEPTION AREAS
**Reception Desk Details**

① PLAN M.308

② ELEVATION - FRONT

③ SECTION -

④ SECTION -

⑤ ELEVATION - LEFT

**Fig. 6** The reception desk shown here is designed in order to provide privacy on three sides with partial privacy on the fourth side. In this example, a right-hand typing return has been provided. Careful consideration should always be given to the height and placement of task lighting in order to ensure that the surface or task below is being lit properly. Many designers do not give this adequate thought. Overall costs of custom-designed reception desks can be reduced by integrating standard metal file compoments into the architectural woodwork.

ELEVATION

# PLAN RECEPTION DESK

½″ = 1′-0″

MARBLE TOP

MARBLE THICKNESS VARIES
SEE PLAN

WOOD BACKUP

¼″ SS DOWEL PIN
EPOXY INTO
WOOD BACKUP
AND MARBLE DIE

CAULKING BEAD

SECURE MARBLE DIE
BASE & TOP TO WOOD
FRAME WITH DOWEL PIN
& ADHESIVE

SECTION
(NO SCALE)

**Fig. 7    A larger reception desk can accommodate work surfaces on three sides, as shown here. With this type of configuration, however, the designer must be concerned with the orientation of the open side. As with all custom reception desks, the designer must anticipate the integration of wiring and electronic equipment within the architectural woodwork.**

① PLAN - RECEPTION DESK (4 - REQUIRED)
SCALE : ¾" = 1'-0"

POLISHED GRANITE COUNTER
& TRIM
3 × 39½"L FIXTURES
AMERICAN WHITE OAK
VENEER WORK SURFACES
STAINED TO MATCH ARCHITECTS
SAMPLE
2-3½"L FIXTURES (TYP. OPT. SIDE)

POLISHED STAINLESS ST'L.
GROMMETS (4) EACH DESK

UNDER COUNTER WOOD
PEDESTALS

NOTES :
ALL FINISH HARDWARE TO BE US 26
ALL PEDESTALS TO HAVE GANG LOCK. MASTER KEY ALL DESKS.
KEY PEDESTALS WITHIN INDIVIDUAL DESKS ALIKE.
ALL GRANITE TO BE : ANDES BLACK GRANITE - POLISHED
FORD N° 40004 OR EQUAL
ALL INTERIOR FABRIC TO BE 'KNOLL TEXTILES'
"MOHAVE" N° W 730/2 - CHAMPAGNE 54"W 93° MOD ACRYLIC/
70% SILK, SPECIAL ACRYLIC BACKING
LEATHER TO BE: SPACE 10002 - N° L01 BY AMERICAN LEATHER
"CAPRI" N° SKN. 2114 SPACE 13002 - N° L04 BY
AMERICAN LEATHER "CAPRI" N° SKN. 1570 - MAHOGANY
SPACE 15002 - L02 BY AMERICAN LEATHER "CAPRI" N° X410
SP. 17002 - L03 BY AMER. LEATHER - "CRYSTALANINE N° CR1806

② ELEVATION - RECEPTION DESK
SCALE: ¾" = 1'-0"

⅛" × ⅜" REVEAL (TYP.)
POLISHED GRANITE (ANDES BLACK
GRANITE) FORD N° 40004 OR EQUAL
FLUSH POLISHED STAINLESS
STEEL TRIM
LEATHER WRAPPED PANELS (TYP.)
FLUSH POLISHED STAINLESS
STEEL TRIM
POLISHED GRANITE
LEVELERS

③ ELEVATION - RECEPTION DESK
SCALE: ¾" = 1'-0"

⅛" TYP.
⅛" × ⅜" REVEAL (TYP.)
POLISHED GRANITE (ANDES BLACK
GRANITE) FORD N° 40004 OR EQUAL
FLUSH POLISHED STAINLESS STEEL
TRIM
LEATHER WRAPPED PANELS (TYP.)
BUTT JOINTS TYP.
FLUSH POLISHED STAINLESS
STEEL TRIM
POLISHED GRANITE (SAME AS ABOVE)
LEVELERS

**Fig. 8** Total privacy of the receptionist's workstation can be achieved through enclosure on all four sides. In addition to enhancing visual privacy, such a design can also provide added security and control by the addition of a door. Such a design might be particularly appropriate for a reception area where the designer might wish to control access by children.

④ ELEVATION - RECEPTION DESK
SCALE: ¾" = 1'-0"

POLISHED GRANITE
FLUSH ST./ST. TRIM
LEATHER WRAPPED PANELS (TYP.)
FLUSH ST./ST. TRIM
POLISHED GRANITE
LEVELERS

BUTT JOINT TYP.

⑥ ELEVATION - RECEPTION DESK (LOW WORK SURFACE)
SCALE: ¾" = 1'-0"

POLISHED GRANITE
FABRIC WRAPPED HOMOSOTE TACK SURFACE
APPLIED FABRIC
AMERICAN WHITE OAK BASE

PENCIL DWR.
BOX DWR.
FILE DWR.

⑤ ELEVATION - RECEPTION DESK (WORK SURFACE)
SCALE: ¾" = 1'-0"

POLISHED GRANITE
FABRIC WRAPPED HOMOSOTE TACK SURFACE
APPLIED FABRIC
AMERICAN WHITE OAK BASE

PENCIL DWR.
BOX DWR.
FILE DWR.

FABRIC @ DOOR EDGE TO BE TUCKED INTO ROUTED EDGE (TYP.)
GLYNN-JOHNSON 32F ROLLER LATCHES (2) W/ STRIKE ON DOOR.
EXPOSED WOOD TO BE AMERICAN WHITE OAK (TYP.)
"SOSS" N°220 HINGES
RUBBER BUMPERS
LEATHER @ DOOR EDGE TO BE TUCKED INTO ROUTED EDGES.

⑦ PLAN-SECTION @ RECEPTION DESK DOOR
SCALE: 3" = 1'-0"

**Fig. 8** *(Continued)*

Fig. 9 A reception desk can often consist of two workstations.

**Fig. 9** *(Continued)*

**Fig. 10** A circular reception desk can make a bold and sophisticated corporate statement. The designer is cautioned, however, to carefully analyze the minimum radius required for chair movement. Custom built-in files and drawers, if also curved, can become costly and sometimes impractical.

**POLISHED GRANITE COUNTER TOP** W/ 5"L × 5"W × 5"D STL. ANGLE SUPPORTS 2'-0" O.C. MAX.
—"ALKCO" LITTLE INCH OR EQUAL
**FABRIC WRAPPED 3/4" HOMOSOTE** TACK SURFACE
**AMERICAN WHITE OAK VENEER** WORK SURFACE & PEDESTAL (TYP.)

**PENCIL DRAWER W/ 50 lb. CAPACITY** DWR. GLIDES - FULL EXTENSION

**"TYDX" MIRROR PULLS (TYP.)** N° SF 5/16" × 3L US26
**BOX DRAWER W/ GLIDES 75 lb. CAPACITY** FULL EXTENSION

**FILE DRAWER W/ ADJUSTABLE** METAL BARS TO ACCOMMODATE LEGAL & LETTER SIZE FOLDERS GLIDES - 150 lb. CAPACITY FULL EXTENSION

**AMERICAN WHITE OAK BASE (TYP.)**

1/8" × 1/8" FLUSH ST./ST. TRIM (CONTINUOUS)

LEATHER WRAPPED WOOD PANELS W/ BUTT JOINTS (TYP.) SECURE W/ METAL CLIPS

1/8" × 1/8" FLUSH ST./ST. TRIM (CONTINUOUS)

POLISHED GRANITE BASE

**VERTICAL SECTION @ HIGH PEDESTAL**
SCALE : 3" = 1'-0"

AMERICAN WHITE OAK VENEER COUNTER
INTERMEDIATE VENEER SUPPORT BRACKETS
AFFIXED FABRIC ON WOOD BACKING
LEATHER WRAPPED PANELS SEE ELEVATIONS FOR BUTT JOINT LOCATIONS
AMERICAN WHITE OAK VENEER ON SOLID BACKING - STAIN 1/8" REVEAL TO MATCH

**VERTICAL SECTION @ LOW WORK SURFACE**
SCALE : 3" = 1'-0"

CONT. ST./ST. TRIM

LEATHER WRAPPED WOOD PANELS - SEE ELEVATIONS FOR LOCATION OF BUTT JOINTS

**VERTICAL SECTION @ LOW PEDESTAL**
SCALE : 3" = 1'-0"

**VERTICAL SECTION @ HIGH WORK SURFACE**
SCALE : 3" = 1'-0"

**Fig. 11** A fully detailed reception desk will require many large-scale vertical sections to explain the various storage, drawer, work surface, lighting, and electrical requirements. Examples of such details are shown here.

CROSS SECTION - DRAWER BASE

CROSS SECTION- BOOK SHELF @ DWR. BASE

CROSS SECTION

**VERTICAL SECTION- RECEPTION DESK**

CORNER DETAIL

SECTION AT COUNTER FRONT

SECTION OF COUNTER @ STATIONARY FILE

**HEAD** 6 9/16"

1/4" SAFETY GLASS WITH 3"⌀ OPENING (POLISHED EDGES)

**SILL**

8 7/8" H.WD. FRAME (OAK)

H.WD. FRAME (OAK) 8 7/8"

DOOR #5

6 3/4" FRAME (OAK)

H.WD. TRIM 5 3/4"

**2A** JAMB DETAIL AT INTERSECTION
CORNER AT DOOR #5
@ 3"=1'-0"

FIN. CLG.

1'-7 1/4" F.O.

FINISHED OPENING 3'-0"

1/4" THICK SAFETY GLASS WITH 3"⌀ CUT-OUT

2A / A-19

FACE OF FINISHED WALL

FLOOR SLAB

ELEVATION OF LOBBY
CONTROL WINDOW @ 1/4"=1'-0"

**2** VERTICAL SECTION THRU LOBBY CONTROL WINDOW
@ 3"=1'-0"

**Fig. 12**  A receptionist's workstation need not be freestanding within a reception area, where security and privacy are of critical importance. A receptionist may be located on the opposite side of a glass partition as shown here. Such a solution is often suggested when the receptionist performs multiple tasks such as typing and answering phones.

## RECEPTION AREAS

Reception Window/Pass-Through

**5** NORTH ELEVATION FROM SPACE NO. 13
SCALE ½" = 1'-0"

LINE OF SUSPENDED CEILING.
GYPSUM WALL BD.
PLASTIC LAM, TEXTOLITE 1614 MARIGOLD.
SLIDING PANEL
3/8" CLEAR LEXAN
OPEN
TOP OF BACK SPLASH.
PLASTIC LAMINATE COUNTERTOP FORMICA, 417-64 HONEYTONE
TEAK W/ WHITE PLAS LAM. EDGE. TEXTOLITE #1480
PLYWOOD STIFFNER
2 DRAWERS FILE 17⅞" W, 30" D, 27⅜" H. BY OTHERS
PLASTIC LAM.
3/4" PLYWOOD BRACE
2½" VINYL BASE

WHITE PLASTIC LAMINATE

**CW 5**

**6** SCALE ½" = 1'-0"

WHITE PLASTIC LAMINATE
TEAK PLASTIC LAMINATE

PLASTIC LAM. BACK SPLASH.
PLASTIC LAM. COUNTER TOP, 7/8" THK.
3½" x 3/4" STIFFNER
3/4" PLYWOOD BRACING
FACE OF WALL
2 DRAWER FILE 17⅞" W x 30" D x 27⅜" H. BY OTHERS.

**7** SCALE ½" = 1'-0"

PLASTIC LAM.

**11** NORTH ELEVATION SPACE # 4A
SCALE 3/8" = 1'-0"

WHITE BIRCH SHELVES. NATURAL LAQUER FINISH
HANG ROD

**12** SCALE 3" = 1'-0"

GARCY B 3335 HANGROD W/ B 3369 SOCKET

**13** COAT & HAT SHELVES PART ELEVATION
SCALE 3" = 1'-0"

BIRCH FILLER
WHITE BIRCH SHELVES NATURAL LAQUER FINISH
GARCY B 3335 HANGROD W/ B 3369 SOCKET.

LINE OF SUSPENDED CLG.

GYPSUM WALL BD.

PLASTIC LAM.
TEXTOLITE 1614 MARIGOLD

REVEALS AND VERTICALS. PAINT TO MATCH WALLS

3/8" CLEAR LEXAN

OPEN

COUNTER TOP
TEXTOLITE 1480 WHITE

PLASTIC LAM
TEXTOLITE 1614 MARIGOLD.

2½" VINYL BASE

**④ SOUTH ELEVATION FROM SPACE NO. 14**
SCALE ½" = 1'-0"

SLIDING DOOR POCKET

SUSPENDED ACOUSTIC TILE
CEILING AT 8'-8" TYP.

PLASTIC LAM.
TEXTOLITE 1614 MARIGOLD

FLUSH BOLT

7/8" THICK PLASTIC LAM. SLIDING DOOR
TEXTOLITE 1614 MARIGOLD

3/8" CLEAR LEXAN

PLASTIC LAM. COUNTER TOP & EDGE
TEXTOLITE 1480 WHITE

TOP OF BACK SPLASH

PLASTIC LAM.
TEXTOLITE 1614 MARIGOLD

2½" VINYL BASE

PLASTIC LAM.
COUNTER TOP
TEXTOLITE 1480 WHITE

1/4" x 3¾" WOOD FRAME
VERTICALS, PAINT
TO MATCH WALLS.

3/8" CLEAR LEXAN

3/16" x 3/8" GROOVE
FOR SLIDING DOOR

½ x 3/8"
HARD WOOD FILLER

CASING BEAD
U.S. GYPSUM # 200A
OR EQUAL

5/8" GYPSUM BD.

METAL STUD

**⑨ SCALE : HALF FULL SIZE**

½ x 3/8"
HARD WOOD FILLER

1/4" x 3¾" VERTICALS

1/8" x 1/8" QUIRK

PLASTIC LAM.

7/8" SLIDING DOOR
PLASTIC LAM.
TEXTOLITE 1614
MARIGOLD

1/8" x 1/4" QUIRK

**⑩ SCALE : HALF FULL SIZE.**

**Fig. 12** (Continued)

275

**ELEVATION FROM SPACE 202**
@ ¼" = 1'-0"

PLASTER

4'-0"

3'-0"

3'-0"

8'-0"

5A
AD-15

DARCY #2040
ALUMINUM SLIDING
DOOR ASSEMBLY
W/ ¼" SLOT PLUNGER LOCK

¼" CLEAR PLATE GLASS

HOLLOW METAL
FRAME

7½"

3'-0"

3'-6" TO FLOOR

SPACE #202

¾"  5⅝"  ¾"

**5A**

21 — EAST ELEVATION
@ ½" = 1'-0"

PLASTIC
LAM.
STAINLESS ST. BRACKET

22 — @ 3" = 1'-0"

2X8 BLOCKING
PLASTIC LAM.
ON ¾" PLYWOOD
PLASTIC LAM.
¼" WOOD SHIM

STAINLESS STEEL
BRACKET

3'-10" TO FINISH FL.
4'-0"
TO FIN. FLOOR

ISOMETRIC OF
STAINLESS STEEL BRACKET
NOT TO SCALE

**Fig. 12** *(Continued)*

PLAN VIEW

DETAIL-WALL SHELF

SECTION

DETAIL: PHONE SHELF

DETAIL-TYP. COATS

Fig. 13   While the reception desk is typically the major element to be designed and detailed for a reception area, other custom-designed components must also be carefully considered. A phone shelf, a wall shelf, a coat hanging area, and a work surface are often items that must be carefully designed and detailed.

# FURNITURE, FURNISHINGS, AND EQUIPMENT
## `Desks and Seating

Furniture, furnishings, and equipment are the basic building blocks in the design of office spaces. The illustrations and dimensional data contained in this part are based on the product lines available from particular manufacturers.

Although the data, to a great extent, are fairly standard throughout the industry, there will be some variations according to manufacturer. Accordingly, although the information presented is adequate for preliminary planning purposes, the designer is cautioned to reconcile preliminary assumptions with the actual dimensional data of the manufacturer whose product is ultimately specified.

Included in the data provided in this part are examples of filing cabinets, storage cabinets, conference tables, desks, and electronic media.

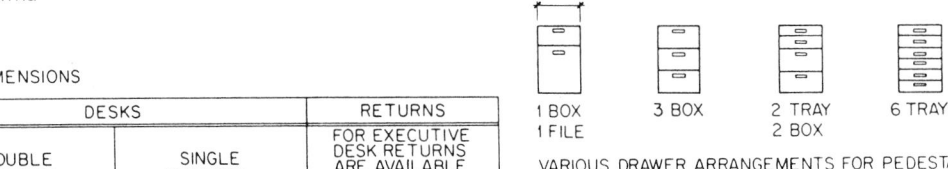

VARIOUS DRAWER ARRANGEMENTS FOR PEDESTALS

**DESK DIMENSIONS**

| | DESKS | | | | RETURNS | |
|---|---|---|---|---|---|---|
| | DOUBLE PEDESTAL | | SINGLE PEDESTAL | | FOR EXECUTIVE DESK RETURNS ARE AVAILABLE AT SAME HEIGHT AS DESK | |
| | STANDARD | RANGE | STANDARD | RANGE | STANDARD | RANGE |
| D | 2'-6" | 2'-0"–3'-3" | 2'-6" | 2'-0"–3'-3" | 1'-6" | 1'-3"–1'-8" |
| H | 2'-5" | 2'-4"–2'-6" | 2'-5" | 2'-4"–2'-6" | 2'-2" | 2'-1"–2'-3" |
| L | 5'-0" | 4'-6"–7'-0" | 5'-0' | 3'-9"–7'-0" | 3'-0" | 2'-0"–5'-0" |

DESKS–SINGLE OR DOUBLE PEDESTAL

WORK TABLES ARE OF SIMILAR DIMENSIONS. FOR EXECUTIVE DESKS WITH RETURNS, RETURNS ARE AVAILABLE AT THE SAME HEIGHT AS THE DESK SURFACE.
A MINIMUM CLEAR WIDTH OF 22" SHOULD BE PROVIDED FOR KNEE ROOM, 24" IS NORMAL.

ARTIST AND DRAFTING DESKS OR TABLES

PEDESTALS FOR SECRETARIAL RETURNS WILL BE REDUCED IN HEIGHT THE EQUIVALENT OF ONE PENCIL DRAWER.

STANDARD SIZE ENGINEERING OR ARCHITECTURAL DRAFTING TABLES ARE 37 1/2"x 43 1/2"D x 60"–72"–84"W x 37"H.

**Fig. 1   Office planning: desks — sizes.**

**CHAIR DIMENSIONS**

| | | SECRETARIAL | | SWIVEL ARMCHAIR | | RIGID ARMCHAIR | | STACK CHAIR | | RIGID AND ADJUSTABLE DRAFTING STOOL | | SIDE CHAIR | |
|---|---|---|---|---|---|---|---|---|---|---|---|---|---|
| | | STD. | RANGE | STD. | RANGE | STD. | RANGE | STD. | RANGE | STD | RANGE | STD. | RANGE |
| W | | 1'-5" | 1'-4"–1'-8" | 2'-4" | 1'-8"–2'-6" | 1'-10" | 1'-6"–2'-3" | 1'-9" | 1'-6"–1'-11" | 1'-6" | 1'-5"–2'-0" | 1'-8" | 1'-4"–2'-0" |
| D | | 1'-7 1/2" | 1'-6-2'-0" | 2'-3" | 1'-8"–2'-6" | 1'-10" | 1'-7"–2'-8" | 1'-9" | 1'-7"–1'-10" | 1'-8" | 1'-6"–2'-0" | 1'-10" | 1'-6"–2'-8" |
| H | | 2'-6" | 2'-5"–2'-10" | 2'-9" | 2'-6" 3'-0" | 2'-6" | 2'-4"–2'-10" | 2'-6" | 2'-4-2'-9" | 3'-0" | 2'-11"–3'-6" | 2'-6" | 2'-4–2'-10" |
| H₁ | | 1'-5" | 1'-4"–1'-8" | 1'-5" | 1'-4"–1'-10" | 1'-6" | 1'-4"–1'-7" | 1'-5" | 1'-5"–1'-6" | 2'-4" | 1'-5"–2'-10" | 1'-6" | 1'-5"–1'-7" |

**LOUNGE CHAIR AND SOFA DIMENSIONS**

| | LOUNGE CHAIR | | SOFA |
|---|---|---|---|
| | STD. | RANGE | |
| W | 2'-6" | 2'-6"–3'-4" | D, H AND H₁ SIMILAR |
| D | 2'-7" | 2'-2"–3'-4" | 2 SEATS-5'-0"–6'-7" |
| H | 2'-6" | 2'-1"–3'-4" | 3 SEATS-6'-0"–7'-6" 4 SEATS-7'-8"–9'-0" |
| H₁ | 1'-3" | 1'-0"–1'-6" | |

**Fig. 2   Office planning: seating — sizes.**

operator
sled base

height range:
33"
arm height range:
25¾"
seat height range:
18"

operator stool

height range:
39¼"-46¾" pneumatic
39¼"-46¾" vecmatic
arm height range:
31"-38¾" pneumatic
31"-38¾" vecmatic
seat height range:
22¾"-29¾" pneumatic
22¾"-29¾" vecmatic

operator

height range:
33"-37" pneumatic
33"-37" vecmatic
34" fixed
seat height range:
16¾"-20¾" pneumatic
16¾"-20¾" vecmatic
17¾" fixed

operator

height range:
33"-37" pneumatic
33"-37" vecmatic
34" fixed
arm height range:
25¾"-29¾" pneumatic
25¾"-29¾" vecmatic
26" fixed
seat height range:
16¾"-20¾" pneumatic
16¾"-20¾" vecmatic
17¾" fixed

mid-manager

height range:
33¾"-37¾" pneumatic
33¾"-37¾" vecmatic
34¾" fixed
seat height range:
17"-21" pneumatic
17"-21" vecmatic
17¾" fixed

mid-manager
sled base

height:
33"
arm height:
25¾"
seat height:
18"

mid-manager

height range:
33¾"-37¾" pneumatic
33¾"-37¾" vecmatic
34¾" fixed
arm height range:
25¾"-29¾" pneumatic
25¾"-29¾" vecmatic
25¾" fixed
seat height range:
17"-21" pneumatic
17"-21" vecmatic
17¾" fixed

high back
mid-manager

height range:
39¾"-43¾" pneumatic
39¾"-43¾" vecmatic
arm height range:
25¾"-29¾" pneumatic
25¾"-29¾" vecmatic
seat height range:
17"-21" pneumatic
17"-21" vecmatic
45 pounds
Shipped Set-Up

manager
sled base

height:
35"
arm height:
25¾"
seat height:
18¾"

executive
manager
sled bases

height:
35"
arm height:
25¾"
seat height:
18¾"

manager
high back

height range:
42"-46" pneumatic
42"-46" vecmatic
arm height range:
25¾"-29¾" pneumatic
25¾"-29¾" vecmatic
seat height range:
17¾"-21¾" pneumatic
17¾"-21¾" vecmatic

grand class
manager
sled bases

height:
33¾"
arm height:
25"
seat height:
18¾"

manager

height range:
34¾"-39¾" pneumatic
34¾"-39¾" vecmatic
35" fixed
arm height range:
25¾"-29¾" pneumatic
25¾"-29¾" vecmatic
26" fixed
seat height range:
17¾"-21¾" pneumatic
17¾"-21¾" vecmatic
18" fixed

grand class
manager

height range:
34¾"-39¾" pneumatic
34¾" fixed
arm height range:
25¾"-29¾" pneumatic
25¾" fixed
seat height range:
17¾"-21¾" pneumatic
17¾" fixed

executive

height range:
42-46" high back
34¾"-39¾" manager
arm height range:
25¾"-29¾"
seat height range:
17¾"-21¾"

50 pounds
Shipped Set-Up

grand class
high back

height range:
42"-46"
arm height range:
25¾"-29¾"
seat height range:
17¾"-21¾"
60 pounds
Shipped Set-Up

Chair types are often associated with certain generic job titles. The designer, however, is cautioned not to make assumptions as to chair selection without a thorough understanding of the tasks the individual is to perform. Ergonomic considerations are to be carefully reviewed in order to select a chair with appropriate attributes, i.e., seat height, adjustability, back and arm support, firmness, etc. Overall chair size must be understood within the context of available clearances and workstation configuration.

# FURNITURE, FURNISHINGS, AND EQUIPMENT
## Chairs

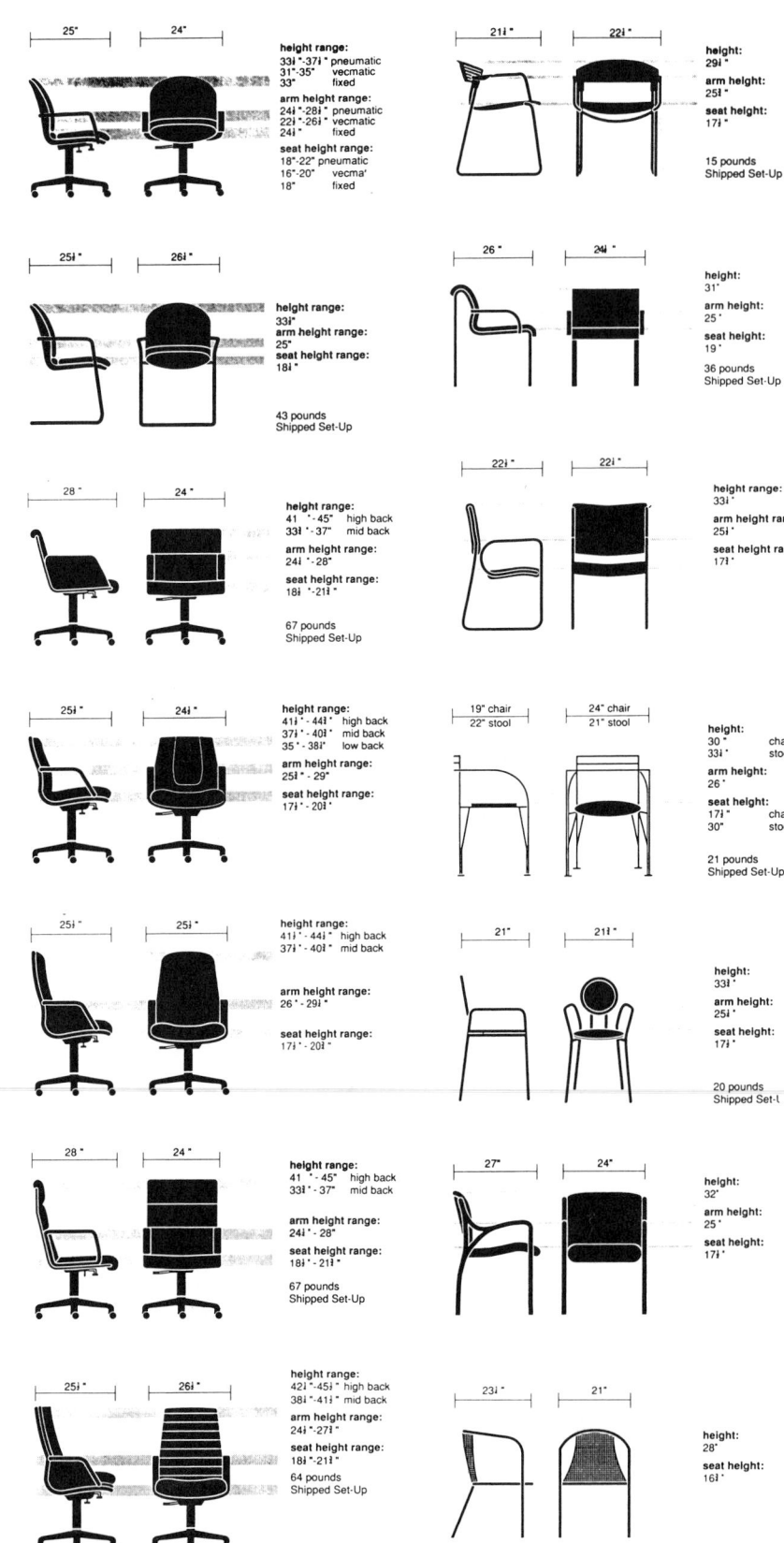

**height range:**
33¼"-37¼" pneumatic
31"-35" vecmatic
33" fixed
**arm height range:**
24¼"-28¼" pneumatic
22¼"-26¼" vecmatic
24¼" fixed
**seat height range:**
18"-22" pneumatic
16"-20" vecma'
18" fixed

**height:**
29¼"
**arm height:**
25¼"
**seat height:**
17¼"

15 pounds
Shipped Set-Up

**height range:**
33¼"
**arm height range:**
25"
**seat height range:**
18¼"

43 pounds
Shipped Set-Up

**height:**
31"
**arm height:**
25"
**seat height:**
19"

36 pounds
Shipped Set-Up

**height range:**
41"-45" high back
33¼"-37" mid back
**arm height range:**
24¼"-28"
**seat height range:**
18¼"-21¼"

67 pounds
Shipped Set-Up

**height range:**
33¼"
**arm height range:**
25¼"
**seat height range:**
17¼"

**height range:**
41¼"-44¼" high back
37¼"-40¼" mid back
35"-38¼" low back
**arm height range:**
25¼"-29"
**seat height range:**
17¼"-20¼"

19" chair / 22" stool
24" chair / 21" stool

**height:**
30" chair
33¼" stool
**arm height:**
26"
**seat height:**
17¼" chair
30" stool

21 pounds
Shipped Set-Up

**height range:**
41¼"-44¼" high back
37¼"-40¼" mid back
**arm height range:**
26"-29¼"
**seat height range:**
17¼"-20¼"

**height:**
33¼"
**arm height:**
25¼"
**seat height:**
17¼"

20 pounds
Shipped Set-U

**height range:**
41"-45" high back
33¼"-37" mid back
**arm height range:**
24¼"-28"
**seat height range:**
18¼"-21¼"

67 pounds
Shipped Set-Up

**height:**
32"
**arm height:**
25"
**seat height:**
17¼"

**height range:**
42¼"-45¼" high back
38¼"-41¼" mid back
**arm height range:**
24¼"-27¼"
**seat height range:**
18¼"-21¼"

64 pounds
Shipped Set-Up

**height:**
28"
**seat height:**
16¼"

**Executive Chairs**

**Tilt-Swivel Chair with Casters**

**Option: CA**

**Non-Swivel Lounge Chair**

**Swivel Lounge Chair**

**Non-Swivel Lounge Arm Chair**

**Swivel Lounge Arm Chair**

**Tilt-Swivel Reclining Arm Chair**

**Ottoman**

**Lounge**

**Non-Swivel Lounge Chair**

**Swivel Lounge Chair**

**Non-Swivel Lounge Armchair**

**Swivel Lounge Armchair**

**Tilt-Swivel Reclining Armchair**

**Ottoman**

**Straight Module**

**Side/Pull-up Chairs**

**Non-Swivel Side Chair**

**Swivel Side Chair**

**Non-Swivel Arm Chair**

**Swivel Arm Chair**

**Tilt-Swivel Arm Chair with Glides**

**Tilt-Swivel Arm Chair with Casters**

**Option: CA**

**Executive Chairs**

**Tilt-Swivel Chair with Glides**

**Lounge Chair**

**Ottoman**

**Lounge Chair and Ottoman**

**Eames™ Chaise**

**Sofa Compact**

**Nelson Sling Sofa**

**Eames Executive Lounge Chairs**

**Executive Swivel Lounge Chair**

**Adjustable Executive Tilt-Swivel Lounge Chair**

**Adjustable Tilt-Swivel**

# FURNITURE, FURNISHINGS, AND EQUIPMENT

**Reception and Lounge Seating**

**straight seating units**

**wedge seating units**

**arms**

**All seats:**
27" height
16" seat height
34" depth

**All tables, 30" bench:**
16" height
34" depth

**Full arm:**
27" height
34" depth

Fig. 3 Reception and lounge seating can assume various sizes, shapes, and configurations. Modular seating units can offer a custom built-in look, and can often incorporate table and storage components. Overall sizes will vary from manufacturer to manufacturer.

Conference tables come in an infinite variety of shapes and sizes. Figures 4 to 6 attempt to provide a representative sampling of such tables, along with dimensional information and seating capacities. The designer is cautioned to use such information as a preliminary planning tool only, and to carefully lay out conference rooms with actual furniture pieces that have been selected. Chair width and spacing will ultimately dictate conference table seating capacity.

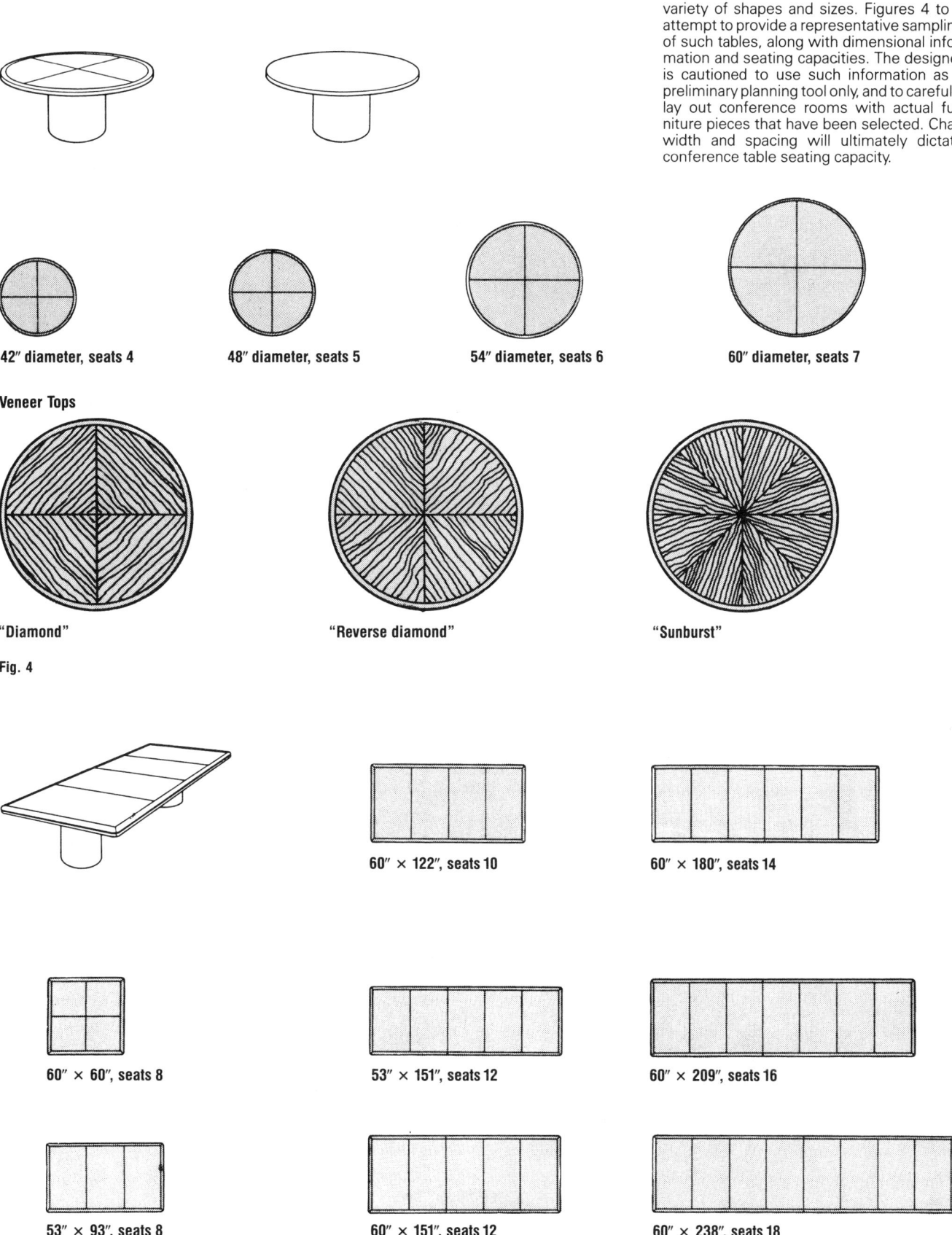

**42″ diameter, seats 4**   **48″ diameter, seats 5**   **54″ diameter, seats 6**   **60″ diameter, seats 7**

**Veneer Tops**

"Diamond"   "Reverse diamond"   "Sunburst"

**Fig. 4**

**60″ × 122″, seats 10**   **60″ × 180″, seats 14**

**60″ × 60″, seats 8**   **53″ × 151″, seats 12**   **60″ × 209″, seats 16**

**53″ × 93″, seats 8**   **60″ × 151″, seats 12**   **60″ × 238″, seats 18**

**Fig. 5**

# FURNITURE, FURNISHINGS, AND EQUIPMENT
`Conference Tables

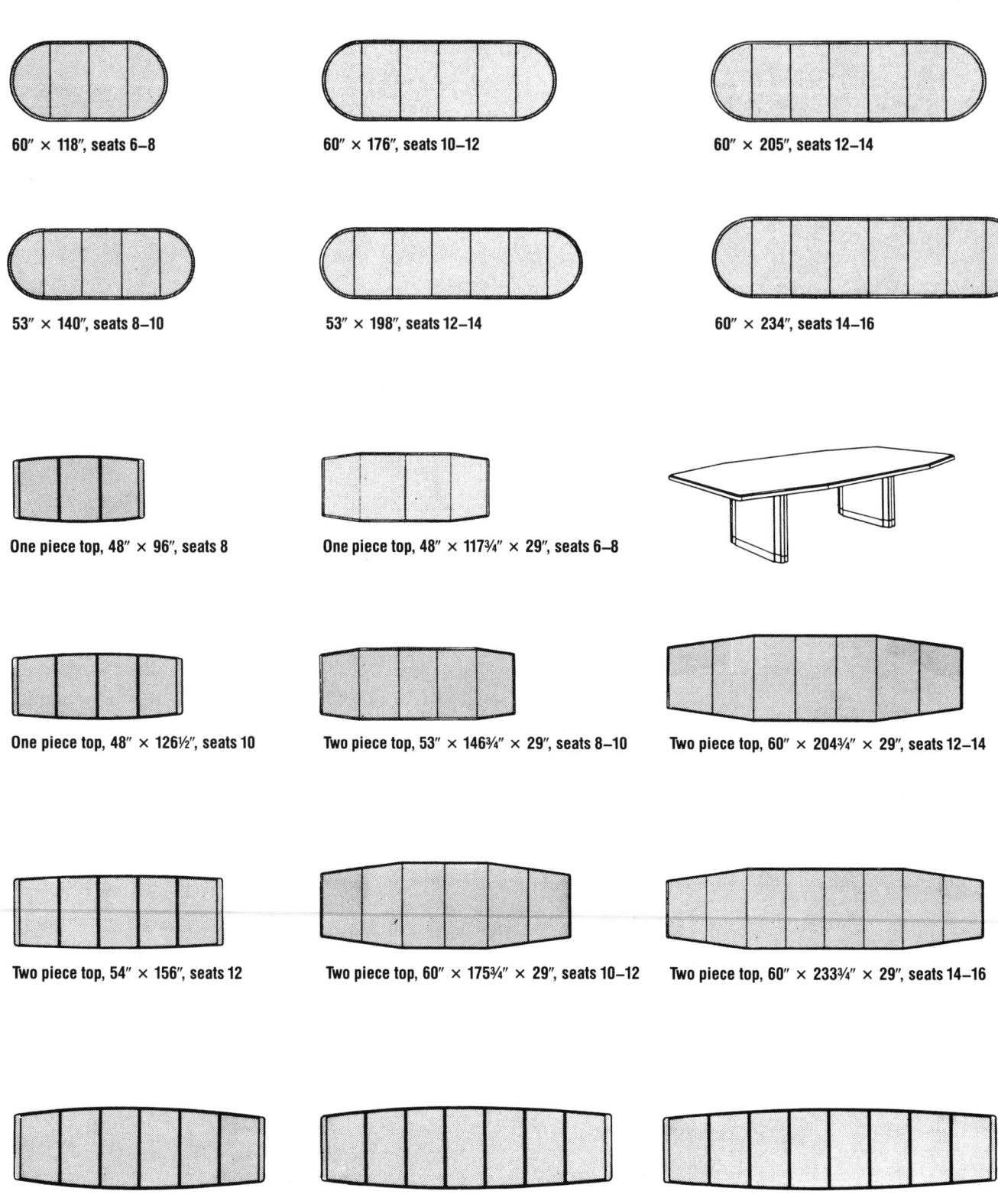

60″ × 118″, seats 6–8

60″ × 176″, seats 10–12

60″ × 205″, seats 12–14

53″ × 140″, seats 8–10

53″ × 198″, seats 12–14

60″ × 234″, seats 14–16

One piece top, 48″ × 96″, seats 8

One piece top, 48″ × 117¾″ × 29″, seats 6–8

One piece top, 48″ × 126½″, seats 10

Two piece top, 53″ × 146¾″ × 29″, seats 8–10

Two piece top, 60″ × 204¾″ × 29″, seats 12–14

Two piece top, 54″ × 156″, seats 12

Two piece top, 60″ × 175¾″ × 29″, seats 10–12

Two piece top, 60″ × 233¾″ × 29″, seats 14–16

Two piece top, 60″ × 185¾″, seats 14

Two piece top, 60″ × 216″, seats 16

Two piece top, 60″ × 245¼″, seats 18

Fig. 6

**TABLE 1   Vertical File Cabinets**

| Description | | Cabinet height | | Outside dimensions | | |
|---|---|---|---|---|---|---|
| | | | | Depth | Width | Height |
| | | 58⅝″ | Letter | 28⁹⁄₁₆″ | 14⅞″ | 58⅜″ |
| | | | Legal | 28⁹⁄₁₆″ | 17⅞″ | 58⅜″ |
| | | 52⅜″ | Letter | 28⁹⁄₁₆″ | 14⅞″ | 52⅜″ |
| | | | Legal | 28⁹⁄₁₆″ | 17⅞″ | 52⅜″ |
| | | | Card | 28⁹⁄₁₆″ | 14⅞″ | 52⅜″ |
| | | 41¼″ | Letter | 28⁹⁄₁₆″ | 14⅞″ | 41¼″ |
| | | | Legal | 28⁹⁄₁₆″ | 17⅞″ | 41¼″ |
| | | 29⅜″ | Letter | 30″ | 14⅞″ | 29⅜″ |
| | | | Legal | 30″ | 17⅞″ | 29⅜″ |
| | | 27⅜″ | Letter | 30″ | 14⅞″ | 27⅞″ |
| | | | Legal | 30″ | 17⅞″ | 27⅞″ |

Standard vertical file cabinets are usually designed to accommodate standard height drawers and half-height file insert drawers (optional). Cabinets are available in letter-size widths (14⅞″) and legal-size widths (17⅛″). Vertical file drawers are usually 12″ high and accommodate front-to-back filing.

Standard cabinets are available in four heights: five-drawer (58⅝″), four-drawer (52⅜″), three drawer (41¼″), and two-drawer (29⅜″ or 27⅜″). The depths of the three-, four-, and five-drawer cabinets are 28⁹⁄₁₆″, while the depth of the 2-drawer cabinets is 30″. Table 1 lists these dimensional data. It should be noted that although adequate for preliminary planning purposes, the data are based on Steelcase cabinets.

### Guidelines for Customizing Vertical Files

Depending on the manufacturer, vertical file cabinets can be customized. Usually two half-height file insert drawers may be substituted for a 12-in-high drawer in any or all positions. Table 2 indicates the dimensions and linear capacities of such insert drawers, while Fig. 7 illustrates basic guidelines for customizing.

**Fig. 7**

## FURNITURE, FURNISHINGS, AND EQUIPMENT
### Vertical File Drawers; Overfile Cabinets; Roll-Away Carts

**TABLE 2   Vertical File Insert Drawers**

| Description | Inside dimensions | | | Linear capacity |
| | Depth | Width | Height | |
| --- | --- | --- | --- | --- |
| Half-height (3x5 or 4x6 cards) | 26⅞" | 6"(2) | 4⅜" | 53⅞"* (2 rows) |
| Half-height (checks) | 26⅞"* | 10¾" | 4⅜" | 26⅞" |
| Half-height (cash) | 8¼" | 3¼" | 1⅞" | Bills |
| | 8½" | 11½" | 1⅞" | Storage |
| | 4⅜" | 2¼" | 1¾" | Coin tray |
| Half-height (box) | 26⅞" | 12¼" | 4¾" | 26⅞" front-to-back |
| | | | | 12¼" side-to-side |
| Half-height (microfilm) | 26¼"* | 4"(3) | 4⅜" | 80¾"* (3 compartments) |
| Full height (letter size) | 26⅞"* | 6"(2) | 10⅛" | 53⅞"* (2 compartments) |
| Full height (letter size) | 26⅞"* | 4"(3) | 10⅛" | 80¾"* (3 compartments) |
| Full height (box) | 26⅞" | 15¼" | 4¾" | — |
| Full height (3x5 cards) | 26⅞"* | 5"(3) | 4½" | 80¾"* (3 compartments) |
| Full height (4x6 cards) | 26⅞"* | 6¼"(2) | 4⅜" | 53⅞" (2 compartments) |
| Full height (legal size) | 26⅞"* | 7½"(2) | 10⅛" | See style no. C |
| Full height (legal size) | 26⅞"* | 5"(3) | 10⅛" | See style no. D |

*Deduct ⅝" when compressor is used.

**TABLE 3   Drawers, Overfile Cabinets, and Roll-Away File Cart**

| Description | Width | Inside dimensions | | | Linear capacity |
| | | Depth | Width | Height | |
| --- | --- | --- | --- | --- | --- |
| 12" Letter-size drawer | — | 27⅜" | 12¼" | 10½" | 27⅜" front-to-back* |
| 12" Legal-size drawer | — | 27⅜" | 15¼" | 10½" | 27⅜" front-to-back |

| Description | Width | Outside/inside dimensions | | | Linear capacity |
| | | Depth | Width | Height | |
| --- | --- | --- | --- | --- | --- |
| Overfile cabinet<br>Fits over two letter-size files | 29¾" | 28⅝"/28½"† | 29¾"/27⅞" | 28⅛"/25⅜" | 55¾" side-to-side on<br>2 shelves (1 adj., ¾" thick) |
| Overfile cabinet<br>Fits over two legal-size files | 35¾" | 28⅝"/28½"† | 35¾"/33⅞" | 28⅛"/25⅜" | 67¾" side-to-side on<br>2 shelves (1 adj., ¾" thick) |
| Overfile cabinet<br>Fits over three letter size files | 44⅝" | 28⅝"/28½"† | 44⅝"/42¾" | 28⅛"/25⅜" | 85½" side-to-side on<br>2 shelves (1 adj., ¾" thick) |
| Overfile cabinet<br>Fits over three legal-size files | 53⅝" | 28⅝"/28½"† | 53⅝"/51¾" | 28⅛"/25⅜" | 103½" side-to-side on<br>2 shelves (1 adj., ¾" thick) |
| Roll-away file cart | | 30¼"/28" | 15⅛"/12⅛" | 22⅞"/13⅜" | 25" Letter/legal |

*Deduct ⅝" when compressor is used.
†Deduct 1½" when ordered with sliding doors.

**TABLE 4   Lateral File Cabinets**

| Description (cabinet inside height) | Cabinet width | Outside/inside dimensions | | |
|---|---|---|---|---|
| | | Depth | Width | Height |
| 60″ | 30″ | 18″/17⅛″* | 30″/28½″ | 64⅝″/60″ |
| | 36″ | 18″/17⅛″* | 36″/34½″ | 64⅝″/60″ |
| | 42″ | 18″/17⅛″* | 42″/40½″ | 64⅝″/60″ |
| 48″ | 30″ | 18″/17⅛″* | 30″/28½″ | 52⅜″/48″ |
| | 36″ | 18″/17⅛″* | 36″/34½″ | 52⅜″/48″ |
| | 42″ | 18″/17⅛″* | 42″/40½″ | 52⅜″/48″ |
| 36″ | 30″ | 18″/17⅛″* | 30″/28½″ | 41¼″/36″ |
| | 36″ | 18″/17⅛″* | 36″/34½″ | 41¼″/36″ |
| | 42″ | 18″/17⅛″* | 42″/40½″ | 41¼″/36″ |
| 24″ | 30″ | 18″/17⅛″* | 30″/28½″ | 28¼″/24″ |
| | 36″ | 18″/17⅛″* | 36″/34½″ | 28¼″/24″ |
| | 42″ | 18″/17⅛″* | 42″/40½″ | 28¼″/24″ |

3″ Module unit

| Loaded Weights | | | | | | | | | | | |
|---|---|---|---|---|---|---|---|---|---|---|---|
| | Cabinet inside height | | | | | | | | | | |
| Description | 24″ | | | 36″ | | | 48″ | | | 60″ | | |
| Cabinet width | 30″ | 36″ | 42″ | 30″ | 36″ | 42″ | 30″ | 36″ | 42″ | 30″ | 36″ | 42″ |
| Loaded weight in pounds | 285 | 336 | 391 | 401 | 475 | 553 | 524 | 645 | 720 | 610 | 725 | 843 |

*Deduct ⅝″ when compressor is used.

**24″**

**36″**

**48″**

**60″**

Standard lateral file cabinets are usually available in three widths — 30″, 36″, and 42″ — and with 12″-high drawers or roll-out shelves. Some cabinets are designed on a 3″ module to accommodate 3″-, 6″-, 9″-, 12″-, and 15″-high drawers and shelves.

Ganging hardware is usually included with each file cabinet. Cabinets should be ganged with adjacent files or bolted to the floor. Counterbalance weights should be used for single-application files.

Table 4 shows the outside and inside dimensions of four lateral file cabinets, and their loaded floor weights based on 12″-high drawers filled to capacity.

It should be noted that the dimensional data and load factors are based on Steelcase cabinets. Although these data are adequate for preliminary planning purposes, it is essential that the data of the equipment being specified are verified with its manufacturer.

# FURNITURE, FURNISHINGS, AND EQUIPMENT

**Lateral File Cabinets**

### Filing Arrangements

Most lateral file drawers are designed for filing both letter-size and legal-size documents, in addition to EDP printouts. Lateral file drawers can usually accommodate materials in a front-to-back (F to B) arrangement or in a side-to-side (S to S) arrangement. In some instances a combination of the two is possible. The actual capacity in linear inches for each arrangement and for each particular drawer or shelf has been calculated and is shown in the "Linear capacity" column in Tables 2, 3, 6, 7 and 8. It should be noted that the dimensional data in Table 5 are based on Steelcase drawers.

**TABLE 5   Filing Arrangements**

| Description | 30" width | 36" width | 42" width |
|---|---|---|---|

Letter/legal, 12" drawer

EDP binders, 15" drawer

EDP folders, 15" drawer

**TABLE 6   Drawers, Shelves, Add-On Cabinets**

| Description | File cabinet width | Style no. | Outside/inside dimensions | | | Linear capacity |
|---|---|---|---|---|---|---|
| | | | Depth | Width | Height | |
| 12" legal fixed shelf with door | 30" | | 16½" | 28½" | 10½"* | 28½" side-to-side |
| | 36" | | 16½" | 34½" | 10½"* | 34½" S to S |
| | 42" | | 16½" | 40½" | 10½"* | 40½" S to S |
| 15" legal fixed shelf with door | 30" | | 16½" | 28½" | 13½" | 28½" S to S |
| | 36" | | 16½" | 34½" | 13½" | 34½" S to S |
| | 42" | | 16½" | 40½" | 13½" | 40½" S to S |
| Center hook filing hanger bar | 30" | | 17" | 28½" | 10⅝" (12" high door)<br>12¾" (15" high door) | 28½" S to S<br>28½" S to S |
| | 36" | | 17" | 34½" | 10⅝" (12" high door)<br>12¾" (15" high door) | 34½" S to S<br>34½" S to S |
| | 42" | | 17" | 40½" | 10⅝" (12" high door)<br>12¾" (15" high door) | 40½" S to S<br>40½" S to S |
| T-bar | 30" | | 17" | 28½" | 10¼" (12" high door)<br>12⅜" (15" high door) | 28½" S to S<br>28½" S to S |
| | 36" | | 17" | 34½" | 10¼" (12" high door)<br>12¾" (15" high door) | 34½" S to S<br>34½" S to S |
| | 42" | | 17" | 40½" | 10¼" (12" high door)<br>12⅜" (15" high door) | 40½" S to S<br>40½" S to S |
| Wire tape rack | 30" | | 17" | 28½" | 7⅛" ( 9" high door)<br>10⅛" (12" high door)<br>13⅛" (15" high door) | 28½" S to S<br>28½" S to S<br>28½" S to S |
| | 36" | | 17" | 34½" | 7⅛" ( 9" high door)<br>10⅛" (12" high door)<br>13⅛" (15" high door) | 34½" S to S<br>34½" S to S<br>34½" S to S |
| | 42" | | 17" | 40½" | 7⅛" ( 9" high door)<br>10⅛" (12" high door)<br>13⅛" (15" high door) | 40½" S to S<br>40½" S to S<br>40½" S to S |
| Add-on cabinet | 30" | 830-610 | 18"/16⅜"* | 30"/28⅛" | 15¾"/13⅛" | 28⅛" S to S |
| | 36" | 836-610 | 18"/16⅜"* | 36"/34⅛" | 15¾"/13⅛" | 34⅛" S to S |
| | 42" | 842-610 | 18"/16⅜"* | 42"/40⅛" | 15¾"/13⅛" | 40⅛" S to S |
| | 30" | 830-710 | 18"/16⅜"* | 30"/28⅛" | 28⅛"/25⅛" | 28⅛" S to S |
| | 36" | 836-710 | 18"/16⅜"* | 36"/34⅛" | 28⅛"/25⅛" | 34⅛" S to S |
| | 42" | 842-710 | 18"/16⅜"* | 42"/40⅛" | 28⅛"/25⅛" | 40⅛" S to S |

*Deduct ⅝" when compressor is used.

# FURNITURE, FURNISHINGS, AND EQUIPMENT
## Storage Cabinets

Standard cabinets often provide a fast, flexible, and economical solution to many storage problems. Table 7 provides dimensional data and capacities for four typical cabinet types. These cabinets are manufactured by Steelcase. The dimensions of cabinets of other manufacturers will differ somewhat. The data in Table 7, however, are adequate for preliminary planning purposes.

**TABLE 7   Storage Cabinets**

| Description | Outside/inside dimensions | | | Linear capacity |
|---|---|---|---|---|
| | Depth | Width | Height | |
| Storage cabinet | 18"/17" | 36"/33⅛" | 41¼"/35⅝" | 99½" side-to-side on 3 shelves (2 adj., 1" thick) |
| | 18"/17" | 36"/33⅛" | 52⅜"/46⅜" | 99½" S to S on 3 shelves (2 adj., 1" thick) |
| | 18"/17" | 36"/33⅛" | 64⅝"/58¾" | 132¾" S to S on 4 shelves (3 adj., 1" thick) |
| | 18"/17" | 36"/33⅛" | 80½"/74½" | 165⅞" S to S on 5 shelves (4 adj., 1" thick) |
| | 24"/23" | 36"/33⅛" | 64⅝"/58¾" | 132¾" S to S on 4 shelves (3 adj., 1" thick) |
| | 24"/23" | 36"/33⅛" | 80½"/74½" | 165⅞" S to S on 5 shelves (4 adj., 1" thick) |
| Wardrobe cabinet | 18"/17" | 36"/33⅛" | 52⅜"/46⅜" | Not for filing |
| | 18"/17" | 36"/33⅛" | 64⅝"/58¾" | Not for filing |
| | 18"/17" | 36"/33⅛" | 80½"/74½" | Not for filing |
| | 24"/23" | 36"/33⅛" | 64⅝"/58¾" | Not for filing |
| | 24"/23" | 36"/33⅛" | 80½"/74½" | Not for filing |
| Wardrobe/storage cabinet | 18"/17" | 36"/33⅛" | 52⅜"/46⅜" | 43¼" S to S on 3 shelves (2 adj., 1" thick) |
| | 18"/17" | 36"/33⅛" | 64⅝"/58¾" | 58" S to S on 4 shelves (3 adj., 1" thick) |
| | 18"/17" | 36"/33⅛" | 80½"/74½" | 58" S to S on 4 shelves (3 adj., 1" thick) |
| | 24"/23" | 36"/33⅛" | 64⅝"/58¾" | 58" S to S on 4 shelves (3 adj., 1" thick) |
| | 24"/23" | 36"/33⅛" | 80½"/74½" | 58" S to S on 4 shelves (3 adj., 1" thick) |
| Wardrobe | 18"/16⅝" | 18"/15⅛" | 41⅛"/35⅞" | 15⅛" on bar |
| | 18"/16⅝" | 18"/15½" | 52¼"/47" | 15½" on bar |
| | 18"/16⅝" | 18"/15⅛" | 64½"/59¼" | 15⅛" on bar |

**TABLE 8   Interior Card Trays**

(For use in vertical or lateral files)

| Description | Style No. | Inside dimensions | | | Linear capacity |
|---|---|---|---|---|---|
| | | Depth | Width | Height | |
| 3 x 5 card | 4335 | 11⅞" | 5" | 3¼" | 10¼" |
| 3 x 5 card | 4337M | 14⅞" | 5" | 3¼" | 13¼" |
| 5 x 8 card | 4355 | 11⅞" | 8⅛" | 4¾" | 11¼" |
| 5 x 8 card | 4357 | 14⅞" | 8⅛" | 4¾" | 13¼" |
| 4 x 6 card | 800-TN-46 | 12" | 6⅛" | 4⅜" | 11⅜" |
| 4 x 6 card | 800-TW-46 | 15" | 6⅛" | 4⅜" | 14⅜" |
| Tab card | 7201 | 11⅞" | 7½" | 3⅝" | 10⅜" |
| Tab card | 7204 | 14⅞" | 7½" | 3⅝" | 13⅜" |
| Coin and bill | 4388 | 8¼" / 5⅞" | 3⅛" / 11¹/₁₂" | 1⅞" / 1⅞" | * / † |
| Coin and bill | 4389 | 7⅞" / 2⅜" | 3¾" / 2¼" | 1⅞" / 1¾" | * / † |

| | | Number of card trays accommodated per 6"-high drawer or shelf | | | |
|---|---|---|---|---|---|
| | | 4337M | 800TW46‡ | 4357 | 7204M |
| 6" high shelves/drawers | 842 DWDV-6 | 7 | 5 | 4 | 5 |
| | 842 SWDV-6 | 7 | 5 | — | 5 |
| | 836 DWDV-6 | 6 | 4 | 3 | 4 |
| | 836 SWDV-6 | 6 | 4 | — | 4 |
| | 830 DWDV-6 | 5 | 3 | 3 | 3 |
| | 830 SWDV-6 | 5 | 3 | 3 | 3 |
| | 830 SWDV-3 | 5 | 3 | — | 3 |

*Dimensions of each of 6 bill compartments.
†Dimensions of each of 5 coin compartments.
‡Card trays cannot be installed in 6"-high shelf located directly below a door. Use 3"-high shelf and refer to guidelines.

# FURNITURE, FURNISHINGS, AND EQUIPMENT

## Storage Components Glossary

**Lower storage/Lateral file**
Free-standing wall- or panel-mounted files with width dimension greater than depth dimension.

**Rails**
Mount in lateral file for drawer suspended filing, front-to-back or side-to-side.

**Media compartment kit**
Can be retrofit or factory assembled to 800/900 Series 6" roll-out shelf. Provides dividers and partitions adjustable for storing a variety of media-cassettes, mini-cassettes, cartridges, floppy disks, and more.

**Storage cabinet**
Storage for general supplies. Available in 2, 3, or 4 adjustable shelves.

**Mobile pedestal**
Supports drawers in several combinations and has casters for mobility.

**T-bar filing for bound printouts**
Accepts EDP printouts in T-bar type binders.

**Overfile cabinet**
For use above lateral or vertical files. Sliding door, lock, and shelf-modifier options.

**Vertical file**
Letter- or legal-size filing cabinet with depth dimension greater than width dimension. For front-to-back filing only.

**Partition**
A double metal wall that mounts into a lateral file drawer to divide drawer.

**Vertical file drawer**
6" high and 12" high drawers for letter or legal-size filing cabinets.

**Personal drawer**
For personal items. An adjustable divider is included. 3" high.

**Wardrobe**
Provides full-width coat rod for hanging clothes mounted beneath full-width shelf.

**Pull-out keyboard shelf**
Attaches beneath work-surface for computer keyboard support and storage.

**Wire tape racks**
Racks can be freestanding or built-in to lateral files for storage of magnetic tapes and disk cartridges on edge. Dividers can be positioned to accommodate media of different thicknesses.

**Bookcase**
Units have adjustable shelves which can accommodate rows of standard ring binders and other bound materials.

**Center hook filing hanging bar**
Accepts printouts and magnetic tape reels with center hooks.

**Combination wardrobe and storage cabinet**
Units are divided – space for hanging clothes and two or three vertically adjustable shelves.

**Compressor**
A spring-loaded plate that supports file material. Can be moved and locked in position. Used in vertical and lateral file drawers, pedestal file drawers and card trays.

**Divider**
Metal plate used to separate and support file material. For lateral file and pedestal file drawers, fixed and roll-out shelves.

**Double-door storage cabinet**
For miscellaneous storage below worksurface. Includes one adjustable shelf and two swing-arm doors.

**File drawer**
For letter- or legal-size documents 12″ and 15″ high. 15″ high drawers can also be used for computer printouts. For front-to-back or side-to-side or combination filing.

**File insert drawers**
For use in vertical files instead of card trays.

**Hanging folder frame**
A metal rod mounted in lateral and vertical files for suspended file material. Can be mounted on partitions for front-to-back filing.

**Interior card trays**
Portable trays in various sizes for common card sizes: 3 x 5, 4 x 6, etc. Compressor included.

**Later file drawer**
3″ tray drawer, 6″ card drawer, and 9″, 12″ and 15″ high file drawers. Letter or legal-size filing. Dividers, three sway blocks, compressor, hanging folder frames, rails, or partitions available.

**Lateral file fixed shelf**
12″ or 15″ high shelves with or without doors and with three dividers.

**Lateral file posting shelf**
Metal pull-out shelf option on 48″ and 60″ interior height lateral files. When not specified, the space will be filled by a posting shelf filler.

**Lateral file roll-out shelf**
3″, 6″, 12″, and 15″ high shelves extend for accessibility.

**Lateral file workshelf**
3″ high roll-out workshelf with laminate surface.

# FURNITURE, FURNISHINGS, AND EQUIPMENT

## Electronic Media Storage

### Microfiche

4" x 6"

**Description** Microfiche is a 4" x 6" film transparency containing multiple rows of greatly reduced page images of any written, printed or graphic material. Image reductions range from 13 up to several hundred times smaller than the originals. A microfiche viewer enlarges the images so that they are readable. Labeling information is written or printed on a narrow strip along the long edge at the top of the microfiche.

Microfiche may be stored in interior card trays, in lateral file 6"-high roll-out shelves, and in a lateral file media compartment.

### Microfilm

1" x 4" diameter reel
(1¼" x 4¼" x 4¼" box)

**Description** Microfilm is roll photographic film on a reel or in a square cartridge that contains images of pages of written, graphic or printed material reduced hundreds of times. A microfilm viewer enlarges the images so that they are readable. Microfilm on a reel is kept in a square plastic or cardboard box for protection and ease of handling. Microfilm is most conveniently stored on edge. Labeling is placed on one of the edges of the reel or box.

Microfilm may be stored in the lateral file media compartment kit, in an interior card tray, and in lateral file 6"-high drawers or shelves.

### Print-out Paper

**Description** Print-out paper, also known as continuous form data processing paper, is used in almost all computer printers and some word processing equipment. The most common types are recognizable by:

■ Small "pin-feed" holes along both edges which are used by the printer to grip and advance the paper.

■ Green or grey-shaded stripes across the paper which serve to organize the printed information.

After printing, the print-out may exist in a "fan-folded" stack or it may be "burst," i.e., separated into individual sheets along the perforations that exist at the fold lines.

If the print-out consists of a significant number of sheets, it may be "bound" for easier handling. Fan-folded printouts *must* be bound along the top or long edge. Print-outs that have been burst may be bound along *either* the long edge *or* the short edge. The binding may consist of only a narrow metal or plastic clamp or it may be include a stiff plastic or fiberboard cover. Frequently the binding may include hooks at both ends so the print-out may be hung from two rails like a hanging file folder. Other hooks may be used to suspend it from special bars or rails.

Identification information may be marked on one of the edges (depending on how the print-out is stored) or on the front sheet of the binding cover.

Print-out paper may be stored in Steelcase lateral and vertical files depending on the paper size. Check the file which will accommodate your paper. Boxed paper can be stored in storage cabinets.

### Cartridges

⅝" x 4" x 6" (cartridge)
⅞" x 4¼" x 6¼" (cartridge in case)

**Description** Cartridges have ¼" wide magnetic tape loaded into a reel-to-reel cartridge generally made of clear plastic with metal back plate. They look similar to an oversize recording cassette. Cartridges come in and are sometimes stored in a "flip-open" plastic or cardboard box. Labels or identification information are located on the long edge or on the side along the long edge of the cartridge or the box.

Cartridges may be stored in interior card trays or in a media compartment kit in lateral file 6"-high drawers or shelves.

## Cassettes

Standard Cassette Case
$1^{1}/_{16}$" x $2^{3}/_{4}$" x $4^{5}/_{16}$"

Mini Cassette Case
$^{7}/_{16}$" x $1^{1}/_{2}$" x $2^{7}/_{8}$"

**Description** Cassettes are available in "standard" and "mini" sizes and consist of magnetic tape loaded into a reel-to-reel configuration in a plastic case. Standard cassettes for electronic equipment are identical in size and appearance to those used for home recording. Cassettes may be used in microcomputers and in word processing or dictation equipment. They come in and are frequently stored in a flip-open plastic case. Labels or identification information may be located on the long edge or side of the cassette or its case.

Cassettes may be stored in a lateral file media compartment kit.

## Disk Cartridges

1" x 10" diameter
3" x 10" diameter
1" x 15" diameter
3" x 15" diameter

**Description** Disk cartridges are round plastic cases which contain a series of rotating platters (or disks) on which data is magnetically recorded. The number of platters in a case varies with the height of the case. In use, the entire case is inserted in a computer disk drive unit where recording arms, which read/record information, enter the case through a slot with a spring door.

Disk cartridges are flat in appearance with an elongated Y-shaped protrusion on the top. They can be stored flat or on edge.

Labels for identification are usually located on the edge of the disk cartridge. Frequently disk cartridges have to be stored in a temperature/humidity controlled environment.

Disk cartridges may be stored in lateral file 6"-high roll-out shelves, storage cabinets, and bookcases.

## Disk Packs

7" x 10" diameter
7" x 15" diameter

**Description** Disk packs are round plastic cases which contain a series of rotating platters (or disks) on which data is magnetically recorded. The number of platters in a unit varies with the height of the plastic case. In use, the entire case is inserted in a computer disk drive unit where recording arms, to read/record information, enter the case through a slot with a spring door. Disk packs are flat on the bottom and upright with the handle on top. Identification is generally located on the edge of the disk pack. These units should be stored in a temperature/humidity controlled environment. Disk packs *must not* be stored one on another.

Disk packs may be stored in storage cabinets, bookcases, and on 3"- and 6"-high lateral file shelves.

## Floppy (Flexible) Disks

8" x 8"
$5^{1}/_{4}$" x $5^{1}/_{4}$"
$3^{1}/_{2}$" x $3^{1}/_{2}$"

**Description** Floppy disks, also called diskettes or flexible disks, are small record-like disks each permanently enclosed in a square, stiff paper envelope. They are used to magnetically record information in all types of small computer and word processing equipment. Labels are placed on the paper envelope.

Floppy disks may be stored in 12"-high lateral file drawers and shelves.

# FURNITURE, FURNISHINGS, AND EQUIPMENT
**Electronic Media Storage**

### Laser Disks

12¼" x 12⅜" jacket
12" diameter
4¾" diameter

**Description**  Laser disks look like long-play record albums complete with a paper protective sleeve. Data are stored and retrieved by laser beam.

Laser disks may be stored in 15"-high lateral file drawers and shelves.

---

### Magnetic, Tab, and Aperture Cards

3¼" x 7⅜"

**Description**  Magnetic cards, also known as mag cards, are a tab-size black plastic card with magnetic material coated on one or both sides. The cards are used to record or reproduce information in word processing equipment. In some cases one or more of the cards will be kept in a paper envelope. Identifying information will be marked on the face of the envelope.

Tab cards, also known as keypunch cards, are 80 column cards or punch cards with small holes in them to represent bits of data. Although they may be stored in a workstation or central storage area, they are usually used and produced in a mainframe computer room or keypunch department, and are stored in specially separated decks. The decks are most frequently identified by markings across the edges of the cards.

Aperture cards are tab cards with a piece of microfilm mounted over a hole in their center. They are most frequently used for microfilm images of engineering or architectural drawings. Aperture card reader/printers enlarge the image on a screen for reference and, if required, reproduce a full-sized copy of the drawing. Identifying information is printed in a narrow band along the top (long edge) of the card.

These cards may be stored in interior card trays and in lateral file 6"-high drawers and roll-out shelves.

---

### Magnetic Tape Reels

1" x 7½" diameter
1" x 8½" diameter
1" x 10½" diameter
1" x 15" diameter

**Description**  Magnetic tape is typically ½" wide and loaded on reels of varying diameters. A flexible plastic strip locks around the outside of the reel to protect the tape and prevent unraveling when it is not in use. This media is used in large tape drive units that are generally found only in computer rooms. The long-term storage of magnetic tapes is subject to strict temperature and humidity requirements to prevent damage. Tapes are labeled both on the side and on the flexible strip that is placed around the edge of the reel. They can be stored flat or on edge. For flat storage, handle like disk cartridges.

Magnetic tape reels may be stored in the lateral file add-on cabinets, storage cabinets, or in free-standing wire racks on lateral file shelves.

---

PLASTIC LAM.
COUNTER TOP

6 FILES @ 3'-0" = 18'-0"

GW
7

9
A-7

10
A-7

METAL FILE CABINETS BY OTHERS

FILLER                    FILLER

(6) NORTH ELEVATION SPACE No. 18
@ 3/8" = 1'-0"

PLASTIC LAM.
COUNTER TOP

GW
6

9
A-7

4 FILES @ 3'-0" = 12'-0"

10
A-7

METAL FILE
CABINETS BY OTHERS

FILLER                    FILLER

(4) NORTH ELEVATION SPACE No. 16
@ 3/8" = 1'-0"

GW
3

PLASTIC LAM.
COUNTER TOP

9
A-7

3 FILES @ 3'-0" = 9'-0"

10
A-7

METAL FILE CABINETS BY OTHERS

FILLER

(8) WEST ELEVATION SPACE No. 12
@ 3/8" = 1'-0"

1'-7"

SCRIBE TO WALL

TEAM PLASTIC LAM.

BACK PLASTIC LAM.
1/2" HARDWOOD FILLER

METAL FILE CABINET

(9) @ 3" = 1'-0"

METAL FILE CABINET
WOOD BLKG.
HARDWOOD VENEER PLYWD
SHOP PRIMED FOR
PAINTING IN FIELD

DIM. VARIES
SEE ELEVATION
SCRIBE TO WALL

(10) @ 1/2 FULL SIZE

## FURNITURE, FURNISHINGS, AND EQUIPMENT

File Countertop with Shelf Light

SECTION **1**
SCALE: 3"=1'-0"

SECTION **2**
SCALE: 3"=1'-0"

SECTION **3**
SCALE: 3"=1'-0"

# FURNITURE, FURNISHINGS, AND EQUIPMENT
**Office Pantry**

PLAN SECTION **4**
SCALE: 3"=1'-0"

Labels: WALNUT VENEER · BLOCKING AS REQ'D · WHITE PLASTIC LAM. BACK, SIDE & TOP · BLOCKING AS REQ'D · WALNUT VENEER · WALNUT VENEER · PATTERN GLASS

PLAN SECTION **5**
SCALE: 3"=1'-0"

Labels: WALNUT VENEER · WALNUT VENEER · BLOCKING AS REQ'D · WHITE PLASTIC LAM. · OPEN SPACE FOR REF. · OAK INTERIOR · OAK INTERIOR · BLOCKING AS REQ'D · PLAS. LAM · PLAS. LAM. · WALNUT VENEER · WALNUT VENEER · WHITE PLAS. LAM. DOORS

**9** NORTH ELEVATION SPACE NO 9 6¼"=1'-0"

**10** EAST ELEVATION SPACE NO 9 6¼"=1'-0"

**13** @ 3"=1'-0"

**14** @ 3"=1'-0"

**11** SOUTH ELEVATION SPACE NO 8 6¼"=1'-0"

**12** @ 3"=1'-0"

**15** @ 3"=1'-0"

**16** ELEVATION OF PULLS 3½ FULL SIZE

**FURNITURE, FURNISHINGS, AND EQUIPMENT**

Island File Counter; Compact Kitchen

### ISLAND FILE COUNTER

### COMPACT KITCHEN

# Hospitality Spaces

Restaurants    307

Bars    346

Hotels    374

The basic components of any restaurant interior are the chair and the table. Depending upon restaurant type, menu, service, table setting, furniture selection, and degree of intimacy required, table size and overall chair space requirements can, and should, vary greatly. A restaurant that encourages rapid turnover of customers will normally provide smaller table top and chair sizes. On the other hand, those restaurants that encourage limited turnover and emphasize the wining and dining experience will typically provide larger table top sizes and larger, more comfortable chairs, with greater distance between table groupings.

There is no agreement among even the most experienced restauranteurs and restaurant designers as to what the optimal table and chair dimensions should be. In addition, many other design factors will influence the final decision, including circulation and egress, accessibility standards, methods of service, and the overall dimensions of any given space.

Figures 1 to 19 provide the designer with restaurant planning standards that have been developed by many experienced architects and interior designers. These drawings not only show the various individual table and chair arrangements, but provide the designer with groupings of these arrangements, as well as an indication of overall size, floor area, and number of persons accommodated. These arrangements, however, should only be utilized for preliminary planning information.

| | O | L | W | A |
|---|---|---|---|---|
| LUXURIOUS | 22" | 18" | 18"–20" | 18" |
| INTERMEDIATE | 19"–20" | 16" | 16" | 18" |
| ECONOMICAL | 17"–18" | 15" | 14" | 18" |

CHAIR DIMENSIONS

CHAIR-AND-TABLE UNITS (OCCUPIED)

| AISLE WIDTHS: | FOR PUBLIC CIRCULATION: 84" MINIMUM CLEAR WIDTH | FOR SERVICE ONLY: 24" MIN. BETWEEN CHAIR BACKS | FOR MAIN ENTRANCE: LARGE AS POSSIBLE |

**Fig. 1**

## RESTAURANTS

**Types and Sizes of Table Arrangements**

72"

30"x 36"

18"      18"

**2 PEOPLE**

66"

24"x 30"

24"

18"      18"

**2 PEOPLE**

60"

24"x 24"

24"

18"      18"

**2 PEOPLE**

78"

42"x 42"

18"      18"

**4 PEOPLE**

72"

36" x 36"

18"      18"

**4 PEOPLE**

66"

30" x 30"

18"      18"

**4 PEOPLE**

60"

42"x 42"

**4 PEOPLE**
LUXURIOUS SEATING SUCH AS
DINING 14 SQ. FT./ PERSON

51"

36"x 36"

**4 PEOPLE**
INTERMEDIATE SEATING CAFETERIA
RESTAURANT 12 SQ. FT./ PERSON

42"

30"x 30"

**4 PEOPLE**
ECONOMICAL SEATING SUCH AS
BANQUET 10 SQ. FT./ PERSON

**SQUARE SPACING**
SERVICE AISLES: SQUARE SEATING 60" MIN. BETW. TABLE
TOPS, 24" AISLE PLUS TWO CHAIRS BACK TO BACK 36"
CHAIRS: 17" TO 18" FROM FLOOR TO SEAT, 17" PREFERRED FOR WOMEN
TABLES: 29" TO 30" HIGH

SERVICE AISLE     SERVICE AISLE

24"  36"  60"  36"  60"  36"

18" 24" 18"   18" 24" 18"

24"  36"  42"  36"

**DIAGONAL SPACING**
SERVICE AISLES: DIAGONAL SEATING
30" MIN. BETW. CORNERS OF TABLE TOPS

SERVICE AISLE     SERVICE AISLE

12"  51"  30"  51"  30"  51"

12"  51"  24"  51"

**Fig. 2**

Fig. 3    Seating for 2.

Fig. 4    Seating for 4.

# RESTAURANTS
### Types and Sizes of Table Arrangements

**Fig. 5** 13 ft × 27 ft, 351 ft², seats 18.

**Fig. 6** 8 ft × 27 ft, 216 ft², seats 12.

**Fig. 7** 33 ft × 11 ft, 363 ft², seats 12.

**Fig. 8** 33 ft × 22 ft, 726 ft², seats 26.

**Fig. 9** 11 ft × 28 ft, 308 ft², seats 12.

# RESTAURANTS

Tables: Design Criteria

Fig. 10   These drawings highlight several critical dimensions that the designer must consider. Aisle circulation must be adequate in width; other clearances to consider include chair depth from edge of table and clearance between chairs. While laying out chair and table arrangements, a designer must anticipate the potential conflict between a patron leaving a seat and a tray-carrying waiter.

Fig. 11   Mixed banquette seating.

Fig. 12   Banquettes for 2, 4, and 6 persons.

Fig. 13   21 ft × 9 ft, 189 ft², seats 12.

Fig. 14   27 ft × 10 ft, 270 ft², seats 12.

# RESTAURANTS
Types and Sizes of Banquette Arrangements

**Fig. 15** 19 ft × 9 ft, 171 ft², seats 12.

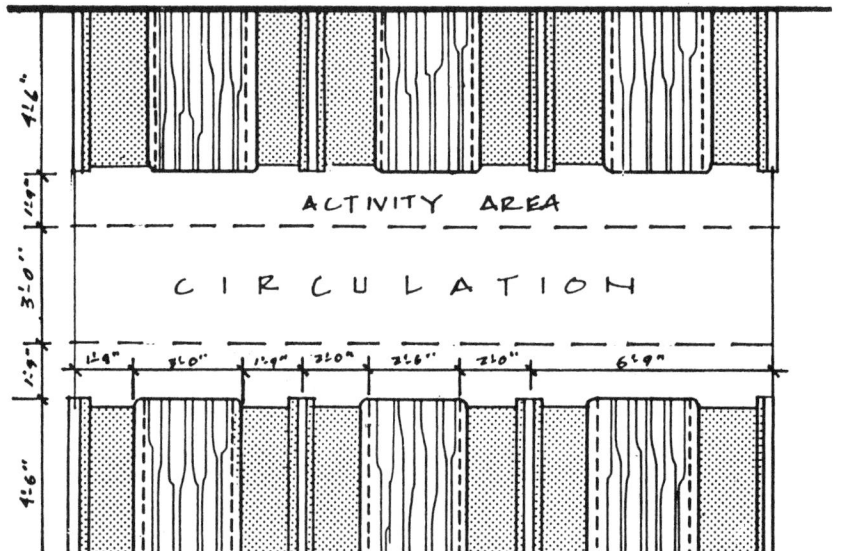

**Fig. 16** 19 ft × 15 ft, 285 ft², seats 24.

**Fig. 17** 21 ft × 19 ft, 400 ft², seats 24.

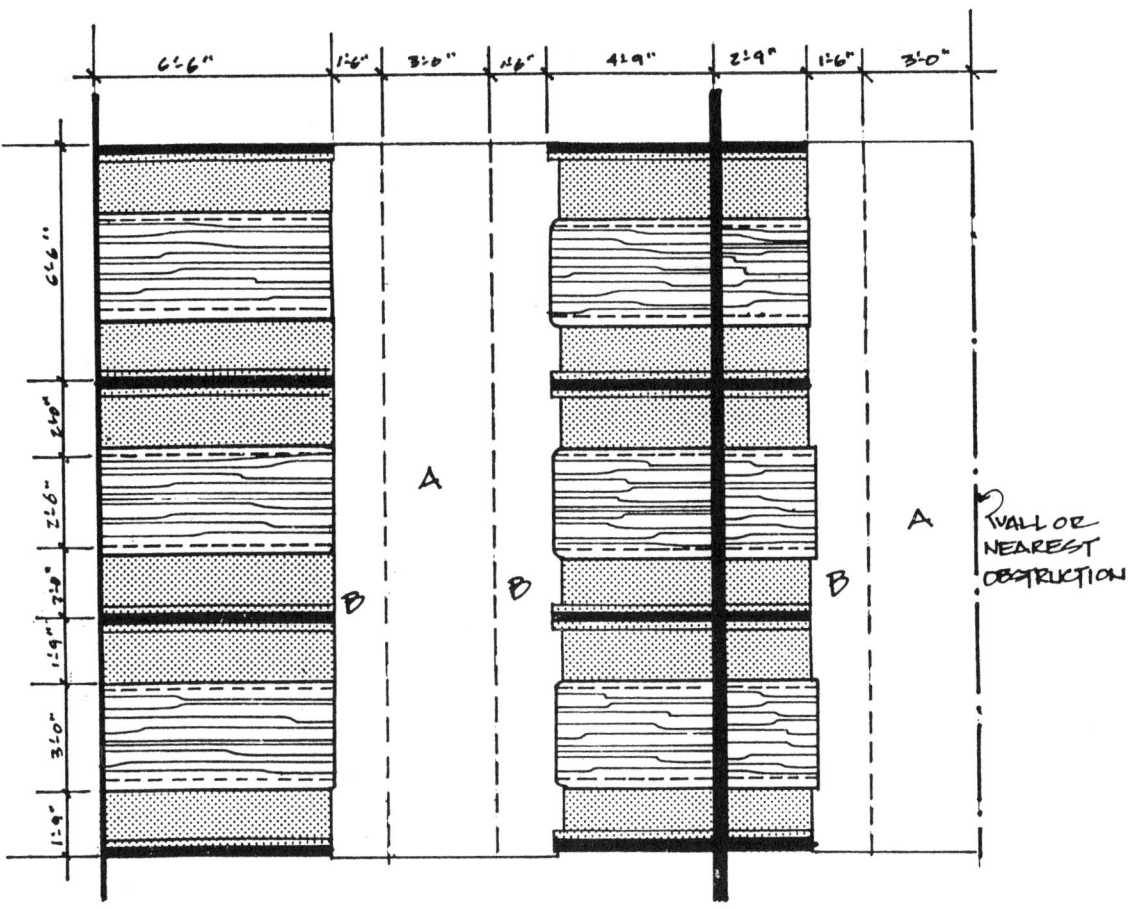

**Fig. 18**   24 ft × 20 ft, 480 ft², seats 36. A = main circulation, B = activity zone.

**Fig. 19**   13 ft × 13 ft, 169 ft², seats 16.

# RESTAURANTS

**Dining Room Seating**

### Restaurant and Dining Room Seating

Dispersed seating suitable for guests with restricted mobility should be available in restaurants, coffee shops, and dining facilities. As a guide, the Uniform Federal Accessibility Standards (UFAS) require a minimum of 5 percent of restaurant seating to be accessible. Accessible aisles should connect the entrance to these seating locations, public restrooms, and self-service areas such as salad bars, condiment stands, or buffet tables. Comfortable seating for waiting should be available to customers near the entrance.

A variety of accessible seating should be available, suitable for large and small dining groups. Small tables may not be accessible to guests in wheelchairs because of the restricted kneespace. Therefore, a party of one or two may require a table usually set up for four. Restaurants or coffee shops with built-in seating, such as booths or banquettes, should also provide some chairs for guests who have difficulty getting into and out of bench seating. These chairs can be removed to seat guests in wheelchairs. Where seating areas are raised on platforms, accessible seating and similar services should be available on the main-floor level or a ramp to the upper level should be provided.

Aisles serving accessible seating should be at least 3'0" wide, which typically requires a 6'0" clearance between parallel tables, or 4'6" between rotated tables. (See Fig. 21.) Aisle widths should also provide room for customers to be seated at tables. At least a 2'6" clear space should be available behind each seating location. This space allows chairs to be withdrawn from the table and staff to assist guests reposition chairs close to the table.

For wheelchair seating, a 3'0" to 3'6" aisle is necessary, depending on the width of the kneespace. (See Fig. 25.) Wheelchairs positioned at tables project approximately 5" further into aisles than most chairs. To allow guests with restricted mobility to turn around, seating arrangements should also include a 5'0" diameter circle or T-shaped clear area at dead-end aisles.

### Dining Tables and Chairs

Accessible seating locations should allow guests with restricted mobility to dine with ambulatory customers. Tables should provide kneespace for customers in wheelchairs, and dining chairs should be coordinated to provide comfortable seating at the same table height.

Dining room chairs should be stable to maintain balance as guests seat themselves, and comfortable to sit in during dinner. Chairs should be light and easy to reposition. The seat should have a slight slant to the rear to transfer body weight to the back of the chair. However, an exaggerated incline makes it difficult to rise. The seat should be approximately 16" deep and at least 16" wide to allow space for customers to reposition themselves during the meal. Padding or cushions on the chair seat should be firm, and the chair back should also be slightly inclined to the rear. To help guests sit and rise, dining chairs should have armrests 7" to 8" above the front edge of the seat. (See Fig. 22.) Supports or cross-bracing should not

**Fig. 20** Restaurants or coffee shops with fixed seating should include some movable seating for guests in wheelchairs and guests who have difficulty getting into and out of the bench seating. Number in parentheses is dimension in centimeters.

**Fig. 21** Aisles serving accessible seating should provide a path at least 3'0" wide for passage and clear space for guests to seat themselves at tables. Numbers in parentheses are dimensions in centimeters.

interfere with kickspace below the seat, so the feet can be positioned to rise. The front edge of the chair seat should be low enough to allow the feet to rest on the floor, but not so low that it is difficult to rise. This is determined by the lower leg length (popliteal height) which varies between 15″ and 20″ for most adults.

The height of the chair seat should be 10½″ to 11½″ below the top of the table. Common seat heights vary between 14″ and 18″. Because the height of wheelchair seats is typically 19″, a relatively high chair seat is necessary to coordinate with the table height. A chair with an 18″ high seat is comfortable for most ambulatory guests and closely approximates the height of a wheelchair seat.

Dining room tables should have a stable surface at a convenient height and kneespace and legroom below the tabletop for customers in wheelchairs. Narrow table configurations allow face-to-face seating, which

reduces the distance between diners, making conversation easier and table lighting more effective. For safety, the corners and edges of the top should be rounded.

Full-height wheelchair kneespace is 2′6″, which requires tabletops to be at least 2′7″ above the floor, too high for most seating. Many wheelchairs now provide adjustable or two-tier armrests, which allow customers to sit close to tables in a kneespace only 2′3″ high. To provide this kneespace, the tabletop (without an apron) should be 2′4½″ to 2′5″ above the floor. This is 11″ to 11½″ above the chair seat, 10½″ to 11″ above the seat of wheelchairs, and convenient for both. This kneespace also permits the armrests of chairs to pass below the tabletop so seated customers can draw close. This combination of tables and chairs is suitable for the majority of wheelchair users and most ambulatory guests.

Footroom is important for customers with wheelchairs or leg braces. The footrests of

wheelchairs are 2½″ to 3″ above the ground and angled slightly forward, which requires 1′7″ of footroom, measured from the edge of the tabletop. The outside width of footrests is only 1′6″, but 2′6″ of side-to-side clearance is necessary to maneuver into position beneath the table. To provide kneespace, table legs should be at least 2′6″ apart, and the tabletop, for face-to-face seating, should be 3′6″ wide. Pedestalbase tables should have low, tapered bases and a minimum diameter of 3′6″, although 4′0″ is preferred.

A portable raised leaf should be available to modify tables for customers in wheelchairs with high armrests. The leaf should be approximately the size of a place setting, 1′4″ by 2′0″, and secured to the underside of an accessible table with clamps. The raised leaf should project 6″ beyond the edge of the table and provide 2′6″ clearance above the floor. (See Fig. 24.)

**Fig. 22**  Dining room chairs should have a seat 10½″ to 11½″ below the top of the table and armrests 7″ to 8″ above the seat. To coordinate with an accessible table, the seat height should be 18″. Numbers in parentheses are dimensions in centimeters.

**Fig. 23**  Accessible tables should provide kneespace at least a 2′3″ high by 2′6″ wide with 1′7″ of footroom. To increase the kneespace height, a raised portable leaf can be provided. (See Fig. 24.) Numbers in parentheses are dimensions in centimeters.

| Kneespace Width | Clearance |
|---|---|
| 2′-6″ (minimum) | 3′-6″ |
| 3′-0″ or greater | 3′-0″ |

**Fig. 24**  A portable raised leaf can be provided for accessible tables to accommodate customers in wheelchairs with high armrests. Numbers in parentheses are dimensions in centimeters.

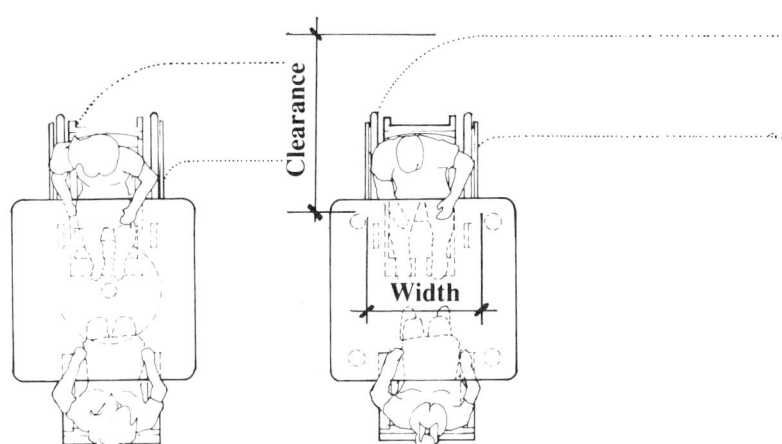

**Fig. 25**  The necessary maneuvering room required to access a kneespace depends on its width.

# RESTAURANTS

**Banquettes: Design Criteria**

Figure 27 shows the basic dimensions for the design of banquette seating. The lack of armrests makes it difficult to define seat boundaries. The user, therefore, tends to establish a territory by assuming a desired sitting posture and placing personal articles next to him or her, such as a briefcase, purse, or package. Since the nature of this type of seating can permit some form of body contact, hidden dimensions and personal space also play an important part in how close the users sharing the banquette will sit.

Because of the many hidden psychological factors involved, the actual efficiency of this seating type in terms of capacity is questionable. Figure 27 indicates two possible seating situations, each dictated by the anthropometrics involved. One arrangement is based on the premise that the user's elbows will be extended, possibly in conjunction with some activity, such as reading, or simply as an attempt to stake out additional territory, as would be the case in the strategic positioning of some personal article on the seat. In this situation it would be reasonable to assume that each user would take up about 30 in, or 76.2 cm, of space. The other diagram shows a more compact seating arrangement. Figure 26 shows a section through a typical banquette.

**SECTION**

**Fig. 26  Banquette seating.**

| | in | cm |
|---|---|---|
| **A** | 18–24 | 45.7–61.0 |
| **B** | 15.5–16 | 39.4–40.6 |
| **C** | 16–17 | 40.6–43.2 |
| **D** | 30 | 76.2 |
| **E** | 24 | 61.0 |

**LOW DENSITY**          **HIGH DENSITY**

**Fig. 27  Banquette seating.**

Banquette seating provides the designer with one of the few opportunities to custom design restaurant seating. While there can be a great variety of aesthetic solutions achieved through use of various materials, ergonomic considerations must be analyzed carefully. Specific attention should be given to depth of seat, slope of seat and back, height of back, and relationship of seat height to table height.

**TYPICAL BANQUETTE DETAIL**
SCALE 1½" = 1'-0"

**④ ELEVATION / CONFERENCE ROOM**

CHROME FINISH
SURFACE MOUNTED
CANOPY LIGHT ?-
@ 16" O.C.

ACOUSTONE CEILING

4" THICK GYP. BOARD
& MET. STUD FASCIA.

SOUND ATTEN. BLANKET

GYPSUM BOARD

BANQUETTE CUSHIONS
TO BE REMOVABLE

CURVED ½" PLYWOOD
BACK ATTACHED TO
CURVED PARTITION.

½" PLYWOOD SPACER
AS REQUIRED. FASTEN
TO WALL.

ENTIRE WOOD FRAME
RIBS, PLYWOOD BY
NICO.

"FABRIC SELECTION"

DACRON FILL

VERY FULL LATEX
FOAM RUBBER
CUSHION FRAME
W/VELCRO FAST.
NER.

PAINT

CARPET (HERE)

¾" PLYWOOD RIBS 1'6" O.C.
SHIM AS REQUIRED TO LEVEL
PLYWOOD CLOSURE

④ AIV-3 / SECTION THRU BANQUETTE
SCALE 1½" = 1'-0"

Seat    Table    Seat
1'-8½"    2'-4"    1'-8½"

PLAN of SEATS 3/8" scale

Table
Wood    Formica

ELEVATION of SEATS

ELEVATION of
SEAT BACK
1" scale

Finished wall

2'-2"

¾" × 2½"

Formica base

Top of wainscot

SECTION
1" scale

3"

3'-0"

Cushions

3'-5"

1" × 1¾"

1¾" × 1¾"

7"

7"

1'-3"

Floor

Banquette seating can be detailed relatively simply, as Figs. 28 to 30 suggest. The simplest form of banquette seating may take the form of a plywood seating platform with a removable seat cushion, or a box cushion seat and back support. Such seating is appropriate in fast food or quick turnover restaurant operations.

PARTIAL PLAN

MAHOG FINISH

MAHOG MOLDING

DYKES MOLDING #121 MAHOG FINISH

¼ CLEAR GLASS W ¾ BEVELED EDGES & ETCHED GRAPHIC BY OTHERS
OR
¼ FROSTED GLASS W ¾ BEVELED EDGES & CLEAR GRAPHIC BY OTHERS

MAHOG FINISH
DYKES MOLDING #121
MAHOG FINISH

BOX CUSHION (SEAT & BACK) BY OTHERS

MAHOG FINISH

¼ RAD. ROUND EDGE

BLOCKING

DYKES MOLDING #131 MAHOG FIN
½ PLYWD BACKING

⑧ DETAIL OF BANQUETTE & LOW PARTITION
A7 SCALE: 1½"=1'-0"

**Fig. 28**

① PLAN: PLYWD. SEAT'G
A6 PLATFORM NR. OFFICE
½"=1'-0"

② PLAN: PLYWD. SEAT'G
A6 PLATFORM @ ENTRY
½"=1'-0"

CONCEAL BRIDGING IN WALL BETWEEN STUDS @ PLY STIFFEN. LOCATIONS

SEAT CUSHION (N.I.C.)

MITER EDGE, SAND DULL.

¾" PLYWD. PAINT W/ SEALER & TWO COATS HI-GLOSS BLACK, SAND BETN. COATS

CONTIN. 2x3 ALL AROUND

2x3 @ 16' O.C.

¾" PLY STIFFENER RIB

⑤ SECTION: PLYWOOD SEATING PLATFORM
A6 1½"=1'-0"

**Fig. 29**

¾"x 6" BIRD'S EYE MAPLE CAP

¾" BIRD'S EYE MAPLE PANEL W. VERT. BLACK REVEAL 2"x¼"

PLASTIC LAMINATE EDGE BLACK FORMICA #904

FABRIC TO BE SELECTED

SLOPE 1½"

¾"x4" BIRD'S EYE MAPLE BASE
CARPET

PLASTIC LAM.

¾"x4" BIRD'S EYE MAPLE BASE

⑥ SECTION OF BANQUETTE
A4 SCALE: 1½"=1'-0"

**Fig. 30**

# RESTAURANTS

**Lunch Counters: Design Criteria**

Figure 31 shows some of the basic clearances required for a typical counter: 36 in, or 91.4 cm, for workspace behind the counter; 18 to 24 in, or 45.7 to 61 cm, for the counter top; and 60 to 66 in, or 152.4 to 167.6 cm, between the front face of the counter and the nearest obstruction. Figure 32 shows a section through the counter and back counter. Most counters are about 42 in, or 106.7 cm, in height. The clearance from the top of the seat to the underside of the counter top and the depth of the counter top overhang are extremely important. Buttock-knee length and thigh clearance are the key anthropometric measurements to consider for proper body fit. Footrest heights should take into consideration popliteal height. In most cases this is ignored, and 42-in counters are provided with 7-in, or 17.8-cm, footrests that are 23 in, or 58.4 cm, below the seat surface, which cannot work. The popliteal height of the larger user, based on 99th percentile data, is only about 20 in, or 50.8 cm. Therefore, the feet dangle unsupported several inches above the footrest and the body is deprived of any stability. The footrest shown in Fig. 32, although higher, only serves a portion of the seated users and is intended primarily for standing patrons. The most logical solution is a separate footrest, integral with the stool.

| | in | cm |
|---|---|---|
| A | 60–66 | 152.4–167.6 |
| B | 18–24 | 45.7–61.0 |
| C | 36 | 91.4 |
| D | 24 | 61.0 |
| E | 12–18 | 30.5–45.7 |
| F | 35–36 | 88.9–91.4 |
| G | 42 | 106.7 |
| H | 30–31 | 76.2–78.7 |
| I | 11–12 | 27.9–30.5 |
| J | 10 | 25.4 |
| K | 12–13 | 30.5–33.0 |

Fig. 31   Lunch counter.

Fig. 32   Lunch counter.

NOTE:

1. ALL WOOD VENEER SHALL BE OAK LEREX.

2. SEE <.C.M. DWG # KO-16 FOR DETAIL OF SERVERY EQUIP. COUNTER.

3. STAINLESS STEEL BASE TO MATCH FINISH OF SERVERY EQUIP. COUNTERTOP.

PLAN

SCALE ¾" = 1'-0"

PLAN

SCALE ¾" = 1'-0"

ELEVATION  C

SCALE ¾" = 1'-0"

ELEVATION  D

SCALE ¾" = 1'-0"

WOOD VENEER FIN.

1'-8"

1'-0"

2'-8"

2"  2"

I"  EQ.  EQ.

WOOD VENEER FIN.

4'-5¾"

1¼"

4¼"

2⅛"

2'-10"

¼"×¾"×¼" ALUM. SLIDE INSERTS

STAINLESS STEEL COUNTER BY OTHERS

ANGLE FRAMES

ANGLE FRAMES

WOOD VENEER FIN.

CERAMIC TILE FLOOR

ST. ST. BASE

CERAMIC TILE FLOOR.

4"

BLOCKING AS REQ'D.

LINE OF SLAB

2"

### SECTION 1

SCALE  3" = 1'-0"

SS. SERVER EQUIP. BY K.C.M. SEE DWG. KD-16

2"

WOOD VENEER FIN.

WOOD VENEER

2'-10"

2"

MINIMUM 'V' JOINT

WOOD VENEER FIN.

5'-0"

BLOCKING AS REQ'D.

4"

S.S. BASE

2"

WOOD VENEER FIN.

### SECTION 2

SCALE: 3" = 1'-0"

### PLAN SECTION 3

SCALE: 3" = 1'-0"

4" FROSTED GLASS

LIGHT FXT. # H

4" PEACH MIRROR W. POL. EDGE

BLOCKING AS REQ'D

RED MAHOGANY OIL FINISH

COUNTER at CASH REGISTER (SHOWN DOTTED)

INTER'M SUPPORTING DIAPHRAGMS VERIFY W. EQUIP. SIZE

BACK BAR EQUIP. & UNDER COUNTER CAB FINISH TO BE RED MAHOGANY OIL FIN. (SHOWN DOTTED) BY PERLICK

RED MAHOGANY OIL FIN.

PROVIDE VERTICAL SLOTS at WING PANELS FOR HEAT RELEASE

FROZEN BEVERAGE DISPENSER BY PERLICK (SHOWN DOTTED)

RED MAHOGANY OIL FINISH

PROVIDE 4 CASTERS FOR REMOVABLE SECTION

③ SECT. of BACK BAR COUNTER W. LIQUER DISPLAY
A9  SCALE: 1½"=1'-0"

④ SECT. of CABINET for FROZEN BEVERAGE DISPENSER
A9  SCALE: 1½"=1'-0"

S/S SHELF BY BASIC

METAL SUPPORTING BRACKETS

BLACK FORMICA FIN at SERV. STAT'N # 111 & # 212, RED LAVANTO MARBLE FIN at BREAD STATION

SET CASH REGISTER INTO MARBLE TOP W. 1'-4½" x 1'-0½" CUT OUT, NEED 10" LEDGE FOR KEY BOARD. (SHOWN DOTTED)

DRAWER

BLACK FORMICA FIN. at SERV. STAT'N # 111 & # 212, RED MAHOGANY OIL FIN at BREAD STATION

ADJ. SHELVES

VERT. PIN HOLES at 2" O.C.

S/S SHELF BY BASIC

METAL SUPPORTING BRACKETS

RED LAVANTO MARBLE TOP, HONED FINISH

TILED WALL

SINK

SINK STAND BY BASIC

ADJ. SHELF

VERT. PIN HOLES at 2" O.C.

⑧ CABINET DETAIL at SERVICE STATIONS # 111 & 212, BREAD ST'N # 113
A9  SCALE: 1½"=1'-0"

⑨ CABINET DETAIL at KITCHEN #112
A9  SCALE: 1½"=1'-0"

EXISTING WINDOW

RED MAHOGANY OIL FINISH

SPEAKER

RED MAHOGANY OIL FINISH

4" FLUTEX GLASS, RIBBED HORIZONTALLY LIGHT FIXTURE # D

RED MAHOGANY, OIL FINISH

TILED WALL

BLACK FORMICA FINISH

ADJUSTABLE SHELVES SEE 6 A9 FOR ELEVAT'N

VERT. PIN HOLES at 2" O.C.

EXISTING WINDOW

RED MAHOGANY OIL FINISH

⑫ DET. of WINDOW SILL CABINET
A9  SCALE: 1½"=1'-0"

⑭ LIGHT/CAB ABOVE COUNTER at KITCHEN # 112
A9  SCALE: 1½"=1'-0"

⑮ DET. of LOW WINDOW SILL CAB. at DINING # 101
A9  SCALE: 1½"=1'-0"  (SIM. DET. at VIP DINING # 211)

⑯ CABINET DET. of GLASS STORAGE
A9  SCALE: 1½"=1'-0"

**① SECT. of FRONT BAR COUNTER**
A9   SCALE: 1½" = 1'-0"

**② SECT. of CASH REGISTER COUNTER at BAR #103**
A9   SCALE: 1½" = 1'-0"

**⑥ CAB. DETAIL of HAMPER UNIT at SERVICE STATION #108**
A9   SCALE: 1½" = 1'-0"

**⑦ CABINET DETAIL at SERVICE STATION #108**
A9   SCALE: 1½" = 1'-0"

**⑫ DETAIL of FLORAL CABINET**
A9   SCALE: 1½" = 1'-0"

**⑤ SECT. of COUNTER at ESPRESSO & ANTIPASTO #109**
A9   SCALE: 1½" = 1'-0"

**A** ELEVATION OF SERVING ISLAND

- FINISHED CEILING
- POLISHED BRASS
- DOWN LIGHTS
- PLEXIGLASS SNEEZE GUARD
- STAINLESS STEEL TRAY INSET
- MARBLE COLUMN
- PLASTIC LAMINATE OR PAINTED GLASS
- 4" ROYER TILE BASE

8'-6"
9"
1'-0"
1'-0"
4"
1'-0"
12'-0"

---

**Section BB**

- FINISHED CEILING
- 1/2" x 1/2" POLISHED BRONZE L
- PLASTIC LAM.
- 2" RAD. TOP & BOTTOM FIN. POLISHED BRONZE
- SUPPORT AS NECESSARY
- POLISHED ALUMINUM
- LIGHTING TO FOLLOW
- 1/2" x 1/2" POLISHED BRONZE L
- PLASTIC LAMINATE

2'-0"
9"
1/2"
1'-0"

**BB** SECTION THRU HOOD

---

**Section CC**

- PLEXIGLASS SNEEZE GUARD SUPPORTS TO BE 1/2" DIAM. POL. BRONZE
- PLASTIC LAMINATE
- POL. BRONZE
- PLASTIC LAM.
- MARBLE TO HAVE 2" RAD TOP & BOTTOM MARBLE TO BE BONDED TO PLYWOOD SUPPORT AS NECESSARY
- 1/2" x 1/2" POL. BRONZE L
- ROYER TILE BASE

1/2" TYP.
2" 2" 2" 2" 2"
1/2"
1'-0"
2'-0"
4"
4"

**CC** SECTION THRU SERVING COUNTER

**Fig. 33  Waiter stations and host/hostess counters can be designed as freestanding elements or integrated into the interior architecture, as shown by these details. Special attention must be given to specific drawer and storage requirements.**

STAINED MAHOGANY VENEER ¾" PLY COUNTER & LIP.

CONTIN. OXIDIZED COPPER STRIP

BRASS ROUND HEAD, PHILLIPS SCREW W/ OXIDIZED COPPER GROMMET

COUNTERS SCREWED TO FLANGE OF STEEL BRACKETS; BRACKETS WELDED TO STEEL POST

STAINED MAHOGANY VENEER ¾" PLY COUNTER & LIP

STAINED ASH VENEER ¾" PLY PANEL W/ ¾" WOOD EDGE BAND

PANEL BOLTED TO PRE-DRILLED ¾" X 1½" STL. CLEAT WELDED TO POST.

1½"Ø STL. PIPE FOOTREST

STL. FOOTREST BRACKET

2" X 2" STL. PIPE BOLTED TO STL. BASE. STL. BASE PLATE BOLTED TO CONC. & SET INTO MORTAR BED

BRASS, ROUND HEAD BOLT W/ OXIDIZED COPPER GROMMET

+2'-3" FIN. FLOOR

NOTE:
ALL STEEL JOINTS TO BE SHOP WELDED & GROUND SMOOTH.
ALL STEEL TO BE 'BLUE' FINISH UNLESS OTHERWISE NOTED.

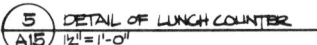

5 / A15  DETAIL OF LUNCH COUNTER  1½" = 1'-0"

6 / A8  LONG PART/SECTION THRU RAISED DINING AREA  ½" = 1'-0"

6 / A8  CROSS SECTION THRU RAISED DINING AREA  ½" = 1'-0"

10 / A8  SECTION @ CURVED SEAT IN SHUFFLE BD. AREA  1½" = 1'-0"

# RESTAURANTS
**Wheelchair Accessibility to Self-Service Areas**

### Self-Service Areas

Salad bars, buffet lines, condiment stands, and other self-service areas should be accessible. Cafeteria or food-service lines should have a minimum width of 3'0", but a width of 3'6" is recommended to permit ambulatory customers to pass customers in wheelchairs.

The tray slide should be 2'10" above the floor, the maximum height for customers in wheelchairs and convenient for ambulatory guests. The tray slide should be continuous, if possible, from the entrance to the cashier. Tray slides restrict access to the counters and therefore should not be wider than necessary (1'0" recommended). In this instance, the reach of a customer in a wheelchair is extended if the wheelchair can be angled or positioned perpendicular to the tray slide. This is possible if the lower face of the counter is recessed to provide low knee-space. (See Fig. 34.)

For guests with a limited range-of-motion, food, beverages, utensils, or other items should be displayed near the edge of the counter where they are easier to see and reach. When duplicate items are displayed, a vertical rather than horizontal arrangement allows customers to select items at the most convenient height. Self-service systems, such as beverage or ice-dispensers, should be easy to operate without fine hand function. Instructions and price information should be prominently displayed in large clear lettering.

Salad bars and buffets should provide a 3'0"-wide clear space for access on all sides and plate slides, or areas to temporarily set plates, at a maximum height of 2'10". This permits customers to serve themselves with one hand, without simultaneously balancing the plate or bowl. Kneespace 2'3" high below the counter or table allows front wheelchair approach, to increase customers' forward reach. Condiments should be located as low and close to the edge of the counter or table as practical. A tilted mirror above the food display at salad bars also aids customers in wheelchairs and children. (See Fig. 35.) For some customers with restricted mobility, poor balance, or limited hand function, it is more difficult to carry a plate. Therefore trays should be available at both salad bars and buffets.

**Fig. 34** Cafeteria lines should be wide enough to accommodate guests in wheelchairs. Food and beverages should be within a convenient vertical and horizontal reach. Numbers in parentheses are dimensions in centimeters.

**Fig. 35** A plate slide is recommended at salad bars and a kneespace at the counter. A mirrored surface above the bar is a further aid to guests in wheelchairs. Numbers in parentheses are dimensions in centimeters.

PLAN
SCALE ¾" = 1'-0"

PLAN
SCALE ¾" = 1'-0"

ELEVATION A
SCALE ¾" = 1'-0"

ELEVATION B
SCALE ¾" = 1'-0"

ELEVATION E
SCALE ¾" = 1'-0"

6 PLAN OF LUNCH COUNTER
A14  ½" = 1'-0"

7 ELEVATION OF LUNCH COUNTER FROM DINING ROOM
A14  ½" = 1'-0"

8 SIDE ELEVATION OF LUNCH COUNTER
A14  ½" = 1'-0"

9 SECTION THRU BAR
A14  ½" = 1'-0"

10 PLAN OF CASHIERS STATION
A14  ½" = 1'-0"

11 SOUTH ELEVATION OF CASHIERS STATION
A14  ½" = 1'-0"

12 WEST ELEVATION OF CASHIER STATION
A14  ½" = 1'-0"

13 EAST ELEVATION OF CASHIER STATION
A14  ½" = 1'-0"

CANTILEVER SNEEZE GUARD TO BE SUPPORTED FROM THIS LEVEL OF TIERED SOFFIT & CONSIST OF A BRUSHED STAINLESS STEEL SUPPORT RING. RING SHALL HAVE A CONSTANT RADIUS. CLEAR ACRYLIC PANELS TO BE ATTACHED TO SUPPORT RING W/ CONCEALED FASTENERS.

TRAY HOLDERS W/ PLASTIC LAMINATE FIN.

FREE STANDING WALL W/ TILE FINISH

**A** ELEVATION OF TYPICAL 'ROTARY SERVING' UNIT

NOTE:
FOOD CONSULTANT SHALL PROVIDE SHOP DWGS. FOR:
- FOOD SERVICE ISLANDS
- ROTARY SERVICE UNITS
- ALL SNEEZE GUARDS
- TRAY STATIONS

TRAY GLIDES TO BE PLACED IN TRAY SLIDE TO FORM A CONTINUOUS PATTERN AROUND 'ISLAND'

TRAY SLIDE TO BE SOLID OAK BUTCHER BLOCK

**B** PARTIAL PLAN OF TYPICAL 'ISLAND'

STAINLESS STEEL
OAK BUTCHER BLOCK
PLASTIC LAMINATE
TILE BASE

2'-6"
3'-6"

**C** PARTIAL ELEVATION

PLASTIC LAMINATE

STAINLESS STEEL EQUIPMENT SURFACE

FLOOR MATERIAL CONTINUED UP BASE OF 'ISLAND'

**DD** SECTION OF TRAY SLIDE

**A** PLAN AT MARBLE COUNTER

POLISH EDGES

DRAINS

MARBLE SHELF ABOVE

FIELD DRILL FOR ELECT.

STAINLESS STEEL ICE PANS BY EQUIP. MAN. CO.

MARBLE JOINTS

MARBLE GRAIN

PAINTED STEEL TUBING

MANVILLE HALOPH-ANE LIGHT FIXTURE

MARBLE SHELF

PLEXI GLASS SNEEZE GUARD

AUBUSSON RED

MARBLE TOP
CERAMIC TILE

QUARRY TILE

**B** ELEVATION

STEEL TUBING 1½" DIAM.

MANVILLE HALOPHANE LIGHT FIXT.

"BRASS" NICKEL'D FACED

MARBLE SHELF

FLUOR. LT. FIXTURE

MILKY PLEXI GLASS

CLEAR PLEXI GLASS

MARBLE TOP

PLASTIC LAMINATE

BRACE

BRACK TILE
QUARRY TILE

BRACE

**CC** SECTION

① SECTION THROUGH CASHIER'S COUNTER

Adjustable shelf & 's.....
height to be determined by
size of equipment (to be verified)

Wood blocking
as req'd.

Removable plastic lam. panel
hardware to be co-ord. w/ arch.

Plastic lam. panels

Space for
electrical wire chase

Ceramic tile on cement
bed w/ waterproofing

Cinder block

Lighting fixture (roberts
step lite systems)

Ceramic tile on cement bed w/waterproofing & '8"th. protin. bd.

② SECTION THROUGH TRAY PICK-UP COUNTER

Tray dispenser

Trays

Plastic lam.
panels

Wood blkg.
as req.

Concrete curb

Ceramic tile on
cement bed w/
waterproofing and
protection bd.

③ SECTION DETAIL - SERVERY TRAYSLIDE
scale

Wen trayslide
metal edge'g
as req.

Pl. lam. trayslide
w/ '8" x 4" thick bar
finish brush st/stl

Kitchen equip.
see kitchen dwg
for information

Removeable
plastic lam. panels
w/ concealed
fasteners
hardware to be
co-ord. w/ arch.

Ceramic tile on
cement bed w/
waterproofing &
'8" th. protection bd.

Lighting fixture type

Waterproofing as req

Mud slab

Concrete curb
w/ sleeve for
all servery equip.
conduit & piping

CONCRETE PAD DETAIL FOR MECH
EQUIP + HOT WATER HEATER
@ ROOM # 4673
CO-ORDINATE SIZE OF PAD W/ EQUIP.

FLOOR SLAB

⑤ CONCRETE PAD DETAIL          1½" = 1'-0"
A320

CERAMIC TILE ON CEMENT BED
WATER PROOFING + PROTECT. BD
CEMENT ROUND CORNER

⑥ CONCRETE CURB @          1½" = 1'-0"
A320  SERVERY COUNTER

LINE OF TRAYSLIDE BEHIND
WOOD TRAYSLIDE NOSING
PLASTIC LAMINATE W/
⅛" REVEALS

RECESSED + CONCEALED
HINGES (GRASS OR EQ.)
CONT. WD. BLOCKING STOP W/
MAGNETIC CATCH + PTR TO
MATCH ADJ. PARTITION
GATE

FLUSH PL. LAM EDGE

⅛" REVEAL

⅛" REVEAL

④ ELEVATION @ SIDE + GATE SERVERY ISLAND          3" = 1'-0"
A320  SIM. FOR CASHIER

ST. STEEL KITCHEN
EQUIP.
SEE KIT. EQUIP DWGS

PLAST. LAM. TRAYSLIDE
W/ FIN. BRUSH ST/STL.

LOW PARTITION
@ SEATING AREA
ONLY

⅛" PLAS. LAM

STORAGE BELOW

HINGED
DOOR
W/ PLASTIC LAM. FIN.

CERAMIC TILE ON
CEMENT BED W/
WATER PROOFING
AND ⅛" THICK
PROTECTION BD.

CO-ORD HARDWARE
W/ ARCH.

LIGHTING FIXTURE
ROBERTS "STEP LITE" SYS.

CINDER BLOCK W/
PROTECT. BD @ TOP

⑦ SECTION THROUGH CONDIMENT COUNTER          3" = 1'-0"
A320  SCALE

ROLLING COUNTER DR.
SLATS #5 FINISH
TO MATCH PL. LAM.
COLOR

COUNTER DOOR:
TYPE CDB-1 MANUAL PUSH-UP
BY COOKSON MTR. BETWEEN JAMBS

PL. LAM.
COVER'D HD.

PL. LAM CLG. • JAMB
SEE 'K' SERIES DWGS.

SILL TO HEAD

① SECTION DET. @ TRAY DROP
A320   SCALE 3"=1'-0"

PLASTIC LAM. COVER'D JAMB

PLASTIC LAMINATE
TRAY DROP. SEE K-SERIES
DWGS FOR INFORMATION.

ALIGN

VK CTY • TILE ON
BAKER BOARD

CERAMIC TILE • WALLS
ON CEMENT BED
WATER PROOF • PROTECT BD

CEMENT ROUNDED CORNERS

⑩ SECTION DETAIL @ TRAY DROP
A320   SCALE 3" = 1'-0"

CERAMIC TILE
@ INTERIOR

SEE K-SERIES DWGS
FOR TRAY DROP-OFF
INFORMATION

PL. LAMINATE
COVERING
JAMB SEE
K-SERIES
FOR FURTHER
INFORMATION
ON JAMB CONST.

PL. LAM TRAY DROP. SEE K-SERIES

⑨ PLAN DETAIL
A320  SCALE 3" = 1'-0"

WD. NOSING @ TRAYSLIDE
TRAYSLIDE
SIDE PANEL TOP - PL. LAM.
GATE PL. LAM.

GRASS
HINGE
MAGNETIC
CATCH

⑪ PLAN SECTION @ GATE
A320

FITTCON STD FORM
CWR - CAS - 020

⑫ SECTION - FITTCON REVEAL
A320  SCALE 3"=1'-0"

LAP ENDS OF TRAYSLIDE TO
PROVIDE SUPPORT IN CLOSED
POSITION

WOOD NOSING & WOOD END
CERAMIC TILE ENDS (TYP)
NOTE:
ALL END PIECES TO BE
PLASTIC LAMINATE - PL.9
UNLESS OTHERWISE NOTED

OPEN @ ENDS

CASHIER'S ADJ
COUNTER

CASHIER'S GATE
2 PIECES - DOOR +
LIFT-UP TRAYSLIDE

⑮ AXONOMETRIC • PLAN  CASHIER'S GATE
A320  SCALE 1½" = 1'-0"

2'-0"

PLASTIC LAM. #B TOP
MAHOG. TRIM

PLASTIC LAM. #B

BLOCKING

$\frac{5}{A11}$ **SECTION thru SERVICE COUNTER**
SCALE: 1½"=1'-0"

VERMONT VERDI-
ANTIQUE MARBLE
HONED FINISH

DRAWER

BIRCH PLYWD. FIN.

MAHOG. VENEERED
PLYWD.

MAHOG. RAISED
PANEL

11"

SHELVING:
PLASTIC LAM. #A W.
MAHOG. EDGE

SUPPORTING BRACKET

PORCELAIN PANEL & ALUM.
MOLDING, ACCESSORIES

MAHOG. FINISH

FOCAL POINT
CROWN MOLDING
MAHOG. FIN.

GYPBD. PT'D

METAL STUDS

1'-3"

PLASTIC LAM. #A

MAHOG. TRIM

BLOCKING

$\frac{16}{A11}$ **SECT. of HOST CABINET**
SCALE: 1½"=1'-0"

PLASTIC LAM. TOP
W. MAHOG. TRIM

DRAWER

PLASTIC LAM. #A

ADJ. SHELF

METAL PIN W. VERT.
HOLES at 2" OC

MAHOG. BASE
PLASTIC LAM. BASE

$\frac{18}{A11}$ **TYP. WAITER'S STATION CABINET**
SCALE: 1½"=1'-0"

$\frac{19}{A11}$ **SECT. of TRASH COUNTER CABINET**
SCALE: 1½"=1'-0"

**23** CONDIMENT CABINETS
SPACE NO. 21 @ 1" = 1'-0"

CW 13

**25** @ 1½" = 1'-0"

NOTE:
ALL PLASTIC LAMINATE
SHALL BE TEXTOLITE
MUSHROOM NO. 1682

**24** @ 1" = 1'-0"

**2** SERVER PLAN @ DINING RM. #4
1" = 1'-0"

**A** SERVER ELEV. @ DINING RM. #4
1" = 1'-0"

**1** TYP. SERVER SECTION
1" = 1'-0"

SEE 62/AB-4
FOR SNEEZE
GUARD DIMS

SEE ELEVATIONS
FOR SNEEZE GUARD
LOCATIONS

FLOURESCENT FIXTURE
"MARCY" # 8071

INTERMEDIATE SUPPORT,
COORD. LOCATION
W/ K.E.C.

WOOD BLOCK'G

BRUSHED S/S COUNTER TOP (BY OTHERS)G.C.
TO COORDINATE W/ K.E.C.

⅜" THICK S/S BRACKET SUBMIT SHOP
DRAW'GS AND SAMPLE TO ISD FOR
APPROVAL PRIOR TO FABRICATION.

¾" DIA. BRUSHED S/S MT'L TUBING

PROVIDE CONT. 1½"X 3½" BLOCK'G AT
BRACKET MOUNT'G HT.

"Z" CLIP (⅛" SHIM SPACE)

⅝" PLYWD. W/ COLOR CORE PLAS. LAM. FACE
AND EDGES & ½2" PLAS. LAM. BACK'G

EQUIP. (BY OTHERS)G.C.
TO COORDINATE ALL
MECH., ELEC. & PLUMB'G
REQUIREMENTS W/
K.E.C.

⅜" PLYWD. W/½2" PLAS. LAM. FIN.

1⅝" MT'L STUD 18" O.C.

1⅝" FLR. RUNNER SECURE TO CONC. PAD

½" BIRCH PLYWD. PT. FINISH

5/16" TILE COVE BASE

½" THIN SET

GROUT AS PER TILE MANUF'R SPEC'N

TILE FIN. FLOOR

MORTAR BED

EXIST'G CONC. SLAB

LIGHT WEIGHT
CONC. PAD

ALIGN

GYP. BD. CEILING

FOR WALL TYPE
SEE CONST. PLAN

½" REVEAL
½" PAINT GRADE

¼" SOLID CORE
PLAS. LAM.

GYP. BD. PAINTED

2'-2"

8'-0" A.F.F.

SILVER & NAPKIN
HOLDER BY K.E.C.

FIXTURE TYPE SEE
LIGHTING FIXTURE
SCHEDULE

CERAMIC TILE

67
AB-4

15'

S.S. COUNTER TOP

½" BIRCH PLY. WD.

6"

SPECIFIED TRASH
CONTAINER
14½" SQ. × 28" h
BY K.E.C.

24"

36"

½" ¼"

BOTTOM OF CABINET
CUT OUT TO HOUSE
TRASH CONTAINER
CUTOUT DIM: 1'-6"±

3"

5"

**Condiment counter**

FOR WALL TYPE SEE
CONSTRUCTION PLAN

PROVIDE REQ'D BLOCKING
FOR SOFFIT

ADDITIONAL LEVEL OF
⅝" GYP. BD.

55
AB-4

2'-0" MT.

10'-0" MT.

¼" REVEAL

⅜" SOLID CORE PLAS. LAM.

2'-0"

8'-0" A.F.F.

SILVER & NAPKIN HOLDER BY K.E.C.

FIXTURE TYPE SEE LIGHTING
FIXTURE SCHEDULE

TOP OF COUNTER CUT OUT TO
HOUSE TRAY DISPENSER

15"

S.S. COUNTER TOP

½" BIRCH PLY WD.

TRAY DISPENSER
BY K.E.C.

30"

6" TILE COVE BASE

G.C. TO VERIFY
EQUIP. CUT-OUT DIMS
W/ K.E.C.

5"

**Section at tray pick-up**

GYP. BD. CEILING

FOR WALL TYPE
SEE CONST. PLAN

¼" REVEAL

½" PAINT GRADE

¾" SOLID CORE
PLAS. LAM.

GYP. BD. PAINTED

2'-2"

8'-0" A.F.F.

SILVER & NAPKIN
HOLDER BY K.E.C.

FIXTURE TYPE SEE
LIGHTING FIXTURE
SCHEDULE

CERAMIC TILE

S.S. COUNTER TOP

½" BIRCH PLY. WD.

SPECIFIED TRASH
CONTAINER
14½" SQ. x 28" H
BY K.E.C.

BOTTOM OF CABINET
CUT OUT TO HOUSE
TRASH CONTAINER
CUTOUT DIM: 1'-6" ±

67
AB-4

15"

6"

24"

36"

5"

S.S. COUNTER TOP

SPRING LOADED
HINGE

S.S. FACE COVER

SOLID CORE
PLAS. LAM.

S.S. LOUVER DOOR

6" TILE COVE BASE

6"

5½"

1½"

3"

**DETAIL SECTION AT
CONDIMENT COUNTER**

SECTION AT STONE COUNTERS

- LINE OF FIN CEILING
- SILICON ADHESIVE AND BRACKETS AS PER MANUF'R SPECIFICATION
- 'NEOPARIUM B' PANELS
- 1⅝" MT'L STUD W/2 LAYERS ⅝" GYP. BD.
- LINE OF WALL BEYOND
- PITTCON # STR - 038-050
- S/S ∠
- EQUIP. G.C. TO COORDINATE ALL DIM. & CLEARANCES W/ K.E.C.
- 1½" POLISHED GRANITE TOP
- ¾" PLYWD. LAMINATED TO GRANITE
- STEEL ∠ AS REQ'D
- ½" BIRCH PLYWD.
- ¾" PLYWD W/ PLAS. LAM. FACE.
- 1⅝" MET'L STUD
- 'NEOPARIUM B' PANEL AND BASE
- SILICON SEAL
- FIN. FLR. EL. 355'-0⅜"

2'-9" HOLD

CONC. PAD

---

- 1⅝" M.S. FRAMING
- LGHT FIX. SEE LIGHT'G SCHDULE
- ½' PLYWD.
- PAINT FLAT WHITE
- SCHEDULED CEILING
- ½' X ½' EGGCRATE LOUVRE WHT. FINISH
- MIRROR MASTIC
- ¼" SHIM SPACE
- 2½" M.S.
- ¾" POLISHED GRANITE (ST-1)
- ½" PLYWD. BACKING
- ¾" POLISHED GRANITE
- STEEL WELDING
- 2½" X 2½" STEEL ∠
- FIN. FLR. ELEV. 355'-⅜"
- COVE TILE BASE TO MATCH CT-4
- CT-4
- MORTAR BED

VERT. SECTION AT
SALAD BAR / GRANITE COUNTER

VERT. SECTION THROUGH CABINET AT SALAD BAR

VERT. SECTION AT CENTER OF SALAD BAR
& PROTECTIVE GLASS GUARD

PATTERNED PERFORATED TOP PAINTED TO MATCH PL. LAM

PL-1 PANEL

ACCESS DOOR PL-1

HORIZONTAL PANEL ATTACHED TO DOOR, H/CUP DISPENSER; IN FRONT OF ENCLOSURE PANEL ONLY.

SS. DOUBLE PAN PANEL W/3" RETURN EACH SIDE; ALIGN W/FACE OF EQUIP.

EQUIP.

SIDE PANEL BEYOND

TUFF TOP

PL-1

10/AB-9

TUFF TOP

PL-1

14/AB-9     15/AB-9

10/AB-9

## HOT FOOD STAND

3/16"W x 3/8"H BRONZE INSERTS

6"

1½"   3½"   3½"   1½"

½"

2½"

TUFFTOP MONOLITHIC CUSTOM CAST SHAPE WITH FACTORY CUTOUTS.

3'-0"

## TRAY SLIDE

## COLD BEVERAGE & DESSERT STAND

SCHED P.LAM MILLWORK

BOTTOM OF MILLWORK ATTACHED TO WOOD BLOCKING BASE

½"

4"

SCHED CERAMIC TILE BASE THINSET

TILE BACKING BOARD

2"x4½" WOOD BLOCKING SECURED TO CONCRETE SLAB

HALF SCALE

## TYPICAL BASE DETAIL @ SERVERY MILLWORK          10

# BARS

### Bar Section Details

The distance between bar and backbar should allow adequate workspace. A minimum of 36 in, or 90 cm, should provide space for one bartender to serve and another to circulate behind. Maximum body depth and maximum body breadth are the primary anthropometric considerations in establishing clearance. A one-bartender operation would require a 30-in, or 75-cm, clearance.

In regard to bar stools, clearance between the stool seats is more critical than center line spacing, and it should allow patrons of larger body size a comfortable side approach and departure from the stool without body contact with the next person. A 12-in, or 30-cm wide stool on 24-in, or 61-cm, centers, which is quite common, will allow only less than 5 percent of male users access to the stool without disturbing the next patron, while a 30-in, or 75-cm, spacing will accommodate 95 percent of the users. The tradeoff however, would be the loss of two seats for every 120 in, or 300 cm, of bar length. A spacing of 12-in stools on 28-in, or 70-cm, centers is suggested as a compromise. The ultimate decision is an individual one and must reconcile human factors with economic viability.

| | in | cm |
|---|---|---|
| A | 54 | 137.2 |
| B | 18–24 | 45.7–61.0 |
| C | 24 | 61.0 |
| D | 30 | 76.2 |
| E | 16–18 | 40.6–45.7 |
| F | 24–30 | 61.0–76.2 |
| G | 30–36 | 76.2–91.4 |
| H | 28–38 | 71.1–96.5 |
| I | 100–128 | 254.0–325.1 |
| J | 42–45 | 106.7–114.3 |
| K | 11–12 | 27.9–30.5 |
| L | 6–7 | 15.2–17.8 |
| M | 7–9 | 17.8–22.9 |
| N | 6–9 | 15.2–22.9 |
| O | 22–26 | 55.9–66.0 |
| P | 60–69 | 152.4–175.3 |
| Q | 36–42 | 91.4–106.7 |

**BAR AND BACK-BAR**

**BAR / SECTION**

Fig. 1

**Fig. 2  Bar/clearances public side.**

To ensure proper circulation and interface, adequate clearances in front of the bar are illustrated in Fig. 2. A customer activity zone of 18 to 24 in, or 45.7 to 61.0 cm, should be provided to allow for seating, standing, and access, in addition to a general circulation zone of at least 30 in, or 76.2 cm. If a supplementary drinking surface or shelf is provided, a smaller activity zone of 18 in is suggested in front of the shelf. The shelf can be 10 to 12 in, or 25.4 to 30.5 cm, deep. Figure 3 shows suggested clearances for 18 or 24 in cocktail tables.

|   | in | cm |
|---|------|-----------|
| A | 76–84 | 193.0–213.4 |
| B | 66–72 | 167.6–182.9 |
| C | 10–12 | 25.4–30.5 |
| D | 18 | 45.7 |
| E | 30 | 76.2 |
| F | 18–24 | 45.7–61.0 |
| G | 76 | 193.0 |
| H | 54–56 | 137.2–142.2 |
| I | 6–9 | 15.2–22.9 |
| J | 7–9 | 17.8–22.9 |
| K | 42–45 | 106.7–114.3 |
| L | 24 | 61.0 |
| M | 29–33 | 73.7–83.8 |
| N | 32–36 | 81.3–91.4 |

**Fig. 3  Cocktail tables/seating for two.**

# BARS

### Bar Shapes: Planning Criteria

Bar shapes, seating capacities, overall dimensions, and "footprints" of bar areas vary greatly. Figures 4 to 22 show examples of bar designs drawn at a scale of ¼" = 1'0". Careful study of these designs would suggest that seating width, spacing, and circulation areas must be given special attention.

**Fig. 4   U shape: 16 ft × 11 ft, 176 ft², seats 9.**

**Fig. 5   Straight/enclosed: 20 ft × 10 ft, 200 ft², seats 9.**

**Fig. 6   Straight bar: 25 ft × 10 ft, 250 ft², seats 8.**

**Fig. 7** Angular: 30 ft × 12 ft, 320 ft², seats 10.

**Fig. 8** Enclosed/rounded end: 22 ft × 9 ft, 198 ft², seats 10.

# BARS
**Bar Shapes: Planning Criteria**

**Fig. 9   L shape: 30 ft × 13 ft, 390 ft², seats 15.**

**Fig. 10   Angular: 16 ft × 16 ft, 256 ft², seats 11.**

**Fig. 11   Octagon/partial: 26 ft × 18 ft, 468 ft², seats 16.**

**Fig. 12   L shape: 27 ft × 20 ft, 510 ft². Bar seating, 17; additional seating, 10.**

## BARS
**Bar Shapes: Planning Criteria**

Fig. 13    Polygon: 36 ft × 11 ft, 396 ft², seats 18.

Fig. 14    U shape: 21 ft × 20 ft, 420 ft², seats 22.

**Fig. 15   Curvilinear bar: 500 ft², seats 25.**

**Fig. 16   Straight bar: 40 ft × 10 ft, 400 ft², seats 24.**

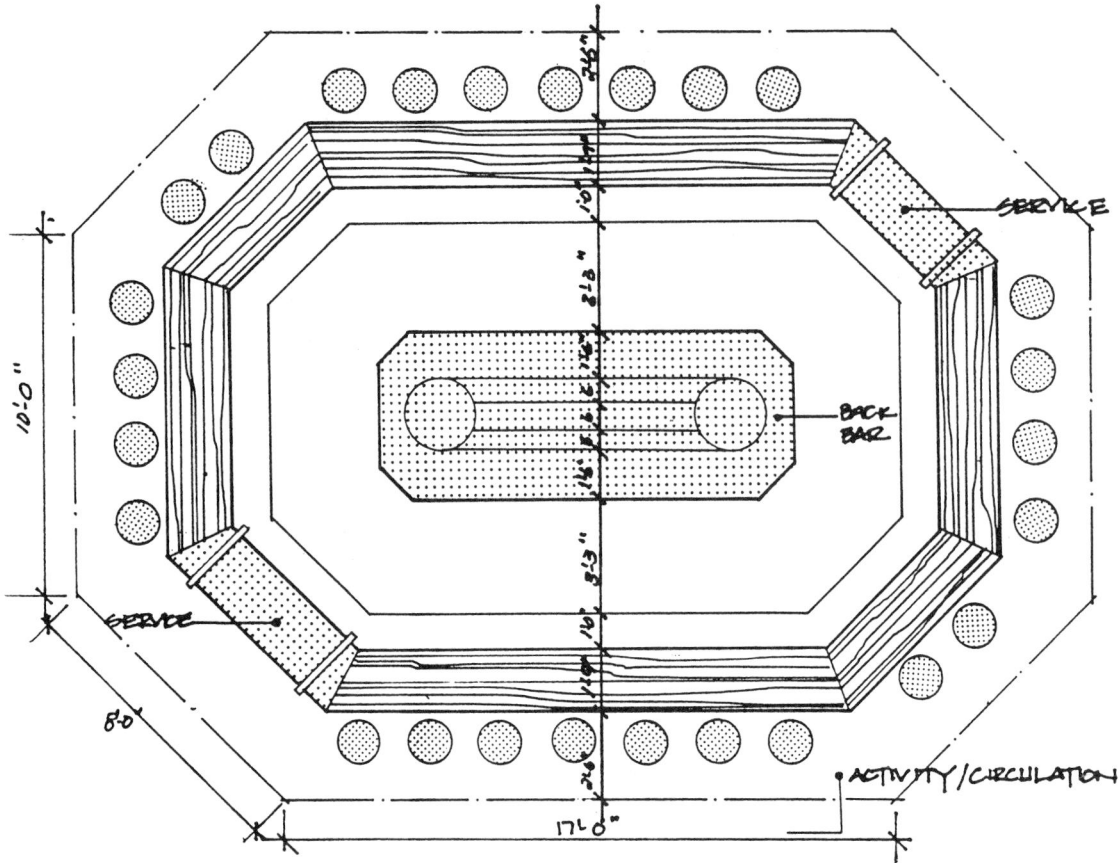

**Fig. 17   Octagon/freestanding: 28 ft × 21 ft, 558 ft².**

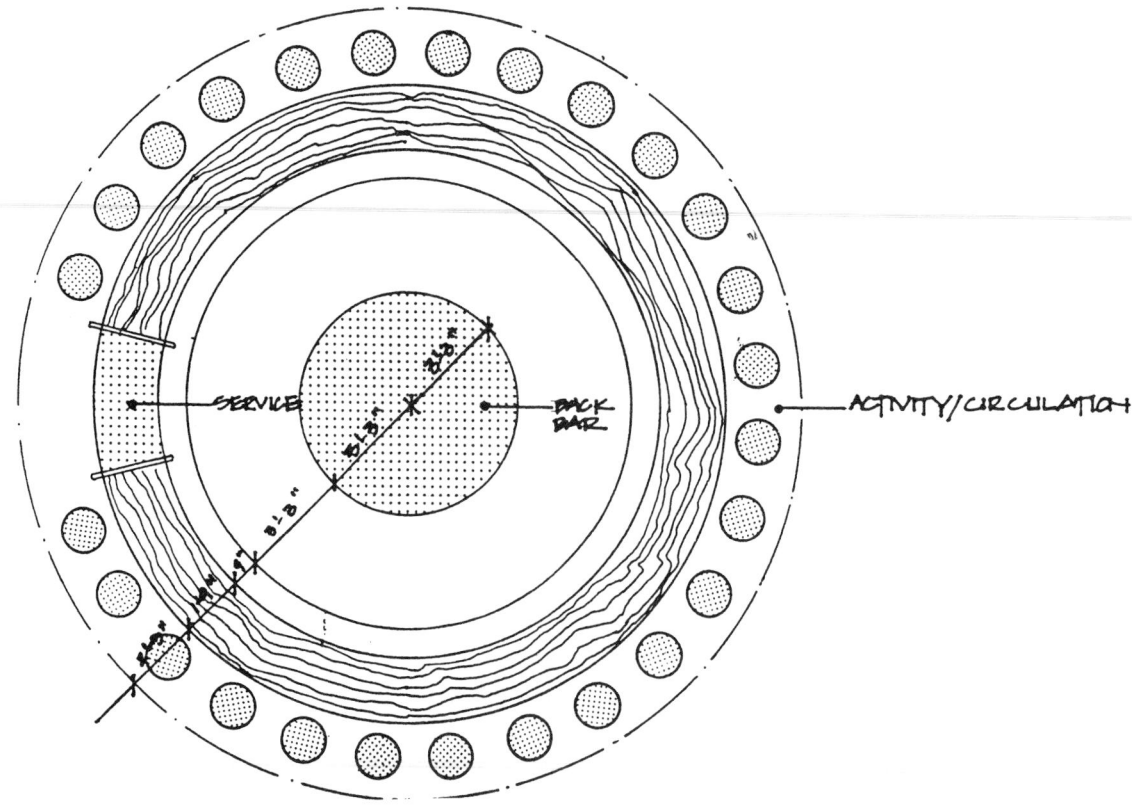

**Fig. 18   Circular/freestanding: 22 ft × 22 ft, 334 ft², seats 26.**

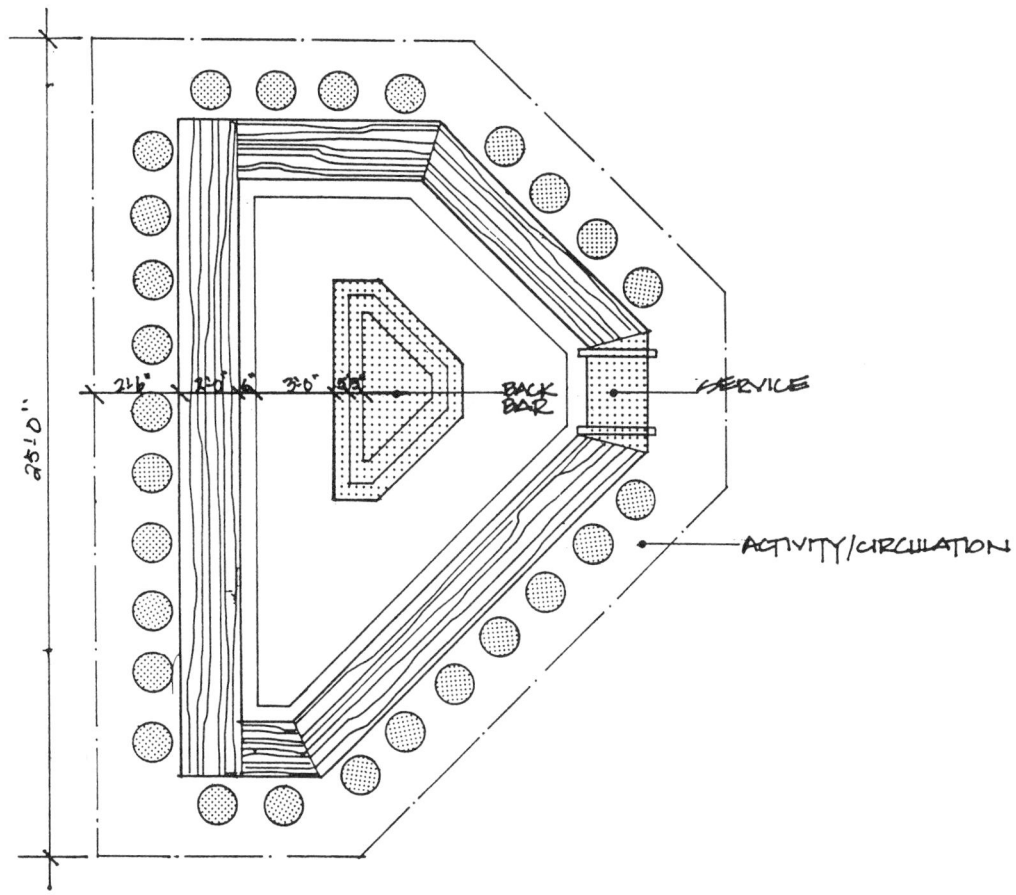

**Fig. 19   Polygon irregular: 20 ft × 25 ft, 360 ft², seats 27.**

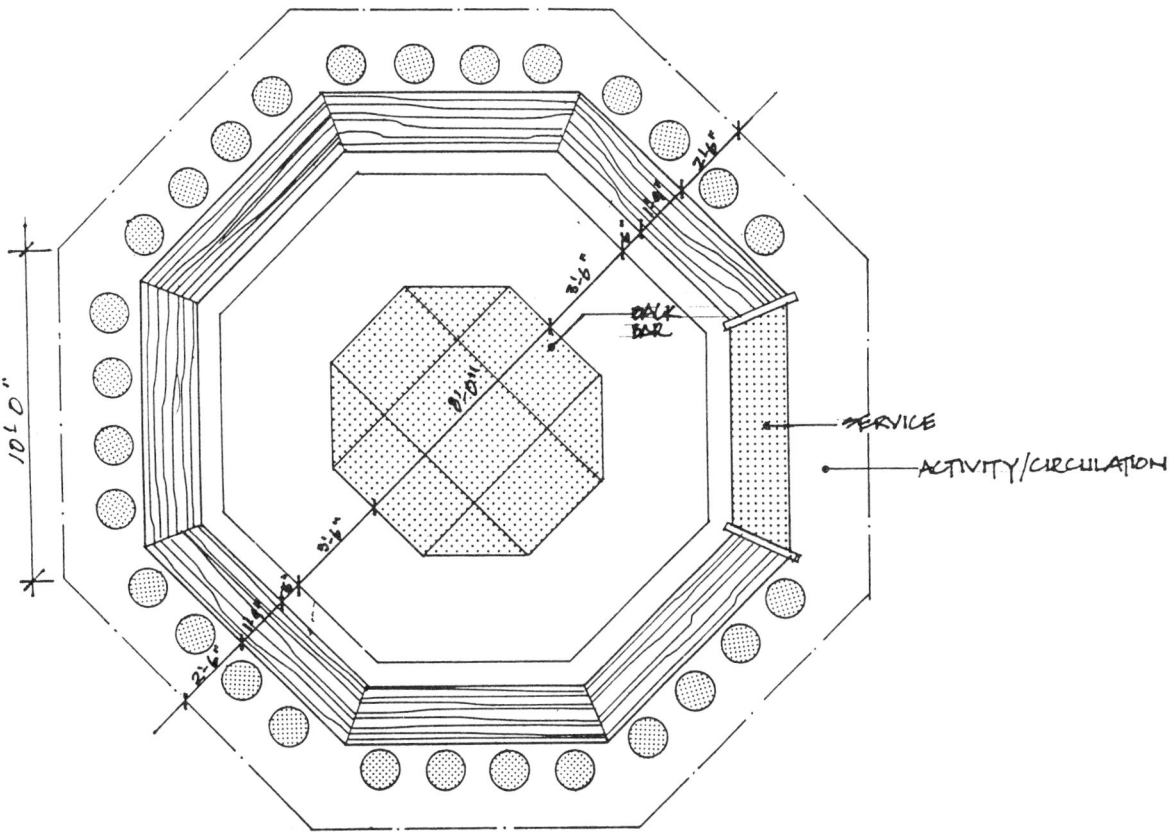

**Fig. 20   Octagon: 25 ft × 25 ft, 429 ft², seats 28.**

# BARS

**Bar Shapes: Planning Criteria**

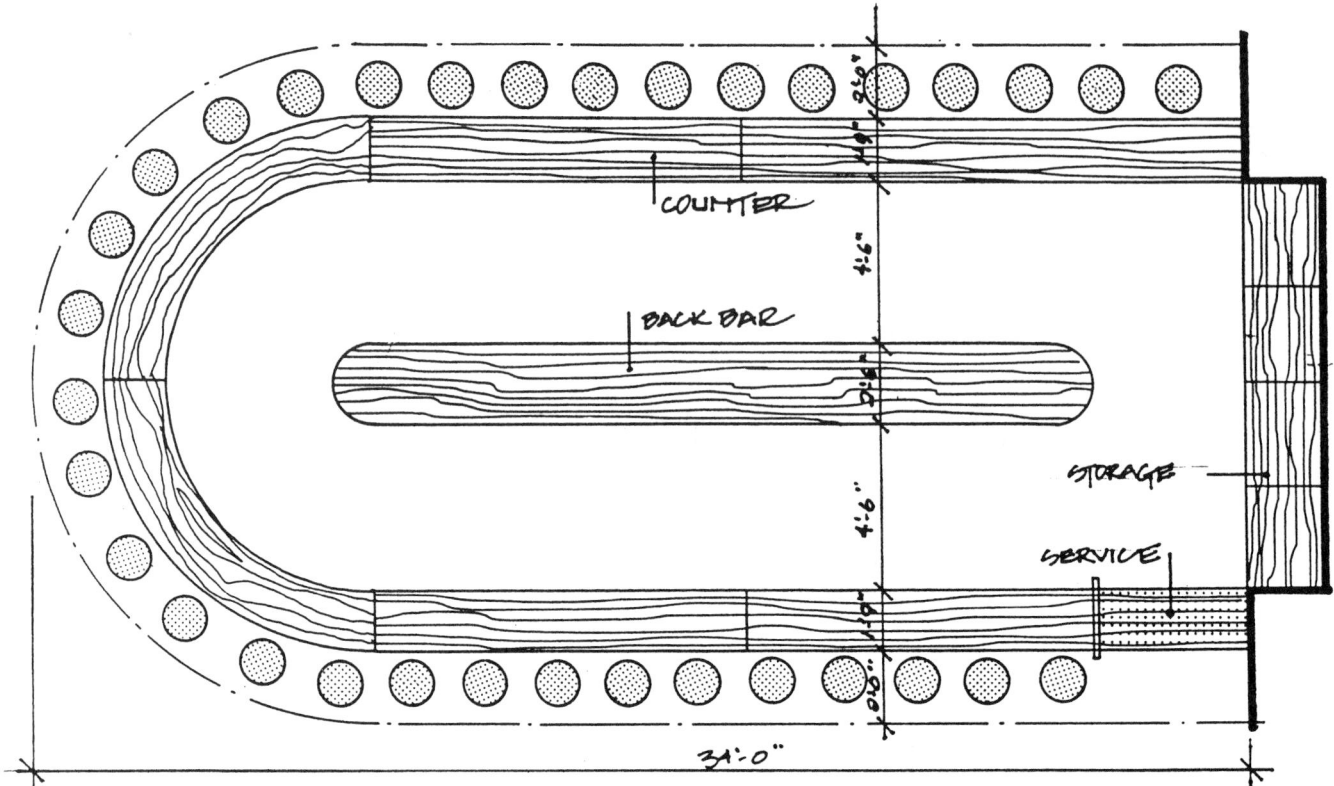

**Fig. 21    Horseshoe/oval end: 34 ft × 19 ft, 546 ft², seats 34.**

**Fig. 22    Racetrack: 50 ft × 19 ft, 750 ft², seats 48.**

The detailing of bars and backbars can vary from the very simple and basic to the complicated and intricate. Figures 23 to 40 provide the designer with selected examples of working drawings from some of the most experienced restaurant and hospitality design firms in the world. Careful review of these drawings would suggest that overall dimensions and clearances vary from detail to detail. In that regard, individual requirements based upon bar type and the hospitality area serviced must be given careful consideration. In addition, local building codes and health codes must be consulted.

 ELEVATION

**Fig. 23**

Section labels and callouts:

**DD SECTION**

GYPSUM BOARD SOFFIT
MAHOGANY WALL PANELS
MAHOGANY PASS-THRU DOOR
MAHOGANY COUNTER
PLASTIC LAMINATE FINISH STORAGE CABINET
QUARRY TILE BASE

MAHOGANY DOOR OVER TV CABINET
MAHOGANY WING CABINET ENCLOSURE
DIRECTION OF GRAIN
PANEL JOINT
MAHOGANY BAR COUNTER
POLISHED BRASS BAR RAIL
STAINLESS STEEL UNDER BAR EQUIPMENT
MAHOGANY FRONT PANEL
POLISHED BRASS FOOT RAIL
¼" QUIRK
MAHOGANY BASE

2'-5½"
8'-5"
3'-6"
6"

**FF SECTION**

LINE OF PLYWOOD BACKING
ANCHOR FRAME TO PLYWOOD
WOOD BLOCKING
¼" CLEAR GLASS MIRROR
1"x1"x⅛" POLISHED BRASS TUBE FRAME
PATTERNED GLASS PANEL
BRASS FINISH SELF TAPPING HEX-HEAD SCREW (TYP.)
NYLON GROMMET (TYP.)
½" x ¾" BRASS ANGLE (TYP.)

CLEAR GLASS SHELF & FRAME BELOW

½"  10"  1½" ¼" ¼"
1"  1½"  1½"  1"
10"

**EE SECTION**

GYPSUM BOARD FASCIA
GYPSUM BOARD SOFFIT
BLOCKING
BLUE TINTED GLASS PANEL
PLYWOOD BACKING
BEVELED GLASS GLUE-CHIP FINISH MIRROR
FABRIC WRAPPED PANELS
PORCELAIN LIGHT SOCKETS W/LAMPS
PATTERNED GLASS FRONT & SOFFIT
1" x 1" POLISHED BRASS FRAME
PATTERNED GLASS SIDE PANELS
LIGHT FIXTURES LOCATED INSIDE GLASS & BRASS UNITS
¼" CLEAR GLASS MIRROR
CLEAR BEVELED GLASS MIRROR
WAINSCOTTING

1" VERIFY
1"8½"
9½"
9½"
9½"
9½"
1'-13¾"  4'-10"
11½"
9½"

**Fig. 23**  *(Continued)*

Fig. 24

# BARS

Bar Plans, Elevations, and Sections

CUT-AWAY

9'-3"

3'-8"

END VIEW

MAHOGANY TOP

STAINLESS STEEL COUNTER

PLAN

2'-2"

4 1/4"   1'-5 3/4"   3"   1"

135°   MAHOGANY TOP

3/4"

2"

MAHOGANY

STEEL BRACKET SUPPORT

FLUORESCENT LIGHT FIXTURE

STAINLESS STEEL LINER AND WORK SURFACE

3/4"

2"

3/4"

LEATHER UPHOLSTERY

FIRM CUSHIONING

3/4" PLYWOOD

METAL CLIPS WELDED TO EDGING

1'-3"

3 1/2"

MIRROR POLISHED RED BRASS EDGE

TRIPOD

3/4"

1 1/2"

AT CORNER

1 1/2"

AT JOINT

PLAN SECTION

STAINLESS STEEL DOOR

2'-5"

2'-6"

3" O.D. MIRROR POLISHED RED BRASS PLATED STEEL COLUMN

1'-10"

STEEL COUPLING THREADED TO RECEIVE THREADED STEEL SLEEVE

10"X10"X5/16" STEEL PLATE WITH FOUR 1/2" EXP BOLTS

1'-0"   8"

MIRROR POLISHED RED BRASS PLATED STEEL PIPE

8"

CALKING

WELDED

GRANITE BASE

EPOXY ADHESIVE

2"

BLOCKING

RUBBER BASE

3"

4"

2" GRANITE FLOOR

PARTIAL VERTICAL SECTION   1 1/2" SCALE

Fig. 25

## SECTION THRU BAR CABINET

## VERTICAL SECTION
## AT METAL POST AND LIGHT BOX

**Fig. 26**

**Plan, Elevation, and Section details:**

A. **PLAN**
- 5'-0"
- 4 EQ PANELS AT 5'-0" EA
- 5'-0"
- 1'-10½"
- 1'-6"
- 2'-0"
- 2'-3"
- 1'-0"
- B
- 3½" Ø BRONZE RAIL
- WOOD COUNTER TOP
- BRONZE INSERT
- BRONZE LIGHT FIXTURE
- C
- 3'-4½" R
- 3½" / 1" / 1'-6" / 1'-6" / 1'-6" / 1'-6" / 1" / 3½"
- BAR EQUIPT. LINE
- C

B. **ELEVATION**
- 5'-0"
- 4 EQ SPACES AT 5'-0" EA = 20'
- 5'-0"
- BRONZE LIGHT FIXTURES W/ BRONZE VERT. SUPPORT
- BRONZE RAIL
- NAT. FIN. WD. PANEL
- BRONZE INSERTS
- BRONZE FOOT RAIL
- VERDE MARBLE BASE
- 3'-6"

CC. **ELEVATION**
- BRONZE LIGHT FIXTURE
- 7/8" WOOD TOP LAMINATED TO 3/4" BACKING
- 2'-3"
- ½" / 4" / 1'-6" / 1" / 3½"
- 1"
- 3½" Ø BRONZE RAIL W/ 1" X 2" BRONZE TUBING CONNECTED TO STEEL SLEEVE THRU BAR FRONT
- 3½"
- 10"
- STEEL SLEEVE & ANGLE BOLTED TO BAR TOP TO SUPPORT LIGHT FIXTURE
- STEEL 'T' 14" X 12" X ¼" TH AT 2'-0" O.C.
- NAT. FIN. WD. PANEL FRONT
- 1" X 4" STEEL TUBE COLUMN 5'-0" O.C. COORDINATE W/ KITCHEN EQUIP.
- 3'-6"
- 3/4" PLYWOOD BACK
- 2 3/8" Ø BRONZE RAIL W/ 1" X 1" BRONZE TUBING CONNECTED TO STEEL SLEEVE THRU BAR FRONT
- STEEL SLEEVE BOLTED TO STEEL ANGLE
- 3"
- 8"
- VERDE MARBLE BASE
- STEEL ANGLE CLIP 9" X 6" X ¼" BOLTED TO FL. 2'-0" O.C.
- 5"
- FINISHED FLOOR

Fig. 28

① SECTION @ FRONT BAR
A15   1½" = 1'-0"

② SECTION THRU BACK BAR @ PASS THRU'
A15   1½" = 1'-0"

③ DETAIL OF BAR THRU NORTH SIDE
A15   1½" = 1'-0"

④ SECTION THRU BACK BAR @ BOTTLE STEPS
A15   1½" = 1'-0"

FOCAL POINT 'CROWN
MOLDING, MAHOG. FIN.

MAHOG. FINISH

DYKES' MOLDING # 141
MAHOG. FINISH

4" CLEAR GLASS BACK
W/ BLACK PLASTIC LAM.
FRONT GRAPHIC TO BE
HAND PAINTED BY OTHERS

LT. FIXTURE # O
GLASS RACK W/ CUT-OUT
FOR GLASS INSERT

2'-6"

5'-6"

3/4" VERMONT VERDI-ANTIQUE
MARBLE, HONED FINISH
SOLID MAHOG. STOCK

LT. FIXT. # U

DYKES' CHICAGO
BAR RAIL # 403
MAHOG. FINISH

ANGLE BRACING

2x6 FIRE-RETARDED
LUMBER

3/4" Ø BRASS STUDS

MAHOG. VENEERED
PLYWD.

BLACK REVEAL

5'-C"

BRASS FOOT-REST

MAHOG. BASE

TILE COVE BASE

QUARRY TILE

9  DETAILS OF BAR COUNTER & GLASS RACK
A-9  SCALE: 1½" = 1'-0"

FOCAL POINT 'CROWN
MOLDING, MAHOG. FIN.

6" CHANNEL REVEAL

1/4" THICK MIRROR

GYP.BD.

FURRING CHANNEL

6'-0"

PLASTIC LAMINATE # B

MAHOG. TRIM

3'-0"

PLASTIC
LAM. # B

10  SECTION OF SERVING COUNTER # 104
A-9  SCALE: 1½" = 1'-0"

**Fig. 30**

① BAR SECTION LOOKING EAST
A6  1⁄8" = 1'-0"

② SECTION THRU BAR COUNTER
A6  1½" = 1'-0"

⑧ SECTION THRU BACK BAR
A6  1½" = 1'-0"

**Fig. 31**

366

① PLAN OF BAR
A14  ½" = 1'-0"

② ELEVATION OF FRONT BAR
A14  ½" = 1'-0"

③ SOUTH ELEVATION OF BAR
A14  ½" = 1'-0"

④ NORTH ELEVATION OF BAR
A14  ½" = 1'-0"

⑤ ELEVATION OF BACK BAR
A14  ½" = 1'-0"

TV SHELF - SEE
DWG. 9/A7

LIGHT MTD. UNDER SHELF

⅛" CL. MIRROR LAMINATE
TO GYP. BD.

BOTTLE STEPS IN ½" PLY.
PAINT W. SEALER & 2 COATS
HI-GLOSS

½" PLY. DIVIDERS TO FORM
8 EQUAL BOTTLE HOLDERS

¾" PLY. TOP & FACE
MITER EDGE SAND DULL

¾" PLY. SHELVES ON ADJUST-
ABLE STEEL BRACKETS

NEW ¾" BIRCH PLY. BAR TOP
& COASTER RAIL.

PLYWOOD KNEE BRACE
AS REQ'D.

KNEE WALL: 2X4's @
16" O.C.

⅛" CORRUGATED
GALV. STEEL FIXED
TO WOOD PLATES
& BLOCKING

1½"ø GALV. STEEL
PIPE

TRIPLE SINK

(6/A7) SECTION THRU' BAR
1"=1'-0"

WINE RACK,
OUTER FRAME IN ¾" PLY
INNER DIVISIONS IN ¼" PLY

BOTTLE STEPS

¼" WHITE PLEXIGLASS ON
CONTIN. WOOD BLOCKING
(¾" X 1½")

¾" PLY HINGED BAR GATE

REFRIGERATOR

EXISTING BEER BOX RE-USED

(7/A7) SECTION THRU' BAR
1"=1'-0"

(1/A7) BAR PLAN
½"=1'-0"

¾" BIRCH PLY. TOP
STAINED FINISH (TUB
W/PAINT, SEAL W/ 2-3
COATS GLOSS GYM SEAL

¼" X ¾" TRIM. PRE-
PAINTED BLACK
HI-GLOSS

¾" WOOD BLOCKING
PRE PAINTED
HI GLOSS

1½" X 1½" WOOD

¾" PLY FACE
PRE PAINTED
HIGH GLOSS

(8/A7) BAR EDGE DETAIL
HALF FULL SIZE

Fig. 33

368

**DETAIL OF BAR COUNTER**
SCALE : 1½"=1'-0"

- 1" MARBLE TOP
- PLASTIC LAM. FORMICA BLACK #909 BIRD EYE MAPLE EDGE
- LIGHT FIXT. 'D'
- SOLID MAPLE
- BIRD'S EYE MAPLE PANEL
- PLYWD PAINTED BLACK LACQUER
- LOCATIONS OF SUPPORTING DIAPHRAGMS TO BE VERIFD W. EQUIPMENT'S DIM.
- BRASS FOOT REST BY SHIP N OUT #115, 2"∅
- 6x6 QUARRY TILE

**DETAIL OF BACK BAR COUNTER**
SCALE : 1½"=1'-0"

- ½" MIRROR POL EDGE W. MET. CHANNEL
- ¼" FROSTED GLASS
- ¼" MIRROR W. P.L. FACE
- LIGHT FIXT. 'T'
- BLOCKING AS REQ'D
- PLASTIC LAM. FORMICA BLACK #909
- 2 ADJ. SHELVES
- VERT. PIN HOLES 2" O.C.

**Fig. 34**

**DETAIL SECTION THRU BAR COUNTER & RAISED FLOOR**
3" = 1'-0"
NOTE : ALL SURFACES INDICATED AS GYP BD. TO BE WOOD PANELLING TO MATCH EXIST'G BAR FRONT

- 2¼" OAK WOOD CAP (TYPICAL)
- BLOCKING AS REQ'D.
- TIVOLI ⅛" DIA. TUBE LT #
- 1⅛"x¾" WD. FRAME
- 2⅝"x1¼" WD. STUD.
- ¼" FROSTED GLASS
- 1⅛" OAK WD. BAR COUNTER
- COUNTER HT.
- 1⅞"x6" HARD WD. MOULDING
- 2"x3⅝" WD. STUD.
- WOOD PANEL
- INSET METAL STRAP TO SUPORT CANTILEVERING BAR COUNTER (AS REQ'D)
- 1⅞"x5⅝" HARD WD. BASE MOULDING
- HARD WD. BASE MOULDING

**Fig. 35**

**SECTION AT BAR**

- 24" OVERALL WITH SANDSTONE
- 23½"
- 21½"
- ¼" SPACE
- 17¼"
- 4"
- 2"
- ¾" SANDSTONE
- ½" EXT. A-C PLYWOOD
- ¼" SETTING SPACE
- 1" RAD.-TYPICAL AT TOP AND BOTTOM
- ¾" SANDSTONE
- 1"x 4" BLOCKING
- ½" EXT. A-C FIR PLYWOOD
- WHITE OAK
- 4" BLOCK WALL
- 11¾"
- ¾" PLYWOOD WITH RIFT CUT W OAK FACE VENEERS
- 40½" TO TOP OF 4" BLOCK WALL
- 28½"
- WHITE OAK PANEL MOULDING
- 1½" x 8" BASE
- 2" (FIN.)

**Fig. 36**

VERTICAL SECTION- LOBBY BAR

VERTICAL SECTION
LIQUOR STORAGE UNIT

VERTICAL SECTION-
DRINK RAIL

SECTION-
PICK UP STATION

**Fig. 37**

2'-0" NTS

3/4" 4"  1'-0 1/4"±  7 1/8"±

3/8"  1 1/8"

ST-2

M-1 GREEN MARBLE
1/2" THICK HARDWD

DYKES # 403 (1 5/8" x 7 5/8")
CHICAGO BAR RAIL

3/4" THICK STIFFENER
BLOCK AS REQUIRED

3/4" THICK HARDWD TRIM

1/2" QUARTER ROUND

RIBBONLITE
1/2" PLYWD
3/4" PLYWD

9" x 9" x 1/4" STEEL
ANGLES AS REQUIRED

3/4"  3 5/8"

5"  6 7/8"±

1'-0"  1"

PL. LAM PL-1

2" x 4" WD STUDS

3/4" EXTERIOR PLYWD
1/2" PLYWD

3/4" FIN. GRADE HARDWD
VENEER PLYWD

DYKES# 233 (3/4" x 2 3/4")

"SHIP N' OUT"
#112-2 COMBINATION
BRACKET W/ 2" Ø TUBING
W/ #140E-2 DOME CAP
ALL COMPONENTS TO
BE POLISHED BRASS
W/ FLUSH CONNECTORS AND
SPACERS - PROVIDE INNER
LINER STL TUBING

6 3/4"

INNER LINER

3/8" MARBLE M-3
3/8" SUBPLYWD

QUARRY TILE

RED OAK SURROUND
RE: OAK FLOOR

3/4"

3/4" SUB PLYWD

5"  1/2"  3/4"

2'-6"  4"

3'-6"

1 / 10·10    BAR SECTION AND ELEVATION

Fig. 38

¼" SOLID MAHOGANY TRIM ST-2

FINISH GRADE MAHOGANY VENEER PLYWD TOP W/ MITERED CORNERS ST-2

MAHOGANY TRIM ST-2

9
1D17

2'-0"

¾" 4" ¼" 1'-3" 4" ¼"

CONTINUE HARDWD @ DRINK WELLS

3/8" RAD

2½"

SOLID MAHOGANY TRIM ST-2

3½"

BLOCK'G AS REQR

6"X6"X¼" STL L AS REQUIRED

RIBBON LITE

MARINE PLYWD FACED WITH PL LAM PL-3

FINISH GRADE HARDWD VENEER PLYWD

SOLID MAHOGANY TRIM ST-2

10"

5"

9"

EYE

2'X4" WOOD STUDS 16" O.C

3'-6"

9
1D17
BAR RAIL DETAIL
HALF SCALE

½"
¼"

M4
POLISHED GRANITE SLAB W/ MITERED CORNERS

POLISHED GRANITE TILES M5

CARPET C

CONCRETE FILL

T-9 QUARRY TILE

7"

7"

½"

2'-0"

SURROUND

5
1D17
BAR SECTION

**Fig. 39**

**BACK BAR SECTION**

**SECTION AT CURVED BAR**

**VERTICAL SECTION AT BAR**

**SECTION AT BAR**

**Fig. 40**

# HOTELS
## Guestroom Plans

It is interesting to note how trends in hotel design have headed off in two directions, especially in regard to the design of rooms. On one hand, an effort is being made to provide more luxurious multipurpose rooms and suites. The hotel room as office away from work or as fantasy sleeping/relaxation environment often results in rooms with work areas, living rooms, and hot tubs, just to name a few of the more popular amenities. On the other hand, there is a trend toward economy accommodations. Hotel rooms are being designed as a place to rest and sleep, a place to feel comfortable and safe at a reasonable cost. Accordingly, these rooms use less floor area and provide less second-ary or frill items. With both of these ap-proaches, however, designers must ensure that the room or suite layouts are accessible to the physically challenged. In that regard, various room layouts and bathroom plans are provided in this section that address this issue.

**Fig. 1** *(a)* Uris Brothers Hotel, New York. *(b)* Americana Hotel, New York, typical tower room. *(c)* Loews N.Y. Motel, typical room. *(d)* Causeway Inn, Tampa, Florida.

CEILING: PT
DOOR FRAME: PT
BATH FLOOR: CT

(a)

(b)

(c)

(d)

Fig. 2 Guestroom plans. *(a)* Typical double-double finishes plan: vinyl wallcovering (WC), paint (P), carpet (C), ceramic tile *(CT)* identified and keyed to legend. *(b)* King-studio (Holiday Inn): standard layout with armoire unit and large lounge area including a convertible sofa. *(c)* Reversed layout (Sheraton, Washington, D.C.): unusual room with bed placed in front of window and lounge area near bathroom. *(d)* Luxury king room (Sheraton Grande, Los Angeles): oversized room with shelf/ledge in place of headboard, large desk surface, and lounge area; four-fixture bathroom.

**Fig. 3   Motel rooms — exterior entrance.**

**Fig. 4   Motel rooms — interior corridor.**

## Guestroom Plans

Accessible guestrooms have design features and floor plans that provide the maneuvering clearances for guests with limited mobility. Figures 5 to 9 show sample plans of guestrooms and bathrooms with the required:

■ Widths and clearances at the entry, connecting, closet, and bathroom doors

■ Maneuvering space in front of the closet, in the sleeping area, and within the bathroom

■ Clearances to use and transfer to fixtures in the bathroom

■ Clearances to open dresser drawers, to maneuver into kneespace at the desk, and to access the bed, bedside table, windows, blinds, and thermostat

Clearances may depend on the design of specific furnishings. The width of the access aisle at the bed is determined by the design of the bedside table. Access to dressers is determined by the width of the drawer. The maneuvering space to turn into the desk is determined by the width of the kneespace.

**(b)**

## 15' Bay-spacing

**(a)**

## 14' Bay-spacing

**Fig. 5   Bay-spacings of** *(a)* **14',** *(b)* **15', and** *(c)* **16' can easily accommodate guests with restricted mobility.**

**(c)**        ## 16' Bay-spacing

### 12' Bay-spacing

**Fig. 6** This alternative 12′0″ bay-spacing design requires the dresser to be offset from the foot of the bed. The bathroom wall is stepped back to provide clearances for the bathroom door and connecting door. The heating/cooling unit projects into the room to allow access to the thermostat. If balconies are provided, a minimum depth of 5′0″ is recommended to allow guests with wheelchairs to turn around.

### 13' Bay-spacing

**Fig. 7** A 13′0″ bay-spacing provides room for wheelchair clearances, including a turning space in front of the closet and at the foot of the beds, an access aisle between the beds, a T-turnaround at the window aisle for access to temperature controls and blinds and drapes, door clearances, and a bathroom that meets ANSI standards.

2'-6" (76)

5'-0" (152)

## Suite with 14' Bay-spacing

**Fig. 8**  Accessible suites should meet the same requirements for accessible guestrooms and guest baths. Because suites are usually more generous in terms of space, providing accessibility is less difficult. If a small kitchenette is included, a kneespace 2′3″ high should be provided below the sink. A countertop height of 2′10″ (2″ lower than standard) is suitable for both ambulatory guests and guests in wheelchairs. A pull-out lapboard at a height of 2′6″ provides a workspace for guests in wheelchairs. The kitchenette should include a 5′0″ turning space.

**Fig. 9**  These two diagrams illustrate the same bathroom plan with the required clearances for door operation and turning space and access to each fixture, including the tub/shower, vanity, and water closet. Clearances for maneuvering space, door operation, and individual fixtures can "overlap." Because of the vertical characteristics of wheelchairs, clearances can include toespace (9″ high) below water closet and kneespace (2′3″ high) below vanities.

The hotel registration desk serves as both a symbol of hospitality for the arriving guest and the operational nerve center for the hotel. With the advent of electronic check-in procedures, credit cards, and computer-aided management, the registration desk has become a sophisticated electronic workstation not unlike a trading table or an airline reservations desk. At the same time, this electronic data processing capability is meant to be maintained at low visibility for reasons of hotel image and confidentiality. Accordingly, the designer must be able to project the appropriate hospitality image while at the same time integrating all of the required technologies. Figures 10 to 13 show examples of architectural working drawings and details that meet many of these requirements.

The design of a front desk or registration desk can take many forms and be constructed with a variety of materials. Regardless of the design vocabulary used or architectural style, certain important design considerations must be observed.

1. The number of persons actively staffing the counterlike facility will dictate both the width and overall depth of the front desk. It is suggested that between 5–7 ft be allocated per staff workstation and that one workstation be allocated for every 125–150 rooms. For every additional 125–150 rooms, an additional workstation should be provided. Peak check-in/check-out loads could require even more staff workstations.

2. The front desk should be easily accessible from and to the main hotel entrance. "Easily accessible" strongly implies clear visibility.

## ENLARGED PARTIAL PLAN
## REGISTRATION COUNTER
## GRAND FLORIDIAN HOTEL

## PARTIAL PLAN
## REGISTRATION COUNTER
## GRAND FLORIDIAN HOTEL

## SECTION AT REGISTRATION DESK
## GRAND FLORIDIAN HOTEL

## SECTION AT COUNTER
## GRAND FLORIDIAN HOTEL

**Fig. 10**

3. Elevators servicing the hotel guest rooms should be readily visible from the front desk. This is not always feasible in extremely large hotels.

4. The front desk should be designed in such a way as to take into consideration the various users it will accommodate. Special attention should be given to the fact that hotel guests may be physically challenged or chairbound. The overall height, writing surfaces, and overhangs should be designed to accommodate a hotel guest seated in a wheelchair.

5. The basic front desk design should avoid, wherever possible, visual obstructions that block sightlines or create blind spots. Accordingly, columns and high walls should be avoided.

6. Equipment and custom elements that are typically incorporated within the front desk include computer monitors/CRTs with keyboards and printer, room racks, reservation racks, information racks, room status displays, mail drawers, key drawers, alpha guest listings, message-waiting display, credit card imprinters, fax and telex, guest/employee paging system, automatic wake-up system, electric receptacles, cable chases, alarm systems, and file and cash drawers.

ELEVATION
AT SELF CHECK MONITOR

SECTION DETAIL
AT SELF CHECK MONITOR

SECTION DETAIL-
SETTEE

ELEVATION/SECTION-
REGISTRATION COUNTER

SECTION-CIRCULAR SETTEE BACK

ELEVATION-REGISTRATION COUNTER

ELEVATION/SECTION-REGISTRATION COUNTER

Fig. 11

**Fig. 12**

383

## PARTIAL ELEVATION-FRONT DESK
## TROPICANA HOTEL

## VERTICAL SECTION
## REGISTRATION DESK TROPICANA HOTEL

## VERTICAL SECTION AT RECEPTION DESK

Fig. 13

384

# Retail Spaces

| | |
|---|---|
| Shops | 387 |
| Banks | 396 |
| Department stores | 401 |

**Fig. 1   Seated customer/high counter height.**

**Fig. 2   Typical sales area/standing customer.**

The essential function of retail spaces is to display and sell merchandise. The design of these spaces involves the manipulation and coordination of architectural, interior design, and merchandising elements as necessary to meet the programmatic needs of the client. It is critical that the space in which the customer and store personnel function is of the highest quality. Ensuring this quality requires a knowledge of the planning and design of the various interior components that constitute the building blocks of retail spaces.

Figure 1 shows the clearances involved for a 42-in, or 106.7-cm, high counter to service a seated user. By filling the recess with an additional display, however, the counter can also be used exclusively as a typical sales counter. It should be noted, however, that although sometimes used for special display situations, such a counter height is not recommended. Both the customer and the sales clerk of smaller body size would find coping with such a height uncomfortable anthropometrically, particularly when one considers that the counter would be higher than the elbow height of slightly over 5 percent of the population. From a merchandising viewpoint, where customer convenience is of paramount importance, it would be unwise to exceed 39 to 40 in, or 99 to 101.6 cm, as a counter height. In addition, the smaller sales clerk forced to tend such a counter for extended periods of time could be subjected to severe backaches and pains. Getting on and off a high stool for elderly and disabled people or those of smaller body size can be not only difficult, but hazardous. Figure 2 illustrates the clearances for a typical sales counter.

|   | in | cm |
|---|---|---|
| A | 26–30 | 66.0–76.2 |
| B | 18–24 | 45.7–61.0 |
| C | 42 | 106.7 |
| D | 28 | 71.1 |
| E | 84–112 | 213.4–284.5 |
| F | 18 | 45.7 |
| G | 18–24 | 45.7–61.0 |
| H | 30–48 | 76.2–121.9 |
| I | 18–22 | 45.7–55.9 |
| J | 35–38 | 88.9–96.5 |
| K | 72 | 182.9 |

Figure 3 shows the clearances required for a medium height display counter. The suggested seat height of 21 to 22 in, or 53.3 to 55.8 cm, requires a footrest for the seated customer. The counter height shown will allow the display to be viewed by both the seated customer and the standing sales clerk. The customer activity zone allows adequate space for the chair. Knee height, buttock-knee length, popliteal height, and eye height sitting are all significant human dimensions to consider in the design of counters to be used by a seated customer.

Figure 4 shows a low 30-in, or 76.2-cm, display counter also for use by a seated customer. The anthropometric considerations are the same. Although the counter height is responsive to the anthropometric requirements of the seated customer, it is less than ideal for the standing clerk. For the standing user's optimum comfort, the counter height should be about 2 or 3 in, or 5 to 7.6 cm, below elbow height. This will allow a person to handle objects comfortably on the counter surface or use the counter as support for his or her arms. The 30-in height is too low to permit such use.

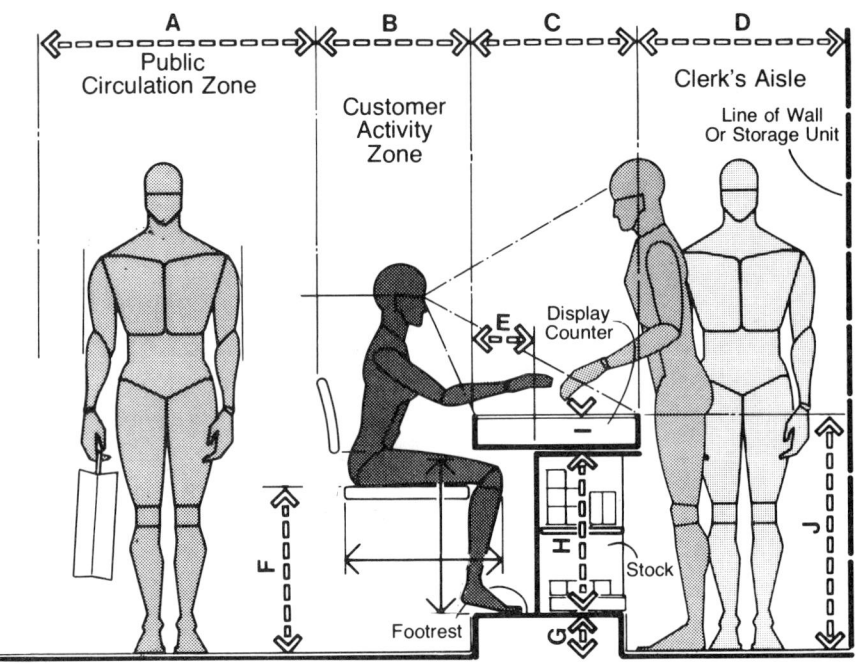

**Fig. 3  Seated customer/desirable counter height.**

|   | in | cm |
|---|---|---|
| A | 36 | 91.4 |
| B | 26–30 | 66.0–76.2 |
| C | 18–24 | 45.7–61.0 |
| D | 30 min. | 76.2 min. |
| E | 10 | 25.4 |
| F | 21–22 | 53.3–55.9 |
| G | 5 | 12.7 |
| H | 23–25 | 58.4–63.5 |
| I | 4–6 | 10.2–15.2 |
| J | 34–36 | 86.4–91.4 |
| K | 30 | 76.2 |
| L | 16–17 | 40.6–43.2 |

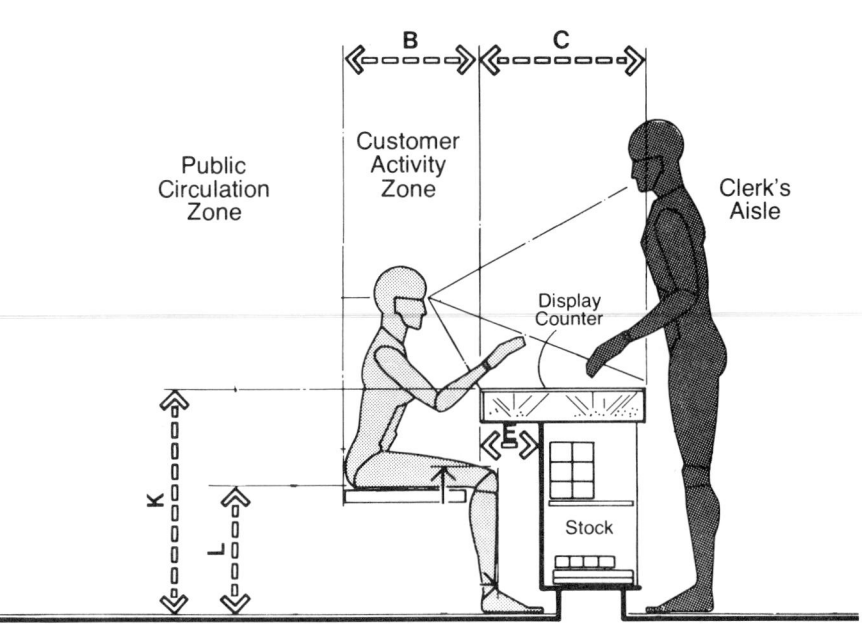

**Fig. 4  Seated customer/low counter height.**

Shelving is probably used more than any other single interior component for the storage and/or display of merchandise. Not only must the merchandise be within reach anthropometrically, but it must be fairly visible as well. The heights established must therefore be responsive to vertical grip reach dimensions as well as to eye height. In establishing height limits, the body size data of the smaller person should be used. Since in retail spaces, departments may cater exclusively to members of one sex or the other, two sets of data are presented. One is based on the body size of the smaller female and the other on the body size of the smaller male. The suggested heights reflect a compromise between reach requirements and visibility requirements.

Figure 6 illustrates the clearances involved in hanging-type merchandise cases. Rod heights should be related not only to human reach limitations, but in certain cases to the sizes of the merchandise displayed. There is usually no conflict in respect to garments.

|   | in | cm |
|---|----|----|
| **A** | 48 max. | 121.9 max. |
| **B** | 30–36 | 76.2–91.4 |
| **C** | 51 min. | 129.5 min. |
| **D** | 66 | 167.6 |
| **E** | 72 | 182.9 |
| **F** | 84–96 | 213.4–243.8 |
| **G** | 20–26 | 50.8–66.0 |
| **H** | 28–30 | 71.1–76.2 |
| **I** | 18–24 | 45.7–61.0 |
| **J** | 18 min. | 45.7 min. |
| **K** | 72 max. | 182.9 max. |
| **L** | 4 | 10.2 |
| **M** | 42 | 106.7 |
| **N** | 26 min. | 66.0 min. |

**Fig. 5  Typical merchandise cases.**

**Fig. 6  Hanging merchandise cases.**

**Section** 3/16" SCALE

ALUMINUM
REGINA

14'-0"

7'-0"+

1/4" SLIDING GL. DOORS

TRANSOM BAR OVER

2-3"

2 3/4"

3/4" GL. DOOR

2"   3'-0 3/8"   2"

**Plan at 2**

*All details at 3" scale*

**Section 1**

WALL

GLASS

SLIDING GL. DOORS

2-3"   5'-6"   11'-6"   2-3"

2'-9"

BULKHEADS DOTTED

CERAMIC TILE FLOOR
WIDE CEMENT JOINTS

**Plan** 3/16" SCALE

METAL CHANNEL

CEILING

1/4" PLATE GLASS

5 1/2"

4" CHANNEL

3 1/2"

5 1/2"

ALUMINUM COVERED

**Section 5**

1/4" PLATE GLASS

2'-3"

3'-0 1/2"

BLOCKING

4" CHANNELS, SET FLAT

2 1/2"

2'-9"

2"x2" ANGLE, CONTINUOUS

2 3/4"

WIRE LATH & PLASTER

CERAMIC TILE

2"x4" FRAMING

3/4" TEMPERED GLASS

7'-0" DOOR

**Section 4**

METAL SADDLE

1/4" PL. GLASS

1 3/4"

4"

**Section 3**

FIN. FLOOR

ELEVATION-SHIRT DISPLAY CASE

VERTICAL SECTION
SHIRT DISPLAY

VERTICAL SECTION
JEWELRY SHOWCASE

VERTICAL SECTION
COSMETIC DISPLAY

REFRIGERATED CASE

REFRIGERATED CASE

CROSS SECTION·DISPLAY CABINET

CEILING MOULDING

TYPICAL TRIM

ISLAND DISPLAY

**PLAN**
SC: 3/4" = 1'-0"

**DETAIL** (D)
SC: 3" = 1'-0"

CUT-OUT IN BACK SIGN HOLDER

(2) 1/4" TH. PLEXI PANELS CEMENTED TO 1/4" TH. CENTER PANEL W/ 1/8" X 1/2" PEXI BAND ON THREE SIDES (TOP OPEN)

1 1/2" TH. PLYWD. CENTER DIVIDER PL. LAM. FIN. ALL SIDES

5/8" X 2' X 5 1/8" QUIRK P.T.M. PL. LAM.

**PART FRONT ELEV.**
SCALE: 3/4" = 1'-0"

**VERTICAL SECTION**
SCALE: 3/4" = 1'-0"

PLEXI GLASS SIGN HOLDERS

1" RADIUS CORNERS

1 1/2" PLYWD. PANEL, PL. LAM. FIN. ALL SIDES

3/8" CL. PLEXI GL. SHELVES W/ CLIPS

3/8" CLEAR PLEXI PANELS

3/4" PLYWD. BASE PL. LAM. FIN. ALL SIDES, WOOD BLOCK'G. AS REQ'D.

F.C. TO PROVIDE FINGER CUT-OUT IN EACH SIGN HOLDER

1/4" THK. PLEXI PANEL CEME-NTED TO 3/8" PANEL W/ 1/8" X 1/2" PLEXI BAND ON (3) SIDES

**DETAIL** (A)
SC: 3" = 1'-0"

3/8" CL. PLEXI SHELVES ON CL. ALLIGATOR CLIPS

CLEAR PLEXI ALLIGATOR CLIP

3/8" TH. CLEAR PLEXI PANELS

**DETAIL** (B)
SC: 3" = 1'-0"

ALLIGATOR CLIP

3/8" CL. PLEXI GL. SHELF

EDGE OF 3/8" CL. PLEXI PANEL

**DETAIL** (C)
SC: 3" = 1'-0"

393

Half Elevation  1/2" SCALE

Section  1/2" SCALE

Section **2**  3"SCALE

Plan thru Counter

Plan above Counter

Section **1**  3" SCALE

COUNTER WITH VERTICAL FRONT
3 4" = 1'-0'

COUNTER WITH SLOPING FRONT
3 4' = 1' 0'

COUNTER WITH RECESSED PURSE SHELF
3 4' = 1'-0'

COUNTER ON WOOD FRAMING
3 4'= 1' 0"

SECTION AT CHECK DESK
(DEPOSIT SLIP AREA)

SECTION AT TELLER COUNTER

VERTICAL SECTION AT TELLERS COUNTER

## VERTICAL SECTION-TELLERS UNITS

## PLAN OF TELLERS COUNTER

VERTICAL SECTION-TELLERS COUNTER

VERTICAL SECTION OF TELLERS COUNTER

VERTICAL SECTION AT TELLERS COUNTER

SECTION AT TELLERS COUNTER

VERTICAL SECTION AT CHECK STAND

VERTICAL SECTION
AT CHECK DESK

HALF PLAN THRU CHECK DESK

LAMINATED PLASTIC TOP

DRAWER

6"

1'-1"

DRAWER

WOOD FRAME
AND BLOCKING

1/4" PLYWOOD

3/4" PLYWOOD

FLOOR

1"

6"

1'-1"

6 1/2"

4 1/2"

6"

5/8"

3"  4"

2'-11"

4'-1"

2'-11"

SPACE FOR
METAL
CABINETS

PLYWOOD DOOR

12 1/2"  5"

LAMINATED PLASTIC

3/4" PLYWOOD

*Edge*  FULL SIZE

*Sections*  3/4" SCALE

*Plan and
Rear Elevation*
3/8" SCALE

WALL LINE

LAMINATED
PLASTIC TOP

WALL LINE

OPEN

2 SHELVES

DRAWER

3 SHELVES

DRAWER

METAL
CABINETS

DRAWER

2 SHELVES

2'-2" OPEN

2'-2" OPEN

2'-2" OPEN

3'-0"

5'-8 1/2"

17'-5"

5'-8 1/2"

3'-0"

**UPPER SECTION** (A)
SCALE: 3" = 1'-0".

2" DIA. HARDWD. TRIM W/ COL. LACQ. FINISH

PL. LAM. FINISH

DOM LOCK

GARCY 4" L. PULL #R 1060

DOM LOCK #301015

3/4" PLYWD. CONST'N. PL. LAM. FINISH

F.C. TO PROVIDE POWER TRAC #L G50, L-G51 OR L-G52 WITH LAMP# L 2717 GIMBAL RING LAMP HOLDER W/ INTEGRAL SOLID STATE 12V TRANSFORMER W/ @5W 12V MR 16 LAMPS.

1/4" CL. GLASS DOOR ON PIVOT HINGES

FABRIC COVER'D. REMOVABLE 1/4" MASONITE PAD BY FIXT. CONT'R.

1 1/4" X 1" X 1/8" ANGLE EXTRUDED ALUM. NO SUBSTITUTE

3/4" PLYWD. DRAWERS 7 PLY TYPE ON FULL EXTENSION GRANT DRAWER SLIDES #555

**PLAN SECTION** (B)
SCALE: 3" = 1'-0".

PROVIDE VENT HOLES

FABRIC COVER'D. PAD.

PL. LAM.

PIVOT HINGE

1/4" CLEAR GLASS DOOR

VARIES SEE PLAN

**SECTION** (1)
SCALE: 3/4" = 1'-0".

CL. GL. DOOR ON PIVOT

1" TYP.

DUPLEX OUTLET ACCESS PANEL SEE DWG. SD-4

F.C. TO PROVIDE ACCESS PANEL TO TRANSFORMER

TYP. TRANSPARENCY SEE DWG. SD-4

1/4" CL. GL. SHELF W/ METAL BRACKETS

FABRIC COVER'D. 1/4" MASONITE PANEL

TYP. DRAWER BASE UNIT OF 3/4" PLYWD. CONSTR'N. PL. LAM. FIN. & GANG LOCKED

NOTE: BACK FIXT. BUILT IN SECTIONS & BOLTED TOGETHER ON SITE.

PL. LAM. FINISH RECESSED BASE

**SECTION** (2)
SCALE: 3/4" = 1'-0".

VARIES

A
S-1B

B
S-1B

1'-10"

PLAN

VARIES

A
S-1B

B
S-1B

1'-10"

1'-10"

1'-10"

PLAN

A
S-1B

GLASS TOP
AND FRONT

A
S-1B

1
S-1A

⅛" x ⅛" CONT. QUIRK

PL. LAM. FIN.
N.F.W. AT MENS

4" H. RECESSED
BASE PL. LAM. FIN.
(N.F.W. AT MENS)

FRONT ELEV.

FRONT ELEV.

2
S-1A

A
S-1B

CUT-OUT FOR
ELECTRIC RECEPTACLE

CUT-OUT FOR
ELECTRIC
RECEPTACLE

A
S-1B

1
S-1A

¼" CLEAR MIRROR
SLIDING DOORS
W/PULL & LOCK

PL. LAM. FIN.
N.F.W. AT MENS
4" H. RECESSED
BASE PL. LAM. FIN.
(N.F.W. AT MENS)

2
S-1A

REAR ELEV.

REAR ELEV.
SCALE: ½" = 1'-0"

1'-10"

¼" CLEAR GLASS
FRONT & TOP
POL. CHR. FIN.
METAL FRAME

⅜" CLR. GL. SHELVES

¼" CL. MIRROR SLIDING
DOORS PL. LAM. FIN.
W/PULL & LOCK
N.F.W. AT MENS

PL. LAM. AT ENDS
N.F.W. AT MENS
FABRIC COV'D. REMOVABLE DISPLAY PAD.

TYP. DRAWER BASE
W/PL. LAM. FIN. &
4"L. PULLS W/LOCK
(N.F.W.) AT MENS

4" H. RECESSED BASE
W/PL. LAM. FIN.
(N.F.W) AT MENS

HALF ROUND WD.
MLDG. COL. LACQ. FIN.

4'-0"

3'-8"

10"

4"

2'-0"

SECTION
SC: ¾" = 1'-0"

SIDE ELEV.

1
S-1A

SIDE ELEV.

2
S-1A

LEVITON #1374W
ELECTRIC RECEPTACLE
W/ 15'-0" LONG CORD &
TWIST LOCK PLUG

LOCK

2" OVERLAP

FELT

1¼"

1¼"

LOCK

¼" MIRROR INTERIOR
PL. LAM. FINISH
FROM OUTSIDE

GARCY STD. #649
W/ BACK CHANNEL
FOR 5'-0" & 6'-0"
LONG SHOWCASES

1'-10"

¼" POL. PLATE GLASS

3/4"

3/4"

## PLAN SECTION ⬡1
SCALE: HALF FULL SIZE.

LEVITON #1374·W
ELECTRIC RECEPTACLE W/
15' L CORD & TWIST LOCK PLUG

1¼"

1¼"

2" OVERLAP

LOCK

1'-10"

¼" CL. MIR. INTERIOR
PL. LAM. FINISH
FROM OUTSIDE

GARCY STD. #649
W/ BACK CHANNEL
FOR 5'-0" & 6'-0"
LONG SHOWCASES.

3/4"

3/4"

¼" POL. PL. GLASS

## PLAN SECTION ⬡2
SCALE: HALF FULL SIZE.

1'-10"

1³/₁₆"

GARCY
#RM4 & RM3

SECURITY CLIPS

5/4"

REFL.
GARCY
#3802

3/8" SHOES

PL. LAM. ON
1/4" CL. MIRROR

SLOTTED
STANDARD
REQUIRED

1/4" POL. PL. GLASS

2'-0"

GARCY #S-2177
SHOE CLOSE ENDS
W/ #2077 WHEELS
GARCY #20700 TRACK

KENSTAN K-40
PLUNGER LOCK

FABRIC COVER'D.
1/4" MASONITE PAD
(NOT SHOWN HERE);
SEE DET. BELOW

1"X1¼"X⅛"
EXTRUDED
ALUM. ANGLE

GARCY
#R-1060 FULL
4" LONG

TYP. DRAWER
7 PLYWD. CONST
ON GRANT
#355 FULL EXT.
SLIDES GANG
LOCKED AS REQ'D.

DOM CAM.
LOCK #310-015

1'-2"

PL. LAM. ON
3/4" PLYWD.
NO SUBSTITUTE

1½"

2"

2"

2"

SOLID WOOD
BASE PL. LAM. FIN.

10'-0" LONG CORD W/
TWIST LOCK PLUG.

# SECTION Ⓐ
SCALE: 3/4" = 1'-0"

# LONG. SECT. Ⓑ
SCALE: 3/4" = 1'-0"

PL. LAM.
REMOVABLE
BUILD-UP

1/4" MASONITE
REMOVABLE DISPLAY PAD.
FABRIC COVER'D BY BURDINES

3"

45°

4"

⅛"

WOOD BLOCK'G.
AS REQUIRED

# DISPLAY PAD DETAIL
SCALE: 1/4" = ONE INCH

SHT. RK. CURTAIN WALL
W/ PAINT. FIN.

CEILING LINE
AT 11'-0" A.F.F.

SEE ELEVATIONS
FOR SPECIFIC
TRIM DESIGN

FASCIA 3/4" PLYWD
W/ PL. LAM. FIN.

3/4" PLYWOOD DOOR
W/ PL. LAM. FIN &
MAGNETIC CATCHES
AT TOP & BOTTOM ON
CONCEALED PIANO
HINGES

WALL CABINET
3/4" PLYWOOD WITH
PL. LAM. FIN.

CUTOUTS IN DOORS
TO ACCOMMODATE
J.V.C. TELEVISION 2E
MODEL NO. C-2526

3/4" FLUSH PLYWOOD
ACCESS PANELS W/
MAGNETIC CATCHES

REMOVABLE BASE
CABINET 3/4" PLYWD.
W/ PL. LAM. FIN.

HINGED DOOR
3/4" PLYWOOD W/
PL. LAM. FIN.

RECESSED BASE
3/4" SOLID WOOD W/
PL. LAM. FIN.

AT ENDS — 7 3/4"    1'-9"    4"  4"    1'-9"    4"  4"

LOCKS

## ELEVATION
SCALE: 3/4"=1'-0"

CEILING LINE
AT 11'-0" A.F.F.

SHT. RK. CURTAINWALL
SEE ELEVATIONS FOR
SPECIFIC DETAILS

SOFFIT & FASCIA
3/4" PLYWD. W/ PL.LAM.FIN.

1/2" DIA. VENT HOLES

COMBINATION AM/PM
G-4000, ANTENNA OUTLETS
2'-0"O.C. HORIZ. BY P.F.C.

1/2" DIA. VENT HOLES

PANEL DOORS, 2'-4 11/16" W. x 4'-7" H.
3/4" PLYWD. W/ PL. LAM. FIN.
ON CONCEALED HINGES AND
CUTOUTS FOR TV's.

3" DIA. WIRE RUN HOLES

CABINET 3/4" PLYWD.
W/ PL. LAM. FIN.

FLUSH ACCESS PANELS
3/4" PLYWOOD W/ PL.LAM.FIN.
ON CONCEALED HINGES AND
MAGNETIC CATCHES

REMOVABLE BASE CABINET
3/4" PLYWOOD W/ PL.LAM.FIN.

COMBINATION AM/PM
G-4000, ANTENNA OUTLETS
2'-0"O.C. HORIZONTALLY,
FURNISHED & INSTALLED BY P.F.C.

3/4" PLYWOOD SHELF W/ PL.LAM.
ON PILASTER STANDARDS

CONCEALED HINGED DOOR
3/4" PLYWD. W/ PL. LAM. FIN.
WITH LOCK AND 4' WIRE PULLS

## SECTION 1
SCALE: 3/4"=1'-0"

PERIMETER
BACKWALL

FABRIC WRAPPED
PANEL

1'-2"

MET. ANGLE AT ENDS

3/8" THK. MILK WHITE
PLEXI-GLASS

1"

2" DIA. HARDWOOD TRIM
COL. LAQ. FIN.

4"

SHELF BOX 3/4" PLYWD.
PL. LAM. FIN. ALL EXP'D.

MET. ANGLES, PAINT WHITE

PAINT INTERIOR WHITE

MODIFIED MET. BRACKET
& CLIP BY P.F.C.

DUPLEX
RECEPT.
BY E.C.

3/8" THK. MILK-WHITE
PLEXI-GLASS

FLUOR. LIGHT STRIP
BY P.F.C.
C.J. LIGHTING #1602

**SHELF DETAIL** Ⓐ
SCALE: 3"=1'-0"

1"    4'-1"    1"

DUPLEX RECEPTACLE
1 PER SHELF BY E.C.

PERIMETER BACKWALL

REMOVABLE PADS W/
FABRIC COV'G BY P.F.C.

FLUOR. LIGHT STRIP
BY PERIM. FIXT. CONTR.

1'-2"

METAL ANGLES
AT ENDS

MODIFIED METAL BRACKET
AT ENDS W/ SHELF CLIPS
BY P.F.C.

SHELF BOX, 3/4" PLYWD.
PL. LAM. FIN.

BULLNOSE TRIM
2" DIA. HARDWOOD

**PLAN SECTION @ SHELF** Ⓑ
SCALE: 1½"=1'-0"

4'-3"

3/4"    3/4"

Ⓐ

1'-3"    2'-1"

REMOVABLE PADS W
FABRIC COV'G

MILK WHITE PLEXI
AT SHELF

SHELF BOX

MILK WHITE PLEXI
AT BASE CABINET

BASE CABINET

**PLAN WHERE SHELVES ABUTT**
SCALE: 3/4"=1'-0"

**SECTION** (1)
SCALE: 3/4"=1'-0"

**SECTION** (2)
SCALE: 3/4"=1'-0"

REMOVABLE PADS W/ FABRIC COV'G

1'-0"

3"

3/4" PLYWD. SHELF ON MET. BRACKET BY P.F.C

FLUOR. LIGHT STRIP BY P.F.C. C.J. LIGHTING #1850-12

DETAIL (A)
SCALE: 1½"=1'-0"

1½"

SECURED TO MET. STUD

1'-0"

REMOVABLE PAD W/ FABRIC COV'G BY P.F.C.

PLUGMOLD #2100 7/8"D. × 1¼"W. BY E.C.

DIVIDER PANEL 3/4" PART. BD.

3"

DETAIL (B)
SCALE: 1½"=1'-0"

3" 6"
6"
1'-0"
1'-0"
1'-0"
1'-0"
2'-6"
8"
2"

FLUOR. LIGHTING FIXT. BY E.C.

SEE ELEVATIONS FOR SPECIFIC DESIGN DETAILS

ACRYLIC DIFFUSER & MET. ANGLES BY P.F.C.

1'-0"

3/4" PLYWOOD SHELF W/ BULLNOSE TRIM PL. LAM. FIN. AND FLUOR. STRIP BY P.F.C.

(A)

DIVIDER PANEL 3/4" PART. BD. W/ PL. LAM. FIN.

RECESSED 4'-6"L. PLUGMOLD BY E.C. W/ OUTLETS 6" O.C.

REMOVABLE PADS W/ FABRIC COV'G BY P.F.C. SEE DWG. 1/P-3

1'-0"

(B)

CONTINUOUS HARWOOD BULLNOSE TRIM 2" DIA. COL. LAQ. FIN.

REMOVABLE SHAM BASE 3/4" PARTICLE BOARD W/ PL. LAM. FIN. ON ALL EXP'D. SURFACES

1 / T-17 SIM.

RECESSED BASE 4" H. 3/4" SOLID WOOD W/ PL. LAM. FIN.

SECTION (1)
SCALE: 3/4"=1'-0"

2 ROWS OF 'Q' TYPE LIGHT FIXTURES SUPPLIE BY OWNER; INSTALLED & CONNECTED B.E.C.

4'-0"

3'-0"

6"

CLG 11'-0"

10'-0" AFF

1'-0"

1'-6"

8'-0" (RECESSED STANDARD)

10'-0"

SHEETROCK BACK WALL W/ WALL COVER'G FINISH B.P.C.

¼" MILK WHITE ACRYLIC LENS ON METAL ANGLES B.F.C.

6'-0"

A —

¼" GL. MIRROR ON MASTIC.

STYLMARK ALUM. ANGLE

PL. LAM. BASE

1'-6"

6"

## SECTION
SCALE ¾" = 1'-0"

MIRROR

6'-0"

PL LAM

A

2"

ELEV
¾" = 1'-0"

1'-6"

2'-0"x6'-0" MIRROR
1'-6"x1'-6" MIRROR

1'-9"

9"  2'-0"  9"

A  PLAN SECT.
N.T.S.

¾"

¾"

2'-0"

1'-6"

¾" FIN PLY.

¼" GL MIRROR ON MASTIC

STYLMARK" ALUM. ANGLE # 120059

¾"

HARD WD EDGE PL LAM. FINISM.

3/4" x 3/4 POL. CHR. METAL TUBING FRAME

1/8" MILK WHITE PLEXI
1/8" POL. PL. CLEAR GLASS

CONT. POL. CHR. HINGES

POL. CHR. SET SCREW LOCK

PLAN

1 1/4"

1/8" x 1 1/4" x 1 1/4" POL. CHROME METAL ANGLE FRAME W/ GROUNDED SMOOTH WELDED JOINTS.

1/8" POL. PL. CLEAR GLASS

3/4" X 3/4" POL. CHR. METAL TUBING FRAME

(VARIES)

1/8" MILK WHITE PLEXI

NOTE: FABRICATED & INSTALLED BY PERIMETER FIXTURE CONTRACTOR (LIGHTS INCLUDED)

1 1/4"

WELDED METAL STOP POL. CHR. FIN.

SECT.

TYPICAL TRANSPARENCY DETAIL

SECTION

SINGLE/DOUBLE
HANG-ROD
WITH OPEN VALANCE

SECTION

SLOPED SHELVING
WITH OPEN VALANCE

SECTION

SINGLE/DOUBLE
HANG-ROD

SECTION

STEPPED SHELVING
MERCHANDISE DISPLAY

TWO (2) SINGLE LAMP FLUORESCENT CHANNELS WITH SURFACE MOUNTED TRACK LIGHT WITH ADJUSTABLE LAMPHOLDER B-1

SHIELDING MATERIAL

STEPPED GLASS SHELVING MERCHANDISE DISPLAY WITH 2"-6" OVERLAP

MERCHANDISE STORAGE

**SECTION**

STEPPED SHELVING
MERCHANDISE DISPLAY

TO BE PAINTED WHITE
SOFFIT NON REFLECTIVE

TRACK LIGHT WITH ADJUSTABLE LAMPHOLDER WITH ACCENT LIGHTS
TWO SINGLE LAMP FLUORESCENT CHANNELS REFLECTOR OPTIONAL C1V3

ALIGN FRONT EDGE OF SHELF WITH FRONT EDGE OF "FACEOUT"

**SECTION**

FEATURE WALL DISPLAY
WITH ILLUMINATED
SOFFIT ᴀɴᴅ ACCENT LIGHT

SINGLE LAMP FLUORESCENT CHANNELS PROVIDE OVERLAP OF 1'-0" AT ENDS SEE DETAIL "C1V3

SHIELDING MATERIAL

ALIGN FRONT END OF SHELF WITH FRONT EDGE OF "FACEOUT"

**SECTION**

FEATURE WALL DISPLAY
WITH RECESSED COVE
IN SOFFIT ᴀɴᴅ TRACK LIGHT.

RECESSED INCANDESCENT WALLWASHER OR DOWN-LIGHT WITH WIDE BEAM

SIGNAGE OR ARTWORK

BANQUETTE SEATING

**SECTION**

FEATURE WALL DISPLAY
DROPPED SOFFIT ABOVE
BANQUETTE SEATING

SECTION

FEATURE WALL DISPLAY
WITH ILLUMINATED
SOFFIT and ACCENT LIGHT

SECTION

FEATURE WALL DISPLAY
WITH RECESSED LIGHT
TROUGH and ACCENT LIGHT

SECTION

FEATURE WALL DISPLAY
WITH RECESSED ACCENT
LIGHT IN DROPPED CEILING

SECTION

FEATURE WALL DISPLAY
WITH RECESSED COVE
IN SOFFIT and ACCENT LIGHT

DRYWALL CONSTRUCTION

TWO (2) SINGLE LAMP FLUORESCENT CHANNELS USE 3'-0" AND 4'-0" LENGTHS ONLY

SOLID REFLECTOR SYMMETRICAL CONFIGURATION

SURFACE MOUNTED TRACK LIGHT WITH ADJUSTABLE LAMPHOLDER 50 W. PAR 38 @ 2'-0" O.C.

DIFFUSER ANGLES

METAL STUD

LIGHT SHIELDING MATERIAL AS SPECIFIED

EQUAL   EQUAL

SHIELDED VALANCE
WITH TWO (2) SINGLE
LAMP FLUORESCENT
CHANNELS AND TRACK
LIGHT WITH INCANDESCENT
"CURTAIN WALL" TYPE

EXISTING WALL

OUTRIGGER BRACKET TO SUPPORT FLUORESCENT CHANNELS AND VALANCE BELOW

TWO (2) SINGLE LAMP FLUORESCENT CHANNELS USE 3'-0" AND 4'-0" LENGTHS ONLY

PERFORATED REFLECTOR (33%) SYMMETRICAL CONFIGURATION

DIFFUSER ANGLES

LIGHT SHIELDING MATERIAL AS SPECIFIED

EQUAL   EQUAL

SHIELDED VALANCE
WITH TWO (2) SINGLE
LAMP FLUORESCENT CHANNELS

DROPPED SOFFIT

SINGLE LAMP FLUORESCENT CHANNELS PROVIDE OVERLAP OF 1'-0" AT ENDS SEE DETAIL CV-3

SHOE DISPLAY

STORAGE BELOW

SECTION
FEATURE WALL DISPLAY
WITH DOUBLE COVE
IN SOFFIT

RECESSED ADJUSTABLE ACCENT LAMP FEATURES A REVOLVING TILT GUIDE BRACKET FOR FLEXIBILITY.

75 W PAR 38 LAMP

LAMP HOUSING

DROPPED CEILING

RECESSED ADJUSTABLE
ACCENT LIGHT

**SECTION**

ACCESS DOOR THRU
MERCHANDISE DISPLAY
"CURTAIN WALL"

TWO (2) SINGLE LAMP
FLUORESCENT CHANNELS
SOLID REFLECTOR
SYMMETRICAL CONFIGURATION
SEE DETAIL "

SHIELDING MATERIAL

ACCESS DOOR TO
MERCHANDISE
STOCKROOM AREAS

**SECTION**

ACCESS DOOR THRU
MERCHANDISE DISPLAY
"OPEN VALANCE"

TWO (2) SINGLE LAMP
FLUORESCENT CHANNELS
SOLID REFLECTOR
SYMMETRICAL CONFIGURATION
SEE DETAIL "

SHIELDING MATERIAL

ACCESS DO TO
MERCHANDISE
STOCKROOM AREAS

DRYWALL CONSTRUCTION

METAL STUD

3/4" PLYWOOD BOX

SINGLE LAMP
FLUORESCENT CHANNEL
USE 3'0" AND 4'0"
LENGTHS ONLY

PERFORATED REFLECTOR
ASYMMETRICAL CONFIGURATION

SHIELDED VALANCE
WITH SINGLE LAMP
FLUORESCENT CHANNEL
CURTAIN WALL TYPE

EXISTING WALL

OUTRIGGER BRACKET
TO SUPPORT FLUORESCENT
CHANNELS AND VALANCE
BELOW

SINGLE LAMP
FLUORESCENT CHANNEL
WITH PERFORATED
REFLECTOR (33%)
ASYMMETRICAL CONFIGURATION
USE 3'0" AND 4'0"
LENGTHS ONLY

CENTERLINE OF LAMP
TO ALIGN WITH
RETURN EDGE OF
WOOD VALANCE

DEPTH VARIES

VALANCE WITH
SINGLE LAMP
FLUORESCENT CHANNEL

SINGLE LAMP FLUORESCENT
CHANNELS TO BE
STAGGERED WITH A
MINIMUM OVERLAP
OF 12" SO AS TO
AVOID SHADOWS CAST
BY SOCKET ENDS.
USE 3'0" AND 9'0" LENGTHS ONLY

INTERIOR TO BE PAINTED
LIGHT VALUE/COLOR

DIFFUSER ANGLES

ACRYLIC DIFFUSER
WITH PRISMATIC LENS

9" - 12"

1'0" - 1'4"

2"

DIRECT COVE
SINGLE/DOUBLE ROW
STAGGERED FLUORESCENT

TWO (2) SINGLE LAMP
FLUORESCENT CHANNELS
USE 3'0" AND 4'0'
LENGTHS ONLY

SOLID REFLECTOR
ASYMMETRICAL CONFIGURATION

DRYWALL CONSTRUCTION

DIFFUSER ANGLES

METAL STUD

LIGHT SHIELDING
MATERIAL AS SPECIFIED

1'-4"

EQUAL        EQUAL

DEPTH VARIES        4"±

SHIELDED VALANCE
WITH TWO (2) SINGLE
LAMP FLUORESCENT CHANNELS
"CURTAIN WALL" TYPE

CEILING TO BE PAINTED
LIGHT VALUE/COLOR

SPLAY LIP / MAINTAIN 1/2"
FROM TOP OF LAMP TO TOP OF LIP

DOUBLE ROW FLUORESCENT
CHANNELS TO BE
STAGGERED AT 50'/
INTERVALS SO AS TO
AVOID SHADOWS CAST
BY SOCKET ENDS

R=1'6"

1'-6" MIN

10"

1'-0" MIN        VARIES

INDIRECT/CURVED COVE
DOUBLE ROW FLUORESCENT

## DEPARTMENT STORES
Wall Display Systems

**WATERFALL**
Average Quantity of
Garments Per Post: 48

**FACE OUT & WATERFALL**

**FACE OUT**
Average Quantity of
Garments Per Post: 46

**POST FACE OUT WITH
STRAIGHT HANGING**
Average Quantity of
Garments Per 4'-0" Section: 94

**STRAIGHT HANGING & FACE OUT**

**STRAIGHT
WITH HANGRAIL FACE OUT**
Average Quantity of Garments
Per 4'-0" Section: 96

**FACE OUT WITH DISPLAY**
Average Quantity of Garments
Per 4'-0" Section: 49

• Compatible with
  universal ½" slotting
• Unique new oval hangrail

**ROD DISPLAYS**
6 or 7 Rods Per
4'-0" Section

- Design continuity
  from wall to floor
  carries theme throughout
  the department or
  the store
- Designed for high
  volume merchandising
- Flexible merchandising
- Designed to be
  compatible with other
  Pam International Systems

**BINNING SYSTEM**

**MULTI-NET SYSTEM**

**BASKETS & SHELVES**

**WOOD OR GLASS SHELVES**

**MULTI-NET PANELS**

**MESH PANEL SYSTEMS**

**GRID WALL PANELS**

- All Multiples/Systems 2™ upright posts are engineered with easily changeable post covers (Pat. Pend.)
- All metal components are coated with a durable, long lasting, baked on epoxy powder finish.

## DEPARTMENT STORES
Rack Display Systems

16" Straight Arms     16" Slant Arms with 8 balls     16" Straight Arm and 16"Slant Arm with 8 Balls     16" Slant Arms with 5 "J" Hooks

**Two-arm costumers**

SPACE SAVER 22" Arms     FOUR WAY RACK     18" Slant Arms with 8 Balls     18" Slant Arms with 5 "J"Hooks

**Four-way racks**

Rectangular Hangrail     REVOLVING     1¼" Dia. Hangrail

36" Dia. 42" Dia.     36" Dia.     36" Dia. 42" Dia.

**Circular racks**

THREE LEVEL
36" Dia.
42" Dia.

OUTRIGGER
All Chrome Wall Fin

14¾" deep
16¾" deep
with adjustable
cornice mount

14¾" deep
Non-adjustable
cornice mount

14¾" deep
16¾" deep

Single Tier
Revolving
Belt Rack

Two Tier
Revolving
Belt Rack

**Specialty racks**

**Outriggers, wall fins**

60" Long

Double Hangrail

Tandem Hangrail

**Rectangular racks**

Folding-60" long
w/15" Pullouts
1" Square Tubing

60" Long
All 1" Square Tubing      12" Pullout

54" High
66" High
74" High

60" Long
All Rectangular Tubing 1¼" Hangrail

1 1/16" tubing with
12" Pullout
Uprights removable for storage.
60" Long

**Rolling racks**

## MEDIUM DUTY-½" SLOTS 1" O.C.

1/16"    13/32"    11/16"

For General Use
The Standard of
Wall Standards
24"
30"
36"
42"
48"

1/16"    ½"    1¼"

For Medium Load
Single or Double
Brackets.
60"
72"
84"

1¼"    1/16"    11/16"

Concealed wall
standard for 5/8"
or less wall panels.
72"
84"
96"

3/32"    13/32"    11/16"

For additional
strength.
60"
72"
84"

3/32"    .080    1¼"    ½"

used for heavier
loads.
60"
72"
84"

## HEAVY DUTY-1" SLOTS 2" O.C.

1/8"    11/16"    7/8"

For your heaviest
load requirements.

60"
72"
84"
76"

1¼"    1/8"    11/16"

Concealed wall
standard for 5/8"
or less wall panels.

72"
84"
96"

Regular Duty Brackets for use with 1" O.C. Slotting.
½ hard steel .093 thickness

.Polished chrome.
Felt lined to prevent
scratching of hangrail

12"

For 1" and 1 1/16" Tube
12"
14"

For 1½" and 1 5/16" Tube
12"
14"
.Satin Zinc.

.Satin Zinc.
12"
14"

.Polished Chrome.
Felt lined to prevent
scratching hangrail

3"

For 1" and
1 1/16" Tube
3"

For 1¼" and
1 5/16" Tube
3"
.Satin Zinc.

3"
.Satin Zinc.

Heavy Duty Brackets for use with 2" O.C. Slotting
½ hard steel .125 Thickness

.Polished Chrome.
Felt lines to prevent scratching of hang rail.

12"

.Satin Zinc.

12"
14"

# Public Restrooms, Toilets, and Coatrooms

Restrooms and toilets                             425
Coatrooms                                        460

## TABLE 1 Minimum Number of Plumbing Fixtures Required by Building Occupancy Type*

| Type of building occupancy | Type of fixture | | | | | |
|---|---|---|---|---|---|---|
| | Water closets | Urinals | Lavatories | Bathtubs or showers | Drinking fountains | Other fixtures |
| Assembly — places of worship† | 1 for ea. sex for ea. 150 persons | Urinals may be provided in toilet rooms in lieu of water closets but for not more than ½ of the required number of water closets | 1 | | | |
| Assembly — other than places of worship (including but not limited to auditoriums, theaters, convention halls) and all spaces classified as F-4 | No. of persons / No of fixtures for each sex<br>1-100   1<br>101-200   2<br>201-300   3<br>301-400   4<br>Over 400, add 1 fixture for ea. sex for ea. additional 200 persons | Urinals may be provided in toilet rooms in lieu of water closets but for not more than ½ of the required number of water closets | No. of persons / No. of fixtures<br>1-200   1<br>201-400   2<br>401-750   3<br>Over 750, add 1 fixture for ea. 500 persons | | 1 for ea. 1,000 persons except that there shall be at least 1 fixture at each assembly floor level or tier | Where motion picture projection booths contain more than 2 projectors, at least 1 water closet and 1 lavatory shall be provided on the same level and within 20 ft. of the booth |
| Dormitories — school or labor, also institutional | 1 for ea. sex for ea. 8 persons | Urinals may be provided in toilet rooms in lieu of water closets but for not more than ½ of the required number of water closets | 1 for ea. 12 persons | 1 for ea. 8 persons; for women's dormitories, 1 bathtub shall be substituted for 1 shower at the ratio of 1 for ea. 30 women | | Laundry trays — 1 for ea. 50 persons |
| Single room occupancies for sleeping accommodations only | 1 for ea. 6 persons | | 1 for ea. 6 persons | 1 for ea. 6 persons | | |
| Dwellings — one- and two-family | 1 for each dwelling unit | | 1 for each dwelling unit | 1 for each dwelling unit | | Kitchen sink — 1 for each dwelling unit |
| Public buildings, offices, business mercantile, storage; warehouses, factories and institutional employees‡ | No. of persons each sex / No. of fixtures<br>1-15   1<br>16-35   2<br>36-55   3<br>56-80   4<br>81-110   5<br>111-150   6<br>1 fixture for ea. additional 40 persons | Urinals may be provided in toilet rooms in lieu of water closets but for not more than ½ of the required number of water closets when more than 35 persons | No. of persons / No. of fixtures<br>1-20   1<br>21-40   2<br>41-60   3<br>61-90   4<br>91-125   5<br>1 fixture for ea. additional 45 persons | | 1 for ea. 75 persons | |
| Public bathing | 1 fixture for ea. sex for ea. 30 persons | Urinals may be provided in toilet rooms in lieu of water closets but for not more than ½ of the required number of water closets | 1/60 | 1/40 | | |
| Schools:<br>Elementary<br>Secondary | 1 fixture for ea. sex for ea. 35 students | Urinals may be provided in toilet rooms in lieu of water closets but for not more than ½ of the required number of water closets | 1/50 pupils<br>1/50 pupils<br>Over 300 pupils: 1/100 pupils | In gym or pool shower rooms, ⅓ pupils of a largest class using pool at any one time | 1/50 persons but at least 1 per floor | |
| Workers' portable facilities | 1/30 workers | 1/30 workers | | | At least 1 per floor equivalent for ea. 100 workmen | |
| Industrial — foundries only | No. of persons / No. of fixtures<br>1-10   1<br>11-25   2<br>26-50   3<br>51-80   4<br>81-125   5<br>1 additional fixture for each additional 45 persons | Where more than 10 men are employed:<br>No. of men / No. of urinals<br>11-29   1<br>30-79   2<br>1 additional fixture for each additional 80 males<br>Urinals may be provided in toilet rooms in lieu of water closets but for not more than ½ of the required number of water closets | No. of persons / No. of fixtures<br>1-8   1<br>9-16   2<br>17-30   3<br>31-45   4<br>46-65   5<br>1 additional fixture for each additional 25 persons | 1 shower for each 15 persons exposed to excessive heat or occupational hazard from poisonous, infectious, or irritating material | 1 for ea. 75 persons | |
| | | | | | | Other fixtures |
| Kitchens for public or employees dining | | | 1 lavatory for the personal use of kitchen employees | | One machine or a 3-compartment sink for the effective washing and sanitizing of all cutlery, dishes and glasses before re-use | |
| Dwellings — multiple or apartment | 1 for each dwelling unit or apartment | | 1 for each dwelling unit or apartment | 1 for each dwelling unit or apartment | Kitchen sink — 1 for each dwelling unit or apartment. Within each dwelling unit, not designed for use by transients, one laundry tray or automatic laundry washing machine; or in a readily accessible location within a general laundry room. 1 two-compartment tray for each 10 dwelling units or 1 automatic laundry washing machine for each 20 dwelling units. | |

*The population used in determining the number of fixtures required shall be based on the number of people to occupy the space but in no case shall the population be less than that determined by allowing 125 sq. ft. of net floor area per person.

†Such facilities may be in adjacent buildings under the same ownership or control, and shall be accessible during periods when the assembly space is occupied.

‡Facilities for employees in a storage building or warehouse may be located in an adjacent building, under the same ownership, where the maximum distance of travel from the working space to the toilet facilities does not exceed 500 ft. horizontally.

## RESTROOMS AND TOILETS
### Plumbing Fixture and Accessory Heights

While Fig. 1 provides specific vertical dimensions of both plumbing fixtures and accessories, the designer is cautioned that every plumbing fixture and accessory must be carefully analyzed in light of the users to be served. Plumbing contractors will follow the manufacturer's recommendations or their own standards unless the designer provides this information on the working drawings. In large-scale projects, it is suggested that the designer carefully provide all fixture mounting heights on all interior elevations or on a separate diagramatic drawing, such as is shown in Fig. 1.

**Fig. 1  Fixture heights.**

**Handicapped Washrooms**

**Fig. 2  Suggested mounting heights for various bathroom accessories.**

**Partition Mounted Units**

**Fig. 3  Typical back to back male/female washroom stalls using partition mounted units to accommodate a handicapped stall and one standard stall. If room permits, grab bars should be placed on all three sides, resulting in a "U"-shaped configuration. Most codes require toilet stall doors to open outward.**

PART ELEVATION

PART PLAN

MEN'S TOILET ROOM

**Fig. 4**  This drawing of a part plan and part elevation of a men's toilet room demonstrates how mounting heights of plumbing fixtures and accessories are indicated. In addition, spacing of plumbing fixtures is indicated by use of a horizontal dimension from centerline to centerline of the lavatories. Many designers prefer to show horizontal dimensions on the plan.  a = recessed waste receptacle,  b = recessed towel dispenser and soap dispenser with shelf.

# RESTROOMS AND TOILETS
## Plumbing Fixture and Accessory Heights

PART ELEVATION

PART ELEVATION

PART PLAN

PART PLAN

WOMEN'S TOILET ROOM

Fig. 5 Mounting heights or vertical dimensions are always taken from the finished floor. When installing accessories on tile walls, the tile module and dimensions should be taken into consideration. a = full length mirror, b = recessed feminine napkin dispenser, c = recessed towel cabinet and waste receptacle, d = recessed soap dispenser with shelf.

PART ELEVATION

PART PLAN

PRIVATE TOILET ROOM

Fig. 6 The mounting heights of plumbing fixtures and accessories for a private toilet are, in many instances, determined by the physical characteristics of the primary user. A person 6′6″ tall might require the mounting height of a lavatory, mirror, or shower head to be higher than usual. Note that any electrical outlets near a lavatory or shower must be specified with a ground fault interrupter. c = first aid cabinet and medicine cabinet.

**MEN**

SIDE ENTRANCE
WHEEL CHAIR
TOILET ENCLOSURE

(This is not preferred)

**WOMEN**

Fig. 7  These drawings show minimum dimensions both for toilet enclosures and between partitions and walls. These layouts are recommendations provided by the General Services Administration, but they may not be in conformity with other codes or desired bathroom layouts, especially in regard to accessibility. Remember, too, that codes provide minimum, not optimal, standards.

LAVATORY

LAVATORY

JAN. CLOSET

**Fig. 8** These working drawings provide both vertical and horizontal dimensions for placement of plumbing fixtures and accessories. Note that accessories are identified or "called out" through the use of letters, which would be coordinated with either a legend or a schedule.

## RESTROOMS AND TOILETS

**Plans**

In multiple-fixtured public toilets, at least one watercloset and lavatory must be designed to conform to barrier-free or accessibility standards.

### LAVATORY

### BRIDE'S ROOM LAVATORY

### LAVATORY

### LAVATORY

### JAN. CLOSET

# MENS TOILET

## RESTROOMS AND TOILETS

**Plans and Elevations**

The women's room shown in Fig. 9 requires approximately 250 ft² for the toilet area and about the same for the vanity area. Wall elevations for the two areas are shown in Fig. 10. The designer should carefully analyze the number of lavatories and water-closets specified for a given facility. Research suggests that most "fixture counts" provided by city or state codes are too low and do not adequately reflect the amount of time that women require. As a result, it is not unusual to see long lines in front of women's rooms, particularly those that service places of public assembly. Note that the plan in Fig. 9 provides supplemental vanity or counter surfaces.

## WOMENS TOILET
## POWDER ROOM

Fig. 9

Fig. 10   Wall elevations for the women's room plan in Fig. 9.

**WOMENS TOILET**
**MENS TOILET**

Fig. 11   This men's room and women's room complex, including a janitor's closet, requires slightly more than 400 ft² of floor area. Corresponding wall elevations are shown in Fig. 12.

Fig. 12   Wall elevations for the men's room and women's room complex shown in Fig. 11.

Fig. 12   *(Continued)*

# RESTROOMS AND TOILETS
**Miscellaneous Elevations**

Fig. 13   These drawings show how some designers indicate the heights of certain fixtures and bathroom accessories.

men's toilet

showers

$\frac{1}{2}'' = 1'-0''$

## TOILET ROOM ELEVATIONS

**Fig. 14** Detailed large-scale wall elevations such as this are required to show materials, accessory mounting heights, the coordination and placement of plumbing fixtures, and even manufacturer's model numbers.

COUNTER DETAIL
$1\frac{1}{2}'' = 1'-0''$

**Fig. 15** The large-scale counter detail shown here provides all the information needed to construct this essential bathroom element. Not only are the construction details carefully defined and described, but all the other design relationships are clearly shown. Note the relationships of the mirror, soap dispenser, and lavatory to the plastic laminate counter. Other lavatory counter details are shown in Figs. 16 to 19.

SECTION

TOILET LAVATORY-TYP.

SEE FLOOR PLAN FOR LOCATION AT SILOS
TOILETS - 103, 104, 132, 96, 216, 297

LAV.-TYP.

SECTION - LAV. COUNTER

SECT./DETAIL
SILO LAVATORIES

Fig. 16

MIRROR IN BRIDES RM. & POWDER RM.

2'-0"

PLASTIC LAMINATE
1¼" HARDWOOD PLYWOOD

2'-6" TO FINISH FL. BACKSPLASH

RECESSED LAVATORY IN BRIDES ROOM #105

METAL 'T' SHAPED BRACKETS ANCHORED TO WALL & UNDERSIDE OF COUNTER 3'-0" ± O.C.

@ 1½" = 1'-0"

CONTINUOUS STAINLESS STEEL SINK TRIM

METAL CLAMPS & BOLTS

LAVATORY IN BRIDES RM. #105

PLASTIC LAMINATE

HARDWOOD PLYWOOD

@ FULL SIZE

VANITY DETAILS

2'-6"

PLASTER

FACE OF VERTICAL FIR BOARDS

PLASTER BEAD

PLASTIC LAMINATE ON 1¼" HARDWOOD PLYWOOD

2'-6" SPACE #207
3'-0" IN PHONE BOOTH TO FINISH FLOOR

METAL 'T' SHAPED BRACKETS ANCHORED TO WALL & UNDERSIDE OF COUNTER 3'-0" O.C.

FACE OF VERTICAL FIR BOARDS IN TELEPHONE BOOTH IN LAVATORY FOYER SPACE #110

PLASTER

COUNTER DETAILS
@ 1½" = 1'-0"

24" x 72" MIRROR

FIBERGLASS ON 5/8" WR GYPB'D.

SOAP DISP.

12 LOCKERS 12"W 56"H 15"D

3'-0"    1'-6"

4'-0"    2'-7"

6'-0"

CER. TILE BASE

223-224-WEST

SCRIBE & CAULK

2'-1"
L.P. ON ¾" W.D.

1x4 FRAME

L 1x3

1x4    L.P.

L 2x2x³⁄₁₆ MITERED, WELDED ANGLE FRAME. LAG BOLT THRU PIPE SPACER TO 4x4 STUD

1'-4"    2'-1"

3/AB  LAVATORY

Fig. 17

443

MIRROR

VERDE ANTIQUE MARBLE TOP, SPLASHES
AND SKIRT, 7/8" THICK, SET IN EPOXY GROUT.
SET SKIRT IN CONT. 304 S.S. 18 GA. #7 FINISH
EASE EXP EDGES OF MARBLE 1/16" R.

3/4" EXT. PLYWOOD

LAVATORY

2-10

2-10

2×6

P.T. #2 SYP FRAMING, BEAM, LEDGER,
JOISTS & CLEATS. PROVIDE JOIST
BETWEEN EA. LAV. 1/2" × 4" LAG
@ EA. STUD, STUDS 16" O.C. BACK & ENDS.

1'-10"

MET. STUD TO FLR.

SEE ELEVS.

7/8"

10 5/8"

12"

2×4 WD STD SCREW TO MET STUD
FULL BEARING IN MET. SHOE

A / 5   LAVATORY COUNTER

---

1/2" GYPSUM WALL BOARD
CERAMIC TILE
4" HIGH SPLASH
PLASTIC LAMINATE ON
3/4" PLYWOOD

2'-0"

6"

WOOD BLOCKING
BACKING GRADE
PLASTIC LAMINATE
LINE OF LAVATORY & HARDWARE
2'-10" SUPPORT CUT AS SHOWN ON
2'-10" SUPPORT BLOCKING
LINE OF END PIECE (COVERED WITH
PLASTIC LAMINATE)

FASTEN THRU TO WOOD BLOCKING
IN ADDITION TO SCREWING INTO
STEEL STUDS @ 16" O.C.

AT MASONRY WALL CONDITION
IN MEN'S TOILET USE LAG BOLTS
AND EXPANSION SLEEVES
(NO WOOD BLOCKING)

SPACE SUPPORTS BETWEEN
EACH LAVATORY

DETAIL @ LAVATORY

---

PLATE GLASS MIRROR
ON 1× WOOD FRAME

1" × 2" DARK BRONZE ANODIZED ALUMINUM
ANGLE

CLEAR SEALANT

MARBLE
TOP AS SPECIFIED

2×6

.064 DARK BRONZE ANODIZED
ALUMINUM APPLIED IN MASTIC

1 1/4"

8 1/2"

2'-1 TO FIN. FLOOR

1'-0"

1/2"  1/2"

DETAIL @ LAVATORY TOP

MIRROR / TOWEL & SOAP DISP.

SHOWER DR.

CERAMIC TILE

4" SPLASH CERAMIC TILE

FOLDING SEAT

5'-2"
8'-2"
2'-5½"
18"
6'-8"

4

cabinet
D/A10

PLAST. LAM. FRONT TOP & BACKSPLASH ON 3/4" PLYWD

1'-9"
4"
5'
2'-5"
2'-10"

SINK

HORIZ. SUPPORT AS REQ'D RM. 10B

3/4" THK. END PANEL · RM. 10B (PLAST. LAM. ALL SURFACES.)

9'-0" (ROOM 110)
8'-4" (ROOM 112)

DRYWALL SOFFIT

(3) 26¼" x 46¼" MIR.

SEC. 1

VINYL ON PLSTR WALL

10½"   2'-5¼"   2'-5¼"   2'-5¼"   10½"   @ RM. # 110
9½"    2'-3¼"   2'-3¼"   2'-3¼"   9½"    @ RM. # 112

*ELEVATION @ VANITY - RMS. 110 & 112*

2'-0" (RM. 112)
2'-0" (RM. 110)
1'-11¼"

PLAS. LAM.

2 x 4's CONT.

2 x 10 CONT.

HILTI · POCKET INTO MASONRY WALL AT ENDS

3/4" THK. FURRING STRIPS

4"
4½"
8½"
1'-0"
3/4"

*SECTION 1*

2'-0"

MIRROR

W/R GWB OVER STUD WALL

CERAMIC TILE - THIN SET

LAMINATED PLASTIC FORMED COUNTER-TOP W/ 4" COVED SPLASH (ONE SIDE & BACK & NON DRIP EDGE)

LAM. PLASTIC FACE TO MATCH TOP

2X SUPPORT FRAME SECURED TO WALL

STEEL BRACKET · STANLEY NO. 796 6" X 18" · OR EQUAL. PROVIDE STUD @ BRACKET. PAINT TO MATCH LAM. PLASTIC · SEE INT. ELEV.

4

2'-10"
2'-5½"
4½"
6"

2½" METAL STUDS
5/8" GYP. BD

BLOCKING

PLASTIC LAM. TOP, EDGE & SPLASH

3/4" PLYWOOD

2X CONT

3/8" ø LAG BOLTS STAGGERED @ 12" O.C.

2X4 LEDGER

4"
6"
2'-" AFF
1'-6"

VANITY DETAIL

Fig. 19

445

## RESTROOMS AND TOILETS

**Lavatory Cabinet Details**

**Fig. 20  Elegantly detailed lavatory cabinets are shown here. Note the use of an exposed oil-finished red mahogany frame or edge surrounding a verdi antique marble top. Complementary telephone shelf details in plan, elevation, and large-scale detail are also shown.**

PLAN

PLAN

FRONT ELEVATION

SIDE ELEVATION

FRONT ELEVATION

SECTION D-D

wall bracket

1" partition

1¼" stile

1" door

honeycomb filler

slide latch

keeper

wall bracket

slide latch

OUTSWING DOOR

handle

INSWING DOOR

E-E

SECTION A-A

E-E

OVERHEAD SUPPORTING MEMBER, & DRILLING OF SAME BY OTHERS

SIDE VIEW
SECTION C-C

CEILING FASTENING
SECTION B-B

Fig. 21

## RESTROOMS AND TOILETS
### Toilet Stall Details

**PLAN**

**PLAN**

**FRONT ELEVATION**

**SIDE ELEVATION**

**FRONT ELEVATION**

**SECTION D-D**

wall bracket

slide latch

wall bracket

1" partition

slide latch

keeper

honeycomb filler

1¼" stile

1" door

handle

OUTSWING DOOR

INSWING DOOR

E-E

**SIDE VIEW**
(SECTION)

**FLOOR FASTENING**
SECTION B-B

EXPANSION SHIELDS MUST BE SET IN SOLID CONCRETE

**SECTION A-A**

**E-E**

Fig. 22

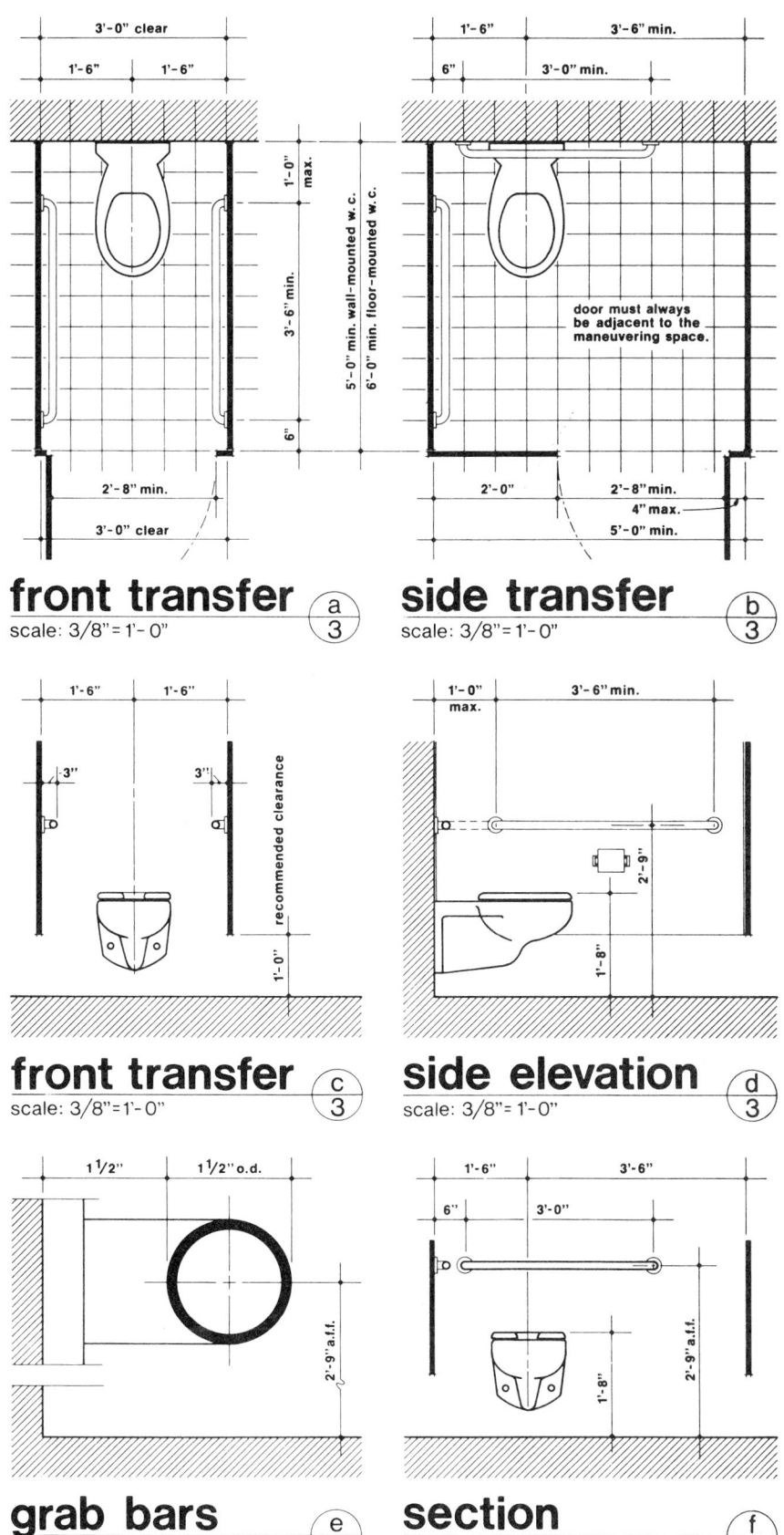

**front transfer** (a/3)
scale: 3/8"= 1'- 0"

**side transfer** (b/3)
scale: 3/8"= 1'- 0"

door must always
be adjacent to the
maneuvering space.

**front transfer** (c/3)
scale: 3/8"=1'- 0"

**side elevation** (d/3)
scale: 3/8"= 1'- 0"

**grab bars** (e/3)
scale: half

**section** (f/3)
scale: 3/8"=1'- 0"

## TOILET AND RESTROOM DESIGN

The design data contained on the following pages are intended to illustrate functional accessibility concepts. Some examples illustrate minimum federal requirements, while others are culled from among the various state standards. Designers are cautioned to consult local standards in their respective jurisdictions.

The current minimum federal standard is ANSI A117.1-1986, published by the American National Standards Institute, Inc. It specifies a stall typified by detail a/3. This "front transfer" type stall requires a watercloset mounted at 1'8" a.f.f., preferably wall hung. Stall doors must be outswinging.

Because a significant portion of people using wheelchairs cannot transfer in this manner, the side transfer stall (b/3) has been developed. Clear stall dimensions and seat heights vary somewhat with jurisdiction. Most standards that address side transfer stalls require lower seat heights with 15"–17" mounting heights being typical.

We recommend locking devices for doors that do not require twisting and grasping motions, avoidance of foot operated flush valves, installation of ceiling or wall-hung partitions as practical, and avoidance of curtains in lieu of doors.

Federal standards mandate grab bars of 1½" o.d. The bars must be securely mounted 1½" clear from the wall or partition. This mounting distance is critical, as it provides a "cradle" for a forearm during transfer or if a user loses her or his grip.

## RESTROOMS AND TOILETS
**Wheelchair Accessible Design**

Lavatories need not be specialized designs to be accessible. Utilization of clearances shown will do much to make lavatories accessible. Because persons with loss of sensation in their legs cannot feel pain (and because they heal at a slower rate), hot water lines and drains must be insulated. Also, under several state codes, faucets are required to be lever, blade, or multi-arm handle operated.

Single lever controls are preferable. Spring-operated faucets must have time delay devices.

At least one mirror must be located with the reflecting surface mounted at 3'4" a.f.f. (3'2" or lower preferable). Where possible, full-length mirrors are preferable.

At least one of each type of toilet accessory must also be located at 3'4" a.f.f. or less. Note that this dimension is measured to the highest control required for operation. Controls that require twisting and grasping motions should be avoided.

Because people that use wheelchairs require increased fluid intake, drinking fountains become more than convenience items. While there is not space here to address all configurations, the following concerns are typical to all: controls should be operable without the need for precise grasping; the faucet should not direct spray away from the user and must be located as near the front edge as practical; the units must be free of sharp edges and corners and overhead obstructions.

## lavatory  (p/3)
scale: 3/8"= 1'-0"

## lavatory  (q/3)
scale: 3/8"= 1'-0"

## mirrors  (r/3)

## accessory  (s/3)
scale: 3/8"= 1'-0"

## d.f.  (t/3)
scale: 1/4"= 1'-0"

## alcove  (u/3)
scale: 1/4"= 1'-0"

## e.w.c.  (v/3)

## d.f.  (w/3)
scale: 1/4"= 1'-0"

## alcove  (x/3)
scale: 1/4"= 1'-0"

## e.w.c.  (y/3)

**urinal** (g/3)

**urinal** (h/3)
scale: 3/8"=1'-0"

**urinal** (i/3)
scale: 3/8"=1'-0"

**clearances** (j/3)
scale: 1/8"=1'-0"

**clear.** (k/3)
scale: 1/8"=1'-0"

**clearances** (l/3)
scale: 1/4"=1'-0"

**clearances** (m/3)
scale: 1/4"=1'-0"

**clearances** (n/3)
scale: 1/4"=1'-0"

**clearances** (o/3)
scale: 1/4"=1'-0"

Urinals, if provided, should have elongated bowls with the opening of the basin located at 19" a.f.f. or less, or mounted level with the main floor. Many state standards specify maximum mounting heights of 15"–16" a.f.f. These lower dimensions are preferable.

The toilet room itself should provide a clear floor area with minimum dimensions of 60" x 60" to facilitate maneuvering wheelchairs. Additionally, provide a minimum of 3'6" clearance in front of accessible toilet stalls to facilitate entry.

Similarly, adequate clearances must be provided at entrances. The spaces shown in details l/3 to o/3 represent typical dimensions specified in state codes. Note, however, that federal and many state standards require 12" clear jamb areas adjoining both sides of all doors. A clearance of 18" or more on the strike side of a door is more effective. In vestibules having doors in series, there must be space for a wheelchair to clear one door prior to opening another.

**Fig. 23  Toilet stalls.**

In Figs. 24 to 30, various generic toilet accessories and grab bar configurations are illustrated. While most manufacturers have similar accessories and grab bars within their catalogs, overall dimensions and methods of installation vary greatly. Placement of accessories in relationship to plumbing fixtures, door swings, and interior circulation is to be carefully studied by the designer.

**Facial tissue dispenser**

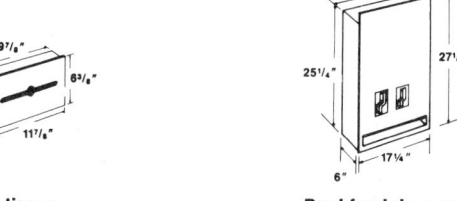

**Dual feminine napkin/ tampon vendor**

**Sanitary napkin disposal**

**Dual feminine napkin/ tampon vendor**

**Sanitary napkin disposal**

**Recessed dual napkin/tampon dispenser and disposal**

**Recessed seat cover and toilet tissue dispenser**

**Wall urn ash tray**

**Toilet seat cover dispenser**

**Liquid soap dispenser**

**Recessed powdered soap dispenser**

**Recessed horizontal soap dispenser and shelf**

**All-purpose unit with concealed towel cabinet**

**Multipurpose unit with mirror, shelf, towel, and liquid soap dispensers**

**Disposal valve soap gun**

**Fig. 24**

# RESTROOMS AND TOILETS
Toilet Accessories

Paper towel dispenser

Paper towel dispenser

Paper towel dispenser and disposal

Paper towel dispenser

Paper towel dispenser

Paper towel disposal

Towel dispenser and Disposa-Valve soap gun

Paper towel disposal

Paper towel disposal

Paper towel dispenser and disposal

Paper towel dispenser and covered disposal

Paper towel dispenser and disposal

Roll paper towel dispenser and disposal

Paper towel dispenser and disposal

Roll paper towel dispenser and disposal

Paper towel dispenser and disposal

Semirecessed waste receptacle

Fig. 25

454

**Ash trays**

**Waste receptacles**

**Shelves**

**Medicine cabinets**

Fig. 26

## RESTROOMS AND TOILETS
**Toilet Accessories**

**Sanitary napkin dispensers**

**Sanitary napkin disposals**

**Combined sanitary napkin dispenser and disposal**

**Hand and hair dryers**

**Paper cup dispenser**

**Paper cup disposal**

**Multipurpose cabinet**

Fig. 27

**Toilet tissue dispensers**

**Paper towel dispensers**

**Soap dispensers**

Fig. 28

## RESTROOMS AND TOILETS
**Grab Bar Configurations**

**left** hand shown
**right** hand opp.

*This dimension 11″ when
1½″ O.D. tubing specified.

left hand shown
right hand opp.

*This dimension 11″ when
1½″ O.D. tubing specified.

**left hand** shown
**right hand** opp.

Projects 3″ below finished floor,
has slip flange at floor.

**bar** swings full 180°

left hand shown
right hand opp.

right hand shown
left hand opp.

right hand shown
left hand opp.

**Fig. 29**

right hand shown
left hand opp.

right hand shown
left hand opp.

right hand shown
left hand opp.

right hand shown
left hand opp.

right hand shown
left hand opp.

right hand shown
left hand opp.

right hand shown
left hand opp.

right hand shown
left hand opp.

36″ from side wall to side wall

**Fig. 30**

# COATROOMS

**Floor Area Requirements**

Coatrooms typically fall into two categories: those that are self-service and those that are controlled by one or more attendants. The latter category of coatroom can be more compact because only one, or perhaps two, attendants have access to the coats. A self-service coatroom must have more space between rows of coats so that several persons can enter and get their coats.

Self-service coatrooms are susceptible to theft of property, particularly expensive outerwear. Therefore, it is desirable that these coatrooms be visible to someone at all times, such as a maitre d' in a restaurant or a receptionist in an office. In those situations where a supervised self-service coatroom is inappropriate or cannot be provided, self-service keyed locks offer a viable alternative. In addition to being able to provide secure coat storage, lockers can also store briefcases, packages, or other encumbrances.

**TABLE 1  Floor Area Requirements for Public Coatrooms**

| Number of coats (capacity) | Floor area (with attendant) | | Floor area (without attendant) | | Floor area (electric conveyor) | |
|---|---|---|---|---|---|---|
| | Min | Max | | | | |
| 50 | 35 | 50 | 40 | 60 | N/A | N/A |
| 100 | 65 | 85 | 80 | 100 | 80 | 100 |
| 150 | 90 | 120 | 110 | 145 | 110 | 125 |
| 200 | 125 | 150 | 150 | 180 | 140 | 150 |
| 250 | 150 | 190 | 180 | 230 | 100 | 110 |
| 300 | 180 | 225 | 215 | 270 | 125 | 140 |
| 350 | 200 | 260 | 240 | 300 | 135 | 150 |
| 400 | 225 | 275 | 270 | 330 | 150 | 160 |
| 450 | 260 | 320 | 310 | 370 | 160 | 175 |
| 500 | 300 | 365 | 425 | 430 | 175 | 190 |
| 750 | 450 | 500 | 540 | 600 | 250 | 275 |
| 1000 | 600 | 650 | 720 | 780 | 325 | 350 |
| 1500 | 800 | 900 | 950 | 1080 | 450 | 480 |
| 2000 | 1000 | 1250 | 1200 | 1500 | 600 | 675 |
| 3000 | 1600 | 1850 | 1900 | 2200 | 1000 | 1150 |

*Note:* The above floor areas are approximate and should only be used for preliminary space planning requirements.

Since the number of coats per linear foot of hanging can vary from 4 to 8, the floor area can vary dramatically. A lightweight overcoat, for example, can measure 1–1.5 inches in width. A medium weight to heavyweight coat might measure from 2 to 4 inches. A fur coat might require a minimum of 4–6 in. The designer must consider the overall size of coatroom based upon the following critical factors: (1) geographic location/climate; (2) attendants required or not required; (3) aisle clearance; (4) peak entry/exit loads for coat retrieval; (5) assumed garment thickness or garments per linear foot; (6) linear feet of counter surface and overhead shelving; and (7) other storage components, i.e., hats, umbrellas, briefcases, packages, etc.

Three basic types of manufactured or prefabricated coat storage units are shown in Figs. 1 to 3. Exact coat storage capacities are provided by the manufacturer. All units can be customized to suit various room configurations. Note the adjoining counter space to speed operations. Coat capacities relative to length are listed in Table 2.

**Fig. 1  Electric carousel coat storage.**

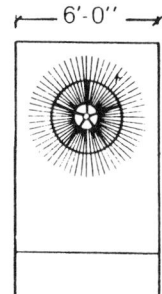

**Fig. 2  Rotating reels coat storage.**

**Fig. 3  Stationary coat storage.**

# COATROOMS

**Electric Checkroom Systems**

**Fig. 4**

**TABLE 2**

| Overall length with garments* | Length of hanging capacity | Coat capacity: no. of slots† |
|---|---|---|
| 7' 5" | 13' 0" | 144 |
| 7'11½" | 14' 1" | 156 |
| 8' 6" | 15' 2" | 168 |
| 9' 1" | 16' 3" | 180 |
| 9' 7" | 17' 4" | 192 |
| 10' 1½" | 18' 5" | 204 |
| 10' 8" | 19' 6" | 216 |
| 11' 2½" | 20' 7" | 228 |
| 11' 9" | 21' 8" | 240 |
| 12' 3½" | 22' 9" | 252 |
| 12'10" | 23'10" | 264 |
| 13' 4½" | 24'11" | 276 |
| 13'11" | 26' 0" | 288 |
| 14' 5½" | 27' 1" | 300 |
| 15' 0" | 28' 2" | 312 |
| 15' 6½" | 29' 3" | 324 |
| 16' 1" | 30' 4" | 336 |
| 16' 7½" | 31' 5" | 348 |
| 17' 2" | 32' 6" | 360 |
| 17' 8½" | 33' 7" | 372 |
| 18' 3" | 34' 8" | 384 |
| 18' 9½" | 35' 9" | 396 |
| 19' 4" | 36'10" | 408 |
| 19'10½" | 37'11" | 420 |
| 20' 5" | 39' 0" | 432 |
| 20'11½" | 40' 1" | 444 |
| 21' 6" | 41' 2" | 456 |
| 22' 0½" | 42' 3" | 468 |
| 22' 7" | 43' 4" | 480 |
| 23' 1½" | 44' 5" | 492 |
| 23' 8" | 45' 6" | 504 |
| 24' 2½" | 46' 7" | 516 |
| 24' 9" | 47' 8" | 528 |
| 25' 3½" | 48' 9" | 540 |
| 25'10" | 49'10" | 552 |
| 26' 4½" | 50'11" | 564 |
| 26'11" | 52' 0" | 576 |
| 27' 5½" | 53' 1" | 588 |
| 28' 0" | 54' 2" | 600 |

*Add 4" minimum clearance to each end and each side when adjacent to walls, columns, obstructions, or other machines.

†This provides 1.1" per coat. In areas or facilities where bulky coats are customary, the actual capacity may be reduced one-third.

**Fig. 5**

122-1-5W

Wall Mounted

Single Face

Double Face

| | Length | Number of Coats | Number of Shelves |
|---|---|---|---|
| **Wall Mounted** | 3'-0'' | 36 | 0 1 2 |
| | 4'-0'' | 48 | 0 1 2 |
| | 5'-0'' | 60 | 0 1 2 |
| **Single Face** | 3'-4'' | 36 | 0 1 2 |
| | 4'-4'' | 48 | 0 1 2 |
| | 5'-4'' | 60 | 0 1 2 |
| **Double Face** | 3'-4'' | 72 | 0 1 2 |
| | 4'-4'' | 96 | 0 1 2 |
| | 5'-4'' | 120 | 0 1 2 |

# COATROOMS

Coatroom Plans, Elevations, and Sections

Fig. 6 A typical coatroom configuration will often consist of a counter with an access door plus the required shelves and hang rods. The overall size of the coatroom will vary with the number and types of coats to be stored. In high-volume coatroom situations, the design should provide appropriate counter space for those persons working behind the counter.

HARDWOOD SHELVES
METAL HANGROD

SEE SCHEDULE

FIN. FL.

8'-0" MAX.

SEE SCHEDULE

NOTE: O.A. OPENING TO BE DIVIDED INTO EQUAL SECTIONS UNLESS OTHERWISE SHOWN

ELEVATION OF UNITS UNDER 8'-0"
1/4" = 1'-0"

ELEVATION OF UNITS OVER 8'-0"
1/4" = 1'-0"

1'-3"

CONTINUOUS VEE BLOCKING SCREW TO WALL & BACK OF SHELF UNIT AS SHOWN

LINE OF DIVIDERS

3/4" VERTICAL DIVIDERS AS REQUIRED

FACE OF WALL

GARCY #A-3369 HANGRAIL SOCKET. NOTE: IN GYPSUM BOARD PARTITIONS PROVIDE WOOD BLOCKING OR SHEET METAL PLATE TO RECEIVE SCREWS

SCRIBE TO WALL

CENTER HANGER AT VERTICAL DIVIDERS. CAPITAL #A-239 SATIN CHROME FINISH

FACE OF WALL

1-1/16" ⌀ SATIN CHROME HANGROD

1'-0"

1 PART ELEVATION
@ 3" = 1'-0"

2 SECTION
@ 3" = 1'-0"

3 SECTION
@ 3" = 1'-0"

NOTE: SEE SHEET 2:2 FOR SCHEDULE

TYPICAL OPEN COAT AREA

SCALE - AS NOTED

# Construction Details and Finishes

Partitions and wall finishes                469
Floors and floor finishes                   516
Doors                                       566
Ceilings                                    641
Stairs                                      660
Fireplaces                                  724
Lighting                                    743

Selecting the appropriate partition or wall type is both a science and an art. In fact, there are so many options available to the designer that it is not unusual to refer to the partition or wall as a system, a combination of framing, sheathing, and finish elements, all working together to meet aesthetic, functional, code, and economic requirements.

In that regard, this section explores the great variety of wall and partition types, examining all of their characteristics with the exception of load bearing capacity and cost of labor and materials. With respect to load bearing or structural capacities, while many of the wall and partition types are able to carry superimposed loads, it is not the intent of this book to discuss structural issues. With respect to cost, too many factors and variables make this a topic that is difficult to analyze with any precision.

Information on both traditional and contemporary partitions and wall types is provided. Many traditional materials and methods of construction, such as solid gypsum plaster and plaster on clay tile, are cited, thus providing information to the designer who is redesigning or altering older structures.

A large portion of this section is devoted to the detailing of contemporary partition systems. In addition to providing examples of partition types, these pages place great emphasis on the detailing of unusual interface conditions that many designers often leave to the contractor to work out in the field. It should be noted that most, if not all, of these details have been selected from the working drawings of outstanding architectural and interior design firms.

While general information has also been provided about acoustics, sound transmission, and fire ratings of various walls and partitions, the designer is cautioned to verify all such information with manufacturers' certified test results, as well as with those building and fire codes having jurisdiction. It also should be noted that while test results may demonstrate a certain fire rating or sound transmission classification, it is important to determine if the results have been accepted by the local building or fire department.

It is often necessary to apply a finish to a wall or partition. Again, both traditional and contemporary methods to apply wood paneling, ceramic tile, and stone are clearly illustrated through the use of architectural details.

Finally, walls and partitions must ultimately meet floors and ceilings, and, of course, have doors and openings penetrate them. While some examples are provided in this section, the designer will also find important information in the sections Floors and Floor Finishes; Doors; and Ceilings, which follow.

## PARTITIONS AND WALL FINISHES

### Characteristics of Interior Partitions

| DRAWING AND DESCRIPTION | FIRE-RATING | SOIL AND DAMAGE RESISTANCE | ACOUSTICS | REMARKS | COST COMPARISON |
|---|---|---|---|---|---|
| 4 inch face brick, tooled joints; Actual thickness, 3⅝ inches; Weight, 40 lbs. per square foot of wall surface | Incombustible, with one hour fire-rating | Good | Very good; transmission loss, 45 decibels | Low maintenance, but limited flexibility; a good-looking wall, but poor light reflection | installation cost  maintenance and insurance cost for 20 years |
| 4 inch concrete block, tooled joints, two coats of paint on each side; Actual thickness, 3⅝ inches; Weight, 30 lbs. per square foot | Incombustible, with one hour fire-rating | Good | Good; transmission loss, 40 decibels | Inexpensive; attractive if constructed neatly; frequently used for corridors, gyms, assembly rooms, etc.; no flexibility | |
| 4 inch cinder block, ¾ inch layer of plaster on each side, 2 coats of paint on each side; Actual thickness, 5¼ inches; Weight, 30 lbs. per square foot | Incombustible, with two hour fire-rating | Poor | Good; transmission loss, 43 decibels | A smooth, dense finish; a good light reflector if painted a light color; no flexibility | |
| 3 inch cinder block, ¾ inch layer of plaster on each side, 2 coats of paint on each side; Thickness, 4½ inches; Weight, 21 lbs. per square foot | Incombustible, with two hour fire-rating | Poor | Good; transmission loss, 39 decibels | A smooth, dense finish; a good light reflector if painted a light color; no flexibility | |
| 4 inch structural facing tile, glazed on each side; Actual thickness, 3¾ inches; Weight, 40 lbs. per square foot | Incombustible, with a fire-rating of less than one hour | Very good | Good; transmission loss, 35 decibels | Used well in classrooms, corridors, also in toilets and showers; care must be taken with the design to avoid bright reflectivity; no flexibility | |
| 4 inch concrete block, 2 coats of vinyl plastic spray over entire surface of each side; Actual thickness, 3¾ inches; Weight, 38 lbs. per square foot | Incombustible, with one hour fire-rating | Good | Good; transmission loss, 40 decibels | Sleek finish, but no flexibility | |
| 2 by 4 inch wood studs, spaced 16 inches apart; metal lath and plaster, 2 coats of paint on each side; Thickness, 4¾ inches; Weight, 20 lbs. per square foot | Combustible | Poor | Good; transmission loss, 39 decibels | Good light reflector, not much flexibility | |

W-1 — WOOD STUDS - 16" O.C. 3/8" 3-PLY PLYWOOD NAILED BOTH SIDES

W-2 — WOOD STUDS - 16" O.C., METAL LATH, GYPSUM SCRATCH & BROWN, WHITE FINISH BOTH SIDES

W-3 — WOOD STUDS - 16" O.C. 1/2" FIBERBOARD, JOINTS FILLED, BOTH SIDES

W-4 — SAME AS W-3, WITH 1/2" SCRATCH, BROWN & WHITE, GYPSUM BOTH SIDES

W-5 — 2" x 4" WOOD STUDS, STAGGERED, 8" O.C. 2" x 6" STUD AT EDGES 1/2" FIBERBOARD NAILED BOTH SIDES

W-6 — SAME AS W-5, WITH 1/2" SCRATCH, BROWN, & WHITE GYPSUM, BOTH SIDES

W-7 — WOOD STUDS - 16" O.C., GYPSUM LATH, ATTACHED WITH STIFF CLIPS 3/8" SCRATCH, BROWN, WHITE GYPSUM PLASTER BOTH SIDES

W-8 — SAME AS W-7, EXCEPT ATTACHED WITH SPRING CLIPS. 1/2" PLASTER BOTH SIDES.

W-9 — 2" SOLID GYPSUM PLASTER ON PERFORATED GYP LATH, 3/4" CHANNEL STUDS, SMOOTH WHITE BOTH SIDES

W-10 — 2" SOLID GYPSUM PLASTER SAME AS W-9 EXCEPT EXPANDED METAL LATH

W-11 — 2 1/2" SOLID GYPSUM PLASTER SAME AS W-10

W-12 — 3" METAL STUDS - 16" O.C., METAL LATH, 1/2" SCRATCH, BROWN, WHITE GYPSUM PLASTER BOTH SIDES

W-13 — TWO PANELS, NOT JOINED; 3/4" CHANNEL STUDS, EXPANDED METAL LATH, SCRATCH, BROWN & WHITE GYPSUM PLASTER BOTH SIDES FACE TO FACE = 10"

W-14 — SAME AS W-13, EXCEPT FACE TO FACE = 4 1/2"

W-15 — 3" x 12" x 30" GYPSUM TILE 1/2" BROWN, WHITE GYPSUM PLASTER BOTH SIDES

W-16 — 3" x 12" x 30" GYPSUM TILE, RESILIENT CLIP, METAL LATH, 3 COATS GYPSUM PLASTER, 2 COATS GYPSUM PLASTER ON TILE, OTHER SIDE (WHITE FIN. BOTH SIDES)

W-17 — 4" BRICK PARTITION, 1/2" BROWN, WHITE FINISH GYPSUM PLASTER BOTH SIDES

W-18 — SAME AS W-17, EXCEPT 8" BRICK PANEL

W-19 — SAME AS W-17, EXCEPT ONE LAYER OF BRICK LAID ON EDGE

W-20 — BRICK LAID ON EDGE, 1" x 2" FURRING, WIRED, & GYPSUM LATH PLUS 1/2" BROWN & WHITE GYPSUM PLASTER BOTH SIDES

W-21 — 3" x 12" x 12" - 3 CELL CLAY TILE, 1/2" BROWN & WHITE GYPSUM PLASTER BOTH SIDES.

W-22 — ANOTHER PANEL BUILT AS NEARLY LIKE W-21 AS POSSIBLE

W-23 — SAME AS W-21 EXCEPT 4" x 12" x 12" 3-CELL TILE

W-24 — SAME AS W-21 EXCEPT 6" x 12" x 12" 3-CELL TILE

W-25 — SAME AS W-21 EXCEPT 8" x 12" x 12" 3-CELL TILE

W-26 — DOUBLE CLAY TILE: 3 3/4" x 12" x 12" 8" x 12" x 12", 1/2" BROWN AND WHITE GYPSUM PLASTER BOTH SIDES

W-27 — DOUBLE PARTITION WITH AIR SPACE. TWO WALLS OF 3" x 12" x 12" 3-CELL CLAY TILE. 1" FLAXLINUM BUTTED TIGHT BETWEEN TILE. NO PLASTER. 1" x 4" FLAXLINUM STRIP AT BOTTOM, SIDES & TOP OF ONE PARTITION

W-28 — PUMICE & PORTLAND CEMENT 2-CELL TILE 4" x 8" x 16" NO PLASTER (VERY POROUS)

W-29 — SAME AS W-28, BUT 1/2" GYPSUM PLASTER ON ONE SIDE ONLY

W-30 — SAME AS W-28, BUT 1/2" GYPSUM PLASTER ON BOTH SIDES

W-31 — GLASS BRICK 3 3/4" x 4 7/8" x 8"

## PARTITIONS AND WALL FINISHES

### Partition and Wall Types

SOUND CONTROL BY
STAGGERED STUDS

SOUND CONTROL-STAGGERED
STUDS AND WALL BOARD

SOUND CONTROL-STAGGERED
STUDS AND BLANKET CENTER

SOUND CONTROL - SIDEWISE
STUDS AND BLANKET CENTER

SOUND CONTROL-BLANKET
OVER GYPSUM BLOCK

SOUND CONTROL-BLANKET
BETWEEN GYPSUM BLOCK

GYPSUM SOLID OR HOLLOW
PARTITION TILE-1

METHOD FOR WALL AND FLOOR
FOR EXTENSION OVER PORCH

TERRA COTTA BLOCK PARTITION
TO HEIGHT OF GLAZED TILE

GYPSUM SOLID OR HOLLOW
PARTITION TILE-2

FRAMING FOR WIDE OPENING
ABOVE SUB-STRUCTURE

TERRA COTTA HOLLOW
PARTITION TILE

HOLLOW MASONRY UNITS

bonding unit

HOLLOW WALLS

CAVITY WALLS

bonded facing

stone facing

brick facing

FACED WALLS

COLUMN OF MASONRY INTEGRAL WITH WALL

ISOLATED COLUMN OF MASONRY

PIERS

MASONRY TIES; MASONRY BACKING

METAL TIES; MASONRY BACKING

METAL TIES; MASONRY BACKING

METAL TIES; FRAME BACKING

VENEERED WALLS

## PARTITIONS AND WALL FINISHES

Modular    Engineer    Economy    Double

Roman    Norman    Norwegian    King Norman    Triple

SCR      SCR      SCR

**Fig. 1  Typical clay brick.**

**Fig. 2  Structural clay tile.**

**Fig. 3  Structural facing tile.**

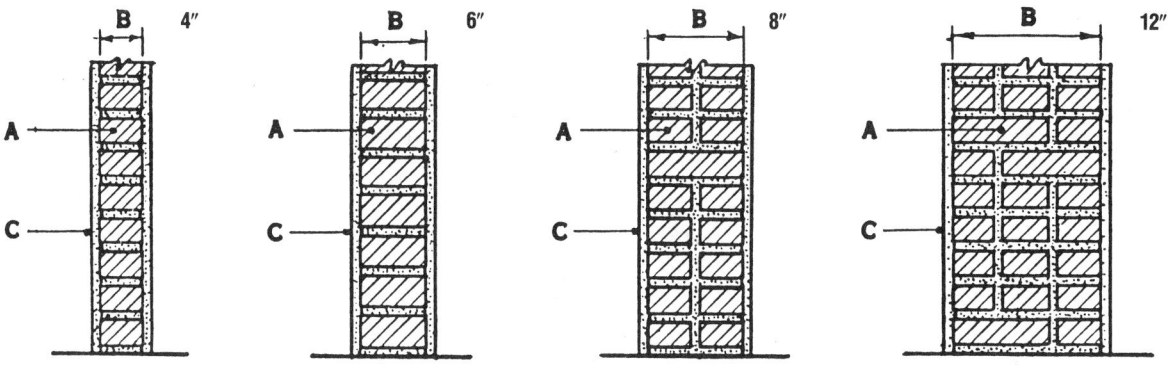

Fig. 4   Solid brick: bearing or nonbearing (sections). A = brick, B = nominal wall thickness, C = finish.

Fig. 5   Hollow brick units: bearing or nonbearing (sections). A = brick, B = nominal wall thickness, C = finish.

Fig. 6   Structural clay tile: bearing (sections). A = structural clay tile, B = nominal wall thickness, C = finish.

## PARTITIONS AND WALL FINISHES

Types of Masonry

**Fig. 7  Faced or veneered construction: bearing (sections).** A = brick; B = sheathing; C = corrosion-resistant metal ties spaced 24 in on centers, vertically and horizontally; D = wood or steel studs; E = plaster or gypsum wallboard; F = masonry bond; G = masonry backing unit.

**Fig. 8  Cavity type: bearing (sections).** A = clay brick, B = corrosion-resistant metal ties spaced to provide one tie to each 3 ft² of wall surface, C = gypsum plaster, D = structural clay load-bearing tile, E = concrete masonry units of load-bearing grade, F = exterior face of wall.

**Fig. 9  Hollow concrete masonry units (sections).** (a) Bearing, (b) Non-bearing. A = concrete masonry units conforming to ASTM, *Standard Specifications for Hollow Load-Bearing Concrete Masonry Units;* B = nominal wall thickness, C = nominal shell thickess, D = gypsum plaster.

Fig. 10    Structural clay tile: nonbearing (sections). A = structural clay tile, B = nominal wall thickness, C = finish, D = fill.

Fig. 11    Gypsum tile or block: nonbearing (sections). A = gypsum block, B = nominal wall thickness, C = finish.

Fig. 12    Structural clay facing tile: nonbearing (sections). A = clay tile, B = nominal wall thickness, C = plaster, D = glazed or smooth-surfaced side of tile.

## PARTITIONS AND WALL FINISHES

**Brick Types and Bonds**

AMERICAN

ROMAN

NORMAN

ENGLISH

HEADER    STRETCHER    BULL HEADER    BULL STRETCHER    QUOINS

PLACEMENT OF BRICK

SIDE
BED
CULL → FACE → END
BED

SIX FACES OF BRICK

CLOSER    KING CLOSER    QUEEN CLOSER

HALF OR BAT    SPLIT    THREE QUARTER

METHODS OF
CUTTING BRICK

STRUCK    RAKED    STRIPPED    FLUSH OR PLAIN CUT

V-SHAPED    CONCAVE OR ROUNDED    WEATHERED    FLUSH AND RODDED

BRICK JOINTS

**COMMON HEADER BOND**
HEADER COURSE EVERY 6TH COURSE
7.88 BRICK PER SQ. FT.

**COMMON FLEMISH BOND**
ALTERNATE FULL HEADERS EVERY 6TH COURSE
7.15 BRICK PER SQ. FT.

**ENGLISH BOND**
HEADER EVERY 6TH COURSE - HALF BRICK
USED FOR HEADER COURSE EXCEPT EVERY 6TH
7.88 BRICK PER SQ. FT.

**BASKET PATTERN**
6.75 BRICK PER SQ. FT.

**FLEMISH CROSS BOND**
ALTERNATE FULL HEADER EVERY 6TH COURSE
7.15 BRICK PER SQ. FT

**ENGLISH CROSS BOND**
CONTINUOUS FULL HEADERS EVERY 6TH COURSE
7.88 BRICK PER SQ. FT.

Full and Half-Height Units

Full, Half and Fractional Size Units

Fig. 13    Designs of standard-size hollow concrete-masonry units.

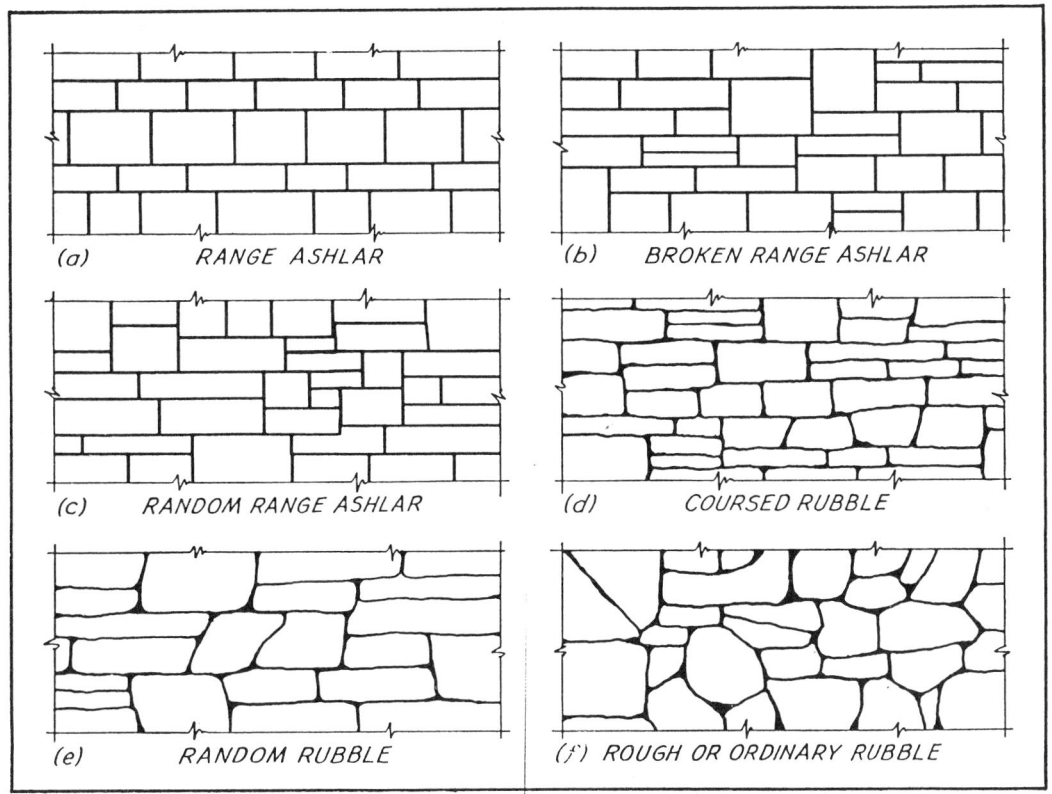

(a)    RANGE ASHLAR

(b)    BROKEN RANGE ASHLAR

(c)    RANDOM RANGE ASHLAR

(d)    COURSED RUBBLE

(e)    RANDOM RUBBLE

(f) ROUGH OR ORDINARY RUBBLE

Fig. 14    Stone ashlar and rubble masonry.

NOTE: UNGLAZED BLOCK TO BE USED ABOVE CLG

NOTE: EXTEND PLASTER TO UNDERSIDE OF STRUCTURE WHERE REQD BY FIRE RATING

UNDERSIDE OF STRUCTURE ABOVE

CLG.

CLG.

4", 6", 8", 12" (NOM)
3⅝", 5⅝", 7⅝", 11⅝" (ACTUAL)

4", 6", 8", 12" (NOM.)
3⅝", 5⅝", 7⅝", 11⅝" (ACTUAL)

4", 6", 8" (NOMINAL)
3⅝", 5⅝", 7⅝" (ACTUAL)

4⅞", 6⅞", 8⅞"

4", 6", 8" (NOMINAL)
3⅝", 5⅝", 7⅝" (ACTUAL)

5¾" 7¾" 9¾"

PLASTER

CERAMIC TILE
SETTING BED
SCRATCH COAT

FLOOR

① CINDER OR CONCRETE BLOCK - UNFINISHED

② GLAZED OR PREFINISHED CONC. OR CINDER BLK.

③ CONC. OR CINDER BLK. PLASTERED BOTH SIDES

④ CONC OR CINDER BLK. PLASTER / CERAMIC TILE SET IN MORTAR

**MASONRY PARTITIONS**

## TYPICAL SIZES AND SHAPES OF CONCRETE BLOCK

Half - Hi

Brick    Frog    Jumbo

BRICK TYPES

Split Face

Slump

Coping

Faced

Shadowal (decorative)

Chimney

Lintel

Pilaster

Sill

Header

Partition

Chimney

Lintel

Pilaster

Screen (decorative)

Control Joint

Solid Top

Grade

Jamb

JAMB BLOCKS

Sash

Stretcher ( 2 core )

Stretcher ( 3 core )

Half - Corner

Double - Corner

Bullnose

Return ( or 'L' ) Corner

UNDERSIDE OF STRUCTURE

BRACE TO STRUCTURE AS REQUIRED

SCHED. FIN. CLG.

1 LAYER 5/8" GYP. BD. ON 2 1/2" METAL STUDS 16" O.C. TO 6" ABOVE FIN. CEIL.

SCHED. FIN. BASE
SCHED. FIN. FLR.

CONT. CONCEALED ACOUSTICAL SEALANT

UNDERSIDE OF STRUCTURE

BRACE TO STRUCTURE AS REQUIRED

1 LAYER 5/8" GYP. BOARD

SCHED. FIN. CEILING

SCHED. FIN. BASE
SCHED. FIN. FLR.

VARIES
RE: A1 DRAWINGS

UNDERSIDE OF STRUCTURE

SCHED. FIN. CEIL.

1 LAYER 5/8" GYP. BD. ON 2 1/2" METAL STUDS

2" SOUND BLANKET

SCHED. FIN. BASE

SCHED. FIN. FLOOR

CONT. CONCEALED ACOUSTICAL SEALANT TOP & BOTTOM

SCHED. FIN. CLG.

2" SOUND BLANKET

1 LAYER 5/8" GYP. BD. ON 2 1/2" METAL STUDS

SCHED. FIN. BASE
SCHED. FIN. FLR.

CONT. CONCEALED ACOUSTICAL SEALANT TOP & BOTTOM

BRACE WITHIN AS REQUIRED

VARIES
RE: A1 DRAWINGS

'G' - CONTINUOUS VAPOR BARRIER @ COMPUTER ROOM
'Ga' - WATER RESISTANT GYP. BD. ON SHOWER RM. SIDE

'G' - WATER RESISTANT GYP. BD.

ACOUSTICAL PARTITION

## PARTITIONS AND WALL FINISHES

Metal Stud and Gypsum Board

Metal stud and gypsum board: braced to slab

Metal stud and gypsum board partition: floor to slab

Metal channels and gypsum board: wall furring

Metal stud and gypsum board partition: floor to slab

Metal stud and gypsum board: underside of ceiling

Labels (upper left detail):
- BRACE AS REQUIRED
- ACOUSTICAL CEIL. LINE
- "J" BEAD TAPE & FLOAT
- 1 LAYER 5/8" GYP. BD. ON 2 1/2" METAL STUDS
- SCHED. FIN. BASE
- SCHED. FIN. FLR.
- CONT. CONCEALED ACOUSTICAL SEALANT

Labels (upper right detail):
- UNDERSIDE OF STRUCTURE
- 1" RIGID INSULATION LAMINATED TO BLOCK
- LINE OF FINISHED CEILING
- 1 LAYER 5/8" G.W.B.
- 2 1/2" METAL STUD 16" O.C.
- FACE OF BASE BLDG. PARTITION
- ADDITIONAL LAYER OF 5/8" GYP. BD. TO TOP OF MILLWK BASE @ F-1 ONLY
- SPACKLE BEAD
- 1/2" REVEAL
- MILLWK. BASE @ F-1 ONLY
- 5" L BOTTOM RUNNER (CONT.) SECURE TO STRUCTURE AS REQ'D
- 1"
- 4 1/8"
- 6"

Metal channels and gypsum board: wall furring

Labels:
- UNDERSIDE OF STRUCTURE
- SCHED. FIN. CEIL.
- 1 LAYER 5/8" GYP. BD.
- SCHED. FIN. BASE
- SCHED. FIN. FLR.
- 2"

Labels:
- BLOCKING AS REQUIRED
- EXP. JOINT FOAM COMPRESSION
- SCHED. FIN. CEIL.
- 8" CMU
- 1 LAYER 5/8" GYP. BD. ON FURRING CHANNEL
- SCHED. FIN. BASE
- SCHED. FIN. FLR.
- GROUT
- 6"

## PARTITIONS AND WALL FINISHES
**Metal Stud and Gypsum Board**

HEAD

1½"

PLAN

5⁄8" GYP. BD.

7⁄8" METAL FURRING CHANNEL

SCHED. BASE

**FUR-OUT GYPSUM B'D ON METAL FURRING CHANNEL**

HARDWOOD TOP CAP W/ SEMI-GLOSS ENAMEL FINISH REVEAL PAINTED TO MATCH PARTITION FINISH

MATCH HEIGHT OF FURNITURE SYSTEM

A.D.S. METAL FLOOR ANCHOR 16" O.C.

SCHED. BASE

**SECTION @ LOW PARTITION**

ALIGN

**SHAFT WALL, TWO HOUR FIRE RATED PARTITION**

UNDERSIDE OF CONCRETE STRUCTURE

2½" SHAFTWALL STUDS

1" SHAFTLINER

1 LAYER 5⁄8" GYP. BD. EACH SIDE

SEALANT TOP & BOTTOM

**Metal stud and gypsum board: shaftwall**

SCHED. CLG.

MOVABLE WALL SYSTEM - GYP. BD. PANELS - PAINTED

SCHED. FLOORING

**Metal stud and gypsum board: movable**

CONTINUOUS CAULKING
STRUCTURAL SLAB
2½" MTL. RUNNER 20. GA.
SOUND ATTENUATION BLANKET 1½" THICK
ACOUSTIC TILE CLG.
CONTINUOUS MTL. PLATE @ A.F.F. FOR SHELVES
2½" MTL STUDS. 16" O.C. WITH ONE LAYER OF ⅜" GYP. BD. ON BOTH SIDES TO UNDERSIDE OF SLAB ABOVE.
⅜" GYP. BD. EXTEND 6" ABOVE CEILING • LOCATED ON CORRIDOR SIDE WHEN USED @ CORRIDOR • LOCATED ON EITHER SIDE @ ALL OTHER AREAS.
CONTINUOUS CAULKING

1 TYPE 1 (TYPICAL PARTITION)

CONTINUOUS CAULKING
STRUCTURAL SLAB
2½" MTL. RUNNER 20.GA.
SOUND ATTENUATION BLANKET - 1½" THICK
ACOUSTIC TILE CLG.
2½" MTL. STUDS. 16" O.C. WITH TWO (2) LAYERS OF ⅜" GYP. BD. ON BOTH SIDE.
CONTINUOUS CAULKING.

2 TYPE 2 (4-LAYER ACOUSTICAL PARTITION)

STRUCTURAL SLAB
CONTINUOUS CAULKING
ACOUSTIC TILE CLG.
2½" MTL STUDS 16" O.C. WITH TWO LAYER OF ⅝" FIRECODE GYP. BD. BOTH SIDES TO UNDERSIDE OF SLAB ABOVE.
CONTINUOUS CAULKING

3 TYPE 3 (2-HOUR FIRE-RATED PARTITION)

STRUCTURAL SLAB
CONTINUOUS CAULKING
1⅝" MTL RUNNER
ACOUSTIC TILE CLG.
SOUND ATTENUATION BLANKET - 1½" THICK
1⅝" MTL STUDS 16" O.C. WITH ONE LAYER OF ⅝" GYPSUM BOARD
EXIST'G WALL/COLUMN
1⅝" MTL RUNNER
CONTINUOUS CAULKING

4 TYPE 4 - EXIST'G WALL/COL. FIRRED OUT
SCALE:

# PARTITION TYPES AND DIMENSIONING SYSTEM

**DETAIL** C
SCALE: 3"=1'-0"

EXPOSED SPLINE GRID

1½" C.R. CHANNEL

ACOUSTICAL PANEL CEILING

PAINT TO MATCH PARTITION

TOP RUNNER

SHT. RK. PANEL ON METAL STUD

NOTE: SECURE TOP RUNNER TO SUSP'D CLG. W/ TOGGLE BOLTS

5/8"  3 5/8"  5/8"

**DETAIL** F
SCALE: 3"=1'-0"

BUILDING WALL

3"

ACOUSTICAL PANEL CEILING

METAL ANGLE PAINT TO MATCH CEILING

SHT. RK. PANEL ON METAL STUD

7/8"  5/8"

**DETAIL** B
SCALE: 3"=1'-0"

TOGGLE BOLT

FURRING CHANNEL CLIP

FURRING CHANNEL

5/8" SHT. RK. CLG.

PAINT TO MATCH PARTITION

TOP RUNNER

SHT. RK. PANEL ON METAL STUD

3/4"

5/8"  3 5/8"  5/8"

**DETAIL** E
SCALE: 3"=1'-0"

DUSTPROOF MEMBRANE

1½" C.R. CHANNEL

5/8" SHT. RK. CEILING

FURRING CHANNEL

BUILDING WALL

7/8"  5/8"

**BASE DETAIL** A
SCALE: 3"=1'-0"

4 7/8"
5/8"  3 5/8"  5/8"

SHEET ROCK PANEL

METAL STUD

4"H. VINYL BASE BY FL'R COV'G CONTR.

FIN. FLOOR

BOTTOM RUNNER

**BASE DETAIL** D
SCALE: 3"=1'-0"

1½"
7/8"  5/8"

SHEET ROCK PANEL

FURRING CHANNEL

BUILDING WALL

4"H. VINYL BASE BY FL'R COV'G CONTR.

FIN. FLOOR

## PARTITIONS AND WALL FINISHES
Metal Stud and Gypsum Board Details

DRYWALL CORNER BEAD

5/8"

3 5/8'

5/8"

TAPE AND JOINT COMPOUND

C  90° CORNER

METAL STUD

5/8'

5/8"  3 5/8"

TAPE AND JOINT COMPOUND

F  "T" CORNER

MODIFIED CORNER BEAD

5/8'

3 5/8"

5/8"

TAPE AND JOINT COMPOUND,

20 GA. METAL GUSSET PLATES 1'-0" LONG SPACED 3'-0" o.c.

B  45° CORNER

METAL STUDS

5/8'

3 5/8"

5/8"

TAPE AND JOINT COMPOUND

E  "CROSS" CORNER

4 7/8"

5/8"  3 5/8"  5/8"

SHEET ROCK

METAL STUDS 2'-0" O.C.

DRYWALL CORNER BEAD

A  PARTITION END DETAIL

5/8'  5/8"

3 5/8'  5/8"

3 5/8"

5/8

5/8"

CONT. METAL ANGLE

TAPE AND JOINT COMPOUND

D  "Y" CORNER

## PARTITIONS AND WALL FINISHES

Metal Stud and Gypsum Board: Partition Conditions

Metal stud and gypsum board: partition to mullion detail

Metal stud and gypsum board: partition to column detail

Metal stud and gypsum board: partition to mullion detail

— SPRAY ON FIREPROOFING

5/8" GYP. BD. ON 2½" METAL STUDS @ 24" O.C. MAX. TO UNDERSIDE OF SLAB.

NOTE: WHEN COLUMN IS ENGAGED BY A 2 HR RATED PARTITION - GYP. BD. TO BE 2 LAYERS W/ CAULK @ PERIMETER.

**8 / A·27  FIREPROOFING @ COL's. - 3HR RATED**
1½" = 1'-0"          UL # X 709

NOTE: SIZE OF COLUMNS VARY.
ON COLUMNS W/ LACING PROVIDE METAL LATH
SEE NOTE 4a,b/A·27

— ATRIUM FACE

ONE LAYER 5/8" FIRECODE 'C' GYP. BD. BOTH SIDES ON 8" 16 GA. METAL FRAMING @ 16" O.C.

1½" CEMENTITIOUS FIREPROOFING SPRAY APPLIED TO 3.4 LB/SQ.YD. METAL LATH - TIE LATH TO COL. W/ #18 SWG GALV. ST'L. WIRE
U.L. DESIGN # X 709

1½" METAL FRAMING W/ ONE LAYER 5/8" FIRECODE GYP. BD.

FOR FINISHED COL. WIDTH, SEE ENLARGED PLAN, DWG. A/B

1'-9½"

FIN. COL. WIDTH U.O.N.

**9 / A·27  TYPICAL COL. FIREPROOFING @ PERIMETER OF ATRIUM**

**Tempered glass**

**Demountable**

① DETAIL FOR FIRE RATED PART'N.
A-109 & A.C. DUCT ABOVE

② SECTION @ METAL DUCT ENCLOSURE
A-109

ONE LAYER GYP. BD. FOR PART'N. ⑧
TWO LAYERS GYP. BD. FOR PART'N. ⑦

③ COLUMN FURRING
A-109

NOTES:
1. DUCT ENCLOSURE TO EXTEND FOR 20' DISTANCE FROM FAN ROOM
2. MAINTAIN ½" MIN. CLEARANCE BETWEEN DUCT AND 1⅝" METAL STUDS.

④ SECTION AT SUPPLY AIR DUCT ENCLOSURE
A-109   NONE

FINISHED CEILING

SEQUENCE OF CONSTRUCTION

STEP ① FASTEN TEMPORARY 2"x 2" ANGLE TO SLAB. FASTEN TOP RUNNER OF PARTITION
TO TEMPORARY ANGLE AND ERECT STUDS. (MAINTAIN 1" AIR SPACE BETWEEN
RUNNER AND SLAB.)

STEP ② APPLY GYPSUM BOARD LAYER(S) TO ONE SIDE OF STUDS.

STEP ③ FASTEN 2"x 2" CONTINUOUS ANGLE (WITH ¼" FELT GLUED TO SIDE) TO SLAB
ONLY (DO NOT SECURE STUDS TO THIS ANGLE).

STEP ④ INSTALL USG SA8 MINERAL WOOL BETWEEN STUDS.

STEP ⑤ REMOVE TEMPORARY ANGLE AND REPLACE WITH 2"x 2" CONTINUOUS ANGLE (WITH
¼" FELT GLUED TO SIDE). FASTEN THIS ANGLE TO SLAB ONLY.

⑤ "SOFT" TERMINATION OF PARTITIONS
A-109  NONE

⑥ TYP. REINF. CORNER DET'L.
A-109   SCALE   3"-1'-0"

493

# PARTITIONS AND WALL FINISHES

## Sound Insulation and Transmission

The resistance of a building element, such as a wall, to the passage of airborne sound is rated by its *sound transmission class* (STC). Thus, the higher the number, the better the sound barrier. The approximate effectiveness of walls with varying STC numbers is shown in the following tabulation:

| STC No. | Effectiveness |
|---|---|
| 25 | Normal speech can be understood quite easily |
| 35 | Loud speech audible but not intelligible |
| 45 | Must strain to hear loud speech |
| 48 | Some loud speech barely audible |
| 50 | Loud speech not audible |

Sound travels readily through the air and also through some materials. When airborne sound strikes a conventional wall, the studs act as sound conductors unless they are separated in some way from the covering material.

### Wall Construction

As the preceding STC tabulation shows, a wall providing sufficient resistance to airborne sound transfer likely has an STC rating of 45 or greater. Thus, in construction of such a wall between the rooms of a house, its cost as related to the STC rating should be considered. As shown in Fig. 5, details *A*, with gypsum wallboard, and *B*, with plastered wall, are those commonly used for partition walls. However, the hypothetical rating of 45 cannot be obtained in this construction.

Good STC ratings can be obtained in a wood-frame wall by using the combination of materials shown in Fig. 5D and E. One-half-inch sound-deadening board nailed to the studs, followed by a lamination of ½-in gypsum wallboard, will provide an STC value of 46 at a relatively low cost. A slightly better rating can be obtained by using ⅝-in gypsum wallboard rather than ½-in. A very satisfactory STC rating of 52 can be obtained by using resilient clips to fasten gypsum backer boards to the studs, followed by adhesive-laminated ½-in fiberboard (Fig. 5E). This method further isolates the wall covering from the framing.

A similar isolation system consists of resilient channels nailed horizontally to 2- by 4-in studs spaced 16 in on center. Channels are spaced 24 in apart vertically and ⅝-in gypsum wallboard is screwed to the channels. An STC rating of 47 is thus obtained at a moderately low cost.

Thus use of a double wall, which may consist of a 2 by 6 or wider plate and staggered 2- by 4-in studs, is sometimes desirable. One-half-inch gypsum wallboard on each side of this wall (Fig. 6A) results in an STC value of 45. However, two layers of ⅝-in gypsum wallboard add little, if any, additional sound-transfer resistance (Fig. 6B). When 1½-in blanket insulation is added to this construction (Fig. 6C), the STC rating increases to 49. This insulation may be installed as shown or placed between studs on one wall. A single wall with 3½ in of insulation will show a marked improvement over an open stud space and is low in cost.

The use of ½-in sound-deadening board and a lamination of gypsum wallboard in the double wall will result in an STC rating of 50 (Fig. 6D). The addition of blanket insulation to this combination will likely provide an even higher value, perhaps 53 or 54.

| WALL DETAIL | DESCRIPTION | STC RATING |
|---|---|---|
| A | ½" GYPSUM WALLBOARD | 32 |
|  | ⅝" GYPSUM WALLBOARD | 37 |
| B | ⅜" GYPSUM LATH (NAILED) PLUS ½" GYPSUM PLASTER WITH WHITECOAT FINISH (EACH SIDE) | 39 |
| C | 8" CONCRETE BLOCK | 45 |
| D | ½" SOUND DEADENING BOARD (NAILED) ½" GYPSUM WALLBOARD (LAMINATED) (EACH SIDE) | 46 |
| E | RESILIENT CLIPS TO ⅜" GYPSUM BACKER BOARD ½" FIBERBOARD (LAMINATED) (EACH SIDE) | 52 |

**Fig. 5   Sound insulation of single walls.**

| WALL DETAIL | DESCRIPTION | STC RATING |
|---|---|---|
| A | ½" GYPSUM WALLBOARD | 45 |
| B | ⅝" GYPSUM WALLBOARD (DOUBLE LAYER EACH SIDE) | 45 |
| C | ½" GYPSUM WALLBOARD 1½" FIBROUS INSULATION | 49 |
| D | ½" SOUND DEADENING BOARD (NAILED) ½" GYPSUM WALLBOARD (LAMINATED) | 50 |

**Fig. 6   Sound insulation of double walls.**

**1** ONE HOUR FIRE RATED PARTITION

**1a** SAME AS **1** BUT WITH SOUND ATTENUATION BLANKET

**2** TWO HOUR FIRE RATED PARTITION

**2a** SAME AS **2** BUT WITH SOUND ATTENUATION BLANKET

**3a** SOUND PARTITION / "CLASS A" /

**4a** SOUND PARTITION / "CLASS B" /

## PARTITIONS AND WALL FINISHES

### Acoustical and Fire-Rated Metal Stud and Gypsum Board

HEAD

PLAN

SCHED.
BASE

- SINGLE LAYER 5/8" G.B.
- DBL. LAYER 5/8" GYP.B.
- 2½" TH. SOUND ATTENUATION INSULATION BLANKET

| 5 | DRYWALL PARTITION. USE TO ALIGN WITH PARTITION 2 @ NON-FIRE RATED AREA |
| 5a | SAME AS 5 BUT WITH SOUND ATTENUATION BLANKET USE TO ALIGN WITH PARTITION 2a & 3a @ NON-FIRE RATED AREA |

HEAD

PLAN

SCHED.
BASE

- UNDERSIDE OF FLOOR CONSTRUCTION, ABV.
- 3½" METAL STUD RUNNER ANCHOR'D, AS REQ.
- SUSP. ACOUST. TILE CEILING & ASSEMBLY (BUILDING STANDARD)
- METAL TRIM ∅, AS REQ W/FITTING SPACER (TYP.)
- 5/8" G.B. ON BOTH SIDES OF 3½" MET. STUDS
- 3½" METAL STUD RUNNER, ANCHOR'D, AS REQ'D
- BASE... SEE FIN. PLAN & SCHEDULE

| 6 | DRYWALL PARTITION TO 6" ABOVE CEILING |
| 6a | SAME AS 6 BUT WITH SOUND ATTENUATION BLANKET / "CLASS C" |

- SUSP. ACOUST. TILE CEILING & ASSEMBLY (BUILDING STANDARD)
- METAL TRIM ∅, AS REQ. W/FITTING SPACER (TYP.)
- 5/8" G.B. - DOUBLE LAYER
- 2½" METAL STUD RUNNER, ANCHOR'D, AS REQ'D
- SCHED. BASE

| 7 | FUR-OUT PARTITION / USE WITH PARTITIONS 2 @ COLUMN ENCLOSURE |
| 7a | SAME AS 7 BUT WITH SOUND ATTENUATION BLANKET |

- UNDERSIDE OF FLOOR CONSTRUCTION ABOVE
- 2½" METAL STUD RUNNER ANCHOR'D, AS REQ.
- SUSP. ACOUST. TILE CEILING & ASSEMBLY (BUILDING STANDARD)
- METAL TRIM ∅, AS REQ. W/FITTING SPACER (TYP.)
- 5/8" G.B.
- 2½" METAL STUD RUNNER, ANCHOR'D, AS REQ'D.
- BASE... SEE FIN. PLAN
- SEALANT

| 8 | FUR-OUT GYPSUM B'D. ON METAL STUDS. CHASE PARTITION & COLUMN ENCLOSURE |
| 8a | SAME AS 8 BUT WITH SOUND ATTENUATION BLANKET |

FACE OF WALL

¼" AIR SPACE HOLD

2" THICK 4LB. DENSITY FIBERGLASS OR MINERAL WOOL ACOUSTICAL BLANKET AS MANUF. BY BALDWIN-EHRET HILL DIV. OF KEENE CORPORATION

¼" HARDWOOD VENEER PLYWOOD PANELS DET A-1 PERFORATED (SEE NOTE) DET A-2 UNPERFORATED SEE SCHEDULE OF INTERIOR FINISHES FOR SPECIES OF WOOD. GLUE PANELS TO PLYWOOD STRIPS.

CONTINUOUS ¼" x 3" PLYWOOD STRIPS NAILED TO 2 x 2 FURRING

2" x 2" WOOD FURRING 24" O.C IN BOTH DIRECTIONS

SHIMS AS REQ'D TO SET FURRING PLUMB & TRUE

2" MIN. HOLD

NOTE: PERFORATED HARDWOOD VENEER PANELS SHALL HAVE ³⁄₁₆" DIA. HOLES ½" O.C. HOLES SHALL BE DRILLED NOT PUNCHED OPEN AREA TO BE AT LEAST 11%

(A-1) PERFORATED HARDWOOD VENEER PLYWOOD FINISH

(A-2) UNPERFORATED HARDWOOD VENEER PLYWOOD FINISH

## ACOUSTIC WALL TREATMENT DETAILS

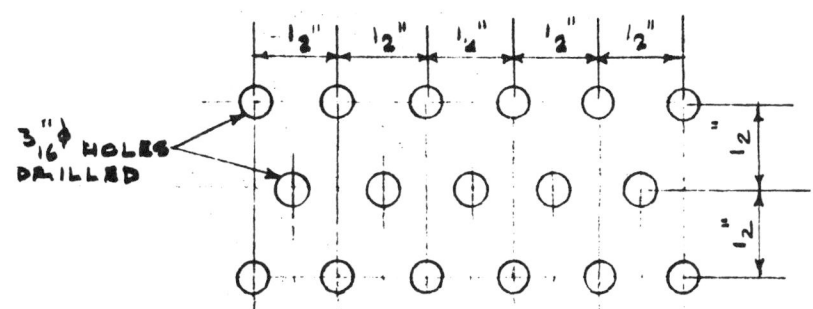

³⁄₁₆"∅ HOLES DRILLED

## PATTERN FOR PERFORATED PLYWOOD

# wood frame partition systems for sound control

| PARTITION SYSTEM | WALL NUMBER | WALL FACE | STC |
|---|---|---|---|
| **single stud walls** Basic construction is 2" x 4" studs 16" o.c. with double top plate and single or double bottom plate. Faces are ⁵⁄₈" thick fire resistive type gypsum board applied, taped and finished in accordance with manufacturer's recommendations. Resilient channels are applied to studs 24" o.c. as shown with a ¹⁄₂"x3" gypsum nailing strip at the bottom. Absorptive material is paper-backed glass fiber or mineral wool batts stapled in the stud space as illustrated. Sound deadening board is sound-rated organic fiber board with a 15-18 pcf density. **no. 3** | 1 | Single gypsum board each side, applied with screws; no resilient channels | 34 |
| | 2 | Single gypsum board laminated and nailed[2] over sound board each side; no channels | 45 |
| | 3 | Single gypsum board applied with screws 1 side; opposite side on resilient channels | 50 |
| | 4 | Single gypsum board laminated and nailed[2] over sound board, opposite side on resilient channels | 52 |
| | 5 | Single gypsum board on resilient channels each side | 53 |
| | 6 | Double ½" gypsum board, base sheet vertical; face sheet horizontal; applied on resilient channels one side | 59 |
| **double stud walls with a common plate** basic construction is a double row of 2"x3" or 2"x4" studs, each row 16" o.c. and each row aligned with an opposite edge of the 2"x6" top and bottom plates. The rows of studs are offset 2" to 8" to prevent any chance contact. Other details and materials are as described for single stud walls. **no. 11** | 7 | Single gypsum board each side, applied with screws (2x3 studs—16" o.c.); no resilient channels | 49 |
| | 8[3] | Single gypsum board laminated and nailed[2] over sound deadening board each side (2x4 studs—16" o.c.); no resilient channels | 49 |
| | 9[4] | Single gypsum board nailed one side. Single gypsum on resilient channels opposite | 50 |
| | 10 | Single gypsum board laminated and nailed[2] over sound deadening board 1 side. Single gypsum board on resilient channels opposite (2x3 studs—16" o.c.) | 53 |
| | 11 | Double gypsum board (½" over ⁵⁄₈") nailed one side; single gypsum board on resilient channels opposite (2x4 studs—24" o.c.) | 56 |
| **double stud walls on separate plates** Basic construction is a double wall of 2"x3" studs on separate plates about 1" apart. Studs of each frame are 16" o.c. with the studs in one frame offset 2" to 8" from those of the other. Other details and materials are as described for single stud walls. **no. 13** | 12 | Single gypsum board each side applied with screws | 51 |
| | 13 | Single gypsum board laminated and nailed[2] over sound board each side | 53 |
| | 14 | Same as wall 13 | 60 |
| | 15 | Single gypsum board laminated and nailed[2] over sound board 1 side; single gypsum board on resilient channels opposite | 58 |
| | 16 | Double gypsum board; nailed each side | 51 |
| | 17 | Double gypsum board each side; outer layer laminated and nailed[2]; base layer nailed | 59 |
| | 18 | Double gypsum board laminated and nailed[2] one side. Single gypsum board on resilient channels opposite | 57 |

[1] Design No. 5—1 Hr. combustible (bearing wall) Underwriters' Lab, Inc. (10)
[2] Face laminated vertically with three 6-inch wide strips of construction adhesive and nailed with about half the usual number of nails.

① OUTWARD & INWARD CORNER DETAIL (TYPICAL)
SCALE: 1/2" = 1'-0"

④ FURRING AT INTERIOR CORNERS
FULL SCALE

② FURRING AT WINDOW JAMB
SCALE: 1/2" = 1'-0"

③ FURRING AT WINDOW JAMB
SCALE: 1/2" = 1'-0"

NOTE: THE ABOVE DETAILS ARE SOLUTIONS FOR THE SAME CONDITION

**Metal "Z" furring and gypsum board: exterior walls**

⑤ FURRING AT DOOR JAMB (TYPICAL @ INTERIOR WALLS)
FULL SCALE

⑥ FURRING AT DOOR JAMB (TYPICAL @ EXTERIOR WALLS)
FULL SCALE

**Metal "Z" furring and gypsum board: door jamb details**

## PARTITIONS AND WALL FINISHES
Wood Veneer Plywood Wall Paneling

¼" HARDWOOD
VENEER
PLYWOOD PANEL

NAIL

CONTINUOUS
¼"x 3" PLYWOOD
STRIPS

1"x 2" FURRING

JOINT

① ② ③

3¼"  ¼"  ¼"

LINE OF CLG.
¼" HARDWOOD VENEER PLYWOOD PANEL
¼" HARDWOOD VENEER PLYWOOD PANEL
WOOD GROUNDS

FACE OF WALL
¼" HARDWOOD VENEER PLYWOOD PANEL
CONTINUOUS ¼"x 3"
PLYWOOD STRIPS NAILED
TO FURRING
1"x 2" FURRING

SEE
INSTALLATION
METHOD

3¼"  ¼"  ¼"

¼" HARDWOOD VENEER
PLYWOOD PANEL

¼" VENEER PLYWOOD
WOOD GROUNDS

HARDWOOD BASE

4"

LINE OF FLOOR

### INSTALLATION METHOD

① FASTEN FURRING TO WALL
WHERE JOINTS IN VENEER
WILL SIT, MAXIMUM 3'-0" ON
CENTER.
NOTE: EXACT SPACING TO BE
DETERMINED BY PANEL SIZES

② NAIL CONTINUOUS ¼"x 3"
PLYWOOD STRIPS TO FURRING

③ GLUE ¼" HARDWOOD VENEER
PLYWOOD PANELS TO ¼" PLYWOOD
STRIPS

## HARDWOOD VENEER PLYWOOD PANEL
SCALE: 3"=1'-0"

CONTINUOUS HARDWOOD PLYWOOD STRIP

LINE OF CLG.

LINE OF ROUGH WALL

HARDWOOD VENEER PLYWOOD PANEL

CONTINUOUS WOOD HANGER STRIPS

CONTINUOUS WOOD USE BLOCKING SPACING TO BE DETERMINED BY PANEL HEIGHT

PANEL DIMENSION

3/4   3/4   3/4

ALTERNATE WOOD HANGER DETAIL

HARDWOOD VENEER PLYWOOD BASE

2"

1½"

1"

¼"

ISOMETRIC OF STEEL PANEL CLIPS

FLOOR LINE

**CONTINUOUS WOOD HANGERS**

HARDWOOD VENEER PLYWOOD STRIP

3/4   1/4   3/4

HARDWOOD VENEER PLYWOOD PANEL

PANEL DIMENSION

PANEL ANCHORING CLIPS - NUMBER REQ'D TO BE DETERMINED BY PANEL SIZE

HARDWOOD VENEER PLYWOOD BASE

4'

**STEEL CLIPS**

**INSTALLATION METHODS**

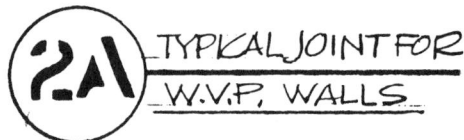

**2A** TYPICAL JOINT FOR W.V.P. WALLS

**2B** WALL/CEILING/FASCIA (TYPE 5) INTERSECTIONS IN SANTUARY/FOYER

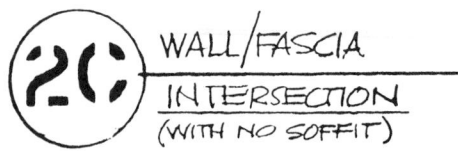

**2C** WALL/FASCIA INTERSECTION (WITH NO SOFFIT)

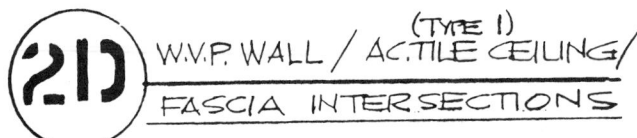

**2D** W.V.P. WALL / AC.TILE CEILING/ (TYPE 1) FASCIA INTERSECTIONS

Fitting ledge is left on cap piece to cover slight variations due to the plaster work. Planed off to suit condition.

Wainscot cap

All woodwork to be best grade, well matched for grain and thoroughly kiln dried.

Cabinet work not to be installed until building is thoroughly dry.

Base

Composition floor.

Concrete

Plaster

Ground

Toggle bolt

Terra cotta block partition

Toggle bolt

Blocking

In some cases the use of the cover mould is specified to avoid the danger of an unsightly joint between cap piece & plaster in case of shrinkage.

Fillet left on cap to cover joint.

Mouldings run solid on rail, with rail routed-out to receive panel. This method, while used in the cheaper class of work, does not allow for any adjustment in panel variations.

Straight panel.

All panelling to fit snug and held secure in manner shown, allowing the panel to expand or contract freely. Panels are never to be nailed fast.

Plaster

Ground

Stud partition.

Base

Sub-base

Floor cover mould

Floor

Blocking

Ground

Panel rail.

Raised moulding.

5-Ply veneered panels are to be recommended for interior work, in preference to solid panels. Exterior panelling should always be solid.

Raised panel.

⅞" thick for large panels.

⅛" to 1¼"

Plaster

Ground

blocking

Stud partition

Blocking

Ground

Floor

Flush moulding

5-Ply panels (one ply is ⅛" in thickness).

Raised panel.

All wainscot, including capping base and in particular the panels to be thoroughly back-painted at the mill, to prevent the wall dampness from injuring or in any way affecting the wainscot after erection.

This dimension should never be less than ⅞"

Floor

Plaster

Ground

Nailing block

Back-plastering

Brick Wall

Blocked fastened to rail

Blocking

Grounds

WAINSCOTING WITH PANEL HAVING RAISED MOULDING

WAINSCOT WITH PANEL HAVING FLUSH MOULD

WAINSCOT WITH PANEL HAVING RAISED MOULD

WAINSCOT WITH PANEL HAVING FLUSH MOULD

## PARTITIONS AND WALL FINISHES

### Wall Paneling Elevation

# Wood Studs or Furring

## Cement Mortar

- CERAMIC TILE
- BOND COAT
- MORTAR BED
- SCRATCH COAT
- METAL LATH
- MEMBRANE
- WOOD STUDS OR FURRING

**Recommended uses**
- over dry, well-braced wood studs or furring
- preferred method of installation over wood studs in showers and tub enclosures

# Metal Studs

## Cement Mortar

- CERAMIC TILE
- DRY-SET OR LATEX-PORTLAND CEMENT MORTAR BOND COAT
- CURED MORTAR BED
- SCRATCH COAT
- METAL LATH
- METAL STUD-MIN.3⅝"

3/4" TO 1"

**Recommended use**
- over metal studs

# Gypsum Board Organic Adhesive

- CERAMIC TILE
- ADHESIVE
- SINGLE OR MULTIPLE LAYER GYPSUM BOARD
- METAL STUDS

**Recommended uses**
- over gypsum board screwed to metal studs, single or double layer installed in accordance with GA-216
- where a gypsum board, non-load-bearing partition is desired with durable, low-maintenance finish
- for fire-resistant, sound-insulated, ceramic-tiled walls (fire-resistance and sound-insulation ratings calculated on partitions before tiling)
- for dry areas in schools, institutions, and commercial buildings

# Wood or Metal Studs
## Gypsum Board
## Dry-Set Mortar or Latex Portland Cement Mortar

- CERAMIC TILE
- DRY-SET OR LATEX-PORTLAND CEMENT MORTAR BOND COAT
- GYPSUM BOARD
- WOOD OR METAL STUDS

**Recommended uses**
- dry interiors over gypsum wall board
- for dry areas in schools, institutions, and commercial buildings

# Glass Mesh Mortar Unit

## Dry-Set Mortar or Latex Portland Cement Mortar

- CERAMIC TILE
- DRY-SET OR LATEX-PORTLAND CEMENT MORTAR BOND COAT
- GLASS MESH MORTAR UNIT
- WOOD OR METAL STUDS

**Recommended uses**
- in wet areas
- over dry, well-braced wood studs or furring
- over well-braced metal studs

# Masonry

## Cement Mortar

- CERAMIC TILE
- BOND COAT
- MORTAR BED
- SCRATCH COAT
- METAL LATH
- MEMBRANE
- MASONRY

3/4" TO 1"

**Recommended use**
- over masonry or concrete on exteriors

## Dry-Set Mortar or Latex-Portland Cement Mortar

- CERAMIC TILE
- DRY-SET OR LATEX-PORTLAND CEMENT MORTAR BOND COAT
- MASONRY

**Recommended use**
- over clean, sound, dimensionally stable masonry or concrete

# Masonry or Concrete

## Cement Mortar Bonded

- CERAMIC TILE
- BOND COAT
- MORTAR BED
- MASONRY

3/8" TO 3/4"

**Recommended use**
- over clean sound, dimensionally stable masonry or concrete

## Cement Mortar

- CERAMIC TILE
- BOND COAT
- MORTAR BED
- SCRATCH COAT
- METAL LATH
- MEMBRANE
- SOLID BACKING: WOOD, PLASTER, MASONRY, OR GYPSUM BOARD

3/4" TO 1 1/2"

**Recommended uses**
- over masonry, plaster, or other solid backing that provides firm anchorage for metal lath
- ideal for remodeling or on surfaces that present bonding problems

## One Coat Method

- CERAMIC TILE
- BOND COAT
- MORTAR BED
- METAL LATH
- MEMBRANE
- SOLID BACKING: WOOD, PLASTER, MASONRY, OR GYPSUM BOARD OVER WOOD OR METAL STUDS

3/8" TO 3/4"

**Recommended uses**
- over masonry, plaster, or other solid backing that provides firm anchorage for metal lath
- ideal for remodeling or on surfaces that present bonding problems
- ideal for remodeling where space limitations exist
- preferred method of applying tile over gypsum plaster or gypsum board in showers and tub enclosures

# Solid Backing

## Organic Adhesive

- CERAMIC TILE
- ADHESIVE
- SOLID BACKING: PLASTER, MASONRY, GYPSUM BOARD, OR GLASS MESH MORTAR UNITS OVER WOOD OR METAL STUDS

**Recommended use**
- interiors over gypsum board, plaster, dimensionally stable masonry, or other smooth surfaces

**Fig. 15   Standard trim shapes and designations (6 by 4¼ in wall tile set in conventional mortar bed).**

**Fig. 16   Standard trim shapes and sizes.**

## PARTITIONS AND WALL FINISHES

**Marble Veneer Wall Finishes**

START OF PLASTER CORNICE

PLASTER

CAP

MARBLE WAINSCOT

DIE

BASE

FACE OF ROUGH WALL

CEMENT BED

CONCRETE FILL

**WALL SECTION - for MARBLE WAINSCOT**
SCALE 3" = 1'0"

ANCHORS

FACE OF ROUGH WALL

PLASTER OF PARIS "SPOTS"

MORTAR BED SHOULD CONSIST OF 1 PART PORTLAND CEMENT TO 3 PARTS CLEAN SHARP SAND

CEMENT BED

CONCRETE FILL

**WALL SECTION MARBLE WALL**
SCALE 3" = 1'0"

FACE OF ROUGH WALL

1½" IS THE VERY LEAST SPACE THAT SHOULD BE ALLOWED FOR MARBLE ASHLAR OR WAINSCOT.
SOME MARBLES REQUIRE "BACKING" UP WITH "LINERS" OR EXTRA THICKNESS & REQUIRE MORE SPACE. THE KIND OF MARBLE DETERMINES THE SPACE REQUIRED

CEMENT BED

CONCRETE FILL

**WALL SECTION - MARBLE ASHLAR WALL & MARBLE CEIL.**
SCALE 1½" = 1'0"

**Fig. 17   Marble treatment for walls and wainscots.**

**Fig. 18  Anchorage details.**

## PARTITIONS AND WALL FINISHES

**Marble and Travertine Veneer Wall Finishes**

Investigate and determine this distance when allowing for wall surface.

Minimum 3/4".

Point up after setting.

Marble cap.

Marble panel.

SCALE·FOR·
DETAILS·3"·1'·0

1/8" brass wire anchor.

Brick filler for setting marble base.

Floor to be of Tennessee marble, free from defects. Set in full bed of 1:3 mortar. To be level through-out.

Mortar floor bed.

Brick wall

·WAINSCOT·&·TRAVERTINE·PANEL·

---

Imitation Travertine stone is used extensively for interior wall surfaces for banks, public buildings, etc.

A good piece of stone is used as a model and from this the negative gelatine form is made. The travertine plaster is then poured into the form to depth of 1/4 to 3/8 to form the stone surface. This is followed or backed with plaster, and reinforced with burlap.

Total thickness from 3/4 to 1". All this work is accomplished at the building.

Travertine plaster surface.
Backing of plaster.
Burlap reinforcement.

Chair rail

Imitation travertine is at times applied to wall like plaster. This method is cheaper but the final result is not as successful by any means as the cast travertine.

Wood base.

Sub-base of marble screwed to ground. Screws to be counter-sunk and waxed to match marble. Alternate, nickle plated round head screws.

1/2" cork floor.

Plaster lump for anchorage.

Terra cotta block partition

Plaster lump for securing stone

Solid er ground

Blocking

·TRAVERTINE·WALL·SURFACE·

---

Joints in travertine cut in after stone is set. After cutting-in, the rough edges and back of joint are neatly repointed. It is a very simple matter to repair travertine as it patches easily.

Specify finished material and see that grain is matched and uniform.

The same conditions which cover the installation of marble also apply to Caen and travertine stone.

All marble shall be cut full with end and side joints rubbed straight and true with sharp angles.

Surface shall be smooth and true and out of wind.

When work is complete, it is to be thoroughly cleaned and washed down. No acid to be used.

Marble floor-minimum thickness 7/8" but for use where traffic is great 1 1/4" is best.

Plaster lumps to secure ashlar.

T.C. block furring

1/8" brass wire used to anchor marble facing to wall two for every stone.

·MARBLE·WALL·BASE·&·FLOOR·

**Fig. 19 Slate panel veneer.**

**Fig. 20 Slate panels applied to concrete wall.**

HEAD

8 9/16"  5/16"  3/4"  1/4"

16 1/2"

1/4" SAFETY GLASS
WITH 3"∅ OPENING
(POLISHED EDGES)

3"∅
CUT-OUT

16 1/2"

8 7/8" H.WD.
FRAME (OAK)

SILL

1 1/4" OAK

3 1/2"
FROM FLOOR

1 7/8"

1/4"

H.WD. TRIM

5 1/4"

3/8"

DOOR #5

6 3/4" FRAME (OAK)

8 7/8"

H.WD. FRAME (OAK)

**2A** JAMB DETAIL AT INTERSECTION—CORNER AT DOOR #5

FIN. CLG.

1-7 1/4"
F.O.

1/4" THICK
SAFETY GLASS
WITH 3"∅ CUT-OUT

3'-0" FINISHED OPENING

3'-6"

2A
A-19

FACE OF
FINISHED
WALL

FLOOR SLAB

ELEVATION OF LOBBY
CONTROL WINDOW

**2** VERTICAL SECTION THRU LOBBY CONTROL WINDOW

VINYL FABRIC
ON PLASTER

GRANT #2620
BI-FOLD HARD-
WARE OR EQUAL

CASING BEAD

OAK EDGE

3/4" OAK PLYWOOD
BI-FOLD DOORS

SCREW & PLUG

OAK FRAME

1/4" HARDWOOD VENEER
PLYWOOD PANEL

HEAD

8'-0"
FIN. JAMB

JAMB

PLYWOOD
BI-FOLD DOOR

IVES # 261 B-4
FLUSH BOLT
OR EQUAL

3/4"

SILL

FLUSH BOLT
DETAIL
@ 1/2 FULL SIZE

CHAPEL

OAK SILL

NOTE:
BI-FOLD DOOR SHALL
BE PAINTED (ON CHAPEL
SIDE ONLY) TO MATCH
COLOR OF VINYL FABRIC

7 5/8"

3/4"  5 5/8"  3/4"  1/4"

SILL

FAMILY ALCOVE

30 BI-FOLD DOOR DETAILS
@ 3"=1'-0"

CORNER BEAD

DOUBLE STRAND 18 GA. TIE WIRE

DOUBLE THICKNESS ½" LONG LENGTH GYPSUM LATH

1½" VERMICULITE OR GYPSUM PERLITE PLASTER

20 GA. GALVANIZED 1" HEXAGONAL MESH

STEEL COLUMN SEE STRUCTURAL DWGS

**4 HR. RATING**

2⅝" | COLUMN DIMENSION | 2⅝"

COLUMN DIM. + 5¼"

DOUBLE STRAND 18 GA. TIE WIRE

CORNER BEAD

STEEL COL. SEE STRUCTURAL DWGS

⅜" PERFORATED GYPSUM LATH

PLASTER: SEE TABLE FOR TYPE ↓ THICKNESS

PLASTER THICKNESS SEE TABLE

**GYPSUM LATH ↓ PLASTER FIREPROOFING**

| PLASTER THICKNESS ↓ TYPE | | |
|---|---|---|
| RATING | THICK. | TYPE |
| 3 HR | 1⅜" | VERMICULITE OR GYPSUM PERLITE |
| 3 HR | 2" | GYPSUM SAND |
| 2 HR | 1⅜" | |
| 1 HR | ½" | ↓ |

CORNER BEAD

DIAMOND MESH METAL LATH

1½" VERMICULITE OR GYPSUM PERLITE PLASTER

¾" CHANNEL BRACKETS LAID FLAT. 2'-0" O.C.

**4 HR RATING**

**METAL LATH ↓ PLASTER FIREPROOFING**

PLASTER (SEE FINISH SCHEDULE)

CORNER BEAD

THICKNESS SEE TABLE

COLUMN SEE STRUCTURAL DRAWINGS

| MATERIAL | THICKNESS IN INCHES | | | |
|---|---|---|---|---|
| | 1 HR | 2 HR | 3 HR | 4 HR |
| BRICK (BURNED CLAY OR SHALE) | 2¼" | 2¼" | 3¾" | 3¾" |
| BRICK (SAND LIME) | 2¼" | 2¼" | 3¾" | 3¾" |
| CONCRETE BLOCK, BRICK, OR TILE EXCEPT CINDER CONCRETE UNITS | 2¼" | 2¼" | 3¾" | 3¾" |
| HOLLOW CINDER OR CONCRETE BLOCK ↓ TILE HAVING A COMPRESSIVE STRENGTH OF AT LEAST 700#/SQIN. OF GROSS AREA | 1½" | 2" | 2" | 2½" |
| SOLID GYPSUM BLOCK PROVIDED THAT TO OBTAIN 4 HR RATING, BLOCKS SHALL BE PLASTERED WITH AT LEAST ½" GYPSUM PLASTER | 1" | 1½" | 2" | 2" |
| HOLLOW OR SOLID BURNED CLAY TILE OR COMBINATION OF TILE ↓ CONCRETE | 1½" | 2" | 2" | 2½" |
| HOLLOW GYPSUM BLOCK, PROVIDED THAT TO OBTAIN A 4 HR. RATING, BLOCKS SHALL BE PLASTERED WITH AT LEAST ½" GYPSUM PLASTER | 3" | 3" | 3" | 3" |

**MASONRY FIREPROOFING**

NOTE: DIMENSION FROM FACE OF COLUMN MAY BE INCREASED IF REQD. TO ALIGN WITH FACE OF ADJOINING PARTITION

## GYPSUM BOARD FIREPROOFING — 2 HR. RATING

FOR 3 HR. RATING ADD 1 ADDITIONAL LAYER OF 5/8" FIRECODE GYPSUM BOARD

1½ HR RATING 3 LAYERS OF GYPSUM BD. (STANDARD)
1 HR. RATING 2 " " " " " " "

SCALE: 3" = 1'-0"

| RATING | PLASTER THICK. | LATH |
|--------|----------------|------|
| 1 HR. | 5/8" | 3.4# DIAMOND MESH METAL LATH |
| 2 HR. | 1" | 3.4# SELF FURRING DIAMOND MESH METAL LATH |
| 3 HR. | 1⅜" | |
| 4 HR. | 1¼" | |

NOTE: N.Y.C. CODE - 4HR RATING MAY BE OBTAINED WITH 1" VERMICULITE PLASTER ON S.F. LATH & BACKFILL OF LOOSE VERMICULITE

## VERMICULITE OR GYPSUM PERLITE FIREPROOFING

2¾" ± 3 HR. RATING
3¼" ± 4 HR RATING
DIMENSIONS VARY
CHECK LOCAL BLDG.
CODE & MANUFACTURERS
SPECIFICATION

## SPRAYED ON FIREPROOFING

## FLOORS AND FLOOR FINISHES

The designer must be familiar with the great variety of floor types, finishes, and patterns in order to specify and detail architectural flooring properly. While some examples of "soft finishes" such as carpeting and resilient flooring are shown, this section explores in depth the installation and detailing of "hard" or architectural finishes.

It is important for the designer to research the various characteristics of the floor finish being specified. While aesthetics and color are obviously important considerations, the designer must also analyze other factors. Among these factors are wear resistance and durability, soil resistance, maintenance, resiliency, flammability, costs of installation, and life cycle cost. Once these factors have been analyzed, the final specification and detailing of the architectural finish must be developed.

Examples of standard patterns are provided, but the designer must become familiar with the infinite number of pattern possibilities. The inherent limitations of materials control their sizes and thicknesses. The patterns of certain materials are dictated by both the thickness of the material and the weight or "dead load" of the material superimposed upon the structure. For example, a large pattern of marble or granite will necessitate a slab of material that will weigh much more per square foot than that of a smaller pattern. This greater weight might have structural consequences, as well as make floor transitions more significant.

Transitions between flooring materials, particularly under doors or at entrances, and transitions between flooring and walls are some of the key material interfaces that have to be detailed. Again, this section provides such information using both traditional and contemporary approaches.

Finally, a portion of this section is devoted to the detailing of raised computer room floors. While not traditionally a floor finish, raised computer room floors seem appropriate for this section. While generic architectural details are provided, the designer should always develop final details in conjunction with the manufacturer(s) being specified.

# FLOORS AND FLOOR FINISHES
## Typical Characteristics of Floor Finishes

| DRAWING AND DESCRIPTION | WEAR RESISTANCE | SOIL RESISTANCE, CLEANING AND MAINTENANCE | RESILIENCY | REMARKS | COST COMPARISON |
|---|---|---|---|---|---|
| ⅛ inch hardened cement finish on concrete slab | Good | Poor; frequent cleaning needed; must be refinished every ten years | Very hard | Cement base costs little, is too hard a floor to be comfortable; infrequently used in classrooms, sometimes used in corridors, shops and inexpensive toilet rooms | installation cost<br><br>maintenance and insurance cost for 20 years |
| ¾ inch terrazzo finish, with ¾ inch cement underbed on a concrete slab | Very good | Very good; needs cleaning once a week with detergent and water | Very hard | Terrazzo base is easy to clean and sanitary, but not resilient and sometimes noisy; seldom used in classrooms, often used in corridors, vestibules, toilets and shower rooms | |
| Ceramic mosaic tile, ¾ inch setting bed on concrete slab | Very good | Very good | Very hard | Used in toilet rooms, showers, food service areas, but seldom used in classrooms | |
| ⅛ inch asphalt tile finish installed in mastic on concrete slab | Poor, usually needs replacing every ten years | Fair; must be cleaned and waxed once a week. | Fair | Low first cost; finish requires careful maintenance | |
| ⅛ inch linoleum finish installed in mastic on concrete slab | Good | Fair; must be cleaned and waxed once a week | Fair | Serviceable; a sanitary floor for classrooms, corridors, assembly and administration rooms | |
| ⅛ inch cork tile floor installed in mastic on concrete slab | Good | Fair; needs frequent cleaning and waxing | Very good | Used primarily in libraries and kindergartens; floor is subject to indentations by chair legs; acoustically good | |
| ⅛ inch rubber tile finish installed in mastic on concrete slab | Good | Fair; needs cleaning and waxing once a week | Very good | Subject to slight indentation by chair legs | |
| ⅛ inch vinyl tile finish installed in mastic on concrete slab | Good | Fair; needs a weekly cleaning and waxing | Very good | Subject to indentation | |
| 25/32 inch maple strip flooring set in ⅛ inch hot asphalt mastic on concrete slab | Very good | Good; requires monthly cleaning with steelwool and a wax finish | Fair | Steel angles necessary to cover expansion joint; used in gymnasiums and playrooms; not suitable for damp areas or climates | |
| 25/32 inch maple finish; 1 by 4 inch cypress subfloor laid diagonally; 2 by 6 inch cypress sleepers, 12 inches apart, set in two ⅛ inch layers of hot asphalt mastic | Very good | Good; requires a monthly cleaning with steelwool and a wax finish; sand and re-finish every 2 years | Excellent | A deluxe gymnasium floor | |

## FLOORS AND FLOOR FINISHES

### Floor Construction Details

**F-1**
2" x 8" JOISTS - 16" O.C.,
1¾₆" OAK FLOORING,
SUB-FLOOR, METAL LATH,
½" GYPSUM PLASTER

**F-2**
1⅜" HARD WOOD FLOOR,
SUB-FLOOR,
2" x 6" WOOD JOISTS,
WOOD LATH,
½" PLASTER

**F-3**
SAME AS F-2,
EXCEPT ½" FIBERBOARD
BETWEEN ROUGH &
FINISH FLOOR

**F-4**
⅜" HARDWOOD FLOOR, SUB-FLOOR,
¾" x 2" NAILING STRIPS (SEE NOTE)
½" FIBERBOARD, SUB-FLOOR,
2" x 6" WOOD JOISTS,
WOOD LATH, ½" PLASTER.

NOTE - ROUGH & FINISH FLOOR NAILED TO NAILERS; NAILERS NOT
NAILED THROUGH FIBERBOARD: MERELY RESTING THEREON.

**F-5**
SAME AS F-4,
EXCEPT ½" FIBERBOARD
BETWEEN ROUGH &
FINISH FLOOR

**F-6**
⅜" HARD WOOD FLOOR,
SUB-FLOOR,
2" x 6" WOOD JOISTS - 16" O.C.
SUSPENDED CEILING -
2" x 4" JOISTS - 16" O.C.
½" FIBERBOARD, ½" PLASTER

NOTE - COMMON END SUPPORT FOR BOTH JOIST SYSTEMS;
NO INTERMEDIATE CONNECTIONS BETWEEN 2x6s & 2x4s.

**F-7**
SAME AS F-6,
EXCEPT ½" FIBERBOARD
ON PRIMARY SUB-FLOOR.
¾" x 2" NAILERS (SEE NOTE WITH F-4)
PLUS ROUGH & FINISH FLOOR.

**F-8**
2" CONCRETE FILL,
STEEL FLOOR SECTION,
SUSPENDED METAL LATH,
½" PLASTER
4½"

**F-9**
SAME AS F-8, EXCEPT
½" EMULSIFIED ASPHALT
APPLIED BEFORE
2" CONCRETE FILL.

**F-10**
BATTLESHIP LINOLEUM,
2½" CONCRETE FILL ON
HIGH-RIB METAL LATH,
8" MAC-MAR JOISTS,
HIGH-RIB METAL LATH,
3 COATS GYPSUM PLASTER

**F-11**
4" REINF. CONCRETE SLAB,
¾" x 2" FURRING,
½" FIBERBOARD LATH,
½" GYPSUM PLASTER

**F-12**
SAME AS F-11,
EXCEPT ¾" x 2" SLEEPERS
PLUS ROUGH & FINISH
FLOOR ADDED, TOP

**F-13**
SAME AS F-12,
EXCEPT ½" FIBERBOARD
PLACED UNDER SLEEPERS

**F-14**
8" COMBINATION FLOOR,
6" x 12" x 12" 3-CELL TILE,
½" TWO-COAT
GYPSUM PLASTER CEILING

**F-15**
SAME AS F-14, EXCEPT
2" CINDER CONCRETE FILL
PLUS 1" CEMENT TOPPING
ADDED FOR FLOOR

**F-16**
6" COMBINATION FLOOR,
4" x 12" x 12" 3-CELL TILE,
¾" x 2" FURRING - 16" O.C.,
½" FIBERBOARD LATH,
½" GYPSUM PLASTER

**F-17**
SAME AS F-16,
EXCEPT ¾" x 2" SLEEPERS
PLUS ROUGH & FINISH
FLOOR ADDED, TOP

**F-18**
SAME AS F-17,
EXCEPT ½" FIBERBOARD
PLACED UNDER SLEEPERS

**F-19**
FINISH & ROUGH FLOOR
ON ¾" x 2" SLEEPERS - 16" O.C.
RESTING ON ½" FIBERBOARD,
6" COMBINATION FLOOR,
4" x 12" x 12" 3-CELL TILE,
SUSPENDED 2" x 4" JOISTS,
PLUS ½" FIBERBOARD LATH,
½" GYPSUM PLASTER

**F-20**
1¾₆" OAK FLOORING NAILED
TO 2" x 2" SLEEPERS - 16" O.C.,
SLEEPERS GROUTED ON 6"
COMBINATION FLOOR (SIM-
ILAR TO F-19), ½" TWO-COAT
GYPSUM PLASTER CEILING

**F-21**
SAME AS F-20,
EXCEPT 2" x 2" SLEEPERS
CARRIED ON
RESILIENT STEEL CLIPS

**F-22**
1½" HYDROCAL ON
½" GYPSUM PLASTERBOARD,
2" x 2" SLEEPERS - 16" O.C.
ON RESILIENT STEEL CLIPS,
6" COMBINATION FLOOR
(SIMILAR TO F-20), ½" TWO-
COAT GYPSUM PLASTER CEILING

By groups of four squares as a unit separated by wider joints, the scale is increased.

A diagonal pattern of square tiles is emphasized by a border.

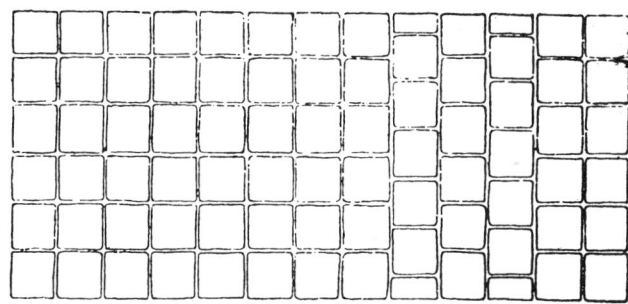

By a few rows of broken joints, an effect of border is produced in a field of square tiles.

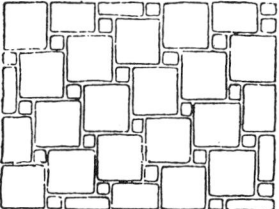

When the small squares are less than one-quarter of the area of the large squares, the pattern runs off at the side.

When the small squares are one quarter of the area of the large squares, the pattern has more repose.

By breaking joints in one course, the border is made wide.

An arrangement adapted to large rooms.

Another way to increase the scale with small tiles.

A decorative pattern that can be made on the job.

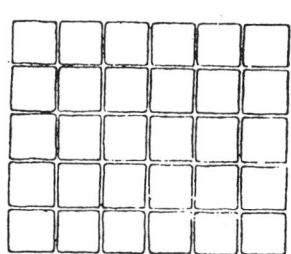

The simplest floor of square tiles is interesting if the joints are in scale.

When square tiles are laid with broken joints, long lines in one direction are the result.

When double squares are laid "basket pattern," the necessary allowance for joints adds interest.

A good pattern for corridors.

Varieties of "herringbone."

Two combinations suggesting plaids.

A simple device for a panel or a floor for a large room.

## FLOORS AND FLOOR FINISHES

**Marble Floor Patterns and Details**

NOTE: Size of marble tiles vary with design. If several varieties are used, the abrasive hardness (Ha) of each should be similar. (ASTM C241).

MARBLE BORDERS

MARBLE TILES

MARBLE BORDERS

FEATURE STRIPS OR JOINTS

MARBLE BORDERS

TYPICAL MARBLE FLOORING DESIGNS    3/8"==1'-0"

MARBLE TILE
DRY SET CEMENT
MORTAR BED
SUB SLAB

[1] MORTAR BED

[3] THIN SET MORTAR

MARBLE TILE
MORTAR BED
REINFORCING
MEMBRANE

[5] MORTAR BED

MARBLE TILE
MORTAR BED
REINFORCING
MEMBRANE

[2] MORTAR BED

MARBLE TILE
ADHESIVE
SUB SLAB

[4] ADHESIVE

MARBLE TILE
ADHESIVE
STRUCTURALLY SOUND WOOD SUBFLOOR

[6] ADHESIVE

METHODS OF INSTALLATION    HALF SIZE

**Fig. 1    Marble flooring details.**

c. Thin marble tile, preferred method

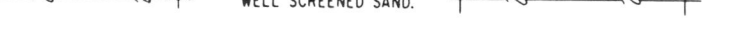

a. Standard floor tile, preferred method   b. Standard floor tile, thin-set method   d. Thin marble tile, thin-set method

**Fig. 2   Marble floor setting methods.**

a. Random rectangular

b. Coursed

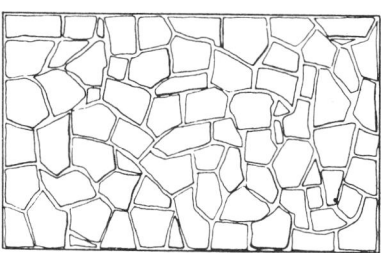

c. Irregular or mosaic

**Fig. 3   Flagging patterns.**

a. On sand bed

Flagging 1 to 1½ in.
Sand bed 4 in.

b. On concrete slab on grade

Flagging ¾ to 1 in.
Setting bed 1 to 1½ in.
Reinforced concrete slab 4 in.
Gravel or cinders 4 in.

c. On wood joist construction

Flagging ¾ to 1 in.
Setting bed 1 to 1½ in.
Reinforced concrete slab 4 in.
Wood subfloor ¾ in.

**Fig. 4   Flagstone setting methods.**

S-1  $3"=1'-0"$

S-2  $3"=1'-0"$

S-3  $3"=1'-0"$

S-4  $3"=1'-0"$

## FLOORS AND FLOOR FINISHES
**Door Saddles**

SADDLE TO MATCH
FRAME WIDTH

DOOR

¾" OFFSET

ZERO #675
BRONZE SADDLE
(SOCIAL HALL)
RESILIENT TILE

CARPET

ZERO #22

ZERO #69

RIXON #25 OFFSET
FLOOR CLOSER

**S-5**   3"=1'-0"

DOOR

ZERO #22
WEATHER STRIP

ZERO #656
ALUM. SADDLE

CONCRETE

RESIL. TILE

**S-6**   3"=1'-0"

DOOR

RESILIENT TILE

QUARRY
TILE

2"x2" ALUMINUM ⊄

**S-7**   3"=1'-0"

DOOR

RESILIENT
TILE

RUBBER REDUCING
STRIP

**S-8**   3"=1'-0"

DOOR

(SEE NOTE #5
THIS SHEET)

DOOR WITH
SOUND-PROTECTIVE
FITTINGS (SEE NOTE #5, THIS SHEET)

CARPET

RUBBER SADDLE

CARPET

2"

**S-9**   3"=1'-0"

## FLOORS AND FLOOR FINISHES

### Saddles/Floor Transitions

1 CARPET TILE TO CARPET
A102  FULL SIZE SCALE

2 VINYL TILE TO CARPET TILE
A102  FULL SIZE SCALE

3 CARPET TILE TO STONE TO CARPET
A102  FULL SIZE SCALE

4 CARPET TO CONCRETE
A102  FULL SIZE SCALE

10 CARPET TILE TO CONCRETE
A102  SEE DETAIL 4 ABOVE... SIM.

5 VINYL TILE TO CARPET
A102  FULL SIZE SCALE

6 VINYL TILE TO CONCRETE
A102  FULL SIZE SCALE

7 CERAMIC TILE TO CARPET
A102  FULL SIZE SCALE

8 CERAMIC TILE TO CARPET TILE
A102  FULL SIZE SCALE.

9 CERAMIC TILE TO VINYL TILE
A102  FULL SIZE SCALE

10 STONE TO CERAMIC TILE
A102  FULL SIZE SCALE

## FLOORS AND FLOOR FINISHES

Floor Finish Transition Details

CARPET.

VINYL REDUCER STRIP BY CARPET CONTRACTOR SUBMIT SAMPLE FOR ARCH' APPROVAL

VINYL TILE

② SECTION @ FLOOR TRANSITION/ CARPET/ VAT
N.T.S.

GRANITE TILE FLOOR. SEE STONE SPEC'
ALUM & EDGE TRIM BY GENERAL CONTRACTOR COORDINATE W/ STONE CONTRACTOR
FLASH PATCH AS REQ'D. BY CPT CONTRACTOR
CARPET FLOORING.

① SECTION @ FLOOR TRANSITION. STONE/ CPT'
1/2 F.S.

CPT TILE

MERCER (OR APPROVED EQUAL) REDUCER STRIP #15. SAMPLE TO BE SUBMITTED FOR ARCH' APPROVAL.

CARPET

④ SECTION @ FLOOR TRANSITION CPT'TILE/CPT'
NTS

DOOR FRAME AS PER SCHEDULE.

1¾" DOOR AS PER SCHEDULE

CARPET AS PER SPECIFICATION

MARBLE SADDLE (BY G.C.)

CERAMIC TILE AS PER SPECIFICATION

2"

③ SECT' @ FLOOR TRANSITION: CPT/C.TILE.
3"=1'-0"

CONC. FLOOR

MERCER (OR EQUALLY APPROVED) EDGE MOULDING STOCK #1 SUBMIT COLOR SAMPLE FOR ARCH' APPROVAL

CARPET

⑥ SECT' @ FLOOR TRANSITION. CPT/CONC.
NTS.

DOOR JAMB BEYOND

CARPET.

WD' SADDLE; NOTCH AS REQ'D (BY G.C.) TO ACCOMODATE DOOR JAMB BEYOND ( WD TO BE AMERICAN WHITE OAK STAINED TO MATCH ENGLISH BROWN OAK. SUBMIT SAMPLE TO MATCH ARCH' SAMPLE.

⑤ SECT' @ WD SADDLE.
NTS

**Vinyl Snap Down Divider**
- ¾" wide removable section for joining carpets

**Vinyl Snap Down Divider**
- 1⅜" wide removable section for joining carpets

**Vinyl Snap Down Edging**
- 1" wide removable section for joining carpet to tile

**Vinyl Snap Down Edging**
- 1¼" wide removable section for joining carpet to tile

**Vinyl Single Flange Track**

**Vinyl 5/16" Glue Down Reducer**
- ¼" butting gauge undercut
- Long flange, smooth taper

**Vinyl Custom Edge**
- For sponge backs
- General purpose edge and cap

**Vinyl 1/4" Square Cove Cap**
- Undercut 1/4"
- Cap for coved carpets and wall paneling

**Vinyl Tile Carpet Joiner**
- Provides smooth carpet/tile transition

**Vinyl 3/16" Glue Down Reducer**
- Undercut, flange, and transition combined
- Undercut 3/16," smooth transition

**Vinyl Carpet Cove Cap**
- Trim for coved carpet
- Undercut 3/16" (flexible)

**Vinyl 9/32" Cap**
- For capping coved carpets, ceramics, and paneling

**Vinyl Tackless Carpet Bar**
- ¼" butting edge to accept tackless strip
- Deep undercut

**Vinyl Tackless Carpet Bar Reducer**
- 1/4" butting edge to accept tackless strip

**Vinyl 1/8" Square Cove Cap**
- Undercut 1/8"
- Cap for coved sheet vinyl

**Vinyl Corner Guard**
- Protects corners and columns from bumps, abrasion. wear

**Vinyl Fillet Strip**
- Superb backing for flashing up the wall
- Black only

**Vinyl Underslung Reducer**
- Binder-bar type edging for resilient flooring
- Undercut .105" for use with 1/16" to 1/8" material

**Vinyl 1/4" Glue Down Reducer**
- 1/4" butting gauge undercut
- Long flange, smooth taper

**Vinyl 1/16" Tile Reducer**
- Beveled edge for resilient flooring material
- 1/16" (.063") butting gauge

**Vinyl 3/32" Tile Reducer**
- Beveled edge for resilient flooring material
- 3/32" (.094") butting gauge

**Vinyl 1/8" Tile Reducer**
- Beveled edge for resilient flooring material
- 1/8" (.125") butting gauge

## BASE TYPES

ELISABETH COIT

Plaster

Wood cap
moulding

Wood
base

6"

Linoleum
floor

**4**

( Cowles Lewis House,
Farmington, Conn.)

Line of studs

Plaster

Wood
base

4¼"

Finish
wood
floor

Line of studs

Plaster

Wood
base

6"

Finish
wood
floor

Line of masonry
support

Plaster line

Metal ground

¼" Plastic
Magnesia
base and
flooring

Cement

¼ Base coat

Concrete
sub-floor

Plaster
wall

Wood shims

Metal
dividing
strip
(patented)

Line of
masonry
support

Terrazzo
base and
floor

McKIM
MEAD
& WHITE

Travertine
wainscot

Marble
Cove and
base

6"

Terrazzo
floor

1½"

**8**

JAMES EPPENSTEIN

Stud line

Wood wall
covering

Plaster

Wood base

4"

Finish
wood floor

**5**

( Le Moyne House )
Washington County
Pennsylvania

Plaster

Line of stud

Wood
base

6"

Finish
wood
floor

( Dorsey House )
Washington County
Pennsylvania

Plaster

Wood
base

Stud
line

8¾"

Finish
wood
floor

Patented metal
edge, sliding
down in place
after material
is laid

Nail

Plaster or other
wall finish

Wood cove,
1½ radius

Linoleum
or
Rubber fl.

Plaster
wall

Wood shims

Metal
dividing
strip
(patented)

Line of
masonry
support

Terrazzo
base and
floor

AYMAR EMBURY II

Wood wainscot
and cap mould

Marble
base

5"

Finish
wood floor

**9**

LAWRENCE J. KLEIN

Line of rough
wall

Wood
paneling

Wood
base

5"

Finish
wood
floor

**6**

N. CHESTER SORENSON

Rough wall

Plaster

20 gauge
metal clips

Wood base

6½"

Finish
wood floor

**7**

( Kingsley House )
New Haven, Conn.

Plaster

Wood
base

Stud
line

8"

Finish
wood
floor

Plaster or
other wall
finish

Stud line

Wood cap
moulding

Wood grounds

Wood cove
1½ radius

Linoleum
or
Rubber fl.

PAUL GERHARDT, JR.

Marble
base and
wainscot

8"

Marble
mldg and
floor

**11**

( Museum of Fine
Arts, Boston )

Wood wainscot
and cap
moulding

Marble
base

6"

Finish wood
flooring

**10**

# FLOORS AND FLOOR FINISHES

Stone Floor Patterns and Details

COLORS SEE SPEC. ON DWG A-210

A - VENDE AVEN POLISHED
B - CIPPOLINO POLISHED
C - ANDES BLACK GRANITE POLISHED
D - ROSSO LEVANTO POLISHED WITHOUT GREEN

① STONE FLOORING PATTERN DETAIL  TYP. FLOORS 37TH THRU 45TH FL.
A310  1/4" = 1'-0"

② STONE DET. @ ELEV. DOOR SILL
A310  1 1/2" = 1'-0"

TYP. STONE FLOORING DET @ LOBBY PANEL WALL
④ A310  3" = 1'-0"

③ STONE FLOORING DET. @ ENTRY DOORS
A310  3" = 1'-0"

TYP. STONE BUTT JOINT DETAIL
⑤ A310  3" = 1'-0"

FULL DEPTH EXPANSION JOINT

TYPICAL CONTROL JOINT
RUSTIC TERRAZZO ~ STRUCTURAL SYSTEM.
OVER GRANULAR FILL

FULL DEPTH EXPANSION JOINT

TYPICAL CONTROL JOINT
RUSTIC TERRAZZO ~ BONDED SYSTEM WITH
SETTING BED ~ OVER STRUCTURAL CONCRETE

FULL DEPTH EXPANSION JOINT

TYPICAL CONTROL JOINT
RUSTIC TERRAZZO OVER SLABS WITH HEATED SPACE
BELOW & OVER INSULATED & WATERPROOFED SLABS

## FLOORS AND FLOOR FINISHES
Terrazzo Floor Construction Details

**SAND CUSHION TERRAZZO OVER
PRECAST CONCRETE TYPE DECK**

**EPOXY, POLYESTER, TERRAZZO FLOOR & BASE**

Fig.5

**TERRAZZO OVER CORRUGATED METAL TYPE FLOOR**

**TERRAZZO OVER CELL TYPE FLOOR**

**POLYACRYLATE TERRAZZO FLOOR & BASE**

Fig.5 Angle or "L" Strips        Single Angle Strip
Two Strips Positioned
Back to Back Directly over saw cuts

## FLOORS AND FLOOR FINISHES
**Terrazzo Base Details**

**PRECAST TERRAZZO BASE**

BLOCK WALL
3/4" TERRAZZO

**POURED TERRAZZO BASE**

BLOCK WALL
TYPE H. SCREED
3/4" TERRAZZO

**FLUSH TYPE**

Sheet Rock
METAL BASE BEAD INSTALLED BY OTHERS
3/8" TERRAZZO
3/4" UNDERBED
R = 1" OR 1½"
VARIES

**SHADOW TYPE**

WALL FINISH
METAL BASE BEAD
3/8" TERRAZZO
3/8" UNDERBED
R = 1" OR 1½"
Not less than 6 inches
VARIES

The Terrazzo base height should be 6 inches or more to use this detail.

**RE-VEAL TYPE**

Wall finish
Metal channel
3/8" terrazzo
Underbed
R-1"
Varies

**SPLAY TYPE**

Sheet Rock
BASE BEAD INSTALLED BY OTHERS
3/8" TERRAZZO
6"
3"
R = 1½"
UNDERBED
VARIES

# TERRAZZO BASE

2 layers Sheet Rock
Metal Base Bead Flush Type
3/8" Terrazzo
Underbed
Galv. Metal Lath anchored to steel studs
R-1" or 1½"
Varies
Steel Stud
varies

metal Re-veal unit furnished and installed by others
Steel Studs
Varies
R-1"
Divider Strip
Underbed
Varies

**Note: Provide Dimension in Space Indicated "Varies"**

**PROJECTING TYPE**

Sheet Rock
METAL BASE BEAD INSTALLED BY OTHERS
3/8" TERRAZZO
5/8" UNDERBED
R-1" OR 1½"
VARIES

PLASTER
FLUSH OR PROJECTING TYPE HERE
3/8" TERRAZZO
5/8" UNDERBED
1/4" SCRATCH COAT BY OTHERS

**VERTICAL TERRAZZO**
SCALE 3"=1'-0"

VAPOR BARRIER.
METAL LATH BY OTHERS
DIVIDER STRIP
SCRATCH COAT BY OTHERS
UNDERBED
TERRAZZO
BASE
STRIP
6"

3/4" FURRING CHANNELS 12" O.C.
2.7 LB DIAMOND MESH LATH
UNDERBED
3/8" TERRAZZO
2½"

**SOLID PARTITIONS**
SCALE 3"=1'-0"

# PRE-CAST TERRAZZO STAIRS

NOTE: Abrasive inserts should be positioned 1/16 inch higher than Terrazzo surface

ABRASIVE INSERTS

¾ UNDERBED

CONCRETE STAIR CONSTRUCTION BY OTHERS

Tread & Riser

ABRASIVE INSERT

⅜ STEEL PLATE DRILLED, TAPPED, WELDED TO REINFORCING BARS

STRINGER

**Self Supported Tread**

# POURED TERRAZZO STAIRS

Abrasive Inserts

½ TERRAZZO TOPPING

MIN. WALL STRINGER IF DESIRED

UNDERBED

CONCRETE STAIR CONSTRUCTION BY OTHERS

Tread & Riser

Stair Channels For Abrasive Inserts

ABRASIVE INSERTS  4½ MIN.  1½ TREAD

ANCHOR AT EACH END

**Tread on Steel Stairs**

½ TERRAZZO TOPPING

REINFORCING

UNDERBED

Tac weld steel rods to metal pan..tie wire mesh to rods....

**Steel Pan-Type**

⅜ TERRAZZO TOPPING

⅝ UNDERBED

TYPE "H" BEAD

PLASTER BEAD BY OTHERS

**Terrazzo Stringer, Curb & Fascia**

MASONRY OR CEMENT PLASTER BACKING BY OTHERS

⅜ UNDERBED

⅜ FINISH

**VERTICAL RUSTIC TERRAZZO**

BACKUP BY OTHERS
A-C GRADE EXT. PLYWD.
CEM. ASB. BOARD
CONC. BLOCK
PRECAST CONC.

⅜ MATRIX & FINISH

**TEXTURED MOSAIC**
**Epoxy, Polyester or Polyacrylate**

539

## FLOORS AND FLOOR FINISHES

Ceramic Tile, Terrazzo, and Brick

5/8" TERRAZZO TOPPING

MORTAR BED BONDED TO SLAB

STRUCTURAL SLAB

DIVIDING STRIP (WITH PROPER ANCHORAGE)

BONDED TERRAZZO

CERAMIC TILE

CEMENT MORTAR SETTING BED

CONCRETE SLAB

CERAMIC TILE SET IN MORTAR

DIVIDING STRIP (WITH PROPER ANCHORAGE)

5/8" TERRAZZO TOPPING

MORTAR BED

LIGHT REINFORCING MESH

TAR PAPER LAPPED 2"

1/4" BED OF SAND

STRUCTURAL SLAB

SAND-CUSHION TERRAZZO

CERAMIC TILE

DRY-SET MORTAR

STRUCTURAL SLAB

CERAMIC TILE IN DRY-SET MORTAR

DIVIDING STRIP

5/8" TERRAZZO TOPPING

STRUCTURAL SLAB

NOTE:
DIVIDER STRIPS TO BE DRAWN & SPECIFIED ON FINAL WORKING DRAWINGS

MONOLITHIC TERRAZZO

CERAMIC TILE

ADHESIVE

STRUCTURAL SLAB

CERAMIC TILE SET IN ADHESIVE

BRICK PAVERS

1" GROUT

CONC. SLAB

BRICK PAVERS

CARPET CUSHION

CARPET

V.A.T.

METAL DIVIDER

CONC. SLAB

CARPET

# FLOORS AND FLOOR FINISHES

Marble, Resilient Tile, Slate, Wood, and Quarry Tile

MARBLE, SLATE OR STONE
CEMENT SETTING BED

NOTE:
OPTIONAL — TAR PAPER, 15 LB FELT,
POLYETHYLENE FILM, OR THIN
BED OF CLEAN WELL SCREENED
SAND

STRUCTURAL SLAB

STONE FLOORING

2⅝₃₂" FINISH WOOD FLOORING
⅝" PLYWOOD SUB-FLOORING
½" AIR SPACE
2"X3" SLEEPERS BEVELED
SPACED 16" O.C.
CEMENT FILL
BUILDING PAPER LAPPED 1"
STRUCTURAL SLAB

WOOD FLOORING

RESILIENT TILE SET IN
TILE CEMENT AS PER
MANUFACTURERS SPECIFICATIONS

STRUCTURAL SLAB

RESILIENT FLOORING

QUARRY TILE
MORTAR BED
STRUCTURAL SLAB

QUARRY TILE

## MORTAR BED METHOD

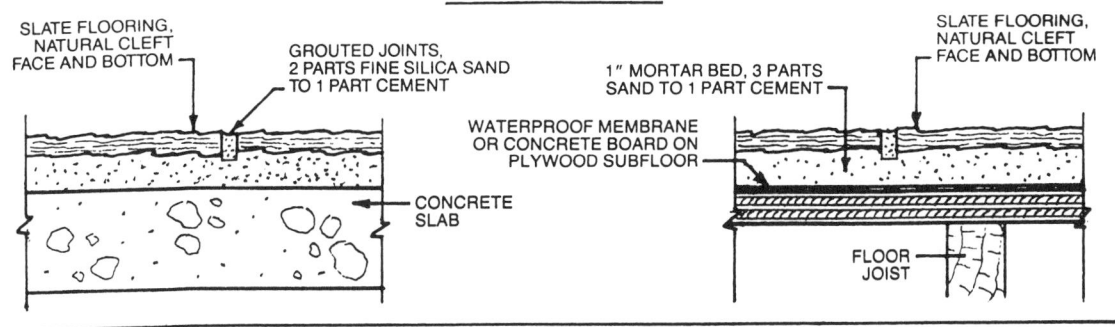

SLATE FLOORING,
NATURAL CLEFT
FACE AND BOTTOM

GROUTED JOINTS,
2 PARTS FINE SILICA SAND
TO 1 PART CEMENT

CONCRETE
SLAB

1" MORTAR BED, 3 PARTS
SAND TO 1 PART CEMENT

SLATE FLOORING,
NATURAL CLEFT
FACE AND BOTTOM

WATERPROOF MEMBRANE
OR CONCRETE BOARD ON
PLYWOOD SUBFLOOR

FLOOR
JOIST

## THINSET METHOD

SLATE FLOORING,
NATURAL CLEFT FACE
AND GAUGED BOTTOM

ACRYLIC LATEX GROUT.
CAN BE TIGHT JOINT
WHEN SLATE IS 1/4"

CONCRETE
SLAB

ACRYLIC LATEX MORTAR BED
APPLIED WITH NOTCHED TROWEL.
DEPTH NOT LESS THAN HALF THE
THICKNESS OF SLATE (MIN. ¼").

PLYWOOD OR CONCRETE
BOARD-TO-PLYWOOD SUBFLOOR

SLATE FLOORING,
NATURAL CLEFT FACE
AND GAUGED BOTTOM

FLOOR
JOIST

## FLOORS AND FLOOR FINISHES
### Wood Floor Construction Details

WOOD FLOOR OVER PRE-CAST GYPSUM
BASE AND CEILING — WOOD JOISTS

CEMENT FLOOR OVER PRE-CAST GYPSUM
BASE AND CEILING — WOOD JOISTS

TILE FLOOR ON FLAT-TOP
AND BEVELLED WOOD JOISTS

SOUND-CONTROL WITH STAGGERED
JOISTS AND SUB-FLOORING

SOUND-CONTROL WITH INSULATION BLANKET
BETWEEN ROUGH AND FINISHED FLOORING

SOUND-CONTROL WITH STAGGERED
JOISTS AND INSULATION BLANKET

PARTITION OVER PARTITION
PARALLEL WITH JOISTS

PARTITION NOT OVER PART-
ITION - ON DOUBLE JOISTS

PARTITION OVER PARTITION
AT RIGHT ANGLES TO JOISTS

Perhaps the most widely used pattern is a $^{25}/_{32}$- by 2¼-in *strip flooring*. These strips are laid lengthwise in a room and normally at right angles to the floor joists. Some type of a subfloor of diagonal boards or plywood is normally used under the finish floor. Strip flooring of this type is tongued-and-grooved and end-matched (Fig. 6). Strips are random length and may vary from 2 to 16 ft or more. End-matched strip flooring in $^{25}/_{32}$-in thickness is generally hollow backed (Fig. 6A). The face is slightly wider than the bottom so that tight joints result when flooring is laid. The tongue fits tightly into the groove to prevent movement and floor "squeaks." All of these details are designed to provide beautiful finished floors that require a minimum of maintenance.

Another matched pattern may be obtained in ⅜- by 2-in size (Fig. 6B). This is commonly used for remodeling work or when subfloor is edge-blocked or thick enough to provide very little deflection under loads.

*Square-edged strip flooring* (Fig. 6C) might also be used occasionally. It is usually ⅜ by 2 inches in size and is laid up over a substantial subfloor. Facenailing is required for this type.

**Fig. 6 Types of strip flooring: *A*, side- and end-matched — $^{25}/_{32}$-in; *B*, thin flooring strips — matched; *C*, thin flooring strips — square-edged.**

**Fig. 7 Application of strip flooring: *A*, general application; *B*, starting strip.**

# FLOORS AND FLOOR FINISHES
## Wood Parquet Floor Patterns

| PRODUCT DESCRIPTION AND PATTERN | *PANEL SIZE | GRADE | *SPECIES |
|---|---|---|---|
| STANDARD Pattern Unfinished—paper-faced | 5/16" x 19" x 19" 16 equal alternating squares | Select & Better | Cherry, Maple, Red Oak, White Oak, Cedar, Pecan, Walnut, Rhodesian Teak, Angelique (Guiana Teak) |
| | 5/16" x 12" x 12" 4 equal alternating squares | Rustic | |
| STANDARD Pattern Unfinished—WebBack or Mesh-Back | 5/16" x 19" x 19" 16 equal alternating squares | Select & Better Rustic Select & Better (Par & Better) | Red Oak, White Oak, Pecan Pecan |
| | 5/16" x 11" x 11" 4 equal alternating squares | Rustic | Red and White Oak |
| STANDARD Pattern Unfinished—WebBack (For Industrial Use) | 5/16" x 19" x 19" 16 equal alternating squares | Select & Better (Par & Better) | Maple, Red Oak White Oak Pecan |
| | 9/16" x 19" x 19" 16 equal alternating squares | Select Rustic & Better Rustic | |
| STANDARD Pattern Unfinished WebBack (For Industrial Use) | 11/16" x 11" x 11" 4 equal alternating squares | Select & Better (Par & Better) | Red Oak, Maple White Oak |
| | ¾" x 12-11/16" x 12-11/16" 4 equal alternating squares | Select & Better (Rustic & Better) | |
| STANDARD Pattern Factory-Finished and Unfinished (Available in various colors) | 5/16" x 6-11/32" x 6-11/32" 5/16" x 2" x 12" (slats) 5/16" x 6" x 6" 5/16" x 6⅜" x 6⅜" 5/16" x 6½" x 6½" individual unit | Select & Better Natural & Better Fireside Rustic Cabin & Better Cabin | Oak, Walnut Pecan, Maple White Oak, Ash |
| STANDARD Pattern Factory-Finished Foam-Back Tile | 5/16" x 6½" x 6½" individual units . . . ⅛" foam, 2 lb. density | Natural & Better Cabin & Better Cabin | Oak, Pecan Maple |
| ANTIQUE TEXTURED (Factory-Finished and Unfinished)—Kerfsawn Various colors available | 5/16" x 6" x 6" individual squares 5/16" x 6⅜" x 6⅜" individual squares 5/16" x 6½" x 6½" individual squares 5/16" x 11" x 11" 4 equal alternating squares | Select Natural & Better Select & Better (Par & Better) Rustic Fireside | Red Oak & White Oak Red Oak & White Oak |
| ANTIQUE TEXTURED (Factory-Finished and Unfinished)—Wire brushed Various colors available | 5/16" x 6⅜" x 6⅜" 5/16" x 6½" x 6½" individual squares | Natural & Better Cabin | Oak |
| MONTICELLO Pattern Unfinished—Paper-Faced— Pre-Finished, Mesh-Back | 5/16" x 6" x 6" individual squares used with 5/16" x ⅞" x 8" pickets 5/16" x 13¼" x 13¼" 4 equal alternating squares 5/16" x 13⅛" x 13⅛" (Factory Finished) | Select & Better (Par & Better) Rustic Natural & Better | Angelique (Guiana Teak) Red Oak, White Oak Black Walnut Ash, Maple |
| HADDON HALL Pattern Unfinished—Paper-Faced— Pre-Finished, Mesh-Back | 5/16" x 14¼" x 14¼" 5/16" x 13¼" x 13¼" 4 equal squares 5/16" x 13⅛" x 13⅛" (Factory Finished) | Select & Better (Par & Better) Rustic Natural & Better | Angelique (Guiana Teak) Red Oak, White Oak Black Walnut |
| HERRINGBONE Pattern Unfinished—Paper-Faced | 5/16" x 2" x 12" individual slats 5/16" x 14⅛" x 18⅛" (Approximate overall) 2 - "V" shape courses wide and 11 slats long | Select & Better (Par & Better) | Angelique (Guiana Teak) Red Oak, White Oak Black Walnut |
| SAXONY Pattern Unfinished—Paper-Faced | 5/16" x 19" x 19" 4 equal squares on diagonal and 8 equal half squares | Select & Better (Par & Better) | Angelique (Guiana Teak) Red Oak, White Oak |
| CANTERBURY Pattern Unfinished—Paper-Faced Pre-Finished, Mesh-Back | 5/16" x 13¼" x 13¼" 4 equal alternating squares with diagonal center slats 5/16" x 13⅛" x 13⅛" | Select & Better (Par & Better) Natural & Better | Angelique (Guiana Teak) Red Oak, White Oak Black Walnut |
| RHOMBS Pattern Unfinished—Paper-Faced | Hexagonal Shape 5/16" x 15⅛" x 15⅛" 12 equal Rhomboids | Select & Better (Par & Better) Rustic | Red Oak & White Oak Angelique (Guiana Teak) Black Walnut |
| BASKET WEAVE Pattern Unfinished—Paper-Faced | 5/16" x 15-1/5" x 19" 4 runs of 3 slats and 5 slats alternating | Select & Better (Par & Better) | Angelique (Guiana Teak) Red Oak, White Oak Black Walnut |
| ITALIAN & DOMINO Pattern Unfinished—Paper-Faced | 5/16" x 19" x 19" 400 equal size pieces butt-jointed | Select & Better (Par & Better) | Black Walnut Angelique (Guiana Teak) Maple, Red Oak White Oak |

Pattern #1
Same length of any size

Pattern #2
Same length of any size

Pattern #3
Same length of any size

Pattern #4
Same length of any size

Pattern #5
Same length of any size

Pattern #6
Same length of any size

Pattern #7
Same length of any size

Pattern #8
Same length of any size

Pattern #9
Same length of any size

Pattern #10
36" and 18" lengths

Pattern #11
36" and 18" lengths

Pattern #12
Same length of any size

Pattern #13
36" and 9" lengths

Pattern #14
9" lengths

Pattern #15
18" and 9" lengths

Pattern #16
18" lengths

Pattern #17
36" and 9" lengths

Pattern #18
9" lengths

Pattern #19
36" and 9" lengths

Pattern #20
18" and 9" lengths

Pattern #21
36" and 27" lengths

Pattern #22
27" and 9" lengths

Pattern #23
Same length of any size

Pattern #24
36" and 9" lengths

Pattern #25
36" and 9" lengths

Pattern #26
36" and 9" lengths

Pattern #27
18" and 9" lengths

Pattern #28
36" and 9" lengths

Pattern #29
9" lengths

Pattern #31
27" and 9" lengths

## FLOORS AND FLOOR FINISHES
Wood Parquet and Plank Floor Patterns

5/16″ x 13-1/4″ x 13-1/4″

5/16″ x 13-1/4″ x 13-1/4″

5/16″ x 13-7/16″ x 13-7/16″

5/16″ x 18″ x 18″

5/16″ x 14-1/4″ x 14-1/4″

5/16″ x 14-1/8″ x 18-1/8″
Slat Length 4-3/4″

5/16″ x 16-1/4″ x 18-1/8″
Slat Length 5-1/2″

5/16″ x 19″ x 19″

5/16″ x 11″ x 11″

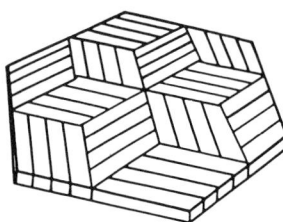

5/16″ x 15-1/8″ x 15-1/8″

5/16″ x 19″ x 19″

5/16″ x 19″ x 19″

5/16″ x 11″ x 16-1/2″

3/4″ x 3″, 5″, & 7″

3/4″ x 3″, 5″, & 7″

3/4″ x 3″, 5″, & 7″″*

3/4″ thick design formed
with 6″ x 6″ blocks and
2-1/4″ x 14-1/4″ pickets

3/4″ x 2-1/4″ single slat.
Lengths: 6-3/4″, 9″, 11-1/4″,
13-1/2″, 15-3/4″, 18″

3/4″ x 3″ single slat.
Lengths: 6″, 9″, 12″, 15″, 18″

3/4″ x 15″ x 15″

3/4″ x 16″ x 16″ Units

WOOD FLOOR OVER CONCRETE
WITH UNDERLAYER OF NAILING CONCRETE

WOOD FLOOR
OVER CONCRETE

FINISHED FLOOR DIRECTLY ON SLEEPERS
SET IN MASTIC CEMENT & NAILED TO CONCRETE

WOOD FLOOR OVER CONCRETE
WITH SUB-BASE OF SLEEPERS & SLEEPER FILL

WOOD BLOCK FLOOR
OVER CONCRETE

WOOD FLOOR
OVER CONCRETE IN MASTIC

CORK TILE FLOOR
OVER CONCRETE

WOOD FLOOR
APPLIED OVER EARTH

## FLOORS AND FLOOR FINISHES
### Floor Construction Sound Insulation

Sound insulation between an upper floor and the ceiling of a lower floor not only involves resistance of airborne sounds but also that of impact noises. Thus, impact noise control must be considered as well as the STC value. Impact noise is caused by an object striking or sliding along a wall or floor surface, such as by dropped objects, footsteps, or moving furniture. It may also be caused by the vibration of a dishwasher, bathtub, food-disposal apparatus, or other equipment. In all instances, the floor is set into vibration by the impact or contact and sound is radiated from both sides of the floor.

A method of measuring impact noise has been developed and is commonly expressed as the *impact noise ratings (INR)*. The greater the positive value of the INR, the more resistant is the floor to impact noise transfer. For example, an INR of −2 is better than one of −17, and one of +5 INR is a further improvement in resistance to impact noise transfer.

Figure 8 shows STC and approximate INR(db) values for several types of floor constructions. Figure 8A, perhaps a minimum floor assembly with tongued-and-grooved floor and 3/8-in gypsum board ceiling, has an STC value of 30 and an approximate INR value of −18. This is improved somewhat by the construction shown in Fig. 8B, and still further by the combination of materials in Fig. 8C.

The value of isolating the ceiling joists from a gypsum lath and plaster ceiling by means of spring clips is illustrated in Fig. 9A. An STC value of 52 and an approximate INR value of −2 result.

Foam-rubber padding and carpeting improve both the STC and the INR values. The STC value increases from 31 to 45 and the approximate INR from −17 to +5 (Fig. 9B and C). This can likely be further improved by using an isolated ceiling finish with spring clips. The use of sound-deadening board and a lamination of gypsum board for the ceiling would also improve resistance to sound transfer.

An economical construction similar to (but an improvement over) Fig. 9C, with a STC value of 48 and an approximate INR of +18, consists of the following: (a) a pad and carpet over 5/8-in tongued-and-grooved plywood underlayment, (b) 3-in fiberglass insulating

| DETAIL | DESCRIPTION | ESTIMATED VALUES | |
|---|---|---|---|
| | | STC RATING | APPROX. INR |
| (16") 2 x 8 | FLOOR 7/8" T. & G. FLOORING CEILING 3/8" GYPSUM BOARD | 30 | −18 |
| 2 x 8 | FLOOR 3/4" SUBFLOOR 3/4" FINISH FLOOR CEILING 3/4" FIBERBOARD | 42 | −12 |
| 2 x 8 | FLOOR 3/4" SUBFLOOR 3/4" FINISH FLOOR CEILING 1/2" FIBERBOARD LATH 1/2" GYPSUM PLASTER 3/4" FIBERBOARD | 45 | −4 |

Fig. 8   Relative impact and sound transfer in floor-ceiling combinations (2- by 8-in joists).

batts between joists, (c) resilient channels spaced 24 in apart, across the bottom of the joists, and (d) ⅝-in gypsum board screwed to the bottom of the channels and finished with taped joints.

The use of separate floor joists with staggered ceiling joists below provides reasonable values but adds a good deal to construction costs. Separate joists with insulation between and a soundboard between subfloor and finish provide an STC rating of 53 and an approximate INR value of −3.

**Sound absorption** Design of the "quiet" house can incorporate another system of sound insulation, namely, sound absorption. Sound-absorbing materials can minimize the amount of noise by stopping the reflection of sound back into a room. Sound-absorbing materials do not necessarily have resistance to airborne sounds. Perhaps the most commonly used sound-absorbing materials is acoustic tile. Wood fiber or similar materials are used in the manufacture of the tile, which is usually processed to provide some fire resistance and designed with numerous tiny sound traps on the tile surfaces. These may consist of tiny drilled or punched holes, fissured surfaces, or a combination of both.

Acoustic tile is most often used in the ceiling and areas where it is not subjected to excessive mechanical damage, such as above a wall wainscoting. It is normally manufactured in sizes from 12 by 12 to 12 by 48 in. Thicknesses vary from ½ to ¾ in, and the tile is usually factory finished ready for application. Paint or other finishes which fill or cover the tiny holes or fissures for trapping sound will greatly reduce its efficiency.

Acoustic tile may be applied by a number of methods — to existing ceilings or any smooth surface with a mastic adhesive designed specifically for this purpose, or to furring strips nailed to the underside of the ceiling joists. Nailing or stapling tile is the normal application method in this system. It is also used with a mechanical suspension system involving small "H," "Z," or "T" members. Manufacturers' recommendations should be followed in application and finishing.

| DETAIL | DESCRIPTION | ESTIMATED VALUES | |
|---|---|---|---|
| | | STC RATING | APPROX. INR |
| A — 2 x 10, 16" | FLOOR<br>  ¾" SUBFLOOR<br>    (BUILDING PAPER)<br>  ¾" FINISH FLOOR<br>CEILING<br>  GYPSUM LATH AND<br>    SPRING CLIPS<br>  ½" GYPSUM PLASTER | 52 | −2 |
| B — 2 x 10 | FLOOR<br>  ⅝" PLYWOOD SUBFLOOR<br>  ½" PLYWOOD<br>    UNDERLAYMENT<br>  ⅛" VINYL-ASBESTOS<br>    TILE<br>CEILING<br>  ½" GYPSUM WALLBOARD | 31 | −17 |
| C — 2 x 10 | FLOOR<br>  ⅝" PLYWOOD SUBFLOOR<br>  ½" PLYWOOD<br>    UNDERLAYMENT<br>  FOAM RUBBER PAD<br>  ⅜" NYLON CARPET<br>CEILING<br>  ½" GYPSUM WALLBOARD | 45 | +5 |

**Fig. 9   Relative impact and sound transfer in floor-ceiling combinations (2- by 10-in joists).**

## FLOORS AND FLOOR FINISHES
Floor Construction Sound Insulation

# conventional wood floor joist systems for sound control

| FLOOR SYSTEM | FLOOR NUMBER | FLOOR COVERING |
|---|---|---|
| **conventional**<br><br>CARPET & PAD<br>⅝" PLYWOOD SUBFLOOR<br>2 x 8 JOISTS 16" O.C.<br>3" GLASS FIBER<br>**FLOOR NO. 3**<br><br>The basic construction is illustrated by floor No. 3 although floors 4 and 5 have 2"x10" joists and ½" subfloor. Except in floor No. 1, the ceiling is fire-resistive type gypsum board applied with screws to resilient channels 24" o.c. Standard carpet is 44-ounce (sq. yd.) gropoint over 40-ounce hair pad. | 1 | ⅛" vinyl asbestos tile on ⅜" plywood underlayment |
| | 2 | .075" vinyl sheet on ⅜" plywood underlayment |
| | 3 | Carpet and pad directly over subfloor |
| | 4 | ²⁵⁄₃₂" oak strip floor over subfloor |
| | 5 | Carpet and pad added to No. 4 |
| **conventional**<br>**With Floated Floor Over**<br><br>½" UNDERLAYMENT<br>½" SOUND BOARD<br>⅝" SUBFLOOR<br>2 x 10 JOISTS 16" O.C.<br>3" GLASS FIBER<br>**FLOOR NO. 8**<br><br>The basic construction is illustrated. Sound deadening board (15-18 p.c.f.) is laid over a ⅝" plywood subfloor, with or without stapling, and ½" T&G underlayment grade plywood glued over the sound board. The ceiling is ⅝" fire-resistive type gypsum board on resilient channels; absorptive material is 3-inch thick glass fiber batts | 6 | Wood block (⁵⁄₁₆") laminated to underlayment |
| | 7 | Carpet and pad |
| | 8 | Vinyl flooring laminated to underlayment applied over sound board with 4-inch circular globs of glue |
| | 9 | Vinyl covering like 8 with sleepers glued between sound board and underlayment |
| | 10 | Oak strip flooring (²⁵⁄₃₂") nailed to 2x3 sleepers glued over sound board strips 1⅞" glass fiber between sleepers |
| | 11 | Vinyl flooring (0.07") on ⅝" T&G plywood underlayment glued to 2x2 sleepers glued to subfloor 16" o.c. Sand fill over subfloor to depth of sleepers (1½"). Balance as in basic construction |
| **conventional**<br>**With lightweight Concrete or Gypsum Cement Added**<br><br>**FLOOR NO. 14**<br>1⅝" LT. WT. CONCRETE<br>⅝" SUBFLOOR<br>3" MINERAL WOOL<br>2 x 10 JOISTS 16" O.C.<br>⅝" GYPSUM BOARD ON R.C.<br><br>The basic construction is illustrated by floor No. 14. The floor topping is 1⅝" thick cellular (foamed) concrete (100 p.c.f.). Ceilings are fire-resistive type gypsum board on resilient channels, 24 inches o.c. Absorptive material is 3" thick mineral wool batts. Floor coverings for impact tests are 44-ounce carpet over 40-ounce hair pad or vinyl floor covering, approximately 0.07 inches thick. Note variations from basic construction drawn in plans 12-16. | 12 | Ceiling nailed to joists; no absorptive material; with carpet and pad........................ |
| | 13 | Ceiling nailed to joists; 3" glass fiber with carpet and pad........................ |
| | 14 | **Basic construction**—(no floor covering) with carpet and pad........................ |
| | 15 | Add ½" sound board between concrete and subfloor with vinyl tile........................<br>with carpet and pad........................ |
| | 16 | Basic construction—but with ¾" thick gypsum concrete in place of 1⅝" thick cellular concrete; ½" gypsum ceiling without floor covering........................ |

The improved resistance to airborne sound transmission gained by isolating the ceiling with resilient channels and adding absorptive material is evident by comparing floors 2 to 5 with No. 1. A 10-point increase in STC reduces the loudness of transmitted noise by one-half. Improved resistance to impact noise transmission is gained by adding carpet and pad as is evident by comparing floor No. 3 with No. 2 or floor No. 5 with 4. An IIC of 51 is often recommended as an acceptable level of impact insulation.

*Standard toe base*

*No-toe base:* Adds a decorative touch to carpeted interiors.

*Butt toe base:* Engineered to butt precisely to ⅛" floor coverings.

*Long toe base:* For special applications. Features a longer toe extending 1" to cover wide irregularities between floor and wall.

**TABLE 1   Cove Base Specifications**

| Type | Sizes available |
|------|-----------------|
| Standard toe base | 2½"   4"   6" |
| No-toe base | 2½"   4"   6" |
| Butt toe base | 4"   6" |
| Long toe base | 4" |

Length: 48"

5/8" Standard Toe Base   No-Toe Base   Butt Toe Base 5/8"   Long Toe Base 1"

Dimensionally stable. Won't shrink.

Sealing lip ensures tight fit.

1/8" thickness.

Flexible. Easy to install.

Ribbed back for long-lasting adhesion.

**TABLE 2   Corner Specifications**

| Type | Length of return | Sizes available |
|------|------------------|-----------------|
| Inside/outside | 2¼" | 2½"   4"   6" |
| Underlap outside | 3" (with underlap) | 4" |
| No-toe outside | 2¼" | 2½"   4" |
| Long toe outside | 2¼" | 4" |

IC Inside   OC Outside   NT OC No-Toe Outside   LT OC Long Toe Outside

UL OC Underlap Outside

## FLOORS AND FLOOR FINISHES

**Ceramic Tile Patterns**

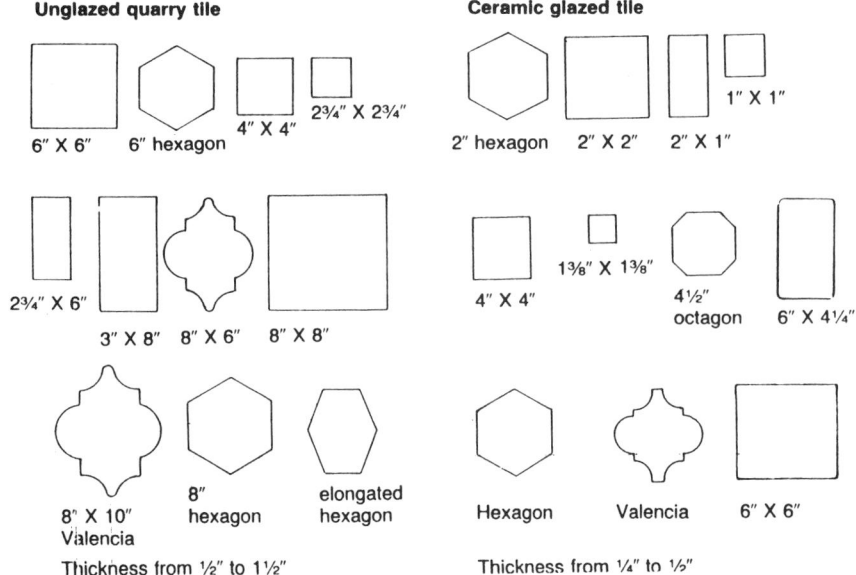

**Fig. 10   Ceramic tile shapes.**

**Fig. 11   Ceramic tile patterns.**

**Serpentine Circles (8 Ft. Module)** Quantity for 100 sq. feet: 3.2 pcs. circle; 70 pcs. small wedge; 256 pcs. medium wedge; 500 pcs. large wedge

**Serpentine Circles (6 Ft. Module)** Quantity for 100 sq. feet: 5.7 pcs. circle; 126 pcs. small wedge; 460 pcs. medium wedge; 280 pcs. large wedge

**Meandering Serpentine** Quantity for 100 sq. feet: 3 pcs. circle; 58 pcs. small wedge; 220 pcs. medium wedge; 610 pcs. large wedge

**Serpentine Fan** Quantity for 100 sq. feet: 106 pcs. small wedge; 290 pcs. medium wedge; 484 pcs. large wedge

# FLOORS AND FLOOR FINISHES

**Ceramic Tile Patterns**

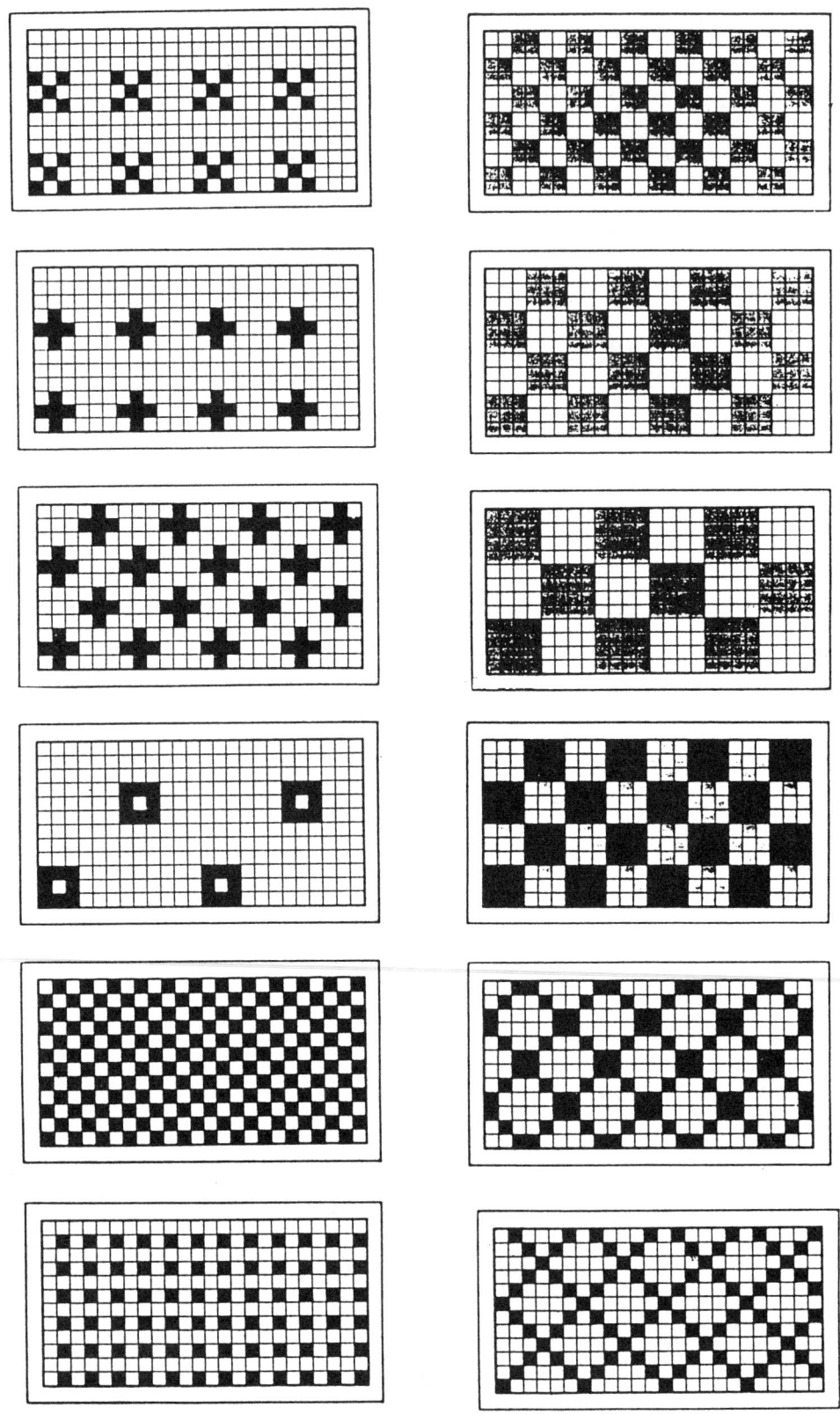

Fig. 12   1×1 overall patterns.

Fig. 13   1 × 1 six-inch borders.

Fig. 14   1 × 1 twelve-inch borders.

## FLOORS AND FLOOR FINISHES
**Ceramic Tile Patterns**

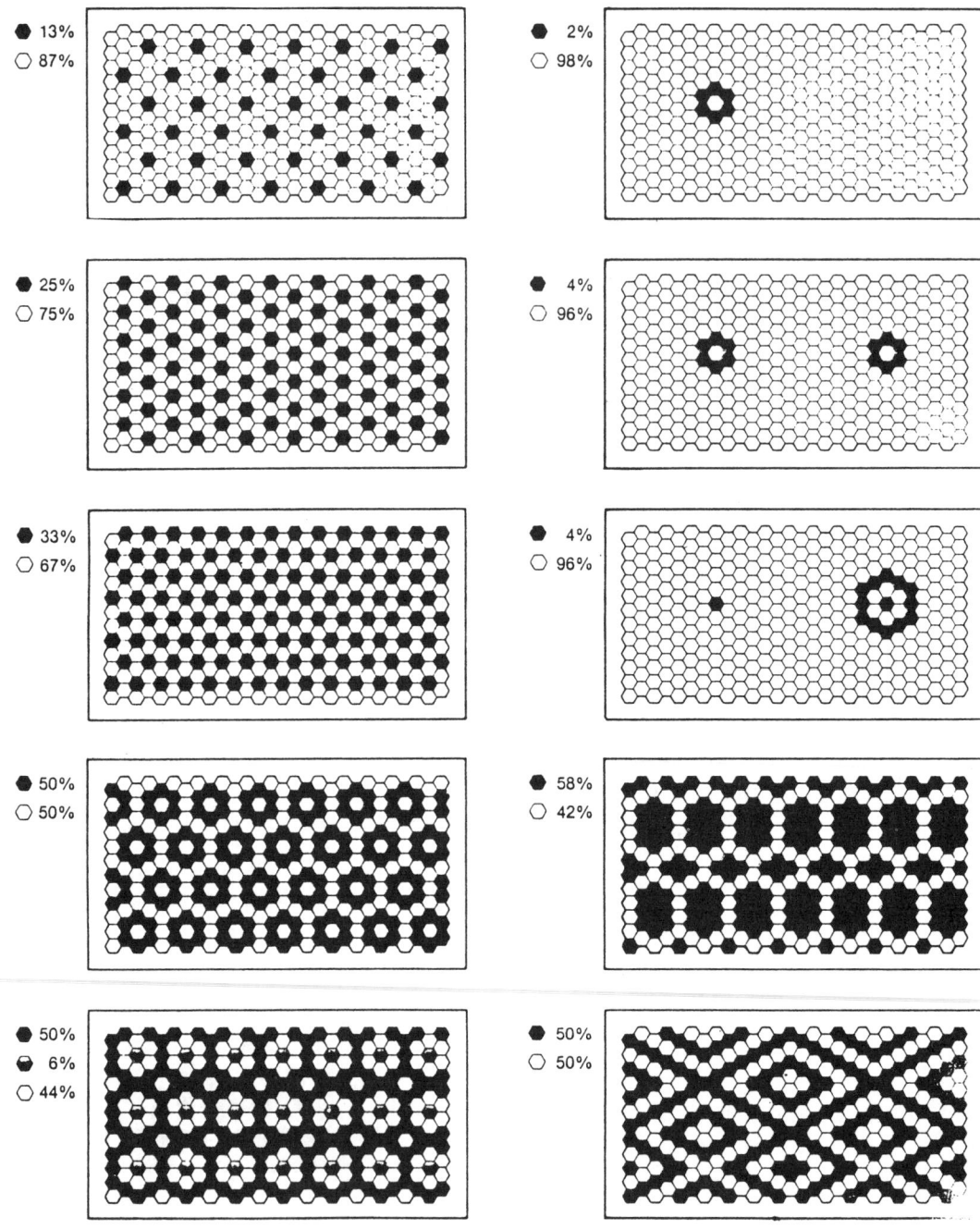

**Fig. 15** 1" hex overall patterns. All patterns master-set 12" × 24" sheets.

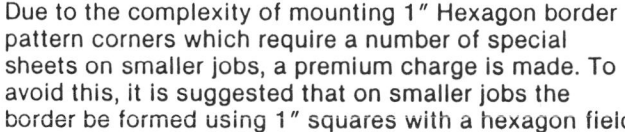

1″ Square Border with
Hexagon Field

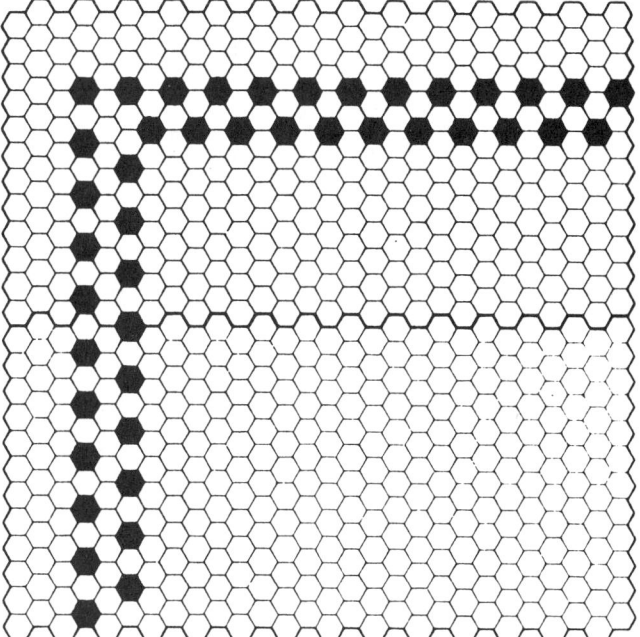

Due to the complexity of mounting 1″ Hexagon border pattern corners which require a number of special sheets on smaller jobs, a premium charge is made. To avoid this, it is suggested that on smaller jobs the border be formed using 1″ squares with a hexagon field.

If a Hexagon border is required, you must provide a plan of the area with dimensions because the Hexagon configuration precludes interchanging sheets. We will provide specific sheets for those areas and setting plans.

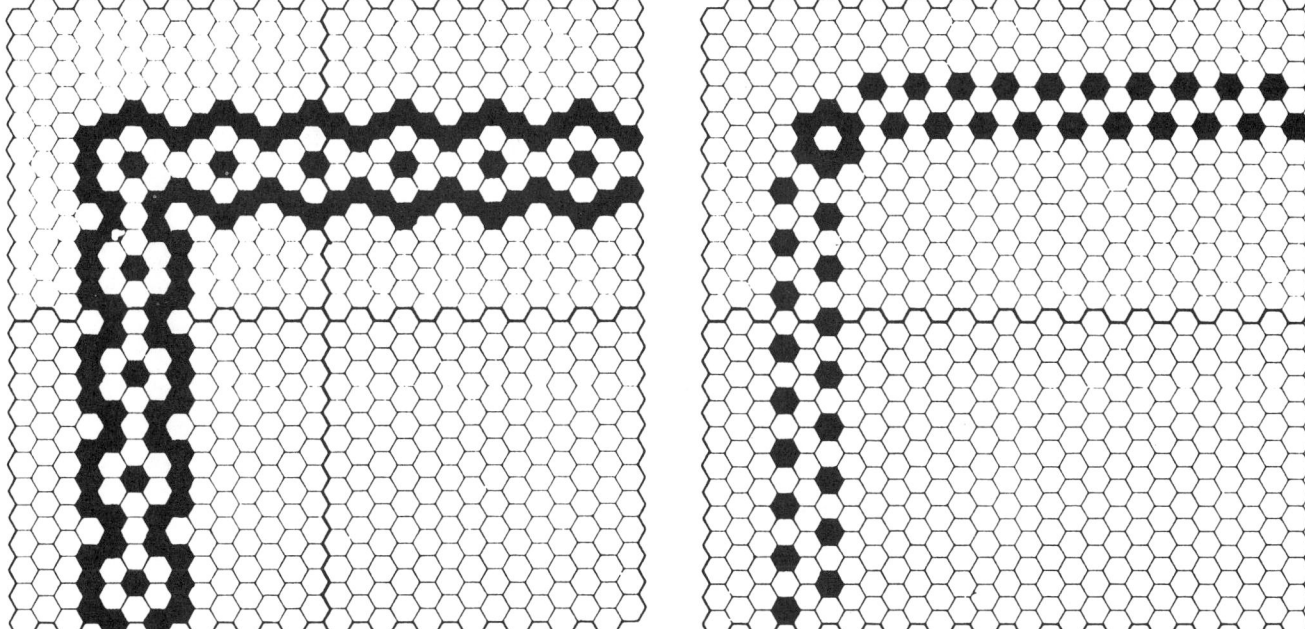

Note that on three of these border patterns a full sheet is used for the corner. Some designs, however, will require a half sheet for the corner as shown in SB-1404. In this case a right and left corner will be on one sheet and the sheet is cut in half before placement.

**Fig. 16    1″ hex border patterns. All patterns master-set 12″ × 24″ sheets.**

# FLOORS AND FLOOR FINISHES

**Ceramic Tile Patterns**

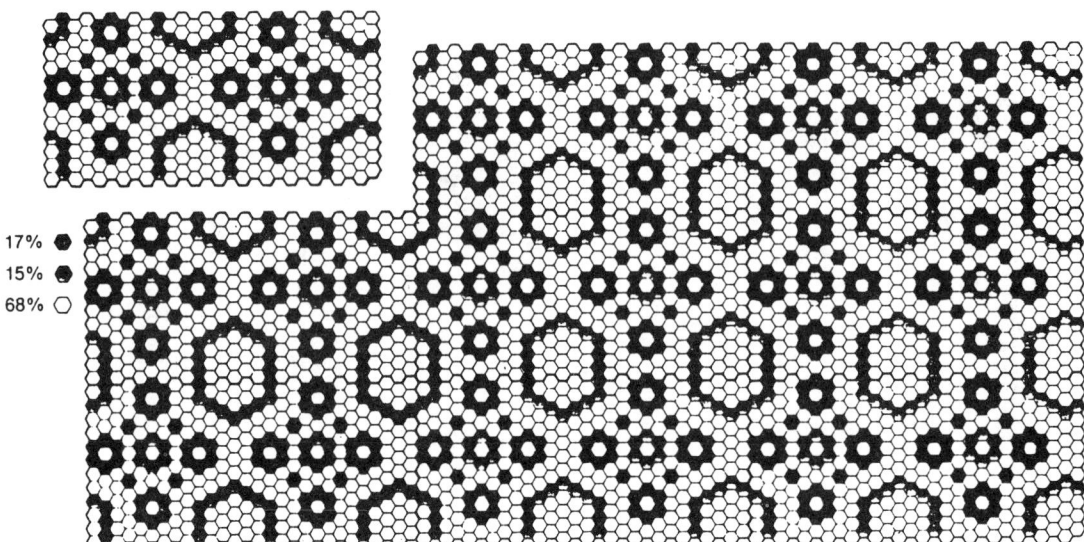

17% ●
15% ●
68% ○

Single sheet repeat pattern. Repeat for overall pattern.

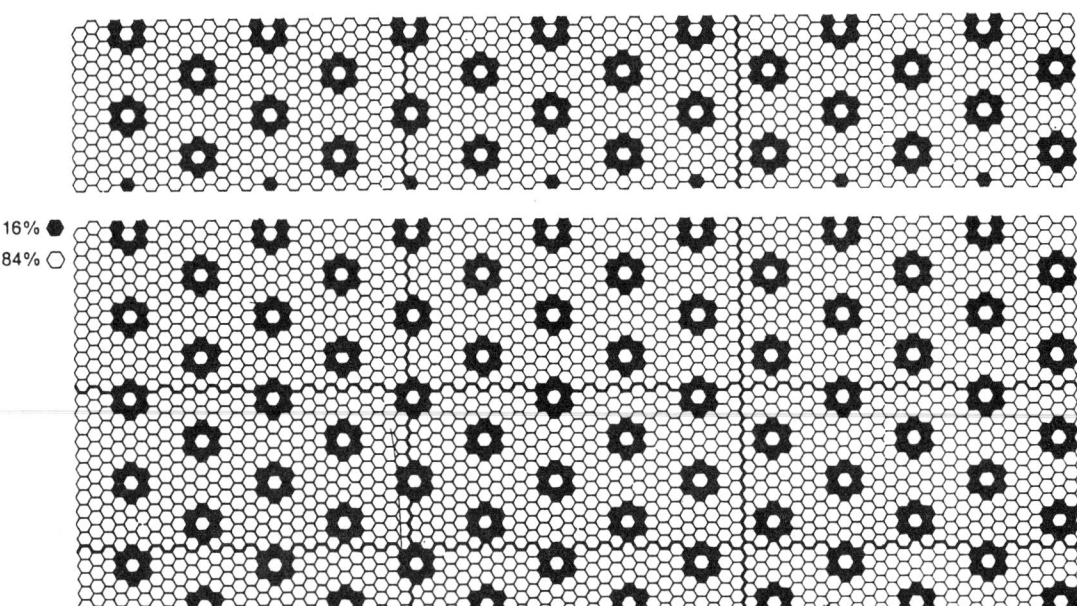

16% ●
84% ○

Three sheet repeat pattern. Three different sheets complete the pattern, then repeat throughout.

**Fig. 17   1″ hex overall patterns. All patterns master-set 12″ × 24″ sheets.**

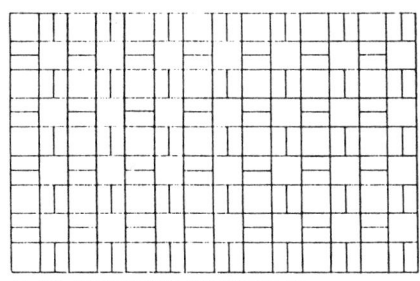

QP-6101 ALTERNATING CHECKERBOARD
Shown: 3⅞" × 8" (50%), 8" × 8" (50%)

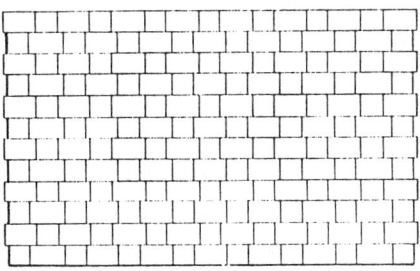

QP-6102 FLEMISH BOND
Shown: 6" × 6" (40%), 6" × 9" (60%)
Also Use: 3⅞" × 3⅞", 3⅞" × 8", or 6" × 6", 6" × 12⅛"

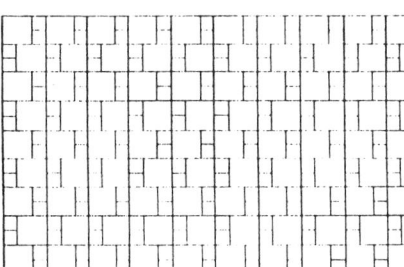

QP-6103 FLEMISH SQUARE BOND
Shown: 3⅞" × 3⅞" (33⅓%), 8" × 8" (66⅔%)

QP-6104 BROKEN JOINT
Shown: 6" × 9" (100%)
Also Use: 3⅞" × 8" or 6" × 12⅛"

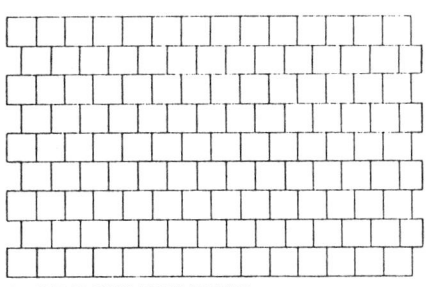

QP-6105 BROKEN JOINT SQUARE
Shown: 8" × 8" (100%)
Also Use: 6" × 6"

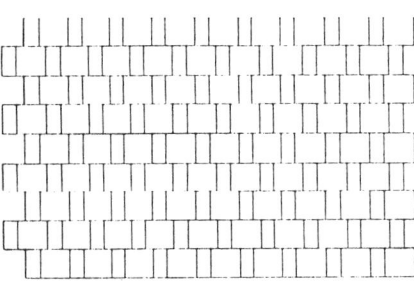

QP-6106 BARRED SQUARE
Shown: 3⅞" × 8" (33⅓%), 8" × 8" (66⅔%)

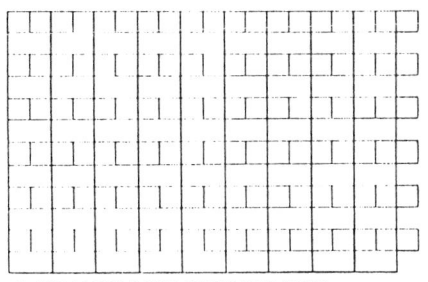

QP-6107 ALTERNATING STRIPE VARIATION
Shown: 6" × 6" (50%), 6" × 12⅛" (50%)
Also Use: 3⅞" × 3⅞", 3⅞" × 8"

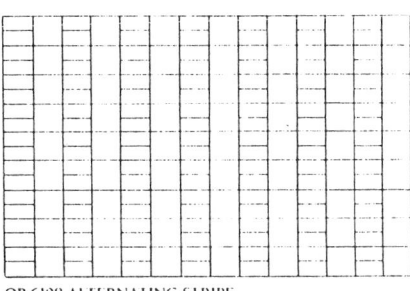

QP-6108 ALTERNATING STRIPE
Shown: 3⅞" × 8" (50%), 8" × 8" (50%)

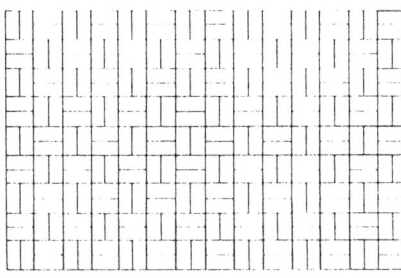

QP-6109 BASKETWEAVE
Shown: 3⅞" × 8" (100%)
Also Use: 6" × 12⅛"

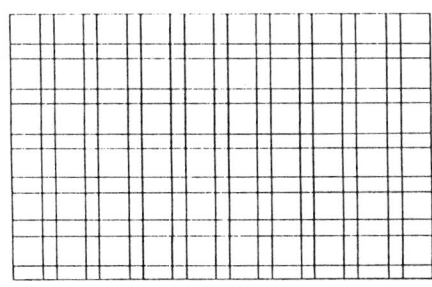

QP-6110 FORMAL RANDOM
Shown: 3⅞" × 3⅞" (11.2%), 3⅞" × 8" (44.4%),
8" × 8" (44.4%)

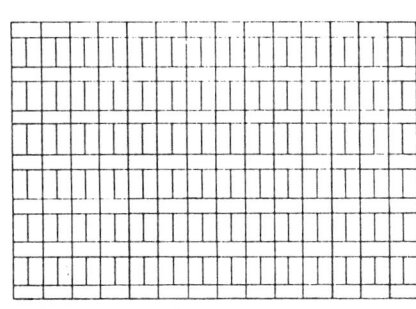

QP-6111 RAILROAD BOND
Shown: 3⅞" × 8" (100%)
Also Use: 6" × 12⅛"

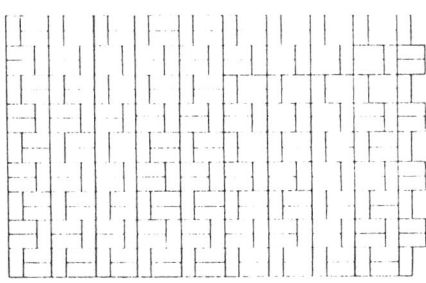

QP-6112 BASKETWEAVE VARIATION
Shown: 3⅞" × 8" (100%)
Also Use: 6" × 12⅛"

## FLOORS AND FLOOR FINISHES
**Basic Quarry Tile Patterns**

**QP-6221 SPIRAL**
Shown: 3¾" × 8" (66⅔%), 8" × 8" (33⅓%)

**QP-6222 INTERLOCKING SPIRAL**
Shown: 3¾" × 8" (100%)
Also Use: 6" × 12⅛"

**QP-6223 BLOCK RANDOM**
Shown: 3¾" × 3¾" (15%), 3¾" × 8" (41%)
8" × 8" (44%)

**QP-6224 VERTICAL HERRINGBONE**
Shown: 3¾" × 8" (100%)
Also Use: 6" × 12⅛"

**QP-6225 PINWHEEL**
Shown: 3¾" × 3¾" (11.1%), 3¾" × 8" (88.9%)
Also Use: 6" × 6", 6" × 12¼"

**QP-6226 BLOCK RANDOM SQUARE**
Shown: 3¾" × 3¾" (25%), 3¾" × 8" (50%)
8" × 8" (25%)

**QP-6227 DOUBLE HERRINGBONE**
Shown: 3¾" × 8" (100%)
Also Use: 6" × 12⅛"

**QP-6228 BLOCK RANDOM VARIATION**
Shown: 3¾" × 3¾" (11.2%), 3¾" × 8" (44.4%),
8" × 8" (44.4%)

**QP-6229 RANDOM SQUARE**
Shown: 3¾" × 3¾" (19⅕%), 8" × 8" (80⅘%)

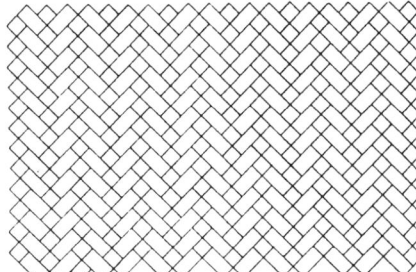

**QP-6230 DIAMOND HERRINGBONE**
Shown: 3¾" × 3¾" (33⅓%), 3¾" × 8" (66⅔%)
Also Use: 6" × 6", 6" × 12¼"

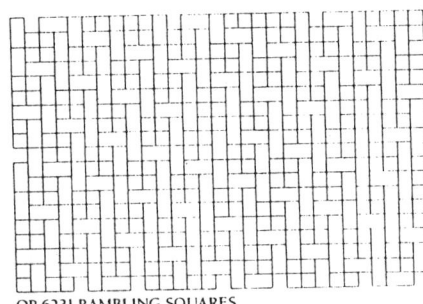

**QP-6231 RAMBLING SQUARES**
Shown: 3¾" × 3¾" (40%), 3¾" × 8" (60%)
Also Use: 6" × 6", 6" × 12¼"

**QP-6232 DIAGONAL STRIPE**
Shown: 3¾" × 8" (50%), 8" × 8" (50%)

**FLOORS**

**STAIRS**

# Wood Subfloor

## Cement Mortar

## Organic Adhesive

## Cement Mortar

CERAMIC TILE
BOND COAT
MORTAR BED NOMINAL 1 1/4"
REINFORCING
CLEAVAGE MEMBRANE
SUBFLOOR

CERAMIC TILE
ADHESIVE
DOUBLE WOOD FLOOR

CERAMIC TILE
BOND COAT
MORTAR BED

**CONCRETE STAIRS**

CERAMIC TILE
BOND COAT
MORTAR BED
REINFORCING

PAN

**METAL STAIRS**

CERAMIC TILE
BOND COAT
MORTAR BED
SCRATCH COAT
METAL LATH
WATERPROOF MEMBRANE

**WOOD STAIRS**          3/4" - 1 1/4"

**Recommended use**

■ over all wood floors that are structurally sound

**Recommended use**

■ over wood floors exposed to residential traffic only

# Wood Subfloor

## Epoxy Mortar and Grout

# Glass Mesh Mortar Units

## Dry-Set Mortar or Latex-Portland Cement

CERAMIC TILE
EPOXY GROUT
EPOXY MORTAR BOND COAT
GAP BETWEEN PLYWOOD SHEETS
DOUBLE WOOD FLOOR

CERAMIC TILE
DRY-SET OR LATEX-PORTLAND CEMENT MORTAR BOND COAT
GLASS MESH MORTAR UNIT
PLYWOOD SUBFLOOR

**Recommended uses**

■ over wood floors where resistance to foot traffic in better residential, normal commercial, and light institutional use is desired with thin-set construction
■ where water, chemical, and stain resistance is desired
■ for tilework exposed to prolonged high temperatures, use high temperature, chemical resistant epoxy mortar, and grout

**Recommended uses**

■ over structurally sound plywood where lightweight construction is a factor
■ where water resistance is desired
■ eliminates necessity of recessing subfloor to accommodate portland cement mortar bed

**CEILINGS, SOFFITS**

CERAMIC TILE
BOND COAT
MORTAR BED ON SUSPENDED METAL LATH & SCRATCH COAT, CONCRETE, OR GLASS MESH MORTAR UNIT

**Recommended uses**

■ over a mortar bed
■ over glass mesh mortar units
■ over clean, sound, dimensionally stable concrete
■ over metal lath attached directly to the bottom of wood joists or trusses; spacing not to exceed 16" on center

# FLOORS AND FLOOR FINISHES
### Ceramic Tile on Concrete Slab Floor Construction Details

## CONCRETE SUBFLOOR

### Cement Mortar Cleavage Membrane

- CERAMIC TILE
- BOND COAT
- MORTAR BED NOMINAL 1¼"
- REINFORCING
- CLEAVAGE MEMBRANE

**Recommended use**
- over structural floors subject to bending and deflection

**Requirements**
- reinforcing mesh mandatory
- motor bed thickness to be uniform, nominal 1¼" thick

### Cement Mortar, Bonded

- CERAMIC TILE
- BOND COAT
- MORTAR BED NOMINAL 1¼"

**Recommended uses**
- on slab-on-grade construction where no bending stresses occur
- on properly cured structural slabs where deflection does not exceed 1/360 of span
- on properly cured structural slabs of limited area

### Dry-Set Mortar or Latex-Portland Cement Mortar

- CERAMIC TILE
- DRY-SET OR LATEX-PORTLAND CEMENT MORTAR BOND COAT

**Recommended uses**
- on plane, clean concrete
- on slab-on-grade construction where no bending stresses occur

### Cement Mortar Epoxy or Furan Grout

- CERAMIC TILE
- EPOXY OR FURAN GROUT
- BOND COAT
- MORTAR BED NOMINAL 1¼"
- REINFORCING
- CLEAVAGE MEMBRANE

**Recommended uses**
- with tile set by Method F111 requiring good stain resistance and resistance to erosion caused by occasional contact with mild chemicals such as found in commercial dining areas, photographic dark rooms, public toilets, public foyers, etc.
- for use with quarry tile and paver tile

### Dry-Set Mortar, Epoxy or Furan Grout

- CERAMIC TILE
- EPOXY OR FURAN GROUT
- DRY-SET OR LATEX-PORTLAND CEMENT MORTAR BOND COAT

**Recommended uses**
- with tile set by Method F112 or Method F113 requiring good stain resistance and resistance to erosion caused by occasional contact with mild chemicals such as found in commercial dining areas, photographic dark rooms, public toilets, public foyers, etc.
- for use with quarry tile and paver tile

### Organic Adhesive or Epoxy Adhesive

- CERAMIC TILE
- ADHESIVE

**Recommended use**
- for use over concrete floors in residential construction only; for heavier service select Method F113

## WATERPROOF MEMBRANE

### Cement Mortar Bed

- CERAMIC TILE
- BOND COAT
- MORTAR BED NOMINAL 1¼"
- REINFORCING
- WATERPROOF MEMBRANE
- CONCRETE OR WOOD SUBFLOOR

**Recommended use**
- wherever a waterproof interior floor is required in conjunction with ceramic tile installed on a portland cement mortar bed

### Thin-Set

- CERAMIC TILE
- DRY-SET OR LATEX-PORTLAND CEMENT MORTAR BOND COAT
- WATERPROOF MEMBRANE: SHEET OR LIQUID APPLIED
- MEMBRANE BOND COAT
- CONCRETE OR CURED MORTAR BED

**Recommended use**
- wherever a waterproof interior floor is required in conjunction with ceramic tile installed in a thin-set method

## FLOORS AND FLOOR FINISHES
### Ceramic Tile on Concrete Slab Floor Construction Details

- CERAMIC TILE
- EPOXY GROUT
- EPOXY MORTAR
- BOND COAT

**Recommended uses**

- for setting and grouting ceramic mosaics, quarry tile, and paver tile
- where moderate chemical exposure and severe cleaning methods are used, such as in commercial kitchens, dairies, breweries, food processing plants, etc.
- for tilework exposed to prolonged high temperatures, use high-temperature, chemical-resistant epoxy mortar and grout

- CERAMIC TILE
- EPOXY GROUT
- EPOXY MORTAR
- BOND COAT
- MORTAR BED NOMINAL 1¼"

**Recommended uses**

- where leveling of subfloor is required
- for setting and grouting ceramic mosaics, quarry tile, and paver tile
- where moderate chemical exposure and severe cleaning methods are used, such as in commerical kitchens, dairies, breweries, food processing plants, etc.
- for tilework exposed to prolonged high temperatures, use high-temperature chemical resistant epoxy mortar and grout

- 1¼" THICK PACKING HOUSE TILE
- ACID RESISTANT GROUT AND MORTAR
- ¼" THICK ACID RESISTANT MEMBRANE
- MORTAR BED OR CONCRETE FILL

**Recommended use**

- for setting 1¼" thick packing house tile in areas of continuous or severe chemical exposure where special protection against leakage or damage to concrete subfloor is required

- CERAMIC TILE
- FURAN GROUT
- RESIN MORTAR
- BOND COAT

**Recommended uses**

- for setting and grouting quarry tile and paver tile
- in kitchens, chemical plants, etc.

### EXPANSION JOINTS
**Vertical and Horizontal**

- CERAMIC TILE
- REINFORCED MORTAR BED
- CLEAVAGE OR WATERPROOF MEMBRANE
- CONCRETE OR WOOD
- SEALANT
- COMPRESSIBLE BACK-UP

- CERAMIC TILE
- BOND COAT
- CONCRETE OR MASONRY
- SEALANT
- BOND BREAKER TAPE
- BACK-UP STRUCTURAL JOINT

- SEALANT DEPTH 1/2 WIDTH
- ROUNDED BACK-UP WITH NO BOND TO SEALANT
- COMPRESSIBLE BACK-UP
- WIDTH 4 TIMES EXPECTED MOVEMENT

- CERAMIC TILE
- MORTAR BED
- CONCRETE
- SEALANT & BACK-UP
- SAW-CUT CONTROL JOINT COLD JOINT

- CERAMIC TILE
- BOND COAT
- CONCRETE
- SEALANT & BACK-UP
- SAW-CUT CONTROL JOINT
- CONTROLED CRACK OR CONTROL JOINT

**Use these details for control, contraction, and isolation joints**

## FLOORS AND FLOOR FINISHES
### Raised Computer Room Floors

ELEVATION FLOOR PROJECTION WITH CLOSURE PLATE AND NOSING

TYPICAL ELEVATED FLOOR

ELEVATED FLOOR AGAINST MASONRY WALL

ELEVATED FLOOR-A CONTINUATION OF EXISTING FLOOR

PARTITION EDGE OF ELEVATED FLOOR

ANGLE CLIP

AIR GRILLE

# DOORS

### Hollow Metal Door Construction

The design, specification, and detailing of a door can have serious consequences for functional considerations such as accessibility and sound transmission. The door is also one of the most important architectural elements with respect to design image and aesthetics. A door can be a major part of design expression: a monumental door to a church or synagogue, the main entrance to a residence, the doors to a corporate board room — all of these doors have symbolic importance.

Doors come in a variety of standard heights, widths, and thicknesses, yet they may also be custom designed, assume a variety of shapes and forms, and be constructed with a variety of materials. The design, specification, and detailing of a door is, in fact, a rather complex task.

A door is typically set within a frame or jamb, but may also be installed within a wall without a frame or jamb. The frame/jamb interface between door and wall partition is another area requiring special attention by the designer.

The design of a door is never complete without the specification of hardware. Hinges, locksets, closers, stops, and thresholds are but a few of the hardware elements that a designer must consider.

This section on doors provides the designer with extensive information on door types, materials, door frames, and materials and methods of door construction and installation. Details show doors and frames installed in all types of walls and partitions, including wood and metal stud, masonry, concrete, and glass.

Of special interest to the designer are examples of less standard door types such as elevator doors, sliding pocket doors, and fabric-covered doors. The majority of the details in this section are taken from the actual working drawings of successfully executed projects.

### PANEL CONSTRUCTION

There are two basic types of panel construction:

*Steel stiffened:* Face sheets supported by steel stiffeners, which are channels, Z-shaped sections, hat-shaped sections, or similar members, positioned vertically. Sheets are attached to these members by spot welding.

*Laminated core:* Sandwich construction employing a core of impregnated kraft paper honeycomb, plastic foam, or structural mineral blocking, to which the steel face sheets are laminated, using a structural adhesive.

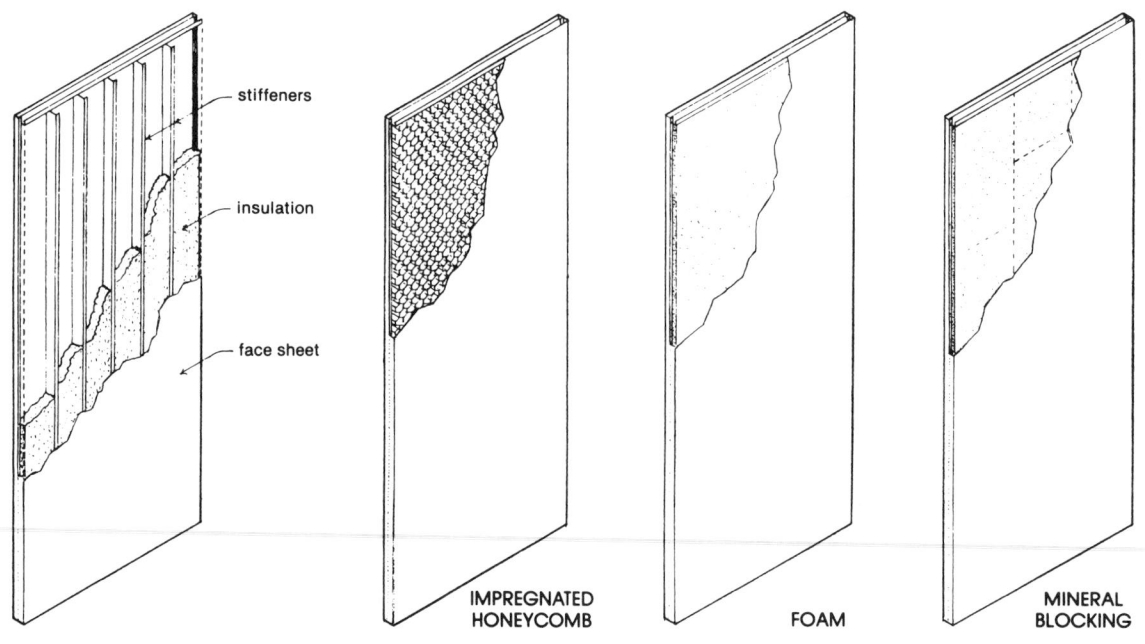

STEEL STIFFENERS — stiffeners, insulation, face sheet

LAMINATED CONSTRUCTIONS — IMPREGNATED HONEYCOMB, FOAM, MINERAL BLOCKING

CHANNEL    ZEE    OFFSET CHANNEL

HAT SECTIONS    HAT SECTIONS

**REPRESENTATIVE STIFFENER SECTIONS**
Other sections used by some manufacturers

## Types of Construction

The four basic types of construction for hollow metal swing doors are illustrated and identified in Fig. 1. The type usually specified in commercial work is the continuously welded edge seam construction, Type A, and it is this type which is the basis of NAAMM Standard HMMA 861.

Most custom hollow metal doors are of the full flush type with continuously welded edges (Type A). When glazed openings, recessed panels, or louvers are to be provided, they are built into the door during fabrication, rather than being cut out of a flush panel door by field modification.

Fire-rated doors may differ in certain details of construction; see NAAMM Standard HMMA 850, Fire-Rated Hollow Metal Doors and Frames.

| FULL FLUSH WITH CONTIN-UOUSLY WELDED EDGE SEAMS (NAAMM STANDARD HMMA 861) | FULL FLUSH WITH UNFILLED EDGE SEAMS (NAAMM STANDARD HMMA 860) | FLUSH STILE AND RAIL | RECESSED PANEL(S) (MANY VARIATIONS) |

**Fig. 1** The top edge of Types A and B doors may have only an inverted channel (standard construction) or may have an additional closing channel. Types C and D have tubular rails and stiles, with no edge seams. S = stile (hinge stile is stile at edge where hinges or pivots are located; lock stile is stile in which a lock or latch is installed; and meeting stile is stile adjacent to another door, in a pair of doors). TR = top rail. CR = center rail. BR = bottom rail. P = panel. P/G = panel or glass.

## DOORS
**Hollow Metal Door Types**

**DIMENSIONS AND HINGE LOCATIONS**

Hinge locations shown represent the industry standard,
but may be altered to suit requirements.

### MOST COMMON SIZES FOR 1¾-INCH THICK DOORS*

| Width of Opening | Height of Opening | | | | |
|---|---|---|---|---|---|
| 2'0" | 6'8" | 7'0" | 7'2" | 7'10" | 8'0" |
| 2'4" | 6'8" | 7'0" | 7'2" | 7'10" | 8'0" |
| 2'6" | 6'8" | 7'0" | 7'2" | 7'10" | 8'0" |
| 2'8" | 6'8" | 7'0" | 7'2" | 7'10" | 8'0" |
| 3'0" | 6'8" | 7'0" | 7'2" | 7'10" | 8'0" |
| 3'4" | 6'8" | 7'0" | 7'2" | 7'10" | 8'0" |
| 3'6" | 6'8" | 7'0" | 7'2" | 7'10" | 8'0" |
| 3'8" | 6'8" | 7'0" | 7'2" | 7'10" | 8'0" |
| 4'0" | 6'8" | 7'0" | 7'2" | 7'10" | 8'0" |

*Sizes shown are for single doors only; for pairs of doors, use twice the width indicated.

OTHER DOOR SIZES: The sizes listed are those most commonly used, but custom hollow metal doors are available in any width, height and thickness desired. It is not uncommon to supply them in widths of 5' or more and/or heights of 10' or more. Standard doors, on the other hand, are generally available from inventory only in the most commonly used sizes.

LISTING DESIGNATION: Always preface the door listing with "SGL" or "PR," followed by the designation of the opening size. For example, a single flush door for a 4'0" × 8'0" frame opening is listed SGL 4080F, and a pair of flush doors for an 8'0" × 8'0" frame opening is listed as PR 8080F.

## REPRESENTATIVE DOOR DESIGNS

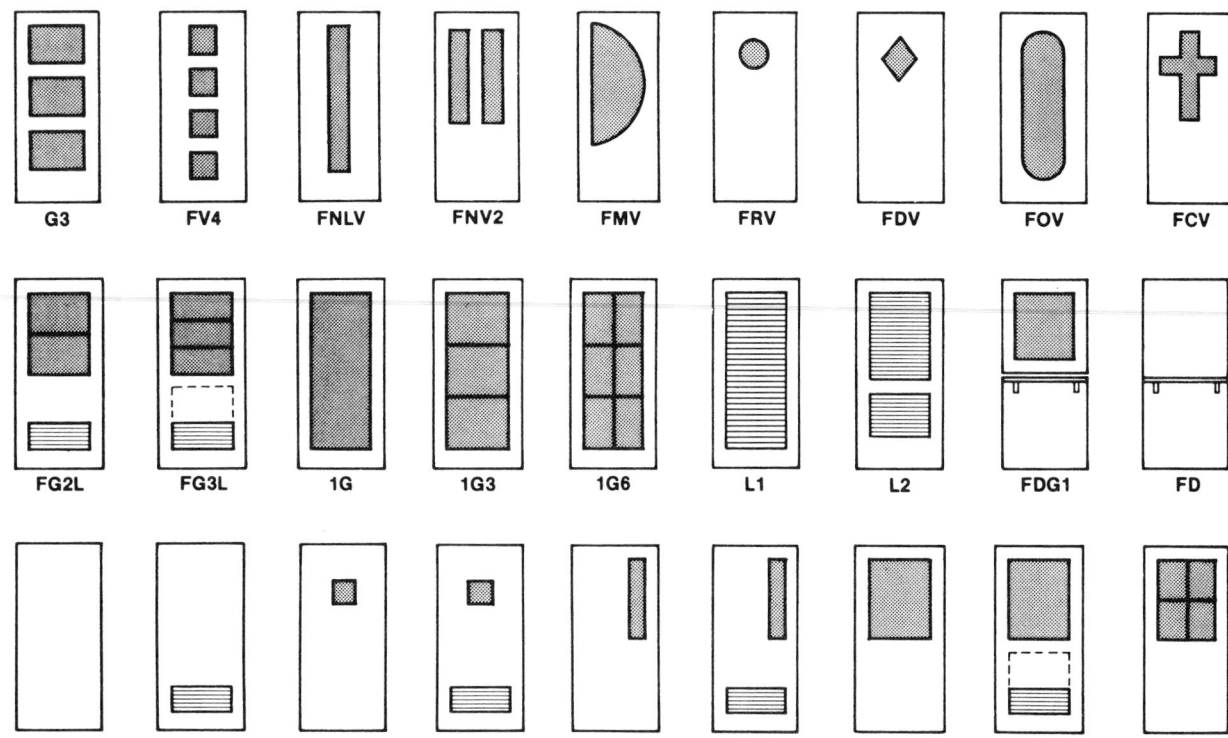

G3 · FV4 · FNLV · FNV2 · FMV · FRV · FDV · FOV · FCV

FG2L · FG3L · 1G · 1G3 · 1G6 · L1 · L2 · FDG1 · FD

F · FL · FV · FVL · FNV · FNVL · FG · FGL · FG4

NOTE: Some manufacturers may use differing designations for some designs

**TYPICAL HARDWARE PREPARATION**

internal
edge strip

7 ga. offset
plate

**A**
**BUTT
HINGE**

¼″ (6.4 mm)
std. backset

continuously
welded
invisible seam

KEY ELEVATIONS

14 ga. plate
each side

9 ga. offset clip

top channel

cutout for
closer as
req'd.

**H**
**MORTISED
CLOSER**
(CONCEALED IN DOOR)

7 ga. plate
welded to
top channel

cutout for
pivot arm

**B**
**TOP
PIVOT**

7 ga. offset
plate

cutout for
pivot arm

**C**
**INTERMEDIATE
PIVOT**

19 ga.
channels
flush with
cutout

**E**
**CYLINDER
LOCK**

**F**
**UNIT LOCK**

cutout for
pivot arm

7 ga. plate
welded to
bottom channel
— may be drilled, for
some types of pivot

**D**
**BOTTOM PIVOT**

ALL REINFORCEMENTS
SECURELY WELDED IN PLACE

14 ga.
plates

12 ga. offset
clip

lock
support
clips

**G**
**MORTISE
LOCK**

12 ga. offset
clip

NOTE: CUTOUTS AND/OR REINFORCEMENTS OF SIMILAR NATURE
ARE PROVIDED FOR ALL OTHER HARDWARE ITEMS SUCH AS FLUSH
BOLTS, SURFACE-MOUNTED CLOSERS, FIRE EXIT HARDWARE, PULLS, ETC.

## DOORS
### Hollow Metal Door Schedules

## DOOR SCHEDULE

Column numbers are for reference here only (14 ← reference here only)

| Opening Number | Door Type | Door Mat'l | No. | Width | Height | Thkns. | Sill Detail | Louver W | Louver H | Glass* | Spec'l. Detail | Frame Type | Frame Mat'l | Jamb | Head | Sill | Fire Rating | Hardware Set | Remarks |
|---|---|---|---|---|---|---|---|---|---|---|---|---|---|---|---|---|---|---|---|
| 101 | F | HM | 1 | 3-0 | 7-0 | 1¾ | 24/17 | - | - | - | - | 1 | HM | 1/17 | 1/17 | - | - | 1 | Contin. aluminum threshold |
| 102 | 1G | AL | 2 | 6-0 | 8-0 | 1¾ | 25/17 | - | - | TEMP | - | 2 | AL | 6/17 | 6/17 | - | - | 8 | |
| 103 | FGL | WD | 1 | 3-0 | 7-0 | 1¾ | 25/17 | - | - | ¼"TEMP | 28/17 | 1 | HM | 1/17 | 1/17 | - | - | 4 | |
| 104 | FG | HM | 1 | 3-0 | 7-0 | 1¾ | 24/17 | - | - | ¼"WIRE | - | 5 | HM | 6/17 | 6/17 | - | C | 6 | |
| 105 | FV | HM | 3 | 4-0 | 7-0 | 1¾ | 24/17 | - | - | ¼"TEMP | - | 2 | HM | 2/17 | 2/17 | - | A | 1 | Mullions 16/17 |
| 106 | F | HM | 2 | 7-0 | 7-0 | 1¾ | 29/17 | - | - | - | - | 3 | HM | 1/17 | 1/17 | - | - | 5 | Transom bar 16/17 |
| 107 | FL | HM | 1 | 3-0 | 7-0 | 1¾ | 24/17 | 23 | 12 | - | - | 1 | HM | 1/17 | 1/17 | - | - | 7 | Plastic faced door |
| 108 | F | WD* | 1 | 2-10 | 7-0 | 1¾ | 24/17 | - | - | - | 28/17 | - | HM | 3/17 | 3/17 | - | - | 4 | Cased opening |
| 109 | - | - | - | - | - | - | - | - | - | - | - | - | HM | 5/17 | 5/17 | - | - | - | |
| 110 | FGL | HM | 1 | 3-0 | 7-0 | 1¾ | 26/17 | 23 | 20 | ¼"TEMP | - | 4 | HM | 1/17 | 1/17 | 25, 19/17 | - | 1 | Side light mullion 16/17 |
| 111 | F | HM | 1 | 3-0 | 7-0 | 1¾ | 24/17 | - | - | - | 3/17 | 1 | HM | 8/17 | 8/17 | - | - | 2 | Sound retardant |

*Use metric units if desired; 1 inch = 25.4 mm, 1 foot = 0.305 m.

**1. Opening Number**
Number all openings individually, with the numbering system reflecting floor numbers if practicable.

**2. Door Type**
Use alphabetical designation for types, as shown on elevation views on facing page. Elevations should show door configurations and all features such as louvers, vision lights, etc. Do not use one elevation with dash lines to indicate variations.

**3. Door Material**
Designate material from which door is made: HM = hollow metal; AL = aluminum; WD = wood. * indicates special facing as noted in Remarks column. Type of core construction should be stated in the specifications.

**4. Nominal Size**
List number of doors per framed opening, plus width, height and thickness of door. State head and jamb clearances in specifications, using Hollow Metal Manufacturers Association recommended standards unless special conditions require otherwise.

**5. Sill Detail**
Reference sill detail, which shows sill clearance, threshold if any, and any special condition. Reference number shows detail number first, followed by sheet number.

**6. Louver**
Note width and height (in inches) of louver panel. Louver types may be either specified or shown in detail drawings.

**7. Glass**
Note thickness and type of glass to be used in glazed opening.

**8. Special Detail**
Reference detail(s) showing special features such as astragal (on pair), dutch door shelf, flush transom panel or other.

**9. Frame Type**
Use numerical designation for type, as shown on elevation views on facing page.

**10. Frame Material**
Designate material from which frame is made, using same symbols as for door materials.

**11. Frame Sections**
Reference details, showing frame sections at head and jamb, and details of such members as transom bars, mullions and other special features.

**12. Fire Rating**
State fire rating, if any, required for opening.

**13. Hardware Set**
State applicable hardware set number as described in specifications.

**14. Remarks**
Note here any special characteristics or required features of the opening, to insure that the contractor or supplier will be properly informed.

# REPRESENTATIVE DETAILS ACCOMPANYING DOOR SCHEDULE

# DOORS
**Hollow Metal Door Schedules**

DOOR SCHEDULE

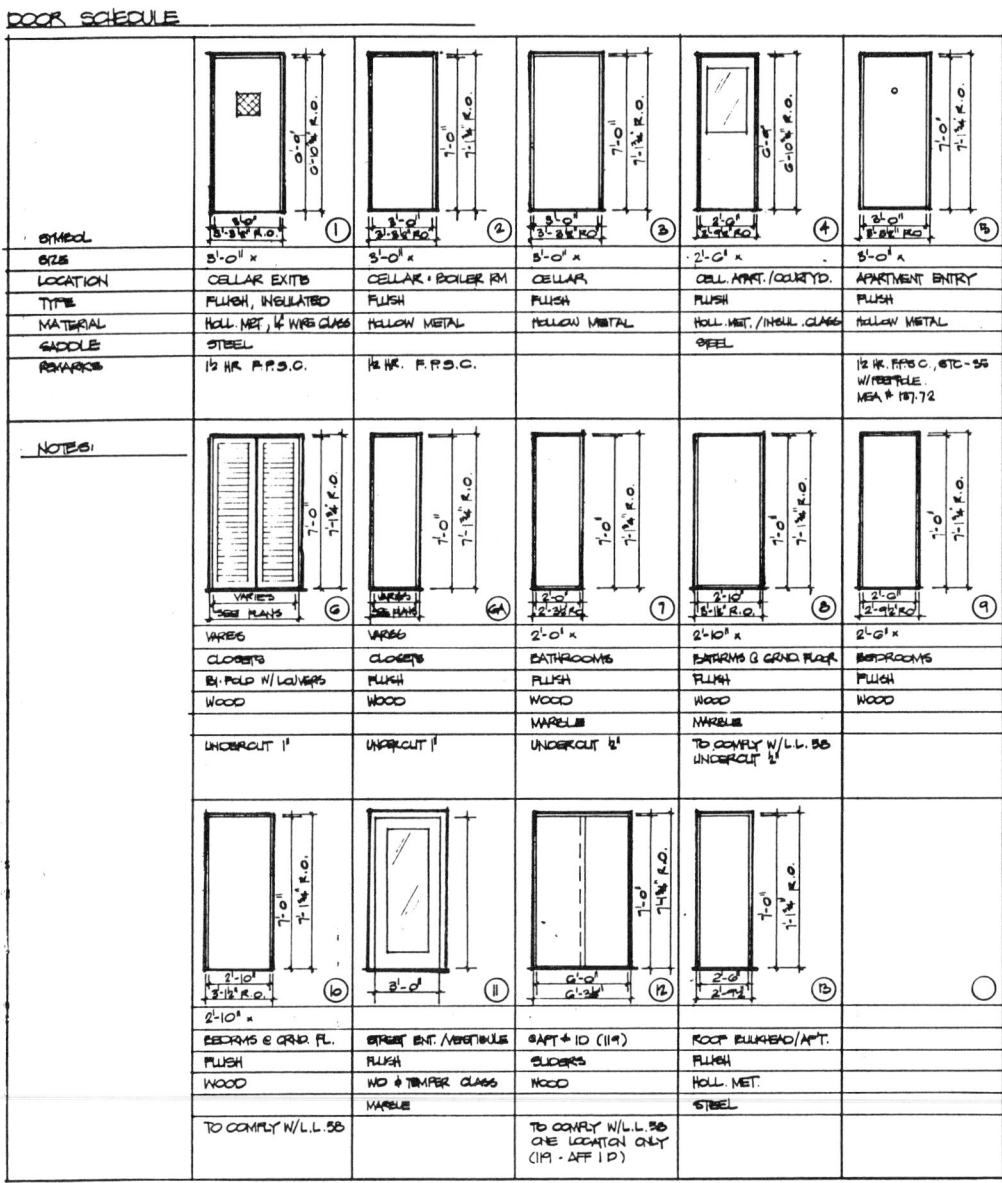

| | ① | ② | ③ | ④ | ⑤ |
|---|---|---|---|---|---|
| SYMBOL | | | | | |
| SIZE | 5'-0" x | 5'-0" x | 5'-0" x | 2'-0" x | 5'-0" x |
| LOCATION | CELLAR EXITS | CELLAR + BOILER RM | CELLAR | CELL. APT./COURTYD. | APARTMENT ENTRY |
| TYPE | FLUSH, INSULATED | FLUSH | FLUSH | FLUSH | FLUSH |
| MATERIAL | HOLL. MET, ¼" WIRE GLASS | HOLLOW METAL | HOLLOW METAL | HOLL. MET./INSUL. GLASS | HOLLOW METAL |
| SADDLE | STEEL | | | STEEL | |
| REMARKS | 1½ HR. F.P.S.C. | 1½ HR. F.P.S.C. | | | 1½ HR. F.P.S.C., STC-35 W/PEEPHOLE. MEA # 157.72 |

NOTES:

| | ⑥ | ⑥A | ⑦ | ⑧ | ⑨ |
|---|---|---|---|---|---|
| | VARIES | VARIES | 2'-0" x | 2'-10" x | 2'-6" x |
| | CLOSETS | CLOSETS | BATHROOMS | BATHRMS @ GRND FLOOR | BEDROOMS |
| | BI-FOLD W/LOUVERS | FLUSH | FLUSH | FLUSH | FLUSH |
| | WOOD | WOOD | WOOD | WOOD | WOOD |
| | | | MARBLE | MARBLE | |
| | UNDERCUT 1" | UNDERCUT 1" | UNDERCUT ½" | TO COMPLY W/L.L. 58 UNDERCUT ½" | |

| | ⑩ | ⑪ | ⑫ | ⑬ | ◯ |
|---|---|---|---|---|---|
| | 2'-10" x | | | 2'-6" x | |
| | BEDRMS @ GRND. FL. | STREET ENT./VESTIBULE | APT # 1D (119) | ROOF BULKHEAD/APT. | |
| | FLUSH | FLUSH | SLIDERS | FLUSH | |
| | WOOD | WD & TEMPER GLASS | WOOD | HOLL. MET. | |
| | | MARBLE | | STEEL | |
| | TO COMPLY W/L.L. 58 | | TO COMPLY W/L.L. 58 ONE LOCATION ONLY (119 - APT 1D) | | |

(a) Masonry with plaster, one or both sides

(b) Two-inch plaster wall

(c) Wood stud and plaster

(d) Two-inch solid dry wall

(e) Steel stud and plaster

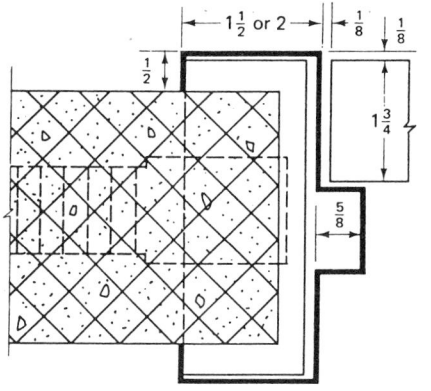

(f) Masonry block. Wrap-around or butt joint

**Fig. 2 Typical jamb installations.**

## DOORS
**Hollow Metal Door Frames**

**BASIC DOOR FRAME PROFILES AND THEIR PARTS**

**VERTICAL FRAME DIMENSIONS**

**TYPICAL BACKBEND or PLASTER STOP PROFILES**

CASED OPENING BLANK JAMB

**HORIZONTAL FRAME DIMENSIONS**

Frame depth to fit any wall thickness or finish    Any face profile may be combined with any backbend profile

splayed jamb    drywall

**REPRESENTATIVE FRAME PROFILES**

HEAD

for corner assembly

STD. CLOSER REINFORCEMENT (if closer used)

HINGE JAMB

STRIKE JAMB

HINGE CUTOUT & REINFORCEMENT

STRIKE CUTOUT & REINFORCEMENT

SPREADER (temporary brace)

### TYPICAL FRAME ASSEMBLY
As shipped

standard floor anchor

90° closed end

45° closed end

floor line

**CUTOFF (SANITARY) STOPS**

**ADJUSTABLE FLOOR ANCHOR**

STRAP & STIRRUP (MASONRY)

(perforated or corrugated strap)

WIRE LOOP (MASONRY)

T-STRAP (MASONRY)

METAL WIRE STUD

SOLID PLASTER

METAL CHANNEL STUD

WOOD STUD

**COMMON TYPES OF JAMB ANCHOR FOR PRE-SET FRAMES**

WOOD STUD

Removable stop

FHMS

FHMS

expansion shell

**1**

FHMS

**2**

Pipe spacer

**3**

mold optional

rough buck 14 ga. min.

CABINET JAMB FIELD ASSEMBLED

SPLIT JAMB PRE-ASSEMBLED

FRAMES WITH ROUGH BUCK

**ANCHORAGE OF FRAMES IN PREPARED OPENINGS**

# DOORS

**Hollow Metal Door Frames**

**FLOOR STILT**

terrazzo or other base mtl.

**FIXED MULLION ANCHOR**

**SPATS**

SPAT

SPAT

May be used with either cutoff or full length stops

**Light gage stainless steel wrap-around covering**

**Stainless steel same thickness as frame and flush with all jamb surfaces**

**CEILING STRUTS**

1¼″ × ¼″ steel strap

anchored to overhead construction

14 ga.

frame head

wedge

carriage bolt in keyhole slot

**ALTERNATE CHANNEL STRUT**

**PLAN**

head

1½″ × 1½″ × 12 ga. or struct'l angles

12 or 14 ga. channel

Used on wide openings to prevent deflection and possible interference with door operation

SHOULD NEVER BE USED IN PLACE OF STRUCTURAL LINTEL

**HEAD REINFORCEMENT**

frame head

4″ ±

**HEAD ADAPTER**

**For frames extending from slab to slab**

adjustable gasket

door

**jamb & head section**

**SOUND BARRIER FRAME**

sheet lead lining

Lead lining in frame provides barrier to x-rays, which travel in straight line, in gap between lead-lined wall and door

**LEAD-LINED FRAME**

A

**KEY ELEVATION**

open ends capped at center of head

**ALTERNATE HEAD SECTIONS "A"**

**JAMB SECTIONS**

**DETAILS OF DOUBLE EGRESS FRAME**

Detail 1 — CONC. OR CINDER BLK

Detail 2 — CONC. OR CINDER BLK

Detail 3 — CONC. OR CINDER BLK. PLASTER BOTH SIDES

Detail 4 — CONC. OR CINDER BLK. PLASTER ONE SIDE

Detail 5 — CONCRETE OR CINDER BLK.

Detail 6 — CONCRETE OR CINDER BLOCK-PLASTER BOTH SIDES

## DOORS
**Hollow Metal Door Frames**

⑦ CINDER OR CONC. BLK. PLASTERED ONE SIDE

⑧ CINDER OR CONC. BLK. - PLASTER / CERAMIC TILE IN CEM. MORTAR

⑨ CINDER OR CONC. BLK - PLASTER / CERAMIC TILE - THIN SET MORTAR

⑩ CINDER OR CONC. BLK. PLASTER & CERAMIC TILE

⑪ GYPSUM BLOCK - PLASTER BOTH SIDES

⑫ MASONRY BLOCK & PLASTER

**13** STEEL STUDS WITH 5/8" GYPSUM BOARD BOTH SIDES

**14** 1 5/8" STEEL STUDS WITH 5/8" GYPSUM BOARD BOTH SIDES

**15** STEEL STUDS WITH 5/8" GYPSUM BD. BOTH SIDES - CERAMIC TILE ONE SIDE

**16** STEEL STUDS - GYPSUM LATH & PLASTER BOTH SIDES

**17**

## DOORS
### Hollow Metal Door Frames

F-1  UNFINISHED MASONRY BLOCK
    @ 3" = 1'-0"

F-2  MASONRY BLK. - CERAMIC TILE ONE SIDE
    @ 3" = 1'-0"

F-3  TRIMMED OP'G. MASONRY BLOCK
    @ 3" = 1'-0"

F-4  MASONRY BLK. PLASTER BOTH SIDES
    @ 3" = 1'-0"

F-5  MASONRY BLK. PLASTER ONE SIDE
    @ 3" = 1'-0"

F-6  HARDWOOD FRAME
    @ 3" = 1'-0"

## DOORS
**Hollow Metal Door Frames**

F-7  MASONRY DR. CERAMIC TILE & PLASTER
@ 3" = 1'-0"

F-8  HARDWOOD FRAME
@ 3" = 1'-0"

F-9  H.M. FRAME - HWD. COVERING
@ 3" = 1'-0"

F-10  HARDWOOD FRAME
@ 3" = 1'-0"

F-11  TYPICAL HARDWOOD MULLION
@ 3" = 1'-0"

F-12  TYPICAL H.M. MULLION
@ 3" = 1'-0"

F-13  HARDWOOD FRAME @ 3"=1'-0"

F-14  HARDWOOD FRAME @ 3"=1'-0"

F-15  EXTERIOR HOLLOW METAL FRAME @ 3"=1'-0"

F-16  EXTERIOR HOLLOW METAL FRAME @ 3"=1'-0"

F-17  TRIMMED OPG. MASONRY BLK. CERAMIC TILE & PLASTER @ 3"=1'-0"

F-18  HARDWOOD FRAME @ 3"=1'-0"

## DOORS
Hollow Metal and Wood Door Frames

F-25  HARDWOOD FRAME
@ 3" = 1'-0"

F-26  HARDWOOD FRAME
@ 3" = 1'-0"

F-27  H.M. FRAME — HWD. COVERING
@ 3" = 1'-0"

F-28  HARDWOOD FRAME
@ 3" = 1'-0"

F-29 HARDWOOD FRAME @ 3" = 1'-0"

F-30 EXTERIOR HOLLOW METAL FRAME @ 3" = 1'-0"

F-31 HOLLOW METAL FRAME @ 3" = 1'-0"

F-32 EXTERIOR HOLLOW METAL FRAME @ 3" = 1'-0"

## DOORS
Hollow Metal and Wood Door Types

F-19  HARDWOOD FRAME
@ 3" = 1'-0"

F-19A  WOOD STUD PARTITION

F-20  HARDWOOD FRAME
@ 3" = 1'-0"

F-21  HARDWOOD FRAME
@ 3" = 1'-0"

F-22  HARDWOOD FRAME
@ 3" = 1'-0"

F-23  HARDWOOD FRAME
@ 3" = 1'-0"

F-24  EXTERIOR HOLLOW METAL FRAME
@ 3" = 1'-0"

D-1

D-2

D-3

D-4

D-6

D-7

D-8

D-9

D-5

D-1

D-2

D-3

D-4

# DOORS

**Door Types**

### FULL MORTISE BUTT HINGE

Two equal square-edged leaves, one mortised into door edge, the other into frame rabbet.

Two bearings, as shown, on regular weight hinges, four on heavy weight.

Typical Uses:

By far the most common type of hinge for both interior and exterior hollow metal and wood swing doors, in all types of buildings.

Usual Sizes (see NOTE below):

heights — 4½″; 5″ for doors over 36″ w. widths — 4½″ for 1¾″ door and 1½″ trim clearance (dimension A); 5″ (or more) for thicker doors or larger clearances.

### HALF MORTISE BUTT HINGE

One square-edged leaf mortised into door edge; the other leaf, bevel-edged, mounted on face of frame.

Typical Uses:

Used with hollow metal or kalamein doors in structural channel frames, usually in industrial type buildings.

Usual Sizes:

4½″, 5″ and 6″ heights.

### HALF SURFACE BUTT HINGE

One leaf, bevel-edged, mounted on face of door; the other leaf, square-edged, mortised into frame rabbet.

Typical Uses:

Used with hollow metal or kalamein doors in hollow metal frames, usually in industrial buildings. Heavy weight type also used on lead-lined doors.

Usual Sizes: 4½″, 5″ and 6″ heights.

### FULL SURFACE BUTT HINGE

Two bevel-edged leaves of differing widths, one surface-mounted on door face, the other on frame face.

Typical Uses:

Used with hollow metal or kalamein doors in structural channel frames, in industrial buildings. Heavy weight type may be used on lead-lined doors.

Usual Sizes: 4½″, 5″ and 6″ heights.

NOTE: Anchor hinges and pivot hinges should be specified for heavy doors and doors with high frequency use, such as entrances to large department stores, office buildings, theaters, banks and schools, or to toilet rooms in schools and airport buildings. Regular weight hinges may be specified for doors with average and low frequency uses such as corridor doors in public buildings and doors in residential buildings.

### ANCHOR HINGE

Heavy weight hinge with each leaf extended at its top edge and bent to form a flange that fastens to top edge of door and to frame head rabbet. May be used as top hinge on heavy doors and doors having high frequency usage.

### THRUST PIVOT UNIT AND HINGE SET

Pivot unit for top of door, with both jamb and top plates for both door and frame. Used, with conventional butt hinges, on wide doors that may be subjected to abnormal abuse. The hinge is almost invisible when door is closed.

### PIVOT REINFORCED HINGE

Heavy weight hinge with added pivot on the same pin. Leaves of pivot are interlocked with hinge leaves. Used with conventional butt hinges on doors subject to abnormal abuse, particularly with overhead closers.

## DOORS

**Hollow Metal Door Hardware: Hinges**

### FULL MORTISE

Both leaves bent; one mortised into frame rabbet, the other into door edge.

### HOSPITAL "SWING CLEAR" TYPES

These hinges have their pins located approximately 2″ beyond the door edge, providing an unobstructed clear frame opening width when the door is open 90″.

They are used on hospital corridor doors to patients' rooms, operating rooms, emergency rooms, or wherever a completely clear opening is required in hospitals, institutional or public buildings.

Swing clear hinges are available only in heavy weight

### HALF MORTISE

One bent leaf mortised into edge of door, one flat, bevel-edged leaf surface-mounted on frame face.

### HALF SURFACE

Offset bevel-edged leaf surface-mounted on door face, bent leaf mortised into frame rabbet.

### FULL SURFACE

Offset bevel-edged leaf surface-mounted on door face, other bevel-edged leaf surface-mounted on frame face.

Full mortised, centered on door thickness. Hinge is completely concealed when door is closed.

Full mortised; door leaf usually centered on door thickness. When door is closed, only the knuckle is visible.

### INVISIBLE HINGE

### OLIVE KNUCKLE HINGE
(PAUMELLE HINGE SIMILAR)

top pivots

intermediate
pivot
(optional)

bottom pivots

ELEVATION

alternative
floor-mounted bottom pivots

PLAN

ELEVATION

PLAN

### OFFSET TYPE

Used on single-acting doors only. Need for intermediate pivot depends upon the size, weight and usage of door; recommendation of hardware manufacturer should be followed. Pivot knuckles visible when door is closed.

### CENTER TYPE

Used at top and bottom of double-acting doors only. Pivots are completely invisible when door is closed.

Pivots are stronger and more durable than hinges and are better able to withstand the racking stresses to which doors are subjected. Their use is generally recommended on oversize doors, on heavy doors such as lead-lined doors, and on entrance doors to public buildings such as schools, theaters, banks, store and office buildings.

NOTE: Because of adjustments that must be made during the installation of doors with bottom pivots, it is recommended that reinforcements be furnished in blank and that drilling and tapping be done in the field by the contractor.

### LOCKS, LATCHES, AND DEADLOCKS

The selection of the proper lock type is very important. The types shown here are those most commonly used, but are by no means the only types available. Their names serve to identify either the type of lock construction or the type of installation. Mortise locks provide the greatest variety of lock functions, the best security, and excellent durability. Another popular type, with rugged construction and easily operated, is the preassembled lock, which is completely assembled at the factory. It does not have as many lock functions as the mortise lock, but can have a separate deadbolt. The bored lock is the least secured type and is not available with a separate deadbolt in the lock.

**MORTISE LOCK**

The mortise lock is so named because it is installed in a prepared recess (mortise) in the door. Working parts are contained in a rectangular case with holes for cylinder and knob spindle. Anti-friction split bolts are available for smooth retraction of the lock bolt. Lock front may be armored to protect against burglars getting at cylinder screws and lock fasteners. Lever handles may be used if desired, and trim may be either sectional or full plate.

**MORTISE DEADLOCK**

This is a mortise lock with a deadlock only. (A deadlock is a lock bolt which has no bevel or spring action, and is operated by a key or thumb turn.) It is often used for locking a door having push or pull plates or for providing added security on doors with cylindrical locks.

**BORED (CYLINDRICAL) LOCK**

This type of lock uses the key-in-the-knob principle. It is installed in a door having one hole bored through the thickness of the door and another bored in from the edge. The assembly must be tight on the door, without excessive play, to avoid binding.

**UNIT LOCK**

This lock is preassembled in the factory and consists of a one-piece extruded or cast brass frame within which all parts are contained. It is installed in a rectangular reinforced notch cut in the door edge. Lever handles may be used in place of knobs.

**BORED (CYLINDRICAL) DEADLOCK**

This is a cylindrical type of lock having a deadbolt only. It fits into the same type of cylindrical cutout as that required for the bored lock.

SECTION          ELEVATION

**Fig. 3   Surface mounted, on hinge face of door.**

Also available with concealed arm

SECTION          ELEVATION

**Fig. 4   Concealed in door, with exposed arm.**

SECTION          ELEVATION

**Fig. 5   Surface mounted, on stop face of door.**

SECTION          ELEVATION

**Fig. 6   Concealed in head, with concealed arm.**

SECTION          ELEVATION

**Fig. 7   Concealed in head, with exposed arm.**

SECTION          ELEVATION

**Fig. 8   Concealed in transom bar.**

# DOORS

**Hollow Metal Door Hardware: Floor Closers**

### OVERHEAD AND FLOOR CLOSERS

Overhead closers (Figs. 3 to 8) are hydraulic devices, containing a piston, fluid chambers, and a spring. When the door is opened the piston is pulled back, the spring is compressed, and the fluid is moved from one side of the piston to the other. With release of the door a reverse action takes place, closing the door. Closing speed is controlled by an adjustable valve or valves. Overhead closers may be installed on either single- or double-acting doors.

Floor closers, generally more durable than overhead closers, provide concealed closing mechanisms often appropriate for doors having a high frequency of use. As shown, the type of closer used depends on whether the door is hung on hinges, offset pivots, or center pivots.

Both overhead and floor closers are available in a range of sizes for various door sizes, locations, and job conditions. The manufacturer's recommendations should always be followed in determining which size and type should be used.

Where surface-mounted closers are specified, internal reinforcement plates shall be provided in the door and frame by the manufacturer. Drilling and tapping for the closer shall be done in the field by the installer. Only after the door is installed and adjusted can the closer be mounted for proper operation. If drilling and tapping have been done at the factory, the necessary field adjustments become difficult if not impossible.

**FOR HINGED DOORS**

**FOR OFFSET PIVOTED DOORS**

single acting

**FOR CENTER PIVOTED DOORS**

either single or double-acting

## PANIC AND FIRE EXIT HARDWARE

### Types of Installation

Panic hardware is tested and labeled for casualty only, fire exit hardware for both casualty and fire resistance. Only the latter may be used where fire rated doors are required. Both types are always releasable from the inside by depressing the crash bar. The mortise type (Fig. 9) and the concealed vertical rod type (Fig. 10) are the least conspicuous, and either of these types is readily applicable to custom hollow metal doors.

Rim and mortise types are used on
Single door
Active door of pair
Both doors of pair with mullion
Vertical rod types are used on
Single door
Active door of pair
Both doors of pair

Where rim type (Fig. 11) or exposed vertical rod (Fig. 12) exit devices are specified, internal reinforcement plates shall be provided in the door and frame by the manufacturer. Drilling and tapping for trim and mounting plates shall be done in the field by the installer. The hardware can then be more readily adjusted for best operation.

In preparing the door for a lock, the drilling of three bolt holes (½" dia. or less) and/or the drilling and tapping for sectional or full trim plates shall be done in the field by the installer and not at the factory. After the lock is installed and adjusted, the trim plate can be applied to suit the final position of the latching device. If thru bolt holes or tapped holes are provided at the factory, this adjustment becomes difficult if not impossible.

The manufacturer shall drill for all function holes, i.e., cylinder, turn piece, and knob.

### Door Coordinators

Coordinators (Figs. 13 and 14) are used on pairs of doors having overlapping astragals and closers. When both leaves are open, the coordinator holds the active leaf open until the inactive leaf is closed, preventing interferences of the astragal.

**Fig. 9   Mortise type exit device.**

**Fig. 11   Rim type exit device.**

**Fig. 10   Concealed vertical rod type exit.**

**Fig. 12   Exposed vertical rod type exit device.**

**Fig. 13   Surface-mounted type door and coordinator.    Fig. 14   Mortised type door coordinator.**

## DOORS

**Hollow Metal Door Hardware**

### FLUSH BOLTS

These bolts are installed on the inactive leaf of a pair of doors to secure it in the closed position to serve as a latching point for the active leaf. They may also be used as auxiliary locking devices for added security. Bolts may be either surface-mounted or flush (concealed rod); only the latter type is illustrated in Fig. 15.

There are many variations of these flush bolts; only the more common types being shown in Fig. 15. Due to the variety of frame construction encountered, the selection of the most appropriate type of strike is particularly important, and clearance at the floor must be very carefully controlled to insure proper engagement.

The manual type (Fig. 15A) requires hand operation of the operating lever for both latching and unlatching. The variable length of the extension rod, however, permits convenient location of the operating mechanism in the door edge. The self-latching types (Fig. 15B and C) latch automatically when the inactive leave is closed, but must be unlatched manually. The automatic type (Fig. 15D) both latches and unlatches automatically when the inactive leaf is closed or opened.

None of these types of flush bolt should be used on doors that are intended to serve as emergency exists. NFPA pamphlet 80 should be consulted for the selection of bolts for fire-rated pairs of doors.

**MANUAL TYPE**          **SELF-LATCHING TYPES**          **AUTOMATIC TYPE**

U.L.-APPROVED BOLTS ARE REQUIRED AT BOTH TOP AND
BOTTOM OF INACTIVE LEAF OR FIRE-RATED PAIRS OF DOORS

**Fig. 15** Except for Type C, only top bolts are shown; bottom bolts are similar in all cases.

## OVERHEAD DOOR HOLDERS

**CONCEALED TYPE**
For single-or double-acting doors

These are devices used to limit and control the swing of the door or hold it in the open position. By controlling the door action they serve to protect against damage to the door and/or hinges caused by abusive usage, and damage to the holder caused by violent opening of the door.

**EXPOSED TYPES**
For single-acting doors only

PUSH LEVER

PULL LEVER ON OPPOSITE FACE

### HOSPITAL DOOR LATCH

Designed primarily for use in hospitals, on corridor doors leading to patient rooms. May also be used on any door requiring push-pull operation, particularly by forearm or elbow, when hands are engaged in carrying objects.

### EMERGENCY DOOR STOP

Intended primarily for use in hospitals, on doors between patient rooms and toilets. This stop permits door to be opened from the stop side in the event that an incapacitated patient should block the normal swing by falling. Door must be hung on center (double-acting) pivots.

## DOORS

**Hardware Locations**

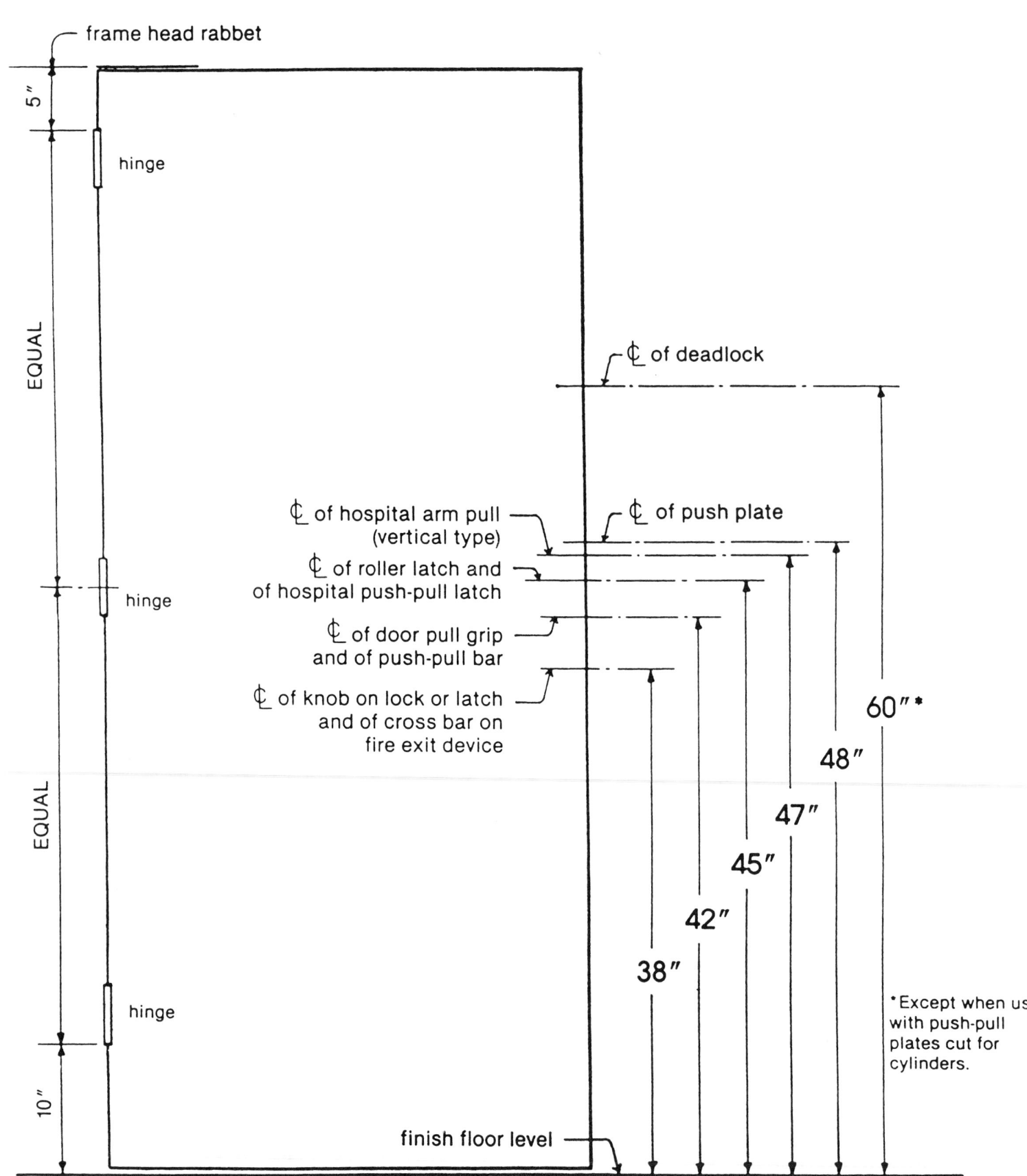

frame head rabbet

5″

hinge

EQUAL

℄ of deadlock

℄ of hospital arm pull
(vertical type)

℄ of push plate

℄ of roller latch and
of hospital push-pull latch

℄ of door pull grip
and of push-pull bar

℄ of knob on lock or latch
and of cross bar on
fire exit device

hinge

EQUAL

60″ *

48″

47″

45″

42″

38″

hinge

10″

*Except when us
with push-pull
plates cut for
cylinders.

finish floor level

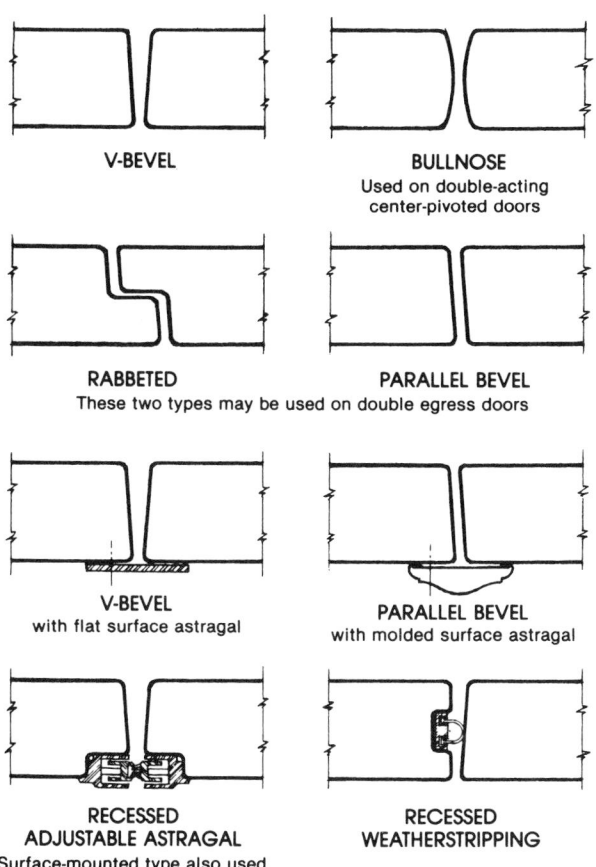

V-BEVEL

BULLNOSE
Used on double-acting
center-pivoted doors

RABBETED

PARALLEL BEVEL

These two types may be used on double egress doors

V-BEVEL
with flat surface astragal

PARALLEL BEVEL
with molded surface astragal

RECESSED
ADJUSTABLE ASTRAGAL
Surface-mounted type also used

RECESSED
WEATHERSTRIPPING

## COMMON MEETING STILE EDGE PROFILES

spot welds

channel or
angle may be
used in place
of plate

**All joint seams continuously welded and ground smooth**

## STILE EDGE DETAILS — TYPE A DOORS

sealed
if desired

STANDARD
Inverted channel

FILLER
CHANNEL

## TOP EDGE DETAILS

HARDWARE REINFORCEMENTS are provided on doors wherever hardware is to be attached, to insure that it is firmly and securely fastened.

STANDARD

FLUSH
(closing channel)

AUTOMATIC
WEATHERSTRIP

**Other designs available as required**

## BOTTOM EDGE DETAILS

transom
panel

filler on
ext. doors,
optional
on others

door

## TOP EDGE DETAILS
## WITH FLUSH TRANSOM PANEL ABOVE

## DOORS

Fire-Protected Wood Doors

1⅜" min. — solid wood core

crossbanding

veneer

**SOLID WOOD CORE FLUSH DOORS**

1⅝" min. — 5-inch min. width battens and brace

2-inch nominal T & G or splined stock not over 6 inches wide

1½" min. — two layers of 1-inch nominal T & G stock not over 6 inches wide, with one layer vertical and the other horizontal, and one layer of asbestos paper between

**BATTENED DOORS**

1⅜" min. — wood panel

sheet iron, copper not less than 28 U. S. gage, fastened on each side to stiles, rails and edges with nails or screws

1⅜" min. — wood panel

⅛-inch asbestos millboard or ⅜-inch gypsum wallboard

sheet iron, copper not less than 28 U. S. gage, fastened to side on which protection is desired, to stiles, rails and edges with nails or screws

**PROTECTED PANEL DOORS**

spring hinge or door closer

on doors less than 1½ inches in thickness, cover latch stile with minimum 28-gage metal

minimum throw of latch ⅜"

min. 8"

min. 4½"

doors more than 5 ft high: minimum 3 butts not less than 4" by 4"

fire-retardant treated wood

fire-retardant treated wood stop, glued and nailed to frame on not more than 6-inch centers

1¾"

½"

1¾"

½"

1⅝-inch minimum actual dimension

TREATED WOOD     UNTREATED WOOD     METAL COVERED     PRESSED OR ROLLED STEEL

**HARDWARE**     **FRAMES**

CONC.
W/E.S.A.
FINISH

HEAD
CHANNEL

CONC.
W/E.S.A.
FINISH

CAULK

CAULK

NORTHROP ARCHITECTURAL
SYSTEMS'
ARCADIA ALUMINUM
SLIDING GLASS DOORS
SERIES 812 W/1" INSUL GLASS;
W/HEAD CHANNEL ;
W/ 1 FIXED JAMB AND
1 LATCHING JAMB ;
W/ INTERLOCKERS ;
ANODIZED ALUM. FINISH
COLOR TO BE SELECTED
BY ARCHITECT

L O B B Y

(102)

1" INSULATING GLASS

CAULK

BLUESTONE
SILL

CARPET

EL. 250'-0"

EL.
250'-8"

CONC.

EL.
.249'-6"

**2A**   @ 3" = 1'-0"

## DOORS
Thresholds

Thresholds are essential for nearly every type of door. Usually a standard section is satisfactory. Where conditions require, special sections may be designed.

Thresholds of plain surface, extruded or rolled.

Thresholds with fluted surface, extruded or rolled.

Thresholds cast with plain or abrasive surface.

Thresholds for weather strips.

Holes for fastening not to exceed 12" o.c. for threshold less than 3" wide. For thresholds over 3" fastenings should not exceed 15" o.c. On wide sills holes may be staggered.

Threshold fastened with screws tapped to steel angle set in floor construction.

Threshold fastened to wood with wood screws.

Threshold fastened with screw in fibre plug or expansive metal anchor. Floor may be cement, terrazzo or similar construction.

Threshold fastened with screws tapped to clips set in cement.

| | | | | | | | | |
|---|---|---|---|---|---|---|---|---|
| THRESHOLD | SIZES | | AND | METAL | | | | |
| FIG. | WIDTH | HEIGHT | CAST | STEEL | BRASS | BRONZE | ALUMINUM | NICKEL SILVER |
| 14 | 2½" | ¼" | | o | o | o | o | o |
| 15 | 3" | ¼" | | o | o | o | o | o |
| 16 | 4" | ½" | | o | o | o | o | |
| 17 | 3" | 5⁄16" | | o | o | o | o | |
| 18 | 4" | ½" | | o | o | o | o | |
| 19 | 5" | ½" | | o | o | o | o | |
| 20 | 6" | 5⁄8" | | | o | o | o | |
| 21 | 7½" | ½" | | | | | o | |
| 22 | 3" | ½" | o | | | | | |
| 23 | 4" | ½" | o | | | | | |
| 24 | 5" | ½" | o | | | | | |
| 25 | 4 3⁄16" | 5⁄8" | | | o | o | o | |
| 26 | 4" 5" 6" | 5⁄8" | o | | | | | |

Cast metal may be iron, aluminum, bronze, or nickel silver, with or without abrasive surface.

These thresholds are representative of a great many sections produced in various metals, widths, heights, and types of surface. For other sections refer to manufacturers' catalogs.

Steel loading door threshold anchored to concrete

Steel shipping door threshold anchored to concrete

Steel shipping door threshold screwed to floor

Elevator door threshold for double doors cast with grooves. Surface may be abrasive or plain of cast iron, aluminum or bronze.

Elevator door threshold for double doors of rolled sections, steel, bronze or aluminum.

Elevator door threshold for single doors cast with grooves. Surface may be abrasive or plain of cast iron, aluminum or bronze.

Thresholds with concealed steel anchors are usually fastened to anchors with flat head machine screws, the anchors independently fastened to the floor construction.

Threshold for single acting floor check.

Threshold for single acting floor check.

Threshold for double acting floor check.

SCALE 1½" = 1'-0"

Threshold for double acting floor check.

Thresholds for floor checks may be obtained in the same metals and sections as standard thresholds or may be designed to fit special conditions.

All thresholds fitted to floor checks must be designed with removable cover plate.

Screw spacing must fit floor check.

Dimension "A" is determined by type of floor check, usually 5¾", 6¾" or 7¾".

Dimension "B" may be same as "A" or less as specified.

**SPECIFY:**
**Type, location**
**Width, length**
**Metal and finish**
**Show detail of**
**special requirements**

SCALE ½" = 1'

Joint strips, also called dividing strips or division bars, used for separation of floors of different materials, may be of steel or non-ferrous metals. They may be of angles or other sections with anchors attached, or of a patented design.

Terrazzo strips for design or pattern work in terrazzo floors are not considered architectural metal.

## DOORS
**Thresholds and Edging Strips**

**T-1**
Ceramic tile adhesive applied or cork tile flooring
Normal floor line
1⅛"
⅛" resilient flooring
5/16"
Screws with expansion shields, one at each end and intermediate ones 8" o.c.
Extruded alum. threshold

**T-2**
⅛" resilient flooring
Normal floor line
1"
Vinyl plastic edging strip

**T-3**
Finished floor line
¼"
½"
Material as required see other dwgs.
Zinc dividing strip

**T-4**
⅛" resilient flooring
Normal floor line
1⅛"
Screws with expansion shields one at each end and intermediate ones 8" o.c.
Solid metal edging strip as required

**T-5**
Marble threshold
⅛" resilient flooring
Normal floor line
Carpet
½"
1"
4"

**T-6**
Aluminum threshold
⅛" resilient flooring
Normal floor line
Carpet
½"
4"
Provide two rows of screws with expansion shields, two at each end and intermediate ones staggered and spaced 12" o.c. in each row.

**T-7**
Neoprene weather strip
⅛" resilient flooring
Normal floor line
Carpet
½" ¾"
4"
Aluminum threshold
Screws with expansion shields, one at each end and intermediate ones 8" o.c.

NOTES:
1. For door swing, see other drawings.
2. For schedule of floor finishes, see other drawings.
3. For gauges of metal see specifications.

8-A52 ELEVATION
A39 · 1/2" 1'-0"

SCHEDULED CEILING

GRANITE VENEER

ALUM. REVEAL

STAINLESS STEEL (S.S.) TRIM BY VAULT DOOR MFG. & INSTALLER

VAULT DOOR BY OTHERS N.I.C.

FIXED S.S. PANEL LAMINATED TO 1/2" PLYWOOD BACKING BY VAULT DOOR MFG. & INSTALLER

GRANITE VENEER

9-A52 SECTION
A52 · 1/2" 1'-0"

ALUM. REVEAL

CONC. VAULT WALL

GRANITE VENEER

SCHED. CEILING

5/8" GYP. BD. ON 7/8" MTL. FURRING

J-BOX REFER TO ELECTRICAL

AIR VENT BY DOOR MFG.

NOTE: ALL EXPOSED ALUM. TO BE BRONZE FINISHED.

DEPRESS SLAB

10'-0" FIN. FLR. TO FIN. CLG.

7'-0 1/8" FIN. FLR. TO GRANITE SOFFIT

6'-7 1/2" VAULT FLR. TO DOOR FR. HEAD

DEPRESS SLAB

12-A52 DETAIL
A39 · 1/2" 1'-0"

4'-3" RECESS

DEPRESS SLAB

CONCRETE VAULT WALL

2'-10" FR. OPNG. (VERIFY)
3'-7" CONC. OPNG. (VERIFY)
2'-10" S.S. PANEL
6'-11" GRANITE DIM.
8'-9 1/4"

5-A52
A52

LIGHT & SOUNDPROOFING FOR WOOD DOOR FRAME

HEAD & STRIKE JAMB    HINGE JAMB    DOOR BOTTOM

LIGHT & SOUNDPROOFING FOR HOLLOW METAL FRAME

HEAD & STRIKE JAMB    HINGE JAMB    ALTERNATE

NOTE: DOOR BOTTOM SIMILAR TO WOOD DOOR ABOVE
FOR SURFACE MOUNTED AUTOMATIC DOOR BOTTOM
USE ZERO #365

The prime functions of the door frame are to hold the door and its controls in the opening, and to trim the opening. But frames often serve other esthetic or functional purposes also, such as trimming a wall opening having no door, or enclosing glazed areas that provide through-wall visibility or admitting light and/or air. Hollow metal frames, which are strong, sturdy, and durable, serve all such functions economically.

The variety of configurations available in custom hollow metal frames is virtually unlimited. Illustrated in Fig. 16 are some of the more common and representative types.

**Fig. 16**

F-11A — H.M. FRAME HWD. TRIM/ONE SIDE — 3"=1'-0"

F-11 — H.M. FRAME HWD. TRIM/ONE SIDE — 3"=1'-0"

F-12 — H.M. EXTERIOR FRAME — 3"=1'-0"

F-13 — HARDWOOD FRAME — 3"=1'-0"

F-14 — #2Y — 3"=1'-0"

F-14A — #2Y — 3"=1'-0"

F-6  H.M. EXTERIOR FRAME
3"=1'-0"

F-7  H.M. FRAME – HARDWOOD/ONE SIDE
3"=1'-0"   SEE DETAIL 4/A-20 FOR DOOR #11

F-8  H.M. FRAME
3"=1'-0"

F-9  H.M. MULLION
3"=1'-0"

F-10  H.M. FRAME
3"=1'-0"

F-10A  H.M. FRAM.

# DOORS

## Door Types and Construction

| | PARTICLE | STAVE | HOLLOW | ACOUSTICAL** STC 31, 36, 38, & 40 | LEAD | STILE AND RAIL |
|---|---|---|---|---|---|---|
| **THICKNESS** | 1⅜", 1¾" | 1⅜", 1¾", 2¼" | 1⅜", 1¾" | 1¾" | 1¾" — lead thickness to ⅜". | 1¾", 2¼" |
| **MAX. SIZE** | 4'0" x 12'0" | 4'0" x 12'0" | 4'0" x 12'0" | 4'0" x 10'0" | 4'0" x 10'0" | 4'0" x 12'0" |
| **CORE** | Mat-formed particle board conforming to ANSI A208.1-1L1. | (21-27 pcf) Low density wood blocks bonded together. One species per core. | Resin impregnated honeycomb — ½" cell. | Special materials and assembly to meet ratings shown. | Divided core. Mat-formed particle board conforming to ANSI A208.1-1M3. Lead over ⅛" reinforced with lead plugs. | Stiles and rails: Low density wood blocks bonded together & to edgebands. Panels: Mill option, mat-formed particle board or edge-glued lumber core. |
| **STILES** | 1¾" face matching or compatible to face veneer, mill option inner-ply. Glued to core. Maximum 5". | ⅛" matching or compatible to face veneer. Glued to core. | 1⅛" x 2 ply Matching or compatible to face veneer, mill option inner-ply. | STC 31 — Stave ⅛", particle 1⅜" matching or compatible to face veneer. Glued to core. STC 36, 38, 40 — 2" Face compatible outer-ply. Glued to core. | 1½" matching or compatible to face veneer. Glued to core. | ⅛" Matching or compatible to face veneer. Glued to stile. |
| **RAILS** | 1⅜" mill option hardwood glued to core standard. Nominal 2½", 5", 8" and 12" optional. | | 2¼" mill option hardwood. | STC 31 — 1⅛" mill option hardwood glued to core. STC 36, 38, 40 — 3". | 2¼" mill option hardwood glued to core. | ½" edgeband compatible to face veneer. Glued to rail. |
| **FACES** | All available domestic and foreign veneers. Medium density overlays. High pressure laminates. | | | | | All available 1/16" sliced hardwood veneers on stiles and rails. Standard veneers on panel faces. |
| **CROSSBANDS** | | Min. 1/16" hardwood. | | | | 1/20" mill option hardwood. |
| **VENEER MATCHING** | | Virtually unlimited in standard veneers, end matching in door and transoms with wood grain plastics. | | | | Limited veneer matching. |
| **PREMACHINING** | | Prefitting, mortise for appropriate hardware. No preparation for surface mounted. | | | | |
| **OPENINGS** | | Min. 5" margins edge of door and adjacent hardware cut-outs. Max. opening 40% of door area or 50% of height. | | | | Min. 5" stiles, minimum 10" bottom rail. Min. 5" top rail. |
| **SPECIAL DETAILS** | | Cut light openings* Install metal and wood louvers, openings, wood beads, and safety glazing. Applied mouldings. Dutch doors and shelves. | Cut light openings* Install metal and wood louvers, wood beads, and safety glazing. Standard beads or architect's detail at light and louver openings. Dutch doors. | Cut light openings* Install metal and wood louvers, openings, wood beads, and safety glazing. Standard beads or architect's detail at light and louver openings. Applied mouldings. Dutch doors and shelves. | Cut light openings* Safety glazing. Standard wood, acoustical and lead lined beads. No applied mouldings. No dutch doors. | Solid sticking or moulding per architect's detail. Wood louvers and safety glazing factory installed. |
| **FINISHING** | | Gardall II, primed, painted, sealed, oiled or waxed as specified. | | | | |
| **WARRANTY** | Interior — Life of original installation. Exterior — 2 years. | Interior — Life of original installation. Exterior — 2 years. | Interior — 1 year. Exterior — Not recommended. | Interior — 1 year. Exterior — Not recommended. | Interior — Life of original installation. Exterior — Not recommended. | Interior — 2 years. Exterior — Not recommended. |
| **STANDARDS** | NWWDA I.S.-1 AWI Section 1300 PC Federal LLLD581 Type I & II. Class 1 | NWWDA I.S.-1 AWI Section 1300 SLC Federal LLLD581 Type I & II, Class1 | NWWDA I.S.-1 | NWWDA I.S.-1 AWI Section 1300 SR — ASTM E90-70 Federal LLLD581 Type IV, Class 4 | NWWDA I.S.-1 AWI-1300-LL and E413-73 Federal LLLD581: Type IV, Class 5 | AWI Section 1400 Federal LLLD581: Type III |

*Footnote on openings — Minimum margins per AWI Section 1300. **No rating guaranteed on doors with lites or pairs.

STILE AND RAIL

LEAD

ACOUSTICAL STC 38

HOLLOW

STAVE

PARTICLE

natural linen

colored linen band    1

ELEVATION

PLAN

natural linen

teak

ELEVATION

PLAN

natural linen

colored linen    3

4

ELEVATION

PLAN

flush veneer doors

5

wood

1

2

4

3

5    metal handle

MISCELLANEOUS HANDLES

6

linen or celophane

ELEVATION

PLAN

Japanese handmade paper

7

7    wood

8    bamboo

8

scale    1'    2'    3'    4'    5'    10'

# DOORS

### Door Types

**Fig. 17  Typical interior doors showing the dimensions of stiles and rails.**

Lock rail heights, width of stiles, and width of rails as noted on all elevations are minimum and maximum dimensions as used by the various manufacturers.

#### STANDARD SIZES OF ONE, TWO, AND SIX PANEL DOORS

| | |
|---|---|
| 2'- 0"x6'- 0", 1⅜" | 2'-10"x6'-10", 1⅜" |
| 2'- 0"x6'- 6", 1⅜" | 3'- 0"x6'- 8", 1⅜" |
| 2'- 0"x6'- 8", 1⅜" | 3'- 0"x7'- 0", 1⅜" |
| 2'- 0"x7'- 0", 1⅜" | 2'- 6"x6'- 6", 1¾" |
| 2'- 4"x6'- 6", 1⅜" | 2'- 6"x6'- 8", 1¾" |
| 2'- 4"x6'- 8", 1⅜" | 2'- 6"x7'- 0", 1¾" |
| 2'- 6"x6'- 6", 1⅜" | 2'- 8"x6'- 8", 1¾" |
| 2'- 6"x6'- 8", 1⅜" | 2'- 8"x7'- 0", 1¾" |
| 2'- 6"x7'- 0", 1⅜" | 2'-10"x6'-10", 1¾" |
| 2'- 8"x6'- 8", 1⅜" | 3'- 0"x6'- 8", 1¾" |
| 2'- 8"x7'- 0", 1⅜" | 3'- 0"x7'- 0", 1¾" |

## ONE AND TWO PANEL DESIGNS

Manufactured in Ponderosa Pine with laminated flat panels of pine, fir, gum, or birch. Moulded C&B, B&C or Ovolo Sticking. Standard thickness of doors 1⅛" or 1¼". Made also in any Hardwood with veneered stiles, rails and panels.

**Fig. 18  Sizes of panelled interior doors.**

#### STANDARD SIZES

4'-0" opening, 2'-0"x6'-8" or 2'-0"x7'-0"
4'-8" opening, 2'-4"x6'-8" or 2'-4"x7'-0"
5'-0" opening, 2'-6"x6'-8" or 2'-6"x7'-0"
5'-4" opening, 2'-8"x6'-8" or 2'-8"x7'-0"

#### CASEMENT DESIGNS

Casement doors can also be divided into:

8 lights (2 wide—4 high) and
12 lights (3 wide—4 high).

Pairs of casement doors in openings less than 5'-0" wide have 3⅛" stiles as shown while pairs in openings 5'-0" wide and wider have 4¼" stiles.

**Fig. 19  Sizes of French or casement doors.**

Fig. 20  Exterior wood doors.

Fig. 21  Interior wood doors.

1    2    3    4

5    6    7    8

LEDGED & BRACED    SINGLE PANEL    TWO PANEL    FOUR PANEL

FIVE X PANEL    SIX PANEL    EIGHT PANEL    EIGHT PANEL

## DOORS
### Wood Door Frames

MASTER BATHROOM

MASTER BEDROOM

2'-4"

PLAN

TYP. TRIM AS PER SCHEDULE

2'-4" DOOR OPN'G

6'-8" DOOR OPN'G

TYP. BASE AS PER SCHEDULE

FIN. FLR.

ELEVATION

28

DETAIL @ JAMB
F.S.

BASE

2"

2"

4¼"

ALIGN

**ELEVATION·SHOWING·SECRET·DOOR·LOCATED·IN·PANELLING·Scale ¼"=1'-0"**

Wood Panelling.

Push button.

Secret door.

Floor line.

Button & ferrule furnished in metal or in wood to match adjoining wood.

Push button

Lock

Push out spring.

Latch

Button releases latch & permits push out spring to throw door open.

**SECTIONAL·PLAN·THRU·SECRET·DOOR·LOCK·Scale 3"=1'-0"**

There are several secret door openers procurable. All patented.

Grounds

Plaster

Dotted lines indicate pins of Walking Beam Pivot.

Jamb & stile & head & rail glued & fastened together at the mill.

**SECTION·THRU·HEAD·&·TOP·RAIL· ON·A-A·Scale 3"=1'-0"**

1¾" built-up door with veneered raised panel thoroughly secured.

5 ply veneered panel.

Raised moulding mitered at corners & thoroughly glued

Hard wood core

This distance to be as little as practicable.

Dotted lines indicate location of floor pivot.

Fin. Floor

**SECTION·THRU·BOTTOM·RAIL·&·AT-TACHED·BASE·ON·B-B·Scale 3"=1'-0"**

Cut door with usual bevel (⅛ in 2") as far as it will go. This releases latch & push spring opens door. To close door, push door in until latch catches.

Strike
Push spring.

Grounds
Studs

Lock

Patented secret lock with no parts visible. To open, push door in firmly & quickly (at latch position) as far as it will go. This releases latch & push spring opens door.

Door or jamb to be rabbeted or stop set back so that door can be pushed in 5/16 of an inch from its normal position when closed.

Alternate: The Offset Pivot hinge. Regular jamb detail used as hinge is so designed that clearance is provided for by hinge for projecting mouldings. The butts of these hinges will show.

Alternate: The Invisible hinge. Use 2-5" butts. Hinge designed for 1¼" clearance. Projecting base requires groove cut similar to detail shown.

Form panel on inside face of door.

Cut of room base & door jamb depends on clearance required when door opens

Dotted line indicates hollow groove in jamb necessary to allow projecting base to clear jamb. Groove to be just high enough to allow base to clear.

Door in opening position.

Pivot

**SECTION·THRU·SECRET·DOOR (SHOWING·BEVEL·CUTS·IN·BASE, JAMB·&·DOOR)·ON·C-C·Scale 3"=1'-0"**

# DOORS
**Exterior Wood Entrance Doors**

**Fig. 22  Door for an architect's office.**

SECTION "A-A"
scale: 1½" = 1'-0"

SECTION "B-B"
scale: 1½" = 1'-0"

ELEVATION
Scale: 3/8" = 1'-0"

**SECTION "A-A"**
Scale: 1½" = 1'—0"

face of wall

2⅞"

1'—0"
Stone Reveal

1⅜"  4⅝"  6"
splay

W. I. Orna Straps

¼" Joints

Corner of Tower  "A"

9" rad  Spring Line

Stone Carved
Corbel (Model)

W. I. Straps
& Hinges

"A"

Sand Blasted
Briar Hill
Limestone

OAK DOOR
'V' cut Joints

"B"  "B"

1⅞"
8¾"  4⅝"    3'—2¾"    4⅝"  1⅞"
splay  Masonry Opng.  splay

Stone Sill

Grade

5
1'—0⅞" Jt.
3½"
1'—0⅜" Jt.
1'—3½"
1'—0⅞" Jt.
8'—5½"
1'—3½"
¾" Jt.
11½"
½" Jt.
10"
¾" Jt.
1'—4¾"

**ELEVATION**
scale: ½" = 1'—0"

3½"
⅛"

Screen Door

4" Bluestone Sill

Horizontal
Grain

2'—7⅞"
2⅞"

2"
frame

⅝" strap

½"

5/16"  2¾"  5/16"
Door

1'—0"
brick

**BASE**

chamfer

bluestone
Sill

6"

1'—0"
stone

4⅝"

face of wall

1⅜"
⅜"
1¾"
base

1¼"  4⅝"  1½"

**SECTION "B-B"**
Scale: 1½" = 1'—0"

# DOORS

**Exterior Wood Entrance Doors**

DETAIL of
W.I. STUD.
Scale: 3" = 1'-0"

furred plaster
ceiling

2¼"

Holes

face of wall

Carving

3⅜"  1¼"  2½"
1⅛"

Leaded Gl. Panel
W.I. Grille

**SECTION "C-C"**
s c a l e :  1½" = 1'—0"

3-¾" slate

Carved Oak Door Head

"C"

¼" Projection

Leaded Glass
Panel-Fixed

W.I. Knocker

Carved Oak

Oak Door
Broad Axed Surface

W.I. Studs

3-2" Door

stone sill

Brick Step

Grade

E L E V A T I O N
S c a l e :  ½" = 1'—0"

3'-2"

Line of Abacus
(above)

Pitch

face of wall

Varies

**SECTION "A-A"**
s c a l e :  1½" = 1'—0"

Carving

W.I. Stud

Wood Saddle

**SECTION "B-B"**
s c a l e :  1½" = 1'—0"

**SECTION "C-C"**
Scale: ¾" = 1'—0"

Flashing

Copper Cov'd Hood

4'-1½" R.

2"x2" Angle frame

2'-1½"

2'-7¾"

Wrought Iron Bracket

Expansion Bolt

**ELEVATION**
Scale: ⅜" = 1'—0"

Copper Covered Wood Hood
Standing Seams

W.I. Bracket

W.I. Brackets

Painted brick

Wood Door

W.I. Hardware

"V" cuts with W.I.
Ornamental Nails
at intersections

stone sill & Terrace

**INTERIOR ELEVATION
OF DOOR** Scale ⅜" = 1'—0"

**SECTION "A-A"**
Scale: ¾" = 1'—0"

stone flagging sill

£ of Door

1'-8"   5"   2'-0"

Pitch

3'-6" Radius
stone flagging

**SECTION "B-B"**
Scale: ¾" = 1'—0"

2⅝"   5⅝"   2¼"

W.I. Nails

Bronze Weatherstrip Saddle
¼" pitch         fin floor

stone terrace

Grade

# DOORS

**Exterior Wood Entrance Doors**

·HALF·INTERIOR·
ELEVATION·OF·
·DOOR· ½"=1'-0"

"1" "1"

2"

**SECTION "1-1"**

T.C. Block

6 T.C.

face of plaster

1'-9"

Concrete

3"

8" 8"

**SECTION "A-A"**
Scale : 1½" = 1'-0"

"A"

wood carving

1'-0"

Adzed Finish
as directed

3'-3¾"

Leaded Glass
Panel (fixed)

"A"

2'-2"

6'-8" (Door)

9"

stucco
finish

Oak Door &
Frame

"B" "B"

3" 3'-4" (Door) 3"

"C"

Brick Sill

ELEVATION·
·SCALE: ½"=1'-0"

Grade

"C"

T.C. Block

8"

furring

Wood Saddle

2"

Concrete

Brick Sill

Line of Wood Trim
(above)

3"

½"

**SECTION "B-B"**
Scale : 1½" equals 1'-0"

**SECTION "C-C"**
Scale : 1½" = 1'-0"

Screen Door

Wood Saddle
Weatherstripped

¼" Pitch

Brick Sill

7"

2

Base Cap

Approx 4'-0"

Stone flagging

## DOORS

**Exterior Wood Entrance Doors**

1½" SCALE · DETAIL · OF · W·I·
STRAP · & · DOOR · KNOCKER ·

ELEVATION
scale: ½" = 1'-0"

SECTION "A-A"
scale: 1½" = 1'-0"

SECTION "B-B"

/cale: 3/8" = 1'-0"

Oak

Lighting Fixture

Spring Line

16" I

12"

1 1/2" R.

2'-6"
/play

12"
/play

W. I. Knocker

Painted Brick

3'-8"

7 1/2"
/play

7 1/2"
/play

4"    Wood    Panels

6'-6"

Fin. Floor

Flag/tone

Bra//
/addle

Terrace Floor

Spring Line

Grind Face
of Brick

Sheathing

Copper
Flashing

2' x 4'
/tud/

Lath &
Pla/ter

2" x 7/8"
Furring
In/ulation

4" Brick

Spring Line

6'-6 1/8"

Brick Jamb /play
/creen Door

Bra//
/addle

Fin. Floor

1'-0"

1 1/8"

4"

2 1/4"

1/2" Pitch

Membrane
Waterproofing

2'/tone

3" Concrete

12"

Concrete Wall

2 1/4"

3/4"

1 1/8"

1 5/8"

· DETAIL · OF ·
· DOOR · PANEL
· /cale: half · full · /ize

## DOORS

**Exterior Wood Entrance Doors**

FLASHING

BLOCKING

HEADER

CASING

HEAD JAMB

EXTERIOR DOOR

COMBINATION DOOR

INSERT

GLASS

A

RABBETED STOP
AND WEATHERSTRIP

CASING

SIDE JAMB

EXTERIOR DOOR

THRESHOLD

B

COMBINATION DOOR

EXTERIOR DOOR

THRESHOLD AND
WEATHERSTRIP

SILL

C

**Fig. 23    Exterior door and frame. Exterior-door and combination-door (screen and storm) cross sections:
*A*, head jamb; *B*, side jamb; *C*, sill.**

HARDWOOD DOOR FRAMES

WOOD PANELS

BASE BELOW

TYP. 1/8" REVEAL W/WOOD

SCHED. DOOR 9¾" PLINTH BELOW

**WOOD DOOR JAMB**

**Wood clad metal door frames**

SCHED MOLDING

WOOD PANEL

TYP. 1/8" REVEAL

SCHED PTN.

VERIFY

HARDWOOD DOOR FRAME

SCHED DOOR

**WOOD DOOR HEAD**

STEEL ANGLES & TIES AS REQ'D

SCHED. PARTITION W/ ELEVATOR FRAME

HARDWD FRAME (SCRIBE TO ELEV. FRAME) W/IND-1 VENEER

LINE OF BASE BELOW

STONE BASE BELOW

STONE PILASTER

**JAMB @ ELEVATOR**

**Marble jamb and head details at elevator**

RE: 16/A8-7 FOR NOTES & DIMENSIONS

STEEL ANGLES & TIES AS REQ'D

EXIST. ELEVATOR FRAME

**HEAD @ ELEVATOR**

F-1  H.M. FRAME - HWD. TRIM
3"=1'-0"

F-2  H.M. MULLION HWD. TRIM
3"=1'-0"
(ALSO TYPICAL AS ASTRAGAL FOR CLASS "B" F.R.S.C. DOORS IN FIREWALL)

F-3  H.M. FRAME - ONE-SIDE HWD. TRIM
3"=1'-0"

F-4  H.M. FRAME - PLAS./BOTH SIDES
3"=1'-0"

F-5  H.M. FRAME - PLAS./ONE SIDE
3"=1'-0"

F-6  H.M. EXTERIOR FRAME
3"=1'-0"

F-7  H.M. FRAME - HARDWOOD/ONE SIDE
3"=1'-0"  SEE DETAIL 4/A-20 FOR DOOR #11

F-8 H.M. FRAME 3"=1'-0"

F-9 H.M. MULLION 3"=1'-0"

F-10 H.M. FRAME 3"=1'-0"

F-11A H.M. FRAME HWD. TRIM/ONE SIDE 3"=1'-0"

F-11 H.M. FRAME HWD. TRIM/ONE SIDE 3"=1'-0"

F-13 HARDWOOD FRAME 3"=1'-0"

F-12 H.M. EXTERIOR FRAME 3"=1'-0"

F-14 #2Y 3"=1'-0"

F-14A #2Y 3"=1'-0"

## DOORS

**Bi-Fold Doors**

VINYL FABRIC
ON PLASTER

GRANT #2620
BI-FOLD HARD-
WARE OR EQUAL

CASING BEAD

OAK EDGE

3/4" OAK PLYWOOD
BI-FOLD DOORS

SCREW & PLUG

OAK FRAME

1/4" HARDWOOD VENEER
PLYWOOD PANEL

### HEAD

PLYWOOD
BI-FOLD DOOR

IVES # 261 B-4
FLUSH BOLT
OR EQUAL

3/4"

SILL

### FLUSH BOLT DETAIL
@ 1/2 FULL SIZE

8'-0"
FIN. JAMB

3/4" 1 1/4"

### JAMB

OAK SILL

FAMILY ALCOVE

**CHAPEL**
(215)

7 5/8"

5 5/8"

3/4"    3/4"  1/4"

### SILL

## BI-FOLD DOOR DETAILS
@ 3" = 1'-0"

10"

PLASTIC LAMINATE
TOP & EDGES & BOTTOM

1 1/4"

DOOR

PIANO HINGE

SHELF ON DROP LEAF
SUPPORT, SELBY HARDWARE
# DLS-1 OR EQUAL

· ELEVATION · OF · SLIDING · DOORS ·

· SECTION · THRU · HEAD · "A-A" ·

· SECTION · THRU · MUNTIN · "D-D" ·

· SECTION · THRU · JAMB · "E-E" ·

· SECTION · THRU · ASTRAGAL · "C-C" ·

· SECTION · THRU · BOTTOM · RAIL · "D-D" ·

## DOORS
### Hardware

Fig. 24 Door clearances.

Hardware for doors may be obtained in a number of finishes, with brass, bronze, and nickel perhaps the most common. Door sets are usually classed as (a) entry lock for exterior doors, (b) bathroom set (inside lock control with safety slot for opening from the outside), (c) bedroom lock (keyed lock), and (d) passage set (without lock).

### Hinges

Using three hinges for hanging 1¾-in exterior doors and two hinges for the lighter interior doors is common practice. There is some tendency for exterior doors to warp during the winter because of the difference in exposure on the opposite sides. The three hinges reduce this tendency. Three hinges are also useful on doors that lead to unheated attics and for wider and heavier doors that may be used within the house.

Loose-pin butt hinges should be used and must be of the proper size for the door they support. For 1¾-in-thick doors, use 4- by 4-in butts; for 1⅜-in doors, 3½- by 3½-in butts. After the door is fitted to the framed opening, with the proper clearances, hinge halves are fitted to the door. They are routed into the door edge with about a 3-16"-in back distance (Fig. 26A). One hinge half should be set flush with the surface and must be fastened square with the edge of the door. Screws are included with each pair of hinges.

Fig. 26 Installation of door hardware: A, hinge; B, mortise lock; C, bored lock set.

Fig. 25 Door details: A, installation of strike plate; B, location of stops.

Determination of the hand of mortise or rim locks

Locks not designated as reversible are made right-hand, left-hand, right-hand reverse bevel, or left-hand reverse bevel.

The hand of a lock is invariably determined from the outside of an entrance door or from the corridor or hall side of a room door. An easy method of determining the hand of a lock is to imagine oneself on that side of the opening from which the lock is controlled or operated by the key. Viewing the opening in this position, note which one of the following is true: (1) If the door swings in and is hinged at your right hand, the lock is right-hand; (2) if hinged at your left hand, the lock is left-hand; (3) if the door swings toward you and is hinged at your right, the lock is right-hand reverse bevel; (4) if hinged at your left hand, the lock is left-hand reverse bevel.

You may find that many locks are marked "reversible," meaning that they are interchangeably right- or left-hand, and in these instances no reference to hand or bevel of lock is necessary. These are locks which operate alike from both sides or locks which can be inverted in order to reverse the locking functions.

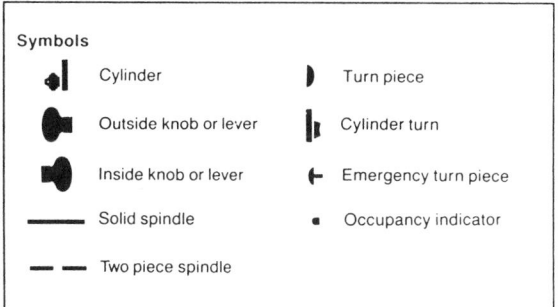

Features of and symbols for door hardware

# DOORS

## Lock Functions

### OFFICE

**For Inner Office and Area Entry Doors.**
- Latchbolt retracted by lever or knob from either side unless outside is locked by stop button.
- When outside is locked, latchbolt is retracted by key outside and lever or knob inside.
- Auxiliary latch deadlocks latchbolt when door is closed.
- Latch holdback available.

### APARTMENT ENTRANCE

**For Apartment House or Office Building Entrance Doors**
- Latchbolt retracted by lever or knob either side unless outside is locked by key from inside.
- When locked, latchbolt retracted by tenant key outside, lever or knob inside.
- Auxiliary latch deadlocks latchbolt when door is closed.

### INSTITUTION

**For Permanently Locked Passage Doors.**
- Latchbolt retracted by key from either side.
- Both levers or knobs always inoperative.
- Auxiliary latch deadlocks latchbolt when door is closed.
- Latch holdback available.

### STORE DOOR

**For Store Entrance Doors.**
- Latchbolt retracted by lever or knob from either side unless outside is locked by stop button.
- When locked latchbolt retracted by key outside and lever or knob inside.
- Deadbolt operated by key from either side.
- Auxiliary latch deadlocks latchbolt when door is closed.

### STORE DOOR

**For Storedoor, Storeroom or Utility Room Doors.**
- Latchbolt retracted by lever or knob from either side.
- Deadbolt operated by key from either side.

### CYLINDER X TURN PIECE

**Deadlock**
- Deadbolt operated by key outside and turn inside.

### DOUBLE CYLINDER

**Double Cylinder Deadlock**
- Deadbolt operated by key from either side.
- Bolt automatically deadlocks when fully thrown.

### CLASSROOM

**Classroom Deadlock**
- Deadbolt operated by key outside.
- Cylinder turn inside will retract deadbolt but will not project it.
- Bolt automatically deadlocks when fully thrown.

### CYLINDER X BLANK

**Deadlock**
- Deadbolt operated by key from one side.
- No trim on opposite side.
- Bolt automatically deadlocks when fully thrown.

### CLASSROOM

- Latchbolt retracted by lever or knob from either side unless outside is locked by key.
- Inside lever or knob always free for immediate exit.
- Auxiliary latch deadlocks latchbolt when door is closed.

### STOREROOM

- Latchbolt retracted by lever or knob inside, by key outside.
- Outside lever or knob always inoperative. Knob is free spinning.
- Auxiliary latch deadlocks latchbolt when door is closed.
- Latch holdback available.

### ENTRANCE

**For Commercial and Residential Entry Doors**
- Deadbolt and latchbolt retracted by lever or knob trim either side unless outside is locked by stop button.
- When locked, key outside and lever or knob inside retracts deadbolt and latchbolt simultaneously. Outside remains locked until stop button is reset to unlocked position.
- Deadbolt operated by key and turn piece. Throwing deadbolt automatically locks stop button.
- Auxiliary latch deadlocks latchbolt when door is closed and locked.

### CONVALESCENT

**For Convalescent or Bedroom Doors**
- Latchbolt retracted by lever or knob from either side when unlocked.
- Deadbolt operated by key outside and turn piece inside.
- Throwing deadbolt disengages outside lever or knob.
- Turning inside lever or knob retracts deadbolt and latchbolt simultaneously for immediate exit and unlocks outside.

### CLOSET

**For Closet, Storeroom, or Utility Room Doors**
- Latchbolt retracted by lever or knob from either side at all times.
- Deadbolt operated by key outside.

### DORMITORY

**For Dormitory or Bedroom Doors.**
- Latchbolt retracted by lever or knob from either side at all times.
- Deadbolt is operated by key outside and by turn piece inside.

### HOTEL

**For Corridor Doors to Guest Rooms.**
- Outside lever or knob always inoperative. Knob is free spinning.
- Latchbolt retracted by guest key outside except when deadbolt is thrown by turn piece inside.
- When thrown occupancy indicator is engaged, all keys inoperative except emergency or display keys.
- Turning inside lever or knob retracts deadbolt and latchbolt simultaneously. Aux. latch deadlocks latchbolt when door is closed.

### HOTEL

**For Corridor Doors to Guest Rooms**
- Same as 85P function except that visual "DO NOT DISTURB" plate replaces occupancy indicator button.

Available for 1¾" doors and escutcheon trim only.

## Non-Keyed Locks — ANSI A156.2 Series 4000

| A. N. S. I. No. | Grade | |
|---|---|---|
| A10S | F75 | 2 |
| C10S | | 1 |
| D10S | | 1 |
| F10N | | 2 |

**Passage Latch:** Both knobs always unlocked

| D12D | F89 | 1 |
|---|---|---|

**Exit Lock:** Unlocked by knob inside only. Outside knob always fixed.

| A20S | | |
|---|---|---|

**Closet Latch:** Outside knob and inside thumbturn are always unlocked.

| A25D | | |
|---|---|---|
| D25D | | |

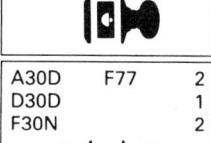

**Exit Lock:** Blank plate outside. Inside knob always unlocked. (Specify door thickness, 1⅜" or 1¾".)

| A30D | F77 | 2 |
|---|---|---|
| D30D | | 1 |
| F30N | | 2 |

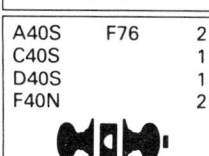

**Patio Lock:** Push-button locking. Turning inside knob releases button. Closing door on A & D series also releases button.

| A40S | F76 | 2 |
|---|---|---|
| C40S | | 1 |
| D40S | | 1 |
| F40N | | 2 |

**Bath/Bedroom Privacy Lock:** Push-button locking. Can be opened from outside with small screwdriver or flat narrow tool. Turning inside knob releases push-button. Closing door on A, C and D series also releases button, preventing lock-out.

| A43D | F79 | 2 |
|---|---|---|

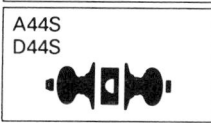

**Communicating Lock:** Turn button in outer knob locks and unlocks knob and inside thumbturn.

| A44S | | |
|---|---|---|
| D44S | | |

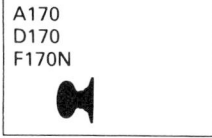

**Hospital Privacy Lock:** Push-button locking. Unlocked from outside by turning emergency turn-button. Rotating inside knob or closing door releases inside button.

## Dummy Trim

| A. N. S. I. No. | Grade | |
|---|---|---|
| A170 | | |
| D170 | | |
| F170N | | |

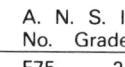

**Single Dummy Trim:** Single dummy trim for one side of door. Used for door pull or as matching inactive trim.

## Keyed Locks — ANSI A156.2 Series 4000

| A. N. S. I. No. | Grade | |
|---|---|---|
| F51N | F81 | 2 |

**Entrance Lock:** Unlocked by key from outside when outer knob is locked by turn-button in inside knob. Inside knob always unlocked.

| D50PD | F82 | 1 |
|---|---|---|

**Entrance/Office Lock:** Push button locking. Pushing button locks outside lever until unlocked with key or by turning inside lever.

| A53PD | F81 | 2 |
|---|---|---|
| C53PD | F82 | 1 |
| D53PD | F82 | 1 |

**Entrance Lock:** Turn/Push button locking: Pushing and turning button locks outside knob requiring use of key until button is manually unlocked. Push button locking: Pushing button locks outside knob until unlocked by key or by turning inside knob.

| A55PD | F92 | 2 |
|---|---|---|
| D55PD | | 1 |

**Service Station Lock:** Unlocked by key from outside when outer knob is locked by universal button in inside knob. Closing door releases button. Outside knob may be fixed by rotating universal button.

| D60PD | F88 | 1 |
|---|---|---|

**Vestibule Lock:** Unlocked by key from outside when outside knob is locked by key in inside knob. Inside knob is always unlocked.

| D66PD | F91 | 1 |
|---|---|---|

**Store Lock:** Key in either knob locks or unlocks both knobs.

| A70PD | F84 | 2 |
|---|---|---|
| C70PD | | 1 |
| D70PD | | 1 |

**Classroom Lock:** Outside knob locked and unlocked by key. Inside knob always unlocked.

| D72PD | F80 | 1 |
|---|---|---|

**Communicating Lock:** Key in either knob locks or unlocks each knob independently.

| A73PD | F90 | 2 |
|---|---|---|
| D73PD | | 1 |

**Dormitory Lock:** Locked or unlocked by key from outside. Push-button locking from inside. Turning inside knob or closing door releases button.

| D76PD | F85 | 1 |
|---|---|---|

**Classroom Hold-Back Lock:** Outside knob locked or unlocked by key. Inside knob always unlocked. Latch may be locked in retracted position by key.

## DOORS
**Lock Functions**

|  | A. N. S. I.<br>No. | Grade |
|---|---|---|
| A79PD | | |

### Keyed Locks
**ANSI A156.2**
**Series 4000**

**Communicating Lock:** Locked or unlocked by key from outside. Blank plate inside.

|  | A. N. S. I.<br>No. | Grade |
|---|---|---|
| A80PD | F86 | 2 |
| C80PD | | 1 |
| D80PD | | 1 |
| F80N | | 2 |

**Storeroom Lock:** Outside knob fixed. Entrance by key only. Inside Knob always unlocked.

|  | | |
|---|---|---|
| D82PD | F87 | 1 |

**Institution Lock:** Both knobs fixed. Entrance by key in either knob.

|  | | |
|---|---|---|
| A85PD | F93 | 2 |
| D85PD | | 1 |

**Hotel-Motel Lock:** Outside knob fixed. Entrance by key only. Push-button in inside knob activates visual occupancy indicator, allowing only emergency masterkey to operate. Rotation of inside spanner-button provides lockout feature by keeping indicator thrown.

|  | A. N. S. I.<br>No. | Grade |
|---|---|---|
| B160N | E2151 | 2 |
| B460P | | 1 |
| B560 | | 1 |

### Deadbolt Locks   ANSI A 156.5

**Single Cylinder Deadbolt Lock:** Deadbolt thrown or retracted by key from outside or by inside turn unit. Bolt automatically deadlocks when fully thrown.

|  | | |
|---|---|---|
| B162N† | E2141 | 2 |
| B462P† | | 1 |
| B562† | | 1 |

**Double Cylinder Deadbolt Lock:** Deadbolt thrown or retracted by key from either side.

|  | | |
|---|---|---|
| B461P | E2161 | 1 |

**One-Way Deadbolt Lock:** Deadbolt thrown or retracted by key only. Blank plate inside.

|  | | |
|---|---|---|
| B463P | E2171 | 1 |

**Classroom Deadbolt Lock:** Deadbolt thrown or retracted by key outside. Inside turn unit will retract bolt only.

|  | | |
|---|---|---|
| B464P | | |

**Cylinder Lock:** Deadbolt thrown or retracted by key from one side. No inside trim.

|  | | |
|---|---|---|
| B180 | E2191 | 2 |
| B480 | | 1 |

**Door Bolt:** Deadbolt thrown or retracted by turn unit only. No outside trim.

|  | A. N. S. I.<br>No. | Grade |
|---|---|---|
| B250PD | E2121 | 1 |

### Deadlatch Locks   ANSI A156.5

**Night Latch:** Deadlocking latchbolt retracted by key from outside or by inside turn unit. Rotating turn unit and activating hold-back feature keeps latch retracted.

|  | | |
|---|---|---|
| B252PD† | E2111 | 1 |

**Double Cylinder Deadlatch:** Deadlocking latchbolt retracted by key from either side. No hold-back feature.

|  | | |
|---|---|---|
| B270D | E2181 | 1 |

**Exit Latch:** Deadlocking latchbolt retracted by inside turn unit only. No outside trim. Rotating turn unit and activating hold-back feature keeps latch retracted.

| Schlage<br>Number | A. N. S. I.<br>No. | Grade |
|---|---|---|
| B245S | | |

### Lever Functions

**Lever Passage Latch:** For use on passage, closet and doors that do not require locking. Rotating either lever retracts latchbolt. (Specify door hand.)

|  | | |
|---|---|---|
| B281<br>B282 | | |

**Single Dummy Trim-Double Dummy Trim:** For use on single or pairs of doors when fixed turn is required. (Specify door hand.)

|  | A. N. S. I.<br>No. | Grade |
|---|---|---|
| E51PD | | |

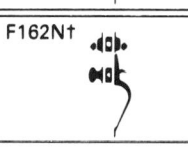

### Grip Handle Sets

**Entrance Lock:** Unlocked by key from outside when thumb-piece is locked by inside turn-button.

|  | | |
|---|---|---|
| F160N | | |

**Entrance Lock:** Deadbolt thrown or retracted by key from outside or by inside turn unit. Latch retracted by thumbpiece from outside or by inside knob.

|  | | |
|---|---|---|
| F162N† | | |

**Double Cylinder Entrance Lock:** Deadbolt thrown or retracted by key from either side. Latch retracted by thumbpiece from outside or by inside knob.

†CAUTION: Double cylinder locks on residences and any door in any structure which is used for egress are a safety hazard in times of emergency and their use is not recommended. Installation should be in accordance with existing codes only.

## Dummy Trim

| A. N. S. I. | |
|---|---|
| No. | Grade |

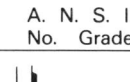

E193

F193N

**Outside and Inside Dummy Trim:** For use as door pull or as dummy trim on an inactive of pair of doors. Fixed thumb-piece and inside knob. Thru bolted dummy cylinder.

**Outside and Inside Dymmy Trim:** For use as door pull or as dummy trim on inactive leaf of pair of doors. Fixed thumbpiece and inside knob. Dummy cylinder with inside plate.

## Interconnected Locks    ANSI A156.12

| No. | Grade |
|---|---|

H110    F95    4

**Entrance—Single Locking:** Deadbolt thrown or retracted by key in upper lock from outside or by inside turn unit. Latchbolt retracted by knob from either side. Turning inside knob retracts deadbolt and latchbolt simultaneously for immediate exit.

H153    F97    4

**Entrance—Double Locking:** Deadbolt thrown or retracted by key in upper lock from outside or by inside turn unit. Deadlatch retracted by key in outer knob when locked by pushing turn-button in inner knob. Outer knob may be fixed in locked position by rotating turn-button. Inside knob retracts deadbolt and deadlatch simultaneously for immediate exit.

H180

**Storeroom Lock:** Bolt may be operated by key from outside or by turn unit from inside. Bolt automatically deadlocks when fully thrown. Lock may be opened by key from outside. Inside knob will retract both latch and deadbolt. Latch automatically deadlocks when door is closed, inside knob always free for immediate exit. Outer knob always fixed.

H185    F100    4

**Hotel-Motel Lock:** Deadbolt thrown or retracted by key in upper lock from outside or by inside turn unit. Deadlatch retracted by key in outer fixed knob. Push-button in inner knob activates visual occupancy indicator, allowing only emergency masterkey to operate. Rotation of inside spanner-button provides lockout feature by keeping indicator thrown. Turning inside knob retracts deadbolt simultaneously for immediate exit.

## Dummy Trim

| A. N. S. I. | |
|---|---|
| No. | Grade |

H170

H172

**Single Dummy Inside Trim:** Snap-on rose and knob. Concealed mounting screws.

**Dummy Trim Inside and Outside:** Snap-on rose and knobs thru-bolted.

## Mortise Locks Non-Keyed    ANSI A156.13 Series 1000

| A. N. S. I. | | |
|---|---|---|
| No. | Grade | |

L9010*    F01    1

**Passage Latch:** Latch bolt retracted by lever or knob from either side at all times.

L9040    F22    1

**Bath/Bedroom Privacy Lock:** Latchbolt retracted by lever or knob from either side unless outside is locked by inside turn piece. Operating inside lever or knob or closing door unlocks outside lever or knob. To unlock from outside, remove emergency button, insert turn piece (furnished) in access hole and rotate.

L0170

**Single Dummy Trim:** Lever or knob on both sides fixed by mounting bar.

L0172*

**Pair Dummy Trim:** Lever or knob on both sides fixed by mounting bar.

L9175**

**Single Dummy Trim:** Lever or knob on one side fixed. Includes lock chassis and armor front.

L9176**

**Pair Dummy Trim:** Lever or knob both sides fixed. Includes lock chassis and armor front.

## Keyed Locks

| A. N. S. I. | | |
|---|---|---|
| No. | Grade | |

L9050*    F04    1

**Office and Inner Entry Lock:** Latchbolt retracted by lever or knob from either side unless outside is made inoperative by key outside or by rotating inside turn piece. When outside is locked, latchbolt is retracted by key outside or by lever or knob inside. Outside lever or knob remains locked until thumbturn is returned to vertical or by counter clockwise rotation of key. Auxiliary latch deadlocks latchbolt when door is closed.

L9060*    F09    1

**Apartment Entrance Lock:** Latchbolt retracted by lever or knob from either side unless outside is locked by key from inside. When locked, latchbolt retracted by key outside or lever or knob inside. Auxiliary latch deadlocks when door is closed.

L9070*    F05    1

**Classroom Lock:** Latchbolt retracted by lever or knob from either side unless outside is locked by key. Unlocked from outside by key. Inside lever or knob always free for immediate exit. Auxiliary latch deadlocks latchbolt when door is closed.

**When armored front is required as strike for inactive door, specify L9177 for single or L9178 for pair of dummy trim. Specify door hand.

**DOORS**

Lock Functions

| A. N. S. I. | | |
|---|---|---|
| L9080 | F07 | 1 |

## Keyed Locks

**Storeroom Lock:** Latchbolt retracted by key outside or by lever or knob inside. Outside lever or knob always inoperative. Auxiliary latch deadlocks latchbolt when door is closed.

| | | |
|---|---|---|
| L9080EL | | |

**Storeroom Lock:** Electrically locked. Outside lever or knob continuously locked by 24V AC or DC. Latchbolt retracted by key outside or by lever or knob inside. Switch or power failure allows outside lever or knob to retract latchbolt. Auxiliary latch deadlocks latchbolt when door is closed. Inside lever or knob always free for immediate exit.

| | | |
|---|---|---|
| L9080EU | | |

**Storeroom Lock:** Electrically unlocked. Outside lever or knob unlocked by 24V AC or DC. Latchbolt retracted by key outside or lever or knob inside. Auxiliary latch deadlocks latchbolt when door is closed. Inside lever or knob always free for immediate exit.

| | | |
|---|---|---|
| L9082 | | |

**Institution Lock:** Latchbolt retracted by key from either side. Lever or knob on both sides always inoperative. Auxiliary latch deadlocks latchbolt when door is closed.

| | | |
|---|---|---|
| L9453 | F20 | 1 |

**Entrance Lock:** Latchbolt retracted by lever or knob from either side unless outside is locked by 20° rotation of thumbturn. Deadbolt thrown or retracted by 90° rotation of thumbturn. When locked, key outside or lever or knob inside retracts deadbolt and latchbolt simultaneously. Outside lever or knob remains locked until thumbturn is restored to vertical position. Throwing deadbolt automatically locks outside lever or knob. Auxiliary latch deadlocks latchbolt when door is closed.

| | | |
|---|---|---|
| L9456 | F13 | 1 |

**Dormitory/Exit Lock:** Latchbolt retracted by lever or knob from either side. Deadbolt thrown or retracted by key outside or inside thumbturn. Throwing deadbolt locks outside lever or knob. Rotating inside lever or knob simultaneously retracts deadbolt and latchbolt, and unlocks outside lever or knob.

| | | |
|---|---|---|
| L9465 | | 1 |

**Closet/Storeroom Lock:** Latchbolt retracted by lever or knob from either side except when deadbolt is extended. Deadbolt extended or retracted by key outside.

| | | |
|---|---|---|
| L9466 | F14 | 1 |

**Store/Utility Room Lock:** Latchbolt retracted by knob or lever from either side except when deadbolt extended. Deadbolt extended or retracted by key from either side.

| | | |
|---|---|---|
| L9473 | F21 | 1 |

**Dormitory/Bedroom Lock:** Latchbolt retracted by knob or lever from either side except when deadbolt is extended. Deadbolt extended or retracted by key outside or thumbturn inside.

| A. N. S. I. | | |
|---|---|---|
| L9485 | | |

## Keyed Locks

**Hotel Lock:** Latchbolt by key outside or by lever or knob inside. Outside lever or knob always fixed. Deadbolt thrown or retracted by inside thumbturn. When deadbolt is thrown, all keys become inoperative except emergency or display keys. Turning inside lever or knob retracts both deadbolt and latchbolt simultaneously. Auxiliary latch deadlocks latchbolt when door is closed.

| | | |
|---|---|---|
| L9486 | F15 | 1 |

**Hotel Lock:** Latchbolt retracted by key outside or by lever or knob inside. Outside lever or knob always fixed. Deadbolt thrown or retracted by inside thumbturn. When deadbolt is thrown, "DO NOT DISTURB" plate is displayed—all keys become inoperative except emergency or display keys. Turning inside lever or knob retracts both deadbolt and latchbolt simultaneously. Auxiliary latch deadlocks latchbolt when door is closed.

| A. N. S. I. | | |
|---|---|---|
| L9460 | F17 | 1 |

## Deadlocks

**Cylinder X Thumbturn:** Deadbolt thrown or retracted by key outside or thumbturn inside.

| | | |
|---|---|---|
| L9462 | F16 | 1 |

**Double Cylinder:** Deadbolt operated by key from either side.

| | | |
|---|---|---|
| L9463 | | 1 |

**Classroom Lock:** Deadbolt thrown or retracted by key from outside. Inside cylinder turn retracts deadbolt but cannot project it.

| | | |
|---|---|---|
| L9464 | F18 | 1 |

**Cylinder Lock:** Deadbolt thrown or retracted by key from one side. No trim on opposite side.

This section provides the designer with information on both suspended ceilings and ceilings directly attached to the structure above. It starts with a review of generic suspension systems and then provides details and discussion of the various suspended ceiling types.

Large-scale details show how, in addition to standard acoustical tiles, other ceiling materials such as plaster, metal panels, baffles, gypsum board, and wood can be attached to suspension systems. A variety of

unusual conditions are also detailed, including curved and vaulted ceilings, wall conditions, light coves, and lighting fixture framing.

The designer is cautioned that in many jurisdictions, suspension systems must attain a higher level of structural integrity than most other architectural elements. For example, wire hangers may not be an acceptable method of suspending channels from the structure above. Rather, steel rods of a minimum diameter or flat bar hangers of a

minimum width and thickness may be required. Local or state codes should always be consulted prior to finalizing such details.

In many situations, the ceiling "skin" takes on further importance beyond aesthetic, acoustical, or visual requirements. It can also be used to complete an envelope that provides a fire-resistive rating to the structural members above. Again, it is necessary to thoroughly investigate the building and fire codes that might govern ceiling design.

### Acoustical Tile and Lay-in Panel Ceiling Suspension Systems

# CEILINGS

Suspension System Types

EXPOSED T GRID SYSTEM

CONCEALED Z BAR SYSTEM

SIDE MOUNTING LEVELING LUG BY FIXTURE MFG. INSTALLATION BY ELECTRICIAN AS PART OF FIXTURE - 2 PER SIDE

WALL MOULDING, CAN BE L OR L

WALL SPRING CLIP

Z BAR COUPLING - P-41

WHERE PURLIN OCCURS AT LIGHT, TOP LIP SHALL BE BENT UP TO PREVENT CLIP FROM SLIDING OFF

FIXTURE VARIES WITH MFG TILE OPENING

DETAIL AT WALL

LOCKING BAR

SECTION "A-A"

LOCKING BAR OR APPROVED EQUAL

WIRE CLIP, #9 SPRING STL OR APPROVED EQUAL

11" × 3/4" × .021 FLAT ANTI-BREATHING SPLINE - 12" O.C. (NOTE: ANGLE OR TEE SPLINE MAY BE USED)

1/2" DIA. GALV. STEEL ROD OR 1/8 × 1" ASPHALT PAINTED FLAT STRAP HANGER, NOT TO EXCEED 4'-6" O.C.

### NOTES

1. IN THE EVENT A LOCKING BAR CANNOT BE INSERTED BECAUSE OF CONTINUOUS OR TANDEM LIGHTS, THE Z BAR SHALL BE SECURED TO THE 1/2" FURRING MEMBER BY MEANS OF A MECH. FASTENING I.E. RIVET, SHEET METAL SCREW, OR OTHER MEANS.

2. THE TOTAL WEIGHT OF A LIGHT FIXTURE AND OTHER EQUIPMENT (AIR BOXES ETC.) AND CEILING MATERIAL SUPPORTED BY THE EXPOSED Z BAR MUST NOT EXCEED THE ALLOWABLE DEFLECTION OF 1/360 OF ITS SPAN. DEFLECTION DATA MUST BE FURNISHED AND CERTIFIED BY THE MANUFACTURER.

3. SURFACE OR PENDENT FIXTURES MUST BE INDEPENDENTLY SUPPORTED FROM 1 1/2" BLACK IRON CHAN. OR FROM FLOOR OR ROOF CONSTRUCTION ABOVE.

12" OR 24"

1 1/2" ELECTRO-GALV. STEEL "Z" BAR

SELF-LEVELING TONGUE & GROOVE JOINT

GAT CLIP #B I.S.L, CAT #16-59-SM (OR OTHER APPROVED MEANS)

1 1/2" C.R. 16 GA. STEEL SUSP. CHANNEL .475# APPROX. 4'-6" O.C. (NOTE: LARGER OR HEAVIER CHAN. MAY BE USED WHEN REQ'D BY BLDG. CODE

EXPOSED Z BAR SYSTEM

## CEILINGS
**Gypsum Board Suspended Ceilings**

| ASSEMBLY | REMARKS |
|---|---|
| **GYPSUM BOARD, ATTACHED** | |

### DIRECT TO FRAMING

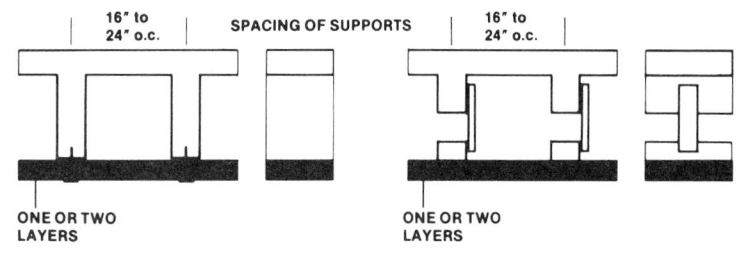

- secured directly to framing members or to solid furring.
- most widely used in residential and light commercial construction.
- two layers may be required for an improved fire resistance rating or for better resistance to sound transmission.
- directly affected by deflection and/or expansion/contraction in supporting framing.

### FURRED-DOWN

- hat-shaped or resilient channels may be used.
- furring will minimize effects of deflection and expansion/contraction in framing upon membrane.
- resilient channels also used to improve resistance to sound transmission.
- furring will also minimize effects of streaking due to temperature differential which may occur with direct attachment.

**GYPSUM BOARD, SUSPENDED**

### PRIMARY SUPPORTS ONLY

- when framing is spaced more than 24 inches on centers, or when a plenum space for mechanical/electrical service lines is required, a suspension/support system consisting of wood or metal sections or special nailing channels is generally provided.
- prefabricated metal suspension systems are available.

### PRIMARY AND SECONDARY SUPPORTS

- primary suspension system may also include a secondary system of furring channels used to align the primary system and/or to provide resilient mounting of the membrane.
- it is a high cost assembly and not widely used.
- resilient furring channels generally used with wood framing.

| ASSEMBLY | REMARKS |
|---|---|
| **PLASTER, ATTACHED** | |

### DIRECT TO FRAMING

16" to 36" o.c.  SPACING OF SUPPORTS  16" to 24" o.c.

METAL LATH    GYPSUM LATH

- metal or gypsum lath secured directly to framing.
- membrane will be directly affected by deflection and/or expansion/contraction in supporting framing.
- metal lath may be backed for machine application of plaster.
- fire resistance ratings for different assemblies have been established.

### FURRED-DOWN

24" to 60" o.c.  SPACING OF SUPPORTS  24" to 60" o.c.

FURRING CHANNELS 16" to 24" on CENTER    FURRING CHANNELS 16" to 24" on CENTER

- furring channels secured to framing, lath supported by furring.
- furring will minimize effects of deflection and expansion/contraction upon membrane.
- large areas of membrane should have expansion joints and should not be restrained at the perimeter.
- corners of openings in gypsum lath membranes should have metal lath reinforcing.

| **PLASTER, SUSPENDED** | |

### PRIMARY SUPPORTS ONLY

16" to 24" o.c.  SPACING OF SUPPORTS  16" to 24" o.c.

OPTIONAL HANGER    OPTIONAL HANGER

METAL LATH    GYPSUM LATH
FURRING CHANNELS 16" to 24" on CENTER    FURRING CHANNELS 16" to 24" on CENTER

- suspended membrane with furring channels only is similar to furred membrane except that furring channels are suspended from, rather than directly attached to, framing members.
- suspension of membrane may be a requirement in some fire resistance rated floor or roof/ceiling assemblies.
- spacing of hangers is quite close and limits the size and/or extent of mechanical/electrical service lines in plenum space.

### PRIMARY AND SECONDARY SUPPORTS

24" to 60" o.c.  SPACING OF SUPPORTS  24" to 60" o.c.

OPTIONAL SUPPORT    OPTIONAL SUPPORT

METAL LATH    GYPSUM LATH
FURRING CHANNELS    FURRING CHANNELS
MAIN CHANNELS    MAIN CHANNELS

- when spacing of framing is wide and/or the number of hangers must be reduced, a primary support system consisting of main carrying channels may be used; the furring channels are then a secondary system, secured to such primary supports.
- for wide hanger spacing, metal joists instead of carrying channels may be used.

| ASSEMBLY | REMARKS |
|---|---|

## EXPOSED GRID: FLAT UNITS

### SQUARE EDGE

- lay-in panels should be secured in place by clips when assembly requires a fire resistance rating; also against uplift due to pressure differential.
- fixtures generally have to be boxed-in for fire resistance rating; fire dampers must be provided at all openings, such as diffusers.
- hangers secured to framing members, structural deck, or to secondary framing system.

### RECESSED EDGE

- clearance required for all lay-in panels for tilting them into place.
- suspension system used is the same as for square edge tile, but tile only available in 2x2 foot size.
- may be used in fire resistance-rated floor or roof/ceiling assemblies; clips to secure tiles in place and opening protection generally required.

## EXPOSED GRID, SHAPED UNITS

### INLAY PANELS, CORRUGATED, RIBBED

- metal panels generally perforated, with sound absorbing blankets.
- plastic panels generally solid; used in luminous ceiling installations.
- corrugated/ribbed metal or plastic panels generally used with main runners only.
- flat plastic panels generally either 2x4 or 2x2 feet in size, used with main runners and cross tees.

### PRE-ASSEMBLED MODULES

- flat pre-assembled modules are also available.
- when pressurized plenum and ventilating tile are used, air return must be ducted through plenum.
- with ventilating plenum, dirt streaking may result unless the membrane is made completely air tight.
- may be used in fire resistance-rated floor or roof/ceiling assemblies.

| ASSEMBLY | REMARKS |
|---|---|
| **CONCEALED GRID, SHAPED UNITS** | |
| **METAL PAN TILE**<br> | • tile may be repeatedly repainted without loss in sound absorbing characteristics.<br>• heating/cooling piping may be incorporated into the system.<br>• combination lighting/infra-red heating fixtures may be integrated into membrane.<br>• secondary suspension system generally required.<br>• tile may be used for supply/return air. |
| **LINEAR PANELS**<br> | • formed prefinished metal panels in long lengths.<br>• air supply/return and lighting fixtures may be integrated into the system.<br>• may be used outdoors in protected locations, such as large soffits, canopies.<br>• some assemblies may be used as required components in fire resistance rated floor or roof/ceiling assemblies.<br>• membranes may be curved perpendicular to direction of panels. |
| **BAFFLES**<br> | • baffles available in shaped metal, with or without sound absorbent material cores, or in faced sound absorbent material.<br>• various arrangements available, such as linear, radial, hexagonal.<br>• used to: provide additional sound absorption in selected locations; for visual interest, or to conceal mechanical/electrical services. |
| **CONCEALED GRID, FLAT UNITS** | |
| **KERFED EDGE**<br> | • tile, generally 12 x 12 inches in size with kerfed edges secured in place by main runners in one direction, and cross tees or splines in the other.<br>• secondary supports, such as carrying channels may be used to reduce spacing of hangers to framing system.<br>• may be used as component in fire resistance rated floor or roof/ceiling assemblies.<br>• special panels available to provide access to plenum. |

# CEILINGS
## Suspended Ceiling Types

**1** — (SQUARE-EDGED) ACOUSTIC TILE ON CONCEALED Z-SPLINE SUSPENSION SYSTEM. TILE TO BE 12"x12"x¾" FIRE-RETARDANT 1-HR RATING. ARMSTRONG FISSURED "TRAVERTONE FIREGUARD" SALFENO DESIGN — OR EQUAL.

Concealed 2-spline system with acoustical tile

**2** — PERFORATED ALUMINUM ACOUSTIC TILE ALUMINUM-CLAD FIRE-RETARDANT CORE (2 HR. RATING) ARMSTRONG "FIREGUARD" — OR EQUAL

Concealed 2-spline system with aluminum-clad acoustical tile

**3** — HARD WHITE GYPSUM PLASTER

Suspended plaster ceiling

**4** — ⅝" GYPSUM BOARD "FIRECODE" (2-HR RATING)

Suspended ceiling with gypsum board

**5** — ¼" PLYWOOD SPACER — ¼" W.V.P. (OAK)

Suspended ceiling with plywood finish

648

WALL FINISH - SEE FINISH PLAN
"W" MOLDING

⅞" FURRING 18" O.C.
CHANNEL CLIP
CHANNEL 1½" - 4'-0" O.C. MAX.
WIRE HANGERS - 4'-0" O.C. MAX.
STEEL ANGLE
CONCRETE SLAB
GYP. BOARD CEILING ⅝"

TYPICAL HUNG GYP. BOARD
CEILING DETAIL

MYLAR-FACED LAY-IN CEILING TILES 2'x2'
MOLDING
T-RUNNER
WIRE HANGER - 4'-0" O.C.
WALL FINISH - SEE FINISH PLAN

TYPICAL LAY-IN TILE
CEILING DETAIL

CROSS TEE
TORSION SPRINGS
MAIN TEE
K-2424 ILLUSIONS CEIL'G PANEL
PERIMETER WALL CHANNEL
SCHEDULED WALL

TYPICAL
CEILING DETAIL

CEILING TILES
Z-SECTION
CHANNEL CLIP
CHANNEL 1½"
WIRE HANGER - 4'-0" O.C. MAX.
MOLDING
SCHEDULED WALL

TYPICAL CONCEALED SPLINE
CEILING DETAIL

Detail 1:
- EXISTING STRUCTURAL STEEL W/SPRAY ON FIRE PROOFING.
- 1½" FURRING CHANNEL, BRACE AS REQUIRED.
- EXISTING WINDOW WALL
- VENT OPENING.
- D.W.C. FURRING CHANNELS.
- 5/8" GYPSUM BD. FASCIA.
- FRY DRYWALL ACOUSTIC MOULDING FDA-G25 OR EQUAL
- SUSPENDED ACOUSTICAL TILE CLG.

CEILING HEIGHT AT 8'-8' DETAIL NO. 1
C.H. AT 8'-0' DETAIL-1A
C.H. AT 7'-6' DETAIL-1B

**1**

Detail 2:
- 1½" FURRING CHANNEL BRACE AS REQUIRED.
- SUSPENDED ACOUSTIC TILE CLG. AT 8'-8' TYP.
- "W" REVEAL MOLDING, WRM 75 (OR EQUAL)
- 3/8" GYPSUM BD. FASCIA.
- D.W.C. FURRING CHANNELS.
- FRY DRY WALL ACOUSTIC MOLDING. FDA-G25 OR EQUAL
- SUSPENDED ACOUSTICAL TILE CLG. CEILING HEIGHT 8'-0' AT DET. NO. 2 CEILING HEIGHT 7'-6' AT DET. NO. 2A

**2**

Detail 3:
- 1½" BLACK IRON
- D.W.C. FURRING CHANNEL
- FLUORESCENT LIGHTING, 2 ROWS, STAGGERED.
- ½" CHANNEL HANGERS.
- D.W.C. FURRING CHANNELS.
- 3/8" GYPSUM BD.
- 12" x ½" LOUVERS. WHITE PLASTIC
- ½" x 3/4" x 1/8" ALUMINUM LS. (ALIGN WITH ELEV. DOOR HEAD.)
- 5/8" GYPSUM BD. FASCIA.
- BRACING AS REQUIRED.
- SUSPENDED ACOUSTIC TILE CLG.
- FRY DRY ACOUSTIC MOLDING FDA-G25 OR EQUAL

CEILING HEIGHT 8'-8'
CEILING HEIGHT 7'-6'

**3**

(4) LIGHT TROUGH & SPRINGLINE EDGE
OF CHAPEL CEILING VAULT @ 5'-4 0"

(5) TYPICAL SPRINGLINE EDGE
OF CHAPEL CEILING VAULTS 3 3'-..

## CEILINGS
**Vaulted Ceiling**

G.R.G. COVE

SCHED MOLDING

MOLDING SUPPORT
RE: 30/AB-3

FACE OF WALL

9'-0"

7 7"

SCALE: 1½" = 1'-0"

HEAD SECTION THRU PORTAL

BEAM BEYOND. G.C. TO COORDINATE
HVAC W/ STRUCTURAL

MTL. STUD FRAMING
& BRACING TO
STRUCTURE AS
REQ'D

RE: 30/AB-3

SHEET METAL
BOOT. RE:
ENG. DWGS.

PROJECTION BEHIND
CURVED VENEER
PLASTER CLG.

ARCH'L SLOT IN GYP. BD.
NO DIFFUSER, PAINT
INSIDE BLACK

SCHED LIGHT FIXTURE
RE: ELECTRICAL

SCHED MOLDING

GYP. BD. COLUMN
BEYOND

12'-0"

1'-2"

VAULTED CEILING WITH
MOULDING FRAMED
COVE LIGHT

6'-1½"
CLEAR

1'-2"

4"

VAULT
FINISH

VENEER
FINISH

JAMB @ PORTAL

G.R.G.

RE: 30/AB-3

SCHED LIGHT
FIXTURE, RE:
ELECTRICAL

SCHED MOLDING

GYP. BD. PILASTER
BEYOND

TO APEX OF CLG.

1'-0"

12'-0"

1'-2"

VAULTED CEILING WITH
MOULDING FRAMED BEAM

(13) DETAIL - SOFFIT IN CAFETERIA AT WINDOW WALL
3" = 1'-0"

(12) DETAIL - SOFFIT IN CAFETERIA
3" = 1'-0"

(14) DETAIL - LINEAR DIFFUSER
F.S.

(10) DETAIL - EDGE @ TYPE "F" FIXTURE
1/2" = 1'-0"

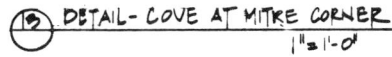

(15) DETAIL - COVE AT MITRE CORNER
1" = 1'-0"

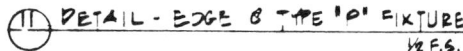

(11) DETAIL - EDGE @ TYPE 'P' FIXTURE
1/2" F.S.

## CEILINGS
Miscellaneous Details of Suspended Ceilings

① SECTION THRU SUSP. CLG.
A-100

② EXPOSED "T" GRID (2'x2')
A-100

③ WINDOW HEAD — ALL FLOOR EXCEPT 2ND FL.
A-100

UNDERSIDE OF EXIST. STRUCTURE
& HANGER AS REQUIRED
6" Ø PENCIL ROD
1½" C BLACK IRON @ 4'-0" O.C.
METAL CLIP
GIAT CLIP

WIRE TIE
T-BAR @ 2'-0" O.C.
W EXPOSED SPLINE
PAINTED

⅞" FURRING CHANNELS @ 16" O.C.
½" GYPBD. PT'D.
CORNER BEAD

MAHOG. TRIM w/ RED MAHOG. STAIN

½" GYPBD. BACKING
METAL TIN CLG. PAINTED

(1) GYPBD. CEILING DETAIL
A10   SCALE : 3" = 1'-0"

(2) METAL TIN CEILING DETAIL
A10   SCALE : 3" = 1'-0"

UNDERSIDE OF EXIST. STRUCTURE
& HANGER AS REQUIRED
4" Ø PENCIL ROD
1½" C BLACK IRON @ 4'-0" O.C.
SNAP BAR FOR FIXT. & METAL CLG. PANEL SUPPORT
T-BAR
SIMPLEX CLG. PANEL

METAL CLIP
BLOCKING AS REQ'D

SLIP MOULD
GYPBD. SOFFIT PAINTED

LIGHT FIXTURE
METAL CLIP

MAHOGANY PANEL
¼" x ¼" BLACK REVEAL
METAL "Z" CLIP
CONT. ANGLE

(3) SIMPLEX METAL CEILING DETAIL
A10   SCALE : 3" = 1'-0"

(4) MAHOG. PANEL CEILING DETAIL
A10   SCALE : 3" = 1'-0"

METAL STUDS
BLOCKING AS REQUIRED
MAHOGANY TRIM

MAHOGANY FINISH

MAHOG. RAISED PANEL

(5) DETAIL OF RAISED MAHOGANY PANEL CEILING
A10   SCALE : 3" = 1'-0"

UNDERSIDE OF EXIST. STRUCTURE
& HANGER AS REQUIRED
6" Ø PENCIL ROD
1½" C BLACK IRON @ 4'-0" O.C.
METAL CLIP
WIRE TIE

T-BAR W EXPOSED SPLINE
ACOUSTIC. TILE (2x4 LAY-IN)
WALL ANGLE

(6) ACOUSTICAL TILE CEILING DETAIL
A10   SCALE : 3" = 1'-0"

# CEILINGS

Suspended Ceilings: Perimeters and Drops

**4** PROJECTION SCREEN
A-109

**5** PERIMETER TROUGH SYSTEM
A-109 @ SERVERY (PTS-4)

**6** CONF. CNTR. CLG. - TYP.
A-109

**7** ELEVATOR LOBBY - SECT.
A-109 REVEAL @ CLG.

**8** WINDOW HEAD @ 2ND FLOOR
A-109

**9** SECT. THRU TWO (2) DIFF. SUSP. CLG'S.
A-109

HANGERS (MAX. SPACING 4'-0" O.C.)
1" x 3/16" FLAT BAR, #8 GAGE WIRE,
3/16" OR 1/4" DIA. MILD STEEL RODS

1 1/2" FURRING CHANNELS 4'-0" O.C.

1 1/2"

3/4"

3"

3/4"

3/4" FURRING CHANNELS 16" O.C.

3.4# FLAT RIB METAL LATH

3/4" GYPSUM PLASTER

NOTE: WHERE FIRE RATING IS REQD. CHECK U.S. GYPSUM CATALOG FOR SPECIFICATIONS

**① PLASTER ON METAL LATH & STEEL FURRING**

HANGERS - SEE DETAIL #1 ABOVE

1 1/2" FURRING CHANNELS 4'-0" O.C.

3/4" FURRING CHANNELS 16" O.C.

1 1/2"

3 3/8"

3/4"

3/8"

1/2"

1/2" GYPSUM PLASTER

3/8" PERFORATED GYPSUM LATH FASTENED TO 3/4" C's WITH METAL CLIPS

NOTE: WHERE FIRE RATING IS REQD. CHECK U.S. GYPSUM CATALOG & ADJUST THICKNESS & SPACING AS REQD.

**② PLASTER ON GYPSUM LATH & STEEL FURRING**

HANGERS - SEE DETAIL #1 ABOVE

1 1/2" FURRING CHANNELS 4'-0" O.C.

1 1/2"

7/8"

3"

5/8"

TYPE "S" SCREWS

5/8" GYPSUM BOARD

METAL FURRING C's CLIPPED OR WIRED WITH 10 GA. TIE WIRE TO 1 1/2" FURRING C's - SPACE 2'-0" O.C.

NOTE: CHECK BLDG. CODE & U.S. GYPSUM CATALOG FOR FIRE RATINGS

**③ GYPSUM BOARD ON STEEL FURRING**

④ — ACOUSTIC TILE CONCEALED ZEE SUSPENSION SYSTEM

⑤ — ACOUSTIC TILE H & T SUSPENSION SYSTEM

⑥ — ACOUSTIC TILE Z & L SUSPENSION SYSTEM

Completed design for an office space

# STAIRS

## Planning Data

Nowhere is the personal safety and comfort of the user more important than in the design of stairs. This section, therefore, provides the planning data necessary to solve most problems of stair design. Various stair types are illustrated, including straight run, long "L," wide "L," double "L," and narrow and wide "U." Stair tables and related diagrams are provided that indicate vertical and horizontal areas, headroom clearances, and tread and riser dimensions for various stair systems. Information concerning nosings, landing widths, etc., is also included. In addition to general planning data, this section includes barrier-free design data as well as actual construction details of wood, steel, and concrete stairs prepared by various design firms.

It should be noted that stair design must conform to local building codes. Most codes require that means-of-egress stairways not be less than 44 in (1118 mm) in width, that the least dimension of landings and platforms not be less than the required width of the stair, and that the minimum headroom in all parts of a stairway not be less than 6 ft 8 in (2032 mm) measured vertically from the tread nosing or from the floor surface of the landing or platform. In one- and two-family dwellings, most codes require that stairways not be less than 3 ft (915 mm) clear in width, and that hand rails not be less than 30 in (762 mm) nor more than 34 in (864 mm) measured vertically from the nosing of the treads and be provided on at least one side of stairways of four or more risers.

## CRITICAL DIMENSIONS AND CLEARANCES

### Stair Table

Dimensions indicated in Fig. 1 and listed in Table 1 determine the vertical and horizontal areas and headroom clearances for stair systems with tread and riser proportions shown. They can be used directly in developing sketches or working drawings and eliminate the need for experimental stair plans or sections. All dimensions refer to face of treads without nosing.

Tabular data refer only to minimum conditions for straight run stairs. All figures may be adjusted according to requirements of design or stair use. For similar dimensional information controlling other types of stairways, see the following pages.

Widths of stairways may vary with these requirements. For passage of furniture, minimum clear widths should be selected from Table 2.

**Fig. 1**

### TABLE 1 Stair Table

(Dimensions in feet and inches)

| Floor to Floor Height | | No. of Risers | Riser R | Tread T | Total Run L | Min. Headroom Y | Handrail X | Clearance C | Partition Above Z* | First Riser Below - U | First Riser Above - V* |
|---|---|---|---|---|---|---|---|---|---|---|---|
| 8'-0" | † | 11 | 8.73" | 8½" | 6'-10½" | 8'-2" | 2'-10" | 5'-8" | -1'-10" | 8'-6" | -1'-7" |
| | † | 12 | 8.00 | 9 | 8-3 | 7-10 | 2-9½ | 5-10½ | -1-8½ | 9-7½ | -1-4 |
| | | 13 | 7.38 | 10¼ | 10-3 | 7-7 | 2-9 | 6-2 | -1-8½ | 11-6 | -1-1½ |
| | | 14 | 6.86 | 11½ | 12-5½ | 7-4 | 2-9 | 6-4 | -1-7 | 13-5½ | -9½ |
| | △ | 15 | 6.40 | 12½ | 14-7 | 7-3 | 2-9 | 6-7½ | -1-6½ | 15-5½ | -7½ |
| | △ | 16 | 6.00 | 13½ | 16-10½ | 7-3 | 2-9 | 6-7½ | -1-9 | 17-6 | -8 |
| 8'-6" | † | 12 | 8.50 | 8½ | 7-9½ | 8-1 | 2-9½ | 5-8½ | -1-3½ | 8-10 | -11 |
| | † | 13 | 7.85 | 9¼ | 9-3 | 7-9 | 2-9½ | 5-10½ | -1-1 | 9-10 | -7½ |
| | | 14 | 7.29 | 10¼ | 11-4½ | 7-6 | 2-9 | 6-2 | -10½ | 12-9 | -4 |
| | | 15 | 6.80 | 11½ | 13-8½ | 7-4 | 2-9 | 6-4 | -10½ | 13-10 | -1½ |
| | △ | 16 | 6.38 | 12½ | 15-7½ | 7-3 | 2-9 | 6-5½ | -7 | 15-5½ | +3¼ |
| | △ | 17 | 6.00 | 13½ | 18-0 | 7-3 | 2-9 | 6-7 | -7 | 17-8 | +5 |
| 9'-0" | † | 12 | 9.00 | 8 | 7-4 | 8-3 | 2-10 | 5-6 | -11 | 8-1 | -8 |
| | † | 13 | 8.31 | 8½ | 8-6 | 8-0 | 2-9½ | 5-9 | -9 | 8-11½ | -5 |
| | | 14 | 7.71 | 9½ | 10-3½ | 7-9 | 2-9½ | 6-0 | -6 | 10-5 | -½ |
| | | 15 | 7.20 | 10½ | 12-3 | 7-6 | 2-9 | 6-2½ | -3 | 11-10 | +4½ |
| | | 16 | 6.75 | 11¾ | 14-8¼ | 7-4 | 2-9 | 6-4 | +2 | 13-11 | +1-0 |
| | △ | 17 | 6.35 | 12½ | 16-8 | 7-3 | 2-9 | 6-5½ | +5 | 15-5½ | +1-4 |
| | △ | 18 | 6.00 | 13½ | 19-1½ | 7-3 | 2-9 | 6-7½ | +6 | 17-8 | +1-6 |
| 9'-6" | † | 13 | 8.77 | 8 | 8-0 | 8-2 | 2-10 | 5-5½ | -3½ | 8-2 | -½ |
| | † | 14 | 8.14 | 9 | 9-9 | 7-10 | 2-9½ | 5-9½ | ±0 | 9-5½ | +5 |
| | | 15 | 7.60 | 9¾ | 11-4½ | 7-7 | 2-9 | 5-11½ | +4½ | 10-7 | +10½ |
| | | 16 | 7.13 | 10¾ | 13-5¼ | 7-5 | 2-9 | 6-2 | +9½ | 12-2 | +1-5½ |
| | | 17 | 6.71 | 11¾ | 15-8 | 7-4 | 2-9 | 6-4 | +1-1½ | 13-11½ | +1-11 |
| | △ | 18 | 6.33 | 12½ | 17-8½ | 7-3 | 2-9 | 6-5½ | +1-5½ | 15-7 | +2-4 |
| | △ | 19 | 6.00 | 13½ | 20-3 | 7-3 | 2-9 | 6-8 | +1-8 | 17-9 | +2-7½ |
| 10'-0" | † | 14 | 8.57 | 8½ | 9-2½ | 8-1 | 2-9½ | 5-8½ | +2 | 8-8 | +6 |
| | † | 15 | 8.00 | 9 | 10-6 | 7-10 | 2-9½ | 5-10½ | +6½ | 9-7 | +11 |
| | | 16 | 7.50 | 10 | 12-6 | 7-7 | 2-9 | 6-1 | +1-1 | 10-11½ | +1-6½ |
| | | 17 | 7.06 | 11 | 14-8 | 7-5 | 2-9 | 6-2½ | +1-7½ | 12-5½ | +2-2½ |
| | | 18 | 6.67 | 12 | 17-0 | 7-4 | 2-9 | 6-5 | +2-0 | 14-3½ | +2-9 |
| | △ | 19 | 6.32 | 12½ | 18-9 | 7-3 | 2-9 | 6-6 | +2-5 | 15-8 | +3-2½ |
| | △ | 20 | 6.00 | 13½ | 21-4½ | 7-3 | 2-9 | 6-7½ | +2-10 | 17-9 | +3-8½ |
| 10'-6" | † | 14 | 9.00 | 8 | 8-8 | 8-3 | 2-10 | 5-5½ | +6 | 8-0 | +9 |
| | † | 15 | 8.40 | 8½ | 9-11 | 8-1 | 2-9½ | 5-8½ | +9½ | 8-10 | +1-1 |
| | | 16 | 7.88 | 9¾ | 11-6¾ | 7-9 | 2-9½ | 5-10½ | +1-3½ | 9-10 | +1-8½ |
| | | 17 | 7.41 | 10 | 13-4 | 7-7 | 2-9 | 6-1 | +1-9½ | 11-0 | +2-3½ |
| | | 18 | 7.00 | 11 | 15-7 | 7-5 | 2-9 | 6-2½ | +2-5 | 12-7½ | +3-0½ |
| | | 19 | 6.63 | 12 | 18-0 | 7-4 | 2-9 | 6-4½ | +2-11 | 14-4 | +3-8½ |
| | △ | 20 | 6.30 | 12½ | 19-9½ | 7-3 | 2-9 | 6-6 | +3-5½ | 15-7 | +4-3½ |
| | △ | 21 | 6.00 | 13½ | 22-6 | 7-3 | 2-9 | 6-7½ | +4-0 | 17-9 | +5-0 |
| 11'-0" | † | 15 | 8.80 | 8 | 9-4 | 8-2 | 2-10 | 5-6 | +1-0½ | 8-1 | +1-2½ |
| | † | 16 | 8.25 | 8¾ | 10-11¼ | 8-0 | 2-9½ | 5-10 | +1-5 | 9-2½ | +1-9 |
| | | 17 | 7.76 | 9½ | 12-8 | 7-9 | 2-9 | 6-0 | +2-0 | 10-3½ | +2-4½ |
| | | 18 | 7.33 | 10¼ | 14-6¼ | 7-6 | 2-9 | 6-1½ | +2-7½ | 11-4½ | +3-1½ |
| | | 19 | 6.95 | 11 | 16-6 | 7-5 | 2-9 | 6-3 | +3-3 | 12-8 | +3-9 |
| | | 20 | 6.60 | 12 | 19-0 | 7-4 | 2-9 | 6-5 | +3-10½ | 14-8 | +4-7½ |
| | △ | 21 | 6.29 | 12½ | 20-10 | 7-3 | 2-9 | 6-6 | +4-5 | 15-8 | +5-3 |
| | △ | 22 | 6.00 | 13½ | 23-7½ | 7-3 | 2-9 | 6-7½ | +5-1 | 17-8 | +6-0 |

*Dimensions given plus or minus, i.e., behind or in front of first riser (see Fig. 1).
*Notes:* Figures in boldface indicate stairs recommended for most interiors.
†indicates stairs allowable only for attics and cellars but not recommended.
△indicates stairs for exterior or monumental use.

## Clearances for Furniture Passage

Width is not always a critical factor of stairway design but is important when the layout involves one or more turns with straight runs. Typical layouts for such stairways include the Long L, Double L, Wide U, Wide L, and Narrow U. (See Fig. 3 for layouts and tabular data on these types.)

Stairways used solely as circulation from floor to floor can be 2'0" wide for comfortable passage of one individual or 3'6" for two, side-by-side. When furniture must be taken up and down, minimum clear widths of straight runs and landings must be carefully selected or corners will constitute obstructions in many instances.

Recommended minimum clear widths as shown in Table 2 are not necessarily the width of stairs, either rough or wall-to-wall. Projections of newels, handrails, or baseboards can obstruct passage of furniture and must be taken into account when determining actual stair widths.

Headroom is also a controlling factor of design. With minimum headroom conditions shown in Table 1, clear widths for furniture passage must be greater in most cases than may be necessary if headroom is unlimited or equal at least to the ceiling heights. This is particularly important at the first riser and at turns, where the under rake of the first stair limits the vertical clearance of the stairway below. Therefore, if stairs must be comparatively narrow and if furniture must be transported over them, headroom, or vertical clearance, must be increased accordingly.

Landing widths may be increased to provide greater turning space for maneuvering furniture. If this is done, minimum clear widths can be proportionately decreased. However, this expedient is not effective unless hallways at either end of the stairway are at least equal to the landing widths. Narrow hallways often offer as great an obstruction to furniture maneuvering as low headroom, narrow runs, or cramped turns.

Open-well stairways give more opportunity to maneuver furniture, since even very bulky but light pieces may often be lifted over rails or newels. In general, a closed-string stair should be wider than an open-string type for the same degree of convenience.

The data in Table 2 reflect safe *average* clearances for transportation of items listed. Dimensions of furniture are subject to wide variations. Consequently, the minimum clear widths recommended here are susceptible to adjustment in certain instances.

MINIMUM HUMAN PASSAGE

(a)

PASSAGE FOR FURNITURE

(b)

**Fig. 2   Minimum stair widths.** *(a)* Stairs designed for comfortable human passage only may be relatively narrow. $W_1$ may be 2'0" but 2'6" is better. $W_2$ should be at least 3'6". *(b)* Furniture passage demands greater width. If stair landing is increased or headroom unlimited, $W_F$ may be decreased. See Table 2.

**TABLE 2   Recommended Minimum Clear Widths of Stairs ($W_F$) for Furniture Movement***

| Furniture | | Min. Headroom ▲ | | Unlimited Headroom | | |
|---|---|---|---|---|---|---|
| Article | Size | Wide U Type | Narrow U Type | Wide and Narrow U | Narrow U only● | |
| | | | | | Stair | Landing |
| Double Bed Box Spring | 4'·6"x 6'·6"x 8" | 3'· 2" | 3'· 2" | 2'· 3" | | |
| Dressing Table | 1'·10"x 4'·0"x 2'·6" | 2'· 5" | 2'· 5" | 2'· 5" | | |
| Bureau | 2'·0"x 4'·0"x 3'·0" | 2'· 8" | 2'· 8" | 2'· 8" | | |
| Chiffonier | 1'·8"x 3'·4"x 4'·8" | 2'· 6" | 2'· 6" | 2'· 6" | | |
| Chest of Drawers | 1'·9"x 3'·4"x 4'·8" | 2'· 7" | 2'· 7" | 2'· 7" | | |
| Divan - Club | 3'·6"x 7'·2"x 2'·9" | 4'· 8" | 4'· 8" | 3'· 4" | 3'·0" | 3'·8" |
| Divan - Average | 3'·0"x 6'·8"x 2'·6" | 4'· 4" | 4'· 4" | 2'·11" | | |
| Piano - Concert Grand | 9'·0"x 5'·4"x 1'·8" | 4'· 8" | 4'· 8" | 3'· 2" ■ | 3'·0" ■ | 3'·4" ■ |
| Piano - Music Room Grand | 7'·3"x 5'·2"x 1'·6" | 3'·10" | 3'·10" | 3'· 0" | | |
| Piano - Drawing Room Grand | 6'·9"x 5'·0"x 1'·4" | 3'· 6" | 3'· 6" | 2'·10" | | |
| Piano - Baby Grand | 5'·8"x 4'·10"x 1'·2" | 3'· 0" | 3'· 0" | 2'· 8" | | |
| Piano - Standard Upright | 2'·2"x 5'·10"x 4'·6" | 4'· 0" | 3'· 9" | 3'· 3" | 3'·0" | 3'·6" |
| Highboy - Large | 2'·0"x 3'·6"x 7'·6" | 4'· 4" | 4'· 4" | 2'·10" | | |
| Highboy - Average | 1'·8"x 3'·4"x 6'·0' | 3'· 6" | 3'· 6" | 2'· 6" | | |
| Secretary - Large | 1'·10"x 3'·8"x 7'·2" | 4'· 0" | 4'· 0" | 2'·10" | | |
| Secretary - Average | 1'·10"x 3'·0"x 6'·10" | 3'·10" | 3'·10" | 2'· 6" | | |
| Sideboard | 1'·9"x 5'·0"x 3'·2" | 2'· 6" | 2'· 6" | 2'· 6" | | |
| Buffet | 2'·1"x 3'·3"x 6'·6" | 4'· 0" | 4'· 0" | 2'·10" | | |
| Dresser | 1'·9"x 6'·0"x 5'·6" | 4'· 4" | 3'· 6" | 3'· 4" | 3'·0" | 3'·8" |
| Table (6 People) | 3'·6"x 5'·0"x 2'·6" | 3'· 2" | 3'· 2" | 3'· 2" | 3'·0" | 3'·4" |
| Table (8 People) | 3'·6"x 7'·0"x 2'·6" | 4'· 8" | 4'· 4" | 3'· 2" | 3'·0" | 3'·4 |
| Table (10 People) Rd. | 6'·4" Diam. | 4'· 8" | 4'· 8" | 3'· 0" | | |
| Desk - Slope Top | 2'·6"x 3'·8"x 3'·4" | 3'· 3" | 3'· 2" | 3'· 2" | 3'·0" | 3'·4" |
| Desk - Flat Top | 3'·0"x 5'·6"x 2'·6" | 3'· 2" | 3'· 0" | 3'· 0" | | |
| Desk - Executive's | 3'·2"x 6'·0"x 2'·6" | 4'· 2" | 4'· 2" | 3'· 1" | 3'·0" | 3'·2" |
| Trunk - Wardrobe | 1'·11"x 2'·6"x 3'·7" | 2'· 5" | 2'· 5" | 2'· 5" | | |

*Clear width between faces of rails, newels, etc., or between rail or newel and finish wall.
*Notes:* ▲ Headroom limited to minimum for comfortable human passage (see Table 1 and text).
  ● Narrow stairs and wide landings.
  ■ Absolute minimum not recommended (see text).

# STAIRS

**Planning Data**

### Purpose

The six diagrams in Fig. 3 represent unit plans for types of nonwinder stairways which are most frequently encountered in the average residential planning problem. Tabular information with each was developed from data contained in Table 1.

Unit plans are drawn to ⅛" scale and therefore can be supplied directly as a check of stair layouts to sketch plans and elevations. Each represents an average condition with a stair pitch well within the comfort zone. The basis is a 9'6" floor-to-floor height with 16 risers each 7.13" in height. Width is 3'0" from wall to wall.

Tabular data with each unit plan indicate dimensional variations which occur when stairways of substantially similar pitches are planned for floor-to-floor heights from 8 to 11 ft.

Width is the only critical dimension missing from this unit plan information. This varies with requirements of design and stair use and should be selected from data in Table 2. Width is a dimension controlling critical clearances on all stairs.

Winders have not been included in these unit plans because they represent a stair condition generally regarded as undesirable. However, use of winders is sometimes necessary due to cramped space. In such instances, winders should be adjusted to replace landings so that the narrow portions of treads at the inside of the turn are at least equal to ¾" T. When this is done, dimensions of $L_1$ and $L_2$ are decreased by approximately ½T, the exact figure depending upon the width selected. The practice of adding a winder-riser to bisect the landing diagonally from the corner of a newel is to be avoided in

all cases for it produces a dangerously narrow step in a particularly undesirable place.

### Application of Unit Plans

Diagrammatic data can be used on sketches as a graphic check as noted. Tabular data can be applied to either sketches or working drawings to eliminate the necessity of developing experimental stairway sections to determine run, proportional rise, horizontal and vertical areas, and location of under-rake minimum headroom.

Dimensional data have been confined to a single pitch for all floor-to-floor heights. The pitch indicated is that most generally desirable for human comfort. Data for other pitches listed as tread and riser proportions in Table 1 can be substituted for values of $L_1$, $L_2$, and M.

| HEIGHT FLOOR TO FLOOR | NO OF RISERS | RISER | TREAD | $L_1$ | M |
|---|---|---|---|---|---|
| 8'-0" | 13 | 7.38 | 10¼" | 10'-3" | — |
| 8'-6" | 14 | 7.29 | 10½" | 11'-4½" | 4½" |
| 9'-0" | 15 | 7.20 | 10½" | 12'-3" | 1'-1½" |
| 9'-6" | 16 | 7.13 | 10¾" | 13'-5¼" | 1'-11¼" |
| 10'-0" | 17 | 7.06 | 11" | 14'-8" | 2'-9½" |
| 10'-6" | 18 | 7.00 | 11" | 15'-7" | 3'-7" |
| 11'-0" | 19 | 6.95 | 11" | 16'-6" | 4'-5" |

| HEIGHT FLOOR TO FLOOR | Nº RISERS | RISER | TREAD | Nº RISERS | $L_1$ | Nº RISERS | $L_2$ | M |
|---|---|---|---|---|---|---|---|---|
| 8'-0" | 13 | 7.38 | 10¼" | 13 | 10'-3" + W | 0 | W | 10'-3" |
| 8'-6" | 14 | 7.29 | 10½" | 13 | 10'-6" + W | 1 | W | 10'-6" |
| 9'-0" | 15 | 7.20 | 10½" | 13 | 10'-6" + W | 2 | 10½" + W | 10'-6" |
| 9'-6" | 16 | 7.13 | 10¾" | 13 | 10'-9" + W | 3 | 1'-9½" + W | 11'-0" |
| 10'-0" | 17 | 7.06 | 11" | 13 | 11'-0" + W | 4 | 2'-9" + W | 11'-4" |
| 10'-6" | 18 | 7.00 | 11" | 13 | 11'-0" + W | 5 | 3'-8" + W | 11'-5" |
| 11'-0" | 19 | 6.95 | 11" | 13 | 11'-0" + W | 6 | 4'-7" + W | 11'-6" |

**Fig. 3**

WIDE "L"

NARROW "U"

DOUBLE "L"

WIDE "U"

| HEIGHT FLOOR TO FLOOR | Nº RISERS | RISER | TREAD | Nº RISERS | L₁ | Nº RISERS | L₂ | M |
|---|---|---|---|---|---|---|---|---|
| 8'-0" | 13 | 7.38 | 10¼" | 7 | 5'-1½" + W | 6 | 4'-3¼" + W | — |
| 8'-6" | 14 | 7.29 | 10½" | 7 | 5'-3" + W | 7 | 5'-3" + W | 4½" |
| 9'-0" | 15 | 7.20 | 10½" | 8 | 6'-1½" + W | 7 | 5'-3" + W | 1'-1½" |
| 9'-6" | 16 | 7.13 | 10¾" | 8 | 6'-3¼" + W | 8 | 6'-3¼" + W | 1'-11¼" |
| 10'-0" | 17 | 7.06 | 11" | 9 | 7'-4" + W | 8 | 6'-5" + W | 2'-9½" |
| 10'-6" | 18 | 7.00 | 11" | 9 | 7'-4" + W | 9 | 7'-4" + W | 3'-7" |
| 11'-0" | 19 | 6.95 | 11" | 10 | 8'-3" + W | 9 | 7'-4" + W | 4'-5" |

| HEIGHT FLOOR TO FLOOR | Nº RISERS | RISER | TREAD | Nº RISERS | L₁ | Nº RISERS | L₂ | M |
|---|---|---|---|---|---|---|---|---|
| 8'-0" | 13 | 7.38 | 10¼" | 7 | 5'-1½" + W | 6 | 4'-3¼" + W | — |
| 8'-6" | 14 | 7.29 | 10½" | 7 | 5'-3" + W | 7 | 5'-3" + W | 4½" |
| 9'-0" | 15 | 7.20 | 10½" | 8 | 6'-1½" + W | 7 | 5'-3" + W | 1'-1½" |
| 9'-6" | 16 | 7.13 | 10¾" | 8 | 6'-3¼" + W | 8 | 6'-3¼" + W | 1'-11¼" |
| 10'-0" | 17 | 7.06 | 11" | 9 | 7'-4" + W | 8 | 6'-5" + W | 2'-9½" |
| 10'-6" | 18 | 7.00 | 11" | 9 | 7'-4" + W | 9 | 7'-4" + W | 3'-7" |
| 11'-0" | 19 | 6.95 | 11" | 10 | 8'-3" + W | 9 | 7'-4" + W | 4'-5" |

| HEIGHT FLOOR TO FLOOR | Nº RISERS | RISER | TREAD | Nº RISERS | L₁ | Nº RISERS | L₂ | M |
|---|---|---|---|---|---|---|---|---|
| 8'-0" | 13 | 7.38 | 10¼" | 13 | 10'-3" + 2W | 0 | W | 10'-3" + W |
| 8'-6" | 14 | 7.29 | 10½" | 12 | 9'-7½" + 2W | 1 | W | 9'-7½" + W |
| 9'-0" | 15 | 7.20 | 10½" | 11 | 8'-9" + 2W | 2 | 10½" + W | 8'-9" + W |
| 9'-6" | 16 | 7.13 | 10¾" | 10 | 8'-0¾" + 2W | 3 | 1'-9½" + W | 8'-3¾" + W |
| 10'-0" | 17 | 7.06 | 11" | 9 | 7'-4" + 2W | 4 | 2'-9" + W | 7'-8" + W |
| 10'-6" | 18 | 7.00 | 11" | 8 | 6'-5" + 2W | 5 | 3'-8" + W | 6'-10" + W |
| 11'-0" | 19 | 6.95 | 11" | 7 | 5'-6" + 2W | 6 | 4'-7" + W | 6'-0" + W |

| HEIGHT FLOOR TO FLOOR | Nº RISERS | RISER | TREAD | Nº RISERS | L₁ | Nº RISERS | L₂ | Nº RISERS | L₃ | M |
|---|---|---|---|---|---|---|---|---|---|---|
| 8'-0" | 13 | 7.38 | 10¼" | 4 | 2'-6¾" + 2W | 4 | 2'-6¾" + W | 5 | 3'-5" + W | — |
| 8'-6" | 14 | 7.29 | 10½" | 4 | 2'-7½" + 2W | 5 | 3'-6" + W | 5 | 3'-6" + W | 4½" |
| 9'-0" | 15 | 7.20 | 10½" | 4 | 2'-7½" + 2W | 5 | 3'-6" + W | 6 | 4'-4½" + W | 1'-1½" |
| 9'-6" | 16 | 7.13 | 10¾" | 4 | 2'-8¼" + 2W | 6 | 4'-5¾" + W | 6 | 4'-5¾" + W | 1'-11¼" |
| 10'-0" | 17 | 7.06 | 11" | 4 | 2'-9" + 2W | 6 | 4'-7" + W | 7 | 5'-6" + W | 2'-9½" |
| 10'-6" | 18 | 7.00 | 11" | 4 | 2'-9" + 2W | 6 | 5'-6" + W | 7 | 5'-6" + W | 3'-7 |
| 11'-0" | 19 | 6.95 | 11" | 4 | 2'-9" + 2W | 7 | 5'-6" + W | 8 | 6'-5" + W | 4'-5" |

**Fig. 3** *(Continued)*

# STAIRS
## Layouts and Dimensions

### Nosings

Nosings extending ¾ to 1½ in (usually 1¼ in) beyond the face of the riser are functionally necessary and are required by most building codes. Nosings may be provided by extending the treads or by sloping the risers. The latter method is customary in concrete stairs because of easier forming, and in any type of stair where carpet is to be installed. This type of nosing is also recommended for stairs to be used by the handicapped.

### Stairway Layouts

Comfortable stairways cannot be designed except in relation to dimensions of the average human figure. As applied to stairways these dimensions and the equivalent of the average comfortable walking stride of about 24 in fix the gradient of stairways, the proportional relation of treads and risers, the height of the handrail, and the minimum necessary headroom.

Figure 4 indicates the influence of human figure dimensions and suggests the desirability of varying ceiling clearances and handrail heights according to variations in stair gradients. These variations are included in Table 3.

Treads and risers in curved stairs should be proportioned on an assumed "line of travel" 18 in from the inner (smaller radius) handrail.

All building codes have strict specifications for stairs which are required exits. The National Building Code of the American Insurance Association and the New York City code both require that treads and risers be proportioned by the formula $T \times R = 70$ to 75, with risers not over 7¾ in high and treads not less than 9 in wide, exclusive of nosings. Minimum stair width for most uses is 44 in, based on two 22-in lanes of traffic. Handrails are required on both sides and may project a maximum of 3½ in into the required width. Winders and open risers are prohibited. The maximum vertical rise permitted between landings is 12 ft; in places of assembly it is 8 ft. Stairs must be designed for a live load of 100 lb/ft².

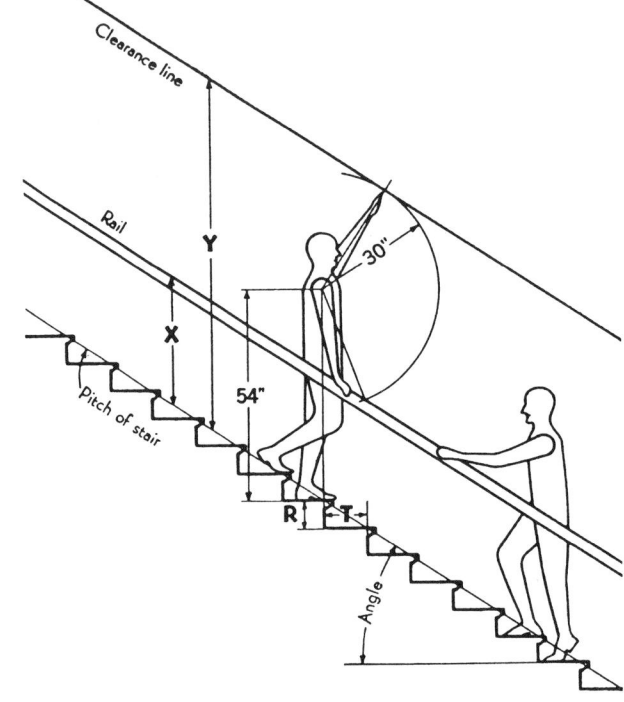

**Fig. 4**

**TABLE 3   Dimensions for Stairways**

| Step dimensions | | Gradient designations | | Headroom * Y in inches | Handrail height X in inches | NOTES |
|---|---|---|---|---|---|---|
| Riser **R** in inches | Tread **T** in inches | Per cent grade | Angle in degrees, minutes | | | |
| 5 | 16 | 31.25 | 17 - 21 | 85 | | 1. 7" by 11" is the proportion by which all steps are laid out |
| 5¼ | 15½ | 33.87 | 18 - 43 | | 33½ | |
| 5½ | 14¾ | 37.28 | 20 - 27 | 86 | | 2. Risers from 5" to 6½" are suitable for exterior and "grand" interior stairs |
| 5¾ | 14 | 41.07 | 22 - 20 | | | |
| 6 | 13½ | 44.44 | 23 - 58 | 87 | | 3. Risers from 6⅜" to 7⅜" are most comfortable and most suitable for interior stairs |
| 6¼ | 13 | 48.07 | 25 - 40 | | | |
| 6½ | 12¼ | 53.06 | 27 - 57 | 88 | 33 | 4. Risers for cellar and attic stairs may be up to 9" high |
| 6¾ | 11¾ | 57.44 | 29 - 52 | | | |
| 7 | 11 | 63.63 | 32 - 28 | 89 | | 5. Width - minimum for single-file travel, 30" |
| 7¼ | 10½ | 69.04 | 34 - 37 | 90 | | |
| 7½ | 10 | 75 | 36 - 52 | 91 | | 6. Width - minimum for comfort, 36" |
| 7¾ | 9½ | 81.57 | 39 - 12 | 93 | | |
| 8 | 9 | 88.88 | 41 - 38 | 94 | 33½ | 7. Width - desirable (for furniture passage etc.), 42" |
| 8¼ | 8½ | 97.05 | 44 - 9 | 96 | | |
| 8½ | 8¼ | 103.02 | 45 - 51 | 97 | | 8. Consult local building codes on all stair problems |
| 8¾ | 8⅛ | 107.07 | 46 - 57 | 98 | 34 | |
| 9 | 8 | 112.5 | 48 - 22 | 99 | | |

Minimum for head clearance only can be safely taken as 84 in. for all gradients; HUD permits 80 in.

Average height of rail 2'-6".

Handrail
Balusters
Easing
Newel
Ease string into base.
Floor line.
Closed string
Plaster soffit.
Plaster
Open string

**· ELEVATION · OF · STAIR ·**

Line of carriage
Nosing line
Variable

**· PLAN · OF · STAIR ·**
Scale ¼"=1'-0"

Riser mitred with string
Cut and mitred string
String line
Baluster
Dove-tail recess in tread to receive baluster.
Return nosing mitred with tread and returned against string

**PARTIAL · PLAN · OF · TREAD ·**
and detail showing mitre of riser and string.

Filler piece between balusters
Baluster
Minimum ⅛"
Tread
Minimum
Carriage string housed to receive tread & riser.
Blocking
Panel.
Variable
Wire lath & plaster

**SECTION · C-C ·** thru closed string, panel & plaster soffit.

Cover mould
Plaster
"A"

Baluster dove-tailed into tread
Minimum ½"
Wall string housed for treads & risers
Wedge
Separate return nosing, mitred at tread
Open, cut and mitred string.
Carriages cut for risers & treads.
Wall string 10" to 12".
Alternate carriage
Wall line.
Blocking Plaster

Average rise = 7" to 7½"
Average run = 10 to 10½"
Sum of the rise and run to be 17½" to 18".
Basement stair may have 8" to 9" risers.

Nosing 1" to 1½"
Run
Minimum thickness of tread to be 1⅛".
Treads to be Oak, Y. Pine or Birch.

Rise

Wall string accurately cut to receive risers & treads & wood wedges as shown. Wedges to be thoroughly glued and driven up tight

Wall string 10" to 12" wide.

"A"

Blocking

**LINE · "A-A" · SHOWING ·**
**SECTION · THRU · WALL ·**
**STRING ·· SECTION ·**
**CONTINUED · ON · AND ·**
**THRU · OUTSIDE · STRING ·**

Alternate carriage construction provides 3"x6" carriages in place of carriages as shown. (Not cut for treads & risers)

Block up riser & tread between strings. Blocks to be glued & screwed in place.

Blocks approx. 2"x2"x6"

Handrail design varies.
Baluster groove.
Baluster

**Half Section on "D-D"** thru handrail.

Wedges

**SECTION · THRU · TREAD · & ·**
**RISER · AND · ELEVATION ·**
**OF · WEDGES · ON · LINE · "B-B" ·**

NO·D·5··DETAILS·OF·MAIN·STAIRWAY··TWO·STORY·COLONIAL·HOUSE

2⁷⁄₈"

GLUE FOR THICKNESS
AS REQD

SOLID MAHOGANY
STAINED

2⁷⁄₈"

### SECTION-HANDRAIL

OAK HANDRAIL

2" ∅ OAK BRACKETS
3 BRACKETS PER
RAIL

OAK PLUGS

FACE OF WALL

2" ∅

1½"  1¾"

0"

## OAK HANDRAIL

BALUSTERS

5"  5"  5"  5"

10"
(TYP)

2½" 2½"   2½" 2½"

2¼" ⁷⁄₈"
⁵⁄₈"

¾"

½"

⁵⁄₈"

VARIES

SOLID MAHOGANY
STAINED
SOLID POPLAR
PRIMED

½" BIRCH PLYWOOD

½" PLYWOOD
VENEER CORE

¼" SHIM SPACE

STEEL

FURRING & SHEETROCK

## PARTIAL ELEVATION STAIR

3"
BRONZE
BRKTS.

4"

4"

⁵⁄₈"

3-0" @ NOSING

¾" 2" ¾"
¼"      ¼"

4'-4"

VARIES

CUT TREAD & RISERS
1/8" CLEAR (TYPICAL)
CARPET TO COVER

³⁄₈"

VARIES ⁵⁄₈"

CARPET COVERING

(STAIR TREAD
3'-7¾" LONG)

½"

¼"    ½" SHIM SPACE
¼" 2"
¾"         STEEL

4"

³⁄₈"

4"

¾"

¾" PLYWOOD   4'-2½"

4'-4"

### SECTION AT STAIRS

2"

8"

10"

10"  10"

STEEL C

6⁷⁄₈"

6⁷⁄₈"

6⁷⁄₈"

³⁄₈"  4"

CARPET

³⁄₄"   1¼"

¼" ½"

¾"  1¼"

¾" FIR PLYWOOD
FIRE TREATED

⁵⁄₈" DRYWALL

1¼"

⁵⁄₈"

6⁷⁄₈"

2"x 4"
CLEAT

5"

3"

1⁵⁄₈"

6⁷⁄₈"

¾"

### TYPICAL SECTION AT STAIRS

STAIR DETAILS

(15) DETAIL OF TREAD & RISER AT STAIR #4
     SCALE: 3/4" = 1'-0"

(16) DETAIL OF STRINGER AT STAIR #4
     SCALE: 1½" = 1'-0"

SECTION THRU. STEPS

## STAIRS
Wood and Steel Stairs

LINE OF 6X6 STL
COLUMN
2X4 CUSTOM WOOD
SILL
2X8 STL. ∠
1 X8 GALV. STL. ZEE
STL. WINDOW FRAME
SEE DWG A15
GALV. METAL FLASHING
CEDAR SIDING
W/ VAPOR BARRIER
ON 3/4" PLY

FLITCH BEAM
(2) 2X12S
1/4" STL PLATE
WOOD BLOCKING
GALV. MET.
FLASHING
LINE OF 6X6
STL COLUMN
BEYOND

2X8 STL C

6"

2" THICK WOOD PLATFORM

10'-7"

2 1/2X6 STL C W/
END PLATE:
BOLT THRU TRUSS

2" Ø STL. POST & HANDRAIL

1" Ø STL. RAIL

VARIES/SEE DWG ⟨4/A16⟩
10-7" TYPICAL TREAD

CUSTOM WOOD TREAD
SCREW THRU BAR ∠ BELOW
FOR PLAN SEE ⟨/A16⟩

1/4" X 2" STL. BAR: WELD TO
STL. ∠ CLIP. (CONTINUOUS)

3X3 STL ∠ CLIPS: WELD
TO STL. C (2" LONG)

1X2 STL ∠: WELD TO STL C (CON)

2 1/2X6 STL C: BOLT TO STL
∠ CLIP W/ STAINLESS STL BOLTS

4X4 STL ∠ CLIP: WELD TO
STL C CLIP.

EL + 2'-0"
FIN. FLOOR

FLOOR: TILE ON MORTAR
BED ON 3/4" PLY SUBFLOOR

4X6 STL C CLIP: BOLT
THRU FLITCH BEAM

FLITCH BEAM: (2) 2X12S
& 1/4" STL PLATE
RUNS @ 6' TO JOISTS
SEE FRAMING PLAN ⟨/A16⟩

2X12 FLOOR JOISTS

11'-1 3/4"

⟨5/A16⟩ SECTIONAL ELEVATION  1 1/2" = 1'-0"

## STAIRS

**Concrete Stairs**

**DD** Section

LEATHER & FELT PADDING GLUED TO WOOD

WOOD CORE

BRONZE CHANNEL (CONT.)

NEOPRENE GASKET

BRONZE SECTION TO RECEIVE SCREW BRACED TO CHANNEL

SELF TAPING SCREW AT 1'-6" O.C.

LEATHER PIPING

3/4" Ø BOLT W/MODIFIED HEAD & NUT

BRONZE BOLT & COVER (3) EACH GLASS SECTION

3/4" CLEAR GLASS

**EE** Section

3/4" GLASS RAIL W/NEOPRENE GASKET

1/4" BRONZE PLATE

3/8" U CONT. GLASS RAIL SHOE

CLIP SPACE

FILL IN CONC. AFTER RAIL SUPPORTS ARE INSTALLED

4 HEAVY MAL. IRON ADJ. INSERTS FOR 3/4" Ø BOLTS SEC. TO CONC. W/ 5/8" Ø X 2'-0" HAIRPINS AT INSERTS

VERTICAL SLOT

6 X 6.5 E

SHIM AS REQUIRED

1" X 1" X 3/16" Δ BLOCKING SUPPORT WELDED TO 1/2" PLATE

3/4" PLASTER ON METAL FURRING

**FF** Section

| A-D | Starting Newels | | A | Overhand Easing |
|---|---|---|---|---|
| E-G | Landing Newel | | AA | 90 degree Up Easing |
| H-I | Starting Step | | BB | Volute |
| J | Stair Tread | | CC | Turnout |
| K | Landing Tread | | DD | Gooseneck 2 Riser |
| L | Risers | | EE | Gooseneck 1 Riser |
| M | Return Nosing | | FF | Gooseneck 1 Riser Ledge Return |
| N | Stair Cove | | GG | Gooseneck Riser with Cap |
| O-R | Turned Balusters | | | |
| S | Wall Rosette | | HH | Gooseneck Riser Tandem Cap |
| T | Plain Cap | | | |
| U | One OPG Newel Cap | | JJ | Starting Easing |
| V | Tandem Cap | | KK | Starting Easing with Return End |
| W | Quarter Turn Cap | | | |
| X | Quarter Turn | | MM | Hand Rail |
| Y | Up Easing | | | |

## STAIRS

**Spiral and Circular Stairs**

### SPIRAL STAIRS

5' diameter — spiral

5' diameter — spiral

6' diameter — spiral

### CIRCULAR STAIRS

8' diameter — circular

11' diameter — circular

9' diameter — circular

15' diameter — circular

13' diameter — circular

15' diameter — circular

*Note:* All drawings left-hand turn (looking down).

thread and riser terrazzo

carborundum mosaic

teak railing

**Plan**

cinder concrete

teak railing

plaster

**Elevation**

# STAIRS

**Spiral Stairs**

1"X1I/2"STEEL BAR FOR HANDRAIL & BALUSTERS

4"LAG SCREWS WITH STAINLESS STEEL WASHERS TO SECURE TUBE RAILINGS

3'-11 1/8"

2'-11"

5'-0"

LAMINATED WOOD LANDING

DETAIL 1 1/2" SCALE

3 5/8"

4'2"

3

3'-0"

6"

4"

3'-9"

3/8" STEEL PLATES CONTINUOUSLY WELDED TOGETHER

6" LALLY COLUMN

ELEVATION 1/4" SCALE

4 5/8"

8'-0"

PLAN 1/2" SCALE

1'-2"

1'-2"

3'-6"

1'-2"

1'-2"

4'-0"

4'-0" RADIUS

WOOD TREAD SCREWED TO STEEL PLATE

FOOTING

2" WOOD TREAD

WELD

WELD

ISOMETRIC OF TYPICAL TREAD 1/2" SCALE

SECTION

FIN. GRADE

3'-0"

4"

3'-0"

4'-0"

5'-0"

1'-0"

12"X12"X5/8" ST. PLATE SECURED WITH FOUR 5/8" DIA. ANCHOR BOLTS

## Types of Stairs

Four types of stairs are defined: straight stairs, circular stairs, curved stairs, and spiral stairs.

Straight stairs are by far the most common type, representing the bulk of the stair market. Though the term "straight" is self-explanatory, for purposes of classification a straight stair is defined as one in which the stringers are straight members. Straight stairs, unlike stairs of the other three types, may be arranged in several different ways:

*Straight run:* Either a single flight extending between floors, as shown in Fig. 5A, or a series of two or more flights in the same line, with intermediate platforms between them, as shown in Fig. 5B.

*Parallel:* Successive flights which parallel each other and are separated only by one or more intermediate platforms, as shown in Fig. 5C.

*Angled:* Successive flights placed at an angle of other than 180° to each other (often 90°), with an intermediate platform between them, as shown in Fig. 5D or E. The type shown in Fig. 5D is often referred to as a "trussed" stair.

*Scissor:* A pair of straight run flights paralleling each other in plan and running in opposite directions on opposite sides of a dividing wall, as shown in Fig. 5F.

Circular stairs are stairs which, in plan view, have an open circular form, with a single center of curvature. They may or may not have intermediate platforms between floors.

Curved stairs are stairs which, in plan view, have two or more centers of curvature, being oval, elliptical, or some other compound curved form. They also may or may not have one or more intermediate platforms between floors.

Spiral stairs are stairs with a closed circular form, having uniform sector shaped treads and a supporting center column.

## Classes of Stairs

The class designation of stairs, as already noted, is a key to the type of construction, the quality of materials, details and finish and, in most cases, the relative cost. As stairs of all classes are built to meet the same standards of performance in respect to load carrying capacity and safety, these class distinctions *do not represent differences in functional value, but in character and appearance.* It is important to recognize that where function is the prime concern, and esthetics are of minor importance, significant economies can be achieved by specifying one of the less expensive classes.

The following four classes of stairs are listed in order of increasing cost (as a general rule); the general construction characteristics of each class are described.

*Industrial class.* Stairs of this class are purely functional in character and consequently they are generally the most economical. They are designed for either interior or exterior use, in industrial buildings such as factories and warehouses, or as fire escapes or emergency exitways. They do not include stairs which are integral parts of industrial equipment.

Industrial class stairs are similar in nature to any light steel construction. Hex head bolts are used for most connections, and welds, where used, are not ground. Stringers may be either flat plate or open channels; treads and platforms are usually made of grating or formed of floor plate, and risers are usually open, though in some cases filled pan type treads and steel risers may be used. Railings are usually of either pipe, tubing, or light steel angle construction.

*Service class.* This class of stairs serves chiefly functional purposes, but is not unattractive in appearance. Service stairs are usually located in enclosed stairwells and provide a secondary or emergency means of travel between floors. In multistoried buildings they are commonly used as egress stairs. They may serve employees, tenants, or the public, and are generally used where economy is a consideration.

Stringers of service stairs are generally the same types as those used on stairs of the industrial class. Treads may be one of several standard types, either filled or formed of floor or tread plate, and risers are either exposed steel or open construction. Railings are typically of pipe construction or a simple bar type with tubular newels, and soffits are usually left exposed. Connections on the underside of the stairs are made with hex head bolts, and only those welds in the travel area are smooth.

*Commercial class.* Stairs of this class are usually for public use and are of more attractive design than those of the service class. They may be placed in open locations or may be located in closed stairwells or in public, institutional, or commercial buildings.

Stringers for this class of stairs are usually exposed open channel or plate sections. Treads may be any of a number of standard types, and risers are usually exposed steel. Railings vary from ornamental bar or tube construction with metal handrails to simple pipe construction, and soffits may or may not be covered. Exposed bolted connections in areas where appearance is critical are made with countersunk flat or oval head bolts; otherwise, hex head bolts are used. Welds in conspicuous locations are smooth, and all joints are closely fitted.

*Architectural class.* This classification applies to any of the more elaborate and usually more expensive stairs, those which are designed to be architectural features in a building. They may be wholly custom designed or may represent a combination of standard parts with specially designed elements such as stringers, railings, treads, or platforms. Usually this class of stair has a comparatively low pitch, with relatively low risers and correspondingly wider treads. Architectural metal stairs may be located either in the open or in enclosed stairwells in public, institutional, commercial, or monumental buildings.

The materials, fabrication details, and finishes used in architectural class stairs vary widely, as dictated by the architect's design and specifications. As a general rule, construction joints are made as inconspicuous as possible, exposed welds are smooth, and soffits are covered with some surfacing material. Stringers may be special sections exposed, or may be structural members enclosed in other materials. Railings are of an ornamental type, and, like the treads and risers, may be of any construction desired.

## General Requirements, All Classes of Stairs

All fixed metal stairs, regardless of class, are of fire-resistant construction and are designed and constructed to carry a minimum live load of 100 pounds per square foot of projected plan area or an alternative concentrated load of 300 pounds applied at the center of any tread span. Railings and handrails are designed and constructed to withstand a minimum force of 200 pounds applied in any direction at any point on the rail.

**Fig. 5**

## STAIRS

**General Purpose Steel Stairs**

SECTION
SCALE ⅛" = 1'-0"

PLAN B-B

LAYOUT FOR:
MULTIPLE STORY
INTERMEDIATE PLATFORM
TWO RUNS PER STORY

PLAN A-A

START-AT POST    WALL STRING    START-AT WALL
SCALE ¾" = 1'-0"

WALL STRING

**SPECIFICATION FOR STAIR AS DETAILED:**
Furnish and erect steel stairs and railings complete as detailed. Strings 10"x1½"x8.4 lb. channels with 1¼"x1¼"x⅛" angle brackets, facias same section bolted to newels and floor construction. Headers of channels bolted or welded to newels and strings. Angle struts placed in wall, bolted to strings and to floor construction. Risers and sub-treads of 14 gauge steel, sub-platforms of 12 gauge steel reinforced with angle or tee stiffeners. Fill, 2" for treads, 3" for platforms, by others. Newels 4" square pipe, railing balusters ½" square spaced 4½" and welded into 1"x½" channels top and bottom with handrail section as shown. All surfaces to be cleaned and painted one shop coat. Shop drawings, to show construction methods and fastenings, are to be approved before fabrication.

**ALTERNATE SPECIFICATIONS:**
**Strings** may be channels, flat plates, or formed plates.
**Tread Brackets** may be other size angles, or bars.
**Riser Brackets** may be omitted.
**Hanger Rods** may be used in place of struts.
**Sub-Treads, Risers** and **Sub-Platforms** may be heavier gauge.
**Newels** and **Railings** may be of other construction as designed by architect.
**Wall Rails**, where required, may have same handrail section as railing.
**Prime Coat** may be red lead, black graphite, zinc chromate, or other approved paint.

SECTION C-C

SECTION F-F

NUMBER OF
RISERS VARIABLE

SECTION K-K

PLAN B-B

PLAN E-E

PLAN J-J

PLAN A-A

PLAN D-D

SCALE $\frac{1}{8}$" = 1'-0"

PLAN H-H

PLAN G-G

LAYOUT FOR:
MULTIPLE STORY
INTERMEDIATE PLATFORMS
PLATFORM AT FLOOR
TWO RUNS PER STORY
Strings and rails finishing against face of rectangular newels, allowing minimum hand clearance between strings and rails. For wider center well, two square newels replace one rectangular newel.

LAYOUT FOR:
MULTIPLE STORY
INTERMEDIATE PLATFORMS
THREE RUNS PER STORY
Open center well allowing intermediate stair runs at 90 degrees. One square newel at each platform.

LAYOUT FOR:
MULTIPLE STORY
INTERMEDIATE PLATFORMS
ONE AND TWO RUNS PER STORY
Arrangement for stairs in corridors, or other restricted spaces, either closed or open well.

# STAIRS

**Steel Stairs**

SECTION
SCALE ⅛"=1'-0"

NUMBER OF RISERS VARIABLE

STRUT

RISERS

RISERS

PLAT. TREADS

DN.

PLAN B-B

ROUGH WELL

ROUGH WELL

UP

PLAN A-A

LAYOUT FOR:
MULTIPLE STORY
INTERMEDIATE PLATFORMS
TWO RUNS PER STORY

SAFETY NOSING

ALTERNATE
TREAD CONSTRUCTION

1¼"⌀ G.P.

1¼" CLEARANCE

2'-7"

FLOOR

ROUGH BEAM

5

4

4

ALTERNATE
TWO POSTS OR
ONE RECTANGULAR
POST

10"×1½" ⌷ - 8.4#

RISE

TREAD

1¼"×1¼"×⅛" L

FLOOR

START - AT POST

3

PLATFORM

FLOOR

1

3

PLATFORM

2

₵ RAILS

3

7

6

7

FLOOR

ROUGH BEAM

6

PLATFORM

BASE

WALL STRING

FLOOR

BASE

PLATFORM

WALL STRING

ANGLE STRUT

SCALE ¾"=1'-0"

ROUGH BEAM

BASE

FLOOR

START - AT WALL

SECTION

NUMBER OF RISERS VARIABLE

ROUGH WELL
TREADS PLAT
STRUT

PLAN A-A

SCALE ⅛"=1'-0"

LAYOUT FOR:
SINGLE STORY
INTERMEDIATE PLATFORMS
THREE RUNS PER STORY

TREAD — GRATING
TREAD — CAST ABRASIVE

ALTERNATE
TREAD CONSTRUCTION

1¼" φ PIPE

WALL RAIL
ENDS RETURNED

FLOOR
ROUGH BEAM

4

1¼" φ PIPE

2'-7"
2'

START-AT POST

SCALE ¾"=1'-0"

TREAD

PLATFORM

3

BASE
FLOOR
ROUGH BEAM

WALL STRING

PLATFORM

3

1

2

PLATFORM
FLOOR PLATE
TREAD
L STRUT
10" x 12 ⊏ 8.4 #
1¼ x 1¼ x ⅜" L
FLOOR
RISE
BASE

WALL STRING

1¼" φ PIPE

WALL RAIL
CLOSED END WITH BRACKET

## STAIRS

**Steel Stairs**

SECTION

NUMBER OF RISERS VARIABLE

SECTION

WALL RAIL OPTIONAL

PLASTER

PLASTER

PLAN A-A

SCALE 1/8" = 1'-0"

PLAN B-B

LAYOUT FOR:
ONE STORY
SINGLE RUN
BETWEEN WALLS

LAYOUT FOR:
ONE STORY
SINGLE RUN
WITH RAILINGS

ROUGH BEAM

CLIPS FOR METAL LATH 15" C.C.

HAND RAIL

SECTION

PLASTER METAL

CLIPS FOR METAL LATH 15" C.C.

10" x 1½ C 8.4#

WALL RAIL

3

BASE

TILE OR LINOLEUM MAY BE USED FOR TREAD COVERING

CLIPS FOR METAL LATH

ROUGH BEAM

WALL STRING-TREAD-RISER

1¼" x 1¼" x 3/8" L

TREAD

RISE

BASE

SCALE 3/4" = 1'-0"

3/16" BENT PL.

10" C - 6.5#

ALTERNATE STRING CONSTRUCTION

WOOD

RUBBER TILE OR LINOLEUM

ALTERNATE TREAD CONSTRUCTION

SUPPORTING BRACKETS ARE OMITTED WHEN TREADS ARE WELDED TO STRINGS

TIRE IRON

HALF OVAL

ALTERNATE RAIL CONSTRUCTION

The platform (Fig. 6) is shown constructed with a steel channel, A, of adequate strength to span the well on line X, through Secs. 1, 2, and 3, and supported at both ends by the wall strings. Newel posts rest on this channel through angle clips, around which the platform plate is cut (Sec. 3). Face strings have welded end plates with flathead screws tapped into the newels (Sec. 2).

The two platforms with two intermediate risers (Fig. 7) are shown constructed with the load carried on line Y by string B, post C, and channel D, which are shown bolted together (Secs. 8, 9, and 10) with through bolts. The load is also carried from post C on line Z in the same manner.

The members at post C may be brought together and welded and the post fitted over the connection, or the entire unit welded.

**Fig. 6**

Plan—One Platform. Load carried on Line X. Wall strings supported on masonry wall.

SCALE $\frac{1}{4}$" = 1'-0"

**Fig. 7**

Plan—Two Platforms with Two Intermediate Risers. Load carried on Line Y and supplemented on Line Z. Wall strings supported by struts.

Stairs are supported by one or more of the following methods, (a) String at floor rests directly on floor construction; (b) String at landing or platform extends into adjacent load-bearing wall; or (c) String at landing or platform is supported by struts extending to the floor below, these being of angles, I-beams or pipes either set in the wall or exposed; or (d) String at landing or platform is supported by rods hung from the floor above, either set in walls or exposed; (e) String paralleling load-bearing wall may have shelf brackets on the back of the strings and set in wall; similar brackets may be used with struts or hanger rods.

SIZE OF CHANNEL VARIES WITH LOAD

ANGLE STRUT (OMIT ON FIG. 6)

_8_    _9_    _6_

_10_

SIZE OF CHANNEL VARIES WITH LOAD

_2_    _3_

TREAD

RISE

_1_

_5_

_4_

_7_

**CONDITIONS ILLUSTRATED:**
Concrete or terrazo fill.
Open unplastered soffit.
Square steel newel posts.
Steel Channel Strings.

683

Width of stair is usually considered center line of rail to finished wall. When wall rail is required allowance should be made for clearance to comply with any legal requirements as to net width.

PLASTER

PLASTER

HAND CLEARANCE.
NOT LESS THAN 1¼

VARIES

USUALLY ONE-HALF
OF STRING WIDTH

ONE-HALF OF
HANDRAIL WIDTH

4"

ROUGH WELL

### METHOD OF ESTABLISHING THE WIDTH OF A STAIR WELL

Height of riser and width of tread vary to fit the type of stair and its use. Legal requirements often limit the minimum tread and maximum rise. A tread of 10" and a rise of 7" to 7½" are considered average. Stairs of easy runs are often 10½" to 11" treads with risers under 7". Stairs used exclusively by maintenance and operating men are often constructed with a rise and tread to equal a pitch greater than 40°. Tread width is always face to face of riser.

TREAD

**ALTERNATE CONSTRUCTION**
Newel set into beam. Plaster finished on center of newel.

DETERMINED BY WIDTH
AND NUMBER OF TREADS

RISER LINE TO ROUGH BEAM
DETERMINED BY ONE-HALF OF
POST WIDTH PLUS CLEARANCE

ROUGH WELL

TREAD

DETERMINED BY WIDTH
AND NUMBER OF TREADS

RISER LINE TO ROUGH BEAM
DETERMINED BY ONE-HALF OF
POST WIDTH PLUS CLEARANCE

WIDTH AT PLATFORM
NOT LESS THAN WIDTH OF STAIR
In some localities laws or ordinances establish a minimum platform width in relation to stair width.

VARIES

1"
4

ROUGH WELL

### METHOD OF ESTABLISHING THE LENGTH OF A STAIR WELL

**REFER TO GOVERNING CODES
TO ESTABLISH DIMENSIONS**

Width of stair is usually measured from inside face of balusters or newel to finished wall. However, governing codes should be consulted for points of measurement.

3½ ″ maximum projection into required egress width. If more than 3½ ″, egress width should be increased by the excess of projection over 3½ ″.

Minimum 1½ ″ hand clearance between rails, and between handrail and wall, or other obstructions.

A minimum clearance of ¼ ″ should be allowed between edge of stringer and wall.

STAIR WELL WIDTH — DISTANCE BETWEEN WALLS

Minimum code requirements are usually measured from finished wall to finished wall. When establishing rough stair well dimensions, allowance should be made for thicknesses of any finish materials to be applied to the rough walls.

Platform width not less than width of stair, usually measured from inside face of balusters or newel to finished wall. However, governing codes should be consulted for points of measurement.

All handrailing heights to meet minimum requirements of governing codes.

A minimum clearance of ¼ ″ should be allowed between edge of stringer and wall.

Varies; recommended minimum 1½ ″.

Length determined by tread run and number of treads required by code.

Varies; recommended minimum 1½ ″.

STAIR WELL WIDTH — DISTANCE BETWEEN WALLS

## REFER TO GOVERNING CODES TO ESTABLISH DIMENSIONS

Height of riser and tread run vary according to governing codes. A tread of 10″ and a rise of 7″ to 7½″ are considered average. Stair treads for more comfortable runs are often 10½″ to 11″ with risers less than 7″. Treads and risers should be so proportioned that the sum of two risers and one tread run is not less than 24″ or more than 26″.

In establishing stair well dimensions, tread run is always face to face of riser.

Platform width not less than width of stair, usually measured from inside face of balusters or newel to finished wall. However, governing codes should be consulted for points of measurement.

A minimum clearance of ¼″ should be allowed between edge of stringer and wall.

Length determined by tread run and number of treads required.

Riser line to rough beam, recommended minimum 1½″.

Varies, recommended minimum 1½″.

STAIR WELL LENGTH — DISTANCE BETWEEN BEAM AND WALL

Provide headroom to meet minimum requirements.

Minimum code requirements are usually measured from finished wall to finished wall. When establishing rough stair well dimensions, allowance should be made for thickness of any finish materials to be applied to the rough walls.

Riser line to rough beam, recommended minimum 1½″

Length determined by tread run and number of treads required.

In some localities, an intermediate platform is required by code when the height between landings exceeds the maximum permitted in a single uninterrupted run.

Length determined by tread run and number of treads required.

Varies

STAIR WELL LENGTH — DISTANCE BETWEEN BEAMS

Steel riser and sub tread with formed nosing, angle supporting brackets.

Steel riser and sub tread with formed nosing, angle supporting brackets.

Steel riser and sub tread with lead filled safety nosing, sanitary cove, angle supporting brackets.

Steel riser and sub tread with abrasive safety nosing, sanitary cove, flat bar supporting brackets.

Steel riser and sub tread with rolled steel or extruded nosing and tile or linoleum tread, angle supporting brackets. Other types of safety nosing or tread covering may be used.

Steel riser and sub tread with marble, or pre-cast tread, angle supporting brackets.

Steel riser and sub-tread with grooved safety nosing and tile or linoleum fill, angle supporting bracket. Other types of safety nosing or tread covering may be used.

Steel floor plate tread, angle tread bracket, with or without steel riser.

Cast metal abrasive tread, with or without steel riser.

Grating Tread.

SCALE 1½" = 1'-0"

Steel riser and sub tread with precast or wood treads, angle supporting brackets.

Steel sub-riser and sub tread with marble tread and riser, angle supporting brackets.

Stairs with concrete or terrazzo fill may be constructed with the top of supporting bracket 2" below the tread surface and 3" below the platform surface. These thicknesses may be less for narrow stairs or where use is limited.

Fill is always considered the distance from string bracket to finish tread.

Treads and riser brackets may be 1¼"x1¼"x³⁄₁₆" or ⅛" angles, welded or riveted to string, or ¼"x1¼" bar welded. Treads and risers are usually bolted to brackets with round head bolts. Cast or grating treads are usually bolted to strings with two ⅜" bolts at each end. Brackets back of risers may be omitted when more economical construction is desired.

## STAIRS
**Tread Sections**

Steel sub-tread and riser with formed nosing at 45 degrees, with or without sanitary cove. Concrete filled tread.

Steel sub-tread and riser with or without sanitary cove, with square formed nosing. Concrete filled tread.

Steel sub-tread and riser with riser sloped to meet formed nosing. Concrete filled tread with resilient tile covering.

Steel sub-tread without riser, concrete filled and reinforced.

Steel sub-tread and riser formed to receive pre-fabricated tread such as pre-cast concrete.

Steel floor plate or aluminum tread plate formed tread and riser.

Steel floor plate or aluminum tread plate formed tread with sheet steel or aluminum riser optional.

Steel or aluminum grating with nosing. End plates welded to grating and bolted to stringer.

Extruded aluminum tread.

Steel channel sub-tread concrete filled.

Flat plate strings with floor plate tread and pipe railing.

Face string at post. Moldings not mitered unless shown or specified mitered.

Steel channel strings with filled pan type tread. The stair should be installed before the face brick or tile walls are built to insure close joints.

Bent plate strings with cast tread, with or without abrasive.

Face string at post. Moldings mitered only when shown or specified mitered.

Steel channel strings with ornamental molding on face string and channel wall string; plastered soffit.

Structural steel channel strings with grating type treads.

Box type face string of two plates and two channels.

Box type face string of channel, plate and moldings; channel wall string.

These string sections include a majority of the various types of strings employed for steel stairs. Other types also are used, and other methods of combining with railings are sometimes desired.

The various types of trim moldings shown are only illustrative of the possibilities of design. The various forms of box type strings shown illustrate several methods of accomplishing this type of construction.

Because of the great number of extrusion and rolling dies now in use for the manufacture of moldings of steel, aluminum, bronze and other metals, the architectural plans should give the manufacturers molding numbers selected. If the moldings shown are designed specially for the project the plans should so state.

Box type face strings.

Box type face string of steel channel and ferrous or non-ferrous exposed face; steel plate wall string.

# STAIRS

**Stringer Sections**

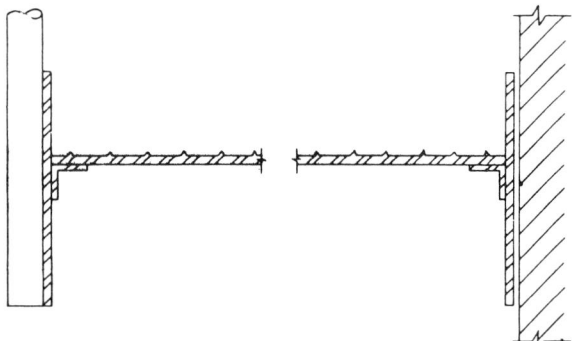

Steel plate stringers, carrier angles, floor plate treads, pipe railing on side of face stringer. Aluminum tread plate may be used when specified. Wall not plastered.

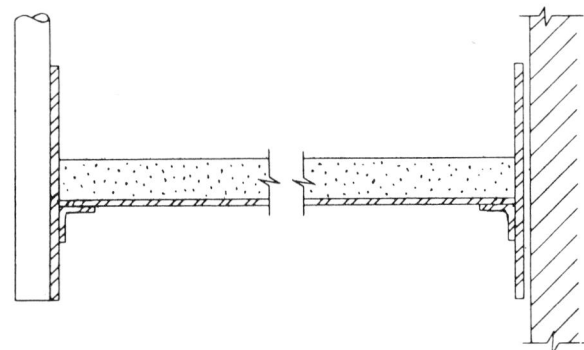

Steel plate stringers, carrier angles, steel sub-tread and riser, concrete filled tread. Pipe railing on side of face stringer, wall not plastered.

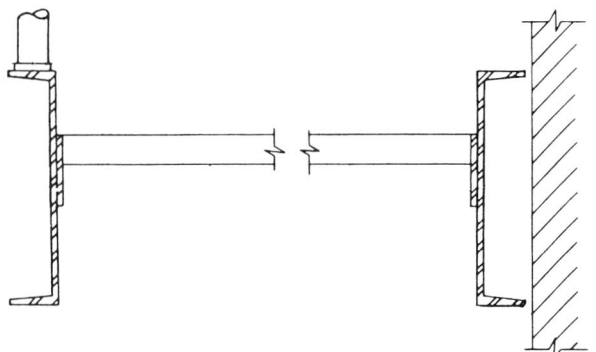

Standard steel channel stringers, grating tread bolted or welded to stringer, pipe railing bolted or welded to top flange of face stringer. Wall not plastered.

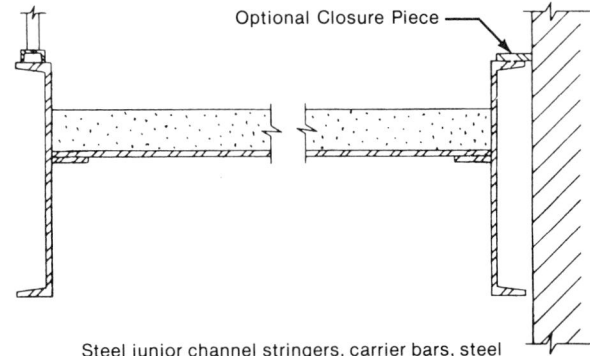

Optional Closure Piece

Steel junior channel stringers, carrier bars, steel sub-tread and riser. Concrete filled tread. Railing with bottom channel fastened to top flange of face stringer. Optional closure piece fastened to top flange of wall stringer in the field. Wall not plastered.

Cast abrasive nosing with short lip, available in iron, bronze or aluminum as specified. Standard drilling with wing anchors, bolts and nuts or drilled as required.

Cast abrasive nosing with deep lip, available in iron, bronze or aluminum as specified. Standard drilling with wing anchors, bolts and nuts or drilled as required.

Extruded aluminum base with epoxy top, containing abrasive. Available in colors. Integral anchors for fresh concrete. Also available drilled to specifications without the anchors.

Extruded aluminum or brass with abrasive filled ribs. Concealed integral anchor runs full length of tread. Also available drilled to specifications, without the integral anchor.

Extruded aluminum with abrasive ribs. Special design for pan stairs with sloped risers. Drilled to specification or furnished with strap anchors or wing anchors.

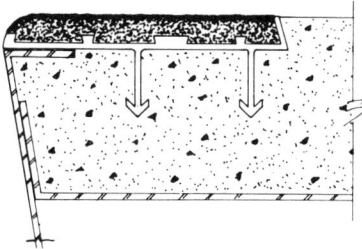

Barrier free design to meet standards for the physically handicapped. Aluminum base with epoxy containing abrasive top. Integral anchors for fresh concrete.

Cast abrasive structural tread, available in iron or aluminum. Integrally cast end lugs for bolting directly to stringers.

Cast abrasive double nosed tread, available in iron or aluminum and is reversible. Supported by carrier angles bolted to tread and either bolted or welded to stringer.

Cast abrasive tread, available in iron or aluminum. Nosing and toe plate can be drilled for attaching flat plate risers. Supported by carrier angles.

# STAIRS
## Handrails

**NOTE:** When the railing and stringer metals are weldable to each other, the railing post can be welded directly to the stringer.

PLAN AT A

PLAN AT B

PLAN AT C

PLAN AT D

Stair platform or landing with pipe railings, railings not connected, for stairwell having minimum clearance. Short newels, supported on header.

Stair platform or landing with pipe railing, one post at return. Lower rail returned into post, two or more posts used at wide wells. Short newels, supported on header.

Stair platform or landing with rectangular or square newel, pipe railing members capped and welded to newel post.

2"x4"x1/8" STAINLESS STEEL HANDRAIL W/ SATIN FINISH

2'-10"

2"

2"

SECT. THRU S.S. HANDRAIL

4"

6"

3"

FACE OF RISER

TOP RISER

BOTTOM RISER

2"x4" STAINLESS STEEL HANDRAIL

BLUESTONE TREADS

HARD LEAD CAULKING

CEMENT GROUT

STEEL SLEEVE 2½"x4½" (INSIDE DIM.) x 8"

STEEL BASE PLATE 4"x6" W/CONTINUOUS WATERTIGHT FILLET WELD

## HANDRAIL

Stair start with square newel, baluster type railing with channel top and bottom, pipe handrail.

Stair start with short newel, parallel bar type railing with end and intermediate posts of square, rectangular or round section, extruded handrail with mitered, forged or cast terminal.

Stair start with square newel, parallel bar type railing with intermediate posts of square, rectangular or round section; extruded or rolled handrail section mitered to form cap over newel.

Square or rectangular newel, pipe rail fitted with offset lug to center on stringer.

Square or rectangular newel, pipe rail fitted with offset lug for positioning inside of stringer.

Section showing fastening for intermediate posts to stringers.

Rectangular newel, pipe rail and stringer welded or bolted to face.

## STAIRS
**Newels and Railings**

PLAN—RAILING

PLAN AT A

HANDRAIL

PLAN—RAILING

PLAN AT B

Ⓐ

Ⓑ

Stair landing, with stringer and fascia at right angle.
Landing extended on down flight to set-forward riser,
producing easement in handrail.

Stair landing with stringers and fascia framed square.
Square railing return, end balusters centered on
newels and landing extended on up flight to set-back
riser.

PLAN—RAILING

PLAN—RAILING

Stair landing with stringers and fascia framed square.
Radius railing return, parallel bar type railing with end
balusters centered on newels. Landing extended on
down flight to set-forward riser.

Stair landing with stringers and fascia framed into full
height newel, baluster railing with channel top and
bottom. Continuous pipe handrail offset from balusters
and newels by brackets.

Figures 9 and 10 indicate typical railings for decks, platforms, balconies, roofs, and similar locations, adapted for residential, apartment, or hotel construction. These railings may be fastened with wood screws or lag bolts to wood, or with expansion bolts to masonry. On roofs or decks the setting of the post bases should be waterproofed.

**Fig. 9**

SPACE FOR ORNAMENT
DESIGN BY ARCHITECT

**Fig. 10**

SECTION

Methods of constructing railing top members.

SCALE 1½" = 1'-0"

**TO SPECIFY:**
Give locations.
Indicate kind of metal.
Specify finish.
Give sizes of members.
Give height.
Provide scale details of ornaments, finials and bases.

Specify method of fastening, or have fabricator provide fastenings best suited to each condition.

Railing with balusters and bottom longitudinal member supporting balusters. Posts extending into masonry.

Railing without bottom longitudinal member, each baluster set in masonry and fitted with slip flange or base. Masonry specifications should specify holes.

## STAIRS
**Ornamental Railings**

**-2-**

Railing panels set between columns or jambs. Posts extended to floor construction for support.

**-1-**

DESIGN BY ARCHITECT

**-3-**

**-4-**

Railing for balcony or mezzanine with double posts and panels. Posts extended to support facia and fastened to floor construction.

**-6-**

Railing for balcony or mezzanine with curved section. Facia fastened to floor construction. Railing fastened to facia.

**-5-**

Center railings are recommended for wide stairs. They may be a single pipe or tubing railing or they may be designed with double rails and panels of interesting design.

*Note:* A number of codes require that railings have a level extension beyond the nosings at the floors as indicated in Fig. 11 by dashed lines. This applies to both wall and center railings.

Center railing of double pipe, posts extended to subtread.

**Fig. 11**

Center railing of single pipe or tubing, round, square or rectangular steel, bronze or aluminum. Posts set into floor as at ends, or extended to subtread and bolted as at center. Flanges loose or fixed.

Center railing of double pipe, posts set into floor.

Railing post set over dowel which is anchored to pan tread and reinforced with structural tee member supported between stringers prior to placing concrete fill.

**PLAN A**
Handrail with square return mitered.

**PLAN B**
Handrail with round return.

**1**

ALTERNATE SECTIONS

HINGED BRACKET

Center railing of two members, with brackets to square or rectangular posts, steel, bronze or aluminum. Posts set into floor as at ends, or extended to subtread and bolted as at center. Flanges loose or fixed.

Center railing of single member centered on top of rectangular post by means of hinged bracket.

Non-ferrous or stainless steel sleeves may be used on exterior rails to prevent staining masonry or concrete.

FLANGE BOLT TO WALL W/ EXPANSION BOLTS

SEE TABLE FOR SPACING

WELDED CONNECTIONS GROUND SMOOTH

WELDED CONNECTIONS GROUND SMOOTH

EQ.

EQ.

3'-0"

FLOOR

3'-0"

FACE OF WALL

## ELEVATION OF WELDED PIPE RAILING
@ 3/8" = 1'-0"

1½" ⌀ PIPE

POST SET IN PIPE OR SHEET METAL SLEEVE, ANCHOR W/CONC. OR SULPHUR. FLANGE MAY BE LOOSE OR FASTENED TO POST.

NOTE: MOLTEN LEAD OR LEAD WOOL MAY BE USED FOR ANCHORING, WHERE THE TENDENCY TO FLOW IS NOT A FACTOR INVOLVING STRENGTH

CONC.

METAL SLEEVE

3"x3"x³⁄₁₆" PL. WELDED TO BOTTOM

5"

1 @ 3" = 1'-0"

1½" ⌀ PIPE

1½" x ¼" PLATE WELDED TO STRINGER

STRINGER

## WELDED PIPE RAILING DETAIL FOR STEEL STAIRS
@ 3" = 1'-0"

| RECOMMENDED POST SPACING FOR PIPE RAILING | |
| --- | --- |
| SIZE OF PIPE | MAXIMUM SPACING |
| ³⁄₄" | 4' |
| 1" | 6' |
| 1¼" | 7' |
| 1½" | 8' |
| 2" | 9' |
| 2½" | 10' |
| 3" | 10' |

## TYPICAL EXTRUDED ALUMINUM AND BRONZE POST SECTIONS

1 ¼″

2 ¾″

2 ¾″

2″
Aluminum only

1 ⁵⁄₈″

2 ¾″
Aluminum only

2″
Aluminum only

Various

Flanges for box and solid stringers.

Flanges for channel stringers.

½″

1½″

Post mounted on box stringer.

Post mounted on channel stringer.

PLAN

Post mounted on concrete step using post anchor.

Sections — Railing posts with brackets.

**Fig. 12**

Elevation; intermediate post set on face of box stringer.

Section; intermediate post set on face of box stringer.

Stair landing with box stringers attached to sides of newel, parallel type bar railing supported by brackets at newels and intermediate posts. Risers offset to allow metal soffits of stair to meet at intersection with soffit of landing. Bottom and top rails must be the same and have symetrical cross section to obtain proper mitered connection.

**Fig. 13 Elevation of Fig. 12: rectangular newel post.**

## STAIRS

Handrail Sections

### TYPICAL EXTRUDED ALUMINUM AND BRONZE HANDRAIL SECTIONS

A = 1-5/8", 1-15/16", 2-1/4"
Aluminum and Bronze

A = 1-3/4", 2-1/8"
Aluminum and Bronze

A = 1.66" and 1.90" typical.
Aluminum and Bronze

**Fig. 14**

A = 2-3/8" Aluminum

A = 1-1/2", 2", 2-1/2" Aluminum

A = 3-1/4, 3-3/4" Aluminum
A = 2-1/4", 2-3/4" Bronze

A = 2-3/4", 3"
Aluminum and Bronze

A = 2-7/8"
Aluminum and Bronze

A = 2-3/4" Aluminum

**Most of these sections can be mounted on channels or flats, secured by screws from below. Some are designed for mounting on handrail brackets. The use of channels instead of solid bars often simplifies the attachment of baluster and ornaments. The channels may be of the same or a different metal.**

### TYPICAL ROLLED STEEL HANDRAIL SECTIONS

A = 1-3/4" Steel

A = 1-15/16", 2-1/4" Steel

A = 1-3/4" Steel

**Fig. 15**

A = 2" Steel

A = 1-3/4" Steel

Various Steel

Various, 1.66" typical Steel

**Most of these sections can be mounted on channels or flats, secured by screws or welding from below. Sometimes they are welded directly to the baluster (see Fig. 15) or attached to handrail brackets (see Fig. 14). The use of channels often simplifies the attachment of balusters and ornaments.**

## REPRESENTATIVE EXTRUDED AND TUBULAR STAINLESS STEEL HANDRAIL SECTIONS

Stainless Steel Extrusion

Stainless Steel (other sizes available)

Stainless Steel

Stainless Steel

Stainless Steel (other sizes available)

Stainless Steel

A = Various
1.66" and 1.90" typical

Stainless tubular handrail sections usually have a wall thickness of .065".

## PLASTIC HANDRAIL COVERINGS

Fig. 16

Fig. 17

Fig. 18

Fig. 19

**TABLE 4   Table of Dimensions for Plastic Handrail Coverings**

| Fig. | A<br>Inside<br>width | B<br>Inside<br>height | C<br>Outside<br>width | D<br>Outside<br>height |
|---|---|---|---|---|
| 16 | 1" | ½" | 1⁵⁄₁₆" | 1³⁄₁₆" |
|  | 1¼" |  | 1⁹⁄₁₆" |  |
|  | 1½" |  | 1¹³⁄₁₆" |  |
| 17 | 1¼" | ¼" | 1⁹⁄₁₆" | ⁹⁄₁₆" |
|  | 1½" | ¼" | 1¹³⁄₁₆" | ⁹⁄₁₆" |
|  | 2" | ³⁄₈" | 2⁵⁄₁₆" | 1¹⁄₁₆" |
| 18 | 1½" | ¼" | 2¾" | ½" |
|  | 2" |  | 3¼" | ⁹⁄₁₆" |
| 19 | 1¼" | ¼" | 1⁵⁄₈" | 1³⁄₁₆" |
|  | 1½" |  | 1⁷⁄₈" | 1⁵⁄₁₆" |

*Caution:* Consult manufacturers for fabrication limitations.

### General Information

Functional and decorative plastic handrail mouldings of polyvinyl chloride plastics are available in a variety of sizes and profiles, several of which are illustrated in Figs. 16 to 19. Consult suppliers' current literature for variations in details and features.

Plastic handrail mouldings are not structural and require bar, tube, or channel members to support vertical and horizontal loads.

Plastic handrail mouldings are produced in a range of colors from subdued to bright, to suit either formal or informal design situations. The color is integral with the plastic,

which is highly resistant to wear, weathering, and corrosion.

The thermoplastic material becomes pliable when heated (not over 165°F), at which time it can be fitted over the support member and conforms to vertical, horizontal, or combined vertical and horizontal curves within certain limitations.

Lateral bends should have a minimum centerline radius of not less than 2 times the width of the plastic section or 2½ to 3 times the width of the support section, whichever is greater. Mitered corners should be used if

sharper turns are required.

Combined vertical and horizontal turns can be formed by twisting the moulding.

The material can be joined by thermal welding, and end caps can be shaped using a knife, a file, or abrasives.

The use of a cleaning solution for removing grease and foreign material is recommended, after which a solvent is used for polishing or removing abrasive scratches. Normal cleaning requires only soap and water.

## STAIRS
**Wall Handrail Brackets**

Wall rail bracket of conventional cast design, malleable iron, aluminum or bronze. 3/8″ bolt into wall.

Wall rail bracket of conventional cast design, malleable iron, aluminum or bronze, 3/8″ stud into wall, tapped into arm of bracket.

Wall rail bracket of extruded aluminum, made to set at right angle to wall rail or set vertically. 3/8″ bolt into wall.

Two-piece wall rail bracket of aluminum. Wall plate bolted into wall through expansion type anchor. Outer sleeve screwed to rail. Outer sleeve fastened to wall plate by set screw.

Wall rail bracket of aluminum with fittings to handrail adjustable to any pitch. 3/8″ stud into wall.

Optional fastening

Wall rail bracket of formed steel. Filler and anchor bolt through gypsum board on masonry. Bracket fastened to filler by three screws or by 3/8″ bolt through center.

Typical steel stair construction

**PLAN · OF · FIRE-TOWER · SHOWING · STEEL · STAIRS · (TYPICAL · FLOOR·)** Scale ⅜"=1′-0"

**DETAIL · FOR · MARBLE · OR · SLATE · TREADS ·** 1½"-1′-0"

**SIDE · VIEW · OF · PIPE · RAIL · AT · NEWEL ·** Scale 1½"-1′-0

**SECTION · C-C · THRU · WALL · STRING ·** Scale 1½"-1′-0"

**SECTION · THRU · RISERS · AND · TREADS ·** Scale 1½"-1′-0"

**SECTION · C-C · THRU · FACE · STRING ·** Scale 1½"-1′-0"

**PLAN · OF · TRUSS · RISER · AT · NEWEL · X · INTER-MEDIATE · LANDING · DETAIL · AT · NEWEL · Y · SIMILAR ·** Scale ¾"-1′-0" ·

**ELEVATION · SHOWING · 12" · TRUSS · RISER ·** Scale ¾"-1′-0"

3"x3"x⅜" steel newel

Metal door

Wall string

Cement finish
Cinder fill
Concrete fill

Allow sufficient space between riser face and steel supports

1¼"x1¼"x³⁄₁₆" Ls

12"x⅜" string bent to 10" width

Treads and risers in section

⅝" Sq. bars 5" o.c.

Metal or Kalamein doors and trim

1⅝" Iron pipe

3"x3"x⅜" steel newel

Plaster line

Face string

Plaster line

1⅝" dia. Iron pipe rail.

Wall pipe rails secured with C.I. brackets 5'-0" o.c.

3"x3"x⅜" Steel newels with C.I. caps and drops.

Wall string opposite side

Truss riser (See detail.)

12"x⅜" Plate string bent 10" wide.
Stock iron moulding for face strings.

SECTION·ON·A-A·SHOWING·CONSTRUCTION·OF·TYPICAL·STEEL·STAIR·
Scale ⅜"=1'-0".

Pipe cap
1⅝" Pipe hand rail

Wall bracket

ELEVATION·OF·BRACKET·& HAND·(WALL)·RAIL·

12"x⅜" Truss Riser

String

SECTION·THRU·TRUSS·RISER·B-B    ¾"=1'-0".

·DETAIL·OF·SPLICE·FOR·STRING·

Non-slip nosing

Nosing anchor

·DETAIL·OF·NON-SLIP·NOSING·FOR·TREAD·    1½"=1'-0".

## STAIRS
### Steel Stairs

¾"x1½" FLAT GALV. STL. HANDRAIL, PT'D

½"x1" FLAT GALV. STL. SUPPORT WELDED TO STRINGER & HANDRAIL

STL. STRINGER PAINTED

(12/A10) DETAIL OF TYP. HANDRAIL at STAIR #1
SCALE: 1½"=1'-0"

GALV. STL PIPE RAILING, 1½"∅ PAINTED, COLOR #A

GALV. STL PIPE RAILING, 1"∅ PAINTED, COLOR #A

VERT. POST WELDED TO STRINGER

STL. STRINGER W. CLADDING PT'D COLOR #A

NOTE: VERTICAL POST AT DINING #105 PLATFORM (SHOWN DOTTED)

(13/A10) DETAIL OF HANDRAIL at STAIR #2
SCALE: 1½"=1'-0"

11" TREAD

HEADER CHANNEL

GALV. STL STRINGER SEE STRUC. DWG FOR SIZE, PT'D COLOR #A

METAL DIAMOND PAN TREAD & RISER

1¼"x1¼"x⅛" ANGLE SUPPORTS WELDED TO STRINGER

GYP BD. PT'D (at STAIR #3 ONLY)

NOTE: FOR OVERALL VERTICAL HEIGHT CONTRACTOR SHOULD VERIFY DIMENSION at JOB SITE

(17/A10) DETAIL OF TREAD & RISER at STAIRS #3 & #5
SCALE: 1½"=1'-0"

1½"∅ GALV. STL. PIPE HANDRAIL WELDED TO BRACKET, PT'D COLOR #A

GYP BD. PT'D COLOR #A

EXPANSION BOLTS

GALV. STL. BRACKET AT 4'-0" O.C. PT'D COLOR #A

METAL SPACER (DOTTED)

STRUCTURAL STL. STUD ANCHORED TO WALL STUDS

(18/A10) DETAIL OF HANDRAIL at STAIRS #3 & #5
SCALE: 3"=1'-0"

## STAIRS
Steel Stairs

### STEEL STAIRS WITH TERRAZZO TREADS

MINIMUM RECOMMENDED THICKNESS FOR TERRAZZO TREAD, RISERS, & STRINGERS

| LENGTH (FT.) | THICKNESS (MIN.) IN. |
|---|---|
| TO 4'-6" | 1½" |
| 4'-6" TO 6'-6" | 1¾" |
| 6'-6" TO 8'-0" | 2" |
| OVER 8'-0" | NOT RECOMMENDED |

### STEEL STAIRS WITH TERRAZZO TREADS AND RISERS

## Construction

Material may be steel, stainless steel, cast iron, or aluminum. Treads are supported in cantilever fashion by the column, each consecutive tread being rotated at a predetermined angle. The platform attaches to the column and is fastened to the floor structure to hold the column secure. The spiral railing is supported by balusters attached to the outer ends of the treads.

## Tread Designs

Fabricators provide several standard types and designs of treads and platforms. These include open riser, closed riser, and cantilever types, with surface of checkered plate, abrasive plate, steel grating, or plain surface to receive wood, resilient flooring, carpet, or other covering. Pan type treads to receive concrete or terrazzo fill are also available.

## Stair Height

Spiral stairs are adaptable to any height, the height being equal to the distance from finished floor to finished floor.

## Stair Diameter

Spiral stairs are available in various diameters from 3'6" to 8'0", normally in 6" increments. A 4'0" diameter is considered minimum for general access purposes; a 5'0" diameter provides a comfortable general purpose stair. Larger diameters are used chiefly for architectural effect. Note that the diameter of the finished well opening should be at least 2" greater than the stair diameter, to provide hand clearance.

## Hand of Stairs

*Left-hand stairs:* User ascends in clockwise direction, with handrail at left.

*Right-hand stairs:* User ascends in counterclockwise direction, with handrail at right.

EXIT AT LOWER FLOOR

Minimum clearance between well opening and handrail is 1"

Well opening may be either square or circular

PLAN AT TOP FLOOR
Left Hand, 30°, Full Circle

PLAN AT TOP FLOOR
Right Hand, 22½°, ¾ Circle

**Fig. 20**

**TABLE 5    Riser Heights for Various Tread Angles**

| Tread angle | Min. height of riser* | Treads per ¾ circle | Treads per full circle |
|---|---|---|---|
| 30° | 8¹⁵⁄₁₆" | 9 | 12 |
| 27° | 8" | 10 | 13 = 351° |
| 24½° | 7⁵⁄₁₆" | 11 | 15 = 367½° |
| 22½° | 6¹¹⁄₁₆" | 12 | 16 |

*Minimum height to attain 6'6" clear headroom using a 90° landing, 2" thick.

**TABLE 6    Chart for Selection of Number and Height of Risers**

| Floor to floor height | Number of risers and height of each in inches | | | | | | | | |
|---|---|---|---|---|---|---|---|---|---|
| | 10 | 11 | 12 | 13 | 14 | 15 | 16 | 17 | 18 |
| 7'0" | 8.4 | 7.6 | 7.0 | | | | | | |
| 7'4" | 8.8 | 8.0 | 7.3 | 6.8 | | | | | |
| 7'8" | 9.2 | 8.4 | 7.7 | 7.0 | | | | | |
| 8'0" | 9.6 | 8.7 | 8.0 | 7.4 | 6.9 | | | | |
| 8'2" | 9.8 | 8.9 | 8.2 | 7.5 | 7.0 | | | | |
| 8'4" | | 9.1 | 8.3 | 7.7 | 7.1 | 6.7 | | | |
| 8'6" | | 9.3 | 8.5 | 7.8 | 7.3 | 6.8 | | | |
| 8'8" | | 9.4 | 8.7 | 8.0 | 7.4 | 6.9 | | | |
| 8'10" | | | 8.8 | 8.2 | 7.6 | 7.1 | 6.6 | | |
| 9'0" | | | 9.0 | 8.3 | 7.7 | 7.2 | 6.7 | | |
| 9'2" | | | 9.2 | 8.5 | 7.9 | 7.3 | 6.9 | | |
| 9'4" | | | 9.3 | 8.6 | 8.0 | 7.5 | 7.0 | | |
| 9'6" | | | | 8.8 | 8.1 | 7.6 | 7.1 | 6.7 | |
| 9'8" | | | | 9.0 | 8.3 | 7.7 | 7.2 | 6.8 | |
| 9'10" | | | | 9.2 | 8.4 | 7.9 | 7.4 | 6.9 | |
| 10'0" | | | | 9.3 | 8.6 | 8.0 | 7.5 | 7.0 | 6.7 |
| 10'2" | | | | | 8.7 | 8.1 | 7.6 | 7.2 | 6.8 |
| 10'4" | | | | | 8.9 | 8.3 | 7.7 | 7.3 | 6.9 |
| 10'6" | | | | | 9.0 | 8.4 | 7.9 | 7.4 | 7.0 |
| 10'8" | | | | | 9.1 | 8.5 | 8.0 | 7.5 | 7.1 |
| 10'10" | | | | | | 8.6 | 8.1 | 7.6 | 7.2 |
| 11'0" | | | | | | 8.7 | 8.2 | 7.8 | 7.3 |
| 11'2" | | | | | | 8.9 | 8.4 | 7.9 | 7.4 |
| 11'4" | | | | | | 9.0 | 8.5 | 8.0 | 7.6 |
| 11'6" | | | | | | | 8.6 | 8.1 | 7.7 |
| 11'8" | | | | | | | 8.7 | 8.2 | 7.8 |
| 12'0" | | | | | | | 9.0 | 8.5 | 8.0 |

WELL OPENING

1" MIN    STAIR DIAMETER    1" MIN

See notes below

Center column

3'0" RESIDENTIAL
3'6" OTHERS

Platform either square, rounded or special shape to fit well opening.

STAIR HEIGHT (FIN FLOOR TO FIN FLOOR)

Base plate either below floor level or anchored to floor.

TYPICAL ELEVATION — RIGHT HAND OPEN RISER STAIR

## STAIRS

**Spiral Stairs**

PLAN AT PLATFORM

**Diameter and head room** Spiral stairs may be made in diameters from 3'6" to 6'0" or greater, with 4'0" usually considered the minimum for easy travel. The well hole should be at least 3" larger in diameter than the stair, for railing clearance. Spiral stairs are usually constructed with 12 or 16 treads to the circle. Head room should be calculated on the basis of three-fourths of a circle. On a 12-tread circle, 9" is approximately the minimum rise, providing 6'9" head room. On a 16-tread circle, 7" rise will provide 7'0" head room. A rise up to 12" per tread may be employed.

CAST METAL SPIRAL STAIR CONSTRUCTION:
Spiral stairs may be constructed with cast metal treads and landings of plain or checkered surface, made with or without abrasive material. Each tread has a collar which slips over a stand pipe of steel. Risers are not desirable as toe room near the stand pipe is limited. The treads are bolted together at the outer edge, either by bolts or by using the railing posts as bolts. Fabricators may have several types of standard design treads and landings which may be satisfactory without preparation of special patterns.

PLATFORM

FRONT ELEVATION

12 TREADS PER CIRCLE—30°
16 TREADS PER CIRCLE—22°30'

RADIUS

TREAD

SECTION

START

PLAN AT START

SCALE $\frac{3}{8}$" = 1'-0"

FRONT ELEVATION

STRUT

UP

PLAN A-A

NUMBER OF RISERS VARIABLE

WALL STRING

FACE STRING

1

2

3

4

5

Circular stairs placed between walls may be built self-supporting at the inner string and be supported by concealed struts or hangers at the outer string. When completely exposed a circular stair may be designed to require few supports between floors.

In constructing a circular stair the overall size of the well and the tread length of the stairs may be adjusted to fit the particular conditions of the structure. Treads should be a minimum width of 8″ at a distance 15″ out from the inside railing. The treads may be of steel, abrasive cast iron, abrasive non-ferrous metal, cement, tile, linoleum, wood, marble or other material.

Landings and platforms may be constructed as part of the stair, and may be supported by beam or cantilever construction. Wall rails and brackets may be constructed with handrail sections matching the railing.

Face strings and railings may be similar to those used on straight stairs but should be designed of shapes adaptable to abrupt curved construction. The small radius to which these are constructed offers possibilities of design that should not be overlooked. Combinations of contrasting metal colors can be effectively employed in such installations.

## STAIRS

**Concrete Stairs**

Plan 3/16" scale

Section 3/16" scale

Section 3/4" scale

Section 3/4" scale

Section 3/4" scale

PIPE HANDRAIL
DETAILS

3/8" HEX. HEAD
EXPANSION BOLT

1 1/4" I. D.

EQUAL

I. D. PIPE
HANDRAIL

STD. MALLEABLE
IRON BRACKET

WELD & GRIND
SMOOTH

STD. C.I.
RETURN

2'-8" AT FACE OF RISER

TYPICAL FLOOR PLAN

UP 14R

DN 14R

CLEARANCE

3'-8" MIN.

NON-SLIP TREADS
(SEE NOTE)

3'-8" MIN. CLEARANCE

DN 14R

UP 14R

HANDRAIL

NON-SLIP TREADS
(SEE NOTE)

3'-8" MIN. CLEARANCE

15'-0 MIN.

₵ OF DOOR

₵ OF DOOR

SECTION THRU STEP

CONCRETE WALL

LINE OF
1ST. RISER

NON-SLIP
TREAD

RISER

3/4" R

3/4" R

CAST TYPE ANCHOR, 12" O.C.

3/4"

1 1/4"

TREAD

SECTION "A-A"

13 TREADS AT 9 5/8" = 10'-5 1/2"

2"

2"

CONSTRUCTION JOINT

TYPICAL FLOOR

BRACKET
HANDRAIL

CONSTRUCTION
JOINT

CONCRETE

14 RISERS

8'-6"

TYPICAL FLOOR

Typical reinforced concrete scissors stair

## STAIRS

Concrete, Steel, and Terrazzo Stairs

1 STAIR DETAIL

1 STAIR DETAIL WITH CARPETING

2 STAIR DETAIL WITH TERRAZZO TREADS & RISERS

STEEL RISER CEMENT TREADS

STEEL RISER TERRAZZO TREADS

ABRASIVE (NON-SLIP) INSERTS

MARBLE RISER ANCHORED
TO STRINGER

MORTAR SETTING BED

MORTAR SETTING BED

**(a)**

MORTAR SETTING BED

STEEL STRINGERS

**(b)**

ABRASIVE (NON-SLIP) INSERTS

MARBLE RISER ANCHORED
TO STRINGER

DOWEL

MORTAR SETTING BED

**(c)**

**(d)**

**Fig. 21** Sections *(a)* and *(b)* are marble treads and risers supported by steel stringers; section *(c)*, marble treads only; section *(d)*, cubic marble treads supported by concrete or steel stringers.

NON-SKID INSERTS INSTALLED AT SHOP

NON-SLIP TREADS

℄ FOR W.I. OR
MARBLE BALUSTERS

KEY TO
MATERIALS

MARBLE
TILE
CEMENT
PLASTER
STEEL

CAP OPTIONAL

STEEL
WALL
STRINGER

WALL
STRINGER

HUNG PL. CEILING

STEEL PANS

TREAD & RISERS

STEEL
STRINGER

FACE
STRINGER

STRIP
LINER

EYE-BOLT AT
EACH JOINT

³⁄₁₆" PIN

STAIR
DETAILS

**Fig. 22** Interior marble details.

## STAIRS

### Slate Treads

Natural Cleft Slate Treads and Risers w/ Back Surface Gauged. Set w/ ¼" min Grouted Joints on Concrete Base. Same for Sand Rubbed Finish. Exposed Edges Honed.

Sand Rubbed Slate Treads and Risers w/ Back Surface gauged, set w/ ¼" min. Grouted Joints on Steel pan. Same for Natural Cleft Finish. Bondage Grooves optional. All exposed Edges Rubbed Smooth.

Natural Cleft or Sand Rubbed Finish Treads Set on Brick or other exposed Base. All Exposed Edges Honed.

**Suggested detail for slate treads and risers, exterior and/or interior**

Sand Rubbed Face/Gauged Back Surface Shown, May Also Be Natural Cleft Face Finish with Gauged Back Surface

Cement Mortar 1:2 Mix Float Off High, Wet Bottom Of Tread, Sprinkle Setting Bed With Portland Cement, Sprinkle With Water And Force Tread Down Onto Setting Bed.

Set Riser With Epoxy Cement.

Bondage Grooves May Be Added For Additional Stability.

**Slate treads and risers set on metal pan stair**

LOBBY SLATE FIN. FL. TO MATCH SLATE TREAD

EXIST. SLAB.

6" [

SECURE TO EXIST. STEEL

1'-0" TREAD TYPICAL

1'-0" TREAD TYPICAL

¼" SLATE

¼" NOSING TYPICAL

+1 6½" RISER TYPICAL HTS.

¼" STEEL RISERS, ANGLES & TREAD PAN

STEEL CHANNEL STRINGER

**A / A-45  DETAIL OF TOP END STAIR #4 @ LOBBY LEVEL**
SCALE: 1½" = 1'-0"

4" SLATE TREAD ON CONC. BED

¼" STEEL TREAD PAN & RISER

1"x1"x¼" STEEL ANGLES

¼" SLATE RISER

STEEL ANGLE WITH EXPANSION BOLT ANCHOR

1'-0" TREAD TYP.

1½" NOSING

6½" RISER TYPICAL VIF

RVT

EX'G FL.

**6 / A-45  DETAIL OF STAIR #4 LANDING**
SCALE: 1½" = 1'-0"

Any potential hazards must be eliminated. Stairs should be "easy going," that is, there must be an appropriate relationship of riser to tread. Treads are of nonslip material which is also extended onto platforms and landings for a distance equal to the width of the stair treads. Double handrails, one higher than the other, are provided on stairs for each line of short or tall pupils. The posts, which support the center handrails of double stairs, are extended high enough above the top handrail to prevent pupils from sliding down.

SECTION 'A-A'

SECTION 'B-B'

PLAN · VIEW·

## STAIRS
**Barrier-Free Design Data**

(c)
**Extension at Bottom of Run**

(d)
**Extension at Top of Run**

(a)
Plan

(b)
**Elevation of Center Handrail**

*NOTE:*

*X is the 12 in minimum handrail extension required at each top riser.*

*Y is the minimum handrail extension of 12 in plus the width of one tread that is required at each bottom riser.*

**Fig. 23   Stair handrails.**

(a)
*Handrail*

(b)
*Handrail*

(c)
*Handrail*

(e)
*Grab Bar*

(d)
*Handrail*

**Fig. 24   Size and spacing of handrails and grab bars.**

**Fig. 25    Usable tread width and examples of acceptable nosings.**

### Steps and Stairs

Steps and stairs should have nonprotruding nosings so that people with stiff joints, braces, artificial legs, or other leg or stability problems will not catch their toes as they climb.

Handrails should be oval or round with 1½"/4 cm hand clearance between the rails and the wall: 1½"/4 cm clearance will provide ease of grip but will prevent the hand or wrist from slipping between the handrail and the wall if the person loses balance. Handrails should be positioned on both sides of steps and stairs and should extend beyond the first and last steps on at least one side and preferably on both to allow people with long leg braces to pull themselves beyond these points. To guard against falls and to help children, some codes require another, lower handrail.

Steps, stairs, and handrails should not be made of slippery material.

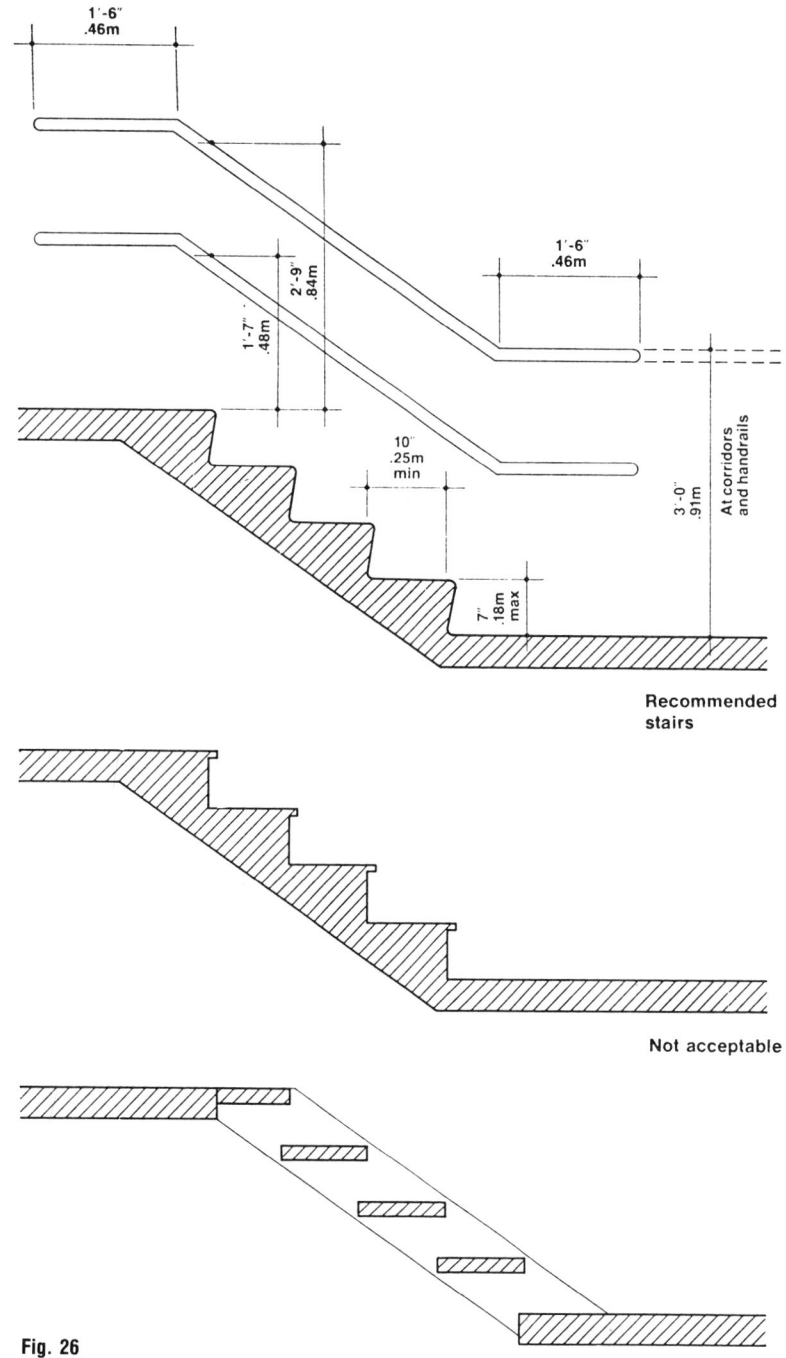

**Fig. 26**

## STAIRS

Ladders

**56° WOOD**

**56° STEEL**

**68° STEEL**

**68° ALUMINUM**

## LADDERS

① ENGINEERS LADDER WITH CAST ABRASIVE TREADS

② VERTICAL LADDER

## OPEN STEEL STAIRS

① STAIR DETAIL (GRATING TREAD)

② CAST ABRASIVE TREAD

| WIDTH OVERALL | CENTER TO CENTER SPACING |
|---|---|
| 5 INCHES | 2 INCHE O.C. |
| 6 | 3 |
| 7 | 3½ |
| 8 | 4 |
| 9 | 5 |
| 10 | 6 |

STANDARD HOLE SPACING FOR CAST ABRASIVE TREAD

| THICKNESS IN INCHES | CAST IRON | CAST ALUMINUM | CAST BRONZE | CAST NICKEL-BRONZE |
|---|---|---|---|---|
| 5/16" | UP TO 6" WIDE | UP TO 8" WIDE | UP TO 8" WIDE | UP TO 8" WIDE |
| 3/8" | 12" | 18" | 18" | 18" |
| 7/16" | 24" | 26" | 24" | 24" |
| ½" | 30" | 36" | 30" | 30" |
| 5/8" | 42" | 42" | 36" | 36" |

THICKNESS LIMITATIONS FOR VARIOUS WIDTH CASTINGS

## STAIRS
**Steel Pan Cement-Filled Stairs**

1 STAIR DETAIL

2 STRINGER DETAIL

3 ABRASIVE SAFETY NOSING

NOTE:
STRINGER DETAIL SIMILAR FOR STAIRS WITH TERRAZZO OR MARBLE TREADS & RISERS

1 SECTION AT LANDING WITH POST

1 SECTION AT CONC. SLAB FLOOR

2 SECTION AT FLOOR

2 SECTION AT LANDING WITHOUT POST

**Slopes and rise** Provide the least practical slope for any ramp or curb ramp subject to the following new construction requirements:

   1. Maximum running slope shall not exceed 1:12 (8.3%)

   2. Maximum rise for any run shall not exceed 2'6" (760 mm)

**Width** Ramps and curb ramps shall have a minimum clear width of 3'0" (915 mm) exclusive of edge protection or flared sides.

**Cross-slope and surface** Cross-slope of ramp surfaces shall not exceed 1:48 (¼ in/ft).

# ramp slope

| slope | maximum rise | | maximum projection | |
|---|---|---|---|---|
| | in | mm | ft | m |
| 1:12 to < 1:16 | 30 | 760 | 30 | 9 |
| 1:16 to < 1:20 | 30 | 760 | 40 | 12 |

## maximum rise & projection
new construction

| slope | maximum rise | | maximum projection | |
|---|---|---|---|---|
| | in | mm | ft | m |
| 1:10 to 1:8 | 3 | 75 | 2 | 0.6 |
| 1:12 to 1:10 | 6 | 150 | 5 | 1.5 |

## maximum rise & projection
alterations to existing construction

**Fig. 27  Examples of edge protection and handrail extensions.**

# FIREPLACES

The function of the fireplace today differs dramatically from its role of years ago. Whereas its original function was primarily to provide heat for warmth and/or cooking, today it serves more as a decorative asset and as the focal point of interior spaces and conversational groupings, providing the esthetic pleasure and comfort of firelight.

Of particular interest to the interior designer is the proportion and scale of the fireplace opening, the treatment of wall surfaces surrounding the fireplace, the design of mantel pieces and hearth extensions, and the array of fireplace accessories available. Accordingly, the information contained in this section addresses these considerations. Drawings include elevations, plans, and details of various fireplaces; elevations of a wide selection of prefabricated mantel types; and a sampling of fireplace accessories including andirons, wrought iron fire sets, and log grates. It should be noted that, aside from their decorative aspects, the fireplace and chimney have important structural implications and require special foundations. Moreover, the fireplace must be designed to carry smoke away safely.

With respect to hearth extensions, most building codes require that for fireplaces having an opening of less than 6 ft² (0.56 m²), the hearth must extend a minimum of 16 in (406 mm) beyond the face of the opening and a minimum of 8 in (203 mm) on each side. For fireplaces whose openings exceed 6 ft², the hearth must extend a minimum of 20 in (508 mm) beyond the face of the opening and 12 in (305 mm) on each side.

Most building codes also require that woodwork or other combustible materials not be placed within 6 in (153 mm) of a fireplace opening, and that combustible material within 12 in (305 mm) of a fireplace opening not project more than ⅛ in for each 1-in distance from such an opening.

Since building codes may vary, it is important that the designer have her or his plans checked for conformance with the applicable local or state codes. Any structural modifications to an existing fireplace and chimney or the design of a new fireplace and chimney should be reviewed by a professional engineer or registered architect.

A fireplace that draws properly can be assured by applying proper principles of design. The size of flue should be adequate and should be based upon the size of the fireplace opening. One rule commonly used is to take one-tenth of the area of the fireplace opening to find the minimum area of the flue. For example, if a fireplace had an opening 3 ft wide by 2 ft 6 in high, it would have an area of 1080 in². One-tenth of 1080 in² equals 108 in². The standard-size flue nearest to this requirement and readily available is a 13- by 13-in flue lining, which has an inside cross-sectional area of 126.56 in². One could also use a 13-in round flue that has a cross-sectional area of 113.0 in².

The front of the fireplace should be wider than the back and the upper part of the back should tilt forward to meet the throat in order to throw heat into the room instead of up the chimney. The arch over the top of the fireplace opening should be only 4 in thick, and the throat should project toward the front as much as possible to form the smoke shelf behind it. The area of the throat should be 1¼ times the area of the flue, with minimum and maximum width of 3 and 4½ in, respectively, so that the narrow throat will cause a quick suction into the flue. The sides of the fireplace above the throat are drawn together to form the flue, which always starts exactly over the center of the width of the fireplace.

The smoke shelf is very necessary to stop back drafts. The depth of the fireplace should be one-half the height of the opening, with a maximum of 24 in. The back should rise one-half the height of the opening before sloping forward and should be two-thirds the opening in width.

The back, sides, and parts of the hearth that are under the fire must be built of heat-resistant materials. Firebrick laid in fire clay is the best combination.

The damper is a large valve that can be adjusted to regulate the draft. Many types of commercial damper units are manufactured. The position of a damper unit is important. The damper is generally set about 8 in above the top of the fireplace opening and is concealed by the brickwork. One advantage of these units is that they are correctly designed and have correctly proportioned throat damper and chamber to provide a form for the masonry and to reduce the risk of failure in the function of the completed fireplace.

The hearth consists of two parts, the front or finish hearth and the back hearth under the fire. The front hearth is simply a precaution against flying sparks and, while it must be noncombustible, it need not resist intense prolonged heat. Because the back hearth must withstand intense heat, it is built of heat-resistant materials. In buildings with wood floors, the hearth in front of the fireplace should be supported on masonry. The front hearth should project at least 16 in from the front of the fireplace.

At the back part of the hearth it is customary to have an ash dump for dropping the ashes into the ash pit, which is generally located in the basement with a door for cleaning out ashes.

CLAY FLUE LINING

SMOKE DOME

METAL DAMPER

FIRE BRICK

ASH DUMP

ASH PIT

SECTION

Ash Dump

FIRE BRICK

PLAN

FINISH FLOOR

HEADERS & LEDGER

JOISTS

FIRE BRICK

ELEVATION

**Fig. 1   Construction details of a typical fireplace.**

**Fig. 2  Construction details of a typical fireplace.**

**TABLE 1  Recommended Dimensions for Fireplaces and Size of Flue Lining Required**
(Letters in column heads refer to Fig. 2; all dimensions in inches)

| Size of fireplace opening | | Depth, d | Minimum width of back wall, c | Height of vertical back wall, a | Height of inclined back wall, b | Size of flue lining required | |
|---|---|---|---|---|---|---|---|
| Width, w | Height, h | | | | | Standard rectangular (outside dimensions) | Standard round (inside diameter) |
| 24 | 24 | 16–18 | 14 | 14 | 16 | 8½ × 13 | 10 |
| 28 | 24 | 16–18 | 14 | 14 | 16 | 8½ × 13 | 10 |
| 30 | 28–30 | 16–18 | 16 | 14 | 18 | 8½ × 13 | 10 |
| 36 | 28–30 | 16–18 | 22 | 14 | 18 | 8½ × 13 | 12 |
| 42 | 28–32 | 16–18 | 28 | 14 | 18 | 13 × 13 | 12 |
| 48 | 32 | 18–20 | 32 | 14 | 24 | 13 × 13 | 15 |
| 54 | 36 | 18–20 | 36 | 14 | 28 | 13 × 18 | 15 |
| 60 | 36 | 18–20 | 44 | 14 | 28 | 13 × 18 | 15 |
| 54 | 40 | 20–22 | 36 | 17 | 29 | 13 × 18 | 15 |
| 60 | 40 | 20–22 | 42 | 17 | 30 | 18 × 18 | 18 |
| 66 | 40 | 20–22 | 44 | 17 | 30 | 18 × 18 | 18 |
| 72 | 40 | 22–28 | 51 | 17 | 30 | 18 × 18 | 18 |

## SECTION WITH DAMPER

FLUE

SMOKE CHAMBER (steel)

Collar to support flue tile

4" (min.)

May be set back

Any Damper

H

D

BACK HEARTH    FRONT HEARTH

Back Hearth may be raised or lowered

Cantilevered Conc Slab

## ELEVATION
Scale ¾" = 1'-0"

FLUE

SMOKE CHAMBER

60°

Limit of Wood Trim

THROAT and DAMPER

12" (Rec. min.)

FIREPLACE OPENING

(min.) W/6     H     (min.) W/6

1'-0" to 1'-4"

8" (Rec. min.)

W

Trimmers

## SECTION WITHOUT DAMPER

FLUE

Corbel to support flue tile

May be set back

4" (min.)

SMOKE SHELF

Parge with mortar to deflect down draft

6" to 8"

Slope Back Wall in a straight plane

H

D

ASH DUMP

20" (Rec min.)

Cinder Conc. Fill

Brick Trimmer Arch

Corbel or line with flue tile

ASH PIT

Ash Pit may receive ashes thru flue tile from more than one fireplace

C.I. Clean-Out Door

Parge for slope

May be left void or expanded to accommodate flue

### PLAN
Scale ⅜" = 1'-0"

2" Limit for Wood Framing

ASH DUMP

D

(min.) W/6     (min.) W/6

20" (Rec. min.)

W

Line of Front Hearth

## MATERIALS

| Location | Material and Thickness |
|---|---|
| FRONT HEARTH | Any Masonry 2" to 4" |
| BACK HEARTH & REFLECTING WALLS | Fire Brick 4" • <br> Soapstone 4" •• <br> Hard-burned Tile 3" •• <br> • (Includes bed) |

## FIREPLACE DIMENSIONS (In Inches)

| | |
|---|---|
| **W** | 24 to 84 |
| **H** | ⅔ to ¾ W |
| **D** | ½ to ⅔ H {16 to 24 (Rec) for Coal / 18 to 24 (Rec) for Wood} |
| **FLUE (Effective Area)** | ⅛ WH for unlined flue <br> ¹⁄₁₀ WH for rectangular lining <br> ¹⁄₁₂ WH for circular lining |
| **T (Area)** | ⁵⁄₄ to ½ FLUE AREA |
| **T (Width)** | 3" minimum to 4½" maximum |

## RECOMMENDED FLUE SIZES (In Inches)

| FIREPLACE WIDTH W | RECTANGULAR FLUES | | | EQUIVALENT ROUND | |
|---|---|---|---|---|---|
| | Nominal or Outside Dimension | Inside Dimension | Effective Area | Inside Diameter | Effective Area |
| 24 | 8½ x 8½ | 7¼ x 7¼ | 41"" | 8 | 50.3"" |
| 30 to 34 | 8½ x 13 | 7 x 11½ | 70"" | 10 | 78.54"" |
| 36 to 44 | 13 x 13 | 11¼ x 11¼ | 99"" | 12 | 113.0"" |
| 46 to 56 | 13 x 18 | 11¼ x 6¼ | 156"" | 15 | 176.7"" |
| 58 to 68 | 18 x 18 | 15¾ x 5¾ | 195"" | 18 | 254.4"" |
| 70 to 84 | 20 x 24 | 17 x 21 | 278"" | 22 | 380.13"" |

## FIREPLACES
Through or Two-Way

**Fig. 3   Fireplace open on both sides.**

**TABLE 2   Table of Dimensions and Equipment (in inches)**

| Width of opening, A | Height of opening, B | Damper height, E | Smoke chamber, F | Old flue size G | Old flue size H | New flue size G | New flue size H | Angle (2 req'd),* J | L | Tee | Ash dump | Ash-pit door |
|---|---|---|---|---|---|---|---|---|---|---|---|---|
| 28 | 24 | 30 | 19 | 13 | 13 | 12 | 16 | A-36 | 36 | 35 | 58 | 12 × 8 |
| 32 | 29 | 35 | 21 | 13 | 18 | 16 | 16 | A-40 | 40 | 39 | 58 | 12 × 8 |
| 36 | 29 | 35 | 21 | 13 | 18 | 16 | 20 | A-42 | 44 | 43 | 58 | 12 × 8 |
| 40 | 29 | 35 | 27 | 18 | 18 | 16 | 20 | A-48 | 48 | 47 | 58 | 12 × 8 |
| 48 | 32 | 37 | 32 | 18 | 18 | 20 | 20 | B-54 | 56 | 55 | 58 | 12 × 8 |

*Angle sizes: A—3 × 3 × 3/16; B—3½ × 3½ × ¼".
Note Y from Fig. 3: The damper and the steel T should not be built-in solid at the ends, but given freedom to expand with heat.

TABLE OF DIMENSIONS AND EQUIPMENT (IN INCHES)

| A | B | C | D | E | F | OLD FLUE SIZES | | | | NEW FLUE SIZES | | | | L | M | STEEL ANGLE J* | PLATE LINTEL K | CORNER POST N |
|---|---|---|---|---|---|---|---|---|---|---|---|---|---|---|---|---|---|---|
| | | | | | | IN G OUT | | IN H OUT | | IN G OUT | | IN H OUT | | | | | | |
| 28 | 26½ | 20 | 14 | 20 | 29¼ | 11¼ | 13 | 11¼ | 13 | 10¼ | 12 | 10¼ | 12 | 36 | 16 | *A-36 | 11×16 | 3φ×26½ |
| 32 | 26½ | 20 | 14. | 20 | 32 | 11¼ | 13 | 11¼ | 13 | 10¼ | 12 | 13½ | 16 | 40 | 16 | *A-42 | 11×16 | 3φ×26½ |
| 36 | 26½ | 20 | 14 | 20 | 35 | 11¼ | 13 | 11¼ | 13 | 10¼ | 12 | 13½ | 16 | 44 | 16 | *A-48 | 11×16 | 3φ×26½ |
| 40 | 29 | 20 | 14 | 20 | 35 | 11¼ | 13 | 15¾ | 18 | 13½ | 16 | 13½ | 16 | 48 | 16 | *B-54 | 11×16 | 3φ×29 |
| 48 | 29 | 24 | 14 | 24 | 43 | 11¼ | 13 | 15¾ | 18 | 13½ | 16 | 13½ | 16 | 56 | 20 | *B-60 | 11×16 | 3φ×29 |

* ANGLE SIZES    *A 3 × 3 × 3/16    *B 3½ × 3½ × ¼

**Fig. 4  Corner fireplace.**

**Fig. 5  A shallow fireplace with a copper hood, built as shown, throws out considerable heat after the hood gets hot. The wall should be of fire-resistant masonry.**

END     FRONT ELEVATION

SECTION

PLAN

DETAIL PLAN AT · A ·

DETAIL SECTION
Scale 3" = 1 foot

PLAN
Scale ¾"=1'-0"

Ash dump

Shelf over

Slate hearth

Base

Wood Cabinet

Fireplace symmetrical on center line

Mirror

Wood frame

Mirror

Mirror

Slate shelf

Damper

Metal plate

Ash dump

Flush

Crab Orchid stone

Slate shelf

Stone

Wood Cabinet

Floor

SECTION   Scale ¾"=1'-0"

ELEVATION   Scale ¾"=1'-0"

ELEVATION   Scale ¾"=1'-0"

Continuous brick pattern
Bricks 1⅜"×7⅞"

Center line

Screen

Flush

Fireplace symmetrical on center

PLAN
Scale ¾"=1'-0"

Carved wood panel

Plan

Wood

Travertine

Brass frame (beaded)

Detail

Brass screen

Floor

Flush hearth

SECTION
Scale ¾"=1'-0"

SECTION
Scale ¾"=1'-0"

Plaster

24 Ga Metal trim

ELEVATION
Scale ¾"=1'-0"

Stone tile
4"x 6"x12"

2'-6"

½"

Floor

PLAN
Scale ¾"=1'-0"

3'-0"

Ash dump

1'-6"

Ash dump
6"x 9"

2" split
fire brick

3½

4'

4'-2"

½"

Cast iron door

Line of grade

Plaster

Mirror

Detail at joint

Mirror

5"

Wood shelf

¾"

24 oz Copper facing

Mahogany
veneer

1'-0"

Seat

2'-9"

2'-10"

Copper

Ash dump

Seat

½"

Grade

ELEVATION   Scale ¾"=1'-0"

SECTION   Scale ¾"=1'-0"

Ash dump

PLAN
Scale ¾"=1'-0"

2'-0"

Access door 10"x12"

1'-8"

2" Split fire brick

Door to
ash dump

1'-6"

1'-5"

Wall line
over

4"

10"

2'-0"

24 oz copper

Cement
hearth

Fireplace symmetrical
on Center line

2'-10"

Seat

2'-10"

½ DESIGN J    ½ DESIGN K
SCALE ½"=1'-0"

SECTION B
SCALE 1½"=1'-0"

SECTION A
SCALE 1½"=1'-0"

SECTION C
SCALE 1½"=1'-0"

½ DESIGN L
SCALE ½"=1'-0"

½ DESIGN M
SCALE ½"=1'-0"

PLAN E
SCALE 1½"=1'-0"

SECTION D
SCALE 1½"=1'-0"

ELEVATION
DESIGN M
SCALE 1½"=1'-0"

KEY TO MATERIALS

| MARBLE | |
| WOOD | |
| PLASTER | |
| WALL TILE | |
| BRONZE | |

# FIREPLACES
**Marble Mantels**

ELEVATION

MARBLE PANELS
ANCHORED TO MASONRY
WITH CONCEALED
WIRE ANCHORS

PLASTER OF PARIS SPOTS

$\frac{7}{8}$" MARBLE

2'$\frac{8}{}$" SETTING SPACE

FACE OF WOOD
PANELING

FACE OF
FINISHED WOOD
CLOSURE STRIP

NAILING STRIPS
ANCHORED TO ROUGH
MASONRY WALL

WOOD
PANELING

PLAN AT "A"

ROUGH
MASONRY
FIRE BRICK
BRICK
HEARTH
FINISHED WOOD
PANEL WALL
MARBLE
HEARTH

ROUGH MASONRY
WALL

STEEL SUPPORT
ANGLE 6"x 6"x $\frac{5}{8}$"
6" LONG-2 REQ'D.

DETAILS

MARBLE
JOINTS
RAISED HEARTH
LINTEL
FIREPLACE OPENING

Section 'A-A'  Elevation
FIREPLACE DESIGN 'A'

Elevation  Section 'B-B'
FIREPLACE DESIGN 'B'

Design 1  Design 2  Design 3  Design 4
MARBLE MANTEL FACING DETAILS

MARBLE
JOINTS
PLANTER
MARBLE ASHLAR
FIREPLACE OPENING
RAISED HEARTH

Side elevation  Front elevation
DETAIL OF CORNER FIREPLACE IN MARBLE

ELEVATION·

·SECTION · B—B

·SECTION · A—A

PLAN

Mantle

ELEVATION ·

Incised Rosette

Adjustable Shelving

Moulded Boarding

Hinged Panel

Tile Facing

¢ of Fireplace

Brick Painted Black

B – B

2"
⅞" Boarding

SECTION · A–A

Tile

# FIREPLACES

**Wood Mantels**

Mantel shelf to be of solid
piece, maximum 2¼" thick.
Shelf, if hard wood finish, must
have moulding run against ends
to cover end grain.

Back paint all finished wood

Columns glued and
screwed to face.

PLAN·OF·COLUMNS·ON·B·B·
Scale 3"=1'-0"

Shelf

If this distance is not
great, one piece of wood may be used

Furring

Variable

Chimney Breast

Damper

Face brick

Floor line

PARTIAL·ELEVATION·
Scale ¾"=1'-0"

SECTION·A·A·THROUGH·MANTEL·
Scale 3"=1'-0"

Mantel shelf

Plaster

All finished wood to
be back painted

Thoroughly blocked
& secured to wall

Adjustable piece
of moulding

PLAN·OF·CORNER·ON·
D·D·Scale 3"=1'-0"

Chimney Breast

Tile

Tile

Return tile 4", &
to be flush with
lining.

Fire Place to
be lined with
soap stone

Floor line

PARTIAL·ELEVATION·
Scale ¾"=1'-0"

SECTION·C·C·THROUGH·MANTEL·
Scale 3"=1'-0"

**Fig. 6**  These wood mantels are readily available.

# FIREPLACES

## Wood Mantels

**Fig. 6** *(Continued)*

# FIREPLACES

**Fireplace Accessories**

Fire set of wrought metal, stand and four tools.

Fire set, polished brass, stand and four tools.

Andirons of wrought metal, smooth or hammered black finish.

Andirons of wrought and cast metal, smooth or hammered black, or polished brass finish.

Fire set, wrought metal, back plate with jamb hooks, five tools.

Fire set, wrought metal stand and three tools.

Crane, pivoted, of wrought metal.

SCALE $\frac{1}{2}" = 1'-0"$

Crane, pivoted, of wrought metal, movable hook.

Crane, pivoted, of wrought metal, ornamental adjustable hook.

Footman, wrought metal.

Trivet, wrought metal.

SCALE $\frac{3}{4}" = 1'-0"$

Fire lighter, kerosene torch, can and drip pan, wrought metal.

Spit with removable clamps. Hand turning crank may be replaced by pulley and operated by weight or spring clock mechanism.

SCALE $\frac{1}{2}" = 1'-0"$

Log grate, wrought metal

Log grate, wrought metal

Log grate, wrought metal

SCALE $\frac{1}{2}" = 1'-0"$

Fender with wire mesh screen.

Fender with stamped grille.

Fender of wrought metal

Fender of wrought metal. Moulding on top may be replaced by padded seat.

**Fig. 7** Fireplaces offer opportunities for the use and display of a variety of metal items of decorative value. These may be selected or designed to match other material in the room. Metals used for wrought and cast fireplace products are usually cast iron, steel in a dark hammered finish, or polished brass. Combinations of these metals and other metals may be used very effectively.

Although lighting design is a discipline in and of itself, the interior designer and architect must be knowledgeable about the interface between lighting elements and the interior architecture. This section, therefore, focuses primarily on the detailing of this interface. Details from actual contract drawings, prepared by various interior design and architectural firms, are provided for the reader's reference. Among the details are those for valence and cove lighting and for the lighting of stairs, columns, and skylights. This section also provides some basic planning data including illuminance values for residences, offices, stores, and industrial spaces.

Bottom of shade at eye level when seated — approx. 40″-42″ off floor.

APPROX. 40″-42″

Exceptions: Sewing, Piano

Light colored shade should transmit light generously.

20″

MIN. 47″

**Fig. 1   Measuring when the lamp is at the side — when sitting, lying down, or playing the piano.**

When bottom of shade is above eye level, lamp stem should be about 10″ behind shoulder — near rear corner of chair

MIN. 47″

**Fig. 2   Measuring when the lamp is behind — when sitting.**

# LIGHTING

**Planning Data: Minimum Shade Heights**

### Recommended Minimum Shade Dimensions

| LAMP TYPE | Top Dia. " | Depth " | Bottom Dia. " |
|---|---|---|---|
| Sr. Floor | 10 | 10 | 18 |
|    Swing Type | 10 | 10 | 16 |
| Jr. Floor — Swing Type | 10 | 9 | 16 |
|    Diffuser Type | 14 | 6 | 16 |
|    Bridge | 8 | 8 | 13 |
| End Table | 8 | 10 | 16 |
| Diffuser Type | 14 | 6 | 16 |
| Sr. Table | 14 | 13 | 16 |
| Wall Lamp | 8 | 8 | 13 |
| Diffuser Type | 4 | 6 | 14 |
| Study Type — pair | 6 | 7 | 10 |
| **Make-Up** — pair | 7 | 7 | 9-10 |
| Double Dresser — pair | 8 | 8 | 12-14 |

Base Height (measure from table to shade bottom)

$+$ Table Height

$=$ Seated Eye Height (approx. 40″-42″ off floor)

### FLOOR LAMPS

Measure from floor to bottom of shade.

### SHADES

Measure top and bottom diameters, and depth vertically through center.

Minimum 15″ to shade bottom. Shade fairly dense, or opaque, in a light but not strong color

Exception: **Make-Up**  White or ivory highly translucent shades

Standing

Seated

Fig. 3  Measuring when the lamp is in front — when studying, sewing, or grooming oneself.

# LIGHTING

**Table Lamps**

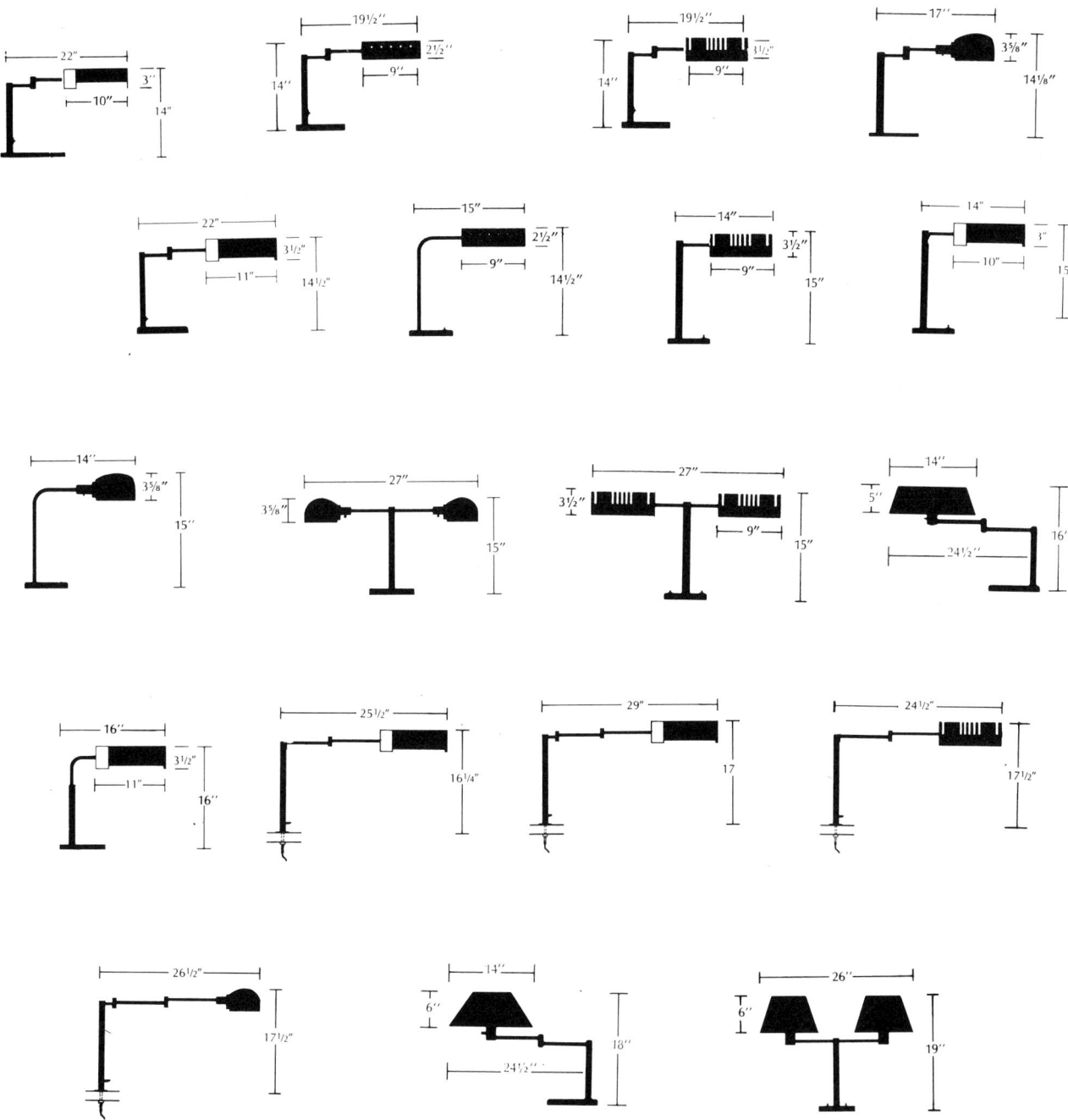

## LIGHTING

**Wall-Mounted Task Lamps**

**Fig. 4   Valance faceboard may be tilted.**

**Fig. 5   With side-mounting channels, no extender is necessary.**

**Fig. 6   Intermediate brackets are required to support long faceboards.**

**Fig. 7   Variation of valance lighting. (If distance between wall and lamp is increased, light will be distributed more evenly, but shielding may be required at the bottom of the faceboard.)**

**Fig. 8   Minimum dimensions for cornice lighting installation.**

**Fig. 9   Cornice lighting with two tubes may require shielding.**

# LIGHTING

Planning Data: Residential Down Lighting

100 WATT

METAL FLANGE

CEILING

2" (50 mm) APERTURE

Fig. 10   Common types of downlights.

ADJUSTABLE SHUTTERS    APERTURE

1" (25 mm)

Fig. 11   Pinhole spot, a recessed downlight with adjustable shutters to shape beam pattern.

LOUVER

Fig. 12   "Eyeball" semirecessed fully adjustable downlight.

CEILING

FURRED DOWN STRUCTURE

WALL

METAL CHANNEL

FLUORESCENT LAMP

PAINT CAVITY WHITE

12" (300 mm)

LOUVERS

14" (300 mm)

Fig. 13   Luminous panel or soffit lighting, used over a kitchen or bathroom counter.

CEILING

L    S

T-BAR SUPPORT    DIFFUSER

Fig. 14   Critical dimensions for luminous panel and luminous ceiling lighting. (S should not exceed 1½ to 2 times L.)

CAVITY OR PLENUM UNOBSTRUCTED FINISHED MAT WHITE 80%

(457 mm)    18"  18"  18"  18"  18"  18"

12" (300 mm)

DIFFUSING TYPE SHIELDING 45% TRANSMITTANCE

WALLS 50%

8' (2.8 m)

9' (2.9 m)

60 fc (600 lx) AVG

FLOOR 25%

30" (760 mm) TABLE AND DESK HEIGHT

12' (3.6 m)    12' (3.6 m)

Fig. 15   Basic relationship for the design of luminous panels. [A light level of 60 fc (600 lx) is produced by seven rows of three 40-W fluorescent tubes on 18-in (457 mm) centers. Light distribution and surface luminance are approximately uniform.]

### TABLE 1   Illuminance Values for Residences*

| Specific visual tasks | Illuminance | |
|---|---|---|
| | Foot-candles | Lux† |
| Dining | 15 | 150 |
| Grooming, shaving, makeup | 50 | 500 |
| Handcraft | | |
|   Ordinary seeing tasks | 70 | 700 |
|   Difficult seeing tasks | 100 | 1000 |
|   Very difficult seeing tasks | 150 | 1500 |
|   Critical seeing tasks | 200 | 2000 |
| Ironing (hand and machine) | 50 | 500 |
| Kitchen duties | | |
|   Food preparation and cleaning | 150 | 1500 |
|   Serving and other noncritical tasks | 50 | 500 |
| Laundry | | |
|   Preparation, sorting, inspection | 50 | 500 |
|   Tub area—soaking, tinting | 50 | 500 |
|   Washer and dryer areas | 30 | 300 |
| Reading and writing | | |
|   Handwriting, reproductions, and poor copies | 70 | 700 |
|   Books, magazines, newspapers | 30 | 300 |
| Reading piano or organ scores | | |
|   Advanced (substandard size) | 150 | 1500 |
|   Advanced | 70 | 700 |
|   Simple | 30 | 300 |
| Sewing (hand and machine) | | |
|   Dark fabrics | 200 | 2000 |
|   Medium fabrics | 100 | 1000 |
|   Light fabrics | 50 | 500 |
|   Occasional—high contrast | 30 | 300 |
| Study | 70 | 700 |
| Table games | 30 | 300 |
| General lighting | | |
|   Conversation, relaxation, entertainment | 10 | 100 |
|   Passage areas, for safety | 10 | 100 |
| Areas other than kitchen involving visual tasks | 30 | 300 |
| Kitchen | 50 | 500 |

*Minimum on the task at all times.
†Lux is an SI unit equal to 0.0929 footcandle.

(11) WD. CONT. LIGHTING @ ALCOVE

(B) WD. SOFFIT @ CONF. ROOMS

STAGGERED (OVERLAP)
LIGHTING UNITS TYPE 'GC'

12"

3"          1'-0"

9¾"

AC. TILE
TYPE 1

PLASTER TYPE-3A

6"

4½"          1'-0"
FASCIA-LIP

DETAIL OF LIGHT COVE RECESS
IN SANCTUARY    @ 3"=1'-0"

# LIGHTING

## Cove Lighting Details

PAINTED GYP. BD. CEILING
PAINTED GYP. BD. FASCIA

COLD CATHODE TUBE
FIXTURE - SEE LIGHTING
SCHEDULE

BLOCKING

PLYWD. PAINTED TO
MATCH DRYWALL

1/2" PLYWD. PLATFORM

CONTINUOUS FILLER STRIP
PAINT TO MATCH DRYWALL

SECURE STUDS TO
SLAB ABOVE

METAL STUDS

DIAGONAL
BRACING

RETURN AIR SLOT

EQ. EQ

SUSPENDED ACC. TILE CEILING

1 5/8" METAL STUD 20 GAGE

5/8" PAINTED GYP.BD. FASCIA & SOFFIT

8' 18'

7'-0" TO FLOOR

**4** DETAIL - LIGHT COVE @ RECEPTION AREA

PAINTED GYP. BD. CEILING
PAINTED GYP. BD. FASCIA

COLD CATHODE TUBE
FIXTURE - SEE LIGHTING
SCHEDULE

BLOCKING

PLYWD. PAINTED TO
MATCH DRYWALL

1/2" PLYWD. PLATFORM

CONTINUOUS FILLER STRIP
PAINT TO MATCH DRYWALL

SECURE STUDS TO
SLAB ABOVE

MASONRY
WALL AT
ELEV. LOBBY

DIAGONAL
BRACING

RETURN AIR SLOT

EQ. EQ

1 5/8" METAL STUD
20 GAGE

PAINTED 5/8" GYP. BD.

8' 14" V.I.F.

8'-0" TO FLOOR

ALIGN W/ EDGE OF GRANITE BELOW

**5** DETAIL - LIGHT COVE @ ELEVATOR LOBBY

SECURE STUD FRAMING TO SLAB ABOVE, TYP.

STAGGERED LAMP FLOURESCENT FIXTURE - SEE LIGHTING SCHEDULE

FRAME GYP.BD COVE W/ STUDS.

PAINT ALL INSIDE SURFACES OF COVE WHITE

EQ. EQ.

9⁵⁄₁₆"

'C.J.' TRIM

SUSPENDED CEILING

PAROBOLIC BAFFLE

CERAMIC WALL TILE IN STATE LOCATIONS

SUSPENDED CEILING

7⁵⁄₁₆" (6" MIN.)

8'-0"

① DETAIL - LIGHT COVE & TYPE "D" FIXTURE AT WALLS
3"=1'-0"

SECURE STUDS & CROSSBRACING TO SLAB ABOVE

CROSSBRACING

WIREWAY

'PAR' WALLWASHER SEE LIGHTING SCHEDULE

PAINT GYP SOFFIT

13"

BAFFLE

CURVED GYP. BD. WALL

15⁷⁄₈"

5"

CORNER BEAD SPACKEL & PAINT

SUSPENDED GYP. BD. CEILING PAINTED

5½"    4"

⑤ DETAIL - LIGHT COVE @ STAIR, TYPE 'K' FIXTURE
3"=1'-0"

SECURE STUD FRAMING TO SLAB ABOVE, TYP.

STAGGERED LAMP FLOURESCENT FIXTURE - SEE LIGHTING SCHEDULE

FRAME GYP.BD COVE W/ STUDS.

PAINT ALL INSIDE GYP.BD SURFACES OF COVE WHITE

GYP.BD WALL, SEE CONST. PLANS FOR WALL TYPE

CROSSBRACING

EQ. EQ.

9⁵⁄₁₆"

7⁵⁄₁₆" (6" MINIMUM)

'C.J.' TRIM

HUNG CEILING

PAROBOLIC BAFFLE

GYP. BD. BLOCKING

METAL STUDS

PAINTED HDWD. FILLER PIECE PAINT TO MATCH ADJ WALLS

1½"

8'-0"

VERIFY DIM. W/ARCHITECT & FURN. MANUF.

OVERFILE STORAGE UNIT (N.I.C.)

2'-4½"

② DETAIL - LIGHT COVE & TYPE "D" FIXTURE AT FILES
3"=1'-0"

SECTION AT LIGHT COVE

Labels (top detail, left):
- EXISTING SLAB
- 2½" 'C' RUNNER SECURE TO SLAB ABOVE
- 2½" MT'L STUD W/DIAG. BRACE TO SLAB ABOVE
- LINE OF FIN. CEILING
- LIGHT FIX. SEE LIGHT FIX. DETAILS.
- WD BLOCKING
- 5/8" GYP. BD. TYP. (PROVIDE SPACKEL BEAD AT ALL EXPOSED CORNERS)
- 1½" MT'L STUD

SECTION AT TROUGH AND SOFFIT
1½" = 1'-0"

Labels (right detail):
- ¼" IMPERIAL PLASTER ON GYP. BD.
- LIGHTING FIXT. TYPE.
- 1⅜" METAL STUDS
- ¾" COLD ROLLED C DIAGNOL BRACE
- ¾" PLASTER ON METAL LATH
- PLASTER REVEAL CHANNEL
- 2 LAYERS 5/8" GYP. BD & ¼" LAYER IMPERIAL PLASTER ON 7/8" FURRING CHANNELS

SECTION AT LIGHT COVE

Labels:
- EXISTING SLAB
- 2½" 'C' RUNNER SECURE TO SLAB ABOVE
- 2½" M.S. W/DIAG. BRACE TO SLAB ABOVE
- LINE OF FIN. CEILING
- RETURN AIR SLOT WITH EGGCRATE LOUVER, WHITE FINISH
- 5/8" GYP. BD. TYP. (PROVIDE CORNER BEAD AT ALL EXPOSED CORNERS)
- LIGHT FIX. SEE LIGHT FIX. DETAILS.
- WD. BLOCKING
- 1½" MT'L STUD

SECTION AT LIGHT COVE, DINING ROOM

Labels:
- EXISTING SLAB
- 2½" 'C' RUNNER SECURED SLAB ABOVE
- 2½" MT'L STUD W/ DIAG. BRACE TO SLAB ABOVE
- 1½" MT'L STUD
- LIGHT FIX. TYPE.
- 5/8" PLYWOOD
- ALUM BAFFLE SEE LIGHTING DETAILS
- GYP. BD. CEILING
- 5/8" GYP. BD. TYP. (PROVIDE CORNER BEAD AT ALL EXPOSED CORNERS.)
- FOR WALL TYPE, SEE CONST. PLAN.

BRACE AS REQ'D

SCHEDULED FIXTURE

2½" M.S. 16" O.C.

UTILITY ANGLE 4'-0" O.C. MAX.

NUT, BOLT & LOCK WASHER
SNAP BAR HANGER
SNAP BAR

18" X 18" PERFORATED METAL
TILE W/ ACOUSTICAL PADS
ABOVE.

¾" PLYWD. PROVIDE MT'L END CAP.
SLIP MOULD SECURE TO PLYWD.
STRUCTURAL SILICON ADHESIVE
AS PER MANUFCT'R'S SPEC'S
"NEOPARIUM 5" TILE.
PITTCON STR 038-050 REVEAL

PROVIDE SPACKEL BEAD
⅝" GYP. BD.

LINE OF WALL BEYOND

---

EX'G. CONCRETE
SLAB

EX'G. JUNIOR
BEAM

EX'G. WALL CONST.

N.Y.C. APPROVED BLACK IRON
HANGER ASSEMBLY

NATIONAL LIGHTING SINGLE
LAMP FLUORESCENT CHANNEL

CUSTOM ALUM. LT. COVE AS
MANF. BY TECHNICAL CEILING
SYSTEMS, INC., 1410 W. LARK
INDUSTRIAL PARK, FENTON,
MISSOURI (314) 343-6372
MED. BRONZE ANOD. FIN.

1½"D X 12"W ALUM. BAFFLE
BLADES @ 1½" O.C. MED. BRONZE ANOD. FIN.

2" X ¾" [ REVEAL INTEGRAL W/COVE

ARMSTRONG "CROSSGATE"
CEILING TILE - ITEM # 2604-
24 X 24" X ¾" SQ. EDGE & TEGULAR
LAY-IN - CONCRETE COLOR

**TYP. LT. COVE @ ELEVATORS**
1
A57
Scale 3"=1'-0"

# LIGHTING

**Fluorescent Cove Lighting Details**

RAPID START T-12 LAMPS IN CONTINUOUS ROW.

GYPSUM BOARD CAVITY. PAINT ALL INTERIOR SURFACES OF CAVITY MATTE WHITE.

ACRYLIC PRISMATIC DIFFUSER

FINISHED CEILING

1/2"x1/2"x1/2" ALUMINIUM EGGCRATE LOUVER PAINTED LIGHT TO MEDIUM VALUE COLOR AS SELECTED BY ARCHITECT.

FINISHED WALL

RAPID START T-12 LAMPS IN CONTINUOUS ROW.

GYPSUM BOARD CAVITY. PAINT ALL INTERIOR SURFACES OF CAVITY MATTE WHITE.

FINISHED CEILING

1/2"x1/2"x1/2" ALUMINIUM EGGCRATE LOUVER PAINTED LIGHT TO MEDIUM VALUE COLOR AS SELECTED BY ARCHITECT.

FINISHED WALL

SCHED. LIGHT FIXTURE

PAINT INTERIOR WHITE

EGGCRATE

SCHED. GYP. BD. PTN.

SCHED. CLG.

FINISHED CEILING

MIRROR

$3" = 1'-0"$

SECTION THRU CONTINUOUS COVE LIGHT

RAPID START T-12 LAMPS IN CONTINUOUS ROW.

GYPSUM BOARD CAVITY. PAINT ALL INTERIOR SURFACES OF CAVITY MATTE WHITE.

WHITE ACRYLIC DIFFUSER

FINISHED CEILING

FINISHED WALL

RAPID START T-12 LAMPS IN CONTINUOUS ROW.

GYPSUM BOARD CAVITY. PAINT ALL INTERIOR SURFACES OF CAVITY MATTE WHITE.

ACRYLIC PRISMATIC DIFFUSER

FINISHED CEILING

FINISHED WALL

RAPID START T-12 LAMPS IN CONTINUOUS ROWS.

GYPSUM BOARD CAVITY. PAINT ALL INTERIOR SURFACES OF CAVITY MATTE WHITE.

4" X 4" X 4" ALUMINUM EGGCRATE LOUVER PAINTED LIGHT TO MEDIUM VALUE COLOR AS SELECTED BY ARCHITECT.

MIRROR

RAPID START T-12 LAMPS IN CONTINUOUS ROWS.

GYPSUM BOARD CAVITY. PAINT ALL INTERIOR SURFACES OF CAVITY MATTE WHITE.

1/2"x1/2"x1/2" ALUMINIUM EGGCRATE LOUVER PAINTED LIGHT TO MEDIUM VALUE COLOR AS SELECTED BY ARCHITECT.

CEILING CONSTRUCTION

RAPID START T-12 LAMPS IN CONTINUOUS ROWS

1/2" X 1/2" X 1/2" ALUMINUM LOUVER. FINISH AS SELECTED BY ARCHITECT.

MIRROR

RAPID START T-12 LAMPS IN CONTINUOUS ROWS.

GYPSUM BOARD CAVITY. PAINT ALL INTERIOR SURFACES OF CAVITY MATTE WHITE.

ACRYLIC PRISMATIC DIFFUSER

FINISHED WALL

FINISHED CEILING

① VANITY LIGHTING SOFFIT DETAIL
3" = 1'-0"

757

## LIGHTING
**Fluorescent Cove Lighting Details**

MATTE PAINT WITH MIN.
REFLECTANCE OF 70%.

2'-6"

1'-0"

⊕ 8'-0" AFF.

1'-0"          6'-0"          1'-0"

SECTION THRU COVE UPLIGHT

MATTE PAINT WITH MIN.
REFLECTANCE OF 70%

1'-0"

3¾"   5"
1'-0"

ENLARGED DETAIL

RECOMMENDED REFLECTANCE
IS BETWEEN 50% and 70%

9"

ALIGN

4"

11"

SECTION THRU COVE

ACOUSTICAL TILE CLG @
9'-11⅝ A.F.S.
USG. 200B METAL TRIM

BRACING AS REQ'D

CHANNEL

FURRING CHANNEL

5/8" GYP. BD. CLG
@ 9'-11"

5/8" GYP. BD.

CHANNEL

TYPE BH LIGHT
FIXTURE

FURRING CHANNEL

BRACING AS REQ'D

1'-0⅝"

10⅝"

9¾"

6⅛"

BLOCKING
AS REQ'D

CHANNEL

WOOD
VENEER

5/8" GYP. BD. CLG
@ 8'-6½"

BOTTOM OF BAFFLE
@ 8'6" A.F.S.

2⅛"  1"  2¼"
5¼"

SECTION
SCALE: ¾"=1'-0"

DRYWALL CONSTRUCTION

METAL STUD

3/4" PLYWOOD BOX

SINGLE LAMP FLUORESCENT CHANNEL USE 3'-0" AND 4'-0" LENGTHS ONLY

PERFORATED REFLECTOR ASYMMETRICAL CONFIGURATION

**SHIELDED VALANCE WITH SINGLE LAMP FLUORESCENT CHANNEL CURTAIN WALL TYPE**

EXISTING WALL

OUTRIGGER BRACKET TO SUPPORT FLUORESCENT CHANNELS AND VALANCE BELOW

SINGLE LAMP FLUORESCENT CHANNEL WITH PERFORATED REFLECTOR (33%) ASYMMETRICAL CONFIGURATION USE 3'-0" AND 4'-0" LENGTHS ONLY

CENTERLINE OF LAMP TO ALIGN WITH RETURN EDGE OF WOOD VALANCE

DEPTH VARIES

**VALANCE WITH SINGLE LAMP FLUORESCENT CHANNEL**

9" - 12"

SINGLE LAMP FLUORESCENT CHANNELS TO BE STAGGERED WITH A MINIMUM OVERLAP OF 12" SO AS TO AVOID SHADOWS CAST BY SOCKET ENDS. USE 3'-0" AND 4'-0" LENGTHS ONLY

INTERIOR TO BE PAINTED LIGHT VALUE/COLOR

DIFFUSER ANGLES

ACRYLIC DIFFUSER WITH PRISMATIC LENS

**DIRECT COVE SINGLE/DOUBLE ROW STAGGERED FLUORESCENT**

R = 1'-6"

CEILING TO BE PAINTED LIGHT VALUE/COLOR

SPLAY LIP/MAINTAIN 1/2" FROM TOP OF LAMP TO TOP OF LIP

DOUBLE ROW FLUORESCENT CHANNELS TO BE STAGGERED AT 50% INTERVALS SO AS TO AVOID SHADOWS CAST BY SOCKET ENDS

1'-6" MIN

10"

1'-0" MIN   VARIES

**INDIRECT/CURVED COVE DOUBLE ROW FLUORESCENT**

DRYWALL CONSTRUCTION

TWO (2) SINGLE LAMP FLUORESCENT CHANNELS USE 3'-0" AND 4'-0" LENGTHS ONLY

SOLID REFLECTOR SYMMETRICAL CONFIGURATION

SURFACE MOUNTED TRACK LIGHT WITH ADJUSTABLE LAMPHOLDER 50 W. PAR 38 @ 2'-0" O.C.

DIFFUSER ANGLES
METAL STUD

LIGHT SHIELDING MATERIAL AS SPECIFIED

EQUAL   EQUAL

**SHIELDED VALANCE WITH TWO (2) SINGLE LAMP FLUORESCENT CHANNELS AND TRACK LIGHT WITH INCANDESCENT "CURTAIN WALL" TYPE**

# LIGHTING

### Miscellaneous Lighting Details

3 ROWS TYPE L

LITELAB CPMC - CLEAR PLASTIC MOUNTING CLIP FOR 3/8" DIA. TUBING SPACED AS REQ'D

TYPE L - LITELAB "XANADU" SERIES 100 LOW VOLTAGE TUBELIGHT 3/8" DIA. WITH 0.40 WATT LAMPS 2" O.C. OPERATED @ 24 VOLTS.

1/4"

5/8"

CORRIDOR SIDE

SECTION @ CORRIDOR CLG.
N.T.S.

**SECTION - TYPE L**
SCALE: 3" = 1'-0"

SCREW LUCIFER LIGHT STRIP IN PLACE AT LEAST TWICE EA. PIECE

LUCIFER LIGHT STRIP FEED AT 12 V. - MOUNT AS SHOWN.

EXISTING CLG.

HS-RI ADAPTOR

12V MR-11 LAMP (FLOOD)

EXISTING WALL

WOOD VENEER BAFFLE

1 1/2"

6"

1/2"

11"

**SECTION - TYPE M**
SCALE: HALF SIZE

RECESSED JUNCTION BOX (OR OUTLET BOX) WITH DUPLEX RECEPTACLE(S) AS REQ'D. SEE REFLECTED PLANS AT RIGHT.

4 1/2"

WOOD VENEER PANEL (BY INTERIOR DESIGNER)

LAMPS: 15 S11 WITH MEDIUM BASE.

PLUG-IN LAMPHOLDER - BRYANT ELECTRIC #N RECEPTACLE TO MEDIUM BASE ADAPTER.

MIRROR

GLASS TOP

**SECTION - TYPE G**
SCALE: 3" = 1'-0"

RECESSED OUTLET BOX W/ DUPLEX RECEPTACLES

LAMPS: 15 S11 WITH MEDIUM BASE ON PLUG-IN LAMHOLDER

**REFLECTED PLAN @ LIVING ROOM**
SCALE: 3" = 1'-0"

RECESSED J-BOX WITH (2) DUPLEX RECEPTACLES

LAMPS: 15 S11 WITH MEDIUM BASE ON PLUG-IN LAMPHOLDER.

**REFLECTED PLAN @ AUDIO VISUAL AREA**
SCALE: 3" = 1'-0"

BLOCKING

LITELAB MICROLUME #MLU-913 VINYL EXTRUDED SNAP-IN HOLDER TO BE FASTENED TO BLOCKING

LITELAB MICROLUME #ML-.75 WITH 1 WATT LAMPS 3/4" O.C. TO BE OPERATED AT 12 VOLTS.

EXISTING CEILING

WOOD VENEER BAFFLES

PROFILE OF WOOD VENEER PANELS AT "LIGHT BOX", MOUNTING DETAIL SAME.

2'-4"
±1'-10"
±1'-11½"
±1'-5½"

LOW VOLTAGE WIRE FED FROM ABOVE

TYPE A - LITELAB MICROLUME #ML-.75, (4) UNITS LENGTHS AS REQUIRED

WOOD VENEER BAFFLE

DUTCH METAL GOLD LEAF PANEL

SECTION-TYPE A

REFLECTED PLAN @ LIGHT BOX-

EXISTING CEILING LINE

(2) LITELAB "MICROLUME" #ML-.75 WITH 1 WATT LAMPS 3/4" O.C. TO BE OPERATED @ 12 VOLTS.

PROVIDE FINISHED WOOD FINS 12" O.C. THIS IS REQUIRED TO PROMOTE AIR CIRCULATION AROUND FIXTURES.

WOOD VENEER PANEL

NOTE: PROVIDE SCREW TERMINAL TYPE CONNECTOR IN LOW VOLTAGE WIRES TO FIXTURES TO ALLOW FOR REPLACEMENT.

NOTE: FIXTURES TO LAY-IN WOODWORK & NOT BE FASTENED DOWN

¼" 4/16"
2¼"
5¼"

SECTION-TYPE B

EXISTING J-BOX

CENTRAL FEED BOX - WIREMOLD #5739A EXTENSION BOX 1" DEEP (OR EQUIVALENT)

WIREMOLD #500 OR #700

WIREMOLD #5733 BOX 3" DIA. X 13/16" DEEP

1/8" IPS NUT

BLANK COVER WITH ½" DIA. HOLE IN CENTER

COMPOUND

2 LAYERS 5/8" SHEETROCK

COMPOUND

CSL RAY SYSTEM FIXTURE STEM

WASHER-FIELD PAINT TO MATCH CEILING

SILICONE ADHESIVE BEAD

SECTION-TYPE C

## LIGHTING
Miscellaneous Lighting Details

OPEN @ TYPE F ONLY

SQUARE OR TRIANGULAR SHAPE GLASS. DIMENSION AS REQ'D. FROST OUTSIDE SURFACE & GRIND EDGES SMOOTH. (TYPE F1)

CABINET WORK - PROVIDE LEFT OUT NOTCH TO REMOVE GLASS.

LAMP: 30R20 @ TYPE F1. 25A-19 SOFT WHITE @ TYPE F.

PORCELAIN SOCKET MOUNTED AS REQ'D BY ELECTRICAL CONTRACTOR ON J-BOX OR CONDUIT STUB OR OTHER CODE METHOD.

RELAY THIS DIMEN. TO CABINETMAKER

- Optional white plastic or frosted glass top
- ¾" wide metal angle brackets on 24" centers
- Toggle bolts or other appropriate fasteners on 16" centers
- Single- or double-lamp fluorescent light strip
- ¾" hardwood faceboard and end returns, finished to suit outside, flat white finish inside

5"–6"

7"–9"

**Wall bracket cross section**

BLOCKING

NESSEN LAMPS 'PICSTICK' #NP43 32" LENGTH WITH (3) 20 WATT HALOGEN LAMPS OPERATED AT 12 VOLTS

FINISH: POLISHED BRASS

PICSTICK MOUNTING PLATE TO BE ATTACHED TO BLOCKING

FOR WIRING ACCESS TO THIS BOX REMOVE BLOCKING MOUNTING SCREWS

CABINET DOOR

CABINET TOP

FASCIA ABOVE CABINET

TYPE J - ALKCO LINEAR INCANDESCENT FIXTURES & LAMPS. #30CM & #50CM LENGTHS REQ'D. SEE LIGHTING PLANS FOR LOCATIONS.

MIRROR DOOR

CABINET

JUNCTION BOX

SOLID CORE DOOR
HARDWOOD FRAME
5/8" GYP. BD.

PLYWOOD SHELVES, SEE A6

"L" MOULD

3/4" PLYWOOD ACCESS DOOR
1'-0" x 8'-4 1/2", PIVOT HINGES

FULL HEIGHT NEON TUBE
TRANSFORMER ABOVE

CONTINUOUS WOOD BLOCK

LINE OF EXISTING PARTITION

**1 — PLAN: NEON/NICHE: ENTRY**
A4   1 1/2" = 1'-0"

POCKET DOOR (TYP.)
EXISTING

5/8" GYP. BD.
"L" MOULD
ALIGN W/ STEP UP TO BOTH 2

3/4" x 2" CONTINUOUS WOOD
BLOCK

7'-3 1/2" NEON TUBE, LOCATE
TRANSFORMER IN CAB. IN
STUDY

**2 — PLAN: NEON NICHE: STUDY**
A4   1 1/2" = 1'-0"

LINE OF EXIST. CLG.
BLOCKING AS REQ'D.
LSI 1 CIRCUIT TRACK

18 GAUGE STEEL BOX
PAINT BLACK

5/8" GYP. BD. CLG.

7'-4 1/2"

NOTE: LOCATE TRANSFORMER
OF REQ'D CAPACITY IN
KITCHEN CABINET ABOVE MICRO

**3 — RECESSED LIGHT TROUGH (KITCHEN)**
A4   3" = 1'-0"

LINE OF EXIST. CEILING
5/8" GYP. BD.

2 1/2" STEEL STUD

RITE ANGLE ELECTRODE
LAMP 1" DIA. BY NAT'L
CATHODE CORP. OR EQUAL.

"J" BEAD OR ANGLE BEAD

5/8" GYP. BD.

7/8" FURRING CHANNEL

7'-4 1/2"

"L" MOULD

**4 — COVE LIGHTING: TYPICAL SECTION**
A4   3" = 1'-0"

3/4" PLYWOOD SIDE PANEL

RIGHT ANGLE ELECTRODE
LAMP 1" DIA. BY NAT'L
CATHODE CORP.

FACE TO ALIGN W/
FACE OF DOOR

3/4" PLYWOOD
PAINT FINISH

RECESSED HALO #H499T
FIXTURE W/ 1420-P TRIM
TO BE FLUSH W/ PLYWOOD

**5 — LIGHT FIXTURE OVER BED: BDRM 1**
A4   3" = 1'-0"

# LIGHTING

Miscellaneous Lighting Details

COLD CATHODE LIGHTING SEE DTL.

BENT SHEET METAL TO SUPPORT GYP. BD.

EXISTING BEAM
1⅝" STL. STUD
⅞" FURRING
⅝" GYP. BD. MOLDING

**11 / A9 DETAIL: COVE LIGHTING IN LIVING ROOM**
3" = 1'-0"

⅝" GYP BD.
1⅝" STL. STUD
COLD CATHODE LIGHTING

RUBBER MOLDING

J-BEAD
⅞" FURRING
BENT SHEET METAL TO SUPPORT GYP. BD.

**12 / A9 DETAIL: COVE LIGHTING IN LIVING, DINING & FAM. RMS.**
3" = 1'-0"

VERIFY

ARCHED SHEET STL. CEILING PANEL
PLYWOOD FRAME
NEON TUBE
FURRING
⅝" GYPSUM BOARD CORNER

**DETAIL: COVE LIGHT @ BAR**
1½" = 1'-0"

1⅝" STL. STUD
⅝" GYP. BD.

LIGHT FIXTURE
J-BEAD
⅞" FURRING

**13 / A9 DETAIL: COVE LIGHTING @ SLOPED WALL & HALL**
3" = 1'-0"

ALIGN

½" PLYWOOD NEON
J-BEAD
⅞" FURRING
1⅝" STL. STUD

**14 / A9 DETAIL: NEON RECESS @ ENTRY**
3" = 1'-0"

TO SLAB ABOVE
NEON TUBE
STEEL STUD
⅞" FURRING
⅝" GYPSUM BOARD

**DETAIL: NEON @ FOYER**
1½" = 1'-0"

STEEL STUD CONSTRUCTION

LINE OF EXISTING CEILING
⅝" GYP. BD.

NEON TUBE
STEEL ANGLE TO GYP. BD.

**DETAIL: COVE LIGHTING**
1½" = 1'-0"

**Lighted wood and glass guardrail**

7″

1″
4″
8″

Handrail 30″ to 34″
Guardrail 36″ to 42″

- Hardwood trim
- Gypsum board backing
- Continuous fluorescent light strips between posts
- Lighting cutoff line
- Support posts 4′ to 6′ to the inside per lamp lengths
- ½″ tempered glass baluster panels

**Lighted low-partition guardrail**

10″

9″

- Hardwood trim
- Continuous cold cathode lamps, exposed or concealed
- Full-width partition at corner
- Metal stud and gypsum board construction

Floor line

**Extruded aluminum light rail**

3½″

5″

- Extruded aluminum top railing
- Continuous fluorescent lamps between support posts
- Support posts 4′ to 6′ to the inside per lamp lengths

Pavement line

6″ maximum   3′   4′   4′

*Elevation of lighted guardrail planter demonstrates the use of combined 3-foot and 4-foot fluorescent light strips to achieve overall lengths in 1-foot multiples. To minimize dark areas between lamps, use strips without end caps and install lamps back to back.*

- 42″-high aluminum handrail
- Hardwood trim
- Gypsum board backing
- Continuous fluorescent, neon, or low-wattage incandescent lamps
- Metal balusters, 6″ on center
- Hardwood vertical supports 4′ to 6′ on center
- Metal-lined planter for set-in pots or direct planting
- Metal stud and gypsum board construction
- Finish floor line

Sight line for shielding lamps from below

**Lighted guardrail planter section**

*Open circulation areas can be illuminated with lighted railings, as shown in this section of a lighted guardrail planter.*

765

# LIGHTING

Stair Lighting Photometrics

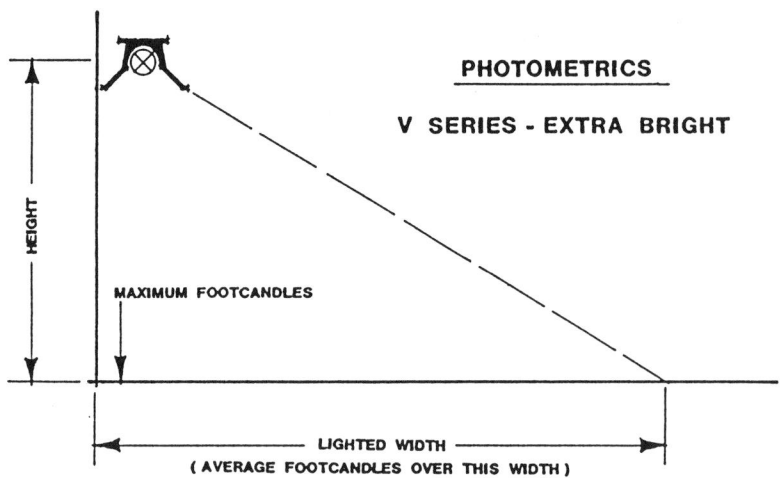

## PHOTOMETRICS

## V SERIES - EXTRA BRIGHT

FOOTCANDLES

| HT. ABOVE FLOOR IN. | LIGHTED WIDTH IN.[1] | AVERAGE[2] | MAXIMUM[3] |
|---|---|---|---|
| 6 | 11 | 5.0 | 13.0 |
| 8 | 14 | 3.8 | 9.8 |
| 10 | 18 | 3.0 | 7.8 |
| 12 | 21 | 2.5 | 6.5 |
| 18 | 32 | 1.7 | 4.4 |
| 24 | 42 | 1.3 | 3.3 |
| 30 | 53 | 1.0 | 2.6 |
| 36 | 63 | 0.8 | 2.1 |

NOTES:

1. LIGHTED WIDTH TO POINT FOOTCANDLE LEVEL FALLS TO 10% OF MAXIMUM

2. AVERAGE FOOTCANDLES OVER LIGHTED WIDTH

3. FOOTCANDLES DIRECTLY BELOW LIGHT FIXTURE

Fig. 16   Surface-mounted step light.

Fig. 17   Recessed step light.

ADJUSTABLE SNAP-ON LAMP REFLECTORS

RITE ANGLE ELECTRODE LAMPS
fabricated to-shape and length of
architectural design
continuous line of light — no shadows

RITE ANGLE ELECTRODE LAMPHOLDERS
94" o.c. max.

LUMINOUS COVER (by others)
to protect lighting from weather and
vandalism. Clear/translucent/acrylic/lexan
as desired with foam gaskets & tamperproof
screws.

7" min. to install lamps

**Wall recessed stair lighting**

**Schematic perspective**

#RP.F FEED
LAMPHOLDER

**ADJUSTABLE SNAP-ON
LAMP REFLECTORS**

2" min.

2 1/2"   3¾" min.
to remove lamp

for stairs over 8' long
continuous line of light

**Typical section through riser (interior)**

LUMINOUS COVER with foam
neoprene gaskets (to protect
lighting from vandalism and
weather)

2" min.

recess at
lampholders
only
94" o.c. max.

2 1/2"

5½"

**Typical section through riser (exterior or interior)**

3" min.

5" min.

DOWNLIGHTING
Assymetrical spread
planters, benches

UPLIGHTING
Assymetrical spread
parapets, dwarf plants

SIDE LIGHTING

desks, counters

TYPICAL DESIGNS/SUGGESTED CONSTRUCTIONS.
Exact construction as required within parameters of
illumination desired, lamps and lampholders.

**Alternate stair lighting designs**

767

# LIGHTING

Stair Lighting Details

Carpeted cast-in-place step light

Exposed cast-in-place step light

Concrete surface-applied bonded extrusion

Wood surface-applied bonded extrusion

Brick steps with recessed light

LIGHT FIXT. #G

COLD SPRING CHARCOAL BLACK GRANITE TREAD FLAMED FINISH

STL. STRINGER W. PAINTED CLADDING

¾" MAHOG. VENEERED PLYWD. ON PIANO HINGE TYPICAL

METAL PAN TREAD & RISER TREAD NOSING TO BE PTD TO MATCH GRANITE

MAHOG. VENEERED PLYWD. W. BRASS STUDS (ON EITHER SIDE OF STAIR #1 ONLY)

10/A10 DETAIL OF TREAD & RISER at STAIRS #1 & #2

11/A10 DETAIL OF STRINGER at STAIRS #1 & #2

OAK EDGE

RED MAHOGANY, OIL FIN.

VERDI ANTIQUE MARBLE TREAD

LIGHT FIXT. #F

TERRAZZO TOPPING

UNDERBED

EXISTING SLAB

⅛" ALUM. DIVIDER

21/A7 DETAIL OF MARBLE STEP

ROUNDED NOSING

CARPET

LIGHT FIXT. N. STEP LIGHT

¾" PLYWOOD TREADS & RISERS

FRAMING AS REQ'D & TO BE FIRE RETARDED WHERE

DETAIL OF STEP LIGHTS at LOUNGE #08

# LIGHTING

**Skylight Lighting Details**

SKYLITE by others

MOUNTING BRACKETS

WIRING & BALLAST TROUGH

Spiral Lamps

LAMP SUPPORT clear plastic

Curb Diameter

Luminous Element (as selected)

**SECTION THRU TYPICAL SKYLITE**

SKYLITE by others

WIRING & BALLAST TROUGH

Adjustable snap-on lamp reflector

M, U or Straight lamps

LAMP SUPPORT clear plastic

Curb Opening

Luminous Element (as selected)

**SECTION THRU TYPICAL SKYLITE**

Feed

**TYPICAL PLAN · 2 SPIRAL LAMPS**
**(without luminous element)**

3" min.

54" max. Curb Opening

**TYPICAL PLAN · U LAMPS**

Max. Curb Opening

**TYPICAL PLAN · STRAIGHT LAMPS**

3" min.

32" max. Curb Opening

**TYPICAL PLAN · M LAMPS**

**Fig. 18  Skylight lighting. Skylight serves as fixture — does not interfere with natural lighting, will not cast shadows on luminous element. Spiral, M, U, and straight lamps fabricated to fit curb opening.**

CL OF EXISTING COL.

2½" X 5" SUPPORTING
ANGLE BRACKETS

LIGHT FIXT. #9
TYP. at COLUMN

EXISTING COLUMN

FROSTED GLASS

RED MAHOGANY FRAMES
& TRIMS, OIL FINISH

CL OF EXISTING COL.

**21** PLAN DETAIL of LIGHTED COLUMN
**A8** SCALE : 1½" = 1'-0"

CL OF COLUMN

NEW LOCATION of
SPRINKLER MAIN
& LAMINATED
EXISTING BEAM
at #1 ROLL COL.
(SHOWN DOTTED)

RED MAHOGANY
FRAMES & TRIMS
OIL FINISH

FROSTED GLASS

RED MAHOGANY
OIL FINISH

RED MAHOGANY
OIL FINISH

LIGHT FIXT. #9

¼" FROSTED
GLASS

RED MAHOGANY
FRAMES & TRIMS
OIL FINISH

BLOCKING
AS REQUIRED

CABINET

**22** ELEVATION of LIGHTED COLUMN
**A8** SCALE : 1½" = 1'-0"

**23** SECTION of LIGHTED COLUMN
**A8** SCALE : 1½" = 1'-0"

• 15" Ø GAL. SHADE

• FROSTED GLASS @ CENTER, MAHOG. @ SIDES

• MAHOG. TRIM

• MAHOG.

3/4" DOWEL W/RUBBER TIP

1/4"

BANQUETTE

NOTE:
• RESIN SHADE SHOWN DOTTED BY SIRMOS HALF SPHERE

FIXTURE IS INSIDE

11/A5  BLOW-UP DETL. OF UPLIGHT • SEE DETL. 12/A5
SCALE: 3"=1'-0"

PLAN VIEW

15" Ø GLASS SHADE
3/4" WD. DOWELS W/RUBBER TIP
FROSTED GLASS INSERT (CENTER PANELS (3) VERT.)
1/2"x1/4" MAHOGANY TRIM
MAHOGANY PANEL
LIGHT FIXTURE INSIDE
3/4" Ø BRASS STUD (ALL FOUR SIDES)
1 1/2" x 1/2" MAHOGANY TRIM
1 1/2" MAHOGANY CAP W/1/2" MAHOG. REVEAL
BANQUETTE
MAHOGANY PANEL
MAHOGANY BASE
1/2" REVEAL W/ ( 4 ) EQUAL MAHOG. PANELS
SEE SPECS.

12/A5  CENTER BANQUETTE @ DINING 09 • SIDE/BACK+ PLAN VIEW • SEE DETL. 11/A5
SCALE: 1/2"=1'-0"

PINE PT'D BLACK
PINE, PT'D RED ⚠

¼" FROSTED
GLASS BENT
TO FORM HALF
CYLINDER

EXISTING COL.

PLYWOOD
PAINTED RED

⚠ CONT. S/S FLAT
DIVIDER

LIGHT FIXT. 'F'
8 PER COLUMN

CONTINUOUS ⚠
S/S CHANNEL
PAINTED RED

PLYWD, PAINTED
RED, TYP. at THESE
3 COLUMNS

EXISTING COLUMN

REMOVABLE QUART.
SECTION FOR
CHANGING LIGHT
FIXTURE

HORIZ. SECTION

8'-6" at CENTER COLUMN, 7'-6" at RIGHT + LEFT COLUMNS

2½"    1'-2"    2½"

¼" FROSTED GLASS
TO FORM HALF CYLINDER

PINE STOP, PAINTED RED

PINE, PAINTED BLACK

REMOVABLE QUART. SECTION

4"

HALF ELEVATION | HALF SECTION

14  DETAIL OF LIGHT COLUMN
A4  SCALE: 1½" = 1'-0"

# LIGHTING

**Ceiling-Mounted Cold Cathode Lighting Details**

### Exposed/sculpture lamp lighting

Cold cathode lighting, an architectural lighting tool with unusual flexibility.

Lamps fabricated to the architectural design, continuous line of light — low brightness — no glare — high efficiency — long life — approaches a permanent light source.

Remote transformers — no wiring troughs, ballasts, ballast failures, or hum. Only 2 leads for up to 120 feet of lamps.

Excellent uniform dimming — no premature flickering of individual lamps as with hot cathode lighting.

#R LAMPHOLDER
95" o.c. max.

4½"

RITE ANGLE ELECTRODE LAMPS
Continuous line of light

RITE ANGLE ELECTRODE LAMPHOLDERS
94" o.c. max.

Clear nylon lamp ties

RITE ANGLE ELECTRODE LAMPS
continuous line of ligth
fabricated to shape of soffit

Stem hanger

Lampholder housing

RITE ANGLE ELECTRODE LAMPHOLDERS

RITE ANGLE ELECTRODE LAMPS — continuous line of light
Double row warm white on dimmer
Clear glass neon on dimmer

RECESSED LAMPHOLDER
95" o.c. max.

2½"

2"

LAMP TIES—for hanging
down lamp only.

Vertical Blinds

RITE ANGLE ELECTRODE LAMPS
Continuous line of light

# Principal types of lamps for general lighting purposes

| Category | Type | Maximum lamp efficacy lm/W | Average life hrs | Characteristic features | Typical application areas |
|---|---|---|---|---|---|
| Incandescent Lamps | Normal incandescent lamps and reflector lamps | 22 | 1,000 | Easy to install, easy to use; many different versions; instant start; low cost price; reflector lamps allow concentrated light beams | General lighting in the home; decorative lighting; localized lighting; accent and decorative lighting (reflector lamps) |
| | Halogen | 27 | 2,000 | Compact; high light output; white light; easy to install; long life compared with normal incandescent lamps | Accent lighting; floodlighting |
| Fluorescent Lamps | Tubular | 104 | 20,000 | Wide choice of light colors; high lighting levels possible; economical in use | All kinds of commercial and public buildings; streetlighting; home lighting |
| | SL* | 61 | 10,000 | Energy-effective; direct replacement for incandescent lamps | Most applications where incandescent lamps were used before |
| | PL* | 80 | 10,000 | Compact; long life; energy-effective | To create a pleasant atmosphere in social areas, local lighting; signs, security, orientation lighting and general lighting |
| Gas-Discharge Lamps | Self-ballasted | 28 | 12,000/16,000 | Long life; good color rendering; easy to install; better efficacy than incandescent lamps | Direct replacement for incandescent lamps; small industrial and public light projects; plant irradiation |
| | High pressure mercury | 63 | 24,000 + | High efficacy; long life; reasonable color quality | Residential area lighting; sports grounds; factory lighting |
| | Metal halide | 94 | 15,000 | Very high efficacy combined with excellent color rendering; long life | Floodlighting, especially for color TV; industrial lighting; road lighting; plant irradiation |
| | High pressure sodium | 125 | 24,000 + | Very high efficacy; extremely long life; good color rendering | Public lighting; floodlighting; industrial lighting; plant irradiation EL: direct replacement for mercury lamps |
| | Low pressure sodium | 200 | 18,000 | Extremely high efficacy; very long life; high visual acuity; poor color rendering: monochromatic light | Many different application areas: wherever energy/cost-effectiveness is important and color is not critical |

## LIGHTING

**Planning Data: Incandescent Bulb Sizes**

### INCANDESCENT BULBS

C-7   Decor C   C-15   S-11

F   P   S   G

CA   A-15-19   A   T

GT   PS   R   ER   EAR

KR   PAR 38   PAR 46 PAR 56 PAR 64   Lumiline

A Bulb designation consists of a letter(s) to indicate the shape and a figure(s) to indicate the approximate major diameter in eights of an inch. Bulbs are measured through their greatest diameter, in eights of an inch. Thus, a F-15 bulb is a flame shape, 15/8 of an inch or 1⅞ inches in diameter.

# BASES

Mini Can
Screw
Mini Can

Candelabra
Cand

E-14 Screw
European Base

Intermediate
Inter

B-15 Bayonet
European Base

B-22 Bayonet
European Base

Single Contact
Bayonet
Candelabra
S C Bay

Double Contact
Bayonet
Candelabra
D S Bay

Candelabra
Prefocus
S C Pf
D C Pf

Single Pin
(T 12 Slimline)

Miniature Bipin
Min. Bipin
(T 5 F Lamp)

Single Pin
(T 6 Slimline)

Single Pin
(T 8 Slimline)

Mini Screw
M S

Screw
Terminal
Scr. Term.

Ext. Mog.    Mogul
End Prong   End Prong
Mog E Pr

Medium
Prefocus
Med Pf

Standard

3 Kon Tact
Medium
3 C Med

Mogul Bipin
Mog Bipin
(T 17 F Lamp)

Rect RSC
Recessed Single
Contact

Disc
(Lumiline)

Recessed
Dbl Contact
(T 12 F Lamp)

Metal Sleeve

Medium 2 Pin

Med Bipost

Medium Bipin
Med Bipin
(T 8 F Lamp)

Medium Bipin
Med Bipin
(T 12 F Lamp)

RSC
Recessed Single
Contact

Mini Can
Socket

Ceramic Tubular

Medium
Side Prong

4 Pin
(Circline)

Mogul Bipost
Mog Bip

Position Oriented
Mogul
Pos Or Mog

Type Q
Axial Lead

Medium
Skirted
Med Skt

Medium
Skirted
Med Skt

Admedium
Skirted
Admed

Mogul
Prefocus
Mog Pf

Mogul
Mog

Three Contact
Mogul
3 C Mog

# OFFICE

## LIGHT LEVEL RECOMMENDATIONS

| Type of Work | Foot Candles* |
|---|---|
| Corridors, lobbies | 10-15-20 |
| Easy tasks (Typed originals, ball-point pen handwriting, large print) | 20-30-50 |
| Medium tasks (Poor copies, medium hard pencil, small print) | 50-75-100 |
| Difficult tasks (Very poor copies, hard pencil writing) | 100-150-200 |

*Choose an illuminance value in the mid-range for your type of activity. Then decide upon a specific value (Same, lower, or higher) within that range by considering the age of the workers and the importance of the work.

## SELECTING THE PROPER FIXTURE

- **Light Output/Efficiency**

  The more light, the fewer fixtures needed in new lighting systems and lower operating cost.

- **Visual Comfort**

  Fixtures should direct light to the task and away from the eyes. The fixture's VCP rating, available from the fixture manufacturer, should be 70 or above.

- **Maintainability**

  Check ease of lamp replacement, cleanability, and permanence of finishes.

- **Fit In Application**

  Should look right and cover the area to be lighted (consider smaller fixtures closer together, such as 2×2s instead of 2×4s, for lower ceilings, or lower light levels or high-panelled work stations).

## STORE

### LIGHT LEVEL RECOMMENDATIONS

| | Circulation | Merchandising | Feature Displays |
|---|---|---|---|
| High Activity Area (Mass Merchandiser) | 30 | 100 | 500 |
| Medium (Family Dept. Store) | 20 | 70 | 300 |
| Low (Boutique. Specialty Stores) | 10 | 30 | 150 |

- **Shielding Materials**

  Comparison of lighting characteristics for typical 2×4 troffer luminaries:

| Shielding Material | Efficiency Range (%) | VCP Range |
|---|---|---|
| Clear Lens | 50-70 | 55-85 |
| Polarizer | 55-60 | 60-70 |
| Deep Cell Parabolic Louver | 45-60 | 70-85 |
| Diffuser | 40-60 | 40-50 |
| Plastic Louver Panel (45°) | 45-55 | 50-70 |
| White Metal Louver (45°) | 35-45 | 65-85 |
| Parabolic Louver Panel (45°) | 40-50 | 99 |
| Toned Lens | 30-60 | 70-85 |
| Dark Metal Louver | 25-40 | 70-90 |

# INDUSTRIAL

## LIGHT LEVEL RECOMMENDATIONS

| | Footcandles Maintained on the Task |
|---|---|
| GARAGES–SERVICE | |
| ☐ repair | 50-100fc |
| ☐ active traffic areas | 10-20fc |
| LOADING PLATFORM | 20fc |
| MACHINE SHOPS AND ASSEMBLY AREAS | |
| ☐ rough bench/machine work, simple assembly | 20-50fc |
| ☐ medium bench/machine work, moderately difficult assembly | 50-100fc |
| ☐ difficult machine work, assembly | 100-200fc |
| ☐ fine bench/machine work, assembly | 200-500fc* |
| RECEIVING & SHIPPING | 20-50fc |
| WAREHOUSES, STORAGE ROOMS | |
| ☐ active-large items/small items, labels | 15fc/30fc |
| ☐ inactive | 5fc |

*Higher illuminance values may be achieved through a combination of supplementary and general lighting.

# 3

# Architectural Woodwork

Standard joinery and casework details     781
Woodwork details     804
Cornices and mouldings     866
Furniture hardware     887

## INTRODUCTION

Most residential and commercial projects require the design of a certain amount of architectural woodwork. Such woodwork may be in the form of built-in furniture, cabinets, display cases, reception desks, credenzas, work counters, kitchen cabinets, etc. The extent of detail necessary to intelligently communicate and identify the scope and character of required woodwork is an important consideration in the preparation of contract drawings. It is necessary, therefore, that the designer have a knowledge of basic wood joinery and understand how to apply it in the preparation of construction details.

Accordingly, the information in this section can be used as a general guide in the detailing of most woodwork items and addresses four areas of concern. The first deals with basic joinery and typical casework details. This information is fundamental to an understanding of the detailing of woodwork. The typical joints illustrated vary in sophistication and structural integrity and represent the most common methods of joining any two wood members. The casework details are intended to illustrate the construction of routine casework and are divided into three categories: exposed face frame, flush overlay, and reveal overlay. The second area deals with custom woodwork and includes details of woodwork items selected directly from contract drawings contributed by various interior design and architectural firms. This information should prove helpful in providing the reader with a more global perspective of how different firms approach the detailing of some common types of woodwork items and the extent of that detailing. The third area of this section deals with standard cornices and mouldings, and is intended to simply provide the designer with dimensional and design information relative to the many standard items available on the market. Since many woodwork items involve some moveable elements, the fourth area of this section deals with furniture hardware.

## Characteristics of Joints

Joints may be divided into four general types: *butted, shiplapped, tongued-and-grooved,* and *mitered.* Used in their simple basic form, none is satisfactory for cabinet work except the tongued-and-grooved type in certain instances. However, when variously combined or when reinforced with gluing and dowels or splines, satisfactory joints can be developed.

**Butt joint** A simple but weak joint that opens easily and may show end wood when used at angles. Strength and range of use is greatly increased by use of the *mortise and tenon* and *dowels* and even more when a *straight spline* is included. Use of a glued *butterfly spline* with a butt joint produces an extremely strong joint. These variations are widely used to produce large flush surfaces of solid wood or backing for veneers.

**Shiplap joint** Stronger than a butt joint but subject to opening from shrinkage. Rarely used in a simple form in cabinet work except for door rebates. It is often moulded to conceal shrinkage in quirks or combined as a *miter and shoulder* for corners. Another variation is the *shoulder joint.*

**Tongue-and-groove joint** A strong joint, widely used for re-entrant angles. Effect of wood shrinkage is concealed when the joint is beaded or otherwise moulded. In expensive cabinet work glued *dovetail* and *multiple tongue-and-groove* are used.

**Miter joints** are weak and difficult to fit if used alone. Joints with *miter brads* are sufficiently strong for short lengths. Joints made in combination with other forms, as a *tongue-and-groove miter,* are tight and sturdy.

## Use of Joints

Use of certain types of joints depends to a large degree upon the type of work and skill involved. The following notes indicate use of joints in various categories, but cannot be regarded as an inclusive check list.

**For panels, shelving, etc.,** or wherever the end of one piece butts against the face of another; *housed joint,* with or without cover mould, or some type of *tongue-and-groove* joint. Omit glue to avoid splitting due to swelling or shrinkage.

**For joining stiles and rails:** *mortise and tenon,* glued in better work. Dowels may be used or hardwood wedges may be driven and glued into ends of tenons in high grade work.

**For re-entrant corners:** *shoulder joints* for inexpensive work. *Tongue-and-groove* is sturdier. Both should be glued, are often screwed together, and may be glued to a rough frame.

**For external corners:** simple *miter* and *quirk and miter* both lack strength. *Miter brads* are practical only for short lengths. *Miter and shoulder* glued and face-screwed or nailed is satisfactory (generally "millwork"). *Miter and spline* is preferable. In high grade work exterior corners are reinforced by gluing to a corner post or short lengths of blocking.

**Glued joints:** when screws, nails, etc., cannot be used, or when fine work is to be veneered, strength of the joint depends on accuracy of milling and total glue surface. Glue surface may be tremendously increased by using multiple or offset tongues and grooves, by forming miter cuts into waves, multiple shoulders, tongues and grooves, etc. Such work is cabinet work. If done by a reliable cabinet maker, a guarantee should be obtained and joint detail and composition of glue left to him or her.

**Mouldings** should be applied in continuous lengths if possible. Use simple miter for necessary joints, cope re-entrant angles unless excessively undercut, miter external corners.

TYPICAL JOINTS

Letters indicate class of woodwork in which joint is commonly used. See text.
A.- Carpentry    B.- Millwork    C - Cabinet Work    D - Furniture

BUTTED....
- Butt *(not recommended)* — A
- Doweled — B
- Splined — C
- Butterfly Spline — C D
- Dove Tail — C D
- Butt *(Mortise & Tenon Dotted)* — B C

SHIPLAPPED
- Shiplap *(sheathing etc.)* — A
- Rebated *(Bead & 'V')* — B
- Shoulder — B
- Shoulder & Bead — B C

TONGUED & GROOVED....
- Tongue & Groove *(Flooring etc.)* — A B
- TG & Bead — A B
- Housed — B C - D
- Tongue & Bead — B
- Tongue & Groove — B C
- Lapped Dove Tail — C
- Tongue & Groove *(Offset)* — C
- Multiple Tongue & Groove — C D

MITERED....
- Miter *(Mouldings & Baseboards)* — A
- Quirk & Miter — A B
- Miter Brads — B
- Miter & Shoulder — B
- Miter & Spline — C
- T & G and Miter — C D

## STANDARD JOINERY AND CASEWORK DETAILS

Typical Joints

**TYPICAL JOINTS**

| | | | |
|---|---|---|---|
| BUTT | TONGUE & GROOVE | SPLINE | HALF LAP |
| HALF LAP | SCARF | FINGER | DOWELED |
| MORTISE & TENON, SLOTTED | MORTISE & TENON, STUB | MORTISE & TENON, BLIND | MORTISE & TENON, THROUGH |
| RABBET | LOCK | DOVETAIL | DOVETAIL DADO |
| DOVETAIL, BLIND | DADO | DADO, BLIND OR STOPPED | DADO, BLIND OR STOPPED |
| MITER | SPLINED MITER | MITER, SHOULDER | MITER, LOCK |

## Terminology

**Spline joint** Used for gluing plywood in width or length. Since the spline serves to align faces, this joint is also used for items requiring site assembly.

**Stub tenon** Joinery method for assembling stile and rail type frames that are additionally supported, such as web or skeleton case frames.

**Conventional mortise and tenon joint** Joinery method for assembling square-edged surfaces such as case face frames.

**Dowel joint** Alternative joinery method for serving same function as conventional mortise and tenon.

**Haunch mortise and tenon joint** Joinery method for assembling paneled doors or stile and rail type paneling.

**French dovetail joint** Method for joining drawer sides to fronts when fronts conceal metal extension slides or overlay the case faces.

**Conventional dovetail joint** Traditional method for joining drawer sides to fronts or backs. Usually limited to flush or lipped type drawers.

**Drawer lock-joint** Another joinery method for joining drawer sides to fronts. Usually used for flush type installation but can be adapted to lip or overlay type drawers.

**Edge banding** Method of concealing plys or inner cores of plywood or particleboard when edges are exposed. Thickness or configuration will vary with manufacturers' practices.

**Through dado** Conventional joint used for assembly of case body members — dado usually concealed by application of case face frame.

**Blind dado** Variation of conventional dado with applied edge "stopping" or concealing dado groove. Used when case body edge is exposed.

**Stop dado** Another method of concealing dado exposure. Applicable when veneer edging or solid lumber is used.

**Exposed end detail** Illustrates attachment of finished end of case body to front frame using butt joint.

**Exposed end detail** Illustrates attachment of finished end of case body to front frame using mitered joint.

**Paneled door details** Joinery techniques when paneled effect is desired. Profiles are optional as is the use of flat or raised panels. Solid lumber raised panels may be used when width does not exceed 10 in. Rim raised panels recommended when widths exceed this dimension or when transparent finish is used.

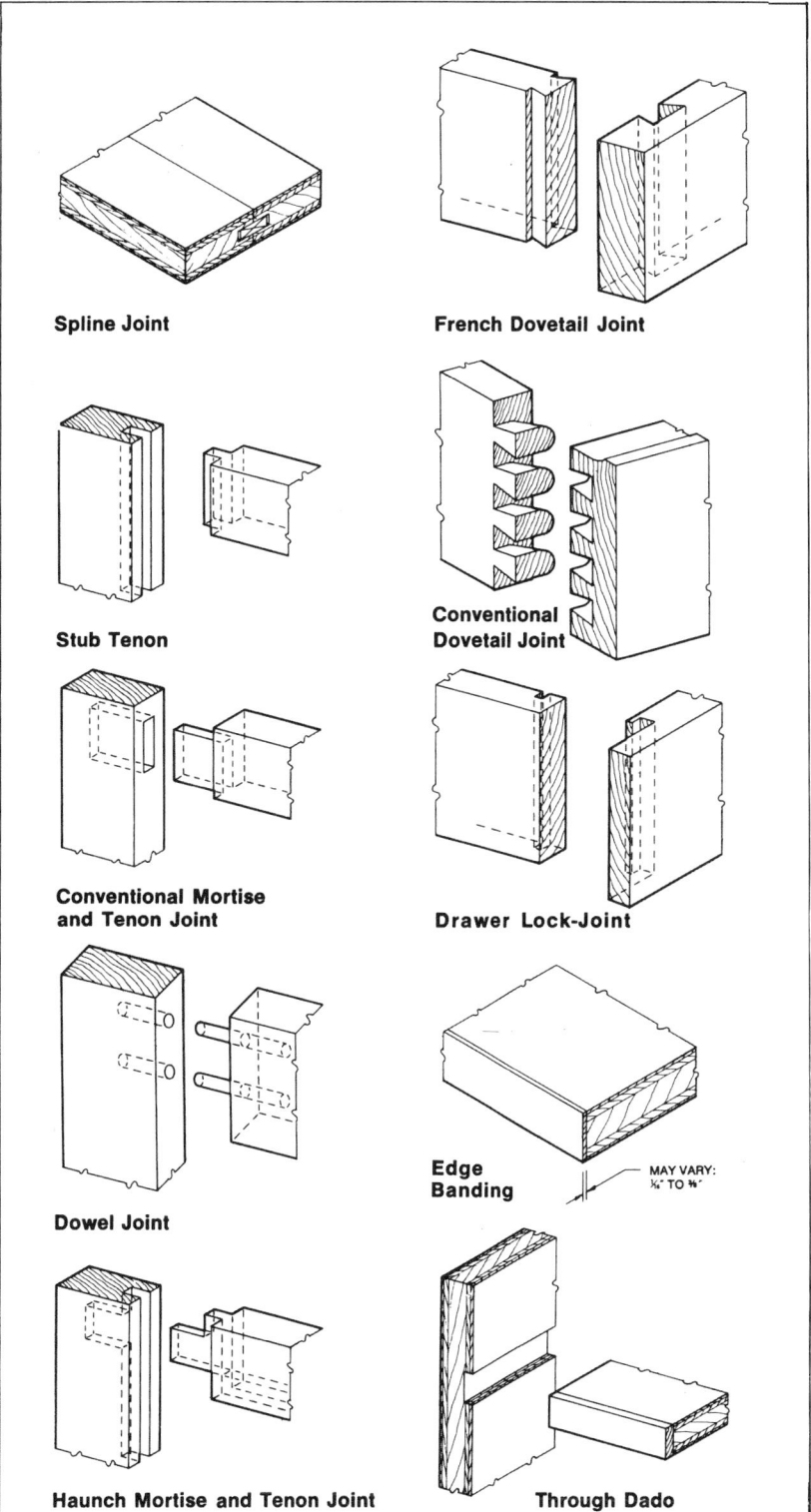

**Spline Joint**

**French Dovetail Joint**

**Stub Tenon**

**Conventional Dovetail Joint**

**Conventional Mortise and Tenon Joint**

**Drawer Lock-Joint**

**Dowel Joint**

**Edge Banding**

MAY VARY: ¼" TO ¾"

**Haunch Mortise and Tenon Joint**

**Through Dado**

## STANDARD JOINERY AND CASEWORK DETAILS

Typical Joints

**Blind Dado**

**Exposed End Detail**

STILE

SOLID RAISED PANEL

SOLID OVOLO STICKING

RAIL

**Paneled Door Detail**

**Stop Dado**

**Exposed End Detail**

STILE

RIM RAISED PANEL

SOLID O.G. STICKING

RAIL

**Paneled Door Detail**

TOP RAIL

STILE

CROSS RAIL

MULLION

BOTTOM RAIL

**Typical Frame Parts**

STILE

FLAT OR RAISED PANEL

APPLIED RAISED MOULDING

RAIL

**Paneled Door Detail**

# TYPICAL
# CABINET CONSTRUCTION

## DIAGRAMMATIC PLAN
(No Scale)

## GROUNDS & COVER MOULD

Ground

Finish Plaster coat
may be omitted
½" (Desirable)

Any Complete Cabinet

Nail Cover
Mould to
ground,
not to
Cabinet

Grounds are carefully
located before erecting

**A**

Grounds   Plaster   Grounds

Housed or shoulder
joint to conceal
possible shrinkage

Framing

Shelf   Shelf

**D**

Stud
Grounds

**E**   Any Trim

Corner Space may be used
for secret storage
Possible door and stop
shown dotted

Finish coat of plaster usually
omitted when concealed

Access Door
if desired

Door Stops
if desired

**C**

Square or round cut
to suit type of hinge

This detail permits easy removal
of articles. Shelves should not
exceed 3'-0" in unsupported length
and may be fixed or adjustable

Ground

Solid or
Plywood
Back-panel

Concealed faces
back-painted

Return against paneling

**A**

Panel
may be
omitted

Tongue & Groove
or Shoulder at
re-entrant angle

Dotted lines in-
dicate applied
stops when used

Drawer
Guide

Dust Panel
or open space below

Drawer
Guide

Stud

Ground

Temporary
Ground

Plaster

Dotted lines indicate
Drawer Runners below

Drawer

**C**

See Also T-SS "Finish – Woodwork–
Cabinet Work – 1"

**E**   Narrow Trim

Linear Trim usually
coped at re-entrant
angle

Any type of Door

Canvas covered
plaster

Any Panel scribed
to wall

Mitered Corners
(Quirk, Shoulder,
Spline, Tongue &
Groove, Shoulder
& Bead Joints)

Linear Trim mitered
at external corner

**A**   **B**

## DRAWER CLEARANCE
## FOR CLOSET CABINET

Drawer

Drawer Guide
Plaster
Studs

Grounds

1⅜" Door

Line of
Drawer
Opened

2"

(min. clearance)

Any trim

## STANDARD JOINERY AND CASEWORK DETAILS
Cabinet Work

**SECTIONAL PLAN**

Back

Sides

Front

When any type of patented drawer slide is used, consult man'f's catalogue for this dimension. The lapped front conceals slide

Dust-Panels & top face of drawer Runners should be flush

Dust Panel & Runner

Runner concealed

**BACK** **FRONTS**

Bottom rabeted to front and sides; secured to front only.
Runners & Guides preferably hardwood; Panels either veneer or solid

### DRAWERS

Lapped Dovetail Joint

Dovetail concealed by joint

Dovetail concealed by moulds

The sides of drawers should be dovetailed to fronts. Usual methods shown

1.     2.

1 Bottomless – For towels, etc.
2 Flush Lattice Bottom – Permits air circulation for linens, etc.

Line of wall

A    B

Guide

**SIDES**

A Guide at side of drawer, fastened to Drawer Runner
B Guide (Hardwood) rabeted into side of Drawer.

For Sliding Doors this space should be slightly greater than depth of wheel grooves to permit the removal of doors

Any suitable type track (See man'f's catalogue)

**SLIDING DOORS**
(Removable)

Flush Front Panel Doors

Felt Backing
Plate Glass Mirror
Removable Mouldings

**DOOR WITH MIRROR**

Miter & Shoulder Joint Removable Mouldings

Tongue & Groove Joint Glass

**DETAILS FOR GLAZED DOORS**

Miter Joint & Hardwood Spline Invisible Hinges Optional

Miter Joint with Miter Brads Integral & Applied Stops

**DETAILS FOR PANELED DOORS**
(Panels may be either plain or ply-wood)

### DOORS

Door

This detail permits the use of different woods

Door

This detail may be used if Cabinet extends to Finish Floor

Any Blocking

Baseboard

Finish Floor

Rough Floor

Door

### BASES

Ceiling Line

Any Blocking

Door

This detail permits use of different woods

For Average Construction

Detail where Cabinet does not extend to Ceiling

Blocking

Back Panel

### CORNICE

Shelf on cleats fastened to grounds in plaster wall

Shelf on nailing strips

When any type of patented Shelf-Adjusters are used, consult man'f's catalogue for recommended dimensions Shelf edge may be Hardwood

Holes 1" O.C.

Adjustable Shelf on Wood Pegs

### SHELVES

Door

Door

Tension Rod with washer & nut concealed by wood plug

Bracket

The Section of a Cabinet above Counter (Upper Section) may be supported as shown.

### SUPPORTS

1 With drawer below
2 With moulding
3 With Backboard
4 Backboard with Cove Corner

Ground

Door
Drawer

1    2    3    4

### COUNTERS

Toe Space with Sanitary Cove

Floor Covering may finish against bottom of Cabinet

3½" (min.)

Any Blocking Rough Floor

Door

Floor Covering butts against base

4" (min.)

Blocking

### TOE SPACE

### Purpose

The following information outlines methods of assembly and installation of common cabinet work, Solutions of typical problems are presented without attempting to detail specific cabinets.

### Assembly

High-grade cabinet and veneered work is assembled as far as possible at the shop. Joints are glued and blocked, and sometimes secured with finishing nails or screws. Carpentry and millwork are generally put together with finishing nails if of soft wood, or with screws if of hardwood. Hardwood should be drilled to prevent splitting before using nails or screws, and heads should be countersunk and concealed by cover moulds, moulding quirks, or putty, plastic wood, or other filler, colored to match the finish. No nails, screws, or joints should be visible unless they are intentionally incorporated in design.

**Shrinkage and warping** effects can be largely eliminated by proper detailing and construction. *Wide flat surfaces* (solid or veneered) should be made up of several narrow strips glued and doweled, splined, or dovetailed together. Cleats may also be screwed or keyed to backs of wide surfaces. *Joints in corners, sheathing, etc.,* should be con- cealed within quirks of moulds (as in moulded tongue-and-groove) or return faces (shoulder joints). *Panels* should be rigidly secured on one side only, and are often left entirely loose. Housed joints, not glued, permit panels to expand and contract without splitting.

**Large moulded surfaces** (such as cornices or mantels) should always be shop-assembled and delivered with scribe-moulds (see "Scribing" below) loosely tacked to assembled units.

### Installation

All grades of woodwork should be preservative treated or back painted before erection, preferably before delivery to the job. Satisfactory priming coats are aluminum paint or white lead in linseed oil, thinned with turpentine or mineral spirits.

**Preparation** On frame walls plaster may be limited to one or two coats, may be recessed between studs, or may be omitted. In the latter case, building paper should be used between woodwork and studs. On masonry, plaster may consist of one or two coats or may be omitted. Masonry surfaces, particularly exterior walls, should be waterproofed or woodwork should be protected by a layer of waterproof paper and should always be furred out. When finish of the interior of cabinets is plaster, either plain or canvas covered, the final coat of plaster is applied after erection of cabinet.

**Grounds** of soft wood for attaching cabinet work must be accurately located, are secured directly to framing members or furring, and must be concealed.

**Blocking** of rough lumber should be erected for supporting raised floors and large or heavy cabinet work, if it can be concealed. Blocking must be accurately placed and secured with nails.

**Shimming** Minor irregularities in blocking, furring, or placement of studs may be corrected by using shims (wedge-shaped pieces of wood, often shingles) to bring completed work to plumb and level lines. Shimming should be concealed.

**Scribing** is the practice of fitting edges of cabinet work accurately to all irregularities of finish plaster, masonry, or other abutting surfaces. Wood mouldings, panel frames, or cabinet returns to be scribed should be provided with a beveled edge.

**Prefabricated woodwork** is generally delivered knocked down for assembly on the job and is erected similarly to custom-made work. Consult manufacturers' data.

Note how wide-faced mould is obtained from minimum stock.

**NAILING TO GROUNDS**

Drill holes before setting screws or driving nails in hardwood. Concealed faces of all millwork should be dampproofed by back-painting.

**CONCEALING ATTACHMENT OF HARDWOODS**

**NAILING IN QUIRKS**

Nail to stiles or rails; avoiding panel

**NAILING PANEL MOULD**

This portion is cut (scribed) on job to conform to irregularities in adjoining plaster or masonry surfaces.

**SCRIBING AGAINST PLASTER OR MASONRY**

This joint typical of millwork

Nailing & gluing a mortise and shoulder provides a strong, reasonably permanent joint

**GLUING AND BLOCKING**

Either Hardwood Dowels or Hardwood Wedges

For wedges, make saw-cut in tenon before assembling. Holes for dowels may be offset to draw joint tight.

**SECURING MORTISE & TENON**

Cope by hand on job unless excessively undercut; if so, use miter. Flat members may be butted or Tongued-and-Grooved

**COPING MOULDINGS RE-ENTRANT ANGLE**

# STANDARD JOINERY AND CASEWORK DETAILS

Plastic-Covered Casework

### Casework Definitions

A. Exposed portions
1. All surfaces visible when doors and drawers are closed.
2. Underside of bottoms of cabinets over 4'0" above finished floor.
3. Cabinet tops under 6'0" above finished floor or if over 6'0" and visible from an upper building level or floor.
4. Visible front edges of web frames, ends, divisions, tops, shelves, and hanging stiles.
5. Sloping tops of cabinets that are visible.
6. Visible surfaces in open cabinets or behind glass for premium grade only.
7. Interior faces of hinged doors for premium grade only.
8. Visible portions of bottoms, tops, and ends in front of sliding doors in custom and premium grades only.

B. Semi-exposed portions
1. Shelves.
2. Divisions.
3. Interior face of ends, backs, and bottoms.
4. Drawer sides, subfronts, backs, and bottoms.
5. The underside of bottoms of cabinets between 2'6" and 4'0" above the finished floor.
6. Interior faces of hinged doors, except premium grade.
7. Visible surfaces in open cabinets or behind glass for economy and custom grades and all rooms designated as storage, janitor, closet, or utility.
8. Visible portion of bottoms, tops, and ends in front of sliding doors in economy grade only.

C. Concealed portions
1. Toe space unless otherwise specified.
2. Sleepers.
3. Web frames, stretchers, and solid subtops.
4. Security panels.
5. Underside of bottoms of cabinets less than 2'6" above the finished floor.
6. Flat tops of cabinets 6'0" or more above the finished floor, except if visible from an upper building level.
7. The three nonvisible edges of adjustable shelves.
8. The underside of countertops, knee spaces, and drawer aprons.
9. The faces of cabinet ends of adjoining units that butt together.

**Fig. 1   Inside surfaces of open shelf cabinets and behind glass are considered exposed for premium grade and tops of tall cabinets and upper cabinets 6 ft above the floor that are exposed from upper levels are considered exposed.**

Fig. 2  Casework construction details — base cabinet.

## STANDARD JOINERY AND CASEWORK DETAILS

**Typical Upper Cabinet Details**

CASEWORK CONSTRUCTION DETAILS — UPPER CABINET AT THE CEILING

(1) PREMIUM
(2) CUSTOM
(3) ECONOMY
(7) CUSTOM & PREMIUM
(8) PREMIUM
(9) CUSTOM
(10) ECONOMY
(4) PREMIUM
(5) CUSTOM
(6) ECONOMY
(11) PREMIUM
(12) CUSTOM
(13) ECONOMY
(14) PREMIUM
(15) CUSTOM
(16) ECONOMY
(17) PREMIUM
(18) CUSTOM
(19) ECONOMY
(20) ALL GRADES
(21) CUSTOM & PREMIUM
(22) ECONOMY
(23) PREMIUM
(24) CUSTOM
(25) ECONOMY
(26) PREMIUM
(27) CUSTOM
(28) ECONOMY
(29) CUSTOM & PREMIUM
(30) PREMIUM
(31) CUSTOM & PREMIUM
(32) ALL GRADES
(33) C & P ECONOMY / ECONOMY / ECONOMY / ECONOMY

**Fig. 3   Casework construction details — upper cabinets at the ceiling.**

## DRAWER DETAILS

① CUSTOM & PREMIUM GRADES

② CUSTOM & PREMIUM GRADES

③ ECONOMY GRADE

④ FLUSH OVERLAY CUSTOM & PREMIUM GRADES

⑤ FLUSH OVERLAY CUSTOM & PREMIUM GRADES

⑥ FLUSH OVERLAY CUSTOM & PREMIUM GRADES

⑦ ECONOMY GRADE

⑧ CUSTOM & PREMIUM GRADES

⑨ CUSTOM & PREMIUM GRADES

⑩ CUSTOM & PREMIUM GRADES

⑪ ALL GRADES (1)

⑫ ALL GRADES

⑬ ALL GRADES

⑭ PREMIUM GRADE

⑮ PREMIUM GRADE

## DRAWER GUIDE DETAILS

⑯ SIDE RUNNER ALL GRADES

⑰ SIDE ALL GRADES

⑱ CORNER ALL GRADES

⑲ CENTER ALL GRADES

(1) Premium Grade requires top edge of sides to be shaped or stop shaped.
(2) Dado not required. Must be securely attached.

**Fig. 4  Drawer details.**

## STANDARD JOINERY AND CASEWORK DETAILS

**Typical Flush Overlay Casework Construction**

# FLUSH OVERLAY TYPE CASEWORK CONSTRUCTION DETAILS

NOTE: GRAIN OF DRAWER FRONTS MAY RUN VERTICALLY OR HORIZONTALLY UNLESS SPECIFIED OTHERWISE.

Sections shown are typical; however, variations are permitted as provided in the standard established for each grade.

Fig. 5   Flush overlay type casework construction details

ELEVATION    SECTION AT DOORS    SECTION AT DRAWERS

¾" THICK
LOCK-MITERED FINISH
BACK WHEN USED AS
PENINSULA

1" IF ADJUSTABLE AND D
LENGTH EXCEEDS 36"

9

PARTICLE BOARD

CORE

1    6    8    2

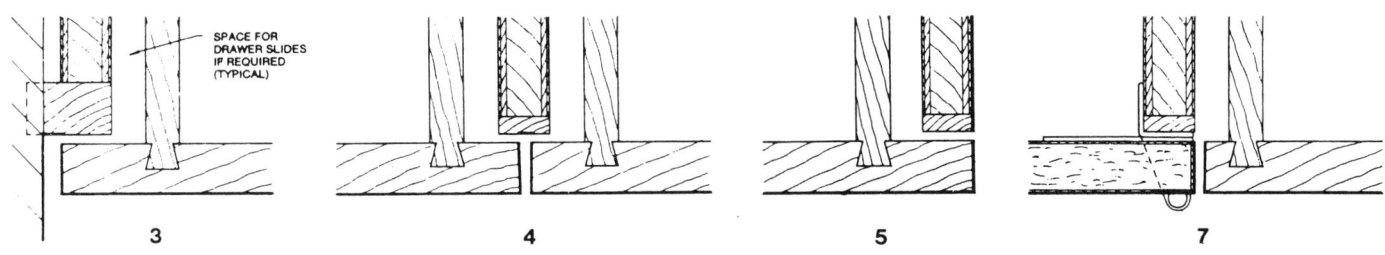

SPACE FOR
DRAWER SLIDES
IF REQUIRED
(TYPICAL)

3    4    5    7

## STANDARD JOINERY AND CASEWORK DETAILS

Typical Flush Overlay Casework Construction

TOP AND BOTTOM RAILS
- MINIMUM 1 INCH (25.40mm)

WIDTH OF STILES
- MINIMUM 1 INCH (25.40mm)

CORE OF MAT-FORMED
COMPOSITION BOARD

COMBINED THICKNESS OF EACH
FACE PANEL
- MINIMUM 1/12 INCH (2.12mm)

FACE VENEER

**Fig. 6  Mat-formed wood particleboard core (7-ply construction illustrated).**

TOP AND BOTTOM RAILS
- MINIMUM 1 INCH (25.40mm)

CORE OF MAT-FORMED
COMPOSITION BOARD

WIDTH OF STILES
- MINIMUM 1 INCH (25.40mm)

COMBINED THICKNESS OF EACH
FACE PANEL
- MINIMUM 1/12 INCH (2.12mm)

FACE VENEER

**Fig. 7  Mat-formed wood particleboard core (5-ply construction illustrated).**

TOP AND BOTTOM RAILS
- MINIMUM 1 INCH (25.40mm)

CORE OF MAT-FORMED
COMPOSITION BOARD

WIDTH OF STILES
- MINIMUM 1 INCH (25.40mm)

FACE PANEL
- MINIMUM 1/8 INCH (3.18mm)

**Fig. 8  Mat-formed wood particleboard core (3-ply construction illustrated).**

TOP, BOTTOM, AND SIDE EDGE
BANDS
- GLUED TO CORE
- MINIMUM 1/2 INCH (12.7mm)

WOOD CORE BLOCKS
- ANY LENGTH
- JOINTS STAGGERED
- BLOCKS GLUED TOGETHER

COMBINED THICKNESS OF EACH
FACE PANEL
- MINIMUM 1/12 INCH (2.12mm)

FACE VENEER

**Fig. 9  Glued block core (5-ply construction illustrated).**

## STANDARD JOINERY AND CASEWORK DETAILS
**Solid Core and Hollow Core Wood Flush Doors**

### SOLID CORE WOOD FLUSH DOORS

TOP AND BOTTOM RAILS
- MINIMUM 1 INCH (25.40mm)

WIDTH OF STILES
- MINIMUM 1 INCH (25.40mm)

WOOD CORE BLOCKS
- ANY LENGTH
- JOINTS STAGGERED
- BLOCKS GLUED TOGETHER

COMBINED THICKNESS OF EACH
FACE PANEL
- MINIMUM 1/12 INCH (2.12mm)

FACE VENEER

**Fig. 10   Framed block glued core (7-ply construction illustrated).**

TOP AND BOTTOM RAILS

WIDTH OF STILES

CENTRAL WOOD BLOCK CORE
- FRAMED BLOCK CORE
  ILLUSTRATED

CORE LINER

COMBINED THICKNESS OF EACH
FACE PANEL
- MINIMUM 1/12 INCH (2.12mm)

FACE VENEER

**Fig. 11   Wood block lined core (7-ply construction illustrated).**

### HOLLOW CORE WOOD FLUSH DOORS

TOP AND BOTTOM RAILS
- MINIMUM 2¼ INCHES (57.2mm)

WIDTH OF STILES
- MINIMUM 1 INCH (25.4mm)

WOOD OR WOOD DERIVATIVE
STRIPS

- STRIPS MAY BE STAGGERED
  OR FULL CORE SIZE
- STRIPS MAY RUN VERTICAL
  OR HORIZONTAL

LOCK BLOCKS
- REQUIRED
- MINIMUM LENGTH 20 INCHES
  (508mm)
- MID POINT OF LOCK BLOCK
  LOCATED AT MID POINT
  OF STILE
- WIDTH AS SPECIFIED IN 3.1.4

COMBINED THICKNESS OF EACH
FACE PANEL
- MINIMUM 1/10 INCH (2.54mm)

FACE VENEER

**Fig. 12   Ladder core (7-ply construction illustrated).**

TOP AND BOTTOM RAILS
- MINIMUM 2¼ INCHES (57.2mm)

WIDTH OF STILES
- MINIMUM 1 INCH (25.4mm)

WOOD OR WOOD DERIVATIVE
STRIPS
- PAPER HONEY COMB MATERIAL
  ILLUSTRATED

LOCK BLOCKS
- REQUIRED
- MINIMUM LENGTH 20 INCHES
  (508mm)
- MIDPOINT OF LOCK BLOCK
  LOCATED AT MIDPOINT OF
  STILE
- WIDTH AS SPECIFIED IN 3.1.4

COMBINED THICKNESS OF EACH
FACE PANEL
- MINIMUM 1/10 INCH (2.54mm)

FACE VENEER

**Fig. 13   Mesh or cellular core (7-ply construction illustrated).**

a.  **FLUSH CABINET DOORS. All WIC Grades.**

**TYPE "1"**
  Veneer / tape banding, 1/16″ maximum.

**TYPE "2"**
  Solid banding.

3 Ply Skin

**TYPE "3" — Medium Density Fiberboard.**
  Banding not required for **Economy and Custom Grades.**
  **Band required for Premium Grade.**

b.  **LIPPED CABINET DOORS.**

**TYPE "4"**
  Veneer / tape banding, 1/16″ maximum, required.

**TYPE "5"**
  Solid banding.

3 Ply Skin

**TYPE "6" — Medium Density Fiberboard.**
  Banding not required for **Economy and Custom Grades.**
  **Band required for Premium Grade.**

c.  **STILE AND RAIL CABINET DOORS. All WIC Grades.**
  TYPE "7", S4S Stop.

  TYPE "8", Solid Stuck.

  TYPE "9", Moulded Stop.

d.  The top and bottom edges of sliding doors do not require an edge band.

# STANDARD JOINERY AND CASEWORK DETAILS

Stile and Rail Joinery Details

**Fin. Ceiling**

2A Veneered Stile and Rail with Concealed Stile and Rail Edges and Panel Rim

B Solid Lumber Stile and Rail with Panel Products and Solid Rims

C Solid Stile and Rail with Lip Moulding and Panel Product with Solid Rim

D Medium Density Fibreboard (MDF) for both Stile and Rails and Panels

Mortise and Tenon Construction

Doweled Construction

3 Inside Corner

4 Outside Corner Splined Joint

4A Optional Outside Corner Lock Mitrers

**Fin. Floor**

1 Vertical Section

**Fig. 14  Full-height stile and rail raised paneling. Stile and rail wall paneling accented by raised panels creates a beautiful effect of traditional architectural woodwork. Framed within the stiles and rails and accented by the shadow lines, this construction offers limitless opportunities for various effects through the use of different wood species and veneer cuts. Each design creates a unique atmosphere complimented by the finely proportioned paneling.**

Elevation

1A) Solid Stile and Rail with Flat Panel Product

B) Solid Stile and Rail with Lip Moulding and Panel Product with Solid Rim

C) Panel Product Stile and Rail and Panel with Raised Moulding

Fin. Floor

2) Vertical Section

**Fig. 15** Flap paneled wainscot. Flat panels set within the frame of the stile and rail create a rich effect of traditional architectural woodwork. Different results can be produced through the use of veneer selections with transparent finish or painted finishes chosen by the architect or designer.

3A) Veneered Stile and Rails with Loose Mouldings, Flat Panel Product or Glass

B) Veneered Stile and Rails with Loose Moulding and Panel Product with Solid Rim

C) Veneered Stile and Rails with Solid Profile Moulding and Panel Products with Solid Rim

D) Solid Lumber Construction Throughout

**Fig. 16** Paneled doors. Stile and rail doors designed to accent the adjacent wall paneling whether traditional or contemporary, or used alone, beautify an entryway or area.

## STANDARD JOINERY AND CASEWORK DETAILS
**Raised Paneling**

Elevation

② Fin. Ceiling

② Top Rail

③ Mullion

④ Bottom Rail

Fin. Floor

⑥ Inside Corner

① Meeting Stiles

⑤ Jamb

⑦ Bottom Rail

**Fig. 17    Full-height contemporary raised paneling. This design, distinguished by its simplicity, is a contemporary expression of the stile and rail construction.**

## PROFILES OF STOCK STICKING FOR SASH & DOORS

SASH & FRENCH DOORS

PANEL DOORS

## STANDARD JOINERY AND CASEWORK DETAILS

**Double Hung Windows**

**Fig. 18   Double hung windows: stock designs. Standard widths are 1′6″, 2′0″, 2′6″, 3′0″, 3′6″, 4′0″, 4′6″, and 5′0″. Standard heights are 2′0″, 2′6″, 3′0″, 3′6″, 4′0″, 4′6″, 5′1″, 5′6″, and 6′0″. Standard thicknesses are 1⅜″ and 1¾″. Stock thickness is 1⅜″. Standard glazing is s.s.b. glass — not bedded.**

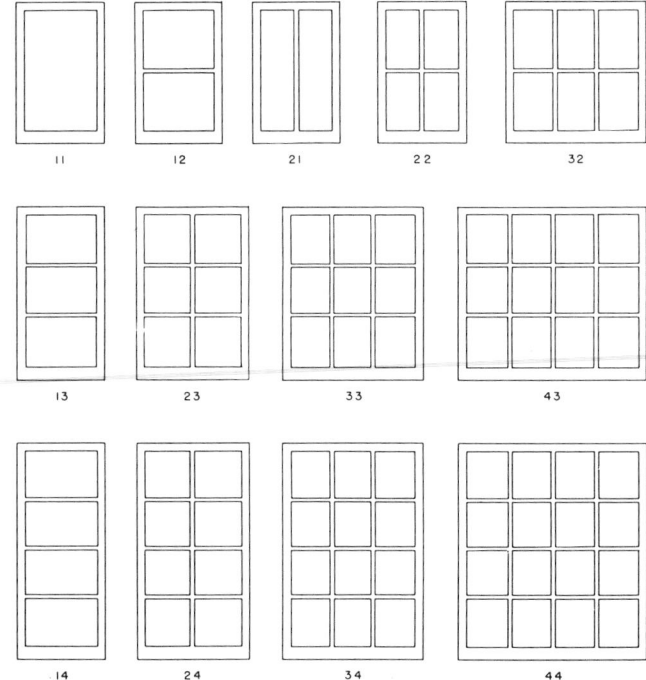

**Fig. 19   Single sash: stock designs. Standard widths are 2′0″, 2′6″, 3′0″, 3′6″, 4′0″, 4′6″, 5′0″, 5′6″ and 6′0″. Standard heights are 2′0″, 2′6″, 3′0″, 3′6″, 4′0″, 4′6″, 5′1″, 5′6″, 6′0″, 6′6″, and 7′0″. Standard thicknesses are 1⅜″ and 1¾″. Stock thickness is 1⅜″. Standard glazing is s.s.b. glass — not bedded.**

**Fig. 20** Casements in pairs: stock designs. Standard widths are 2′6″, 3′0″, 3′6″, 4′0″, 4′6″, and 5′0″. Standard heights are 2′0″, 2′6″, 3′0″, 3′6″, 4′0″, 4′6″, 5′1″, 5′6″, and 6′0″. Standard thicknesses are 1⅜″ and 1¾″. Stock thickness is 1⅜″. Standard glazing is s.s.b. glass — not bedded.

**Fig. 21** Windows and sash: typical diamond light cut-ups.

ELEVATION ·
/cale : ½" = 1'-0' ·

B — B
3" = 1'-0'

C — C
3" = 1'-0'

TYPICAL
PANEL
HEAD

DETAIL·ON·LINE·A–A

ELEVATION

PLAN·A·A

PLAN AT B

ELEVATION AT·D·    SECTION·C·C

# PANELED WAINSCOT

ELEVATION

PLAN AT·A·

Wood Mold

Plaster

Ceiling

Face of Plaster Wall

ELEVATION

PLAN

ELEVATION AT·B·    SECTION·C·C

# FRENCH PANELING

ELEVATION

Scale : ¾" - 1'-0"

PLAN

¾" - 1'-0"

fin plaster ceiling

"B" wood cornice

"B"

2⅛"

1¼"

10½"

Spring Line

2⅛"

9"

plaster back

"C"

9"

3'-4½"

"C"

9"

1'-11"
Opening

"A"

9"

2⅛"

plaster

wood

wood

wood
chair rail

7'-8½"

plaster

"A"

2'-10"

1'-6"

3"

4"

4"

5"

wood
base

fin floor

**E L E V A T I O N**
Scale  ¾" = 1'—0"

fin ceiling

**SEC "C-C"**

Note.
Scale of sections
equals one half
full size

**·SEC·"A-A"·**     **SEC·"B-B"·**

plaster back

¼" plate groove

Wood Shelves

4½" R.

6¾"

1'2" R

1¼" 1⅜" ¾" 2⅛"          1'-11"          2⅛" ¾" 1⅜" 1¼"

3'-3"

**P L A N**
¾" = 1'—0"

⅜" SCALE · ELEVATION · DOOR BACK ·
Showing · book shelving · and · secret
Door · to · a · silver closet ·

⅜" SCALE PLAN
of
BOOK SHELVES
& SECRET DOOR

· VERTICAL · SECTION ·   · ELEVATION ·
· THROUGH · DOOR ·    OF PILASTER
· Scale:   1½" = 1'-0"

· SECTION · ON · LINE · "A-A" · THRU · SHELVING ·
scale : 1½" = 1'-0"

· SECTION · ON · LINE · "B-B" · THRU · CUPBOARD ·
Scale: 1½" ~ 1'-0"

Framing & blocking

Cold rolled steel adjustable shelf supports. ¼" adjustment. Finish as desired.

2" 1⅜" 10"±

·SECTION·HEAD·&·SHELF·"A-A"·

Metal corner beads

Framing

Support clips snap into place in standard

·SECTION·THRU·JAMB·D-D·

Support standards

Framing

NOTE: Scale for details 1½"=1'-0". Scale for elevations ¼"=1'-0".

·SECTION·THRU·SILL·"A-A"·

Metal lath & plaster
Framing & blocking

2¼"

Keep span between vertical supports about 30", never more than 38". ¾" to ⅞" thick shelving. If spans are greater, increase thickness of shelving and vertical supports.

7" 10"± 8"

·SECTION·THRU·HEAD·C-C·

Veneered back

2¼"

Cabinet under book shelves.

Veneered panel

2¼"

Framing

8½"

Fin Flr

·SECTION·THRU·BASE·C-C·

BUILT-IN·BOOKCASES·BOTH·SIDES·OF·ROOM·DOORWAY·

4'-0"

3'-0"

Opening between rooms
Flr. Line

Variable

2'-9"

3'-0"

Floor line

·BUILT-IN·BOOKCASES·WITH·CABINETS·UNDERNEATH·

Small books, rarely used, at top

Area for books often used

Variable

2'-6"  ⅞"

Place large books, seldom used, at bottom

Flr. line

° BUILT-IN · BOOKCASE · BATTERY · FORMATION ·

Metal lath & plaster
Framing & blocking

In design of book cases, keep in mind type of books the shelves are to accommodate. For the home a 5½" to 10" shelf is sufficient. For the office, business, etc. having big books greater depth is required.

10"±

· SECTION · THRU · HEAD · D·D ·

Framing
Metal corner bead.

Veneered back

· SECTION · THRU · JAMB · E-E ·

The use of adjustable shelf supports is recommended

PLASTER WITH FAUX PAINTING

EXISTING PLYWOOD BULKHEAD

Fin. Flr.

Framing
Base

· SECTION · THRU · BASE · D-D ·

SECTION - BOOKCASE UNIT

ELEVATION

PLAN

SECTION

FULL SIZE SECTION ·B·      F.S. SECTION ·A·

## VERTICAL SECTION
## LIBRARY CABINETS

## VERTICAL SECTION-LIBRARY BOOKCASE

ELEVATION AT BAR

ELEVATION
AT PORTAL

VERTICAL SECTION AT BAR

ELEVATION AT BAR

① ELEVATION SPACE NO. 7
③ 1/2" = 1'-0"

④ @ 1½" = 1'-0"

⑤ @ 1/2 FULL SIZE

⑥ @ 3" = 1'-0"

Fig. 1   *(Continued)*

# WOODWORK DETAILS

**Storage Cabinets**

3/4" PLYWOOD
1/4" PLYWOOD

1/2" PLYWOOD

2'-4"

1⅛"

3/4" ADJUSTABLE SHELVING

DRAWER SLIDE

DOOR

1/2" PLYWOOD

3'-5"

2¾"

3"
4"

2¾"

3"
4"

3"
4"

4"

2½"

ASPHALT TILE

*Section* **A**   1½" SCALE

SHELVES AND DRAWERS

SHELVES

COATS

SHELVES

2'-4"

3/4" PLYWOOD

1⅛" DOORS

*Plan*
3/8" SCALE

*Section* **B**
3/8" SCALE

*Elevation*
3/8" SCALE

1/2" PLYWOOD PANELS

1/2" PLYWOOD SOFFIT

11'-10"

ADJUSTABLE SHELVES

DOORS NOT SHOWN

ADJUSTABLE SHELVES

A

POLE

B

ADJUSTABLE SHELVES 12" DEEP

1'-4"

DRAWERS

6'-8"

10'-0"

3/4" SUPPORTING PARTITIONS DOTTED

1⅛" TOP

SINK

2'-0"

3/4" DOOR

SECTION A·A     ELEVATION     SECTION B·B

DETAIL PLAN C     PLAN     DETAIL PLAN D     DETAIL SECTION

# WOODWORK DETAILS

**Bar Sink**

UPPER PLAN

BASE CABINET WIDTH OR WALL AS FAR
AS DOOR TRIM LESS THICKNESS OF
ROOM BASE.

EXISTING BAR
SINK RELOCATED

2'-0"

LOWER PLAN

ALIGN CAB'T. TOP & DOOR
TRIM

TRIM TO MATCH
THAT OF LIBRARY

BRIGHT CHROME NARROW
EDGE STANDARDS &
BRACKETS

FORMICA
SHELVES
ENTIRE

1'-0"     1'-0"

¼" POL. & GLASS
MIRROR

FORMICA

FORMICA

LINE OF DOOR TRIM
& FORMICA JUNCTION

STILES & RAILS SAME SIZE
FOREWARD OF DOOR TRIM

LINE OF DOOR TRIM

FORMICA

1'-5"

PANEL          6 DRAWER

ICE MAKER
AS SELECTED
BY OWNER

FILLER PIECE WIDTH OF BASE
TO MATCH CABINET BETWEEN
CAB'T & DOOR TRIM.

SHELF ADJ @ 1"

½" THICK FILLER PIECE
MATCHING FIN. OF TRIM &

THICKNESS OF DOOR TRIM

STILES (& RAILS) SAME
WIDTH ALL AROUND &
MEASURED HERE FOREWARD
OF DOOR TRIM

3'-2"

PR. DOORS          DOOR

13"

CLOSE-IN TOE SPACE
AT ENDS.

MATCH TO EXISTING
LIBRARY BASE

15⅛"
VERIFY

15⅞"
VERIFY

4"

ELEVATION

SIDE
ELEVATION

VERTICAL FIR
T/G BOARDS

GB
AD-15

GLASS SLIDING DOORS
ADJUSTABLE GLASS SHELVES

PLASTER

GC
AD-15

GA
AD-15

CARPET

2'-4"

5'-0"

9'-6"

2'-2"

## ELEVATION OF GIFT DISPLAY CASE

VERTICAL FIR
T/G BOARDS

STANDARDS

2'-7"

2 1/2"

2 1/2"

1/4" BULLETIN BOARD CORK
COLOR TO BE SELECTED
BY ARCHITECT

OAK

SLIDING GLASS DOORS

10'-0"

POLISH BRASS

1 1/2"    1/2"

VERTICAL FIR BOARDS

3'-0"

6'-0"

6'-4 1/2" R.B.O.

2 1/4"

C DISPLAY CASE

GA

1'-3"

¾" ¾"

PLASTER ON M.L.

¾" ¾"

10½"

¾" 2½"

2×3

6'-0" FLUORESCENT STRIP

½" × ½" PLASTIC LOUVER (WHITE)

1½"

1¾"

¾" ¾"

½"

9¼"

2½"

1"

REMOVABLE OAK STOP

SLIDING GLASS DOORS

10"

3/8" PLATE GLASS SHELVES POLISH EDGES

BULLETIN BOARD CORK COLOR TO BE SELECTED BY ARCHITECT

4'-9¾"

5'-0"

**613**

@ 3" = 1'-0"

2'-2"

½" × ½" PLASTIC LOUVER (WHITE)

4¼"

OAK FRAME

LOCK

1¾"

6'-0" FLUORESCENT STRIP

2×3

10¼"

¾" ¾"

2½"

¼"

1"

½"

2'-2"

2×3

**6C**

@ 3" = 1'-0"

CB
AD-15

SLIDING GLASS DOORS

ADJUSTABLE GLASS SHELVES

GD
AD-15

OAK
HANDRAIL

CE
AD-15

### ELEVATION OF GIFT DISPLAY CASE
### SPACE NO. 202
@ 1/4" = 1'-0"

STANDARDS
(4) REQD

2 1/2"

BULLETIN
BOARD CORK

1'-3"

PLASTER

3/4"

1/2"   1 3/4"   6'-4 1/2"

**6D**  @ 3"=1'-0"

1 1/2"   6'-9"

7'-0" M.O.

SLIDING
GLASS DOORS

LOCK

0'-0" FLUORESCENT LAMP

CASING
BEAD

(2X3)
2 1/2"

PLASTER ON MTL.

3/4"   10 1/4"   3/4"

3/4"

1'-3"

**6E**  @ 5"=1'-0"

**PLAN OF WALL-CABINET #1**

**ELEVATION OF WALL-CABINET #1**

**DETAILS OF WALL-CABINET #1 - HORIZONTAL TRANSITIONS & INTERSECTIONS. @ 3"=1'-0"**

Fig. 2

DETAIL OF FASCIA LIP — 1G

GLASS DOOR TRACK — 1D
@ FULL-SIZE

TYPICAL STILE @ HINGE END — 1E
@ 3"=1'-0"

VERTICAL SECTION — WALL-CABINET #1 — 1C
@ 3½"=1'-0"

Fig. 2   *(Continued)*

## WOODWORK DETAILS
**Work Counter**

Fig. 3   Countertop.

Fig. 4   Back counter.

**Fig. 5   Word processing counter.**

**Fig. 6   Cashier counter.**

**Fig. 7   Base and work counter.**

**Fig. 8   Walkup counter.**

SCRIBE TO WALL

PLASTIC LAM. INSET

POLISHED BRASS STRIP

SOLID WOOD
PAINT TO MATCH
PLAM

POLISHED BRASS PULLS.
TYDIX: ⌐ 5/8 × 2. (US3.)

PLASTIC LAMINATE DOORS. SEE
DOOR SCH. FOR HINGE TYPE
ALL PLASTIC LAMINATE
SURFACES TO BE PL-5

ADJUSTABLE PLASTIC LAMINATE
SHELF ON METAL PINS. PROVIDE
HOLES AT 1"O.C. SIDEWALLS
AS INDICATED.

PLASTIC LAMINATE
ON 3/4" PLYWOOD
ALL INT. SURFACES.

BLOCKING AS REQ'D.

ALIGN W/ ADJACENT DOORS

**3** CONF RM. CREDENZA @ RM. 45'B
A351A                                   NTS

ACOUSTICAL CLG. TILE

FULL HT DOOR.

2½" METAL STUDS SECURED
TO SLAB ABOVE

SHELF STANDARD @ 24"O.C.
SECURED TO METAL STUDS
KNAPE + VOGT Nº. 87.
SHELF BRACKET - KNAPE + VOGT Nº. 187

3/4" PLYWD. SHELF - ROUTE
SHELF AROUND STANDARD

NOTE: PROVIDE HORIZONTAL
BRAC'G FOR METAL STUDS.
1½" CR CHANNEL SECURED
TO STUDS TO ELIMINATE
HORIZONTAL MOVEMENT
OF METAL STUDS.

NOTE: SHELVES TO BE
FINISHED @ ALL FACES
AND EDGES W/ PLASTIC
LAMINATE AS PER SPEC.

**5** SHELF UNIT
A351A                          3/4"=1'-0"

FLATCUT
MAHOGANY VENEER ON
3/4" PLYWOOD (TYP.)

1/4" REVEAL
HOLD BACK

OPEN

2" ⌀ BRASS GROMMET

HARDWOOD EDGE

WOOD BLOCKING

2 × 6 WOOD ANCHOR BLOCK

**4** DET. SECTION THRU TELEPHONE COUNTER
A351A                     1½" = 1'-0"

(SEE PLAN)

MOUNT AS REQD

PLASTIC LAM FILE TOP
WITH 4 FINISHED EDGES

FILES BY OTHERS

**6** TYP. SECTION THRU FILE COUNTER TOP
A351A                                HALF SCALE

*THIS DWG. INDICATES BASIC PROFILE
ONLY. SEE SPECIFIC ELEVATIONS
FOR LENGTH, HEIGHT + DEPTH OF
CABINET WORK

CONTINUOUS ALUMINUM ⌐ AT WALL
BLOCK AS REQ'D.

2" ⌀ BRASS (PLASTIC) GROMMET

ALL SURFACES TO BE PLASTIC
LAMINATE

INTERMEDIATE AND/OR END PANEL
TO BE FLUSH W/ FACE OF TOP.

**12** TYP. COUNTER UNIT - TAX LIBRARY + LITIGATION CENTER
A351A                                                        NTS

TYP. FILE LIGHT
SEE DETAIL 2/A8-2
SWITCHED AT WALL

CLEAR LACQUER FIN.
BIRCH/PLYWOOD
ALL AROUND

PAINT REVEALS
(P-1)

COLOR LACQUER
TO MATCH P.1
OVERFILE
(5) SELBY
CONCEALED
SPRING
HINGE
T & B,
MAG. CATCH

ADJ. SHELF
ON PILASTER
STDS. 4 CLIPS

PAINTED FILLER

FILES (N.I.C.)
G.C. TO INSTALL,
BOLT & LEVEL
CABINETS.

¾" PLYWOOD SHIM
BASE CONT.

PAINT FIN.

OVERFILE

FIN. CLG.

VENEER PANEL (W-1)
TOP & SIDES

COLOR
LACQUER
TO MATCH
(P-1)

DET. 5.4

FOR
OVERFILES
CONST. SEE
DETAIL
12/A81

FILE END
PNL

FILES
(N.I.C.)

DETAIL

Fig. 9   Wall unit with overhead cabinets.

Fig. 10   Free-standing island unit.

1"∅ VENTS @ 6" O.C.

2' FLUOR. UNIT. TYPE "GC"

PAINT ALL SURFACES WHITE

½" x ½" PLASTIC LOUVER (WHITE)

¾" W.V.P. (OAK)

¾" x ¾" x ¼" L

¼" POL. PLATE GLASS

11¾"

10½" SHELF

½" POL. PLATE GLASS SHELF POLISHED EDGES

GARCY #Y78 BRACKETS GARCY #U378 STANDARDS SET FLUSH

¼" CORKBOARD (COLOR TO BE SELECTED BY ARCHITECT)

2' LONG LTG. UNIT TYPE "GC-1"

7½"

36¾" ACCESS PANEL

5¾"

6"

14"

8'-4"

33"

4'-0"

6¾"

2'-6"

FINISH FLOOR

① **LOBBY DISPLAY CABINET #1**
**VERTICAL SECTION @ 3"-1'-0"**

(E.O. TO BE VERIFIED ON JOB)

H.WD. TRIM

ACCESS PANEL

WD. TRIM

GLASS SHELF

11¾"

¾" W.V.P. (OAK)

VERTICAL CONDUIT

¾" W.V.P. WALL

1¼" 2¾" 3⅝" (VERIFY) 3⅝" 2⅛" ¾"

¼" QUARK

① **LOBBY DISPLAY CABINET #1**
**HORIZONTAL SECTION @ 3"-1'-0"**

GRANITE TOP, 1/8" BEVELED EDGE. (G-2)

2½" × 3½" × 3/8" STL. & VERT. SUPPORT SLAB TO SLAB @ 32" O.C.

BLACK
2" Ø GROMMET BY DOUG MOCKETT

1'-8¼"

WELDED CONNECTION

2½" × 3½" STL. &

PEARWOOD VENEER FINISH BOTH SIDES OF DOOR

ADJ. SHELF ON PLASTER STDS. BY CAROY

3'-0" (TYP.) ONLY
2'-0" (W.) 22½"

PROVIDE CUT-OUT FOR ELEC. & TEL. OUTLETS

CLEAR LACQUER FIN. BIRCH VENEER / PLYWOOD ALL AROUND TONE TO MATCH PEARWOOD. TOP & BOT. SELECT HINGES & MAG. CATCH

9"

# WALL HUNG
# CREDENZA

VENEER WD PANEL (W-1) ON ¼" CLIP SPACE

1" GRANITE, 1/8" BEVELED EDGE G-2

2½" × 3½" × 3/8" STEEL & VERTICAL @ 32" O.C., SLAB TO SLAB

¾"

V.I.F.

1/16"

4"

2'-6" A.F.F.

PROVIDE CLIP & FOR ATTACHMENT TO SLAB

¾" PLYWOOD SHIM TO LEVEL

2" × 2" STL. & WELDED TO VERT. CHANNEL

4"

# COUNTER TOP

EXISTING A.C. TILE

EXISTING W.V.P.

NEW PLANTER GUARD-RAIL CABINET

W.V.P.

EXISTING DOORS

EXISTING

14'-2"± (EXISTING)

4
A-19

EAST
3

BASEMENT LEVEL

## ENTRY FOYER

1'-6"

H.WD TRIM

3/4"

3/4"

8 3/4"

3/4" W.V.P.

PLANTER

3/4"

TOP OF EXIST'G. BALUSTRADE RAILING

PRESSURE-MAGNETIC CATCH

CENTER DIVIDER

3/4" W.V.P. DOOR PANEL

LOCK

3'-8"

29 3/4"

30 1/2" (VERIFY)

ADJUSTBLE SHELVING

EXISTING BALUSTRADE

2"x2" FURRING

3/4" W.V.P. (OAK)

STORAGE

3/4"

12"±

3/4"

3 3/4"

3/4"

ELEY. 15.2'

3/4"

3/4"

4"  BASE

4"

EXISTING STAIR LANDING

1"

(OAK) H.WD

## 4  SECTION THRU PLANTER-CABINET

**3B** ELEVATIONS OF BOOK & SHAWL CABINETS
@ 1/4"=1'-0"

**3C** PLAN OF BOOK & SHAWL CABINETS
@ 1/4"=1'-0"

**3D** TYPICAL STILE DETAIL
@ 3"=1'-0"   BOOK & SHAWL CABINETS

Fig. 11

Fig. 11 *(Continued)*

ELEVATION OF STORAGE
CLOSETS 4'-0" OR LESS IN LENGTH
@ 1/4" = 1'-0"

ELEVATION OF STORAGE
CLOSETS OVER 4'-0" IN LENGTH
@ 1/4" = 1'-0"

ELEVATION OF UNIT
@ 1/4" = 1'-0"

ELEVATION OF UNIT
@ 1/4" = 1'-0"

**7** NORTH ELEVATION SPACE Nº 19
@ ½" = 1'-0"

**4** @ 3" = 1'-0"

BIRCH NATURAL LACQUER FINISH

HARDWOOD VENEER PLYWOOD
SCRIBE TO WALL

1" x 1" x ⅛" ALUMINUM "F"

BIRCH NATURAL
LACQUER FINISH

2½" WIDE
PULLS POLISHED
CHROME U.S. 26 FINISH

DRAWERS
ON GRANT
#329 FULL
EXTENSION
DRAWER
SLIDES

LACQUER
FINISH COLOR
TO BE SELECTED
BY DESIGNER

FILE DRAWER

**5** @ 3" = 1'-0"

HARDWOOD VENEER PLYWOOD
SCRIBE TO WALL

1" x 1" x ⅛" ALUMINUM ANGLE "F"

**6** @ 3" = 1'-0"

ALUMINUM
PENDAFLEX
BARS

DRAWER
SIDES

**7** @ FULL SIZE

**Fig. 12   Credenza.**

PLASTIC LAM.
COUNTER TOP

METAL FILE
CABINETS BY OTHERS

FILLER          FILLER

CW G

4 FILES @ 3'-0" = 12'-0"

**4** NORTH ELEVATION SPACE No. 16
@ ½" = 1'-0"

SCRIBE TO WALL

TEAK PLASTIC LAM.

BACK PLASTIC LAM.
½" x ½" HARDWOOD FILLER

METAL FILE CABINET

**9** @ 3" = 1'-0"

METAL FILE CABINET
WOOD BLKG.

HARDWOOD VENEER PLYWD
SHOP PRIMED FOR
PAINTING IN FIELD

DIM. VARIES
SEE ELEVATION
SCRIBE TO WALL

**10** @ ½ FULL SIZE

**Fig. 13   File countertop.**

**NOTES:**

1. STEEL DRAWERS SHALL HAVE GRANT 338 FULL EXTENSION DRAWER SLIDES

2. FILE DRAWER SHALL HAVE GRANT 329 FULL EXTENSION DRAWER SLIDES

ALL PLASTIC LAMINATE FOR THESE ITEMS TO BE: PARKWOOD #51202E INDIA TEAK

ALL INTERIORS TO HAVE NATURAL LACQUER FINISH

FIN. CLG. @ 8'-0"

PLAS LAM.
(L-1)

1 ADJ SHELF
CLEAR LACQUER
BIRCH PLYWOOD PILASTER
STDS.

P. LAMINATE
(L-1)

UNDERCABINET
LIGHT SWITCHED
@ WALL

1'-2"

1'-6"

P LAMINATE (L-1)

1 1/4"

1'-11 3/4"

CLEAR LACQUER
BIRCH PLYWOOD
ON PILASTER STDS

2'-8"

CONCEALED
SELF
HINGES
T & B,
MAG. CATCH

CERAMIC TILE
@ TILE FLOOR
OR VINYL BASE
@ VCT FLOOR.

NOTE: SEE 9/AB-1 FOR
CABINET WITH DRAWER

MAHOGANY
LOOSE FILLER

1'-1"

BEVELED CLEAT
FIXED TO CABINET

ADJUSTABLE
SHELVES

2'-2"

2'-1 1/2"

SLIP JOINT ON
RIGHT OF
EXPANSION JOINT

BEVELED
CLEAT FIXED
TO WALL

SLIP JOINT
RIGHT OF
EXPANSION
JOINT

SLIP JOINT
RIGHT OF
EXPANSION
JOINT

HPDL COUNTER TOP

HPDL WITH
MAHOGANY
TRIM

(2) 3/4" ADJUSTABLE
SHELVES W/
HARDWOOD EDGE

1'-9 3/4"

1'-8 1/2"

SLIP JOINT
RIGHT OF
EXPANSION JOINT

PLAIN SAWN
HONDURAS
MAHOGANY
LOOSE BASE

3/4" 1/4" 1'-8" 3" 2" 3/4" 1/4"

2'-0"

# PANTRY CABINETS

# VERTICAL SECTION-PANTRY CABINETS

Pulpit
3′9″ High x 3′6″ Wide x 1′8½″ D

Table
2′7″ High x 5′0″ Long x 2′ D

Center Pulpit Chair
4′ High x 2′2½″ Wide x 1′10″ D

Side Pulpit Chair
3′9″ High x 2′2½″ Wide x 1′10″ D

Communion Chair
3′4″ High x 1′8½″ Wide x 1′7½″ D

Flower Stand
2′6″ High x 1′3″ Square

Pulpit
4′0″ High x 3′6″ Wide x 1′8″ D

Table
2′9″ High x 6′0″ Long x 2′0″ D

Flower Stand
2′0″ High x 1′2″ Square

Pulpit
3′9″ High x 3′4″ Wide x 1′8″ D

Table
2′9″ High x 6′0″ Long x 2′0″ D

Flower Stand
2′0″ High x 1′2″ Square

Clergy Pew End

Pulpit
4′0″ High x 3′8″ Wide x 1′9″ D

Table
2′9″ High x 4′6″ Long x 2′0″ D

Flower Stand
2′0″ High x 1′2″ Square

Clergy Pew End

**Fig. 15** Fully upholstered seat. All exposed surfaces of the seat and back are fully upholstered.

**Fig. 16** Combination upholstered/wood seat. An upholstered seat with a wooden back (either solid or veneer laminate).

**Fig. 17** All wood seat. Either solid wood or veneered seat and back. Generally the most expensive option. Wood seats and back can be contoured for increased comfort.

**Cup holder**

**Card and pencil holder**

**Wood, with bonded foam, upholstered pad**

**Metal, with bonded foam, upholstered pad**

**Fig. 18** Pew accessories.

**Fig. 19** Screens are adaptable for many uses in the sanctuary. They serve as modesty screens in front of the first row of pews, or they can be adapted for use as communion rails, as choir boxes, or as wainscoating.

## WOODWORK DETAILS
Sanctuary Doors and Miscellaneous Details

SECTIONS-SANCTUARY DOORS

ELEVATION - SANCTUARY DOORS

PLAN AT INTERSECTION
OF CHANCEL RAIL AND COLUMN

SECTION
AT SANCTUARY COLUMN

SECTION
AT WAINSCOAT

TREFOIL LAYOUT

¾" R

¾"

SOLID OAK

¾" OAK VENEERED PLYWOOD

1½" RADIUS

3"

¾" PLYWOOD

FINISHED OAK FACE

② FULL SIZE SECTION THRU BIMAH TOP

4'-0"

② OAK TOP TO BE ADJUSTABLE WITH TILT & HOLD MECHANISM

3" DIAM. BULLNOSE

DARK STAINED OAK

CYLINDER LOCK

9"   2'-6"   9"

BRASS PULLS "EPCO" OR EQUAL

OAK DOORS

ADJ. 1" SHELF WITH SOLID NOSING

CONCEALED INSET HINGE TOP & BOTTOM

WEIGHTED BASE FOR STABILITY

LEVELER

4" HIGH, 3" RECESSED BASE, DARK OAK STAIN

④ FRONT ELEVATION (EAST SIDE)
SCALE: 1½" = 1'-0"

③

2'-6"

FINISHED, SOLID OAK EDGE

OAK TOP

PROVIDE & INSTALL BRASS ADJUSTING HARDWARE TO TILT & HOLD TOP FROM 0° (HORIZONTAL POSITION) TO 15°

5"   3"

6"   1'-6"   6"

④

OAK ADJUSTABLE SHELF

2'-6"   3'-6"

4'-0"

LINE OF CABINET BELOW TOP

1½"   2'-3"   1½"

CARPET

3"

4"

② ②

① PLAN OF BIMAH TOP
SCALE: 1½" = 1'-0"

③ SIDE ELEVATION (SOUTH SIDE)
SCALE: 1½" = 1'-0"

843

**ELEVATION FRONT VIEW** ⑤

STYLED FOR HINGE MOUNTING BEYOND BRACE AS REQ'D.

HARDWARE ; " BALDWIN BRASS No 4929, 4932, USE BACK PLATES 4735, 4737 OR EQ.

MENU POCKET/HOLDER

NOTE; PANEL MOULDINGS SHOULD ALIGN TO EACH OTHER, SEE NOTE ①

2'x¾" HARDWOOD BASE (ALL EDGES MITRED.)

**ELEVATION SIDE** ②

DYKES O.G. MOULDING No 142, TYP.

ALL EXTERNAL CORNERS TO BE MITRED. ALL JOINTS TO BE GLUED

¾" HALF ROUND W/ROUNDED EDGES

3" FRONT DRAWER TO OPERATE ON SIDE MOUNTED METAL TRACKS, GRANT, OR EQ.

2"x2" BLOCKING

(4) 4" SOLID WOOD BRACKET TO BE GLUED & NAILED

NOTE; PROVIDE HOLES FOR TELEPHONE & ELECTRICAL WIRES AS NECESSARY.

2"x8" BLOCKING

1¼" BLOCKING

**SECTION** ③

**ELEVATION BACK VIEW** ①

WIRE FOR PHONE ON THIS SIDE.

CABINET TOP TO HAVE VENEERED EDGES.

LOCATE DRAWER PULLS SYM. ABOUT HORIZONTAL C.L's.

1'-11½" DRAWER (MAINTAIN ⅛" CLEARANCE ON SIDES) TYP. MOULDING DETAIL, AS PER. CABINET DET. ⑦

2¾" X4" BUILT UP WOOD BRACKET TYP.

① NOTE; TOP OF DOOR DOES NOT ALIGN TO PANEL MOULDING

1¼" TYP.

DOOR PULLS AE; "BALDWIN BRASS No. 4929, 4932, USE BACK PLATES 4735, 4737.

LOCATE DRAWER PULLS SYM. ABOUT HORIZONTAL C.L.

2⅝" "SCALLOP" MOULDING DYKES #344 OR EQ. TYP.

(4) ¼" X3¾" LATTICE MATERIALS FOR PLATE BETWEEN BRACKET & PLASTER

½" REVEL, TYP.

## SECTION VIEW THRU LECTERN STANDS

## PLAN VIEW OF LECTERN STANDS

## CROSS SECTION @ PODIUM

## PLAN SECTION

1/8" · 2'-8" · 1/8"

20/F4-2

19 / F4-2

18 / F4-2

1/8" 3"     3" 1/8"

1/8" 2 DIM 'B' SEE

17 / F4-2 — LECTURN PLAN

2'-8"

EQ   EQ   EQ

DIM 'B'

WD.2

WD.1

WD.1

EQ 'B'

4'-0"

6"

18 / F4-2 — FRONT VIEW

EQ 'B'   EQ 'B'

WD.2

WD.1

W.1

EQ 'B'

6"

19 / F4-2 — M.317 SIDE VIEW

6/F4-3   3" 4½"

PLASTIC GROMMETS

ADJ. SHELF

POLISHED BRONZE BAR

CASTERS

1"  2½"

1"  4"  2"  3"  3"

4'-0"

7½"

20 / F4-2 — M.317 SECTION

## VERTICAL SECTION- BOARDROOM TABLE

## SECTION

FIXED PANEL

SLOT FOR WIRE WAY

VOICE ACTIVATED MICROPHONE

MAHOGANY TOP

MAHOGANY BULLNOSE

1/8" @ 3/16" THICK TUBING OUTRIGGER

#14 FLAT HEAD WOOD SCREWS

1/4" PARTICLEBOARD PAINT BLACK

REMOVABLE PANEL ON LOCKING BLOCKS

MAHOGANY

SLOT FOR WIRE WAY

LOOSE BASE & REMOVABLE PANEL ABOVE

CARPET

FLOOR BLOCKING

## CROSS SECTION AT BOARDROOM TABLE

PARTIAL PLAN
OF BENCH

SECTION
D-D

TYPICAL SECTION
THRU REAR BENCH

SEAT AND BACK SUPPORT

SECTION THRU JUDGES BENCH

SCREEN · ABOVE · SEAT

BALUSTER

SOLID 8½"
CEILING BEAM
ADZED
PLAS CEILING
CHAMFERED
ELEV.

MOULDED · BOARDING · SEAT · BACK
BOARD NOT ADZED

BALUSTER
SCALE 1½" = 1'0"
TURNED

CHAMFERED
APPROX LINE OF POST FROM SCREEN
OUTLINE OF SEAT ENDS
SEAT BACK SLOPED
CEILING BEAM
SECTION 8½
SOLID
CHAMFERED
PROFILE OF POST ONE PIECE
POST
SCALE 1½" = 1'0"
FACE OF POST
CHAMFERED
WOOD BASE

FRONT VIEW
OUTLINE OF SEAT ENDS

SEC TREAD NOSING
SEAT SLOPE
SEC · THRU · SEAT
SEAT END SIDE VIEW
END OF SCREEN
SCALE 3" = 1'0"
SEAT · END
FRONT VIEW
FINISH FLOOR

**DETAIL · OF · STAIR · SCREEN · & · SEAT · MAIN · HALL ·**

Line of window stool.

·PART·PLAN·OF·WINDOW·SEAT·
·Scale ⅜"=1'-0"·

Provide flush lifts to raise seat cover.

Corner line of plaster

Wall

Furring

Plaster

SECTION·THRU·CORNER·"B-B"·
·Scale 3"=1'-0"·

Base

Return of seat.
1'-2"

End Panel

Seat cover may be designed as a continuous top member, hinged at back.

Pitch seat back as shown.

Pitch seat 1" towards rear.

Block to hold removable seat panels, which act as covers for storage compartment under seat.

If compartment is not desired eliminate lining, detail seat in one piece and eliminate panel rests.

Supports across at panel points and both ends.

Line of window stool.

Panel back

Seat line

Panel

Base

·PARTIAL·ELEVATION·OF·WINDOW·
·SEAT·  ·Scale ¾"=1'-0"·

Rough frame

5 ply veneered panel.

Fin. Floor line

SECTION·THRU·WINDOW·SEAT·ON·"A-A"· Scale 3"=1'-0"

Exterior wall line

Furring

Plaster

Rough frame

⅞" lining

Line of Finished Floor.

Line of sub-floor.

PLAN OF
RAIL AND GATE

ELEVATION OF
RAIL AND GATE

SECTION
A - A

SECTION
B - B

SECTION
C - C

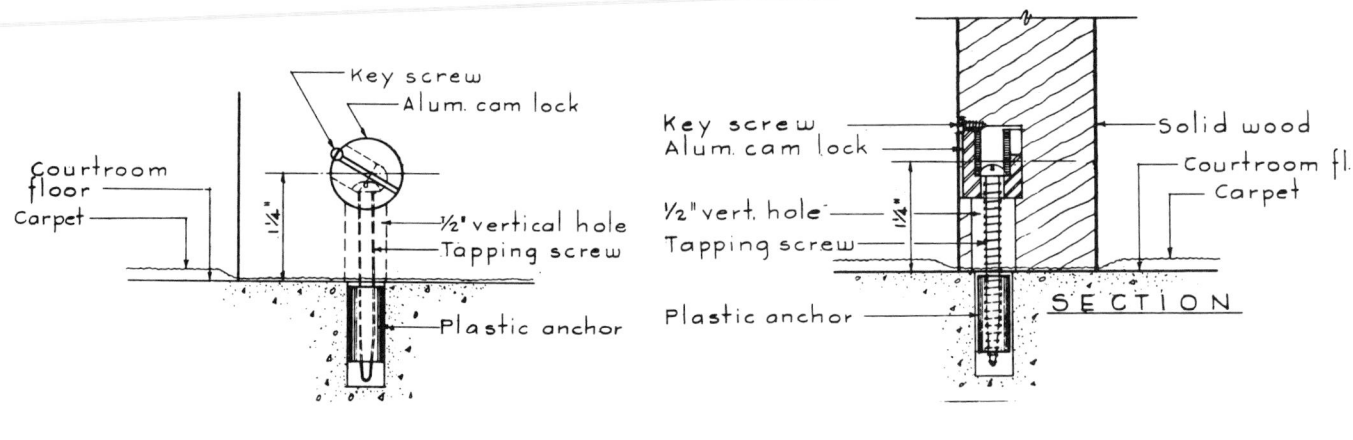

ELEVATION

CAM LOCK ASSEMBLY

SECTION

DETAIL-HIDDEN DOOR

HEAD DETAIL

DETAIL-HIDDEN PASS THROUGH DOOR

DETAIL

ELEVATION–FRONT ENTRY

JAMB DETAIL AT ENTRY

ELEVATION OF SPECIAL DOOR

SECTION "A" TYPICAL DOORS

JAMB DETAIL AND DOOR DETAIL

SECTION

SECTION

SECTION

## CREDENZA

## VERTICAL SECTION AT TELLERS COUNTER

## VERTICAL SECTION-RECEPTION DESK

**TYPICAL TRIM AND CORNICE**

Wood Crown Moulding 3/4" x 5 1/2"

Woodbeaded Edge Back Band 3/4" x 3 1/2"

3/4" Mahogany

3/4" Panel Mould

1/2" Plywood

3/4" Mahogany

1/8" Lauan Panel

Chair Rail 1 x 2 1/2"

Toe Moulding 3/16" x 1"

**SECTION-TYPICAL CEILING MOULDINGS**

Blocking

Solid Mahogany Crown

Wall

**SECTION AT ENTABLATURE**

Structural Framing & Plywood Cladding

Light Fixtures and Grille for Light Fixture

27'-5" Above Finished Floor

21'-2" Above Finished Floor

4'-1" Projection from Base to Finish Wall

**PANELING**

FIN: PLASTER CEILING

BLOCKING

2"X 4" STUDS
16" O.C.

5 7/8"

SECTION THRU
CORNICE

FURRING

SECTION
THRU PANEL
MOULD

SECTION
THRU CHAIR
RAIL

FURRING

PLASTER

FIN FL.

FIN ROUGH FLOOR

SECTION THRU BASE

## DETAIL OF WOOD CORNICE AND PANELING

PLASTER

FINISH PLASTER CEILING

$3\frac{1}{8}$"

$3\frac{7}{8}$"

5"

BLOCKING

$12\frac{3}{4}$"

ELEVATION OF CORNICE

$3\frac{3}{4}$"

$\frac{7}{8}$"

$\frac{7}{8}$"

$\frac{5}{8}$"

FACE OF
BOARDING

ROUGH STUD

PLASTER

BOARDING VARIED WIDTHS

WALL
SECTION

MATERIAL - KNOTTY PINE
STAINED, SHELLACED & WAXED

$1\frac{3}{4}$"

·SECTION OF BOARD·MOULD·

FINISH WOOD FLOOR

·DETAIL·OF·WOOD·WALL·&·CORNICE·LIBRARY·

## DETAIL-FIREPLACE MANTEL

## DETAIL AT COLUMN CAPITAL

## DETAILS AT COLUMN

·SECTION· ·B· ·ONE HALF INCH ELEVATION·

CORNICE

ROSS RAIL

DOOR

FUEL SHAFT

BASE

·SECTION ·B·
$\frac{1}{4}$ FULL SIZE·
MATERIAL—KNOTTY PINE
STAINED AND WAXED·

HEAD

SHELVES

BOOKCASE

DIV. BAR

FUEL SHAFT

FACE OF BRICK

SLATE FACING

DOOR

PLAN ·A·
$\frac{1}{4}$ FULL SIZE

MATERIAL—WALLS AND RAILING KNOTTY PINE STAINED WALNUT CRYSTALS LIGHT FINISH WAXED FLOOR AND STAIR OAK

·¾"SCALE·ELEVATION·

MOULD POST & BEAM

HAND RAIL

BALUSTER
SCALE 1½"·1'0"

CORNICE
SCALE 3"·1'0"

PANEL MOULD

UPPER NEWEL

HANDRAIL REMOVABLE ON PLATFORM

HANDRAIL

FACE OF PANEL

SCALE 3"·1'0"
FRONT VIEW 5"
SIDE VIEW 4"

OUTER·STRING  STAIR·
BALUSTER
TREAD

BASE  LOWER NEWEL

## SHOWCASE SECTION

REMOVABLE TRAYS

ADJ. SHELVES

## VERTICAL SECTION-DISPLAY CASE

SATIN STAINLESS STEEL FRAME

LIGHT

3/8" GLASS

SATIN CHROME

SATIN CHROME

SHELF SIZE

1/4" ADJUSTABLE SHELF

INTERIOR OF CABINET
PAINTED TO MATCH
EXTERIOR SEMI-GLOSS BLACK

MARBLE

BALLAST

## VERTICAL SECTION
## JEWELRY CASE

1/4" PLEXIGLASS
MIRROR

1/4" GLASS
MIRROR

APPLIED
3 x 1 5/8
MOULDING

BALLAST

## PLAN SECTION JEWELRY CASE

PAINT TO
MATCH HPDL

VERTICAL SECTION
AT DISPLAY CASE

TYPICAL VERTICAL SECTION
AT WALL UNIT

VERTICAL SECTION
SHIRT DISPLAY

SECTION AT BAR

VERT. SECTION AT BAR
& OVERHEAD CABINETS

SECTION AT BACK BAR

# FINISHING MATERIALS

| GENERIC TYPE | RECOMMENDED USAGE | CHARACTERISTICS |
|---|---|---|
| **System #1**<br>Lacquers | For all wood surfaces except medium to heavy acid areas; Interior use. | Good coverage; Easy to apply; Sands easy; Poor water resistance. |
| Catalyzed Lacquers | For wood surfaces requiring medium acid resistance; Interior use. | Tough wearing surface; Good water resistance; Can be repaired. |
| **System #2**<br>Varnishes | For all wood surfaces; Interior use; Exterior use — spar varnishes. | Good build; Tends to amber with age; Slow drying. |
| Conversion Varnishes | For all wood surfaces; Some acid resistance; Interior use. | Good build and solids; Can be repaired. |
| **System #3**<br>Polyurethane | For all wood surfaces; Interior use. | Tough surface; Excellent wear and abrasion resistance; Can be repaired. |
| Catalyzed Polyurethane | For all wood surfaces; High acid resistance; Interior use. | Tough surface; Excellent wear and abrasion resistance; Can be repaired. |
| **System #4**<br>Epoxy | For all wood surfaces; High acid resistance; Interior use. | Very hard surface; Excellent wear and abrasion resistance; Limited pot life; High water resistance. |
| **System #5**<br>Penetrating Oils | For all wood surfaces; Performs well on Oak, Teak, Walnut, etc. | Easy to apply; Makes touch-up easy; Average wear and abrasion qualities; Easy to repair. |
| **System #6**<br>Synthetic Enamels | Most wood and wood product surfaces; Interior use; Most colors available. | Good coverage; Tough wearing; Can be re-coated or repaired; Easy to apply. |
| **System #7**<br>Vinyl Lacquer | For all wood products; Interior use; Light acid resistance. | Tough surface; Good wearing; Resists light chemicals. |
| Catalyzed Vinyl | For all wood products; Interior use; Excellent for residential kitchens, etc.; Better acid resistance. | Tough surface; Good wearing; Repairs not easy. |
| **System #8**<br>Fire Retardant Coatings (Intumescent) | For surfaces of wood products requiring flame spread protection. (See WIC Technical Bulletin No. 423 — Section 19.) Interior use only.<br>UL Rated-UL-723; NFPA-255; and ASTM E-84; Tested for flame spread, fuel contributed, and smoke developed. | Leaching will result if exposed directly to high humidity or direct water. Can be coated with compatible overcoat system or waterproofing materials. Available for transparent and opaque finishes. |

# CORNICES AND MOULDINGS
### Deep Sculpt and Crown Mouldings

**Deep Sculpt Mouldings**

**Crown Mouldings**

# CORNICES AND MOULDINGS

**Crown Mouldings**

# CORNICES AND MOULDINGS

Miscellaneous Mouldings

### Chair Rail Mouldings

### Picture/Mirror Hanging Mouldings

### Door Trim Moulding

### Panel and Trim Mouldings

CWS1134  11/16 x 3 1/4
CWS1115  11/16 x 2 3/4
CWS1114  9/16 x 2 5/8
CWC1113  9/16 x 2 1/2
CWS1111  9/16 x 2 1/4
CWS1112  9/16 x 2 1/4

CWS1110  9/16 x 1 5/8
CWC1116  9/16 x 3 1/2
CWC1142  11/16 x 5 1/4
CWS1140  11/16 x 4 5/8
CWS1138  11/16 x 4 1/4
CWS1136  11/16 x 3 5/8
CWC1132  2 1/2 x 11/16

CWC 1426  1 1/16 x 2 1/2
CWC 1434  1 5/8 x 1 1/8
CWC 1414  1 5/8 x 11/16
CWC 1402  1 3/8 x 5/8

Solid Crowns

## CORNICES AND MOULDINGS
**Crown Mouldings**

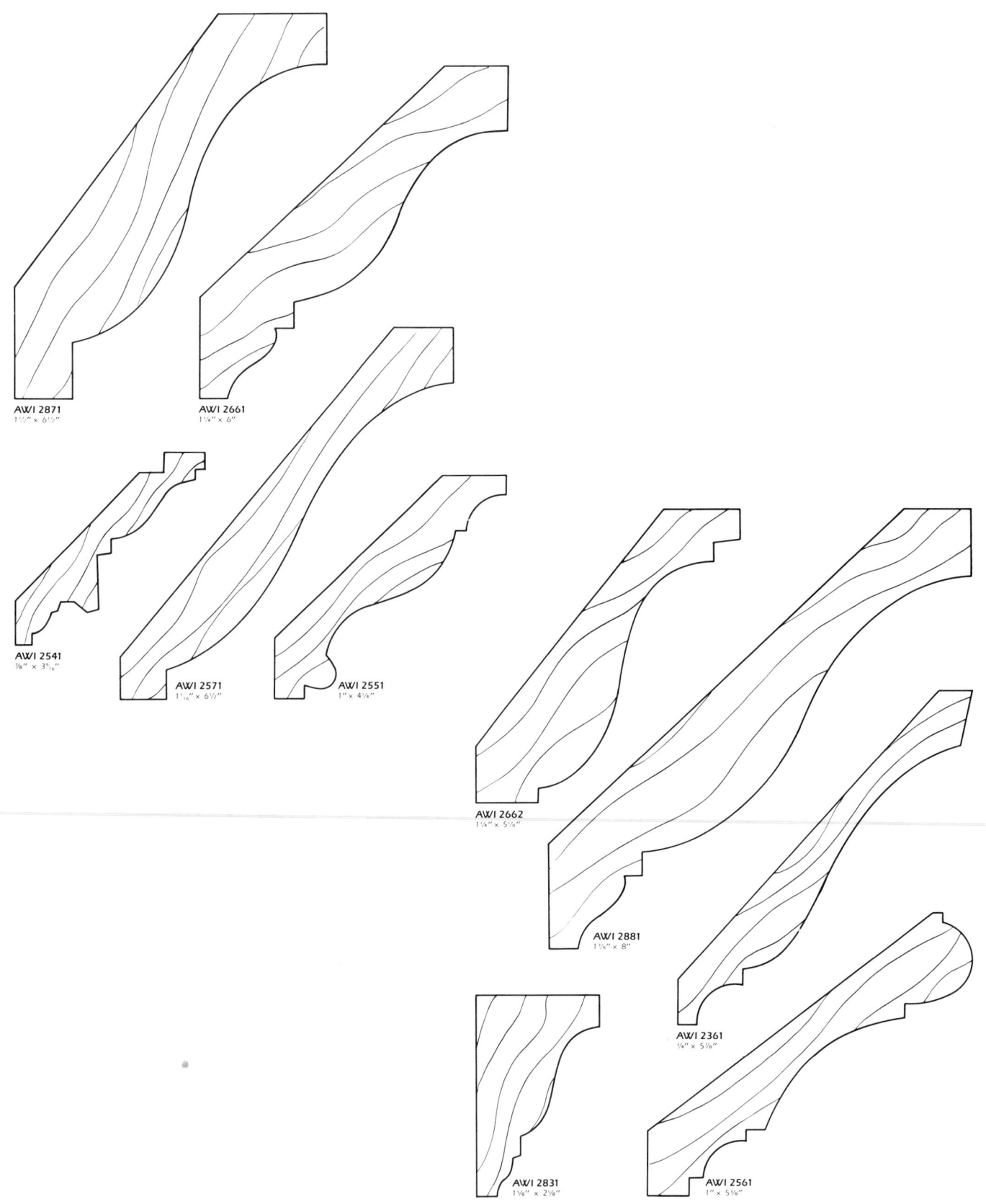

AWI 2871
1½" × 6½"

AWI 2661
1¼" × 6"

AWI 2541
⅞" × 3⁵⁄₁₆"

AWI 2571
1¹⁄₁₆" × 6½"

AWI 2551
1" × 4¼"

AWI 2662
1¼" × 5⅛"

AWI 2881
1⅛" × 8"

AWI 2361
¼" × 5⅞"

AWI 2831
1⅛" × 2⅛"

AWI 2561
1" × 5⅛"

AWI 5821
1 5/8″ × 1 3/4″

AWI 5832
1 5/8″ × 2 3/8″

AWI 5822
1 3/8″ × 1 5/8″

11/16 x 1 3/4

11/16 x 1 3/4

11/16 x 1 3/8

**Picture Moulds**

AWI 5522
1 1/16″ × 2″

AWI 5831
1 7/16″ × 2 1/2″

AWI 5521
1″ × 2″

**Picture Mouldings**

11/16 x 2 1/16

11/16 x 1 3/8

**Picture Frame**

AWI 11421
3/4″ × 1 1/8″

AWI 11521
1 1/16″ × 1 1/2″

AWI 11522
3/8″ × 1 11/16″

7/8 x 1 7/8

11/16 x 1 5/8

AWI 11631
1 1/4″ × 2 3/16″

AWI 11831
1 7/16″ × 2 5/8″

AWI 11941
2 3/8″ × 4″

**Back Bands**

1 1/8 x 2 1/4

1 x 2 1/2

**Step Moulds**

873

# CORNICES AND MOULDINGS

**Miscellaneous Mouldings**

1 1/8 x 5 1/2 & 1 1/8 x 7 1/2

Pilaster

3/16 x 1 3/4

Tongue and Groove Siding

11/16 x 1 3/4

Fluted Pilaster

1 5/16 x 2

1 5/8 x 1 1/2

1 1/8 x 1 1/4

1 1/4 x 2

1 1/2 x 2

1 11/16 x 1 7/8

1 1/16 x 2

1 3/32 x 2

2 1/4 x 1 1/2

1 7/8 x 2

**Brick Moulds**

1 5/8 x 1 1/16          11/16 x 1 5/8

Drip Caps

3/8  1 1/2

3/8 x 2

3/8 x 2

3/8 x 1 3/4

**Mullion Centers**

5/8 x 3/4      3/8 x 1/2

**Nosings**

3/4 x 1 3/4

5/8 x 1 3/4

**Sash Stops**

1 x 1      3/4 x 3/4

**Skew Back**

7/16 x 3/4    9/16 x 1/2    3/8 x 3/8

**Sash Beads**

1/4 x 3/4    1/4 x 5/8

**Shelf Edge**

1/4 x 3/4

**Screen**

3/4 x 7/16

11/16 x 1 3/8

11/16 x 1 3/4

3/8 x 1 3/8

3/8 x 1 5/8

**Astragals**

3/8 x 1

9/32 x 1 3/8

9/16 x 1 1/8

11/16 x 1 5/8

**Panel Mouldings**

1 5/16 x 2 3/8

**"T" Astragal**

5/8 x 1 1/8

**Sanitary Cap**

15/16

1 1/8

7/8

3/4

1/2 x 1 1/8

**Back Band**

1 1/4x2 1/2

15/16

1 1/8

7/8

1/2 x 3/4

**Parting Strip**

**Cornerguards**

# CORNICES AND MOULDINGS

**Base Mouldings**

11/16 x 4 1/4    11/16 x 3 1/2    11/16 x 2 1/2    11/16 x 3 1/2    9/16 x 3 1/2    9/16 x 3 1/4    7/16 x 3    1/2 x 3    11/16 x 2 1/2    1/2 x 2 1/4    7/16 x 2 1/4

9/16 x 3 1/2    11/16 x 3 1/2    9/16 x 3 1/4    1/2 x 3    7/16 x 3    9/16 x 2 1/4    7/16 x 2 1/4

9/16 x 5 1/4    9/16 x 4 1/4

1 1/8 x 1 1/8    7/8 x 7/8    3/4 x 3/4    11/16 x 11/16    5/8 x 5/8

**Quarter Round Moulds**

1/2 x 3/4    7/16 x 3/4    7/16 x 11/16    1/2 x 3/4    1/2 x 1/2    3/8 x 3/8    1/4 x 1/4

**Base Shoe & Floor Moulds**

AWI 1861
1½" × 5⅞"

AWI 1561
1" × 6"

AWI 1661
1¼" × 6"

AWI 1461
¼" × 6"

AWI 1441
¼" × 4"

AWI 1451
¾" × 4½"

AWI 1551
1" × 4⅛"

AWI 1552
1" × 5"

AWI 6421
¾" × 1⅝"

AWI 6422
¾" × 1⅜"

AWI 6521
⅞" × 1⅛"

AWI 6531
1" × 2¼"

AWI 1341
¾" × 3½"

AWI 1342
1" × 3½"

AWI 1343
1" × 3½"

AWI 1344
1" × 3½"

11/4 x 2

3/4 x 11/2

11/16 x 13/8

11/16 x 11/4

11/16 x 11/8

5/8 x 3/4

3/4 x 17/8

3/4 x 19/16

11/16 x 15/8

5/8 x 13/8

11/16 x 13/8

11/16 x 11/8

5/8 x 11/4

**Base Cap Moulds**

# CORNICES AND MOULDINGS

**Casings**

11/16 x 2 1/4

5/8 x 2 1/4

11/16 x 2 1/4

5/8 x 2 3/8

11/16 x 2 1/2

9/16 x 2 1/4

3/4 x 2 1/2

5/8 x 2 1/4

11/16 x 2 1/2

11/16 x 2 1/4

11/16 x 2 5/8

11/16 x 2 1/4

11/16 x 3 1/2

11/16 x 2 1/2

11/16 x 3 1/2

11/16 x 2 1/2

5/8 x 3 1/4

1/2 x 3 1/4

9/16 x 3 1/4

9/16 x 3 1/4

11/16 x 3 1/2

11/16 x 2 1/4

11/16 x 2 1/4

11/16 x 2 3/8

11/16 x 2 1/2

11/16 x 2 5/8

AWI 4551
1 1/16" × 4 1/8"

AWI 4552
1" × 4 9/16"

AWI 4661
1 3/4" × 5 3/16"

AWI 4662
1 1/4" × 5 1/8"

AWI 4861
1 3/8" × 5 9/16"

AWI 4641
1 3/8" × 3 1/2"

AWI 4531
1" × 3"

AWI 4532
1" × 2 1/4"

AWI 4851
1 3/8" × 4 3/4"

AWI 4862
1 3/16" × 5 1/2"

AWI 4842
1 15/16" × 3 3/8"

AWI 4321
5/8" × 1 1/4"

AWI 4841
1 3/8" × 3 1/2"

AWI 4332
3/4" × 2 1/2"

AWI 4842
1 1/4" × 4"

AWI 4331
1" × 2 1/4"

AWI 4431
3/4" × 2 1/2"

AWI 4441
5/8" × 3 1/2"

AWI 4533
1 1/2" × 2 1/2"

# CORNICES AND MOULDINGS

**Beaded Casings**

11/16 x 2 1/4
11/16 x 2 1/4
11/16 x 2 1/4
11/16 x 2 1/2
11/16 x 2 1/2
11/16 x 2 1/2
11/16 x 2 3/4
11/16 x 2 3/4
3/4 x 2 1/4
11/16 x 3 1/4
11/16 x 3 1/4
11/16 x 3 1/4
9/16 x 3 1/4

11/16 x 3 1/2
1 1/4 x 4 3/4
7/8 x 4 3/4
2 1/4 x 5 1/2
1 1/4 x 6 1/8

**Specialty casings**

5/8 x 5/8

11/16 x 11/16

3/4 x 5/8

7/8 x 11/16

11/16 x 1 1/8

3/4 x 1 1/8

3/4 x 3/4

7/8 x 3/4

11/16 x 1 11/16

1 1/2 x 1 1/2

9/16 x 1 5/8

11/16 x 2 1/2

9/16 x 2 1/2

11/16 x 2 1/2

3/4 x 2 3/4

11/16 x 3 1/4

1/2 x 1/2

1 x 3/8

9/16 x 1 5/8

9/16 x 2

9/16 x 1 3/4

9/16 x 2 1/4

9/16 x 2 3/4

9/16 x 3 1/4

AWI 3531
1 1/16" × 3"

AWI 3542
1 1/16" × 3 15/16"

AWI 3651
1 1/8" × 4 1/4"

AWI 3561
1 1/16" × 5 1/2"

3/4 x 9/16

1/4 x 9/16

3/4 x 9/16

1 5/8 x 9/16

1 1/2 x 2 9/16

**Bed Moulds**

# CORNICES AND MOULDINGS

**Panel Mouldings**

AWI 12631
1¼" × 3"

AWI 12531
1" × 2½"

AWI 12522
1" × 2"

AWI 12523
1" × 1½"

AWI 12321
¹¹⁄₁₆" × 1¹⁵⁄₁₆"

AWI 12322
¹¹⁄₁₆" × 1½"

AWI 12521
⅞" × 2"

AWI 12421
¹³⁄₁₆" × 1½"

AWI 12422
¹³⁄₁₆" × 1⁵⁄₁₆"

AWI 12423
¾" × 1¼"

AWI 12424
¹¹⁄₁₆" × 1⁵⁄₁₆"

AWI 12323
¹¹⁄₁₆" × 1⅜"

AWI 12221
⁹⁄₁₆" × 1⅜"

11/16 x 2 5/8

9/16 x 2 1/2

1/2 x 2 1/4

3/4 x 2

5/16 x 3 9/16

11/16 x 3

11/16 x 3

11/16 x 3

11/16 x 2 1/2

9/16 x 2 1/2

AWI 10461
3/4" × 6"

AWI 10462
3/4" × 5 3/8"

AWI 10463
13/16" × 5 7/16"

AWI 10431
3/4" × 2 1/2"

AWI 10421
13/16" × 1 5/8"

AWI 10432
3/4" × 2 1/2"

Handrails

Baluster

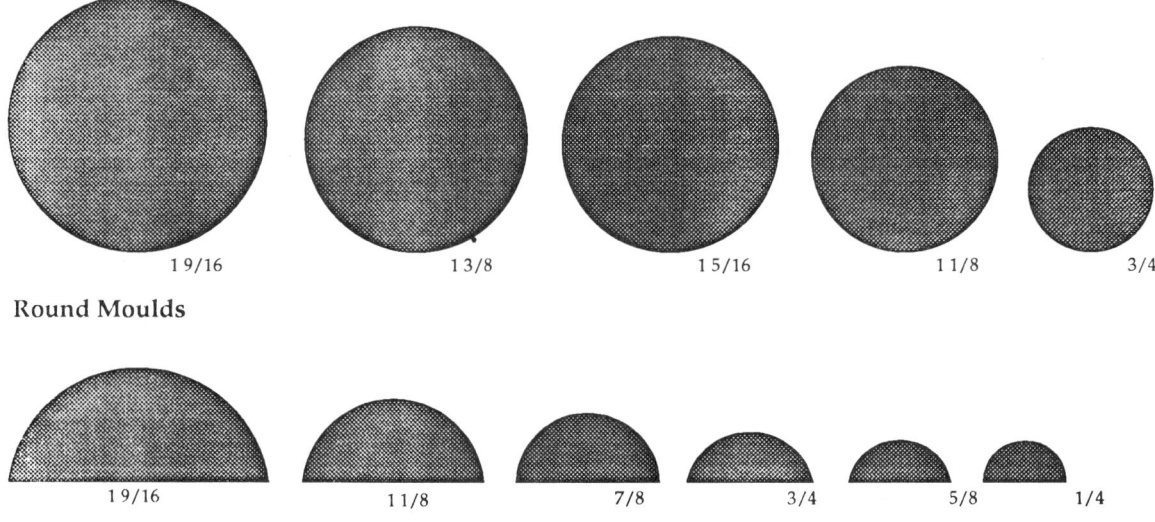

Round Moulds

Half Rounds

## CLAM SHELL MOULDINGS

11/16 x 1 5/8

9/16 x 2 1/8

11/16 x 2 1/4

11/16 x 2 1/4

9/16 x 2 1/4

11/16 x 2 1/4

5/8 x 2 1/4

9/16 x 2 1/4

11/16 x 2 1/2

11/16 x 2 1/4

9/16 x 2 1/4

9/16 x 2 1/4

## STOP MOULDINGS

Lattice

1/4 x 3/4

1/4 x 7/8

1/4 x 1 1/8

1/4 x 1 3/8

1/4 x 1 5/8

1/4 x 2 5/8

1/4 x 3 5/8

3/8x1 1/8

3/8x1 1/8

1/2x1 3/8

Sanitary

1/2x1 5/8

1/2x1 5/8

1/2x1 1/8

Sash

3/8x3/4

3/8X7/8

3/8x1 1/16

3/8x1 5/16

3/8x 1 5/8

3/8x2 1/4

Clam Shell

3/4x1 5/8

3/4x1 3/8

Sash

7/16x1 5/8

7/16x1 3/8

7/16x1 1/8

Sash

3/8X3/4

3/8X7/8

3/8X1 1/8

3/8X1 3/8

3/8X1 5/8

3/8X2 1/4

Colonial

# CORNICES AND MOULDINGS
**Hand-Carved Brackets**

Flute & Lyre
10½"W x 11"H

Bracket
6½"W x 12½"H x 5¼"D.

Bracket
8"W x 12"H x 4"D.

Left & Right Scroll
8¼"W x 11½"H

Bracket
4½"W x 13"H x 9½"D.

Bracket
4"W x 8½"H x 1¾"D.

Bracket
2¾"W x 12"H x 7"D

Bracket
7½"W x 14"H x 7½"D

1

A

B

2

3

4

5

6

7

8

**TABLE 1   Butt Hinges**

| No. | Type | Comments |
|---|---|---|
| 1 | Standard brass butt: A, solid drawn type; B, pressed pattern | General usage |
| 2 | Back flap hinge | With wide plates for table leaves and rebated or rabbeted fallflaps |
| 3 | Strap hinge | For narrow sections |
| 4 | Lift-off butt | For doors which have to be removed from time to time without disturbing setting |
| 5 | Loose pin hinge; ball-tipped hinge | Where it is necessary to throw door clear of carcass frame with the whole or the hinge knuckle protruding |
| 6 | Stopped hinge | Opens through 90° only for box lids, etc. |
| 7 | Piano hinge | Continuous strip form for supporting long lengths; supplied in drilled and countersink or undrilled blanks |
| 8 | Clock case hinge | One plate is wider to allow for a projecting door |

## FURNITURE HARDWARE

**Hinges**

1

2

3

4

5

6

7

8

9

10

11

## FURNITURE HARDWARE
### Hinges

### Left- and Right-Hand Hinges

Hinges with screw-mounted flanges should be viewed as if in mounted condition with the countersunk screw holes facing you. If the female flange is uppermost on the left, the hinge is a left-hand hinge and vice versa.

### Cranked Hinges and Their Uses

The position of the door relative to the side panel can vary considerably, being decided at the design stage in accordance with the final effect required. A wide variety of hinge types has developed from variations in door mounting methods, which must be coordinated at the design stage.

#### Straight hinge

For butting, flush or front-hung doors. The barrel is positioned centrally between the two flanges.

#### Crank B

Mounting with set-back doors. One flange is cranked by an amount equivalent to the thickness of the material.

#### Crank C

Similar to crank B but for forward-set doors.

#### Crank D

Mounting with rebated doors with flanges of non-uniform width (reduced female flanges).

#### Crank L1

Mounting with butting front-hung doors
Door opening range 270°.
Crank features internal roll.

### Butt Hinge Designations

Butt hinges for cupboards, windows, and doors, and hinges with mortise-type flanges should be viewed with the barrel facing you. If the female flange is positioned on the left of the barrel, it is a left-hand hinge and vice versa.

The same rule applies to hinges with symmetrical flanges.

#### Butt hinge

The hinge is made with offset flanges for mortised mounting. The door-mounted flange is secured with screws or pins from the rear or front (giving exposed heads).

#### Double butt hinge

Suitable for mounting two doors · to a single centre panel. The door opening range is 180° each (centre flange only mortised).

## FOLDING TABLE HINGE

Functional diagram

Self-supporting hinge,
for folding and sewing machine tables,
flush-mounted

Functional diagram
(seen from below)

Folding table hinge,
flush-mounted

Functional diagram

Card table hinge
Two-way table-leaf hinge,
flush-mounted

## FLAP HINGES

Flap closed

Flap open

Specimen mounting

Flap closed

Flap open

Flap closed

Flap open

## FURNITURE HARDWARE
### Mitred and Concealed Hinges

### MITRED HINGE

The hinges are suitable for wooden doors and side panels from 16 mm to 22 mm in thickness, chamfered at an angle of 45°.

Door closed

Door open

For the first time a concealed hinge is available for modern furniture incorporating 45° mitre angles.

An all-metal mitred hinge, specially designed to enable door and carcase edges to meet at an angle of 45°.

Since both bosses have the same adjustment facilities, the complete hinge can be adjusted in three directions, vertically, laterally and from front to back.

### CONCEALED HINGES

Specimen installation of a butting, flush-fitting cupboard door. Doors may, however, be set back or forward if preferred, provided the housing recesses are appropriately offset. If doors are set back, care must be taken to ensure that the opening angle is restricted as little as possible.

Side panel
Door
Hinge

Side panel
Hinge
Door

Door closed          Door open

Specimen installation of a butting, front-hung door, fitting flush with the cupboard side in the conventional manner. Doors may, however, be hung with inset edge if preferred, provided the housing recesses are offset accordingly. It is important in such cases to ensure that centre doors are not mounted with groove gap clearance.

Side panel
Door
Hinge

Side panel
Hinge
Door

Door closed          Door open

Specimen installation of a butting, front-hung, flap-type door. On opening, the flap projects downwards by its own thickness. Thus, if doors or other panels are situated below the flap, a degree of clearance exceeding the flap thickness will be necessary.

Flap-door
Lower shelf
Hinge

Hinge
Flap-door
Lower shelf

Flap closed          Flap open

Specimen installation joining two panels. In this way folding doors can be constructed for furniture or room dividers:

Panel
Hinge
Hinge
Panel          Panel

Panel
Hinge
Panel

Typical folding door     Door closed     Door open

28
18
52
Min. wood thickness 24

26
15
80
Wood thickness up to 24

Dimensions in mm.

Dimensions in mm

Pivot hinge, without stop
**Hollow drawn,** with one short flange

Material thickness
8.0 x 2.25 mm

Pivot hinge, without stop
**Smooth drawn,** with one short flange

Material thickness
9.0 x 3.0

Corner pivot hinge, without stop
With outer knuckle, **straight**

Material thickness
1.0 x 2.0

Corner pivot hinge, without stop
With outer knuckle, **cranked**

Pivot hinges for writing bureau drop leaf mounting,
smooth drawn.

Dimensions in mm.

## FURNITURE HARDWARE

### Glass Door Hinges

For flush-fitted doors

One upper and one lower hinge per mounting

Drilling diagram (top)

For flush-fitted doors

One left and one right hinge per mounting

For flush-fitted doors

One left and one right hinge per mounting

For flush-fitting doors

For front-hung doors

For front-hung doors

One left and one right hinge per mounting

One pull per mounting

### Magnetic Pressure Catches

Dimensions in mm.

Vertical mounting

| Length (mm) | Internal carcase height (mm) | Distance A (mm) | Distance C (mm) |
|---|---|---|---|
| 250 | 300 to 400 | 240 | Determine by trial mounting |
| 325 | 350 to 450 | 308 | |
| 450 | 400 to 500 | 430 | |

Horizontal mounting

| Length (mm) | Internal carcase height (mm) | Distance A (mm) | Distance C (mm) |
|---|---|---|---|
| 250 | 300 to 400 | 65 | Determine by trial mounting |
| 325 | 350 to 450 | 100 | |
| 450 | 400 to 500 | 150 | |

Vertical mounting

| Length (mm) | Internal carcase height (mm) | Distance A (mm) | Distance C (mm) |
|---|---|---|---|
| 160 | 250 to 350 | 127 | Determine by trial mounting |
| 190 | 300 to 400 | 151 | |
| 220 | 350 to 450 | 175 | |
| 250 | 400 to 500 | 198 | |
| 280 | 450 to 550 | 222 | |

Horizontal mounting

| Length (mm) | Internal carcase height (mm) | Distance A (mm) | Distance C (mm) |
|---|---|---|---|
| 160 | 200 to 300 | 82 | Determine by trial mounting |
| 190 | 230 to 330 | 105 | |
| 220 | 260 to 360 | 127 | |
| 250 | 290 to 430 | 148 | |
| 280 | 320 to 460 | 171 | |

| Length (mm) | Internal carcase height (mm) | Distance A (mm) | Distance C (mm) |
|---|---|---|---|
| 150 | min. 130 | 70 | Determine by trial mounting |
| 200 | min. 170 | 105 | |
| 250 | min. 210 | 140 | |

Dimensions in mm.

## FURNITURE HARDWARE
### Lid Stays

| Length (mm) | Lid height (mm) | Distance A (mm) | Distance C (mm) |
|---|---|---|---|
| 250 | up to 300 | 170 | Determine by trial mounting |
| 325 | up to 450 | 205 | |
| 450 | over 450 | 275 | |

| Length (mm) | Distance A (mm) | Distance B (mm) | Distance C (mm) |
|---|---|---|---|
| 145 | Determine by trial mounting depending on opening angle of lid. | | |
| 260 | | | |
| 330 | | | |

This raised marker must always be lowermost on either side.

| Length (mm) | Carcase depth (mm) | Distance A (mm) | Distance C (mm) |
|---|---|---|---|
| 200 | 210 | 150 | Determine by trial mounting |
| 250 | 260 | 180 | |
| 300 | 310 | 230 | |

| Length (mm) | Distance A (mm) | Distance C (mm) |
|---|---|---|
| 130 | 150 | Determine by trial mounting |
| 250 | 260 | |

Dimensions in mm.

## Extension type

Soft-Roller systems are capable of varying degrees of extension, depending on design. Basically, three types are employed:

### E — Single extension

The withdrawal distance offered by single extensions is designed to be less than the installation length. Drawers cannot be opened clear of the carcase.

### V — Full extension

The full extension model incorporates a pull-out distance as great as, or greater than, the installation length.
Drawers can be opened completely clear of the carcase.

### T — Telescopic extension

Telescopic extensions are fully extending systems. Their particular design is such that all the elements travel on a central axis resulting in a particularly neat, space-saving, compact assembly.

## Mounting method

An indication as to how the rails are secured to the drawer or pull-out element.

### A — Base mounted

### S = Side mounted

### N = Groove mounted

### T = Shelf mounted

Single extensions with friction bearing mounted nylon rollers

Telescopic extensions guided by means of ball cages

## FURNITURE HARDWARE
Magnetic and Spring Catches; Bolts

Magnetic catches, screw-mounted

Magnetic catches, mortised

clip-fit

Magnetic catches, (heat resistant)

Magnetic catches, for double doors

Magnetic catches, for metal doors

Magnetic catches, for installation in series-drilled holes

Elbow catches, screw-mounted

Twin roller catches, screw-mounted

Roller catches, screw-mounted

Twin ball catches

Glass door/ shelf catches

Ball catches, with stop plate or ball headed screw

Ball catches, mortised

Plinth spring catches, screw-mounted and press-fit

Spring catches, screw-mounted

Flexa-Touch drawer latch

Magnetic push-latches, surface-mounted or mortised

Pulls and counterplates for magnetic push latches

Furniture bolts, screw-mounted and press-fit

Flush bolts, barrel bolts, tower bolt

| Automatic door bolt | Rim locks | Lever-type rim locks | Inlaid-and Inlaid flap locks |
|---|---|---|---|
|  |  |  |  |

| Mortise locks | Sliding door locks pushbutton cylinders | Central locking cylinders | Espagnolette locks |
|---|---|---|---|
|  |  |  |  |

| Central locking systems with anti-tilt mechanism | Cylinder modul system | Glass door locks | Lever locks |
|---|---|---|---|
|  |  |  |

Locker locks |

## FURNITURE HARDWARE
**Shelf Supports**

Shelf supports, pin mounted

...Plug-in, Ø 3 mm hole

...Plug-in, Ø 5 mm hole

...Plug-in, Ø 4 mm hole

Shelf supports, plastic

Shelf supports, with added screw fastening

Shelf suppports, with spling clip

...Plug-in, Ø ¼ in. hole

Shelf supports, with sleeves (steel)

Shelf supports, with sleeves (plastic)

...Plug-in, Ø 6 mm hole

Shelf retainers, in Ø 5 mm hole

Shelf retainers, in Ø 5 mm hole

Glass shelf supports, in 5 Ø mm holes

Glass shelf supports, in Ø 5 mm holes

Shelf supports, screw-in type

Shelf supports, surface-mounted

Shelf support systems, screw-mounted

Shelf supports systems, groove-mounted

Mirror mount, for mirror with backing panel

## WARDROBE RAILS AND SUPPORTS

OVA wardrobe rails
and supports

Shoe racks

Universal storage rack
Pull-relief plug

Single and double hooks,
pew hooks

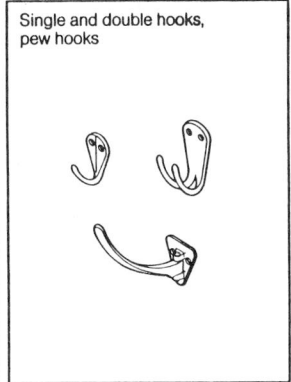

Ø 18 mm, Ø 20 mm,
Ø 25 mm wardrobe rails
and supports

Wardrobe lifts,
hanging rails

Cloakroom, wall and
ceiling hooks, nylon

Cloakroom fittings
Thiefproof cloakroom fittings

Nylon tubular rails and coat
hangers

Cloakroom hooks, wood

Wardrobe rails

Tie rails and hat racks

Hat and coat hooks

Wardrobe hanging bars
and rails

## CASTORS AND GLIDES

**Twin-Wheel Castors**
Audio and
Audio-Stop

**Enclosed Castors**

**Furniture Glides**

**Furniture Glides**
Cylindrical

**Furniture Legs**
**Furniture Glides**

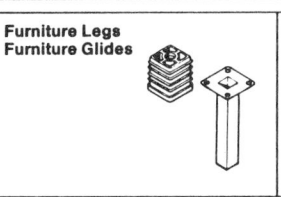

**Bed Box Castors**
**Ball Castors**

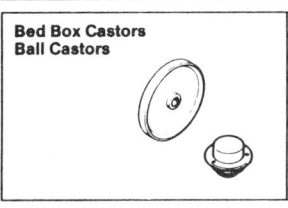

**Coal Box Castors**
**Light Duty**
**Swivel Castors**

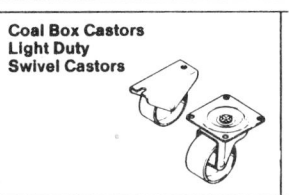

# FURNITURE HARDWARE
## Furniture Glides

**knock-in furniture glides**

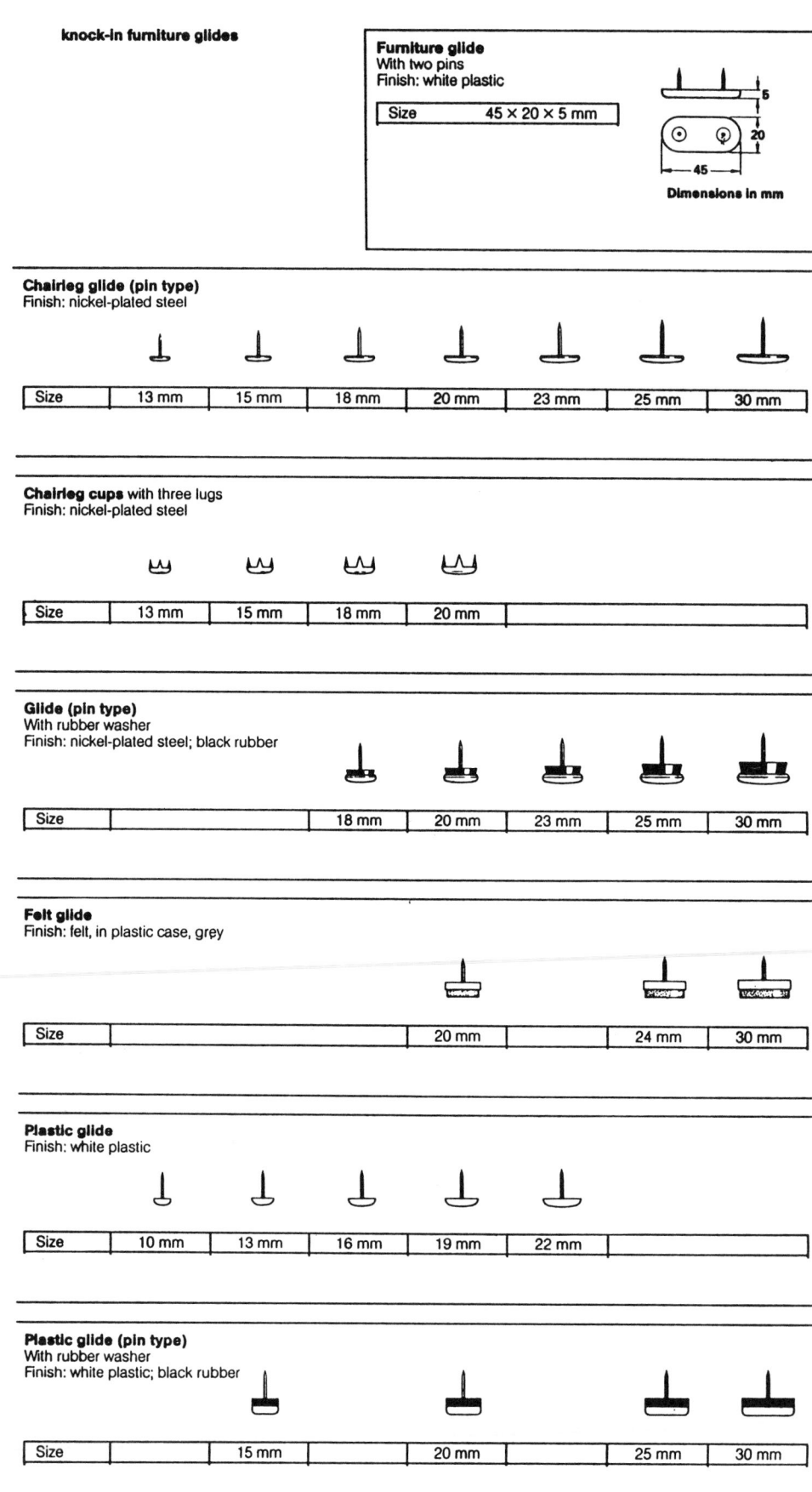

**Furniture glide**
With two pins
Finish: white plastic

| Size | 45 × 20 × 5 mm |
|------|----------------|

Dimensions in mm

**Chairleg glide (pin type)**
Finish: nickel-plated steel

| Size | 13 mm | 15 mm | 18 mm | 20 mm | 23 mm | 25 mm | 30 mm |
|------|-------|-------|-------|-------|-------|-------|-------|

**Chairleg cups** with three lugs
Finish: nickel-plated steel

| Size | 13 mm | 15 mm | 18 mm | 20 mm | | | |
|------|-------|-------|-------|-------|--|--|--|

**Glide (pin type)**
With rubber washer
Finish: nickel-plated steel; black rubber

| Size | | 18 mm | 20 mm | 23 mm | 25 mm | 30 mm |
|------|--|-------|-------|-------|-------|-------|

**Felt glide**
Finish: felt, in plastic case, grey

| Size | | 20 mm | | 24 mm | 30 mm |
|------|--|-------|--|-------|-------|

**Plastic glide**
Finish: white plastic

| Size | 10 mm | 13 mm | 16 mm | 19 mm | 22 mm | |
|------|-------|-------|-------|-------|-------|--|

**Plastic glide (pin type)**
With rubber washer
Finish: white plastic; black rubber

| Size | | 15 mm | | 20 mm | | 25 mm | 30 mm |
|------|--|-------|--|-------|--|-------|-------|

# Specialties

| | |
|---|---|
| Plantscaping | 906 |
| Signage and graphics | 931 |
| Audio-visual systems | 949 |
| Auditorium seating | 961 |
| Security | 977 |
| Color theory | 998 |
| Window treatments | 1015 |
| Elevators | 1060 |
| Indoor recreation | 1069 |
| Accessories | 1075 |

In most instances, the design process requires a knowledge of, or at the very least, an awareness of, certain specialized elements that can contribute heavily to the success or failure of a project in terms of aesthetics or function, or both. These elements may take the form of manufactured "off-the-shelf" products or consist of design theories, standards, and guidelines for certain areas of expertise. Accordingly, this section deals with ten such elements, ranging from plantscaping to accessories.

Information can be found concerning the height, spacing, and diameter of indoor trees and floor plants. Also included are planting standards, details, and maintenance information. The section dealing with signage and graphics provides information on signage systems, symbols, mounting heights, and locations. Other sections provide data on audio-visual systems, including projection room layouts and details, and auditorium seating arrangements and sightlines. The section dealing with security includes information on door and window hardware, mailbox rooms, lighting, and security systems. Still other sections provide information on color theory and window treatments, including draperies and curtains, shutters and shades, and rods, holdbacks, and ties.

## DESIGNING WITH PLANTS

Any successful design uses plants that are compatible not only in an aesthetic design sense, but also in their growing requirements. No matter how beautiful the design, if neighboring plants are not matched to the correct growing conditions, parts of the design will either deteriorate or require elaborate maintenance. The aesthetic design considerations involve choosing the proper variety of plant textures, heights, and spacing to give the desired effect. The growing considerations involve the proper matching of light intensity, soil, and water, as well as proper container size, to the plant environmental requirements.

Of all the growing conditions, the most important is the light intensity. It is easy to underestimate the amount of available light, since the human eye can easily see in 20 footcandles of light, while even the plant needing the lowest light requires 50 to 75 footcandles to remain healthy. If the light intensity is to be below 100 footcandles, even these "low-light" plants must be slowly acclimatized prior to installation.

No matter if the space to be planted is a small office, a large interior garden, or a cafeteria, the first step is to ascertain the actual level of the existing or planned lighting. To allow maximum creativity in the planting design, the light intensity should be considered in the initial planning stages, especially in large areas such as those in shopping malls or corporate interior gardens. Adding the needed lighting fixtures after the initial electrical installation is often expensive or impossible. In smaller-scale situations, such as offices or homes, extra light fixtures should be added or the plants should be chosen according to the available light. If the plants do not have the proper light intensity, they will die. The lower the light intensity below the minimum needed by the species, the faster they will do so.

Since the light source (incandescent, fluorescent, sun, or other) is not important, but the light intensity is, accurate intensity measurements are essential. For these measurements we recommend the General Electric Model 213 or 214 light meter or its equivalent. The measurements must be made at the level of the plant foliage; they must be made several times a day on several days typical of the location if sunlight is used; and they must take curtains, tinted glass, and other light-shielding devices into account. Only light hitting the top of the leaves is effective. While underlighting with spotlights can create dramatic effects, it does very little to help the plant.

After the light intensity is determined, the plants should be selected from the appropriate light-level group (see Fig. 7), consistent with the design aims. Plants that will be growing near one another should also have similar water requirements (also given in Fig. 7). If plants with different watering requirements must be close, they should be kept in their own growing containers so they can be watered separately.

An interior planting designer creates the mood through the interplay of plant texture and plant height, working only with those plants that will live under the predetermined light intensity. Color cannot really be used as a design element, since the average interior light intensity is seldom more than 100 footcandles and brightly colored plants or blooming flowers need up to 1000 footcandles. If flowering plants are used where the lighting conditions are normal, they will generally have to be replaced every few days.

### Plant Texture

The good designer will provide for design variety through the clever use of plant texture. The term is used here to describe the general structure, shape, and appearance of the plant, regardless of height. It includes the size, shape, edging, and thickness of the plant's leaves, as well as its overall shape and the arrangement and number of leaves on the plant.

Five general rules concerning texture should be kept in mind.

1. Juxtapose fragmented foliage (such as that of a palm) with solid foliage (say, that of a dracaena).

2. Avoid too much of the same type of foliage (e.g., large flat leaves) in one area, unless a border or hedge effect is desired.

3. An exception to these previous rules on groupings is the palm. Although all palms have similar foliage, they vary slightly in color and interest, so that different types of palms may be planted together.

4. To create interest, mix small-leaved with large-leaved plants, and narrow-leaved with broad-leaved plants.

5. When using plants as specimens, especially as interior design elements in offices or homes, pick the plant with the background fabric, carpet, or wallpaper in mind. For example, a "busy" foliage plant will fight with a "busy" fabric.

### Plant Height

Plant height not only determines the scale of the design, but it adds variety to the plant groupings. There are six general rules regarding plant height selection to keep in mind.

1. In the plant grouping, build up with the low plants in front. If the grouping can be seen from all sides, the grouping must be well balanced throughout and built up to the center height.

2. If a plant has canes with no lower foliage, try to place the lower plants in front to conceal the absence of foliage of the taller plants in the rear.

3. Uneven sizes throughout a grouping add more interest than consistent levels of foliage.

4. If a single plant is desired to hide a column or some other object, be sure that the plant height, including its container, is about three-fourths the height of the object to be concealed.

5. Keep the scale of the surroundings in mind when choosing the plant height. A 3-foot plant is fine next to a desk, but a plant of at least 6 feet should be selected if it is to be viewed when entering a room.

6. By convention, interior plant heights are measured from the bottom of the root ball or planter, while exterior plant heights are measured from the top of the root ball. The reason is that interior plants are usually placed in a container or raised planter, and the total available height from floor to ceiling is fixed.

### Plant Spacing

Under certain conditions, the plants of an interior landscaping design will grow. Therefore, any possible change in the plant size must be considered by the designer. If the lighting intensity is at or below the recommended level, there will be little or no plant growth and the plant size and relationships will change little over time. If the lighting intensity is well above the required level, there will be plant growth, with different plant species growing at different rates.

Unlike outdoor plants, indoor tropical plants seldom grow outward; most of their growth occurs upward. The main exceptions are the *Ficus* family, the schefflera, and the *Philodendron Selloum,* which will spread somewhat outward. If a full plant design is desired, the required number of plants should be placed close together at the time of installation since future growth will seldom fill in the bare spots.

Even if the light intensity is high enough, before the plant can grow significantly, its root system must be able to expand. Thus, the best way to ensure that the size relationships of the plants do not change is to keep them in their original growing containers and not to replant them into a growing medium. If they are kept in the original containers, they will become pot-bound and future growth will be automatically limited.

Plant material is sold on the basis of height or growing-container size, and one must be familiar with the particular species to know what the spread will be. For each plant species considered here, Fig. 1 lists the height range for each plant in each standard growing-container size and gives a recommended minimum center-to-center plant spacing. This recommended spacing is based on experience with the plant's branching habits and growth patterns and will give a full plant design. If an open or a less full design is called for, the spacing should be increased.

When the plants are to be displayed in individual planters or decorative containers, each plant, still in its growing can, is placed directly into the planter or container, on top of a layer of drainage material of the appropriate depth. However, many standard planters have lips that reduce the interior diameter to less than the overall diameter. This inner diameter should be larger than the growing cans diameter so that the plant can be placed directly into it without being repotted and risking the attendant danger of root damage. To emphasize this requirement, Fig. 2 gives the standard planter diameter needed for each standard size of growing container. The size of the lip changes when a nonstandard type is used. If space is limited, this measurement should be carefully checked.

**INDOOR TREES**

| Species | Height Range | Recommended Center-to-Center Plant Spacing | Growing Can Diameter |
|---|---|---|---|
| Fiddle-leaf fig (Ficus lyrata) | 3- 4 ft | 24-36 in | 10 in |
| | 4- 6 ft | 30-42 in | 14 in |
| | 6-11 ft | 42 in & up | 17 in |
| Indian laurel (Ficus retusa) | 5- 7 ft | 42-54 in | 14 in |
| | 7- 9 ft | 48-60 in | 17 in |
| | 9-12 ft | 60 in & up | 22 in |
| Rubber plant (Ficus elastica cv. 'Decora'), tree standard | 4-5 ft | 48-60 in | 10 in |
| | 5-6 ft | 54-66 in | 12 in |
| | 6-7 ft | 60-72 in | 14 in |
| Rubber plant (Ficus elastica cv. 'Decora'), bush type | 1½-2 ft | 12-18 in | 6 in |
| | 2 -2½ ft | 12-24 in | 8 in |
| | 3 -4 ft | 24-36 in | 10 in |
| | 4 -5 ft | 36-48 in | 12 in |
| | 4 -5 ft | 48-60 in | 14 in |
| Weeping fig (Ficus benjamina) | 3- 4 ft | 24-36 in | 10 in |
| | 4- 5 ft | 30-42 in | 12 in |
| | 5- 7 ft | 36-48 in | 14 in |
| | 6- 8 ft | 48-60 in | 17 in |
| | 9-10 ft | 60 in & up | 22 in |
| | 9-12 ft | 60 in & up | 28 in |
| | 10-12 ft | 72 in & up | 36 in |
| Norfolk Island pine (Araucaria heterophylla) | 1½-2 ft | 18-30 in | 6 in |
| | 2 -3 ft | 24-36 in | 8 in |
| | 3 -5 ft | 30-42 in | 10 in |
| | 4 -5 ft | 36-48 in | 12 in |
| | 4 -6 ft | 42-54 in | 14 in |
| | 6 -7 ft | 54-66 in | 17 in |
| Schefflera (Brassaia actinophylla) | 3- 4 ft | 36-48 in | 10 in |
| | 4- 5 ft | 36-48 in | 10 in |
| | 5- 7 ft | 55-66 in | 14 in |
| | 7- 8 ft | 60-72 in | 17 in |
| | 8- 9 ft | 60 in & up | 22 in |
| | 9-12 ft | 72 in & up | Metal tubs |

**FLOOR PLANTS**

| | | | |
|---|---|---|---|
| Bamboo palm (Chamaedorea erumpens) | 3-4 ft | 30-42 in | 10 in |
| | 4-6 ft | 36-48 in | 12 in |
| | 5-7 ft | 42-54 in | 14 in |
| | 7-9 ft | 48-60 in | 17 in |
| Corn plant (Dracaena fragrans cv. 'Massangeana') | 1½-2 ft | 24-30 in | 6 in |
| | 3½-4 ft | 24-36 in | 10 in |
| | 4½-6 ft | 30-42 in | 12 in |
| | 5 -7 ft | 36-48 in | 14 in |
| Corn plant bush (Dracaena fragrans cv. 'Massangeana') | 1 -1½ ft | 18-24 in | 6 in |
| | 1½-2½ ft | 18-30 in | 8 in |
| | 3 -4 ft | 24-36 in | 10 in |
| | 4 -5 ft | 30-42 in | 14 in |
| | 5 -7 ft | 36-48 in | 17 in |
| Dwarf date palm (Phoenix Roebelenii) | 2-3 ft | 30-42 in | 10 in |
| | 3-4 ft | 36-48 in | 12 in |
| | 4-5 ft | 42-54 in | 14 in |
| | 5-6 ft | 48-60 in | 17 in |
| | 5-6 ft | 54-66 in | 22 in |

Fig. 1   Spacing recommendations.

# PLANTSCAPING

Plant Height, Spacing, and Diameter

| Species | Height Range | Recommended Center-to-Center Plant Spacing | Growing Can Diameter |
|---|---|---|---|
| Dwarf dragon tree *(Dracaena marginata)* | 3-4 ft | 24-36 in | 10 in |
| | 4-5 ft | 30-42 in | 12 in |
| | 5-7 ft | 36-48 in | 14 in |
| | 7-9 ft | 48 in & up | 17 in |
| Dwarf schefflera *(Brassaia arboricola)* | 1 -1½ ft | 18-24 in | 6 in |
| | 1¼-2½ ft | 30-42 in | 8 in |
| | 3 -4 ft | 36-48 in | 10 in |
| | 4 -5 ft | 42-54 in | 14 in |
| False aralia *(Dizygotheca elegantissima)* | 1¼-2 ft | 18-30 in | 6 in |
| | 3 -4 ft | 30-42 in | 10 in |
| | 5 -7 ft | 36-48 in | 14 in |
| | 7 -8 ft | 42-54 in | 17 in |
| Green dracaena *(Dracaena deremensis* cv. 'Janet Craig') | 1 -1½ ft | 18-24 in | 6 in |
| | 1¼-2½ ft | 18-30 in | 8 in |
| | 3 -4 ft | 24-36 in | 10 in |
| | 4 -5 ft | 30-42 in | 14 in |
| | 5 -7 ft | 36-48 in | 17 in |
| Green pleomele *(Dracaena reflexa)* | 1¼-2 ft | 12-18 in | 6 in |
| | 3 -4 ft | 18-30 in | 10 in |
| | 4 -5 ft | 30-45 in | 14 in |
| | 5 -6 ft | 36-48 in | 17 in |
| Kentia palm *(Howea Forsterana)* | 3-4 ft | 36-48 in | 10 in |
| | 4-5 ft | 42-54 in | 12 in |
| | 5-8 ft | 48-60 in | 14 in |
| Lady palm *(Rhapis excelsa)* | 3-4 ft | 36-48 in | 10 in |
| | 4-5 ft | 42-54 in | 12 in |
| | 5-7 ft | 48-60 in | 14 in |
| Mock orange *(Pittosporum Tobira)* | 1¼-1½ ft | 24-36 in | 10 in |
| | 1½-2½ ft | 30-42 in | 12 in |
| | 2 -3 ft | 36-48 in | 14 in |
| Narrow-leaved pleomele *(Dracaena angustifolia honoraii)* | 3-4 ft | 24-36 in | 12 in |
| | 5-6 ft | 30-42 in | 14 in |
| | 6-7 ft | 36-48 in | 17 in |
| Neantha bella palm *(Chamaedorea elegans)* | 1 -1½ ft | 18-30 in | 6 in |
| | 1¼-2½ ft | 24-36 in | 8 in |
| | 2¼-3½ ft | 30-42 in | 10 in |
| | 4 -5 ft | 36-48 in | 14 in |
| Ponytail *(Beaucarnea recurvata)* | 1½-2 ft | 24-36 in | 10 in |
| | 2 -3 ft | 30-42 in | 12 in |
| | 3 -4 ft | 36-48 in | 14 in |
| | 4 -5 ft | 42-54 in | 17 in |
| Reed palm *(Chamaedorea Seifrizii)* | 4-6 ft | 36-48 in | 12 in |
| | 6-7 ft | 42-54 in | 14 in |
| | 7-9 ft | 48-60 in | 17 in |
| Self-heading philodendron *(Philodendron Selloum)* | 3 ft | 30-42 in | 10 in |
| | 4 ft | 42-54 in | 14 in |
| | 5 ft | 54-66 in | 17 in |
| Southern yew *(Podocarpus macrophyllus* var. Maki) | 4-5 ft | 36-48 in | 10 in |
| | 5-6 ft | 42-54 in | 12 in |
| | 5-6 ft | 48-60 in | 14 in |
| | 6-7 ft | 54-66 in | 17 in |

**Fig. 1** *(Continued)*

| Species | Height Range | Recommended Center-to-Center Plant Spacing | Growing Can Diameter |
|---|---|---|---|
| TABLE OR DESK PLANTS—GROUND COVER | | | |
| Boston fern (*Nephrolepis exaltata* cv. 'Bostoniensis') | 1 ft | 24–30 in | 6 in |
| | 1 –1½ ft | 30–36 in | 8 in |
| | 1½–2 ft | 36–42 in | 10 in |
| Common philodendron (*Philodendron scandens oxycardium*) | 1 ft | 18–24 in | 8 in |
| | 1¼–1½ ft | 24–30 in | 10 in |
| | 1¼–1½ ft | 24–36 in | 12 in |
| Chinese evergreen (*Aglaonema commutatum* var. maculatum) | 1¼–1½ ft | 18–24 in | 6 in |
| | 1½–2 ft | 24–30 in | 8 in |
| | 2 –2½ ft | 30–36 in | 10 in |
| Dumb cane (*Dieffenbachia maculata* cv. 'Rudolph Roehrs') | 1 ft | 18–24 in | 6 in |
| | 2 ft | 24–30 in | 8 in |
| | 3 ft | 30–36 in | 10 in |
| | 3 –3½ ft | 36–42 in | 12 in |
| | 3½–4 ft | 42–48 in | 14 in |
| Golden pothos (*Epipremnum aureum* or *Scindapsus aureus*) | 1 ft | 12–18 in | 6 in |
| | 1 ft | 18–24 in | 8 in |
| | 1¼–1½ ft | 24–30 in | 10 in |
| | 1¼–1½ ft | 30–36 in | 12 in |
| Grape ivy (*Cissus rhombifolia*) | 1 ft | 18–24 in | 6 in |
| | 1 –1¼ ft | 18–30 in | 8 in |
| | 1¼–1½ ft | 24–36 in | 10 in |
| | 1¼–1½ | 24–36 in | 12 in |
| Jade plant (*Crassula argentea*) | 1 ft | 18–24 in | 8 in |
| | 2 ft | 24–36 in | 10 in |
| | 2 –2½ ft | 30–42 in | 12 in |
| | 2½–3½ ft | 36–48 in | 14 in |
| Prayer plant (*Maranta leuconeura*) | 1 ft | 18–24 in | 8 in |
| | 1 ft | 24–30 in | 10 in |
| | 1–1½ ft | 24–30 in | 12 in |
| Swedish ivy (*Plectranthus australis*) | 1 ft | 18–24 in | 6 in |
| | 1 –1¼ ft | 18–30 in | 8 in |
| | 1¼–1½ ft | 24–36 in | 10 in |
| | 1¼–1½ ft | 24–36 in | 12 in |
| Wax plant (*Hoya carnosa*) | 1 ft | 12–18 in | 6 in |
| | 1 ft | 18–24 in | 8 in |
| | 1 ft | 24–30 in | 10 in |
| White flag (*Spathiphyllum* cv. 'Clevelandii') | 1¼–1½ ft | 24–36 in | 6 in |
| | 2 –3 ft | 30–42 in | 8 in |
| | 2½–3½ ft | 36–48 in | 10 in |
| | 3 –4 ft | 48–54 in | 14 in |
| White-striped Dracaena (*Dracaena deremensis* cv. 'Warneckii') | 1¼–1½ ft | 18–24 in | 6 in |
| | 2 ft | 24–30 in | 8 in |
| | 3 –4 ft | 24–36 in | 10 in |
| | 4 –5 ft | 30–42 in | 12 in |
| | 4 –7 ft | 36–48 in | 14 in |
| Green dracaena (*Dracaena deremensis* cv. 'Janet Craig') | 1 –1½ ft | 18–24 in | 6 in |
| | 1¼–2½ ft | 24–30 in | 8 in |
| | 3 –4 ft | 30–42 in | 10 in |
| Neantha bella palm (*Chamaedorea elegans*) | 1 –1½ ft | 18–30 in | 6 in |
| | 1½–2½ ft | 24–36 in | 8 in |
| | 2½–3½ ft | 30–42 in | 10 in |
| Self-heading philodendron (*Philodendron Selloum*) | 1 ft | 18–24 in | 6 in |
| | 2 ft | 24–36 in | 8 in |
| | 3 ft | 30–42 in | 10 in |

**Fig. 1** *(Continued)*

| Plant Growing Container Diameter | Recommended Planter Exterior Diameter |
|---|---|
| 4 in | 6 in |
| 6 in | 8 in |
| 8 in | 10 in |
| 10 in | 12 in |
| 11 in | 14 in |
| 12 in | 14 in |
| 13 in | 16 in |
| 14 in | 16 in |
| 17 in | 18–22 in |
| 22 in | 24 in |

**Fig. 2** Planter selection. These recommendations are based on the fact that most standard planters have either a 1-inch lip or no lip at all. Because the growing cans sometimes have ridges or have become deformed, it is always best to allow for a little extra leeway, even for planters with no lip. Some manufacturers, however, put 2-inch lips on their planters, a possiblity that should be checked. If the planter is an automatic watering type, the inside and outside diameters will be quite different, depending on the manufacturer.

# PLANTSCAPING
## Design Guidelines

### Writing Specifications

The interior landscaping business is very competitive, and a common practice is for the architect or designer to send out the landscaping specifications for bids. Unless the specifications for the job are well-written, however, there are many ways for the contractor to cut corners and still be within the specifications. Consequently, the final installation may not be what the designer had in mind. The lowest bid is not necessarily the best bargain, unless the specifications are very tightly written or unless the architect is dealing with a well-established landscape contractor with a reputation for high-quality work.

The following are some suggested guidelines to use in writing specifications. If they are observed, the bids received will accurately reflect the design requirements of the job.

1. Specify the plant heights within a 6-inch bracket. For example, designate 5 to 5½ feet or 5½ to 6 feet. If the specification were simply "5 to 6 feet," the supplier could use all 5-foot plants, which are considerably less expensive than 6-foot plants.

2. For corn plants, dwarf dragon trees, and the like, specify the number of canes and approximate number of foliage heads, as well as the height. The difference in cost between a two-cane and a three-cane corn plant of the same height is not minor.

3. For reed palms, bamboo palms, and the like, specify the number of stems desired, five to six being medium full.

4. For the green dracaena and white-striped dracaena, list the number of main foliage stems desired. They range from one to three stems.

5. For ficus trees, it should be specified whether the bush style or standard tree style is desired. In the bush style, the plant has multiple stems (ranging from two to five in number) branching out from the base of the plants. The standard tree or "lollipop" style has one main 5- to 6-foot stem with a sheared, ball-shaped foliage head.

6. Small plants should be specified as to single plants or combinations or several plants. Examples are dumb cane, Chinese evergreen, and white flag.

7. If ivy trailers are desired, their length should be specified. The trailers take up to eight months to grow, depending on the length, so the designer must plan for these up to a year before installation. Examples are grape ivy, swedish ivy, golden pothos, common philodendron, and wax plant.

8. Specifications should call for plant cleaning and spraying before installation.

9. Perlite should be specified as the drainage material for both planters and decorative containers. Styrofoam, which is much cheaper, is often used but has little long-term value.

10. The amount of ingredients in large planters (soil mixture, drainage material, soil separator) should be specified, as should the composition of each of the ingredients.

11. If bark chips, moss cover, or other soil coverings are desired, they should be specified.

12. Special attention should be given to the description of specimen plants, including the number of heads, stems, or canes, and any unusual stem structure that is desired. If canes with character (such as angle and peculiarity of growth), tufts of foliage at various heights, or other unusual features are wanted, they should be specifically mentioned.

13. If the landscape contractor will not maintain the plants after installation, provision should be made for a training program for the maintenance crew. Also, the contractor should provide for two weeks' initial maintenance of the plants and replacement of any that fall below specifications during the period.

14. If the landscape contractor is to maintain the plants after the installation (usually the best all-around solution), such an agreement should be reached before the plants are installed and a maintenance contract should be signed. This contract should include a provision for the replacement of any plant that falls below specifications because of faulty maintenance. This stipulation gives the contractor incentive for professional-quality maintenance.

15. If a large garden is planned and the landscape contractor is given design responsibility for it, the contractor should provide a floor plan of the garden for the designer's approval, before the installation.

16. If the architect or designer provides the landscape contractor with a detailed planting floor plan and the contractor finds it impossible to meet all the specifications (because of unavailability of certain species, etc.), the contractor and the designer or architect should agree in writing on any changes.

### USE OF INTERIOR PLANTS AND PROCEDURES

The general rule of interior planting design is to vary the plant heights, shapes, and textures to give the desired design feeling consistent with the available light level and planting space. The best way to learn to apply this rule to specific situations is to study successful designs.

Interior planting designs have usually been found to fall into one of two categories: (1) interior gardens, both large and small, such as those seen in residential and hotel lobbies, corporate headquarters reception areas, and enclosed shopping mall public spaces; and (2) open plan or specimen design, like office landscaping designs and designs that use individual plants as living sculptures. In both categories of design, the main requirements to be considered are the available light intensity, the scale of the design, and the client's wishes and budget. After these basic requirements are determined, however, the design considerations are somewhat different for the two types of design.

### Interior Gardens

Interior gardens are planting areas, sometimes contained in built-in planters, that have a variety of plants and that convey their design feeling through plant arrangements rather than through individual plant specimens. Small gardens generally contain only a single grouping of plants, act as a single design element, and have uniform lighting and watering requirements throughout. Large gardens have a variety of plant groupings and varying design feelings among the groupings, and they can encompass areas of different lighting and watering requirements. Since any garden conveys its effects through the juxtaposition of different plants, a single dominant plant cannot be considered a garden from the design point of view, even if it is in a built-in planter with ground-cover plants.

In designing any built-in planter, enough planter depth must be provided to allow the root ball or the planting can to be covered with soil and to rest on 4 to 8 inches of drainage material. Since soil and gravel are expensive, it is best not to overdesign the planter, by making it larger than necessary, and not to buy too much soil to fill in between the plants. (For example, a depth of 1½ to 2 feet is usually enough for most small gardens.) Figure 1 lists the size of the growing can for different sizes of plants of each species. The depth of the largest growing can, plus the depth of the drainage material, yields the minimum planter depth for the garden. The volume of the planter minus the total volume of all the growing cans indicates the amount of additional soil and drainage material to be provided.

If the planter is already in place, its depth may limit the size of the plants that may be used. Since soil must reach to the top of the root ball or can, the only way to utilize too shallow a planter is to put the large plant in the center and to build up from the edge inward. The planter must be wide enough to slant the soil gradually so that the slope is not too great.

**Small gardens** While a garden may be large enough to have only a single design function, that function can be quite varied, provided that the lighting intensity is appropriate. It can serve as a small glen or a space separator, or it can be simply a large decorative planter. The garden can be airy and open or it can be dense and closed. Planter depth of 1½ to 2 feet is usually sufficient.

Also, some small gardens can be designed to be changed with the seasons. Often, flowering plants, such as chrysanthemums or azaleas, are used, but the plants must then be replaced every two weeks. If the seasonal or flowering plant changes are desired, the plants should be left in their containers so that they may be easily moved. Some care should be given to the planter design so that the growing cans are not obvious and do not detract from the arrangement.

Creative additions of volcanic rocks, small ponds, or fountains can be quite attractive and set off and enhance the plants. However, with the usually limited space in the small garden, these additions can produce a crowded or overdone appearance. Overcrowding will give a jungle effect that is rarely desired.

Just as in other design fields, good proportion and good sense will create a pleasing design that is neither overlooked or overbearing.

**Large gardens** Large gardens are simply larger versions of small gardens, but their very size opens up more design possibilities, since they may be subdivided into related sections. The shape, height, and texture of the planters may be varied from section to section. The plants may be chosen to reflect varying design moods and functions. The lighting and watering requirements may differ between sections. In fact, variety is often necessary for good large-garden design, since a large mass of similar plants or plant groupings will create the impression of a monotonous forest or field.

Because large indoor gardens usually are in areas of high ceilings, the light level must be very carefully considered. Just the presence of windows or skylights does not guarantee enough light. In addition, if the light sources are distant from the plants, the taller plants may effectively block some of the light from reaching the lower plants and foliage.

When large areas are to be planted, there is a tendency to use rocks, pools, gravel, or fountains to cut down the plant costs and simplify the maintenance. Care is essential when using these elements to prevent the plant arrangement from looking bare and sterile.

Large gardens are most commonly used in shopping malls. The skilled designer will take this illumination into account, as well as design the garden to enhance the shopper's view of the stores.

The designer will always remember that large gardens achieve their effectiveness by both the proper variation of plant groupings and the proper variation of plants within the groupings.

**Procedures for planting gardens** As pointed out earlier, a successful garden needs proper planting, since improper procedures can inflict severe damage. Correct planting involves not only correct technique and design but also correct organization.

The techniques of proper drainage, spacing, and handling will ensure that the plants remain healthy once they are installed. Experienced supervision of the installation staff will be important in this regard, since a large installation of expensive plants is no place for the on-the-job training of the supervisor.

Proper planning and organization will ensure that the plants remain healthy between unloading and planting. If the plants are left on an unheated loading dock or stored in an unlighted or unheated room until they are installed, irreversible damage may occur.

**Drainage** Overwatering of plants leads to root rot and is often more harmful than underwatering. To minimize this danger, the planter or container should be installed with proper drainage. The simplest technique is to provide a porous reservoir below the planting soil; any excess water will then drain into it from the root ball and be slowly fed back to the soil as the soil dries out.

To prepare the planter or decorative container, the drainage material is poured into the bottom and leveled. The plant growing can is placed on top of the drainage layer and surrounded with more of the drainage material. For the smaller plants (in pots 6 inches or less in diameter), a 1-inch depth of drainage material is usually enough. For the larger plants, a layer of 3 to 4 inches is suggested. For very large gardens, about one-third of the planter depth should be the drainage layer, provided it leaves enough room for the root ball or planting can.

The drainage material can be perlite (a readily available synthetic material) alone or

mixed with small pebbles or gravel. The perlite is suggested since it is porous enough to feed back the excess water to the soil as the soil dries out. If only gravel or pebbles are used, the excess water will sit and stagnate in the reservoir and will not be fed back to the plants.

Even with the proper drainage layer, overwatering is possible if so much excess water is used that it fills up the reservoir. The water level in a small container can be determined by tapping the container at various intervals and listening for the change in sound. In large planted areas, it is wise to provide for "dipstick" readings of the water level. To take such a reading, rigid hollow plastic tubes, with a cloth over their lower ends, are "planted" at intervals along with the plants. The hollow tubes reach from the top of the container to just above the drainage layer and the cloth on the bottom prevents soil or drainage material from entering the tube. A dipstick is lowered into the tube until it touches the cloth. If the stick, upon removal, shows more than ½ inch of water, there is too much water in the bottom of the planter.

If gravel is used as part of the drainage material, it should be ⅜ inch to ½ inch in diameter. Under no circumstances should limestone be used, since it is alkaline and will raise the pH of the water to a level that is too high for most tropical plants.

**Soil separator** If the plants are removed from their growing cans and replanted in growing soil, it is usually best to use a soil separator between the drainage layer and the planting soil. The separator is a semiporous sheet, often composed of fiberglass wool, which serves to keep the soil from falling into the drainage material. If the separator is not used, soil will clog the drainage material. Fiberglass wool of building material grade should not be used, as it contains chemicals that will damage the plant (Fig. 3).

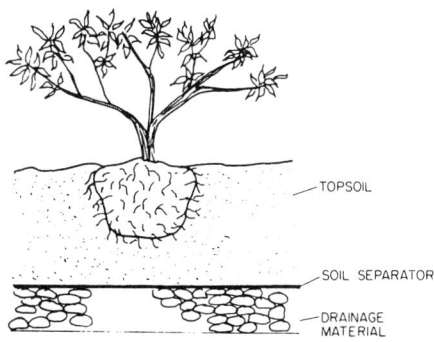

**Fig. 3   Soil separation.**

**Planting medium** Because the root systems of tropical plants are much finer than those of outdoor plants, pure topsoil is too heavy and too easily compacted to be used as a planting medium. It will constrict the plant roots and will retain too much water.

For the common tropical plants discussed here, we recommend the use of the foliage plant mix developed by Cornell University. Because it is easiest to calculate the quantity of needed soil in terms of the volume of the planter to be filled, the formula given here is

for 1 cubic yard of soil. For conversion purposes, 1 cubic yard equals 21.7 bushels, 765 liters, or 27 cubic feet.

*Sphagnum peat moss:* ½ cu yd = 383 lit
*Vermiculite #2:* ¼ cu yd = 191 lit
*Perlite, medium fine:* ¼ cu yd = 191 lit
*Ground limestone, dolomitic:* 0.85 gal = 13.5 cup = 3.2 lit
*Superphosphate 20 percent solution:* 0.21 gal = 3.4 cup = 0.79 lit
*10-10-10 fertilizer:* 0.32 gal = 5.1 cup = 1.2 lit
*Iron sulphate:* 0.11 gal = 1.7 cup = 0.41 lit
*Potassium nitrate:* 0.11 gal = 1.7 cup = 0.41 lit

While this Cornell foliage plant mix gives the best all-around results, a simpler mix that gives good results in most cases is as follows:

⅓ by volume sterilized commercial mix of peat moss and vermiculite
⅓ by volume sterilized topsoil
⅓ by volume perlite

This mix is particularly effective for container planting. If it is to be used in a larger garden planting, such as a shopping mall garden, more perlite should be added for improved drainage.

The peat and topsoil mix is considerably heavier than the Cornell mix and both are heavier wet than dry. If the garden is not situated at grade level, this weight can be an important consideration. Figure 4 gives guidelines to be used in estimating the weight of the planting medium.

**Planting organization** The basic ingredients for a large planting installation are drainage material, planting medium, soil separator, plant material, material-handling equipment, light, water, and labor. Organization of all these ingredients is important since every one must be ready and available for a successful installation. Arrangements for all these factors should be made ahead of time, and they should be ready and waiting when the plants are delivered.

The amount of interior volume in the planters and containers determines the amount of needed drainage material, soil separator, and planting medium. If detailed blueprints are not available, actually measuring the planters is generally a good way to obtain this volume. The relationship between planting medium, drainage material, and soil separator can be determined using the guidelines of the previous subsection. If the plants are to be left in their cans (as generally recommended), the space between the plants is filled with drainage material. If they are removed from their cans, the space between plants is filled with planting medium. In either case, the amount of volume displaced by the plants is simply the sum of the volume contained in the growing cans. Information for each standard size of growing container is given in Fig. 5.

The installation should not be started unless all lights and water connections are operating, as the plants will need both light and water during the installation — especially the light. If the plants are delivered dry, they should be watered in their cans unless they are to be planted at once and watered immediately after planting. If the plants are removed from their cans and placed into dry planting medium, they and the planting medium should be thoroughly watered immedi-

# PLANTSCAPING
**Plant Use and Procedures**

ately afterward.

Fewer design mistakes will be made if the plants are installed one section at a time, under the direction of a supervisor familiar with the design of the section. If the installation is in an office building, it may be necessary to arrange for a workroom and a freight elevator with access both to the loading dock and the workroom. Depending on the exact arrangements, a crew of four to six workers per supervisor is generally optimum.

It is recommended that each section be planted in the following order. First, leftover building material and other debris are removed from the planting areas. Second, drainage material is added to the proper depth and leveled. Third, the plants, either in or out of their growing containers, are placed on top of the drainage material and the soil separator if present, and arranged according to the design. The spaces between the plants are then filled in with drainage material or planting medium, depending on whether the plants are in or out of their growing containers. If planting medium is used, it should be lightly compacted to prevent its settling later. (If the light intensity is below specifications and periodic replacement of the plants is expected, the plants should be left in their cans.)

After the spaces between the large plants have been filled in, the groundcover, if any, is planted. The use of decorative bark or marble chips on top of the soil is not recommended as they easily mix with the soil and are hard to remove if the plants are replaced.

After all the spaces have been filled, the plants should be thoroughly watered and the maintenance schedule begun. If dry planting medium is used, it should be watered thoroughly several times during the first week to ensure that it is completely wet.

**Removing plants from cans or burlap**  A healthy root system is necessary for the maintenance of a healthy plant. It is the new, very fine, feathery roots that are the most important and also the most easily damaged. This damage is very likely if the soil between the fine roots is dislodged in the course of repotting. Whether the tropical plants are delivered in growing cans or with their roots wrapped in burlap, the root system must be handled with care.

The best procedure for removing a plant from its container is to lean the pot on its side, tap on the container sides and bottom, and carefully slide out the plant. In large container-grown plants (in 17-inch or larger cans), the root system may be held very tightly in the can. In this case, a can cutter, which works on either metal or rubber cans, may be the most gentle way of removing the can. Once the can is removed, the root ball of soil and roots should be scored by making ¼-inch-deep vertical cuts at 3-inch intervals around the root ball from top to bottom. If the can removal and ball scoring are done near the planting site, the exposed root system is subjected to minimum handling.

Very large plants and trees are frequently field-grown rather than container-grown. The root balls of such plants will come wrapped in burlap. When planting them, only the upper half of the burlap should be removed. The lower portion will disintegrate in the soil after the plant is installed.

| Planting Bed Material | Dry Weight | Wet Weight |
|---|---|---|
| Cornell foliage mix | 12-18 lb/cu ft | 25-35 lb/cu ft |
| Peat/topsoil mix | 38-42 lb/cu ft | 70-90 lb/cu ft |
| Topsoil (loam) | 80-100 lb/cu ft | 100-120 lb/cu ft |
| Gravel | 120-135 lb/cu ft | 120-135 lb/cu ft |
| Sand | 95-110 lb/cu ft | 120-130 lb/cu ft |

*Note:* For conversion to metric system: 1 lb = 0.454 kg; 1 cu ft = 0.028 cu m.

**Fig. 4  Planting material weight. These figures are the normal weight for each of the materials in both the dry and the wet state. The exact weight depends on the degree of compaction of the material.**

| Pot Size | Soil Volume | Pot Diameter x Height |
|---|---|---|
| 6 in | 1 gal | 6½ in x 6 in |
| 8 in | 2 gal | 8 in x 7 in |
| 10 in | 3 gal | 10 in x 9½ in |
| 12 in | 4 gal | 11 in x 10½ in |
| 14 in | 7 gal | 13½ in x 12 in |
| 17 in | 10 gal | 17 in x 16 in |
| 22 in | 20 gal | 21 in x 17 in |
| 30 in | 35 gal | 29 in x 17' in |
| 32 in | 65 gal | 32 in x 22 in |
| 36 in | 95 gal | 36 in x 24 in |

*Note:* For conversion to different units, use the following factors. 1 gal = .00495 cu yd = .0038 cu m = .134 cu ft = 3.79 lit; 1 in = 2.54 cm.

**Fig. 5  Pot-size and volume proportions.**

**Rock formations and decorative pools**  Natural elements, such as rock formations, decorative pools, water fountains, and waterfalls, can add an artistic touch and turn an unimaginative large planting arrangement into a full garden. Unfortunately the overuse of such design elements is tempting, since they are usually inexpensive compared with the cost of filling the same area with plants. Provided they are not overused, they can serve as natural sculpture or as the answer for areas with too little light to support plants or where conditions limit the variety of plants that can be used.

In rock formations, volcanic rock is the most commonly used type because it is much lighter than ordinary rock. This weight factor can be of considerable importance when the weight of the garden must be limited. This type of rock is also easy to shape with a hammer and chisel.

Although a large decorative pool or fountain must be custom-designed, there are small fiberglass pools that can be purchased in a variety of sizes and are available in kidney, free-form, or rectangular shapes. They are usually no longer than 6 feet, but they are of a standard 16-inch depth, which is deep enough to accommodate any water plants, recirculating pump, and a filter tray with mat and gravel. Their high-capacity, low-pressure pumps are usually adequate for small fountains and waterfalls.

If decorative pools are used, some thought might be given to using water plants in them. These plants are very attractive and can be easily grown indoors. As with all plants, different species have different growing and flowering habits. A reputable dealer should be consulted for information.

The use of fish in pools should be carefully studied in light of the plant maintenance requirements. Fertilizer, plant chemicals, and limestone runoff from the planting area may enter the circulating water system and kill the fish. Fish can be an attractive design element, but their maintenance requirements must be considered along with the maintenance requirements of the plants.

**Open Plan and Specimen Design**

Modern offices are sometimes sterile places in which to work. The introduction of live plants into such an environment is one way of making the space seem less austere and more comfortable without disrupting the integrity of the original design. For windowless offices, plants provide an attractive natural setting appreciated by the occupants. For offices and other windowed areas, the plants provide a transition which makes indoors and outdoors seem to flow together.

In all locations, however, the light intensity must be at the proper level before the plants are introduced. The intensity cannot be taken for granted, since artificial lighting designed for office vision is seldom enough for any but the lowest-light plant species. Even a large window will not provide enough light if it has an overhang or a northern exposure. If the light intensity cannot be directly measured or calculated from detailed ceiling plans, one must assume the worst and use only low-light material. There is sometimes a tendency to use plants to fill in otherwise forgotten spots, such as corners, stairwells, and hallways. Such areas are often poorly lit and no plant will survive there unless additional lighting is installed.

In large areas with barely enough light, the usual design problem is how to arrange the limited number of low-light species so that different areas stand out from one another. Design interest can be accomplished by using different types of foliage (for example, fragmented and solid) in the different areas, varying the plant sizes among the areas or using specimen plants selectively.

Specimen plants usually have fuller foliage or an unusual stem structure and hence appear to be different from other plants of that species. The true specimen plants are more expensive than ordinary plants of the same species, but can solve many a design problem. However, a plant with fuller foliage than most will also require more light than most to maintain the foliage.

If the office has floor-to-ceiling walls, the best design procedure is to select specimen plants that act as living sculptures. Since these plants are used for visual emphasis, the plant height and container size should conform to the scale of the rest of the interior design. The plant texture and container finish should blend with each other and with the wall and floor treatments. The particular plant specimen chosen should have an inherently interesting shape and texture.

If the office area is very large or is designed along an "office landscaping" plan with movable partitions, the plants can become an integral part of the design. They can be used with the partitions as space dividers and are excellent for indicating the importance of the space. They also may be effective in relating widely separated areas with one another. They break the monotony of the partitions with both color and texture. They act as sound absorbers. Also, specimen plants can be used in the office landscaping scheme for visual emphasis.

**Planting into individual planters** Individual decorative containers are used for individual plants or small plant groupings. The plants are left in their growing containers and placed directly into the decorative planter on top of 4 to 6 inches of perlite as the drainage material. The decorative planter or container must be tall enough to accommodate the growing can and the perlite, and wide enough to accommodate the width of the growing can. The space between the growing can and the inner wall of the planter can be filled with additional perlite. (See Fig. 2 for size-selection guidance.) As a decorative finishing, bark chips or sheet moss may be placed on the surface of the soil in the growing can. This decorative cover can be easily removed if the plant is replaced and it does not mix with the soil, as sometimes happens in large gardens.

Removing the plant from the growing can and repotting it directly into the planter is not generally recommended. Replacing the plant, if necessary, is a messy job unless drainage material and soil separator are added to the bottom of the container. Also, once removed from its growing container, the plant may take up to four weeks to adjust fully to its new environment.

## CONTAINERS

### Decorative Containers: Different Types

A plant container should be more than decorative. Its proper selection is the first element of proper maintenance, since the container must provide the plant roots with sufficient growing room and with adequate drainage.

All small to medium-size plants are received from the grower in growing containers, usually metal cans or rubber tubs. Large plants are either in large growing containers or their root balls are wrapped in burlap. As a rule, these growing cans provide the proper volume of soil for the size of the plant and have a hole in the bottom for drainage. There is seldom any need to remove the plant from its growing container, especially since rough handling of the root system can shock the plant. Only the smaller plants, such as ivy, can be repotted without much disturbance of the root system. If it is absolutely necessary to repot a larger plant, it should be done carefully as outlined earlier, and it should be always into a larger volume of soil, never into a smaller volume.

The decorative container should be chosen so that its inside dimensions are large enough that the plant-growing container can be dropped directly into it. In addition, it should be deep enough for the growing container to rest on at least 2 inches of perlite or other drainage material, and leave about 1 inch between the top of the growing can and the top of the decorative container. Some care must be taken in the choice since the interior dimensions of the decorative container are often not uniformly related to the exterior dimensions. For example, some fiberglass containers have a large lip which limits the size of the growing can that can be dropped directly into them. Also some containers have a large false bottom, which makes the interior depth much less than the outside height.

With these simple size-selection rules in mind, the proper decorative container can be selected using Fig. 6 as a guide. This figure lists the decorative pros and cons of the most common types of containers.

### Excess Water in Container

Overwatering of plants is more harmful than underwatering. This problem is most likely to occur when the plants are in individual decorative containers that do not allow the excess water to flow off. To minimize this danger, we have recommended that a plant in a decorative container be double-potted. In the bottom of the decorative container, below the plant growing can, there should be at least 2 inches of perlite or other drainage material to act as a reservoir for excess water. Nevertheless, if the plant is continually overwatered, this reservoir will fill up and lead to root rot because the roots are in a pool of water.

If the plant soil is continually wet to the touch, excess water may be the problem. The water level in the container may be determined by tapping the sides of the container. If the water level indicates excess water, the container is tilted on its side, the plant gently pulled from the container, and the excess water drained from the perlite. If the perlite is completely saturated or appears old, it must be discarded and replaced with new drainage material. If the plant has been sitting in a pool of water for some time, the root ball should be allowed to dry before repotting.

If a very large container or garden has been overwatered and there is no way to drain out the excess water, not really much can be done short of using a small electric pump. One must simply avoid watering the plant or garden at all until the soil has begun to dry out and feels dry to the touch.

# PLANTSCAPING

Plant Containers

### Automatic Watering Devices

In areas where regular maintenance would be difficult, the use of automatic watering devices can be of considerable help. Even when they are used, however, the plant must be checked periodically to see that the device is working properly, that its water reservoir is full, and that no other maintenance problems have developed.

Automatic watering devices are either external to the container or are built into the planter. The external devices tend to work well only with small plants, and also, they are likely to detract from the design. For these reasons, the built-in type of device is preferred. The planters with this type come in both cylindrical and rectangular shapes and in several colors. The planter has a hollow space within its double-wall sides which serves to hold a three- to four-week water supply, feeding the water to the plant soil by a wick mechanism, sensor, or capillary action. Most types have a float to indicate the amount of water remaining in the reservoir.

Since the soil must be in contact with the wick or capillary tubes for the device to work, the plant must be removed from its original growing can and repotted directly in the planter. As the soil never dries out, the plant must be watched for symptoms of overwatering. Because different plants use water at different rates under different humidity and temperature conditions, a timetable should be kept for each container so the maintenance staff will know when to refill each reservoir.

The use of automatic watering devices will not eliminate maintenance personnel, but it will reduce the number of workers needed. One person can handle many more plants, devoting more time to cleaning and trimming, since the reservoir has to be refilled only every month or so. Occasionally, however, one will find a client who will resist the use of the automatic devices because he or she likes the assurance of seeing a person with a watering can once a week.

The use of the automatic watering devices is expected to increase in the future as more architects and designers become aware of them and convince their clients of their usefulness, and as the manufacturers produce more colors and styles and improve the efficiency of the devices.

| Container Type | Pros | Cons |
|---|---|---|
| Fiberglass | Large selection of sizes, shapes, and colors. Light weight, easy to move. Some types have casters. Reasonable prices. Many manufacturers. | Easily scratched. Some types have large lips. |
| Ceramic | Large selection of sizes, shapes, colors, and textures. Rich appearance. Can be put on casters. | Expensive. Easily broken in shipping and handling. |
| Metal | Large selection of sizes and styles. Rich appearance. Polished or brushed finish. | Expensive. |
| Baskets, traditional | Good range of styles and textures. Combines well with all furniture styles. Reasonable prices. | Limited sizes. Tend to sag. Need saucer under plant can to prevent water spillage. |
| Baskets woven around metal | Good texture range. Reasonable prices. Do not sag. Need no saucers. Combine well with all furniture styles. | Sizes limited. |
| Plastic | Least expensive. Good for table plants. Versatile. | Available mostly in green or white. Sizes largely limited to standard pot sizes. Need saucers underneath. Cheap appearance. |
| Hanging planters (Heavy; must be used with a rotating hook which can support the weight and allow for easy plant access.) | Available in ceramic, fiberglass, plastic, and metal. Ceramic in various shapes and textures, metal in various finishes. Plastic and fiberglass are inexpensive. All are versatile. | Makes plants susceptible to drafts from heating and air conditioning. Difficult to water without spilling on floor. Metal very expensive. All need inner pot to allow for drainage. Ceramic is porous and presents condensation problem. |

Fig. 6  Comparison of container types.

| Design Type | Plant Name | Watering Requirements |
|---|---|---|
| **HIGH-LIGHT PLANTS—150 FOOTCANDLES AND UP** | | |
| T | Fiddle-leaf fig (Ficus lyrata) | W |
| T | Indian laurel (Ficus retusa) | W |
| T | Rubber plant (Ficus elastica cv. 'Decora') | W |
| T | Weeping fig (Ficus benjamina) | W |
| T | Norfolk Island pine (Araucaria heterophylla) | LF |
| T | Schefflera (Brassaia actinophylla) | W |
| FP | Dwarf date palm (Phoenix Roebelenii) | LF |
| FP | Dwarf schefflera (Brassaia arboricola) | W |
| FP | False aralia (Dizygotheca elegantissima) | W |
| FP | Lady palm (Rhapis excelsa) | W |
| FP | Mock orange (Pittosporum Tobira) | W |
| FP | Ponytail (Beaucarnea recurvata) | LF |
| FP | Southern yew (Podocarpus macrophyllus var. Maki) | LF |
| DTP | Jade plant (Crassula argentea) | LF |
| DTP | Swedish ivy (Plectranthus australis) | MF |
| DTP | Wax plant (Hoya carnosa) | MF |
| **MEDIUM-LIGHT PLANTS—100 TO 150 FOOTCANDLES** | | |
| T | Indian laurel (Ficus retusa) | W |
| T | Schefflera (Brassaia actinophylla) | W |
| T | Weeping fig (Ficus benjamina) | W |
| FP | Bamboo palm (Chamaedorea erumpens) | MF |
| FP | Corn plant (Dracaena fragrans cv. 'Massangeana') | W |
| FP | Dwarf date palm (Phoenix Roebelenii) | LF |
| FP | Dwarf dragon tree (Dracaena marginata) | LF |
| FP | Dwarf schefflera (Brassaia arboricola) | W |
| FP | Green dracaena (Dracaena deremensis cv. 'Janet Craig') | W |
| FP | Green pleomele (Dracaena reflexa) | W |
| FP | Kentia palm (Howea Forsterana) | W |
| FP | Narrow-leaved pleomele (Dracaena angustifolia honoraii) | W |
| FP | Neantha bella palm (Chamaedorea elegans) | W |
| FP | Reed palm (Chamaedorea Seifrizii) | MF |
| FP | Self-heading philodendron (Philodendron Selloum) | LF |

| Design Type | Plant Name | Watering Requirements |
|---|---|---|
| DTP | Boston fern (Nephrolepis exaltata cv. 'Bostoniensis') | W |
| DTP | Chinese evergreen (Aglaonema commutatum var. maculatum) | LF |
| DTP | Common philodendron (Philodendron scandens oxycardium) | W |
| DTP | Dumb cane (Dieffenbachia maculata cv. 'Rudolph Roehrs') | LF |
| DTP | Golden pothos (Epipremnum aureum) | LF |
| DTP | Grape ivy (Cissus rhombifolia) | W |
| DTP | Prayer plant (Maranta leuconeura) | W |
| DTP | Swedish ivy (Plectranthus australis) | W |
| DTP | White flag (Spathiphyllum cv. 'Clevelandii') | W |
| DTP | White-striped dracaena (Dracaena deremensis cv. 'Warneckii') | W |
| **LOW-LIGHT PLANTS—50 TO 100 FOOTCANDLES** | | |
| FP | Corn plant (Dracaena fragrans cv. 'Massangeana') | W |
| FP | Dwarf dragon tree (Dracaena marginata) | LF |
| FP | Green dracaena (Dracaena deremensis cv. 'Janet Craig') | W |
| FP | Green pleomele (Dracaena reflexa) | W |
| FP | Kentia palm (Howea Forsterana) | W |
| FP | Neantha bella palm (Chamaedorea elegans) | W |
| FP | Reed palm (Chamaedorea Seifrizii) | W |
| FP | Self-heading philodendron (Philodendron Selloum) | W |
| DTP | Chinese evergreen (Aglaonema commutatum var. maculatum) | LF |
| DTP | Common philodendron (Philodendron scandens oxycardium) | W |
| DTP | White Flag (Spathiphyllum cv. 'Clevelandii') | W |

**A Final Word about Lighting Intensity** The preceding lighting-intensity recommendations are based on experience and the assumption that these levels will be provided eight hours a day, five days a week, and that the plants have been fully acclimatized. If light can be provided for more hours each day or more days each week, the plant material will look its best for longer periods. On the other hand, often the energy costs of the longer lighting exposure are more than the costs of plant replacement. However, if the plants are not to be maintained by the landscape contractor with a plant replacement guarantee, provision should be made for giving the plants light exposure seven days a week.

**Fig. 7** Growing requirements. Design type: T = tree; FP = floor plant; DTP = desk or table plant or ground cover. Watering requirements: W = water weekly; MF = water more frequently, as required; LF = water less frequently, as required.

# PLANTSCAPING
**Typical Plants**

### (False) Aralia

A plant of grace and elegance with narrow, ribbonlike, notched leaves of dark green, usually born on slender, single stems. The aralia is attractive if two or three plants are planted together in one pot. It grows very quickly, so prune the stem tips from time to time to prevent the foliage from thinning at the bottom.

**Temperature**   The aralia is tolerant of warm temperatures if there is plenty of humidity.

**Light/sun**   The plant likes a semisunny to semishady window; an east or west window is ideal.

**Water/humidity**   Keep the soil damp but not soggy. The false aralia likes a humid atmosphere. Place your plant on a pebble tray and mist the foliage daily.

**Soil**   The soil should be equal parts loam, sand, and peat moss.

**Special care**   You can rejuvenate leggy plants by drastically cutting the stems back to four to six inches from the pot. Do this in the spring and leave the plant in a sheltered location, being sure to fertilize and water frequently.

### African Violet

The African violet, a longtime favorite houseplant, does insist on more care and attention, but its beautiful blossoms make the effort worthwhile.

**Temperature**   African violets are more contented and grow best within a temperature range of 65 to 80 degrees. Be careful that your plants are not in an open window or a draft.

**Light/sun**   The African violet enjoys a place in an east or west window. Direct sun is too strong, unless filtered through a curtain. Excess sun will cause spotting and loss of color, and too little light causes elongated stems and no blooms.

**Water/humidity**   African violets should be watered from the saucer underneath in the morning with *lukewarm* water. Water when the soil begins to dry out. Do not keep it soggy. If the air is dry in your home, place the potted plant in a tray of moistened pebbles.

**Soil**   The soil should be porous for good drainage and should contain ample organic matter such as compost or peat moss. Commercial African violet soil mixture is specially prepared for these plants; however, add sand or perlite to ensure adequate drainage. A plastic pot is less likely to cause the lower leaves to rot where they touch the pot.

**ASPARAGUS FERN**
*Asparagus sprengeri*

### Asparagus Fern — Emerald Feather

The bright feathery green of this delightful plant is best displayed in a hanging container. The long branches drape gracefully and are studded with tiny white flowers that ripen into red-orange berries.

**Temperature**   Asparagus fern is not fussy about temperatures, but prefers a range of 60 to 68 degrees.

**Light/sun**   The bright filtered sun of an east or west window is a good location for this plant.

**Water/humidity**   Soak the soil in the pot thoroughly and allow it to become dry to the touch before rewatering.

**Soil**   A well-drained potting soil or a mixture of equal parts of loam, peat moss, and sand or perlite.

**How to start new plants**   Allow the berries to ripen and when dry sow the seeds they contain. Asparagus fern can usually be grown from seed quite well.

**AVOCADO**
*Persea americana*

### Avocado

The avocado comes easily from seed and is grown for its ornamental foliage. It makes a nice tree for your indoor garden. Allow the plant to reach the desired height and then begin regular pinching to force branching and encourage bushy growth.

**Temperature**  Temperatures between 60 and 70 degrees suit the avocado well.

**Light/sun**  Keep your avocado in bright light but protected from direct sun. Avocados are easily sunburned, especially when they are first moved outside.

**Water/humidity**  Use tepid water and keep the soil moist. Place the plant on a pebble tray to raise the humidity level around it. This plant likes a fair amount of humidity and benefits from regular misting. Any signs of browning or crispness at the tips and along the edges of the leaves means the plant needs more humidity.

**Soil**  Use a mixture consisting of equal parts of sand, loam, and peat moss.

**BOSTON FERN**
*Nephrolepis exaltata*

### Boston Fern

Exaltant is a good adjective for this family of ferns that can fill a corner with rich green foliage. These ferns are excellent for hanging baskets. Initially the ferns may need a lot of attention until the right combination of environmental factors is achieved, but the effort is well worth it. The leaflets grow on a midrib that is covered with fine brown hairs and vary from smooth-edged to feathery and even ruffled. A mature fern can have fronds ranging in length from two to three feet and two to three inches across.

**Temperature**  With lots and lots of humidity, ferns will do well in house temperatures in the 60 to 70 degree range.

**Light/sun**  Ferns need a location with good bright light, but this means filtered sunlight. *Avoid direct sunlight.*

**Water/humidity**  It is essential that the roots of the ferns never dry out at any time. Soak the soil regularly. Clay pots and hanging baskets can be soaked in a bucket or the sink for half an hour and then drained. The soil should be checked daily to make sure that it is not drying out. Humidity is the most important ingredient to successful fern growing. Place pots of ferns on a pebble tray. Mist the foliage daily with room temperature water.

**Soil**  Ferns need a soil that is loose and easily penetrated by their dense root system. The soil mixture should be rich in peat moss and organic matter with a liberal amount of sand for drainage. A sprinkling of charcoal mixed in the soil helps to keep the soil from becoming sour from the frequent waterings. When potting ferns, place a layer of bits of broken pots or gravel in the bottom of the pot. Ferns do not take kindly to having their roots tampered with, so be careful not to damage them when repotting.

**CHINESE EVERGREEN**
*Aglanonema modestum*

### Chinese Evergreen

This beautiful foliage plant has waxy dark green leaves. The leaves grow on a canelike stem and are oblong, tapering to a thin tip. Some of the varieties are variegated with splashes of creamy white or yellow. Under optimal conditions, it will produce a flower spike surrounded by a white spathe. The flower is similar to a calla lilly. The great thing about this plant is that it will adapt to a variety of environments which makes it a good plant for a beginner or a difficult location.

**Temperature**  A range of 60 to 70 degrees suits this plant well.

**Light/sun**  A shady spot, an artificial light, or any other location will suit this plant. The Chinese evergreen is an excellent plant for a north window.

**Water/humidity**  Keep the soil moist but not soggy. To avoid waterlogged soil, allow the surface soil to become dry to the touch before rewatering. The Chinese evergreen can be grown in water. The roots are attractive so a clear glass container shows them off to best advantage. It is important to wash the leaves regularly to keep them dust free.

**Soil**  The soil should be equal parts of garden loam, peat moss, and sand.

Dracaena sanderiana

Dracaena marginata

Dracaena deremensis "Warneckei"

### Dracaenas

There are several varieties of dracaenas which vary in foliage color, variegation, and size. Here are three that are commonly available.

*Dracaena deremensis "Warneckei":* is a good choice for a location without much light. The gray green foliage is striped with white and gray.

*Dracaena marginata:* has clusters of narrow deep green leaves edged with red and gray stems strongly marked with leaf scars. This variety will reach a height of five or six feet.

*Dracaena sanderiana:* resembles a corn plant in the brightness of the green and the size and shape of the leaves with the difference that the leaves are striped with white.

**Temperature**   Moderate household temperatures in the 60 to 70 degree range suit these plants best. It is important to keep plants away from heating vents.

**Light/sun**   The marginata and sanderiana should get only filtered sun or bright light. The Warneckei will fare well in a spot with very little light; it will flourish when more light is available.

**Water/humidity**   These plants all like soil that is kept evenly moist but not soggy. Soak the soil in the pot thoroughly and then rewater when the soil surface feels dry to the touch. Humidity is a must. Brown crispy leaf tips and margins mean too little moisture in the air. It is a good idea to place the dracaenas in pebble trays and mist the foliage daily.

**Soil**   Commercial potting soil is adequate but added drainage material such as sand or perlite is advisable.

**DUMB CANE**
Dieffenbachia maculata

### Dumb Cane

The cool-looking foliage of this plant is yellow-green, mottled with white. The leaves are pointed ovals that become quite large as the plant matures. The dieffenbachia is known as the "mother-in-law" plant or the dumb cane because when a piece of the stem is placed on the tongue it causes temporary numbness and loss of speech. All joking aside, *this plant is poisonous.*

**Temperature**   The dieffenbachia prefers warm temperatures and will tolerate hot dry places with added humidity.

**Light/sun**   This plant does well in an east or west window where it can bask in the sun for a few hours.

**Water/humidity**   The soil should be allowed to dry out for a few days before rewatering. The plants indicate a need for water when the leaves show signs of dropping. Regular misting keeps the foliage dust-free and luxuriant.

**Soil**   A porous soil of equal parts loam, peat moss, and sand is fine.

**GARDENIA**
Gardenia radicans floraplena

### Gardenia

The gardenia is a handsome foliage plant with intensely fragrant blooms, but it has an extremely temperamental nature. It is a challenging plant to grow successfully indoors. The most frequently available varieties are *Gardenia radicans floraplena,* a low spreading plant with small double flowers, and *Gardenia florida,* which blooms in summer.

**Temperature**   The temperature must be kept above 65 degrees to maintain healthy foliage and flower buds. These plants hate drafts. Loss of flower buds is often due to sudden changes in temperature.

**Light/sun**   The gardenia needs lots of light, but avoid strong sun that might burn the leaves.

**Water/humidity**   The soil must be kept constantly moist without becoming soggy. Submerge the pot in a bucket of lukewarm water and allow it to soak for half an hour or until the soil is moist on the surface. Do not allow the pot to sit in water as that will cause the roots to rot. Gardenias need very high humidity at all times. Place the pot in a tray of moistened pebbles. Mist the foliage daily with tepid water. Leaf or bud drops indicate the air is too dry.

**Soil**   Potting soil should be a mixture of equal parts peat moss, loam and well-decayed manure with sand or perlite added for drainage.

**GRAPE IVY**
*Cissus rhombifolia*

### Grape Ivy

Grape ivy is a climber or trailer. The olive colored green leaves look a bit like those of holly without the stiffness or the sharp tips. The leaves form attractive groups of three and are accompanied by furry tendrils.

**Temperature** The plant is fairly tolerant of a wide temperature range. Increase the amount of humidity as the temperature goes up.

**Light/sun** Grape ivy will do all right in low light and is often used in low light areas. But it flourishes with bright light or filtered sunlight.

**Water/humidity** Soak the pot and soil thoroughly and then allow the soil to become dry to the touch before rewatering. Mist frequently and wash the foliage regularly to remove dust and restore the luster of the leaves.

**Soil** A potting soil that is rich in organic matter is the best. Be sure to add plenty of drainage material to the soil mixture.

**JADE PLANT**
*Crassula arborescens*

### Jade Plant

The jade plant is a tough plant well-suited to the hot dry conditions so prevalent in office and apartment buildings. The rounded leaves are in pairs on the branched treelike stem. A plant that is six to eight years old will produce clusters of lacy-looking star-shaped flowers.

**Temperature** Temperatures ranging from 65 to 75 degrees are fine. Lower and higher temperature will be tolerated.

**Light/sun** The jade plant will require full sunlight with shade at midday if possible. A west or south window would be good locations. If you put the plant outside in the summer, place it in a lightly shaded spot.

**Water/humidity** The soil should remain dry for several days between waterings. The fleshy leaves soak up the soil water and store it for future use. Too much water will cause stem and root rot and certain death.

**Soil** The jade plant will do well in rich garden soil that has coarse sand or fine bits of broken pots added to it for drainage. Each year give the pot a top dressing of humus. A new pot will be necessary only after about three or four years.

**NORFOLK ISLAND PINE**
*Araucaria excelsa*

### Norfolk Island Pine

The delightful symmetry of this evergreen makes it a desirable house plant. The branches grow in tiers of six, each tier representing a year's growth. The bright green needles are soft and pleasant to touch.

**Temperature** The ideal temperature is between 50 and 60 degrees. High temperatures are tolerated when sufficient humidity is available.

**Light/sun** The filtered sun of an east or west window is best. Yellowing of the needles might mean too much sun.

**Water/humidity** Provide the plant with a well-drained soil and pot. Water thoroughly and allow the soil surface to become dry before rewatering. Daily misting is necessary for the warmer temperatures of most houses and offices. A pebble tray will help to add more moisture to the air around the plant.

**Soil** Garden loam mixed with equal parts of sand and peat moss makes a suitable potting mixture. Repot the Norfolk Island pine only when it has become potbound (the pot is crammed with roots). This would be about every two or three years.

**PARLOR PALM**
*Chamaedora elegans*

### Parlor Palm

The palm trees are not the easiest plants to grow. However, once you have discovered their basic needs they are a delightful addition to your indoor garden. This palm grows to about four feet tall. It is most attractive when two or three plants are grouped together in a pot. The long feathery fronds grow out of a single stem. Other varieties to try are *C. seifrizii, C. erumpens,* and *C. costarincana.*

**Temperature** The best growing temperatures for palms range between 60 and 75 degrees.

**Light/sun** Palms are good plants for locations without much light. They do not like direct sun light.

**Water/humidity** During the active growing season, between March and October, the palm needs moist soil but it will not tolerate soggy soil. In the winter months, allow the soil to dry on the surface before rewatering. If the foliage shows signs of browning and drying on the tips, it needs more humidity. Misting regularly is recommended to keep the foliage healthy.

**Soil** The palm needs well-drained soil of equal parts rich garden loam, peat moss, and sand. It will need repotting only every two or three years. It prefers being a bit potbound.

**COMMON PHILODENDRON**
*Philodendron oxycardium*

### Philodendron

By nature, the philodendron is a climbing plant, but it also trails. It looks best on a bracket beside the window frame, and for good effect must be kept strongly pinched back so that the plant is full of bushy young growth and does not deteriorate into two or three stringlike stems.

**Temperature** Normal house or office temperatures are fine.

**Light/sun** The philodendron is quite hardy and robust and will grow almost anywhere. However, it will fare better in a well-lighted area.

**Water/humidity** The plant should be kept evenly moist and never allowed to dry out. Be certain water does not remain in the saucer after watering. The foliage should be misted daily and the leaves cleaned of accumulated dust.

**Soil** Potting soil mixed with perlite, vermiculite, or sand and peat moss is recommended.

**WINDOWLEAF PHILODRON**
*Philodendron pertusum "Monstera deliciosa"*

### Windowleaf Philodendrom

This philodendron has large heart-shaped leaves that are slashed irregularly. It is an enthusiastic climber and needs a piece of bark or totem for support. The aerial roots can be inserted in the soil or encouraged to attach to the totem. Keep the growing tips pinched back so that the plant doesn't get leggy.

**Temperature** The windowleaf prefers temperatures between 65 and 70 degrees.

**Light/sun** Bright light is best for this plant. However, avoid putting the plant in a location where the plant would get direct sun.

**Water/humidity** Soak the plant thoroughly and allow the soil surface to remain dry for a day or two before rewatering. Mist the foliage daily and wash the leaves weekly to remove dust.

**Soil** A soil mixture of equal parts garden loam, peat moss, and sand is fine.

**PURPLE PASSION PLANT - VELVET PLANT**
*Gynura aurantica*

## Purple Passion Plant — Velvet Plant

The strikingly rich royal purple coloring and velvety texture of the foliage and stems attract many growers. The green leaves and stems are covered with tiny purple hairs. The straggly growth habit is best kept in check by frequent pruning.

**Temperature**   The purple passion plant likes temperatures in the 65 to 70 degree range.

**Light/sun**   Direct or partial sun will promote the color.

**Water/humidity**   It is important that the velvet plant not dry out. Keep the soil evenly moist at all times. A humid atmosphere is important to keep the brilliant color. Mist the foliage frequently and place the pot in a tray of moistened pebbles to raise the humidity.

**Soil**   Use potting soil of equal parts garden loam, peat moss, and sand. This plant will also grow in water.

## Rubber Tree Plant

This house plant with dark green glossy leaves can grow to be four feet high with a little care and not too much water.

**Temperature**   Due to its hardy nature, the plant does well in any normal household temperature.

**Light/sun**   The plant will do well in almost any light, but a well-lighted area is best for the rich green foliage characteristic of the rubber tree plant.

**Water/humidity**   Water only when the soil is completely dry all through the pot. You should set the entire pot in a bucket when watering, so that moisture can penetrate the deepest roots. Clean the leaves every two weeks or so with a damp cloth. Do not artificially shine the leaves as this clogs the plant's pores and does not allow it to breathe!

**Soil**   Soil should be a well-drained mixture of equal parts of sand, peat moss, and garden loam. If pot is plastic or rubber, be sure to provide plenty of drainage material in the bottom of the pot.

**RUBBER TREE PLANT**
*Ficus elastica decora*

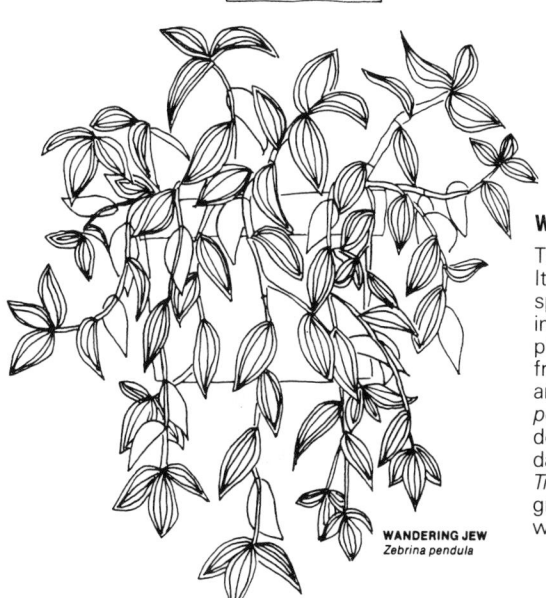

## Wandering Jew

This is a particularly attractive hanging plant. It is hardy and easy to grow with only one special requirement, which is regular pinching to keep it full and bushy. There are several plants called Wandering Jew, distinguished from each other by their different colorings and markings. The illustration is a *Zebrina pendula*. The leaf is a pointed oval with a deep purple underside, and the upperside is dark green striped with pale silvery-green. *Tradescantia fluminensis* has small oval green leaves marked with white, silver and white, or yellow.

**Temperature**   These plants prefer warm temperatures.

**Light/sun**   Bright indirect sunlight keeps the foliage brilliant. Avoid direct sunlight as they are susceptible to sunburn.

**Water/humidity**   Water generously, keeping the soil moist at all times. During the winter months it will not need quite as much water.

**Soil**   This plant grows in a well-drained potting soil, or water.

**WANDERING JEW**
*Zebrina pendula*

### Schefflera — Umbrella Tree

If you are looking for a tree for your indoor garden, a schefflera is a good choice. It has handsome deep green leaves that radiate out from a long slender stalk rather like the ribs of an umbrella.

**Temperature**  The umbrella tree does well in a room where the temperature ranges from 55 to 75 degrees.

**Light/sun**  The schefflera does not like direct sunlight. It grows best in good light from a shaded window.

**Water/humidity**  When watering your schefflera, soak the pot thoroughly and then allow the soil to dry before rewatering. The plant likes a humid atmosphere and responds well to daily misting with warm water. This is essential if the plant is in a room with forced hot air heat. This plant needs a pebble tray.

**Soil**  The soil mixture for the umbrella tree should be equal parts of peat moss, garden soil, and sand. The pot should have a layer of gravel or bits of broken pots underneath the soil to ensure good drainage.

**SCHEFFLERA - UMBRELLA TREE**
*Schefflera venulosa*

### Snake Plant

Seen in many homes and offices, this spikey, banded plant will take almost any abuse.

**Temperature**  Normal household temperatures are best, *but* do not allow the plant to become suddenly chilled!

**Light/sun**  The snake plant is a good low light plant but needs sun in order to bloom.

**Water**  The plant likes the dryness of the home and should never be overwatered. The leaves should be cleaned with clear water every two weeks.

**Soil**  Garden loam, peat moss, and sand mixed together provides the best soil for the snake plant.

**SNAKE PLANT**
*Sansevieria trifasciata*

### Spider Plant

With its green and white foliage, the spider plant makes one of the best hanging plants. The graceful trailing runners have plantlets and white star-shaped flowers. There are all-green varieties but the more commonly seen one has a green leaf striped with white.

**Temperature**  The plant lives best in a warm location.

**Light/sun**  This lovely plant does very well hanging in indirect sun or a moderately lighted area.

**Water/humidity**  The spider plant should be allowed to dry out before rewatering. Drying leaf tips usually indicates lack of humidity. To tidy up the plant just snip these off.

**Soil**  The plant grows contentedly in a rich soil composed of garden loam, sand, and peat moss.

**SPIDER PLANT**
*Chlorophytum elatum vittatum*

### Zebra Plant

The zebra plant is one of the showiest house plants one can grow. Its spike of waxy yellow flowers and deep shiny green leaves veined in white makes it a striking specimen.

**Temperature**   The zebra plant needs warm temperatures free from drafts.

**Light/sun**   The plant wants bright light but not direct sunlight.

**Water/humidity**   It is important never to allow the soil to dry out. Set the pot in a pebble tray and mist the foliage daily.

**Soil**   The zebra plant likes loose soil consisting of one part garden loam, one part sand or perlite, and two parts peat moss.

SOIL LEVEL — 3"

NURSERY CONTAINER (MAJOR PLANT)

PLANTING MEDIUM (SEE SPECS)

3" CRUSHED STONE DRAINAGE LAYER

MINOR PLANT

CONTRACTOR SHALL CUT VERTICAL SLITS IN CONTAINER PRIOR TO PLANTING

DECORATIVE PLANTER - FIBERGLASS OR CUSTOM WOOD; SEE PLANS

SOIL SEPARATOR

TYPICAL PLANTING DETAIL

FOR APPLICATION
OF STANDARDS,
SEE SPECS

① PLANT STANDARDS: OVERALL PLANT HEIGHT
NOT TO SCALE

THIS DETAIL APPLIES TO
ALL SHRUBS OVER 5' HIGH

② PLANT STANDARDS: CANE HEIGHT
NOT TO SCALE

③ TREE PLANTING DETAIL
NOT TO SCALE

④ SHRUB PLANTING DETAIL
NOT TO SCALE

ZAMIA LEFT IN NURSERY POTS

MOSS @ VOIDS

10" NURSERY POT

"PROMIX - B"

FIBERGLASS PLANTER

"FALSE" PLANTER

SOIL SEPARATOR

3" CRUSHED STONE

DZYGOTHEGA PLANTED IN FIBERGLASS CONTAINERS

MOSS COVERING ALL EXPOSED SOIL AND VOIDS

"PROMIX - B" PLANTING MEDIA

ROOT BALL

SOIL SEPARATOR

3" CRUSHED STONE

PLANTING DETAIL IN "FALSE" PLANTER

STUDS
1'0 O.C.

HARDWOOD CORNER

1½"x½"x½" OR 1½"x1½"x¼" STEEL ANGLE
4" LEGS W/ BEVELED HOLE FOR WL #12
FLATHEAD WOOD SCREWS AS SHOWN

2'x2"(NOM.) WOOD STUDS

ELASTOMERIC MEMBRANE

⑧ PLANTER CORNER STUD DETAIL

½" SQUARE HARDWOOD CORNER
MOLDING W/ ⅜" RADIUS
ROUTED EDGE

⑨ PLANTER CORNER DETAIL

3/16" ROUNDED EDGE (TYPICAL)

HARDWOOD CAP (SHOWN FULL SCALE)

1½"x #12 FLATHEAD WOOD SCREWS
@ 6' O.C. (STAGGER AS SHOWN)

3d FINISHING NAILS, COUNTERSINK
AND FILL HOLES W/ PLASTIC WOOD

2"x2"(NOM.) WOOD TOP PLATE

1½" WIDE STEEL CORNER BRACE 4" LEGS,
BEVELED HOLES TO RECEIVE 4-#12
FLAT HEAD WOOD SCREWS

3d FINISHING NAILS @ 4" O.C. VERT.
COUNTERSINK AND FILL HOLES.

ELASTOMERIC WATERPROOFING
20 GAUGE MINIMUM

½" MARINE PLYWOOD GLUE TO STUDS
W/ WATERPROOF GLUE

2'x2"(NOM.) WOOD STUD @ 1'0" O.C.

½" BIRCH PLYWOOD, GLUE TO STUD
W/ WATERPROOF GLUE

3d FINISHING NAILS @ 4" O.C. VERT.
COUNTERSINK AND FILL HOLES W/
PLASTIC WOOD

1½"x1½" STEEL ANGLE CORNER BRACE
4" LEGS BEVELED HOLES FOR 1½x #12
FLATHEAD WOOD SCREWS AS SHOWN
BELOW, SEE ⑧

3d FINISHING NAILS, COUNTERSINK
AND FILL HOLES W/ PLASTIC WOOD (TYP.)

2"x2"(NOM.) WOOD BOTTOM PLATE

2"(NOM.) WOOD
JOIST

½" BIRCH PLYWOOD, GLUE TO JOIST
W/ WATERPROOF GLUE

2"(NOM.)x2" WOOD
JOIST @ 1'0" O.C.

3d FINISHING NAILS, COUNTERSINK
AND FILL HOLES W/ PLASTIC WOOD

⑦ PLANTER SECTION.

**SECTION of PLANTER @ WINDOW**

**FLOOR LEVEL PLANT WITH FLOOR @ FINIS EXTERIOR GRADE**

**FRONT ELEVATION** SCALE ¼"=1'-0" **SECTION D-D**

**PLAN B-B** SCALE ¼" = 1'-0"

**PLAN A-A of ROOM DIVIDER W/ PLANTER**

**SECTION C-C**

**Fig. 8** Detail 1: In this window planter, the plants are placed directly in the earth or growing medium filling the planter and continue to grow and blossom there. The entire planter is contained within a galvanized steel pan with drain. The 6-in-high perforated pipe allows for drainage of excess water over a long period of time before the entire planter has to be cleaned out and started anew. Detail 2: This is a simple floor-level planter where the drainage can easily be connected to the building's drainage system. Here also, plants are installed and grow naturally until a complete planting change is required. Detail 3: A room divider planter for the Ackermann residence, Southampton, New York, consists of a planter-bookcase combination. Here the plants remain in their clay pots and are inserted in the planter with or without gravel or some other type of filler. The entire planter is pitched toward one end, where the drain empties into a small container which catches any extra water.

# PLANTSCAPING

## Planters

**Section of window planter in a south wall**

**Planter for a warm climate**

**Planter for a restaurant or store**

**Floor planter**

**Fig. 9   Detail 1:** The plants remain in their own clay pots. The use of pea gravel at top and only 4 in of ¾-in gravel at bottom permits easy changes of the plants. To take care of watering and drainage, the copper pan is simply sloped to one side and two screened drains are connected, trapped, and joined to a waste line. This takes care of any excess water, as it is eliminated by gravity drainage. **Detail 2:** This planter is for areas where freezing does not occur, and the drainage of excess water can be taken care of by simply extending small pipes directly to the exterior. **Detail 3:** In this planter the plants remain within the planter and excess water is carried off by a screened pipe at the bottom. Pea gravel is used as a 1-in topping so that odds and ends dropped into the planter can easily be removed. **Detail 4:** A planter in a commercial lobby or entrance is shown in this detail. The plants are permanently installed and the tall drainage pipe takes care of any top applied water. The white sand at the top is to bring contrast to the colors of the plants.

6'-0"

2½" x 1½" MEMBERS
(PHILLIPINE MAHOGANY)

2¾" 10¼" 10¼" 2¾"

## FRONT ELEVATION

1'-11½"

2½"

(4) PHILLIPS HEAD METAL
SCREWS COUNTERSUNK
IN STEEL STRAP

(8) "TAMPRUF" WOOD METAL SCREWS
FOR ¼"Ø HOLE (ALL SCREWS CENTERED
IN MEMBERS) (IN 3"x ½" STEEL STRAPS)

STEEL STRAP, 3/8" x 3" @ PEDESTAL
3/8" x 1" @ CENTER OF BENCH AND
2¾" FROM EACH END

3"x 3"x 3/16" STEEL TUBE

4"x 12"x 3/8" STEEL PLATE

EXPANSION SHIELDS & BOLTS INTO EXISTING CONCRETE

(12) "TAMPRUF" WOOD
METAL SCREWS
FOR ¼"Ø HOLE

(3) ALLENHEAD
BOLTS

1'-6"

1" R

1¼"

4½" 1½" 1½" 4½"

6" 6"

## SECTION

**929**

2½ X 1¾" MEMBERS
(PHILLIPINE MAHOGANY)
INTERNAL ⅜" ⌀ GALVANIZED
STEEL ROD W/ PLUGGED ENDS

FRONT ELEVATION

(3) ⅜" ⌀ INTERNAL GALVANIZED RODS

SLOPED RECESSED SPACER (¼" RECESS)
(½" X 2 X 6")

ENDS PLUGGED (1" ⌀ TYP)
⅜" X 3" X 22⅛" STEEL PLATE
5/16" ⌀ EYE BOLT, NUTS & WASHER
¼" ⌀ X 1½" L · #14 PAN/PHILIPS HEAD WOOD SCREW

2" X 4" X 3/16" STEEL TUBE
⅜" X 3" X 12" STEEL PLATE
EXPANSION SHIELDS & BOLTS INTO EXISTING CONCRETE

SECTION

## SIGNAGE SYSTEM DESIGN CRITERIA

Initial consideration should be directed toward determining the basic parameters required in developing the sign system. Each of them merits discussion here.

### Performance Requirements

Signs usually must be designed to meet specific performance requirements. The good designer will determine how a system is to perform within given space relationships. The sign system may function entirely on its own merit, or it may be supplemented by staff personnel at major decision-making locations, such as the main lobby and reception areas. Sign devices may become decorative amenities to be featured within the environment, or they may be subtle and low-key elements of minor importance. Supergraphics may be considered in certain areas simply as an art form, or as a functional graphic device presented in large scale for emphasis of context. Certainly, a combination of the two is feasible. These are only several performance considerations that should be addressed prior to the development of the signage system. The designer must evaluate the needs of the client, the unique traffic flow requirements and mounting restrictions dictated by the structure, and the basic performance requirements desired of the signing devices to be utilized.

### Usage Considerations

The general nature of the building complex often defines how signs are to be used. They may be given an appearance of being fixed and an integral part of the architecture by the appropriate selection of materials, colors, and mountings, or they may appear changeable and temporary should need so dictate. Some signage requires constant change to properly relate information to people or people to facility, while most sign devices are considered permanent fixtures within a given space. The designer is responsible for determining how signs are to be used most effectively, and at the same time, for enhancing the environment.

### Durability Requirements

Prior to the selection of materials for a signing system, durability requirements must be considered. The vast assortment of materials available for signs covers a wide spectrum of durability from soft plastics to metals. The sign copy and background material should be evaluated both individually and jointly when considering durability requirements.

### Vandalism Considerations

Signs located in controlled spaces are often free from destructive vandalism; however, in many instances vandalism becomes rampant and uncontrolled. There are no materials that may accurately be labeled "vandal-proof." However, some materials are more vandal-resistant than others. Where vandalism is of prime importance, only materials and graphic techniques engineered to resist destruction should be considered.

### Flexibility to Accommodate Changes and Additions

Modern architectural structures are designed to accommodate inner spacial changes to meet tenant needs. Partition systems, prehung door units, room dividers, and modular furniture have ensured ease of change in officescapes. The sign system may also require alterations to preserve continuity. Changes and additions to a sign system should be considered by the designer prior to the selection of materials, graphic techniques, and mounting methods to be used.

### Readability Factors

Sign readability is determined by the letter style selected, size of copy, interletter spacing, copy position relevant to background, colors, and angle of observance.

**Letter style**  Letter styles are classified as sanserif and serif. Sanserif letters, such as Helvetica, are more contemporary than serif letters, such as Clarendon (Fig. 1). Each letter style has its own unique personality and flavor. Printers carry alphabets in most letter styles, including lowercase letters as well as uppercase (Fig. 2). Test results indicate that messages starting with an initial uppercase letter and followed by lowercase characters are more recognizable than messages formed with uppercase characters only. Lowercase letters have more "personality" because their shape is varied by ascenders and descenders, resulting in characteristic word forms that are much easier to recognize than all-uppercase word forms. Also, people are more accustomed to reading text in upper- and lowercase than in all uppercase. The proper selection of a particular alphabet should be carefully considered, not only from a legibility point of view, but also from a "personality" standpoint. The letter style should make a concise and meaningful impression in the environment it serves.

**Readability**  Readability is directly related to the size of copy. Visibility studies indicate that 1-inch-high Helvetica Medium, for example, is readable from a distance of 40 feet. Using this as a measure for comparison, 1-inch-high Clarendon style would be readable from a somewhat lesser distance, approximately 25 feet. The distance visibility per 1-inch height may be used as a guideline to determine distance readability for larger letters; that is, 2-inch-high Helvetica Medium will be readable at 80 feet, and 3-inch-high at 120 feet. This direct proportion may be helpful for determining copy (text) sizes for signs used in pedestrian situations. However, the direct proportion may not hold true for vehicular traffic applications where many other factors are involved. The designer must exercise caution after selecting the alphabet and copy size to make certain the lettering will fit properly on the sign background. The sign size should be determined using the longest line of copy and the maximum number of copy lines that may be required.

**Letters and line spacing**  Interletter spacing and interline spacing of copy greatly affect the overall readability of a sign. Message legibility and ease of recognition are increased when proper visual relationships are established between individual characters, words, and lines of copy. Copy with spacing too tight becomes very difficult to read; copy with too open spacing tends to break the message down into fragments (Fig. 3). Proper spacing depends largely on the distance from which the message is to be read. Messages to be read at close distances should employ tighter spacing than messages that will be read at greater distances. Spacing is also affected by the angle at which the message is to be viewed: Greater angles of observance require wider interletter spacing to prevent the characters of the message from appearing to run together.

**Copy position**  The position of copy on the sign background influences the overall readability. Signs on which copy occupies most of the background are not as readable as signs that have sufficient background material surrounding the copy to form a visual barrier separating the message from the environment (Fig. 4 and 5).

Emphasis should be placed on selecting an appropriate sign size to best accommodate the sign message. There are nine basic copy placement positions to be considered in determining the important relationship of copy to sign background. They are: upper left, upper centered, upper right, centered left, centered, centered right, lower left, lower centered, and lower right. Traditionally, the most popular placement selections have been the centered and upper left positions.

**Color**  Color of copy and sign background greatly affect readability. Strong contrasting colors are more readable than less dramatic color combinations. White copy on a black background offers the greatest contrast and readability. Color also influences the apparent relationship between the copy size and the background. For example, white copy on a black field appears larger than black copy on a white field, although letter height, size, and copy position remain the same in both examples (Fig. 6).

Colors in a signage system should also relate harmoniously with the pallet of colors selected for the building and its environment. The designer may choose to select colors that blend with the environment or vibrant primary colors that accent the sign system and perhaps contrast with the architectural color scheme.

# Helvetica Medium
# Clarendon
Fig. 1

# HELVETICA MEDIUM
# CLARENDON
Fig. 2

Architectural Signage Systems
Architectural Signage Systems
Architectural Signage Systems
Fig. 3

Fig. 4

Fig. 5

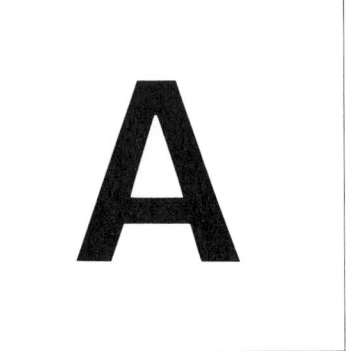

Fig. 6

**The viewing angle** The angle of observance is influential in the design of a signage system, since it affects interletter spacing and overall readability. Normally, interior signs are viewed chiefly from a straight-on position; however, exterior signs are frequently seen from more than one angle. Signs to be read from vehicles moving at varying speeds with different angles of observance may require a compromise in letter spacing to best communicate the message.

### Multilingual Needs

The jet age is a contributing factor in bringing people together from all over the world to visit and transact business. Transportation terminals and public facilities that may be used by visitors unaccustomed to reading English should employ sign systems that bridge any visual communication gap. Multilingual messages in English and the dominant foreign languages used by visitors may be combined and presented on one sign background. However, sign design and graphic formats become very critical to prevent confusion. A more popular solution involves the use of pictorial symbols as word substitutes. Pictographic signs are bold, recognizable images not bound by language barriers.

### Regulatory Considerations

The designer should become aware of regulations governing signs. Federal regulations concerning safety signs are enumerated in Occupational Safety and Health Administration (OSHA) publications. American National Standards Institute (ANSI) publishes standards concerning signage for the physically handicapped. Underwriters' Laboratory (UL) issues standards applicable to illuminated signs. State and local codes contain regulatory information concerning sign sizes, mounting locations and heights, quantities of signs allowable in various zoning areas, and other restrictions relating to exterior signs. These rules, and those of other regulatory bodies, should be taken under advisement prior to completing a comprehensive signage program.

### Need for Illumination

Many signs are required to relate their messages after dark as well as during natural daylight. The careful designer will determine which signs require artificial illumination and decide on the method of illumination. Signs can be externally illuminated by readily available stock fixtures produced by many manufacturers, or they can be internally illuminated. Fluorescent lighting is the most common source of internal illumination, although metal arc lamps, incandescent lamps, and neon are frequently employed.

### Need for a Graphics Manual

Many signage programs are developed for institutions that have a continuing need not only to maintain, but also to augment or change, their signage systems. The preparation of a signage manual containing all the information required to create additional signs or components would benefit the client and ensure continuity in the system as changes and additions are made. The designer should determine this potential need and include the manual with other documents developed for the signage program.

### SIGN TYPES CATEGORIZED BY FUNCTION

Signage systems should be logically broken down into various types of signs to be utilized on a particular project. Many categories of sign types may be developed, but one of the most conclusive listings is based on function. The following discussion of signage system components, including sign requirements for specific applications, covers these functions.

### Exterior Signs

Exterior sign system components are normally viewed from vehicles or by pedestrians who have parked their vehicles and are walking toward their destination.

**Primary identification** All architectural projects require some form of identification that is both easily readable and recognizable. A person's first association with a building is the identifying device selected to "label" the structure. The importance of the first impression created by this device should be recognized. A sign that produces an image in keeping with the environment it serves reflects the quality of the people associated with that environment. Major corporations spend large sums of money on corporate identity programs to ensure the visual image presented to the public best reflects corporate philosophy and product desirability. Equal emphasis should be placed upon the image presented by the device employed to identify an architectural structure.

**Secondary identification** Many complexes containing more than one basic structure require secondary identification signs to properly identify the various elements within the complex. A systems approach to design will provide continuity in the relationship of primary to secondary identification signs.

**Vehicular advance notice** A system of road signs suitably located in advance of decision-making points will allow vehicular traffic to execute the proper decisions smoothly and safely at the appropriate times.

**Vehicular directional** Intersections and parking facility entrances are major decision-making locations requiring directional devices to guide drivers toward their destination.

**Traffic regulatory and control** Vehicular traffic can be systematically controlled by employing signing devices. Traffic codes are usually clear as to what signs are required, where they are to be located, and the height at which they are to be mounted. Usually, colors, sizes, and shapes are standardized by the traffic authorities. Stop, yield, and speed limit signs are representative of this classification of signs.

**Instructional** Frequently, signs are required to instruct vehicular and pedestrian traffic. These notices must be properly installed in carefully selected locations to be effective. Examples include parking procedures, delivery and service directions, and the like.

**Informational** Signs are required to present information that is both relevant to the location and important to the viewer. This information may pertain to parking rates, hours of operation, and security, or it may relate to items of interest within the environment.

**Decorative** Decorative graphics may be employed to enhance the beauty or decor of a particular area; form, color, and design may be utilized to create interest and to become features of the exterior landscape.

## Interior Signs

Interior sign system components should assist visitors to travel from the building entrances throughout the complex until they reach their desired destination.

**Identification** Multiple-occupancy buildings require tenant identification; frequently, buildings with only one tenant will also utilize identification in the main lobby or reception areas to reinforce the corporate signature. Criteria for multiple-tenant signage are very important and should be included in lease documents to provide for visual continuity and architectural harmony. When individuals are allowed to implement their own desires concerning signage, each will attempt to outdo the other, resulting in clutter, confusion, and visual pollution. Signs that are too big, too gaudy, too competitive, and poorly conceived and executed will become commonplace unless controls on tenant identification are established and enforced.

**Primary directory** Information relevant to one's location within a complex should be clearly enumerated on the primary directory, usually located in a very visible area of the main lobby. Alphabetized listings of tenants, departments, and individuals should be concise and should designate the floor and room numbers. Such directories may be flush or recessed wall mounts, horizontal projected wall mounts, or pedestal or kiosk mounts, and internally illuminated or not, depending upon the ambient lighting conditions.

**Elevator lobby floor directory** High-rise structures require well-positioned signage that not only identifies each individual floor, but also serves as a secondary directory system for that floor. Frequently, the floor identification, directory, and corridor directional signage may be included in one device. When a visitor exits from an elevator on a chosen floor, a sign showing the floor number and also the direction of the office or room number sought is both helpful and reassuring.

**Pictorial "you are here" indicators** Pictorial schematic maps may become an integral part of directory systems, or they may be utilized separately as visual aids in depicting one's intended passage through a complex. Hospitals, sports complexes, and transportation centers, are good examples of structure that may require pictorial maps to supplement word messages. Caution will be exercised by the expert designer to keep the pictorial map simple and correctly oriented in the building according to where the viewer is standing, and to evaluate the need of color coding as part of the visual aid. Too frequently, designers employ a complicated color-coded system that becomes very confusing to the viewer and, in fact, compromises the effectiveness of the system.

**Primary directional** The maze that often results from interior corridor layouts creates many decision-making points for a visitor. Primary directional signs may be ceiling-mounted, wall-mounted, or floor-mounted as kiosk-type units in open areas. Areas with heavy pedestian traffic should have directional signs located so that people do not obstruct the line of sight to the sign device.

Normally, ceiling-suspended or kiosk-type units are the best choice to enhance visibility.

**Secondary directional** Directional signs should be considered in locations where traffic flow and corridor layouts do not demand primary directional devices but do require some guidance for direction control. Corridors within suites of offices and corridors that change direction should be considered as decision-making points that may require a secondary directional signage device.

**Area identification** Specific areas within a complex should be properly identified. These areas may be tenant spaces, divisions, or departments. When occurring along main corridors, they are usually designated by wall-, door-, or transom-mounted devices. Ceiling-suspended signs are a good solution in open office spaces.

**Room identification** Wall- or door-mounted room identification signs are required to "label" the function of a particular room. Work functions are properly identified within tenant areas, while service and maintenance functions should be suitably designated in most situations.

**Desk identification** Reception areas may require a sign device located on a desk or counter to identify a particular service or individual rendering assistance to visitors. Such signs may be permanently affixed or removable, and may provide for changeable name inserts.

**Personnel identification** Persons rendering a service to the public, such as nurses, maintenance personnel, and food service personnel, generally are identified by name badges or pins.

**Regulatory and control signs** Signs that authorize or prohibit certain functions are required, frequently by law or code, to inform people using the facility. Examples include signs for the handicapped and signs relevant to no smoking areas, elevator capacities, "no entry" areas, fire control, and "authorized personnel only" areas. These signs are usually mounted on doors or their adjacent walls; they may employ colors which deviate from the standard colors used in the comprehensive signage system to emphasize a dangerous situation or the need for caution.

**Exits** Exit signs are required by codes to designate exits effectively in times of emergency. Supplemental devices are used to give additional information pertaining to a particular exit such as "Emergency Exit Only" and "Alarm Sounds When Door Is Opened." OSHA-approved exit signs are standard items manufactured by many lighting companies, and are generally provided by the electrical contractor.

**Information exhibit cases** Notices, posters, attractions, and promotional pieces should be contained within an appropriately designed case to control the display of this type of information. Standard units featuring vinyl-covered cork panels housed within extruded aluminum frames with lockable doors are available from many directory manufacturers.

**Decorative features** Decorative designs may be reproduced on walls as interior features. Reproduction processes include appliqués, painting, and screen printing on location; or mural processes, which are applied much like wall-coverings, may be considered. Doors may also receive supergraphic treatments in which copy may become an integral part of the design.

**Dedicatory plaques** Building dedication plaques should be carefully conceived and implemented, using materials that reflect favorably upon the talents involved in the realization of the project. Historically, these plaques have been bronze or aluminum castings. However, modern technology has provided photographic methods and photochemical processes which offer the designer a freedom of size, format, letterform, and color not available in the casting operation.

**Donor recognition** Buildings constructed in part by contributions from donors require special recognition for the donors. Hospitals, performing arts centers, and service institutions rely on gifts to assist in financing buildings, additions, and furnishings, and usually stipulate that donors will be remembered and recognized in some prestigious location in the building. The designer is responsible for establishing controls and developing a system that fulfills promises made by those soliciting funds, while allowing flexibility to expand the system as future needs may dictate. Location selection is very important in the overall effectiveness of the donor recognition signage.

**Mechanical, instrumentation, and control system markings** Many industrial and mechanical installations require equipment, control, and pipe markings to meet codes, assist maintenance and service personnel, and ensure safety. Often, these locations are not public spaces, and require an industrial, rather than an architectural, approach to signage. Elevator floor-indicator panels, however, should receive special attention and be considered in a comprehensive signage program.

## CONCEPTUAL DESIGN OF THE SIGN FACE

Emphasis will not be placed on the graphic design of each sign required in a comprehensive signage program. However, the following considerations will help to ensure continuity, correctness, and aesthetic acceptability.

**Alphabet selection** An alphabet must be carefully chosen that best exemplifies the graphic image to be portrayed to the public without compromising legibility and performance requirements. More than one alphabet may be selected should need dictate. However, good design practices should be maintained in choosing the family of alphabets to be employed.

**Interletter, word, and line spacing** Each alphabet has its own "personality" and visual impact; therefore, spacing between characters, words, and lines of copy must be carefully developed to give the best legibility and visual harmony possible (Fig. 8).

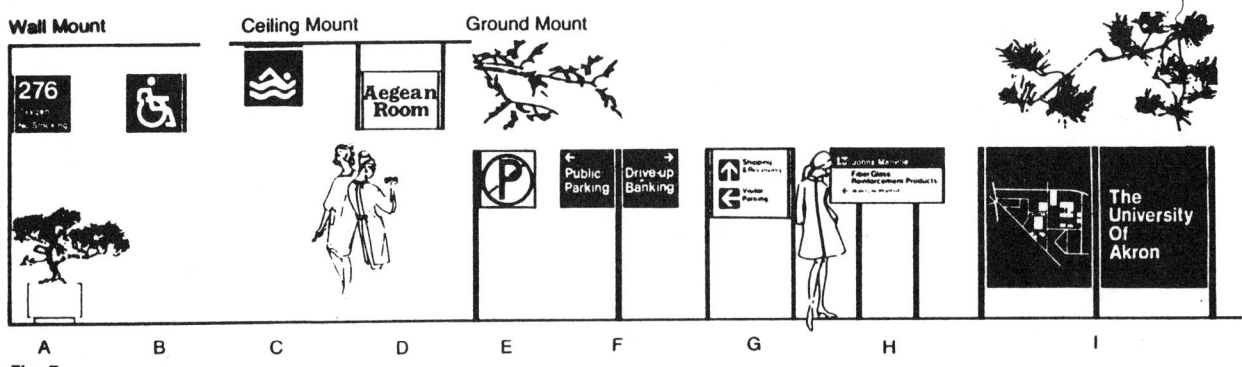

Fig. 7

# Architectural Signage Systems
## Planning · Design · Implementation

Fig. 8

Fig. 9

**These Doors Should Not Be Opened Except During An Emergency**

Fig. 10

**Emergency Exit Only**

Fig. 11

**Arrow selection** Directional arrows should be designed to reflect the "personality" of the letterform selected. Stroke width and size relationships are important considerations (Fig. 9).

**Copy determination** The message for each sign must be accurately determined and the copy condensed to the fewest words that will still relay the desired message. Wordy signs are frequently misread or not read at all. The message must be concise, clear, and informative (Fig. 10 and 11).

**Copy placement format** The placement of copy on a sign face may take one of the nine basic positions or a custom format for special situations (Fig. 12).

**Size determination of the sign face** After the copy for each sign is in final form, the sign with the greatest amount of copy is selected from each of the sign types utilized and the desired copy height is determined for each type. This height should be based upon the distance from which the sign will be read and the graphic design portrayed. Using this letter height, the message should be laid out with photographic type or transfer lettering to scale, incorporating the copy placement and spacing requirements. The most pleasing shape and size for the message to be contained are then determined, realizing that this particular layout is for the maximum copy required for that particular sign type. A shape and size format should be chosen that works well as a module which can be proprotioned and become applicable to the entire family of

sign types. While this may be ideal, frequently the proportional system is not applicable. An example of each sign type should be drawn to scale and fully dimensioned to serve as a production guide for signs within that type. (Fig. 13).

**Color selections** Selection is then made of the copy and background colors that offer good contrast and harmoniously blend with the prominent colors in the environment. It is also wise to consider any corporate colors required by the client.

## SIGNAGE SYSTEM DEVELOPMENT CHECKLIST

The completed sign schedule, location plans, scaled drawings of typical examples from each sign type, construction or assembly details or both, mounting details, and specifications form the documents required to bid competitively or to negotiate signage projects. Well-prepared documents prevent individual interpretation by vendors and result in comparable competitive bids.

The following systematic approach to the design and development of a comprehensive signage program will serve as a guideline to problem solving, employing the concepts contained in this chapter. This checklist may be expanded or condensed to meet individual project parameters. The basic systematic thought process, however, is applicable to all projects.

1. Develop the signage system design criteria based on:

a. Performance requirements
b. Usage considerations
c. Durability requirements
d. Vandalism considerations
e. Flexibility to accommodate changes and additions
f. Readability factors
g. Multilingual needs
h. Regulatory considerations
i. Need for illumination
j. Need for graphics manual for ongoing implementation and system maintenance

2. Study the traffic flow patterns, determine all sign locations, and draw the location symbols on the site and floor plans.

3. Evaluate and select the sign types required from the following list, categorized by function, that meet the design criteria:

a. Exterior sign types:
Type A – Primary identification
Type B – Secondary identification
Type C – Vehicular advance notice
Type D – Vehicular directional
Type E – Traffic regulatory and control
Type F – Instructional
Type G – Informational
Type H – Decorative

b. Interior sign types:
Type I – Primary identification
Type J – Primary directory
Type K – Elevator lobby floor directories
Type L – Pictorial "You Are Here" indicators
Type M – Primary directional
Type N – Secondary directional

Type O – Area identification
Type P – Room identification
Type Q – Desk identification
Type R – Personnel identification
Type S – Regulatory and control
Type T – Exit
Type U – Information exhibit cases
Type W – Dedicatory
Type X – Donor recognition
Type Y – Mechanical, instrumentation, and control system markings
Type Z – Other (to be specified by designer)

4. Select the best signing devices for each sign type designated above from the following lexicon of signage system components

that most effectively satisfy the design criteria established:

a. Elevated pylons
b. Monolithic sign structures
c. Panel and post assemblies
d. Illuminated sign cabinets
e. Directory and informational systems
f. Die-cut pressure-sensitive lettering
g. Dimensional graphics
h. Plaque signage
i. Environmental graphics
j. Other (to be defined by the designer)

5. Conceptually design the sign face for each sign type selected, indicating:

a. Alphabet selection
b. Interletter, word, and line spacing
c. Arrow selection

d. Copy determination
e. Copy placement format
f. Size determination of copy and sign face
g. Color selections

6. Complete the location plans by filling in the symbol indicating sign number and type.

7. Prepare scaled drawings of typical examples from each sign type.

8. Prepare the detailed sign schedule.

9. Prepare typical construction and assembly details, mounting details, and engineering drawings for wind loading, foundations, and illumination.

10. Prepare detailed specifications for all materials, techniques, and components required in the system.

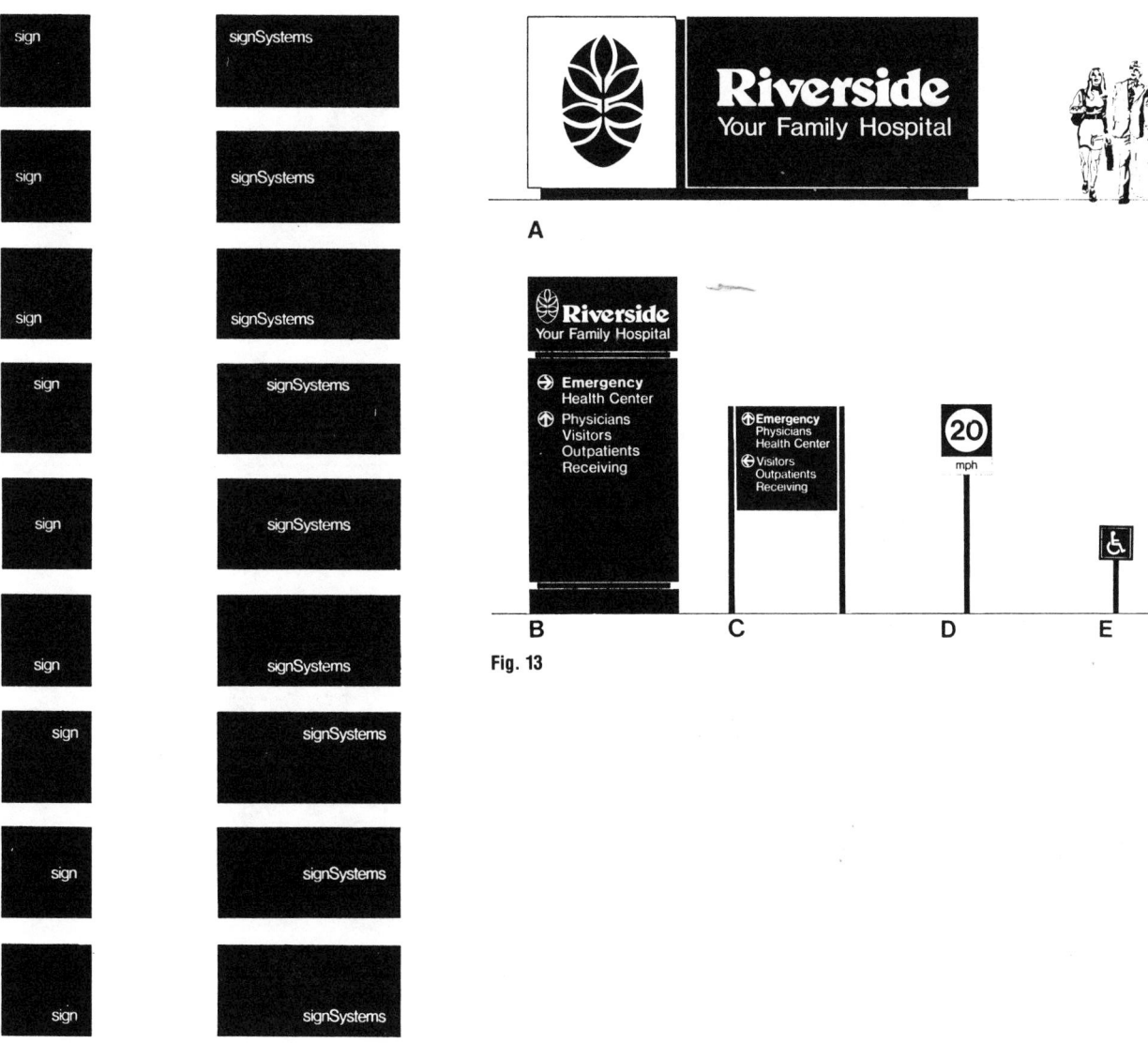

Fig. 12

Fig. 13

## STANDARD SIGN SYSTEM

## CODE SIGNS

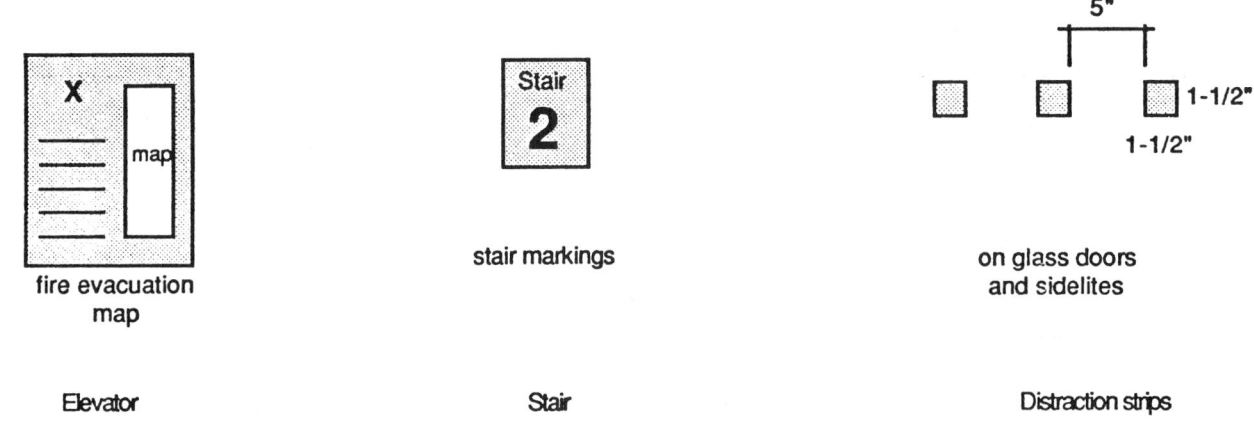

## STANDARD MOUNTING HEIGHTS AND LOCATIONS

### Sign Type

DIRECTIONAL (CEILING-HUNG)

### Material Choices

MDO board, acrylic

### Finishes

Painted, plastic laminate, metal laminate

### Graphics

Vinyl die cuts, silkscreen, dimensional applied letters

### Standard Mounting Detail

1. Threaded rod: pendant, flush
2. Scissor clip

10" x 24"

12" x 48"

12" x 72"

**Standard sizes**

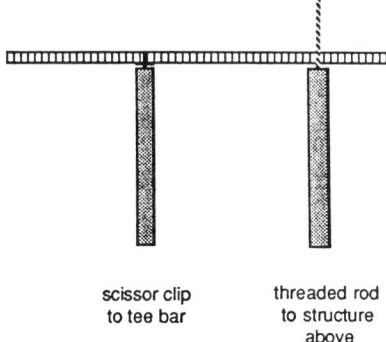

scissor clip to tee bar

threaded rod to structure above

**Section**

### Sign Type

DIRECTIONAL (WALL-MOUNTED)

### Material Choices

Acrylic, aluminum, acrylic with metal laminate face

### Finishes

Painted acrylic or aluminum, natural aluminum or brass (satin or polished), laminates available in standard laminate finishes

### Graphics

Silkscreen, front surface or reverse

### Standard Mounting Materials

1. Backpanel: backplate with countersunk screws with shields; magnetic, form, or vinyl tape with adhesive
2. Strips: vinyl tape

* should not exceed 36" high

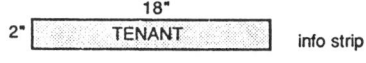

2"  18"  TENANT  info strip

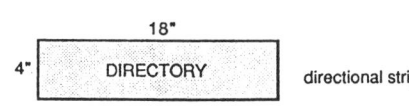

4"  18"  DIRECTORY  directional strip

**Standard sizes**

header strip

1/4" acrylic backplate

information strip

Wall Fasteners

**Section**

### Sign Type

AREA DESIGNATION (WALL-MOUNTED)

### Material Choices

Acrylic, aluminum, acrylic with metal laminate face

### Finishes

Painted acrylic or aluminum, natural aluminum or brass (satin or polished), laminates available in standard laminate finishes

### Graphics

Silkscreen, front surface or reverse; vinyl die cuts

### Standard Mounting Materials

Vinyl or magnetic tape, foam tape, silastic adhesive

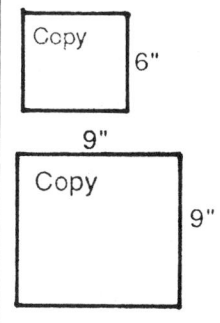

6"  Copy  6"

9"  Copy  9"

12"  Copy  12"

**Standard sizes**

acrylic sign

adhesive & tape mount

**Section**

## SIGNAGE AND GRAPHICS

### Sign Type

ROOM IDENTIFIER (WALL-MOUNTED)

### Material Choices

Acrylic, aluminum, acrylic with metal laminate face

### Finishes

Painted acrylic or aluminum, natural aluminum or brass (satin or polished), laminates available in standard laminate finishes

### Graphics

Silkscreen, front surface or reverse

### Standard Mounting Materials

Vinyl tape, foam tape, magnetic tape, silastic adhesive

**Standard sizes**

acrylic sign

adhesive &
tape mount

**Section**

### Sign Type

ROOM IDENTIFIER, CHANGEABLE MESSAGE (WALL-MOUNTED)

### Material Choices

Holder, acrylic; insert, vinyl

### Finishes

Painted (surface or subsurface)

### Graphics

Silkscreen or vinyl die cuts

### Standard Mounting Materials

Vinyl tape, foam tape, silastic adhesive

**Standard sign sizes**        **Standard insert sizes**

**Elevation and section**

### Sign Type

FRAMED PLAQUE SIGNS, WALL-MOUNTED (previous plaque types are insertable into standard frame signs)

### Material Choices

Molded acrylic, aluminum, brass

### Finishes

Painted, satin, polished

### Standard Frame Mounting Materials

1. Frame: screw mount, tape and adhesive
2. Insert: adhesive or magnetic tape, Velcro, magnet

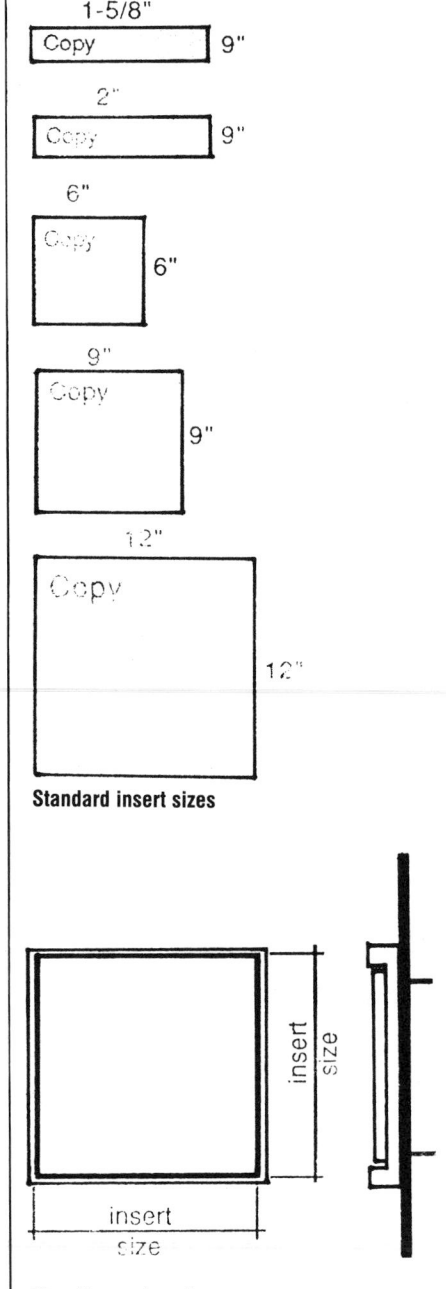

**Standard insert sizes**

**Elevation and section**

**Sign Type**

COUNTERTOP/FLAG MOUNT

**Extrusion Material**

Aluminum

**Insert Material**

Acrylic, aluminum, acrylic with metal laminate

**Graphics**

See area and room plaques

**Standard Mounting Details**

1. Counter: free-standing with extruded aluminum base
2. Flag mount: countersunk screws and shields

counter top

**Standard sizes**

wall mount

**Elevation and section**

**Sign Type**

DESKBAR (DESK TOP)

**Material Choices**

Aluminum, molded acrylic

**Finishes**

Painted, satin, polished

**Graphics**

Vinyl die cuts; silkscreen on acrylic plaque, front surface or reverse

**Standard Mounting Detail**

Free-standing on desks or countertops

 2" x 9"

 1-5/8" x 9"

**Standard sizes**

*Note:* Changeable face available by using acrylic sign plaque.

**Sign Type**

CUT LETTERS: FLUSH, PROJECTED

**Material Choices**

Acrylic, acrylic with metal laminate face, brass, aluminum

**Finishes**

Polished, painted, brushed, sand blasted

**Standard Mounting Details**

Adhesive mount, flush pin mount, standoff mount

**Standard Letter Sizes**

Varies from 2" to 18"

Front View

Projected Mount
(least vandal resistant)      Flush Mount

**Sections**

# Medical

**Nursing Homes**
**Medical Complexes**
**First-Aid Centers**

Picto'grafics not shown:
1.516 Parking    1.413 Health
1.372 Playroom    2.531 Warning
1.150 Library or Reading   1.147 Chest

Hospital
Pharmacy
Dental Care
Wheelchair

 1.508

 1.518

1.184

 1.188

X-Ray
Physiotherapy
General Medicine, Female
General Medicine, Male

 1.146

1.148

 1.440

 1.450

Coronary Care
Hematology
Urology
Eye

 1.446

 1.417

 1.448

 1.123

Podiatry
Mental Health
Ear, Nose & Throat
Oxygen

 1.129

1.473

 1.137

 1.368

Shower
Isolation
Nursery
Laboratory

 1.376

1.411

 1.302

 1.359

Conference
Occupational Therapy
Rehabilitation
Ambulatory Patients

 1.406

1.347

 1.483

 1.152

# Commercial

**Shopping Centers**
**Stores & Shops**
**Eating Facilities**
**Community Services**

Picto'grafics not shown:
| 1.218 | Concrete Mixer | 1.226 | Flatbed Truck | 1.314 | Vegetable Produce |
| 1.219 | Cushman Vehicle | 1.250 | Pickup Truck | 1.363 | Newspaper Vendor |
| 1.222 | Dump Truck | 1.304 | Basket | 1.370 | Record Store |
| | | | | 1.394 | Cooking |

Cocktail Lounge
Pub
Coffee Shop
Liquor Store

1.344

1.361

1.360

1.307

Mens' Furnishings
Furniture
Cinema
Camera Store

1.352

1.315

1.126

1.338

Gift Shop
Florist
Dress Shop
Shoe Store

1.339

1.393

1.321

1.375

Restaurant
Soda Fountain
Grocery Store
Tobacco Shop

1.354

1.341

1.337

1.316

Bookstore
Record Shop
Fuel
Toy Shop

1.305

1.455

1.336

1.372

Theater
Van
Beauty Salon
Barber Shop

1.449

1.290

1.192

1.149

## SIGNAGE AND GRAPHICS

**Commercial and Travel Symbols**

# Travel

Picto'grafics not shown:

1.350    Motel
1.266    Seaplane Base

**Airport**
**Departures**
**Arrivals**
**Car Rentals**

1.253

1.255

1.254

1.202

**Bus**
**Subway**
**Train**
**Taxi**

1.208

1.268

1.278

1.203

**Monorail**
**Ferry**
**Cable Car**
**Automobile**

1.239

1.225

1.215

1.201

**Lost & Found**
**Porter**
**Locker**
**Fuel**

1.310

1.319

1.308

1.336

**Baggage Claim**
**Customs**
**Immigration**
**Money Exchange**

1.303

1.125

1.464

1.532

**Motorcycle**
**Moving Sidewalk**
**Lodging**
**Ice Cubes**

1.241

1.145

1.173

1.353

# Recreation and Sports

**Sports Arenas**
**Parks**
**Recreation Facilities**
**Amusement Parks**

Picto'grafics not shown:
| | | | |
|---|---|---|---|
| 1.112 | Curling | 1.138 | Hockey | 1.471 | Wintersports |
| 1.115 | Dancing | 1.183 | Tobogganing | 1.387 | Outdoor Recreation |
| 1.140 | LaCrosse | | | |

Campers
Picnic Area
Midway
Trailer Train

 1.276

 1.366

 1.313

 1.185

Water
Swimming
Canoeing
Sailing

 1.492

 1.177

 1.217

1.265

Marina, Boating
Life Preserver
Snowmobiling
Camping

 1.401

 1.357

 1.267

 1.385

Judging
Bicycling
Women's/Girl's Toilet
Fishing

 1.370

 1.211

 1.910

 1.334

Skiing
Soccer
Ice Skating
Football

 1.172

  1.176

 1.181

1.130

Hunting, Shooting
Golf
Baseball
Tennis, Badminton

 1.170

 1.133

 1.105

1.182

## SIGNAGE AND GRAPHICS

**Universal Symbols**

# Universal

**Applicable to any building or facility**

Picto'grafics not shown:

| | | | | | |
|---|---|---|---|---|---|
| 1.110 | Children | 1.372 | Playroom | 1.493 | Smoke |
| 1.144 | Man with boy | 1.410 | Church | 1.516 | Parking |
| 1.340 | Fragile | 1.472 | Synagogue | 1.488 | Keep Dry |
| | | 1.469 | Police | 1.155 | Janitor |

Entry
Exit
Ramp up
Ramp down

1.403

1.404

1.461

1.462

Emergency
Women's Toilet
Men's Toilet
Stairs

4.412

1.189

1.143

1.377

Handicapped
No Smoking
Telephone
Escalator

1.188

3.316

1.365

1.328

Elevator
Down
No Parking
Drinking fountain

1.311

1.402B

3.516

1.139

Mail Box
Check Room
Up
No Entry

1.326

1.317

1.402A

3.463

Shower
Waiting Room
Telegraph Office
Information

1.376

1.151

1.327

1.530

**International symbol of accessibility**

**Alternate** GOTHIC NO. 3

Americana

*Americana* ITALIC

Aster

Avant Garde GOTHIC MEDIUM

Baker Danmark 2

Baker Sans MONO REGULAR

*Baskerville* BOLD ITALIC

Bodoni

Bookman

*Caledonia* BOLD ITALIC

Caslon BOLD

Century SCHOOLBOOK

**Century** SCHOOLBOOK BOLD

Cheltenham MEDIUM

Columbus

COPPERPLATE GOTHIC LIGHT

Craw Clarendon BOOK

**Craw Clarendon**

Craw Modern

Delta MEDIUM

Eastern Souvenir MEDIUM

Eurostile

**Eurostile** BOLD

Eurostile EXTENDED

**Eurostile** BOLD EXTENDED

Firmin Didot

Folio MEDIUM

Folio MEDIUM EXTENDED

Fortuna LIGHT

**Franklin Gothic**

Futura MEDIUM

**Futura** DEMIBOLD

**Garamond** BOLD

Gerstner Program MEDIUM

Gill Sans

**Harry** FAT

Hellenic WIDE

Helvetica LIGHT

Helvetica

**Helvetica** MEDIUM

Helvetica MEDIUM OUTLINE

Horizon MEDIUM

**Karen** BOLD

Korinna

**Korinna** BOLD

Lydian

Melior

**Melior** SEMIBOLD

MICROGRAMMA NORMAL

**MICROGRAMMA** BOLD

**MICROGRAMMA** BOLD EXTENDED

Modula MEDIUM

**News Gothic** BOLD

Olive ANTIQUE

Optima

**Optima** SEMIBOLD

Palatino

**Palatino** SEMIBOLD

**Permanent** MEDIUM

Perpetua ROMAN

Plantin

Quorum MEDIUM

Romana NORMAL

**Schadow** ANTIQUA SEMIBOLD

Serif Gothic REGULAR

**Serif Gothic** BOLD

Solitaire BOLD

Souvenir LIGHT

*Souvenir* MEDIUM ITALIC

Standard MEDIUM

**Stymie** BOLD

Times ROMAN

**Times** ROMAN BOLD

Trooper ROMAN LIGHT

**Trooper** ROMAN

Univers 55

*Univers 56*

**Univers 65**

**Univers 67**

Univers 53

Univers 63

Univers 55 OUTLINE

Univers 65 OUTLINE

Univers 83 OUTLINE

Venus MEDIUM

**Venus** EXTRABOLD

**Venus** EXTRABOLD CONDENSED

**Venus** BOLD EXTENDED

**Walbaum** MEDIUM

Weiss ROMAN EXTRABOLD

**Windsor**

Windsor OUTLINE

# Clarendon Medium
abcdefghijklmnopqrstuvwxyz
ABCDEFGHIJKLM
NOPQRSTUVWXYZ
0123456789 !"#$%&'*()"+¢£:?-=;/,.

# Optima Regular
abcdefghijklmnopqrstuvwxyz
ABCDEFGHIJKLM
NOPQRSTUVWXYZ
0123456789 !"$%&'()"¢£:?-;/,.

# Helvetica Medium
abcdefghijklmnopqrstuvwxyz
ABCDEFGHIJKLM
NOPQRSTUVWXYZ
0123456789 ®!"#$%&'°()"+¢£:?-=;/,.

# Times New Roman
abcdefghijklmnopqrstuvwxyz
ABCDEFGHIJKLM
NOPQRSTUVWXYZ
0123456789 !"#$%&'()+¢£:?-=;,.

## General Symbols Extended

Fig. 14    General type styles with maximum readability. ½″ cap height is legible up to 25′, ¾″–1″ cap height is legible up to 50′, 1–2″ cap height is legible up to 100′.

## DESIGNING THE SYSTEM

The formulation of a communications program is based on the functional requirements delineated in the feasibility study. The presentation modes to be utilized are a part of such a program. They might include slides, films, videotape, and a sound-recording and playback system. The detailed design of the facility includes the selection of basic equipment, possible modification of that equipment, and provision for additional optical elements, as well as the engineering of the electrical control circuitry and the design of the electromechanical devices that may be needed.

The implementation of a proposed A-V system is not merely an exercise in mechanical assembly. It is a highly complex process of logistics that involves providing specific functional requirements within architectural and economic constraints. Careful engineering and balancing of the alternatives available will generally achieve optimum results.

A large number of variables is encountered in every A-V design problem. As an example, the dimensions of the presentation room have a significant effect on the audience size, the acoustic characteristics, the size of the projected image, the choice of equipment, and the location and the interrelationship of the components.

The A-V consultant who is responsible for the program planning, the design, and the engineering of this complex, multifaceted discipline should be intimately familiar with the problems of fabrication, installation, and operation of such systems. This knowledge will enable the consultant to plan a facility whose execution will not create difficulties and whose construction and operation can be effected without costly changes. However, even when the consultant has experience as an adviser to members of the architectural and engineering professions, the creation of a well-integrated facility is not necessarily assured. His or her work and the completed facilities should be viewed and evaluated.

## Optical Aspects

It is of critical importance for an A-V system to have the ability to display bright, sharp images to all viewers and to maintain the stability and consistency of those images in a simple and straightforward manner. The picture quality is a function of a number of factors requiring careful attention during all phases of the project. These include:

■ The quality of the original photography or artwork

■ The density, contrast, and sharpness of the actual material being projected

■ The output intensity of the projector light source

■ The optical characteristics of each projection unit

■ The optical characteristics of the integrated system

■ The ratio of the projection distance to the image size

■ The centering integrity of the light path from the material being projected to its image on the screen

■ The characteristics of the projection screen or other viewing surface

## Projection Engineering

**Room size** Ideally, the dimensions of the viewing room should be an outgrowth of the estimate of the audience size that was established in the original A-V study. In many cases, however, the A-V design engineer must utilize a predetermined space. Given the characteristics of that space, the designer can determine the ideal audience size for each type of seating arrangement, and also ascertain whether a front or rear projection mode is feasible and what the image size should be.

The type of relationship that is desired between the person making the presentation and the audience will determine the seating configuration: theatre, lecture, or conference format. That configuration will in turn dictate the number of viewers that can be comfortably seated for optimum viewing (Fig. 1).

As an illustration, a room 20 feet by 32 feet can accommodate about 49 people in a theatre configuration (Fig. 2); in a lecture arrangement, the audience size would be 24 (Fig. 3); a U-shaped table would seat 18 (Fig. 4); and 15 people could fit comfortably at a conference table (Fig. 5). Circular and multi-use arrangements (Figs. 6 and 7) are additional examples of the relationship of seating configuration and audience size.

Other seating configurations have been devised for other types of communication program modes, each with a direct rela-tionship between room size and audience size. The audience size is also affected by the angle of view between each member of the audience and the screen (Fig. 1).

Whenever the A-V design engineer has the opportunity of establishing the dimensions of the presentation room, he or she should be aware of the important fact that a longer projection throw for a particular image size results in more even light distribution and sharpness as well as a better angle of view. Consequently a larger audience can be accommodated than would be possible using a system with a short projection distance and a narrower angle of view. This question of projection distance applies to both front and rear projection systems. However, as the throw is normally quite short when a rear projection screen is used, this factor of design in rear projection facilities is an extremely critical planning element.

Distortion, sometimes called "keystoning," will result if the viewing surface is not precisely parallel to the plane of the image being projected. Therefore, the light path, which is usually perpendicular to the projected material, must be carefully controlled in relation to the projector and the screen. The size of the audience and the room, as well as the mode of projection, will determine whether the screen will be vertical or at an angle (Fig. 8). Normally, a rear projection screen will permit a vertical viewing surface.

**Fig. 1  The interrelationship of projection distance, image size, and viewing area.**

## AUDIO-VISUAL SYSTEMS
**Typical Projection Room Layout and Sightlines**

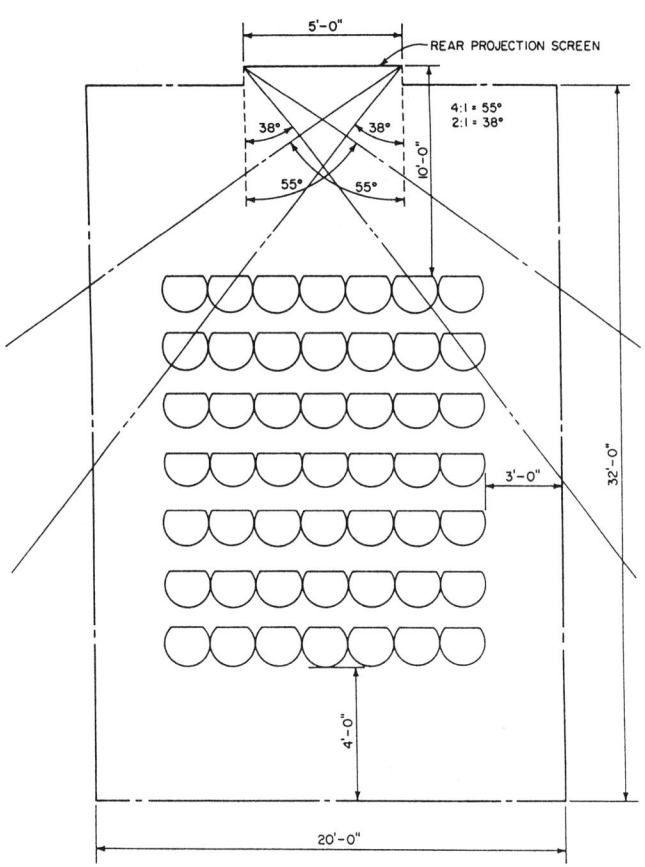

**Fig. 2   A room 20 feet by 32 feet, seating 49 people in theatre style.**

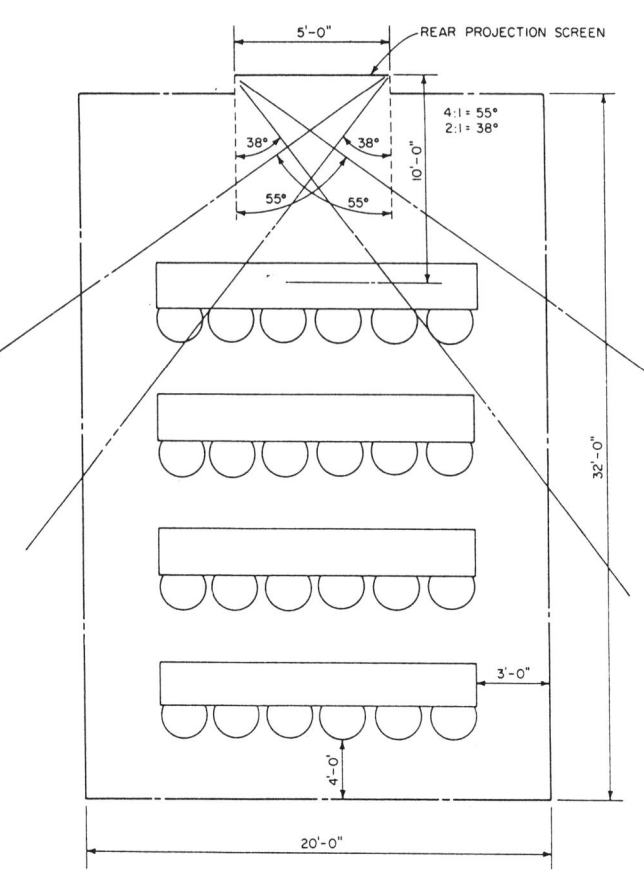

**Fig. 3   A room 20 feet by 32 feet, seating 24 people in lecture style.**

**Fig. 4   A room 20 feet by 32 feet, seating 18 people at a U-shaped table.**

**Fig. 5   A room 20 feet by 32 feet, seating 15 people at a boat-shaped conference table.**

**Fig. 6** A room 20 feet by 24 feet, seating 13 people at a circular table. With the depth increased to 32 feet, from 7 to 14 observers can also be accommodated.

**Fig. 7** A modified classroom arrangement including both lecture and separate tables.

**Fig. 8** Cross section of a theatre-style auditorium with stepped seating showing both front and rear projection. Note that the projected light beam is perpendicular to the screen in both cases.

## AUDIO-VISUAL SYSTEMS
**Planning Guideline Summary**

**Screen image area** The most useful screen is one that is square, as it will permit both vertical and horizontal images, as well as square ones, of course (Fig. 9). A single image format will need one such screen, while a dual format will have a viewing surface that is the width of two images placed side by side (Figs. 9 and 10).

It is an easy matter to determine the minimum image size necessary for a room of a given size. For a front projection screen the minimum size is the distance between it and the farthest viewer divided by 6. For a rear projection screen, the division factor is 7.5. As illustration: When the distance between the front projection screen and the last row of viewers, is 45 feet, the minimum image size would be 7.5 feet; with a rear projection screen, the minimum image should be 6 feet. These calculations assume that the original artwork from which the projection materials are made meets the generally accepted basic minimum standards.

**Front projection** The projector in a front projection system transmits the image in the form of a light beam to an opaque screen where it is reflected back to the viewers, creating the image. As the screen reflects any light falling on its surface, the general light level in the room during a presentation must be extremely low. If the full color and contrast of the projected image is to be retained, the ambient light should be no greater than 0.3 percent of the average screen brightness.

Projectors are generally noisy and should be separated from the audience to avoid distractions. If the space is available, a separate projection booth can be built behind the room's rear wall. Besides insulating the viewers from unwanted sound and light spill, this arrangement provides the opportunity for equipment to remain in place ready for use. There are other possible arrangements when space is constricted (Figs. 11, 12, and 13).

Creating an A-V front projection system that is both aesthetically pleasing and functionally efficient requires a high level of technical expertise and design skill. The results of such a combination can be effective yet unobtrusive. Fig. 16 provides an example of a multimedia front projection system that is compatible with the decor of the room and its formalized seating arrangement.

**Rear projection** The image in a rear projection system is focused on the back of a translucent screen and is visible to the audience on the other side. Since the light passes through the screen rather than being reflected off its front surface, there can be a reasonable light level in the viewing room during the presentation without affecting the quality of the image. It is only in the immediate vicinity of the screen that the room lights need be dimmed.

As is the case with all projection systems, for minimum distractions the equipment should be separated from the audience. This can be effected by means of a separate projection booth or by an enclosed cabinet within the viewing room. A separate room usually requires more space, but it may be the best solution for a particular situation. A cabinet within the viewing room permits front access to the projectors, enabling the

**Fig. 9   A square screen will permit horizontal, vertical, and square images to be shown.**

**Fig. 10   A dual-image format uses a screen that is a double square — giving the same flexibility of image shape for each of the two images or for a single central image.**

presenter to load the equipment without assistance.

While technical expertise and design skill are needed for the creation of a front projection A-V system, they are even more important for a system intended for rear projection, as a rear-mode arrangement has more inherent problems to overcome.

A rear projection system utilizing the indirect deep method in a separate projection booth requires a considerable amount of space. In addition, if more than one projector is used in such a system, either the projectors must be optically aligned each time a change is made (as there is only one true screen axis), or they are permanently positioned a little off axis, resulting in a slight "keystone" or distortion effect in the projected image (Fig. 17).

For good image clarity, the distance between the image source and the screen must be at least twice the picture size. To achieve

this clarity within a limited amount of space, the folded light-path method can be used (Figs. 18 and 19). As the name implies, the light path from the projector is "folded" by means of a large mirror, usually placed some distance away. This arrangement has the advantage of reducing the depth required behind the screen while retaining an adequate projection distance. As a further advantage, several projectors can be aligned in optically true positions by the use of a movable mirror with preset position stops.

The use of the folded light-path method of projection and a movable mirror can also be engineered in a cabinet that is directly accessible from the presentation room for "hands-on" operation by the person making the presentation. Both single-image and side-by-side dual-image systems can be designed in this manner (Figs. 20 and 21).

A great number of variations are possible using the same basic engineering concepts.

These variations can accommodate different functional requirements, spatial limitations, and image-quality parameters. Figures 14, 15, 22, and 23 illustrate some of the possible arrangements. User requirements and job conditions will guide the A-V engineer in the design of a specific system.

## The Optical Design Factor

A projection system — of whatever nature — is only as good as the quality of the image on the screen. The clarity, sharpness, resolution, and angle of view that can be expected are a direct result of the thought and care that go into the optical design of the system. The more complex the system becomes, the more critical is the system optics. The need for larger images, sharper images, multiple images, multiple image sources and the existence of physically constraining parameters all add to the conflicting requirements that must be satisfied. And they must be satisfied if an acceptable image quality is to be achieved.

## The Sound System

The quality and the functional characteristics of the sound system that is part of an audiovisual facility are as important as the quality and functional characteristics of the optical system. The two aspects of a facility are mutually complementary and the one should not be neglected in relation to the other if the goal of an effective and useful facility is to be attained.

The quality of the sound, as perceived by the listener, will be influenced by such factors as:

    The sensitivity of controls
    The quality of the amplifiers
    The quality of the speakers
    The location of the speakers
    The elimination of extraneous sounds
    The overall acoustical characteristics of the space

The design factors that govern the functional characteristics of the sound system might include the following:

*Sound sources:* voice, movie soundtrack, videotape, audiotape

    Telecommunication facilities for outside program sources

    Mixing and control requirements

    Quantity and placement of speakers

*Room size and function:* conference room, classroom, auditorium

    Provision for flexibility and future expansion

## The Remote-Control System

Most people who make informational presentations are not audiovisual specialists. Their primary concern is with the material they are presenting and not with the mechanics of how it is to be presented. As a result, any control devices they may be required to operate should be simple and logical. The presenter should be asked to make only a minimum of effort to determine how to manipulate the controls in order to achieve a desired result. The fewer operations necessary to reach a particular goal, the better. For example, in order for a change to be made from one presentation mode to another, it may be necessary to alter the ambient room lighting, reposition a mirror, turn one machine

**Fig. 11   A typical rear-access equipment arrangement for front projection.**

**Fig. 12   A rear-access reduced-depth arrangement of equipment for front projection.**

**Fig. 13   A front-access equipment cabinet for front projection.**

**Fig. 14**   An arrangement of two enclosed rear projection systems serving a single large room.

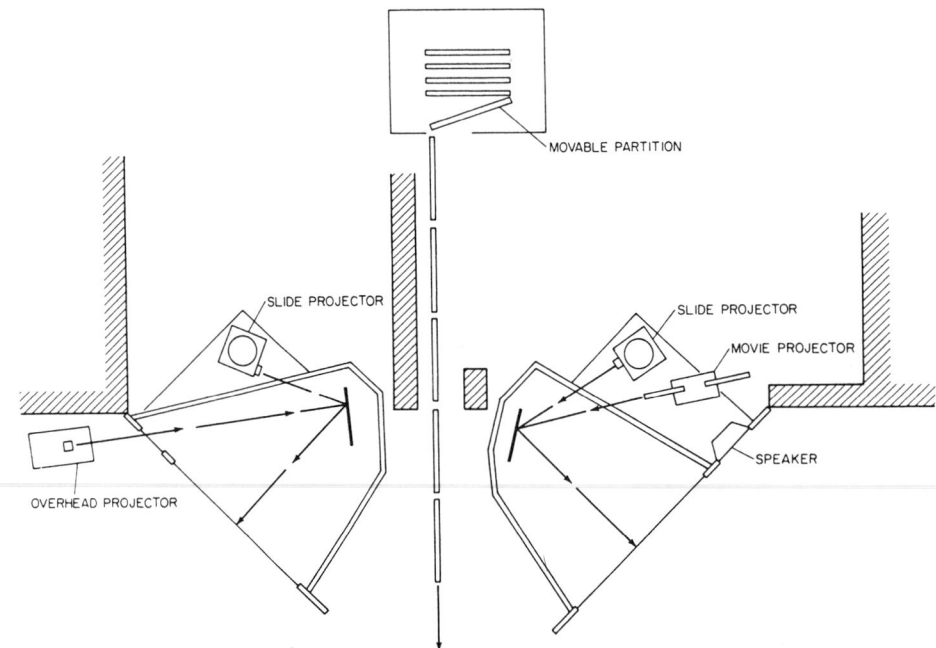

**Fig. 15**   The two enclosed and pivoted rear projection systems positioned to serve the two separate rooms that are created when a hidden dividing partition is extended.

off and then another on. If all these things can be accomplished merely by flipping one clearly marked switch, the presenter is freed from mechanical distractions and can concentrate full attention on the message being delivered. The location and spacing of the various switches on the panel, as well as the use of nomenclature unmistakable to a non-technical person, are important parts of the design of a remote-control system that will aid the presenter in the use of the audiovisual facility.

Other considerations that may affect the design of a remote-control system include:

The seating configuration

The room lighting

The number of control points required

The use of a lectern incorporating a control module

The number and type of functions to be controlled

The degree of automation required to meet system objectives

## SUMMARY

An audiovisual presentation facility is made up of many components and subsystems which are interdependent and must perform as an integrated unit. Regardless of its size or scope, the A-V system must be conceived, designed, and installed to function as a totality – as a single entity that works with optimum efficiency and effectiveness in an unobstrusive manner.

In order to achieve this goal – that of developing a logical and workable solution to any particular communication problem – careful and detailed preliminary investigations must be made. These will determine the functional requirements that make up the design program. From this program, the space needs for the equipment and for the audience can be established early enough in the development of the project to avoid undesirable procrustean solutions later. The selection, adaptation, manufacture, assembly, and installation of equipment and components should be carefully coordinated to ensure their functional integrity and performance.

Ultimately, a successful audiovisual system is one that serves as a logical and natural extension of the human capabilities of the person using it. It should respond easily and unobtrusively to the communicator's needs, and it should reproduce the material being communicated with the highest possible degree of fidelity.

## RECAP

### Front Projection

1. Viewing distance factor is 6. (For example, if image size is 5 feet the alphanumerics

would be clear at a maximum distance of 30 feet to a viewer with a 20/40 vision if characters are 3/16 inch on 6- by 9-inch original copy area.)

2. Advantages
   a. Good angle of view
   b. Good for checking laboratory quality of all projectuals
   c. Virtually no apparent falloff to the sides
3. Disadvantages
   a. High ceilings are required to utilize a square screen to accommodate vertical as well as horizontal images.
   b. Distraction occurs when the presenter or viewers interrupt the light beam.
   c. Any ambient light adversely affects image quality. The room must be relatively dark to achieve the desired picture contrast.
   d. An overhead projector cannot be used most effectively.

### Rear Projection (Rigid or Flexible Material)

1. Viewing distance factor is 7.5. (For example, if image size is 5 feet the maximum viewing distance would be 37.5 feet.)
2. Advantages
   a. A 20 percent smaller image than is required by front projection permits minimum standards to be met in low-ceilinged rooms.
   b. Can be used in higher ambient light conditions.
   c. No distracting light beam. (Presenter can more comfortably point at details).
   d. In a brighter room, the presenter easily maintains eye contact.
   e. An overhead projector can be used, so that neither it nor the presenter blocks the image from the viewers.
3. Disadvantages
   a. The inherent grain and directional quality of the rear screen eliminate it as a viewing medium to determine laboratory quality of projectuals.
   b. The projection system must be designed to overcome apparent illumination falloff at the sides and improve the angle of view.
   c. Mirrored image is required for proper use.
   d. More space is required than with front projection.
   e. Usually costs more.

### Seating

(Plan should permit several arrangements.)

1. A U- or V-table layout provides for best

viewing and viewer/presenter interaction (lowest audience capacity).

2. Conference table (boat-shape or oval) provides good interaction for conferences but not so good as the U- or V-table layout for audiovisual communication.

3. Random seating style (usually with writing tablets) is frequently selected for high-level visitor presentations. It permits larger capacity and creates a more luxurious atmosphere than the two arrangements above.

4. Classroom style (shallow tables parallel to front wall with chairs behind) is the next best method but less conducive to student interaction.
   a. Stepped, curved seating (lecture hall) provides unobstructed viewing.
   b. When classroom style is contemplated, study and programmed-learning carrels should be considered.

5. Auditorium style provides the largest capacity seating and is generally used for large group-orientation and overview types of presentation.

### Rear Projection System Factors

1. The physical center of all projector lenses must be in perfect alignment with the physical center of the screen to eliminate any "keystone" effect. (For dissolve mode, 2° off center vertically is permitted.)

2. A front-surface mirror should be used to reverse the image so the equipment can be loaded much as it is for front projection; slides in magazines need not be reversed, and special reversed prints are not needed for motion pictures. The use of a mirror can also extend the projection distance appreciably by folding the light path. Remember, the longer the projection distance, the better the viewing angle. Minimum projection distance should be at least 2 times the image size.

3. The screen-image area should be considered to be square to accommodate vertical and horizontal images unless the system is to be used for a special, limited requirement.

4. Apparent light falloff at the sides can be diminished or eliminated by increasing the projection distance and projector illumination. Another minor contributor is slide density. A dense or underexposed slide reduces the amount of light transmission. This condition increases apparent light falloff.

## AUDIO-VISUAL SYSTEMS
Equipment Arrangement

**Fig. 16** A custom-designed recessed front-access equipment cabinet for a multi-image front projection system.

**Fig. 19** An indirect rear projection arrangement using the folded-light-path method and the minimum recommended 2 to 1 ratio of projection distance to image size. This permits a flexible equipment arrangement within tight space limitations.

**Fig. 17** A deep, indirect-method, rear projection arrangement using the minimum recommended ratio of 2 to 1 between projection distance and image size.

**Fig. 18** An indirect rear projection arrangement using the folded-light-path method, resulting in a ratio of 3.5 to 1 within the same depth. This improves the image quality and increases the possible viewing angle as well as allowing rear projection of overhead transparencies with the overhead projector in the presentation room.

**Fig. 20** A front-access rear projection arrangement using the folded-light-path method for single-image presentations.

**Fig. 21** A front-access rear projection arrangement using the folded-light-path method for dual-image presentations.

**Fig. 22** A rear-access rear projection arrangement using the folded-light-path method for dual-image or single central-image presentations.

**Fig. 23** A rear projection arrangement for dual-image and single central-image presentations utilizing both deep indirect projection and the folded-light-path method.

## AUDIO-VISUAL SYSTEMS

Typical Projection Room Layout

16'0''
MIN

5'0''

### 5'0''x5'0''  REAR PROJECTION SCREEN

**Front wall supplied with system.**

19'3''
MIN

5'0''

### 5'0''x10'0''  REAR PROJECTION SCREEN

**Front wall supplied with system.**

20'-0"

WALL BY OTHERS

STATIONARY
REVERSING
MIRROR

EQUIP.
RACK

OVERHEAD PROJECTOR W/
TRANSPARENCY CHANGER

35MM SLIDE
PROJECTOR

5'-6"

DRY-MARKER
BOARD

5'-0" X 5'-0"
REAR PROJECTION
SCREEN

DRY-MARKER
BOARD

EQUIP. ACCESS
DOOR

EQUIP. ACCESS
DOOR

20'-0"

WALL BY OTHERS

OVERHEAD &
35MM SLIDE
PROJECTOR

REVERSING
MIRROR

OVERHEAD PROJECTOR
W/ TRANSPARENCY
CHANGER

5'-6"

5'-0" X 5'-0" REAR
PROJECTION SCREEN

35MM SLIDE
PROJECTOR

EQUIP. ACCESS
DOOR

EQUIP. ACCESS
DOOR

5'0''x10'0'' REAR
PROJECTION SCREEN

SECTION

EQUIP. RACK

OPERATOR
POSITION

EQUIP. RACK

CONSOLE MOUNTED
VIDEO PROJECTOR

CONSOLE MOUNTED
VIDEO PROJECTOR

A/V
STORAGE
CABINET

MASTER
CNTRL.
STATION

WORK
TABLE

PROJECTION ROOM

SCREENWALL
SPEAKER

DUAL 6'-0" X 6'-0"
REAR PROJECTION
SCREENS

SCREENWALL
SPEAKER

## TYPICAL CONFIGURATION

EQUIP. RACK

CONSOLE MOUNTED.
COLOR VIDEO
PROJECTOR

A/V
STORAGE
CABINET

MASTER
CONTROL
STATION

WORK
TABLE

PROJECTION ROOM

SCREENWALL
SPEAKER

6'-0" X 6'-0" REAR
PROJECTION SCREEN

SCREENWALL
SPEAKER

## TYPICAL CONFIGURATION

**TYPICAL CONFIGURATION**

**TYPICAL CONFIGURATION**

Sight line studies vary depending on the particular event and seating configuration. The following are some basic design elements. (*Note:* Remember to review and verify slope, riser heights, tread depths, etc., with pertinent national and local code requirements.)

The visibility profile shown in Fig. 1:

*Angle A:* Shifting position to look between heads in row immediately in front of spectator and over all other heads.

*Angle B:* Shifting position to look between heads of two rows immediately in front of spectators and over all other heads.

Generally, the variables considered in determining these angles are:
- 3'8" eye level in the seated position
- 5" minimum eye clearance
- Row spacing and row rise

Angle A is commonly used in determining floor slope for auditorium, performing arts or theater type seating configurations. When angle A profile is used in conjunction with a staggered seating arrangement (chairs staggered or alternated in arrangement of sizes opposite every other row) it allows unobstructed view of spectators to a determined focal point at screen on stage. The final analysis is to have all sight lines to intersect the desired focal point (usually 5'6" elevation either at screen or 12'0" back from front of stage).

Angle B is most commonly used in determining riser or stepped applications for gymnasium, arena, or stadium type seating configurations. When the angle B profile is used (generally associated with an aligned seating arrangement) it allows unobstructed view of spectators to a determined focal point at court line or line of play. The final analysis is to have all the critical sight lines to intersect the focal point or line of play at generally a 3'0" elevation.

Legal responsibility lies with the owners and users of equipment in acquiring acceptance with local officals. The following are some basic guidelines.

### Standard Seating

1. Row spacing shall provide a clear space of not less than 12" (30.5 cm) from the back of one chair to the front of the most forward projection of the chair directly behind it when measured with the self-rising seat in the up position.

2. Rows of chairs shall not exceed 14 chairs between aisles and exceed seven chairs from an aisle to a row end.

3. Aisles serving 60 seats or less shall be a minimum of 30" (76 cm) wide. Aisles serving more than 60 seats shall be at least 3' (91 cm) wide when serving seats on one side and at least 3'6" (107 cm) wide when serving seats

on both sides. These minimum widths, measured at the point furthest from an exit, cross aisles, or foyer shall be increased 1½" (3.8 cm) for each 5' (152 cm) in length toward the exit, cross aisle, or foyer. Where egress is possible in either direction, aisles shall be uniform in width. Dead end aisles are not allowed over 20'0" (61.0 m) in length.

4. Cross aisles, foyer or exit widths shall be not less than the sum of the required width of the widest aisle plus 50% of the total required width of the remaining aisles that it serves.

### Continental Seating

1. Row spacing shall provide a clear space of not less than: 18" (45.7 cm) between rows of 18 chairs or less; 20" (50.8 cm) between rows of 35 chairs or less; 21" (53.3 cm) between rows of 45 chairs or less; 22" (55.9 cm) between rows of 45 chairs or more to a maximum of 100 chairs per row, measured from the back of one chair to the front of the most forward projection of the chair directly behind it with the self-rising seat in the up position.

2. There shall be exits of 66" (168 cm) minimum clear width along each side aisle of the chair rows for each five rows of chairs.

3. Aisles shall not be less than 44" (112 cm) in clear width.

**Fig. 1**

## AUDITORIUM SEATING
**Row Length**

Row length = ℄ to ℄ + (2A) measured at the Chair Size Line

(3) @ 20" = 5'-0"

A ←→ ← → A

℄        ℄        ℄        ℄

20"       20"       20"

CHAIR
SIZE
LINE →

*Note:* End dim. A varies 2" to 3" for end tablet arm applications.

**EXAMPLE:**
(3) 20" chairs = 5'-4" row length.

| | DIMENSIONS: Center line to center line (℄ to ℄) | | | | | | | | | | |
|---|---|---|---|---|---|---|---|---|---|---|---|
| **QTY** | **SIZE** | | | | | **QTY** | **SIZE** | | | | |
| | **18"** | **19"** | **20"** | **21"** | **22"** | | **18"** | **19"** | **20"** | **21"** | **22"** |
| 2 | 3'-0" | 3'-2" | 3'-4" | 3'-6" | 3'-8" | 32 | 48'-0" | 50'-8" | 53'-4" | 56'-0" | 58'-8" |
| 3 | 4'-6" | 4'-9" | 5'-0" | 5'-3" | 5'-6" | 33 | 49'-6" | 52'-3" | 55'-0" | 57'-9" | 60'-6" |
| 4 | 6'-0" | 6'-4" | 6'-8" | 7'-0" | 7'-4" | 34 | 51'-0" | 53'-10" | 56'-8" | 59'-6" | 62'-4" |
| 5 | 7'-6" | 7'-11" | 8'-4" | 8'-9" | 9'-2" | 35 | 52'-6" | 55'-5" | 58'-4" | 61'-3" | 64'-2" |
| 6 | 9'-0" | 9'-6" | 10'-0" | 10'-6" | 11'-0" | 36 | 54'-0" | 57'-0" | 60'-0" | 63'-0" | 66'-0" |
| 7 | 10'-6" | 11'-1" | 11'-8" | 12'-3" | 12'-10" | 37 | 55'-6" | 58'-7" | 61'-8" | 64'-9" | 67'-10" |
| 8 | 12'-0" | 12'-8" | 13'-4" | 14'-0" | 14'-8" | 38 | 57'-0" | 60'-2" | 63'-4" | 66'-6" | 69'-8" |
| 9 | 13'-6" | 14'-3" | 15'-0" | 15'-9" | 16'-6" | 39 | 58'-6" | 61'-9" | 65'-0" | 68'-3" | 71'-6" |
| 10 | 15'-0" | 15'-10" | 16'-8" | 17'-6" | 18'-4" | 40 | 60'-0" | 63'-4" | 66'-8" | 70'-0" | 73'-4" |
| 11 | 16'-6" | 17'-5" | 18'-4" | 19'-3" | 20'-2" | 41 | 61'-6" | 64'-11" | 68'-4" | 71'-9" | 75'-2" |
| 12 | 18'-0" | 19'-0" | 20'-0" | 21'-0" | 22'-0" | 42 | 63'-0" | 66'-6" | 70'-0" | 73'-6" | 77'-0" |
| 13 | 19'-6" | 20'-7" | 21'-8" | 22'-9" | 23'-10" | 43 | 64'-6" | 68'-1" | 71'-8" | 75'-3" | 78'-10" |
| 14 | 21'-0" | 22'-2" | 23'-4" | 24'-6" | 25'-8" | 44 | 66'-0" | 69'-8" | 73'-4" | 77'-0" | 80'-8" |
| 15 | 22'-6" | 23'-9" | 25'-0" | 26'-3" | 27'-6" | 45 | 67'-6" | 71'-3" | 75'-0" | 78'-9" | 82'-6" |
| 16 | 24'-0" | 25'-4" | 26'-8" | 28'-0" | 29'-4" | 46 | 69'-0" | 72'-10" | 76'-8" | 80'-6" | 84'-4" |
| 17 | 25'-6" | 26'-11" | 28'-4" | 29'-9" | 31'-2" | 47 | 70'-6" | 74'-5" | 78'-4" | 82'-3" | 86'-2" |
| 18 | 27'-0" | 28'-6" | 30'-0" | 31'-6" | 33'-0" | 48 | 72'-0" | 76'-0" | 80'-0" | 84'-0" | 88'-0" |
| 19 | 28'-6" | 30'-1" | 31'-8" | 33'-3" | 34'-10" | 49 | 73'-6" | 77'-7" | 81'-8" | 85'-9" | 89'-10" |
| 20 | 30'-0" | 31'-8" | 33'-4" | 35'-0" | 36'-8" | 50 | 75'-0" | 79'-2" | 83'-4" | 87'-6" | 91'-8" |
| 21 | 31'-6" | 33'-3" | 35'-0" | 36'-9" | 38'-6" | 51 | 76'-6" | 80'-9" | 85'-0" | 89'-3" | 93'-6" |
| 22 | 33'-0" | 34'-10" | 36'-8" | 38'-6" | 40'-4" | 52 | 78'-0" | 82'-4" | 86'-8" | 91'-0" | 95'-4" |
| 23 | 34'-6" | 36'-5" | 38'-4" | 40'-3" | 42'-2" | 53 | 79'-6" | 83'-11" | 88'-4" | 92'-9" | 97'-2" |
| 24 | 36'-0" | 38'-0" | 40'-0" | 42'-0" | 44'-0" | 54 | 81'-0" | 85'-6" | 90'-0" | 94'-6" | 99'-0" |
| 25 | 37'-6" | 39'-7" | 41'-8" | 43'-9" | 45'-10" | 55 | 82'-6" | 87'-1" | 91'-8" | 96'-3" | 100'-10" |
| 26 | 39'-0" | 41'-2" | 43'-4" | 45'-6" | 47'-8" | 56 | 84'-0" | 88'-8" | 93'-4" | 98'-0" | 102'-8" |
| 27 | 40'-6" | 42'-9" | 45'-0" | 47'-3" | 48'-6" | 57 | 85'-6" | 90'-3" | 95'-0" | 99'-9" | 104'-6" |
| 28 | 42'-0" | 44'-4" | 46'-8" | 49'-0" | 51'-4" | 58 | 87'-0" | 91'-10" | 96'-8" | 101'-6" | 106'-4" |
| 29 | 43'-6" | 45'-11" | 48'-4" | 50'-9" | 53'-2" | 59 | 88'-6" | 93'-5" | 98'-4" | 103'-3" | 108'-2" |
| 30 | 45'-0" | 47'-6" | 50'-0" | 52'-6" | 55'-0" | 60 | 90'-0" | 95'-0" | 100'-0" | 105'-0" | 110'-0" |
| 31 | 46'-6" | 49'-1" | 51'-8" | 54'-3" | 56'-10" | —— | —— | —— | —— | —— | —— |

**EXAMPLE:**
4 rows (3 spaces) at 33″ = 8'-3″

ROW SPACE *

CLEAR SPACE *

See elevation drawings for envelope dimensions

CHAIR SIZE LINE

4 rows (3 spaces) at 33″ = 8'-3″

See elevation drawings for dimensions

***Notes:**
1. Refer to applicable building codes.

2. Spacing varies with tablet arm applications.

3. Row space dimension will be the sum of "clear space" (see building codes) plus "chair envelope" (see chair dimensions) plus any additional space as desired for convenience to permit patron easy access to concessions, restrooms, etc.

| OVERALL SPACING OF CHAIRS (back to back) | | | | | | | | | | | |
|---|---|---|---|---|---|---|---|---|---|---|---|
| Number of seating rows (spaces + 1) | ROW SPACE DIMENSIONS | | | | | | | | | | |
| | 32″ | 33″ | 34″ | 35″ | 36″ | 37″ | 38″ | 39″ | 40″ | 41″ | 42″ |
| 2 | 2'-8″ | 2'-9″ | 2'-10″ | 2'-11″ | 3'-0″ | 3″-1″ | 3'-2″ | 3'-3″ | 3'-4″ | 3'-5″ | 3'-6″ |
| 3 | 5'-4″ | 5'-6″ | 5'-8″ | 5'-10″ | 6'-0″ | 6'-2″ | 6'-4″ | 6'-6″ | 6'-8″ | 6'-10″ | 7'-0″ |
| 4 | 8'-0″ | 8'-3″ | 8'-6″ | 8'-9″ | 9'-0″ | 9'-3″ | 9'-6″ | 9'-9″ | 10'-0″ | 10'-3″ | 10'-6″ |
| 5 | 10'-8″ | 11'-0″ | 11'-4″ | 11'-8″ | 12'-0″ | 12'-4″ | 12'-8″ | 13'-0″ | 13'-4″ | 13'-8″ | 14'-0″ |
| 6 | 13'-4″ | 13'-9″ | 14'-2″ | 14'-7″ | 15'-0″ | 15'-5″ | 15'-10″ | 16'-3″ | 16'-8″ | 17'-1″ | 17'-6″ |
| 7 | 16'-0″ | 16'-6″ | 17'-0″ | 17'-6″ | 18'-0″ | 18'-6″ | 19'-0″ | 19'-6″ | 20'-0″ | 20'-6″ | 21'-0″ |
| 8 | 18'-8″ | 19'-3″ | 19'-10″ | 20'-5″ | 21'-0″ | 21'-7″ | 22'-2″ | 22'-9″ | 23'-4″ | 23'-11″ | 24'-6″ |
| 9 | 21'-4″ | 22'-0″ | 22'-8″ | 23'-4″ | 24'-0″ | 24'-8″ | 25'-4″ | 26'-0″ | 26'-8″ | 27'-4″ | 28'-0″ |
| 10 | 24'-0″ | 24'-9″ | 25'-6″ | 26'-3″ | 27'-0″ | 27'-9″ | 28'-6″ | 29'-3″ | 30'-0″ | 30'-9″ | 31'-6″ |
| 11 | 26'-8″ | 27'-6″ | 28'-4″ | 29'-2″ | 30'-0″ | 30'-10″ | 31'-8″ | 32'-6″ | 33'-4″ | 34'-2″ | 35'-0″ |
| 12 | 29'-4″ | 30'-3″ | 31'-2″ | 32'-1″ | 33'-0″ | 33'-11″ | 34'-10″ | 35'-9″ | 36'-8″ | 37'-7″ | 38'-6″ |
| 13 | 32'-0″ | 33'-0″ | 34'-0″ | 35'-0″ | 36'-0″ | 37'-0″ | 38'-0″ | 39'-0″ | 40'-0″ | 41'-0″ | 42'-0″ |
| 14 | 34'-8″ | 35'-9″ | 36'-10″ | 37'-11″ | 39'-0″ | 40'-1″ | 41'-2″ | 42'-3″ | 43'-4″ | 44'-5″ | 45'-6″ |
| 15 | 37'-4″ | 38'-6″ | 39'-8″ | 40'-10″ | 42'-0″ | 43'-2″ | 44'-4″ | 45'-6″ | 46'-8″ | 47'-10″ | 49'-0″ |
| 16 | 40'-0″ | 41'-3″ | 42'-6″ | 43'-9″ | 45'-0″ | 46'-3″ | 47'-6″ | 48'-9″ | 50'-0″ | 51'-3″ | 52'-6″ |
| 17 | 42'-8″ | 44'-0″ | 45'-4″ | 46'-8″ | 48'-0″ | 49'-4″ | 50'-8″ | 52'-0″ | 53'-4″ | 54'-8″ | 56'-0″ |
| 18 | 45'-4″ | 46'-9″ | 48'-2″ | 49'-7″ | 51'-0″ | 52'-5″ | 53'-10″ | 55'-3″ | 56'-8″ | 58'-1″ | 59'-6″ |
| 19 | 48'-0″ | 49'-6″ | 51'-0″ | 52'-6″ | 54'-0″ | 55'-6″ | 57'-0″ | 58'-6″ | 60'-0″ | 61'-6″ | 63'-0″ |
| 20 | 50'-8″ | 52'-3″ | 53'-10″ | 55'-5″ | 57'-0″ | 58'-7″ | 60'-2″ | 61'-9″ | 63'-4″ | 64'-11″ | 66'-6″ |
| 21 | 53'-4″ | 55'-0″ | 56'-8″ | 58'-4″ | 60'-0″ | 61'-8″ | 63'-4″ | 65'-0″ | 66'-8″ | 68'-4″ | 70'-0″ |
| 22 | 56'-0″ | 57'-9″ | 59'-6″ | 61'-3″ | 63'-0″ | 64'-9″ | 66'-6″ | 68'-3″ | 70'-0″ | 71'-9″ | 73'-6″ |
| 23 | 68'-8″ | 60'-6″ | 62'-4″ | 64'-2″ | 66'-0″ | 67'-10″ | 69'-8″ | 71'-6″ | 73'-4″ | 75'-2″ | 77'-0″ |
| 24 | 61'-4″ | 63'-3″ | 65'-2″ | 67'-1″ | 69'-0″ | 70'-11″ | 72'-10″ | 74'-9″ | 76'-8″ | 78'-7″ | 80'-6″ |
| 25 | 64'-0″ | 66'-0″ | 68'-0″ | 70'-0″ | 72'-0″ | 74'-0″ | 76'-0″ | 78'-0″ | 80'-0″ | 82'-0″ | 84'-0″ |
| 26 | 66'-8″ | 68'-9″ | 70'-10″ | 72'-11″ | 75'-0″ | 77'-1″ | 79'-2″ | 81'-3″ | 83'-4″ | 85'-5″ | 87'-6″ |
| 27 | 69'-4″ | 71'-6″ | 73'-8″ | 75'-10″ | 78'-0″ | 80'-2″ | 82'-4″ | 84'-6″ | 86'-8″ | 88'-10″ | 91'-0″ |
| 28 | 72'-0″ | 74'-3″ | 76'-6″ | 78'-9″ | 81'-0″ | 83'-3″ | 85'-6″ | 87'-9″ | 90'-0″ | 92'-3″ | 94'-6″ |
| 29 | 74'-8″ | 77'-0″ | 79'-4″ | 81'-8″ | 84'-0″ | 86'-4″ | 88'-8″ | 91'-0″ | 93'-4″ | 95'-8″ | 98'-0″ |
| 30 | 77'-4″ | 79'-9″ | 82'-2″ | 84'-7″ | 87'-0″ | 89'-5″ | 91'-10″ | 94'-3″ | 96'-8″ | 99'-1″ | 101'-6″ |
| 31 | 80'-0″ | 82'-6″ | 85'-0″ | 87'-6″ | 90'-0″ | 92'-6″ | 95'-0″ | 97'-6″ | 100'-0″ | 102'-6″ | 105'-0″ |

# AUDITORIUM SEATING

**Chair Dimensions**

## AUDITORIUM SEATING
### General Seating Arrangement

Seating arrangements in an assembly space will either be identified as "multiple-aisle" or "continental." These terms are commonly found in design standards manuals, building codes, and similar architectural reference documents. Each is unique with specific guidelines governing row size, row spacing, and exitways.

Basically, a multiple-aisle arrangement (Fig. 2) will have a maximum of 14–16 chairs per row with access to an aisleway at both ends. If an aisle can be reached from one end of a row only, the seat count may then be limited to 7 or 8. It should be noted here that the maximum quantities will always be established by the governing building code.

In a continental arrangement (Fig. 3) all seats are located in a central section. Here the maximum quantity of chairs per row can greatly exceed the limits established in a multiple-aisle arrangement. In order to compensate for the greater length of rows allowed, building codes will require wider row spacing, wider aisles and strategically located exit doors.

Although more space would appear to be called for, a continental seating plan is often not any less efficient than a multiple-aisle arrangement. In fact, carefully planned, a continental arrangement can frequently accommodate more seating within the same space. For early planning an average 7.5 sq. ft. per person may be used. This will include both the seating area and space necessary for aisleways.

**Fig. 2  Multiple-aisle arrangement.**

**Fig. 3  Continental arrangement.**

## Design Considerations

1. Layout per applicable building and life safety codes, regulations, and ordinances.

2. Allow sufficient distance between aisles for desired quantity and size of chairs plus end space.

3. Space rows to allow for proper seat to back clear space.

4. Determine radius or straight rows and locate by the chair size line.

5. Allow 1" minimum clearance from either side or rear of chair to any adjacent side wall, end walls, etc.

6. Provide adequate sightlines for either sloping or stepped (riser) floor configurations.

7. Seating area should be free of obstructions.

8. To allow for sufficient aisle illumination: Aisle lights are generally located in the end panel standards at least every other row. Locate aisle light junction box 6" from the standard.

9. Provide adequate floor or riser materials for sound anchorage.

**TYPICAL PLAN OF SEATING AND TERMINOLOGY**

# AUDITORIUM SEATING
## Row Seating

**Seat Widths** Seating comfort is initially established by individual chair widths. Available sizes range from 18" to 24", however, all may not be produced by a single manufacturer. The most commonly used chair widths are 20", 21", and 22". It should be noted that these dimensions are nominal, being measured from center to center of the support legs. If seating comfort is a high priority, thought must be given to a particular width and the space taken up by chair arms to determine an actual size. Usually, smaller sizes of 18" and 19" have limited application due to the minimum clear width provided. Typically, all manufacturers size their chairs along an imaginary line which may be referred to as a "datum line", "chair radius line" or a similar name. For accurate planning in an assembly area, this line must be identified so as not to over or underestimate the potential of a row of chairs.

**Row Spacing** Row spacing or "back to back" spacing of seats is also very important in developing a comfortable assembly area. A minimum dimension occasionally used is 2'-8" (32"). This spacing provides marginal clearance between a seated person's knees and the back of the chair in the next forward row. At the same time, however, it will require that a seated person stand to permit the passage of another individual. As the row spacing is increased to 3'-0" (36"), seating comfort is dramatically improved and passage along a row of seated persons is accomplished with less disruption.

**Floor Design** Seating comfort will also be affected by the design of the assembly space floor. Flat or less steeply sloped floors will usually allow a person to extend their knees and legs even under minimum row spacing dimensions. Here an individual can take advantage of the open area under a seat and the free space created by the pitched back of a chair. As the floor slope is increased, this "free" space diminishes. The extreme condition exists where a large elevation change between rows is combined with a minimum row spacing. An example would be a 12" high riser and a 32" wide row spacing. At this point, it becomes necessary to consider increasing the back to back dimension to provide more leg room.

The "free" space under a chair is also lost when a row of seats is located directly behind a low wall. In this case a recommended minimum clearance would be 11" measured from seat edge in the lowered position to face of wall. The back to back dimension of a row of seats abutting a rear wall should also be carefully studied. Normally, the pitched back of a chair will overlap a riser face, automatically reducing the width of that row unless succeeding rows are similarly positioned. Where a rear wall exists the recommended procedure is to increase the dimension of the last row sufficiently to accommodate any overlap plus a minimal space between the wall and top edge of the chair back.

Visibility in an assembly space is a function of seat location. As stated earlier, building codes, comfort guidelines, floor design and the overall form of an assembly space will play a part in seating arrangements. This information combined with a basic understanding of sightline analysis and related planning guidelines can result in achieving an acceptable, if not optimum, level of viewing for spectators.

Perhaps film projection requires the most critical sightline analysis, since poor seat location will result in distorted images. For this activity the seating parameters are established by the screen or image size. An angle of 30° up to 45° measured perpendicular to the far and near edges of the screen can establish a side to side seating limit, while the screen or image height may determine the maximum distance. The minimum dimension or closest recommended seat will also be set by the screen height. (It should be noted that these figures are approximate and apply principally to flat screen projection.)

# AUDITORIUM SEATING
### End Stage; ¾ Arena

| Basic Theater Form | End Stage |
| --- | --- |
| Quantity of Seats | 55 |
| Seating Area | 450 Sq. Ft. |
| Space per Seat | 8.23 Sq. Ft. |
| Row Spacing | 2'-9" |
| Most Distant Seat | 22'-0" |
| Stage Elevation | None |
| Floor Design | Flat / One Riser 8" |

| Basic Theater Form | ¾ Arena |
| --- | --- |
| Quantity of Seats | 56 |
| Seating Area | 622 Sq. Ft. |
| Space per Seat | 11.1 Sq. Ft. |
| Row Spacing | 3'-3" |
| Most Distant Seat | 32'-0" |
| Stage Elevation | None |
| Floor Design | Risers 4" |

| Basic Theater Form | End Stage |
| --- | --- |
| Quantity of Seats | 80 |
| Seating Area | 700 Sq. Ft. |
| Space per Seat | 8.75 Sq. Ft. |
| Row Spacing | 3'-6" |
| Most Distant Seat | 25'-0" |
| Stage Elevation | 3'-6" |
| Floor Design | Risers 6" |

| Basic Theater Form | End Stage |
| --- | --- |
| Quantity of Seats | 92 |
| Seating Area | 956 Sq. Ft. |
| Space per Seat | 10.4 Sq. Ft. |
| Row Spacing | 3'-0" |
| Most Distant Seat | 37'-0" |
| Stage Elevation | 12" |
| Floor Design | Flat |

## AUDITORIUM SEATING
**End Stage**

| Basic Theater Form | End Stage |
| --- | --- |
| Quantity of Seats | 99 |
| Seating Area | 953 Sq. Ft. |
| Space per Seat | 9.62 Sq. Ft. |
| Row Spacing | 3'-5" |
| Most Distant Seat | 32'-0" |
| Stage Elevation | 12" |
| Floor Design | Risers 12" |

| Basic Theater Form | End Stage |
| --- | --- |
| Quantity of Seats | 105 |
| Seating Area | 903 Sq. Ft. |
| Space per Seat | 8.6 Sq. Ft. |
| Row Spacing | 3'-0" |
| Most Distant Seat | 35'-0" |
| Stage Elevation | 5" |
| Floor Design | Risers 12" |

| Basic Theater Form | ¾ Arena |
|---|---|
| Quantity of Seats | 108 |
| Seating Area | 1200 Sq. Ft. |
| Space per Seat | 11.1 Sq. Ft. |
| Row Spacing | 3'-0" |
| Most Distant Seat | 45'-0" |
| Stage Elevation | Varies |
| Floor Design | Risers 12" |

Up to
Projection
Room

Speaker's
Podium

Projection
Screen

| Basic Theater Form | End Stage |
|---|---|
| Quantity of Seats | 120 |
| Seating Area | 1088 Sq. Ft. |
| Space per Seat | 9.1 Sq. Ft. |
| Row Spacing | 3'-3" |
| Most Distant Seat | 41'-0" |
| Stage Elevation | 1'-6" |
| Floor Design | Iscidomal Slope |
| | 2.4°, 4.7°, 7.1° |

# AUDITORIUM SEATING

**End Stage; Wide Fan**

| Basic Theater Form | End Stage |
|---|---|
| Quantity of Seats | 180 |
| Seating Area | 1218 Sq. Ft. |
| Space per Seat | 6.8 Sq. Ft. |
| Row Spacing | 2'-8" |
| Most Distant Seat | 50'-0" |
| Stage Elevation | 1'-6" |
| Floor Design | Iscidomal Slope |
| | -1° to 10° |

| Basic Theater Form | Wide Fan |
|---|---|
| Quantity of Seats | 253 |
| Seating Area | 1790 Sq. Ft. |
| Space per Seat | 7.1 Sq. Ft. |
| Row Spacing | 3'-0" |
| Most Distant Seat | 48'-0" |
| Stage Elevation | None |
| Floor Design | Risers—Varying |
| | Height 10½" to 16" |

| Basic Theater Form | End Stage |
|---|---|
| **Quantity of Seats** | 430 |
| **Seating Area** | 2586 Sq. Ft. |
| **Space per Seat** | 6.0 Sq. Ft. |
| **Row Spacing** | 2'-8¾" |
| **Most Distant Seat** | 58'-0" |
| **Stage Elevation** | 2'-6" |
| **Floor Design** | Sloped 7.1° |

| Basic Theater Form | End Stage |
|---|---|
| **Quantity of Seats** | 224 |
| **Seating Area** | 1660 Sq. Ft. |
| **Space per Seat** | 7.4 Sq. Ft. |
| **Row Spacing** | 2'-9" |
| **Most Distant Seat** | 60'-0" |
| **Stage Elevation** | None |
| **Floor Design** | Sloped 7.1°/Risers 13¾" |

## AUDITORIUM SEATING
Wide Fan

| Basic Theater Form | Wide Fan |
|---|---|
| Quantity of Seats | 208 |
| Seating Area | 1557 Sq. Ft. |
| Space per Seat | 7.5 Sq. Ft. |
| Row Spacing | 2'-8" |
| Most Distant Seat | 48'-0" |
| Stage Elevation | 5" |
| Floor Design | Risers 14" |

| Basic Theater Form | Wide Fan |
|---|---|
| Quantity of Seats | 207 |
| Seating Area | 1428 Sq. Ft. |
| Space per Seat | 6.9 Sq. Ft. |
| Row Spacing | 3'-4" |
| Most Distant Seat | 40'-0" |
| Stage Elevation | 2'-3" |
| Floor Design | Sloped 6.6° |

## CONTROL OF GROUNDS

Fencing can be a very effective means of limiting access to secondary exits and to vulnerable ground-level dwellings. Fencing functions as a control by requiring entry through a single, limited, highly visible area. The fencing surrounding most single-family homes does not have locked gates. It is intended primarily to protect children, pets, and gardens, and to define the area immediately around the home as the private outdoor space of that household. Any intrusion into the area within the fence is therefore noticeable. As a security measure, such fencing, used symbolically, is of minimal value against premeditated crime, but it does make criminal intent visible and so is an important deterrent.

A conventional use of fencing in multifamily complexes is to limit access to backyards and windows of a housing cluster. On conventional city blocks, backyards of row housing are accessible only through one of the houses. However, in many superblock designs, such backyards are left open to public access. In this situation, addition of a limited amount of fencing can protect a large group of homes (see Fig. 1). This approach can also subdivide the superblock and so create small, natural clusters.

### The Lobby

Improving visibility is the most important ingredient in providing a naturally secure lobby. It is crucial that a tenant entering a building be able to see what is going on in the lobby from the outside. Hidden nooks and blind curves provide perfect hiding places. Where such features cannot be removed structurally, the use of mirrors, windows, and improved lighting may ease the situation.

Ideally, a person walking down a path to enter a building should be able to see anyone standing in the lobby and elevator waiting area. In fact, it is often advantageous if the arriving person can see into the elevator from across the lobby.

## CONTROL OF INTERIOR PUBLIC SPACES OF MULTIFAMILY DWELLINGS

The most vulnerable locations in multifamily buildings are the interior public spaces: lobbies, elevators, stairwells, and corridors. These are areas open to the public but without the attending surveillance given a public street by passersby and police. The crimes that occur in these interior public spaces are the most fearful types of crimes, involving acts of personal confrontation such as robbery, assault, and rape. Limiting access to these spaces through the use of a doorman or intercom/door lock system can be of substantial benefit.

Lobby visibility discourages a number of different kinds of crime. Crimes of personal confrontation may be deterred primarily because the potential victim can readily perceive and avoid a suspicious person in the lobby. The potential criminal must also fear the possibility that another tenant or the police may be viewing the crime in the well-lit open area.

**Fig. 1 Use of fencing to define and secure large semiprivate areas.**

Mailbox crime — generally the theft of checks — can be deterred when mailboxes are located in a highly protected area of the lobby. This protection can consist of placing the mailboxes behind an intercom or in a locked mailroom. It is essential that the mailboxes be visible from as many different viewpoints as possible. Improved visibility in this context can be a significant deterrent to crime.

Some managers designate an area of the lobby as a legitimate resting place, where chairs and other lounging items are provided. Lounging may aid security, particularly if the building includes a high proportion of elderly. The best locations for such seating are areas with high visibility. Often tenant patrols use this space as a station and provide still another dimension of security.

A bulletin board is an inexpensive device that can improve lobby security by providing a diversion. If, for example, a tenant enters the lobby and sees someone she doesn't recognize waiting for an elevator, she may need a reasonable excuse for not taking the same elevator. The bulletin board provides the tenant with a natural excuse to pause and survey the situation.

The area around the main entry to a multifamily building should be clearly distinguished from the public walkway which leads to it. A person entering through the main door should feel distinctly that he is entering a space controlled by the residents of the building. The main entry should be well lit and clearly visible from outside.

Entry doors should be constructed of a transparent material covering as large an area as possible. In vandalism-prone areas, the main entry doors should be made of unbreakable glass or other similar, very sturdy transparent material. Because of the need for good visibility, replacing glass panels with metal or other material should be avoided. For window walls and doors where the incidence of vandalism is extreme, glass panels less than 2 feet from the ground and higher than 7 feet from the ground may be replaced by solid materials.

### Fire Doors and Fire Stairs

Secondary exit doors are the weakest link in security of buildings. An ideal secondary exit door would be one that allows exit but not entrance. Unfortunately, there is no acceptable emergency exit system that allows egress only.

In the design of any security system there is a continuing clash between the need for security against crime and the need for safety in case of fire. Fire doors are frequently used for entry and exit by criminals. Installation of panic hardware and the absence of exterior hardware sometimes prevent criminal use. These measures will not suffice, however, where tenants do not cooperate in avoiding use of secondary exits and ensuring they are kept closed.

To a large extent, the design and location of secondary fire exits determine tenant attitudes about the exits. For example, a building's main entry may face the street, but the parking lot may be to the rear of the building. If the secondary exit is also at the rear and close to this destination, the temptation to use the fire door as an entry or exit will be difficult to resist. Similarly, security is decreased in buildings where the main entries face the interior of the project while the fire doors face the surrounding streets with their parking and shopping facilities. Where the fire exit does not represent any shortcut or improved convenience to the tenant, it is far more likely to remain closed. A securely designed building is one in which the fire door exits to an area that is less convenient or desirable than the area outside the main door.

In cases of persistent breaks in security of secondary exits, it is possible to modify the building plan at the ground level and open a new doorway in a better location. However, this improvement is costly and can only be done where architecturally possible.

Another architectural modification to improve security involves making a fire exit into a legitimate secondary entry and developing a security system that protects both the main and secondary entries. If a fire door exits to a parking area, for example, this modification may be more successful than efforts to prevent tenants from using that exit. If the main entry is equipped with an intercom system, the secondary entry should be similarly equipped and made easily surveillable through the use of lighting and windows.

Other mechanisms can be used to limit access to and prevent circulation through the emergency exit system. A fire exit passageway, for example, can be modified by installing a second door inside the building a short distance from the existing exterior door. Both doors should be equipped with hardware so that they can be opened only from the inside. The point of this system is that it is unlikely that both doors will be propped or jammed open at the same time. A tenant entering an open exterior fire door which leads only to the locked second door will have to exit and use another door. A few experiences of this kind will convince most tenants that it is probably more convenient to go directly through the main entrance. This double-door system generally does not conflict with fire codes.

An extension of this concept is to have the fire door on each floor above ground level openable from the corridor only. Thus, once someone has gone into a stairwell he can only exit at the ground level. This system may be somewhat inconvenient to tenants accustomed to moving easily between floors, but it does create roadblocks for anyone attempting to enter the building from the ground-level exit door.

The improvements outlined above are generally applicable to all dwellings. In buildings which have such security personnel, additional measures are possible.

A doorman or security guard can only be effective if he controls all access to the building, including access through fire doors. In a well-designed building, the doorman can see the fire doors from his position at the main entry. Where this is not possible, an inexpensive and effective solution is to install panic hardware with an alarm, and make sure the doorman can hear and respond to the alarm. Where the doorman or guard has access to closed-circuit TV, this may be used to monitor the fire doors. If the doorman can also be given a device for controlling the secondary door, it becomes very difficult for a criminal to use the fire entry.

### Elevators

There are virtually no structural modifications that can improve security within elevators. The only possible improvements are use of mirrors, communication devices, emergency buttons, or an electronic surveillance system.

Security modifications to other areas of a building improve security within the elevator. If the elevator waiting area and the elevator cab are a visible extension of the lobby, the residents are afforded some protection. Similarly, if the fire door and fire stairs are secure, there is less chance of a criminal entering the elevator on an upper floor. In this sense, the safety of the elevator is dependent upon the general security of the building.

## SECURING THE DWELLING

Illegal entry into dwelling units is traditionally prevented by use of hardware. However, there are building design features which in themselves limit access, improve surveillance, and promote neighbor recognition.

### Windows

Ground-level windows are generally most vulnerable to illegal entry and breakage. (All windows whose lower ledges are less than 7 feet off the ground should be considered ground level.) There are three ways to discourage criminal entry through ground-floor windows: design ground-floor areas which need few windows; house activities on the ground floor which hold no interest to the burglar; and assign the grounds immediately adjacent to the building for the use of the neighboring resident and fence off the grounds for his protection.

Elaborate architectural details — protruding ledges, for example — often increase the vulnerability of lower windows. Fences, garbage containers, and parked cars, when located near windows, are used as stepping stones to an otherwise inaccessible window. Care should be taken to prevent this type of situation.

Most windows above the ground floor are relatively inaccessible, with very important exceptions. Fire escapes make windows accessible. Little can be done to modify fire escapes, except in terms of hardware, because of fire safety and fire codes. One solution is to ensure that the ladder from the lowest fire escape is at least 12 feet above the ground. The ground area under the fire escape should be highly visible.

Another point of entry to the fire escape is the roof, which can be secured with panic hardware and possibly patrolled. The roof also provides possible entry to windows or balconies on the top floor. Therefore, security of the roof is quite essential, particularly to top-floor residents. Other accessible windows are those located diagonally across from a stairwell window. The criminal can open a stairwell window and cross from the stairwell into the units. It is not advisable to board up stairwell windows, as they provide the security of visibility to the stairwell and may have a fire safety function.

Accessible windows are also those located above or near door canopies. Criminals can reach the canopy by climbing onto it from the ground or from a stair or hall window.

### Doors

Security of doors, beyond the hardware aspect, depends upon surveillance and neighbor recognition. An experienced burglar needs just a few seconds to enter a locked apartment door equipped with minimal hardware. Within this interval, the crucial factors are: Will the intruder be seen or heard by tenants, will the viewer perceive that the potential criminal is in fact an intruder, and will the viewer respond by calling authorities or in some way challenge the criminal?

Physical design can directly influence the opportunity for surveillance of doors. Cor-

ridors that are open to view, either single loaded or with windows, are more easily surveillable by residents and police. Thus the opportunity for the criminal to attempt entry undetected is reduced.

In most single-family homes (detached or row) where the entrance door is on the street, the only means of improving surveillance is to avoid placing trees and shrubs where they hide the doors and windows, and to locate lighting to improve visibility around these openings.

In multiple-family dwellings, the apartment doors, located on interior corridors, are generally difficult to keep under surveillance. Any windows, mirrors, or lighting that allow someone inside an apartment or outside the building to view the hallway and doors can be helpful.

## HARDWARE

This section describes hardware devices that secure the individual residential dwelling and the multifamily dwelling. Much of this material is intended to prevent burglary. However, some of the measures, particularly those directed at multifamily dwellings, will also deter forcible entry, robbery, and vandalism.

### THE RESIDENTIAL DWELLING

#### Door Materials

The major security tests of door material are its ability to withstand efforts to force entry by brute strength and its ability to retain securely the locking devices attached. Materials most commonly used for doors are wood, aluminum, steel, and glass, often in combination with hardboard, fiberboard, asbestos, and plastic. The two most common door designs are panel and flush. Panel doors consist of vertical and horizontal members framing rectangular areas in which opaque panels, panes of glass, or louvers are located. Flush doors consist of flat panels running the full height and width of the door. (See Fig. 2.)

Solid-steel flush doors, although most secure, are rarely used except in very high-security areas such as banks and prisons. Steel-clad doors, which are flush doors constructed of 24-gauge sheetmetal facing bonded to a nonresinous, kiln-dried wood interior, provide an optimum weight-strength situation for ordinary residential use. Hollow steel doors (1¾-inch flush type) are satisfactory in multiple-dwelling buildings. Aluminum doors can provide sufficient protection but may be comparatively expensive.

While less strong than steel-clad doors, wood doors can be secure. All exterior wooden doors should be of solid-core construction with a minimum thickness of 1¾ inches. Although flush doors provide better security, if panel doors are desired for aesthetic reasons, the panels should have a minimum ½-inch thickness (see Fig. 3). Both hollow-core wood doors and thin-wood panel doors are unacceptable where security is a factor.

### Door Frames

The sides and top of a doorway are provided with a door frame which holds the door in position. The side members of the door frame are called jambs; the top member is called the head (see Fig. 4). The strike is the portion of the jamb which is cut out or drilled out to allow installation of a metal plate, which accepts the latch or bolt from the door lock (see Fig. 5).

Wooden frames provide an unacceptable level of security unless they are at least 2 inches thick. Metal-covered wood frames provide an optimum cost-security investment when used in combination with metal-covered wood doors. If a hollow steel frame is used, the residual air space behind the frame should be filled with a crush-resistant material such as cement grout, especially in the area of the strike (see Fig. 6). This will prevent an intruder from wedging a crowbar between the door and frame and crushing the frame to free the lock.

For doors swinging in, rabbeted jambs should be used. These are jambs containing a metal extension that protrudes beyond the edges of the closed door, thus preventing tampering in the area of the strike (see Fig. 7).

For doors without rabbeted jambs, an L-shaped piece of angle-iron at least 2 feet long, mounted in the area of the strike, gives extra protection (see Fig. 8). The iron acts as a lip which protects the strike from attack.

**FLUSH    ONE PANEL    TWO PANELS**

Fig. 2    Door types.

1¾" MINIMUM

½" MINIMUM

Fig. 3    Panel door.

HEAD

JAMB

Fig. 4    Door frame.

Fig. 5    Door strike.

CEMENT FILLER BEHIND STRIKE TO PREVENT FORCING OF THE FRAME

Fig. 6    Hollow metal door frame.

RABBET

Fig. 7    Rabbeted jamb.

# SECURITY

**Doors and Hardware**

For doors opening out, a flat metal plate, called an escutcheon plate, can be mounted to the face of the door in the area of the lock. This plate, which extends beyond the edge of the door and fits flush with the jamb when the door is closed, will protect the lock from attack in the area of the strike (see Fig. 9).

All plates located on the outsides of doors should be attached with tamper-resistant connectors such as round-headed carriage bolts or one-way screws.

### Door Hinges and Closers

Spring hinges close the door automatically by using spring force. A spring hinge prevents a criminal from slipping in behind a resident who has neglected to close the door immediately upon entering. Also, spring hinges prevent the resident from leaving the door open when he exits. Door closers (see Fig. 10) serve the same purpose. These are for more heavy duty and are commonly used in lobbies and commercial facilities.

Hinges should be mounted on the inside of the door so that burglars cannot remove the door from the hinges to enter. If hinges must be placed on the outside, they should have nonremovable pins. Pins can be made nonremovable by peening the straight end or by drilling and tapping a machine screw into the middle portion of each pin from the inside of the open hinge (see Fig. 11). Doors with outside hinge pins can also be protected by screwing two screws halfway into the jamb edge of the door. One screw is placed near each hinge, and a receiving hole is drilled into the jamb for each screw. These protruding screws hold the door when it is closed, even if the hinge pins are removed.

**Fig. 8  Protective angle-iron for doors opening in.**

**Fig. 9  Escutcheon plate for doors opening out.**

**Fig. 10  Door closer.**

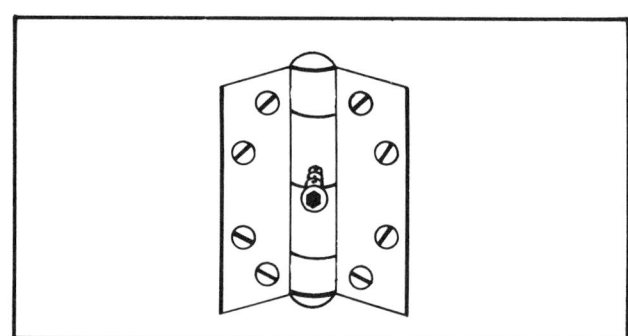

**Fig. 11  Nonremovable hinge pin.**

## Door Locks

Locks must withstand or seriously delay not only a simple forced entry but also sophisticated criminal attack. Locks may also guard against window entry-door exit crimes.

Parts of the a lock are defined as follows:

*Cylinder:* A cylinder is that part of the lock into which the key is inserted. If the proper key is used, the cylinder will allow the key to turn, thus moving a bolt or latch.

*Deadbolt:* A deadbolt (or bolt lock) is a heavy metal bar which moves horizontally into the strike of the door jamb, thus locking the two together. It is called a deadbolt because it cannot be pushed back unless the knob is turned by the correct key.

*Latch:* A latch (or spring lock) is the part of the lock that keeps the door in a closed position by extending into the strike automatically when the door is closed. The latch is most often operated by the doorknob. Most latches can be pushed back by external pressure without having to turn the doorknob.

*Deadlatch:* In a deadlatch, the latch is positively held in the projected position by an automatic mechanism which is depressed against the strike plate (see Fig. 12).

*Strike:* The strike is the portion of the jamb where a metal plate has been placed to receive the deadbolt and/or the latch (see Fig. 5).

*Stopworks:* Stopworks consist of two buttons located under the latch. Pressing the top button in allows the doorknob to turn freely and operate the latch, from both inside and out. Pressing the lower button in allows the inside doorknob to operate the latch, but "freezes" the outside doorknob.

*Throw:* The throw of a lock is the length (in inches) that the deadbolt extends beyond the face of the lock.

**Primary locks**  Primary locks operate in conjunction with the latch. There are two major types: mortise locks and cylindrical or bore-in tubular locks (commonly called key-in-the-knob locks).

Mortise locks (see Fig. 13) are more common than key-in-the-knob locks and will provide good security. All mortise locks with latches should contain a deadbolt with at least a 1-inch throw constructed of case-hardened steel, brass or zinc alloy, or bronze. Federal FF-H 106a heavy-duty series 86 mortise locks or 185 latch and 190K modified deadbolts are recommended. The deadbolt and latch should be key-operated from the exterior and operated from the inside by a device not requiring a key.

Mortise locks with latches used in residences should not contain an automatic spring latch with stopworks. Although stopworks prevent the outside knob from being turned, they leave the premises open to easy entry because they do not prevent the latch from being pushed back. An intruder need only insert a credit card into the strike area, push back the spring latch, and open the door (called "loiding" or "shimming" the lock). In locks without stopworks, the deadbolt (which cannot be loided) must be thrown by the key of the resident. Eliminating the stopworks prevents the resident from relying on the stopwork and latch mechanism alone.

Key-in-the-knob locks (see Fig. 14) are less secure than mortise locks. Although inex-

**Fig. 12  Deadlatch.**

**Fig. 13  Mortise lock.**

pensive due to easy installation, key-in-the-knob locks can be easily gripped by a tool and twisted until they break. A key-in-the-knob lock can include a deadbolt, at a comparable to slightly higher price than a mortise lock.

**Secondary locks**  A secondary lock (rim lock) operates independently of the latch. "Secondary" is perhaps a poor name, since this type of lock is essential for good security. Secondary locks are usually mounted above the primary lock at shoulder level. They are operated by a key from the outside, and by a turnbolt from the inside. Both mortise and secondary locks may require keys to open them from inside and outside — useful where access to premises may be gained through a small opening other than the door (window transom), since this will prevent the thief from using the door to remove large objects or to escape.

There are three major types of secondary locks: spring bolt, horizontal deadbolt, and vertical deadbolt. The spring bolt lock operates much the same as the primary door latch. Because the bolt must be spring loaded and bevelled to allow automatic latching, the bolt can be easily opened. A button (slide stop) may be set to deadlock the bolt. However, the button must be set from the

inside and can only be used when another means of egress is available. The spring bolt is not recommended as a secondary lock (see Fig. 15).

Horizontal bolt rim locks operate much the same as deadbolts on primary locks. While horizontal deadbolts afford much better protection than spring bolts, they still can be easily overcome. By inserting a crowbar between the door and the jamb, the intruder can pry them apart to release the bolt from the strike. For this reason, the longer the throw of the deadbolt, the greater protection it affords. However, throws of over 1½ inches may have excessive cantilever. The recommended minimum throw is 1 inch (see Fig. 16).

Vertical bolt deadlocks should be used as secondary locks wherever possible. These utilize two deadbolts that fit vertically into eyeholes or sockets attached to the jamb. This creates a firm bond between the door and the jamb. The vertical bolt deadlock made by Segal is highly recommended, both for its pressed-steel construction and for its ability to hold up under heavy use (see Fig. 17). For additional security, a pick-resistant cylinder should be installed in a good vertical deadbolt body. This combination provides excellent security.

Fig. 14.   Key-in-knob lock.

Fig. 15   Spring bolt.

Fig. 16   Horizontal bolt.

Fig. 17   Vertical bolt.

Fig. 18   Buttress door lock.

Fig. 19   "Magic Eye" lock with thumb turn.

Fig. 20   Buttress door lock with deadbolt.

**Fig. 21  Double-bar lock.**

UNLOCKED POSITION

SPRINGS →

PINS →
BARREL →

LOCKED POSITION

**Fig. 22  Cylinders.**

The locks discussed so far rely on the rigidity of an existing door frame to resist attacks on the lock. Since older buildings may contain weak door frames, a buttress-type door lock is advisable. Locks of this type include a bar set against a plate on the door and into a receptacle in the floor, thus forming a triangular buttress (see Fig. 18). Most of these locks can be operated only by a key from the outside. The Magic Eye Company buttress lock can be operated from the outside by a key and from the inside by a turnbolt to prevent accidental locking (see Fig. 19). One model contains a heavy-duty deadbolt as well as the buttress bar, and affords still further protection (see Fig. 20).

The double-bar lock may also be used to increase the strength of a door, by means of two steel bars that extend up to 2½ inches into each side of the jamb (see Fig. 21). The cyclinder is protected on the outside by an escutcheon plate to prevent forcible removal. A pick-resistant cylinder can be installed for added protection. The Fox Police Lock and the Fichet Locking Bar are examples of high-quality double-bar locks.

**Cylinders**  Regardless of the type of lock purchased, the cylinder is critical in providing protection. It must withstand efforts by sophisticated criminals such as lock pick experts.

The cylinder is the part of the lock into which the key is inserted. The most common type of cylinder is the pin tumbler which operates as follows: As the key is inserted, spring-loaded pins are raised to the proper position to allow the barrel and the key to turn; the turning causes the bolt or latch (or both) to move. If the wrong key is used, the pins will line up incorrectly and prevent the barrel from turning (see Fig. 22).

Recently, cylinders have become available which utilize special keyways and keys to make the cylinder pick proof or pick resistant (see Fig. 23). Medeco, Illinois Duo, Sargent, Keso, Eagle Three Star, Mela, Fitchet, and Miracle Magnetic are highly pick resistant. Such cylinders provide improved security, but may require registered keys that can be duplicated only at the factory upon receipt of a signed request. A compromise is the use of a key type whose blank is not available normally, but for which spare blanks are kept for replacements.

Of all cylinders on the market, Medeco has proven most difficult to overcome. Medeco utilizes twisting tumblers operated by a key with angular or criss-cross cuts. Only if the proper key is inserted will the pins twist the exact amount needed to allow the barrel to turn.

If special keyway cylinders are deemed unnecessarily secure or costly (Medeco cylinders cost about two times the next adequate), the cylinder used should be of solid-bar-stock bronze and machined for a tight fit.

The cylinders of a master-key system of locks are constructed so that individual keys fit only one lock, but a single master key can open all locks in the system. Use of a master-key system makes maintenance and other authorized access simpler, but the dangers of improper use of a lost or stolen master key far outweigh the benefits.

From a security standpoint, a cylinder should have at least six pins. This often results in the cylinder being longer than the thickness of the door. In mortise locks (which are recessed into doors), a six-pin cylinder often extends slightly beyond the surface of the door, thus making it susceptible to forcible removal by use of a gripping tool. To prevent use of such a tool, protruding cylinders should be protected by one of the following:

*Spinner ring:* A hardened steel ring that forms a collar around the cylinder and which spins freely around the cylinder when gripped (see Fig. 24).

*Bevelled-ring cylinder guard:* A case-hardened steel ring that prevents the cylinder from being gripped by a tool because of its bevelled shape (see Fig. 25). Scotsman makes a flat, very secure, cylinder guard ring.

*Escutcheon plate:* A metal plate mounted to the door, which covers all of the cylinder except the core (the part where the key is inserted), thus protecting the cylinder from attack. The escutcheon plate should be constructed of malleable cast iron and attached to the door with one-way screws. Machine bolts should not be used to mount escutcheon plates on mortise locks, as the increased pressure can have an adverse effect on the mechanism (see Fig. 26).

**Sliding Doors**

Sliding doors opening onto a ground-level patio or accessible balcony (on the first floor or top floor, or adjacent to other balconies) should be constructed so the movable section of the door slides on the inside of the fixed portion. Sliding doors should be break resistant (plate glass) and equipped with a vertical-bolt Segal lock (see Fig. 27), which uses a hook-type bolt to grip door and frame together, or a Loxem Sli-door lock that hoods at top and bottom (see Fig. 28).

**Fig. 24  Spinner ring.**

**Fig. 25  Bevelled ring.**

**984  Fig. 23  Keyways.**

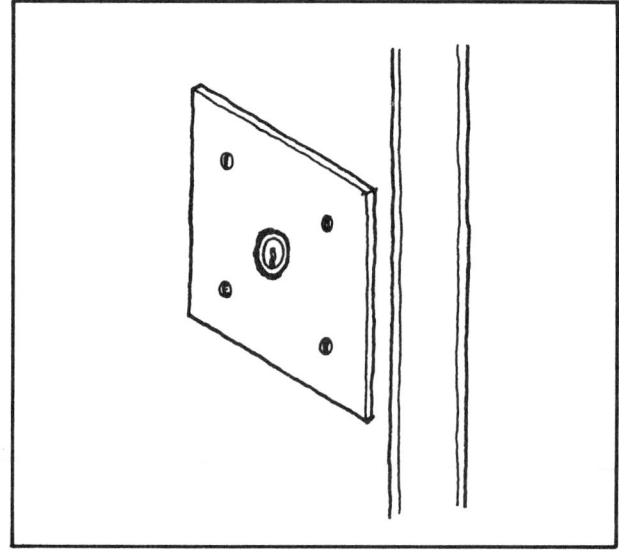

**Fig. 26  Escutcheon plate covering cylinder mortise lock.**

**Fig. 27   Segal lock.**

**Fig. 28   Loxem Sli-door lock.**

**Fig. 29   Flush bolt on double door.**

### Doors with Large Glass Panels

Exterior doors containing panes of glass are not recommended for security. French doors that open out should have hinges with nonremovable pins. The vertical stile incorporating the lock should withstand a concentrated horizontal load of 300 pounds. The doors should contain a mortise-type lock that is key operated from the inside and outside. The lock should contain a pin-tumbler cylinder with at least six pins (a pick-resistant cylinder can be used for extra protection).

Even when fitted with key-operated locks inside and outside, doors with large panes of glass are a security problem. Use of break-resistant glass substitutes is one modification. Bars or metal grilles, while providing good security, may be aesthetically unacceptable. Alarms may also be used on these vulnerable doors.

### Double Doors

On double doors, the active leaf should be equipped with a mortise-type lock. The inactive leaf should be equipped with flush bolts with at least a ¾-inch throw at head and foot (see Fig. 24).

### Private Garage Doors

Many rolling overhead doors operated by electric motors offer adequate security because the motors are controlled by a key switch inside the garage or by a low-power radio transmittor. Manually operated doors should be provided with slide bolts on the bottom bar (see Fig. 30). Chair-operated doors should be provided with a cast-iron keeper and pin for securing the hardened-steel chain.

### Door Interviewers

Interviewers are devices installed on an opaque door to allow residents to see and hear who is outside the door without opening it.

**Fig. 30   Slide bolt on garage door.**

An optical interviewer (peephole) should be installed on each door that provides entry into private dwellings. Many types of interviewers are available, ranging in diameter from two-tenths of an inch to 3 inches. Optics of the interviewer include one-way glass, plastic, and wide-angle glass.

Interviewers with openings of over one-quarter of an inch are not recommended. Larger interviewers can easily be punched out to allow insertion of tools to open the door from the inside. Someone also may stick a knife, wire, or gun through the hole while the person is looking through it. Interviewers are located approximately 4 feet 9 inches from the floor (see Fig. 31). The best interviewers contain a double glass for safety. Wide-angle glass allows maximum visibility. Although a wide-angle lens does produce a curved, "fisheye" image, clarity of the image is not impaired. If wide-angle glass is not used, the person outside cannot be seen unless he is standing in a direct line with the interviewer (see Fig. 32).

Instead of an optical interviewer, a case-hardened steel chain which fits into a horizontally mounted slide track on one end of the door jamb may be installed (see Fig. 33). The chain allows the door to open slightly (preferably not more than 2 inches) to permit easy conversation without fully unlocking the door. These chains should be used for interviewing only, not to protect a locked door. The swing of the door, even if only 2 inches, allows the criminal to exert strong force with momentum, which breaks most chain devices. The interviewing space also allows insertion and use of tools. Some slide chains have a locking mechanism which prevents use of a thumb tack (or piece of tape) and rubber band to pull back the slide mechanism and remove the chain from the track. Even when equipped with a locking mechanism, steel chains and slides are readily overcome by simple tools and brute force.

### Window Materials

Because windows contain large sections of glass, they naturally impose a security problem. Windows most vulnerable are those on the first floor (or otherwise accessible from the ground) and those leading to fire escapes. Less vulnerable, but still easily reached, are windows over a canopy (as above a main entrance), windows adjacent to stairwell windows, and windows on the top floor.

### Window Locks

Among the common window locks are the crescent sash lock, often standard on residential windows; various friction or pressure devices, such as the thumb-screw latch; pin-type latches, such as the simple steel pin-in-the-hole device; and the slide-bolt latch. All of these devices can easily be overcome, especially if an intruder is willing to risk the noise of breaking a small section of the glass. (See Figs. 34, 35, 36, and 37.)

Normal windowpane glass is approximately one-eighth of an inch thick, extremely brittle, and breaks easily. Plate glass is usually one-quarter of an inch thick and tempered to withstand an accidental knock. Plate glass is used for larger areas because of its greater strength and because the initial cost is worth the extra protection. Tempered

**Fig. 31 Interviewer location.**

**Fig. 32 Interviewer angles.**

**Fig. 33 Chain lock.**

glass has a thin, hardening coating and, while no stronger than plate glass, will not cut someone who breaks it.

Several companies have developed unbreakable, transparent polycarbonate materials which look like glass but are very difficult to break. GE's Lexan, for example, is guaranteed unbreakable. It costs two to three times as much as glass and has low resistance to scratching. An improved material, Lexan MR-4000, is slightly more expensive but is much less easily scratched. These polycarbonate materials have not yet been extensively used for private dwellings.

Another type of durable "glass" is fabri-

cated much like the safety glass used in automobiles: two layers of high-quality glass are bonded together with a layer of tough vinyl between. This is sold by one company as Secur-lite. While Secur-lite can eventually be broken, the noise and trouble required to do so are considerable deterrents.

Oversized glazed areas should be avoided. Anything beyond standard size (6 feet by 8 feet for glass, for example) is expensive and may be difficult to obtain.

The only reliable devices are those with a key-operated locking mechanism. Yale and Ideal Security manufacture a window lock which is a modification of the pin-type lock. It

can be locked in either of two positions, one of which allows the window to be open slightly at the bottom for ventilation (see Fig. 38). Fox makes a window lock combining a pin-type lock and a hasp and padlock. Although somewhat unsightly, it provides excellent protection. Ideal Security manufactures a modification of the crescent sash lock which requires a key to operate.

All of these devices provide adequate security for normal residential use. A set of keys should be convenient to the window for use in emergencies but far enough away so that a burglar cannot reach them.

Fig. 34  Crescent sash lock.

Fig. 36  Pin latch.

Fig. 35  Thumb screw lock

Fig. 37  Slide bolt.

### Window Bars, Grilles, and Gates

Where tighter security is desired, metal bars, grilles, and gates have proven most reliable. If a wire mesh grille is used, the metal should be at least one-eighth of an inch in diameter and the openings should not exceed 2 inches (see Figs. 39 and 40). The grille should be attached to the window frame with machine or roundhead bolts which cannot be removed from the outside.

If bars are used, they should be placed not more than 5 inches apart. The bars should have a diameter of at least three-quarters of an inch and be set at least 3 inches into the masonry.

Sliding gates afford excellent protection and can be pushed aside or opened for emergency exit. The gates should be set in tracks on the top and bottom to prevent them from being pulled or pried away from the window (see Fig. 41). Protect-A-Guard gates are highly recommended for residential and commercial use.

All of these devices should be installed inside the window for maximum security.

### Skylights

The best protection for skylights is installation of metal bars, grilles, or mesh. Bars should be made of steel not less than three quarters of an inch in diameter and should be placed not more than 5 inches apart (see Fig. 42). If mesh is used, it should be at least one-eighth of an inch thick and the spaces should not be greater than 2 inches. Mesh should be secured firmly by machine or roundhead bolts that cannot be removed from the outside.

If metal is undesirable, a securely fastened hasp and padlock will discourage entry and exit through the roof, if the glass is not removed.

Both hook-in-eye and sliding-bolt devices are unacceptable security measures for skylights.

**Fig. 39    Mesh window grille.**

**Fig. 40    Wire mesh dimensions.**

**Fig. 38    Keyed window lock.**

**Fig. 41    Window guard.**

## MULTIFAMILY DWELLINGS

### Lobby Doors and Walls

All lobby entrance doors should provide maximum visibility of the lobby. This often requires large glass areas in the lobby doors. Where there is a high degree of vandalism and crime, use of Lexan is recommended. In all cases, oversized glass sheet should be avoided. Glazed areas should be divided so that sheets larger than 6 by 8 feet are not needed. The doorframe should be constructed of rugged, heavy-duty metal. The vertical jamb incorporating the lock should withstand a concentrated load of 500 pounds and be a minimum of 5 inches thick so that it can receive heavy-duty mortise lock sets.

The main outer lobby door should have a key-operated lock with a pin-tumbler cylinder containing at least six pins. The key for this lock should not open any other door (such as an apartment door) as this makes the lobby-door cylinder susceptible to picking. An anti-friction latch (see Fig. 43) and a sturdy door closer should be used in conjunction with the lock.

Lobby doors, especially if locked or equipped with intercoms, should open out for fire safety and to reduce vandalism (tenants who have misplaced their keys can kick an in-swinging door hard enough to break the locking mechanism).

### Secondary Exits

In multifamily dwellings, exit doors leading to fire stairwells on each landing should have self-locking deadlatches to allow free egress while prohibiting entry. The stairside surface of the door should be free of hardware to prevent access to one floor from another via the stairwell. Hardware should limit access to the roof or ground-floor exits via the stairwell.

Panic hardware, if required, should be in the form of vertical-bolt latches on the top and bottom of the door. This hardware makes the door more sturdy and makes entry from the outside difficult (see Fig. 44).

Doors leading into the buildings from garage areas should have self-locking dead-latches with a minimum throw of one-half inch that allow free egress but require a key for entry into the building. The door should be protected in the area of the strike. All exit doors should be equipped with a self-closing apparatus that can be adjusted to the desired tension.

Since fire doors are required by law to be operable from the inside, they are often a means of escape. Exit alarms (see Fig. 45) bring immediate attention to fire doors that are opened when there is no apparent fire. A panic bar or other device simultaneously opens the door and sounds a local alarm. However, effectiveness of the alarm as a security measure depends upon the speed and consistence of response to the signal.

Exit alarms on fire exits leading to roofs keep burglars from using the roof for escape or for access to top-floor apartments. However, the alarm may prove more a nuisance than a good security measure if teenage vandalism is prevalent. Teenagers often set off the alarm to harass the local official, who must respond to the signal and reset the alarm.

**Fig. 42   Skylight protection.**

**Fig. 43   Antifriction latch bolt.**

### Elevators

In most middle-income multifamily dwellings, vandalism of elevators is relatively rare. However, in many high-crime areas and low-income housing developments, this vandalism is reaching a critical level. In New York City Housing Authority projects, vandalism to elevators and elevator equipment is responsible for almost 60 percent of elevator outages. Parts of the elevator most commonly vandalized are the hall buttons, indicator lights, hatch door glass, hatch door interlock, and buttons located inside the cab, especially the emergency and light switches.

Hall buttons are most commonly vandalized because of their accessibility. Impatient tenants push the buttons excessively and often kick or smash them in frustration. To prevent damage to the button and the electrical contacts inside, a stainless steel mushroom-type button should be used (see Fig. 46). The shape of the button prevents the contacts from being damaged by the button's being pushed too heavily against them. Another stainless steel button has been developed on the same principle, except that the stopper is inside the mechanism so that the button has the more familiar stunted-cone appearance.

Use of indicator lights for the lobby, the cab, and the other floors should be decided by the management. In some projects, indicator lights are so vandalized that it is easier to eliminate them. In other developments, indicator lights dampen user impatience and the result is less wear and tear on the buttons. If indicator lights are used, they should be protected by a heavy-duty plastic shield.

There are two types of elevator doors: swing and slide. This nomenclature refers to the doors on each floor; the cab door is always a slide door. Slide doors, which are automatic, are becoming increasingly popular despite higher initial cost, because they increase protection against vandalism. Swing doors are inconvenient and more subject to vandalism (short-circuiting of door interlocks, jamming of closing mechanisms, and joyriding on top of cabs).

# SECURITY

## Elevators

In many older elevators (especially the swing-door type), the hatch and cab door contain small glass windows which allow people to see inside before entering and allow passengers to see what floor they're passing. In high-crime areas, this glass has proven more dangerous than helpful. Vandals smash the glass readily, even if wire glass is used. The opening left when the glass is broken presents a very dangerous situation. Hatch door glass should be eliminated by welding or bolting a piece of metal over the opening. Where this is prohibited by a strict building code, a variance is often granted in a high-crime area. A less desirable modification is to install a heavy steel grille over the opening and replace the glass with Lexan.

Interlocks are more commonly vandalized on swing-door elevators. Causes of damage are excessive pulling on the elevator door while the cab is at another floor and short circuiting due to water or urine damage. The latter problem can be solved by installing interlocks with hydrophilic (non-water-absorbing) contacts. When damaged, this type of interlock requires replacement of only the contact plates rather than the entire mechanism. Damage caused by excessive pulling may be alleviated by signs cautioning tenants against such pulling. Closing mechanisms (keepers) can be made to fit more securely when the bolt is in place to prevent too much play in the door.

The emergency stop button presents a problem because it is often misused. The button may be activated to stop the elevator between floors to commit crimes such as mugging, rape, and drug abuse. Because every elevator has several automatic safety mechanisms that prevent if from falling freely down the shaft, the stop button is primarily a psychological comfort to passengers. Wherever possible, the stop button should be eliminated. The building code requirement for stop buttons is being challenged in New York and several other cities. If code change is unlikely, a variance should be applied for where elevator crime is common. A constant-pressure alarm switch is also somewhat better than the conventional toggle switch.

Fig. 45   Exit alarm.

Fig. 44   Vertical bolt on exit door.

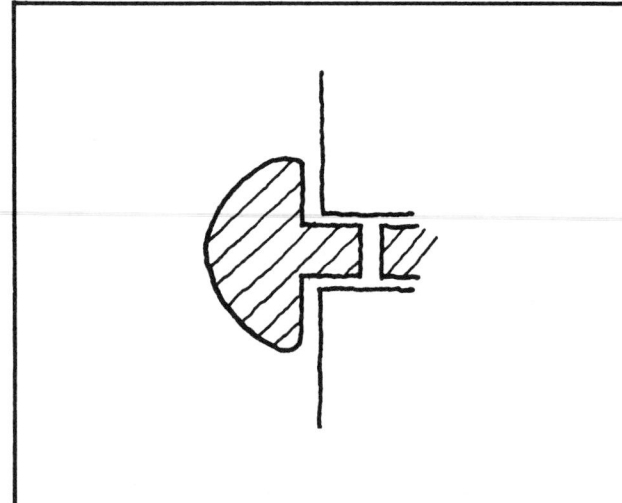

Fig. 46   Mushroom button.

Secer Light and Kendall are among the manufacturers of elevator dome lights that are highly vandal resistant (see Fig. 47). They are constructed of durable steel and contain a shatterproof plastic plate to protect the bulb. Where use of these lights is economically prohibitive, Lexan or an equivalent should be used to protect the light bulb.

Aside from vandalism, joyriding on top of elevator cabs is becoming prevalent in high-crime areas. Injury occurs most often when children are struck by the counterweight when the cab and counterweight pass each other. In other cases, children are crushed between cabs, struck by dividing beams, or squashed under a cab in the pit.

There are numerous means of access to elevator roofs and shafts: door interlocks are jammed by using simple household tools;

emergency stop switches are abused; and roof escape hatch doors are forced. Once on top, children often abuse passengers inside the cabs and interfere with normal elevator operation.

It is difficult to prevent crime by modifying elevator equipment. Restricted access to the building through the use of a buzzer-reply system, tenant patrol groups, or doormen is more likely to be effective. Closed-circuit television and audio-intercom systems mounted on elevators are other possible crime control devices.

A common device used to increase visibility in an elevator is a convex mirror placed in the upper back corner of the elevator. This allows a person to see if anyone is waiting inside the elevator *before* he walks into a possible assault situation (see Fig. 48).

An elevator modification that may deter crime is the up-discharge, down-collect system. When controlled in this way, an elevator will only stop for a person who has selected "up" (discharge) at the ground-floor level. Passengers on the upper floor can only enter the elevator on its way down (collect). The advantage is that a person entering the elevator on the first floor can be assured that the elevator will not stop at another floor to allow a suspicious person to enter. Such a system may be inconvenient for residents—a person wishing to go from the fifth to the seventh floor would have to travel down to the ground floor and then up again. The system is far from foolproof, as criminals can operate in other ways; but the modification is inexpensive and may deter crime in buildings without security personnel.

**Fig. 47   Unbreakable light fixture.**

**Fig. 48   Elevator mirror.**

# SECURITY

Garages, Secondary Entries, and Mailbox Rooms

### Garage Doors and Secondary Entries

Doors to interior garages provide a means of entry that circumvents many security 'precautions. If access to the building is to be limited, entry through the garage door must be carefully controlled.

The most practical solution is to have a locked door which tenants can open but which automatically closes behind them, usually within 15 seconds. A large number of manufacturers provide such self-closing doors. The major variation is the means for opening the garage door. Radio-controlled devices, requiring each auto to have a transistor, are expensive and far from foolproof. If a device is stolen from one car, all the devices should be replaced (an expensive procedure). A convenient and less elaborate system has a key-operated switch mounted on the driver's side of the garage, allowing the driver to use a key without leaving his car.

Despite these controls, the garage door should be monitored by tenants, security personnel, or electronic equipment if a build-ing is to retain a high level of security.

A door leading directly from a parking area to the building interior must be treated the same as a main entry. Such a door will be used continually, and requires equivalent security measures.

The secondary lock recommended for storage rooms containing valuables is the Fox double-bar lock.

### Mailboxes and Mailbox Rooms

Mailboxes are a major target for criminals within multifamily dwellings, particularly in low-income communities. The mail includes welfare, social security, and veterans' checks as well as others. These checks are particularly vulnerable because they arrive on set days of the month.

The bank of mailboxes should be located in the most secure and easily surveyed space available. Some brands of mailboxes do provide security, but any mailbox can be opened in the 10 minutes required to force open the door. If there is any control of access to the building (intercom or doorman), mailboxes should be located inside the protected area.

Mailboxes may be located in a locked room. Such a room must contain a large window to make it visible from the lobby, and be lighted 24 hours a day to reduce its potential as a location for muggings and other crimes. The door to a mailbox room should have sturdy self-locking hardware. Where back-loading mailboxes (generally secure) are used, a separate mail-loading room is often provided (see Fig. 49).

The better mailboxes are constructed of 16-gauge metal. The doors are tightly fitted and without holes to prevent prying them open and to prevent matches from being dropped in. The metal may be corrugated for additional strength. Cylinder locks with at least five pins should be used. Door size should be kept to a minimum to further limit the possibility of prying doors open (see Fig. 50). American and Gorth manufacture such mailboxes.

Fig. 49   Mailroom and loading room.

## LIGHTING

Good lighting in a residential development permits adequate visibility and surveillance. Generally, the higher the lighting level, the better the security. An appropriate level of lighting should be provided in each area; the light should be without excessive glare and generate no heavy shadows; and lighting should be resistant to vandalism and easy to maintain.

Fluorescent lamps are tubular glass lights that require special current-control devices called ballasts. Operating costs of fluorescent lamps are significantly lower than for incandescent bulbs: fluorescent tubes typically produce 3 to 4 times as much light per watt and operate 7 to 10 times longer than incandescent bulbs (due in part to lower operating temperatures).

### Interior Lighting

Lobbies, elevators, stairwells, and corridors must be well lit. Interior lighting normally requires only conventional incandescent bulbs, but low-glare or "frosted" incandescent or fluorescent luminaries are preferable. Low wattages of 25 to 200 watts generally suffice. It is usually desirable to install low-wattage fixtures at close intervals to minimize shadows and glare.

The most common problem of interior lighting is vandalism. Naked bulbs provide maximum illumination at minimal installation cost, but they are so often and so easily broken that maintenance costs are very high, and crime is encouraged by lack of lights. Recessed lighting suffers less from accidental breakage and vandalism. Transparent bulb protectors allow nearly total passage of light, but since the bulb can be seen, a vandal will likely try to break it. Translucent bulb covers are therefore preferable, even though some of the light is blocked by the cover.

Secer and Kendall have developed fixtures that are vandal resistant. They are made of plastic and come in a variety of shapes and sizes.

### Exterior Lighting

All heavily used spaces such as paths, entries, and parking areas should be lit by 5- to 10-foot candles. Higher fixture locations have a variety of advantages. As a general rule, the useful ground coverage of an elevated light fixture is roughly twice the height of the fixture. Thus, a 150-watt incandescent lamp mounted 8 feet above the ground can provide adequate light for 16 feet along a walk. Higher luminaries are safer from vandalism. However, lighting fixtures mounted higher than the second floor may create a feeling of being in a "compound."

A variety of specialized, high-intensity light sources can illuminate large outdoor areas such as recreation facilities and parking lots. Mercury-vapor and sodium-vapor lamps are available in sizes up to 1500 watts; the eerie bluish light of early mercury-vapor lamps may be avoided by selecting one of the newer "color-corrected" models. Once again, the point is to provide an appropriate level of light without creating glare or shadows.

Lamp and fixture breakage can be controlled in part by installing fixtures of tough, break-resistant plastic. The spherical, white glass fixtures so common today are less vulnerable, though not as tough as the more expensive plastic models.

A final comment on lighting is specifically relevant to a building or residential development inhabited primarily by the elderly. The pupil in the human eye gradually decreases in size due to advancing age. As a result, about twice as much actual brightness is required to create the same degree of brightness on the retina of a 60-year-old as on the retina of a 20-year-old (the ratio reaches 3 by age 75). Therefore, lighting levels in residences for the elderly should be well in excess of conventional standards and much higher than what seems adequate to a (younger) management staff.

**Fig. 50   Mailboxes.**

# SECURITY

## Electronic Systems

Electronic security equipment includes alarms designed to detect unauthorized entrance; closed-circuit television systems, apartment-to-lobby intercom locks, and various audio equipment. While the initial cost of many of these systems is high, each could reasonably be installed in moderate-income residential complexes and could prevent future need for more costly measures.

### ALARMS

An alarm performs two functions: it detects the presence of an intruder, and it reports the intrusion. The quality of an alarm mechanism is measured by its ability to perform these two functions.

A wide range of devices detect intrusion of a criminal into a building. These fall roughly into two categories: contact devices and motion-detection devices.

### Contact Devices

Contact devices are mechanical switches that detect movement or perhaps the breakage of glass. A common type consists of a contact on the door (or window) and a contact on the frame. When the door is closed, the two contacts form part of an electrical circuit. When the door is opened, the contact is broken, the ciruit is opened, and the alarm circuit is activated (see Fig. 51). A similar device, called a string-pull alarm, employs a slight variation in that the opening of the door pulls a string, which closes a switch that trips the alarm. Many contact devices are purely mechanical (as just described), while others include magnetic and mercury switches.

Usefulness of a contact depends upon its sensitivity (how much the device can be jarred without being activated) and its reliability. Most situations call for a device sufficiently sensitive that a skilled burglar cannot enter without setting off the alarm, but not so delicate that an innocent jostling will disturb it.

Foil strips are a related mechanism used primarily to detect breakage of glass in windows and doors. A delicate strip of metal foil is glued or taped to the glass. The foil strip acts as one long, continuous electrical circuit. If the glass is broken, the foil is broken, which interrupts the circuit and activates the alarm. Foil can be circumvented if it is possible to break the glass or release a lock without breaking the foil. Primarily because of their unattractiveness, foil strips are seldom installed in residences.

Contact devices can be made part of a lock mechanism (see Fig. 52). This type of alarm is set off whenever an attempt is made to force or pick the lock.

Contact devices themselves are very inexpensive; a simple magnetic contact pair costs about $2. But each contact device can protect only one opening; therefore, even a single-family house requires several devices to protect all points of entry. In addition, it is often expensive to install the alarms and connect them to an alarm-reporting device.

Contacts may be hidden so criminals cannot locate and dismantle them easily. Hiding an alarm system lessens its value as a deterrent, but increases the criminal's chances of being apprehended while com-

Fig. 51    Contact switch on door.

Fig. 52    Lock alarm.

Fig. 53    Ultrasonic detector.

mitting a crime. Since deterrence is the primary goal of residential security efforts, it is quite common to advertise the existence of an alarm without revealing the location of the mechanisms. This advertising is sometimes done where no alarm system exists. Considering the minimal expense involved in such a ruse, it may be worth the cost, but even very unsophisticated criminals can pick out such fake systems.

Heat-sensitive devices are sometimes combined with contact switches to provide an inexpensive fire-security alarm system.

### Motion-Detection Devices

These devices detect the motion of an intruder as he moves about the protected space. This detection can be accomplished in a variety of ways. Seismographic devices are turned on by vibrations or weight upon the floor (these devices have been perfected so they are not triggered by a passing truck). Photoelectric cells ("seeing-eye" mechanisms) use a beam of light to detect any motion across a protected span. Ultrasonic devices send inaudible sound waves through a room (see Fig. 53). Movement by an intruder changes the pattern of reflected sound waves and thus triggers an alarm. Increased sensitivity improves the effectiveness of each of these systems, but also raises their costs.

Motion detectors are far more expensive than contact devices, but one motion device can protect an entire area, regardless of the number of points of entry. Installation costs are often minimal, as the detection device need not be connected to any part of the structure. Motion detectors are most useful in spaces not used during scheduled periods of time, such as in commercial establishments which are totally empty at night and in homes left empty during vacation. More expensive motion-detection devices can protect limited areas, such as a single door or window.

### Alarm Reporting Systems

The term "alarm-reporting system" describes the mechanism that receives the message of an intrusion and reacts. Essentially, there are only two kinds of alarm-reporting systems: Intrusion is reported either by a loud alarm on the premises (called a local alarm) or via wires to a security force which is prepared to react when notified (called a central alarm or silent alarm).

A local alarm has a bell or buzzer connected to the intrusion device which produces a loud audio signal on the premises when the alarm is activated. This is the simplest type of alarm and can be installed readily. The deterrent effect is dependent upon the burglar's being intimidated and driven off immediately by the noise. Noise of the local alarm can also stop a crime in progress and aid in apprehension if someone responds to the alarm. Local alarms are often operated by batteries (see Fig. 54). Instead of an alarm being sounded, lights in the building can be turned on by an alarm system, or lights and alarm can both be activated.

This local system also protects people sleeping in a house by alerting them that a break-in is being attempted. Generally, keys are required to shut off local alarms.

**Fig. 54  Local alarm.**

CONTACT SWITCH SENSOR

A central alarm-reporting system sounds an alarm at a remote point usually connected to the detection device by wires (telephone lines are used in many cases). The remote point is sometimes the residence of the owner of a protected business establishment and sometimes the local police station; but generally, it is the headquarters of a private protective agency. These agencies have guards stationed at this headquarters who will respond to the alarm signal. Usefulness of the alarm system is dependent upon the speed and reliability of the response.

A local alarm signal is often activated at the same time as a central alarm, thus simultaneously frightening the criminal and alerting the authorities. If only a central alarm-reporting system is activated, the criminal is not warned that an alarm has been sent. This system (called a "silent" alarm) increases the possibility of apprehension while eliminating the possibility of driving the intruder off with noise.

A variation on this central-alarm arrangement is to utilize regular city police to respond to the central alarm. In high-income, low-density, high-burglary-risk communities, the city police allow alarms to be hooked up to the police headquarters, where the dispatcher serves as monitor. Another arrangement is for the detection device to trigger a tape-recorded message that is automatically telephoned to the police, telling them the location of a burglary in progress.

The single major problem of all alarm systems is the possibility of false alarms. They can be caused by defects in the intrusion-detection device or the reporting system. False alarms diminish the credibility of the entire system.

If neighbors experience repeated false alarms, if security guards are called out unnecessarily, or if police are accidentally telephoned a tape-recorded message, response by all of these persons slows dramatically and will eventually cease. Thus, the intrusion device must be designed so that it is not accidentally activated by noncriminal occurrences.

Related to the false alarm issue is the question of how the alarm is turned off. The most common method is for the alarm to operate after a 20-second delay; that is, the alarm will not sound for 20 seconds after a contact is broken or motion detected, allow-

ing the resident a brief period in which to switch off the entire system. The switch can be simply a button located in a hidden place. A key-operated switch is more secure, but the possibility of false alarms increases because residents often forget or cannot locate their keys. However, the turnoff mechanism should not be so simple or accessible that the criminal can activate it.

### Selecting Alarm Systems

The security alarm business is large and complex. It is therefore impossible to specify manufacturers or even types of alarm systems for general use. The quality of installation and the maintenance program that backs up the system are crucial elements that should outweigh initial price in the selection of equipment. The best advice is to deal with firms that have a verifiable history of quality installation, a reliable guarantee/warranty record, and an established repair and maintenance program.

The concept of a consistent "level of security" avoids excessive expenditures for one piece of equipment while other means of entry are unprotected. Equipment characteristics should fit specific installation situations. It is often difficult to install contact switches in older houses because window frames often have warped or buckled. String-pull devices have to be set from the inside and therefore cannot be used for a normal exit door.

Selection of alarm equipment should be based on specific system characteristics desired: Is deterrence of crime or apprehension of criminals the primary goal? Should the system be visible to deter attempted burglary, or should it be hidden to increase the likelihood of apprehending a burglar?

### CLOSED-CIRCUIT TELEVISION

When used in residential settings, closed-circuit television (CCTV) is intended to provide "electronic windows"; that is, a visual surveillance where physical design has obviated unaided surveillance. The purpose is to create an environment in which residents know that normal restraints of surveillance by citizens and their authorized agents exist, albeit aided by electronics. While initially costly, CCTV often reduces security personnel requirements or obviates the need for expensive redesign of existing structures.

Electronically aided surveillance is not equal to personal surveillance. A corrective response to a detected crime is obviously a step further away if the viewer sees the crime on a TV receiver rather than on the spot. The deterrent of having a policeman or other person on hand is lost. There is also the possibility of equipment malfunction. But CCTV has a quality of its own: being watched while unable to ascertain who, if anyone, is doing the watching is somehow unnerving, and definitely is a deterrent. A remotely controlled surveillance camera can be fitted with an automatic panning device so that the camera swings from side to side continuously, even when no one is monitoring the system.

### CCTV System Requirements

In general, a CCTV system should perform at approximately the same level as commercial broadcast receivers. Specific equipment and the quality of image needed are determined by characteristics of the area under surveillance, schedules of operation, makeup of the monitoring staff and their expected responses to emergencies, and use of special equipment.

American and foreign manufacturers have TV cameras suitable for security work. All equipment should meet the standards of the Electronic Industries Association for CCTV. Service and maintenance are generally more difficult and expensive than installation; therefore, the capability and reputation of a local supplier is crucial. City police or traffic departments often have had experience with manufacturers, suppliers, and maintenance operations. To encourage reliance on the system by users, and to prevent criminals from taking advantage of a lapse, the CCTV system should break down as infrequently as possible and be repaired quickly in the event of a breakdown.

Picture resolution depends primarily on camera quality and lighting levels: Higher lighting levels permit the use of less sensitive, less expensive cameras.

The entire system should operate unattended. This requires electronically stable equipment, meaning, for example, that no one should be required to constantly adjust the lens of the camera.

It is difficult to project costs of CCTV systems because of the variety of system sizes and configurations and the range of equipment costs. Camera prices start as low as $200, but more sophisticated models, such as those sensitive to very low light levels, cost up to $10,000 each. Complicated accessories including zoom lenses, remote pan (side-to-side movement) and tilt (up-and-down movement) mechanisms, and low-light equipment can increase installation and maintenance costs tremendously. The cost of monitoring equipment can be as low as the cost of a conventional television receiver, but more specialized and sensitive equipment is far more expensive.

### Camera Locations

Locations of a CCTV camera and the light level at that point are key cost-effectiveness factors. A camera's location defines the area to be observed by the camera, and the nature of the location greatly influences the camera's vulnerability to theft and vandalism.

**Fig. 55   Recessed camera.**

Available lighting dictates the type of camera needed to produce a final image of adequate quality. Of course, supplemental lighting may be provided at additional cost.

The camera must be able to view an area that is significant in terms of crime control. Wide-angle or other special lenses should be avoided by choosing a different camera location. Most importantly, the camera itself must be protected from theft and vandalism. This means that the body and lens of the camera should be in an inaccessible place. A mirror is often used to reflect the image into the lens, so that the expensive lens will not be broken by pointed instruments, thrown objects, or bullets (see Fig. 55). All interior cameras should be placed inside sturdy housings which are installed with tamper-proof connectors. Cameras must be accessible for maintenance and repair, however.

A number of locations meet all of these requirements. An elevator in a high-rise building is often protected by CCTV. The camera is generally mounted on the outside of the elevator cab wall so that the image passes via a mirror in a corner of the elevator to the protected lens. In case of camera failure, the elevator must be stopped so that the camera maintenance man can step onto the top of the cab and reach over the side to repair the units. This is not overly inconvenient for repairmen, but it does make access to the camera more difficult for a potential thief.

Building lobbies are another common location of interior cameras. Lobby cameras are commonly hung from the ceiling or recessed into the ceiling. The elevated locations require that the repairmen use a ladder. Use of a ladder, however, would make a thief very conspicuous.

Outdoor locations usually depend upon inaccessibility to protect equipment from theft and vandalism. Cameras are located atop steel poles or on poles extending from roofs or walls. An alternative is to place the camera in a wall or window of an accessible apartment.

### Lighting for CCTV Systems

Lighting plays a key role in the cost and effectiveness of a CCTV system. For camera locations inside buildings, it is almost always less expensive to raise the light level than to use low-light-level equipment. The required lighting level is only slightly higher than normal for building interiors, can be achieved without glare, and has an intrinsic value as a crime deterrent.

Exterior lighting can be very expensive. Cameras used outdoors are almost always more flexible and sensitive, being capable of adapting to full sun, cloudiness, and dusk. But as indicated earlier, camera costs rise dramatically for low-light-level equipment. While increasing of lighting levels is also expensive, well-designed extra lighting again has an intrinsic value as a crime deterrent.

### Monitoring of CCTV Systems

Effectiveness of CCTV depends on the nature and quality of monitoring. Many people may be used as monitors: city police, project security personnel, members of organized tenant patrols, tenants acting as individuals, and various combinations of these groups. The choice depends principally upon availability of personnel and their monitoring costs.

City police will monitor CCTV systems only if they believe it is the most efficient use of manpower. Thus an area being surveyed must suffer large numbers of crimes to warrant hiring a policeman or civilian whose function is simply sitting, watching, and adjusting. Crime reduction or criminal apprehension through CCTV monitoring would have to be substantial to justify continued use of such manpower. Police use of CCTV systems is generally limited to shopping districts and city-center areas. Police normally monitor large systems that include several cameras (each equipped with pan, tilt, and zoom capability) and a monitoring console, so that the viewer can watch activity in several places at once and adjust his equipment to concentrate on a particular place, incident, or individual.

Commercial and industrial facilities often hire private security personnel to monitor CCTV systems. Guards are used less frequently in residential complexes. The major advantage of use of guards is that a single guard can control several entrances to a building or complex of buildings. Usually the guard can see all entrance doors, the lobby, and the elevator interiors on the monitor screens. He can be given audio contact with the lobby area. With the use of an intercom system, he can also control garage and front door entrances. He can also be given the ability to stop the elevator in midflight. Thus the security guard can see and hear every person entering the premises; he can prevent them from entering; and he can even exert some control after they enter.

It is also possible to staff a monitoring panel with members of tenant patrols. Use of volunteer personnel eliminates payment of guard salaries. Because they are personally acquainted with the project residents, tenant monitors can easily pick out strangers and perhaps distinguish a minor argument among friends from an impending fight.

But, there are serious drawbacks in using tenant monitors. It is difficult to guarantee the performance of unpaid people. The novelty of working with TV monitors will wear off quickly, and declining interest increases the likelihood of patrol members simply not showing up. Additionally, tenant patrol members are not equipped or empowered to take much action. The tenant monitoring the CCTV has no real authority over police or security personnel. Finally, there is the problem of tenant patrol members using their position to harass or intimidate other tenants.

An alternative is in-apartment tenant monitoring. Tenants of a building or housing project can monitor CCTV on their home TV screens. By connecting CCTV equipment to a master antenna within a building, tenants can have the option of tuning into unused TV channels to monitor lobby, elevator, playground, or parking lot activity. Tenants may watch CCTV when they are expecting someone to arrive, or when a child is playing within viewing range of a camera in a playground area. Older people may watch for less specific reasons. Obviously, this does not assure continuous monitoring, but if one or more of 200 tennats is watching, it would be risky for intruders to take chances.

An in-apartment tenant monitoring system requires that a cable TV or master antenna system be in operation in the building. CCTV is clearly most suited to large, high-rise dwellings. Picture quality of the CCTV systems should be comparable to that of commercial broadcasting to promote tenant usage. While some picture disintegration may be acceptable in a conventionally monitored CCTV system, there should be no distortion in a system designed for in-apartment monitoring. It is desirable (and generally not expensive) to install a microphone system so that sound accompanies the TV picture, which makes the system more interesting and enjoyable.

It is possible to organize a voluntary in-apartment monitoring program to improve coverage. A tenant organization could arrange for persons to watch CCTV in their homes during specified hours. Such a scheduled system would promote better coverage and facilitate participation because there would be no requirement that residents leave their apartments.

Also, CCTV monitors should be placed where responsible individuals, such as management staff and patrolling guards, are at work or pass by continually.

## INTERCOM SYSTEMS

Most urban multifamily dwellings are equipped with buzzer-reply systems to limit access to the building to tenants and to people who have been interviewed by tenants on an intercom system. A typical buzzer-reply intercom system in an apartment building functions as follows: A panel located outside the lobby entrance door lists the names and apartment numbers of all tenants in the building. Next to each tenant's name is a call button that when pressed rings a bell or buzzer within that tenant's apartment. The tenant responds to the call by walking to a panel mounted on the wall of his apartment and speaking via an intercom system to the person outside the door. When identification is satisfactorily established, the tenant pushes a button on the panel which momentarily allows the entrance door to be opened without a key. Because the costs involved in installing wiring for such a system in an existing building are very high, buzzer-reply systems should be installed in all new buildings during the construction phase.

A modified version of the traditional buzzer-reply system has recently come into use. Local telephone companies install and service front-door intercom systems that use existing telephone wires instead of a separately wired system. The panel mounted outside the lobby door differs from a conventional panel in that it is supplied with a telephone receiver, and the list of residents has a three-digit number next to each name. A person wishing to enter the building dials the appropriate three-digit number, which makes the phone of the tenant buzz (not ring). The tenant then speaks with the person over the phone. If recognition is established, the tenant dials "4" to open the front door. If a tenant is speaking on the phone when the buzzer sounds, he can depress the receiver once, speak to the person in the lobby, buzz him in by dialing "4," and then depress the receiver again to return to his initial telephone conversation. For tenants without telephones, a special unit that can be used only for the intercom can be installed. Fees for installation and service are billed by the phone company and added to the tenants' monthly rent.

## ELEVATOR AUDIO SYSTEMS

Use of audio systems in elevators is rapidly increasing. An elevator audio system is an uncomplicated sound-transmission installation consisting of a microphone and speaker located in the elevator cab and connected to similar devices near the elevator doors on each floor. The system allows someone inside the elevator to speak to anyone standing in the elevator waiting area, and vice versa. In office buildings or high-income residential buildings, an additional connection is made so that a doorman, guard, or maintenance man can respond to persons inside the elevator. In low-income housing, the equipment in the cab is simply connected to the elevator on each floor.

Some systems are designed to remain on at all times, but most require the person in the cab to push a button before he can talk to the outside location. A continuous voice relay system reassures the elevator rider that he can communicate with the outside if any trouble arises, whereas the need to push a button limits the usefulness of a noncontinuous audio system in crime situations. Any elevator audio device is useful when breakdowns occur and someone is trapped inside the cab.

**Primary colors** The longest extended slices on the color wheel (Fig. 1) show the three primary colors — red, yellow, and blue. They're called primary because all the other colors come from combinations of these three colors.

**Secondary colors** Mix any two primary colors and you get the secondary colors:
Orange (red and yellow)
Violet (red and blue)
Green (blue and yellow)

**Tertiary colors** All of the other six colors on the wheel are called tertiary, or intermediate, colors. They are a mixture of the primary colors plus an adjacent secondary color. Thus:
Yellow orange (yellow and orange)
Yellow green (yellow and green)
Blue green (blue and green)
Blue violet (blue and violet)
Red violet (red and violet)
Red orange (red and orange)

Color has three dimensions: the *hue*, distinguishing one color from another — such as red, green, blue, etc.; the *value*, denoting lightness or darkness; and the *tone* or *intensity*, which is the brightness or dullness.

These hues, values, and intensities can appear to change when different ones are used together. Two or more light values combined afford little contrast; nor will darker values in combination provide much interest. But, when a light value is used with a dark, the light appears lighter while the dark appears darker. White is the lightest of all colors, and values range from it through varying gradations of gray to black. Colors that are nearer white in value are called *tints* and colors that are closer to black in value are called *shades*.

Intensities or tones also have similar effects. A brightly upholstered chair will appear brighter and will stand out when used with a carpet of dull color, as it will produce a spot of interest. In contrast, a few dull-colored pieces of furniture will sink into the background if the room contains brighter-colored rugs, draperies, and other furnishings.

Contrasting or opposite hues will emphasize one another. Red with green will make the red look redder and the green appear more orange, while the red-purple will take on a bluish tone.

There are many ways of combining colors for interest. Related color schemes such as reds, purples, and blues together can produce very pleasing effects. Contrasting hues, such as blues with oranges, can also be combined to give more vibrant results.

Some people enjoy excitement. Warm colors such as yellow, orange, and red are exciting because they are associated with things like sunshine, fire, heat, and even blood. Warm colors tend to "advance," and a predominantly warm-colored wall will seem to come forward. They are especially effective in rooms that are on the east or north side of a house, because light entering from those directions seems to be a cool light. The warm colors and cool light complement each other and make the room seem cozier and warmer.

Cool colors are those associated with water, verdure, and the sky — blues, greens, and violets. These tend to "recede," and under most conditions, light, cool-colored walls will create an illusion of greater space. They are good choices for rooms on the south and west side of the house, since these areas receive a lot of sunlight all year around. Theirs is a cooling effect in the warm-light areas, another complementary association.

Black, white, gray, and brown — and the tones of the latter two, known as griege and beige — are not considered to be colors so much as *neutrals*. In practice, they are the "no-color" colors, which are used with other colors to modify them or to contrast with them. But they are far from being negative. As you work with color, you will find that all colors are influenced by the company they keep. This is particularly true of the tints, shades, and so-called neutral colors. A juxtaposition of two muted colors, such as a gray and a tan, will bring out latent greens, lavenders, and pinks you did not see before. Colors also have visual weights. Dark and bright appear heavy, while light or dull seem to weigh less. Remember that a dominant color is the one that "controls" a room, while the others are accents.

### Basic Color-Scheme Planning

Successful decorating often depends on how well the total effect is anticipated. Here are four types of schemes that professional decorators have in mind when they start to plan a job. They are no guarantee of perfect results, but they do make an unwieldy subject easier to handle.

**Monochromatic** This scheme is built around one color, using it somewhere in its full intensity, and then varying it with a number of shades, and tints of the same color. For example, in a monochromatic scheme of yellow, the range could be from dark shades of gold, through clear yellow, to light, pale-yellow tints. A monochromatic color scheme can be restful, create a feeling of spaciousness, and provides a good background for art objects, collections or similar decorations. But generally, when employing a monochromatic color scheme, the interest of the room comes through by using a variety of textures and patterns.

**Analogous or related** Because it's the easiest color scheme to work with, an analogous scheme is the one that enjoys the greatest popularity at the present time. It is based on two or three colors, such as yellow, yellow orange, and red orange, that lie close to each other on the color wheel, with "relief" provided by tints and shades of the same that have been tinged with adjacent greens or vermilion. The analogous color scheme is restful and refreshing also, and the colors are more interesting because of their variations in intensity and value. It is the kind of color scheme that is easily changed; a slight shift of emphasis here and there is all that is necessary to completely change the character of the room.

**Complementary or contrasting** This scheme, which is rapidly coming into favor, uses colors that are opposite each other on the color wheel — blue and orange, red and green, yellow and violet. One color is usually a primary color and the other a secondary color. Using such contrasting colors will give a lively and vibrant room, but it is a color scheme that must be used with caution. One color should always dominate, with the others being primarily dramatic accents. The "shock" impact of a complementary color scheme can be softened by selecting unexpected shades and tints of the two colors. That is, a vivid color and its complement can be quieted, if you prefer, by graying them, or reducing their values. Employing a pair of opposites in this manner means that there will be both cool and warm colors in a room, which makes a mutually complementary association. A complementary color scheme tends to make a room seem smaller.

**Accented** This is a combination of adjacent, related, or analogous colors — call them what you will — accented by a bold touch of color from the opposite side of the wheel. An example would be a scheme ranging through a number of strong, soft, and grayed yellows, spiked with purple or violet.

There are also other color schemes, such as *triad* and *split-complementary* that you can adapt from the color wheel, but the four suggested above are the easiest to visualize and to carry out.

In whatever basic scheme you use do not forget the neutrals: black, white, the grays, and browns — to which you might add metallic gold and silver. Since they will appear, of themselves, in the wood and metal of your furnishings, they must at all times be considered for the part they play in the total effect. If you wish, the neutrals can constitute a fifth, and very sophisticated, color scheme of their own! But usually they must be more or less just "accepted," and played up or played down by the colors you combine them with. Incidentally, some black and white is an asset to almost any color scheme, but too many and indefinite neutrals, used with stronger colors, tend to compromise a color scheme and make it look confused or merely drab. It is best to think of any neutral as a distinctive note of color, whether it is the fieldstone of a fireplace or a hardwood floor.

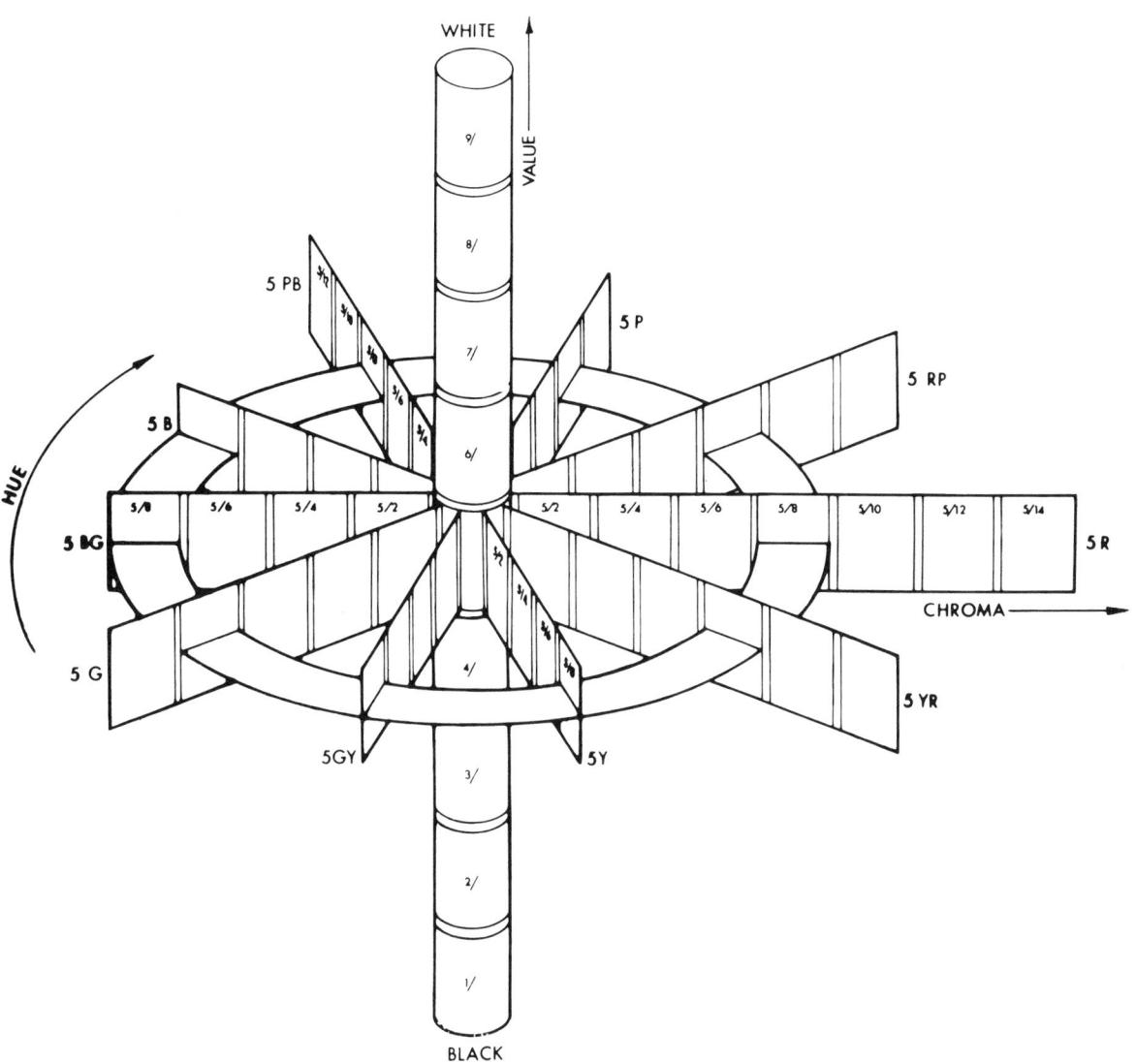

**Fig. 1** The basic wheel with a three-dimensional projection of the attributes of color — hue, value, and intensity — as shown in their relation to one another. The circular band represents the hues: G, green; B, blue; P, purple; R, red; and Y, yellow. The upright center axis is the scale of value. Paths leading from the center indicate color intensity.

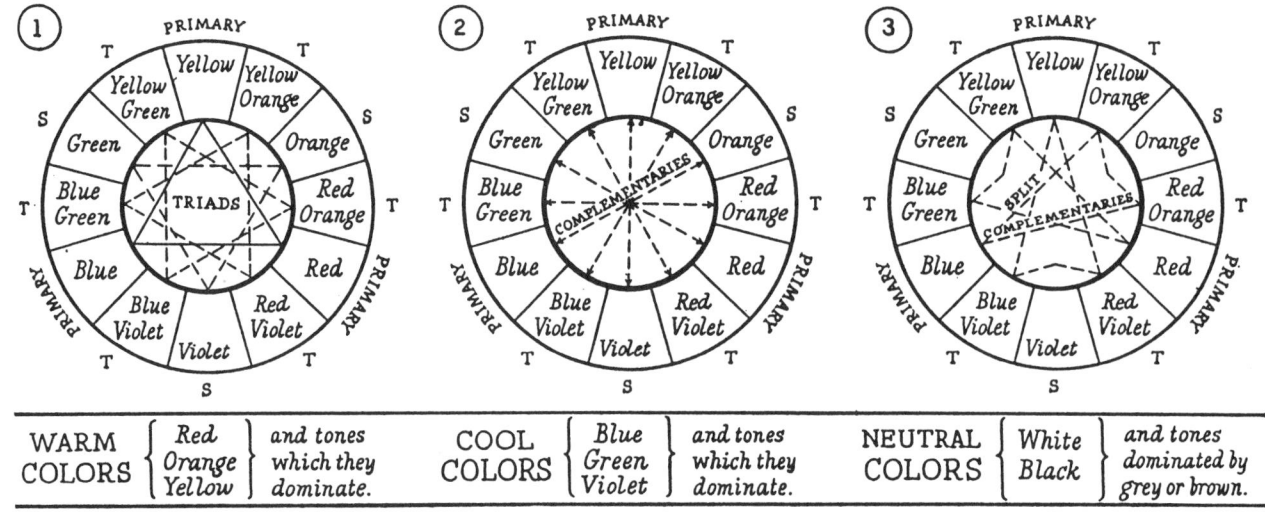

| WARM COLORS | { Red Orange Yellow } | and tones which they dominate. | COOL COLORS | { Blue Green Violet } | and tones which they dominate. | NEUTRAL COLORS | White Black | and tones dominated by grey or brown. |

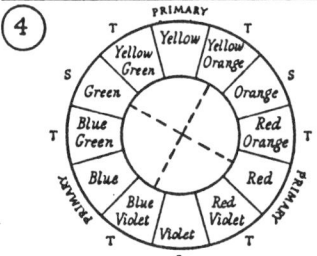

**EXAMPLES OF ANALOGOUS (RELATED) COLOR SCHEMES**

## DIRECTIONS FOR USING COLOR COMBINATION CHARTS

COLOR WHEEL NUMBER 1 illustrates color combinations in which the three primaries are used together, or the three secondary colors, or three tertiary colors. The three points of each triangle link the colors used in this TRIAD COLOR SCHEME. The rule for success is to use only one of them in a strong, bright tone, in small areas, with the other two in softened (or grayed) tones.

COLOR WHEEL NUMBER 2 illustrates the color pairs which are effective together through contrast. This is called the COMPLEMENTARY COLOR SCHEME. As the arrows indicate, the pairs are exactly opposite each other on the wheel. One should be used in a bright tone for smaller areas, the other in grayed tones and larger areas.

COLOR WHEEL NUMBER 3 illustrates the use of a color with the two which are next to its opposite on the wheel, one on each side. This SPLIT COMPLEMENTARY COLOR SCHEME follows the rule for complementaries, and may include the direct contrast color also, if desired. For example, yellow may be used with blue-violet, and red-violet, with or without the true violet shade which comes between them.

To avoid confusion, not all of the triangles are indicated. Cut a piece of paper the size of the triangle and lay it with the top point at any color you choose. The other points will rest on the correct colors.

COLOR WHEEL NUMBER 4 illustrates how an ANALOGOUS COLOR SCHEME is developed by using colors which are related because they are side by side on the wheel. Any group can be used, all around the wheel, as indicated by the dotted lines. For an accent color you can use a contrast color opposite any one of your group. For instance, in the yellow-orange to red group, complementary blue could be used for accent (shown on color wheel 2).

Black, white, gray and other definitely neutral tones can be used with any combination of colors.

## BASIC PRINCIPLES FOR WORKING OUT A COLOR SCHEME

1. DOMINANT OR CONTROLLING COLOR

   Decide on your dominant or controlling color, which may dominate by covering a large area or by strength of color in a smaller area. Decide whether your foundation or background color is to be the dominant or a secondary color. Plan to use a large amount of quiet background color, a small amount of bold, strong color. All large foundation areas should be in light or grayed tones.

2. GRAYING

   Clear colors are gayer, more cheerful, but grayed tones are more restful, their harmonies more subtle. Mixing gray with bright colors brings them into relation with other colors in the room. As . . . red and yellow in bright tones seem to clash. Mixed with gray, they become rose and tan and go very well together. Use this principle also in buying materials. Avoid too much graying. It gives muddy tones, dirty grays, flat greens. A little gray goes far.

3. RELIEF AND CONTRAST COLORS

   Decide on relief and contrast colors and bring them into all parts of the room composition. Remember the order in the amount of space allowed each one—foundation, then relief, then contrast. All colors—including background colors—should be keyed to the dominant color. Soften strong contrast colors with white. Contrast is less in lighter tints. Soften darker contrasts with gray.

4. ACCENT COLORS

   Use pure bright intense colors only in accessories, etc. Distribute them so they will not be spotty. The smaller the area the brighter the color may be. The larger the area the softer the tone should be. Don't use large amounts of pure bright color.

5. KEYING

   This is another means of creating harmony. A key color is the one about which the color scheme is built—the dominant, or controlling color. All other colors in the room must be "keyed" with it—harmonized. Two colors in which any part of a third color is present will be linked together. Example: To key red and yellow to each other, mix them both with a little of the third primary hue—blue. Violet and green will result, and these are harmonious to use with your strong tones. Remember this principle in buying as well as mixing colors. A lovely print or art object will have these tones keyed for you, and you can use them for your own composition. The safe rule is to avoid too many colors and too strong tones except as accents, etc. Most colors will "go together" if you soften them.

## WHAT DECORATORS MEAN
## WHEN THEY USE THESE COLOR TERMS

**HUE:** Each section in the color wheel is called a hue. To change a hue, another color (not black, white or pure gray) must be added to it. Every hue has a different wave length from every other hue. Mixed with its complement equally it produces gray.

**PRIMARY COLORS:** Also called "normal," also "fundamental." Primaries are the three pigment colors which cannot be produced by any mixture of other pigments. These are red like that of a geranium flower, yellow like that of ripe lemons, blue like the deep clear hue of a sunny southern sky.

**SECONDARY COLORS:** Secondaries are the three colors which are produced by mixing two of the three primaries in equal amounts. Red + yellow = orange; red + blue = purple (or violet); yellow + blue = green.

**TERTIARY COLORS:** Tertiaries are the colors produced by mixing a primary with a secondary, the exact shade depending upon the proportion. Red + orange produces shades such as russet, burnt orange, coral, etc. Red + purple—mulberry, amethyst, orchid, etc. Blue + purple—heliotrope, periwinkle, lavender, etc. Blue + green—turquoise, aquamarine, bottle green, etc. Yellow + orange—maize, primrose, flame, etc. Yellow + green—jade, Nile, olive, chartreuse, etc. Mixtures of complementaries not included because these produce shades of gray—a neutral. Some authorities consider, also, the shades produced by mixing two secondaries as tertiaries, such as slate, citron, buff, sage, etc.

**COMPLEX COLORS:** All colors which are made up of more complicated mixtures than those producing secondary and tertiary colors are called complex.

**NEUTRAL COLORS:** Black and white are considered neutral. Also all those tints and shades in which tones of gray or brown predominate.

**TINTS:** The light tones resulting when white is mixed with a color. Much white makes a color cold.

**SHADES:** The dark tones resulting when black is mixed with a color. Much black deadens the color.

**TONE:** Each hue has many tones. By tone—or tonal value—we mean the relative strength of the hue as it approaches black or white at the opposite ends of the value scale. Mixed with white, a color is "pale" in tone; mixed with black, it is "dark" in tone. The upper and lower extremes of any color would be white (or very pale gray), and black.

**CHROMA:** This term is used interchangeably with value, tonal value, and intensity. The chroma of a color such as yellow is "light"; the chroma of a color such as Navy blue is "dark." When a color fades, it loses chroma.

**LUMINOSITY:** This term is used to describe a quality of warm clear colors in light-reflecting tones and finishes, such as light golden-yellow. Clear white is also luminous. Literally "luminous" are only metals in gold, silver, platinum, or clear plastics.

| COLOR | SUGGESTED COLOR GROUPS TO USE WITH IT |
|---|---|
| RED | Green, gray, blue (for accent) |
| SCARLET | Light blue, ecru (or Navy and taupe) |
| CRIMSON | Pearl gray, mauve |
| GARNET | Sapphire blue, mauve, pearl gray |
| CARDINAL | Marine blue, turquoise, gray |
| WINE | Black, old blue, beige |
| ROSE | Flesh, light blue, green |
| OLD ROSE | Blue in various shades |
| CEDAR ROSE | Blue, cream |
| PINK | Green, orchid, blue for accent |
| ORANGE | Violet, light blue, indigo for accent |
| BURNT ORANGE | Electric blue, light brown |
| SALMON | Turquoise, lavender |
| HENNA | Peacock green, royal blue, gray |
| PEACH | Rust, blue, tan |
| MAIZE | Powder blue, pink |
| YELLOW | Violet, blue, green |
| PRIMROSE | Lavender, dusty rose, soft green |
| SOFT YELLOW | Brown, French blue |
| GOLD | Soft gray-green, deep red |
| DARK GREEN | Brown, beige (or sage green and gold) |
| MYRTLE | Heliotrope, yellow |
| SOFT GREEN | Rosewood, deep violet |
| TARRAGON | Heliotrope, pearl gray |
| CHINESE JADE | Rose, ivory |
| NILE | Cornflower, orange |
| LIGHT GREEN | Rose, dark green, mauve |
| BLUE | Yellow, sand, orange for accent |
| COPENHAGEN BLUE | Burgundy, gray |
| FLEMISH BLUE | Olive-green, cardinal |
| LIGHT BLUE | Orchid, champagne |
| DEEP PURPLE | Orange, gray |
| VIOLET | Green, light and dark shades |
| LAVENDER | Green, mauve, gray |
| HELIOTROPE | Light blue, cream |
| HYDRANGEA | Old rose, primrose yellow |
| MAUVE | Emerald green, dark red, brown |
| BROWN | Orange, tan, cardinal for accent |
| GRAY | Violet, crimson, lavender. |

# COLOR AREAS AND SAMPLES

## PROPORTIONATE SAMPLE SIZES

| | | |
|---|---|---|
| 1. | WALLS | 24" x 24" |
| 2. | FLOOR | 18" x 18" |
| 3. | DRAPERIES | 16" x 16" |
| 4. | CEILING | 14" x 14" |
| 5. | COUCH, ETC. | 12" x 14" |
| 6. | WOODWORK | 10" x 14" |
| 7. | LARGE CHAIR | 8" x 8" |
| 8. | LARGE CHAIR | 6" x 8" |
| 9. | SMALL CHAIR | 6" x 7" |
| 10. | ACCESSORIES | 6" x 7" |
| 11. | ACCENTS | 5" x 6" |
| 12. | TRIMMINGS | 5" x 6" |

VARIED as used here means choice of light, dark, or medium tones, clear or grayed colors.

## POINTS TO REMEMBER IN MATCHING SAMPLES FOR COLOR

1. Use larger samples if possible, especially in patterned materials, but keep approximate proportions of chart. Sizes are determined according to area and interest. Ceiling and floor areas, for example, are equal—but floor interest is greater, hence the larger sample. If several items are the same color add them to make one sample.

2. Make allowance for texture. Soft rough surface in paint, paper, or fabric makes colors appear darker. Hard glossy surfaces appear lighter.

3. Make allowance for distance. Colors look brighter when they are close; farther away they seem softer, grayed by atmosphere. Colors which match exactly 1 ft. away may seem quite different at 15 ft. This is important in a large high-ceilinged room.

4. Make allowance for proximity. When side by side: Complementary colors brighten each other; related colors, when both light or both dark, deaden each other; neutral colors brighten clear colors, but pure strong primary colors deaden neutrals such as grays, browns, etc.; light and dark tones brighten each other, especially white for dark colors and black for light tones; one color may seem to change another's hue as when a strong clear color gives a tinge of its complementary to a neutral—red, for example, may give a greenish cast to gray unless a little red has been mixed with the gray.

5. Make allowance for proportion. The larger the area the darker the color will appear. Choose a wall color slightly lighter than you really want it. Don't decide exact shade of a painted wall until all other materials have been chosen. It is easier to match paint to fabric and paper than the other way around.

WALLS MEDIUM TO LIGHT

FLOORS DARK TO MEDIUM

DRAPERY VARIED

CEILING LIGHT

LARGE COUCH BED SOFA VARIED

WOOD-WORK VARIED

LARGE CHAIR VARIED

LARGE CHAIR

SMALL CHAIR BRIGHT

ACCESSORIES

ACCENTS BRIGHT

TRIMMINGS

| 1 | 2 | 3 | 4 | 5 | 6 | 7 | 8 | 9 | 10 | 11 | 12 |

# COLOR COMBINATION CHARTS

S = SECONDARY . . . . . T = TERTIARY

# COLOR THEORY
## Munsell System of Color

One of the best-known and widely respected systems of color standardization used in the United States today is that developed by Albert H. Munsell. He became greatly interested in the practical application of color and was disturbed by the fact that the popular names for colors did not describe them adequately for professional purposes. They are named after flowers or plants, such as violet, indigo, old rose, primrose; after fruits, such as peach, pomegranate, grape, avocado, plum; after places such as french blue, naples yellow, or prussian blue; or after persons, such as Davy's gray or Hooker's green.

Essentially the system consists of an orderly arrangement of colors in the shape of a three-dimensional color solid. The system is based on a color circle of ten major hues made up of five principal hues, red, yellow, green, blue, and purple, and five intermediate hues, yellow-red, green-yellow, blue-green, purple-blue, and red-purple. Each hue is indicated by a symbol as follows:

Red: R
Yellow: Y
Green: G
Blue: B
Purple: P
Yellow-red: YR
Green-yellow: GY
Blue-green: BG

Purple-blue: PB
Red-purple: RP

Each of the above major hues has been given a value of 5 in the inner scale around the hue circle (see Fig. 2, hue symbols), i.e., 5 R, 5 YR, 5 Y, 5 GY, 5 G, 5 BG, 5 B, 5 PB, 5 P, and 5 RP. Between each of the major hues are values of 2.5, 10, and 7.5 for rough indication of hue. The outer scale of the hue circuit is divided into 100 segments to provide greater accuracy for indicating hue where needed.

In the Munsell color tree each hue (H) is allotted ten segments of the hue circle, making 100 hues, and these hues form the horizontal center, or equator, of the color solid. The center segment of each color is considered the true color, and the remaining segments in each hue section vary according to their proximity to adjoining colors; for example, as red gets closer to yellow it contains more yellow, and this is indicated by the numerical designation.

The value (V) notation denotes the lightness or darkness of a hue, which is determined by a neutral core at the center of the hue circle. The core contains ten gradations from a supposedly perfect white (one having 100 percent reflectance) at the top to 0, a perfect black (having 0 percent reflectance) at the bottom.

The chroma (C) notation indicates the saturation of the hue, or the strength of the color. The chroma scale extends outward from the central core or axis, and the increments vary from 0 at a neutral gray to as high as 16, according to the amount of saturation produced by a given hue at a given value level. Since colors vary in chroma, or saturation, some colors extend farther from the neutral axis than others, and the solid is therefore not symmetrical. Pure red, with a chroma of 14, for instance, extends farther than blue-green, with a chroma of only 6 (see Fig. 1).

A Munsell notation indicating hue, value, and chroma (H V/C) might be given as follows:

Vermilion: 5R 5/14
Rose: 5R 5/4

With this information it is possible to describe exactly any given hue and to locate its place in the color solid. Furthermore, as Munsell stated, one can "select one familiar color, and study what others will combine with it to please the eye," by the use of three typical paths: one vertical, with rapid change of value; another lateral, with rapid change of hue; and a third, inward, through the neutral center, to seek out the opposite color field. All other paths are combined by two or three of these typical directions in the color solid.

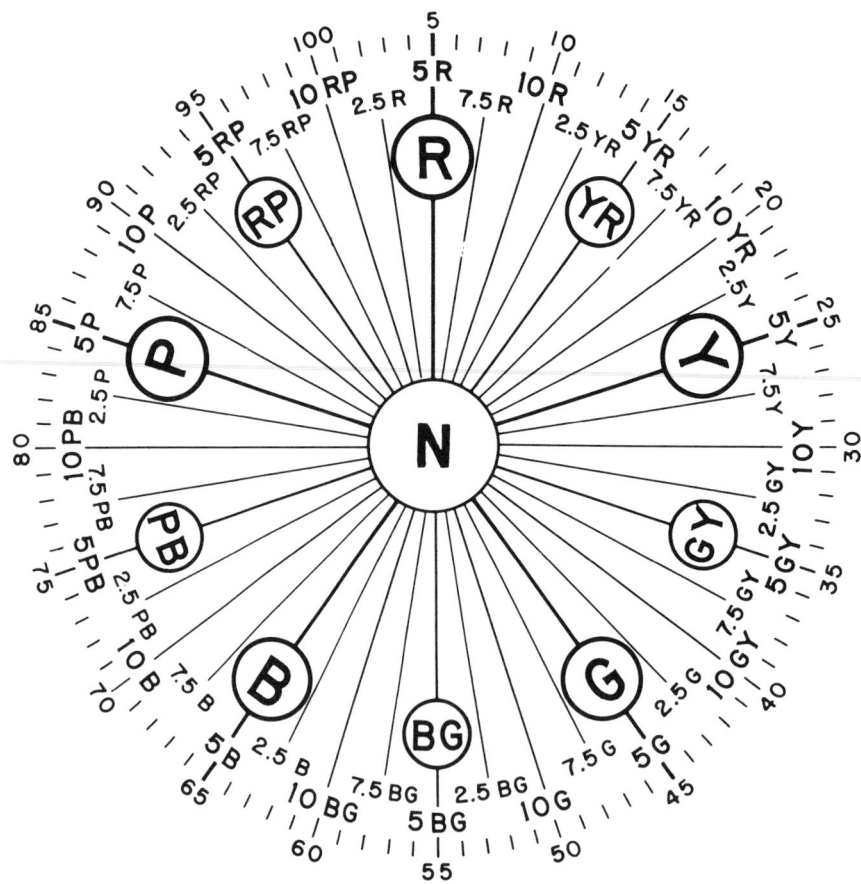

**Fig. 2 Munsell hue symbols and their relation to one another.**

# THE RED FAMILY

REPRESENTATIVE MEMBERS OF THE RED FAMILY . . . FLESH . . . DUSTY-PINK . . . SHELL-PINK . . . ROSE . . . DUSTY ROSE . . . OLD ROSE . . . CARDINAL OR CRIMSON . . . RASPBERRY . . . RED-BURGUNDY OR WINE RED . . . MAROON . . . ETC.

CHARACTERISTICS . . . Warm, advancing . . . Cheerful, hospitable, active . . . In strong tones, stimulating, bold, vital, dramatic, exciting.

WHAT THEY CAN DO . . . Make objects seem closer, larger . . . Make room seem smaller by bringing background closer . . . Focus attention on wall or object . . . Bring life, brightness, warmth, to drab, dark or too-cool rooms.

CORRECT USES . . . In light tints, charming background for fairly light, large rooms . . . In bright tones, highly decorative when used for comparatively small areas, as in accessories, accents, etc. . . . In darker shades, rich and warm for draperies, carpets, upholstery, especially in large rooms with heavy furniture.

CAUTION . . . Do not use too much red—especially in clear, bright tones, and in light rooms . . . Safer to soften a little by "graying," except when used for accent . . . Do not use the Red Family for background of a room that is small or crowded . . . Do not use bright red for large objects, unless you want to call attention to them . . . Do not forget when using the Red Family to include cool colors in your color schemes . . . It takes two cool colors, or a large area of one cool color, to balance red.

## SUGGESTED COLOR SCHEMES IN WHICH MEMBERS OF RED FAMILY PLAY A DOMINANT ROLE

| DOMINANT COLOR | MAJOR WALL COLOR | MAJOR FLOOR COLOR | DRAPERIES AND UPHOLSTERY | ACCENT COLORS | REMARKS |
|---|---|---|---|---|---|
| SHELL-PINK | Shell-pink | Light Blue | Off-white background, powder-blue and shell-pink in pattern | Italian Red | Charming for bedroom. In slightly darker tones of same colors, could be adapted to living rooms. Feminine feeling |
| MELON PINK (like Pompeiian terra cotta) | Melon Pink | Brown | Light tan background, melon-pink with green olive in design | Green Olive | Good for living or dining room with mahogany or walnut furniture |
| VENETIAN PINK | Venetian Pink | Patterned rug, soft tones, green, mauve, red | Draperies, yellow and white stripes / Upholstery, green and dull pink stripes | Red | Good for living room with 18th Century furniture |
| DUSTY PINK | Dusty Pink Woodwork, cocoa brown | Deep Brown | Draperies, pale aquamarine (dusty pink curtains) / Chair and bed covers, cocoa and pink stripes with cocoa brown trimming | White | Interesting for modern bedroom with furniture in cocoa tones |
| BOIS DE ROSE | Bois de Rose | Sage Green | Draperies, pearl gray, trimmed with bois de rose / Upholstery, pale gray with sulphur yellow | Green and Sulphur yellow | Living room color scheme with feminine feeling |
| DAWN ROSE | Dawn Rose | Dark Green | Neutral background, dawn rose and leaf-green in pattern | Wet Leaf-green | Attractive for bedroom |
| LIGHT ROSE | Light Rose | Deep Blue-green | Draperies, dusty rose background, blue-green and foliage tones in design / Upholstery, blue, blue-green and green, plain, pattern and stripes | Blue | Suitable for fairly large room with average light |
| ROSE (1) | Warm Gray | Rose Taupe | Draperies, rose / Upholstery, rose and cream stripes | Blue or Green | Appropriate for almost any living or bedroom |
| ROSE (2) | Oyster White | Rose Red | Draperies, oyster white / Upholstery, oyster white with reds, blues and soft green | Red | Charming for bedroom or woman's living room |
| ASHES OF ROSES | Ashes of Roses | Cafe au lait | White | Strong Blue | Adaptable to bedroom or living room |
| DUSTY ROSE (1) | Deep dusty Rose | Brown | Lighter dusty rose, white and brown | Silver | Good color scheme for living room or dining room |
| DUSTY ROSE (2) | Pickled wood | Pinkish Beige | Draperies, dusty rose / Upholstery, foam green and natural | Pale Green | Adaptable to living room, traditional or modern |
| OLD ROSE (1) | Old Rose | Warm Gray | Blue and pale yellow, with touch of old rose | Jade Green | This color scheme is charming and delicate, suitable for bedrooms and dressing rooms |
| OLD ROSE (2) | Paper, Old Rose, cream and gray | Mulberry | Old rose and gray | Blue and Silver | With woodwork painted warm gray, this scheme would be attractive for bedroom or dressing room |
| OLD ROSE (3) | Paper, Blue and rose pattern | Ivory | Draperies, ivory background, rose, blue and green in pattern / Upholstery, old rose, and drapery fabric | Green | Attractive for formal living room |
| RED (1) | Soft grayed Green | Patterned rug with red background | Draperies, pale gray background, red in pattern / Upholstery, plain green, red and green stripes | Blue and Orange | Suitable living room or dining room |

# COLOR THEORY
**Color Families: Red**

| Color | Walls / Paper | Floor | Draperies / Upholstery | Accent | Remarks |
|---|---|---|---|---|---|
| RED (2) | Paper, granite flecked with red | Patterned rug, red predominating | Chintz, red predominating in pattern | Green and Pewter | Good for Early American room, with pine or maple |
| RED (3) | Paper, red toile design; woodwork, white | Hooked rugs; Floors, painted blue | Draperies, textured beige; Upholstery, textured beige trimmed with red | Blue (chairs painted blue) | Colonial type living room or library |
| RED (4) | Old white; Woodwork, dark green | Red rug | Red and white brocade | Green | Living room in period feeling with walnut furniture |
| RED (5) | Paper, light background, red with green and brown in pattern | Dark blue | Red | Blue | Early American dining room, with pine and maple |
| SOFT RED (1) | Neutral | Soft Red | Draperies, blue-green background, deep red in design; Upholstery, blue-green | Yellow | Nice for living room |
| SOFT RED (2) | White | Rug, blue, red and white pattern | Draperies, linen color with red in pattern; Upholstery, chair seats, blue | Silver | 18th Century dining room |
| CRIMSON (1) | Bone white | Crimson | White background, floral design in red and soft green | White | Mahogany furniture of very nice design would be lovely with white walls |
| CRIMSON (2) | Soft Gray | Crimson | Draperies, white, gray and crimson; Upholstery, white, trimmed with crimson | Black | A smart sophisticated color scheme |
| CRIMSON (3) | Slate Gray | Soft Crimson | Draperies, bluish white, trimmed with soft crimson; Upholstery, bluish white | Gold | Adaptable to modern styles |
| CHINESE RED | Grayed soft Green | Chinese Red | Draperies, grayed soft green; Upholstery, deep beige | Light Beige | Good for living room or dining room |
| LACQUER RED (1) | Gray | Brown | Gray and lacquer red | Green | Colorful living room with some red lacquer furniture |
| LACQUER RED (2) | Paneling, Red Lacquer, silver trim | Black | Silver gray, with red and black in design | Silver | Modern library |
| ITALIAN RED | Yellow | Floor, stained dark; Patterned rug in old reds and dark blues, red predominating | Draperies, Italian red damask. Upholstery, red damask, yellow, glazed chintz with white ground and red in design | Gold | Living room English in feeling; also good for Federal American |
| CRANBERRY RED | Paper with light ground and cranberry pattern; Paneled fireplace end painted blue | Deep soft red | Draperies, rose; Upholstery, blue, and chintz-like wallpaper pattern | Green | Cheerful living room color scheme |
| WINE RED (1) | Green | Wine Red | Draperies, wine red; Upholstery, grayed green and off white | Crystal | Attractive for living room with cool North or East light |
| WINE RED (2) | Soft grayed Blue | Deep Gray | Draperies, wine red; Upholstery, wine red, grayed white and blue | Silver | For fairly formal living room, average size |
| WINE RED (3) | Paper in yellow, pale gray and white | Dark Wine Red | Draperies, Ruby taffeta; Upholstery, glazed maroon chintz with yellow flowers; Chair seats, bright yellow leather | Gold | Specially appropriate for Victorian dining room |
| AMERICAN BEAUTY | Linen color | Fawn | Draperies, fawn and American beauty; Upholstery, American beauty, fawn, blue and gray | Blue | Dramatic color scheme for fairly large living room |
| RED DAHLIA | Gray | Red Dahlia | Draperies, light neutral background with dahlia and melon green in pattern; Upholstery, melon green | Larkspur Blue | Adaptable to various types of living rooms |
| OLD RED | Soft light shade; Old Red | Deep Old Red | Draperies, old red, beige and white stripes; Upholstery, light tan | Copper | Warm, colorful plan for a room inclined to be cold |
| BURGUNDY (1) | Pale clear yellow | Burgundy | Draperies, white, valance and trimming; Upholstery, burgundy and white | Gold | Rich color scheme for formal room |
| BURGUNDY (2) | Burgundy | Darker Burgundy | Burgundy and natural | Chartreuse | For large room, living room or library |
| BURGUNDY (3) | Warm Gray with pinkish cast | Burgundy | Draperies, primrose yellow; Upholstery, pale grayed blue and white | White | Good for any room not too small or too sunny |
| BURGUNDY (4) | Beige with pinkish cast | Burgundy | Draperies, beige background, shell pink and burgundy in pattern; Upholstery, shell pink | Grayed White | Same as above |

# THE ORANGE FAMILY

REPRESENTATIVE MEMBERS OF THE ORANGE FAMILY . . . IVORY . . . PEACH . . . CORAL . . . BEIGE . . . RUST . . . TERRA COTTA . . . WARM BROWN.

CHARACTERISTICS . . . Always warm, advancing . . . Cheerful, welcoming, gay, vibrant, glowing . . . In strong tones, akin to red . . . In softer tones, a good mixer.

WHAT THEY CAN DO . . . In slightly less degree, Orange repeats the activities of the Red Family . . . Effec- tive for "toning" up a room in too dull or quiet colors, or warming a cold room.

CORRECT USES . . . Best in off shades, except for accent . . . In softened tones, excellent background color for dark or cold rooms . . . Wonderful accent color in proper combinations.

CAUTION . . . Do not use too much of the clear color . . . In large areas it has the disturbing quality of red . . . Do not use for background of small rooms unless you want it to be very "cozy."

## SUGGESTED COLOR SCHEMES IN WHICH MEMBERS OF ORANGE FAMILY PLAY A DOMINANT ROLE

| DOMINANT COLOR | MAJOR WALL COLOR | MAJOR FLOOR COLOR | DRAPERIES AND UPHOLSTERY | ACCENT COLORS | REMARKS |
|---|---|---|---|---|---|
| IVORY | Ivory Woodwork, Ivory | Floor, painted ivory Rug, Jade Green | Ivory background, rose and blue green in pattern | Rose and Jade Green | Charming for bedroom or lady's sitting room with ivory painted furniture |
| PEACH (1) | Peach | Peach | Apple green | Bittergreen | Attractive for bedroom, modern or traditional |
| PEACH (2) | Peach | Old Green | Draperies and upholstery, peach, with old blue | Old Blue | For a room that needs warming up, with cool touches |
| PEACH (3) | Peach | Warm Brown | Draperies, brown and coral stripes Upholstery, brown background, with coral, beige and tan | Copper | Modern color scheme appropriate for living room or library |
| PEACH (4) | Paper, shades of yellow, through peach to brown | Brown | Draperies, brown Upholstery, light and dark peach | Yellow | Good modern living room color scheme |
| PEACH (5) | Floral pattern paper, white ground, peach and green | Rust | Draperies, peach Upholstery (chair seats), green | Green | Very good for late Colonial dining room with Duncan Phyfe style furniture |
| PEACH (6) | Yellowish Pink | Eggplant | Draperies, peach background, blue in design Upholstery, peach and blue | Coral and yellow | Good color scheme to lighten dark bedroom |
| APRICOT | Apricot | Rose and Cream | Draperies, old rose Bed and furniture covering, apricot, trimmed with black | Orchid | Charming for young girl's room |
| CORAL (1) | Paper, silver ground, coral-rose design; Woodwork, coral | Aquamarine | Aquamarine | Aquamarine and Silver | Charming for woman's bedroom |
| CORAL (2) | Coral Woodwork, soft Blue | Gray Blue | Draperies, off-white background rose and green in design, Coral valance; Bed and furniture covering, copper rose and same chintz used for hangings | Off-white | Attractive for bedroom with furniture painted blue |
| WARM BEIGE (1) | Warm Beige | Warm Beige | Brown and Copper | Bright Green | Modern living room or library |
| WARM BEIGE (2) | Pink and Beige wallpaper | Warm Beige | Draperies, old white and beige Upholstery, dusty pink and pale olive green | Terra Cotta | Restful living room color scheme |
| WARM BEIGE (3) | Warm Beige | Warm Beige | Draperies, burgundy background, white and beige in design; Upholstery, burgundy and natural | White | Good for living room, library, or man's bedroom |
| WARM BEIGE (4) | Warm Beige | Dark Taupe | Draperies, russet (beige glass curtains) Upholstery, brown with tan cushions | Tan | Restful, chromatic color scheme |
| WARM BEIGE (5) | Beige with pink cast | Light warm beige | Brown, beige and white stripes or checks | Sky Blue | Appropriate for informal living room or boy's room |
| HENNA (1) | Grass cloth, tan and gold | Henna and black | Henna, green and gray | Gold | Living room or man's bedroom |
| HENNA (2) | Mint Green Woodwork, Cream | Henna | Draperies, henna with valance of bedspread material Bedspread, henna, light and dark green and tan stripes Upholstery, same combination in patterned material | White | Man's bedroom |
| TERRA COTTA | Pink Terra Cotta | Eggplant | Draperies, pinkish yellow, trimmed with terra cotta Upholstery, bois de rose | Pale Green | Charming for dining room in Directoire feeling with furniture painted yellow and gold |
| COPPER (1) | Pine paneled | Floor, Pine Rugs (hooked) in tones of orange, yellow, green | Draperies, copper toned background with orange, yellow and green in pattern | Blue and copper | Appropriate for living room in Early American feeling with Early American style furniture |
| COPPER (2) | Rough plaster with oak paneling | Oak plank floor Patterned rug, tones of brown, green, copper | Draperies, copper colored, coarsely woven material Upholstery, neutral green, trimmed with brown and copper | Green | Good color scheme for large, formal, English-style living room, with furniture in natural oak and walnut |
| BURNT ORANGE | Neutral Woodwork, walnut | Rug, greenish background, with burnt orange and henna | Burnt orange and henna | Blue | Good for dining room with walnut furniture |
| WARM BROWN (1) | Tobacco Brown | Warm Beige | Chintz in clear yellow, beige and warm brown in design | White | Modern living room or library |
| WARM BROWN (2) | Tan | Warm Brown | Draperies, copper and topaz; Upholstery, warm browns | Orange, French Blue | Appropriate for boy's room |
| WARM BROWN (3) | Yellow Brown | Orange Brown | Burnt orange and apple green | Greenish Blue | Restful, cheerful color scheme for library |
| WARM BROWN (4) | Pale Yellow | Orange Brown | Shades of warm browns and orange | Silver | Attractive for modern living room or dining room |

# COLOR THEORY

**Color Families: Yellow**

## THE YELLOW FAMILY

REPRESENTATIVE MEMBERS OF THE YELLOW FAMILY . . . CREAM . . . BUFF . . . STRAW . . . CANARY . . . GOLD . . . TAN . . BROWN.

CHARACTERISTICS . . . Warm, somewhat advancing . . . The sunlight color—gay, happy, bright, cheerful . . . In light tones, luminous, radiant.

WHAT THEY CAN DO . . . Diffuse and increase light by reflection, making dark rooms seem lighter and brighter . . . In pale tints, yellow lights up a small room without making it seem smaller because reflective radiance of yellow balances its advancing quality as a warm color.

CORRECT USES . . . Excellent background for all average rooms . . . In light tints, best wall-background for poorly lighted rooms . . . In clear, bright tones, safe accent color almost everywhere.

CAUTION . . . Do not use yellow without testing under artificial light, and providing lamp shades to offset color changes . . . Don't use in wide expanses in a very sunny room . . . Don't use bright tones without restful combination color.

### SUGGESTED COLOR SCHEMES IN WHICH MEMBERS OF YELLOW FAMILY PLAY A DOMINANT ROLE

| DOMINANT COLOR | MAJOR WALL COLOR | MAJOR FLOOR COLOR | DRAPERIES AND UPHOLSTERY | ACCENT COLORS | REMARKS |
|---|---|---|---|---|---|
| CREAM | Cream Woodwork, cream | Patterned rug, mulberry, green and cream | Draperies, green, cream trimming / Upholstery, green and green yellow | Mulberry | Appropriate for bedroom, especially in Directoire feeling with cream and gold furniture |
| BUFF | Buff | Buff | Copenhagen blue and burgundy | Orange, Tete de Negre | Glowing color scheme for living room or man's bedroom |
| PALE YELLOW (1) | Pale Yellow | Soft Beige | Draperies, light yellow background, soft reds, greens and blue in pattern / Upholstery, soft blue, chintz of draperies | Green and Red | Good color scheme for medium-sized dark room |
| PALE YELLOW (2) | Pale Yellow | Pale Yellow | Turquoise | Coral | Colorful for bedroom or small sitting room |
| BRIGHT LEMON (1) | Bright Lemon | Beige | Draperies, beige background, yellow green and lavender / Seat covers, wet leaf green | Wet Leaf Green | This color scheme will brighten up a dark dining room |
| PALE LEMON (2) | Pale Lemon Yellow Woodwork, white | Tobacco Brown | Draperies, white with yellow trimming / Upholstery, emerald green; some pieces white, yellow, dull orange | Orange | Suitable for living room with north light |
| JONQUIL YELLOW (1) | Jonquil Yellow | Gray | Draperies, white, trimmed with Chinese red / Upholstery, warm gray and white | Chinese Red | Charming for living room, modern or traditional |
| JONQUIL YELLOW (2) | Jonquil Yellow | Soft Blue-Green | Draperies, white and yellow / Upholstery, soft blue, green and white | White | Good for any room without too much light |
| YELLOW (1) | Yellow | Brown | Blue and apple green | Black | Good for room with cold light |
| YELLOW (2) | Yellow | Brown | Dutch blue and white | Bright Red | Attractive for informal living room |
| YELLOW (3) | Marbleized yellow paper Woodwork, deep green | Deep Green | Draperies, green, yellow trimming / Chair seat upholstery, yellow | Blue | Charming for dining room, especially in Directoire feeling |
| YELLOW (4) | Paper in Yellow and Ivory stripes, divided by narrow plum lines | Yellow Tan | Draperies, gray background, yellow, plum and rose in pattern / Upholstery, blue and light tan | Old Gold | Good combination for dark maple woodwork |
| GRAYED YELLOW | Grayed Yellow | Brown | Draperies, brown and beige stripes / Upholstery, yellow, beige, moss green | White | Pleasant for living room or man's bedroom |
| SOFT YELLOW | Soft Yellow | Deep Brown | Draperies, yellow / Upholstery, cinnamon brown | Chartreuse | Attractive and restful for library or living room |
| EMPIRE YELLOW | Slate Gray | Lime Green | Draperies, Empire yellow / Upholstery, Strong clear yellow | Silver | Suitable for living room or dining room |
| CITRON YELLOW | Citron Yellow | Citron Yellow | Coral | Silver | Modern or traditional living room |
| LEMON YELLOW | Lemon Yellow | Tete de Negre | Brown and henna | Orange | Distinctive for modern living room |
| SULPHUR YELLOW | Sulphur Yellow | Olive Green | Shades of green and sulphur | Coral | Colorful modern living room |

| | Deep Yellow | Red | | Gold | |
|---|---|---|---|---|---|
| DEEP YELLOW | Deep Yellow | Red | Draperies, gold damask / Upholstery, plum, wine red, gold with red, blue, lavender in pattern | Gold | Suitable for period room with Queen Anne, Sheraton, and other Georgian style furniture |
| MUTED GOLD | Caramel | Bleached wood, rubbed with gold and waxed | Draperies, soft caramel taffeta, trimmed with brown / Upholstery, brown and yellow | Ebony | Unusual modern living room scheme where there is plenty of light |
| GOLD (1) | Yellow, flat finish Woodwork, Olive Green | Old gold carpet | Draperies, old gold, trimmed with green / Upholstery, olive green and paprika | Light Green | Charming for modern living room with blond wood |
| GOLD (2) | Gray and pale Yellow paper | Harvest Gold and Gray | Draperies, oyster white, trimmed with multi-color fringe / Upholstery, rust-shot silk | Brass | Traditional or modern dining room |
| TAN (1) | Neutral Tan | Dark Tan | Draperies, burnt orange / Upholstery, brown and burnt orange | Rich Chocolate | Good with natural wood tones |
| TAN (2) | Tan linen color | Light and dark Tan | Draperies, tan and rose stripes / Upholstery, linen color with rose, tan, gray and blue in pattern | Rose | Attractive for living room or library with walnut woodwork and furniture |
| TAN (3) | Tan | Brown Taupe | Dark green and vermilion | Brown | Rich, warm color scheme for living room or library, especially with walnut furniture and paintings |
| TAN (4) | Brownish Tan | Floor, Oak Multi-colored scatter rugs | Draperies, brown with red, yellow and blue pattern / Upholstery, old red and yellow chintz | Blue | Suitable for bedroom with oak furniture in Early English feeling |
| BROWN (1) | Brown paneled | Deep Brown | Beige background with brilliant gold, scarlet and orange tones of fall foliage | Blue | Attractive for living room with plenty of light |
| BROWN (2) | Pine paneled | Pine | Old chintz in blue and brown | Silver and Pewter | Dining room in French Provincial style |
| BROWN (3) | Warm Beige with brown cast | Brown | Draperies, brown, beige and dusty pink / Upholstery, brown and off-white | White | Appropriate for modern living room |
| BROWN (4) | Pine paneled | Hooked Rugs | Yellow, copper and blue chintz | Green | Suitable Early American living room with maple furniture |
| BROWN (5) | Chalk White | Brown | Turquoise | Peach | Charming bedroom color scheme |
| SABLE BROWN (1) | Sable Brown | Off-white | Draperies, off-white with turquoise / Upholstery, shell pink and off-white | Turquoise | Distinctive modern living room |
| SABLE BROWN (2) | Sable Brown | Deep warm Beige | Draperies, bright yellow / Upholstery, plain chartreuse with white pattern | Earth Brown | Same as above |
| CHESTNUT BROWN | Fawn | Chestnut Brown | Champagne background, beaver, turquoise and apricot in pattern and trimming | Turquoise | Appropriate for living or dining room |
| TAWNY BROWN | Tawny Brown Pine | Light beige and taupe | Blue on light ground | Yellow | Good for dining room in French period feeling |
| GOLDEN BROWN | Knotty Pine | Golden Brown Navajo rug | Draperies, colorful hunting print / Upholstery, red leather | Blue and Green | Library or Den |
| NUT BROWN | Nut Brown Pine | Moss Green | Draperies, dark linen / Upholstery, green, brown and white | Yellow | Restful living room color scheme |
| TOBACCO BROWN | Tobacco Brown | Beige | Clear yellow chintz with beige and dark brown in design | White | Suitable modern dining room with much sunlight |
| CHOCOLATE BROWN | Chocolate Brown | Eggshell | Draperies, white / Upholstery, chartreuse, brown and eggshell | Chartreuse | Interesting modern color scheme for living room or dining room |
| DARK BROWN (1) | Deep Beige | Dark Brown | Draperies, pale, clear blue / Upholstery, cinnamon brown | Pale Clear Blue | Good for dining room or living room |
| DARK BROWN (2) | Light Chartreuse | Dark Brown | Light tan and brown | White | Good for modern living room |
| BROWNS | Light Brown | Deep Brown | Draperies, off-white / Upholstery, Wedgwood green and off-white | Gold | Suitable for living or dining room |

# THE GREEN FAMILY

REPRESENTATIVE MEMBERS OF THE GREEN FAMILY ... NILE ... LETTUCE ... PEA ... GRASS ... SEA ... OLIVE ... BOTTLE ... ETC.

CHARACTERISTICS ... Cool, receding—except when mixed with a warm color ... Most restful color ... Friendly with all other colors, refreshing, versatile ... Endless variety of tones and combinations.

WHAT THEY CAN DO ... In light, soft tints, makes rooms seem larger because the wall seems farther away ... Makes objects seem farther away, therefore smaller ... Brings atmosphere of rest and relaxation to room.

CORRECT USES ... One of best background colors for average rooms, especially where restfulness is important ... Great corrective value for rooms too small or too warm ... Suitable in proper tones for background in any part of room—floor, walls, ceiling.

CAUTION ... Do not use in quantity in cold, dark or overlarge rooms—choose warm, advancing colors for backgrounds, keeping green for smaller areas.

## SUGGESTED COLOR SCHEMES IN WHICH MEMBERS OF GREEN FAMILY PLAY A DOMINANT ROLE

| DOMINANT COLOR | MAJOR WALL COLOR | MAJOR FLOOR COLOR | DRAPERIES AND UPHOLSTERY | ACCENT COLORS | REMARKS |
|---|---|---|---|---|---|
| PALE GREEN (1) | Pale Green | Dark Green | Draperies, off-white background, with pale blues, greens, and mauve in pattern / Upholstery, darker blue | Mauve and Violet | Appropriate for average living room and bedroom |
| PALE GREEN (2) | Pale Green | Plum | Draperies, natural linen color, with flowered plum and green in design / Upholstery, plum, gold, green | Gold | Especially good for traditional living room |
| LIGHT GREEN (1) | White | Light Green | Draperies, white with dark green pattern / Upholstery, dark green and white | Yellow | Pleasant color scheme for modern room |
| LIGHT GREEN (2) | Pickled Pine | Light Green | Draperies, off-white and light green / Upholstery, light green | Brown | Attractive for living room or library |
| LIGHT GREEN (3) | Off-white | Soft Light Green | Shell-pink, green and off-white | Crystal | Charming and cool for small living room or sitting room |
| APPLE GREEN (1) | Apple Green | Plum | Draperies, apple green / Upholstery, gold, yellow and ivory | Gold | Good for small living room |
| APPLE GREEN (2) | Apple Green | Yellow Green | Gray, blue, and touches of light yellow | Light Yellow | This combination makes cool room |
| APPLE GREEN (3) | Pale Apple Green | Floor, brown walnut Rug, blue and tan | Draperies, royal blue background, with rose and green leaves in pattern / Upholstery, same drapery chintz, also rose, antique salmon, apple green and cream stripes | Black, gold, white and ruby | Early American living room with maple or cherry furniture |
| SOFT GREEN (1) | Soft Green | Deeper Green | Draperies, plum background with beige and green in pattern / Upholstery, plum, beige and green | Orange | Restful Color Scheme |
| SOFT GREEN (2) | Soft Grayed Green | Deeper Green | Draperies, corn yellow / Upholstery, grayed green and off-white | Pine Green | Adaptable to living room, dining room or bedroom |
| SOFT GREEN (3) | Pale Soft Grayed Green | Ivy Green | Draperies, soft grayed green / Upholstery, golden yellow and white | Lacquer Red | Excellent to add feeling of space to small room |
| FOAM GREEN | Slate Gray | Foam Green | Draperies, lemon yellow and white / Upholstery, lemon yellow and gray | Gold | Good modern color scheme |
| IVY GREEN | Clear Beige | Ivy Green | Draperies, beige with light and dark green floral design / Upholstery, same chintz and some clear beige | Black | Appropriate for living room |
| DEEP LIME | Deep Lime | Deep Lime | White, green and melon pink | White | Dramatic modern scheme, especially good with blond wood |

| Color Family | | | | | |
|---|---|---|---|---|---|
| NILE GREEN | Nile Green | Green | Glazed chintz with green background and white in design, red lining and trimming | Crystal | Cool, airy bedroom |
| MINT GREEN | Pure White Woodwork, white | Painted Mint Green, spatter-dashed with turquoise and yellow | Turquoise, yellow and mint green | White | Adaptable for informal living room, dining room or bedroom |
| JADE GREEN | Pale Jade | Dark Blue | Draperies, blue / Upholstery, blue and jade green | Silver | Attractive for modern living room |
| SAGE | Slate Gray | Soft Deep Sage | Gray and blue with green touches | Silver | Excellent color to make small sunny room seem larger and cooler |
| BOTTLE GREEN | Pale Apricot | Bottle Green | Green, apricot and topaz | Topaz | Good for living room or dining room |
| CHARTREUSE GREEN | Chartreuse Green | Shades of Tete de Negre | Draperies, chartreuse green / Upholstery, shades of heliotrope | Silver | Modern bedroom. Good with furniture painted chartreuse |
| CHARTREUSE GREEN | Gray | Chartreuse | Chartreuse and bright blue | Silver | Adaptable to any modern room |
| TURQUOISE | Light Turquoise | Patterned rug, Green with Moss Rose | Draperies, turquoise, green and rose stripes / Upholstery, turquoise | Rose | Attractive for bedroom with mahogany furniture |
| BLUE GREEN (1) | Deep Cream | Blue Green | Apple green, greenish blue, touch of burnt orange | Burnt Orange | Versatile color scheme for average room |
| BLUE GREEN (2) | Blue Green | Blue Green | Draperies, light grayish tan background, turquoise, rose and green in pattern / Upholstery, same print and some soft rose | Green | Very restful for living room or bedroom |
| BLUE GREEN (3) | Dull Blue Green | Rug, light field, red violet and green leaves in pattern | Draperies, white / Upholstery, red violet | Dark Green | Dining room in period feeling with walnut furniture |
| WET LEAF GREEN | Deep Lime | Bronze | White background, wet leaf green, down rose and bright lemon in pattern | Rose | Sophisticated modern color scheme |
| DEEP GREEN (1) | Deep Green | Gray | Draperies, sky blue chintz with rose and green pattern / Upholstery, emerald green and gray | Gold and Rose | Suitable for living room or man's bedroom |
| DEEP GREEN (2) | Gray and White paper, Block pattern | 'Deep Green | Draperies, yellow / Upholstery, yellow flowers and pale green leaves on gray background | White and Green | Modern living room or dining room |
| DEEP GREEN (3) | Green, lighter than carpet | Deep Soft Green | Draperies, off-white / Upholstery, off-white and Wedgwood green | Yellow | Very cool and fresh |
| DEEP GREEN (4) | Greenish Gray | Deep Green | Draperies, apple green / Upholstery, grayed greens and white | Salmon | Good combination to make small room seem larger |
| DEEP GREEN (5) | Deep Soft Green | Light Brown | Golden yellow and white | White | Modern or traditional setting |
| GEORGIAN GREEN | Deep Georgian Green | Deep Green | Draperies, soft golden yellow / Upholstery, golden yellow and deep green | Gold | Very cool and restful for period living room or library |
| DARK GREEN (1) | Ivory Green | Dark Green | Draperies, white with dark green pattern / Upholstery, off-red, off-white and dark green | Black | Subtle color combination. Good for living room or dining room |
| DARK GREEN (2) | Warm Gray | Dark Green | Draperies, dark green or gray background / Upholstery, light green | Yellow | Cool and restful for living room |
| DARK GREEN (3) | Dark Green | Tan | Draperies, chintz in blue-green and soft red / Upholstery, same chintz, also some soft red | Copper | Charming for sunny living room |
| GREEN OLIVE | Green Olive | Red-Coral | Lime green, red-coral, antique white | Coral and White | Daring modern color scheme. Good with traditional or modern furniture in light finish |

# COLOR THEORY

## Color Families: Blue

## THE BLUE FAMILY

REPRESENTATIVE MEMBERS OF THE BLUE FAMILY . . . PALE . . . BABY . . . SKY . . . POWDER . . . smaller because they seem more distant . . . In dark tones, make lighter contrast colors more luminous. NAVY . . . MIDNIGHT . . . ETC. CORRECT USES . . . In light tones, excellent background for small, dark, warm rooms . . . Good combining CHARACTERISTICS . . . Coldest, most receding, unless mixed with warm colors . . . Serene, quiet, "spa- color, especially in soft tones . . . Effective background for many other colors. cious" . . . Much-loved hue . . . Too much of it in dull tones may be depressing. CAUTION . . . Do not use in quantity in cold or dark or over-large rooms . . . Do not use too much in dull WHAT THEY CAN DO . . . Make room seem larger, cooler, more airy and spacious . . . Make objects look shades . . . Do not use without some warm bright accent color.

### SUGGESTED COLOR SCHEMES IN WHICH MEMBERS OF BLUE FAMILY PLAY A DOMINANT ROLE

| DOMINANT COLOR | MAJOR WALL COLOR | MAJOR FLOOR COLOR | DRAPERIES AND UPHOLSTERY | ACCENT COLORS | REMARKS |
|---|---|---|---|---|---|
| PALE BLUE (1) | Pale Blue | Dark Blue | Tan draperies and upholstery | Silver | Modern color scheme for bedroom with furniture in lemon color |
| SKY BLUE | Garden Sky Blue | Champagne | Champagne, sky blue and orchid | Orchid | Modern color scheme, good with light natural finish woods |
| POWDER BLUE (1) | Powder Blue | Delft Blue | Draperies, canary yellow / Upholstery, yellow and powder blue | Off-white | Cool and fresh for bedroom |
| POWDER BLUE (2) | Powder Blue | Powder Blue | White draperies and upholstery | Peach | Dainty feminine bedroom |
| LARKSPUR BLUE (1) | Larkspur Blue | Pale Gray | Draperies, wine, trimmed with white / Upholstery, deep blue and white | Deep Blue and Wine | Good modern living room combination |
| LARKSPUR BLUE (2) | Larkspur Blue | Blue | Neutral background, blue and pink in pattern | Red Dahlia | Any period room with enough light |
| BLUE (1) | Pale Blue, deep Rose and ivory paper | Blue | Blue, gold and rose with touches of black—in stripes or plain | Black | Attractive for traditional living room |
| BLUE (2) | Faded Blue (middle value) | Floor, dark Brown / Carpet, Gray and Yellow | Draperies, old yellow / Upholstery, yellow, old yellow, and touch of Venetian red, also some blue | Blue | Bedroom with Directoire feeling and walnut furniture |
| BLUE (3) | Striped wallpaper in tones of light and medium blue and White | Dark Blue | Draperies, blue with white in pattern and trimming / Upholstery, lemon yellow | Dark Blue | Good for small, low-ceilinged but light room |
| HYDRANGEA BLUE (1) | Pale Hydrangea Blue | Eggplant | Draperies, peach background with white, copper, gold and hydrangea blue in design / Upholstery, same chintz, also old blue | Old Blue | Good for room with strong light, especially with 18th Century furniture |
| HYDRANGEA BLUE (2) | Hydrangea Blue | Deeper Blue | Draperies, salmon pink / Chair seats, black and gold | Gold | Dining room with Directoire feeling |
| COPENHAGEN BLUE | Copenhagen Blue | Burgundy | Gray with blue and burgundy | Rose and Silver | Attractive for traditional living room |
| PENCIL BLUE | Lemon Yellow | Pencil Blue | Blue background with yellow in pattern and trim | Silver | Setting for dining room with modern furniture |

| Color | Walls / Woodwork | Floor / Rug | Draperies / Upholstery | Accents | Room Use |
|---|---|---|---|---|---|
| MEDIUM BLUE (1) | Blue | Mulberry ground | Draperies, cherry red; Upholstery, chintz in blue, rose and mauve, some pieces in cherry red and gold | Gold | Good for living room, especially in 18th Century French feeling |
| MEDIUM BLUE (2) | Blue | Mole | Lavender, gray, and some rose | Rose | Adaptable for lady's bedroom in lighter blues, also to living room in darker shades of duller blues |
| MEDIUM BLUE (3) | Cream | Blue | French Blue | Jade Green | Good for south living room or bedroom |
| DUSTY BLUE | Dusty Blue | Dark Burgundy | Draperies, gray, trimmed with soft blue; Upholstery, soft blue and gray | Crystal | Restful for living room or dining room |
| SOFT DULL BLUE | Ivory | Soft Dull Blue | Ivory background with blue, rose and green in design, some pieces in old rose | Green | Bedroom or informal living room |
| OLD BLUE | Old Blue | Deeper Blue | Faded Pink, or chintz with blue, green and pink | Green | Charming for living room or bedroom |
| GRAYED BLUE | Gray Blue | Deeper grayed Blue | Yellow, white, and gold | Red | Dining room in Directoire feeling with mahogany |
| TURQUOISE BLUE | Pale Turquoise Blue | Turquoise | Draperies, golden yellow; Upholstery, golden yellow and white | White | Any room not too large or too dark |
| TURQUOISE BLUE | Grayed Turquoise | Grayed Turquoise | Wine and ivory | Polished Brass | Dignified but friendly living room |
| GREEN BLUE | Green Blue | Plum rug; flowered pattern | Draperies, peach; Upholstery, green-blue with some plum | Peach | Simple living room in French Provincial feeling |
| ROYAL BLUE (1) | Walls, Silver Woodwork, Royal Blue | Floor, painted Gray Rug, Blue | Draperies, blue, trimmed with silver; Upholstery (chairs), silver and blue leather | Silver and Black | Distinctive modern dining room |
| ROYAL BLUE (2) | Old White | Royal Blue | Clear yellow | Silver | Modern living or dining room |
| ROYAL BLUE (3) | Dull White | Rug, Deep Blue ground with honey-yellow in pattern | Draperies, royal blue; Chair Seats, royal blue Morocco | Silver | Attractive for modern dining room, especially with lemon wood furniture |
| DEEP BLUE (1) | Pale Amethyst | Deep Blue | Deep blue, trimmed with gold | Amethyst and Gold | Cool and charming for living room not too dark |
| DEEP BLUE (2) | Deep Blue Woodwork, Ivory | Dark Blue rug with Tan and Rose in pattern | Draperies, dull ivory; Upholstery (chairs), ivory or rosy red leather | Red | Colorful for dining room with plenty of light |
| DEEP BLUE (3) | Deep Blue | Deep Blue | Draperies, deep sea blue; Upholstery, canary yellow | White | Modern living room or dining room |
| DEEP BLUE (4) | Pale Yellow | Natural | Draperies, deep sea blue (gold gauze glass curtains); Upholstery, deep blue | White | Good when blue is dominant color in a dark room |
| DEEP BLUE (5) | Creamy White | Blue | Draperies, deep blue; Upholstery, yellow with dash of white | Gold, Rose-Pink and Blue | Good for bedroom, furniture painted blue with flower decorations, and some smaller oyster white pieces |
| GARDEN POOL BLUE | Ivory | Garden Pool Blue | Draperies, garden pool blue; Chair Seats, red leather | White and Silver | Dramatic modern living room with furniture in rich mahogany or walnut tones |
| DARK BLUE | Cream and beige paper | Dark Blue rug with rose and tan in pattern | Draperies, linen color with blues, greens and rosy reds in pattern; Chair Seats, dark blue | Blue and Silver | Good for dining room where light is needed |

# COLOR THEORY

## Color Families: Violet/Purple

# THE VIOLET (OR PURPLE) FAMILY

REPRESENTATIVE MEMBERS OF THE VIOLET FAMILY . . . ORCHID . . . LAVENDER . . . MAUVE . . . . . . . Create restful, quiet atmosphere when used in soft tones.
VIOLET . . . PLUM . . . PURPLE. . . . CORRECT USES . . . In light, soft tints, excellent wall and ceiling background for an average room . . .
CHARACTERISTICS . . . Cool when mixed with blue, warm when mixed with red . . . In pure form, cold Strong shades good for accent . . . In deep, soft tones, attractive for carpets, upholstery, draperies.
and formal . . . In purple tones, rich and dignified but not friendly . . . May be depressing. CAUTION . . . Do not use blue tones of violet in cold, dark, over-large rooms . . . Be careful when using
WHAT THEY CAN DO . . . Add to impression of room size and coolness, especially when mixed with blue strong shades for dominant color . . . Do not use without some warm contrast.

## SUGGESTED COLOR SCHEMES IN WHICH MEMBERS OF VIOLET FAMILY PLAY A DOMINANT ROLE

| DOMINANT COLOR | MAJOR WALL COLOR | MAJOR FLOOR COLOR | DRAPERIES AND UPHOLSTERY | ACCENT COLORS | REMARKS |
|---|---|---|---|---|---|
| ORCHID (1) | Orchid | Blue | Champagne, orchid and blue | Black and Silver | Attractive for living room |
| ORCHID (2) | Paneled paper in Orchid and Pale Yellow | Mulberry | Green, yellow and orchid chintz | Green | Cool, airy bedroom |
| LAVENDER (1) | Lavender | Lavender with mauve border | Gray, light blue and touches of jade green | Jade Green | Good for sunny room |
| LAVENDER (2) | Lavender, Blue and White paper | Plum | Lavender | Rose | Feminine bedroom |
| LAVENDER (3) | Pale Lavender | Rose | Pink, lavender and white | Lavender | Bedroom with warm light |
| HELIOTROPE (1) | Gray | Beige | Heliotrope draperies and upholstery | Violet and Silver | Lovely color scheme for woman with gray hair |
| MAUVE (1) | Gray | Mauve | Light blue, Nile green, some rose | Rose | Good for sunny bedroom |
| MAUVE (2) | Paneled wall painted Pale Mauve | Deep Violet | Mauve and yellow | Crystal and Sepia | Especially attractive for Louis XVI style bedroom with walnut furniture |
| HELIOTROPE (2) | Pearl Gray | Heliotrope | Draperies, heliotrope trimmed with silver Upholstery, Tarragon green, gray and heliotrope | Green | Cool and restful living room |
| VIOLET | Dove Gray | Black and White | Draperies, violet Upholstery, coral and old gold | Silver and Black | Attractive with silver gray painted woodwork and violet lines, also white and gold furniture |
| MULBERRY (1) | Dusty Mulberry | Mahogany | Draperies, clear blue chintz with mulberry and brown in pattern Upholstery, clear blue | White | Very good for traditional living room or dining room |
| MULBERRY (2) | Dusty Mulberry | Ebony | Draperies, creamy peach chintz with gray, old rose and ebony design Upholstery, creamy peach | Black | Good for sunny living room or dining room |
| MULBERRY (3) | Scenic paper Woodwork, walnut | Deep Mulberry | Mulberry | Orange | Traditional dining room |
| PURPLE | Paper in Gray and soft Purple stripes | Gray | Purple, with blue, green and gray | Burnt Orange | Hall or living room |

**TABLE 1   Reflective Values**

| Color | Approx. percent of reflection |
|---|---|
| White, dull or flat | 75–85 |
| White, gloss | 85–90 |
| Light tints | |
| Cream or eggshell | 79 |
| Ivory | 75 |
| Pale pink and pale yellow | 75–80 |
| Light green, light blue, light orchid | 70–75 |
| Soft pink, light peach | 69 |
| Light beige, pale grey | 70 |
| Medium tones | |
| Apricot | 56–62 |
| Pink | 64 |
| Tan, yellow gold | 55 |
| Light greys | 35–50 |
| Medium turquoise | 44 |
| Medium light blue | 42 |
| Yellow green | 45 |
| Old gold, pumpkin | 34 |
| Rose | 29 |
| Deep tones | |
| Cocoa brown, mauve | 24 |
| Medium green, medium blue | 21 |
| | 20 |
| Unsuitable dark colors | |
| Dark brown, dark grey | 10–15 |
| Olive green | 12 |
| Dark blue, blue green | 5–10 |
| Forest green | 7 |
| Natural wood tones | |
| Birch and beech | 35–50 |
| Light maple | 25–35 |
| Light oak | 25–35 |
| Dark oak, cherry | 10–15 |
| Redwood | 10–15 |
| Black walnut, mahogany | 5–15 |

Recommended ceiling values should be in the range of 60–90%. Floor reflection values should be in the range of 15–35%. Overall reflection values of a room should be in the 35–60% range.

**Safety Color Guides**

Physical hazards:
   *Red:* Fire protection equipment and apparatus; danger; stop
   *Orange:* Dangerous parts of moving machinery
   *Yellow:* Physical hazards that might cause stumbling, falling, etc.
   *Green:* Safety – first-aid dispensary or kits, stretchers, safety deluge showers, etc.
   *Blue:* Caution against movement or use of equipment being worked on such as elevators, scaffolding, etc.
   *Black and White:* Traffic direction; sanitation

Equipment in industrial plants:
   *Red:* Fire protection systems and equipment
   *Orange:* Dangerous materials, nonflammable, such as acids, alkalis, toxic materials, gases, oxygen
   *Yellow:* Dangerous materials, flammable, such as fuel oil, gasoline, kerosene, alcohol, propane, butane, acetylene, hydrogen, and solvent
   *Green:* Safe materials, such as drinking water, service water, brine
   *Blue:* Protective materials
   *Violet:* Valuable materials
   *Black:* Electrical conduit

# COLOR THEORY
### Color Effect

## TABLE 2

| | Color Effects of White Fluorescent Lamps | | | | | | |
|---|---|---|---|---|---|---|---|
| | Cool* White | Deluxe* Cool White | Warm† White | Deluxe† Warm White | Daylight | White | Soft White— Natural |
| Lamp appearance; effect on neutral surfaces | White | White | Yellowish white | Yellowish white | Bluish white | Pale yellowish white | Pinkish white |
| Effect on "atmosphere" | Neutral to moderately cool | Neutral to moderately cool | Warm | Warm | Very cool | Moderately warm | Warm, pinkish |
| Colors strengthened | Orange, yellow, blue | All nearly equal | Orange, yellow | Red, orange, yellow, green | Green, blue | Orange, yellow | Red, orange |
| Colors grayed | Red | None appreciably | Red, green, blue | Blue | Red, orange | Red, green, blue | Green, blue |
| Remarks | Blends with natural daylight | Best overall color rendition; simulates natural daylight | Blends with incandescent light | Excellent color rendition; simulates incandescent light | Usually replaceable with CW | Usually replaceable with CW or WW | Usually replaceable with CWX or WWX |

| | Color Effects of Mercury and Filament Lamps | | | | |
|---|---|---|---|---|---|
| | Mercury | White Mercury | Color-Improved Mercury | Deluxe White Mercury | Filament |
| Lamp appearance; effect on neutral surfaces | Greenish blue white | Greenish white | Yellowish white | White | Yellowish white |
| Effect on "atmosphere" | Very cool, greenish | Moderately cool, greenish | Warm, yellowish | Moderately cool | Warm |
| Colors strengthened | Yellow, green, blue | Yellow, green, blue | Yellow, green | Orange, yellow, blue | Red, orange, yellow |
| Colors grayed | Red, orange | Red, orange | Blue | Green | Blue |
| Remarks | Poor overall color rendering | | Color rendering often acceptable, but not equal to any white fluorescent | Color rendering good; compares favorably with CWX fluorescent | Excellent color rendering |

\* Greater preference at higher levels.

† Greater preference at lower levels.

Windows are available in many types, each having advantages. The principal types are double-hung, casement, stationary, awning, and horizontal sliding. They may be made of wood or metal. Heat loss through metal frames and sash is much greater than through similar wood units. Glass blocks are sometimes used for admitting light in places where transparency or ventilation is not required.

Insulated glass, used both for stationary and moveable sash, consists of two or more sheets of spaced glass with hermetically-sealed edges. This type has more resistance to heat loss than a single thickness and is often used without a storm sash.

Wood sash and door and window frames should be made from a clear grade of all-heartwood stock of a decay resistant wood species or from wood which is given a preservative treatment. Species commonly used include ponderosa and other pines, the cedars, cypress, redwood, and the spruces.

### Double-Hung Windows

The double-hung window is perhaps the most familiar window type. It consists of an upper and lower sash that slide vertically in separate grooves in the side jambs or in full-width metal weatherstripping. This type of window provides a maximum face opening for ventilation of one-half the total window area. Each sash is provided with springs, balances, or *compression weatherstripping* to hold it in place in any location. Compression weatherstripping, for example, prevents air infiltration, provides tension, and acts as a counterbalance; several types allow the sash to be removed for easy painting or repair.

The *jambs* (sides and top of the frames) are made of nominal 1-inch lumber; the width provides for use with dry-wall or plastered interior finish. Sills are made from nominal 2-inch lumber and sloped at about 3 in 12 for good drainage. Sash are normally 1⅜ inches thick and wood combination storm and screen windows are usually 1⅛ inches thick.

Sash may be divided into a number of lights by small wood members called *muntins*. A ranch-type house may provide the best appearance with top and bottom sash divided into two horizontal lights. A colonial or Cape Code house usually has each sash divided into six or eight lights. Some manufacturers provided preassembled dividers which snap in place over a single light, dividing it into six or eight lights. This simplifies painting and other maintenance.

Assembled frames are placed in the rough opening over strips of building paper put around the perimeter to minimize air infiltration. The frame is plumbed and nailed to side studs and header through the casings or the blind at the sides. Where nails are exposed, such as on the casing, use the corrosion-resistant type.

Hardware for double-hung windows includes the sash lifts that are fastened to the bottom rail, although they are sometimes eliminated by providing a finger groove in the rail. Other hardware consists of sash locks or fasteners located at the meeting rail. They not only lock the window, but draw the sash together to provide a "windtight" fit.

Double-hung windows can be arranged in a number of ways — as a single unit, doubled (or mullion) type, or in groups of three or more. One or two double-hung windows on each side of a large stationary insulated window are often used to effect a window wall. Such large openings must be framed with headers large enough to carry roofloads.

### Casement Windows

*Casement windows* consist of side-hinged sash, usually designed to swing outward because this type can be made more weathertight than the inswinging style. Screens are located inside these outswinging windows and winter protection is obtained with a storm sash or by using insulated glass in the sash. One advantage of the casement window over the double-hung type is that the entire window area can be opened for ventilation.

Weatherstripping is also provided for this type of window, and units are usually received from the factory entirely assembled with hardware in place. Closing hardware consists of a rotary operator and sash lock. As in the double-hung units, casement sash can be used in a number of ways — as a pair or in combinations of two or more pairs. Style variations are achieved by divided lights. Snap-in muntins provided a small, multiple-pane appearance for traditional styling.

Metal sash are sometimes used but, because of low insulating value, should be installed carefully to prevent condensation and frosting on the interior surfaces during cold weather. A full storm-window unit is sometimes necessary to eliminate this problem in cold climates.

### Stationary Windows

Stationary windows used alone or in combination with double-hung or casement windows usually consist of a wood sash with a large single light of insulated glass. They are designed to provide light, as well as for attractive appearance, and are fastened permanently into the frame. Because of their size (sometimes 6 to 8 feet wide), 1¾-inch-thick sash is used to provide strength. The thickness is usually required because of the thickness of the insulating glass.

OPERATION                                    VENTILATION          REMARKS

Double-hung window: upper and lower sections slide vertically to open; spring balance; lock at meeting rail

Substantial airflow, but not directed well; drafty without a shield

No parts project even when open; sometimes difficult to open if schoolroom has usual shelving at sill level; usually a glass deflector is installed to prevent drafts

Casement window: with fixed glass section at bottom, two swing-out sections at top; crank-operated

Substantial airflow, but not directed well; drafts are difficult to avoid

Easily operated; shades can be drawn without obstruction when window is open (but they will billow in breeze); these windows must be placed carefully—there is danger of children running into them outdoors if open; rarely used in schools

Projected window: with fixed upper section of glass, vent (hopper type) at bottom opening in; crank-operated

Adequate airflow in most climates; well directed, not drafty

Easily operated, can be used with shades or blinds closed over most of its area; view is unobstructed, even when window is closed

Projected window: with sections opening out at top, in at bottom; crank-operated

Very good airflow, both in quantity and quality (not drafty)

Easily operated; does provide some ventilation even when partially shaded; view through this type is almost unhindered with few obstructions at eye level

Awning window: four horizontal sections project out; crank-operated

Large quantities of airflow are easily controlled, with fairly good draft control

Can be opened quite wide even during rainstorms; is easily operated; shades can be drawn without obstruction; framing does obstruct outdoor view somewhat whether window is open or closed

Sliding window with lower fixed section

Substantial airflow, but hard to control, drafty

No parts project either inward or outward when open, but window is sometimes difficult to slide with the usual schoolroom shelf at sill level

Combination window: upper section is of glass block, supported on angle and channel girts attached to columns; lower section is half fixed glass, and half hopper (crank-operated)

Adequate, well directed air flow for most climates

Some types of glass block refract light to ceiling, providing good light distribution across classroom and eliminating need for shades or blinds; however, designer must take care to use properly; this type does not always meet brightness tests for good schoolroom lighting

| TYPE | | DESCRIPTION |
|---|---|---|

## SIDE HINGED

### CASEMENT

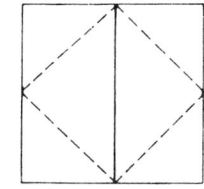

| | |
|---|---|
| **materials** | • wood, steel, aluminum |
| **use** | • common in residences and apartments |
| **operation** | • rotary crank or lever operators hold the vent open to desired position, up to 180°, but usually 90° |
| **note** | • available also as a single vent |
| | • generally allow exterior of glazing to be cleaned from inside when outswinging. |
| | • provide 100 percent opening in the ventilation area |
| | • will be subject to wind pressures when opened. |

### CASEMENT-HOPPER

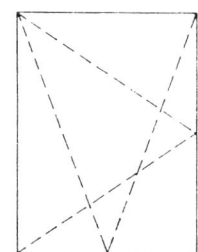

| | |
|---|---|
| **materials** | • wood, aluminum |
| **use** | • especially appropriate for high-rise, life safety installations |
| **operation** | • sophisticated hardware |
| **note** | • no protection from rain when open |
| | • available to limited extent as "tilt and turn" type which acts as a bottom hung window in normal use, but which can be converted by use of secondary hinges into a side-hung, inswinging type, allowing for easy cleaning. |

### CASEMENT-COMBINATION

| | |
|---|---|
| **materials** | • wood, aluminum, steel in varied quality grades |
| **use** | • commonly known as the "classroom window" |
| **operation** | • combination of in-swinging hopper and out-swinging casement vents offer flexibility for ventilation control |

## BOTTOM HINGED

### HOPPER

| | |
|---|---|
| **materials** | • wood, aluminum and steel |
| **use** | • where vent will not interfere with interior conditions |
| | • lower cost utility quality is commonly used for residential basements |
| **note** | • no protection from rain when open |

| TYPE | DESCRIPTION |
|------|-------------|

## BOTTOM HINGED, continued

**HOPPER-SPECIAL**

 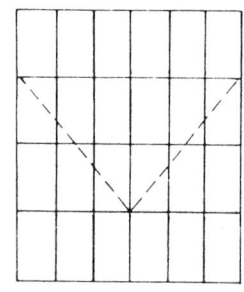

**materials** • steel, stainless steel
**use** • in commercial and industrial buildings where appearance is not of major importance and resistance to forced entry is
 • to prevent forcible exit; sometimes called "guard" windows
**operation** • combined with fixed lights or with projecting vents above, which offer high and low openings that are best for natural-air circulation (due to principles of stratification)
 • separate vent frames usually swing in as hoppers
 • jalousie-like vents also available
 • frames often reinforced with steel rods
**notes** • vents limited in size
 • muntins usually separate openings of 88 inches square

**HOPPER-MULTIPLE**

 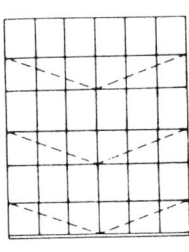

**materials** • steel
**use** • in housing for mental patients, to provide protection against exit while minimizing appearance of restraint
**note** • vents have a maximum clear opening of about 6 inches

## TOP HINGED

**AWNING**

 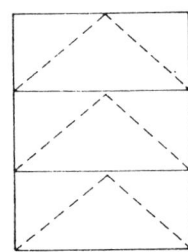

**materials** • wood, steel, aluminum
**use** • multiple assemblies are used mostly in steel for industrial buildings
 • separate units are commonly combined with fixed lights, or with hoppers for maximum stratification ventilation (These are available also in wood and aluminum.)
**operation** • are out-swinging projected windows that create a "canopy" against rain penetration
 • when in multiple, vertical stacks, the mechanical operation will allow for the bottom vent to open before the other vents, which will then open in unison

**PROJECTED**

 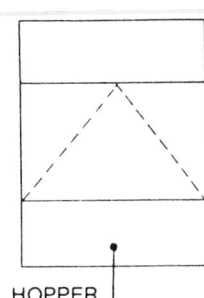

OPTIONAL HOPPER

**materials** • steel or aluminum
**use** • medium quality grade is called "intermediate" and is commonly used in commercial, institutional and industrial type buildings
 • architectural windows are frequently used for schools, hospitals, office buildings, etc.
**operation** • similar to awning windows but with optional fixed glass lights and/or hoppers.

**JALOUSIE**

**materials** • wood, steel, aluminum
**use** • primarily for sunrooms, porches, and the like where protection from the weather is desired with maximum fresh air
**operation** • multiple vents combine unobstructed vision with controlled ventilation
 • the louvers are fully adjustable and can be set in any position
**note** • can be fitted with storm sash on the inside to provide more weather tightness
 • screens, interchangeable with storm sash, are furnished
 • various types of glass, including obscure and colored, often are used for privacy or decoration

| TYPES | DESCRIPTION |
|---|---|

## GLIDING

### DOUBLE-HUNG

**materials** • wood, aluminum, steel in
different designs and weights to meet various service
requirements for all types of buildings

**use** • with combination of fixed windows for maximum window
openings
• use in buildings other than residential and light commercial
has been declining

**operation** • top and bottom openings optimize natural stratification
ventilation

**note** • also available in single-hung (only one sash operating) and
triple hung (three operable sash)

---

### SLIDING

**materials** • wood, aluminum (with various coatings and claddings)

**use** • mostly in residential buildings

**operation** • provide only one half of opening for ventilation;
• sash height to width ratio should not exceed 1 to 2 for good
operation

**note** • sash usually removable for cleaning and may be very large

---

### DUAL-VENT

**materials** • aluminum

**use** • mostly in hospitals

**operation** • essentially two sets of double-hung sash—air circulates
through the bottom outer sash and then through the top
inner sash

**note** • provides ventilation while protecting from rain and drafts
• check cost

---

## PIVOT

### VERTICAL PIVOT

**materials** • wood, aluminum and steel

**use** • mostly in air conditioned buildings

**operation** • consists of large vent, usually pivoted in the center of the
head and sill of the main frame, which rotates 180° or 360°
around its vertical axis for cleaning

**note** • not primarily designed for ventilation, although may be held
open up to 4'' with special hardware (unless unlocked by
maintenance personnel)

| TYPES | DESCRIPTION |
|---|---|

## PIVOT, continued

### HORIZONTAL PIVOT

 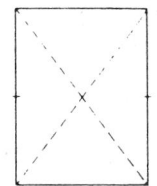

**operation** • similar to vertically pivoted but rotates around a horizontal axis

### INDUSTRIAL PIVOT

 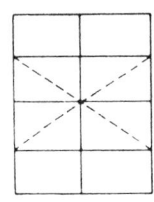

**materials** • steel, aluminum
**use** • often used horizontally and vertically to form entire walls
• lower cost for use in industrial and utilitarian buildings
**note** • mechanical operators are available

## SPECIAL

### CONTINUOUS

 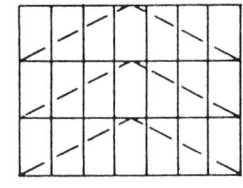

**materials** • steel
**use** • for top lighting and ventilation in monitor and sawtooth roof construction
**operation** • hinged at the top to the structural-steel framing members of the building and swing outward at the bottom
• two-floor lengths are connected end to end on the job
**note** • mechanical operators may be either manual or motor-powered

### AUSTRAL

 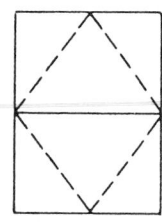

**materials** • wood and steel
**use** • schools, hospitals and other institutional buildings
• upper and lower sash counterbalanced on arms pivoted to frame
• upper and lower sash operate simultaneously
**note** • difficult to screen, shade or curtain

### REVERSIBLE

**materials** • wood and steel
**use** • residential and industrial buildings
**operation** • similar to double-hung in appearance, but may be tilted for better control of ventilation, or reversed for cleaning
**note** • not universally available

### CUSTOM TYPES
### VARIOUS CONFIGURATIONS

**materials** • aluminum, steel, stainless steel
**use** • special types for windows in houses of worship, mausoleums, and memorial buildings
**operation** • various arrangements available

1. Round Top
over casements

2. Full Round
with operating center

3. Round Top
with authentic divided lites

4. Separated
Round Top

5. Eyebrow
with Gothic divided lites

6. Round Top
over double-hung

7. Simulated
Round Top

8. Round Top
with quarter panes

9. Transom Round Top.

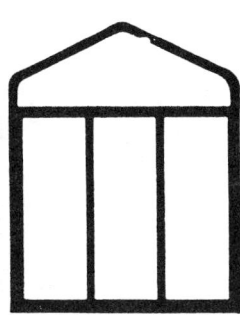

10. 3 point Round Top

11. Quarter Rounds

12. Round Top
over picture window

13. 12 foot Round Top
with decorative divided lites

14. Inverted
corners

15. 12 foot wide Round Top
with operating center

16. Ovals

17. Spider Web

18. Gothic head

19. Rounded casements

20. Rounded double
hung with Gothic
lite pattern.

# WINDOW TREATMENTS

**Window Types**

Two-light window,
the all-purpose window

Two-light window,
three lights over one light

Two-light window,
divided twelve lights

Two-light window, divided
sixteen lights

Two-light window,
six lights over one light

Two-light window,
four horizontal lights high

Two-light window,
six lights over nine

Two-light window, eight
lights over twelve

SASH OPG.

SASH OPG.

SASH OPG.

SASH OPG.

3"

**Typical styles of windows**

CASING
HEAD JAMB
HINGED SASH
SCREEN OR STORM SASH

*A*

SILL

*B*

SASH
SCREEN OR STORM SASH
SILL

*C*

**Fig. 1   Projected window. Cross sections:** *A*, head jamb; *B*, horizontal mullion; *C*, sill.

HEADER
DRIP CAP
CASING
HEAD JAMB
STORM SASH
SASH

*A*

GLASS
MUNTIN
PUTTY

*B*

SASH RAIL
STORM SASH
SILL

*C*

**Fig. 2   Stationary window. Cross sections:** *A*, head jamb; *B*, muntin; *C*, sill.

# WINDOW TREATMENTS

### Window Types: Double-Hung and Casement

**Fig. 3  Double-hung windows. Cross sections:** *A*, head jamb; *B*, meeting rails; *C*, side jamb; *D*, sill.

**Fig. 4  Outswinging casement sash. Cross sections:** *A*, head jamb; *B*, meeting styles; *C*, side jambs; *D*, sill.

**Fig. 5   Double-hung metal windows. Cross sections:** *A*, head; *B*, side jamb; *C*, sill.

**Fig. 6   Solid-section steel outswinging casement sash. Cross sections:** *A*, head jamb; *B*, side jamb; *C*, sill.

### Wood Trim

The casing around the window frames on the interior of the house should be the same pattern as that used around the interior door frames. Other trim which is used for a double-hung window frame includes the sash stops, stool, and apron (Fig. 7A). Another method of using trim around windows has the entire opening enclosed with casing (Fig. 7B). The stool is then a filler member between the bottom sash rail and the bottom casing.

The *stool* is the horizontal trim member that laps the window sill and extends beyond the casing at the sides, with each end notched against the plastered wall. The *apron* serves as a finish member below the stool. The window stool is the first piece of window trim to be installed and is notched and fitted against the edge of the jamb and the plaster line, with the outside edge being flush against the bottom rail of the window sash (Fig. 7A). The stool is blind-nailed at the ends so that the casing and the stop will cover the nailheads. Predrilling is usually necessary to prevent splitting. The stool should also be nailed at midpoint to the sill and to the apron with finishing nails. Face-nailing to the sill is sometimes substituted or supplemented with toenailing of the outer edge to the sill (Fig. 7A).

The casing is applied and nailed as described for doorframes, except that the inner edge is flush with the inner face of the jambs so that the stop will cover the joint between the jamb and casing. The window stops are then nailed to the jambs so that the window sash slides smoothly. Channel-type weather stripping often includes full-width metal sub-jambs into which the upper and lower sash slide, replacing the parting strip. Stops are located against these instead of the sash to provide a small amount of pressure. The apron is cut to a length equal to the outer width of the casing line (Fig. 7A). It is nailed to the window sill and to the 2- by 4-inch framing sill below.

When casing is used to finish the bottom of the window frame as well as the sides and top, the narrow stool butts against the side window jamb. Casing is then mitered at the bottom corners (Fig. 7B) and nailed as previously described.

**Fig. 7**  Installation of window trim: *A*, with stool and apron; *B*, enclosed with casing.

## CURTAINS

Curtains are soft window coverings that generally are shirred (gathered onto a rod) or have headings attached to solid-wood rods, round or oval metal rods, or café rods rather than cord-operated traverse rods. Curtains may be either stationary fabric panels or slid open and closed by hand. They are flexible in that they can be short or long, layered or tiered, or used alone or in combination with other soft, or with hard treatments. *Curtain* is traditionally a term for informal treatments, such as café curtains. However, curtains also may be quite formal, as are shirred and elegant tied-back fabric treatments.

Even though curtains are generally thought to be shirred treatments, other headings might be included in this category. Indeed, there is a crossover of terminology between draperies and curtains. Generally draperies are installed on cord-operated traverse rods, although they may be stationary pleated panels. Curtains may be installed on traverse rods (as in a pleated café curtain, for example), and headings such as the pencil pleat; drawstring pencil pleat; shirred, spaced pencil pleat; alternate pencil pleat; ruffled shirring tape heading; and smocked heading may be called either curtain or drapery treatments.

## DRAPERIES

Draperies are made with pleats. They are hung with drapery hoods onto carriers of conventional, architectural, or decorative traverse rods or into the rings of wood rods or café curtain rods; or they may thread onto spring-system traverse rods. Generally draperies are either hung straight to the floor or tied back. Thus they operate, or "draw," by opening and closing with a cord or a wand or by hand. The exception is tied-back draperies, which sometimes are let down at night. However, tied-back draperies are trained to tie back at an angle and therefore should not be handled to any extent. Draperies draw in a pair and meet in the center (center-meet) or draw one way from left to right or from right to left. One-way draw draperies require one-way traverse rods.

Draperies that hang at a doorway rather than at a window are called portières. They may be pleated in any fashion or shirred. They may be placed on a traverse rod, but historically (and they were used extensively in the Victorian era), they were tied-back stationary panels made of a heavy fabric that were let down when privacy or insulation was needed.

Draperies can be made of any fabric. The selection will depend on the style, use, and needs. Sheer fabrics do best as diffusers of glare and as providers of daytime privacy. Medium- to heavyweight fabrics are excellent choices for overdraperies and plain tieback draperies. Lining fabrics are the right weight for privacy liners or underdraperies. If a drapery is given a ruffled edge or a banding, that trim should be a lightweight, semi-crisp, flexible fabric, not a heavy, stiff fabric or a sheer, slippery fabric.

CROWN MOLDING @ CURTAIN POCKET

# WINDOW TREATMENTS

**Curtains/Draperies**

### TABLE 1 Draperies

| Period style | Fabric | Colors | Design | Upholstery fabrics |
|---|---|---|---|---|
| Early English Tudor Jacobean Charles II | Crewel, embroideries, hand-blocked linen, silk and worsted damask, velvet, brocade | Full-bodied crimson, green, and yellow | Large bold patterns: tree branch, fruits, flowers, oak leaf, animals, heraldic designs | Tapestry, leather, needlework, velvet, brocade |
| Anglo-Dutch William & Mary Queen Anne | Crewel, embroideries, hand-blocked linen, silk and worsted damask, velvet, brocade, India print | Full-bodied crimson, green, and yellow | Large bold patterns: tree branch, fruits, flowers, oak leaf, animals, heraldic designs | Tapestry, leather, needlework, velvet, brocade |
| Early Georgian Chippendale | Crewel, embroideries, hand-blocked linen, silk and worsted damask, velvet, brocade, Indian print | Full-bodied crimson, green, and yellow | Jacobean motifis, classic medallions and garlands | Tapestry, leather, needlepoint, velvet, brocade |
| Late Georgian Adam Hepplewhite Sheraton Empire Federal | Brocade, damask, chintz, taffeta, satin, toile de jouy | Delicate subdued hues of rose, yellow, mauve, green, and gray | Classic designs, small in scale: garlands, urns, floral, animals, etc. | Damask, brocade, velour, satin, petit point, leather in libraries |
| Louis XIV Louis XV Louis XVI | Silk, satin, damask, taffeta, muslin, brocade, toile de jouy | Delicate powder blue, oyster white, pearl, rose, pale greens, mauve, yellow | Stripes sprinkled with ribbons, flowers, medallions, lyres, and other classic motifs | Petit point, satin, moire, velour, chintz, damask, brocade, tapestry |
| Spanish renaissance | Velvet, damask, crewel, India print, printed and embroidered linen | Rich vigorous colors, red, green, and gold | Bold patterns in classic and heraldic designs; also arabesques | Leather, tapestry, velvet, linen, brocatelle |
| Early colonial | Crewel, embroideries, hand-blocked linen, silk and worsted damask, velvet, brocade | Full-bodied crimson, green, and yellow | Large bold patterns: tree branch, fruits, flowers, oak leaf, animals, heraldic designs | Tapestry, leather, needlepoint, velvet, brocade |
| Early American | Toile de jouy, damask, chintz, organdy, cretonne | All colors, but more subdued than in early period | Scenic, birds, animals, floral | Haircloth, mohair, linen, chintz, velours |
| Modern | Textured and novelty weaves, all fabrics | All colors, bright to pastel | Solid colors, modern designs, stripes | All fabrics, novelty weaves, plastics |
| French provincial | Chintz, cretonne, hand-blocked linen, velvet | Subdued colors, pastel shades | Screen prints, block prints | Solid colors, textured weaves, tapestry |
| Victorian | Velvet, brocade, damask | Turkey red, other rich colors | Solid colors, formal patterns | Haircloth, needlework |

18th-century colonial: tieback damask drapery with balled fringe

18th-century colonial: staggered tieback with plain edge asymmetric panels

18th-century colonial: swagged valance over bishop sleeve draperies over holdback

Federal: tieback panels with fringed raised valance of contrasting color

Federal: waterfall over holdback with draped valance

Federal: asymmetric tieback with fringed valance

Federal: heavy valance over straight draperies

# WINDOW TREATMENTS
Curtains/Draperies of Georgian and Directoire Periods

Georgian: tieback drapery with Austrian valance with fringes

Georgian: tieback heavy woven drapery with fabric-covered heading — sheer curtains behind

Georgian: tieback drapery with tapered French pleat heading

Late Georgian: curved fabric cartridge valance over holdback draperies

Late Georgian: gilt wood cornice over fixed lambrequins and sheer curtains

Late Georgian: gilt metal cornice over fixed tieback draperies and sheer curtains

Directoire: tieback draperies with contrasting edging on decorative brass rod

Directoire: fringed overdrapery valance on fringed sleeved tiebacks and fringed drapery

Directoire: painted stepped wood cornice over swag with twin cascades and tieback draperies

**Mid-19th-century Victorian: central swag with twin cascades over heavy draperies with braided tieback over sheer undercurtain**

**Late-19th-century Victorian: looped festoon over decorative brass rod**

**Late-19th-century Victorian: neo-Greek-style cornice with fringed valance over tieback fringed fabric with lace undercurtains**

**Fringed finger festoon over brackets
over straight line draperies with sheer
undercurtains**

**Fringed fabric valance with cascades over
bishop sleeve draperies**

Cafe curtains

Ruffled tieback curtains

Fringed segmented valance with ruffled trim
— tieback draperies over café curtains

Fabric-wrapped-pole draped valance

Café curtains with gathered valance and ball fringe trim

**Tieback draperies with ruffles on center arch rod — pleated shade beneath**

**High tieback draperies with ruffled multirow valance — woven shade beneath**

**Full-length straight draperies with ruffled valance — decorative bows**

**Shirred, ruffled balloon valance over ruffled, shirred heading on narrow rod**

**Shirred heading on brass pole — fixed draperies with rosette tieback**

**Shirred heading on brass pole — fixed panel draperies**

**Shirred balance with shirred tieback draperies over blinds**

**Penta balloon valance over ribbon tieback draperies**

**Shirred valance with horizontal accent banding — tieback draperies with matching edge banding**

**Bishop sleeve fringed-tip valance with ribbon tieback draperies**

**Triple-row fringed heading with shirred tieback draperies**

**Fabric-covered straight cornice over paired tieback draperies and scalloped curtain on brass rod**

**Pinch pleated draperies with horizontal tiebacks over standard roller shades**

# WINDOW TREATMENTS
Curtains/Draperies

Café curtains with scalloped edges on
brass rods

Single pleated draperies over paired double hung windows with tab
headed café curtains on rod

Fabric-covered cornice board valance — ribbon tiebacks on
drapery

Ruffled valance heading over brass rod with straight draperies
over scalloped café curtain

Simple traditional swag with
cascade draperies

Rosette tieback priscilla curtains
with continental heading

Scalloped café curtains on brass rod
with pleated valance

Bow tieback curtains with fringed trim
and gathered valance

Bow tieback gathered curtains
on brass rod

**Overlapping swag on rod with ball-fringed cascades**

**Swag with bow and assymmetric cascades**

**Symmetrical swags and cascades with center rosette**

**Symmetrical draped swag over brass rod**

**Asymmetrical swag drapery over brass rod with sheer curtain**

**Symmetrical draped swag on rod with ties at end over sheer or solid curtain**

**Triple-tail cascades with dual swags and rosette holds**

**Swag over rod with rosette holds**

**Swag, draped valance, cascading ends**

## WINDOW TREATMENTS

**Curtains/Draperies**

**Asymmetrical double-rod-supported swags and draperies —
contemporary**

**Symmetrical long cascades and swags with center swag
and bishop sleeve draperies**

**Overlapped double swag thrown over door-high holdbacks,
with draperies billowed at floor**

Flared cornice box with geometric trimmed
scallops over reverse swags and asymmetric
floor-tip cascades

Trimmed cornice box over asymmetric
tieback drapery

Symmetrical box-pleated draperies on brass rod with double-tiered rosette holdbacks

# WINDOW TREATMENTS
Curtains/Draperies

**Pleated shade**

**Miniblind — custom fitted**

**Wooden shutters**

**Rounded valance with drapery**

**Double swags with balloon drapery**

**Double swags with cascades and drapery**

**Shirred curtain with sunburst**

**Pleated shade with shirred curtain**

**French pleats with shaped top under curtain**

Semiformal box pleats, evenly spaced

Cartridge pleat, evenly spaced

Triple pleat heading, evenly spaced

Shirred heading on a narrow rod

Shirred heading gathering on a wide rod

Ruffled shirred heading on an extra- wide rod

Pencil heading on a wide rod

Shirred heading gathered on an extra-wide rod

Cluster heading, spaced evenly

Ruffled shirred heading on a narrow rod

Standard heading on a narrow rod

Spaced pencil pleats heading on a wide rod

# WINDOW TREATMENTS

**Headings**

**Triple shirred heading with ruffle gathered on 3 narrow rods**

**Decorative heading on a wide rod**

**Triple shirred heading gathered on 3 narrow rods**

**Grouped French pleats**

**Scalloped heading with rings and bows**

**Tab heading spaced evenly on rod**

**Scalloped heading with rings**

**Double butterfly pleat heading**

**Single butterfly pleat heading**

**French pleats with scalloped heading**

**Straight**

**Tapered**

**Banded**

**Tapered with welting**

**Oversized welting**

**Shirred with welting**

**Shirred with braided trim**

**Braided**

**Rosette**

**Fringed with welting**

**Scalloped**

**Frilled**

**Twin ruffles**

**Straight with scallops**

**Twin welting with box pleating**

**Rosette with cascade**

**Ruffles**

**Bow/ribbon**

**Bow with welting and tassel**

**Tapered with welting, rosette, and tassels**

1045

# WINDOW TREATMENTS

**Tiebacks and Holdbacks**

**Leaf motif**

**Decorative holdback**

**Scalloped with welting**

**Layered with pleats**

**Decorative with tassel**

**Decorative bow and ribbon**

**Square holdback with insert**

**Decorative knob with 2 inserts**

**Decorative knob holdback with tassel**

**Stylized rosette**

**Decorative knob with inserts**

**Decorative knob holdback with two tassels**

**Decorative bow holdback**

**Standard knob with cascade**

**Decorative knob with circular insert and cascade**

## MOUNTS

Flush mount — closed top

Outside mount — open top

Outside mount — closed side

Flush mount — open top

Outside mount — closed top

Inside mount bracket

## BRACKETS

Flush extra-projection bracket

Base-mounted extra-projection bracket

Curved bracket

Support bracket

Curved support bracket

Double rod bracket

## COUPLERS

Extra-projection base-mounted coupler

Base-mounted coupler

# WINDOW TREATMENTS
Finials, Rings, and Hooks

### FINIALS

### RINGS

Plain ring    Round eyelet ring    Oval eyelet ring    Square eyelet ring    Round clip-on ring    Oval clip-on ring    Rounded-end clip-on ring

### HOOKS

Metal and plastic hooks for standard tapes

Metal hooks for decorative tapes

Flat curtain rod

Double flat curtain rod

Cafe curtain rod

Fluted wood rod

Tension rod with adjustable screw

Sash rods

Separated curtain rod

Extra wide telescoping projection rod

Swinging arm separated rod

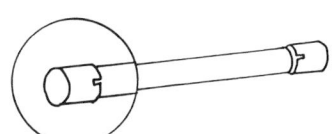

Polyvinyl chloride (PVC) with end caps
curtain rod

Wide telescoping curtain rod

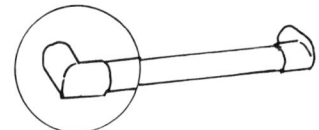

PVC pipe with elbows for projection

## WINDOW TREATMENTS

**Traverse Rods**

Conventional single hung traverse rod — A, projecting end brackets; B, end housing; C, telescoping rod; D, center support; E, master carriers; F, carriers; G, end bracket; H, cord; I, tension pulley

Double traverse rod

One-way traverse rod with two center supports

Double traverse rod with valence

**TABLE 2  Fabric Panel Widths and Pleating Guidelines**

| Desired pleated panel coverage | Flat fabric without hems | Hemmed flat fabric | Number of 4" flat spaces between pleats | Number of pleats | Width of fabric in each pleat |
|---|---|---|---|---|---|
| 16" | 43" | 39" | 4 | 5 | 3⅛" |
| 20" | 51" | 47" | 5 | 6 | 3¼" |
| 24" | 59" | 55" | 6 | 7 | 3⅜" |
| 28" | 67" | 63" | 7 | 8 | 3½" |
| 32" | 75" | 71" | 8 | 9 | 3½" |
| 36" | 83" | 79" | 9 | 10 | 3⁹⁄₁₆" |
| 40" | 91" | 87" | 10 | 11 | 3⅝" |
| 44" | 99" | 95" | 11 | 12 | 3⅝" |
| 48" | 107" | 103" | 12 | 13 | 3⅝" |
| 52" | 115" | 111" | 13 | 14 | 3⅝" |
| 56" | 123" | 119" | 14 | 15 | 3¾" |
| 60" | 131" | 127" | 15 | 16 | 3¾" |
| 64" | 139" | 135" | 16 | 17 | 3¾" |
| 68" | 147" | 143" | 17 | 18 | 3¾" |
| 72" | 155" | 151" | 18 | 19 | 3¾" |
| 76" | 163" | 159" | 19 | 20 | 3¾" |
| 80" | 171" | 167" | 20 | 21 | 3¾" |
| 84" | 179" | 175" | 21 | 22 | 3¾" |
| 88" | 187" | 183" | 22 | 23 | 3¾" |
| 92" | 195" | 191" | 23 | 24 | 3¾" |
| 96" | 203" | 199" | 24 | 25 | 3¾" |
| 100" | 211" | 207" | 25 | 26 | 3¾" |
| 104" | 219" | 215" | 26 | 27 | 3¾" |
| 108" | 227" | 223" | 27 | 28 | 3¾" |
| 112" | 235" | 231" | 28 | 29 | 3¾" |
| 116" | 243" | 239" | 29 | 30 | 3¾" |
| 120" | 251" | 247" | 30 | 31 | 3⅞" |
| 124" | 259" | 254" | 31 | 32 | 3⅞" |
| 128" | 267" | 263" | 32 | 33 | 3⅞" |

**TABLE 3  Rod Lengths Needed for Various Widths of Windows and Stackback Spaces**

| If the glass is | The stackback* should be | Your rod length and drapery coverage should be (add for overlaps and returns) |
|---|---|---|
| 38" | 26" | 64" |
| 44" | 28" | 72" |
| 50" | 30" | 80" |
| 56" | 32" | 88" |
| 62" | 34" | 96" |
| 68" | 36" | 104" |
| 75" | 37" | 112" |
| 81" | 39" | 120" |
| 87" | 41" | 128" |
| 94" | 42" | 136" |
| 100" | 44" | 144" |
| 106" | 46" | 152" |
| 112" | 48" | 160" |
| 119" | 49" | 168" |
| 125" | 51" | 176" |
| 131" | 53" | 184" |
| 137" | 55" | 192" |
| 144" | 56" | 200" |
| 150" | 58" | 208" |
| 156" | 60" | 216" |
| 162" | 62" | 224" |
| 169" | 63" | 232" |
| 175" | 65" | 240" |
| 181" | 67" | 248" |
| 187" | 69" | 256" |

*For one-way draws, deduct 7" from stackback.
*Note:* Figures are based on average pleating and medium-weight fabric. For extra bulky fabrics, add to stackback to compensate for the additional space they require.

# WINDOW TREATMENTS
Shades

Overlapping trimmed valance over scalloped shade

Banded valance over Roman shade

Shirred cornice box over tri-part balloon shade

Twin bow cloud shade with gathered heading

Inset flush Roman shade with horizontal folds

Tri-part Austrian shade with ruffled trim

Inset flush bottom pull Roman shade with horizontal folds

**Pleated shade**

**Crenellated edge**

**Shirred shade**

**Rolldown shade**

**Rolldown shade**

**Pulldown shade**

**Outside mount**

**Inside mount**

**Drapery style**

**Angle top**

**Cathedral canopy**

**Spring roller shade**

**Café curtain**

**Corner installation**

Fig. 8 Woven wood blinds. These blinds have horizontal or vertical reeds — long slats of wood from ¼ to 1 inch width — that are held together by decorative vertical yarns. They range in designs from those that are made mostly from exposed wood to those that are mainly yarns of several colors creating various interesting effects. Woven wood blinds can be used with many window treatments including draperies and café curtains, and such shade types as Roman-fold, spring-rolls, cord and pulley, and duo-fold. Top treatments include canopies, valances, and arches, while scallops, fringes, and trims are suitable for the bottom. Because woven wood blinds add color and texture to a window, they are particularly adaptable to the "natural" look in decorating.

Louvers: 1⅛",
2½", 3½", 4½";
thickness: 1¼";
width of stile: 2";
width: 8" to 36" in
¼" increments

Louvers: 1⅛",
2½", 3½", 4½";
thickness: 1¼";
width of stile: 2";
width: 8" to 36" in
¼" increments.

Louvers:
2½".

Fan top (nonadjustable
louvers); louvers: 2½";
thickness: 1¼".

Louvers: 2½"; thickness: 1¼".

Louvers: 2½"; thickness:
1¼".

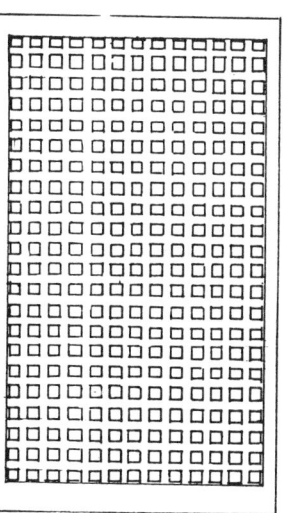

Louver grid. Standard:
4' x 8" unframed; standard
framing: 1¹⁄₁₆" wide x 2¼"
thick.

Traditional/Dixie panel;
louvers: 1¼"; thickness: 1⅛".

**Fig. 9**  Inside shutters can be used next to windows in place of curtains. Some are put under curtains or draperies; others are used café style either above or beneath café curtains. Shutters may be made from wood or metal. Natural wood tones are often used to enhance the beauty of the shutters. The inside section may be made from any of the following materials: fabric mesh, cane, grill cloth, or screening.

**STANDARD DOUBLE HUNG WINDOW**

Hanging hinges are mortised

Window Casement

Window stop Distance "A" MUST be 7/16" or greater for solid square fit. (see cross section below)

**CROSS SECTION OF LOUVER**
1-1/4" louver 1/4" to 1/8 taper

Louvers are attached to tilt control rail with coated pins for Extra strong hold.

Headrail 11/16"
1 of multiple dowel
upper louver light blind

Stile 13/16"x1-1/2"

1-1/4" louvers spaced on 1" centers.

1"

5/16"

Louver projection: 5/16" from back of panel

In the interest of space head and bottom rails are shown smaller in

Lower louver light blind
1 of multiple dowels
Bottom rail 11/16"

Bottom Rail

Predrilled light blind Hanging Stop showing mounting position on window stop behind shutters.

Installation surface on window stop MUST be 7/16" or greater (see distance "A" cross section below)

Heavy duty (0.050) offset brass finish hinge is adjustable up and down, left and right allowing for perfect alignment of shutters on any window

**CROSS SECTION     IMPORTANT:**
Distance "A" on window stop MUST be 7/16" or greater for solid, square installation of hanging stop.

Glass Pane

WINDOW SASH

3/4" x 5/8" Hanging Stop

2 X 4 STUD

2 X 4 STUB

SHEETROCK WALL

Measure to point X if window stop IS NOT removed

lock rail →

**2-panel single hung**

lock rail →

**2-panel single hung**

lock rail →

**Bi-fold single hung**

**Bi-fold double hung**

Bracket installs either inside casement on window stop moulding (see position a below) or on the outside of window casement (see positions b, c, or d)

Installation bracket 3"x3½"

Stop Moulding

POSITION a below shows bracket installed inside of the window casement (IBM). Distance "a" on stop moulding must measure 2 3/8" or greater for solid square fit.

POSITION a and c shows bracket installation on the face of casement (OBM).

POSITION d shows bracket installation on the wall beyond or above the casement. In this position bracket will allow 1/2" projection in order that blind will clear casement.

**CROSS SECTION OF TYPICAL DOUBLE HUNG WINDOW**

AUTHENTIC DOUBLE FLUTED WOODEN FASCIA HIDES ALL OPERATIONAL HARDWARE.

**FRONTVIEW:** Tiltor Hardware with long life wormgear.

Tiltor Cords

Authentic 2" Slats (select Alaskan yellow cedar) gracefully rounded at ends.

Authentic Wooden Tassels

Molded Wooden Bottom Rail matches Tilt Rail

Headrail/Tilt rail

Multi stop cord lock

Installation Bracket 3" projection x3½" height

1½"cotton web tape available in many traditional colors.

Lift Cord #4-½" cotton cord with nylon reinforced center.

1/2"

Bracket projection allows 1/2" clearance from behind blind.

3"

IBM measurement
OBM measurement
OBM measurement
OBM measurement

**STANDARD DOUBLE HUNG WINDOW**

Hanging hinges are mortised

Window Casement

Window stop Distance "A" MUST be 9/16" or greater for solid square fit. (see cross section below)

**CROSS SECTION OF LOUVER**
2-1/2"x3/8" Flat Louver with radius edges

Louvers are attached to tilt control rail with coated pins for Extra strong hold.

Headrail 15/16"
1 of multiple dowels
upper louver light blind
Stile 1-1/8"x2"

Bottom Rail

2-1/2" louvers spaced on 2" center
3/4"

Lower louver light blind
1 of multiple dowels
Bottom rail 15/16"

1-1/8"

Predrilled light blind Hanging Stop showing mounting position on window stop behind shutters.

Installation surface on window stop MUST be 9/16" or greater (see distance "A" cross section below)

Heavy duty (.065) offset brass finish hinge is adjustable up and down, left and right allowing for perfect alignment of shutters on any window.

**CROSS SECTION    IMPORTANT:** Distance "A" on window stop MUST be 9/16" or greater for solid, square installation of hanging stop.

Glass Pane

1-1/4" x 3/4" Hanging Stop

WINDOW SASH

Measure to point X if window stop IS NOT removed.
Measure to point Y if window stop IS removed.

# WINDOW TREATMENTS
Guidelines

## DECORATIVE RODS

### Measuring for Most Windows

**Outside mount** Decorative rods should be mounted on the wall. Measure width of glass; if total glass exposure is desired, add for stackback (see Table 4). Rods should be hung so that drapery headings (pleated tops of panels) are at least 4" above the glass, so they can't be seen from the outside.

### Figuring Stackback

Stackback is the amount of wall space needed if open panels are to clear the glass completely. This dimension, added to the window opening, gives you the proper rod length.

Begin by measuring the window opening, then consult Table 4. Find your opening measurement and read across for the right rod length.

### TABLE 4 Stackback: Average Pleating and Medium Weight Fabric

| Window opening | Stackback* | Rod length |
|---|---|---|
| 24" | 21" | 45" |
| 30" | 23" | 53" |
| 36" | 25" | 61" |
| 42" | 26" | 68" |
| 48" | 29" | 77" |
| 54" | 30" | 84" |
| 60" | 31" | 91" |
| 66" | 32" | 98" |
| 72" | 34" | 106" |
| 78" | 36" | 114" |
| 84" | 37" | 121" |
| 90" | 38" | 128" |
| 96" | 39" | 135" |
| 102" | 42" | 144" |
| 108" | 44" | 152" |
| 114" | 45" | 159" |
| 120" | 48" | 168" |

*Deduct 7" for one-way draw.

### Measuring for Special Windows

**Sliding doors** Measure as for outside mounted rod. Convert rod from two to one-way draw.

**Corner and bay windows** Decorative rods may be used at these windows. However, it is best to consult your dealer or designer about the measuring.

## Layered Treatments

Decorative traverse rods are often used for overtreatments. If the undertreatment is inside mounted or is an outside mounted mini-blind, pleated shade, Romanette woven wood or a cafe curtain, set the brackets for maximum clearance. Drapery returns will be 4½".

If you are using an undercurtain, you will want a utility curtain rod. It comes with its own bracket-supports.

If you are using underdraperies, double brackets are available. They hold both rods and automatically align the headings. Over-drapery returns will be 6" to 7".

If using a decorative rod over an outside mounted vertical blind or a woven wood shade other than Romanette, special brackets are available. Overdrapery returns will be 6" to 7".

## PLEATED SHADES

### Measuring for Most Windows

INSIDE MOUNT    OUTSIDE MOUNT

**Inside mount** Measure width at top, center and bottom. Use narrowest measurement. Shades will be made narrower to slip inside easily. Measure length from inside top of opening to sill. A 1⅝" deep recess is needed for flush mounting. 2¼" for Duette in ¾.

**Outside mount** Measure width of opening. Add at least 1½" on each side for overlap. Measure from top of frame to sill or 1½" below opening if there is no sill. (If brackets are to go above window frame, add an extra 1½" for bracket bases.)

**Ceiling mount** Measure desired width and length of blind. Overlap window openings by at least 1½" on each side.

### Measuring for Special Windows

**Multiple shades** At very wide or sectioned windows and at sliding doors, it's wise to use two shades hung from one headrail. Make a drawing of the window; include measurements of glass, woodwork and overall size. Your dealer will do the rest.

**Corner windows** Inside-mounted shades need no special measuring instructions. If outside or ceiling-mounted shades are used, they can be overlapped. Make a drawing of the windows; include measurements of glass, woodwork and overall size. Your dealer will do the rest.

**Other special windows** Bays and other unusual windows can frequently be fitted for pleated shades. Make a drawing of the window; include measurements of glass, woodwork and overall size. Or ask your dealer to do the measuring for you.

## Layered Treatments

Pleated shades are most often used with an undertreatment. If inside mounted, no extra projection is needed for the overtreatment. If outside mounted, the overtreatment must have a clearance of 2½" to clear the headrail. A cornice used over pleated shades should have a 4½" return.

STACK UP

### TABLE 5 Stack Chart

| Shade length | Stack |
|---|---|
| 24" | 1¾" |
| 36" | 1⅞" |
| 48" | 2" |
| 60" | 2⅛" |
| 72" | 2¼" |
| 84" | 2⅜" |
| 96" | 2½" |

Measurements are from top of headrail to bottom of bottom rail.

## CONVENTIONAL TRAVERSE RODS

### Measuring for Most Windows

**Outside or ceiling mount** Conventional rods may be mounted on the wall or ceiling. Measure the width of glass; if total glass exposure is desired, add for stackback (see Table 4). Rods should be hung so that drapery headings (pleated tops of panels) are at least 4" above the glass, so they can't be seen from the outside.

### Figuring Stackback

Stackback is the amount of wall space needed if open panels are to clear the glass completely. This dimension, added to the window opening, gives you the proper rod length.

Begin by measuring the window opening, then consult Table 4. Find your opening measurement and read across the right rod length.

### Measuring for Special Windows

**Sliding doors** Measure as for outside mounted rod. Use a one-way draw rod.

**Corner and bay windows** Measure each window as if it were set flat into the wall. At corners, run one rod into the corner and butt the other into it. At bays, butt all rods. Use either one or two-way draw rods for corners. For bays, use three two-way rods or two one-ways with a two-way in the center.

CORNER WINDOW

BAY WINDOW

## Layered Treatments

Conventional traverse rods come in sets specifically for layered treatments. If you are using an undercurtain, you will want a traverse and plain rod set; both rods are on one set of brackets. Overdrapery returns will be 4½" to 5½".

If you are using underdraperies, use a double traverse rod set. Again, one set of brackets holds both rods. Overdrapery returns will be 5½" to 6½".

If the undertreatment is inside mounted or is an outside mounted mini-blind, pleated shade, Romanette woven wood or a cafe curtain, use a single rod and set the brackets for maximum clearance. Drapery returns will be 4½".

If the undertreatment is an outside-mounted vertical blind or a woven wood shade other than Romanette, special extender plates for brackets and supports are available. Overdrapery returns will be 5½" to 6½".

Remember, whenever you change the clearance of the brackets, you also change the drapery return.

## VERTICAL BLINDS

### Measuring for Most Windows

INSIDE MOUNT

OUTSIDE MOUNT

**Inside mount** Measure width at top, center and bottom. Use narrowest measurement. Verticals will be made slightly narrower to slip inside easily. Measure length from inside top of opening to sill. A minimum 3¼" recess is required for track; 4½" if open vanes are to be flush with front of opening.

**Outside mount** Measure width of opening. Add for stackback (see Tables 6 and 7). Measure from a point 2½" above top of frame to sill or floor; deduct ¾" for clearance.

Minimum projection of front of vane from wall is 5"; maximum is 6½". Minimum clearance of back of vane from wall is 1"; maximum is 2½".

**Ceiling mount** Measure desired width and length of verticals; deduct at least ¾" for floor clearance.

**Cirmosa 2000** Ask your designer, decorator, or store to measure for you.

## Measuring for Special Windows

**Sliding doors** Use a one-way draw. Measure width from trim to trim. Add to this measurement desired extra width for overlap beyond door. If total glass exposure is desired, also add for stackback (see Tables 6 and 7). Measure from a point 2½" above door trim to floor; deduct ¾" for clearance.

## Layered Treatments

When layered, verticals are most often used as an undertreatment. If inside mounted, no extra clearance is needed for the overtreatment. If outside mounted, the overtreatment must have a clearance of 6" to clear the open vanes. A cornice used over verticals should have a 6" return.

## Figuring Stackback

Stackback is the amount of wall space needed if open verticals are to clear the glass completely. This dimension, added to the window opening, gives you the proper track length.

Begin by measuring the window opening, then consult Table 6 or 7 for the type of treatment you desire — one- or two-way draw. Find your opening measurement and read across for the right track. *(Note: Stackback figure for two-way draw is total stack; one-half of this is on each side of the window.)*

If your window opening is somewhere in between the measurements in the tables, go to the next smallest opening. Add the stackback listed there to your opening dimension.

**TABLE 6  Two-Way Draw Stackback**

| Window opening | Stackback | Track |
|---|---|---|
| 24" | 9" | 33" |
| 30" | 10" | 40" |
| 36" | 11" | 47" |
| 42" | 12" | 54" |
| 48" | 14" | 62" |
| 54" | 15" | 69" |
| 60" | 16" | 76" |
| 66" | 17" | 83" |
| 72" | 19" | 91" |
| 78" | 20" | 98" |
| 84" | 21" | 105" |
| 90" | 22" | 112" |
| 96" | 23" | 119" |
| 102" | 25" | 127" |
| 108" | 26" | 134" |
| 114" | 27" | 141" |
| 120" | 29" | 149" |

**TABLE 7  One-Way Draw Stackback**

| Window opening | Stackback | Track |
|---|---|---|
| 24" | 7" | 31" |
| 30" | 8" | 38" |
| 36" | 9" | 45" |
| 42" | 11" | 53" |
| 48" | 12" | 60" |
| 54" | 13" | 67" |
| 60" | 14" | 74" |
| 66" | 15" | 81" |
| 72" | 17" | 89" |
| 78" | 18" | 96" |
| 84" | 19" | 103" |
| 90" | 20" | 110" |
| 96" | 21" | 117" |
| 102" | 22" | 124" |
| 108" | 23" | 131" |
| 114" | 25" | 139" |
| 120" | 26" | 146" |

## MINI BLINDS

### Measuring for Most Windows

**Inside mount** Measure width at top, center and bottom. Use narrowest measurement. Blinds will be made slightly narrower to slip inside easily. Measure length from inside top of open to sill. A 1⅜" deep recess is needed for flush mounting of Mono-Rail minis; however, a difference of ¼" is not objectionable.

**Outside mount** Measure height and width of area to be covered. It is recommended that blinds overlap window opening by at least 1½" on each side. Measure from top of frame to sill or 1½" below opening if there is no sill.

INSIDE MOUNT

OUTSIDE MOUNT

**Ceiling mount** Measure desired width and length of blind. Overlap window openings by at least 1½" on each side.

**TABLE 8  Stack Chart**

| Blind length | Mini stack | Micro stack |
|---|---|---|
| 36" | 3" | 3¼" |
| 48" | 3½" | 3¾" |
| 60" | 4" | 4¼" |
| 72" | 4¼" | 4¾" |
| 84" | 4¾" | 5¼" |
| 96" | 5¼" | 5¾" |
| 108" | 5½" | 6¼" |

Measurements are from top of headrail to bottom of bottomrail.

# ELEVATORS
## Elevator Types and Planning

### ELEVATOR TYPES

*Hydraulic:* For low-rise buildings — speeds up to 200 ft/min. Ideal where design limitations preclude overhead supports and machine rooms. Economical to install and maintain; no penthouse or load-bearing walls required.

*Geared traction:* For low- to medium-rise buildings — speeds up to 400 ft/min. Recommended for all types of buildings where higher speeds are not essential.

*Gearless traction:* Recommended for high-rise applications requiring the ultimate in service — speeds of 500 ft/min and up.

### ELEVATOR PLANNING

#### Starting Point Recommendations for All Types of Buildings

When preparing schematics for a particular type of building, select the quantity, capacity, and speed from one of Tables 1 to 4 and keep in mind that generally speaking:

- Passenger elevators should be wide and shallow with center-opening or single slide doors.
- Service elevators should be narrow and deep with two-speed doors.
- Combination passenger/service elevators should be almost square with either center-opening or two-speed center-opening doors.
- Freight elevator size and shape should be determined by the dimensions of goods to be carried and by the loading/unloading methods used. Doors should be of the vertical bi-parting type.

The data contained in Tables 1 to 4 are based upon the following criteria.

**Office buildings** 100 square feet per person; an interval of 30 sec.; net rentable area = 80% of gross area; 5 minute carrying capacity of 12% of building population; typical floor heights were estimated at 12' and the main floor at 18'. When the building exceeds 250,000 square feet total, it is suggested that consideration be given to the use of separate freight elevators which are not included in Table 1.

**Hospitals** 5 minute vehicular demand = .04 × the number of beds; interval of 35–50 seconds for vehicular traffic; visitor and staff population = 3 × number of beds; 5 minute carrying capacity equal to 12% of building population.

**Hotels** Registration during conventions = 1.5 × the total number of rooms; maximum 1 hour peak is 1.15 × total registrations; 5 minute carrying capacity = 10% of total 1 hour peak load.

**Apartments** Population est. @ 2 persons per bedroom; 5 minute carrying capacity of 7%; maximum waiting interval of 60–90 seconds; average of 9'0" floor height. Further, Table 4 applies only for average or middle income apartments. For applications beyond the scope of the table such as local-express arrangements, luxury apartment buildings and other considerations, please consult your local elevator company representative.

*Note:* If a restaurant or general assembly area is located in your building (on any but the main floor) and is not served by a separate elevator, the information contained in Tables 1 to 4 may not apply.

**TABLE 1 Office Buildings — Passenger Elevators Only**

| Number of Floors, Including Main | GROSS SQUARE FOOTAGE/FLOOR | | | |
|---|---|---|---|---|
| | 5000 Sq. Ft. | 8000 Sq. Ft. | 12000 Sq. Ft. | 16000 Sq. Ft. |
| 5 floors | 2 Elev. 2500# @ 250 fpm | 2 Elev. 2500# @ 250 fpm | 3 Elev. 2500# @ 250 fpm | 3 Elev. 2500# @ 300 fpm |
| 6 to 8 floors | 3 Elev. 2500# @ 350 fpm | 3 Elev. 2500# @ 350 fpm | 3 Elev. 2500# @ 400 fpm | 4 Elev. 2500# @ 400 fpm |
| 9 to 12 floors | 4 Elev. 2500# @ 400-500 fpm | 4 Elev. 2500# @ 400-500 fpm | 4 Elev. 3000# @ 500 fpm | 5 Elev. 3500# @ 600 fpm |
| 13 to 15 floors | 4 Elev. 2500# @ 600 fpm | 4 Elev. 2500# @ 600 fpm | 5 Elev. 3000# @ 700 fpm | 6 Elev. 3500# @ 700 fpm |
| 16 to 19 floors | 5 Elev. 2500# @ 700 fpm | 6 Elev. 2500# @ 700 fpm | * | * |
| 20 to 22 floors | 5 Elev. 2500# @ 800 fpm | 6 Elev. 3000# @ 800 fpm | * | * |

* Because of the complexities such as local and express arrangements and service requirements inherent in taller and larger buildings, we suggest you contact your Armor representative when the limitations of this chart are exceeded.

**TABLE 2 Hospitals**

| Number of Floors | BEDS/FLOOR | | | |
|---|---|---|---|---|
| | Up to 20 Beds | 21 to 30 Beds | 31 to 40 Beds | 41 to 50 Beds |
| Up to 6 Floors | 3 Elev. 4500# @ 200 fpm | 4 Elev. 2-3000# @ 300 fpm 2-4500# @ 300 fpm | 5 Elev. 2-3000# @ 350 fpm 3-4500# @ 350 fpm | 5 Elev. 2-3000# @ 350 fpm 3-4500# @ 350 fpm |
| 7 to 9 floors | 6 Elev. 3-3000# @ 500 fpm 3-4500# @ 500 fpm | 7 Elev. 3-3000# @ 500 fpm 4-4500# @ 500 fpm | 8 Elev. 4-3000# @ 500 fpm 4-4500# @ 500 fpm | 9 Elev. 4-3000# @ 500 fpm 5-4500# @ 500 fpm |
| 10 to 12 floors | 7 Elev. 3-3000# @ 500 fpm 4-4500# @ 500 fpm | 8 Elev. 4-3000# @ 500 fpm 4-4500# @ 500 fpm | 9 Elev. 4-3000# @ 500 fpm 5-4500# @ 500 fpm | 10 Elev. 4-3000# @ 500 fpm 6-4500# @ 500 fpm |

NOTE: The number of elevators listed above will most likely be reduced if automatic cart and/or container handling equipment for food. laundry, surgical instrument and central supply distribution is used.

**TABLE 3 Hotel Buildings — Passenger Elevators Only**

| Number of Floors | UNITS/FLOOR | | | |
|---|---|---|---|---|
| | Up to 14 Units | 15 to 20 Units | 21 to 28 Units | 29 to 32 Units |
| 4 to 5 floors | 2 Elev. 3000# @ 150 fpm | 2 Elev. 3000# @ 175 fpm | 2 Elev. 3000# @ 200 fpm | 2 Elev. 3000# @ 200 fpm |
| 6 to 9 floors | 2 Elev. 3000# @ 300 fpm | 2 Elev. 3000# @ 350 fpm | 2 Elev. 3000# @ 400 fpm | 3 Elev. 3000# @ 300 fpm |
| 10 to 12 floors | 3 Elev. 3000# @ 300 fpm | 3 Elev. 3000# @ 350 fpm | 4 Elev. 3000# @ 350 fpm | 4 Elev. 3000# @ 350 fpm |
| 13 to 15 floors | 4 Elev. 3000# @ 350 fpm | 4 Elev. 3000# @ 350 fpm | 4 Elev. 3000# @ 350 fpm | 4 Elev. 3000# @ 350 fpm |
| 16 to 20 floors | 4 Elev. 3000# @ 350 fpm | 4 Elev. 3000# @ 400 fpm | 4 Elev. 3000# @ 400 fpm +1 Service 3500# @ 400 fpm | 4 Elev. 3000# @ 400 fpm +2 Service 3500# @ 400 fpm |

NOTE: Because of the complexities such as local and express and service requirements inherent in taller and larger hotels, we suggest that you contact your Armor representatives when the limitations of this chart are exceeded.

**TABLE 4 Apartment Buildings — Passenger Elevators Only**

| Number of Floors Including Main | BEDROOMS/FLOOR | | | |
|---|---|---|---|---|
| | 10 Bedrooms | 16 Bedrooms | 22 Bedrooms | 30 Bedrooms |
| 6 floors | 1 Elev. 2000# @ 150 fpm | 1 Elev. 2000# @ 150 fpm | 2 Elev. 2000# @ 150 fpm | 2 Elev. 2000# @ 150 fpm |
| 12 floors | 2 Elev. 2000# @ 200 fpm | 2 Elev. 2000# @ 200 fpm | 2 Elev. 2500# @ 250 fpm | 3 Elev. 2500# @ 250 fpm |
| 18 floors | 3 Elev. 2000# @ 350 fpm | 3 Elev. 2000# @ 350 fpm | 3 Elev. 2500# @ 350 fpm | 4 Elev. 2500# @ 350 fpm |
| 25 floors | 3 Elev. 2500# @ 400 fpm | 3 Elev. 2500# @ 400 fpm | 4 Elev. 2500# @ 400 fpm | * |
| 32 floors | 3 Elev. 2500# @ 500 fpm | 4 Elev. 2500# @ 500 fpm | * | * |
| 40 floors | 4 Elev. 2500# @ 700 fpm | * | * | * |

## HYDRAULIC ELEVATORS

Ideal for use in buildings up to six floors. Supported and raised by a powerful hydraulic plunger, the Oildraulic is renowned for smooth performance, quiet operation, and accurate floor leveling. And since it's supported from below, no vertical load is placed on the building. That means hoistways can be of lighter construction and no penthouse is needed. The machine room can be located nearly anywhere to let you maintain a flat roof line *and* save money on construction.

HOISTWAY PLAN

RIGHT HAND DOOR SHOWN; LEFT HAND AVAILABLE

### RECOMMENDED SIZES AND CAPACITIES

| TYPE BUILDING | APART-MENT | AVERAGE OFFICE/HOTEL | | LARGE OFFICE/STORE | |
|---|---|---|---|---|---|
| MODEL | FLEET-WOOD 21-H | PLAN 1 MARQUIS-25 | PLAN 2 MARQUIS-25 | SEVILLE-30 | SEVILLE-35 |
| CAPACITY (IN POUNDS) | | | | | |
| DIMENSIONS | 2100 ♿ | 2500 ♿ | 2500 ♿ | 3000 ♿ | 3500 ♿ |
| A[1] | 5'-8" | 6'-8" | 6'-8" | 6'-8" | 6'-8" |
| B[1] | 4'-3" | 4'-3" | 4'-3½" | 4'-9" | 5'-5" |
| C | – | 3'-6" | 3'-6" | 3'-6" | 3'-6" |
| D[2] | 7'-4" | 8'-4" | 8'-4" | 8'-4" | 8'-4" |
| E | 5'-9" | 5'-9" | 6'-8¾" | 6'-3" | 6'-11" |
| F | 15'-0" | 17'-0" | 17'-0" | 17'-0" | 17'-0" |
| G | 3'-0" | 3'-6" | 3'-6" | 3'-6" | 3'-6" |

[1] Inside dimensions.
[2] Single car dimensions.
♿ These models meet minimum size for handicapped use.
   Hoistway dimensions are based on no provisions for seismic conditions and 8'-0" O.A. nominal cab height.
   Standard speeds available: 75, 100, 125 150 FPM.

**POWER UNIT (MACHINE) LOCATION:** The most desirable machine room location is on the lowest floor, adjacent to the elevator hoistway. It may, however, be located remote from hoistway if necessary. Typical size for one-car installation: 7'-10" x 5'-6" x 8'-0" high; for two cars: 10'-9" x 6'-6" x 8'-0" high. Enclosure to meet local code requirements must be provided. A sound-isolated machine room is recommended for quietest operation. Adequate heating and ventilation of machine spaces must be provided.

### TRACTION ELEVATORS

For use in buildings over six floors. They can serve up to 27 landings and can be used in office buildings, apartment complexes, dormitories, hotels, and other structures. These elevators can travel up to 1000 ft/min and are ideal for high-rise buildings of all kinds.

TEMPERATURE RANGE:
50°F MIN.
90°F MAX. TRAFLOMATIC
100°F MAX. COMPUTAMATIC

4" SLAB
BY OWNER

MACHINE BEAMS BELOW SLAB BY ELEVATOR CONTRACTOR³

LADDER TO PIT
BY OWNER

■ 8'-6" COMPUTAMATIC®
7'-6" TRAFLOMATIC

HOISTWAY PLAN

RIGHT HAND DOOR SHOWN: LEFT HAND AVAILABLE

| RECOMMENDED SIZES AND CAPACITIES | | | | |
|---|---|---|---|---|
| TYPE BUILDING | SMALL OFFICE/ APARTMENT | AVERAGE OFFICE/HOTEL | LARGE OFFICE/STORE | |
| MODEL | SPF21-H ♿ | SPF25 ♿ | SPF30 ♿ | SPF35 ♿ |
| CAPACITY (IN POUNDS) | | | | |
| DIMENSIONS | 2100 | 2500 | 3000 | 3500 |
| A[1] | 5'-8" | 6'-8" | 6'-8" | 6'-8" |
| B[1] | 4'-3" | 4'-3" | 4'-9" | 5'-5" |
| C | – | 3'-6" | 3'-6" | 3'-6" |
| D[2] | 7'-4" | 8'-4" | 8'-4" | 8'-4" |
| E | 6'-8" | 6'-8" | 7'-2" | 7'-10" |
| F | 15'-0" | 17'-0" | 17'-0" | 17'-0" |
| G | 3'-0" | 3'-6" | 3'-6" | 3'-6" |

[1] Inside dimensions
[2] Single car dimensions
♿ These models meet minimum size for handicapped use.

Hoistway dimensions are based on 1" out of plumb, no provisions for seismic conditions, and no occupied space below hoistway. If these conditions cannot be met, then consideration must be given for additional required space.

| MINIMUM PIT, OVERHEAD, MACHINE ROOM DIMENSIONS | | | | |
|---|---|---|---|---|
| CAPACITY (IN LBS.) | DIMENSIONS | SPEED (FEET PER MINUTE) | | |
| | | 200 | 350 | 450 |
| 2100 | L | 16'-0" | 16'-0" | – |
| | O | 15'-4" | 15'-4" | – |
| | P[4] | 5'-0" | 5'-0" | – |
| 2500 | L | 16'-0" | 16'-0" | 16'-0" |
| | O | 15'-4" | 15'-4" | 16'-4" |
| | P[4] | 5'-0" | 5'-0" | 6'-6" |
| 3000 | L | 16'-0" | 16'-0" | 16'-0" |
| | O | 15'-4" | 16'-0" | 16'-4" |
| | P[4] | 5'-0" | 5'-0" | 6'-6" |
| 3500 | L | 16'-0" | 16'-0" | 16'-0" |
| | O | 15'-4" | 16'-0" | 17'-6" |
| | P[4] | 5'-0" | 5'-0" | 6'-6" |

Overhead "O" based on 8'-0" O.A. nominal cab height.
[3] Machine beams designed per ANSI/ASME code A17.1 and does not include floor weight and loads on floor.
[4] 6'-0" min. "P"  travel above 250'-0" SPF21 SPF25 ⎫
travel above 225'-0" SPF30       ⎬ for speeds up to 350 F/M
travel above 200'-0" SPF35       ⎭

## HOISTWAY PLAN

RIGHT HAND DOOR SHOWN: LEFT HAND AVAILABLE

HOIST BEAM BY OWNER

TEMPERATURE RANGE:
50°F MIN.
90°F MAX. TRAFLOMATIC
100°F MAX. COMPUTAMATIC

4" SLAB BY OWNER

MACHINE BEAMS BELOW SLAB BY ELEVATOR CONTRACTOR⁴

LADDER TO PIT BY OWNER

■ 8'-6" COMPUTAMATIC•
7'-6" TRAFLOMATIC

### RECOMMENDED SIZES AND CAPACITIES

| TYPE BUILDING | SMALL OFFICE/APARTMENT | | AVERAGE OFFICE/HOTEL | | LARGE OFFICE/STORE | |
|---|---|---|---|---|---|---|
| **DIMENSIONS** | CAPACITY (IN POUNDS) | | | | | |
| | 2000 ⚹ | 2100 ⚹ | 2500 ⚹ | 3000 ⚹ | 3500 ⚹ | 4000 ⚹ |
| A[1] | 6'-0" | 5'-8" | 6'-8" | 6'-8" | 6'-8" | 7'-8" |
| B[1] | 3'-7" | 4'-3" | 4'-3" | 4'-9" | 5'-5" | 5'-5" |
| C | 3'-0" | — | 3'-6" | 3'-6" | 3'-6" | 4'-0" |
| D[2] | 7'-8" | 7'-4" | 8'-4" | 8'-4"▲ | 8'-4"▲ | 9'-4"▲ |
| E[3] | 6'-0" | 6'-8" | 6'-8" | 7'-2" | 7'-10" | 7'-10" |
| F | 15'-8" | 15'-0" | 17'-0" | 17'-0"• | 17'-0"• | 19'-0"• |
| G | — | 3'-0" | 3'-6" | 3'-6" | 3'-6" | 4'-0" |

[1] Inside dimensions  [2] Single car dimensions  [3] Add 3" when speed = 500 FPM or above
▲ Add 2" when speed = 1000 FPM  • Add 4" when speed =1000 FPM

Hoistway dimensions are based on 1" out of plumb, no provisions for seismic conditions, and no occupied space below hoistway. If these conditions cannot be met then consideration must be given for additional required space.

### MINIMUM PIT, OVERHEAD, MACHINE ROOM DIMENSIONS

| CAPACITY (IN LBS.) | DIMENSIONS | SPEED (FEET PER MINUTE) | | | | | | |
|---|---|---|---|---|---|---|---|---|
| | | 200 | 350 | 450 | 500 | 700 | 800 | 1000 |
| 2000 | L | 16'-0" | 16'-0" | 16'-0" | | | | |
| | O | 15'-4" | 15'-4" | 16'-4" | | | | |
| | P[5] | 5'-0" | 5'-0" | 6'-6" | | | | |
| 2100 | O | 16'-0" | 16'-0" | 16'-0" | | | | |
| | O | 15'-4" | 15'-4" | 16'-4" | | | | |
| | P[5] | 5'-0" | 5'-0" | 6'-6" | | | | |
| 2500 | L | 16'-0" | 16'-0" | 16'-0" | 16'-6" | 16'-6" | | |
| | O | 15'-4" | 15'-4" | 16'-4" | 18'-6" | 20'-6" | | |
| | P[5] | 5'-0" | 5'-0" | 6'-6" | 10'-1" | 11'-5" | | |
| 3000 | L | 16'-0" | 16'-0" | 16'-0" | 17'-0" | 17'-0" | 18'-0" | 18'-0" |
| | O | 15'-4" | 16'-0" | 16'-4" | 18'-6" | 20'-6" | 20'-6" | 20'-0" |
| | P[5] | 5'-0" | 5'-0" | 6'-6" | 10'-1" | 11'-5" | 11'-6" | 11'-6" |
| 3500 4000 | L | 16'-0" | 16'-0" | 16'-0" | 17'-0" | 17'-0" | 18'-0" | 18'-0" |
| | O | 15'-4" | 16'-0" | 17'-6" | 18'-6" | 20'-6" | 20'-6" | 20'-6" |
| | P[5] | 5'-0" | 5'-0" | 6'-6" | 10'-1" | 11'-5" | 11'-6" | 11'-6" |

NOTE: These dimensions are for general application to custom designed elevators.
Overhead "O" based on 8'-0" O.A. nominal cab height.
⁴ Machine beams designed per ANSI/ASME code A17.1 and does not include floor weight and loads on floor.

## CENTER-OPENING DOORS

These permit quickest entry and exit, thus speeding elevator service, and provide an attractive balanced appearance both in the hallway and inside the elevator car. They should always be used in high-speed applications.

REFER TO "D" DIM. ON APPROPRIATE HOISTWAY PLAN.

SPACE REQUIRED 2H + 9"=J

$\frac{J-C}{2}$   C   $\frac{J-C}{2}$

C
FRAME OPENING

DETAIL 2 (TYP.)          DETAIL 2 (TYP.)

NOTE: H=opening in 2" increments only (use next higher even dimension for odd size door).
C=actual frame opening

## TWO-SPEED SLIDING DOORS

Doors of this type provide the widest possible opening width for small cars but do not afford the entry and exit speed of center-opening doors. The two doors move in the same direction, one sliding behind the other.

REFER TO "D" DIM. ON APPROPRIATE HOISTWAY PLAN.

SPACE REQUIRED 1½H + 14"=J

J−C−9½"   C   9½"

C
FRAME OPENING

DETAIL 2 (TYP.)          DETAIL 3 (TYP.)

Right hand entrance shown. Left hand available where required.

NOTE: H=opening in 2" increments only (use next higher even dimension for odd size door).
C=actual frame opening

## SINGLE SLIDING DOORS

This is the most economical type of elevator door, and also the slowest. The single door moves either to right or left from one side of the elevator car, the opening being limited by the width of the door and car.

REFER TO "D" DIM. ON APPROPRIATE HOISTWAY PLAN.

SPACE REQUIRED 2H + 14½"=J

J−C−9½"   C   9½"

C
FRAME OPENING

DETAIL 2 (TYP.)          DETAIL 3 (TYP.)

Right hand entrance shown. Left hand available where required.

NOTE: H=opening in 2" increments only (use next higher even dimension for odd size door).
C=actual frame opening

VERTICAL SECTION
(TYPICAL)

* FOR ALTERNATE SILL SUPPORT- (See Detail 4) MINIMUM FLOOR HEIGHT EQUALS FRAME OPENING PLUS 1'-1" + S

8'-6" MIN. (FLOOR TO FLOOR HEIGHT*)

7'-0" FRAME OPENING

2"

DETAIL 1 (TYP.)

DETAIL 4 (TYP.)

## DRYWALL CONSTRUCTION

3 1/2" MINIMUM

DETAIL 1

2"

DETAIL 2          DETAIL 3

3 1/2" MIN.          3 1/2" MIN.

2"          2"

**NOTE:** These diagrams show minimum wall thickness and construction detail required in order to supply UL Label on entrances with no cutouts.

## MASONRY CONSTRUCTION

VARIES

DETAIL 1

2"

DETAIL 2          DETAIL 3

VARIES          VARIES

2"          2"

### DETAIL 4 — SILL SUPPORTS

4"

4" x 4" x 3/8" ANGLE

2"

ROUGH SILL LINE
**RECOMMENDED**

4"

2"
S

ROUGH SILL LINE
**ALTERNATE**

*CENTER OPENING AND SINGLE SLIDING DOORS*

5-1/2"

5" x 5" x 3/8" ANGLE

2"

ROUGH SILL LINE
**RECOMMENDED**

5-1/2"

2"
S

ROUGH SILL LINE
**ALTERNATE**

*TWO-SPEED DOORS*

**Floor plan of elevator cars** The floor area of elevator cars shall provide space for wheelchair users to enter the car, maneuver within reach of controls, and exit from the car. Acceptable door opening and inside dimensions shall be as shown in Fig. 1. The clearance between the car platform sill and the edge of any hoistway landing shall be no greater than 1¼ in (32 mm).

**Illumination levels** The level of illumination at the car controls, platform, and car threshold and landing sill shall be at least 5 footcandles (53.8 lux).

**Car controls** Elevator control panels shall have the following features:

1. Buttons. All control buttons shall be at least ¾ in (19 mm) in their smallest dimension. They may be *raised* or flush.

2. Tactile and visual control indicators. All control buttons shall be designated by *raised* standard alphabet characters for letters, arabic characters for numerals, or standard symbols as shown in Fig. 3(*a*), and as required in ANSI A17.1-1978 and A17.1a-1979. The call button for the main entry floor shall be designated by a *raised* star at the left of the floor designation [see Fig. 3(*a*)]. All *raised*

designations for control buttons shall be placed immediately to the left of the button to which they apply. Applied plates, permanently attached, are an acceptable means to provide *raised* control designations. Floor buttons shall be provided with visual indicators to show when each call is registered. The visual indicators shall be extinguished when each call is answered.

3. Height. All floor buttons shall be no higher than *48 in (1220 mm), unless there is a substantial increase in cost, in which case the maximum mounting height may be increased to 54 in (1370 mm),* above the floor. Emergency controls, including the emergency alarm and emergency stop, shall be grouped at the bottom of the panel and shall have their centerlines no less than 35 in (890 mm) above the floor [see Fig. 3(*a*) and (*b*)].

4. Location. Controls shall be located on a front wall if cars have center opening doors, and at the side wall or at the front wall next to the door if cars have side opening doors [see Fig. 3(*c*) and (*d*)].

**Car position indicators** In elevator cars, a visual car position indicator shall be provided above the car control panel or over the door

to show the position of the elevator in the hoistway. As the car passes or stops at a floor served by the elevators, the corresponding numerals shall illuminate, and an audible signal shall sound. Numerals shall be a minimum of ½ in (13 mm) high. The audible signal shall be no less than 20 decibels with a frequency no higher than 1500 Hz. An automatic verbal announcement of the floor number at which a car stops or which a car passes may be substituted for the audible signal.

**Emergency communications** If provided, emergency two-way communication systems between the elevator and a point outside the hoistway shall comply with ANSI A17.1-1978 and A17.1a-1979. The highest operable part of a two-way communication system shall be a maximum of 48 in (1220 mm) from the floor of the car. It shall be identified by a raised or recessed symbol and located adjacent to the device. If the system uses a handset, then the length of the cord from the panel to the handset shall be at least 29 in (735 mm). The emergency intercommunication system shall not require voice communication.

(a)

**Fig. 1   Minimum dimensions of elevator cars.**

NOTE: The automatic door reopening device is activated if an object passes through either line A or line B. Line A and line B represent the vertical locations of the door reopening device not requiring contact.

**Fig. 2   Hoistway and elevator entrances.**

numeral height

control diameter

3/4
19

5/8
16

7 ○   8 ○
5 ○   6 ○
main entry floor   ★1 ○   2 ○
S ○   B ○
door closed
door open
emergency alarm
emergency stop
octagon symbol shall be tactual, but the X is not

**(a)**
**Panel Detail**

**(b)**
**Control Height**

**(c)**
**Alternate Locations of Panel with Center Opening Door**

**(d)**
**Alternate Locations of Panel with Side Opening Door**

Fig. 3   Car controls.

## 2ND FLOOR ESCALATOR. Nº 1 & 2
SCALE 1/4" = 1'-0"

ESCAL-AIRE #2 DOWN TO 1ST FL

ESCAL-AIRE #1 UP TO 2ND FLOOR

ESCALATOR WELL RAILING - "BLUMCRAFT" RAILGLASS 1/2" TH. "HERCULITE" TEMPERED PLATE GLASS WITH ALUM. TOP RAIL RG 200 BASE TO BE FASTENED TO STRUCTL. STEEL FRAMING IN ACCORDANCE WITH MFGRS APPROVED SHOP DWGS. SEE DWG A-17

## SECTION A-A.
SCALE 1/4" = 1'-0"

FIN. 2ND FL. EL. 30.75
NEW 33 WF 200
NEW 10 B 15
NEW 14 B 22
NEW 33 WF 200

STAINLESS STEEL FASCIA
1/2" STRUCTURAL GLASS

ESCAL-AIRE #1
ESCAL-AIRE #2

STAINLESS STEEL ESCAL. SOFFIT
STAINLESS STEEL ESCAL. SOFFIT
STAINLESS STL.?

FIN 1ST FL. EL.17.25
EXIST 27 WF 94
EXIST 27 WF 94
NEW 10 WF 45
NEW 14 B 36
NEW 4 WF
NEW 10 WF 45
NEW 14 WF 43
NEW 14 WF 26

1" VERMICULITE PLASTER ON METAL LATH FIREPROOFING TO MAINTAIN INTEGRITY OF 3 HR. RATED ENCLOSURE

CRAWL SPACE
CRAWL SPACE EL. 11.33
MECHANICAL EQUIPMENT ROOM
TO EDGE OF LOWER SUPPORT
CELLAR FLOOR EL. 8.0

**Fig. 4** Wheelchair lift. In certain installations where ramps may be impossible due to space limitations, small mechanical wheelchair lifts can be installed to overcome level changes. Manufactured lifts have a lift range from two to several feet and are either electro-mechanical, hydraulic, or pneumatically operated. Lifts can be semi-enclosed and equipped with entrance interlocks for safety, and either key-operated for limited use or button-type. "Dead-man" controls are recommended for safety.

| HEIGHT "H" | "L" |
|---|---|
| 67¼ | 48 |
| 91¼ | 72 |
| 115¼ | 96 |
| 139¼ | 120 |
| 163¼ | 144 |

**FAN SHAPED BACKBOARD**

**COURT LAYOUT**

**RECTANGULAR BACKBOARD**

**Fig. 1 NCAA basketball.** The color of the lane space marks and neutral zone marks shall contrast with the color of the bounding lines. The midcourt marks shall be the same color as the bounding lines. All lines shall be 2 in wide (neutral zone excluded). All dimensions are to inside edge of lines except as noted. Backboard shall be of any rigid weather-resistant material. The front surface shall be flat and painted white unless it is transparent. If the backboard is transparent, it shall be marked with a 3-in wide white line around the border and an 18 x 24-in target area bounded with a 2-in wide white line. [High school recommended court is 84 x 50 ft with a 10-ft unobstructed space on all sides (3 ft minimum). Collegiate recommended court is 94 x 50 ft with a 10-ft unobstructed space on all sides (3 ft minimum).]

**COURT LAYOUT**

**Fig. 2 AAU basketball court.** All dimensions are to inside edge of lines except as noted. All lines to be .05 m (2″) wide. Backboard shall be of any rigid weather-resistant material. The front shall be flat and painted white unless it is transparent. If the backboard is transparent, it shall be marked with a .05-m-wide white line around the border and a .45 x .59-m target area bounded with a .05-m-wide white line.

## INDOOR RECREATION

**One-, Three-, and Four-Wall Handball**

**ELEVATION**

**COURT LAYOUT**

**Fig. 3** One-wall handball. Playing court is 20'0" wide by 34'0" long plus a required 11'0" minimum width of surfaced area to the rear and a recommended 8'6" minimum width on each side. Courts in battery are to be a minimum of 6'0" between courts. Court markings: 1½-in-wide lines painted white, red, or yellow.

**Fig. 4** Handball court layout — four-wall. All court markings to be 1½ in wide and painted white, red, or yellow.

**Fig. 5** Handball court layout — three-wall. All court markings to be 1½ in wide and painted white, red, or yellow. Playing court is 20'0" wide by 40'0" long plus a minimum 10'0" to the rear of the three-wall court. Overhead clearance required is 20'0" minimum.

FLOOR PLAN

11,000 SQ. FT.

SECTION A-A

Fig. 6   Gymnasium plan and section.

## INDOOR RECREATION

**Tennis and Paddle Tennis**

**COURT LAYOUT**

**ISOMETRIC SHOWING NET**

**Fig. 7** Tennis court. All measurements for court markings are to the outside of lines except for those involving the center service line which is equally divided between the right and left service courts. All court markings to be 2 in wide.

**ISOMETRIC SHOWING NET**

**Fig. 8** Paddle tennis court. All measurements for court markings are to the outside of lines except for those involving the center service line, which is equally divided between right and left service court. All court markings to be 1½ in wide.

**COURT LAYOUT**

**COURT LAYOUT**

**ISOMETRIC SHOWING NET**

**Fig. 9   Badminton court.** All measurements for court markings are to the outside of lines except for those involving the center service line which is equally divided between right and left service courts. All court markings to be 1½" wide and preferably white or in color. Minimum distance between sides of parallel courts to be 5'0".

**ISOMETRIC SHOWING NET**

**Fig. 10   Volleyball court.** All measurements for court markings are to the outside of lines except for the centerline. All court markings to be 2 in wide except as noted.

**COURT LAYOUT**

**COURT LAYOUT**

**COURT MARKING DETAIL**

**Fig. 11** Shuffleboard court. All dimensions are to centers of lines and to edge of court. Maximum line width 1½ in, minimum ¾ in. Playing court is 6′0″ x 52′0″ plus a recommended minimum of 2′0″ on each side or 4′0″ between courts in battery.

| NO. OF OPENINGS | | FOR 3-4 & 5 WIDE NESTS | | All dimensions in inches. | |
|---|---|---|---|---|---|
| SINGLE | DOUBLE | SUGGESTED ARRANGEMENT | ROUGH OPENING | CABINET | NET OVERALL WIDTH |
| 3 | 6 | 3 | 17¾ | 16¾ | 18¾ |
| 4 | 8 | 4 | 23¼ | 22¼ | 24¼ |
| 5 | 10 | 5 | 28¹¹⁄₁₆ | 27¹¹⁄₁₆ | 29¹¹⁄₁₆ |
| 6 | 12 | 3-3 | 36½ | 35½ | 37½ |
| 7 | 14 | 3-4 | 42 | 41 | 43 |
| 8 | 16 | 4-4 | 47½ | 46½ | 48½ |
| 9 | 18 | 4-5 | 52¹⁵⁄₁₆ | 51¹⁵⁄₁₆ | 53¹⁵⁄₁₆ |
| 10 | 20 | 5-5 | 58⅜ | 57⅜ | 59⅜ |
| 11 | 22 | 4-3-4 | 66¼ | 65¼ | 67¼ |
| 12 | 24 | 4-4-4 | 71¾ | 70¾ | 72¾ |
| 13 | 26 | 4-5-4 | 77³⁄₁₆ | 76³⁄₁₆ | 78³⁄₁₆ |
| 14 | 28 | 5-4-5 | 82⅝ | 81⅝ | 83⅝ |
| 15 | 30 | 5-5-5 | 88¹⁄₁₆ | 87¹⁄₁₆ | 89¹⁄₁₆ |
| 16 | 32 | 4-4-4-4 | 96 | 95 | 97 |
| 17 | 34 | 5-4-4-4 | 101⁷⁄₁₆ | 100⁷⁄₁₆ | 102⁷⁄₁₆ |
| 18 | 36 | 5-4-4-5 | 106⅞ | 105⅞ | 107⅞ |
| 19 | 38 | 5-4-5-5 | 112⁵⁄₁₆ | 111⁵⁄₁₆ | 113⁵⁄₁₆ |
| 20 | 40 | 5-5-5-5 | 117¾ | 116¾ | 118¾ |
| 21 | 42 | 4-4-5-4-4 | 125¹¹⁄₁₆ | 124¹¹⁄₁₆ | 126¹¹⁄₁₆ |
| 22 | 44 | 5-4-4-4-5 | 131⅛ | 130⅛ | 132⅛ |
| 23 | 46 | 5-5-3-5-5 | 136½ | 135½ | 137½ |
| 24 | 48 | 5-5-4-5-5 | 142 | 141 | 143 |
| 25 | 50 | 5-5-5-5-5 | 147⁷⁄₁₆ | 146⁷⁄₁₆ | 148⁷⁄₁₆ |
| 26 | 52 | 5-4-4-4-4-5 | 155⅜ | 154⅜ | 156⅜ |
| 27 | 54 | 5-4-5-4-5-4 | 160¹³⁄₁₆ | 159¹³⁄₁₆ | 161¹³⁄₁₆ |
| 28 | 56 | 5-5-4-4-5-5 | 166¼ | 165¼ | 167¼ |
| 29 | 58 | 5-5-4-5-5-5 | 171¹¹⁄₁₆ | 170¹¹⁄₁₆ | 172¹¹⁄₁₆ |
| 30 | 60 | 5-5-5-5-5-5 | 177⅛ | 176⅛ | 178⅛ |
| 31 | 62 | 5-4-4-5-4-4-5 | 185¹⁄₁₆ | 184¹⁄₁₆ | 186¹⁄₁₆ |
| 32 | 64 | 5-5-4-4-4-5-5 | 190½ | 189½ | 191½ |
| 33 | 66 | 5-5-4-5-4-5-5 | 195¹⁵⁄₁₆ | 194¹⁵⁄₁₆ | 196¹⁵⁄₁₆ |
| 34 | 68 | 5-5-5-4-5-5-5 | 201⅜ | 200⅜ | 202⅜ |
| 35 | 70 | 5-5-5-5-5-5-5 | 206¹³⁄₁₆ | 205¹³⁄₁₆ | 207¹³⁄₁₆ |
| 36 | 72 | 5-5-4-4-4-4-5-5 | 214¾ | 213¾ | 215¾ |
| 37 | 74 | 5-5-5-4-4-4-5-5 | 220³⁄₁₆ | 219³⁄₁₆ | 221³⁄₁₆ |
| 38 | 76 | 5-5-5-4-5-5-5-5 | 225⅝ | 224⅝ | 226⅝ |
| 39 | 78 | 5-5-5-4-5-5-5-5 | 231¹⁄₁₆ | 230¹⁄₁₆ | 232¹⁄₁₆ |
| 40 | 80 | 5-5-5-5-5-5-5-5 | 236½ | 235½ | 237½ |
| 41 | 82 | 4-4-5-5-5-5-5-4-4 | 244⁷⁄₁₆ | 243⁷⁄₁₆ | 245⁷⁄₁₆ |
| 42 | 84 | 5-5-5-4-4-4-5-5-5 | 249⅞ | 248⅞ | 250⅞ |
| 43 | 86 | 5-5-5-5-3-5-5-5 | 255¼ | 254¼ | 256¼ |
| 44 | 88 | 5-5-5-5-4-5-5-5-5 | 260¾ | 259¾ | 261¾ |
| 45 | 90 | 5-5-5-5-5-5-5-5-5 | 266³⁄₁₆ | 265³⁄₁₆ | 267³⁄₁₆ |

## ACCESSORIES

### Mail Collection Boxes

19 1/4" H x 14 3/8" W x 6" D

17 1/8" H x 14 1/16" W x 16 1/8" D

30" H x 18" W x 12" D

36" H x 20" W x 12" D

**Contemporary**
30" H x 18" W x 10" D

**Classic Bronze**
36" H x 19" W x 10" D

**Letterslot**
6 1/2" H x 14" W

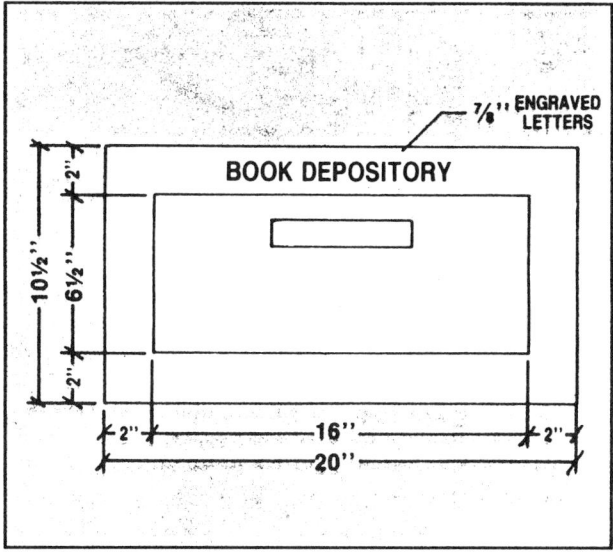

**Book Depository**
10 1/2" H x 20" W

**Plate Front**
26"H x 39"W

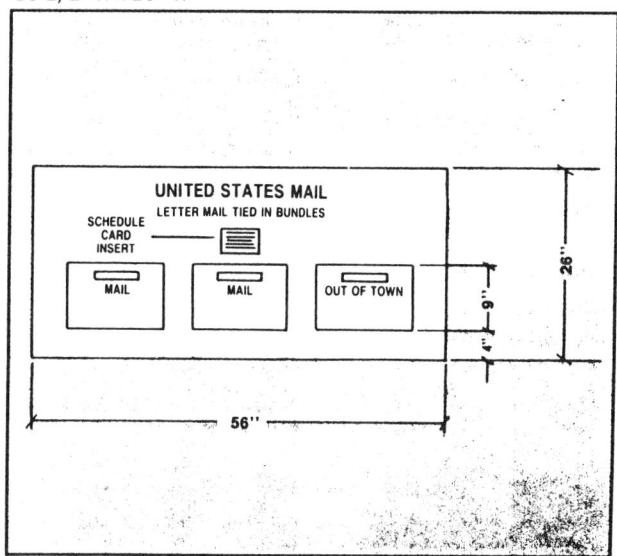

**Plate Front**
26" H x 56" W

## ACCESSORIES

Mail Chutes, Parcel Lockers, and Key Cabinets

**Wide Chute**

**Wide Chute**

**Twin**

**Horizontal Parcel Lockers**

### Key Storage Cabinet

The safest way to keep keys stored in one central secure location. Available in four different sizes, holding from 32 to 128 keys.

**Holds 32 Keys**
9 1/4" H  x  13 5/8" W

**Holds 64 Keys**
16 5/16" H  x  13 5/8" W

**Holds 96 Keys**
23 1/4" H  x  13 5/8" W

**Holds 128 Keys**
30 1/4" H  x  13 5/8" W

### Key Keeper

For use in a mail room (rear loading) installation. The arrow lock is accessed by the postman to retrieve the mail room door key, and stored safely when not in use.

Cluster

Cluster

Free-standing

Free-standing

Wall-mounted

Wall-mounted

Free-standing

Wall-mounted

## ACCESSORIES

**Types of Grilles**

Cast metal grille of unit design, cast in one piece. Grille size is governed by unit sizes plus width of border.

Cast metal grille of Renaissance design, ferrous or non-ferrous metal.

Cast metal grille of unit design, units cast separately and built into frame. Grille size is governed by unit sizes plus width of border.

Cast metal grille panels of various sizes cast in units and fitted into cast or wrought metal frame.

Cast metal grille of unit design. Units cast separately and built into grille spaces. Grille size must conform to unit sizes plus widths of bars and borders.

Cast metal grille for ventilator opening; may be fitted with metal screen and may be formed to curved wall or cove.

Cast metal grille for ventilator opening of special architectural form.

**Fig. 1** Cast metal grilles may be designed and built in various combinations. They may be made in small units cast separately or as one complete piece.

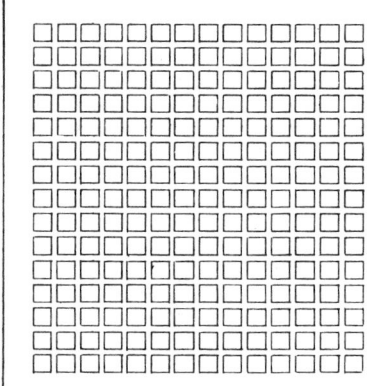

Stamped metal grille, square holes. Holes may be from ¼″ to 1½″ or larger, in ⅛″ steps, with bars or frets from ⅛″ to ⅜″ or greater.

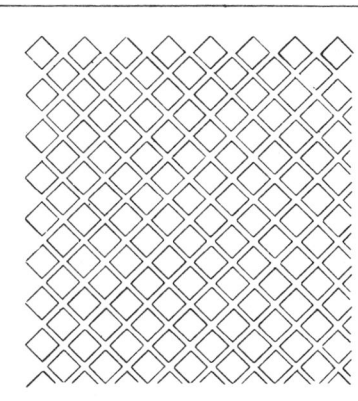

Stamped metal grille, square holes diagonally arranged.

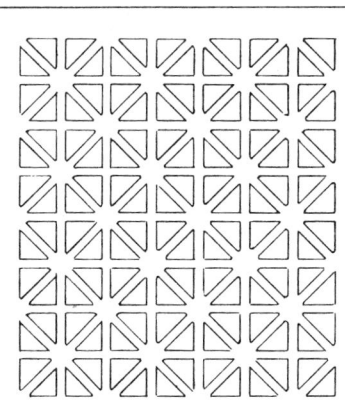

Stamped metal grille, Grecian or Union Jack design, made in a number of unit sizes and variations.

Stamped metal grille, shell or fish scale design, made in several unit sizes and variations.

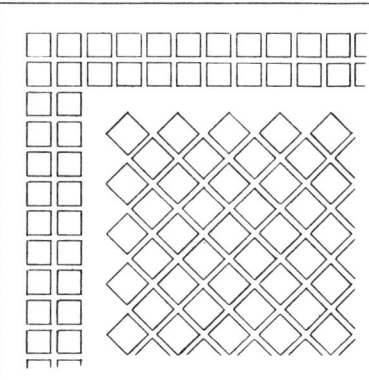

Stamped metal grille, square holes arranged to form plain border with diagonal center.

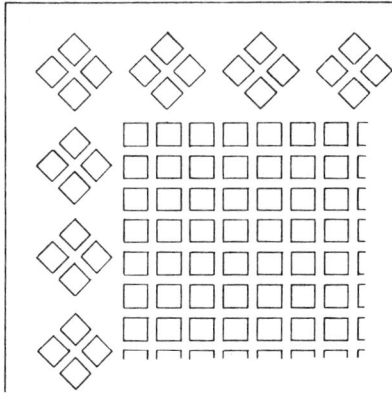

Stamped metal grille, square holes arranged to form diagonal border, with plain center.

Foundation or Bulkhead Grille

Foundation or Bulkhead Grille

Screwdriver Operated Catch

Lock and Dead Bolt

SCALE 1½″ = 1'-0″ AND ½″ = 1″

PROVIDE STOP AS REQUIRED

Thumb Latch

SPECIFY:
**Sizes of holes or unit stampings**
**Thickness**
**Metal and finish**
**Approximate width of margins**
**Method of fastening**
**Hinges and locks where required**
**Invisible hand hole doors.**

**Fig. 2** Stamped metal grilles are produced in a great variety of designs, metals, thicknesses, and sizes. Percentage of free area of stamped grilles may vary from about 25% to over 70%, with a great many designs in the 55% to 65% range. Margin widths can be made to accord with requirements of particular installations, consideration being given to duct openings and overall dimensions. Metal may be steel, painted or otherwise finished, bronze, aluminum, monel metal, or other nonferrous metals, in thicknesses from 16 gauge to ¼″.

Perforated Metal Grilles

Perforated Metal Grilles

GRILLE 3 PANELS

Flat Band Frame

Moulding and
Angle Frame

Tee Bar Frame

- 1 -          - 2 -

Grille of perforated sheets set into
frame of channel, angle, and mouldings.

Reversed Angle Frame

SCALE $\frac{1}{2}$" = 1

Moulding and angle
frame to swing in fixed
frame.

**SPECIFY:**
**Pattern of perforations**
**Metal**
**Finish**
**Gauge or thickness**
**Give frame details**

Fig. 3  Perforated metal grilles may be obtained in several designs and are produced of 19 gauge steel in sheets of standard sizes. Sheets may be cut to any size and placed in frames of metal or other material. Perforated metal grilles are used for vent openings, panels, covers, shelves, partitions, cabinets, metal furniture, boxes, machinery guards, enclosures and many other purposes. They are also available in many other patterns in any ferrous or nonferrous metal that can be perforated, and in thicknesses from about 24 gauge in the smaller perforations to ¼" or ⅜" in the larger perforations.

Wrought metal grille of heavy close construction, for radiator or ventilator openings.

Wrought metal grille for railing or ornamental construction.

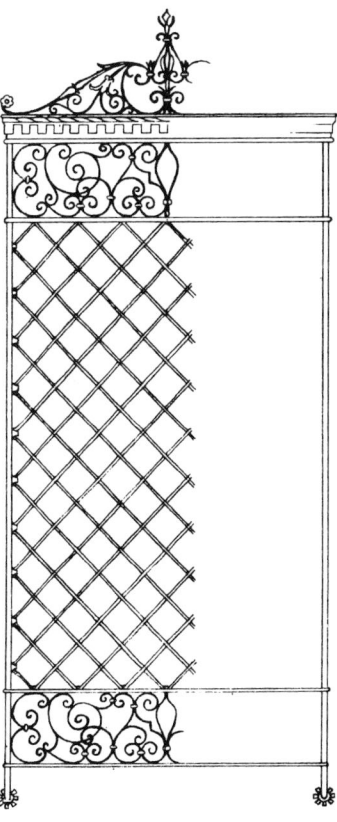

Wrought metal grille for glass door.

Wrought metal grille of light construction, with silhouette work, leaves, flowers, and husks, for arch decoration.

Wrought metal grille of sheet and flat bars, for ventilating opening.

Wrought metal grille for counter.

Wrought metal grille for large window or opening.

**Fig. 4** Design of wrought metal grilles includes the use of other metal forms, such as sheets, extruded mouldings, castings, and stampings. Thus, in addition to plain bar sections and forged items, use is made of the unlimited number of extruded mouldings in non-ferrous metals; stamped leaves, rosettes, and ornaments of many kinds; cast iron, bronze, nickel silver, and aluminum items of every character; and rolled or drawn sections of many shapes.

Grille of round or square vertical bars welded to horizontal bars set in masonry.

Grille with anchors set in masonry and grille bolted or riveted to anchors.

Grille with short alternate vertical bars, angle clips fastened to opening jambs.

Grille, with ornament between bars, set in masonry opening.

Grille of welded construction set on face of wall.

Grille of welded construction set on face of wall.

| A | B | C | D | E | F | G |

Methods of forming vertical bars.

**Fig. 5** Window grilles are of plain construction when used for protection only, and when used for ornamental effect, may be designed with many unique and interesting ideas. Window grilles may be set in the masonry openings or on the face of the wall, with either plain or ornamental brackets or supports. They may also be attached to window frames, or may be arranged to swing, with hinges and locks. Material sizes in window grilles may vary according to the degree of protection required, and in proportion to the size of the grille.

**Fig. 6** Methods of fastening grilles. Cast and stamped metal grilles may be fastened by screws or hinges and locks to walls of wood, plaster, marble, or other material in a variety of ways, depending upon the type of the grille, the type of framing to be used around the grille, and the appearance or effect desired. These methods show a number of ways in which cast and stamped grilles may be fastened. In selecting the method desired, consideration should be given to whether or not the grille will require frequent removal. The size and weight of the grille will have a bearing upon the size of frames, screws, and hinges.

## ACCESSORIES
### Grille Fastening Methods

Two members crossed, one member cut and welded to the other.

Two members crossed, each member halved. Pin may be countersunk or peined.

Two members crossed, one member split permitting other to pass through.

Two members crossed, one member laid upon the other, with round-head or countersunk rivet.

Two members crossed, one member punched permitting other to pass through.

Two members crossed, each member crimped.

Two members crossed, each member flattened, with round head rivet.

Two members linked.

Formed members welded to sides of straight member.

Formed members banded to sides of straight member.

Formed members terminated and banded to sides of straight member.

One member cut and welded to side of other.

One member set into punched hole in other member and welded.

One member set against other member and attached by flat head tapped screw.

One member attached to side of other member by angle clips bolted or riveted.

Formed member with knife edge, welded to side of straight member.

Formed member with blunt end welded to side of straight member.

Corner members welded.

Corner members fitted, with two flat head tapped screws.

Corner members bolted through angle clips.

Corner members with welded gusset plates.

Formed member attached to the other member by band in slot.

Two parallel members attached by spool and pin.

A   B   C   D   E   F

Methods of splitting members and forming into scrolls, ends, ornaments, or structural elements.

SCALE 1½" = 1'-0"

**Fig. 7** Wrought metal grilles are fabricated by the use of a great many different methods of crossing and joining members. Some of the more widely employed of these methods are shown here.

## VINYL WALL PROTECTION GUARDS

## ALUMINUM WALL PROTECTION GUARDS

## FLUSH-MOUNTED CORNER PROTECTION GUARDS

## ACCESSORIES
**Vinyl Wall Protection Guards**

Ceiling height — flush mount

Wainscot installation — surface mount

## VINYL HANDRAILS

## ALUMINUM HANDRAILS

TYPE ①

TYPE ③

TYPE ②

3A    3B

FIXED COVER

UPPER ALIGNMENT CLIP, FACTORY ASSEMBLED TO REMOVABLE COLUMN COVER

LOWER ALIGNMENT CLIP, FACTORY ASSEMBLED TO FIXED COLUMN COVER

SNAP-FORM® ASSEMBLY

REMOVABLE COVER

MOUNTING BRACKET

**COLUMN ASSEMBLY**

PERSPECTIVE

EXISTING STEEL COLUMN 4" DIA.

FIXED COVER

5"

FIRE PROOF EXISTING COLUMN AS PER LOCAL CODE

REMOVABLE COVER

7"

**COLUMN COVER**

7" DIAMETER

EXISTING STEEL COLUMN 7" DIA.

FIXED COVER

8"

REMOVABLE COVER

10"

**COLUMN COVER**

10" DIAMETER

MOUNTING BRACKET

5/16" HOLE

5/16" x 1/2" ADJUSTMENT GROOVE

ALIGNMENT CL'PS

SNAP-FORM® ASSEMBLY

3/16" THICK

SLIGHT V-GROOVE

**JOINT DETAIL**

PLAN

## ACCESSORIES

**Column Covers**

ADDITIONAL BRACING ABOVE COLUMN COVERS BY OTHERS

TOP SLIDER BRACKETS

SOFTFORMS® METAL STUDS

SCREW FASTEN COVERS TO METAL STUDS

REINFORCED JOINT COMPOUND

EMBEDDED REINFORCED TAPE

CURVED TROWEL

SKIM COAT

SANDPAPER

PLUMB STUDS WITH LEVEL

TEMPLATE FOR STUD ALIGNMENT

BOTTOM BRACKETS

ROLLED ALUMINUM 1/8" THICK

SOFTFORMS® FIN

TAPE & SPACKLE

#6 FLAT HEAD FULL THREADED SELF TAPPING SCREWS

SOFTFORMS® 16 GAUGE MTL STUD

7/8"

2 1/2"

7/8"

**SERIES 100K TYPICAL JOINT DETAIL**

NO SCALE          SECTION

UPPER COLUMN COVER

POP-RIVET UPPER COLUMN COVER FIN TO JOINER PLATE 6" O.C.

PITTCON WILL PROVIDE POP-RIVET GUN, DRILL BIT & ALUMINUM POP-RIVETS

3"

SPECIFY OUTSIDE DIAMETER — MINIMUM 14"

EXISTING STEEL COLUMN WITH FIREPROOF INSULATION

**SOFTFORMS® COLUMN COVERS**

SECTION

CONDITION 1 — COLUMN PASSES THROUGH CEILING; REQUIRES INSTALLATION PRIOR TO FINISHING CEILING.

**A** PASSES THROUGH GPDW CEILING WITHOUT REVEAL

**B** PASSES THROUGH GPDW CEILING WITH REVEAL

**C** PASSES THROUGH LAY-IN TILE CEILING WITHOUT REVEAL

CONDITION 2 — COLUMN INSTALLED BETWEEN FIXED CEILING AND FLOOR

**D** FLUSH TO CEILING

**E** REVEAL BOARD AT CEILING

**F** SCRIBE RING AT CEILING

**G** REVEAL BOARD AT FLOOR

**H** FLUSH TO FLOOR

**I** SCRIBE RING AT FLOOR

**ACCESSORIES**

Column Covers

EXISTING
STEEL
COLUMN
WITH
FIREPROOF
INSULATION

TAPE &
SPACKLE

SO 60A
REFER PAGE
SS 33.1

METAL ANGLE
OR WOOD SECTION

½" OR ⅝"
GPDW

EXISTING
STEEL
COLUMN
WITH
FIREPROOF
INSULATION

SOI-9-150
REFER PAGE
SS 38.0

TAPE &
SPACKLE

1¼" x 1¼"
MTL ANGLE

TWO OFFSET
2½" MTL
STUDS

½" OR ⅝"
GPDW

EXISTING
STEEL
COLUMN
WITH
FIREPROOF
INSULATION

SON-9-150
REFER PAGE
SO 27.0

METAL CLADDING
OR
CONTRASTING
PAINT

TAPE &
SPACKLE

TWO OFFSET
2½" MTL
STUDS

½" OR ⅝"
GPDW

EXISTING
STEEL
COLUMN
WITH
FIREPROOF
INSULATION

THREE
QUARTER
COLUMN
COVER

PARTIAL
COLUMN
COVER

REFER TO
SOFTFORMS®
SERIES 100
COLUMN
COVER
BROCHURE

MTL
STUD

TAPE &
SPACKLE

½" OR ⅝"
GPDW

## 3-ARM HIGH-TRAFFIC MANUAL AND ELECTRIC TURNSTILES

DETAIL "B"

CUP

ANCHOR BOLT

FINISHED FLOOR

CONCRETE

HALF SCALE

ANCHOR

**Vertical section**

1.18
1.19
3.87
24.63

2" DIA. SHOWN CONDUIT WIRE HOLES - 2 TYP.

**Plan**

A — A'

SEE DETAIL "B"

FINISHED FLOOR

**Side elevation**        **Front elevation**

25"
15½"

**Plan**

Socket Plug

3.5"
1.5"

Square Socket for Yokes & Turnstiles

1.75" O.D.

**Anchor details**

Socket Plug

3.5"
1.365"

Round Socket for Posts

1.5" O.D.

27"
39¾"

**Side elevation**

55°
90°
34"

**Front elevation**

## ACCESSORIES
Turnstiles

### 4-ARM MANUAL AND ELECTRIC TURNSTILES

**Basic customer security**

**Enhanced security**

**Maximum security**

| right hand | left hand | clockwise | counterclock |

**Rotation guide**

### HIGH-SECURITY TURNSTILES

4¾" TYP.

**Manual**

**Electric**

### 3-ARM MANUAL AND ELECTRIC TURNSTILES

**Post-mounted**

**Tandem (post-mounted)**

**Wall-mounted**

**Portable**

**Plan of electric type configuration**

**Emergency — quick release**

**Finger latch**

**MODEL BA-1**
Break-away finger latch features an adjustable tension setting. SAME mounting as Gate Finger.

**Triple rail — finger latch**

**Triple rail — alarm system**

**Double rail**

**Double rail — flip sleeve latch**

**Double rail — aisle closure with flip sleeve latch**

**Single rail — cart security with flip sleeve latch**

**Single section welded rail — electrically controlled gate latch, wheelchair access**

**Single section welded rail — self-closing or self-opening**

NOTES: FOR DIFFERENT FOUNTAIN INSTALLATION HEIGHT, DIMENSIONS MARKED BY (✱) MUST BE ADJUSTED ACCORDINGLY.

✱ THIS IS A DUAL PURPOSE DRINKING WATER FACILITY; THE DIMENSIONS NOTED (✱) ARE RECOMMENDED HEIGHTS ONLY. WHEN INSTALLING THIS UNIT, LOCAL, STATE OR FEDERAL CODES SHOULD BE ADHERED TO AND DIMENSIONS ADJUSTED ACCORDINGLY.

**17-19**
430-485

**9** min
230

**27** min
685

**36** max
915

**8** min
205

**6** max
150

*equipment permitted in shaded area*
**(a)**
**Spout Height and
Knee Clearance**

**48** min
1220

**17-19**
430-485

**30** min
760

**24** max
610

**(b)**
**Clear Floor Space**

**30** min
760

**48** min
1220

**(c)**
**Free-Standing
Fountain or Cooler**

**30** min
760

*not to exceed
fountain depth*

**48** min
1220

**(d)**
**Built-In
Fountain or Cooler**

**Drinking Fountains and Water Coolers**

# General Reference Data

| | |
|---|---|
| Space planning | 1106 |
| Human factors | 1110 |
| Floor and wall covering | 1122 |
| Fabric | 1130 |
| Electrical | 1132 |
| Columns, capitals, and entablatures | 1135 |
| Nails, screws, and bolts | 1136 |
| Mathematical data and formulas | 1139 |

This section provides a variety of time-saving reference material in the form of tables, charts, formulas, and planning guidelines. Included are area requirements for the preliminary space planning of various building types and human factors data related to anthropometrics, space, and acoustics. Also included are a number of tables for determining carpet and wall covering yardage quantities. In addition, a series of tables dealing with electrical data provides typical amperage ratings for office and electronic equipment and for residential appliances. Still other tables and charts contain mathematical data relative to functions of numbers, metric system conversions, and areas of plane figures.

# SPACE PLANNING
### Area Requirements By Use

The first portion of Table 1 shows some of the planning guidelines for several types of office use. Of course, usable areas per employee vary greatly depending on the type of work performed and types of support space and common areas required, such as file rooms, data processing, conference rooms, and so forth.

### Rules of Thumb

*Office use:* 125 to 150 net sq. ft. area per person.
*Retail space:* 30 net sq. ft. per person on ground floor; 50 net sq. ft. per person on upper floors.
*Classrooms:* 20 net sq. ft. per pupil.

**TABLE 1    Space Planning By Building Type**

| Building/Use Type | Sq. Ft. per Unit | | Area Basis |
|---|---|---|---|
| Office buildings, all types | 100–250 | net | usable |
| Work station, minimum clerical | 40 | person | usable |
| Work station, clerical with VDT | 55 | person | usable |
| Work station, with visitor space | 65 | person | usable |
| Work station, supervisor | 100 | person | usable |
| Manager, private office | 150–225 | person | usable |
| Law firm | 450 | attorney | total usable |
| Law firm library | 25–30 | attorney | usable |
| Law firm conference | 25–30 | attorney | usable |
| Insurance company, branch | 100 average | work station | usable |
| Insurance company, branch Total, includes common areas and circulation | 155–165 | employee | total usable |
| Energy company | 255 | employee | total usable |
| Conference and dining rooms | 15 | person | net |

| Restaurants | | | |
|---|---|---|---|
| Dining areas (includes dining room but not waiting, coat room, etc.) | | | |
| Banquet | 10–15 | seat | net |
| Cafeteria, college | 12–15 | seat | net |
| Cafeteria, commercial | 16–18 | seat | net |
| Counter service | 18–20 | seat | net |
| Table service, hotel or restaurant | 15–18 | seat | net |
| Table service, minimum | 11–14 | seat | net |

**Kitchens**

*Meals per Hour*

| Type | < 200 | 200–400 | 400–800 | 800–1300 |
|---|---|---|---|---|
| Cafeterias | 7.5–5.0 | 5.0–4.0 | 4.0–3.5 | 3.5–3.0 |
| Hotels | 18.0–4.0 | 7.5–3.0 | 6.0–3.0 | 4.0–3.0 |
| Restaurants | 7.0–4.0 | 5.0–3.6 | 5.0–3.6 | 5.0–3.0 |
| Serving and service areas | | | | |
| Cafeterias | 6 | person | | net |
| Restaurants | 5 | person | | net |
| Add to totals space for food storage, administration, waiting. | | | | |

**TABLE 1** Space Planning By Building Type *(Continued)*

| Building/Use Type | Sq. Ft. per Unit | | Area Basis |
|---|---|---|---|
| Night clubs | 25 | person | net |
| Bars | 18 | person | net |
| Hotel | | | |
| 1.5 persons per room without extensive conferencing facilities | 550–600 | room | gross |
| | **Retail** | | |
| Large stores | 30–50 | person | net |
| | **Cultural** | | |
| Public library | | | |
| Stack space | 0.08 | bound vols. | net |
| Reading rooms | 20–35 | user | net |
| Staff space | 100 | staff person | net |
| Overall | 50 | person | net |
| Museums, exhibition areas | 15 | person | net |
| Theater and assembly areas | | | |
| Seating area, fixed seats | 7.5 | seat | net |
| Seating, movable seating | 15 | seat | net |
| Theaters, fixed seating (Does not include stage, lobby, etc.) | 8–12 | seat | net |
| Stage/backstage Performing arts theater | 100% | seating area | |
| Lobbies | 3 | person | net |
| Lobbies | 30% | seating area | |
| **Educational** | | | |
| Elementary | | | |
| The following figures are based on the number of students in the particular space listed. | | | |
| Small classrooms | 20–30 | student | net |
| Library | 40 | student | net |
| Art room | 40 | student | net |
| Secondary | | | |
| The following figures are based on the number of students in the particular space listed. | | | |
| Cafeteria | 12–15 | student | 1/3 of total |
| Small classrooms | 20–25 | student | net |
| Large classrooms | 15 | student | net |
| Art classrooms | 50–60 | student | net |
| Home economics | 50–60 | student | net |
| Laboratory classrooms | 55–70 | student | net |
| Library | 40 | student | 20% of total |
| Music rooms | 30–35 | student | net |
| Physical education | 125 | student | net |
| Shops/vocational rooms small | 50 | student | net |
| Shops/vocational rooms wood, metal, etc. | 120–140 | student | net |
| University | | | |
| Classrooms, small | 20 | student | net |
| Classrooms, large | 12–15 | student | net |

TABLE 1    Space Planning By Building Type *(Continued)*

| Building/Use Type | Sq. Ft. per Unit | | Area Basis |
|---|---|---|---|
| Lecture halls | 9–12 | seat | net |
| Dormitory, no dining | 160 | student | net |
| Dormitory, no dining | 210–240 | student | gross |
| Dormitory, dining | 235–260 | student | gross |
| Food service, table service | 18–26 | seat | net, all areas |
| Food service, cafeteria | 14–19 | seat | net, all areas |
| Laboratories | 34–45 | student | net |
| Laboratory storage | 6–10 | student | net |
| Library | | | |
| Book stacks, less than 300,000 volumes | 0.10 | volume | net |
| Book stacks, 300,000–1,000,000 volumes | 0.7–0.8 | volume | net |
| Book stacks, over 1,000,000 volumes | 0.5 | volume | net |
| Reading, study | 25–35 | station | net |
| (provide stations equal to 25% to 40% of student population): | 6.25–10 | student | net |
| Total service space | 25% | of reading | net |
| **Residential** | | | |
| Apartments | 250 | Occupant | net |
| Senior citizen housing | | | |
| Living units | 300–380 | 1-person unit | net |
| Living units | 350–425 | 2-person unit | net |
| Living units | 400–600 | unit | gross |
| Dining, lounge, lobby, administration, etc. | 33%–45% of living unit space, gross area | | |
| **Health Care Facilities** | | | |
| General hospital | 1000 | bed | gross |
| Medical center | 1100 | bed | gross |

The above figures are based on *usable* square footage, which in the language of leasing includes the area within the boundaries of the leased space. Most building owners lease space based on the *rentable* area, which includes a tenant's prorated share of common areas such as toilet rooms, elevator lobby, public corridors, and so on. The multiplying figure can be obtained from the building owner, or a figure of 1.1 to 1.15 can be used as an estimated multiplying factor.

TABLE 2    Gross to Net Ratios for Common Building Types

| Building Type | Multiplying Factor | Building Type | Multiplying Factor |
|---|---|---|---|
| Office | 1.25–1.35 | Library reading space | 1.5 |
| Retail | 1.35 | Museum | 1.2 |
| Bank | 1.4 | Theater | 1.3–1.7 |
| Restaurant, table service | 1.4–1.5 | School, classroom | 1.5–1.65 |
| Restaurant, cafeteria | 1.5 | School, dormitory | 1.5–1.8 |
| Bars, nightclubs | 1.3–1.4 | School, laboratory | 1.7 |
| Hotel | 1.4–1.6 | School, gymnasium | 1.4–1.45 |
| Public library | 1.25–1.3 | Apartment | 1.25–1.5 |
| Library stack space | 1.1–1.3 | Hospital | 1.5–1.85 |

## LIBRARY PLANNING

Libraries represent a unique building type in that a majority of space is devoted to housing books and not people. The number of volumes to be housed becomes the primary planning parameter, rather than numbers of people. For a detailed layout of book stacks, you can use the figures given in Table 3. For preliminary planning, the following general guidelines are useful.

### Rules of Thumb

*Public library:* 12–18½ volumes per sq. ft.

*Law library:* 5–7 volumes per sq. ft.

To stack space, add a "configuration loss" of from 6% to 20%, to account for inefficiencies in stack layout.

*Minimum aisle between open stacks:* 3 ft. 0 in.

*Staff spaces:* 100 net sq. ft. per person.

*Reading room seating:* 15–35 sq. ft. per person plus 6% configuration loss.

*Net/gross multiplier:* 1.25.

Maximum of 15,000–20,000 sq. ft. per floor.

**Example**  A 100,000 volume public library is planned. How much space should be devoted to open stacks?

Plan about 15 volumes per sq. ft. (100,000 ÷ 15 = 6667 sq. ft.). Add a configuration loss of 10%, to give a total area of 6667 + 667, or 7333 sq. ft. of stack space.

**TABLE 3  Library Shelving — Volumes per Linear Foot of Shelf Based on Subject**

(Standard stack section 3 ft wide x 7½ ft high with 7 shelves)

| Subject | Volumes per foot of shelf | Volumes per single face section |
|---|---|---|
| Art (excluding oversize) | 7 | 147 |
| Circulating, nonfiction | 8 | 168 |
| Economics | 8 | 168 |
| Fiction | 8 | 168 |
| General literature | 7 | 147 |
| History | 7 | 147 |
| Law | 4 | 84 |
| Medical | 5 | 105 |
| Periodicals, bound | 5 | 105 |
| Public documents | 5 | 105 |
| Technical and scientific | 6 | 126 |
| Average for overall estimating | | 125 |

These figures should be reduced by at least 10% to avoid overcrowding and to allow for expansion.

## APPROPRIATENESS

It is essential, due to the many variables involved, that the data selected be appropriate to the user of the space or furniture to be designed. It becomes necessary, therefore, for the intended user population to be properly defined in terms of such factors as age, sex, occupation, and ethnicity. If the user is an individual, or constitutes a very small group, it may, in certain situations, be feasible to develop your own primary anthropometric data by actually having individual body measurements taken. Surely, if one is prepared to take the time to be fitted for a dress or a suit, one should be willing to spend the time to be fitted for an interior environment or components of that environment, particularly since, in most cases, the latter will reflect a far greater financial investment. The measurements, in the event individual data are generated, should, however, be taken with proper instruments by a trained observer. In situations where specific body dimensions or other data for a particular user population are unavailable, and both time and funds prevent undertaking sophisticated studies, an engineering anthropometrist can be consulted to discuss the statistical methods of obtaining the necessary information.

## "AVERAGE MAN" FALLACY

As suggested previously, a very serious error in the application of data is to assume that the 50th percentile dimensions represent the measurements of an "average man" and to create a design to accommodate 50th percentile data. The fallacy in such an assumption is that by prior definition 50 percent of the group may suffer. There simply is no "average man." Depending on the nature of the design problem, the design should usually be conceived to accommodate the 5th or the 95th percentile, so that the greatest portion of the population is served.

Dr. H.T.E. Hertzberg, one of the country's most distinguished research physical anthropologists, in discussing the so-called average man, indicated, "there is really no such thing as an 'average' man or woman. There are men who are average in weight, or in stature, or in sitting height, but the men who are average in two dimensions constitute only about 7 percent of the population; those in three, only about 3 percent; those in four, less than 2 percent. There are no men average in as few as 10 dimensions. Therefore, the concept of the 'average' man is fundamentally incorrect, because no such creature exists. Work places to be efficient should be designed according to the measured range of body size."

## REACH, CLEARANCE, AND ADJUSTABILITY

The selection of appropriate anthropometric data is based on the nature of the particular design problem under consideration. If the design requires the user to reach from a seated or standing position, the 5th percentile data should be utilized. Such data for arm reach indicates that 5 percent of the population would have an arm reach of short (or shorter) dimension, while 95 percent of the population, the overwhelming majority, would have longer arm reaches. If the design

in a reach situation can accommodate the user with the shortest arm reach, obviously it will function for the users with longer reaches as well; it is equally obvious that the opposite is not true, as shown in Fig. 1(a).

In designs where clearance is the primary consideration, the larger or 95th percentile data should be used. The logic is simple. If the design will allow adequate clearance for the users with the largest body size, it would also allow clearance for those users with smaller body size. Here, too, it can be seen from Fig. 1(b) that the opposite is not true.

In other situations it may be desirable to

provide the design with a built-in adjustment capability. Certain chair types, adjustable shelves, etc., are examples of such. The range of adjustment should be based on the anthropometrics of the user, the nature of the task, and the physical or mechanical limitations involved. The range should allow the design to accommodate at least 90 percent of the user population involved, or more.

It should be noted that all the foregoing examples were used primarily to illustrate the basic logic underlying the selection of the body dimensions involved and the particular percentiles to be accommodated. Wherever possible, however, it is naturally more desir-

**Fig. 1** *(a)* People of smaller body dimensions and, correspondingly, the lower-range percentile data should be used to establish dimensions where reach is the determining factor. *(b)* Larger-size people and, correspondingly, the high percentile range data should be used in establishing clearance dimensions.

**Fig. 2   Body measurements of most use to the designer of interior spaces.**

### Adult Male and Female Miscellaneous Structural Body Dimensions in Inches and Centimeters by Age and Selected Percentiles

| | | A | | B | | C | | D | | E | | F | | G | |
|---|---|---|---|---|---|---|---|---|---|---|---|---|---|---|---|
| | | in | cm | in | cm | in | cm | in | cm | in | cm | in | cm | in | cm |
| **95** | MEN | 36.2 | 91.9 | 47.3 | 120.1 | 68.6 | 174.2 | 20.7 | 52.6 | 27.3 | 69.3 | 37.0 | 94.0 | 33.9 | 86.1 |
| | WOMEN | 32.0 | 81.3 | 43.6 | 110.7 | 64.1 | 162.8 | 17.0 | 43.2 | 24.6 | 62.5 | 37.0 | 94.0 | 31.7 | 80.5 |
| **5** | MEN | 30.8 | 78.2 | 41.3 | 104.9 | 60.8 | 154.4 | 17.4 | 44.2 | 23.7 | 60.2 | 32.0 | 81.3 | 30.0 | 76.2 |
| | WOMEN | 26.8 | 68.1 | 38.6 | 98.0 | 56.3 | 143.0 | 14.9 | 37.8 | 21.2 | 53.8 | 27.0 | 68.6 | 28.1 | 71.4 |

A CROTCH HEIGHT
B ELBOW HEIGHT
C EYE HEIGHT
D SHOULDER BREADTH
E MIDSHOULDER HEIGHT SITTING
F BUTTOCK-TOE LENGTH
G EYE HEIGHT SITTING

### Adult Male and Female Functional Body Dimensions in Inches and Centimeters by Age, Sex, and Selected Percentiles

| | | A | | B | | C | | D | | E | | F | |
|---|---|---|---|---|---|---|---|---|---|---|---|---|---|
| | | in | cm | in | cm | in | cm | in | cm | in | cm | in | cm |
| **95** | MEN | 38.3 | 97.3 | 46.1 | 117.1 | 51.6 | 131.1 | 35.0 | 88.9 | 39.0 | 86.4 | 88.5 | 224.8 |
| | WOMEN | 36.3 | 92.2 | 49.0 | 124.5 | 49.1 | 124.7 | 31.7 | 80.5 | 38.0 | 96.5 | 84.0 | 213.4 |
| **5** | MEN | 32.4 | 82.3 | 39.4 | 100.1 | 59.0 | 149.9 | 29.7 | 75.4 | 29.0 | 73.7 | 76.8 | 195.1 |
| | WOMEN | 29.9 | 75.9 | 34.0 | 86.4 | 55.2 | 140.2 | 26.6 | 67.6 | 27.0 | 68.6 | 72.9 | 185.2 |

A THUMB TIP REACH EXTENDED
B BUTTOCK-HEEL LENGTH
C VERTICAL REACH HEIGHT SITTING
D THUMB TIP REACH
E SIDE ARM REACH
F VERTICAL GRIP REACH

able to accommodate the greatest percentage of the user population. In this regard, there is no substitute for common sense. If a shelf can just as easily be placed an inch or two lower, without significantly impacting on other design or cost factors, thereby accommodating 98 or 99 percent of the user population, obviously that is the correct design decision.

The clearances shown in Fig. 3 are intended to introduce general guidelines for barrier-free design. While we have utilized the wheelchair as our design subject, it does not represent the largest number of disabled. However, it is usually the most demanding for which to design. To provide practical limits for this design, we have chosen to plot the range of reach for the short female to the tall male. The overlapping areas of ability for the handicapped and the non-handicapped demonstrate the field of good design practice common to both.

When planning for accessibility, it is important to consider the attitude at which the wheelchair approaches the object desired. Reach limits differ for frontal and side reach. Because of this, range of reach is plotted for each. The elevation targets represent the maximum height at which controls requiring manual dexterity should be located.

Wheelchairs vary in size. They are fitted to their users in much the same manner as clothing is. A range of sizes is given, with the dimensions for the "typical" collapsible, manual chair indicated. Electrically powered wheelchairs require more space. Further, the wheelchair must be considered in its "occupied" state, as the user imparts additional space requirements with arms and feet as well as basic maneuvering space.

We consider the basic space requirement for an occupied wheelchair to function to be 3 ft wide by 4 ft deep. This same space will accommodate most people who use canes, crutches, and walkers. Blind people using the cane technique for perceiving obstacles can also be accommodated in this space. For a person in a wheelchair to make a complete turn, an area of approximately 5 ft by 5 ft is required. As the elevations of surrounding surfaces change, so do the space requirements. The length of time that one is confronted by close quarters also affects the required clearance. An opening through a wall may be 2 ft 8 in clear as it represents only a short time involvement. As travel distance and traffic increase, passage width must also.

The complexity of space also affects minimum clearance. To make a simple 90° turn, adjoining passages 3 ft wide are required (and 3 ft 6 in preferred if a normal walking is to be maintained). A 180° turn around a fixed partition requires more space.

As clearances relate to general circulation requirements, space needs again increase with traffic speed and volume. Narrow corridors (4 ft) should be restricted to basically short, one-directional traffic patterns. Generally, maintain at least 5 ft clearances or more as determined by code.

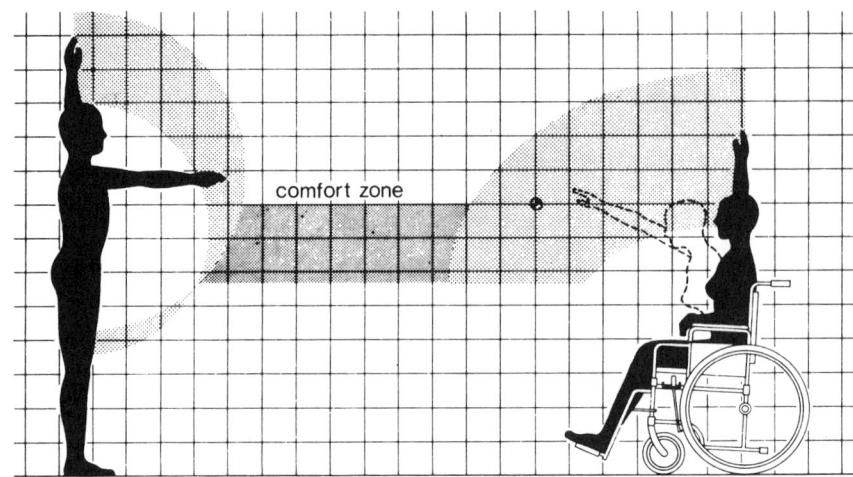

comfort zone

# range of reach

scale: 3/8" = 1'-0"

(a 1)

# range of reach

scale: 3/8" = 1'-0"

(b 1)

3'-0"

19"-31"
26" typ.

3'-6"    4'-0"

6"    6"    1'-0"

2'-3"

# wheelchair

scale: 3/8" = 1'-0"

(c 1)

# cane technique

scale: 3/8" = 1'-0"

(d 1)

**Fig. 3**

**clearance**
scale: 3/8"= 1'- 0"

e 1

**openings**
scale: 3/8"= 1'- 0"

f 1

**360° turn**
scale: 3/8"= 1'- 0"

g 1

**90° turn**
scale: 1/4"= 1'- 0"

h 1

**180° turn**
scale: 1/4"= 1'- 0"

j 1

**one-way**
scale: 3/8"= 1'- 0"

k 1

**two-way**
scale: 3/8"= 1'- 0"

m 1

**Fig. 3** *(Continued)*

Handgrip

Back Upright

Tire

Handrim

Wheel

Spokes

Brake

Axle

Tipping Lever

Wheelbase

Caster Wheel

Back Upholstery

Armrest

Arm

Skirtguard

Seat Rail

Seat Upholstery

Crossbrace

Hanger Bracket

Heel Loop

Footplate

**Fig. 4**

eye level

handle

desk arm

armrest

lap

seat

toe

36
915

30
760

8
205

19
485

27
685

43–51
1090–1295

**Overall length: 40″ to 50″**

26
660

18
455

42
1065

6
150

NOTE: Footrests may extend further for very large people.

**Fig. 5   Dimensions of adult-sized wheelchairs.**

**Width: open, 24″ to 25″; closed, 10″**

(a)
Clear Floor Space

(b)
Forward Approach

(c)
Parallel Approach

NOTE: x ≤ 24 in (610 mm).

NOTE: x ≤ 15 in (380 mm).

(d)
Clear Floor Space in Alcoves

NOTE: If x > 24 in (610 mm), then an additional maneuvering clearance of 6 in (150 mm) shall be provided as shown.

NOTE: If x > 15 in (380 mm), then an additional maneuvering clearance of 12 in (305 mm) shall be provided as shown.

(e)
Additional Maneuvering Clearances for Alcoves

**Fig. 6** Minimum clear floor space for wheelchairs.

**(a)**
**Front Approaches — Swinging Doors**

NOTE: x = 12 in (305 mm) if door has both a closer and latch.

**(b)**
**Hinge Side Approaches — Swinging Doors**

NOTE: x = 36 in (915 mm) minimum if y = 60 in (1525 mm); x = 42 in (1065 mm) minimum if y = 54 in (1370 mm).

NOTE: y = 48 in (1220 mm) minimum if door has both a latch and closer.

**(c)**
**Latch Side Approaches — Swinging Doors**

NOTE: y = 54 in (1370 mm) minimum if door has closer.

NOTE: y = 48 in (1220 mm) minimum if door has closer.

NOTE: All doors in alcoves shall comply with the clearances for front approaches.

**(d)**
**Front Approach — Sliding Doors and Folding Doors**

**(e)**
**Slide Side Approach — Sliding Doors and Folding Doors**

**(f)**
**Latch Side Approach — Sliding Doors and Folding Doors**

NOTE: All doors in alcoves shall comply with the clearances for front approaches.

**Fig. 7    Maneuvering clearances at doors.**

Fig. 8    Two hinged doors in series.

**(a) Side Reach Possible**

**(b) Forward Reach Required**

*Height to highest operable parts which are essential to basic operation of telephone.*

**Fig. 9  Mounting heights and clearances for telephones.**

**(a) Forward Reach Possible**

**(b) Side Reach Possible**

**Fig. 10  Control reach limitations.**

## TYPES OF SPACE

Besides needing enough space in order to move about and perform various tasks, people react to space in a variety of ways. Several researchers have defined the space surrounding the individual in terms of the limits within which people categorically respond (see Figs. 11 and 12). *Intimate space* is that area in which a person tends not to allow anyone to intrude unless intimate relationships are expected. *Personal space* is that area within which a person allows only selected friends or fellow workers with whom personal discussion is mandatory. *Social space* is that area within which the individual expects to make purely social contacts on a temporary basis. And, finally, *public space* is that area within which the individual does not expect to have direct contact with others. Obviously, the more intimate the spatial relationship becomes, the more people resist intrusion by others. Personal space factors are important in establishing the privacy requirements for architectural design.

## Distance Relationships Among People
(Hall)

### Intimate   Personal   Social   Public

½–1½ ft.

1½–4 ft.

4–12 ft.

12 ft. & more

**Fig. 11**

INTIMATE
1.5'

PERSONAL
4.0'

SOCIAL
12.0'

PUBLIC

**Fig. 12**

## TYPICAL SUBJECTIVE RESPONSES TO SELECTED SPATIAL FEATURES

Although few research data have been generated with regard to how people respond to specific spatial factors (at least in terms of being able to prescribe precise, quantitative guidelines), it is important for the designer to reflect on potentially negative reactions that often result when a given space is not made compatible with what the user expects in terms of the size, shape, organization, color, and illumination of a particular space. The considerations listed in Table 4 are suggested as a checklist for the designer.

**TABLE 4**

| Space Characteristic | Probable Response |
|---|---|
| Size (generally volume) | If the space is too small for the number of people, furnishings, equipment, or other objects that occupy it, people will consider it to be crowded. Although they may accept a crowded condition on a temporary basis, they will object to living or working in such a space for extended periods of time. If the space is too large for the people, furnishings, equipment, or other objects that occupy it, people will consider it "unfriendly," inconvenient, and/or overly demanding in terms of communicating, travel distance, maintenance, etc. Although they may accept the "barnlike" atmosphere for temporary periods, they will object to living or working in such a space for extended periods of time. |
| Shape (generally proportion) | If the space is out of proportion (too narrow, wide, long, high, etc.) for the intended use, people will consider it awkward and often distracting or oppressive. Although they may accept proportional distortion on a short-term basis (i.e., as they pass through briefly), they will object to living or working in such a space for extended periods of time. If the space contains such distortions as all curved surfaces, acute wall junctures, and too many projections or surface changes, people will consider it confusing and difficult to maneuver in and/or furnish. Although they may accept such distortions (or even consider them interesting) on a temporary or one-time basis, they will object to living or working in such a space for extended periods of time. It should also be noted that blind people depend on the constant proportions of right-angle corners to aid them in negotiating a space; such individuals are easily confused by curved surfaces, walls that are not at right angles, and periodic projections that imply they may have reached a turning point. When a ceiling is extremely high relative to the lateral dimension of a space, people feel as though they are working in a pit and that the walls are closing in on them. When a ceiling is extremely low and the space in front of the observer is very long, people feel as though the room is "endless" or as if they will hit their heads unless they duck. |
| Color and illumination | If a space is dark (unless this is required for a particular operation, such as a motion picture presentation), people tend to become lethargic and less active, or they may feel anxious. As a rule, the less bright a room is, the less cheerful it seems. A small space will seem even smaller. If a space is too bright, people will feel overly exposed, or they will complain of glare or thermal discomfort (even though actual glare in terms of accepted light levels or inappropriate thermal conditions for comfort are not present). If there are too many different colors, too large expanses of very saturated color, or too many and too "busy" patterns of color within a space, most people become irritated after more than a brief exposure to the space. If there is too little color, no visual pattern, or no other decorative "break" in the visual environment, people will find the space monotonous, boring, and eventually irritating to the point of wanting to escape. Although isolated points of highly reflective surface provide interest, all-metallic and highly reflective surface treatments create both subjective and directly objective interference for most people who have to work in the space. |
| Windows | Generally, most people do not like to live and work in a space that is devoid of windows. First and foremost, people seem to need visual contact with the outside world. Too many windows, on the other hand, can cause the following possible negative reactions: too much glare, too much exposure (fishbowl effect), lack of protection from outside elements, true anxiety (caused by floor-to-ceiling glass at high elevations). |
| Space organization | The internal components within a space and the traffic corridors and entrance and exit locations will seem either well organized or badly organized. The furnishings, partitions, decorative objects, etc., will appear as being either organized or disorganized, depending on the observer's ability to comprehend what things are and where they are with respect to his or her vantage point. Key behavioral response issues are: apparent capability to find one's way to specific locations, apparent ease for interacting and communicating with others with whom the individual must associate, apparent privacy provisions necessary to perform individual tasks. Although these are sometimes conflicting needs, the people who use a space will perform on the basis of how well each of these factors has been executed for *them*, not for the designer or the boss. The organization of internal space components obviously interacts with all the other space characteristics; i.e., the individual perceives and reacts to the combined effects of size, shape, color and illumination, windows, and organization simultaneously. A significant behavioral response will be an individual's interpretation of whether sufficient options are available for local modification of his or her own portion of the space. Even though people may never require a modification, they react to their own space in terms of permanently established restrictions that eventually elicit the feeling that the space is too small, the wrong shape, too dark, or isolated from the rest of the world, for example. |
| Furnishings | As a general rule, people are sensitive to improperly proportioned furniture, i.e., furniture that is too large, too small, or the wrong shape for the space in which it is placed. Although the designer normally tries to select furnishings that are properly proportioned for the space he or she has created, this may ultimately restrict the efficiency of the individual (e.g., a desk or storage cabinet may be too small). Thus, although the general visual proportions of furniture in relation to space must be taken into account to avoid negative observational responses, shortchanging the individual in terms of specific furniture and use requirements soon stimulates an even stronger negative response. |

**TABLE 5  Comparison of Sound Pressure Levels and Loudness Sensations**

| Sound Pressure Level (decibels—A scale) | Source | Sensation |
|---|---|---|
| 130 | Jet Aircraft at 100' / Bass Drum at 3' / Auto Horn at 3' | Physical Pain |
| 120 | | |
| 110 | Thunder, Artillery, Nearby Riveter | Deafening |
| 100 | Elevated Train / Discotheque | |
| 90 | Loud Street Noise / Noisy Factory | Very Loud |
| 80 | Truck Unmuffled / Police Whistle | |
| 70 | Cocktail Party / Noisy Office / Average Street Noise | Loud |
| 60 | Average Radio / Average Factory | |
| 50 | Noisy Home / Inside General Office | Moderate |
| 40 | Face to Face Conversation / Quiet Radio | |
| 30 | Quiet Home / Private Office | Faint |
| 20 | Empty Auditorium / Quiet Conversation | |
| 10 | Rustle of Leaves / Whisper / Soundproof Room | Very Faint |
| 0 | Threshold of Audibility | |

**Decibel Scale for Sounds**

Physical damage (jet takeoff) — 120

Painful (siren) — 100

Deafening (power mower) — 80

Very Loud (cocktail party) — 60

Loud (traffic) — 40

Moderate (conversation) — 20

Faint (rustling leaves) — 0

**Fig. 13**

**TABLE 6  Speech-Interference Levels that Barely Permit Reliable Conversation**

| Distance between talker and listener, ft | Speech-interference level, dB | | | |
|---|---|---|---|---|
| | Normal | Raised | Very loud | Shouting |
| 0.5 | 71 | 77 | 83 | 89 |
| 1.0 | 65 | 71 | 77 | 83 |
| 2.0 | 59 | 65 | 71 | 77 |
| 3.0 | 55 | 61 | 67 | 73 |
| 4.0 | 53 | 59 | 65 | 71 |
| 5.0 | 51 | 57 | 63 | 69 |
| 6.0 | 49 | 55 | 61 | 67 |
| 12.0 | 43 | 49 | 55 | 61 |

**TABLE 7  Speech Interference Levels (SIL) and Noise Criteria (NC) Recommended for Rooms**

| Type of room | Maximum permissible level (measured in vacant rooms | |
|---|---|---|
| | SIL | NC |
| Secretarial offices, typing | 60 | 50–55 |
| Coliseum for sports only (amplification) | 55 | 50 |
| Small private office | 45 | 30–35 |
| Conference room for 20 | 35 | 30 |
| Movie theater | 35 | 30 |
| Conference room for 50 | 30 | 20–30 |
| Theaters for drama, 500 seats (no amplification) | 30 | 20–25 |
| Homes, sleeping areas | 30 | 20–25 |
| Assembly halls (no amplification) | 30 | |
| Schoolrooms | 30 | 25 |
| Concert halls (no amplification) | 25 | 15–20 |

# FLOOR AND WALL COVERING

Length and Width of Carpet Roll Converted to Area

**TABLE 8  Length and Width of Carpet Roll Converted to Area**

| | Width of carpet roll | | | | | | | | | | Width of carpet roll | | | | | | | | | |
| | 9 ft | | | 12 ft | | | 15 ft | | | | 9 ft | | | 12 ft | | | 15 ft | | |
| Length, ft | ft² | yd² | m² | ft² | yd² | m² | ft² | yd² | m² | Length, ft | ft² | yd² | m² | ft² | yd² | m² | ft² | yd² | m² |
|---|---|---|---|---|---|---|---|---|---|---|---|---|---|---|---|---|---|---|---|
| 2 | 18 | 2 | 1.67 | 24 | 2.67 | 2.23 | 30 | 3.33 | 2.79 | 51 | 459 | 51 | 42.64 | 612 | 68 | 56.86 | 765 | 85 | 71.07 |
| 3 | 27 | 3 | 2.51 | 36 | 4 | 3.34 | 45 | 5 | 4.18 | 52 | 468 | 52 | 43.48 | 624 | 69.33 | 57.97 | 780 | 86.67 | 72.46 |
| 4 | 36 | 4 | 3.34 | 48 | 5.33 | 4.46 | 60 | 6.67 | 5.57 | 53 | 477 | 53 | 44.31 | 636 | 70.67 | 59.09 | 795 | 88.33 | 73.86 |
| 5 | 45 | 5 | 4.18 | 60 | 6.67 | 5.57 | 75 | 8.33 | 6.97 | 54 | 486 | 54 | 45.15 | 648 | 72 | 60.20 | 810 | 90 | 75.25 |
| 6 | 54 | 6 | 5.02 | 72 | 8 | 6.69 | 90 | 10 | 8.36 | 55 | 495 | 55 | 45.99 | 660 | 73.33 | 61.32 | 825 | 91.67 | 76.64 |
| 7 | 63 | 7 | 5.85 | 84 | 9.33 | 7.80 | 105 | 11.67 | 9.76 | 56 | 504 | 56 | 46.82 | 672 | 74.67 | 62.41 | 840 | 93.33 | 78.04 |
| 8 | 72 | 8 | 6.69 | 96 | 10.67 | 8.92 | 120 | 13.33 | 11.15 | 57 | 513 | 57 | 47.66 | 684 | 76 | 63.55 | 855 | 95 | 79.43 |
| 9 | 81 | 9 | 7.52 | 108 | 12 | 10.03 | 135 | 15 | 12.54 | 58 | 522 | 58 | 48.49 | 696 | 77.33 | 64.66 | 870 | 96.67 | 80.83 |
| 10 | 90 | 10 | 8.36 | 120 | 13.33 | 11.15 | 150 | 16.67 | 13.94 | 59 | 531 | 59 | 49.33 | 708 | 78.67 | 65.77 | 885 | 98.33 | 82.22 |
| 11 | 99 | 11 | 9.20 | 132 | 14.67 | 12.26 | 165 | 18.33 | 15.33 | 60 | 540 | 60 | 50.17 | 720 | 80 | 66.89 | 900 | 100 | 83.61 |
| 12 | 108 | 12 | 10.03 | 144 | 16 | 13.38 | 180 | 20 | 16.72 | 61 | 549 | 61 | 51 | 732 | 81.33 | 68 | 915 | 101.67 | 85.01 |
| 13 | 117 | 13 | 10.87 | 156 | 17.33 | 14.47 | 195 | 21.67 | 18.12 | 62 | 558 | 62 | 51.84 | 744 | 82.67 | 69.12 | 930 | 103.33 | 86.40 |
| 14 | 126 | 14 | 11.71 | 168 | 18.67 | 15.61 | 210 | 23.33 | 19.51 | 63 | 567 | 63 | 52.68 | 756 | 84 | 70.23 | 945 | 105 | 87.79 |
| 15 | 135 | 15 | 12.54 | 180 | 20 | 16.72 | 225 | 25 | 20.90 | 64 | 576 | 64 | 53.51 | 768 | 85.33 | 71.35 | 960 | 106.67 | 89.19 |
| 16 | 144 | 16 | 13.38 | 192 | 21.33 | 17.84 | 240 | 26.67 | 22.30 | 65 | 585 | 65 | 54.35 | 780 | 86.67 | 72.46 | 975 | 108.33 | 90.58 |
| 17 | 153 | 17 | 14.21 | 204 | 22.67 | 18.95 | 255 | 28.33 | 23.69 | 66 | 594 | 66 | 55.18 | 792 | 88 | 73.58 | 990 | 110 | 91.97 |
| 18 | 162 | 18 | 15.05 | 216 | 24 | 20.07 | 270 | 30 | 25.08 | 67 | 603 | 67 | 56.02 | 804 | 89.33 | 74.69 | 1005 | 111.67 | 93.37 |
| 19 | 171 | 19 | 15.89 | 228 | 25.33 | 21.18 | 285 | 31.67 | 26.48 | 68 | 612 | 68 | 56.86 | 816 | 90.67 | 75.81 | 1020 | 113.33 | 94.76 |
| 20 | 180 | 20 | 16.72 | 240 | 26.67 | 22.30 | 300 | 33.33 | 27.87 | 69 | 621 | 69 | 57.69 | 828 | 92 | 76.92 | 1035 | 115 | 96.15 |
| 21 | 189 | 21 | 17.55 | 252 | 28 | 23.41 | 315 | 35 | 29.26 | 70 | 630 | 70 | 58.53 | 840 | 93.33 | 78.04 | 1050 | 116.67 | 97.55 |
| 22 | 198 | 22 | 18.39 | 264 | 29.33 | 24.53 | 330 | 36.67 | 30.66 | 71 | 639 | 71 | 59.36 | 852 | 94.67 | 79.15 | 1065 | 118.33 | 98.94 |
| 23 | 207 | 23 | 19.23 | 276 | 30.67 | 25.64 | 345 | 38.33 | 32.05 | 72 | 648 | 72 | 60.20 | 864 | 96 | 80.27 | 1080 | 120 | 100.33 |
| 24 | 216 | 24 | 20.07 | 288 | 32 | 26.76 | 360 | 40 | 33.44 | 73 | 657 | 73 | 61.04 | 876 | 97.33 | 81.38 | 1095 | 121.67 | 101.73 |
| 25 | 225 | 25 | 20.90 | 300 | 33.33 | 27.87 | 375 | 41.67 | 34.84 | 74 | 666 | 74 | 61.87 | 888 | 98.67 | 82.50 | 1110 | 123.33 | 103.12 |
| 26 | 234 | 26 | 21.74 | 312 | 34.67 | 28.99 | 390 | 43.33 | 36.23 | 75 | 675 | 75 | 62.71 | 900 | 100 | 83.61 | 1125 | 125 | 104.52 |
| 27 | 243 | 27 | 22.57 | 324 | 36 | 30.10 | 405 | 45 | 37.63 | 76 | 684 | 76 | 63.55 | 912 | 101.33 | 84.73 | 1140 | 126.67 | 105.91 |
| 28 | 252 | 28 | 23.41 | 336 | 37.33 | 31.21 | 420 | 46.67 | 39.02 | 77 | 693 | 77 | 64.30 | 924 | 102.67 | 85.84 | 1155 | 128.33 | 107.30 |
| 29 | 261 | 29 | 24.25 | 348 | 38.67 | 32.33 | 435 | 48.33 | 40.41 | 78 | 702 | 78 | 65.22 | 936 | 104 | 86.96 | 1170 | 130 | 108.70 |
| 30 | 270 | 30 | 25.08 | 360 | 40 | 33.44 | 450 | 50 | 41.81 | 79 | 711 | 79 | 66.05 | 948 | 105.33 | 88.07 | 1185 | 131.67 | 110.09 |
| 31 | 279 | 31 | 25.92 | 372 | 41.33 | 34.56 | 465 | 51.67 | 43.20 | 80 | 720 | 80 | 66.89 | 960 | 106.67 | 89.19 | 1200 | 133.33 | 111.48 |
| 32 | 288 | 32 | 26.76 | 384 | 42.67 | 35.68 | 480 | 53.33 | 44.59 | 81 | 729 | 81 | 67.73 | 972 | 108 | 90.30 | 1215 | 135 | 112.88 |
| 33 | 297 | 33 | 27.59 | 396 | 44 | 36.79 | 495 | 55 | 45.99 | 82 | 738 | 82 | 68.56 | 984 | 109.33 | 91.42 | 1230 | 136.67 | 114.27 |
| 34 | 306 | 34 | 28.43 | 408 | 45.33 | 37.90 | 510 | 56.67 | 47.38 | 83 | 747 | 83 | 69.40 | 996 | 110.67 | 92.53 | 1245 | 138.33 | 115.66 |
| 35 | 315 | 35 | 29.26 | 420 | 46.67 | 39.02 | 525 | 58.33 | 48.77 | 84 | 756 | 84 | 70.23 | 1008 | 112 | 93.65 | 1260 | 140 | 117.06 |
| 36 | 324 | 36 | 30.10 | 432 | 48 | 40.13 | 540 | 60 | 50.17 | 85 | 765 | 85 | 71.07 | 1020 | 113.33 | 94.76 | 1275 | 141.67 | 118.45 |
| 37 | 333 | 37 | 30.94 | 444 | 49.33 | 41.25 | 555 | 61.67 | 51.56 | 86 | 774 | 86 | 71.91 | 1032 | 114.67 | 95.88 | 1290 | 143.33 | 119.84 |
| 38 | 342 | 38 | 31.77 | 456 | 50.67 | 42.36 | 570 | 63.33 | 52.95 | 87 | 783 | 87 | 72.74 | 1044 | 116 | 96.99 | 1305 | 145 | 121.24 |
| 39 | 351 | 39 | 32.61 | 468 | 52 | 43.48 | 585 | 65 | 54.35 | 88 | 792 | 88 | 73.58 | 1056 | 117.33 | 98.11 | 1320 | 146.67 | 122.63 |
| 40 | 360 | 40 | 33.44 | 480 | 53.33 | 44.59 | 600 | 66.67 | 55.74 | 89 | 801 | 89 | 74.41 | 1068 | 118.67 | 99.22 | 1335 | 148.33 | 124.03 |
| 41 | 369 | 41 | 34.28 | 492 | 54.67 | 45.71 | 615 | 68.33 | 57.13 | 90 | 810 | 90 | 75.25 | 1080 | 120 | 100.33 | 1350 | 150 | 125.42 |
| 42 | 378 | 42 | 35.12 | 504 | 56 | 46.82 | 630 | 70 | 58.53 | 91 | 819 | 91 | 76.09 | 1092 | 121.33 | 101.45 | 1365 | 151.67 | 126.81 |
| 43 | 387 | 43 | 35.95 | 516 | 57.33 | 47.94 | 645 | 71.67 | 59.92 | 92 | 828 | 92 | 76.92 | 1104 | 122.67 | 102.56 | 1380 | 153.33 | 128.21 |
| 44 | 396 | 44 | 36.79 | 528 | 58.67 | 49.05 | 660 | 73.33 | 61.32 | 93 | 837 | 93 | 77.76 | 1116 | 124 | 103.68 | 1395 | 155 | 129.60 |
| 45 | 405 | 45 | 37.63 | 540 | 60 | 50.17 | 675 | 75 | 62.71 | 94 | 846 | 94 | 78.6 | 1128 | 125.33 | 104.79 | 1410 | 156.67 | 130.99 |
| 46 | 414 | 46 | 38.46 | 552 | 61.33 | 51.28 | 690 | 76.67 | 64.10 | 95 | 855 | 95 | 79.43 | 1140 | 126.67 | 105.91 | 1425 | 158.33 | 132.39 |
| 47 | 423 | 47 | 39.30 | 564 | 62.67 | 52.40 | 705 | 78.33 | 65.50 | 96 | 864 | 96 | 80.27 | 1152 | 128 | 107.02 | 1440 | 160 | 133.78 |
| 48 | 432 | 48 | 40.13 | 576 | 64 | 53.51 | 720 | 80 | 66.89 | 97 | 873 | 97 | 81.10 | 1164 | 129.33 | 108.14 | 1455 | 161.67 | 135.17 |
| 49 | 441 | 49 | 40.97 | 588 | 65.33 | 54.63 | 735 | 81.67 | 68.28 | 98 | 882 | 98 | 81.94 | 1176 | 130.67 | 109.25 | 1470 | 163.33 | 136.57 |
| 50 | 450 | 50 | 41.81 | 600 | 66.67 | 55.74 | 750 | 83.33 | 69.68 | 99 | 891 | 99 | 82.78 | 1188 | 132 | 110.37 | 1485 | 165 | 137.96 |
| | | | | | | | | | | 100 | 900 | 100 | 83.61 | 1200 | 133.33 | 111.48 | 1500 | 166.67 | 139.36 |

### TABLE 9  Paperhanging Walls and Ceilings

| Size of room, ft | Height of ceiling | | | Yards of border | Rolls of ceiling |
| | 8 ft | 9 ft | 10 ft | | |
| | Single rolls for walls | | | | |
|---|---|---|---|---|---|
| 4 × 8 | 6 | 7 | 8 | 9 | 2 |
| 4 × 10 | 7 | 8 | 9 | 11 | 2 |
| 4 × 12 | 8 | 9 | 10 | 12 | 2 |
| 6 × 10 | 8 | 9 | 10 | 12 | 2 |
| 6 × 12 | 9 | 10 | 11 | 13 | 3 |
| 8 × 12 | 10 | 11 | 13 | 15 | 4 |
| 8 × 14 | 11 | 12 | 14 | 16 | 4 |
| 10 × 14 | 12 | 14 | 15 | 18 | 5 |
| 10 × 16 | 13 | 15 | 16 | 19 | 6 |
| 12 × 16 | 14 | 16 | 17 | 20 | 7 |
| 12 × 18 | 15 | 17 | 19 | 22 | 8 |
| 14 × 18 | 16 | 18 | 20 | 23 | 8 |
| 14 × 22 | 18 | 20 | 22 | 26 | 10 |
| 15 × 16 | 15 | 17 | 19 | 23 | 8 |
| 15 × 18 | 16 | 18 | 20 | 24 | 9 |
| 15 × 20 | 17 | 20 | 22 | 25 | 10 |
| 15 × 23 | 19 | 21 | 23 | 28 | 11 |
| 16 × 18 | 17 | 19 | 21 | 25 | 10 |
| 16 × 20 | 18 | 20 | 22 | 26 | 10 |
| 16 × 22 | 19 | 21 | 23 | 28 | 11 |
| 16 × 24 | 20 | 22 | 25 | 29 | 12 |
| 16 × 26 | 21 | 23 | 26 | 31 | 13 |
| 17 × 22 | 19 | 22 | 24 | 28 | 12 |
| 17 × 25 | 21 | 23 | 26 | 31 | 13 |
| 17 × 28 | 22 | 25 | 28 | 32 | 15 |
| 17 × 32 | 24 | 27 | 30 | 35 | 17 |
| 17 × 35 | 26 | 29 | 32 | 37 | 18 |
| 18 × 22 | 20 | 22 | 25 | 29 | 12 |
| 18 × 25 | 21 | 24 | 27 | 31 | 14 |
| 18 × 28 | 23 | 26 | 28 | 33 | 16 |
| 20 × 26 | 23 | 28 | 28 | 33 | 17 |
| 20 × 28 | 24 | 27 | 30 | 34 | 18 |
| 30 × 34 | 27 | 30 | 33 | 39 | 21 |

Allowance for waste is included in all figures.
Deduct one roll for every 36 sq ft of openings.
Deduct one roll for every 2 doors.
Deduct for windows as area of each opening.
One roll of wallpaper equals 36 sq ft (24 ft by 18 in.).

### TABLE 10  Covering Capacity

| Material | Surface or use | Coverage per gallon, sq ft |
|---|---|---|
| Exterior Painting | | |
| Priming paint | Wood | 450 |
| | Metal | 500 |
| Flat house paint | Over primer | 500 |
| | Repainting 1 coat | 400 |
| Oil paint | Masonry | 300 |
| | Concrete | 250 |
| | Stucco (smooth) | 200 |
| | Stucco (rough) | 150 |
| Stain | Wood shingle siding, first coat | 150 |
| | Wood shingle siding, second coat | 200 |
| Interior Painting | | |
| Priming paint | Wood | 500 |
| Metal primer | Metal | 600 |
| Undercoat (enamel) | Over primer | 400 |
| Flat | Finish coat | 500 |
| Semigloss enamel | Finish coat | 450 |
| Satin-gloss enamel | Finish coat | 450 |
| Gloss enamel | Finish coat | 400 |
| Floor enamel | Floors | 500 |
| Aluminum paint | Aluminum, first coat | 600 |
| | Aluminum, second coat | 700 |
| Spar varnish | Finishing woodwork | 600 |
| Clear gloss varnish | Finishing woodwork | 600 |
| Lacquer | Over stain | 450 |
| Interior stain | Woodwork, first coat | 500 |
| | Woodwork, second coat | 600 |
| | Woodwork, third coat | 700 |
| Miscellaneous | | |
| Barn red oil paint | Repaint barn | 450 |
| Rust inhibitor (zinc paint) | Metal | 650 |
| Furniture sealer and stain | Unpainted furniture | 600 |

### TABLE 11  Flooring Tile

(Net covering capacity per 100 sq ft)

| Tile size, in. | No. of pieces per 100 sq ft | No. of pieces per sq ft |
|---|---|---|
| 6 × 6 | 400 | 4.00 |
| 6 × 12 | 200 | 2.00 |
| 9 × 9 | 178 | 1.78 |
| 12 × 12 | 100 | 1.00 |
| 12 × 24 | 50 | 0.50 |
| 18 × 18 | 45 | 0.45 |
| 18 × 24 | 34 | 0.33 |
| 18 × 36 | 23 | 0.23 |
| 36 × 36 | 11 | 0.11 |

# FLOOR AND WALL COVERING
## Wall Areas of Rooms

### TABLE 12  Wall Area of Rooms (8-ft ceiling), ft²

| Feet | 3 | 4 | 5 | 6 | 7 | 8 | 9 | 10 | 11 |
|---|---|---|---|---|---|---|---|---|---|
| 3 | 96 | 112 | 128 | 144 | 160 | 176 | 192 | 208 | 224 |
| 4 | 112 | 128 | 144 | 160 | 176 | 192 | 208 | 224 | 240 |
| 5 | 128 | 144 | 160 | 176 | 192 | 208 | 224 | 240 | 256 |
| 6 | 144 | 160 | 176 | 192 | 208 | 224 | 240 | 256 | 272 |
| 7 | 160 | 176 | 192 | 208 | 224 | 240 | 256 | 272 | 288 |
| 8 | 176 | 192 | 208 | 224 | 240 | 256 | 272 | 288 | 304 |
| 9 | 192 | 208 | 224 | 240 | 256 | 272 | 288 | 304 | 320 |
| 10 | 208 | 224 | 240 | 256 | 272 | 288 | 304 | 320 | 336 |
| 11 | 224 | 240 | 256 | 272 | 288 | 304 | 320 | 336 | 352 |
| 12 | 240 | 256 | 272 | 288 | 304 | 320 | 336 | 352 | 368 |
| 13 | 256 | 272 | 288 | 304 | 320 | 336 | 352 | 368 | 384 |
| 14 | 272 | 288 | 304 | 320 | 336 | 352 | 368 | 384 | 400 |
| 15 | 288 | 304 | 320 | 336 | 352 | 368 | 384 | 400 | 416 |
| 16 | 304 | 320 | 336 | 352 | 368 | 384 | 400 | 416 | 432 |
| 17 | 320 | 336 | 352 | 368 | 384 | 400 | 416 | 432 | 448 |
| 18 | 336 | 352 | 368 | 384 | 400 | 416 | 432 | 448 | 464 |
| 19 | 352 | 368 | 384 | 400 | 416 | 432 | 448 | 464 | 480 |
| 20 | 368 | 384 | 400 | 416 | 432 | 448 | 464 | 480 | 496 |
| 21 | 384 | 400 | 416 | 432 | 448 | 464 | 480 | 496 | 512 |
| 22 | 400 | 416 | 432 | 448 | 464 | 480 | 496 | 512 | 528 |
| 23 | 416 | 432 | 448 | 464 | 480 | 496 | 512 | 528 | 544 |
| 24 | 432 | 448 | 464 | 480 | 496 | 512 | 528 | 544 | 560 |
| 25 | 448 | 464 | 480 | 496 | 512 | 528 | 544 | 560 | 576 |

| Feet | 12 | 13 | 14 | 15 | 16 | 17 | 18 | 19 | 20 |
|---|---|---|---|---|---|---|---|---|---|
| 3 | 240 | 256 | 272 | 288 | 304 | 320 | 336 | 352 | 368 |
| 4 | 256 | 272 | 288 | 304 | 320 | 336 | 352 | 368 | 384 |
| 5 | 272 | 288 | 304 | 320 | 336 | 352 | 368 | 384 | 400 |
| 6 | 288 | 304 | 320 | 336 | 352 | 368 | 384 | 400 | 416 |
| 7 | 304 | 320 | 336 | 352 | 368 | 384 | 400 | 416 | 432 |
| 8 | 320 | 336 | 352 | 368 | 384 | 400 | 416 | 432 | 448 |
| 9 | 336 | 352 | 368 | 384 | 400 | 416 | 432 | 448 | 464 |
| 10 | 352 | 368 | 384 | 400 | 416 | 432 | 448 | 464 | 480 |
| 11 | 368 | 384 | 400 | 416 | 432 | 448 | 464 | 480 | 496 |
| 12 | 384 | 400 | 416 | 432 | 448 | 464 | 480 | 496 | 512 |
| 13 | 400 | 416 | 432 | 448 | 464 | 480 | 496 | 512 | 528 |
| 14 | 416 | 432 | 448 | 464 | 480 | 496 | 512 | 528 | 544 |
| 15 | 432 | 448 | 464 | 480 | 496 | 512 | 528 | 544 | 560 |
| 16 | 448 | 464 | 480 | 496 | 512 | 528 | 544 | 560 | 576 |
| 17 | 464 | 480 | 496 | 512 | 528 | 544 | 560 | 576 | 592 |
| 18 | 480 | 496 | 512 | 528 | 544 | 560 | 576 | 592 | 608 |
| 19 | 496 | 512 | 528 | 544 | 560 | 576 | 592 | 608 | 624 |
| 20 | 512 | 528 | 544 | 560 | 576 | 592 | 608 | 624 | 640 |
| 21 | 528 | 544 | 560 | 576 | 592 | 608 | 624 | 640 | 656 |
| 22 | 544 | 560 | 576 | 592 | 608 | 624 | 640 | 656 | 672 |
| 23 | 560 | 576 | 592 | 608 | 624 | 640 | 656 | 672 | 688 |
| 24 | 576 | 592 | 608 | 624 | 640 | 656 | 672 | 688 | 704 |
| 25 | 592 | 608 | 624 | 640 | 656 | 672 | 688 | 704 | 720 |

### TABLE 13  Wall Area of Rooms (9-ft Ceiling), ft²

| Feet | 3 | 4 | 5 | 6 | 7 | 8 | 9 | 10 | 11 |
|---|---|---|---|---|---|---|---|---|---|
| 3 | 108 | 126 | 144 | 162 | 180 | 198 | 216 | 234 | 252 |
| 4 | 126 | 144 | 162 | 180 | 198 | 216 | 234 | 252 | 270 |
| 5 | 144 | 162 | 180 | 198 | 216 | 234 | 252 | 270 | 288 |
| 6 | 162 | 180 | 198 | 216 | 234 | 252 | 270 | 288 | 306 |
| 7 | 180 | 198 | 216 | 234 | 252 | 270 | 288 | 306 | 324 |
| 8 | 198 | 216 | 234 | 252 | 270 | 288 | 306 | 324 | 342 |
| 9 | 216 | 234 | 252 | 270 | 288 | 306 | 324 | 342 | 360 |
| 10 | 234 | 252 | 270 | 288 | 306 | 324 | 342 | 360 | 378 |
| 11 | 252 | 270 | 288 | 306 | 324 | 342 | 360 | 378 | 396 |
| 12 | 270 | 288 | 306 | 324 | 342 | 360 | 378 | 396 | 414 |
| 13 | 288 | 306 | 324 | 342 | 360 | 378 | 396 | 414 | 432 |
| 14 | 306 | 324 | 342 | 360 | 378 | 396 | 414 | 432 | 450 |
| 15 | 324 | 342 | 360 | 378 | 396 | 414 | 432 | 450 | 468 |
| 16 | 342 | 360 | 378 | 396 | 414 | 432 | 450 | 468 | 486 |
| 17 | 360 | 378 | 396 | 414 | 432 | 450 | 468 | 486 | 504 |
| 18 | 378 | 396 | 414 | 432 | 450 | 468 | 486 | 504 | 522 |
| 19 | 396 | 414 | 432 | 450 | 468 | 486 | 504 | 522 | 540 |
| 20 | 414 | 432 | 450 | 468 | 486 | 504 | 522 | 540 | 558 |
| 21 | 432 | 450 | 468 | 486 | 504 | 522 | 540 | 558 | 576 |
| 22 | 450 | 468 | 486 | 504 | 522 | 540 | 558 | 576 | 594 |
| 23 | 468 | 486 | 504 | 522 | 540 | 558 | 576 | 594 | 612 |
| 24 | 486 | 504 | 522 | 540 | 558 | 576 | 594 | 612 | 630 |
| 25 | 504 | 522 | 540 | 558 | 576 | 594 | 612 | 630 | 648 |

| Feet | 12 | 13 | 14 | 15 | 16 | 17 | 18 | 19 | 20 |
|---|---|---|---|---|---|---|---|---|---|
| 3 | 270 | 288 | 306 | 324 | 342 | 360 | 378 | 396 | 414 |
| 4 | 288 | 306 | 324 | 342 | 360 | 378 | 396 | 414 | 432 |
| 5 | 306 | 324 | 342 | 360 | 378 | 396 | 414 | 432 | 450 |
| 6 | 324 | 342 | 360 | 378 | 396 | 414 | 432 | 450 | 468 |
| 7 | 342 | 360 | 378 | 396 | 414 | 432 | 450 | 468 | 486 |
| 8 | 360 | 378 | 396 | 414 | 432 | 450 | 468 | 486 | 504 |
| 9 | 378 | 396 | 414 | 432 | 450 | 468 | 486 | 504 | 522 |
| 10 | 396 | 414 | 432 | 450 | 468 | 486 | 504 | 522 | 540 |
| 11 | 414 | 432 | 450 | 468 | 486 | 504 | 522 | 540 | 558 |
| 12 | 432 | 450 | 468 | 486 | 504 | 522 | 540 | 558 | 576 |
| 13 | 450 | 468 | 486 | 504 | 522 | 540 | 558 | 576 | 594 |
| 14 | 468 | 486 | 504 | 522 | 540 | 558 | 576 | 594 | 612 |
| 15 | 486 | 504 | 522 | 540 | 558 | 576 | 594 | 612 | 630 |
| 16 | 504 | 522 | 540 | 558 | 576 | 594 | 612 | 630 | 648 |
| 17 | 522 | 540 | 558 | 576 | 594 | 612 | 630 | 648 | 666 |
| 18 | 540 | 558 | 576 | 594 | 612 | 630 | 648 | 666 | 684 |
| 19 | 558 | 576 | 594 | 612 | 630 | 648 | 666 | 684 | 702 |
| 20 | 576 | 594 | 612 | 630 | 648 | 666 | 684 | 702 | 720 |
| 21 | 594 | 612 | 630 | 648 | 666 | 684 | 702 | 720 | 738 |
| 22 | 612 | 630 | 648 | 666 | 684 | 702 | 720 | 738 | 756 |
| 23 | 630 | 648 | 666 | 684 | 702 | 720 | 738 | 756 | 774 |
| 24 | 648 | 666 | 684 | 702 | 720 | 738 | 756 | 774 | 792 |
| 25 | 666 | 684 | 702 | 720 | 738 | 756 | 774 | 792 | 810 |

**TABLE 14  Wall Area of Rooms (10-ft Ceiling), ft²**

| Feet | 3 | 4 | 5 | 6 | 7 | 8 | 9 | 10 | 11 | Feet | 12 | 13 | 14 | 15 | 16 | 17 | 18 | 19 | 20 |
|------|-----|-----|-----|-----|-----|-----|-----|-----|-----|------|-----|-----|-----|-----|-----|-----|-----|-----|-----|
| 3 | 120 | 140 | 160 | 180 | 200 | 220 | 240 | 260 | 280 | 3 | 300 | 320 | 340 | 360 | 380 | 400 | 420 | 440 | 460 |
| 4 | 140 | 160 | 180 | 200 | 220 | 240 | 260 | 280 | 300 | 4 | 320 | 340 | 360 | 380 | 400 | 420 | 440 | 460 | 480 |
| 5 | 160 | 180 | 200 | 220 | 240 | 260 | 280 | 300 | 320 | 5 | 340 | 360 | 380 | 400 | 420 | 440 | 460 | 480 | 500 |
| 6 | 180 | 200 | 220 | 240 | 260 | 280 | 300 | 320 | 340 | 6 | 360 | 380 | 400 | 420 | 440 | 460 | 480 | 500 | 520 |
| 7 | 200 | 220 | 240 | 260 | 280 | 300 | 320 | 340 | 360 | 7 | 380 | 400 | 420 | 440 | 460 | 480 | 500 | 520 | 540 |
| 8 | 220 | 240 | 260 | 280 | 300 | 320 | 340 | 360 | 380 | 8 | 400 | 420 | 440 | 460 | 480 | 500 | 520 | 540 | 560 |
| 9 | 240 | 260 | 280 | 300 | 320 | 340 | 360 | 380 | 400 | 9 | 420 | 440 | 460 | 480 | 500 | 520 | 540 | 560 | 580 |
| 10 | 260 | 280 | 300 | 320 | 340 | 360 | 380 | 400 | 420 | 10 | 440 | 460 | 480 | 500 | 520 | 540 | 560 | 580 | 600 |
| 11 | 280 | 300 | 320 | 340 | 360 | 380 | 400 | 420 | 440 | 11 | 460 | 480 | 500 | 520 | 540 | 560 | 580 | 600 | 620 |
| 12 | 300 | 320 | 340 | 360 | 380 | 400 | 420 | 440 | 460 | 12 | 480 | 500 | 520 | 540 | 560 | 580 | 600 | 620 | 640 |
| 13 | 320 | 340 | 360 | 380 | 400 | 420 | 440 | 460 | 480 | 13 | 500 | 520 | 540 | 560 | 580 | 600 | 620 | 640 | 660 |
| 14 | 340 | 360 | 380 | 400 | 420 | 440 | 460 | 480 | 500 | 14 | 520 | 540 | 560 | 580 | 600 | 620 | 640 | 660 | 680 |
| 15 | 360 | 380 | 400 | 420 | 440 | 460 | 480 | 500 | 520 | 15 | 540 | 560 | 580 | 600 | 620 | 640 | 660 | 680 | 700 |
| 16 | 380 | 400 | 420 | 440 | 460 | 480 | 500 | 520 | 540 | 16 | 560 | 580 | 600 | 620 | 640 | 660 | 680 | 700 | 720 |
| 17 | 400 | 420 | 440 | 460 | 480 | 500 | 520 | 540 | 560 | 17 | 580 | 600 | 620 | 640 | 660 | 680 | 700 | 720 | 740 |
| 18 | 420 | 440 | 460 | 480 | 500 | 520 | 540 | 560 | 580 | 18 | 600 | 620 | 640 | 660 | 680 | 700 | 720 | 740 | 760 |
| 19 | 440 | 460 | 480 | 500 | 520 | 540 | 560 | 580 | 600 | 19 | 620 | 640 | 660 | 680 | 700 | 720 | 740 | 760 | 780 |
| 20 | 460 | 480 | 500 | 520 | 540 | 560 | 580 | 600 | 620 | 20 | 640 | 660 | 680 | 700 | 720 | 740 | 760 | 780 | 800 |
| 21 | 480 | 500 | 520 | 540 | 560 | 580 | 600 | 620 | 640 | 21 | 660 | 680 | 700 | 720 | 740 | 760 | 780 | 800 | 820 |
| 22 | 500 | 520 | 540 | 560 | 580 | 600 | 620 | 640 | 660 | 22 | 680 | 700 | 720 | 740 | 760 | 780 | 800 | 820 | 840 |
| 23 | 520 | 540 | 560 | 580 | 600 | 620 | 640 | 660 | 680 | 23 | 700 | 720 | 740 | 760 | 780 | 800 | 820 | 840 | 860 |
| 24 | 540 | 560 | 580 | 600 | 620 | 640 | 660 | 680 | 700 | 24 | 720 | 740 | 760 | 780 | 800 | 820 | 840 | 860 | 880 |
| 25 | 560 | 580 | 600 | 620 | 640 | 660 | 680 | 700 | 720 | 25 | 740 | 760 | 780 | 800 | 820 | 840 | 860 | 880 | 900 |

# FLOOR AND WALL COVERING

**Panel Conversion Chart**

**TABLE 15  Standard Modular Panel Conversion Chart**
(For plywood, architectural woodwork, sheathing, plastic laminate, gypsum board, and other modular wall components)

| No. of units | Size (areas in square feet) | | | | No. of units | Size (areas in square feet) | | | |
|---|---|---|---|---|---|---|---|---|---|
| | 4' x 8' | 4' x 10' | 4' x 12' | 4' x 14' | | 4' x 8' | 4' x 10' | 4' x 12' | 4' x 14' |
| 10 | 320 | 400 | 480 | 560 | | | | | |
| 11 | 352 | 440 | 528 | 616 | 36 | 1152 | 1440 | 1728 | 2016 |
| 12 | 384 | 480 | 576 | 672 | 37 | 1184 | 1480 | 1776 | 2072 |
| 13 | 416 | 520 | 624 | 728 | 38 | 1216 | 1520 | 1824 | 2128 |
| 14 | 448 | 560 | 672 | 784 | 39 | 1248 | 1560 | 1872 | 2184 |
| 15 | 480 | 600 | 720 | 840 | 40 | 1280 | 1600 | 1920 | 2240 |
| 16 | 512 | 640 | 768 | 896 | 41 | 1312 | 1640 | 1968 | 2296 |
| 17 | 544 | 680 | 816 | 952 | 42 | 1344 | 1680 | 2016 | 2352 |
| 18 | 576 | 720 | 864 | 1008 | 43 | 1376 | 1720 | 2064 | 2408 |
| 19 | 608 | 760 | 912 | 1064 | 44 | 1408 | 1760 | 2112 | 2464 |
| 20 | 640 | 800 | 960 | 1120 | 45 | 1440 | 1800 | 2160 | 2520 |
| 21 | 672 | 840 | 1008 | 1176 | 46 | 1472 | 1840 | 2208 | 2576 |
| 22 | 704 | 880 | 1056 | 1232 | 47 | 1504 | 1880 | 2256 | 2632 |
| 23 | 736 | 920 | 1104 | 1288 | 48 | 1536 | 1920 | 2304 | 2688 |
| 24 | 768 | 960 | 1152 | 1344 | 49 | 1568 | 1960 | 2352 | 2744 |
| 25 | 800 | 1000 | 1200 | 1400 | 50 | 1600 | 2000 | 2400 | 2800 |
| 26 | 832 | 1040 | 1248 | 1456 | 51 | 1632 | 2040 | 2448 | 2856 |
| 27 | 864 | 1080 | 1296 | 1512 | 52 | 1664 | 2080 | 2496 | 2912 |
| 28 | 896 | 1120 | 1344 | 1568 | 53 | 1696 | 2120 | 2544 | 2968 |
| 29 | 928 | 1160 | 1392 | 1624 | 54 | 1728 | 2160 | 2592 | 3024 |
| 30 | 960 | 1200 | 1440 | 1680 | 55 | 1760 | 2200 | 2640 | 3080 |
| 31 | 992 | 1240 | 1488 | 1736 | 56 | 1792 | 2240 | 2688 | 3136 |
| 32 | 1024 | 1280 | 1536 | 1792 | 57 | 1824 | 2280 | 2736 | 3192 |
| 33 | 1056 | 1320 | 1584 | 1848 | 58 | 1856 | 2320 | 2784 | 3248 |
| 34 | 1088 | 1360 | 1632 | 1904 | 59 | 1888 | 2360 | 2832 | 3304 |
| 35 | 1120 | 1400 | 1680 | 1960 | 60 | 1920 | 2400 | 2880 | 3360 |

ESTIMATING THE AMOUNT OF HARDWOOD STRIP FLOORING REQUIRED

An allowance for side-matching, plus 5% for end-matching and normal waste are incorporated in these percentages.

Take the Square Footage and ADD the percentage below opposite the size strip flooring to be used.

| When using | 3/4x1-1/2" Strip ADD | 55% |
|---|---|---|
| | 3/4x2" | 42-1/2% |
| | 3/4x2-1/4" | 38-1/3% |
| | 3/4x3-1/4" | 29% |
| | 3/8x1-1/2" | 38-1/3% |
| | 3/8x2" | 30% |
| | 1/2x2-1/2" | 38-1/3% |
| | 1/2x2" | 30% |

Above percentages are for laying flooring straight across the room. Additional flooring should be estimated for diagonal applications and bay windows or other projections.

-------------------------------------------------------------------

CONVERTING SQUARE FEET OF FLOOR SPACE
To Board Feet of Strip Flooring Required.

| FLOOR SPACE | BOARD FEET REQUIRED | | (5% Cutting Waste Included) | | |
|---|---|---|---|---|---|
| Square Feet | 3/4x2¼" | 3/4x1½" | 3/4x3¼" | 1/2x2" | 3/8x1½" |
| 5 | 7 | 8 | 6 | 7 | 7 |
| 10 | 14 | 16 | 13 | 13 | 14 |
| 20 | 28 | 31 | 26 | 26 | 28 |
| 30 | 42 | 47 | 39 | 39 | 42 |
| 40 | 55 | 62 | 52 | 52 | 55 |
| 50 | 69 | 78 | 65 | 65 | 69 |
| 60 | 83 | 93 | 77 | 78 | 83 |
| 70 | 97 | 109 | 90 | 91 | 97 |
| 80 | 111 | 124 | 103 | 104 | 111 |
| 90 | 125 | 140 | 116 | 117 | 125 |
| 100 | 138 | 155 | 129 | 130 | 138 |
| 200 | 277 | 310 | 258 | 260 | 277 |
| 300 | 415 | 465 | 387 | 390 | 415 |
| 400 | 553 | 620 | 516 | 520 | 553 |
| 500 | 692 | 775 | 645 | 650 | 692 |
| 600 | 830 | 930 | 774 | 780 | 830 |
| 700 | 968 | 1085 | 903 | 910 | 968 |
| 800 | 1107 | 1240 | 1032 | 1040 | 1107 |
| 900 | 1245 | 1395 | 1161 | 1170 | 1245 |
| 1000 | 1383 | 1550 | 1290 | 1300 | 1383 |

(a) Velvet weave

(c) Axminster weave

(b) Wilton weave

(d) Tufted process

Fig. 14

Carpets are manufactured in three different ways: woven, knitted, or tufted.

**Woven carpet** The surface pile and backing of woven carpet are interwoven at the same time, creating a single fabric. Due to the interweaving, which locks all of the yarns together in the single woven fabric, the pile yarns cannot be pulled out. Some carpet weaves presently available are velvet, wilton, and axminster. Velvet is best suited for solid-color carpet; however, tweeds, stripes, and salt-and-pepper effects can be produced on velvet looms. The usual velvet is a solid-color carpet with smooth surface and even pile. Sometimes the pile is cut to produce a plushlike surface [see Fig. 14(a)]. It may also be had in loop pile, or twist.

Wilton weave comes in almost unlimited numbers of textures and sculptured effects, as well as patterns. The pile is sometimes cut, sometimes left uncut; a combination of cut and uncut may also be obtained. In multicolor wiltons, one color may be seen on the surface pile, while other colors are hidden in the body of the carpet. Embossed and sculptured effects are also made by the wilton looms, and cut and uncut pile can be combined with cut pile for the top level, with loops at other levels. Another variation is to have some pile yarn straight and others twisted [see Fig. 14(b)].

In the axminster weave, which is similar in appearance to handweaving, we find a complete flexibility in the use of color. In this method each tuft is inserted separately and while solid-color carpets can be made by this method, it is nearly always used for multicolored pattern carpet such as orientals, or modern and geometric designs [see Fig. 14(c)].

**Tufted carpet** In the tufted process, which was only recently perfected, the tufts are attached to a previously made backing, as compared with the methods described above in which the backing and pile are integral. The tufts are held in place by a heavy coating of latex applied to the backing, which is usually cotton, jute, or kraft cord. By the use of this method, a wide variety of textures is possible. For example, the tufted pile can be made in several levels; it can be cut or uncut; and carved or striated effects can be obtained. The pile can be looped or plush. Tufted carpets are made in multicolor patterns with an increasing number of textural effects and refinements [see Fig. 14(d)].

FINISH HARDWARE LOCATION FOR
ALL TYPES of DOORS

# HOME-DECORATING FABRIC CHART

In the chart below are listed the fabrics usually classified as primarily decorating materials. In addition to these, practically all dress materials may be used, and are often woven in extra widths for this purpose. Among these are: light weight cottons such as cambric, challis, chambray, gingham, muslin, percale, poplin, seersucker, silkaline all used for informal draperies, bed coverings, dressing tables, etc.; stiff fabrics such as buckram and crinoline for interlining curtain tops, valances, etc.; cottons such as Canton flannel used for interlinings, and sateen for linings; heavy utility cottons such as crash, denim, drill, gabardine, pique, all suited to certain types of draperies, couch covers, etc.; sheer cottons such as cheesecloth, dimity, plain and dotted Swiss, lace, lawn, organdy, voile, all used for glass curtains, bed coverings, etc.; pile fabrics such as corduroy, panne velet, velour, velvet, velveteen, all excellent for upholstery, draperies, etc.; silk fabrics such as faille, moire (watered silk), pongee and shantung, satin, taffeta, all used for draperies, bed coverings, slipcovers, sometimes upholstery; sheer silks such as chiffon for glass curtains, lamp shades, etc.

| FABRIC | DESCRIPTION | SUITABLE FOR |
|---|---|---|
| **ARMURE** | Ribbed silk, cotton, rayon (sometimes wool), fabric with small design on the surface. | Draperies. Medium-weight upholstery. |
| **ARTIFICIAL LEATHER** | Available under many trade names. A woven cotton fabric, coated with nitrocellulose preparation and stamped surface to simulate different kinds of leather. | Medium-weight upholstery. Panels. Other decorative uses. |
| **BATIK** | Javanese process of coloring fabrics by blocking out various parts of the pattern with wax before dyeing. | Curtains and panels. Other decorative effects. |
| **BOBBINET** | Net with hexagonal openings. Originally handmade with a bobbin. | Glass curtains. Dressing table skirts, etc. |
| **BROCADE** | Rich, colorful fabric with embroidery effects on taffeta, twill, satin or damask weave background. Gold or silver metal threads sometimes introduced in the figures. Brocade is also the name designating a certain type of Jacquard weave. | Draperies. Medium-weight upholstery. Especially good for rooms of Queen Anne, Chippendale, Hepplewhite or Sheraton furnishings of 18th Century. |
| **BROCATELLE** | A heavy fabric with general characteristics of damask, but figures more raised and velvety in quality giving embossed effect. | Draperies on very large studio-size windows. Heavy-weight upholstery. |
| **BROCHE** | Brocade with small floral pattern. | Lined or unlined draperies. Medium-weight upholstery. |
| **BURLAP** | Coarse, plain-weave fabric made of jute or hemp. Comes in variety of colors and widths. Inexpensive. | Drapery or upholstery purposes. |
| **CALICO** | Light-weight cotton fabric in plain weave. May be printed, plain or patterned, in deep colors. Designs usually small. (Also for dresses.) | Curtains, draperies, bedspreads, comfortables. Excellent with Early American or French Provincial furnishings. |
| **CANDLEWICK** | Cotton yarn used for hand tufting on muslin sheeting. Yarn may be white or in color and design simple or elaborate. | Bedspreads, draperies, and other decorative purposes. |
| **CANVAS** | A coarse, firm cotton or linen material, rough finish, plain weave. May be bleached, unbleached, starched, dyed, or printed. | Awnings, couch covers, etc.; also used for stiff interlining as at top of draperies. |
| **CASEMENT CLOTH** | Light, plain, and usually neutral in color. Made in cotton, linen, mohair, silk, wool or rayon. Sometimes comes in small figures. | Fine for draw-curtains; also glass curtains in sheer textures. |
| **CELLOPHANE** | Glossy, transparent synthetic product woven on warp threads of cotton. Often woven in with other materials and used for many novelty effects. | Draperies in modern interiors. Trimmings, etc. |
| **CHENILLE** | Various types of fabrics woven with chenille yarn of silk, wool, mercerized cotton, or rayon. | Draperies. Yarn used for tufting, fringes, etc. |
| **CHEVRON CLOTH** | Fabric with broken twill weave forming chevron pattern. | Draperies, etc. |
| **CHINTZ** | A firm plain weave cotton fabric usually printed in gay pattern, but may be had in plain colors. May be semi-glazed or fully glazed. Some chintz has special finish so that it will retain glaze after washing. Glazed chintz is more resistant to dirt, while its shiny surface and stiff texture adds to its charm. There are many grades of chintz, and many have soil-resistant special finish. | May be formal or informal in pattern. Suitable to any room according to pattern, quality and treatment. Used for draperies, upholstery, slip covers, lamp shades, etc. |
| **CRETONNE** | Cotton or linen fabric named for French town of Creton, with plain, rep or damask weave background printed in large designs. Does not muss easily and can be washed often. | Draperies, upholstery, slip covers, bed covers, etc. Often more formal than chintz. |
| **CREWEL EMBROIDERY** | A type of wool embroidery worked on unbleached cotton or linen ground in large floral, bird, or tree designs. | Draperies and upholstery. Used extensively during Jacobean period. |
| **DAMASK** | The name originated with the beautiful silks woven in Damascus during the 12th Century. Damasks are now made of linen, cotton, wool, or any of the synthetic fibers, or combinations of the two. In taffeta weave on satin ground, this fabric in flat woven pattern is usually reversible. Damask is also the name given to a kind of Jacquard weave. | In silk or cotton it is used for draperies and upholstery. Appropriate for Queen Anne, Chippendale, Hepplewhite or Sheraton furnishings of 18th Century. |
| **DRUID'S CLOTH** | A fabric of loosely twisted cotton yarn, or cotton mixed with jute, in basket weave. Something like monk's cloth but not as rough in texture. | Draperies. Couch covers. |
| **DUCK** | Heavy plain weave cotton fabric. | Outdoor cushions, etc. |
| **FELT** | A material made by matting together, under heat or pressure, woolen fibers, mohair, cowhair, or mixed fibers. | Upholstery and couch covers. Rugs. |

# HOME-DECORATING FABRIC CHART CONTINUED

| FABRIC | DESCRIPTION | SUITABLE FOR |
|---|---|---|
| FILET NET | Cotton or linen net with square mesh. Hand netted filet has a knot at each corner of square mesh. | Curtains, tablecloths, scarves, etc. |
| FORTUNY PRINTS | Fabrics produced in Venice by a secret printing process which gives cotton cloth the effect of antique brocades and damasks. Comes in beautiful color combinations. | Draperies. Wall hangings, screens, etc. |
| FRIAR'S CLOTH | Like druid's cloth but with finer basket weave. | Same as druid's cloth. |
| FRISE | Uncut pile fabric of wool, mohair, cotton or linen. Patterns may be printed or produced by using yarns of different colors, or by cutting some of the loops to give sculptured effect. Very durable. | Upholstery. |
| GAUZE | Thin, sheer transparent fabric of plain weave, sometimes printed. May be all silk, or cotton, linen, wool, mohair, synthetic fibers, or combinations. | Glass curtains. |
| HAIR CLOTH | A fabric with warp of cotton, worsted, or linen, and horsehair weft, woven plain, striped or patterned. May now be obtained in colors and variety of woven designs. | Upholstery. Used extensively in England and America during middle of 19th Century. |
| HOMESPUN | Coarse hand-woven woolen, cotton or linen fabrics. Also trade name given to imitations made on power looms. | Curtains and upholstery in informal rooms. Bedspreads in cotton. |
| INDIA PRINTS | Printed cotton cloth with clear colors and characteristic designs of India or Persia. Handprinted with many colors on white or natural background. | Draperies. Wall hangings. Bed coverings, etc. |
| JASPE | Fabrics having warp threads of different colors giving material streaked or mottled effect, resembling jasper. | Draperies and other decorative effects. |
| LAME | A fabric with silk and metal threads in plain weave or with a woven pattern. | Drapery. Panels. |
| LAMPAS | A fabric similar to damask in appearance and brocatelle in weave. Generally all silk with multi-colored pattern on plain background, often classic in design. | Used as damask is used. |
| MARQUISETTE | Sheer cloth in gauze weave of cotton, silk, rayon, often with woven figure. It comes in wide range of colors, and may be dyed or printed. | Excellent for glass curtains. Fluffy, dainty, tailored spreads. |
| METALASSE | Fabric with brocaded pattern in raised, padded or blistered effect. | Draperies. |
| MOHAIR | Various types of fabrics made from the fleece of the Angora goat. Most durable of all textiles. Now woven in combination with cotton, linen, silk or wool into many types of plain, twill or pile fabrics. | Very durable and widely used for upholstery. |
| MONK'S CLOTH | Heavy cotton fabric of coarse basket weave. | Drapery material. |
| MOQUETTE | Pile fabric resembling frise, woven on Jacquard loom with small set pattern in different colors. | Used for upholstery in mohair, wool, or heavy cotton. |
| NINON | A semi-transparent fabric of silk or rayon. | Glass curtains. |
| PLUSH | High pile fabric resembling fur, made of silk, wool, cotton or any synthetic fiber. Pile may be cut or uncut. | Upholstery. |
| REP | Plain weave fabric of heavy rib made of silk, cotton or wool, or synthetic fibers. Unpatterned and reversible. | Draperies. Upholstery. |
| SAIL CLOTH | Stout, firm, plain weave cotton material similar to canvas in construction but lighter. Has a stiff, hard texture and is printed in gay, bright colors. | Draperies. Slip covers. Bedspreads, etc. |
| SLIPPER SATIN | Sleek, smooth very heavy satin in rayon or silk; may be slightly stiff because of thickness. | Drapery and upholstery, bed coverings, etc. Suitable in formal and period rooms for draperies. |
| SCRIM | Fabric of coarse two-ply yarns in plain, open weave. Often mercerized. | Curtains, bedspreads, etc. |
| STRIE | Term used to designate fabric with uneven streaked effect. This process gives two-toned appearance to taffeta, satin, etc. | According to fabric. |
| TERRY CLOTH | Light cotton fabric similar to bath toweling. Woven with uncut loops. May be dyed or printed, in designs of one or two colors. Rich texture and reversible. | Draperies. Draw-curtains. |
| THEATRICAL GAUZE | Loosely woven, transparent plain-weave fabric of cotton or linen. Obtainable in brilliant as well as soft colors. Inexpensive. | Glass curtains. |
| TOILES DE JOUY | Printed cotton material with repeat designs showing landscapes, or historical scenes. Reproductions of famous printed fabric woven at Jouy, near Paris, France. Designs and figure groups usually in colors on white or cream background. | Draperies, wall hangings, upholstery, bed coverings. Excellent for French, English and American period rooms of late 18th Century and early 19th Century; also French Provincial. |
| TWEED WEAVES | Term applied to a large group of woolen goods made from worsted yarns, woven in plain, twill, or herringbone twill weaves in homespun type. | Draperies and upholstery. Very good for modern or masculine rooms. |
| VELOUR | Really a French word for velvet. Through common usage, a short-pile velvet. | Same as velvet. |

## ELECTRICAL

**Office and Electronic Equipment**

**TABLE 16   Typical Amperage Ratings**

| Equipment | Amperage |
|---|---|
| **Electronic Equipment'** | |
| Video Display Terminals (Detached Keyboards) | |
| Normal maximum | 2.50 |
| Burroughs/MT 983 TP110 | .08 |
| Digital/VT 278 Decmate | 1.25 |
| Form-Phase Systems/8115-2 | .48 |
| Harris/8680A | 1.00 |
| Hewlett-Packard/2382A | .75 |
| IBM/3101 | 1.20 |
| IBM/3278 or 3276 | 1.33 |
| IBM/3279 | 2.50 |
| IBM/5251 Model 11 | 2.10 |
| IBM/6580 | 4.80 |
| ITT Courier/2790-2A | 1.50 |
| Perkin/Elmer/1251 | 1.30 |
| Prime/PT-45 | 1.00 |
| Raytheon/PTS100 | .80 |
| Sperry-Univac/UTS20 (313) | .50 |
| Texas Instruments/940/200 | 2.00 |
| Texas Instruments/DS990 | 2.20 |
| Wang/5503 | 3.00 |
| Xerox/8000 Series | .50 |
| Video Display Terminals (Integrated Keyboard) | |
| Normal maximum | 3.00 |
| Hewlett-Packard/HP-9845A | 4.50 |
| Lear Siegler/ADM31 | .50 |
| NCR/7900-01 | .60 |
| Perkin-Elmer/550B | .80 |
| Tektronics/4112 | 3.00 |
| Wang/5536 | 2.00 |
| Printers (Stand Alone) | |
| Digital Equipment/LA-120AA | 3.00 |
| Wang/5503 | 4.00 |
| Xerox/8000 Print Server | 11.00 |
| Printers (Desk Top) | |
| Normal maximum | 3.50 |
| Centronics/7030 | 1.50 |
| Digital Equipment/Decwriter IV | 1.30 |
| Form-Phase Systems/8125 | 1.60 |
| Hewlett-Packard/7221B | 1.00 |
| Hewlett-Packard/HP7240A | 2.50 |
| IBM/3287 | 2.36 |
| IBM/5256 | 4.70 |
| Epson/FX 185 | .70 |
| NEC/3510 | 2.50 |
| ITT Courier/8700 | 1.60 |
| Lear Siegler/300 Series | 1.60 |
| Perkin-Elmer/650 | 1.50 |
| Raytheon/PTS 1200 3472 | 1.50 |
| Sperry-Univac/0786 | 4.00 |
| Tektronix/4612 | 3.30 |
| Texas Instruments/Omni-800 810R0 | 5.00 |
| Wang/5531-2 w/floor mount | 1.70 |
| Wang/5577 (DW-20 Series) | 1.20 |

| Equipment | Amperage |
|---|---|
| **Electronic Equipment** | |
| Memory Storage Devices (Desk Top) | |
| Wang/5503 Disk | 4.00 |
| Xerox/8000 NS | 12.00 |
| Digital Equipment/RX02 | 3.00 |
| Hewlett-Packard/8290 ZM | 1.00 |
| Hewlett-Packard/9895A | 1.60 |
| Sperry-Univac/8406 | 1.50 |
| Texas Instruments/WD-500 | 3.00 |
| Bell/Western Electric/Dataphone 300/1200 | .08 |
| **Office Equipment*** | |
| General | |
| Typewriter | 1.50 |
| Transcriber | .15 |
| Microfiche | .85 |
| Manuscript holder | .75 |
| Calculator | .25 |
| A.C. adapter | .05 |
| Electric eraser | .25 |
| Pencil sharpener | .25 |
| Fan | 1.00 |
| Space heater (1,000 watts) | 8.50 |
| Space heater (1,250 watts) | 10.50 |
| Space heater (1,500 watts) | 12.50 |
| Coffee pots | 10.00 |
| Copy machine | 15.00 |
| Clock | .03 |
| CRT (average) | 1.50 |
| Printer (average) | 3.50 |
| Lighting | |
| Adjustable task light | .80 |
| 2″ task light (20 watt) | .27 |
| 2″ task light (30 watt) | .40 |
| 2″ task light (40 watt) | .48 |
| 2″ task light (35 watt, energy-saving ballast) | .38 |
| Indirect ambient light | |
| (30 watt/2 lamp) | .68 |
| (30 watt/3 lamp) | 1.08 |
| (40 watt/2 lamp) | .80 |
| (40 watt/3 lamp) | 1.28 |
| (35 watt/2 lamp) | .63 |
| (35 watt/3 lamp with energy-saving ballast) | 1.01 |
| HID light (400 watt) | 4.00 |
| (250 watt) | 2.50 |
| (175 watt) | 1.80 |
| PLP light (20 watt) | .65 |
| (40 watt) | .80 |

*Note:* These figures are for quick reference only. For specific information consult the manufacturer.

*Some appliances — such as large copiers, coffee makers, or space heaters — require most of the current available on a 20-amp circuit. It is recommended that such devices be supplied with their own receptacle, directly from the building. This leaves the capacity of Series 9000 circuits available for the more dynamic requirements of the office occupants.

Receptacle required if any
wall width is 2 ft or more

Walls with sliding
glass doors or
floor-to-ceiling
windows must be
counted as wall
space requiring
receptacles

Wall
receptacles

Floor receptacles must be
close to wall to count as
required spaced receptacles

**Fig. 15   From any point along wall, at floor line, a receptacle must be not more than 6 ft away.**

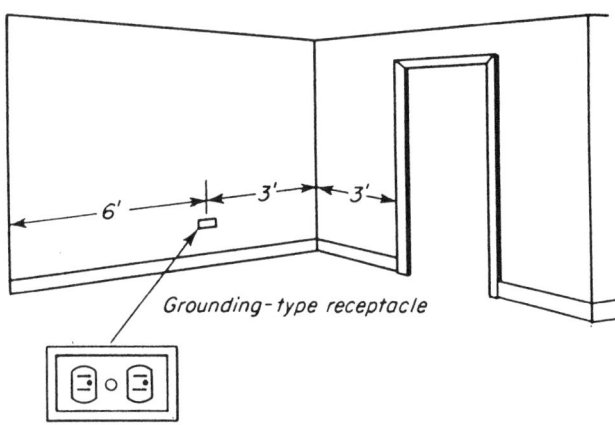

Grounding-type receptacle

**Fig. 16   Location of the receptacle as shown will permit the plugging in of a lamp or appliance located 6 ft on either side of the receptacle.**

## Receptacle required at each counter space wider than 12 in.

Wall receptacles    Counter space

**COUNTER SPACES** in kitchen and dining rooms such as shown by arrows (above) must be supplied with receptacles if they are over 12 in. wide Appliances are frequently used even on narrow counter widths; this requirement is designed to remove the dangerous practice of stretching cords across sinks, behind ranges, etc., to feed such appliances.

## Inaccessible receptacles.

This receptacle is
rendered inaccessible
by refrigerator

therefore another receptacle
must be installed to serve
counter top

Counter top

Refrigerator

**RECEPTACLE LOCATED** behind an appliance, making the receptacle inaccessible, does not count as one of the required "counter-top" receptacles. (Neither does it count as one of the appliance-circuit receptacles required to be located every 12 ft.)

**Fig. 17   Countertop receptacles are needed and must be accessible.**

(Combination switch
and receptacle)

LOCATION of receptacle will vary, depending upon available wall space. Arrows show several possibilities. A receptacle in a medicine cabinet or in the bathroom lighting fixture does not satisfy this rule.

**Fig. 18   Receptacle required adjacent to wash basin in residence.**

### TABLE 17  Residential Appliance, Load, and Circuit Chart*

| Appliance | Typical wattage | Voltage needed | Amps load | Wires and size† | Size fuse or breaker‡ | Type of circuit and comments |
|---|---|---|---|---|---|---|
| Range | 12,000 | 115/230 | 52 | 3#6 | 50A | Separate circuit—grounded |
| Countertop range | 6,000 | 115/230 | 26 | 3#10 | 30A | Separate circuit—grounded |
| Oven built-in | 5,000 | 115/230 | 22 | 3#10 | 30A | Separate circuit—grounded |
| Dishwasher | 1,200 | 115 | 10 | 2#12 w/grd§ | 20A | These two can be connected on one |
| Waste disposal | 500 | 115 | 5 | 2#12 w/grd | 20A | circuit; must be grounded. |
| Broiler | 1,500 | 115 | 13 | 2#12 | 20A | Two or more 20-amp circuits needed |
| Fryer | 1,300 | 115 | 11 | 2#12 | 20A | for these appliances depending on |
| Coffeemaker | 800 | 115 | 7 | 2#12 | 20A | number used at once. A 115/230 V |
| Refrigerator | 400 | 115 | 4 | 2#12 | 20A | "splitwired" circuit provides capac- |
| Toaster | 1,100 | 115 | 10 | 2#12 | 20A | ity of two ordinary circuits at any |
| Frypan | 1,200 | 115 | 10 | 2#12 | 20A | outlet. Ask your wiring inspector |
| Roaster | 1,500 | 115 | 13 | 2#12 | 20A | about this. |
| Clothes dryer | 5,000 to 9,000 | 115/230 | 25 | 3#10 to 3#6 | 30A to 45A | Separate circuit—grounded. |
| Washer | 500 | 115 | 9 | 2#12 w/grd | 20A | Grounded—advise fused outlet for motor protection. |
| Hand iron | 1,000 | 115 | 9 | 2#12 w/grd | 20A | A 20-A circuit will carry |
| Hot plate | 1,500 | 115 | 13 | 2#12 w/grd | 20A | only one of these in addition |
| Ironer | 1,650 | 115 | 15 | 2#12 w/grd | 20A | to washer. |
| Workshop | —— | 115 | — | 2#12 | 20A | Separate circuit grounded. |
| Portable heater | 1,500 | 115 | 13 | 2#12 | 20A | Use on general-use circuits. |
| Television | 300 | 115 | 3 | 2#14 | 15A | |
| Portable lights—(up to) | 300 | 115 | 3 | 2#14 | 15A | |
| Lighting, general (each) | 100 | 115 | 1½ | 2#14 | 15A | (Not over 9 per circuit, including convenience outlets.) |
| Air conditioner (window unit) | 1,500 | 115 or 230 | 13 or 7 | 2#12 w/grd | 20A | Requires separate circuit; 230 volt operation preferred. |
| Air conditioner (central unit) | 3,400 | 115/230 | 20 | 3#10 | — | Check manufacturer's recommendations; should be grounded. |
| Water system | 500 | 115 | 5 | 2#12 w/grd | 20A | Separate circuit—grounded. Provide motor protection (230V. for ½ hp. or larger). |
| Heating plant | 600 | 115 | 6 | 2#12 w/grd | 20A | Separate circuit—grounded. Provide motor protection. |
| Electric heaters (built-in) | 750 to 4,500 | 230 | — | — | — | Wiring should be planned with heating. Provide separate circuits for heating. |
| Water heater | 1,500 to 4,500 | 230 | 7 to 20 | 2#12 w/grd 2#10 w/grd | 20A to 30A | Separate circuit—grounded. |

† Wire sizes are for copper wire. For aluminum, use next larger size.

‡ Fustats advised in place of ordinary fuses up to 30 amp as they do not blow on harmless short-time overloads and cannot be replaced by a larger size.

§ W/grd means with groundwire. This is usually a bare wire run inside the same cable but can be installed separately. Portable equipment is grounded through the third prong on the plug. Permanent equipment is grounded by direct connection of the third wire to the frame of the appliance.

* Courtesy Agricultural Extension Service, South Dakota State University.

### TABLE 18  Typical Office Amperage Loads

| | |
|---|---|
| CAD station* | 10.00–20.00 |
| Calculator | .25 |
| Coffee pot* | 8.50–15.00 |
| Clock | .03 |
| Radio | .03 |
| Stereo | .33 |
| Tape recorder | .07 |
| Laser printer* | 6.00–10.00 |
| Desktop copier* | 10.00–15.00 |
| Electric eraser | .25 |
| Fan | 1.10 |
| Freestanding copier* | 15.00–20.00 |
| Pencil sharpener | 1.00 |
| Task light (4') | .67 |
| Adding machine | .35 |
| Letter opener | 1.90 |
| Dictaphone | .25 |
| Telecopier | .50 |
| Word processor | 1.50– 3.00 |
| Postage meter | 2.80 |
| Tape dispenser | 1.80 |
| Personal computer | 3.50– 8.00 |
| Desktop printer | 1.50– 5.00 |
| CRT | 1.00– 3.00 |
| Space heater* | 12.50 |
| Typewriter | 1.50 |
| Microfiche reader | .85 |
| Transcriber | .15 |
| A.C. adapter | .05 |
| 100-W lamp | .80 |

*Some appliances such as coffee pots, copiers, printers, and heaters consume most of the amperage available on a circuit. It is recommended that these devices be connected directly to the building power supply, leaving flexibility for other circuit planning.

### TABLE 19  Common House Circuits

| Type | Wire size | Ampere rating of fuse or circuit breaker | Volts | Load capacity in watts | Use of circuit | Types of outlets |
|---|---|---|---|---|---|---|
| General purpose | minimum #14 recommended #12 | 15 20 | 115–120 | 1725–1800 | Installed lighting, outlets for lamps and low wattage appliances all over the house | Those for attached light fixtures; ordinary convenience outlets |
| Appliance | minimum #12 recommended #10 | 20 25 | 115–120 | 2300–2400 2875–3000 | Portable appliances in kitchen, dining room, work room, laundry | Ordinary or grounded convenience outlets |
| Individual appliance | #12 | 20 | 115–120 | 2300–2400 | Automatic washer, refrigerator, freezer | Ordinary or grounded convenience outlets |
| Individual power | #6 or #8 | 30–60 | 220–240 | 6600–14400 | Range, water heater, clothes dryer | Receptacle for plug with 3 heavy prongs or appliances may be attached |

**doric**

**ionic**

**corinthian**

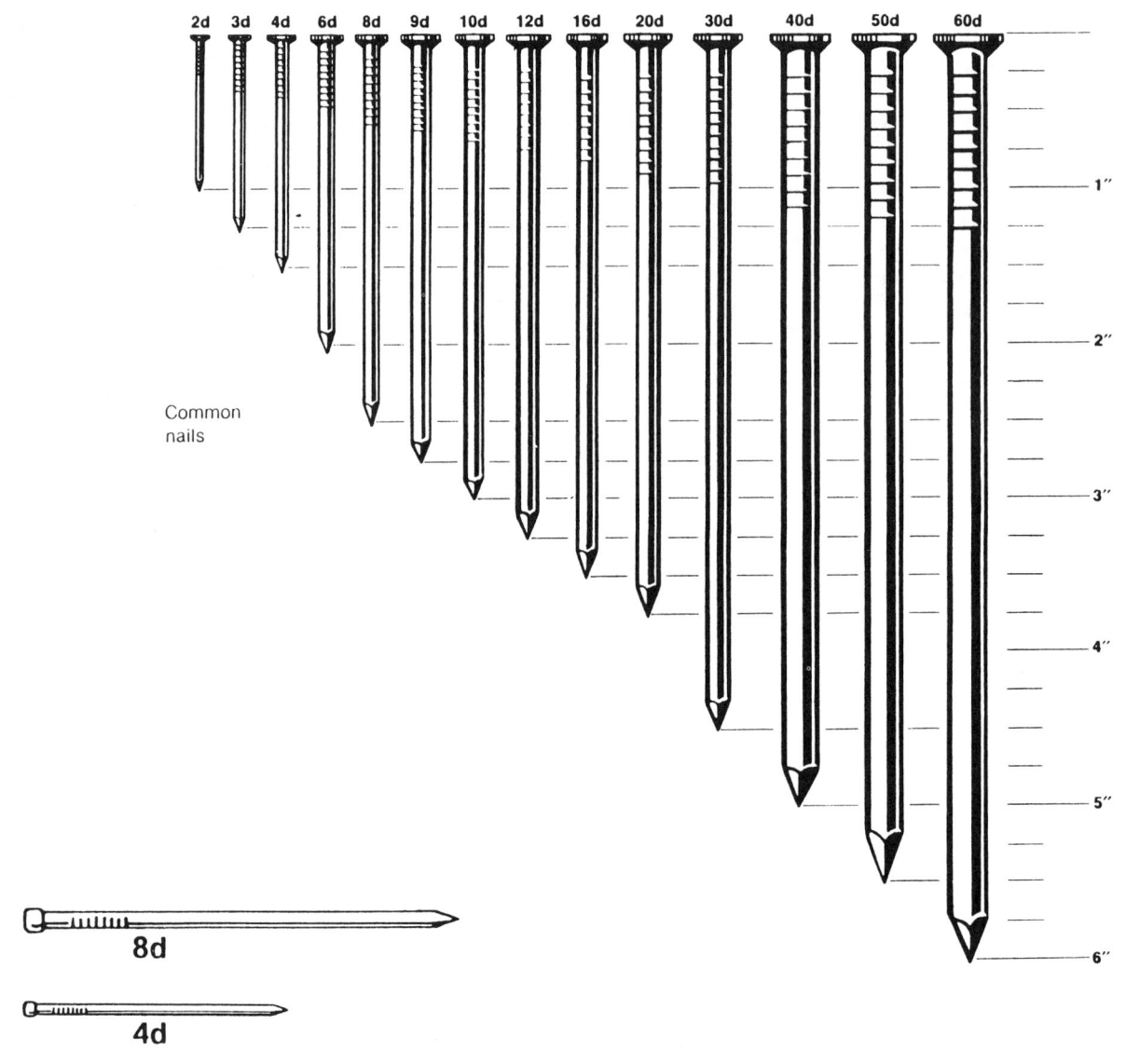

Common nails

**8d**

**4d**

Finishing nails

| Nos. | 1 | 1-1/2 | 2 | 2-1/2 | 3 | 4 | 6 | 8 | 10 | 12 | 14 | 16 | 18 | 20 | 22 | 24 |
|------|---|-------|---|-------|---|---|---|---|----|----|----|----|----|----|----|----|
| Ins. | 3/16'' | 7/32'' | 1/4'' | 5/16'' | 3/8'' | 7/16'' | 1/2'' | 9/16'' | 5/8'' | 11/16'' | 3/4'' | 13/16'' | 7/8'' | 15/16'' | 1'' | 1-1/8'' |

# STANDARD TACK SIZES
ESTABLISHED LENGTHS OF TACKS MEASURED UNDER THE HEAD

Barbed: for fastening shingles or other flexible materials

Boat spike: long spike used in timber construction

Brad: finishing nail less than 1 inch long

Box: for nailing thin dry wood close to edge

Cement-coated box: coated with resin that increases holding power

Casing: similar to finishing, but with dulled point to penetrate thin trim without splitting

Common: for rough and heavy construction

Concrete: hardened steel nail with diamond point

Fluted concrete: hardened steel nail with fluting to increase holding power

Escutcheon pin: small nail used to attach escutcheons

Fence: large-head nail for holding weathered boards

Finishing: slender nail that can be set below surface

Cut finishing: finishing nail used in historic restoration

Blunt flooring: nail with blunt tip to prevent splitting hardwood flooring

Cut flooring: for historic restoration

Drive-screw flooring: nail with screw-drive to increase holding power

Annular drywall: for attaching drywall to framing; rings increase holding power

Gutter spike: for attaching gutter to fascia

Hinge: for attaching large hinges such as for barn doors

Annular hinge: hinge with rings to increase holding power

Lath: small nail for installing wood lath

Offset head: for use with power nailer

Parquet flooring: thin nail to prevent splitting parquet

Pole barn: large spike for attaching framing to poles

Roofing: for attaching asphalt roofing to underlayment

Built-up roofing: for attaching roofing felt

No-leak roofing: nail with rubber gasket to seal metal roofing

Scaffold: nail with double head to make nail easy to pull for temporary fastening

Shingle: for attaching cedar shingles

Cut shingle: used in historic restoration

Siding: used to install beveled wood siding

Screw-thread siding: nail with a screw thread to increase holding power

Cement-coated sinker: used to install underlayment

Slating: used to attach roofing slates

Ring shank underlayment: nail with rings to increase holding power

Spike: common nail 4-1/2 inches or longer

### SCREWS

Flat head wood screw:
for fastening wood to wood

Oval head wood screw:
decorative

Round head wood screw:
used with washer

Sheet metal screw:
for thin metal

Oven head machine screw:
older design

Oval head machine screw:
attractive

Lag bolt:
for heavy loads in wood

Carriage bolt:
bolt will not turn

Hex head bolt:
for heavy loads

Square head bolt:
replaced by hex head

Round head bolt:
older design

Stove bolt:
finishes flush

Fillister head cap screw:
small, strong-headed

Fillister head machine screw:
small, strong-headed

Step bolt:
bolt won't turn

Plow bolt:
for steel to steel

### SCREW AND BOLT HEADS

Slotted

Phillips

Combination
Phillips/slotted

Square

Frearson

Internal torx

Clutch

External torx

Tamper-proof

Tamper-proof

Tamper-proof
hexagon

Tamper-proof
torx

### WASHERS

Flat USS

Flat SAE

Finish

Torque

Internal-
tooth

External-
tooth

Internal-external-
tooth

Split-
lock

## LINEAR MEASURE

### Measures of Length

| | |
|---|---|
| 12 inches | = 1 foot |
| 3 feet | = 1 yard |
| 5½ yards = 16½ feet | = 1 rod, pole or perch |
| 40 poles = 220 yards | = 1 furlong |
| 8 furlongs = 1760 yards = 5280 feet } | = 1 mile |
| 3 miles | = 1 league |
| 4 inches | = 1 hand |
| 9 inches | = 1 span |

### Nautical Units

| | |
|---|---|
| 6080.20 feet | = 1 nautical mile |
| 6 feet | = 1 fathom |
| 120 fathoms | = 1 cable length |
| 1 nautical mile per hr. | = 1 knot |

### Surveyor's or Gunter's Measure

| | |
|---|---|
| 7.92 inches | = 1 link |
| 100 links = 66 ft. = 4 rods | = 1 chain |
| 80 chains | = 1 mile |
| 33⅓ inches | = 1 vara (Texas) |

### Length Equivalents

| Centimeters | Inches | Feet | Yards | Meters | Chains | Kilometers | Miles |
|---|---|---|---|---|---|---|---|
| 1 | 0.3937 | 0.03281 | 0.01094 | 0.01 | 0.0₃4971 | 10⁻⁵ | 0.0₅6214 |
| 2.540 | 1 | 0.08333 | 0.02778 | 0.0254 | 0.001263 | 0.0₄254 | 0.0₄1578 |
| 30.48 | 12 | 1 | 0.3333 | 0.3048 | 0.01515 | 0.0₃3048 | 0.0₃1894 |
| 91.44 | 36 | 3 | 1 | 0.9144 | 0.04545 | 0.0₃9144 | 0.0₃5682 |
| 100 | 39.37 | 3.281 | 1.0936 | 1 | 0.04971 | 0.001 | 0.0₃6214 |
| 2012 | 792 | 66 | 22 | 20.12 | 1 | 0.02012 | 0.0125 |
| 100000 | 39370 | 3281 | 1093.6 | 1000 | 49.71 | 1 | 0.6214 |
| 160935 | 63360 | 5280 | 1760 | 1609 | 80 | 1.609 | 1 |

Subscripts after any figure, 0₃, 9₄, etc., mean that that figure is to be repeated the indicated number of times.

## MEASURES OF AREA

| | |
|---|---|
| 144 square inches | = 1 square foot |
| 9 square feet | = 1 square yard |
| 30¼ square yards | = 1 square rod, pole or perch |
| 160 square rods = 10 square chains = 43,560 sq. ft. = 5645 sq. varas (Texas) } | = 1 acre |

640 acres = 1 square mile = 1 "section" of U. S. Govt. surveyed land

### Area Equivalents

| Square Meters | Square Inches | Square Feet | Square Yards | Square Rods | Square Chains | Roods | Acres | Square Miles or Sections |
|---|---|---|---|---|---|---|---|---|
| 1 | 1550 | 10.76 | 1.196 | 0.0395 | 0.002471 | 0.0₃9884 | 0.0₃2471 | 0.0₆3861 |
| 0.0₃6452 | 1 | 0.006944 | 0.0₃7716 | 0.0₄2551 | 0.0₅1594 | 0.0₆6377 | 0.0₆1594 | 0.0₉2491 |
| 0.09290 | 144 | 1 | 0.1111 | 0.003673 | 0.0₃2296 | 0.0₄9184 | 0.0₄2296 | 0.0₇3587 |
| 0.8361 | 1296 | 9 | 1 | 0.03306 | 0.002066 | 0.0₃8264 | 0.0002066 | 0.0₆3228 |
| 25.29 | 39204 | 272.25 | 30.25 | 1 | 0.0625 | 0.02500 | 0.00625 | 0.0₅9766 |
| 404.7 | 627264 | 4356 | 484 | 16 | 1 | 0.4 | 0.1 | 0.0001562 |
| 1012 | 1568160 | 10890 | 1210 | 40 | 2.5 | 1 | 0.25 | 0.0₃3906 |
| 4047 | 6272640 | 43560 | 4840 | 160 | 10 | 4 | 1 | 0.001562 |
| 2589998 | ....... | 27878400 | 3097600 | 102400 | 6400 | 2560 | 640 | 1 |

(1 hectare = 100 ares = 10,000 centiares or square meters)

Subscripts after any figure 0₃, 9₄, etc., mean that the figure is to be repeated the indicated number of times.

## VOLUMETRIC MEASURE

### Measures of Volume

| | |
|---|---|
| 1728 cubic inches | = 1 cubic foot |
| 27 cubic feet | = 1 cubic yard |
| 1 cord of wood | = 128 cu. ft. |
| 1 perch of masonry | = 16½ to 25 cu. ft. |

### Liquid or Fluid Measure

| | |
|---|---|
| 4 gills | = 1 pint |
| 2 pints | = 1 quart |
| 4 quarts | = 1 gallon |
| 7.4805 gallons | = 1 cubic foot |

(There is no standard liquid barrel; by trade custom, 1 bbl. of petroleum oil, unrefined = 42 gal.)

### Dry Measure

| | |
|---|---|
| 2 pints | = 1 quart |
| 8 quarts | = 1 peck |
| 4 pecks | = 1 bushel |

1 std. bbl. for fruits and vegetables = 7056 cu. in. or 105 dry quarts, struck measure

### Board Measure

1 board foot = { 144 cu. in. = volume of board 1 ft. sq. and 1 in. thick.

No. of board feet in a log = $[\frac{1}{4}(d-4)]^2 L$, where $d$ = diam. of log (usually taken inside the bark at small end), in., and $L$ = length of log, ft. The 4 in. deducted are an allowance for slab. This rule is variously known as the Doyle, Conn. River, St. Croix, Thurber, Moore and Beeman, and the Scribner rule.

### Volume and Capacity Equivalents

| Cubic inches | Cubic feet | Cubic yards | U. S. Apothecary liquid ounces | U. S. quarts Liquid | U. S. quarts Dry | U. S. gallons Liquid | U. S. gallons Dry | Bushels U. S. | Liters (l) |
|---|---|---|---|---|---|---|---|---|---|
| 1 | 0.0₅5787 | 0.0₄2143 | 0.5541 | 0.01732 | 0.01488 | 0.0₂4329 | 0.0₂3720 | 0.0₃4650 | 0.01639 |
| 1728 | 1 | 0.03704 | 957.5 | 29.92 | 25.71 | 7.481 | 6.429 | 0.8036 | 28.32 |
| 46656 | 27 | 1 | 25853 | 807.9 | 694.3 | 202.0 | 173.6 | 21.70 | 764.6 |
| 1.805 | 0.001044 | 0.0₄3868 | 1 | 0.03125 | 0.02686 | 0.007813 | 0.006714 | 0.0₃8392 | 0.02957 |
| 57.75 | 0.03342 | 0.001238 | 32 | 1 | 0.8594 | 0.25 | 0.2148 | 0.02686 | 0.9464 |
| 67.20 | 0.03889 | 0.001440 | 37.24 | 1.164 | 1 | 0.2909 | 0.25 | 0.03125 | 1.101 |
| 231 | 0.1337 | 0.004951 | 128 | 4 | 3.437 | 1 | 0.8594 | 0.1074 | 3.785 |
| 268.8 | 0.1556 | 0.005761 | 148.9 | 4.655 | 4 | 1.164 | 1 | 0.125 | 4.405 |
| 2150 | 1.244 | 0.04609 | 1192 | 37.24 | 32 | 9.309 | 8 | 1 | 35.24 |
| 61.02 | 0.03531 | 0.001308 | 33.81 | 1.057 | 0.9081 | 0.2642 | 0.2270 | 0.02838 | 1 |

Subscripts after any figure, 0₃, 9₄, etc., mean that that figure is to be repeated the indicated number of times.

## MEASURES OF WEIGHT

### Weights
(The grain is the same in all systems)

### Avoirdupois Weight

| | |
|---|---|
| 16 drams = 437.5 grains | = 1 ounce |
| 16 ounces = 7000 grains | = 1 pound |
| 100 pounds | = 1 cental |
| 2000 pounds | = 1 short ton |
| 2240 pounds | = 1 long ton |
| 1 std. lime bbl., small | = 180 lb. net |
| 1 std. lime bbl., large | = 280 lb. net |

Also (in Great Britain):

| | |
|---|---|
| 14 pounds | = 1 stone |
| 2 stone = 28 lb. | = 1 quarter |
| 4 quarters = 112 lb. | = 1 hundredweight (cwt.) |
| 20 hundredweight | = 1 long ton |

### Troy Weight

| | |
|---|---|
| 24 grains | = 1 pennyweight (dwt.) |
| 20 pennyweights = 480 grains | = 1 ounce |
| 12 ounces = 5760 grains | = 1 pound |

1 Assay Ton = 29,167 milligrams, or as many milligrams as there are troy ounces in a ton of 2000 lb. avoirdupois. Consequently, the number of milligrams of precious metal yielded by an assay ton of ore gives directly the number of troy ounces that would be obtained from a ton of 2000 lb. avoirdupois

### Apothecaries' Weight

| | |
|---|---|
| 20 grains | = 1 scruple ℈ |
| 3 scruples = 60 grains | = 1 dram ℨ |
| 8 drams | = 1 ounce ℥ |
| 12 ounces = 5760 grains | = 1 pound |

### Mass Equivalents

| Kilograms | Grains | Ounces Troy and apoth. | Ounces Avoirdupois | Pounds Troy and apoth. | Pounds Avoirdupois | Tons Short | Tons Long | Tons Metric |
|---|---|---|---|---|---|---|---|---|
| 1 | 15432 | 32.15 | 35.27 | 2.6792 | 2.205 | 0.0₂1102 | 0.0₃9842 | 0.001 |
| 0.0₄6480 | 1 | 0.0₂2083 | 0.0₂2286 | 0.0₃1736 | 0.0₃1429 | 0.0₇7143 | 0.0₇6378 | 0.0₇6480 |
| 0.03110 | 480 | 1 | 1.09714 | 0.08333 | 0.06857 | 0.0₄3429 | 0.0₃3061 | 0.0₄3110 |
| 0.02835 | 437.5 | 0.9115 | 1 | 0.07595 | 0.0625 | 0.0₄3125 | 0.0₄2790 | 0.0₄2835 |
| 0.3732 | 5760 | 12 | 13.17 | 1 | 0.8229 | 0.0₃4114 | 0.0₃3673 | 0.0₃3732 |
| 0.4536 | 7000 | 14.58 | 16 | 1.215 | 1 | 0.0005 | 0.0₃4464 | 0.0₃4536 |
| 907.2 | 140₆ | 29167 | 320₃ | 2431 | 2000 | 1 | 0.8929 | 0.9072 |
| 1016 | 15680₄ | 32667 | 35840 | 2722 | 2240 | 1.12 | 1 | 1.016 |
| 1000 | 15432356 | 32151 | 35274 | 2679 | 2205 | 1.102 | 0.9842 | 1 |

Subscripts after any figure, 0₃, 9₄, etc., mean that that figure is to be repeated the indicated number of times.

# MATHEMATICAL DATA AND FORMULAS
### Metric Conversion Tables

## METRIC WEIGHT

Avoirdupois

| | | | | |
|---|---|---|---|---|
| 1 milligram (mg) | | = | 0.0154 | gr. |
| 1 centigram (cg) | = 10 mg | = | 0.1543 | gr. |
| 1 decigram (dg) | = 10 cg | = | 1.5432 | gr. |
| 1 gram (g) | = 10 dg | = | 15.4323 | gr. |
| 1 dekagram (dag) | = 10 g | = | 0.3527 | oz. |
| 1 hectogram (hg) | = 10 dag | = | 3.5274 | oz. |
| 1 kilogram (kg) | = 10 hg | = | 2.2046 | lb. |
| 1 quintal (q) | = 100 kg | = | 220.46 | lb. |
| 1 metric ton (M.T.) | = 10 q or 1,000 kg | = | 2,204.62 | lb. |

## AVOIRDUPOIS WEIGHT

Metric

| | | | |
|---|---|---|---|
| 1 grain (gr.) | | = | 0.0648 g |
| 1 dram (dr.) | = 27.34375 gr. | = | 1.7718 g |
| 1 ounce (oz.) | = 16. dr. | = | 28.3495 g |
| 1 pound (lb.) | = 16 oz. | = | 453.5924 g or 0.4536 kg |
| 1 hundredweight (cwt.) | = 100 lb. | = | 45.3592 kg |
| 1 short ton (s.t.) | = 2,000 lb. | = | 907.18 kg or 0.9072 M.T. |

## WOOD MEASUREMENTS

| | Customary | Metric |
|---|---|---|
| 1 board foot (bd. ft.) | = 144 cu. in. (1 ft. x 1 ft. x 1 in.) = | .00236 m³ |
| 1 cord foot (cd. ft.) | = 16 cu. ft. (4 ft. x 4 ft. x 1 ft.) = | .4528 m³ |
| 1 cord (cd.) | = 8 cd. ft. (4 ft. x 4 ft. x 8 ft.) = | 3.625 m³ |
| | Metric | Customary |
| 1 stere | 1 m³ | 1.3079 cu. yd. or 0.2759 cord |

## LENGTH AND DISTANCE

| Customary | | Metric |
|---|---|---|
| 1 inch (in.) | | = 2.54 cm |
| 1 foot (ft.) | = 12 in. | = 30.48 cm |
| 1 yard (yd.) | = 3 ft. | = 0.9144 m |
| 1 rod (rd.) | = 5½ yd. | = 5.0292 m |
| 1 furlong (fur.) | = 40 rd. or ⅛ mi. | = 201.168 m |
| 1 statute mile (mi.) | = 5,280 ft. | = 1.6093 km |
| 1 league | = 3 mi. | = 4.8280 km |
| Metric | | Customary |
| 1 millimeter (mm) | | = 0.03937 in. |
| 1 centimeter (cm) | = 10 mm | = 0.3937 in. |
| 1 decimeter (dm) | = 10 cm | = 3.937 in. |
| 1 meter (m) | = 10 dm | = 39.37 in. |
| 1 dekameter (dam) | = 10 m | = 393.7 in. |
| 1 hectometer (hm) | = 10 dam | = 328.0833 ft. |
| 1 kilometer (km) | = 10 hm | = 0.62137 mi. |

## SURFACE OR AREA

| Customary | | Metric |
|---|---|---|
| 1 square inch (sq. in.) | | = 6.4516 cm² |
| 1 square foot (sq. ft.) | = 144 sq. in. | = 0.0929 m² |
| 1 square yard (sq. yd.) | = 9 sq. ft. | = 0.8361 m² |
| 1 square rod (sq. rd.) | = 30¼ sq. yd. | = 25.293 m² |
| 1 acre (A.) | = 160 sq. rd. | = 0.4047 ha |
| 1 square mile (sq. mi.) | = 640 A. | = 258.998 ha or 2.5899 km² |
| Metric | | Customary |
| 1 square millimeter (mm²) | | = 0.002 sq. in. |
| 1 square centimeter (cm²) | = 100 mm² | = 0.1549 sq. in |
| 1 square decimeter (dm²) | = 100 cm² | = 15.499 sq. in. |
| 1 square meter (m²) | = 100 dm² | = 1.549 sq. in. |
| 1 square dekameter (dam²) | = 100 m² | = 119.6 sq. yd. |
| 1 square hectometer (hm²) | = 100 dam² | = 2.4710 A. |
| 1 square kilometer (km²) | = 100 hm² | = 247.104 A. or 0.3861 sq. mi. |

## METRIC LAND MEASUREMENTS

| | Metric | Customary |
|---|---|---|
| 1 centiare (ca) | | = 1.549 sq. in. |
| 1 are (a) | = 100 ca | = 119.6 sq. yd. |
| 1 hectare (ha) | = 100 a | = 2.4710 A. |
| 1 square kilometer (km²) | = 100 ha | or 0.3861 sq. mi. |

## VOLUME MEASUREMENTS

| Customary | | Metric |
|---|---|---|
| 1 cubic inch (cu. in.) | | = 16.387 cm³ |
| 1 cubic foot (cu. ft.) | = 1,728 cu. in. | = 0.0283 m³ |
| 1 cubic yard (cu. yd.) | = 27 cu. ft. | = 0.7646 m³ |
| Metric | | Customary |
| 1 cubic millimeter (mm³) | | = 0.00006 cu. in. |
| 1 cubic centimeter (cm³) | = 1,000 mm³ | = 0.0610 cu. in. |
| 1 cubic decimeter (dm³) | = 1,000 cm³ | = 0.0353 cu. ft. |
| 1 cubic meter (m³) | = 1,000 dm³ | = 1.3079 cu. yd. |
| 1 cubic dekameter (dam³) | = 1,000 m³ | = 1,307.9 cu. yd. |
| 1 cubic hectometer (hm³) | = 1,000 dam³ | = 1,307,9000 cu. yd. |

## METRIC CAPACITY MEASUREMENTS

| | Metric | Customary |
|---|---|---|
| 1 milliliter (ml) | | = 0.0610 cu. in. |
| 1 centiliter (cl) | = 10 ml | = 0.6102 cu. in. |
| 1 deciliter (dl) | = 10 cl | = 6.1025 cu. in. |
| 1 liter (l) | = 10 dl | = 61.025 cu. in. |
| | | or 1.057 liquid qt. |
| | | or 0.908 dry |
| 1 dekaliter (dal) | = 10 l | = 610.25 cu. in. |
| 1 hectoliter (hl) | = 10 dal | = 6,102.50 cu. in. |
| 1 kiloliter (kl) | = 10 hl | = 35.315 cu. ft. |
| | | or 264.178 gal. |
| | | or 28.38 bu. |

## HOUSEHOLD CAPACITY MEASUREMENTS

| | Customary | | | Metric |
|---|---|---|---|---|
| 1 teaspoon | | = | ⅙ fl. oz. | = 4.9 ml |
| 1 tablespoon | = 3 teaspoons | = | ½ fl. oz. | = 14.8 ml |
| 1 cup | = 16 tablespoons | = | 8 fl. oz. | = 236.6 ml |
| 1 pint | = 2 cups | = | 16 fl. oz. | = 473.2 ml |
| 1 quart | = 2 pints | = | 32 fl. oz. | = 946.4 ml |
| 1 gallon | = 4 quarts | = | 128 fl. oz. | = 3.785 l |

## LIQUID CAPACITY MEASUREMENTS

| | Customary | | Metric | |
|---|---|---|---|---|
| 1 gill (gi.) | | = | 7.219 cu. in. | = 0.1183 l |
| 1 pint (pt.) | = 4 gi. | = | 28.875 cu. in. | = 0.4732 l |
| 1 quart (qt.) | = 2 pt. | = | 57.75 cu. in. | = 0.9463 l |
| 1 gallon (gal.) | = 4 qt. | = | 231 cu. in. | = 3.7853 l |
| 1 barrel (liquids) (bbl.) | = 31.5 gal. | = | 4.21 cu. ft. | = 119.24 l |
| 1 barrel (petroleum) (bbl.) | = 42 gal. | = | 5.61 cu. ft. | = 158.98 l |
| Imperial | Customary | | | Metric |
| 1 imperial quart | = 1.2009 U.S. qt. | = | 69.355 cu. in. | = 1.13649 l |
| 1 imperial gallon | = 1.2009 U.S. gal. | = | 277.420 cu. in. | = 4.54596 l |

## DRY CAPACITY MEASUREMENTS

| | Customary | | Metric | |
|---|---|---|---|---|
| 1 pint (pt.) | | = | 33.600 cu. in. | = 550.60 cm³ |
| 1 quart (qt.) | = 2 pt. | = | 67.20 cu. in. | = 1,101.21 cm³ |
| 1 peck (pk.) | = 8 qt. | = | 537.61 cu. in. | = 8,809.85 cm³ |
| 1 bushel (bu.) | = 4 pk. | = | 2,150.42 cu. in. | = 0.035239 m³ |
| 1 barrel (bbl.) | | = | 4.08 cu. ft. | = 0.115627 m³ |
| Imperial | Customary | | | Metric |
| 1 imperial dry quart | = 1.032 U.S. qt. | = | 69.354 cu. in. | = 1,136.5 cm³ |
| 1 imperial bushel | = 1.032 U.S. bu. | = | 1.284 cu. ft. | = 0.03636 m³ |

# MATHEMATICAL DATA AND FORMULAS
### Fraction, Decimal, and Metric Conversion Tables

## DECIMAL OF AN INCH AND OF A FOOT

| Fractions of Inch or Foot | | Inch Equivalents to Foot Fractions | Fractions of Inch or Foot | | Inch Equivalents to Foot Fractions | Fractions of Inch or Foot | | Inch Equivalents to Foot Fractions | Fractions of Inch or Foot | | Inch Equivalents to Foot Fractions |
|---|---|---|---|---|---|---|---|---|---|---|---|
| | .0052 | 1/16 | | .2552 | 3 1/16 | | .5052 | 6 1/16 | | .7552 | 9 1/16 |
| | .0104 | 1/8 | | .2604 | 3 1/8 | | .5104 | 6 1/8 | | .7604 | 9 1/8 |
| 1/64 | .015625 | 3/16 | 17/64 | .265625 | 3 3/16 | 33/64 | .515625 | 6 3/16 | 49/64 | .765625 | 9 3/16 |
| | .0208 | 1/4 | | .2708 | 3 1/4 | | .5208 | 6 1/4 | | .7708 | 9 1/4 |
| | .0260 | 5/16 | | .2760 | 3 5/16 | | .5260 | 6 5/16 | | .7760 | 9 5/16 |
| 1/32 | .03125 | 3/8 | 9/32 | .28125 | 3 3/8 | 17/32 | .53125 | 6 3/8 | 25/32 | .78125 | 9 3/8 |
| | .0365 | 7/16 | | .2865 | 3 7/16 | | .5365 | 6 7/16 | | .7865 | 9 7/16 |
| | .0417 | 1/2 | | .2917 | 3 1/2 | | .5417 | 6 1/2 | | .7917 | 9 1/2 |
| 3/64 | .046875 | 9/16 | 19/64 | .296875 | 3 9/16 | 35/64 | .546875 | 6 9/16 | 51/64 | .796875 | 9 9/16 |
| | .0521 | 5/8 | | .3021 | 3 5/8 | | .5521 | 6 5/8 | | .8021 | 9 5/8 |
| | .0573 | 11/16 | | .3073 | 3 11/16 | | .5573 | 6 11/16 | | .8073 | 9 11/16 |
| 1/16 | .0625 | 3/4 | 5/16 | .3125 | 3 3/4 | 9/16 | .5625 | 6 3/4 | 13/16 | .8125 | 9 3/4 |
| | .0677 | 13/16 | | .3177 | 3 13/16 | | .5677 | 6 13/16 | | .8177 | 9 13/16 |
| | .0729 | 7/8 | | .3229 | 3 7/8 | | .5729 | 6 7/8 | | .8229 | 9 7/8 |
| 5/64 | .078125 | 15/16 | 21/64 | .328125 | 3 15/16 | 37/64 | .578125 | 6 15/16 | 53/64 | .828125 | 9 15/16 |
| | .0833 | 1 | | .3333 | 4 | | .5833 | 7 | | .8333 | 10 |
| | .0885 | 1 1/16 | | .3385 | 4 1/16 | | .5885 | 7 1/16 | | .8385 | 10 1/16 |
| 3/32 | .09375 | 1 1/8 | 11/32 | .34375 | 4 1/8 | 19/32 | .59375 | 7 1/8 | 27/32 | .84375 | 10 1/8 |
| | .0990 | 1 3/16 | | .3490 | 4 3/16 | | .5990 | 7 3/16 | | .8490 | 10 3/16 |
| | .1042 | 1 1/4 | | .3542 | 4 1/4 | | .6042 | 7 1/4 | | .8542 | 10 1/4 |
| 7/64 | .109375 | 1 5/16 | 23/64 | .359375 | 4 5/16 | 39/64 | .609375 | 7 5/16 | 55/64 | .859375 | 10 5/16 |
| | .1146 | 1 3/8 | | .3646 | 4 3/8 | | .6146 | 7 3/8 | | .8646 | 10 3/8 |
| | .1198 | 1 7/16 | | .3698 | 4 7/16 | | .6198 | 7 7/16 | | .8698 | 10 7/16 |
| 1/8 | .1250 | 1 1/2 | 3/8 | .3750 | 4 1/2 | 5/8 | .6250 | 7 1/2 | 7/8 | .8750 | 10 1/2 |
| | .1302 | 1 9/16 | | .3802 | 4 9/16 | | .6302 | 7 9/16 | | .8802 | 10 9/16 |
| | .1354 | 1 5/8 | | .3854 | 4 5/8 | | .6354 | 7 5/8 | | .8854 | 10 5/8 |
| 9/64 | .140625 | 1 11/16 | 25/64 | .390625 | 4 11/16 | 41/64 | .640625 | 7 11/16 | 57/64 | .890625 | 10 11/16 |
| | .1458 | 1 3/4 | | .3958 | 4 3/4 | | .6458 | 7 3/4 | | .8958 | 10 3/4 |
| | .1510 | 1 13/16 | | .4010 | 4 13/16 | | .6510 | 7 13/16 | | .9010 | 10 13/16 |
| 5/32 | .15625 | 1 7/8 | 13/32 | .40625 | 4 7/8 | 21/32 | .65625 | 7 7/8 | 29/32 | .90625 | 10 7/8 |
| | .1615 | 1 15/16 | | .4115 | 4 15/16 | | .6615 | 7 15/16 | | .9115 | 10 15/16 |
| | .1667 | 2 | | .4167 | 5 | | .6667 | 8 | | .9167 | 11 |
| 11/64 | .171875 | 2 1/16 | 27/64 | .421875 | 5 1/16 | 43/64 | .671875 | 8 1/16 | 59/64 | .921875 | 11 1/16 |
| | .1771 | 2 1/8 | | .4271 | 5 1/8 | | .6771 | 8 1/8 | | .9271 | 11 1/8 |
| | .1823 | 2 3/16 | | .4323 | 5 3/16 | | .6823 | 8 3/16 | | .9323 | 11 3/16 |
| 3/16 | .1875 | 2 1/4 | 7/16 | .4375 | 5 1/4 | 11/16 | .6875 | 8 1/4 | 15/16 | .9375 | 11 1/4 |
| | .1927 | 2 5/16 | | .4427 | 5 5/16 | | .6927 | 8 5/16 | | .9427 | 11 5/16 |
| | .1979 | 2 3/8 | | .4479 | 5 3/8 | | .6979 | 8 3/8 | | .9479 | 11 3/8 |
| 13/64 | .203125 | 2 7/16 | 29/64 | .453125 | 5 7/16 | 45/64 | .703125 | 8 7/16 | 61/64 | .953125 | 11 7/16 |
| | .2083 | 2 1/2 | | .4583 | 5 1/2 | | .7083 | 8 1/2 | | .9583 | 11 1/2 |
| | .2135 | 2 9/16 | | .4635 | 5 9/16 | | .7135 | 8 9/16 | | .9635 | 11 9/16 |
| 7/32 | .21875 | 2 5/8 | 15/32 | .46875 | 5 5/8 | 23/32 | .71875 | 8 5/8 | 31/32 | .96875 | 11 5/8 |
| | .2240 | 2 11/16 | | .4740 | 5 11/16 | | .7240 | 8 11/16 | | .9740 | 11 11/16 |
| | .2292 | 2 3/4 | | .4792 | 5 3/4 | | .7292 | 8 3/4 | | .9792 | 11 3/4 |
| 15/64 | .234375 | 2 13/16 | 31/64 | .484375 | 5 13/16 | 47/64 | .734375 | 8 13/16 | 63/64 | .984375 | 11 13/16 |
| | .2396 | 2 7/8 | | .4896 | 5 7/8 | | .7396 | 8 7/8 | | .9896 | 11 7/8 |
| | .2448 | 2 15/16 | | .4948 | 5 15/16 | | .7448 | 8 15/16 | | .9948 | 11 15/16 |
| 1/4 | .2500 | 3 | 1/2 | .5000 | 6 | 3/4 | .7500 | 9 | 1 | 1.0000 | 12 |

## METRIC CONVERSION FACTORS

### METRIC TO AMERICAN

Millimeters $\div$ 25.4 = inches
Centimeters $\times$ 0.3937 = inches
Meters $\times$ 39.27 = inches
Millimeters $\times$ 0.003281 = feet
Centimeters $\times$ 0.03281 = feet
Meters $\times$ 3.281 = feet
Meters $\times$ 1.094 = yards
Kilometers $\times$ 0.621 = miles
Kilometers $\times$ 3280.7 = feet
Square millimeters $\div$ 645.1 = square inches
Square centimeters $\div$ 6.451 = square inches
Square meters $\times$ 10.764 = square feet
Square kilometers $\times$ 247.1 = acres
Hectares $\times$ 2.471 = acres
Cubic centimeters $\div$ 16.383 = cubic inches
Cubic meters $\times$ 35.315 = cubic feet
Cubic meters $\times$ 1.308 = cubic yards
Cubic meters $\times$ 264.2 = gallons
Liters $\times$ 61.022 = cubic inches
Liters $\times$ 0.2642 = gallons
Liters $\div$ 28.316 = cubic feet
Hectoliters $\times$ 3.531 = cubic feet
Hectoliters $\times$ 2.84 = bushels
Hectoliters $\times$ 0.131 = cubic yards
Hectoliters $\times$ 26.42 = gallons
Kilograms $\times$ 2.2046 = pounds
Kilograms $\div$ 1102.3 = tons

### AMERICAN TO METRIC

Inches $\times$ 25.4 = millimeters
Inches $\times$ 2.54 = centimeters
Inches $\times$ 0.0254 = meters
Feet $\times$ 304.8 = millimeters
Feet $\times$ 30.48 = centimeters
Feet $\times$ 0.3048 = meters
Yards $\times$ 0.9143 = meters
Miles $\times$ 1.6093 = kilometers
Feet $\div$ 3280.7 = kilometers
Square inches $\times$ 645.1 = square millimeters
Square inches $\times$ 6.451 = square centimeters
Square feet $\div$ 10.764 = square meters
Acres $\div$ 247.1 = square kilometers
Acres $\div$ 2.471 = hectares
Cubic inches $\times$ 16.383 = cubic centimeters
Cubic feet $\div$ 35.315 = cubic meters
Cubic yards $\div$ 1.308 = cubic meters
Gallons (231 cu. in.) $\div$ 264.2 = cubic meters
Cubic inches $\div$ 61.022 = liters
Gallons $\times$ 3.78 = liters
Cubic feet $\times$ 28.316 = liters
Cubic feet $\div$ 3.531 = hectoliters
Bushels $\div$ 2.84 = hectoliters
Cubic yards $\div$ 0.131 = hectoliters
Gallons $\div$ 26.42 = hectoliters
Pounds $\div$ 2.2046 = kilograms
Tons $\times$ 1102.3 = kilograms

## METRIC MEASURES

| Linear | Liquid and Dry | Weights |
|---|---|---|
| 10 millimeters = 1 centimeter | 10 milliliters = 1 centiliter | 10 milligrams = 1 centigram |
| 10 centimeters = 1 decimeter | 10 centiliters = 1 deciliter | 10 centigrams = 1 decigram |
| 10 decimeters = 1 METER (m) | 10 deciliters = 1 LITER (l) | 10 decigrams = 1 GRAM (g) |
| 10 meters = 1 decameter | 10 liters = 1 decaliter | 10 grams = 1 decagram |
| 10 decameters = 1 hectometer | 10 decaliters = 1 hectoliter | 10 decagrams = 1 hectogram |
| 10 hectometers = 1 kilometer | 10 hectoliters = 1 kiloliter | 10 hectograms = 1 kilogram |

# MATHEMATICAL DATA AND FORMULAS
## Areas of Plane Figures

### Square

Diagonal $= d = s\sqrt{2}$.
Area $= s^2 = 4b^2 = 0.5d^2$.
Example. $s = 6$; $b = 3$. Area $= (6)^2 = 36$ Ans.
$\quad\quad d = 6 \times 1.414 = 8.484$ Ans.

### Rectangle and Parallelogram

Area $= ab$ or $b\sqrt{d^2 - b^2}$
Example. $a = 6$; $b = 3$.
Area $= 3 \times 6 = 18$ Ans

### Trapezoid

Area $= \frac{1}{2}h(a + b)$
Example. $a = 2$; $b = 4$; $h = 3$.
$\quad\quad$ Area $= \frac{1}{2} \times 3(2 + 4) = 9$. Ans.

### Trapezium

Area $= \frac{1}{2}[a(h + h^1) + bh^1 + ch]$
Example. $a = 4$; $b = 2$; $c = 2$; $h = 3$; $h^1 = 2$.
Area $= \frac{1}{2}[4(3 + 2) + (2 \times 2) + (2 \times 3)] = 15$.
$\quad\quad\quad\quad\quad\quad\quad\quad\quad\quad\quad\quad$ Ans.

### Triangles

Both formulas apply to both figures
Area $= \frac{1}{2}bh$.
Example. $h = 3$; $b = 5$.
$\quad\quad$ Area $= \frac{1}{2}(3 \times 5) = 7\frac{1}{2}$. Ans.

Area $= \sqrt{S(S - a)(S - b)(S - c)}$ when $S = \frac{a + b + c}{2}$

Example. $a = 2$; $b = 3$; $c = 4$.
$\quad\quad S = \frac{2 + 3 + 4}{2} = 4.5$

Area $= \sqrt{4.5(4.5 - 2)(4.5 - 3)(4.5 - 4)} = 2.9$.
$\quad\quad\quad\quad\quad\quad\quad\quad\quad\quad\quad\quad$ Ans.

### Regular Polygons

$$\text{Area} \begin{cases} 5 \text{ sides} = 1.720477\ S^2 = 3.63271\ r^2 \\ 6\quad`` = 2.598150\ S^2 = 3.46410\ r^2 \\ 7\quad`` = 3.633875\ S^2 = 3.37101\ r^2 \\ 8\quad`` = 4.828427\ S^2 = 3.31368\ r^2 \\ 9\quad`` = 6.181875\ S^2 = 3.27573\ r^2 \\ 10\quad`` = 7.694250\ S^2 = 3.24920\ r^2 \\ 11\quad`` = 9.365675\ S^2 = 3.22993\ r^2 \\ 12\quad`` = 11.196300\ S^2 = 3.21539\ r^2 \end{cases}$$

$n$ = number of sides; $r$ = short radius;
$S$ = length of side; $R$ = long radius.
Area $= \frac{n}{4}S^2 \cot\frac{180°}{n} = \frac{n}{2}R^2\sin\frac{360°}{n}$
$\quad\quad = nr^2\tan\frac{180°}{n}$

### Spandrel

Area $= 0.2146r^2 = 0.1073c^2$
Example. $r = 3$
Area $= 0.2146 \times 3^2 = 1.9314$. Ans

### Parabola

$l$ = length of curved line = periphery $- s$
$l = \frac{s^2}{8h}[\sqrt{c(1+c)} + 2.0326 \times \log(\sqrt{c} + \sqrt{1+c})]$

in which $c = \left(\frac{4h}{s}\right)^2$

Area $= \frac{2}{3}sh$
Example. $s = 3$; $h = 4$
Area $= \frac{2}{3} \times 3 \times 4 = 8$. Ans.

### Ellipse

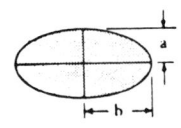

Area $= \pi\,ab = 3.1416ab$

Circum. $= 2\pi\sqrt{\frac{a^2 + b^2}{2}}$ (close approximation)

Example. $a = 3$; $b = 4$.
Area $= 3.1416 \times 3 \times 4 = 37.6992$. Ans.

Circum. $= 2 \times 3.1416\sqrt{\frac{(3)^2 + (4)^2}{2}}$
$\quad\quad\quad = 6.2832 \times 3.5355 = 22.21$ Ans.

### Circle

$\pi = 3.1416$; $A$ = area; $d$ = diameter; $p$ = circumference or periphery; $r$ = radius.

$p = \pi d = 3.1416d$. $\quad\quad p = 2\sqrt{\pi A} = 3.54\sqrt{A}$

$p = 2\pi r = 6.2832r$. $\quad\quad p = \frac{2A}{r} = \frac{4A}{d}$

$d = \frac{p}{\pi} = \frac{p}{3.1416}$ $\quad\quad d = 2\sqrt{\frac{A}{\pi}} = 1.128\sqrt{A}$

$r = \frac{p}{2\pi} = \frac{p}{6.2832}$ $\quad\quad r = \sqrt{\frac{A}{\pi}} = 0.564\sqrt{A}$

$A = \frac{\pi d^2}{4} = 0.7854d^2$ $\quad\quad A = \frac{p^2}{4\pi} = \frac{p^2}{12.57}$

$A = \pi r^2 = 3.1416r^2$ $\quad\quad A = \frac{pr}{2} = \frac{pd}{4}$

### Circular Ring

Area $= \pi(R^2 - r^2) = 3.1416(R^2 - r^2)$
Area $= 0.7854(D^2 - d^2) = 0.7854(D - d)(D + d)$
Area $=$ difference in areas between the inner and outer circles.
Example. $R = 4$; $r = 2$.
Area $= 3.1416(4^2 - 2^2) = 37.6992$. Ans.

### Quadrant

Area $= \frac{\pi r^2}{4} = 0.7854r^2 = 0.3927c^2$.

Example. $r = 3$. $c$ = chord.
Area $= .7854 \times 3^2 = 7.0686$. Ans.

### Segment

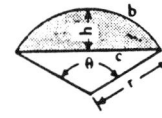

$b$ = length of arc. $\quad \theta$ = angle in degrees
$c$ = chord $= \sqrt{4(2hr - h^2)}$
Area $= \frac{1}{2}[br - c(r - h)]$
$\quad\quad = \pi r^2\frac{\theta}{360} - \frac{c(r - h)}{2}$

When $\theta$ is greater than $180°$ then $\frac{c}{2} \times$ difference between $r$ and $h$ is added to the fraction $\frac{\pi r^2\theta}{360}$
Example. $r = 3$; $\theta = 120°$; $h = 1.5$
Area $= 3.1416 \times 3^2 \times \frac{120}{360} - \frac{5.196(3 - 1.5)}{2}$
$\quad\quad = 5.5278$. Ans.

### Sector

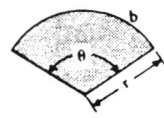

Area $= \frac{br}{2} = \pi r^2\frac{\theta}{360°}$
$\quad \theta$ = angle in degrees; $b$ = length of arc.
Example. $r = 3$; $\theta = 120°$
Area $= 3.1416 \times 3^2 \times \frac{120}{360} = 9.4248$. Ans.

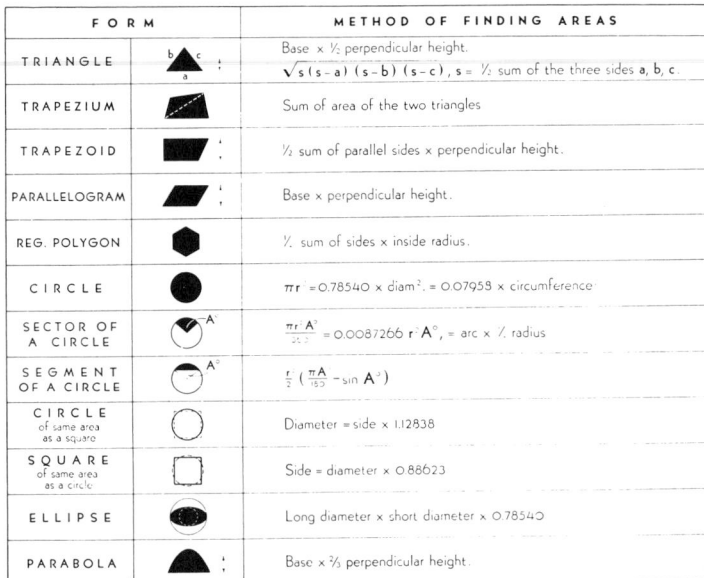

| FORM | | METHOD OF FINDING AREAS |
|---|---|---|
| TRIANGLE | | Base $\times \frac{1}{2}$ perpendicular height. |
| | | $\sqrt{s(s-a)(s-b)(s-c)}$, $s = \frac{1}{2}$ sum of the three sides a, b, c. |
| TRAPEZIUM | | Sum of area of the two triangles |
| TRAPEZOID | | $\frac{1}{2}$ sum of parallel sides $\times$ perpendicular height. |
| PARALLELOGRAM | | Base $\times$ perpendicular height. |
| REG. POLYGON | | $\frac{1}{2}$ sum of sides $\times$ inside radius. |
| CIRCLE | | $\pi r^2 = 0.78540 \times$ diam$^2$. $= 0.07958 \times$ circumference$^2$ |
| SECTOR OF A CIRCLE | | $\frac{\pi r^2 A°}{360} = 0.0087266\ r^2 A°$, $=$ arc $\times \frac{1}{2}$ radius |
| SEGMENT OF A CIRCLE | | $\frac{r}{2}\left(\frac{\pi A}{180} - \sin A°\right)$ |
| CIRCLE of same area as a square | | Diameter $=$ side $\times$ 1.12838 |
| SQUARE of same area as a circle | | Side $=$ diameter $\times$ 0.88623 |
| ELLIPSE | | Long diameter $\times$ short diameter $\times$ 0.78540 |
| PARABOLA | | Base $\times \frac{2}{3}$ perpendicular height. |

**TABLE 20   Functions of Numbers**

| NO. | SQUARE | CUBE | SQUARE ROOT | CUBE ROOT | LOGARITHM | 1000 x RECIPROCAL | NO. = DIAMETER | |
|-----|--------|------|-------------|-----------|-----------|-------------------|--------|------|
| | | | | | | | CIRCUM. | AREA |
| 1 | 1 | 1 | 1.0000 | 1.0000 | 0.00000 | 1000.000 | 3.142 | 0.7854 |
| 2 | 4 | 8 | 1.4142 | 1.2599 | 0.30103 | 500.000 | 6.283 | 3.1416 |
| 3 | 9 | 27 | 1.7321 | 1.4422 | 0.47712 | 333.333 | 9.425 | 7.0686 |
| 4 | 16 | 64 | 2.0000 | 1.5874 | 0.60206 | 250.000 | 12.566 | 12.5664 |
| 5 | 25 | 125 | 2.2361 | 1.7100 | 0.69897 | 200.000 | 15.708 | 19.6350 |
| 6 | 36 | 216 | 2.4495 | 1.8171 | 0.77815 | 166.667 | 18.850 | 28.2743 |
| 7 | 49 | 343 | 2.6458 | 1.9129 | 0.84510 | 142.857 | 21.991 | 38.4845 |
| 8 | 64 | 512 | 2.8284 | 2.0000 | 0.90309 | 125.000 | 25.133 | 50.2655 |
| 9 | 81 | 729 | 3.0000 | 2.0801 | 0.95424 | 111.111 | 28.274 | 63.6173 |
| 10 | 100 | 1000 | 3.1623 | 2.1544 | 1.00000 | 100.000 | 31.416 | 78.5398 |
| 11 | 121 | 1331 | 3.3166 | 2.2240 | 1.04139 | 90.9091 | 34.558 | 95.0332 |
| 12 | 144 | 1728 | 3.4641 | 2.2894 | 1.07918 | 83.3333 | 37.699 | 113.097 |
| 13 | 169 | 2197 | 3.6056 | 2.3513 | 1.11394 | 76.9231 | 40.841 | 132.732 |
| 14 | 196 | 2744 | 3.7417 | 2.4101 | 1.14613 | 71.4286 | 43.982 | 153.938 |
| 15 | 225 | 3375 | 3.8730 | 2.4662 | 1.17609 | 66.6667 | 47.124 | 176.715 |
| 16 | 256 | 4096 | 4.0000 | 2.5198 | 1.20412 | 62.5000 | 50.265 | 201.062 |
| 17 | 289 | 4913 | 4.1231 | 2.5713 | 1.23045 | 58.8235 | 53.407 | 226.980 |
| 18 | 324 | 5832 | 4.2426 | 2.6207 | 1.25527 | 55.5556 | 56.549 | 254.469 |
| 19 | 361 | 6859 | 4.3589 | 2.6684 | 1.27875 | 52.6316 | 59.690 | 283.529 |
| 20 | 400 | 8000 | 4.4721 | 2.7144 | 1.30103 | 50.0000 | 62.832 | 314.159 |
| 21 | 441 | 9261 | 4.5826 | 2.7589 | 1.32222 | 47.6190 | 65.973 | 346.361 |
| 22 | 484 | 10648 | 4.6904 | 2.8020 | 1.34242 | 45.4545 | 69.115 | 380.133 |
| 23 | 529 | 12167 | 4.7958 | 2.8439 | 1.36173 | 43.4783 | 72.257 | 415.476 |
| 24 | 576 | 13824 | 4.8990 | 2.8845 | 1.38021 | 41.6667 | 75.398 | 452.389 |
| 25 | 625 | 15625 | 5.0000 | 2.9240 | 1.39794 | 40.0000 | 78.540 | 490.874 |
| 26 | 676 | 17576 | 5.0990 | 2.9625 | 1.41497 | 38.4615 | 81.681 | 530.929 |
| 27 | 729 | 19683 | 5.1962 | 3.0000 | 1.43136 | 37.0370 | 84.823 | 572.555 |
| 28 | 784 | 21952 | 5.2915 | 3.0366 | 1.44716 | 35.7143 | 87.965 | 615.752 |
| 29 | 841 | 24389 | 5.3852 | 3.0723 | 1.46240 | 34.4828 | 91.106 | 660.520 |
| 30 | 900 | 27000 | 5.4772 | 3.1072 | 1.47712 | 33.3333 | 94.248 | 706.858 |
| 31 | 961 | 29791 | 5.5678 | 3.1414 | 1.49136 | 32.2581 | 97.389 | 754.768 |
| 32 | 1024 | 32768 | 5.6569 | 3.1748 | 1.50515 | 31.2500 | 100.531 | 804.248 |
| 33 | 1089 | 35937 | 5.7446 | 3.2075 | 1.51851 | 30.3030 | 103.673 | 855.299 |
| 34 | 1156 | 39304 | 5.8310 | 3.2396 | 1.53148 | 29.4118 | 106.814 | 907.920 |
| 35 | 1225 | 42875 | 5.9161 | 3.2711 | 1.54407 | 28.5714 | 109.956 | 962.113 |
| 36 | 1296 | 46656 | 6.0000 | 3.3019 | 1.55630 | 27.7778 | 113.097 | 1017.88 |
| 37 | 1369 | 50653 | 6.0828 | 3.3322 | 1.56820 | 27.0270 | 116.239 | 1075.21 |
| 38 | 1444 | 54872 | 6.1644 | 3.3620 | 1.57978 | 26.3158 | 119.381 | 1134.11 |
| 39 | 1521 | 59319 | 6.2450 | 3.3912 | 1.59106 | 25.6410 | 122.522 | 1194.59 |
| 40 | 1600 | 64000 | 6.3246 | 3.4200 | 1.60206 | 25.0000 | 125.66 | 1256.64 |
| 41 | 1681 | 68921 | 6.4031 | 3.4482 | 1.61278 | 24.3902 | 128.81 | 1320.25 |
| 42 | 1764 | 74088 | 6.4807 | 3.4760 | 1.62325 | 23.8095 | 131.95 | 1385.44 |
| 43 | 1849 | 79507 | 6.5574 | 3.5034 | 1.63347 | 23.2558 | 135.09 | 1452.20 |
| 44 | 1936 | 85184 | 6.6332 | 3.5303 | 1.64345 | 22.7273 | 138.23 | 1520.53 |
| 45 | 2025 | 91125 | 6.7082 | 3.5569 | 1.65321 | 22.2222 | 141.37 | 1590.43 |

## MATHEMATICAL DATA AND FORMULAS

Functions of Numbers

**TABLE 20   Functions of Numbers** *(Continued)*

| NO. | SQUARE | CUBE | SQUARE ROOT | CUBE ROOT | LOGARITHM | 1000 x RECIPROCAL | NO. = DIAMETER | |
|---|---|---|---|---|---|---|---|---|
| | | | | | | | CIRCUM. | AREA |
| 46 | 2116 | 97336 | 6.7823 | 3.5830 | 1.66276 | 21.7391 | 144.51 | 1661.90 |
| 47 | 2209 | 103823 | 6.8557 | 3.6088 | 1.67210 | 21.2766 | 147.65 | 1734.94 |
| 48 | 2304 | 110592 | 6.9282 | 3.6342 | 1.68124 | 20.8333 | 150.80 | 1809.56 |
| 49 | 2401 | 117649 | 7.0000 | 3.6593 | 1.69020 | 20.4082 | 153.94 | 1885.74 |
| 50 | 2500 | 125000 | 7.0711 | 3.6840 | 1.69897 | 20.0000 | 157.08 | 1963.50 |
| 51 | 2601 | 132651 | 7.1414 | 3.7084 | 1.70757 | 19.6078 | 160.22 | 2042.82 |
| 52 | 2704 | 140608 | 7.2111 | 3.7325 | 1.71600 | 19.2308 | 163.36 | 2123.72 |
| 53 | 2809 | 148877 | 7.2801 | 3.7563 | 1.72428 | 18.8679 | 166.50 | 2206.18 |
| 54 | 2916 | 157464 | 7.3485 | 3.7798 | 1.73239 | 18.5185 | 169.65 | 2290.22 |
| 55 | 3025 | 166375 | 7.4162 | 3.8030 | 1.74036 | 18.1818 | 172.79 | 2375.83 |
| 56 | 3136 | 175616 | 7.4833 | 3.8259 | 1.74819 | 17.8571 | 175.93 | 2463.01 |
| 57 | 3249 | 185193 | 7.5498 | 3.8485 | 1.75587 | 17.5439 | 179.07 | 2551.76 |
| 58 | 3364 | 195112 | 7.6158 | 3.8709 | 1.76343 | 17.2414 | 182.21 | 2642.08 |
| 59 | 3481 | 205379 | 7.6811 | 3.8930 | 1.77085 | 16.9492 | 185.35 | 2733.97 |
| 60 | 3600 | 216000 | 7.7460 | 3.9149 | 1.77815 | 16.6667 | 188.50 | 2827.43 |
| 61 | 3721 | 226981 | 7.8102 | 3.9365 | 1.78533 | 16.3934 | 191.64 | 2922.47 |
| 62 | 3844 | 238328 | 7.8740 | 3.9579 | 1.79239 | 16.1290 | 194.78 | 3019.07 |
| 63 | 3969 | 250047 | 7.9373 | 3.9791 | 1.79934 | 15.8730 | 197.92 | 3117.25 |
| 64 | 4096 | 262144 | 8.0000 | 4.0000 | 1.80618 | 15.6250 | 201.06 | 3216.99 |
| 65 | 4225 | 274625 | 8.0623 | 4.0207 | 1.81291 | 15.3846 | 204.20 | 3318.31 |
| 66 | 4356 | 287496 | 8.1240 | 4.0412 | 1.81954 | 15.1515 | 207.35 | 3421.19 |
| 67 | 4489 | 300763 | 8.1854 | 4.0615 | 1.82607 | 14.9254 | 210.49 | 3525.65 |
| 68 | 4624 | 314432 | 8.2462 | 4.0817 | 1.83251 | 14.7059 | 213.63 | 3631.68 |
| 69 | 4761 | 328509 | 8.3066 | 4.1016 | 1.83885 | 14.4928 | 216.77 | 3739.28 |
| 70 | 4900 | 343000 | 8.3666 | 4.1213 | 1.84510 | 14.2857 | 219.91 | 3848.45 |
| 71 | 5041 | 357911 | 8.4261 | 4.1408 | 1.85126 | 14.0845 | 223.05 | 3959.19 |
| 72 | 5184 | 373248 | 8.4853 | 4.1602 | 1.85733 | 13.8889 | 226.19 | 4071.50 |
| 73 | 5329 | 389017 | 8.5440 | 4.1793 | 1.86332 | 13.6986 | 229.34 | 4185.39 |
| 74 | 5476 | 405224 | 8.6023 | 4.1983 | 1.86923 | 13.5135 | 232.48 | 4300.84 |
| 75 | 5625 | 421875 | 8.6603 | 4.2172 | 1.87506 | 13.3333 | 235.62 | 4417.86 |
| 76 | 5776 | 438976 | 8.7178 | 4.2358 | 1.88081 | 13.1579 | 238.76 | 4536.46 |
| 77 | 5929 | 456533 | 8.7750 | 4.2543 | 1.88649 | 12.9870 | 241.90 | 4656.63 |
| 78 | 6084 | 474552 | 8.8318 | 4.2727 | 1.89209 | 12.8205 | 245.04 | 4778.36 |
| 79 | 6241 | 493039 | 8.8882 | 4.2908 | 1.89763 | 12.6582 | 248.19 | 4901.67 |
| 80 | 6400 | 512000 | 8.9443 | 4.3089 | 1.90309 | 12.5000 | 251.33 | 5026.55 |
| 81 | 6561 | 531441 | 9.0000 | 4.3267 | 1.90849 | 12.3457 | 254.47 | 5153.00 |
| 82 | 6724 | 551368 | 9.0554 | 4.3445 | 1.91381 | 12.1951 | 257.61 | 5281.02 |
| 83 | 6889 | 571787 | 9.1104 | 4.3621 | 1.91908 | 12.0482 | 260.75 | 5410.61 |
| 84 | 7056 | 592704 | 9.1652 | 4.3795 | 1.92428 | 11.9048 | 263.89 | 5541.77 |
| 85 | 7225 | 614125 | 9.2195 | 4.3968 | 1.92942 | 11.7647 | 267.04 | 5674.50 |
| 86 | 7396 | 636056 | 9.2736 | 4.4140 | 1.93450 | 11.6279 | 270.18 | 5808.80 |
| 87 | 7569 | 658503 | 9.3274 | 4.4310 | 1.93952 | 11.4943 | 273.32 | 5944.68 |
| 88 | 7744 | 681472 | 9.3808 | 4.4480 | 1.94448 | 11.3636 | 276.46 | 6082.12 |
| 89 | 7921 | 704969 | 9.4340 | 4.4647 | 1.94939 | 11.2360 | 279.60 | 6221.14 |
| 90 | 8100 | 729000 | 9.4868 | 4.4814 | 1.95424 | 11.1111 | 282.74 | 6361.73 |

# Credits

## 1. Planning and Design of Interior Spaces

### Residential Spaces

**Pages 5–28:** *House and Garden's Complete Guide to Interior Decoration,* edited by Richardson Wright, Simon and Schuster, New York, 1942 (copyright renewed 1970 by The Condé Nast Publications Inc.).

**Pages 29–42:** Gottshall, Franklin H., *How to Design and Construct Period Furniture,* Bonanza Books, New York, 1989.

**Page 43:** *The House and Home Book of Interior Design,* McGraw-Hill, New York, 1976.

**Page 49:** *New Spaces for Learning,* Educational Facilities Lab, New York, 1966.

**Pages 56–60:** Ramsey, Charles George, and Harold Reeve Sleeper, *Architectural Graphic Standards,* 2d Edition, Wiley, New York, 1936.

**Pages 62, 63, 81, 83, 84, 196, 197, 199:** *Architectural Forum,* October 1937.

**Pages 65–68, 71, 72, 96, 118–124, 164:** Thompson, Robinson, Toraby.

**Page 69:** Verna Cook Salomonsky, Architect.

**Page 70:** Ulrich Franzen, Architect; *Selected Architectural Details,* Reinhold, New York.

**Pages 73–76:** Parrish Hadley Associates.

**Page 80:** U.S. Department of Housing and Urban Development, Washington, D.C.

**Pages 82, 104, 105, 152:** *House Planning Handbook,* 2d Edition, MWPS–16, Midwest Plan Service, Ames, Iowa, 1988 (reproduced with permission).

**Pages 85, 86:** Lehigh Furniture Company.

**Pages 88, 89, 153, 154:** *Manual of Acceptable Practices,* U.S. Department of Housing and Urban Development, Washington, D.C.

**Pages 89, 201:** *Internal Spaces of the Dwelling,* Canada Mortgage and Housing Corporation, 1984.

**Pages 90–93, 125–127, 135, 166, 167:** Bromley/Jacobsen.

**Page 94:** Knobloch, Philip G., *Good Practice in Construction,* Pencil Points Press, New York, 1931.

**Page 95:** *Comparative Architectural Details,* Pencil Points Series (Francis Y. Joannes, Architect), 1935.

**Page 97:** Gensler Associates; ISD; Bromley/Jacobson.

**Pages 98, 99:** *American Architect and Architecture,* January 1937.

**Pages 100, 101, 149, 150, 206:** Panero, Julius, and Martin Zelnik, *Human Dimension & Interior Space,* Whitney Library of Design/Watson-Guptill Publications, New York, 1979.

**Pages 102, 103, 202–204:** *Time-Saver Standards: A Manual of Essential Architectural Data,* F. W. Dodge Corporation, New York, 1946.

**Pages 106–108:** Kohler.

**Pages 109, 110, 114, 170 (bottom):** Eljer.

**Pages 111–113, 115, 116, 170 (top):** American Standard.

**Pages 117, 194, 198:** Hornbostel, Caleb, *Architectural Detailing Simplified,* Prentice-Hall, Englewood Cliffs, N.J., 1986.

**Pages 128, 156:** *A Design Guide for Home Safety,* U.S. Department of Housing and Urban Development, Washington, D.C., 1972.

**Page 129:** Space Design Group.

**Pages 130, 131:** Marble Institute of America.

**Pages 132–134, 136:** *Handbook for Ceramic Tile Installation,* Tile Council of America, Princeton, N.J., 1987.

**Pages 137–140, 181–186:** *Adaptable Housing,* Office of Policy Development and Research, U.S. Department of Housing and Urban Development, 1987.

**Pages 141, 142, 179, 180:** New York City Building Code.

**Pages 143, 146, 147, 178:** *Uniform Federal Accessibility Standards,* 1985-494-187, U.S. Government Printing Office, Washington, D.C., 1985.

**Pages 144, 187:** *Handbook for Design,* Veterans Administration, Washington, D.C.

**Pages 145, 148, 165, 168, 169, 188, 189, 191, 192:** Jerry Caldari, Architect.

**Page 151:** De Chiara, Joseph, and John Hancock Callender (eds.), *Time-Saver Standards for Building Types,* 2d Edition, McGraw-Hill, New York, 1980.

**Page 155:** Formica Corporation.

**Pages 157, 158, 172, 173:** Merillat.

**Pages 159, 160:** St. Charles.

**Pages 161–163:** Triangle Pacific Corporation.

**Page 171:** Euroflair by Frigidaire.

**Pages 174, 175:** *Manual of Millwork,* Woodworking Institute of California.

**Page 193:** *Pencil Points,* April 1934.

**Page 195:** Putnam Rolling Ladder Company.

**Pages 196, 200, 205:** De Chiara, Joseph (ed.), *Time-Saver Standards for Residential Development,* McGraw-Hill, New York, 1984.

**Page 199:** *Design Solutions,* Architectural Woodworking Institute, Summer 1989.

**Page 207 (top):** *Council Notes,* University of Illinois.

**Page 207 (bottom):** *Architectural Forum,* October 1938.

**Page 208 (left):** General Services Administration.

**Page 208 (right):** Illinois Agricultural Experiment Station.

**Pages 209, 213, 214:** *Pencil Points,* 1935.

**Pages 210 (top), 215:** Bertram Bassuk, FAIA.

**Pages 210 (bottom), 211 (top), 212:** ISD.

**Page 211 (bottom):** Charles D. Flayhan Associates.

**Page 216:** Schulte.

**Pages 217–220:** Closet Maid Systems.

## Office Spaces

**Pages 223, 224, 231, 232, 241, 249, 260:** Panero, Julius, and Martin Zelnik, *Human Dimension & Interior Space,* Whitney Library of Design/Watson-Guptill Publications, New York, 1979.

**Pages 225, 226, 243–245:** Pulgram, William L., and Richard E. Stonis, *Designing the Automated Office,* Whitney Library of Design/Watson-Guptill Publications, New York, 1984.

**Pages 236, 237, 240, 259, 266, 267, 271:** Gensler Associates.

**Pages 238, 263, 268, 269, 274, 275, 298, 299, 303, 304 (top):** Charles D. Flayhan Associates.

**Pages 239, 264, 277:** ISD.

**Page 242:** Intergraph Corp., Interiors.

**Pages 246–248:** *Interiors,* November 1985.

**Pages 250, 251:** Lehigh Furniture Company.

**Page 252:** Howe Furniture Corp.

**Pages 256, 283–295:** Steelcase.

**Page 256:** Panero Zelnik Associates.

**Pages 257, 258, 270, 272:** *Design Solutions,* Architectural Woodworking Institute, Spring 1986.

**Page 262:** Will Ching, Planning and Design.

**Page 265:** Marble Institute of America.

**Pages 273, 276:** Bertram Bassuk, FAIA.

**Page 278:** De Chiara, Joseph, and John Hancock Callender (eds.), *Time-Saver Standards For Building Types,* 2d Edition, McGraw-Hill, New York, 1980.

**Pages 279, 280, 281:** Herman Miller.

**Page 282:** Vecta.

## Hospitality Spaces

**Pages 307, 308:** *Architectural Record,* 1943.

**Page 312:** *Architectural Forum ; Manual of Acceptable Practices,* U.S. Department of Housing and Urban Development, Washington, D.C.

**Pages 316, 317, 330, 377–380:** Davies, Thomas D., Jr., and Kim A. Beasley, *Design For Hospitality: Planning for Accessible Hotels and Motels,* Nichols Publishing, New York, 1988.

**Pages 318, 322, 346, 347:** Panero, Julius, and Martin Zelnik, *Human Dimension & Interior Space,* Whitney Library of Design/Watson-Guptill Publications, New York, 1979.

**Pages 319, 325, 326, 328, 338, 359, 365, 368, 369:** Toni Chi and Associates.

**Pages 319, 320:** Panero Zelnik Associates.

**Pages 321, 329, 332, 363, 364, 366, 367, 369:** Jerry Caldari, Architect.

**Pages 323, 324, 331:** Space Design Group.

**Pages 327, 333, 334:** *Interiors,* October 1985.

**Pages 335–337:** Gensler Associates.

**Page 339:** Charles D. Flayhan Associates.

**Pages 340–345:** ISD.

**Pages 357, 358, 362:** *Interiors,* July 1985.

**Page 360:** *Selected Architectural Details,* Reinhold, New York.

**Pages 361, 369, 370, 373, 381, 382:** *Design Solutions,* Architectural Woodworking Institute, Spring 1990.

**Pages 371, 372:** Hochheiser-Elias Design Group.

**Pages 374, 376:** De Chiara, Joseph, and John Hancock Callender (eds.), *Time-Saver Standards for Building Types,* 3d Edition, McGraw-Hill, New York, 1990.


## Retail Spaces

**Pages 387–389:** Panero, Julius, and Martin Zelnik, *Human Dimension & Interior Space,* Whitney Library of Design/Watson-Guptill Publications, New York, 1979.

**Pages 390, 394, 400:** *Selected Architectural Details,* Reinhold, New York.

**Pages 391, 392, 396–399:** *Design Solutions,* Architectural Woodworking Institute, Winter 1987, Summer 1988.

**Pages 393, 401–411:** Walker Group/CNI.

**Page 395:** Marble Institute of America.

**Pages 412–417:** Panero Zelnik Associates.

**Pages 418–422:** PAM International Co., Inc.


## Public Restrooms, Toilets, and Coatrooms

**Page 425:** New York City Building Code.

**Pages 427–430:** General Services Administration.

**Pages 431–438, 465:** Bertram Bassuk, FAIA.

**Page 439:** William Morgan, FAIA.

**Pages 440–445:** DeChiara, Joseph, *Handbook of Architectural Details for Commercial Buildings,* McGraw-Hill, New York, 1980.

**Page 446:** Toni Chi and Associates.

**Pages 447, 448:** American Sanitary Partition Corporation.

**Pages 449–451:** *Access America,* Architectural and Transportation Barriers Compliance Board, Washington, D.C., 1980.

**Page 452:** *Uniform Federal Accessibility Standards,* 1985-494-187, U.S. Government Printing Office, Washington, D.C., 1985.

**Page 453:** A & J Washroom Accessories.

**Pages 454–457:** Parker/Nutone.

**Pages 458, 459:** American Specialties, Inc.

**Pages 461–463:** Railex.

**Page 464:** Jerry Caldari, Architect.


## 2. Construction Details and Finishes

**Pages 471, 472, 518, 542, 547, 660–664, 727:** *Time-Saver Standards: A Manual of Essential Architectural Data,* F. W. Dodge Corp., New York, 1946.

**Pages 470, 517:** McQuade, Walter (ed.), *Schoolhouse,* Simon and Schuster, New York, 1958.

**Pages 473, 475–477:** New York State Building Code.

**Pages 474, 478, 565:** Hornung, William J., *Reinhold Data Sheets,* Reinhold, New York, 1965.

**Pages 480, 487, 489, 491, 497, 500–502, 512–515, 522–526, 532, 540, 541 (top), 577–579, 581–588, 601, 606, 608, 609, 614, 617, 629, 630–632, 648, 657, 658, 692 (bottom), 698, 708, 714, 721, 722, 751 (bottom):** Bertram Bassuk, FAIA.

**Pages 481–483, 484 (bottom), 490 (bottom), 629, 649, 651 (top), 652, 754, 755 (top):** ISD.

**Pages 484 (top), 485, 488, 492, 493, 495, 496, 529, 530, 534, 564, 653, 654, 656, 751 (top), 752, 753:** Gensler Associates.

**Pages 486, 580, 605, 659, 669 (top):** William Morgan, FAIA.

**Pages 490 (top), 650, 651 (bottom):** Charles D. Flayhan Associates.

**Pages 491, 754 (top), 755 (bottom):** Michael Lynn Associates.

**Pages 494, 543, 548, 549, 627, 628, 634:** Anderson, L. O., *Wood-Frame House Construction,* Department of Agriculture Handbook No. 73, U.S. Government Printing Office, Washington, D.C., 1970.

**Pages 498, 550:** *Wood Frame Design,* Western Wood Products Association.

**Pages 499, 504, 758, 759:** Panero Zelnik Associates.

**Pages 503, 508, 510, 616, 633, 665, 704, 705, 738:** Knobloch, Philip G., *Good Practice in Construction,* Pencil Points Press, New York, 1931.

**Pages 505, 506, 561–563:** *Handbook for Ceramic Tile Installation,* Tile Council of America, Princeton, N.J., 1988.

**Pages 507, 554–560:**   American Olean Tile.

**Pages 509, 520, 715, 733–735:**   Marble Institute of America.

**Page 519:**   Radford, William, *Architectural Details,* R. D. Radford, Chicago, 1938.

**Pages 521, 749, 750:**   Callender, John Hancock (ed.), *Time-Saver Standards for Architectural Design Data,* 6th Edition, McGraw-Hill, New York, 1982.

**Pages 527, 528 (top):**   Walker Group/CNI.

**Pages 531, 551:**   Roppe Rubber Corp.

**Page 533:**   *American Architect and Architecture,* May 1932.

**Pages 535–539:**   National Terrazzo and Mosaic Association, Inc.

**Page 541:**   Buckingham Virginia Slate Co.

**Page 544:**   American Parquet Association.

**Page 545:**   Hoboken Wood Flooring Co.

**Page 546:**   Tarkett.

**Page 553:**   Franciscan Tile Company.

**Pages 566–571, 574–576, 589–599, 607:**   Hollow Metal Manufacturers Association.

**Pages 572, 670, 671, 706:**   Jerry Caldari, Architect.

**Page 573:**   *Methods and Materials of Commercial Construction.*

**Page 600:**   *New York State Construction Handbook.*

**Pages 602, 603, 678–684, 687, 689, 695, 696, 710, 711, 742:**   Baker, Earl P., and Harold S. Langland, *Architectural Metal Handbook,* National Association of Ornamental Metal Manufacturers, Washington, D.C., 1947.

**Page 604:**   General Services Administration.

**Page 610:**   Eggers Industries.

**Pages 611, 675:**   Raymond, Antonin, *Architectural Details,* Architectural Book Publishing Co., Inc., 1947.

**Pages 612, 666:**   Burbank, Nelson L., *House Construction Details,* 3d Edition, Simmons-Boardman Publishing Corp., New York, 1952.

**Page 615:**   Thompson, Robinson, Toraby.

**Page 618:**   *Progressive Architecture,* April 1971.

**Pages 620–626:**   *Comparative Architectural Details,* Pencil Points Series (Frank J. Forster, Architect), 1935.

**Pages 637–640:**   Schlage.

**Pages 641–643:**   New York City Building Code.

**Pages 644–647:**   Sweet's Catalog.

**Pages 655, 707, 769, 771–773:**   Toni Chi and Associates.

**Page 667:**   *Design Solutions,* Architectural Woodworking Institute.

**Page 668:**   Simon B. Zelnik, FAIA.

**Page 672:**   *Interiors,* April 1985.

**Page 673:**   Feirer, John L., *Cabinet Making and Millwork,* Charles A. Bennet Co., Peoria, Ill.

**Page 674:**   Ascente.

**Page 676, 712:**   *Selected Architectural Details,* Reinhold, New York.

**Pages 677, 685, 686, 688, 690, 691, 692 (top), 693, 694, 697, 699–703, 709:**   National Association of Architectural Manufacturers.

**Page 713:**   New York City Housing Authority.

**Page 716:**   Slate Institute.

**Page 717:**   *Manual of School Planning,* New York City Board of Education.

**Pages 718, 719, 723:**   *Uniform Federal Accessibility Standards,* 1985-494-187, U.S. Government Printing Office, Washington, D.C., 1985.

**Page 720:**   Lapeyre Stair.

**Page 726:**   *Farmers Bulletin #1889,* U.S. Department of Agriculture, Washington, D.C., 1971.

**Pages 728, 729:**   *Handbook of Successful Fireplaces,* Dunley Bros. Co., Cleveland, Ohio, 1961.

**Page 731:**   *Pencil Points* (Ely Jacques Kahn, Architect), October 1938.

**Page 732:**   *Pencil Points* (Richard Neutra, Architect), 1938.

**Page 736:**   *Pencil Points* (Frank Forster, Architect).

**Page 737:**   *Pencil Points* (Walker & Gillette, Architects).

**Pages 739–741:**   Architectural Paneling, Inc.

**Pages 743, 744, 778:**   General Electric Company.

**Pages 745–748:**   Nessen Lamp Company.

**Pages 756, 757:**   Horton Lees Lighting Designs, Inc.

**Pages 760–762:**   Space Design Group.

**Pages 763, 764:**   Bromley/Jacobsen.

**Page 765:**   *Architectural Lighting,* September 1987.

**Pages 766, 768:**   Roberts Step Lite Systems, Inc.

**Pages 767, 770, 774:**   National Cathode Corp.

**Page 775:**   Philips Lighting Co.

**Pages 776, 777:**   Just Bulbs Ltd.

## 3. Architectural Woodwork

**Pages 781, 785–787:** *Time-Saver Standards: A Manual of Essential Architectural Data,* F. W. Dodge Corp., New York, 1946.

**Pages 782–784, 788–797, 801–803:** Woodworking Institute of California.

**Pages 798–800, 872, 873, 877, 879, 881–883:** Architectural Woodwork Institute.

**Page 804:** Leroy P. Ward, Architect.

**Page 806:** *Comparative Architectural Details,* Pencil Points Series (Frank J. Forster, Architect), 1935.

**Page 807:** *Comparative Architectural Details,* Pencil Points Series (Evans, Moore, Peterson & Woodbridge, Architects), 1935.

**Pages 812, 813, 839 (right), 842, 845, 847, 848, 849 (bottom), 853–856, 859, 862–864:** *Design Solutions.*

**Pages 814, 815:** Space Design Group; ISD.

**Page 816:** *Selected Architectural Details,* Progressive Architecture (Perkins & Wills, Architects).

**Pages 808–810, 851:** Knobloch, Philip G., *Good Practice in Construction,* Pencil Points Press, New York, 1931.

**Page 818:** Thompson, Robinson, Cecil, Inc.

**Pages 819–823, 829, 831–835:** Bertram Bassuk, FAIA.

**Pages 824, 828, 836–838:** Charles D. Flayhan Associates.

**Page 825:** ISD.

**Page 826, 827, 830, 839 (left), 846:** Gensler Associates.

**Pages 840, 841:** Winebarger Church Furniture.

**Page 843:** Panero Zelnik Associates.

**Page 844:** Hochheiser-Elias.

**Pages 849 (top), 852:** General Services Administration.

**Page 850:** Roger H. Ballard, Architect.

**Page 857:** Hyde and Shepherd, Architects.

**Page 858:** Howard and Frenaye, Architects.

**Pages 860, 861:** *Comparative Architectural Details,* Pencil Points.

**Page 865:** *Manual of Millwork,* Woodworking Institute of California.

**Pages 866–870, 886:** Architectural Paneling, Inc.

**Pages 871, 873–878, 880–885:** Camden Window and Millwork.

**Pages 887–889:** Joyce, Ernest, *Encyclopedia of Furniture Making,* Sterling Publishing Co., Inc., New York, 1987.

**Pages 890–902:** Hafele.

## 4. Specialties

**Pages 906–915:** Everett Conklin and Susan Korner, in Alpern, Andrew (ed.), *Handbook of Specialty Elements in Architecture,* McGraw-Hill, New York, 1982.

**Pages 916–922, 923 (top):** *The Green Scene,* National Park Service, U.S. Department of the Interior, Washington, D.C., 1973.

**Pages 923 (bottom), 924–926, 929, 930:** Engel/GGP.

**Pages 927, 928:** Hornbostel, Caleb, *Architectural Detailing Simplified,* Prentice-Hall, Englewood Cliffs, N.J., 1986.

**Pages 931–935, 940, 941, 943, 945–948:** Fred T. Knowles, in Alpern, Andrew (ed.), *Handbook of Specialty Elements in Architecture,* McGraw-Hill, New York, 1982.

**Pages 936–939:** Designers Sign Company/Frank Rispoli.

**Pages 942–944:** U.S. Department of Transportation, Washington, D.C.

**Pages 949–957:** Jerome Menell, in Alpern, Andrew (ed.), *Handbook of Specialty Elements in Architecture,* McGraw-Hill, New York, 1982.

**Pages 961–964:** Hussey Seating Company.

**Pages 965, 966, 968–976:** J.G. Furniture Systems.

**Page 967:** *Design Guide for Music and Drama Centers,* Department of the Army, Washington, D.C., 1981.

**Pages 977–997:** *A Design Guide for Improving Residential Security,* U.S. Department of Housing and Urban Development, Washington, D.C., 1973.

**Pages 998, 1002, 1028:** *The House and Home Book of Interior Design,* McGraw-Hill, New York, 1979.

**Pages 999, 1013, 1014:** Halse, *The Use of Color in Interiors,* McGraw-Hill, New York, 1968.

**Pages 1000, 1001, 1003–1012:** Derieux, Mary, and Isabelle Stevenson, *The Complete Book of Interior Decorating,* Greystone Press, New York, 1950.

**Pages 1023–1026:** Anderson, L. O., *Wood-Frame House Construction,* Department of Agriculture Handbook No. 73, U.S. Government Printing Office, Washington, D.C., 1970.

**Page 1016:** McQuade, Walter (ed.), *Schoolhouse,* Simon and Schuster, New York, 1958.

**Pages 1017–1020:** Sweet's Catalog.

**Page 1021:** Marvin Windows.

**Pages 1056–1059:** Kirsch.

**Page 1060:** Armor Elevator.

**Pages 1061–1064:** Dover Elevator Co.

**Pages 1065, 1066, 1102:** *Uniform Federal Accessibility Standards,* 1985-494-187, U.S. Government Printing Office, Washington, D.C., 1985.

**Page 1067:** Panero Zelnik Associates.

**Pages 1067–1074:** *Outdoor Sports Facilities,* Departments of the Army, Navy, and Air Force, Washington, D.C.

**Page 1068 (top):** Mace, Ronald L., *An Illustrated Handbook of the Handicapped Section of the North Carolina State Building Code,* Raleigh, N.C., 1974.

**Pages 1075–1078:** Cutler Manufacturing.

**Page 1079:** Phillips and Brooks, Inc.

**Pages 1080–1086:** Baker, Earl P., and Harold S. Langland, *Architectural Metal Handbook,* National Association of Ornamental Metal Manufacturers, Washington, D.C., 1947.

**Pages 1087–1089:** Brown Manufacturing Co.

**Page 1090:** Bertram Bassuk, FAIA.

**Pages 1091–1096:** Pittcon Softforms.

**Pages 1097–1099:** Alvarado Manufacturing Co.

**Pages 1100–1101:** Haws.

## 5. General Reference Data

**Pages 1106–1109:** Ballast, David Kent, *Architect's Handbook of Formulas, Tables, and Mathematical Calculations,* Prentice-Hall, Englewood Cliffs, N.J., 1988.

**Pages 1110, 1111:** Panero, Julius, and Martin Zelnik, *Human Dimension & Interior Space,* Whitney Library of Design/Watson-Guptill Publications, New York, 1979.

**Pages 1112, 1113:** *Access America,* Washington, D.C.

**Pages 1114 (top):** Sister Kenny Institute.

**Pages 1114 (bottom), 1115–1118:** *Uniform Federal Accessibility Standards,* 1985-494-187, U.S. Government Printing Office, Washington, D.C., 1985.

**Pages 1119, 1120:** Woodson, W. E., *Human Factors Design Handbook,* McGraw-Hill, New York, 1981.

**Page 1121:** *Building for People,* U.S. Department of Commerce, Washington, D.C.

**Pages 1123–1125:** Foster, Norman, *Practical Tables for Building Construction,* McGraw-Hill, New York, 1963.

**Page 1128:** Halse, *The Use of Color in Interiors,* McGraw-Hill, New York, 1968.

**Page 1129:** Hornbostel, Caleb, *Architectural Detailing Simplified,* Prentice-Hall, Englewood Cliffs, N.J., 1986.

**Pages 1130, 1131:** Derieux, Mary, and Isabelle Stevenson, *The Complete Book of Interior Decorating,* Greystone Press, New York, 1950.

**Pages 1132, 1134:** Steelcase.

**Page 1133:** *National Electrical Code Book,* McGraw-Hill, New York, 1981.

**Page 1135:** Indiana Limestone Institute.

**Pages 1137, 1138:** Wing, Charles, *The Visual Handbook of Building and Remodeling,* Rodale Press, 1990.

**Pages 1139–1142:** *Time-Saver Standards: A Manual of Essential Architectural Data,* F. W. Dodge Corp., New York, 1946.

# Index

Accessible bathrooms, 143–148, 317, 380, 449–452
Accessible design, 317, 330, 377–380, 449–452, 1065, 1066, 1068, 1102
(*See also* Barrier-free design)
Accessories, 1075–1102
  chalkboards, 1090
  column covers, 1091–1096
  drinking fountains, 1100–1102
  fireplaces, 742
  grilles, 1080–1086
  guards, protection, 1087–1088
  handrails, 1089
  key cabinets, 1078
  letter boxes, 1075
  lockers, parcel, 1078
  mail chutes, 1078
  mail collection boxes, 1076
  mail drops, 1077
  telephone booths, 1079
  turnstiles, 1097–1099
  water coolers, 1100–1102
Accessory heights, toilets, 117, 128
Acoustical partitions, 494–498
Adaptable bathrooms, 137–142
Adaptable kitchens, 181–185
Aisle types, center-cross, 961–976
Altars, 840
Anthropometric data:
  bars, 346, 347
  bathrooms, 100, 101
  closets, 206
  conference room, 249
  electronic workstations, 241, 242
  library, 190
  reference data, 1110–1113
  retail spaces, 387–389
Architectural woodworking, 804–865
  altars, 840
  bar sinks, 818
  bars, 346, 347, 358–362, 364–366, 368–373, 864
  base cabinets, 837
  benches, 849
  book and prayer shawl cabinets, 832, 833
  bookcases, 808–812
  cabinet doors, 797
  casework, 788–794
  clothes storage, 835
  coat closet, 835
  corner cupboards, 806, 807
  cornices, 856–861
  counters:
    teller's, 396–400, 855

Architectural woodworking, counters (*Cont.*):
    work, 824–826
  display cases, 819–823, 829, 862, 863
  door finishes, 865
  file countertop, 836
  finishes, 865
  hidden door, 853
  lecterns, 843–846
  lobby display, 829
  mouldings, 856–861
  overfile cabinets, 827, 828
  paneling, 804, 805, 860, 861
  pantry cabinet, 839
  pass-through vision panel, 275, 276
  pews, 841
  planter/storage cabinets, 831
  raised panel door, 794, 799, 801, 854
  sanctuary door, 842
  sash, 801
  screen, 850
  storage shelves, 834
  storage walls, 816
  tables, conference, 847, 848
  trader's wall, 814, 815
  wardrobes, 817
  window seat, 851
  windows, 802, 803
  wood paneling, 804, 805
  wood railing and gate, 852
  wood stairs, 665–671, 673
Area requirements, 1106–1109
Areas of planes, 1142
Astragals, 875
Audio-visual systems, 950–960
  equipment, 48, 953, 960
  front projection, 952
  optical design factors, 953
  planning guidelines, 952–955
  projection rooms, 951–960
  rear screen, 952
  remote control, 953
  sound system, 953
Auditorium seating, 961–976
  arrangements, 966, 970–976
  chair dimensions, 962, 964, 965
  continental, 961
  design considerations, 961, 966, 968, 969
  dimensions, 962, 964, 965
  layouts, 961–976
  row length, 962
  row spacing, 963
  screen sightlines, 969
  screen sizes, 952
  seat widths, 962, 965

Auditorium seating (*Cont.*):
  sightlines, 950, 951, 961
  terminology, 967
  visibility, 969
Awning windows, 1016, 1018

Backbar, 347
Badminton court, 1073
Bank teller's counters, 396–400, 855
Banquet seating, 252
Banquette seating, 313–321
  design criteria, 313–315, 318
  details of, 319–321
Bar configurations, 348–356
Bar details, 346, 347, 358–373
Bar sink cabinet, 818
Bar stool spacing, 348–356
Barrier-free design:
  bathrooms, 143–145, 317, 380
  drinking fountains, 1102
  elevators, 1065
  kitchens, 178–189
  ramps, 723
  restrooms, 449–452
  stairs, 718, 719
  toilets, 449–452
  water coolers, 1102
  wheelchairs, 1114
  (*See also* Accessible design)
Bars, 346–373
  anthropometric data, 346, 347
  backbar, 347
  bar cabinet, 361
  bar shapes, planning criteria, 348–356
  bar stool spacing, 348–356
  bottle steps, 363, 368, 369
  clearances, public side, 347
  cocktail tables, 347
  customer activity zone, 347
  dimensions of, 348–356
  elevations of, 357, 362, 367
  front- and backbar, 348–356, 358, 359, 364, 366–369
  glass racks over, 365, 370
  leaning, 347
  planning criteria, 346, 347, 358–362, 364–366, 368–373
  plans, elevations, and sections, 358–373
  sections through, 346, 347, 356–362, 364–366, 368–373
  standing, 347
  working drawings of, 358–373
Base cabinets, 789, 792, 794, 837
Base cap mouldings, 877

Base details, 532, 533, 538
Base mouldings, 532, 533, 786
Base types, 532, 533, 538
  carpet, 532
  ceramic, 532
  marble, 533
  quarry tile, 532
  resilient, 532, 551
  stone, 533
  terrazzo, 538
  vinyl, 532
  wood, 533
Baseboards, 532, 533, 786
Basketball court, 1069, 1071
Bathrooms, 100–148
  accessible design of, 143–148, 380, 449–452
  accessories, 117, 128
  adaptable design of, 137–142
  anthropometric considerations, 100, 101
  barrier-free, 143–148, 380, 449–452
  bathtub and shower details, 132–134
  bathtub types, 113, 114
  bathtub walls, tile, 132, 133, 136
  bidet, 116
  compartmented plans, 103, 105
  controls, 128
  countertops, 125–127, 130, 131
  custom designs, 106–108
  five-fixture plans, 103
  four-fixture plans. 103, 119, 120
  half, 102, 121
  heights, 117, 128
  lavatory types and dimensions, 109–112
  planning data and fixture arrangement, 100, 101
  plans, elevations, and details, 118–124
  powder room, 102, 121
  three-fixture plan, 102, 118
  tile tubs, 132–134
  two-fixture plan, 102
  typical plans and fixture arrangements, 102–105
  vanities, 125–127, 129–131
  watercloset types and dimensions, 115, 116
  wheelchair accessible, 144–148, 380, 449–452
  whirlpool bath details, 113, 135
  (See also Restrooms and toilets)
Bathtubs:
  grab bars
  sizes, 113, 114
  tile, 132, 133, 136
  types, 113, 114
  walls, 132, 133, 136
  wheelchair accessible, 143–148, 317, 380, 449–452
  whirlpool, 113, 135
Bedroom closets, 96–99, 220
Bedrooms, 87–99
  built-in furniture, 90–95, 97
  clearances and arrangements, 87–89
  closets, 96–99
  furniture, 56
  planning data, 87–89
  walk-in closets, 96
Beds and mattresses, 46
Benches, 841, 849–851, 929, 930

Bi-fold doors, 513
Bidet types and dimensions, 116
Billiard tables, 197
Blinds, woven wood, 1054
Bolts, 898, 1138
Bookcases, 808–812
Booth seating, restaurant, 316
Brackets, curtain, 1047
Bricks:
  bonds, 478
  floors, 540
  joints, 478
  partitions and walls, 473–478
  types, 478
Bulbs, light, 775–777
Butt hinges, 887, 890

Cabinet doors, 797
Cabinet hardware, 887–901
  castors and glides, 901
  coat and hat hooks, 901
  drawer runners, 897
  flap stays, 895
  latches, 898
  lid stays, 896
  locks, 899
  magnetic and spring catches, 898
  shelf supports, 900
  wardrobe rails and supports, 901
Cabinet types:
  base, 837
  book and prayer shawl storage, 832, 833
  coat closets, 835
  corner cupboard, 806, 807
  display, lobby, 829
  file, 285–289
  kitchen, 154–169
  overfile, 827, 828
  pantry, 839
  storage, 290
Cabinets, kitchen, 149–169
  clearances above work surface, 149, 150, 153–156
  dimensions for, 156–164
  styles of, 159, 160
Cafeteria counters, 329, 333–338, 340–345
Carousel coat storage, 461, 462
Carpet:
  area conversion, 1122
  construction, 1128
  edgings, 531
  stair finishings, 714
  transitions, 522, 523, 525–527, 529, 530
Casement/hopper windows, 1017
Casement windows, 803
Casework, 788–794
  custom, 789–791, 797
  definitions, 788
  drawer details, 791
  economy, 789–791, 797
  flush overlay, 792–794
  premium, 789–791, 797
Cashier counter, 825
Casings, 878–880
Ceilings, 641–659
  acoustical, 641–643, 647–650, 654–659

Ceilings (Cont.):
  concealed spline, 647
  curved, 651, 652
  exposed T grid, 642
  exposed Z bar, 643
  gypsum board, 644
  lay-in tile, 642, 643, 646, 654, 658, 659
  plaster, 645, 648, 652, 657
  plywood finish, 648
  reflected ceiling plan, 659
  suspended, 641–653
  suspended, concealed spline, 642
  vaulted, 651, 652
Ceramic floors, 552–563
Ceramic tile:
  ceilings, 561
  concrete slabs, 562, 563
  expansion joints, 563
  floors, 540, 561–563
  installation details, 561–563
  shapes, 507
  soffits, 561
  stairs, 561
  wall finishes, 505–507
  wood subfloors, 561
Chair dimensions, 278–281
Chair rails:
  marble, 508
  wood, 870, 883
Chairs, office, 59, 278–281
Chairs, residential, 5–45, 51–55, 59
  20th century classic, 51–55
Chalkboard, 1090
Checkroom systems, 460–463
Children's furniture, 44
Closers, door, 591, 593, 594
Closets:
  bedroom, 206–209, 213, 214, 218
  children's, 218
  foyer/front entry, 219
  housekeeping/utility room, 217
  linen, 216
  master bedroom, 206–209, 213, 214, 218
  narrow and deep, 207
  pantry, 217
  reach-in, 207
  shallow and wide, 207
  split, 206, 207
  standard, 207, 208
  U-shaped walk-in, 206, 207
  walk-in, 206, 207
  wardrobe, 817
Closets/storage areas, 206–220
  anthropometric considerations, 206
  details, 835
  female, 206
  garment dimensions, 208
  male, 206
  rod lengths and heights, 207
  shelf heights, 206, 208
  shelf space and lighting, 207
  walk-in, 206, 207
  wire shelving systems, 216–220
Clothes dimensions, hanging, 208
Coat shelf details, 210–212, 463, 835
  carousel, 461, 462

Coat shelf details (*Cont.*):
  electric, 461, 462
  fixed/stationary capacities, 461, 463
  rotating reels, 461, 462
Coatroom systems, 461–463
Coatrooms, 460–465
  coat capacity, 462
  floor area requirements, 460
  plans, elevations and sections, 464
  public, 460–465
  shelves for, 465
Cocktail tables, 347
Cold cathode, 774
Collection boxes, 1076
Color, 999–1013
  areas and samples, 1001
  effects of lighting on, 1014
  hues, 998–1002
  intensities, 998–1002
  Munsell system of color, 1002
  reflective values, 1013
  values, 998–1002
Color combinations, 1000, 1001
  charts, 1000
Color families:
  blue, 1010, 1011
  green, 1008, 1009
  orange, 1005
  red, 1003, 1004
  violet/purple, 1012
  yellow, 1006, 1007
Color reflectivity, 1013
  values, 1013
Color schemes, 1000, 1001
  planning, 998
Color terms, 1001
Color theory, 998–1014
Color wheel, 1002
Colors:
  accented, 998
  analog or related, 998, 1000
  color wheel, 999
  combinations, 1001
  complementary or contrasting, 998
  cool, 1000
  monochromatic, 998
  neutral, 1000
  primary, 998
  safety color guide, 1013
  secondary, 998
  tertiary, 998
  value scale, 999
  warm, 1000
Columns:
  capitals and entablatures, 1135
  covers, 1091–1096
  fireproofing of, 514, 515
Computer floors, 564, 565
Computer workstations, 241–248
Concealed hinges, 892
Conference rooms, 248–259
  anthropometric data, 249
  clearances for, 249
  credenzas, 259
  heating unit, enclosures in, 259
  layouts, 254, 255

Conference rooms (*Cont.*):
  planning data, 249–255
  seating capacities, 249–255, 283, 284
  table sizes, 249–255, 283, 284
Conference tables, 283, 284
  bases, 256
  boat-shaped, 251–254
  circular, 249, 250, 253, 254
  clearances around, 249
  details of, 256–258
  edge details of, 256
  race track, 252
  rectangular, 251, 252
  room sizes for, 254, 255
  round, 249, 250, 253, 254
  shapes of, 250–253, 283, 284
  sizes, 249–255, 283, 284
  wood edge treatments, 256
Containers, plant, 831, 912
Continental seating, 961
Corner cupboards, 806, 807
Corner guards, 1087, 1088
Cornices, 856–858, 861
  (*See also* Mouldings)
Couches, 5, 9, 13, 17, 21, 25, 26, 45, 57, 77–79
Counters:
  cafeteria, 329, 333–338, 340–345
  cashier, 335, 337, 825
  condiment, 339, 341, 342
  file, 298, 299, 303
  file countertop, 824–828
  kitchen, 154–169, 792, 794
  lavatory, 125–127, 130, 131
  lunch, 322
  pick-up, tray, 337, 341
  plastic laminate, 174
  retail, 387–389, 391, 392, 394–402
  salad bar, 334, 340, 343, 344
  self-service, 329
  servery, 343, 345
  service, 338
  serving, 340–344
  sink, 175
  telephone, 825
  teller's, 396–400, 855
  walkup, 825
  word processing, 825
  work, 824–826
Courts:
  badminton, 1073
  basketball, 1069, 1071
  handball, 1070
  paddle tennis, 1072
  shuffleboard, 1074
  tennis, 1070, 1072
  volleyball, 1073
Cove lighting, 413–417, 751–759
  cold cathode, 752, 774
  mechandise display, 407–409, 412–417
  retail stores, 407–409, 412–417
Cove mouldings, 881
Covering capacities and quantities:
  carpet, 1122
  floor tile, 1123
  paint, 1123
  panel, 1126

Covering capacities and quantities (*Cont.*):
  wood flooring, 1127
Credenzas, 826, 830, 855
Crown mouldings, 866–868, 871, 872
Cupboard, corner, 806, 807
Curtains, 5, 6, 9, 10, 13, 14, 17, 18, 20–22, 24–26, 28, 1027–1041
  café, 1033, 1036
  colonial style, 1029
  Federal style, 1029
  headings, 1043
  pocket, 1027
  rods, 1048–1051
  ruffled, 1033, 1034, 1036
  shirred, 1034
  (*See also* Draperies)

Decibel scale for sounds, 1121
Decimal conversion tables, 1141
Desks, 7, 8, 12, 16, 20, 24, 27, 30, 58
  lamps, 744, 747
  reception, 260, 262–272, 855
  registration, 381–383
  workstations, 223–235
Dining room/ period furniture, 6, 7, 10, 11, 13, 15, 18, 19, 22, 23, 26–29, 31, 36–38, 40–41
Dining room seating, 316
Dining room sizes, 83, 85
Dining rooms, 80–86
  furniture arrangements, 80
  furniture clearances, 80–84
  furniture dimensions, 50, 56
  seating, 85, 86
  tables, 80–86
Display cases, 387–393, 402–404, 408, 409, 819–823, 829, 862, 863
  cosmetic, 391, 402–404
  feature walls, 412–417
  island, 392
  jewelry, 391
  refrigerated, 392
  shelving, 407–409, 412–414, 422
  shirt, 391
  television, 405, 406
Display systems:
  binning, 419
  rack, 419–421
  wall, 418, 419, 422
Door frames, 571–587, 607–609
Door hardware, 568, 569, 589–598, 634–643, 1129
  installation of, 569, 1129
  location of, 1129
Door jambs:
  hollow metal, 571, 573–582, 585, 586
  marble, 629
  wood, 581–586, 608
Door schedules, 570–572
Door trim, 854
Doors, 566–641, 842, 853, 854
  acoustical, 610
  bank vault, 605
  bi-fold, 513
  casement, 612
  closers, 591, 593, 594
  construction details, 610

Doors (*Cont.*):
  edges, 599
  entrance, 618–628
  exterior, 613, 617–628
  fire-protected, 600
  flush, 795, 796
  frames, 571–587, 607–609
    hollow metal, 571, 573–582, 585, 586
  French, 612
  hardware, 568, 569, 589–598, 634–664, 1129
  hidden, 853
  hinges, 568, 598
  hollow metal, 566–599
  laminated, 566
  lead-lined, 610
  lightproofing, 576, 606
  paneled, 612, 613, 615, 616
  particle board, 610
  raised panel, 842, 853, 854
  saddles, 522–528
  sanctuary, 842
  sash, 801
  schedules, 570–572
  screen, 611
  secret, 616, 808
  shoji, 611
  sizes, 568
  sliding, 601, 611
  sound proofing, 576, 606
  stave, 610
  stile and rail, 610
  thresholds, 602–604
  wood, 573, 587, 588, 600, 610–628, 632–634
  wood-clad, 582, 584, 608
Double hung windows, 802
Down lighting, 749, 750
Draperies, 5, 6, 9, 10, 13, 14, 17, 18, 20–22,
    24–26, 28, 1027–1042
  bishop sleeve, 1035
  cascade, 1037
  colonial, 1029
  colors, 1028
  design, 1028
  Directoire, 1030
  fabric, 1028
  Federal, 1029
  finials, 1048
  full-length, 1029–1032, 1034, 1035
  Georgian, 1030
  hardware, 1046–1051
  headings, 1043, 1044
  historical styles, 5, 6, 9, 10, 13, 14, 17, 18,
    20–22, 24–26, 28
  holdbacks, 1034
  hooks, 1048
  late Georgian, 1030
  late Victorian, 1031
  mid-19th-century Victorian, 1031
  mounts, 1047
  neo-Greek, 1031
  panel widths, 1051
  period styles, 1028–1032
  rings, 1048
  rods, 1049, 1050
  single pleated, 1036
  stackback requirements, 1058

Draperies (*Cont.*):
  swags, 1029–1031, 1038–1040, 1042
  upholstery, 1028
Drawers:
  capacities of, 286–291
  card file, 291
  details, 785, 789–791, 797
  glossary, 292, 293
  insert, 286
  lateral file, 287, 287
  legal file, 285
  letter file, 285
  linear capacities of, 286–291
  with shelves and add-on cabinets, 289
  vertical file, 285, 286
Dresser, 97
Drinking fountains, 1100–1102
Drywall partitions, 481–496

Electrical:
  amperage ratings, 1132, 1134
  appliance loads, 1134
  circuits, 1134
  receptacle location, 1133
  requirements, 1132–1134
Electronic media storage, 294, 295
Electronic workstations, 241–248
  administrative, 244, 245
  analyst/programmer, 245
  anthropometrics, 241, 242
  area requirements, 243–245
  computer requirements, 241, 242
  data retrieval, 243
  managerial, 245
  planning data, 241–248
  secretarial, 243
  shared tasks, 243
  square footage for, 243, 245
  task profiles, 243–245
  trading desk details, 246–248
  word processing, 244
Elevators:
  barrier-free considerations, 1065, 1066, 1068
  doors, 1064
  geared traction, 1060
  gearless traction, 1061
  hydraulic, 1061
  low and mid rise, 1061
  passenger, 1060–1066
  planning guidelines, 1060
  security of, 978, 989–991
  selection of, 1060
  traction high rise, 1062, 1063
  wheelchair lifts, 1068
Escalators, 1067
Exit doors, security of, 989

Fabrics:
  characteristics and suitability of, 1130, 1131
  types, 1130, 1131
Face out display systems, 413, 414, 418
Family/recreation rooms, 196–199
  arrangement and clearances, 196, 197
  recreational activities, 196, 197
File cabinets, 285–289
  card file drawers, 281

File cabinets (*Cont.*):
  dimensions of, 285–287
  drawer types in, 285–289
  insert drawers, 286
  lateral, 287, 288
  legal file drawers, 285
  letter file drawers, 285
  linear capacities in, 286
  overfile, 286
  roll-away, 286
  vertical, 285
  weights of, load, 287
File storage, details of, 298, 299
Fire doors, 600
Fireplaces, 68–71, 724–742
  accessories for, 742
  construction details of, 725, 729
  dimensions of, 725–729, 804
  flue sizes of, 726–729
  mantels, 68–71, 520, 521, 730–741, 804, 859
  planning data, 724–729
Fireproofing, 514, 515
Fixture heights plumbing, 117
Flagstone, 520
Floor:
  raised, 564, 565
  sound rated, 548–550
Floor construction:
  details, 516–565
    computer floors, 564, 565
    marble, 521
    slate, 541
    terrazzo, 535–541
    wood, 542–550
    wood on concrete slab, 547
    wood strip flooring, 543
  sound insulation, 548–550
Floor finishes:
  bases, 532, 533, 786
  brick, 540
  ceramic tile, 519, 540, 541, 552–568
  characteristics of, 517
  edgings, 531
  marble, 541
  parquet, 544–546
  quarry tile, 541
  resilient tile, 541, 551
  saddles, 522–526
  slate, 541
  terrazzo, 535–541
  transitions, 527–530
  wood, 541, 544, 547
Floor lamps, 743, 745
Floor patterns:
  ceramic tile, 519, 552–563,
  marble, 520, 521
  stone, 534
  tile, 519
Flushbolts, 596
Folding table hinges, 891
French doors, 801
French paneling, 805
Functions of numbers, 1144
Furniture arrangements, living room, 61
Furniture clearances:
  dining rooms, 50, 56, 80–84

Furniture clearances (*Cont.*):
living room, 50, 57, 63
Furniture dimensions:
audio-visual equipment, 48
bedroom, 56
beds and mattresses, 46
bookcases, 808–812
chairs, 45, 51–55, 59
chaise lounges, 45
chests, 58
children's furniture and tables, 44
convertible sofas, 47
couches, 5, 9, 13, 17, 21, 25, 26, 45, 57,
77–79
desks, 58
dining room, 50, 56
highboys, 58
love seats, 45
lowboy, 58
mattresses and beds, 46
pianos, types and sizes, 199
secretary, 58
settees, 57
sofa beds, 47
sofas, 5, 9, 13, 17, 21, 25, 26, 45, 57, 77–79
tables, 44, 45, 50, 60,
television sets, 50
20th century classic chairs, 51–55
wall beds, 47
waterbeds, 47
Furniture, furnishings, and equipment,
278–304
chair dimensions, 278–281
chair types, 278–281
conference tables, 282–284
counter tops with base cabinets, 303
desks, 7, 8, 12, 16, 20, 24, 27, 30, 58
file cabinets, 285–289
file counter tops, 298, 304
kitchen, compact, 304
lounge seating, 282
office pantry details, 300–303
overfile cabinet, 299
reception seating, 282
storage cabinets, 290
Furniture glides, 902
Furniture hardware, 890–901
Furniture types/styles, 5–43
American, 17th century colonial, 5–8, 29, 30
American, 18th century colonial, 9–12, 29, 30
American, 18th century Federal, 13–16
American, late 18th–early 19th century
Federal, 13–16
Brothers Adam, 39, 40, 17–24
Chippendale, 36
colonial, 5–16, 24, 30
Directoire and Empire, 25–28
Duncan Phyfe, 31
English 16th century Jacobean, 32
English, 17th century Jacobean, 33
English 17th century William and Mary, 34
English 18th century Georgian, 17–20, 36
English 18th century late Georgian, 21–24,
37, 38
English 18th century Queen Anne, 35
Federal, 13–16

Furniture types/styles (*Cont.*):
French, 17th and 18th century Louis XIV,
XV, and XVI, 41
Georgian, 17–24, 36–38
Hepplewhite, 37
Jacobean, 32, 33
late Georgian, 39, 40
Louis XIV, XV, and XVI, 41
Queen Anne, 35
Sheraton, 38
Spanish, 42
table of, 43
William and Mary, 34
Furring of:
columns, 488, 491
walls, 483, 484, 498, 499
wood, 497

Garage doors, 992–995
Gardens:
drainage, 911
interior, 910
large, 910
planting procedures, 910–913
small, 910
(*See also* Plants; Plantscaping)
General offices, 223–230
area allocations, 225, 226
basic workstations, 223–226
groupings, 224
minimum square footage, 225, 226
multiple workstations, 227–230
open workstations, 225, 226
screened workstations, 225, 226
square footage for, 225, 226
task profiles, 225, 226
U-shaped workstation, 224
Glass door cabinet hinges, 894
Glass partitions, 492
Glass shelving details, 402–404, 407, 408, 409,
413, 414
Gliding windows, 1019
Grab bars, 458, 459
Grilles, 1080–1086
Guards, wall protection, 1087, 1088
Guestroom plans, 374–380
accessible, 377–380
Gymnasium, 1071
Gypsum board partitions, 481–496

Handball courts, 1070
Handrail details, 665–669, 671, 672, 681, 682,
692, 707, 718, 719
Hardware:
bolts, 898, 1138
cabinet, 887–902
catches, 898
closet, 901
coordinators, 595
door, 568, 569, 589–598, 634–640
door closers, 593–594
door holders, 593–594
door stop, emergency
fire exit, 595
flush bolts, 596
furniture, 887

Hardware (*Cont.*):
hand of lock, 635
hinge locations, 568
hinges, 589–591, 634, 887–894
hospital door latch, 597
installation in wood door, 534
locations of, 634, 1129
lock functions, 635
lockset types and descriptions, 592, 636–640
panic, 595
wood door, 534, 592, 636–640
Headings, drapery, 1043, 1044
Hearths, 726–729
Highboy, 58
Hinge types:
anchor, 589
butt, 887, 890
concealed, 892
flap, 891, 895
folding table, 891,
full mortise butt, 589, 590
full surface butt, 589, 590
full surface-swing clear, 590
glass door, 894
half mortise, 589, 590
half mortise butt, 589, 590
half surface butt, 589, 590
hospital "swing" clear, 590
invisible, 590
mitred, 892
pivot, 888, 889, 893
Hinges, 887–894
Holdbacks, 1045, 1046
Hollow metal door frames, 571–582, 585,
586
anchorage of, 575, 577
details, 571, 573, 577–586
light and soundproofing of, 576
profiles, 574, 575, 576, 599
typical jamb installations, 571, 573, 577–586
schedules, 570–572
wood and metal, 582, 584
Hollow metal door hardware, 569, 589–598
Hollow metal doors, 566–599
construction types, 567
designs of, 568, 571
dimensions of, 568
edge treatments, 599
hardware, 569, 589–598
hinge locations, 568, 598
laminated construction, 566
sizes of, 568
steel stiffened, 566
Hospitality spaces, 307–383
bars, 346–373
guestroom plans, 374–380
hotel room plans, 374–380
hotels, 374–383
restaurants, 307–345
Hotel room plans, 374
accessible, 377–380
Hotels, 374–383
accessible bathrooms, 143–148, 317, 380,
449–452
accessible guestroom plans, 377–380
guestroom plans, 374–380

Hotels (*Cont.*):
  reception desk, 384
  registration desks, 381–383
  room layouts, 374–380

Indoor recreation, 1069–1073
Indoor trees, 907
Interior plants, 906–930

Jalousie window, 1018
Jambs:
  hollow metal, 571, 573–582, 585, 586
  marble, 629
  wood, 581–586, 608
Joinery details, 781–803
Joinery types, 781–803
  stile and rail, 503, 610, 798, 799, 805, 813
Joint, 781–784
  butted, 781, 782
  cabinet, 785–793
  characteristics, 781
  furniture, 781–784
  mitered, 781, 782
  shiplapped, 781, 782
  terminology, 783
  tongue and groove, 781–786
  typical, 781–784

Kitchen layouts:
  adaptable, 178–189
  broken U, 151–153
  corridor, 151–153
  L-shaped, 151–153
  U-shaped, 151–153
Kitchens:
  accessible, 178–189
  adaptable, 181–185
  anthropometric data, 149, 150
  appliances, 171–173
  barrier free design, 178–189
  cabinet details, 154–169
  cabinet types and dimension, 156–164
  clearances, 149, 150, 153–156
  compact, details of, 304
  countertops, 174, 175
  heights and equipment, 153
  layouts of, 151–153
  microwave cabinets, 163
  minimum counter frontage, 153
  planning information, 149, 150–155
  plans, elevations and details, 176, 177
  sink types and dimensions, 170
  space criteria, 153
  storage and cabinets, 154, 155
  storage requirements, 154, 155
  typical layouts, 151, 152
  wheelchair accessible designs, 178–189

Ladders, 720, 721
Lamp (bulb) types, 774–778
Lamps (portable), 743–748
  desk, 744, 747
  floor, 743, 745
  minimum shade dimensions, 743–748
  personal, 743, 744
  table, 744–746

Lamps (portable) (*Cont.*):
  wall-mounted task, 748
Laundry room locations, 202, 203
Laundry/bathroom combinations, 202
Laundry/kitchen combinations, 204
Laundry/sewing combinations, 200–205
Laundry/sewing rooms, 200–205
  sewing center clearances, 205
  washer/dryer arrangements, 200, 201
Lavatory clearances, 100–103
Lavatory counter details, 441–446
Lavatory countertops, 441–446
Lavatory heights, 100, 101, 450
  wheelchair accessible, 450
Lavatory types and dimensions, 109–112
Lectern, 843–846
Letterboxes, 1075
Lettering typestyle, 947,948
Libraries/studies, 190–196
  anthropometric data, 190
  bookcases, 808–812
  capacities of, 190
  details of, 192–195
  heights of, 190
  plans, elevations, and details, 191–194
  rolling ladders for, 195
  volumes per linear foot, 190
Lid stays, 895
Light cove details, 413–417
Lighting, 743–778, 1014
  cold cathode ceiling mounted, 774, 752
  cove, 413–417, 751–759
  feature walls, 412–417
  handrail lighting, 765
  lighted column, 771–773
  merchandise, 407–409, 412–417
  miscellaneous, 760–764
  nosings and treads, 766–769
  planning data, 743, 744, 749, 750, 774–778
  retail stores, 407–409, 415–417
  skylite lighting, 770
  stair lighting, 766–769
Lighting levels, 750
  industrial, 778
  office, 778
  plants, 915
  residential, 750
  store, 778
Lighting plan, 659
Lighting types:
  cornice, 749
  downlighting, 749, 750
  valence, 415–417, 749
Living rooms, 61–79
  bars in, 72
  circulation, 62
  conversation area, 62–64
  fireplaces, 69–71
  floor plan of, 67, 68, 73–76
  furniture arrangments, 61
  furniture clearances, 63
  furniture dimensions, 50
  media cabinet details, 65, 66
  planning considerations, 61–63
  plans, elevations, and details of, 67, 76
  sofas, 77–79

Living rooms (*Cont.*):
  television viewing areas, 64
Locks, 592
  bored, 592
  bored cylindrical deadlock, 592
  functions of, 631–640
  furniture, 899
  mortise, 592
  mortise deadlock, 592
  unit, 592
Locks, latches, and deadlocks, 592, 636–640
Lockset functions, 636–640
Lockset types and descriptions, 592, 636–640
Lounge seating, 261, 281, 282
Lowboy, 58
Lunch counters, 322

Mail chutes, 1078
Mail drops, 1077
Mailboxes, 1076
Mantels, 68–71, 520, 521, 733, 735, 736,
  738–741
  marble, 733–735
  wood, 736–741, 804
Marble:
  ceilings, 509
  details, 68–71, 520–521, 733, 735, 736,
    738–741
  patterns, 520, 521
  walls, 508–510
Marble flooring, 519, 520, 521
Marble jambs, 629
Marble stairs, 715
Masonry partitions and walls, 473–480
Mathematical data and formulas, 1139–1144
Mattress types and sizes, 46
Mattresses and beds, 46
Measurement conversion tables, 1139–1144
Media rooms, 65, 66
Medical symbols, 940
Men's toilet room, 427, 433, 436, 437, 440
Metal stud and gypsum board, 481–496
Metric conversion tables, 1140
Mirrors, triple, 410
Modular panel conversion chart, 1126
Mortar beds, 132, 541, 561–563
Mouldings, 856–858, 861, 866–886
  backbands, 873
  baluster, 884
  base, 876, 877
  base cap, 877
  base shoe, 876
  brackets, wood, 886
  brick, 874
  casings, 878, 879, 880
  chair rail, 870, 883
  clam shell, 885
  colonial, 885
  corner guards, 875
  cove, 881
  crown, 866, 867, 868, 871, 872
  deep sculpt, 866, 867
  door trim, 869, 870
  floor, 876
  half round, 884
  handrail, 884

Mouldings (*Cont.*):
  lattice, 885
  mirror, 870
  miscellaneous, 873–875
  panel, 870, 882
  picture, 870, 873
  pilaster, 874
  round, 824
  sanitary, 875, 885
  sash, 875, 885
  step, 873
  stop, 885
  trim, 870
  (*See also* Cornices)
Mounting heights, telephone, 1079
Mounts, curtain rods, 1047
Munsell color system, 1002

Nail types and sizes, 1136, 1137
Newels and railings, 665, 666, 673, 692, 693,
    694, 699, 703, 705
Nosings, stair lighting in, 766–769
Nosings and treads, abrasive, 687, 688, 691,
    715, 722

Office spaces, 223–304
  conference rooms, 248–259
  electronic workstations, 241–248
  furniture, furnishings, and equipment,
      278–304
  general offices and multiple workstations,
      223–230
  pass-through windows, 512
  private, 231–240
  room arrangements, 233–235
  reception areas, 260–277
  workstation types, 223–232
Open workstations, 225, 226
Overfile cabinet, 827, 828

Paddle tennis court, 1072
Panel conversion chart, 1126
Panel mouldings, 503
Paneled door:
    details of, 784, 799, 801, 854
    frame parts of, 784
Paneled wainscot, 503, 799
Paneled walls, 798, 799, 800, 801, 804, 805,
    813, 814, 842, 856–861, 860, 861
Paneling, 500–504, 804, 805, 860, 861
  French, 804, 805
  raised, 503, 800
  wood, 500–504, 736, 737
Panic hardware, 595, 596
Pantry cabinets, 839
Parquet flooring, 544–546
Partitions and wall finishes, 469–515
Partition types:
    metal stud and gypsum board, 481–496
    toilet, 447, 448
Partitions, 470–499
  acoustical, 494–498
  brick, 473–478
  concrete block, 480, 483
  drywall, 481–496
  fire-rated, 495

Partitions (*Cont.*):
  glass, 492
  gypsum board, 481–496
  interior, 470–499
  marble, 508–510
  masonry, 473–478, 480, 483
  miscellaneous types, 493
  piers, 473
  plaster, 470–473, 475–477, 508–511
  slate, 511
  sound transmission, 494–498
  stone, 479, 508–511
  wood stud, 472, 473, 494, 498
Pass-through windows, 275, 276
People, distance relationships, 1119, 1120
Period furniture:
  American, 17th century Colonial, 5–8, 29, 30
  American, 18th century Colonial, 9–12, 29,
      30
  American, 18th century Federal, 13–16
  American, late 18th century–early 19th
      century Federal, 13–16
  Brothers Adam, 39, 40
  Chippendale, 36
  Colonial, 5–16, 29, 30
  Directoire and Empire, 25–28
  Duncan Phyfe, 31
  English 16th century Jacobean, 32
  English 17th century Jacobean, 33
  English 17th century William and Mary, 34
  English 18th century Georgian, 17–20, 36
  English 18th century, late Georgian, 21–24,
      37, 38
  English 18th century Queen Anne, 35
  Federal, 13–16
  French, 17th and 18th century Louis XIV,
      XV, and XVI, 41
  French, late 18th century–early 19th century,
      25–28, 41
  Georgian, 17–24
  Hepplewhite, 37
  Jacobean, 32, 33
  late Georgian, 39, 40
  Louis XIV, XV, and XVI, 41
  Queen Anne, 35
  Sheraton, 38
  Spanish 16th and 17th century, 42
  table of, 43
  William and Mary, 34
Pews, 841
Pianos, 199
  photometrics, 766
Picture mouldings, 870, 873
Pivot hinges, 888, 889, 893
Pivot windows, 1019, 1022
Plant containers, 831, 912
Planters, 831
  diameters, 906–909, 912
  window, 927, 928
Planting, 911, 912, 916–928
  bed material, 411, 912, 916–923
  details, 923–928
  medium, 911, 912, 916–923
  standards, 906–915
Plants, 906–930
  design guidelines for, 906–915

Plants (*Cont.*):
  diameters of, 906–909
  floor, 907
  heights of, 906–909
  high light level, 915
  light and sun requirements, 916–923
  low light level, 915
  medium light level, 915
  procedures for planting, 910–913
  requirements, 906–915
  soil requirements, 911, 912, 916–923
  spacing, 906–909
  species, 907
  specifications, 910
  temperature requirements of, 913–916
  texture, 906
  trees, indoor, 907
  typical, 916–923
  water and humidity requirements, 916–923
  water requirements, 915
Plantscaping, 906–930
  design guidelines, 906–915
  specifications, 910
Plaques, 936–939
Pleated shades, 1053
  measurements, 1058
Pleats, 1051, 1043, 1044
Plumbing fixtures, 107, 109–116
Pools, 912
Pot sizes, 906–909, 912
Projection, 950–960
  distances, 953
  front, 952
  rear, 952
Projection room layouts, 950–960
Projection screens, 949–960

Quarry tile, 541

Railings, 665–669, 671, 672, 681, 682, 692, 707,
    718
Raised floors, 564–565
Raised paneling, 503
Raised wood panels, 503
Ramps, 723
  barrier-free, 718, 719, 723
Rear projection, 952
Receptacles, electrical, 1133
Reception areas:
  planning data, 260, 261
  receptionists' workstation in, 262–276
  seating arrangements, 261
Reception desks, 260, 262–272, 855
  hotel, 381–384
Reception rooms: 260–277
  seating, 261
Reception window detail, 273–276, 512
Recreation, indoor, 196, 197
Reference data, general, 1105–1144
Reflected ceiling plans, 760
Reflective values, color, 1013
Registration desks, 381–383
Residential spaces, 5–219
  bathrooms, 100–148
  bedrooms, 87–99
  closet/storage areas, 206–220

Residential spaces (*Cont.*):
dining rooms, 80–86
family/recreation rooms, 196–199
kitchens, 149–189
laundry/sewing rooms, 200–205
libraries/studies, 190–195
living rooms, 61–79
period furniture, 5–43
Resilient floors, 541, 551
Restaurants, 307–345
accessible design, 317, 330
banquette seating, 313–316, 318–321
booth seating, 316
cafeteria/servery, 333–345
condiment cabinet, 339, 341, 342
counter details, 333–337
counter details, 323–327, 329, 331, 333–338,
340, 343–345
counters, 323–327
dining room seating, 316
host cabinet, 338
lunch counters, 322
design criteria, 322
maitre d' station, 338
salad bar serving counter, 840, 844
seating, 313–316, 318–321
self-service counter, 329
servery counter, 843, 845
service counter, 338
table spacing, 308–316
trash counter, 338
tray pickup, 341
Restrooms and toilets, 425–465
accessible design, 317, 430, 449–452
accessories, 453–457
accessory heights, 426–429, 431, 433,
435–441, 450, 452
clearances for wheelchair access, 317,
449–452
(*see* Bathrooms; Hotels)
fixture requirements, fixture count, 425
grab bar configurations, 458, 459
lavatory counter details, 442–446
lavatory heights, wheelchair accessible, 450
plans and elevations, 430–441
plumbing data, 425
plumbing fixture heights, 426–429, 431, 433,
435–441
public, 425–465
show facility for accessibility, 147
toilet accessories, 453–459
toilet stall details, 447, 448
toilet stalls, accessible, 449–452
vanity details, 441–446
wheelchair accessible, 317, 430, 449–452
women's toilet/powder room, 430, 434–437
Retail spaces, 387–422
anthropometric considerations, 387–389
back island details, 401
banks, 396–400
binning, 419
counter heights, 387–389, 391, 392, 394–402
department stores, 401–423
display cases, 387–393, 402–404, 408, 409,
862, 863
faceouts, 413, 414, 418

Retail spaces (*Cont.*):
feature walls, 412–417
garment capacities, 418
lighting, 407–409, 412–417, 759
planning data, 387–389
rack display systems, 420–421
refrigerated case, 392
sales counters, 387–389, 391, 392,
394–402
shelving, 407–409, 412–414, 422
shops, 387–395
showcases, 387–393, 402–404, 408, 409
storefronts, 390
triplicate mirror, 410
valance and cove lighting, 415–417
wall display systems, 418, 419
Risers, 671, 686–688, 708, 713–716, 719
Rock formations, 912
Rod display system, 421
Rods:
drapery-curtain, 1048–1050
traverse, 1050
Roll-in showers, 140
Rolling ladders, 195
Row length and spacing, 961–969, 970–976

Saddles, 522–528
under doors, 522–528
Salad bar counter, 340
Sales counters, 387–389, 391, 392, 394–402
Sash, profiles of, 801
Screens:
projection, 952
shoji, 611
Screw types, 1138
Seat widths, 968
Seating arrangements, 966, 970–976
auditorium, 961–976
standard, 961
Seating:
continental, 961
multiple, 966
Secondary entries, security of, 989
Security, 977–997
alarms, exit, 995
bars, grills, and gates, 988
closers, 980
control of grounds, 977, 978
cylinders, 981, 983, 984
doors, 977–986
electronic systems, 994, 996, 997
elevators, 978, 989–991
exit doors, secondary, 989
fire doors and fire stairs, 977
garage doors, 992–985
general control guidelines, 977, 978
hardware, 979–986
hinges, 980
lighting, 993
lobby spaces, 977
locks, 981, 986, 987
mailbox rooms, 992, 993
multifamily dwelling, 977
public spaces of multiple dwelling, 977
secondary entries, 989
skylights, 988

Security (*Cont.*):
sliding doors, 984
window and hardware, 978, 986–988
Security alarms, 994–997
Serving counter, 329, 333–338, 340–345
Settees, 5, 9, 17, 25, 33, 57
Sewing equipment, arrangement of, 205
Sewing machines, heights and clearances, 205
Sewing rooms, 205
planning of, 205
Shades, window, 1052–1054
lamp, 743–746
Shelf and hanging pole, 835
Shelf edge, 826, 830, 834, 835
Shelf heights:
closets, 835
storage, 826, 834
Shelf light details, 298
overhead file storage details, 827, 828
Shelf supports, 900
Shelf types:
coat, 277
coatrooms, 465
phone, 277
wall, 277
wire basket and shelving system, 216–220,
419
Showcase types:
cosmetic display, 391, 402–404
island display, 392
jewelry, 391, 401
refrigerated, 392
shirt display, 391
Shower floor details, 132, 133
Shower seat design, 132
Shower wall details, 132
Showers:
grab bars for, 140, 142, 144, 147
roll-in, 140, 144, 147
wheelchair accessibility, 140
Shuffleboard court, 1074
Shutter details, 1057
Shutters, 1055–1057
Sign types, 931–948
area designation-wall mounted plaques, 937
ceiling hung, 937
code, 936
counter top, 939
cut letters, 939
design criteria, 931–935
desk top, 939
directional, overhead, 937
directional, wall mounted, 937
framed wall-mounted plaques, 938
room identifier, 938
Signage:
celing hung, 937
checklist for, 934, 935
counter top, 939
desk bar, 939
desk top, 939
directional, 937
flag mount, 939
framed wall-mounted plaques, 938
room identifier, wall mounted, 938
symbols, 940–946

Signage (*Cont.*):
  type and mounting heights, 936–939
Signage and graphics, 931–948
Signage system design criteria, 931–936, 949
  graphic symbols, 940–946
  mounting heights, 936
  mounting materials, 937
  standard sizes, 936–939
  types, 936–939
Sinks, kitchen, 170
Skylights, lighting, 770
Slate flooring, 541
Slate stairs, 716
Sliding windows, 1019
Sofa beds, 47
Sofa dimensions, 45
Sofas, 77–79
Sofas, chairs, tables, and stools, 45
Soffits (*see* Ceilings)
Sound control partitions, 494–498
Sound insulation, floor construction, 548–550
Sound insulation and transmission details,
    494–498, 548–550
Sound levels, 1121
Sound transmission, partitions, 494–498, 1121
  floor construction, 548–550
Space planning area requirements, 1106–1109
Specialties, 903–1102
  audio-visual systems, 949–960
  auditorium seating, 961–976
  chalkboards, 1090
  color theory, 998–1014
  column covers, 1091–1096
  drinking fountains, 1100–1102
  elevators, 1060–1068
  fireplaces, 742
  guards, protection, 1087–1088
  grilles, 1080–1086
  handrails, 1089
  indoor recreation, 1069–1074
  key cabinets, 1078
  letter boxes, 1075
  lockers, parcel, 1078
  mail chutes, 1078
  mail collection boxes, 1076
  mail drops, 1077
  plantscaping, 906–930
  security, 977–997
  signage and graphics, 931–948
  telephone booths, 1079
  turnstiles, 1097–1099
  watercoolers, 1100–1102
  window treatments, 1015–1059
Spiral stairs, 674, 676, 709, 710
Sports, indoor, 1069–1074
Stair finishes:
  carpeting, 714
  ceramic tile, 561
  concrete, 713, 714, 722
  marble, 715
  slate, 716
  terrazzo, 539, 708, 712, 714
  wood, 665–671
Stair lighting, 766–769
Stairs:
  barrier-free design data, 718, 719

Stairs (*Cont.*):
  circular, 675, 711
  classes of, 677
  clearances, 660–664, 686
  critical dimensions, 660–664, 686
  details of, 665–672, 678–784, 687–699,
      703–708, 712–716, 721, 722
  floor to floor heights, 660
  handrail heights, 664
  handrails, 664–673, 692–702, 717, 718, 765
  headroom, 660, 664
  layout of, 664
  length of, 686, 661–663
  lighting of, 766–769
  minimum width of, 661
  nosings and treads, 664, 687, 688, 691, 708,
      713–716, 722, 766–769
  number of risers, 660, 662, 663
  oval, 674, 676, 709, 710
  pitch of, 664
  planning data, 660–664, 677, 717
  platform, 683
  riser calculations, 660
  spiral, 674, 676, 709, 710
  steel, 670, 671
  stringers, 689, 690
  treads, 687–688, 719
  types, 682, 683
    circular, 674–676, 709–711
    concrete, 672, 712–714
    double L, 662
    L-shaped, 662, 663
    ladders, 720, 721
    oval, 675
    scissor, 713
    spiral, 674–676, 709–711
    steel, 678–683, 722
    straight run, 662
    U-shaped, 663, 717
  width, 661–663, 685
  wood, details of, 665–671, 673
Stairway layouts (*see* Stairs)
Standards and brackets, 422
STC (sound transmission classifications),
    494–498
  floor construction, 548–550
Steel stairs, 670, 671
  details of, 670, 671
Storage:
  closet, 826, 834, 835
  coatroom, 461–463
  electronic media, 294, 295
  overhead file, 827, 828
  registration desks, 381–384
  residential, 206–220
Storage cabinets, 290
  dimensions of, 816
  glossary of, 292, 293
  wardrobe, 817
Storage components, 292, 293
Storage shelves, 834
Storage walls, 816
Stores:
  department, 401–422
  shops, 387–395
Straight run stairs, 662

Stringers, steel, 666, 667, 671, 678, 680–686,
    692–694, 703–708
Strip flooring, 1127
  estimating of wood, 1127
Study, 190–194
Suspended ceiling types, 641–659
  concealed spline, 647
  miscellaneous details, 653–655
  perimeters and drops, 656
Suspension system types, 641–643
Swags, 1029–1031, 1038–1040, 1042
Symbols:
  commercial, 941, 942
  medical, 940
  recreation/sports, 445
  travel, 943, 944
  universal, 946

Tables, 44, 50, 60
  banquet, 252
  boardroom, 847, 848
  conference, 283, 284
  design criteria for restaurants, 312
  dining room, 80–86
  restaurant. 307–316
Table arrangements, restaurants, 307–311
Table lamps, 744
Table sizes:
  billiards, 197
  conference room, 249–255, 283, 284
  ping pong, 197
  pool, 197
  spacing in
Tack sizes, 1136
Task lights, wall-mounted, 748
Telephone stations, 277, 1079
Telephone:
  clearances, 1079, 1118
  mounting heights, 1079
Television viewing areas, 49
Teller's counters, 855
Tennis court, 1070, 1072
Terrazzo, 536–540
  base, 538
  flooring, 536, 537, 540
  stairs, 539
Theater seating, 961–976
Thresholds, 522–528
Tiebacks, 1045, 1046
Tile walls, 132–134, 505–507
Toilet accessories, 143–148, 317, 380, 449–459
Toilet partitions, 447, 448
Toilet stalls:
  accessible, 449
  grab bars, 143–148, 449, 452, 458, 459
Trader's wall, 814, 815
Trading desk details, 246–248
Treads, 671, 686–688, 708, 713–716
  barrier-free, 719
  cement, 713, 714, 722
  concrete, 683, 686–688
  marble, 687, 715
  metal, 687
  slate, 716
  terrazzo, 708, 714
  wood, 671, 687

Trees, indoor, 907
Trim (*see* Mouldings)
Turnstiles, 1097–1099
Typeface styles, 947, 948

Units of measurement, 1139, 1140

Valance and cove lighting, 749
Vanities, 125–127, 129–131
   countertop details, 125–127, 130, 131
Veneer:
   marble, 508, 509
   slate, 511
Vertical blinds, 1059
Vertical circulation (*see* Elevators)
Vinyl cove base, 532, 551
Volleyball court, 1073

Wainscot:
   flat paneled, 798–800
   marble, 508–510
   slate, 511
   wood, 500–502, 805
Waiter station, 328
Wall areas of rooms, 1124, 1125
Wall beds, 47
   wall board partitions, 481–496
Wall finishes, 500–511
   ceramic tile, 505–507
   marble, 508–510
   paneling, 500–504
   slate, 511
   wood, 500–504
Wall-mounted task lights, 748
Wall paneling:
   stile and rail, 503
   wallpaper area conversion, 1123
Wall protection guards, 1087, 1088
Wall types (*see* Partitions)
Wall unit details, private offices, 236–239
Wallpaper covering, 1123–1125
Walls:
   marble, 508–510
   slate, 511
   terrazzo, 539
Washer/dryer arrangements, 200, 201
Waterbeds, 47
Waterclosets, 115, 116
   wheelchair access, 143–148, 317, 380,
      444–452
   grab bars for, 143–148, 458, 459
Wheelchair:
   accessible bathrooms, 143–145, 317, 380,
      449–452
   adaptable kitchens, 181–185
   clearances for, 1114–1118
   elevators, 1065
   lifts, 1068
   restaurants, 317, 330

Wheelchair (*Cont.*):
   terminology, 1114
Whirlpool baths, 113, 135
Window bars, grilles and gates, 1080–1086
Window treatments, 1015–1059
   brackets, 1047
   curtains, 1027–1041
   draperies, 1027–1041
   guidlines, 1058, 1059
   mounts, 1047
   shades, 1052–1054
   shutters, 1055, 1056
Window types, 1015–1026
   austral, 1020
   awning, 1016, 1018
   bottom hinged, 1017
   casement, 1015, 1024, 1025
   casement hopper, 1017
   custom shapes, 1021
   double hung, 1015, 1016, 1019, 1022, 1024,
      1025
   dual vent, 1019
   gliding, 1019
   Gothic, 1021
   hopper, 1017, 1018
   jalousie, 1018
   metal, 1018, 1020
   oval, 1021
   pivot, 1019, 1020
   projected, 1018
   reversible, 1020
   round top, 1021
   side hinged, 1017
   sliding, 1019
   special, 1020
   stationary, 1023
   top hinged, 1018
   two-light, 1022
   wood, 1017–1026
Windows, 1015–1026
   pass-through, 275, 276
   reception, 273–276, 512
   security of, 978, 986–988
Windows and hardware, 1015–1026
Wire shelving systems, 216–220
Women's toilets, 430, 434–437
Wood:
   board feet of, 1127
   door frames, 608, 609
   floor construction, 542–550
   flooring types, 544–547
   joinery details, 781–787
   paneling, 661, 804, 805, 860
   parquet, 544–546
   railing and gate, 852
   railings, 665–671
   stairs, 665–671, 673
   strip flooring, 543
   windows, 802, 803

Woodwork details, 804–865
   altars, 840
   bar sinks, 818
   bars, 346, 347, 358–362, 364–366, 368–373,
      864
   base cabinets, 837
   benches, 849
   book and prayer shawl cabinets, 832, 833
   bookcases, 808–812
   cabinet doors, 797
   casework, 788–794
   clothes storage, 835
   coat closet, 835
   corner cupboards, 806, 807
   cornices, 856–861
   counters, teller's, 855
   counters, work, 824–826, 836, 855
   display cases, 819–823, 829, 862, 863
   door finishes, 865
   drawers, 791
   file countertop, 836
   finishes, 865
   hidden door, 853
   lecterns, 843–846
   lobby display, 829
   overfile cabinets, 827, 828
   moulding, 856–861
   paneling, 804, 805, 860, 861
   pantry cabinet, 839
   pass-through vision panel, 275, 276
   pews, 841
   planter/storage cabinets, 831
   raised panel door, 794, 799, 801, 854
   sanctuary door, 842
   sash, 801
   screen, 850
   storage shelves, 834
   storage walls, 816
   tables, conference, 847, 848
   teller's counters, 855
   trader's wall, 814, 815
   wardrobes, 817
   window seat, 851
   windows, 802, 803
   wood paneling, 804, 805
   wood railing and gate, 852
   wood stairs, 665–671, 673
   work counters, 824–826
Workstation types, 223–232
   basic, 223–226
   electronic, 241–248
     anthropometrics of, 241, 242
   executive, 231, 232
   general, 223–230
   multiple, 227–229
   receptionist, 260
   trading desks, 246, 247
   trading tables, 248
   wood stud partitions, 472, 473, 494, 498

## About the Editors

JOSEPH DE CHIARA is a practicing architect and city planner in New York City. He has taught at Columbia University, Pratt Institute, Cooper Union, the New York Institute of Technology, and the State University of New York at Farmingdale. He is coauthor of *Time-Saver Standards for Site Planning* and the author of *Handbook of Architectural Details for Commercial Buildings* and *Time-Saver Standards for Building Types*, all published by McGraw-Hill. De Chiara received a Bachelor of Architecture degree from Pratt Institute and a Master's degree in Urban Planning from Columbia University.

JULIUS PANERO, AIA, ASID, is a practicing architect, interior designer, and Professor of Interior Design at the Fashion Institute of Technology in New York City. He has taught interior design for the past 32 years and was a former chairperson of the interior design department at FIT. A graduate of Pratt Institute, where he received a Bachelor of Architecture, and Columbia University, where he received a Master of Science in Urban Planning, Panero is a member of the American Institute of Architects and the American Society of Interior Designers.

Licensed to practice architecture in New York, Panero is a principal in the architectural and consulting firm of Panero Zelnik Associates, Architects/Interior Designers. He is coauthor of *Human Dimension & Interior Space*, a sourcebook of design reference standards. In 1986, he was awarded the prestigious ASID Joel Polsky Prize for this book. He is also the author of *Anatomy for Interior Designers* and a contributing author to the *Time-Saver Standards* series.

MARTIN ZELNIK, AIA, ASID, IDEC, is a practicing architect, interior designer, and Professor of Interior Design at the Fashion Institute of Technology in New York City, where he has taught interior design for the past 23 years. He served as chairperson of the interior design department from 1983 to 1986. He is a graduate of Brandeis University, where he received a Bachelor of Fine Arts degree, and

Columbia University, where he earned a Master of Architecture degree. Zelnik is a member of the Interior Design Educators Council, the American Society of Interior Designers, and the American Institute of Architects; has served as a special consultant to the National Council of Interior Design Qualifications; and holds certification with the National Council of Architectural Registration Boards.

He has been a principal in the New York City–based architectural and consulting firm of Panero Zelnik Associates, Architects/Interior Designers, for over 18 years. The firm specializes in institutional, religious, and transportation facilities, and corporate interiors. Zelnik is coauthor of *Human Dimension & Interior Space*, a sourcebook of design reference standards. In 1986, he was awarded the prestigious ASID Joel Polsky Prize for this book.